TEACHER'S EDITION

Addison-Wesley

Earth Science

Robert E. Fariel

Alva T. Stanworth Junior High School, Elmont, New York

Robert W. Hinds

Slippery Rock University of Pennsylvania

David B. Berey

Educational Consultant, New York, New York

Consulting Author

Bonnie B. Barr

State University of New York College at Cortland

CONSULTANTS AND CONTRIBUTORS

Gene Ammarell
Education Director, Fiske Planetarium and Science Center, University of Colorado, Boulder, Colorado

Charles R. Ault, Jr.
Assistant Professor, Science Education, Indiana University, Bloomington, Indiana

Richard Benz
Science Chairman, Wickliffe High School, Wickliffe, Ohio

Thomas H. Callen II
Program Resource Manager, Albert Einstein Planetarium, the Smithsonian Institution, Washington, D.C.

Ronald E. Charlton
Science Coordinator, Mount Lebanon School District, Pittsburgh, Pennsylvania

Jeff Davis
Science Teacher, Tomlin Junior High School, Plant City, Florida

Keith Emrick
Science Teacher, Mesa High School, Mesa, Arizona

Kathleen Kaye Gulley
Science Teacher, Pike High School, Indianapolis, Indiana

Marion S. Hacker
Science Teacher, Wedgwood Middle School, Fort Worth, Texas

Harold Pratt
Science Coordinator, Jefferson County Public Schools, Lakewood, Colorado

▲▼ Addison-Wesley Publishing Company

Menlo Park, California • Reading, Massachusetts • Don Mills, Ontario • Wokingham, England
Amsterdam • Sydney • Singapore • Tokyo • Madrid • Bogotá • Santiago • San Juan

About the Authors

Robert E. Fariel is a science supervisor and teacher of earth science at Alva T. Stanforth Junior High School, Elmont, New York. He has served on the Executive Board of the New York State Science Supervisors Association, and is currently serving as executive secretary of the National Science Supervisors Association. He is also a member of the National Association of Geology Teachers.

Mr. Fariel received a B.S. degree from SUNY at Cortland and an M.S. degree from Hofstra University. He is a recipient of the Jenkins Memorial Scholarship, awarded by the Parent-Teacher Association. He has written articles for the National Science Supervisors Association and has also contributed to the teacher's edition of *Earth Science: Patterns in Our Environment*.

Robert W. Hinds is Professor of Geology and former chairman of the department of geology at Slippery Rock University of Pennsylvania. He also serves as a director and vice president of academics of The Marine Science Consortium, Inc. In addition, he worked on the preparation of museum exhibits on invertebrate fossils for the American Museum of Natural History (New York City).

Dr. Hinds received a B.S. degree from Brigham Young University, an M.S. degree from Louisiana State University, and a Ph.D. degree from Columbia University. He is the recipient of a Penrose grant from the Geological Society of America and a certificate of academic achievement from the Smithsonian Institution.

David B. Berey is an educational consultant, Adjunct Associate Professor at Adelphi University, Garden City, New York and a former science teacher and director of science K-12. Mr. Berey has served as an instructional redesign consultant to school districts. He is experienced in the designing, implementing, and directing of computer-based science educational programs.

Mr. Berey has received a B.S. degree and M.S. degree from the University of Kansas, and has done doctoral study at New York University. He is an author of science books, of the New York State Earth Science Syllabus, and of junior high school science syllabuses.

ISBN 0-201-25040-3

BCDEFGHIJKL-VH-8921098

Teacher's Edition Table of Contents

The Addison-Wesley Earth Science Program T4

Scope and Sequence of Concepts and Skills T20

Software for Earth Science T26

Audiovisual Materials for Earth Science T37

Conducting a Safe Classroom and Laboratory T46

Developing Your Own Activities T47

Master Materials List T48

Page numbers in red indicate annotated student pages.

Chapter 1 **Studying the Earth** 2
Planning Guide 2A
Teacher's Notes 2C

Chapter 2 **Earth Materials** 56
Planning Guide 56A
Teacher's Notes 56C

Chapter 3 **The System of the Earth and the Moon** 114
Planning Guide 114A
Teacher's Notes 114C

Chapter 4 **Beyond the Earth** 168
Planning Guide 168A
Teacher's Notes 168C

Chapter 5 **The Atmosphere** 230
Planning Guide 230A
Teacher's Notes 230C

Chapter 6 **Weather and Climate** 284
Planning Guide 284A
Teacher's Notes 284C

Chapter 7 **The Earth's Fresh Water** 334
Planning Guide 334A
Teacher's Notes 334C

Chapter 8 **The Ocean** 366
Planning Guide 366A
Teacher's Notes 366C

Chapter 9 **The Earth's Changing Surface** 422
Planning Guide 422A
Teacher's Notes 422C

Chapter 10 **The Restless Crust** 468
Planning Guide 468A
Teacher's Notes 468C

Chapter 11 **The Earth's Geologic History** 522
Planning Guide 522A
Teacher's Notes 522C

Chapter 12 **Environmental Concerns** 580
Planning Guide 580A
Teacher's Notes 580C

Addison-Wesley Earth Science supports you in

Planning

Chapter Planning Guides help you organize and design your course to meet your needs.

Teaching

The easy-to-use and easy-to-follow teaching guide guarantees effective and efficient instruction.

Understanding

Comprehensible content encourages your students to think scientifically.

Applying

Applications and hands-on experiences involve students in their learning.

Meeting needs

Success for all students is built in with lots of opportunities for all levels of ability.

Flexibility

More options support your individual teaching style.

Addison-Wesley Earth Science *is one of a series.*
Also available:
Addison-Wesley Life Science;
Addison-Wesley Physical Science;
Addison-Wesley Introduction to Physical Science.

Planning

Addison-Wesley Earth Science

1 Meet individual needs with each feature and component identified as **Core, Enrichment,** or **Reinforcement.**

2 Plan labs and activities to fit your needs and your school's laboratory facilities.

3 Organize your teaching to meet your style and your students' abilities. Each task is indexed and cross-referenced to save you time.

4 Interleaved teacher notes provide ready access to information for each chapter.

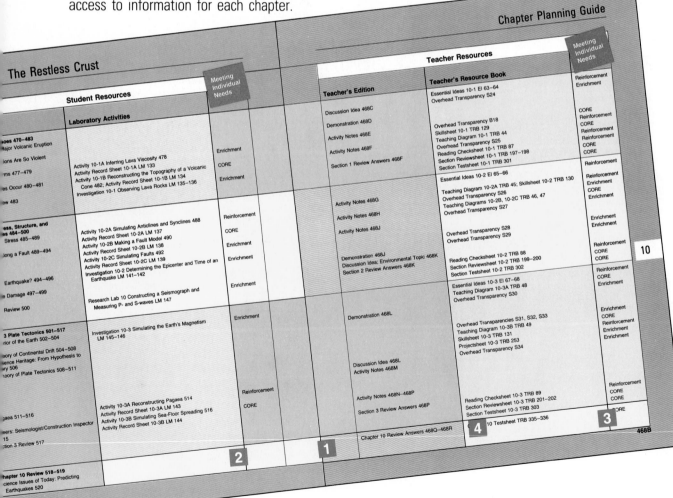

helps you to plan each lesson effectively.

1 Demonstrations motivate students to be curious about the concepts.

2 Learner Objectives define the students' learning goals for each chapter section.

3 Concept Summaries highlight the main ideas and help you coordinate these ideas with your curriculum requirements.

4 Student Misconceptions identify and help correct faulty understanding of scientific principles.

5 Environmental Topics link classroom learning with current concerns in the real world.

6 Discussion Ideas help you involve the students in the learning.

7 Answers help you evaluate student responses to **Thinking Skills, Activities,** and **Reviews.**

8 Science Background information prepares you for class discussions and students' questions.

9 Activities—including materials, time, and group size—can be planned completely in advance.

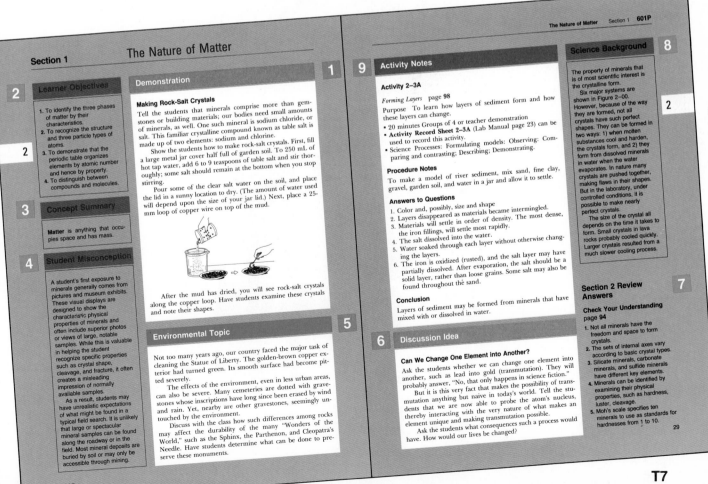

Section 1 — The Nature of Matter

2 Learner Objectives

1. To identify the three phases of matter by their characteristics.
2. To recognize the structure and three particle types of atoms.
3. To demonstrate that the periodic table organizes elements by atomic number and hence by property.
4. To distinguish between compounds and molecules.

3 Concept Summary

Matter is anything that occupies space and has mass.

4 Student Misconception

A student's first exposure to minerals generally comes from pictures and museum exhibits. These visual displays are designed to show the characteristic physical properties of minerals and often include superior photos or views of large, notable samples. While this is valuable in helping the student recognize specific properties such as crystal shape, cleavage, and fracture, it often creates a misleading impression of normally available samples.

As a result, students may have unrealistic expectations of what might be found in a typical field search. It is unlikely that large or spectacular mineral samples can be found along the roadway or in the field. Most mineral deposits are buried by soil or may only be accessible through mining.

1 Demonstration

Making Rock-Salt Crystals

Tell the students that minerals comprise more than gemstones or building materials; our bodies need small amounts of minerals, as well. One such mineral is sodium chloride, or salt. This familiar crystalline compound known as table salt is made up of two elements: sodium and chlorine.

Show the students how to make rock-salt crystals. First, fill a large metal jar cover half full of garden soil. To 250 mL of hot tap water, add 6 to 9 teaspoons of table salt and stir thoroughly; some salt should remain at the bottom when you stop stirring.

Pour some of the clear salt water on the soil, and place the lid in a sunny location to dry. (The amount of water used will depend upon the size of your jar lid.) Next, place a 25-mm loop of copper wire on top of the mud.

After the mud has dried, you will see rock-salt crystals along the copper loop. Have students examine these crystals and note their shapes.

5 Environmental Topic

Not too many years ago, our country faced the major task of cleaning the Statue of Liberty. The golden-brown copper exterior had turned green. Its smooth surface had become pitted severely.

The effects of the environment, even in less urban areas, can also be severe. Many cemeteries are dotted with gravestones whose inscriptions have long since been erased by wind and rain. Yet, nearby are other gravestones, seemingly untouched by the environment.

Discuss with the class how such differences among rocks may affect the durability of the many "Wonders of the World," such as the Sphinx, the Parthenon, and Cleopatra's Needle. Have students determine what can be done to preserve these monuments.

9 Activity Notes

Activity 2–3A

Forming Layers page **98**
Purpose To learn how layers of sediment form and how these layers can change.
- 20 minutes Groups of 4 or teacher demonstration
- **Activity Record Sheet 2–3A** (Lab Manual page 23) can be used to record this activity.
- Science Processes: Formulating models: Observing: Comparing and contrasting; Describing; Demonstrating.

Procedure Notes
To make a model of river sediment, mix sand, fine clay, gravel, garden soil, and water in a jar and allow it to settle.

Answers to Questions
1. Color and, possibly, size and shape
2. Layers disappeared as materials became intermingled.
3. Materials will settle in order of density. The most dense, the iron fillings, will settle most rapidly.
4. The salt dissolved into the water.
5. Water soaked through each layer without otherwise changing the layers.
6. The iron is oxidized (rusted), and the salt layer may have partially dissolved. After evaporation, the salt should be a solid layer, rather than loose grains. Some salt may also be found throughout the sand.

Conclusion
Layers of sediment may be formed from minerals that have mixed with or dissolved in water.

6 Discussion Idea

Can We Change One Element into Another?

Ask the students whether we can change one element into another, such as lead into gold (transmutation). They will probably answer, "No, that only happens in science fiction."

But it is this very fact that makes the possibility of transmutation anything but naive in today's world. Tell the students that we are now able to probe the atom's nucleus, thereby interacting with the very nature of what makes an element unique and making transmutation possible.

Ask the students what consequences such a process would have. How would our lives be changed?

8 Science Background

The property of minerals that is of most scientific interest is the crystalline form.

Six major systems are shown in Figure 2–00. However, because of the way they are formed, not all crystals have such perfect shapes. They can be formed in two ways: 1) when molten substances cool and harden, the crystals form, and 2) they form from dissolved minerals in water when the water evaporates. In nature many crystals are pushed together, making flaws in their shapes. But in the laboratory, under controlled conditions, it is possible to make nearly perfect crystals.

The size of the crystal all depends on the time it takes to form. Small crystals in lava rocks probably cooled quickly. Larger crystals resulted from a much slower cooling process.

7 Section 2 Review Answers

Check Your Understanding page **94**

1. Not all minerals have the freedom and space to form crystals.
2. The sets of internal axes vary according to basic crystal types.
3. Silicate minerals, carbonate minerals, and sulfide minerals have different key elements.
4. Minerals can be identified by examining their physical properties, such as hardness, luster, cleavage.
5. Moh's scale specifies ten minerals to use as standards for hardness from 1 to 10.

29

Teaching

Addison-Wesley Earth Science

1 **Addison-Wesley Earth Science** is organized in Units, Chapters, and Sections to make planning and teaching easier and more effective.

2 **Learner Objectives** help you develop lesson plans and focus instruction.

3 **Caption questions** provide starting points for class discussions.

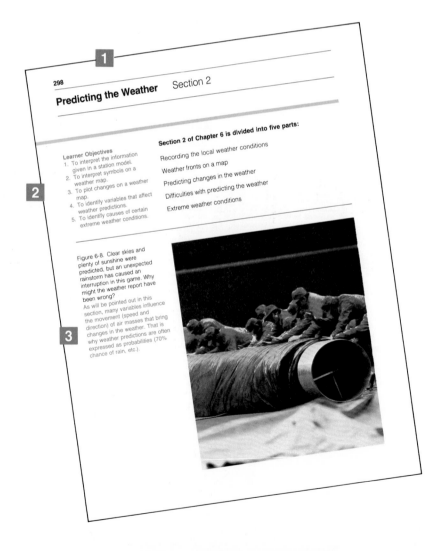

298

Predicting the Weather   Section 2

Learner Objectives
1. To interpret the information given in a station model.
2. To interpret symbols on a weather map.
3. To plot changes on a weather map.
4. To identify variables that affect weather predictions.
5. To identify causes of certain extreme weather conditions.

Section 2 of Chapter 6 is divided into five parts:

Recording the local weather conditions

Weather fronts on a map

Predicting changes in the weather

Difficulties with predicting the weather

Extreme weather conditions

Figure 6-8. Clear skies and plenty of sunshine were predicted, but an unexpected rainstorm has caused an interruption in this game. Why might the weather report have been wrong?
As will be pointed out in this section, many variables influence the movement (speed and direction) of air masses that bring changes in the weather. That is why weather predictions are often expressed as probabilities (70% chance of rain, etc.).

lets you teach successfully and efficiently.

1 **Answers** (in blue) make it easy to evaluate student performance.

2 **Library Research** topics provide starting points for written projects.

3 **Teacher annotations** (in red) provide suggestions and information to help you teach and motivate students.

4 **Check Yourself** is a quick quiz at the end of each section that directs student attention to the main topics.

5 **Overhead Transparencies** are colorful options that add flexibility to your teaching day.

6 **Teaching Diagram** masters can be used for demonstrations, for quizzes, or to emphasize key concepts.

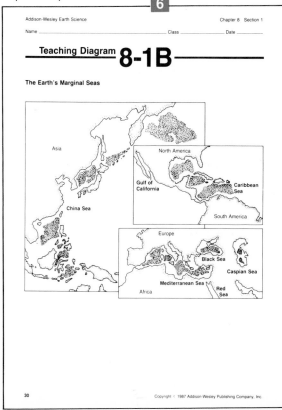

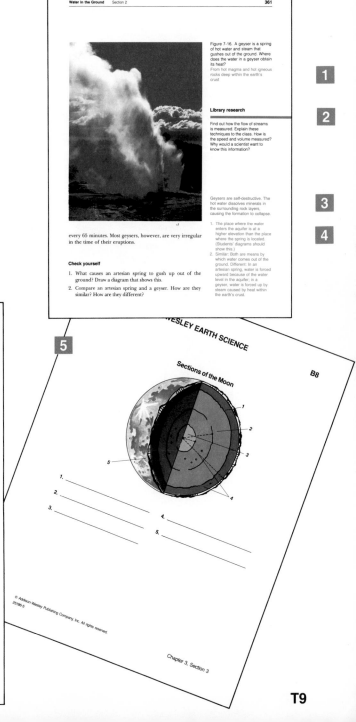

Understanding

Addison-Wesley Earth Science

1 Illustrations, diagrams, tables, graphs, and maps help students absorb and visualize information and data.

2 Many of the captions ask questions that motivate students to interpret and analyze visual clues.

3 New science words are boldfaced, defined in context, and cross-referenced in the glossary to aid in understanding concepts.

4 Phonetic pronunciations are provided for vocabulary words when needed.

5 Margin questions focus students' attention on important information.

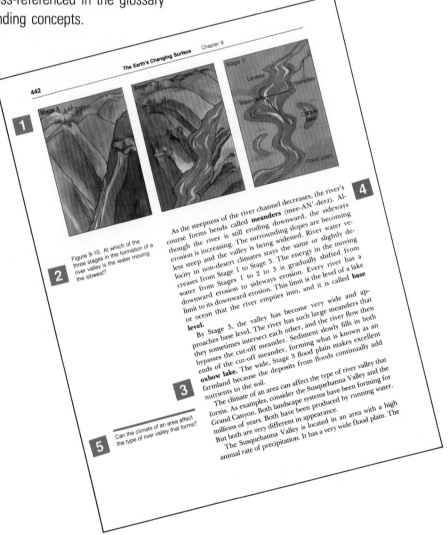

The Earth's Changing Surface — Chapter 9

442

Stage 1 · Stage 2 · Stage 3

Levees · Tributaries · Meanders · Oxbow lake · Flood plain

Figure 9-10. At which of the three stages in the formation of a river valley is the water moving the slowest?

As the steepness of the river channel decreases, the river's course forms bends called **meanders** (mee-AN'-derz). Although the river is still eroding downward, the sideways erosion is increasing. The surrounding slopes are becoming less steep and the valley is being widened. River water velocity in non-desert climates stays the same or slightly decreases from Stage 1 to Stage 3. The energy in the moving water from Stages 1 to 2 to 3 is gradually shifted from downward erosion to sideways erosion. Every river has a limit to its downward erosion. This limit is the level of a lake or ocean that the river empties into, and it is called **base level.**

By Stage 3, the valley has become very wide and approaches base level. The river has such large meanders that they sometimes intersect each other, and the river flow then bypasses the cut-off meander. Sediment slowly fills in both ends of the cut-off meander, forming what is known as an **oxbow lake.** The wide, Stage 3 flood plain makes excellent farmland because the deposits from floods continually add nutrients to the soil.

The climate of an area can affect the type of river valley that forms. As examples, consider the Susquehanna Valley and the Grand Canyon. Both landscape systems have been forming for millions of years. Both have been produced by running water. But both are very different in appearance.

The Susquehanna Valley is located in an area with a high annual rate of precipitation. It has a very wide flood plain. The

Can the climate of an area affect the type of river valley that forms?

T10

focuses on understanding and thinking skills.

1 A three-stage process for developing **Thinking Skills** helps students identify, analyze, and synthesize information.

2 Featured skills include classifying, observing, comparing, inferring, analyzing, and evaluating.

3 Skills are applied specifically to earth science concepts in related text.

4 **Activities** throughout the text encourage students to practice using these thinking skills.

5 **Critical Thinking** questions in the text margins help develop problem-solving and decision-making skills.

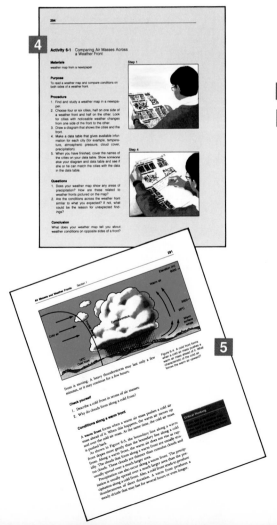

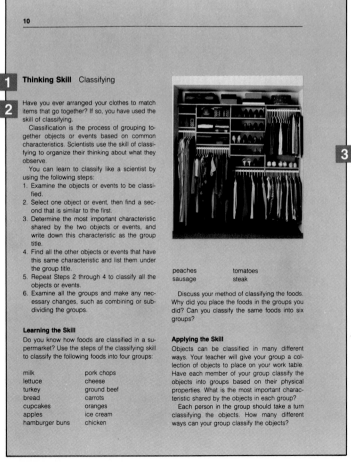

1 **Thinking Skill** Classifying

2 Have you ever arranged your clothes to match items that go together? If so, you have used the skill of classifying.

Classification is the process of grouping together objects or events based on common characteristics. Scientists use the skill of classifying to organize their thinking about what they observe.

You can learn to classify like a scientist by using the following steps:

1. Examine the objects or events to be classified.
2. Select one object or event, then find a second that is similar to the first.
3. Determine the most important characteristic shared by the two objects or events, and write down this characteristic as the group title.
4. Find all the other objects or events that have this same characteristic and list them under the group title.
5. Repeat Steps 2 through 4 to classify all the objects or events.
6. Examine all the groups and make any necessary changes, such as combining or subdividing the groups.

3

peaches   tomatoes
sausage   steak

Discuss your method of classifying the foods. Why did you place the foods in the groups you did? Can you classify the same foods into six groups?

Learning the Skill

Do you know how foods are classified in a supermarket? Use the steps of the classifying skill to classify the following foods into four groups:

milk	pork chops
lettuce	cheese
turkey	ground beef
bread	carrots
cupcakes	oranges
apples	ice cream
hamburger buns	chicken

Applying the Skill

Objects can be classified in many different ways. Your teacher will give your group a collection of objects to place on your work table. Have each member of your group classify the objects into groups based on their physical properties. What is the most important characteristic shared by the objects in each group?

Each person in the group should take a turn classifying the objects. How many different ways can your group classify the objects?

T11

Applying

Addison-Wesley Earth Science

1 Frequent hands-on **Activities** develop valuable process skills and aid students in understanding concepts.

2 **Activity Record Sheets** are organized for meaningful data collection and analysis.

3 Additional **Investigations** can enrich students' hands-on experience.

4 Optional **Research Labs** provide students with opportunities to develop hypotheses, and to design and conduct experiments.

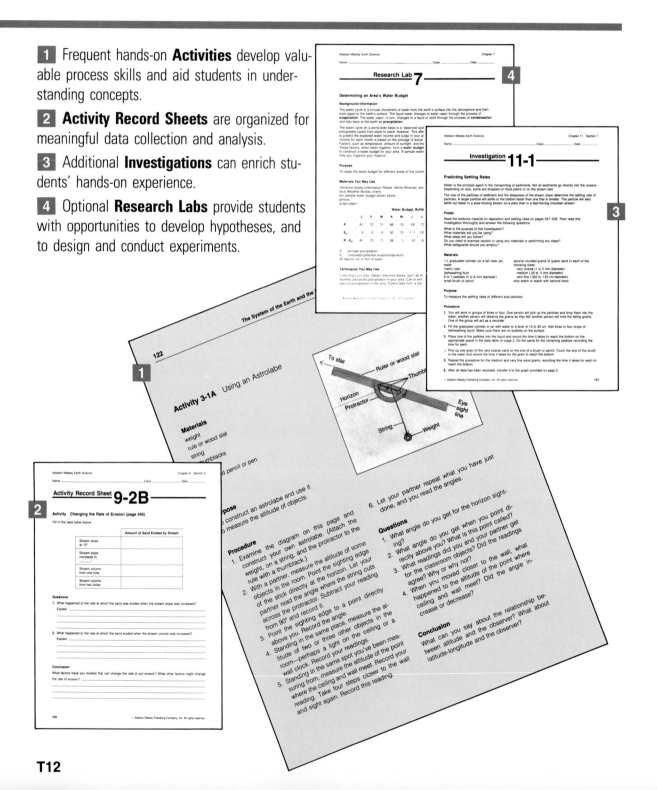

involves students with applications to the real world.

1 **Science Issues of Today** encourage debate and creative thinking about the environment and technology.

2 **Career** options show students a wide range of job opportunities in which earth science skills are utilized.

3 **Our Science Heritage** features explain how discoveries are applied in some of today's technology.

4 **Apply Your Knowledge** questions in the Chapter Reviews encourage students to integrate chapter concepts.

5 **Find Out on Your Own** topics challenge students to independent discovery.

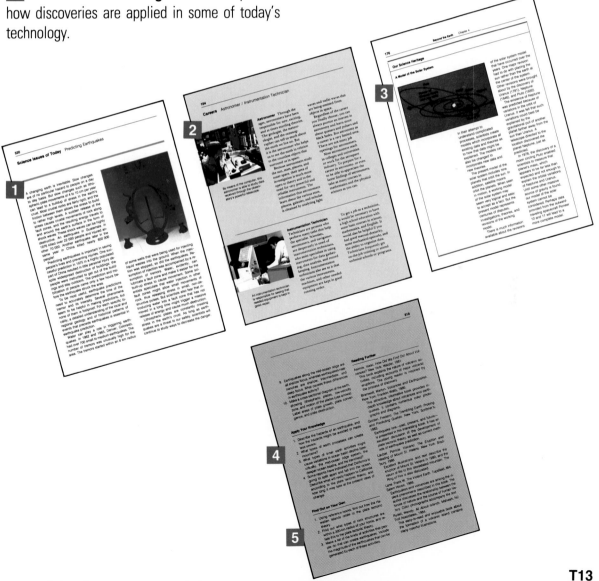

Meeting Needs

Addison-Wesley Earth Science

1 **Reinforce** basic skills and reteach essential concepts.

2 **Core** needs are developed with frequent review and practice.

3 **Enrich** and extend chapter concepts to further challenge students.

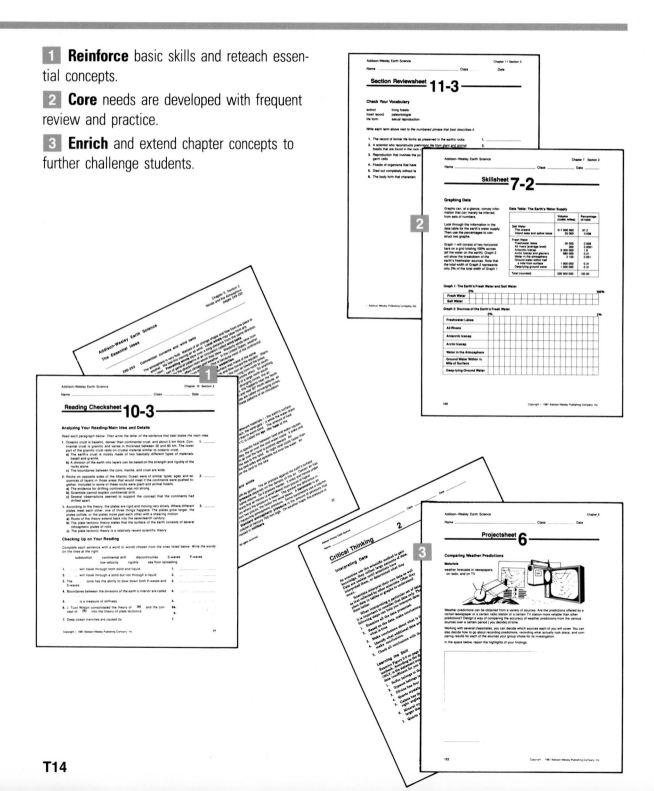

meets the needs of your students.

1 Frequent **Reviews** develop recall, analysis, synthesis, and application skills.

2 **Section Tests, Chapter Tests,** and **Semester Tests** provide a convenient way to evaluate concept understanding, data interpretation, and comprehensive knowledge.

3 **Testing Software** is available for a fast and easy way to create your own tests.

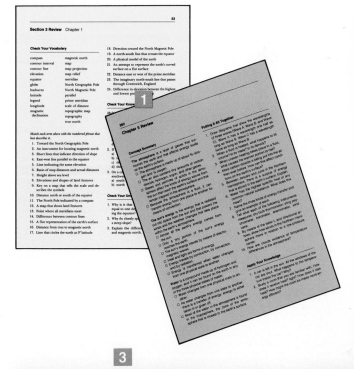

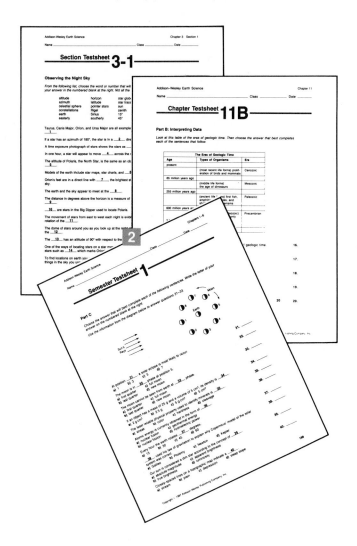

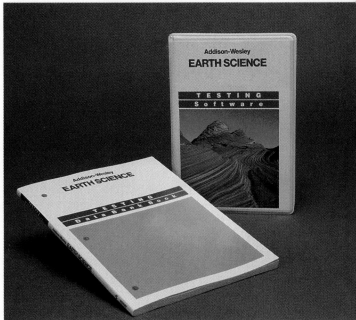

Flexibility

Addison-Wesley Earth Science

Comprehensibility

Addison-Wesley Earth Science

1 Readability is controlled at grade level for junior high school students.

2 Vocabulary is developed in context, phonetically spelled, and cross-referenced in the glossary.

3 Captions and margin questions help students grasp the main ideas and principles.

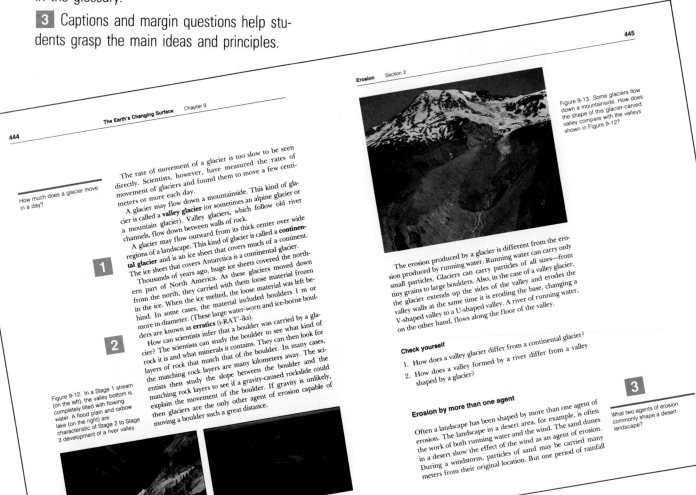

assures comprehensibility for your students.

1 **Reading Checksheets** encourage students to analyze their reading and develop comprehension skills.

2 **Essential Ideas** worksheets summarize the most important concepts.

3 Supplemental materials assist students at all levels in understanding earth science topics.

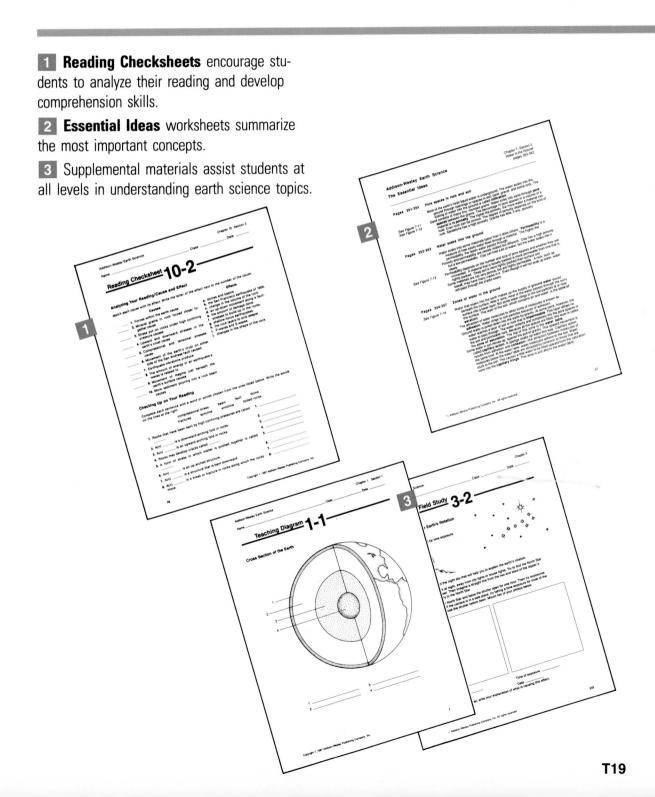

Scope and Sequence of Addison-Wesley Earth Science

Chapter & Section	Main Concepts	Skills
Chapter 1	**Studying the Earth**	
1-1 Learning About the Earth	**Learning** involves gathering data through observation, processing and classifying data, and forming inferences on the basis of relationships drawn from the data. **The earth** is the sum total of all earth materials and all earth processes. **Earth science** involves all the different sciences that study particular earth materials and processes.	To display data on average height in graphic form
1-2 An International System of Measuring	**The metric system** is an accurate international system of measuring that is based on multiples of ten.	To measure length, volume, and mass, using base units in the SI system To find the mass of four different amounts of water
1-3 Mapping the Earth's Surface	**Maps** are graphic representations of all or part of the earth's surface.	To locate some places on the earth using latitude and longitude To find the north-south line using shadows cast by the sun
Chapter 2	**Earth Materials**	
2-1 The Nature of Matter	**Matter** is anything that occupies space and has mass.	To show how the input of heat energy changes water from a solid to a liquid to a gas To use the periodic table to identify 10 mystery elements
2-2 Minerals	**Minerals** are naturally occurring, inorganic, crystalline solids.	To learn a way of classifying minerals by their physical properties To test unidentified mineral specimens for physical properties
2-3 Rocks	Most **rocks** are combinations of two or more minerals.	To learn how layers of sediment form and how these layers can change To use a key to determine the class of a rock sample

Chapter & Section	Main Concepts	Skills
Chapter 3	**The System of the Earth and the Moon**	
3-1 Observing the Night Sky	The **celestial sphere** is a useful model of the night sky.	To construct an astrolabe and use it to measure the altitude of objects
		To find your latitude by measuring the altitude of Polaris
		To follow the paths of four stars across the sky during one evening
3-2 Earth Motions	**The earth's rotation** is the turning of the earth on its axis once a day	To simulate the Coriolis effect
	The earth's axis is the imaginary line around which the earth spins.	To show how the revolution of the earth and the inclination of the earth's axis cause the seasons
	The earth's revolution is the orbiting of the earth around the sun once a year.	
	The earth's inclination is the tilting of the earth's axis 23.5° off the vertical.	
3-3 The Moon	The **moon,** which is the earth's only natural satellite, is like the earth in some ways and unlike the earth in other ways.	To use indirect measurement to calculate the diameters of a classroom clock and the moon

Chapter & Section	Main Concepts	Skills
Chapter 4	**Beyond the Earth**	
4-1 The Solar System	The **solar system** is the sun and all the objects that revolve around the sun.	To draw a model of the solar system
4-2 The Stars	The **sun** is the star that provides the earth's energy and is the star around which all the planets revolve.	To calculate the distance between the earth and the sun
	A **star** is a light- and heat-producing celestial object that has evolved from a cloud of dust and gas.	To illustrate apparent brightness and magnitude, using light bulbs
		To see how parallax displacement works
4-3 The Galaxies and Beyond	A **galaxy** is an enormous group of stars that is held together by gravitational attraction.	To imitate the action of an expanding universe
	The universe probably came into being through an explosion called the **Big Bang.**	

Chapter & Section	Main Concepts	Skills
Chapter 5	**The Atmosphere**	
5-1 Heat and the Atmosphere	**The atmosphere** is a layer of gases that surrounds the earth and that affects energy levels on the earth's surface.	To see how the angle of incoming light affects energy received To see how the angle of light coming from the sun affects heating at the earth's surface
5-2 Winds and the Atmosphere	**The sun's energy** is the energy that is radiated out into space from the sun and that powers the winds and the weather changes that take place within the earth's atmosphere.	To trace the movement of a convection current in a fluid To compare the specific heats of water and sand or soil
5-3 Moisture and the Atmosphere	**Water** is a compound made up of hydrogen and oxygen, and it can be found on the earth in any of the three physical states of matter.	To use a sling psychrometer to find the relative humidity of the air To find the dew-point temperature of the air you are breathing

Chapter & Section	Main Concepts	Skills
Chapter 6	**Weather and Climate**	
6-1 Air Masses and Weather Fronts	An **air mass** is a large body of air that moves as a unit and that has more or less uniform characteristics throughout. A **weather front** is the boundary between two air masses and often produces a change in the weather.	To read a weather map and compare conditions on both sides of a weather front
6-2 Predicting the Weather	A **station model** is a clear and simple way of recording weather conditions at a particular weather station. A **weather map** is a representation of weather conditions over an area of the earth's surface.	To predict weather patterns based on weather maps To understand how severe weather conditions occur and how they affect people
6-3 Climate	**Climate** is the average weather conditions, primarily moisture and air temperature, that occur in one place over a year or longer.	To compare climates at three different locations To see how plants of the same kind are affected by different climates

Chapter & Section	Main Concepts	Skills
Chapter 7	**The Earth's Fresh Water**	
7-1 Water on the Ground	In the **water cycle,** water is continually recycled between the earth's surface and the atmosphere, changing form (through evaporation, condensation, and freezing) because of different atmospheric conditions.	To graph an amount of rainfall and the resulting amount of stream discharge To see evidence of the part transpiration plays in the water cycle
7-2 Water in the Ground	**Infiltration** is the process by which water sinks into the ground. **Porosity** is the total volume of the pore spaces in a material. **Permeability** is the ease with which water flows through a material.	To see if you can make a needle stay on the surface of water To build a model of a water table
Chapter 8	**The Ocean**	
8-1 The Bottom of the Ocean	**Oceans and seas** cover nearly 71% of the earth's surface. The **ocean bottom** has a varied topography.	To calculate the density of two different materials and then compare their elevations above water as they float To take soundings of an underwater surface you cannot see and to use the results to reconstruct topographic features of the underwater surface
8-2 Properties of Ocean Water	**Physical properties of ocean water** affect the ocean environment.	To see what happens when salt water evaporates
8-3 The Circulation of Ocean Water	**Ocean water movements** affect the ocean environment, the coastline, and the climate.	To use a rope to imitate the motion of a wave To compare the absorption of heat by different materials

Chapter & Section	Main Concepts	Skills
Chapter 9	**The Earth's Changing Surface**	
9-1 Weathering	**Weathering** is the breaking down and wearing away of earth materials.	To look at relationships between soils and rocks
	Physical weathering occurs when earth materials are reduced in size.	To compare weathering rates in different rocks
	Chemical weathering occurs when new substances are formed from earth materials.	
9-2 Erosion	**Erosion** involves the transport of weathered earth materials from one place to another.	To study the factors that affect the rate of soil erosion
9-3 Deposition	**Deposition** occurs when particles of earth materials are deposited by an agent of erosion.	To examine a geologic core sample
		To learn where erosion and deposition patterns occur in a stream
		To infer geologic history by comparing two model core samples
Chapter 10	**The Restless Crust**	
10-1 Volcanoes	**Volcanic activity** occurs when lava, gas, or solid fragments come out of a vent in the earth's crust.	To infer lava viscosity from volcanic materials
		To learn to translate a topographic map of a volcanic cone into a profile view
10-2 Stress, Structure, and Earthquakes	**Folded structures** are caused by shape changes in rocks.	To study the relationship between synclines and anticlines
	Faults are breaks in the earth's crust along which the rocks have moved.	To make a model of a geologic fault
	Earthquakes are caused by movement along a fault or by volcanic activity.	To simulate a variety of geologic faults
10-3 Plate Tectonics	The **interior of the earth** is made of layers of different densities and rigidity.	To study the relationships between the present continents and Pangaea
	The theory of continental drift states that the continents have moved around the surface of the earth over the top of the oceanic crust.	To simulate sea-floor spreading
	The sea floor spreading theory states that ocean basins spread apart as the ocean crust grows at the mid-ocean ridges.	
	The plate tectonic theory states that the earth's lithosphere is constantly forming and being destroyed, and that the continents are slowly carried around on top of the lithosphere.	

Chapter & Section	Main Concepts	Skills
Chapter 11	**The Earth's Geologic History**	
11-1 Unraveling the Rock Record	An **assumption** is the taking for granted that a certain process or scientific law remains constant through time and place. **Theories** are working statements intended to be tested, modified, added to, or replaced. The **rock record** is the history of the earth as recorded in its crustal rocks.	To examine the principle of superposition To learn to examine a geologic cross-section for clues to faunal succession
11-2 Dating the Rock Record	**Absolute age determinations** estimate the age of the earth in years. Such age determinations have been made in many ways. **Geologic time** is a method of age determination that dates the earth's history not by years but by eras and periods of time.	To simulate half-life decay of radioactive elements
11-3 A Parade of Life Forms	The **fossil record** is the record of former life forms as preserved in the earth's rocks.	To learn to distinguish between a fossil mold and a fossil cast To distinguish different types of fossils and infer their original environments
Chapter 12	**Environmental Concerns**	
12-1 Using Earth Materials	**Earth materials** consist of all the matter found on earth.	To learn three ways to separate earth materials To learn about the supply of and demand for the world's metal ores
12-2 Preserving the Environment	The **earth's resources** are limited and must be preserved because they are necessary for all life on earth.	To see if a recycling program can pay for the cost of waste disposal and provide an affordable source of raw materials To select the best fuel for a new power plant on the imaginary planet Klar

Software for Earth Science

Addison-Wesley
Information Laboratory Software

Addison-Wesley's Information Laboratory software enables you to teach computer literacy, learning skills, and earth science at the same time. The software is easy and fun to use. With only minimum instruction, students will be exploring this powerful database on their own. Because it covers every topic in Addison-Wesley *Earth Science*, the Information Laboratory can be useful every day of the school year.

Over 900 **data cards** make up the heart of the software. Each card contains facts and descriptions about an earth science topic, such as glaciers or constellations. Many cards also have illustrations. The cards are linked together in hierarchical arrangements. The user can enter these hierar-

chies at any level and have access to **decks** of related cards.

The Information Laboratory also helps teachers meet individual needs. Blackline-master **searchsheets**, written at three levels of student ability, are provided to guide students through information searches covering subject areas in the text.

Information Laboratory is designed to run on any Apple II series computer. An enhanced version is now available to run on the Apple IIGS. It features color graphics, pull-down menus, and the ability to manipulate illustrations. Both versions of the Information Laboratory come complete with disks, tutorials, and searchsheets.

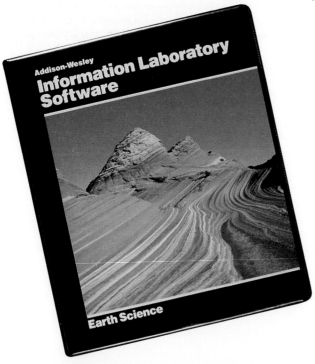

Addison-Wesley Testing Software

Addison-Wesley Earth Science Testing Software provides you with a convenient and flexible way to create tests. This makes it easy for you to evaluate student performance based on the material you cover in class. All you need is an Apple IIe or IIc, a printer, and Addison-Wesley Earth Science Testing Software.

The testing data base contains over 1,000 questions. You can easily browse through those questions in the Data Bank Book. You can use the questions as they exist or change them to meet your specific needs.

You can also add your own questions. This allows you to customize tests according to your state or district objectives. Finally, multiple versions of any given test can be made for classroom use.

Step-by-step instructions are provided with the program to guide you each step of the way.

Required Hardware: Apple II+, IIe, or IIc
64 K RAM
printer

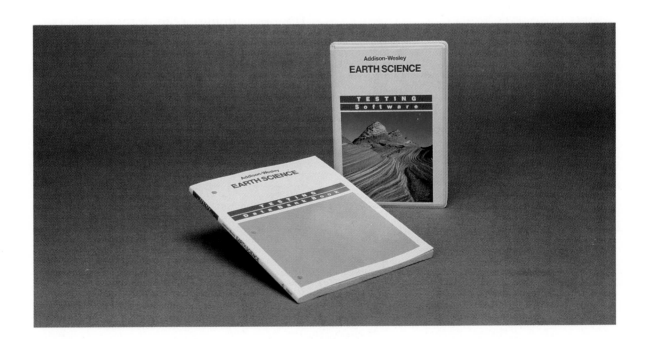

Selecting Earth Science Software

Educational software for earth science falls into several categories.

- Tutorial software teaches a concept step-by-step. Some rely heavily on graphics and animation, while other software is basically a reading experience.

- Simulation software depicts a process or an activity graphically.

- Instructional games use the motivation of fun and competition to teach concepts or to pass on information.

When evaluating software, consider the following points.

- Is the software a tutorial, a simulation, or an instructional game?

- Is the software designed for the remediation, reinforcement, or introduction of new material?

- Is the software interactive? Does it require the student to key in information and "work" with the computer or is this software mainly looked at or read?

- Is there documentation (written material) to accompany the software?

- Are the instructions on the screen or in the documentation clear and easy to follow?

- Does the software do something that could not be done in a text or workbook?

- Is there too much emphasis on attractive graphics and animation and not enough on science content?

- Are there positive rewards for correct answers and nonjudgmental responses for incorrect answer?

- Are the readability and concept levels appropriate for your students?

Ordering Software

Each publisher may have different ordering policies. Consider the following points before ordering software.

- Is the software compatible with the type, model, and memory capacity of your computer?

- Does the program come with a backup disk?

- Does the publisher offer a 30-day evaluation period during which time you can preview the software?

- Does the publisher have a policy for replacing defective disks?

- Is there a telephone hotline service available for technical assistance should it be needed?

- Does the publisher have a quantity discount policy?

- Does the publisher have a networking policy?

Earth science software is distributed by equipment supply houses as well as by software distributors.

For preplanning, write to the suppliers for further information about the software you wish to purchase. You may wish to request catalogs, order forms, and the latest prices.

Sources of Software Reviews

Educational Computing Journals

AEDS Journal
Association for Educational Data Systems
1201 Sixteenth Street, N.W.
Washington DC 20036

AEDS Monitor
Association for Educational Data Systems
1201 Sixteenth Street, N.W.
Washington DC 20036

Classroom Computer Learning
2451 East River Road
Dayton OH 45439

The Computing Teacher
International Council for Computers in Education
1787 Agate
University of Oregon
Eugene OR 97403

Educational Computer
Box 535
Cupertino CA 95015

Electronic Education
1311 Executive Center Drive
Suite 220
Tallahassee FL 32301

Electronic Learning
902 Sylvan Avenue
Englewood Cliffs NJ 07632

Journal of Computers in Mathematics & Science Teaching
Box 4455
Austin TX 78765

Microcomputers in Education
5 Chapel Hill Drive
Fairfield CT 06432

Review Journals

Booklist
50 East Huron Street
Chicago IL 60611

Courseware Report Card
150 West Carob Street
Compton CA 90220

Digest of Software Reviews: Education
1341 Bulldog Lane Suite C
Fresno CA 93710

Peelings II (Apple)
Box 699
Las Cruces NM 88004

School Library Journal
205 East 42nd Street
New York NY 10017

School Microwave Reviews
Dresden Associates
Box 246
Dresden ME 04342

Computer Journals

BYTE
70 Main Street
Peterborough NH 03458

Creative Computing
39 East Hanover Avenue
Morris Plains NJ 07950

Infoworld
530 Lytton Avenue
Suite 303
Palo Alto CA 94301

Interface Age
16704 Marquardt Avenue
Cerritos CA 90701

Microcomputing
80 Pine Street
Peterborough NH 03458

Nibble (Apple)
Box 325
Lincoln MA 01773

Personal Computing
50 Essex Street
Rochelle Park NJ 07662

SoftSide
10 Northern Boulevard
Northwood Executive Park
Amherst NH 03031

Softalk Magazine (Apple)
7250 Laurel Canyon Boulevard
North Hollywood CA 91603

Software Producers and Distributors

Apple Computer, Inc.
20525 Mariani Avenue
Cupertino CA 95014

Cambridge Development Lab
1696 Massachusetts Avenue
Cambridge MA 02138

Carolina Biological Supply Co.
2700 York Road
Burlington NC 27215

CBS Software
CBS, Inc.
Greenwich CT 06836

Datatech Software Systems, Inc
19312 E. Eldorado Drive
Aurora CO 80013

Diversified Educational Enterprises
752 Main Street
Lafayette IN 47901

Educational Activities, Inc.
Box 392
Freeport NY 11520

Focus Media, Inc.
839 Stewart Avenue
Box 865
Garden City NY 11530

IBM
3301 Windy Ridge Parkway
Marietta GA 30067

J & S Software
14 Vanderventer
Port Washington NY 11050

MECC (Minnesota Educational Computing Corporation)
3490 Lexington Avenue N.
St. Paul MN 55126

Micro–Ed, Inc.
8108 Eden Road
Eden Prairie MN 55344

Micro Learningware
Route 1, Box 162
Amboy MN 56010

Nasco
901 Janesville Avenue
Fort Atkinson WI 53538

Nationwide Computer Products
Box 61
3180 South Pennsylvania Avenue
Morrisville PA 19067

Opportunities for Learning, Inc.
20417 Nordhoff Street
Room VP5
Chatsworth CA 91311

Orange Cherry Media
P.O. Box 390
Pound Ridge NY 10576

Quantum Technologies, Inc.
P. O. Box 1396
Englewood CO 80150

Scholastic Software
730 Broadway
New York NY 10003

Schoolmasters
745 State Circle
Ann Arbor MI 48106

Title of Software Program
Explorer Metros: A Metric Adventure

Correlates to Chapters

1   5   6

of *Addison-Wesley Earth Science*

Producer/Distributor Sunburst Communications, 39 Washington Avenue, Pleasantville NY 10570

Copyright 1982   **Price** $49.00

Grade Levels 4–9

Compatible Hardware Apple (48K)

Subject Area(s) Metric Measurement, Mass, Capacity, Length, Temperature

Type of Program Simulation, Problem Solving

Features Graphics,   Animation

Student Materials 1 record sheet

Documentation 27 pages—introduction, objectives, program description, suggestions for classroom use, student and teacher record sheets, information about Explorer Metros: Editor

Program Description This program gives students the opportunity to use their knowledge of the metric system, their decision-making skills, and their mathematical skills. "Explorer Metros" is a rocket ship on a journey to explore a space colony near Mars in 1993. Once at the space colony, the student has eight hours in which to make decisions about twelve encounters. Each encounter describes a problem. Solving the problem depends on the student's correct understanding of the metric measurement given in that situation. Incorrect answers use time more rapidly.

This program can be used over and over again because the values for the metric measurements change every time the program is run. Twenty-seven different encounters are possible.

Overall this program provides a very motivating and interesting way for a student to review his or her knowledge of the metric system.

Title of Software Program
Planetary Construction Set

Correlates to Chapters

1   3   4

of *Addison-Wesley Earth Science*

Producer/Distributor Sunburst Communications, 39 Washington Avenue, Pleasantville NY 10570

Copyright 1985   **Price** $59.00

Grade Levels 7-up

Compatible Hardware Apple (48K)

Subject Area(s) Stars, Planets, Measurements

Type of Program Tutorial, Drill and Practice, Problem Solving

Features Graphics

Student Materials Logbooks, activity sheets

Documentation 51 pages—introduction, objectives, overview, suggestions for classroom use

Program Description *Planetary Construction Set* is designed to familiarize students with the scientific process—the ability to generate hypotheses, design experiments, gather and analyze data, and draw conclusions.

There are six selections: Cadet's Briefing, Cadet's Mission, Captain's Briefing, Captain's Mission, Descriptions, End. The briefing sequences introduce students to scientific information they will need to know to perform the missions. Students should take notes to prepare themselves to carry out the mission.

The Cadet's Mission is to build planets through experimental determination of such variables as star type, planet mass, planet distance, planet atmosphere, planet inclination, and number of satellites. The Captain's Mission is to design a planet that will sustain a particular life form. The alien selected determines the difficulty of the mission. By pressing the H key, students can receive instant help if they have a problem while building a planet.

Title of Software Program
Earth Science

Correlates to Chapters

1   2   4   10

of *Addison-Wesley Earth Science*

Producer/Distributor Orange Cherry Media, P.O. Box 390, Pound Ridge NY 10576

Copyright 1983   **Price** $78.00

Grade Levels 7–12

Compatible Hardware Apple (48K)

Subject Area(s) Scientific Method, The Earth, Erosion, Rocks, Mountains, Earthquakes, Volcanoes, Solar Energy

Type of Program Tutorial, Instructional Game

Features Graphics, Sound, Color

Student Materials None

Documentation 8 pages—introduction, objectives, review of material in program, examples of review questions

Program Description The program consists of two disks. The lessons are the Changing Face of the Earth, Rocks and Mountains, Questions and Answers About the Earth, Energy from the Sun.

The Changing Face of the Earth teaches such concepts as the age of the earth, how the earth was formed and how it is changing, layers of the earth, erosion, and faults.

In Rocks and Mountains, the program gives examples of each type of rock (igneous, sedimentary, and metamorphic) and how each type of rock is created, followed by a series of questions.

In Questions and Answers About the Earth, the student may select from six categories of questions: the Earth in Space, the Earth We Live On, the Changing Face of the Earth, Rocks and Riches from the Earth, Earthquakes, Volcanic Eruptions.

Energy from the Sun teaches students concepts and practical applications of solar energy.

Title of Software Program
The Earth Through Time and Space

Correlates to Chapters

3   4   11

of *Addison-Wesley Earth Science*

Producer/Distributor Educational Activities, P.O. Box 392, Freeport NY 11520

Copyright 1986   **Price** $59.95

Grade Levels 5–9

Compatible Hardware Apple (48K)

Subject Area(s) The Planet Earth, Solar System, Fossils

Type of Program Tutorial, Simulation

Features Graphics, Animation, Sound

Student Materials Worksheets

Documentation 8 pages—overview, objectives, answer key

Program Description The program begins with a geological history of the earth, The Earth Through Time. It describes how the earth developed and presents theories of its age through geological and fossil records. There is a colorful graphic time line illustrating the major events in geological history.

The last two lessons, The Earth and the Moon and Exploring Our Solar System, explore the planets, their orbits, characteristics, and satellites. Animated sequences demonstrate lunar and solar eclipses, the moon's phases, and the effect of the moon on the earth's tides. Students manipulate a robot space-probe through the solar system to identify and explore each planet. These journeys include the planets' positions within the solar system, their relative and absolute sizes, their sizes with respect to the sun, their satellites, their atmospheric composition, and the shapes and duration of their orbits around the sun.

Title of Software Program
Surface Water, Moisture in the Atmosphere, Ground Water (Earth Science Series)

Correlates to Chapters

5   6   7

of *Addison-Wesley Earth Science*

Producer/Distributor IBM, 3301 Windy Ridge Parkway, Marietta GA 30067

Copyright 1984   **Price** $49.00 Each

Grade Levels 9–12

Compatible Hardware IBM (128K)

Subject Area(s) Water, Pollution, Conservation

Type of Program Tutorial, Simulation, Problem Solving

Features Animation, Graphics, Color

Student Materials None

Documentation 44 pages—description of program, learning objectives, synopsis, supplemental questions/answers, glossary, index.

Program Description *Surface Water, Moisture in the Atmosphere,* and *Ground Water* are designed to help students learn about the processes at work in the physical environment and to identify how these processes affect people and the environment.

Surface Water illustrates how water moves over the surface of the earth in the form of overland flow and stream channel flow, ways in which lakes evolve, stream patterns, and processes of erosion, transportation, and deposition, and describes the results of damming, urbanization, and so on.

Moisture in the Atmosphere explains how moisture moves through the atmosphere; the ways in which humidity is expressed, affects human comfort, and changes; how dew, frost, fog, clouds, and raindrops form, how clouds are classified, and the ways in which air can lift and collect to form clouds.

Ground Water describes how water moves into the ground and is stored, why some rocks make good aquifers and others do not, how artesian aquifers and flowing wells are created, and the relationship between the water table and springs, wells, lakes, and rivers.

Title of Software Program
Water and Weather

Correlates to Chapters

5   6   7   8

of *Addison-Wesley Earth Science*

Producer/Distributor Focus Media, Inc., 839 Stewart Avenue, Garden City NY 11530

Copyright 1983   **Price** $89.00

Grade Level 7–12

Compatible Hardware Apple (48K)

Subject Area(s) Water Cycle, Humidity, Clouds, Precipitation

Type of Program Tutorial, Instructional Game

Features Animation, Graphics

Student Materials None

Documentation 39 pages—learning objectives, synopses of the games, teaching suggestions, student suggestions, background information, follow-up questions and answers

Program Description This program's three lessons—The Water Cycle, Humidity, Clouds and Precipitation—consist of a series of questions and a game. Each time a correct answer is given, the student is given a chance to play the game. Each time an incorrect answer is given, the student is asked if he or she wants some help.

In the first game the student can select from one to twenty questions related to the water cycle. Each time a student answers a question correctly, the screen becomes a shooting gallery, and the student can acquire points by hitting a moving target.

Humidity, the second game, involves an auto race, in which the student can either race against the computer or against another student.

Title of Software Program
Quakes (Science Volume 3)

Correlates to Chapter

10

of *Addison-Wesley Earth Science*

Producer/Distributor MECC, 3490 Lexington Avenue North, St. Paul MN 55112

Copyright 1980   **Price** $49.00

Grade Levels 7–12

Compatible Hardware Apple (48K)

Subject Area(s) Earthquakes

Type of Program Tutorial, Simulation, Problem Solving

Features Graphics, Color Optional

Student Materials Activity sheets

Documentation 21 pages—description, objectives, background information, lesson plans, suggested activities, and sample screens

Program Description *Quakes* has three parts: An Explanation, A Lesson, and A Quake. The Explanation introduces the student to a number of terms associated with earthquakes. The Lesson guides students through the calculations necessary to find the location of an earthquake. The Quake gives the student a chance to locate the epicenter of a "real" earthquake. Data about the primary and secondary waves is given from three seismographic stations. It is then up to the student to locate the epicenter using the information given and the locator box on the screen. Once the student is satisfied that he or she has moved the locator box to the epicenter, the space bar is pressed. The computer then tells the student how close or how far off he or she was.

Graphics are used to show the primary and secondary waves on the seismographs.

Title of Software Program
Weather

Correlates to Chapters

5 6 7 8 9

of *Addison-Wesley Earth Science*

Producer/Distributor Educational Activities, Inc., P.O. Box 392, Freeport, NY 11520

Copyright 1983   **Price** $59.00

Grade Levels 5–12

Compatible Hardware Apple (48K), Commodore 64, TRS-80

Subject Area(s) Air Pressure, Humidity, Temperature and Wind

Type of Program Tutorial

Features Graphics, Animation

Student Materials None

Documentation 10 pages—introduction, program description, objectives, sample screens, teaching strategies, management system, and operating instructions for the computer

Program Description This program contains three lessons: Air Pressure, Humidity, and Temperature and Wind. The topics covered include barometers, wind, high and low pressure, wind speed, wind direction, anemometers, water droplets, water vapor, evaporation, how clouds are created, rain, relative humidity, precipitation, the water cycle, wind patterns, and Fahrenheit and Celsius scales. Each topic is clearly defined as it is introduced. Many of the words are shown with pronunciation keys. The lessons present the information, continually ask questions, and support the learner with positive feedback throughout the tutorial. In response to both correct and incorrect answers, the computer comments are quite humorous. A ten-question quiz follows each lesson.

Title of Software Program
Earthquakes and Volcanoes
(Exploring Science II)

Correlates to Chapter

10

of *Addison-Wesley Earth Science*

Producer/Distributor Queue, Inc., 562 Boston Avenue, Bridgeport CT 06606

Copyright 1983   **Price** $34.95

Grade Levels 4–8

Compatible Hardware Apple (48K)

Subject Area(s) Volcanoes, Earthquakes

Type of Program Tutorial, Drill and Practice

Student Materials None

Documentation 12 pages—objectives, description of programs, operating instructions, classroom management instructions

Program Description This program is a good introduction to terminology and concepts in the earth science field. A menu lists the ten lessons from which the student can choose: Introduction, Inside Volcanoes, Volcanic Regions I and II, Volcanic Rocks, Earthquakes, Cause of "Quakes," Tsunamis, Seismographs, and Review.

Each lesson consists of a series of brief paragraphs describing an earth science term or concept. Each paragraph is followed by a multiple choice question based on the reading. If the student chooses an incorrect answer, he or she receives an explanation. A percentage of answers correct is given at the end of each lesson.

A special classroom management system may be purchased. It enables teachers to view an individual student's progress, review groups of students' achievements, and produce hard copies of both sets of data.

Title of Software Program
Dinosaur Dig

Correlates to Chapter

11

of *Addison-Wesley Earth Science*

Producer/Distributor Mindscape, 3444 Dundee Rd., Northbrook IL 60062

Copyright 1984   **Price** $49.95

Grade Levels 4–8, 9–12

Compatible Hardware Apple (48K), Commodore 64, IBM

Subject Area(s) Dinosaurs, Fossils

Type of Program Tutorial, Simulation, Educational Game

Features Graphics, Sound, Animation, Color

Student Materials 2 keyboard overlays

Documentation 17 pages—introduction, computer instructions, background information

Program Description This program has two disks. The first disk is the tutorial that allows students to learn about and compare different types of dinosaurs and discover some of their habits and characteristics. The graphics dramatically illustrate the facts and concepts concerning prehistoric life. The material on disk 1 prepares the student for the activities on disk 2.

The second disk contains five games. Dino Discovery—select a specific dinosaur to see and learn about. Dino Dig—identify dinosaurs from a series of clues given one at a time. Dino Flash—identify dinosaurs from a series of electronic flash cards. Dino Encounters: Fact or Fable—choose the dinosaurs that lived in the same time period and learn more about the Mesozoic Era. Who's Biggest?—choose the dinosaur that weighs the most.

Dinosaur Dig is a fun, motivating program that helps students to learn about dinosaurs.

Title of Software Program
Volcanoes

Correlates to Chapter

11

of *Addison-Wesley Earth Science*

Producer/Distributor Earthware Computer Services, P.O. Box 30039, Eugene OR 97403

Copyright 1982 **Price** $49.50

Grade Levels 7–12

Compatible Hardware Apple (48K)

Subject Area(s) Volcanoes

Type of Program Simulation, Instructional Game, Problem Solving

Features Animation, Graphics, Sound, Color Optional

Student Materials Two reference manuals containing instructions and worksheets, two maps.

Documentation 14 pages—instructions, objectives, sample program output, operating instructions, pretest, posttest, teacher's information, background information, follow-up activities, glossary.

Program Description *Volcanoes* is a game of strategy and cooperation that takes place in fictional Wrangelia, where volcanoes are plentiful and unstable. Armed with a map, a handbook, and a research budget, the student simulates the role of a volcanologist, learning first-hand how volcanologists predict volcanic activity, warn the local residents, and stay within an allocated budget.

The program teaches volcanic terminology and provides students practice in determining and obtaining the results of remote sensing surveys, interpreting bar graphs, keeping careful records, and interpreting scientific observation.

Volcanoes is an interesting, entertaining learning experience, with many surprises accompanied by graphics.

Title of Software Program
Energy House

Correlates to Chapter

12

of *Addison-Wesley Earth Science*

Producer/Distributor Minnesota Educational Computing Corp. (MECC), 3490 Lexington Ave. North, St. Paul, MN 55126

Copyright 1983 **Price** $40.00

Grade Levels 4–8

Compatible Hardware Apple (48K)

Subject Area(s) Energy Conservation

Type of Program Simulation, Problem Solving

Features Graphics, Sound, Animation

Student Materials 8 activity sheets

Documentation 56 pages—description, objectives, background information, command list, sample run of the program, and other teacher resources.

Program Description In *Energy House*, students move through rooms of a house to determine where energy is being lost, misused, or wasted. As the student corrects an energy waster, the energy efficiency of the house increases.

The student begins by getting directions and by choosing the number of rooms he or she wants to visit. As each room appears, the student types the commands he or she wants to correct the energy wasters (TURN OFF stereo). A thermometer shows the energy efficiency percentage in each room. Each command uses up five minutes of time whether it is a correct answer or not. The student has two hours to find all the energy wasters in the seven rooms.

The graphics and animation are fun. Students get to see windows close, lights turn off, and so on.

At the end of the program, the student's success is stated in terms of his or her energy efficiency.

Audio-Visual Materials for Earth Science

Selecting Audio-Visual Materials

All the films listed on the next few pages are in color and are available in a 16-mm format unless otherwise specified. The major film suppliers offer their films in a video format as well.

The films listed are at a level appropriate for seventh grade earth science students. However, it is always a good idea to preview films yourself before showing them to the class. You are the best judge of what is suitable for—and what will hold the attention of—your own class.

New science films are reviewed in *Science Books & Films,* a magazine published five times per year by the American Association for the Advancement of Science, Washington, DC.

Addison-Wesley Video Lessons for Earth Science

This set of seven video lessons has been developed and produced to accompany *Addison-Wesley Earth Science.* The videos are designed to allow you to present difficult concepts and skills effectively, and they provide flexibility in teaching. Each video lesson covers one class period and includes a teacher's guide with suggestions for follow-up activities.

Mineral Identification
Probing the Solar System
Weather Patterns
The Earth's Fresh Water
Plate Tectonics
Exploring the Earth's History
Laboratory Safety

Distributors and Producers of Audio-Visual Materials for Earth Science

Addresses of distributors of earth science films are given below. Before purchasing or borrowing from a distributor, check local film libraries for the film or video you wish to use.

BFA Educational Media
468 Park Avenue South
New York, NY 10016

Britannica Learning Materials
425 N. Michigan Ave.
Chicago, IL 60611

Coronet/MTI Film & Video
108 Wilmot Rd.
Deerfield, IL 60015

Encyclopaedia Britannica Educational Corp.
425 N. Michigan Ave.
Chicago, IL 60611

Eye Gate Media
3333 Elston Ave.
Chicago, IL 60618

Films for the Humanities & Sciences
P.O. Box 2053
Princeton, NJ 08543

Focus Media, Inc.
16 S. Oaks Blvd.
Plainview, NY 11803

Guidance Associates
Communications Park, Box 3000
Mount Kisco, NY 10549

Hubbard Scientific Co.
P.O. Box 104
1946 Raymond Dr.
Northbrook, IL 60062

International Film Bureau, Inc.
332 S. Michigan Ave.
Chicago, IL 60604

Modern Talking Picture Service
500 Park Street
St. Petersburg, FL 33709

NASA Public Relations
Washington, DC 20546

National Audio-Visual Center
National Archives and Records Service
General Services Administration
Order Section GD
Washington, DC 20409

National Geographic Society
Educational Services
17th & M Sts. NW
Washington, DC 20036

NOAA/Dept. of Commerce
Motion Picture Service
12231 Wilkins Ave.
Rockville, MD 20852

Time-Life Film & Video
Time & Life Bldg.
1271 Avenue of the Americas
New York, NY 10020

Ward's Natural Science Establishment, Inc.
5100 W. Henrietta Rd.
P.O. Box 92912
Rochester, NY 14692

Ztek Co.
P.O. Box 54790
Lexington, KY 40555

Chapter 1   **Studying the Earth**

A Geologist (Hawkhill Associates, 125 E Gilman St., Madison WI 53703; 80 frame filmstrip with cassette; part of the *People in Science Today Series*)

The challenges of field work, office work, and the laboratory are discussed in presenting the types of work done by geologists.

How Much Does the Earth Weigh? (Journal Films, Inc. 930 Pitner, Evanston IL 60202; 1980; 12 1/2 min)

Describes the mass, volume, and density of four main constituents of the earth: sand, rocks, soil, and water. Explains differences between weight, mass, density, and force of gravity.

Latitude and Longitude (Lucerne Films Inc., 37 Ground Pine Rd., Morris Plains NJ 07950; 9 min; also available in video)

Using animation and models, this film explains latitude and longitude, and illustrates how to use these dimensions to locate a ship at sea.

Meters, Liters, Grams (Syracuse University Film Rental Center, 1455 E. Colvin St., Syracuse NY 13210; 11 min)

Discusses base units of length, volume, and mass, and the use of prefixes.

School Lab Safety (Handel Film Corp., 8730 Sunset Blvd., W. Hollywood CA 90069; 1981; 20 min)

Alerts high school students to potentially hazardous situations that might occur in a biology, chemistry, or physics laboratory. Helpful in establishing the proper environment for a laboratory.

The Scientific Method in Action (Syracuse University Film Rental Center, 1455 E. Colvin St., Syracuse NY 13210; 19 min)

Simple examples show the scientific method in action. Includes historical material on Salk and Galileo.

Scientific Methods & Values (Hawkhill Associates Inc., 125 E. Gilman St., Madison WI 53703; 1984; part of the Time, Space & Spirit Series; 2 filmstrips with 2 cassettes)

An excellent introduction to the nature of science and scientists. Part one traces scientific contributions over the past 2500 years. Part two emphasizes how scientists do research.

The Search for Solutions (The Search for Solutions Booking Center, 708 Third Ave., New York NY 10017)

Nine free-loan films that come in sets of three. A unique program based on the joy of discovery in science. Excellent in involving students in the processes of science.

Think Metric (Syracuse University Film Rental Center, 1455 E. Colvin St., Syracuse NY 13210)

Humor is introduced in the "metric games." Uses Olympics-type setting to illustrate different metric units.

Chapter 2   **Earth Materials**

Chemistry: Elements, Compounds and Mixtures, 2nd ed. (Coronet/MTI Film & Video, 108 Wilmot Rd., Deerfield IL 60015; 1983; 20 min)

Part of a basic science series for young people. Draws the distinctions among elements, compounds, and mixtures through images that raise awareness of the forms of matter found in the world. Teachers will find the film a useful aid in reinforcing the concepts.

Explaining Matter: Chemical Change, 2nd ed. (Encyclopaedia Britannica Educational Corp., 425 N. Michigan Ave., Chicago IL 60611; 1982; 13 min)

Presents a simple and good discussion of what constitutes chemical changes and relates this information to an elementary discussion of atomic structure and chemical bonding. Suitable for introducing the subject of chemical changes at the junior-high level.

Identifying Minerals: Searching for Clues
(Focus Media Inc., 16 S. Oaks Blvd., Plainview
NY 11803; 1980; 2 color filmstrips with cas-
settes. 12–22 min or 89–91 frames each)

Attractive and useful filmstrips that define and discuss, with clear examples,
physical properties used to identify minerals. Designed so that a student can
view them and then be ready to walk
into a classroom or laboratory and perform the mineral identification tests.

Minerals and Rocks, 2nd ed. (Encyclopaedia
Britannica Educational Corp., 425 N. Michigan
Ave., Chicago IL 60611; 1979; 15 min)

High-quality photography and visual
techniques highlight the wide variety of
minerals and rocks that exist on the
earth.

Rocks That Form on the Earth's Surface
(University of California Extension Media Center,
2223 Fulton St., Berkeley CA 94720; 1965;
16 min)

Investigates processes that produce sedimentary rock. Emphasizes sandstone
and shale as examples of clastic rocks.

Rocks That Originate Underground (University of California Extension Media Center,
2223 Fulton St., Berkeley CA 94720; 1966;
23 min)

Investigates the origin of igneous and
metamorphic rocks and shows the indirect, scientific ways of studying the conditions that created underground rocks.

Unconventional Gas Resources (National Audio-Visual Center, National Archives and Records Service, General Services Administration,
Order Section GD, Washington DC 20409;
1980; 29 min)

Excellent film that looks at four unconventional sources of natural gas: eastern
shales, coal, western gas sands, and gulf
geopressured aquifers.

Chapter 3   The System of the Earth and the Moon

About Time (Visual Aids Service, University of
Illinois, Champaign IL 61820; Part 1 is 29 min;
Part 2 is 26 min)

The measurement of time is presented
through the story of Planet Q, where the
concept of time is unknown. Explains
how time is devised.

Controversy Over the Moon (Encyclopaedia
Britannica Educational Corp., 425 N. Michigan
Ave., Chicago IL 60611; 16 min)

Two geologists analyze data and discuss
theories about the origin of moon craters. Uses photographs, samples, and
models.

The Earth in Motion (Encyclopaedia Britannica Educational Corp., 425 N. Michigan Ave.,
Chicago IL 60611; 11 min)

Shows the apparent rotation of the sky,
then demonstrates the earth's rotation
and revolution. The seasons are also explained.

How to Measure Time (Visual Aids Service,
University of Illinois, Champaign IL 61820; 11 min)

Film shows that to measure time accurately you have to count it in some way.
Animation shows the earth circling the
sun, a kind of clock that measures time
in periods of one year.

How We Know the Earth Moves (BFA Educational Media, 2211 Michigan Ave., Santa Mon-
ica CA 90404; 10 min)

Uses models and animation to demonstrate both the earth's rotation and
revolution.

Latitude, Longitude, and Time Zones
(Coronet/MTI Film & Video, 108 Wilmot Rd.,
Deerfield IL 60015; 14 min)

Uses models and animation to explain
parallels, meridians, and their use in describing location. Also demonstrates the
earth's rotation and time zones.

Target Moon (ACI Films Inc., 35 W. 45th St.,
New York NY 10036; 24 min)

Provides documentation of attempts to
travel to the moon and surveys the principles of space flight.

Chapter 4   **Beyond the Earth**

Exploration of the Planets (NASA Public Relations, Washington DC 20546; 25 min)

Depicts principal features of the planets and plans for their exploration. Contains information about orbits and gravity.

Is Anyone Out There? The Quest for Extraterrestrial Life (Knowledge Unlimited, Box 52, Madison WI 53701; 1984; 1 filmstrip, 39 frames, with optional cassette)

Presents the scientific and philosophical aspects of the debate on extraterrestrial life.

Orbital Shapes and Paths (Journal Films Inc., 930 Pitner, Evanston IL 60202; 1984; part of the Space Science Series; 10 min; also available in video)

Explains the simple relationships among orbital parameters and then shows elliptical orbits and circularization. Equatorial orbits and ground tracks for inclined orbits are illustrated through animation, and satellite coverage of the earth is shown.

The Solar System (International Film Bureau, 332 S. Michigan Ave., Chicago IL 60604; 21 min)

Utilizes time-lapse photography, diagrams, and animation to describe the solar system and its relation to the Milky Way. Also includes a history of the Ptolemaic system and data on radio and optical astronomy.

The Solar System and Beyond (National Geographic Society, Educational Services, 17th & M Sts. NW, Washington DC 20036; 1985; 4 filmstrips, 55 frames each, with 4 cassettes)

Describes the sun, the earth and moon, the nine planets, the asteroids, comets, and meteorites, and the stars and galaxies. Excellent quality and accurate information.

Three Degrees (New York Telephone Film Library, West Glen Film, 1430 Broadway [9th floor], New York NY 10018; 25 min)

A re-creation of the experiments that helped confirm the "Big Bang Theory" of the origin of the universe.

Chapter 5   **The Atmosphere**

The Atmosphere in Motion (Encyclopaedia Britannica Educational Corp., 425 N. Michigan Ave., Chicago IL 60611; 1981; 20 min)

Convection cells, the Coriolis effect, and the composition and structure of the atmosphere are revealed through the use of demonstrations, laboratory models, and special-effects animation.

Cloud Formation (BFA Educational Media, 468 Park Ave. South, New York NY 10016; 1986; 15 min; also available in video)

Illustrates what happens in the atmosphere through photography and simple laboratory experiments. Introduces dew point and its relationship to condensation of water vapor and the formation of fog, clouds, and dew. Also describes conditions on the windward and leeward sides of mountain ranges.

Earth: Its Water Cycle (Coronet/MTI Film & Video, 108 Wilmot Rd., Deerfield IL 60015; 1974; 11 min)

Dramatic scenes of actual cloud formation.

The Energy Balance (Coronet/MTI Film & Video, 108 Wilmot Rd., Deerfield IL 60015; 1986; part of the Atmospheric Science Series; 15 min; also available in video)

Introduces the principles governing variations in the earth's temperature over extended periods. Covers ice-core boring techniques, the discovery of an ancient catastrophic ice age, the possible effects of vulcanism and meteorite impact, and the "greenhouse effect."

What Makes Rain? (Encyclopaedia Britannica Educational Corp., 425 N. Michigan Ave., Chicago IL 60611; 1975; 22 min)

A good investigation of the processes that produce rain and other forms of precipitation. An interesting mixture of laboratory demonstrations, aerial photographs, and simple experiments.

What Makes Weather? 2nd ed. (Encyclopaedia Britannica Educational Corp., 425 N. Michigan Ave., Chicago IL 60611; 1982; 14 min)

Vivid satellite footage, helpful animation, live action, and time-lapse photography graphically examine the movement of winds and air masses.

Chapter 6 Weather and Climate

Above the Horizon (Ward's Natural Science Establishment, Inc., 5100 W. Henrietta Rd., P.O. Box 92912, Rochester NY 14692; 1965; 21 min)

A fast-moving introduction to meteorology and atmospheric sciences. Spectacular footage of hurricanes, tornadoes, and other extreme weather phenomena.

Antarctica: Exploring the Frozen Continent (Encyclopaedia Britannica Educational Corp., 425 N. Michigan Ave., Chicago IL 60611; 1979; 22 min)

A magnificent panorama of the flora and fauna of this frozen world. A source of insight into this geographical area.

Global Forecasting (Coronet/MTI Film & Video, 108 Wilmot Rd., Deerfield IL 60015; 1986; part of the Atmospheric Science Series; 14 min; also available in video)

Portrays the duties of a meteorologist and the operations of a weather service. Stresses that international cooperation is necessary to gain a complete global picture of atmospheric circulation.

Storms: The Restless Atmosphere (Encyclopaedia Britannica Educational Corp., 425 N. Michigan Ave., Chicago IL 60611; 1974; 22 min)

A good overview of the origins and methods of study of thunderstorms, tornadoes, and hurricanes.

The Story of Climate, Weather & People (Hawkhill Associates Inc., 125 E. Gilman St., Madison WI 53703; 1985; part of the Time, Space & Spirit Series; 1 filmstrip, 80 frames, with 1 cassette)

Traces the history of climatology, relating its development to the other sciences and to improved technology. Covers major causes of weather, the complexity of weather forecasting, and long-term climatic changes.

Weather Forecasting, 2nd ed. (Encyclopaedia Britannica Educational Corp., 425 N. Michigan Ave., Chicago IL 60611; 1981; 22 min)

Focuses on the work of a meteorologist in an actual weather station. Shows how data from many sources are combined to give the most accurate possible prediction of a region's weather.

Weather Systems in Motion (Coronet/MTI Film & Video, 108 Wilmot Rd., Deerfield IL 60015; 1986; part of the Atmospheric Science Series; 14 min; also available in video)

Illustrates the development and migration of cyclones, fronts, air masses, and hurricanes, using satellite time-lapse photography. Characteristics and origins of air masses are discussed and portrayed on a map. Excellent photography and narration.

Chapter 7 The Earth's Fresh Water

Ground Water: The Hidden Reservoir (Wiley and Sons, P.O. Box 063, Somerset NJ 08873; 19 min)

Follows ground water from its origin in rain water to when it comes out of the ground in the form of springs.

Living Water (Hartley Film Foundation Inc., Cat Rock Rd., Cos Cob CT 06807; 1986; 15 min; also available in video)

Illustrates the role of water in maintaining life and sculpting landscapes. Conveys a sense of wonder about the unique role of water on this planet.

The Physics and Chemistry of Water (Visual Aids Services, University of Illinois, Champaign IL 61820; 21 min)

Explains how the water molecule is formed, what the properties of water are, and how it functions as a solvent.

The Rise and Fall of the Great Lakes (National Film Board of Canada, 680 Fifth Avenue, New York NY 10016)

Tells the story of the geologic formation of the Great Lakes. Outstanding film.

The River Must Live (Shell Oil Co., 450 N. Meridan St., Indianapolis IN 46204; 15 min)

A photographic essay of causes, effects, and some solutions for water pollution.

The Ways of Water (Encyclopaedia Britannica Educational Corp., 425 N. Michigan Ave., Chicago IL 60611; 13 min)

The water cycle in its various stages is shown occurring in nature. Filmed on the Olympic Peninsula in the state of Washington.

Chapter 8   The Ocean

Oceanography: The Science of the Sea
(Encyclopaedia Britannica Educational Corp.,
425 N. Michigan Ave., Chicago IL 60611; 1984;
6 filmstrips, average of 75 frames each, with 6
cassettes)

Effectively covers introduction to oceanography, chemical and physical oceanography, biological oceanography, plate
tectonics and the origin of the ocean
bases, ocean sediments and earth history, and the ocean's resources. Outstanding photography and clear narration.

The Restless Sea   (Coronet/MTI Film & Video,
108 Wilmot Rd., Deerfield IL 60015; 1979;
35 min)

A widely used introduction to oceanography that exposes viewers to physical,
chemical, geological, and biological aspects of the field and also to how oceanographers study them.

Riches From the Sea   (National Geographic
Society, Educational Services, 17th & M Sts.
NW, Washington DC 20036; 1984; 23 min; also
available in video)

Explores the resources of the oceans, especially of the continental shelf. Raises
the ecological, legal, and esthetic issues
surrounding the use of ocean resources.

Sea Area Forties   (Modern Talking Picture Service, 2323 New Hyde Park Rd., New Hyde Park
NY 11040; 1975; 29 min)

Exciting film that shows the construction
and placement of an offshore oil platform in the North Sea. Excellent photography and breathtaking scenery.

The Sea: Mysteries of the Deep   (Encyclopaedia Britannica Educational Corp., 425 N.
Michigan Ave., Chicago IL 60611; 1979; 22 min)

Presents some of the myths and stories
surrounding life in the oceans and seas.

Waves on Water   (Encyclopaedia Britannica
Educational Corp., 425 N. Michigan Ave., Chicago IL 60611; 16 min)

Explains how waves are created and
demonstrates that even though waves
travel, the water does not move.

Chapter 9   The Earth's Changing Surface

***Erosion and Weathering: Looking at the
Land***   (Encyclopaedia Britannica Educational
Corp., 425 N. Michigan Ave., Chicago IL 60611;
1981; 17 min)

Outstanding photography documents
the effects of physical and chemical
weathering on structures and on rock.

How We Know About the Ice Ages   (rev.)
(BFA Educational Media, 468 Park Ave. South,
New York, NY 10016; 1985; 16 min; also avail-
able in video)

Uses excellent photography, art work,
and narration to introduce the historical
and scientific aspects of glaciation.

The Land That Came In From the Cold   (Journal Films Inc., 930 Pitner, Evanston IL 60202;
1980; 13 min)

Excellent sequential photographs of topographic changes and biotic succession
that follow a receding glacier (in Glacier
National Monument, southeast Alaska).

Night of the Sun   (National Audio-Visual Cen-
ter, National Archives and Records Service,
General Services Administration, Washington
DC 20409; 1981; 20 min)

Excellent but superficial coverage of continental glaciation and the resultant landforms that are found today throughout
the northern United States and Canada.
Useful in any introductory geology or
earth science course.

Rivers: The Work of Running Water   (Encyclopaedia Britannica Educational Corp, 425 N.
Michigan Ave., Chicago IL 60611; 1981; 22 min)

Focuses on the physical erosion force of
running water and its consequences,
with examples drawn from the Colorado
and Mississippi River Basins. Aestheti-
cally appealing photography.

Soil,   Understanding Our Earth Series, rev.
(Coronet/MTI Film & Video, 108 Wilmot Rd.,
Deerfield IL 60015; 1978; 12 min)

An excellent introduction to soil science.
A generally well-organized treatment of
an important aspect of earth science.

Chapter 10   The Restless Crust

An Animated Atlas of the World (Coronet/ MTI Film & Video, 108 Wilmot Rd., Deerfield IL 60015; 1986; 7 min; also available in video)

An animated film that explains weather, earthquakes, mountain formation, and continental drift, and illustrates how the processes at work on the early earth continue to operate today. Humor underlines the content and lightens the film.

Boundary of Creation (NOAA/Dept. of Commerce, Motion Picture Service, 12231 Wilkins Ave., Rockville MD 20852; 1975; 28 min)

A report on project FAMOUS (French-American Mid-Ocean Undersea Study), in which direct observations of the Mid-Atlantic Rift were made by manned submersibles. A primer on plate tectonics.

Continents Adrift, rev. (American Educational Films, P.O. Box 5001, 132 Lasky Dr., Beverly Hills CA 90212; 1979; 16 min)

The theory of continental drift is used to show the scientific method in action. Highly recommended for students of earth science.

Predictable Disaster (Time-Life Film & Video, Time & Life Bldg., 1271 Avenue of the Americas, New York NY 10020; 1976; 32 min)

A much-needed film for earth science geology courses. Excellent coverage of earthquakes, plate tectonics, and plate processes.

Volcanoes, Earthquakes, and Other Earth Movements (Journal Films, Inc., 930 Pitner, Evanston IL 60202; 1980; 16 min)

Highly recommended film that makes use of animation, models, and on-site observation. Includes all evidence for plate tectonics.

When the Earth Moves (Modern Talking Pictures Service Inc., 500 Park St., St. Petersburg FL 33709; 1981; 26½ min)

One of the best documentaries on geologic hazards. Includes coverage of earthquakes, landslides, vulcanism, subsidence, and flooding.

Chapter 11   The Earth's Geologic History

Digging Into the Past (Coronet/MTI Film & Video, 108 Wilmot Rd., Deerfield IL 60015; 1976; 14 min)

The highly complex and potentially boring topic of scientific archaeology is made understandable and exciting for the young viewer because the subjects of the film are junior high school students.

Fossils: Exploring the Past (Encyclopaedia Britannica Educational Corp., 425 N. Michigan Ave., Chicago IL 60611; 1978; 16 min)

A succinct overview of the activities of paleontologists, both in the field and in the laboratory. Presents paleontology as an exciting science. Highly recommended for a career day.

The Great Dinosaur Discovery ed. ver. (Brigham Young University, Audio Visual Services, 101 FB Fletcher Bldg., Provo UT 84602; 1976; 25 min)

Highly recommended film about the discovery and reconstruction of dinosaurs. Few films show the principles of vertebrate paleontology as well as this one. Shows the excitement of discovery and the development of hypotheses.

Message in the Rocks (Time-Life Film & Video, Time & Life Bldg., 1271 Avenue of the Americas, New York NY 10020; 1981; 57 min)

A marvelous up-to-date film that applies nuclear science to the dating of earth rock, lunar samples, and meteorite material.

Prehistoric Times, rev. (Coronet/MTI Film & Video, 108 Wilmot Rd., Deerfield IL 60015; 1976; 10 min)

A fast-moving, interesting film that presents a view of earth history as if it were fact rather than an interpretation of collected information. Incorporates geologic research with other scientific research.

Stephen Jay Gould: His View of Life   (Time-Life Film & Video, Time & Life Bldg., 1271 Avenue of the Americas, New York NY 10020; 1984; prod. NOVA; 57 min; also available in video)

Presents a biographical sketch of Gould, a Harvard University paleontologist who proclaims the virtues of the punctuated equilibrium model of evolution. An overview of the facts and theories of evolution as seen through the eyes of this gifted scientist, teacher, and part-time philosopher.

Chapter 12   **Environmental Concerns**

Acid Rain   (Time-Life Films & Video, Time & Life Bldg., 1271 Avenue of the Americas, New York NY 10020; 1985; prod. NOVA; 57 min video)

A comprehensive, yet cautious look at what is known about acid rain, its effects and probable causes, as well as what is being done about it. Excellent scope, quality, and clarity.

Air Pollution: A First Film;   rev. (Phoenix Films & Video, Inc., 268 Park Ave. South, New York NY 10016; 1984; 12 min; also available in video)

Covers the sources of air pollution and gives a simple view of the relevant atmospheric chemistry and meteorology. Documents the harmful effects of air pollution as well as general strategies for reducing air pollution.

Choices   (The Conservation Foundation, 1717 Massachusetts Ave. NW, Washington DC 20036; 1980; 29 min)

An overview of the issues involved in resource management of forests and rangelands. Describes the many possible uses of land areas as well as efforts to strike a balance among them.

Energy: New Sources,   2nd ed. (Churchill Films, 662 N. Robertson Blvd., Los Angeles CA 90069; 1980; 24 min)

Surveys the new energy sources of greatest potential: solar, geothermal, nuclear fusion, and synfuels from coal and shale.

Nuclear Energy   (National Geographic Society, Educational Services, 17th and M Sts., NW, Washington DC 20036; 1981; 23 min)

A current and accurate presentation of the many-faceted question of the future of fission nuclear power. Contains information on the history, risks and benefits, economics, and safety of nuclear power methods.

Rubbish to Riches   (AIMS Instructional Media, 6901 Woodley Ave, Van Nuys, CA 91406; 11 min)

Demonstrates the potential of converting trash from a waste material to a valuable resource. A professional production oriented to a general audience.

The Sky's the Limit   (University of California Extension Media Center, 2223 Fulton St., Berkeley CA 94720; 1980; 23 min)

An excellent introduction to the subject of air pollution. A most worthwhile film for students beginning to be aware of social and community problems.

Vanishing From the Earth   (National Geographic Society, Educational Services, 17th & M Sts. NW, Washington DC 20036; 1986; 3 filmstrips, 53 frames each, with 3 cassettes)

Explores the causes and consequences of extinction and suggests how endangered species might be saved. Superb photography provided.

Conducting a Safe Classroom and Laboratory

The materials recommended for use in the activities and investigations are generally safe and non-toxic. However, even everyday items such as candles, knives, and glass jars can be dangerous if not handled carefully. Instruct your students not to use the laboratory unsupervised. Always caution students about any possible danger whenever setting up or performing an activity.

Safety goggles and aprons should always be worn in a lab, or whenever activities require them. Safety notes have been included wherever necessary, but it is impossible for the author to know all the special hazards that might exist in each individual classroom.

It is important to keep safety in mind at all times. Insist that everyone using the lab observe all of the following safety rules.

Glassware. Heat substances only in a heat-resistant glass container. (Pyrex® and Kimax® are the most common trademarks for such products.) Never handle broken glass with bare hands; use heavy gloves or a dustpan and brush. Try to avoid breakage by placing glass objects in secure places where they are not likely to fall or be knocked over.

Chemicals. This program does not recommend that the students handle caustic or dangerous chemicals. However, all chemicals should be handled carefully. Read all caution labels on bottles and follow the directions strictly. Avoid keeping strong acids in your classroom. When diluting an acid, always add the acid to the water— very slowly, stirring constantly with a glass rod. And never allow students to taste a substance unless you know it is safe.

Heat and flames. Never allow papers or other flammable substances anywhere near flames. Make sure students do not have loose clothing or hair near flames. Do not use a flame in an open draft. Keep an emergency supply of water and sand nearby to extinguish fires. Do not try to put out a fire from a leaking alcohol lamp with water; use sand or baking soda.

Do not let water get onto hot-plate coils. Do not heat any substance when the label cautions against it. *Anyone heating a liquid should wear safety goggles.*

Field trips. It is a good idea to look into all possible hazards before going on a field trip. Discuss these with your students in advance. Adequate adult supervision is a must.

Electricity. Students should be cautioned about the dangers of house current, which is the source of power for lamps, hot plates, and other appliances that will be used from time to time. Wires and plugs for these devices should be in good condition and should not be allowed to get wet.

Waste disposal. Solutions containing copper sulfate are water pollution hazards if dumped indiscriminately down the drain. Collect these solutions in separate labeled containers after their use in the activities. Reuse these solutions the following year. Otherwise you may precipitate the copper by adding sodium phosphate with stirring to the copper solution until the color is removed. Allow the precipitate to settle for 24 hours. Pour off the liquid; air dry the precipitate and dispose of them in the normal manner.

All other liquids recommended for use with this program can be flushed down the drain. Solids can be disposed of in the normal waste container.

Developing Your Own Activities

The activities and investigations described in this program include thorough instructions. All state a precise purpose and carefully outline a procedure for achieving the stated purpose. For example, the purpose might be to solve a problem, such as determining factors that affect the rate of soil erosion, or to make a model that demonstrates certain scientific phenomena, such as a convection cell.

In addition to forming teaching models and solving problems, activities can be used to show the behavior of things under certain circumstances, to measure certain results, to arouse students' curiosity, and to motivate them to read or experiment or to directly observe nature around them.

Teachers who are comfortable working with earth science content often develop their own original activities. In so doing, they are able to customize their course so that it meets all of their students' needs and helps to foster inquiry and reinforce learning in a special way. For example, one earth science teacher wanted his students to recognize the relationship of the sun to our directions, north and south. He developed an activity similar to the one on page 52 of the student text. It helps students gain a skill they can use long after leaving the classroom.

Some activities may come from something that you observe quite by accident. One teacher happened to be sliding a foam-plastic cup of coffee back and forth on a table in the faculty lounge one day. She noticed some unusual waves that formed on top of the coffee. These were stationary waves caused by the vibrations of the cup against the table. They were the best example of standing waves she had seen. From this experience, she developed an activity on earthquake waves for her students.

When planning your own activities it is important to keep safety in mind at all times. Avoid dangerous substances, or circumstances that could lead to an accident. Make students conscious of the need for safety and review good safety procedures with them.

Always provide your students with step-by-step directions in which you detail the purpose, set-up of equipment, procedure, observations to be recorded, conclusion, and required clean-up. Careful planning is the most important factor in ensuring the success of an activity or investigation.

List all the materials that you need and be sure to get them together well in advance. Always have a "dress rehearsal." Try the activity first, going through every step of the procedure, perhaps with several students after school. It is surprising how many apparently simple processes do not work as expected. Writing clear directions may also be a challenge.

Make sure that students accept cleaning up after the activity as their responsibility. Always include clean-up as part of the activity and an important prerequisite to doing more activities in the future.

We at Addison-Wesley urge that you think seriously about developing some of your own activities and would be very much interested in hearing from you about them.

Master Materials List

The following list gives the quantities needed for a class of 30. The numbers in parentheses after the quantities indicate the chapter and section of the activity or investigation.

Material	Activity	Investigation
adding machine tape	8 m (4-1 CORE)	1 roll (11-2), (11-3)
alcohol burner (optional)		5 (2-1)
aluminum scrap, small fragments		small amounts (Chapter 12)
astrolabe (made for activity 3-1A)	5 shared (3-18 CORE)	
balance (laboratory), with masses	1-3 shared (1-2A CORE), (1-2B), (8-1A CORE), (8-2A CORE), (9-1B CORE)	1-3 shared (1-2), (7-1), (8-2)
balloon, medium-large	15 (4-3 CORE)	
balsa wood block	8 (8-1A CORE)	
bar magnet	1-3 shared (10-3B CORE)	small number (10-3) 1-3
barometer		shared (6-1)
beaker, 250 mL	8-15 (7-1A CORE), 8 (7-2A), 5 (7-2B CORE), 30 shared (9-1B CORE)	
beaker, 600 mL		10 (7-2)
beaker, heatproof, 1000 mL	8 (5-2A CORE)	8 (8-2)
board, flat	5 small pieces (1-3B)	
bucket	3 shared (9-2 CORE), (9-3B CORE)	
bunsen burner	8 (5-2A CORE)	3-5 shared (5-2)
butcher paper, or plain wrapping paper		30 m (4-1)
calculator		5-10 (10-2)
candle		5 (2-1)
cardboard, heavy	5 (1-3B), 30 (3-3 CORE), 16 (10-3B CORE)	5 (3-3), 8 (5-2)
cardboard tube (e.g., paper towel)		30 (4-3)
cellophane tape	small amount (5-18 CORE), (10-3B CORE)	small amount (5-2)
chalk	5 (1-3B), (8-3A CORE)	
clam shell	(11-3B CORE)	
clock or watch that indicates seconds	1-5 shared (5-1B CORE), (5-3A CORE), (11-1A), (12-1B CORE)	1-5 shared (4-1), (4-2), (7-2), (9-3), (11-1)
coins		
assorted	10 shared (1-2A CORE)	
dime	64 shared (3-3 CORE), (11-2 CORE)	
nickel	(3-3 CORE)	
penny	10 (2-1A CORE), (3-3 CORE), (12-1B CORE)	
colored pencils (different colors)	20 (1-1A CORE), (3-2B), 60 (6-2A CORE), (7-1A CORE), (8-3A CORE), (10-3B CORE)	
column clamp		5 (7-2)
column outlet		5 (7-2)
construction paper, black	10 strips (5-1B CORE)	

Material	Activity	Investigation
container, large, plastic (e.g. milk/bleach)	10 (8-2), 10 (8-2A CORE), 5 (9-2 CORE)	
small, with lid	8 (11-2 CORE)	
shallow, box-like	10 (11-3A)	
shoebox-size (e.g., aquarium)	8 (5-2A CORE), 16 (5-2B)	
tall, clear, with lid		10 (9-3)
convex lens	1-3 shared (4-2A)	
copper sulfate solution		small amount (2-1)
crab carapace	10 (11-3B CORE)	
crayon	(3-2C)	8 (3-3), 1-3 boxes shared (5-1)
cup, plastic	8 (11-3A)	
dilute (10%) hydrochloric acid*	small quantity (2-3B CORE), (9-1B CORE)	20 drops (2-2)
dishpan	8 (8-1A CORE), 5 (8-3B)	
dishwashing liquid		several drops (11-1)
drawing compass	1-3 shared (4-1 CORE)	5-10 (10-2)
drinking glass	1 (5-3B)	
eyedropper	8 (1-2B), (2-3B CORE), (7-2A)	
filter paper (or paper towel)	10 (8-2A CORE)	5 (2-1)
fish line, nylon		15 m (4-2)
flashlight	1 (3-1C), (5-1A)	
flowerpot (or similar container for growing plant)	8 (6-3B)	16 (6-3), 20-40 (Chapter 12)
food coloring (blue or red)	several drops (3-2A CORE), (11-3A)	
fork	8 (7-2A), (8-1A CORE)	
fossil samples		
brachiopod	10 (11-3B CORE)	
casts	10-20 (11-3B CORE)	
molds	10-20 (11-3B CORE)	
petrified wood	10 (11-3B CORE)	
trilobite	10 (11-3B CORE)	
funnel	(8-2A CORE)	
glue, or rubber cement	small amount (10-3A)	
graduated cylinder	(1-2A CORE), (1-2B), (8-1A CORE), (9-1B CORE), (11-3A)	5 (1-2), (10-1), (11-1)
graph paper	(1-1A CORE), (1-2B), (3-2B), (5-1A), (6-3A CORE), (7-1A CORE), (8-3A CORE), (10-1B CORE)	8 (11-1)
grass clippings		small amount (Chapter 12)
gravel	small amount (7-2B CORE)	small amount (7-1), (7-2)
grease pencil (optional)	5 (7-2B CORE)	
gummed labels, circular	300 (4-3 CORE)	
hardwood block	8 (8-1A CORE)	
heat lamp	1-3 shared (8-3B)	
hot plate		1-3 shared (8-2)
hot water	small amount (2-3)	
hydrometer, aquarium		1-3 shared (8-2)
index card		32 (5-2)
ice, chips or cube	small amount (5-3B)	
crushed	several cups (3-2A CORE)	
cubes	20-25 (5-2A CORE)	
iron filings	small amount (2-3A), (12-1A)	small amount (10-3)
iron, scrap, small fragments		small amount (Chapter 12)

Material	Activity	Investigation
jar, large and clear	5 (7-2B CORE), 8 (8-1A CORE), 10 (8-2A CORE), (12-1A)	5 (2-1)
large, clear, wide-mouthed, with lid		10 (7-1), (9-1)
tall (over 20 cm) and clear		8 (11-1)
knitting needle	8 (3-2C)	
leaf and/or twig	10 (11-3)	
lens holder	1-3 shared (4-2A)	
light bulbs, assorted wattage	several shared (4-2B CORE)	
same wattage	2 shared (4-2B CORE)	
light socket, with long cord	4-6 shared (4-2B CORE)	
light source (e.g., lamp)	3-5 shared (3-2C), (5-1B CORE), (5-2B)	3-5 shared (5-1)
light source stand	(5-2B)	3-5 shared (5-2)
magazines, old, for illustrations		10-20 (5-3)
magnet	(2-2B), (12-1A)	
magnetic compass	(10-3B CORE)	1-3 shared (1-3), (3-3), (5-2)
magnifying glass	(2-2B), (2-3B CORE), (9-1A)	small number (10-1)
map	(1-3A CORE), (6-2A CORE), (6-3A CORE), (10-3A)	
marking pencil, or crayon	5 (9-2 CORE), (10-2A)	5 (9-1), (9-3), (11-2), (11-3) (Chapter 12)
masking tape	(3-3 CORE), (9-2 CORE)	small amount (3-3), (9-1)
mass, 2-kg		1 (9-2)
measuring cup	5 (9-2 CORE)	5 (9-3)
metal weight, small, no lead	8 (8-1)	
meter stick	3-5 shared (1-2A CORE)), (3-3 CORE), (4-1 CORE), (4-2A), (8-3A CORE)	3-5 shared (4-2), 6-10 (11-2), (11-3)
meter stick support	1-3 (4-2A)	
milk carton, half gallon	8 (4-1)	1 (9-2)
mineral specimens		
calcite	10 (2-2A CORE), 5 (2-2B)	
carnotite (optional)	10 (11-2)	
feldspar, orthoclase	10 (2-2A CORE), 5 (2-2B)	
fluorite	10 (2-2A CORE), 5 (2-2B)	
galena	10 (2-2A CORE), 5 (2-2B)	
gypsum	10 (2-2A CORE), 5 (2-2B)	
magnetite	10 (2-2A CORE), 5 (2-2B)	
mica	10 (2-2A CORE), 5 (2-2B)	
pyrite	5 (2-2B)	
quartz	10 (2-2A CORE), 5 (2-2B)	
uraninite (optional)	10 (11-2)	
modeling clay	small amount (4-2C), (5-1B CORE), (5-2)	500mL (7-2)
colored or plaster of Paris		
dark-colored		small amount (10-1)
light-colored		small amount (10-1)
three different colors	(10-2B)	
nail, iron/steel	5 (1-3B), 10 (2-2A CORE), (2-3B CORE)	10 (2-2)
thin (brad)		
needle	16 (7-2A)	56 (5-2)
newspapers, old	several (6-2B)	

Material	Activity	Investigation
pail, plastic		1 (8-3)
paper, scrap, small pieces		small amount (Chapter 12)
paper clip		10 (4-2)
paper cup	5 (3-2A CORE)	24 (5-2)
colored	8 (5-2)	
paper holder	1-3 (4-2A)	
paper towel	small amount (8-1B)	5 (1-2), (2-1), (8-1), (8-3), (9-1)
pebbles	several (9-3B CORE)	50-60 (11-1)
petroleum jelly	small amount (11-3A)	
Phillips screwdriver		8 (5-2)
picture of moon craters	(4-1)	
pie plate, glass	8 (12-1A)	
pie tin, aluminum	5 (3-2A CORE), 8 (7-2A)	
pin	5 (3-2A CORE)	
pinch clamp		5 (7-2)
plant, potted/transplanted small plants, local vegetation	20-30 (6-3B), 8 (7-1B)	10-20 (6-1), (7-1)
plaster of Paris	moderate amount (11-3A)	
plastic bag, large, with tie	8 (7-1B)	
plastic column		small number (Chapter 12)
plastic-foam ball, 5-7 cm in diameter	8 (3-2C)	
2-3 cm diameter	10 (8-3A CORE)	
plastic food wrap		small amount (7-1), (7-2)
plastic sheet	5 (9-2 CORE)	
playing cards	20 (11-1A)	
poster paint, two colors	small amount (6-1)	
potassium permanganate	small amount (5-2A CORE)	
potting soil		moderate amount (Ch. 12)
powdered clay		small amount (7-2), (9-3), (11-1)
protractor	1-3 shared (1-3B), 15 (3-1A CORE), 5 (9-2 CORE)	
pushpin (optional)	16 (4-1)	
razor blade, single edge (or sharp knife)	1-3 shared (10-3B CORE)	
ring stand		5 (7-2)
rocks, common (back yard/roadside)	20-30 shared (1-1B CORE), (9-1A)	
rock fragments/chips		
dolomite chips	small amount (9-1B CORE)	
granite chips	small amount (9-1B CORE)	small amount (9-1)
limestone chips	small amount (9-1B CORE)	
marble chips	small amount (9-1B CORE)	small amount (9-1)
sandstone	small amount (9-1B CORE)	small amount (9-1)
rock specimens		
aa (or close-up photograph)	10 (10-1A)	
andesite (or close-up photograph)		10 (10-1)
assorted	20-30 shared (2-3B CORE)	
basalt (or close-up photograph)		10 (10-1)
dolomite rock		10 (2-2)
limestone		10 (2-2)
pahoehoe (or close-up photograph)	10 (10-1A)	
rhyolite (or close-up photograph)		10 (10-1)
rod, metal or hard plastic	1-3 shared (2-3B CORE), (12-1A)	
rope, small diameter	65 m (8-3A CORE)	
rotating platform, 30 cm diameter	1-3 shared (3-2A CORE)	
rubber band		small number (7-1)
rubber cement, or glue		small amount (10-3)
rubber stopper, 1-hole, #6		10 (4-2)
rubber (or plastic) tubing	small amount (9-3B CORE)	small amount (7-2)
ruler, metric	3-5 shared (1-2A CORE), (3-1A CORE), (4-1), (6-3B), (8-1B)	3-5 shared (1-2), (1-3), (3-3), (11-1)

Material	Activity	Investigation
safety glasses/safety gloves		10 (9-1)
safety match		5 (2-1)
salt	small amount (8-2A CORE), (12-1A)	
sand	small amount (2-3A), (7-2B CORE), moderate amount (9-3B CORE), (12-1A)	moderate amount (9-3)
coarse		small amount (7-2)
dark-colored	moderate amount (8-3B)	
fine	moderate amount (9-2 CORE)	moderate amount (9-3)
light-colored quartz, medium and fine	moderate amount (8-3B)	small amount (11-1)
sandy soil	small amount (5-2B)	small amount (7-1)
scissors	10 shared (10-3A)	
screwdriver	8 (11-3A)	
seashells	10-20 (11-3A)	
sewing needle	10 (7-2)	
shadow-stick board (made for activity 1-3B)		
shiny can	15 (5-3)	
silt		small amount (9-3)
sling psychrometer	1-3 shared (5-3A CORE), (5-3B)	
soap powder	small amount (7-2A)	
soil sample (back yard/roadside)	5-8 shared (9-1A)	
spectroscope		1 shared (5-1)
spoon	(5-2A CORE), (8-3B)	small number (11-3)
standard mass, 200 g, with hook		3-5 shared (4-2)
stick, pointed (or dowel)	8 (1-3B)	
stirring rod	(11-3A)	
stopwatch (optional)		1-3 shared (7-2), (9-3), (11-1)
streak plate	8 (2-2B)	
stream table (optional)	1 shared (9-3B CORE)	
string	small amount (1-3A CORE), (3-1A CORE), moderate amount (8-1B)	moderate amount (8-1), (9-2)
sulfur, powdered		small amount (8-2), (2-1)
table salt	small amount (2-3A)	small amount (8-2)
tagboard, white, 15 cm × 15 cm	10 (4-2A)	
tape measure, metric (optional)	1-3 shared (4-1)	
teasing needle (optional)	1-3 shared (9-1)	
test tube, heat resistant	16 (2-3A)	8 (2-1)
test-tube holder		8 (2-1)
test-tube rack	3-5 shared (2-3A)	
thermometer	6-8 shared (2-1A), (5-1B CORE), (5-3B)	6-8 shared (5-2)
heat proof		3-5 shared (8-2)
quick-response	3-5 shared (8-3B)	
thread spool, wooden	16 (5-2)	10 (11-2), (4-2)
thumbtacks	small number (1-3A CORE), 45 (3-1A CORE)	small number (5-2)
timer (optional)	1-3 shared (8-3B)	
toothpick	small quantity (4-2C), (9-1A)	
tracing paper	30 (10-3A)	
tripod stand	3-5 shared (5-2A CORE)	
trough, plastic or metal	5 (9-2 CORE)	
tub of opaque solution, specially prepared	5-8 (8-1B)	moderate amount (8-1)
twig and/or leaf	10 (11-3)	
vinegar	small amount (2-2B)	

Material	Activity	Investigation
warm water	small amount (5-3B), (12-1A)	
water	small amount (1-2A CORE), (1-2B), (2-3A), (3-2A CORE), (5-2A CORE), (5-2B), (5-3A CORE), (5-3B), (7-2A), (7-2B CORE), (8-1A CORE), (8-3B), (9-1B CORE), (9-2 CORE), (11-3A), (12-1A)	small amount (1-2), (7-1), (8-2), (9-3), (11-1)
waxed paper	1 roll (10-3B CORE)	1 roll (9-2)
weather map from newspaper	15 (6-1 CORE), 30 (6-2A CORE)	
weight, hooked	15 (3-1A CORE)	
weight (does not contain lead)	8 (8-1B)	moderate number (8-1)
white paper, rough		8 (5-1)
smooth		8 (1-1), 5 (5-1)
wind vane		3-5 shared (6-1)
wire, thin	1 m (10-2B CORE)	
wire gauze, small piece	8 (5-2A CORE)	
wire screen, small piece	8 (9-1B CORE)	
wood block	5 (1-2A CORE), (5-1B CORE), (9-2 CORE), (9-3B CORE)	5 (7-2), 1 (8-3)
wooden spoon (optional)	1-3 shared (8-3B)	
wood, lightweight slat, 50 cm		24 (5-2)
30 cm	15 (3-1 CORE)	
wood, small piece	20 (10-2B CORE)	
carbonized	8 (11-3B CORE)	
petrified	8 (11-3B CORE)	small amount (5-2)
woodworking glue		
world map or globe	1-3 shared (1-3A CORE), (6-3 CORE), (10-3B)	

Suppliers of Laboratory Equipment

Catalogs from distributors/suppliers will provide you with the most up-to-date information about sources, availability, costs, and alternative equipment that might better fit your needs. The following suppliers are frequently cited as sources of scientific supplies and equipment.

Carolina Biological Supply Co.
2700 York Rd.
Burlington, NC 27215

Central Scientific Co. (CENCO)
11222 Melrose Ave.
Franklin Park, IL 60131

Damon/Instructional Systems Div.
80 Wilson Way
Westwood, MA 02090

Delta Education, Inc.
P.O. Box M
Nashua, NH 03061-6012

Fisher Scientific Co.
Educational Materials Division
4901 W. LeMoyne St.
Chicago, IL 60651

Frey Scientific Co.
905 Hickory Ln.
Mansfield, OH 44905

Geoscience Resources, Inc.
2990 Anthony Rd.
P.O. Box 2096
Burlington, NC 27215

McKilligan Supply Corp.
435 Main St.
Johnson City, NY 13790

Merrell Scientific Division
Educational Modules Inc.
1665 Buffalo Rd.
Rochelle, NY 14624

MMI Space Science Corp.
2950 Wyman Parkway
P.O. Box 19907
Baltimore, MD 21211

Nasco
901 Janesville Ave.
Fort Atkinson, WI 53538

Nasco West Inc.
P.O. Box 3837
Modesto, CA 95352

Sargent-Welch Scientific Co.
7300 N. Linder Ave.
Skokie, IL 60077

Schoolmasters Science
745 State Circle
P.O. Box 1941
Ann Arbor, MI 48106

Science Kit and Boreal Labs
777 E. Park Dr.
Tonawanda, NY 14150

Sunstone Publications
P.O. Box 788
Cooperstown, NY 13326

Trippensee Planetarium Co.
301 Cass St.
Saginaw, MI 48602

Ward's Natural Science Establishment, Inc.
5100 West Henrietta Rd.
P.O. Box 92912
Rochester, NY 14692-9012

Teaching Notes

Addison-Wesley
Earth Science

⋏ **Addison-Wesley Publishing Company**

Menlo Park, California

Reading, Massachusetts

New York

Don Mills, Ontario

Wokingham, England

Amsterdam

Bonn

Sydney

Singapore

Tokyo

Madrid

Bogotá

Santiago

San Juan

Addison-Wesley

Earth Science

Authors

Robert E. Fariel

Alva T. Stanforth Junior High School
Elmont, New York

Robert W. Hinds

Slippery Rock University of Pennsylvania
Slippery Rock, Pennsylvania

David B. Berey

Educational Consultant
New York, New York

Consulting Author

Bonnie B. Barr

State University of New York College at Cortland
Cortland, New York

Consultants

Gene Ammarell
Fiske Planetarium and Science Center
University of Colorado
Boulder, Colorado

Charles R. Ault, Jr.
Indiana University
Bloomington, Indiana

Richard Benz
Wickliffe High School
Wickliffe, Ohio

Thomas H. Callen II
Albert Einstein Planetarium
National Air and Space Museum
The Smithsonian Institution
Washington, D.C.

Ronald E. Charlton
Mount Lebanon School District
Pittsburgh, Pennsylvania

Jeff Davis
Tomlin Junior High School
Plant City, Florida

Keith Emrick
Mesa High School
Mesa, Arizona

Eddie L. Green
Palmer High School
Palmer, Texas

Kathleen Kaye Gulley
Pike High School
Indianapolis, Indiana

Marion S. Hacker
Wedgwood Middle School
Fort Worth, Texas

Harold Pratt
Jefferson County Public Schools
Lakewood, Colorado

Cover Photo: Weathered Sandstone, Paria Canyon Wilderness Area, Arizona-Utah
(© Tom Bear/DRK Photo)

ISBN 0-201-25039-X

BCDEFGHIJKL-KR-8921098

Contents

1 Unit 1 **Beginning Earth Science**

2 Chapter 1
Studying the Earth

4 Section 1
Learning About the Earth

5 The scientific method

8 *Activity 1-1:* Graphing Data

10 Thinking Skill: Classifying

12 *Our Science Heritage:* How Did We Find Out the Earth Is Round?

15 What is the earth?

18 What is earth science?

20 Section 1 Review

21 Section 2
An International System of Measuring

22 The International System of Units (SI)

25 Measuring length

26 Measuring mass

28 Determining volume

30 *Activity 1-2A:* Using Base Units to Measure

31 Determining density

32 *Activity 1-2B:* Graphing the Density of Water

33 Measuring the earth

34 Section 2 Review

35 Section 3
Mapping the Earth's Surface

36 Latitude and longitude

39 Map projections

41 Colors and symbols on maps

42 *Activity 1-3A:* Locating Places on the Earth

43 North on a map

44 A scale of distances

45 Topographic maps

48 *Careers:* Earth Scientist/Cartographer

49 Different ways to find north

52 *Activity 1-3B:* Using a Shadow Stick to Find a North-South Line

53 Section 3 Review

54 Chapter 1 Review

56 Chapter 2
Earth Materials

58 Section 1
The Nature of Matter

59 Matter

61 *Activity 2-1A:* Solids, Liquids, and Gases

62 Elements and atoms

65 *Our Science Heritage:* How Did We Learn About Metals?

66 The periodic table

70 *Activity 2-1B:* Using the Periodic Table

72 Isotopes

73 Compounds and molecules

75 Compounds made of ions

77 Mixtures

79 Section 1 Review

80 Section 2
Minerals

81 What are minerals?

84 Silicate minerals

86 Nonsilicate minerals

87 What to look for in a mineral

90 *Activity 2-2A:* Grouping Minerals by Hardness

92 *Activity 2-2B:* Using Physical Properties to Identify Minerals

94 Section 2 Review

95 Section 3
Rocks

96 Where does rock come from?

96 Igneous rock

98 *Activity 2-3A:* Forming Layers

99 Sedimentary rock

100 Metamorphic rock

101 The rock cycle

103 What to look for in a rock

104 *Activity 2-3B:* Determining the Class of a Rock

108 *Careers:* Geophysicist/Technical Secretary

109 Section 3 Review

110 Chapter 2 Review

112 *Science Issues of Today:* The Search for Mineral Resources

114 Chapter 3
The System of the Earth and Moon

116 Section 1
Observing the Night Sky

117 Models of the night sky

118 Locating some constellations

120 *Our Science Heritage:* How Are Astronomy and Astrology Related?

121 Azimuth and altitude

122 *Activity 3-1A:* Using an Astrolabe

124 *Activity 3-1B:* Finding the Altitude of Polaris

126 *Activity 3-1C:* Plotting the Paths of Four Stars

127 A celestial latitude and longitude

128 Section 1 Review

129 Section 2
Earth Motions

130 The earth rotates

132 Evidence of the earth's rotation

134 *Activity 3-2A:* Simulating the Coriolis Effect

137 The time of day

142 The earth revolves

144 Evidence of the earth's revolution

146 The seasons

147 *Activity 3-2B:* Simulating the Seasons on Earth

151 Natural timekeepers

153 Section 2 Review

154 Section 3
The Moon

155 Characteristics of the moon

158 *Activity 3-3:* A Way to Calculate the Diameter of the Moon

159 Phases and eclipses of the moon

162 Information from the *Apollo* program

164 *Careers:* Astronomer/Instrumentation Technician

165 Section 3 Review

166 Chapter 3 Review

168 Chapter 4
Beyond the Earth

170 Section 1
The Solar System

171 The birth of the solar system

172 A sun-centered system

176 *Our Science Heritage:* A Model of the Solar System

177 The inner planets

182 Asteroids and meteoroids

184 *Activity 4-1:* Constructing Scale Models of the Solar System

185 The outer planets

190 Comets

192 Section 1 Review

193 Section 2
The Stars

194 Characteristics of the sun

196 Characteristics of other stars

198 *Activity 4-2A:* Calculating the Distance to the Sun

202 Different kinds of stars

205 The Hertzsprung-Russell diagram

206 *Activity 4-2B:* Observing Magnitudes of Light Bulbs

207 Clusters of stars

208 *Activity 4-2C:* Observing Parallax Displacement

209 How far away are the stars?

211 Section 2 Review

212 Section 3
The Galaxies and Beyond

213 The Milky Way galaxy

214 Other galaxies and superclusters

216 *Careers:* Geoscience Librarian/Solar Energy Firm Owner

217 Beyond the galaxies

218 Thinking Skill: Observing

220 *Activity 4-3:* Simulating an Expanding Universe

222 Looking at the universe

225 Section 3 Review

226 Chapter 4 Review

228 *Science Issues of Today:* Improvements in Astronomic Observations

Unit 3   Air in Motion

230   Chapter 5
The Atmosphere

232   Section 1
Heat and the Atmosphere

233   Energy from the sun

235   Energy moves by conduction

236   *Our Science Heritage:* How Does the Sun Produce Energy?

238   Energy moves by convection

239   Energy moves by radiation

242   Temperatures around the earth

244   *Activity 5-1A:* Changing the Angle of Incoming
Energy

246   *Activity 5-1B:* Measuring the Effect of the Angle
of Incoming Energy

248   Section 1 Review

249   Section 2
Winds and the Atmosphere

250   Convection currents and wind belts

252   *Activity 5-2A:* Forming Convection Currents

254   Specific heat and convection currents

255   Atmospheric pressure and winds

257   The density of the atmosphere

259   Reading an atmospheric pressure map

260   *Activity 5-2B:* Comparing Differences in Specific
Heat

262   Section 2 Review

263   Section 3
Moisture and the Atmosphere

264   Energy and the states of water

266   Water vapor in the atmosphere

268   *Activity 5-3A:* Finding the Relative Humidity

269   When does condensation occur?

270   *Careers:* Weather Forecaster/Weather Technician

272   *Activity 5-3B:* Finding the Dew-Point Temperature

274   Condensation near the earth's surface

276   Condensation in the atmosphere

279   Precipitation

281   Section 3 Review

282   Chapter 5 Review

284   Chapter 6
Weather and Climate

286   Section 1
Air Masses and Weather Fronts

287   Air moves in masses

289   Variations within an air mass

290   Conditions along a cold front

291   Conditions along a warm front

292   Thinking Skill: Inferring

293   A front on top of a front

294   *Activity 6-1:* Comparing Air Masses Across a
Weather Front

295   Stationary and moving fronts

297   Section 1 Review

298   Section 2
Predicting the Weather

299   Recording the local weather conditions

301   Weather fronts on a map

304   *Activity 6-2A:* Plotting Changes on a Weather
Map

305   Predicting changes in the weather

306   Difficulties with predicting the weather

308   Extreme weather conditions

309   *Activity 6-2B:* Tracking Severe Weather
Conditions

314   Section 2 Review

315   Section 3
Climate

316   General types of climates

318   Factors that affect temperature

321   Factors that affect moisture

323   *Careers:* Climatologist/Air-conditioning Mechanic

325   *Our Science Heritage:* Did Glaciers Really Cross
the Sahara?

325   Climate graphs

326   *Activity 6-3A:* Plotting a Climate Graph

328   *Activity 6-3B:* Observing Effects of Climate
Changes

329   Section 3 Review

330   Chapter 6 Review

332   *Science Issues of Today:* Preventing Disasters
from Sudden Weather Changes

334 Chapter 7
The Earth's Fresh Water

336 Section 1
Water on the Ground

337 Water recycles

339 *Our Science Heritage:* Water and Ancient Civilizations

340 Water collects on the ground

342 Water runs off the ground

344 *Activity 7-1A:* Comparing Rainfall and Stream Discharge

346 Water leaves the earth's surface

348 *Activity 7-1B:* Observing Transpiration from a Plant

349 Section 1 Review

350 Section 2
Water in the Ground

351 Pore spaces in rock and soil

352 Water soaks into the ground

354 Zones of water in the ground

356 *Activity 7-2A:* Observing the Cohesion of Water Molecules

357 Water comes out of the ground

358 *Activity 7-2B:* Simulating the Water Table

362 *Careers:* Hydrologist/Heavy-Equipment Operator

363 Section 2 Review

364 Chapter 7 Review

366 Chapter 8
The Ocean

368 Section 1
The Bottom of the Ocean

369 The major oceans

370 Marginal seas

372 Sounding the ocean bottom

374 The topography of the ocean bottom

375 *Our Science Heritage:* The *Nautilus* and the *Challenger*

378 *Activity 8-1A:* Comparing the Density and Elevation of Floating Objects

381 Resources of the ocean bottom

382 *Activity 8-1B:* Taking and Using Soundings

384 Section 1 Review

385 Section 2
Properties of Ocean Water

386 Salinity

388 *Activity 8-2:* Evaporating Salt Water

389 Temperature and density

391 Sea ice

392 Thinking Skill: Analyzing

394 Water pressure

395 Water absorbs light

398 Resources of ocean water

399 Section 2 Review

400 Section 3
The Circulation of Ocean Water

401 Directions of motion in a wave

402 *Activity 8-3A:* Simulating Wave Motion

404 The beginning, middle, and end of a wave

405 *Careers:* Marine Geologist/Computer Operator

407 Effects of wave action

409 Tides

411 Surface ocean currents

414 Deep ocean circulation

416 *Activity 8-3B:* Simulating Effects of Heat Absorption on the Earth's Surface

417 Section 3 Review

418 Chapter 8 Review

420 *Science Issues of Today:* Aquaculture to Help Meet the World's Hunger

421 Unit 5   **Landscapes**

422 Chapter 9
The Earth's Changing Surface

424 Section 1
Weathering

425 Physical weathering

426 Chemical weathering

428 Mixed weathering

429 Rates of weathering

431 From rock to soil

432 *Activity 9-1A:* Comparing Rates of Chemical Weathering

434 *Activity 9-1B:* Comparing Samples in a Soil Profile

435 *Careers:* Geographer/Civil Engineering Technician

436 Section 1 Review

437 Section 2
Erosion

438 Erosion by running water

440 *Our Science Heritage:* Travel and World Geography

441 The formation of a river valley

443 Erosion by glaciers

445 Erosion by more than one agent

447 Controlling erosion

448 Thinking Skill: Comparing

450 *Activity 9-2:* Changing the Rate of Erosion

452 Section 2 Review

453 Section 3
Deposition

454 Deposition by running water

456 *Activity 9-3A:* Analyzing a Core Sample

457 Stream erosion and deposition

458 *Activity 9-3B:* Stream Erosion and Deposition Patterns

459 Deposition by wind

461 Deposition by glaciers

462 *Activity 9-3C:* Comparing Core Samples

465 Section 3 Review

466 Chapter 9 Review

468 Chapter 10
The Restless Crust

470 Section 1
Volcanoes

471 The power of a major volcanic eruption

475 Why some eruptions are so violent

477 Volcanic landforms

478 *Activity 10-1A:* Inferring Lava Viscosity

480 Where volcanoes occur

482 *Activity 10-1B:* Reconstructing the Topography of a Volcanic Cone

483 Section 1 Review

484 Section 2
Stress, Structure, and Earthquakes

485 Rocks under stress

488 *Activity 10-2A:* Simulating Anticlines and Synclines

489 Movement along a fault

490 *Activity 10-2B:* Making a Fault Model

492 *Activity 10-2C:* Simulating Faults

494 What is an earthquake?

497 Earthquake damage

500 Section 2 Review

501 Section 3
Plate Tectonics

502 The interior of the earth

504 The theory of continental drift

506 *Our Science Heritage:* From Hypothesis to Theory

508 The theory of plate tectonics

511 Pangaea

514 *Activity 10-3A:* Reconstructing Pangaea

515 *Careers:* Seismologist/Construction Inspector

516 *Activity 10-3B:* Simulating Sea-Floor Spreading

517 Section 3 Review

518 Chapter 10 Review

520 *Science Issues of Today:* Predicting Earthquakes

521 Unit 6 **Past, Present, and Future**

522 Chapter 11
The Earth's Geologic History

524 Section 1
Unraveling the Rock Record

525 Uniformitarianism

526 Assumptions in science

527 The principle of superposition

528 *Activity 11-1A:* Verifying the Principle of
Superposition

530 The principle of original horizontality

532 The principle of faunal succession

534 *Activity 11-1B:* Reading a Rock Record

535 Darwin's theory of evolution by natural selection

538 Interpreting rock formations

540 Section 1 Review

541 Section 2
Dating the Rock Record

542 Early scientific investigations

544 *Our Science Heritage:* Smith, Cuvier, and Geologic Time

545 Radiometric dating

546 *Careers:* Petrologist/Refinery Operator

548 Thinking Skill: Evaluating

550 The amino acid method

552 Geologic time

556 *Activity 11-2:* Approximating Half-Life Decay

557 Section 2 Review

558 Section 3
A Parade of Life Forms

559 The fossil record

563 Precambrian life forms

564 *Activity 11-3A:* Making a Fossil Mold

566 Paleozoic life forms

571 Mesozoic life forms

574 Cenozoic life forms

576 *Activity 11-3B:* Distinguishing Fossils and Inferring Ancient Environments

577 Section 3 Review

578 Chapter 11 Review

580 Chapter 12
Environmental Concerns

582 Section 1
Using Earth Materials

583 Using minerals and rocks

587 *Activity 12-1A:* Separating Earth Materials

589 Using fossil fuels

591 Using the wind and the sun

593 Using water

596 Using atoms

600 *Activity 12-1B:* Simulating Ore Reserves and
World Demand

601 Section 1 Review

602 Section 2
Preserving the Environment

603 Taking from the earth

604 *Our Science Heritage:* Improving the Environment

608 Heaping up upon the earth

609 *Activity 12-2A:* Considering the Economics of
Recycling

612 A suitable environment for life

613 *Careers:* Range Manager/Petroleum Geologist

615 *Activity 12-2B:* Evaluating Alternative Energy
Sources on Klar

616 Section 2 Review

617 Chapter 12 Review

619 *Science Issues of Today:* Extinction Patterns and
Rates

621 Appendix

632 Glossary

648 Index

656 Acknowledgments

Special Interest Topics

Thinking Skills

10   Classifying
218   Observing
292   Inferring
392   Analyzing
448   Comparing
548   Evaluating

Science Issues of Today

112   The Search for Mineral Resources
228   Improvements in Astronomic Observations
332   Preventing Disasters from Sudden Weather Changes
420   Aquaculture to Help Meet the World's Hunger
520   Predicting Earthquakes
619   Extinction Patterns and Rates

Careers

Careers are listed by page number, chapter-section, and career.

48   1-3   Earth Scientist
48   1-3   Cartographer
108   2-3   Geophysicist
108   2-3   Technical Secretary
164   3-3   Astronomer
164   3-3   Instrumentation Technician
216   4-1   Geoscience Librarian
216   4-1   Solar Energy Firm Owner
270   5-3   Weather Forecaster
270   5-3   Weather Technician
323   6-3   Climatologist
323   6-3   Air-conditioning Mechanic
362   7-2   Hydrologist
362   7-2   Heavy-Equipment Operator
405   8-3   Marine Geologist
405   8-3   Computer Operator
435   9-1   Geographer
435   9-1   Civil Engineering Technician
515   10-3   Seismologist
515   10-3   Construction Inspector
546   11-2   Petrologist
546   11-2   Refinery Operator
613   12-2   Range Manager
613   12-2   Petroleum Geologist

Our Science Heritage

Our Science Heritage entries are listed by page number, chapter-section, and title.

12   1-1   How Did We Find Out the Earth Is Round?
65   2-1   How Did We Learn About Metals?
120   3-1   How Are Astronomy and Astrology Related?
176   4-1   A Model of the Solar System
236   5-1   How Does the Sun Produce Energy?
325   6-3   Did Glaciers Really Cross the Sahara?
339   7-1   Water and Ancient Civilizations
375   8-1   The *Nautilus* and the *Challenger*
440   9-2   Travel and World Geography
506   10-3   From Hypothesis to Theory
544   11-2   Smith, Cuvier, and Geologic Time
604   12-2   Improving the Environment

Activities

Activities

Activities are listed by page number, chapter-section, and title.

8	1-1	Graphing Data
30	1-2A	Using Base Units to Measure
32	1-2B	Graphing the Density of Water
42	1-3A	Locating Places on the Earth
52	1-3B	Using a Shadow Stick to Find a North-South Line
61	2-1A	Solids, Liquids, and Gases
70	2-1B	Using the Periodic Table
90	2-2A	Grouping Minerals by Hardness
92	2-2B	Using Physical Properties to Identify Minerals
98	2-3A	Forming Layers
104	2-3B	Determining the Class of a Rock
122	3-1A	Using an Astrolabe
124	3-1B	Finding the Altitude of Polaris
126	3-1C	Plotting the Paths of Four Stars
134	3-2A	Simulating the Coriolis Effect
146	3-2B	Simulating the Seasons on Earth
158	3-3	A Way to Calculate the Diameter of the Moon
184	4-1	Constructing Scale Models of the Solar System
198	4-2A	Calculating the Distance to the Sun
206	4-2B	Observing Magnitudes of Light Bulbs
208	4-2C	Observing Parallax Displacement
220	4-3	Simulating an Expanding Universe
244	5-1A	Changing the Angle of Incoming Energy
246	5-1B	Measuring the Effect of the Angle of Incoming Energy
252	5-2A	Forming Convection Currents
260	5-2B	Comparing Differences in Specific Heat
268	5-3A	Finding the Relative Humidity
272	5-3B	Finding the Dew-Point Temperature
294	6-1	Comparing Air Masses Across a Weather Front
304	6-2A	Plotting Changes on a Weather Map
309	6-2B	Tracking Severe Weather Conditions
326	6-3A	Plotting a Climate Graph
328	6-3B	Observing Effects of Climate Changes
344	7-1A	Comparing Rainfall and Stream Discharge
348	7-1B	Observing Transpiration from a Plant
356	7-2A	Observing the Cohesion of Water Molecules
358	7-2B	Simulating the Water Table
378	8-1A	Comparing the Density and Elevation of Floating Objects
382	8-1B	Taking and Using Soundings
388	8-2	Evaporating Salt Water
402	8-3A	Simulating Wave Motion
416	8-3B	Simulating Effects of Heat Absorption on the Earth's Surface
432	9-1A	Comparing Rates of Chemical Weathering
434	9-1B	Comparing Samples in a Soil Profile
450	9-2	Changing the Rate of Erosion
456	9-3A	Analyzing a Core Sample
458	9-3B	Stream Erosion and Deposition Patterns
462	9-3C	Comparing Core Samples
478	10-1A	Inferring Lava Viscosity
482	10-1B	Reconstructing the Topography of a Volcanic Cone
488	10-2A	Simulating Anticlines and Synclines
490	10-2B	Making a Fault Model
492	10-2C	Simulating Faults
514	10-3A	Reconstructing Pangaea
516	10-3B	Simulating Sea-Floor Spreading
528	11-1A	Verifying the Principle of Superposition
534	11-1B	Reading a Rock Record
556	11-2	Approximating Half-Life Decay
564	11-3A	Making a Fossil Mold
576	11-3B	Distinguishing Fossils and Inferring Ancient Environments
587	12-1A	Separating Earth Materials
600	12-1B	Simulating Ore Resources and World Demand
609	12-2A	Considering the Economics of Recycling
615	12-2B	Evaluating Alternative Energy Sources on Klar

Working Safely in the Science Classroom

The materials required for the earth science activities have been carefully selected and are generally safe. However, accidents can happen when materials are handled carelessly. It is important that you follow each of the safety precautions listed.

General Safety Precautions

1. Make sure that your teacher is present and knows what you are doing while you are working on activities.
2. Read all the instructions and caution notices carefully; follow them exactly.
3. Pay close attention to the laboratory activity that you are doing. Do not be distracted by others.
4. When working with chemicals or flames, always wear safety goggles and other protective clothing.
5. Know the locations in your classroom of safety equipment, such as fire extinguishers and first-aid kits.

Special Safety Precautions

Glassware and sharp objects Heat substances only in heat-resistant glassware. Clean up broken glass with heavy gloves or a dustpan and brush. Handle sharp knives with care.

Chemicals Read all caution labels on bottles and follow the directions strictly. Never taste a substance. Keep your hands away from your face when handling chemicals. Do not breathe fumes. Wash your hands before leaving the lab.

Heat and Flames Keep papers or other flammable substances away from flames. Tie back hair and loose clothing.

Sunlight Never look directly at the sun. Never use binoculars or a telescope to observe the sun directly.

Emergency Procedures

Emergency	What to do
Burns	Flush with cold water until the burning sensation subsides.
Cuts	If bleeding is severe, apply pressure directly to the wound. If the cut is minor, allow it to bleed briefly and wash it with soap and water.
Eye injury	Flush eye immediately with running water. Do not allow the eye to be rubbed. Remove contact lenses.
Fire	Disconnect all electric circuits. Use a fire blanket or fire extinguisher to smother the fire. CAUTION: Never aim a fire extinguisher at a person's face.

Beginning Earth Science

Unit 1

Scientists surveying the earth's surface are constantly adding to our store of knowledge of the physical properties of our planet.

The earth can be considered as both old and new. The physical earth is billions of years old. But your understanding of and interaction with the physical earth is as new as today.

The physical earth is made up of matter—atoms, molecules, elements, and compounds that are present as liquids (the water you drink), gases (the air you breathe), and solids (the rocks and minerals in the earth beneath your feet).

Earth science involves interaction between people and the physical earth. Sometimes that interaction makes use of only a person's senses; sometimes it also makes use of the latest technology. By means of your senses, you have already learned much about the physical earth. You have a whole lifetime in which to learn more.

Chapter 1
Studying the Earth

Chapter 2
Earth Materials

Chapter 1 Studying the Earth

Student Resources		Meeting Individual Needs
Student Text	**Laboratory Activities**	
Section 1 Learning About the Earth 4–20 The Scientific Method 5–14	Activity 1-1 Graphing Data 8 Activity Record Sheet 1-1 LM 1 Investigation 1-1 Making Observations and Inferences LM 3–4 Research Lab 1 Forming and Testing a Hypothesis LM 13–14	CORE Enrichment Enrichment
Thinking Skill: Classifying 10 Our Scientific Heritage: How Did We Find Out the Earth Is Round? 12 What Is the Earth? 15–17 What Is Earth Science? 18–19 Section 1 Review 20		
Section 2 An International System of Measuring 21–34 The International System of Units 22–24 Measuring Length 25–26 Measuring Mass 26–28 Determining Volume 28–29 Determining Density 31 Measuring the Earth 33 Section 2 Review 34	Activity 1-2A Using Base Units to Measure 30 Activity Record Sheet 1-2A LM 5 Activity 1-2B Graphing the Density of Water 32 Activity Record Sheet 1-2B LM 6 Investigation 1-2 Determining Density LM 7–8	CORE Reinforcement Enrichment
Section 3 Mapping the Earth's Surface Latitude and Longitude 36–39 Map Projections 39–41 Colors and Symbols on Maps 41–43 North on a Map 43–44 A Scale of Distances 44–45 Topographic Maps 45–47 Careers: Earth Scientist/Cartographer 48 Different Ways to Find North 49–51 Section 3 Review 53	Activity 1-3A Locating Places on the Earth 42 Activity Record Sheet 1-3A LM 9 Activity 1-3B Using a Shadow Stick to Find a North-South Line 52; Activity Record Sheet 1-3B LM 10 Investigation 1-3 Finding the Magnetic Declination for Your Location LM 11–12	CORE Enrichment Enrichment
Chapter 1 Review 54–55		

1

Teacher Resources		Meeting Individual Needs
Teacher's Edition	**Teacher's Resource Book**	
Demonstration 2C Activity Notes 2D	Letter to Parents El 1; Essential Ideas 1-1 El 3–4 Projectsheet 1-1 TRB 225	Enrich./Rein. Enrichment
Teaching Thinking Skills 2E		
Environmental Topic 2F Discussion Idea 2F Section 1 Review Answers 2F	Teaching Diagram 1-1 TRB 9 Overhead Transparency B1 Skillsheet 1-1 TRB 103 Reading Checksheet 1-1 TRB 61 Section Reviewsheet 1-1 TRB 143–144 Section Testsheet 1-1 TRB 275	CORE CORE Reinforcement Reinforcement CORE CORE
	Essential Ideas 1-2 El 5–6	Reinforcement
Demonstration 2G Discussion Idea 2G	Teaching Diagram 1-2 TRB 10	Reinforcement
Activity Notes 2H Environmental Topic 2J Activity Notes 2K	Overhead Transparency S1 Skillsheet 1-2 TRB 104	Reinforcement Reinforcement
Section 2 Review Answers 2K	Reading Checksheet 1-2 TRB 62 Section Reviewsheet 1-2 TRB 145–146 Section Testsheet 1-2 TRB 276	Reinforcement CORE CORE
Activity Notes 2L Discussion Idea 2M	Essential Ideas 1-3 El 7–8	Reinforcement
Demonstration 2N	Skillsheet 1-3 TRB 105	Reinforcement
Creative Writing Idea 2N		
Activity Notes 2P	Overhead Transparency S2	Reinforcement
Section 3 Review Answers 2P	Reading Checksheet 1-3 TRB 63 Section Reviewsheet 1-3 TRB 147–148 Section Testsheet 1-3 TRB 277	Reinforcement CORE CORE
Chapter 1 Review Answers 2Q–2R	Chapter 1 Testsheet TRB 317–318	CORE

1

1-1

Learner Objectives

1. To distinguish the various processes by which people learn anything at all.
2. To construct a simple graph, based on collected data.
3. To name the major divisions/parts of the earth's structure.
4. To relate the major parts of the earth's structure to the three states of matter.
5. To relate the major parts of the earth's structure to the various branches of earth science.

Concept Summary

Learning involves gathering data through observation, processing and classifying data, and forming inferences on the basis of relationships drawn from the data.

The earth is the sum total of all earth materials and all earth processes.

Earth science involves all the different sciences that study particular earth materials and processes.

Demonstration

Why Indirect Observations Are Necessary

Have three bowls ready on a table. Put hot water (as hot as you can stand to put your hands in) in a bowl at one end and cold water in a bowl at the other end. Ask one student to put a hand in the hot water for a minute or two. Ask another student to put a hand in the cold water at the same time. Put warm water in the third bowl. Then have the students simultaneously take their hands from the hot and cold water and put them in the warm water.

Ask the two students to describe the temperature in the third bowl. The student whose hand was in cold water will probably say the warm water is hot, while the student whose hand was in hot water will probably say it is cold.

Ask: What does this demonstration tell us about our sense of touch? (Answers will probably vary. Part of the discussion should focus on the inability of the sense of touch to accurately measure temperature.)

Ask: How could we measure the temperature of the water? (with a thermometer) If you haven't already measured the temperature of the water, it might be helpful to do so.

Tell students that in Section 1 they will read about direct observation through the senses and indirect observation through instruments.

Activity Notes

Activity 1-1

Graphing Data   page **8**

Purpose   To display data on average height in graphic form.

- **CORE** 20 minutes Individuals
- **Activity Record Sheet 1-1** (Lab Manual page 1) can be used to record this activity.
- Science Processes: Interpreting data; Comparing and contrasting; Predicting using graphs.

Advance Preparation

Depending on student needs and available time, you might wish to introduce coordinates and coordinate graphing in a separate lesson or two. The students will use coordinates again when they study latitude and longitude in Section 3 of this chapter.

Procedure Notes

It might be necessary to explain that not all graphs need to start at (0.0). You might also point out that some data may fall along a straight line (as in Activity 1-2B, Graphing the Density of Water, page 32) or along a smooth curve (as in Activity 6-3A, Plotting a Climate Graph, page 326).

Answers to Questions

1. Answers will vary.
2. Answers will vary; graphing can either prove or disprove predicted relationships.
3. 8–13
4. 8–16
5. Answers may vary, but most students will say the graph was easiest to use.
6. Trends based on average heights

Conclusion

Students should conclude that putting data into the form of a graph makes it easier to see relationships. Since individual conclusions can vary, ask students to support their answers.

Science Background

Scientists obtain information about the earth's interior in several different ways. The most important method involves measuring the speed at which different kinds of earthquake waves travel through various portions of the earth. The rate of transmission varies with the temperature, density, and composition of the material.

Recently, geophysicists have learned how to use this information to construct three-dimensional maps of the earth's mantle and core. The technique is similar to that employed by radiologists in a CAT scan. Their findings suggest that the molten magma in the mantle is divided into two layers, each of which has a separate pattern of circulation. The core also consists of two parts: a liquid outer core and a solid inner core.

Other kinds of observations also provide information about the earth's interior. The existence of the earth's magnetic field indicates that the core probably contains large quantities of magnetic materials such as iron and nickel. Use of an instrument called a gravitometer shows very slight differences in the gravitational pull, indicating different substances under the ground. Measurements of electric current through various portions of the earth provide another way of probing its interior.

1-1

Learning About the Earth

1-1

The seemingly abstract nature of the scientific method leaves many students feeling insecure. Yet, whenever students have attempted to make sense out of everyday events and observations, they have employed the scientific method.

Removing the scientific method from the content area of science may help students see the practical nature of this process. Have students try this exercise.

Provide students with the following data: Kim is a new student at school. She spends every available minute during the school day studying or working on homework. She does not socialize very much. Kim is not involved with any sports or clubs. She goes home immediately after school every day.

Ask students to form several hypotheses about Kim's pattern of behavior. Try to elicit as many explanations as possible. Ask them to determine what would have to be done to test each hypothesis.

Introduce this new data: Kim was seen delivering newspapers in her neighborhood. Ask students to reevaluate their hypotheses in light of this new data.

By analyzing a more familiar situation for patterns, forming hypotheses to explain the patterns, evaluating how the data fits the hypotheses, and reevaluating their hypotheses in light of new data, students will become more comfortable in applying this process to "scientific" information.

Teaching Thinking Skills

Classifying   page **10**

Earth scientists classify minerals, landforms, climates, clouds, soils, and nearly everything else they study. Classification is one of the most important foundations of any science. It not only organizes the objects to be studied, but also provides much information about them.

Advance Preparation

Have ready 20 to 40 common classroom or household objects, and 20 to 40 common natural objects, such as rocks, shells, leaves, feathers, and bones.

Procedure Note

Learning the Skill can be done individually, in groups, or by the class as a whole. Whichever method is used, discussion of the classification process should follow.

Applying the Skill

This is designed as a group activity. Give each group approximately the same number of varied objects to classify. It may be helpful to walk around the room as the groups are doing the actvity and ask questions about the classifying process. After all the groups have classified their objects, ask them to report to the class on their various classification schemes. Determine the most common classification groups used and ask the students to give each group a name. Discussion should follow.

Possible Student Responses

The groups used to classify the foods in *Learning the Skill* will vary. A possible set of four groups is meat, dairy, produce, and baked goods. A possible set of six groups is vegetables, grains, dairy, poultry, meat, and fruit.

Discussion

Discussion of the food classification activity can begin with the questions on the skill page under *Learning the Skill*. Then ask how the most important properties of the six groups were different from those of the four groups.

Discussion of the activity in *Applying the Skill* may focus on the following questions: What does grouping objects into sets tell you about their common properties? Did you find that you gave names to your groups even before you were asked to? Why or why not? What information about the group does a name give?

Environmental Topic

Environmental issues are global concerns. Nuclear proliferation with its threat of global annihilation, air pollution with its potential for diminishing the quality of the air we breathe, and species extinction with its concurrent risk to the human species are concerns that know no borders.

Allow the class to generate other environmental issues that affect us all. Encourage students to speculate about how we can move toward greater world involvement in dealing with these concerns. For example, one of the most pressing environmental issues is the depletion of ozone in the upper atmosphere. Ozone is vitally important to life on earth, because it is the only component of the atmosphere that is capable of absorbing harmful ultra-violet radiation from the sun. It is possible that a dramatic increase in ultra-violet radiation could result in a dramatic increase in skin cancers.

What is causing the ozone layer to disappear? Evidence indicates that chlorofluorocarbons (compounds used in refrigerator coolants and aerosol sprays) break down in sunlight and react with ozone to decompose it.

Have the class form hypotheses regarding the depletion of the ozone layer and discuss how they would test their hypotheses. One potential hypothesis: The presence of chlorofluorocarbons is associated with a decrease in the amount of ozone in the upper atmosphere. One potential test: Periodically measure the relative amounts of ozone and chlorofluorocarbons in the air over several months' time. You may want to mention the Multinational Airborne Antarctic Ozone Experiment begun in 1987 and some of its findings.

Discussion Idea

How Do We Study the Earth?

Ask students what they expect to learn from their study of earth science. Ask them to turn to the Table of Contents and look through the contents. Point out that several different sciences make up the study of earth science.

Ask students what questions about the earth, the atmosphere, the solar system, etc., come to mind as they look at the chapter and section titles. Some of their questions can be the start of the "Unanswered Questions" chart described on page 7. Tell students that questions and observations lead to inferences, hypotheses, experiments, and theories—the scientific method. Students will learn more about all these terms in Section 1.

Section 1 Review Answers

Check Your Understanding
page **20**

1. An indirect observation uses instruments that can measure accurately, based on fixed standards. It also uses instruments that can magnify, amplify, and be used for detailed analyses of substances.
2. An observation is merely sense data. An interpretation is a way of explaining an occurrence. It goes beyond data and involves some kind of thought process and speculation.
3. A chemical property involves some kind of interaction with another substance.
4. Life is found in parts of the lithosphere, hydrosphere, and atmosphere.
5. Earth science involves different sciences, each investigating certain aspects of the entire earth.

1-1

1-2

Learner Objectives

1. To understand the usefulness of the International System of Units (SI).
2. To learn/review the base units and prefixes used in SI.
3. To use the SI system to make measurements.
4. To put data in graph form.
5. To learn how scientists were able to calculate various measurements of the earth.

Concept Summary

The **metric system** is an accurate international system of measuring that is based on multiples of ten.

Demonstration

The Need to Standardize Units of Measurement

Walk the width or length of the classroom, using your foot length as a measure. Record the distance in "feet" on the board. Have a student do the same and record the distance. Ask: Why are standard systems of measurement important?

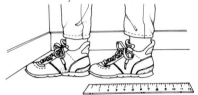

Tell students that in the past, systems of measurement were not always standard and were based on human dimensions and on practical activities. The 12-inch foot is based on the average size of a man's foot; the 4-inch hand, still used to measure horses, is based on an earlier measurement, the palm. The acre was based on the amount of land two oxen could plow in one day.

Tell students that Section 2 explains the International System of Units, a standard system of measurement.

Discussion Idea

The Importance of Standardized Measurements in Earth Science

Ask: How are measurements used in earth science? (Possible answers include measuring the distance to the sun, the thickness of rock formations, the size of a mineral crystal.) Point out that such measurements might be made using millimeters, meters, and kilometers.

Ask students how measurements of the earth are used in daily life. (They might think of using geographic and topographic maps.) Point out that mapping will be discussed in Section 3.

Explain that time involves a system of measurements, too, and that time is important in earth science—in determining the ages of the earth, various life forms, and even the solar system. Point out to students that the International System uses the second as the base unit for time, although it is not a measurement based on units of 10. Ask students if they can guess why. (They might say that time was already more standardized than other measurements or that time is based on natural processes like the rotation of the earth.) Tell students that in Chapter 3, time will be discussed in more detail.

Activity Notes

Activity 1-2A

Using Base Units to Measure   page **30**

Purpose   To measure length, volume, and mass, using base units in the SI system.

- **CORE** 20 minutes Pairs of students
- **Activity Record Sheet 1-2A** (Lab Manual page 5) can be used to record this activity.
- Science Processes: Measuring; Comparing: Reasoning.

Advance Preparation

Before doing this activity, you may wish to review with students the use of a balance to measure mass. You also might want to predetermine the mass of the coins to be used so that students can verify their measurements.

Procedure Notes

Instruct students about the meniscus, the curved upper surface of a column of liquid, formed when measuring the volume of a liquid using a graduated cylinder. For this activity, either the top or the bottom of the meniscus can be used, as long as consistency is maintained throughout the set of readings that are conducted.

If the students' measurements differ from their classmates', ask them to account for these differences.

Answers to Questions

Parts A, B, and C:

Answers to measurement questions will vary, depending upon the objects or volumes measured.

Part D:

1. Answers will vary, depending on skill in using the balance, quality of the balance, etc.
2. Students can find the mass and volume of 100 sheets and then divide the results by 100 to get the answer for 1 sheet.

Conclusion

Instruments help make your observations more accurate. However, the observer's skill at using the instrument and the quality of the instrument can affect measurement.

Science Background

The importance of the metric system in measurement is not that it is more accurate than other systems, for the British system of measurements can produce just as great a degree of accuracy. The principal advantage is 1) that it is easier to work with (being based on 10s) and 2) that certain relationships exist between systems of units. For example, 1 cm^3 of water at sea level and 4°C has a mass of 1 g. This relationship makes it easy to solve problems involving mass, volume, linear measurement, and temperature.

1-2

1-2

Student Misconception

Few students realize that the decimal number system, from which the metric system is derived, is just one of several number systems currently in use. Each number system relies on a particular "base" or the fundamental unit upon which the number system is founded. For example, the decimal system is dependent on the base 10, as in five-tenths ($^5/_{10}$) of twenty-tenths ($^{20}/_{10}$).

The hexadecimal system, as the name implies, relies on base 16. This system is ideally suited as a communication link between the computer and the human. The various computer languages (Fortran, Cobal, Pascal, etc.) are translations of hexadecimal code for the particular application the programmer has in mind.

The binary, or base 2, system of 1's and 0's is the fundamental language of the computer's internal dialogue. With 1's and 0's, the on and off positions of the computer microswitches, the computer is capable of performing the dizzying calculations for which it is indispensable. It is the product of binary code work that is relayed through hexadecimal code to the decimal code that we witness on the computer screen.

Using coins, tokens, or toothpicks, have the students total an imaginary grocery bill in binary, hexadecimal, and decimal codes, and determine which is the easiest to handle. Review with the students why the binary and hexadecimal number systems are not suited for this task.

Environmental Topic

Most of us are unaware of the total amount of garbage that is produced weekly by a large city. Help students develop a sense of the environmental problem created by trash disposal. Have them calculate the volume of garbage produced by New York City in one week. Ask students to imagine a rectangular structure two stories high, one football field wide, and 1 km long. On the board, calculate the volume of this week-long accumulation of trash. Before calculating the volume, it would be helpful for the class to convert the measurements given into meters: 1 story = 4 m, 1 football field = 300 m, and 1 km = 1000 m. Ask students to compare this volume with the volume of a more familiar object.

On a global scale, students might consider the idea of dumping the world's trash into space. Acquaint students with the cost factor (the cost of a fleet of spaceships sufficient for the task would exceed the gross national product of the United States) and the fact that outerspace would never "fill up."

Activity Notes

Activity 1-2B

Graphing the Density of Water　page **32**

Purpose　To find the mass of four different amounts of water.

- 20 minutes Groups of 4 or teacher demonstration
- **Activity Record Sheet 1-2B** (Lab Manual page 6) can be used to record this activity.
- Science Processes: Measuring; Communicating through graphs; Analyzing data; Comparing; Generalizing.

Advance Preparation

If Activity 1-1, Graphing Data, has not been done previously, you may wish to first introduce coordinate graphing in a separate lesson, depending on student needs and available time.

The students' accurate reading of a graduated cylinder and accurate use of a meniscus to measure liquid are essential for this activity.

Procedure Notes

Before calculating the densities in Step 8, have students connect the points of their graphs, beginning at (0,0) and extending through the last point plotted, (50,50). Unlike the graph in Activity 1-1, the points of this graph fall along a straight line.

Discuss with students how the graph could be used to find the mass of different volumes of liquid such as 120 mL of water.

Answers to Questions

1. The answers will be very nearly the same for all volumes of water (1.0 g/mL).
2. For the copper bar, volume is usually measured in cm^3 or m^3, since the copper bar is a solid.

Conclusion

The density of water is 1.0 g/mL, no matter what the volume. Graphing is useful in predicting—another process of science. From the graph, students can tell, without measuring, that if the mass of water is 25 g, the volume is 25 mL; if the volume is 80 mL, the mass is 80 g; and if the volume is 40 mL, the mass is 40 g.

Section 2 Review Answers

Check Your Understanding
page **34**

1. 1) The metric system (SI) is based on unchanging standards. 2) Multiples and subdivisions of base units are multiples of ten. 3) The base units of length, mass, and volume are interrelated. 4) The metric system is used internationally for scientific purposes. 5) An international committee exists to monitor the system and make adjustments as needed.
2. Weight varies with the pull of gravity; mass does not.
3. $Density = \dfrac{Mass}{volume} = \dfrac{36\ g}{9\ cm^3}$
   $= 4\ g/cm^3$
4. The variation between circumferences is not great enough to affect the overall shape of a model of the earth.
5. 1) $C = \pi D$
   $C = 3.1 \times 10\ cm$
   $C = 31\ cm$

   2) $2r = D$
   $2r = 10\ cm$
   $r = \dfrac{10\ cm}{2}$
   $r = 5\ cm$

   3) $A = 4\pi r^2$
   $A = 4 \times 3.1 \times (5\ cm)^2$
   $A = 4 \times 3.1 \times 25\ cm^2$
   $A = 310\ cm^2$

1-2

Mapping the Earth's Surface

1-3

Learner Objectives

1. To understand the usefulness of latitude and longitude for describing the location of any point on the earth.
2. To distinguish among the various kinds of models of the earth's surface.
3. To become familiar with the various conventions used on maps.
4. To infer shape and elevation from a topographic map.
5. To distinguish between magnetic north and true north.

Concept Summary

Maps are graphic representations of all or part of the earth's surface.

Activity Notes

Activity 1-3A

Locating Places on the Earth   page **42**

Purpose   To locate some places on the earth using latitude and longitude.

- **CORE** 10 minutes Pairs of students
- **Activity Record Sheet 1-3A** (Lab Manual page 9) can be used to record this activity.
- Science Processes: Observing; Communicating through co-ordinates; Identifying; Reading a map.

Advance Preparation

Compile a list that states the latitude and longitude of several familiar and unfamiliar cities so that you can do some practice examples with the students.

Procedure Notes

Give latitude and longitude coodinates of several cities and ask students to locate and verbally identify the cities. Latitudes and longitudes may be expressed separately, or in the form of an ordered pair of coordinates similar to those used in graphing. Students should then find the latitude and longitude of the specific cities listed in the activity.

Answers to Questions

1. Pittsburgh, Indianapolis, Denver, Salt Lake City, etc.
2. Africa, South America
3. El Paso, Phoenix, Tucson, Los Angeles, San Francisco, etc.
4. Adelaide
5. Alaska

Conclusion

Latitude and longitude provide a system of coordinates that allows location of any point on earth.

Going Further

The epicenter of an earthquake is described in terms of lati-tude and longitude. The coordinates of the epicenters of ma-jor earthquakes may be found in almanacs or some encyclo-pedias. You may wish to give students such data and have them plot the coordinates on a world map. You might then discuss why earthquakes occur more often in some regions than in others. This information may be used later, when studying earthquakes in Chapter 10.

Discussion Idea

Location Is a Prime Factor in Determining Climate

Ask students if they have ever found their way to a new location by using a map. Have they ever helped their parents read a road map while on vacation? Can it be difficult at times? (Road signs don't always say what you'd expect; not all roads, features, etc. can be included on maps.)

Using a globe or world map, follow the 40° N parallel and read aloud the names of major cities along it. Ask students what they know about the climates of these cities (Denver, Salt Lake City, Philadelphia, Lisbon, Madrid, Ankara, Peking, etc.). Ask them if cities at the same north or south latitude have the same kind of climate. (Answers will vary.) Tell them that, for instance, the average annual precipitation for Denver is 13 inches and for Philadelphia is 40 inches. The average annual temperature in Denver 10°C; in Philadelphia, it is 12.5°C.

Tell students that they will learn more about climate later on in Chapter 6. In Section 3 of Chapter 1, they will learn about latitude and longitude as a way of locating places on earth.

Science Background

Gerardus Mercator was a Flemish geographer who was born in 1512. Sea commerce was expanding greatly during this era, and navigators needed a flat map showing minimum distortion. Mercator's map projection has minimal distortions at the equator, but increasingly larger distortions toward the poles. This was not much of a problem at that time, because shipping routes were mostly limited to the tropical and temperate zones.

The Mercator projection is responsible for some misconceptions about global geography. For example, it does not show that Africa is considerably larger than the Soviet Union. In the Miller cylindrical projection, which is a modification of the Mercator projection, the exaggeration of areas in high latitudes is not as great.

1-3

1-3

Student Misconception

Topographic maps show the shape of the earth's surface, which is covered by elevations and depressions of various magnitudes. Contour lines reflect a change in elevation in a progressive manner, as values increase with elevation above sea levels. Thus contour lines provide a means of visualizing surface features without requiring a three-dimensional model.

Students generally have difficulty reading topographic maps because they cannot visualize the three-dimensional effect of a two-dimensional model. Most confusing is distinguishing between a *downslope,* a change in the direction of slope, and a *depression,* a basin or lowered area between elevated parts of the earth. Many students will misperceive that a decrease in elevation represents a depression. Depressions are indicated by the presence of hachures accompanying a regular decrease in elevation, while downslopes are indicated by a regular decrease in elevation and no hachures. The drawing of rough profiles may help students develop a better sense of reading topographic maps. By comparing a simple contour map of a hill with one of a volcanic cone having a caldera (crater), students can observe the differences in markings used to indicate downslopes and depressions.

Demonstration

How Maps Differ

Collect as many different kinds of maps of your community as you can—if possible, a city/town street map, a state road map, a U.S. Geological Survey topographic map (available in bookstores, sporting goods/backpacking stores, and directly by mail from USGS), a special-use map (for example, one showing recreational areas or campsites), and a Landsat map. Put the maps up around the classroom and give students a chance to examine them.

Ask students if they were able to locate familiar places such as their school, their street, the state capital, or a particular mountain, river, lake, or bay. Ask if they noticed what kinds of scales and symbols were used on each map.

Have the students compare and contrast the map types. Discuss the location of north, the symbols, scale, and familiar features. (On some topographic maps, students can locate their homes.)

Tell students they will learn more about topographic maps and how maps are made in Section 3.

Creative Writing Idea

After students have begun to understand how the two-dimensional topographic map relates to the three-dimensional world, offer them the following writing assignment.

Take an imaginary five-day hike from west to east across the center of the Topographic Map of Orr Mountain, page 626 in the Appendix. Write a letter to your sister describing the slope of the land you cross each day. Be specific, detailing the experience of climbing up slopes versus climbing down. Choose where you would camp each night and describe the topography. If you cross water, describe the shape of the valley that holds the water.

This assignment may be simplified by having students cross the map in Figure 1-31, on page 47 in the textbook.

Activity Notes

Activity 1-3B

Using a Shadow Stick to Find a North-South Line   page **52**

Purpose To find the geographic north-south line using shadows cast by the sun.

- 2½ hours Class demonstration
- **Activity Record Sheet 1-3B** (Lab Manual page 10) can be used to record this activity.
- Science Processes: Observing; Constructing a model; Collecting and analyzing data; Inferring.

Advance Preparation

For permanency, it is recommended that a wooden board, dowel, and nail be used.

Procedure Notes

After preparation in class, students can take turns leaving class to make the necessary markings, or they can do the activity on a nonschool day. If a camera that produces instant pictures is available, photos can be taken every 15 minutes. The photos can be used in a class discussion of the activity.

The north-south line in this activity can be used for Investigation 1-1 (Lab Manual pages 3–4) and Investigation 3-1 (Lab Manual pages 35–36).

Answers to Questions

1. The shadow will be shortest around noon (1:00 p.m. if DST), but can vary because of location or time of year.
2. The shadow moves from west to east.
3. The sun is at its highest point when the shadow is shortest.

Conclusion

It is expected that students will mention the rotation of the earth, the relationship between time and position of the sun, etc.

Section 3 Review Answers

Check Your Understanding
page **53**

1. As you travel north or south from the equator, 1° of longitude represents a shorter distance because the meridians get closer as they near the poles. Parallels, however, do not get closer to each other.
2. The difference in elevation between two contour lines is the same. As the distance between contour lines decreases, the slope has to become steeper, as shown in a diagram like the following.

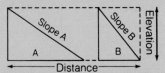

3. True north is toward where the meridians meet at the North Geographic Pole. Magnetic north is toward the North Magnetic Pole.
4. 1 cm = 10 km

1-3

Chapter Vocabulary

Section 1

direct observation
instrument
indirect observation
data
classifying
physical property
chemical property
inference
hypothesis
theory
crust
mantle
Mohorovicic discontinuity (Moho)
core
outer core
inner core
lithosphere
hydrosphere
atmosphere
biosphere
geology
meteorology
oceanography
hydrology
astronomy
petrology

Section 2

SI
meter
weight
mass
derived unit
volume
density
circumference

Chapter 1 Review Answers

Putting It All Together   page 54

1. 1) Observation is the basis of all scientific knowledge. Through our five senses, we obtain data through direct observation. 2) Instruments extend our senses and enable us to gather, through indirect observation, data that our senses could not detect on their own. 3) Evidence is data based on observation and that is offered in support of a particular idea or explanation. 4) Classifying puts similar objects or events into groups so that they can be considered according to common properties or other relationships. 5) An inference is a possible explanation or interpretation of what has been observed. 6) A hypothesis is a possible answer to a question and provides a focus for further testing and investigation. 7) A theory is a stronger explanation than a hypothesis because a theory is based on several hypotheses that have been tested and become generally accepted. Though based on strong evidence, a theory is still not proof that something is true.

2. 1) The lithosphere is the solid, outer part of the earth upon which we live. 2) The hydrosphere is all the water on the earth's surface and in the atmosphere. 3) The atmosphere is the blanket of air that surrounds the earth. 4) The biosphere includes those parts of the atmosphere, hydrosphere, and lithosphere in which life is found.

3. 1) Geology studies the lithosphere. 2) Meteorology studies conditions in the atmosphere. 3) Oceanography is concerned with the oceans (part of the hydrosphere). 4) Hydrology is concerned with the entire hydrosphere. 5) Astronomy deals with the earth in relation to the stars and planets that are observed from the earth.

4. A good measuring system 1) is based on unchanging standards, 2) uses basic units of measure that are easy to work with, and 3) is accepted and used by many people all over the world.

5. a. 742 cm = 7.42 m
   b. 1055 mm = 1.055 m
   c. 0.85 m = 85 cm
   d. 6.82 m = 682 cm
   e. 0.43 m = 430 mm
   f. 128 cm = 1280 mm

6. The mass of an object is the amount of material in that object and is the same no matter where the object is. The weight of an object is dependent upon and varies with the force of gravity on that object. That is why the same object has the same mass on both the earth and the moon, but it weighs only 1/6 as much on the moon because the force of gravity on the moon is only 1/6 as strong as the force of gravity on the earth.

7. To find the volume of an irregularly shaped object, submerge the object in water and measure the amount of water that is displaced by the submerged object. Since 1 mL (liquid volume) of water is displaced by 1 cm^3 (solid volume), a displacement of 30 mL of water means that the submerged object has a volume of 30 cm^3.

Chapter 1 Review Answers (continued)

Putting It All Together

8. density $= \dfrac{\text{mass}}{\text{volume}}$

$2 \text{ g/cm}^3 = \dfrac{\text{mass}}{16 \text{ cm}^3}$

mass $= (16 \text{ cm}^3) \times (2 \text{ g/cm}^3) = 32 \text{ g}$

9. 1) Meridians run north and south; parallels run east and west. 2) Meridians are numbered in degrees east or west of the prime meridian; parallels are numbered in degrees north or south of the equator. 3) Meridians meet at the poles; parallels are always the same distance from each other.

10. a) A map is flat, but a globe is round. b) Because a map can cover only a small portion of the earth's surface, it can show more detail than a globe; but a map of the entire earth will necessarily be distorted in some way. c) A topographic map uses contour lines that indicate contours and changes in elevation.

Apply Your Knowledge page 54

1. Without inferences, science would be limited to the immediate present of direct and indirect observations. By means of inference, the mind is able to look for and analyze patterns and interrelationships among observations, to speculate about possible causes and effects, to draw conclusions, to formulate and test hypotheses, and all the other processes associated with the world of science as we now understand it.

2. $D = \dfrac{M}{V}$ 　　$2.7 \text{ g/cm}^3 = \dfrac{54 \text{ g}}{20 \text{ cm}^3}$

When you halve the volume, you halve the mass. But the density remains the same.

$\dfrac{27 \text{ g}}{10 \text{ cm}^3} = 2.7 \text{ g/cm}^3$

3. Since there are 360° of latitude, 1° of latitude $= 40\ 000 \div 360 = 111.111$.

4. a) The contour interval is 50 m. b) C is higher than D. The hachure lines indicate that D is in a depression. c) Route 2 involves the steepest climb (indicated by the shortest distance from the lowest to the highest contour lines). Route 3 is the gentlest climb (indicated by the longest distance from the lowest to the highest contour lines). If students want to consider the distance to D inside the depression, point out that 1) it is a depression, not a climb, and 2) the only thing you can tell about the depression is that it is less than 50 m (otherwise another contour line would be used).

5. A topographic map, which shows changes in elevation, would indicate possible gradient problems (up and over or around hills, etc.). Presence of other features would also have to be considered. For example: buildings, forests, swamps, lakes, rivers.

Chapter Vocabulary

Section 3

globe
parallel
latitude
meridian
longitude
prime meridian
equator
map
map projection
legend
scale of distance
topographic map
topography
contour line
elevation
map relief
contour interval
hachures
compass
North Magnetic Pole
magnetic north
North Geographic Pole
true north
magnetic declination

Chapter 1

Studying the Earth

Section 1
Learning About the Earth

You learn about the earth in the same way you learn about anything else. You begin with data obtained through your five senses. You then process that information to make inferences and to form ideas about how and why things happen.

The earth is made up of all three states of matter: solid, liquid, and gas. Different sciences study various aspects of the earth. Earth science is really a combination of sciences.

Section 2
An International System of Measuring

Objects like a roof or house are made up of matter, which has certain physical properties. Among the properties of matter are size, mass, volume, and density. By using both accurate measurements and mathematical formulas, the size, mass, volume, and density of even the earth itself can be calculated.

Section 3
Mapping the Earth's Surface

The earth's surface is huge and varied. For thousands of years, people have been studying the earth they live on. During that time, representations of the earth's surface have increased in detail, in area, and in accuracy.

There are many different kinds of representations or models of the earth's surface. Each kind has advantages and disadvantages. You are probably already familiar with many of the different kinds of models of the earth's surface.

Have students list major developments in forms of transportation (e.g. back of animal, sailboat, sailing ship, steamship, railroad, airplane, spacecraft). Then discuss the kinds of information about the earth that were made possible as a result of each.

By means of a single view from space, you can learn more about the earth than earlier people could learn in an entire lifetime. From the photograph on the left, what can you tell about the earth? How could this same information be obtained if people could observe the earth only from its surface?

Learning About the Earth   Section 1

Section 1 of Chapter 1 is divided into three parts:

The scientific method

What is the earth?

What is earth science?

Figure 1-1. If you were walking along this beach, what could you learn through your sense of touch? through your sense of sight? through your other senses? Answers to the caption question will vary.

Learner Objectives
1. To distinguish the various processes by which people learn anything at all.
2. To construct a simple graph, based on collected data.
3. To name the major divisions/parts of the earth's structure.
4. To relate the major parts of the earth's structure to the three states of matter.
5. To relate the major parts of the earth's structure to the various branches of earth science.

From earliest childhood, each of us has been learning many things about the world around us. At first, our world was very small. But because we can always learn more about the things and people around us, our world can become increasingly larger.

This earth science text will help to expand your world. You will learn what other people have discovered about the earth you live on. You will learn names for many of the earth features and processes that are within your experience. You will become more aware of ordinary, everyday earth materials.

At the beginning of this text, it might be a good idea to consider how it is that we learn anything at all. Each of us has been learning for quite some time now. So it certainly cannot hurt to try and figure out what it is that we've been doing. In the process, we might even become better at it, too!

The scientific method

New vocabulary: direct observation, instrument, indirect observation, data, classifying, physical property, chemical property, inference, hypothesis, theory

The **scientific method** is a way of describing "how scientists find out." Scientists have a very special way of learning what is based on experimenting. In this section you will also learn about the *processes of science*, such as observing, classifying, inferring, and hypothesizing. Through the centuries, these observations have been collected from every place that people have been able to explore or study.

How are these kinds of observations made? When you use your sense of sight, your sense of touch, your sense of hearing, or maybe even your sense of smell or taste, you are making a **direct observation.** In some instances, you will use more than one of your senses at the same time. For example, you see a wave break on the beach. At the same time, you hear its thundering noise as it hits the beach. You may even feel the spray or smell the salt in the air. These are all direct observations.

Indirect observations   Our senses have limitations. We are unable to measure accurately the observations we make. And in some cases, we are unable to make any observation at all

If you have a world map that can be placed on a bulletin board, you could establish a class map. Students bring in news articles of earth science events, which are posted on the bulletin board. Strings run from articles to locations on map. This creates interest, teaches geography, and helps students learn about earth science.

The processes of science also include predicting, using numbers, measuring, making models, interpreting data, estimating, defining operationally, and others.

What do you use to make a direct observation?
Throughout this text, answers to margin questions are underlined in color.

Figure 1-2. Because of telescopes like this, scientists are able to see stars and galaxies that could never be seen otherwise. Why can a telescope be called an instrument?
Because it obtains information that our senses would not be able to pick up on their own. (All questions asked in the captions throughout this book are answered in the text the students read, usually on the same page as the caption.)

Additional Activities:

1. It has been said that the other senses of blind people are extra keen. Have students research this. Maybe they know a blind person and can find out about that person's ability to obtain information through the senses.
2. Students can watch their favorite TV program five minutes blindfolded and five minutes with the sound off. Which is more meaningful to understanding the show, sound or sight?

Earthquakes occur around the world daily. Most are never mentioned in the newspapers because the quakes do not release enough energy for us to feel them. A seismograph not only detects these minor quakes, but can also be used to determine their location and depth.

What are indirect observations?

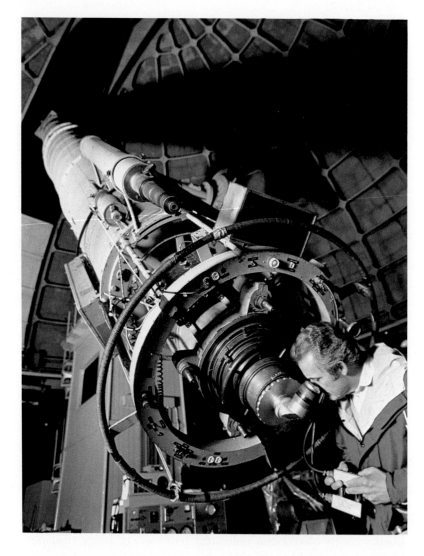

all because the event or thing is not strong enough to be heard, seen, or felt. Sometimes the event is too slow or too fast for our senses to detect. A minor earthquake is a good example of an event that might go unnoticed by observers because of the limitations of their senses.

How then are we able to measure and detect events or make observations if our senses have limitations? Scientists have invented **instruments** that allow us to measure according to standard units of measurement. They have also invented instruments that detect, magnify, and record information that our senses are unable to pick up. These instruments extend our senses beyond their limits. They allow us to make **indirect observations**—that is, observations that could not normally be made.

Collecting data   All sciences begin with observations, both direct and indirect. These observations are then collected and recorded. A collection of observations is known as **data.**

When scientists observe and record data, the data can be presented in a variety of forms. Data can be presented in a written description of what was observed, in chart form (as in Table 1-1), or in the form of a graph.

Collecting data is very important because it enables us to see relationships.

Classifying data   Scientists make data meaningful by using processes such as classifying. **Classifying** is the grouping of similar events or objects, based upon observed properties, or characteristics. It provides a method of understanding the relationships among observations, and in turn, understanding the complexity of nature. Classifying also provides scientists

What is a collection of observations known as?
A good all-year activity is to make a chart entitled "Unanswered Questions." When students ask a question that can't be answered immediately, they get to write that question on the chart. This encourages questions. It also encourages others to find out what the answers are. If they find the answer to a question, they get to put their name after the question.

Average Height of Males and Females		
Age of Male or Female	Average Height of Females	Average Height of Males
8 years old	126.4 cm	127.0 cm
9 years old	132.2 cm	132.2 cm
10 years old	138.3 cm	137.5 cm
11 years old	144.8 cm	143.3 cm
12 years old	151.5 cm	149.7 cm
13 years old	157.1 cm	156.5 cm
14 years old	160.4 cm	163.1 cm
15 years old	161.8 cm	169.0 cm
16 years old	162.4 cm	173.5 cm
17 years old	163.1 cm	176.2 cm
18 years old	163.7 cm	176.8 cm
19 years old	163.8 cm	176.9 cm
20 years old	163.8 cm	176.9 cm

Table 1-1. This table presents, in chart form, average heights for males and females from 8 to 20 years old. Because people mature at their own rates, it is likely that a particular person will differ in height from the average for her or his age group.
Because junior-high students are concerned about their size, etc., it is important that they understand that these figures are merely averages. It is also important that they realize that people mature at different rates.

Science Process: Interpreting data
See also Activity Record Sheet 1-1 (Lab Manual
page 1)

CORE   20 minutes   Individuals or
                                   small groups

Activity 1-1 Graphing Data

Materials

graph paper

2 pencils, each of a
  different color

Table 1-1 on page 7 of
  this text

Purpose

To display data on average height
in graphic form.

Procedure

1. Look at Table 1-1. This data table gives the
   average heights, in centimeters, for females
   and males between the ages of 8 and 20.
2. List all the relationships you see between the
   average heights of females and their ages.
3. Do the same for males.
4. Make a list of all the relationships you see
   between the heights of males and females.
5. Graph the data from the data table on a
   graph similar to the one shown. When you
   connect your plotting points, do the males in
   one color and the females in another. Make
   a key or code for the colors so that your
   graph will be easy to read and understand.

Questions

1. Because of making your graph, can you add
   any more relationships to your list?
2. Were any of the relationships you listed
   wrong? right?

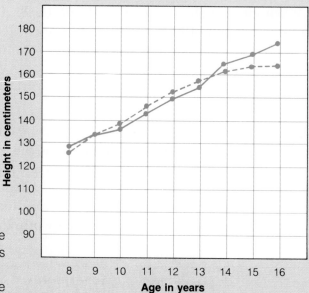

Key - - - = females   ———— = males

3. Between what ages do females grow fastest?
4. Between what ages do males grow fastest?
5. Which was easiest to use to answer questions 4 and 5—the data table, your lists, or
   your graph?
6. Not all males over 16 are 173.5 cm. Not all
   females over 14 are 160.4 cm. What, then,
   do the heights in Table 1-1 indicate?

Conclusion

Did graphing the data help you to see relationships among the data? If so, how?

Answers to Questions:
1. Answers will vary.
2. Answers will vary; graphing can either prove or
   disprove prior relationships.
3. 8-13
4. 8-16
5. Graph, but again answers might vary
6. Trends based on average heights

Conclusion:
It is expected that students will conclude that putting
data into the form of a graph will make it easier to
see relationships. Since individual conclusions can
vary, ask students to support their answers with
evidence or supportive reasoning.

Figure 1-3. Silver needs frequent polishing to keep it shiny. What causes silver to lose its shine? The formation of silver sulfide, which tarnishes the silver.

with a method for communicating their ideas to one another.

As you know, there are many different substances on the earth. Scientists can classify these substances according to their properties. Different substances often have different physical and chemical properties. A **physical property** (FIZ′-uh-kul PROP′-er-tee) is a feature of the substance itself. The color, softness, and shininess of silver, for example, are all physical properties of silver.

A **chemical property** (KEM′-uh-kul PROP′-er-tee) is a feature of the way that one substance reacts with another substance. Silver, for example, needs frequent polishing to keep it shiny. That is because silver readily combines with sulfur (from hydrogen sulfide in the air) to form a dark-colored substance called silver sulfide. The fact that silver tarnishes by forming silver sulfide is a chemical property of silver.

Is the tarnishing of silver a physical or a chemical property of silver?

Making inferences Scientists make inferences from the data gained through observations of properties and processes. An **inference** (IN′-fer-ins) is an interpretation of the data. By inferring, the scientist suggests causes or explanations for what has been observed. A scientist must make inferences that are directly supported by the collected data. To do otherwise would result in incorrect conclusions.

For example, huge impressions shaped like dinosaur feet have been found in some rocks. Observing such impressions leads to the inference that a dinosaur was present before the rock layer formed. This inference may or may not be correct. More observations and information would be needed before you could be reasonably sure that the inference is true.

Thinking Skill Classifying

Have you ever arranged your clothes to match items that go together? If so, you have used the skill of classifying.

Classification is the process of grouping together objects or events based on common characteristics. Scientists use the skill of classifying to organize their thinking about what they observe.

You can learn to classify like a scientist by using the following steps:

1. Examine the objects or events that you will be classifying.
2. Select one object or event, then find a second that is similar to the first.
3. Determine the most important characteristic shared by the two objects or events, and write down this characteristic as the group title.
4. Find all the other objects or events that have this same characteristic and list them under the group title.
5. Repeat Steps 2 through 4 to classify all the objects or events.
6. Examine all the groups and make any necessary changes, such as combining or subdividing the groups.

Learning the Skill

Do you know how foods are classified in a supermarket? Use the steps of the classifying skill to classify the following foods into four groups:

milk	pork chops
lettuce	cheese
turkey	ground beef
bread	carrots
cupcakes	oranges
apples	ice cream
hamburger buns	chicken

peaches	tomatoes
sausage	steak

Discuss your method of classifying the foods. Why did you place the foods in the groups you did? Can you classify the same foods into six groups?

Applying the Skill

Objects can be classified in many different ways. Your teacher will give your group a collection of objects to place on your work table. Have each member of your group classify the objects into groups based on their physical properties. What is the most important characteristic shared by the objects in each group?

Each person in the group should take a turn classifying the objects. How many different ways can your group classify the objects?

Figure 1-4. These dinosaur bones are in a rock layer that is millions of years old. What can be inferred from these bones? We can infer that a dinosaur was present before the rock layer formed.

Ask students to devise questions that would strengthen their inference; for example, How deep are the bones buried? What kind of material are they found in? Where geographically were they found?

Making inferences is a key process of science and in the study of the earth. As you proceed in studying earth science, you will be presented with observations. In some cases, you will be making observations. It is important that you ask questions about those observations. Every question you ask may lead to a different set of inferences or to more questions.

Forming a hypothesis   All observations made by scientists are directed toward a better understanding of how things work, what they are like, how they began, how they change, and how they relate to one another. Basically, scientists are constantly seeking answers and explanations. Questions such as "How can we find out when an earthquake is going to occur?" give focus to scientific investigation. A possible answer or solution to a problem is called a **hypothesis** (hī-POTH'-uh-sis).

Scientists often must use a variety of techniques in their search for the solutions to different problems and questions. The two main techniques that scientists use in forming hypotheses are called the deductive method and the inductive method. In the deductive method, the scientist proposes a hypothesis based on experience and on some logical explanation of the way a particular phenomenon may occur. After the hypothesis is formed, the scientist tests it by collecting data and making observations. The collected data are then analyzed to determine whether they agree or disagree with the original hypothesis.

You might have students make up a hypothesis and explain how they could test it. Or you might give students a hypothesis, such as "It always rains when the barometer drops." Students then plan ways to test the validity of the hypothesis.

Our Science Heritage

How Did We Find Out the Earth Is Round?

Students can test Aristotle's conclusion, based on the earth's curved shadow on the moon. How, for example, do the shadows caused by a curved surface and a straight-edged surface appear when cast onto a sphere?

Through the ages, the earth has been thought to be flat, pear shaped, and perfectly round. What evidences led to the conclusion that the earth is round?

Back in the fourth century B.C., Aristotle offered the earth's shadow during a lunar eclipse as evidence that the earth is round. When a lunar eclipse takes place, the earth passes between the sun and the moon. This causes a shadow of the earth to appear on the surface of the moon. Aristotle noticed that the earth's shadow is curved.

Aristotle obtained another evidence of the earth's

roundness by observing stars from different places. If, for example, you observe a star at an angle of 45° above the northern horizon and then move south, the star will appear to get lower in the sky. If the earth's surface were flat, then the star would always appear at 45° above the horizon.

Based on Aristotle's assumptions, Eratosthenes actually determined the circumference of the earth in the second century B.C. He did this by comparing the length of shadows in two different places at the same time.

Even much later, in Columbus's time, there was still doubt about the earth's shape. One argument used to support the earth's roundness had to do with a ship's "disappearing" over the horizon. As a ship sailed away from an observer, the ship gradually disappeared, with the lower parts disappearing before the sails and masts.

Many other evidences of the earth's shape have, of course, been offered between Aristotle's lifetime and the present day. Depending on your interest, you might research some of these other evidences on your own.

In the **inductive method,** the scientist first collects a lot of data without trying to test any preconceived ideas. By then classifying and analyzing the data, the scientist reaches some conclusion that allows the formation of a hypothesis. This hypothesis explains the data in the simplest and most logical form. Often the deductive and inductive methods are used together, with one leading to the other.

Because a hypothesis is only a possible answer, the scientist then makes additional observations and performs more experiments to determine whether or not the hypothesis is the most accurate answer to the question. Additional observation and experimentation are the true tests of a hypothesis.

No matter how many observations and experiments are conducted, however, a hypothesis can never be proven absolutely true. But hypotheses are strengthened and become better accepted the more they are tested without being proven false. The basic nature of science is, in part, that scientists try to disprove their hypotheses. When a hypothesis cannot be proven false after many years of testing, the hypothesis becomes so strong that it can become a theory.

A hypothesis is often made when patterns can be seen in observations. Such a pattern may be developing between radon gas and earthquakes. Russian and Chinese scientists, for example, have noticed that the amount of radon gas in wells sometimes increases before earthquakes. Before a 1979 earthquake in Southern California, increased amounts of radon

Figure 1-5. Scientists try to predict when and why events such as the eruption of Mount St. Helens take place. How do such questions affect scientific investigation? They may lead to different sets of inferences or to more questions, either of which helps to clarify the focus of the investigation.

Showing students a graph of sunspots or tides or some other recurring event can be used to show patterns and to form a basis for predictions.

Library research

How have scientists added to our knowledge of the earth's shape? Names to consider: Parmenides, Aristotle, Eratosthenes, Picard, Picher, Newton, Cassini, MacLaurin, Clairants, Alexander Clarke, and more recent scientists.

You might wish to use this example/approach to further an understanding of scientific methods of investigation, the validity of conclusions based on observations, or the writing up of investigations.

1. Direct observation uses only the five senses; indirect observation uses instruments.
2. A hypothesis is a possible answer formulated by scientists to give focus to further investigation and experimentation. A theory is a scientific explanation that is based on generally accepted hypotheses that have been tested many times.

were observed. Such a developing pattern of observations could lead to a hypothesis like "An increase in radon gas always precedes an earthquake." Such a hypothesis, according to the scientific method, would have to be tested to see if it is true.

From hypothesis to theory   A **theory** (THEE′-uh-ree) is a way of explaining how or why something happened. It may develop from one or more hypotheses that have become accepted through repeated testing. Just like hypotheses, however, theories can never be proved true. They are subject to change whenever new evidence shows they are incorrect.

The following sample procedure shows how a hypothesis might be set up and tested.

Problem: How can we find out when an earthquake is going to occur?

Evidence (based on observations): Isolated reports show increased amounts of radon gas before an earthquake.

Hypothesis: An increase in radon gas always precedes an earthquake.

Test: Carefully monitor radon gas concentrations in all major earthquake areas throughout the world, perhaps over a period of twenty years.
A. Note whether there is an increase of radon gas before each earthquake that occurs.
B. Note whether there is an increase in radon gas in areas where no earthquakes occur.

The data obtained during the test period can perhaps lead to a general theory about the causes of earthquakes. The theory can then be further refined by testing other hypotheses, such as "Certain events in space can cause earthquakes" or "Heavy rains on a fault plane can cause earthquakes."

Check yourself

1. What is the difference between a direct observation and an indirect observation?

2. What is the relationship between a theory and a hypothesis? Is either considered to be a proof?

New vocabulary: crust, mantle, Mohorovicic discontinuity (Moho), core, outer core, inner core, lithosphere, hydrosphere, atmosphere, biosphere

What is the earth?

Many people think of the earth as a ball of rock and soil. Maybe there was a time when you did, too. The earth is more than just rock and soil. The earth is made up of all three forms of matter. Part of the earth is solid. Part of the earth is liquid. And part of the earth is gas.

Much of what you learn about the earth this year will relate to the earth's structure. The earth's structure can be thought of as having four divisions or layers. From the inside out, the earth consists of an interior, a lithosphere, a hydrosphere, and an atmosphere.

Figure 1-6. The earth is composed of all three states of matter. Where in this scene would you find a solid, a liquid, and a gas?
In the scene pictured on the left, a solid can be found in rock and soil (visible and also beneath the vegetation); a liquid can be found in the water in the river, in the condensation in the clouds, and in water droplets on the objects splashed by the river water; a gas can be found in the invisible water vapor present in the air.

See also Teaching Diagram 1-1 (TRB page 9).

Figure 1-7. We live on the earth's lithosphere, which covers the earth's interior. Compared to the earth's interior (the inner core, outer core, and mantle), how thick is the lithosphere?

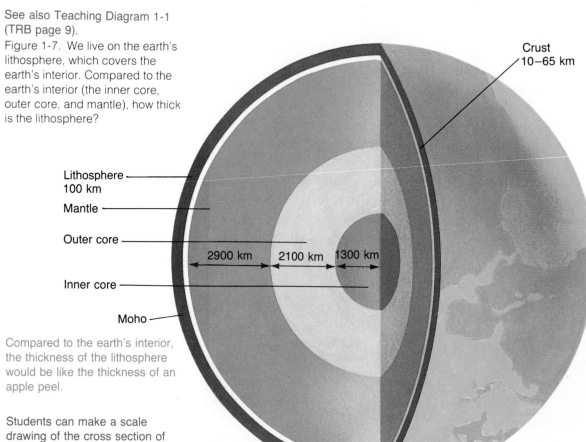

Crust
10–65 km

Lithosphere
100 km

Mantle

Outer core

2900 km   2100 km   1300 km

Inner core

Moho

Compared to the earth's interior, the thickness of the lithosphere would be like the thickness of an apple peel.

Students can make a scale drawing of the cross section of the earth, showing the divisions between the parts. A possible scale for them to use would be 1 cm = 400 m.

Library research

The interior of the earth is thought to have an inner core, an outer core, and a mantle. How do these regions differ from each other?

Check yourself answers for bottom of facing page:
1. The lithosphere includes solid crustal rock and soil; the hydrosphere is liquid water; the atmosphere is mostly gas.
2. There is a constant exchange of energy and materials among the different spheres.

Scientists believe that the interior of the earth is made of different layers (see Figure 1-7). The outermost layer is called the **crust,** and it is made of rock and soil. The crust extends from the continents to the ocean basins and varies from 10 to 65 kilometers (km) in thickness. The layer beneath the crust is called the **mantle.** It is about 2900 km thick and is made of heavy rocks. There is a boundary layer between the crust and the mantle because crustal rock is less dense than mantle rock. This boundary is called the **Mohorovicic discontinuity,** usually shortened to **Moho.**

The innermost layers of the earth are called the **core.** The **outer core,** about 2100 km thick, consists of liquid iron and metal; the **inner core,** about 1300 km thick, consists of solid iron and nickel.

The **lithosphere** (LITH′-uh-sfir) consists of the crust and the upper mantle. It is about 100 km thick. The word *litho-sphere* comes from two Greek words that mean "stone" *(lithos)* and "ball" *(sphaira)*. Compared to the thickness of the entire earth (about 6300 km), the thickness of the lithosphere would be like the thickness of the skin of an apple.

The word *hydrosphere* (HĪ′-druh-sfir) comes from the Greek words for water *(hudor)* and ball. The earth's **hydrosphere** is composed of all the oceans and inland seas, lakes, and streams. The hydrosphere is all the water found on earth. It includes the water that is below the ground and the water that is found in the atmosphere.

The word *atmosphere* (AT′-muh-sfir) comes from the Greek words for vapor *(atmos)* and ball. The earth's **atmosphere** is the blanket of air, dust, water droplets, ice particles, etc. that completely covers the earth's lithosphere and hydrosphere. We actually live at the bottom of an ocean of air. As you go up into the atmosphere, the air thins out very quickly.

The earth's atmosphere is divided into zones or regions. Figure 1-8 shows only one of the ways that scientists divide the atmosphere. Where the atmosphere actually ends and outer space begins is still not defined.

Another of the earth's zones is called the **biosphere** (BĪ′-uh-sfir). The word *biosphere* comes from the Greek words for life *(bios)* and ball. The biosphere is not really a division of the earth's structure. Rather, the biosphere includes part of the earth's lithosphere, hydrosphere, and atmosphere. The biosphere is the region near the earth's surface where all life is found.

One of the most important ideas to remember throughout your study of earth science is that there is a constant exchange of energy and materials among the lithosphere, atmosphere, and hydrosphere. This exchange of energy and materials takes place at their boundaries or between each sphere.

Check yourself

1. How do the lithosphere, hydrosphere, and atmosphere show that the earth is made of solid, liquid, and gas?

2. What is constantly happening at the boundaries of the different spheres?

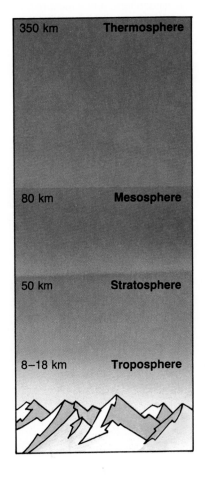

Figure 1-8. The earth's atmosphere is divided into zones or regions. What zone meets the earth's crust?
The troposphere

It is here that most earth changes that we have knowledge of take place. At these boundaries, we are able to observe changes both directly and indirectly.

Check yourself answers appear at the bottom of the facing page.

Is earth science a single science
or does it involve many different
sciences?

Critical Thinking

Into which specialized science
group would you place the
study of clouds? the study of
the sun?

Meteorology; astronomy

Pairs of students might be
interested in doing a project.
Each pair could take a branch of
earth science, such as geology,
and then prepare a chart of the
sub-branches. Such research is
good for career-related
considerations.

Does earth science also involve
the sciences of chemistry,
physics, and biology?

What is earth science?   New vocabulary: geology, meteorology, oceanography, hydrology, astronomy, petrology

What is earth science? Each of the pictures in Figure 1-9 represents one area of science that makes up earth science. Earth science is more than a study of the surface of the earth and all its changes. Earth science is concerned with knowledge of the entire earth. Earth science is therefore concerned with the earth's lithosphere, hydrosphere, and atmosphere. As such, earth science involves many different sciences.

Earth science involves geology. **Geology** (jee-OL′-uh-jee) is the science that deals with the earth's lithosphere. Geology is concerned with the structure of the lithosphere, its composition, and what causes it to change.

Earth science involves meteorology. **Meteorology** (meet′-ee-uh-ROL′-uh-jee) is the science that deals with the earth's atmosphere. Meteorology is concerned with the composition and structure of the atmosphere. It is also concerned with the many changes that are constantly taking place in the atmosphere.

Earth science involves oceanography and hydrology. Oceanography and hydrology are sciences that deal with the earth's hydrosphere. **Oceanography** (ō′-shuh-NOG′-ruh-fee) is concerned with the properties and processes of the earth's oceans. **Hydrology** (hī-DROL′-uh-jee) is concerned with the earth's entire hydrosphere, including the water below the earth's surface and the water in the earth's atmosphere.

The study of earth science really goes way beyond the earth itself. It also includes astronomy. **Astronomy** (uh-STRON′-uh-mee) is the science that deals with stars and planets. Astronomy is concerned with the size, composition, structure, and movement of stars and planets.

Geology, meteorology, oceanography, hydrology, and astronomy are only five of the sciences that investigate the earth. Each of those five sciences also involves the sciences of chemistry, physics, and biology. In addition, each of the major "earth sciences" is divided into very specific and specialized sciences. A geologist, for example, may be a specialist in the study of rocks. The part of geology that specializes in rocks is called **petrology** (puh-TROL′-uh-jee), from the Greek words *petros*, meaning rock, and *logos*, meaning word, thought, or branch of study.

As you can see, then, there are really many earth sciences. In the course of this text, you will see how these various sciences blend together to form a unified presentation of our current knowledge of the earth. Also, twelve career pages, one in each chapter, will give you a better idea of what work in some of the more specialized earth sciences involves.

If, in the future, you decide to learn more about a particular aspect of the earth, you will take courses in the individual sciences that deal in greater detail with those areas of the earth that interest you most.

Check yourself

Check yourself answers appear at the top of facing page.

1. Why does the study of earth science involve many different sciences?

2. How does the study of astronomy differ from the study of the other four major earth sciences?

Figure 1-9. The stars (the Pleiades cluster in the constellation Taurus), the bathyscaphe *Trieste,* the volcano (Del Fuego Volcano near the city of Antigua, Guatemala), the snow, and the tornado represent five earth sciences. Which earth science could be represented by each picture?
The stars—astronomy; the bathyscaphe—oceanography; the volcano—geology; the snow—hydrology; the tornado—meteorology (Del Fuego Volcano means "volcano of fire." On the edge of the city of Antigua is another volcano called *Volcan de Agua*—"volcano of water.")

Section 1 Review   Chapter 1

Use **Reading Checksheet 1-1** TRB page 61
Skillsheet 1-1 TRB page 103
Section Reviewsheet 1-1 TRB pages 143–144
Section Testsheet 1-1 TRB page 275

Check Your Vocabulary

19 astronomy

2 atmosphere

5 biosphere

12 chemical property

9 classifying

22 core

26 crust

20 data

8 direct observation

14 geology

1 hydrology

18 hydrosphere

15 hypothesis

13 indirect observation

4 inference

24 inner core

10 instrument

6 lithosphere

25 mantle

16 meteorology

21 Mohorovicic discontinuity

11 oceanography

23 outer core

17 petrology

3 physical property

7 theory

Match each term above with the numbered phrase that best describes it.

1. The science concerned with the earth's entire hydrosphere

2. The blanket of air that covers the earth's lithosphere and hydrosphere

3. A feature of a substance in itself

4. An interpretation of observations

5. The region where all life is found

6. Consists of the crust and upper mantle

7. Based on strong evidence that several generally accepted hypotheses are correct

8. Information received by the senses

9. Grouping similar objects or events

10. Used to extend our senses when observing

11. The science concerned with the oceans

12. A feature of the way one substance reacts with another substance

13. An observation that requires the use of an instrument

14. The science concerned with the earth's lithosphere

15. Possible answer to a problem, based on observations

16. The science concerned with the earth's atmosphere

17. The part of geology that specializes in rocks

18. The entire liquid or water part of the earth

19. The science concerned with stars and planets

20. A collection of observations

21. Boundary in the earth between crust and mantle

22. The innermost layers of the earth

23. Layer of the earth consisting of liquid iron and other metals

24. Layer of the earth consisting of metals

25. Layer of the earth made of heavy rocks

26. Outermost layer of the earth's surface

Check Your Knowledge

Multiple Choice: Choose the answer that best completes each of the following sentences.

1. All sciences begin with ? .
   a) theories
   b) observations
   c) classifying
   d) hypotheses

2. Among the lithosphere, atmosphere, and hydrosphere, there is ? .
   a) an increase in radon gas
   b) a constant exchange of energy and materials
   c) a layer that has some properties of both solids and liquids
   d) a ball of rock and soil

Check Your Understanding

1. Explain how an indirect observation can be more accurate than a direct observation.

2. Explain why the name of this book could be *Earth Sciences* rather than *Earth Science*.

An International System of Measuring Section 2

Section 2 of Chapter 1 is divided into six parts:

The International System of Units (SI)

Measuring length

Measuring mass

Determining volume

Determining density

Measuring the earth

Learner Objectives
1. To understand the usefulness of the International System of Units (SI).
2. To learn/review the base units and prefixes used in SI.
3. To use the SI system to make measurements.
4. To put data in graph form.
5. To learn how scientists were able to calculate various measurements of the earth.

Figure 1-10. These roofers must make accurate measurements to make a roof that does not leak. If you were roofing a house like this one, what kinds of measurements would you need? What instruments could you use to make the measurements? You would need to measure length in several directions. You could use a meter stick or a measuring tape such as the roofer in the photo is using.

Additional Activity
(for previous page):
Have students measure the width
and height of several doors in
different places. Comparing
measurements, which dimensions
were used as a standard size for
a number of doorways? How
many standard sizes were
observed?

Questions like these appear often
in the running text. Their purpose
is largely to get students thinking
about what the answer might be,
in terms of their own experience.
The text then goes on to answer
the question. If you do not see an
annotation answer for a question
in the running text, most likely the
question is answered by the text
that immediately follows the
question.

Simple observation in science is fine for providing certain kinds of information. But for other kinds of information, some kind of instrument is also needed.

Let us say your friends want a bulletin board for the hallway in their apartment. They want the biggest bulletin board that will fit on the wall between the door to the kitchen and the door of the hall closet. What can you do if you want to get them that bulletin board?

You could go to the store and look at the different size bulletin boards. You could then buy the one that looks like it might fit. But you would be taking a chance. You could easily buy one that will not fit the way your friends want it to.

How can you be sure the one you buy will fit? You can measure the space on the wall. You can then tell the person at the store how big a space you want to fill. The person at the store will then know exactly what size bulletin board to give you to best fill the space.

The International System of Units (SI)

New vocabulary: SI, meter

It is helpful to be able to measure the length of a wall, the width of a doorway, or the height of a shelf. But people have also wondered about the measurements of larger objects, too. How high, for instance, is a certain tree or a certain mountain? How big, even, is the earth itself? To find the answers to questions like these, a very good system of measurement is needed.

What makes a system of measurement good? First of all, a good system of measurement must be based on standards of measure that never change. Secondly, the basic units of measure should be easy to work with. And thirdly, the system of measurement needs to be accepted and used by many people all over the world.

What do the initials SI stand for?

A present-day system of measurement that meets the requirements for a good system is called the International System of Units. Its initials are **SI,** after its name in French, *le Système International d'Unités*.

The International System of Units, which was agreed upon in 1961, is based on a form of the metric system. The metric system traces back to France in 1790. A committee was formed

to decide on a single system of measurement that could be used throughout all of France. For ease of use, the new system was to be based on multiples of ten. Also, there was to be an inter-relationship among the basic units for length and volume and mass.

For the new measuring system, a standard for measuring length was needed. It was decided that the size of the earth itself would somehow be used. To arrive at a standard for measuring length, the distance between the North Pole and the equator was divided by ten million. The resulting length was called a **meter,** from the Greek word *metron,* which means a measure. This length was then marked on a metal bar that for a long time served as the standard to be used in making other meter-length measures. Later, it was found that the length of the meter was not exactly one ten-millionth of the distance between the North Pole and the equator. But the measure was retained as a standard unit.

The metric system developed by the French was not immediately accepted by other people. It took many years before it came to be widely used. By the 1950s, many varieties of metric measures were in use. There was clearly a need, on a world-wide scale, for the International System of Units.

The International System of Units uses seven base units, shown in Table 1-2. As a student, you will probably have the

Figure 1-11. A meter stick is divided into 100 cm. Into how many smaller units is each centimeter divided?
Each centimeter is divided into 10 smaller units (millimeters).

It is *not* important that students learn to convert. Simply help them establish a sense of relationship by stating a few common equivalencies. For example:
  4 liters ≈ 1 gallon
1 meter ≈ 1 yard
  20°C ≈ 70°F

Additional Activity:
Students can bring in labels of products that show metric measures. Some students might construct a graph showing the relationship between grams and ounces (to illustrate the conversion factor).

Base Units of the International System of Units (SI)		
Name	Property Measured	Symbol
meter	length	m
kilogram	mass	kg
second	time	s
ampere	electric current	A
kelvin	temperature	K
candela	luminous intensity (brightness)	cd
mole	number of particles of a substance	mol

Prefixes Used with SI Base Units		
Prefix	Symbol	Value Numbers
mega	M	1 000 000 times the base unit
kilo	k	1 000 times the base unit
hecto	h	100 times the base unit
deka	da	10 times the base unit
deci	d	0.1 times (1/10 of) the base unit
centi	c	0.01 times (1/100 of) the base unit
milli	m	0.001 times (1/1000 of) the base unit
micro	μ	0.000001 times (1/1 000 000 of) the base unit

Table 1-2. The International System of Units (left) uses seven base units. Which two will you probably have most need of?

Table 1-3. The SI system (right) uses prefixes to indicate quantity. The prefixes make it easier and faster to multiply, divide, and make conversions.
See also Teaching Diagram 1-2 (TRB page 10).

most need for the units of length and mass. Some of the other base units are used mainly in specialized sciences. The symbols for ampere and kelvin are capital letters because those base units are named after people who lived in the past.

Along with the base units, the SI system uses prefixes to indicate quantities. The prefixes, given in Table 1-3, make the SI system easier and faster to work with when it comes to multiplying and dividing. It also makes it easier to convert from one unit to another.

The prefixes most commonly used by students are kilo (k), centi (c), and milli (m). If you look at a meter stick, you will see that 1 m = 100 cm = 1000 mm. A centimeter (1 cm) is therefore one hundredth of a meter. A millimeter (1 mm) is one thousandth of a meter.

Note that one of the base units, the kilogram, already has a prefix. The kilogram actually is 1000 (kilo) grams. But the gram was not chosen as the base unit because of its very small amount.

Check yourself

1. What makes a system of measurement good?

2. What are the two most common base units used by students?

3. Why are prefixes used with base units?

4. When the metric system was first being set up at the end of the eighteenth century, what distance on the earth was used as the standard for a meter length?

Measuring length

Marks on a metal bar no longer provide the standard for a meter length. Even under very carefully controlled conditions, the size of the metal bar was found to be not perfectly constant. The standard now used is not even a physical object. The standard is based on the wavelength of a special kind of light. However, there is no need for you to worry about this. For practical purposes, an accurate ruler or measuring tape is the only standard you will need for measuring length.

Today, many of the road signs in the United States give distances in kilometers as well as miles. The United States has been slow to adopt the metric system, however. In Canada and most other countries, the distances are given only in kilometers.

One nice thing about the metric system is that you don't have to worry about remembering the answers to questions like these:

How many inches are in a foot?   12 in.

How many feet are in a yard?   3 ft

Figure 1-12. How do the units of distance on these road signs differ?
The road sign on the left (located in Ontario, Canada) gives distances in kilometers. The road sign on the right (located in California) gives distances in both miles and kilometers.

Library research

The United States is one of the last countries to adopt the metric system. Prepare a report on the Metric Conversion Act of 1975. How much progress in using metric has occurred in the United States since 1975?

1. 100 cm in 1 m; *centi* means 100
2. 1000 mm in 1 m; *milli* means 1000

Which base unit is the only one whose standard is still a physical object?

How many feet are in a mile?   5280 ft

How many yards are in a mile?   1760 yds

Which is longer—316 yards or 950 feet?   950 ft is longer.

With the metric system, the prefix tells you how many. In the case of kilometers, the prefix *kilo* tells you it's one thousand times the base unit, meter(s). And to go from kilometers to meters to centimeters is easy, too. All you have to do is move the decimal point. For example, 95 km = 95 × 1000 m = 95.000. m.

Even though a new measuring system may have clear advantages, it is not easy to get people to change over from their old system. A measuring system is so much a part of a person's way of thinking that to suddenly have to start thinking in different units is very difficult.

Check yourself

1. How many cm are in 1 m? What does the prefix *centi* mean?

2. How many mm are in 1 m? What does the prefix *milli* mean?

Measuring mass

New vocabulary: weight, mass

As indicated in Table 1-2, the base unit for measuring mass is the kilogram. The standard for the kilogram is a special metal cylinder that is kept by the International Bureau of Weights and Measures in Paris, France. An exact copy of that cylinder is kept as a standard in the United States. The kilogram is the only base unit whose standard is still a physical object.

In everyday speech, the term *weight* is used to mean mass. But strictly speaking, weight and mass are not the same thing. The following example illustrates the difference between mass and weight.

Weight is the pull of gravity on nearby objects. On the earth, weight is the pull of the earth's gravity on objects near or on the surface of the earth. On the moon, weight is the pull of the moon's gravity on objects near the surface of the moon. Weight can vary depending on gravity. **Mass** is the amount of material in something. It is the same everywhere.

The 1-kg mass in Figure 1-13 is hanging from the same spring scale on the earth and on the moon. But the 1-kg mass weighs less (only ⅙ as much) on the moon. This is because the moon's gravity is not as strong as the earth's. The moon's gravity does not pull as strongly on the mass and spring.

But the 1-kg mass has not changed. It has just as much material, or mass, in it on the moon as it has on the earth.

Now suppose we take a lump of clay and put it on a beam balance with the 1-kg mass, as shown in Figure 1-14. On the earth, the clay and the 1-kg mass balance, so the mass of the clay on the earth is 1 kg. What would the mass of the clay be on the moon?

When we take the same clay, 1-kg mass, and beam balance to the moon and set it up, we find that the clay and the 1-kg

Does a 1-kg mass weigh the same on the earth and on the moon?

Question is answered in next paragraph.

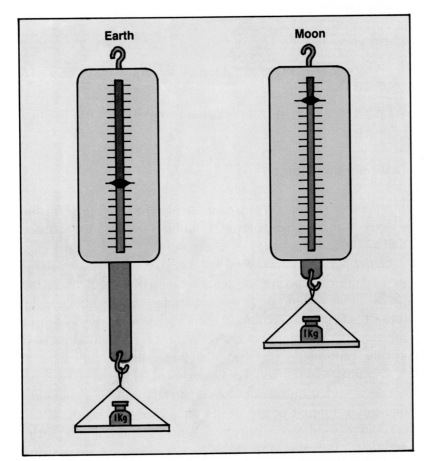

Figure 1-13. A spring scale is used to measure weight. Why does a 1-kg mass weigh only 1/6 as much on the moon as it does on the earth?
As explained in the text, weight depends on the force of gravity and the moon's gravity is only ⅙ as strong as the earth's gravity.

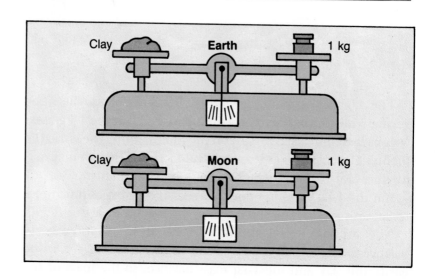

Figure 1-14. A beam balance is used to measure mass. Does a 1-kg mass balance the same mass of clay on the moon as it does on the earth?
Yes, a 1-kg mass balances the same mass of clay on both the earth and the moon.

How can you tell that the mass of the 1-kg mass in Figure 1-14 is the same on the earth as on the moon?

1. Because the moon's gravity is only ⅙ as strong as the earth's

2. 3 kg, regardless of the force of gravity

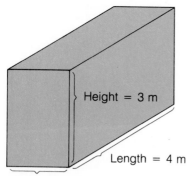

Height = 3 m

Length = 4 m

Width = 2 m

Volume = length × width × height
Volume = 4 m × 2 m × 3 m
Volume = 24 m³ or 24 cubic m

Figure 1-15. Volume is a derived unit. How is a derived unit different from a base unit?
A derived unit is made up of two or more base units.

mass balance each other there, too. The mass of the clay has not changed. It balances the same 1-kg mass on both the earth and the moon. We can see from this little experiment that weight is really a measure of the pull of gravity and that weight changes as the pull of gravity changes.

Check yourself

1. Why would a person weighing 60 kg on the earth weigh 10 kg on the moon?

2. What would be the mass of an object if it were balanced by a 3-kg mass?

Determining volume

New vocabulary: derived unit, volume

It is possible to combine two or more base units. You then have a **derived unit** such as volume. **Volume** is the amount of space that an object takes up.

Figure 1-15 shows how the volume of a rectangular solid is derived by multiplying the length times the width times the height. The volume of a spherical solid can be obtained by using the formula Volume = $\frac{4}{3}\pi r^3$, where r is the length of the radius. The volume of a solid is most frequently expressed in cubic centimeters (cm³) or cubic meters (m³).

A graduated cylinder like those shown in Figure 1-16 is often used to determine the volume of the inside of a container that holds a liquid or gas. A set of marks on the side of the cylinder is used to measure the volume of the liquid in the cylinder. The volume of the liquid is measured by pouring the liquid into the graduated cylinder and recording the mark on the cylinder that corresponds to the middle of the top level of the liquid. The volume of the liquid may be expressed in liters (L) or milliliters (mL). Milliliters are used when only a small amount of liquid is being measured.

Some solid objects cannot be measured with a ruler. But there is an easy way to find the volume of objects like these, too. It is called the water displacement method. The object is submerged in water, causing the water level to rise. The new level of the water is equal to the volume of the water plus the volume of the object. To calculate the volume of the object, you subtract the original volume of the water level reading from the water level reading with the object submerged in the water. 1 mL (liquid volume) equals 1 cm^3 (solid volume). Therefore, if a solid displaces 30 mL of water, it has a volume of 30 cm^3.

Check yourself

1. How would you find the volume of a block of wood?

2. How would you find the volume of an irregular-shaped object such as a rock?

Length: meter, centimeter
Mass: gram, kilogram
Volume: liter, milliliter

1. If a regular shape, measure its length, width, and height; then multiply the length times the width times the height. If irregular, measure the volume of water it displaces when submerged.
2. Its volume is equal to the volume of water it displaces when submerged.

Figure 1-16. This graduated cylinder is an instrument that measures liquid volume in milliliters (mL). It can also be used to measure the volume of some solids. What is the volume of the stone that was lowered into the water in the cylinder on the right? The volume of the submerged stone is 20 cm^3.

To make accurate measurements of the height of a column of liquid, it is important that students be aware of the fact that the level of a liquid can be either convex or concave. Such a curved surface is called a meniscus. When students take liquid measurements, they must be sure that they use the same part of the meniscus (either the top or the bottom) when calculating changes that involve the same sample.

Science Process: Measuring
See also Activity Record Sheet 1-2A (Lab Manual page 5)

CORE   20 minutes   Pairs of students

Activity 1-2A   Using Base Units to Measure

Materials

meter stick or metric rule   water
graduated cylinder   coins
balance   wooden blocks

Purpose

To measure length, volume, and mass, using base units in the SI system.

Procedure

A. Length
On a sheet of paper, construct three lines equal to these lengths: 20 cm, 4.5 cm, and 24 mm.

Question

Have another student measure your lines. Did you make them the right length?

B. Volume of a Solid
Find the volume of a wooden block by measuring the length, width, and height. Multiply these three measurements to find the volume.

Question

What is the volume of the solid in cm^3?

C. Volume of a Liquid
Examine the graduated cylinder with water in it.

Question

What is the volume in mL?

D. Mass
Using a balance, find the mass of each of several coins.

Questions

1. How do your findings compare with those of a classmate?
2. How could you find the mass and volume of the paper you are writing on? The paper does not have enough mass to get a reading on the balance. It does not have enough thickness to measure with a ruler.

Conclusion

How do instruments affect observation?

Step C

Step D

Figure 1-17. The rock sinks in water, but floats on the mercury. What does this observation suggest about the densities of each object?
The rock is denser than water, and less dense than mercury.

Determining density

New vocabulary: density

You know that certain materials are more "dense" than other materials. You would expect a certain volume of iron, for example, to weigh more than the same volume of wood. Iron is more dense than wood.

Density is the mass of 1 cm^3 of a material. To find the density of a material, you must find its mass and its volume. You then divide its mass by its volume.

To find the density of a material, what two measurements must you find first?

$$\text{density} = \frac{\text{mass}}{\text{volume}}$$

Let's say, for example, that a certain block of copper has a volume of 8 cm^3. Its mass is 72 g. The density of copper would be expressed as the mass (in grams) of 1 cm^3 of copper.

$$\text{density of copper} = \frac{72 \text{ g}}{8 \text{ cm}^3} = 9 \text{ g/cm}^3$$

In your study of earth science, you will see how differing densities of air masses cause winds. You will also see how differing densities of water cause ocean currents.

Check yourself

1. How could you determine the density of an object?

2. Suppose a metal bar had a mass of 24 g and a volume of 3 cm^3. What would be its density? Show your work.

1. Calculate its mass and volume; then divide the mass by the volume.

2. density $= \dfrac{24 \text{ g}}{3 \text{ cm}^3} = 8 \text{ g/cm}^3$

Science Processes: Measuring; Communicating through graphs
See also Activity Record Sheet 1-2B (Lab Manual page 6)

20 minutes

Groups of 4

Activity 1-2B   Graphing the Density of Water

Materials

balance
graduated cylinder
water
eyedropper
graph paper

Purpose

To find the mass of four different amounts of water.

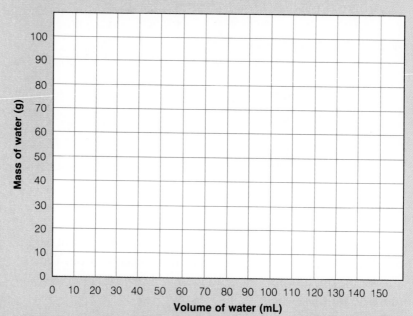

Procedure

1. Find the mass of an empty graduated cylinder. Record the measurement.
2. With your teacher, construct a data table for each mass and volume of water.
3. Put 10 mL of water into the graduated cylinder. (By using an eyedropper, you can make the measurement more accurate.)
4. Find the combined mass of the graduated cylinder and the water in it.
5. Calculate the mass of only the 10 mL of water and record your finding.
6. Empty the graduated cylinder and repeat the procedure, using 20 mL, 30 mL, and 50 mL of water. Each time, find the mass of only the water.
7. After you have found the mass and volume of each amount, plot the data on a piece of graph paper. Following the samples on this page, indicate volume of water (in mL) across the bottom of the graph. Indicate mass of water (in g) up the left side of your graph.

8. On your graph, plot the mass for each amount of water. Then calculate the density for each volume of water. Use the formula

$$\text{density} = \frac{\text{mass in g}}{\text{volume in mL}}$$

for 10 mL, 20 mL, 30 mL, and 50 mL.

Questions

1. Are your calculations of density the same for all four volumes?
2. The unit of density for the water is g/mL. How does this compare with the unit of density used for the copper bar? Why should there be a difference in the units?

Conclusion

Do different volumes of water have different densities? What can the graph tell you about the relationship between volume of water and density of water?

You may want to introduce students to the concept of π by having them measure the diameter and circumference of cans, lamp shades, and other round objects. (Do not explain exactly what the students are determining so that they have the opportunity to discover this concept on their own.) Have them divide the circumference by the diameter and write the results on the board. In most cases, the results will be close to 3.1. This is a good time to discuss error in measurement and, with interested students, to calculate percentage of error.

Measuring the earth

New vocabulary: circumference

Circumference is the distance around a circular object. Scientists know the circumference of the earth. They obtained this information from very accurate measurements of the pull of gravity, from space flights, and from photographs taken from space. The earth's circumference, if measured around the equator, is 40 076 km. The earth's circumference, if measured through the Poles, is 40 008 km.

Because of the difference in the two circumferences, you can see that the earth is not perfectly round. There is a slight flattening at the Poles. And there is a slight bulge at the equator. But these slight differences in the shape of the earth are very small compared to the overall size of the earth. They are so small that if you were asked to draw a picture of the earth, you would draw a circle. If you were asked to make a model of the earth, you would make a round globe.

Once the earth's circumference is known, its radius, its diameter, its surface area, and its volume can be calculated. Scientists used mathematical formulas to obtain these measurements because it is obviously impossible to measure them directly. Figure 1-18 shows the formulas that can be used to obtain various earth measurements.

Scientists have even calculated the density of the earth. As shown in Figure 1-18, scientists could calculate the volume of the earth once they knew its circumference. But how could they obtain its mass? They certainly could not put the earth on a balance. They were able to use the earth's force of gravity to obtain its mass. Scientists were able to calculate the force with which the earth attracts objects to its surface. Using this information, they calculated the density of the earth to be 5.5 g/cm^3.

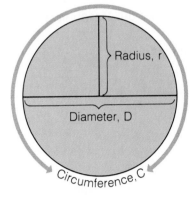

Radius, $r = \dfrac{C}{2\pi}$

Diameter, $D = 2r$

Circumference, $C = \pi D$

Surface area, $A = 4\pi r^2$

Volume of a sphere, $V = \dfrac{4}{3}\pi r^3$

Figure 1-18. Once the earth's circumference is known, other earth measurements can be calculated by using mathematical formulas. What is the relationship between diameter and radius? The diameter is twice the radius

What density did scientists calculate for the entire earth?

1. From the pull of gravity, from space flights, and from photographs taken from space
2. The earth's radius, diameter, surface area, and volume
3. They could calculate its volume once they calculated its circumference; they were able to calculate its mass by using the force of gravity.

Check yourself

1. How have scientists obtained the information needed to calculate the earth's circumference?

2. Once the earth's circumference is known, what four other earth measurements can be calculated?

3. How were scientists able to calculate the earth's density?

Section 2 Review   Chapter 1

Use **Reading Checksheet 1-2** TRB page 62
   Skillsheet 1-2 TRB page 104
   Section Reviewsheet 1-2 TRB pages 145–146
   Section Testsheet 1-2 TRB page 276

Check Your Vocabulary

3 circumference   1 meter

5 density   4 SI

8 derived unit   7 volume

6 mass   2 weight

Match each term above with the numbered phrase that best describes it.

1. A standard unit of length originally based on the distance between the North Pole and the equator

2. The pull of gravity on an object

3. The distance around a circle or ball

4. Initials for International System of Units

5. The mass of 1 cm^3 of a material

6. The amount of material in something

7. The amount of space that an object takes up

8. A unit of measure obtained from two or more base units

Check Your Knowledge

Multiple Choice: Choose the answer that best completes each of the following sentences.

1. The __?__ is the base unit used for measuring length.
   a) kilogram   c) centimeter
   b) meter   d) liter

2. The prefix kilo (k) means __?__.
   a) one hundred
   b) one one-thousandth
   c) ten
   d) one thousand

3. The __?__ is the only unit of measure that contains a prefix and that is a base unit.
   a) centimeter   c) gram
   b) kilogram   d) millimeter

4. Measuring the amount of water displaced by a submerged object is a way of determining the __?__ of the object.
   a) height   c) volume
   b) density   d) weight

5. If a solid displaces 30 mL of water, it has a volume of __?__
   a) 60 cm^3 c) 30 cm^2
   b) 30 cm^3 d) 30 cm

Check Your Understanding

1. Explain why the metric system is a good system of measurement.

2. Describe the difference between mass and weight.

3. The mass of a rock is 36 g. The volume of the rock is 9 cm^3. Explain how to find the density of the rock? What is the density of the rock?

4. Explain why a model of the earth would be round even though the earth is not perfectly round.

5. Using 3.1 as π, find the circumference, radius, and surface area of a ball with a diameter of 10 cm. Show your work.

Mapping the Earth's Surface   Section 3

Section 3 of Chapter 1 is divided into seven parts:

Latitude and longitude

Map projections

Colors and symbols on maps

North on a map

A scale of distances

Topographic maps

Different ways to find north

Learner Objectives

1. To understand the usefulness of latitude and longitude as coordinates for describing the location of any point on the earth.
2. To distinguish among the various kinds of models of the earth's surface.
3. To become familiar with the various conventions used on maps.
4. To infer shape and elevation from a topographic map.
5. To distinguish between magnetic north and true north.

Figure 1-19. The surface of the earth is huge and varied. Over the centuries, models of the earth's surface have been developed with increasing accuracy and detail. If you were making a model of this section of the earth's surface, what features would you feel you had to include?

Answers will vary. In discussion, bring out the need to represent the linear outlines (the shape of the coastline, for example). Also discuss the different elevations that can be seen and ask students if they can think of ways in which these could be indicated on a model? (They can, for example, be represented on a topographic map or a globe. Topographic maps will be discussed in this section of Chapter 1.)

What is a globe?

New vocabulary: globe

A **globe** is a physical model of the earth. Because the earth is almost a perfect sphere, globes are the only true representations of the earth. But a globe may be only the size of a basketball. The surface area of the earth, on the other hand, covers almost 513 000 000 km². Detail and accuracy of particular places and features are impossible to provide on such a globe. For close-up representations of sections of the earth, there are maps that show this detail and accuracy.

Latitude and longitude   New vocabulary: parallel, latitude, meridian, longitude, prime meridian, equator

"Meet me on Main Street and we can walk to the movies together." Probably the first thought that comes to your mind is "whereabouts on Main Street?" If the other person had said, "Meet me at the corner of Main Street and Second Avenue, in front of the drug store," you would have known exactly where to go.

This method of giving locations works well as long as there are streets that can be identified. But what happens out in the country or in a strange land, or even out on the ocean? How are people able to locate places on earth?

The place where Main Street and Second Avenue cross is called an intersection. Intersections called coordinates can also be plotted for any point on the earth's surface. A system of reference points, or coordinates, can be established by drawing two sets of lines or rings around the earth.

Using latitude and longitude to pinpoint locations on the earth is described in the text that follows. Some students may have knowledge of dead reckoning or the use of stars, buildings, or other landmarks. If students know these other methods, they might explain them to the class. Also, students may have parents who have taken navigation classes for boating, and they might be willing to share the information with the class.

Figure 1-20. Intersections are useful for describing locations. How would you describe the location of the A on the map? A is at the corner (intersection) of Main Street and Second Avenue.

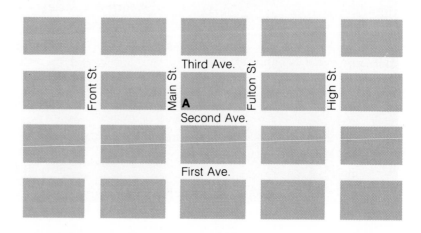

One set of rings runs east-west around the earth, parallel to the equator. These east-west lines, or rings, are called **parallels.** Parallels enable a person to measure the latitude of any point on earth. **Latitude** is the distance any point is north or south of the equator.

Another set of imaginary lines runs north-south. They cross the equator at right angles, and they meet at the North and South Poles. These north-south lines are called **meridians.** Meridians enable a person to measure the longitude of any point on earth. **Longitude** is the distance that any point is east or west of the prime meridian.

Latitude and longitude were introduced by a Greek philosopher, Ptolemy, about 150 A.D. The present system of numbering the parallels and meridians, however, goes back only to 1884. At that time, a group of astronomers was meeting in Washington to discuss how to calculate time around the world. They decided to use Greenwich, England, the site of an important observatory, as the starting point for calculating time. In doing so, they also agreed that an imaginary line passing through Greenwich, England, would be called the **prime meridian.**

Parallels are numbered in degrees north and south of the equator. As shown in Figure 1-22, the **equator,** which is the beginning line for latitude, has a latitude of 0°. Beginning at

Figure 1-21. This photograph shows the original Royal Greenwich Observatory at Greenwich, England. What does that observatory have to do with our being able to describe locations in terms of latitude and longitude?
Longitude is measured in degrees east or west of the prime meridian, which passes through Greenwich, England.

When and by whom were latitude and longitude first used?

In discussing parallels, have students consider that parallel lines never meet. They are equidistant from each other at all times.

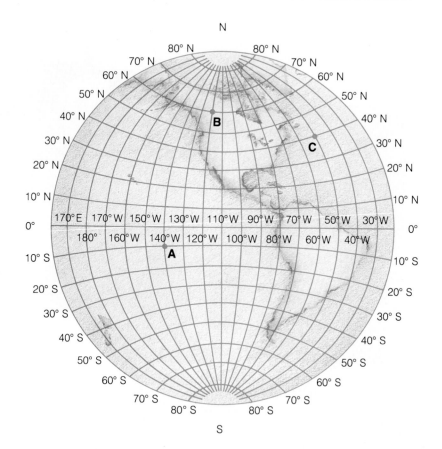

Figure 1-22. Any location on the earth can be described in terms of latitude north or south of the equator and longitude east or west of the prime meridian. How can you identify points A, B, and C, using latitude and longitude? A is at 10° S, 140° W. B is at 60° N, 120° W. C is at 40° N, 50° W.

See also Teaching Diagram 1-3A (TRB page 11).

To calculate the length of 1° latitude at the equator, divide the circumference (40 000 km) by 360° (approximately 111 km/1° latitude).

How are meridians numbered?

In latitude, minutes and seconds are not to be confused with the minutes and seconds used in measuring time. Both are systems based on ¹⁄₆₀ of a larger unit, but the larger unit is different in each case. In time, the larger unit is an hour. In latitude, the larger unit is a 90° angle. (Latitude is based on the angle from the center of the earth to two points on the same north-south line on the horizon—the equator and the location of the point whose latitude is being calculated.)

the equator, the parallels of latitude are numbered from 0° (the equator) to 90° north (the North Pole) and from 0° (the equator) to 90° south (the South Pole). Note that it is impossible to have a latitude greater than 90°. Note also that it is necessary to indicate north (N) or south (S) latitude because latitude can have the same value either side of the equator.

Meridians are numbered in degrees east and west of the prime meridian, which passes through Greenwich, England. Starting at the prime meridian, each meridian is numbered from 0° to 180° east (E) or from 0° to 180° west (W). No place on earth can have a longitude greater than 180°. Because longitude can have the same value either side of the prime meridian, the direction east or west must also be indicated.

The length of 1° of latitude at the equator is about 111 km. The length of 1° of longitude at the equator is about 111 km. Therefore, the area contained within just 1° latitude by 1° longitude at the equator (about 111 km × 111 km) covers more than 12 000 km². If you were lost and a plane were looking for you, your chances of being found in so large an area are not very good. For greater accuracy, degrees can be divided into sixty smaller units called minutes. And each minute can be divided into sixty units called seconds. This is similar to the meter being divided into centimeters and centimeters being divided into millimeters.

As shown in Figure 1-22, the meridians get closer and closer as you travel north or south from the equator. At the equator, 1° of longitude is equal to about 111 km. At 40° north or south latitude, however, 1° of longitude is equal to about only 79 km.

On the other hand, each parallel is almost an equal distance from every other parallel. One degree of latitude is therefore equal to about 111 km at the equator and at every other place on earth. The reason why parallels are not exactly the same distance apart from each other is that the earth's surface is slightly flattened at the polar regions.

Check yourself

1. Explain how latitude and longitude provide a system of coordinates for locating places on the earth's surface.

2. What is the starting point for measuring latitude? for measuring longitude?

3. Why is it necessary to use N and S when describing latitude and E and W when describing longitude?

Map projections
New vocabulary: map, map projection

Maps are representations, on a flat surface, of all or part of the earth's surface. It is impossible to put the earth's curved surface on a flat surface accurately. Therefore, map projections have been devised. A **map projection** is an attempt to represent the earth's curved surface on a flat surface.

Many different ways can be used to try to project curved parallels and meridians onto a flat surface. But no way is perfect. Some map projections are very accurate for the sizes of the continents. Other map projections are accurate for the shapes of the continents. Still other map projections are accurate for distances and directions on the earth's surface.

Library research

Find the exact location in longitude and latitude of your school.

Longitude is based upon the rate of rotation of the earth. The earth (360°) rotates once every 24 hours, or 15° each hour. Therefore, 1° of longitude would be the distance the earth rotates in 4 minutes.

1. Latitude provides one coordinate, distance north or south of the equator; longitude provides the second coordinate, distance east or west from the prime meridian.
2. The equator; the prime meridian
3. Because latitude can be either north or south of the equator and longitude can be either east or west of the prime meridian

Figure 1-23. On a globe, each parallel is an equal distance from every other parallel. On the map projection to the right, what happens to distances between parallels north or south of the equator when lines of latitude and longitude are projected onto a cylinder?

As parallels get nearer the poles, the distance between parallels increases.

Library research

Planes flying from San Francisco to Japan or from New York to London do not fly due west or due east. They follow a "great circle." Find out why.

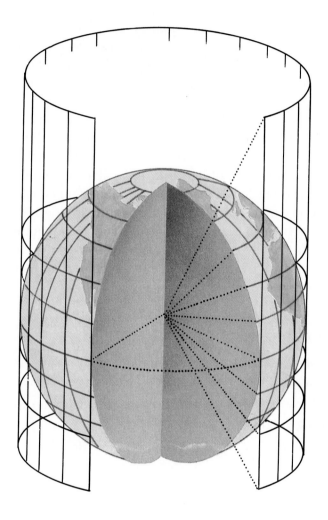

What is the most commonly used map projection for mapping small sections of the earth?

Figure 1-24 shows a Mercator projection of the earth. In that projection, note the size of the island of Greenland. It appears larger than the continent of South America. In reality, however, South America is almost three times longer, in a north-south direction, than Greenland. The Mercator projection is accurate for direction. But the Mercator projection is inaccurate for size and distance, and at the higher latitudes the distortion becomes even greater. But even with this distortion, continents can be recognized by their general shapes.

The most commonly used projection for mapping small sections of the earth is the polyconic projection. The polyconic

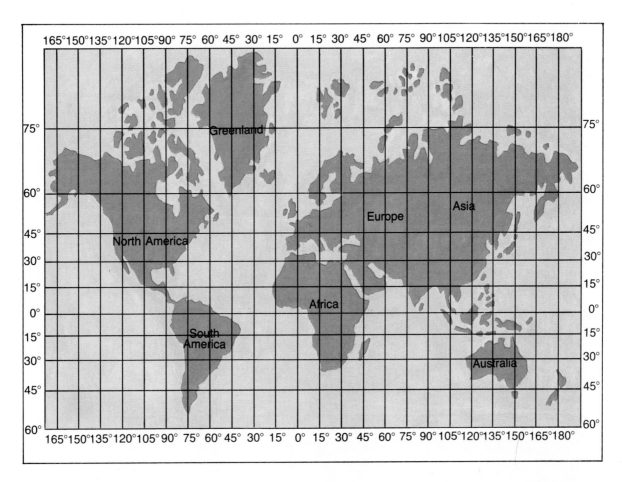

projection is most nearly accurate for distance, direction, size, and shape.

Check yourself

1. How is a map similar to a globe? How is it different?

2. In a Mercator projection, how are distances affected at the higher latitudes?

Colors and symbols on maps

New vocabulary: map relief

Symbols on maps make it easier to identify features. These symbols are often in different colors. Figure 1-25 lists the basic colors used on maps. It also lists what the colors represent and gives some examples.

Figure 1-24. On this Mercator projection of the earth, how accurate is the size of Greenland?
The relative size of Greenland is not accurate. It appears larger on the Mercator projection than on a map drawn to scale.

1. Similar: Both represent all or part of the earth's surface; Different: A globe's surface is curved; a map is on a flat surface.
2. At higher latitudes, relative size and distance on a Mercator projection are exaggerated and inaccurate.

Science Processes: Observing; Communicating
through coordinates
See also Activity Record Sheet 1-3A (Lab Manual
page 9)

CORE   10 minutes   Pairs of students

Activity 1-3A   Locating Places on the Earth

Materials

globe or world map
piece of string

Purpose

To locate some places on the earth using latitude and longitude.

Procedure

Using the piece of string, if necessary, and a
map or globe, answer questions 1-5.

Questions

1. Philadelphia is located at 40° north latitude
   (40° N). Name some other major cities on the
   same parallel.

2. The equator is 0° latitude. Which continents
   does the equator pass through?
3. Denver, Colorado, is located exactly on the
   105° west meridian (105° W). Vancouver,
   British Columbia, is almost on 125° W. Name
   two major cities that are located between
   105° W and 125° W.
4. Which city in Australia is on the same longitude as Tokyo, Japan?
5. Which state in the United States is on the
   same latitude as Finland?

Conclusion

How do latitude and longitude help locate
places on the earth?

Step 3

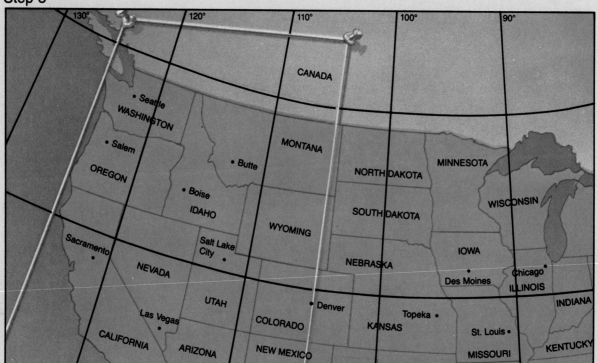

Color Codes Used on Maps		
Color	Type of Item Indicated by Each Color	Sample Map Symbol(s) for Each Color
blue	water features	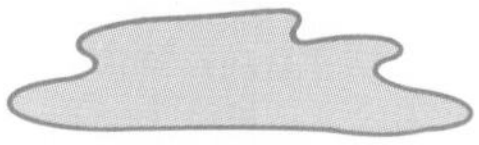
red	major roads	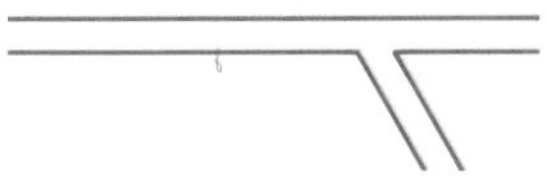
green	vegetation	
black	objects made by people	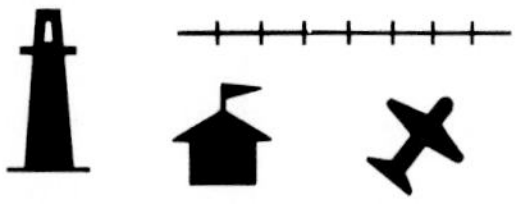
brown	land elevations	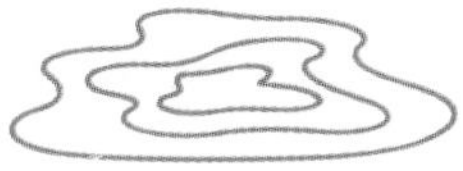

Figure 1-25. Map symbols are often easy to understand. Which sample map symbol stands for each of these: orchard, railroad, hill or mountain, highway, school, lake?

orchard = sample symbol on right for green

railroad = sample symbol on top right for black

hill or mountain = sample symbol for brown

highway = sample symbol for red

school = sample symbol in the middle for black

lake = sample symbol for blue

Symbols vary from one map to another. Sometimes colors also vary. But somewhere on every map is a **legend** that indicates the scale of the map and that may describe the symbols used on that map. Symbols are usually easy to understand, even without a legend. Being able to recognize map symbols and colors is a useful skill.

Check yourself

1. Why are symbols on a map useful?

2. Why are different colors for map symbols useful?

1. Symbols are an economical and direct way to identify recurring features on a map or globe.
2. Colors increase the kinds of information that can be indicated by a symbol. Colors also make an immediate visual impression.

North on a map

On most maps, there is a symbol that indicates north. Generally, the symbol looks like an arrow and is identified. On a map, it is also generally understood that north is toward the top of the map. Why is this so? As illustrated in Figure 1-26, the boundaries of most maps are nothing more than two parallels and two meridians. Meridians, as you have learned, run in a north-south direction. Parallels run east-west.

In the Northern Hemisphere, latitude increases from the "bottom" (0°) to the "top" (90°). In the Southern Hemisphere, just the opposite happens. It is important to stress that north is not up. Up refers to space as away from the earth. Terms such as "up north" are wrong.

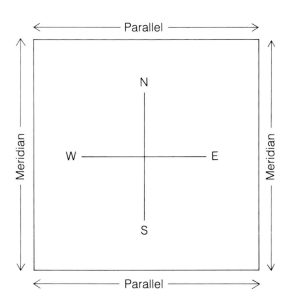

Figure 1-26. How do meridians and parallels affect the position of north on a map?
In general, they cause north to be toward the top of a map.

Figure 1-27. Northeast is halfway between north and east. Where is southeast?
Southeast is halfway between south and east.

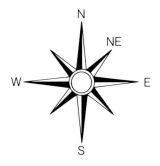

1. It is generally understood that north is toward the top of a map unless otherwise indicated.

2. East is toward the right; northwest is toward the upper left corner of a square map.

You've probably also heard of such compass directions as northeast and southwest. Where are these directions? As shown in Figure 1-27, northeast is halfway between north and east. Southwest is halfway between south and west.

Check yourself

1. How would you know which direction is north on a map if no symbol is shown?

2. In general, which direction is toward the right on a map? Which direction is toward the upper left corner on a square map?

A scale of distances

New vocabulary: scale of distances

Maps can be used to find distances between different places. Maps, therefore, frequently contain a scale of distances. A **scale of distances** is a ratio that shows how a distance on the map compares to the actual distance on the earth's surface.

A *proportional scale of distances* is expressed in numbers, either as a fraction (1/100 000) or a ratio (1:000 000). That tells the reader that 1 unit of measure on the map equals 100 000 of the same units of measure on the earth's surface. If the unit of measure is centimeters, then 1 cm on the map equals 1 km on the earth's surface.

A *word scale of distances* is also commonly used. For example, "One centimeter equals ten kilometers." That tells the user of

Why do maps frequently contain a scale of distances?

Additional Activity:
Students can use the graphic scale to measure some pre-measured lines. A ditto or overhead projector can be used. If an overhead is available, the technique of using a graphic scale can be shown. The measuring of curved lines can also be shown.

the map that a distance of 1 cm on the map is equal to 10 km on the earth's surface.

If you were asked to find the distance between two points on a road map, you would probably use a graphic scale of distances. A *graphic scale of distances* consists of a line that is divided into equal parts. Each part of the line is marked in some type of units. Figure 1-28 shows an example of a graphic scale of distances in kilometers.

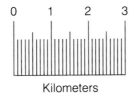

Kilometers

Figure 1-28. On a map containing this scale of distances, 1 cm on the map is equal to 1 km actual distance on the earth's surface. What is this kind of scale of distances called?
A graphic scale of distances

Check yourself

1. What are three different ways in which a scale of distances can be expressed?

2. Suppose you needed to find the distance between two points on a road map. What feature on a road map would make it easy for you to do this?

3. Look at the graphic scale of distances in Figure 1-28. What actual distance on the earth's surface would be indicated by 2.5 cm ?

1. 1) words; 2) numbers, either as a fraction or a ratio; 3) a graphic scale
2. A graphic scale of distances
3. 2.5 km

Topographic maps   New vocabulary: topographic map, topography, contour line, elevation, contour interval, hachure, map relief

The earth's surface is not all the same level. The earth's surface has many ups and downs. It has plains, mountains, valleys, and many other features which you have seen. There are maps that show the ups and downs and the shapes of the earth's surface features. These maps are called **topographic maps.** The word *topographic* comes from two Greek words that mean a place *(topos)* and a representation by means of lines *(grapha)*.

The shapes and elevations, or the **topography**, of a place can be indicated on a map in a number of ways. But the most accurate way is to use contour lines. A **contour line**, which is colored brown, connects places that have the same **elevation**, or

What are topographic maps?

the same height above sea level. Land elevation is always measured from sea level, which is zero elevation. Contour lines
also indicate the shape of land features at various elevations.
Map relief is the difference in elevation between the highest
and lowest points on a topographic map.

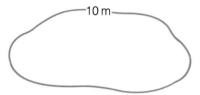

Figure 1-29. On a topographic
map, this drawing indicates an
oval-shaped elevation that is 10 m
above sea level. How can you tell
that the elevation is oval shaped?
Because of the shape of the
contour line, which indicates all
places having the same elevation

Contour lines are not drawn for every separate elevation
above sea level. Contour lines are drawn only at certain regular
intervals of elevation. Each interval, which is called the contour
interval, might be 5 m apart, or 10 m apart, or even 20, 25, 50,
or 100 m apart. The **contour interval** is the difference in elevation between any two contour lines on a topographic map.
The contour interval in Figure 1-30 is 10 m.

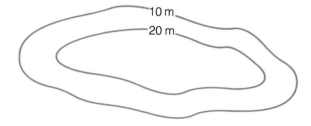

Figure 1-30. The contour interval
is the difference in elevation
between contour lines. In this
drawing, what is the contour
interval?
The contour interval is 10 m.

Figure 1-31 shows another feature that is possible to show on
a topographic map. Location Z on the map is a hole or depression. This is shown on the map by means of the short brown
lines that are drawn from the contour line. These little lines,
which indicate direction of slope, are called **hachures**, pro-
nounced either (huh-SHOORZ′) or (HASH′-oorz).

There is another feature that you will notice on topographic
maps. It is not necessary to number every contour line. In
some cases, all those numbers would clutter the map and make
it unreadable. One solution is to number only every fifth contour line and to make that numbered line a darker brown.

Is it necessary to number every
contour line?

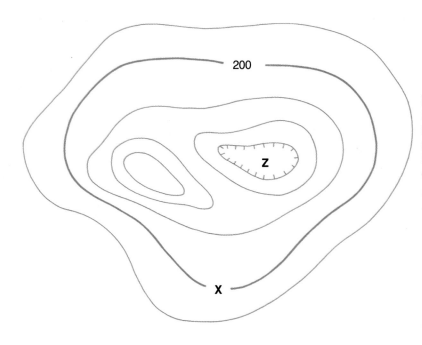

Figure 1-31. The short brown lines around Z are called hachures. What do they indicate about location Z?
Location Z is a hole or depression.

See also Teaching Diagram 1-3B (TRB page 12).

Here are a few simple rules about contour lines and contour intervals.

1. Contour lines always make a closed circle. If a contour line ends on the side of a map, it would be continued on the next map.

2. Contour lines inside the closed contour lines are always higher, unless otherwise indicated by hachures.

3. Contour lines can never cross. Contours for an overhang are an exception to this rule.

4. Closely spaced contour lines indicate a steep slope. Contour lines that are far apart indicate a gentle slope.

5. A contour interval is always an even multiple, such as an interval of 10 or 20.

6. Once established, the contour interval on a map never changes.

7. Contour lines always bend toward the higher elevation when they cross a stream.

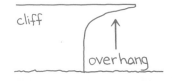

What do closely spaced contour lines indicate?

Check yourself

1. How does a topographic map differ from other kinds of maps?

2. Why do contour lines indicate changes in shape as well as elevation?

1. A topographic map indicates elevations, giving a three-dimensional aspect to the map.
2. A contour line, by connecting points of the same elevation, also indicates the shape of the landform at that elevation.

48

Careers   Earth Scientist / Cartographer

For further information about a
career as an earth scientist,
contact:

American Geological Institute
5202 Leesburg Pike
Falls Church, Virginia 22041

Earth science related careers are
many and varied. This aerospace
worker is preparing equipment
for a wind-tunnel test.

Earth Scientist As you will discover in the course of this book, careers related to earth science are many and varied.

Within earth science, there are careers for people who want to become specialists in a particular earth science. Oceanographers, petroleum geologists, and aeronautical engineers are examples of people who do this kind of work.

Within earth science, there are careers for people who enjoy working with machines, instruments, and other technical equipment. Aerospace workers, weather technicians,

and air-conditioning mechanics are just a few examples.

Within earth science, there are careers for people who enjoy other kinds of work. Building inspectors, owners of solar energy firms, and technical secretaries are examples of these kinds of people.

For further information about a
career as a cartographer, contact:
American Congress on
Surveying and Mapping
210 Little Falls Street
Falls Church, Virginia 22046

To draw accurate maps,
cartographers use very precise
instruments.

Cartographer Cartographers (kar-TOG'-ruh-ferz) are people who are involved in one or more phases of map making, which include planning, researching, designing, and drawing maps.

Cartographers make all kinds of maps. Topographic maps, geologic maps, road maps, and aeronautical maps are just some of the kinds of maps needed by various groups of people.

If you are interested in maps and in communicating information through technical drawings, then maybe you would like to learn more about map making.

Since maps constantly need revision, cartographers are in demand. They are employed by the U.S. government in several different agencies. Highway departments, mining and oil companies, and map-making firms are also in need to cartographers.

To become a cartographer you should have several years of high school mathematics. Drafting and photography would also be helpful. Not all jobs in the field of cartography require a college education.

Different ways to find north

New vocabulary: compass, North Magnetic Pole, magnetic north, North Geographic Pole, true north, magnetic declination

Suppose you did not have a map with a north indicator or a map with parallels and meridians. Are there any other ways to find north?

You can use the shadow of a stick or pencil to find north. If you have ever observed the shadows of trees, buildings, or even people, you probably have noticed that shadows change in length throughout the day. When during the day do you think that you will find the longest shadows? When do you think that you will find the shortest shadows?

In the Northern Hemisphere, the sun is always directly south of you when a shadow is the shortest. This is very close to noon, by the clock, every day. By observing a shadow when it is the shortest, you can tell where south is located. North, then, would be directly in line with the shadow. The shadow at its shortest provides you with a north-south line.

Figure 1-32 shows how you can use the hour hand of a watch to find north. Place the watch flat on the ground with the hour hand pointing in the direction of the sun. South is the point halfway between the hour hand and the 12 on your watch dial. (If you are on daylight-saving time, then you must use the 1 rather than the 12 on your watch dial.) Again, once you have found south, north will be exactly opposite.

You can also use a special instrument called a **compass** to find north. If you do use a compass, however, you will need to make some type of adjustment or correction. This is because the earth has more than one North Pole.

One of the earth's North Poles is called the **North Magnetic Pole.** The direction from where you are to the North Magnetic Pole is called **magnetic north.** As shown in Figure 1-33, a compass needle points to magnetic north.

The earth's other North Pole is called the **North Geographic Pole.** The North Geographic Pole is the point where all the meridians meet. The direction from where you are to the North Geographic Pole is called **true north.** True north is the north that is used for finding and for giving the location of places on the earth.

The North Magnetic Pole is located in northwestern Canada, about 1600 km from the North Geographic Pole. That is why

Library research

The earth is like a huge magnet. Prepare a report on the earth's magnetism.

As part of the students' experience, they should realize that shadows are long in the morning, become shorter until noon, and then increase in length until sunset.
Solar noon and noon by the clock differ. This difference is explained in Chapter 3.
Students can try this on their own. Or, if time permits, go outside and try it with students.

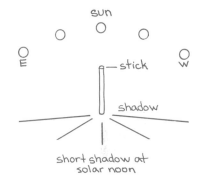

Toward which north does a compass needle point?

Students might ask if there is a South Magnetic Pole. The answer is yes. The earth is like a big magnet.

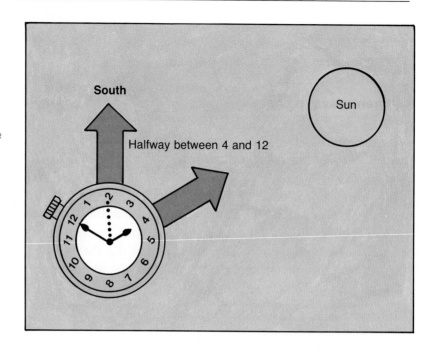

Figure 1-32. How can a watch be used to find north and south?
As described in the text, place the watch flat on the ground with the hour hand pointing toward the sun. South is the point halfway between the hour hand and the 12 on the watch face (the 1, if you're on daylight-saving time).

Check yourself answers:
1. If standard time, N is opposite the direction the hour hand is pointing; if daylight-saving time, N is opposite the direction halfway between the hour hand (12) and the 1.
2. A compass points toward the North Magnetic Pole (magnetic north) rather than the North Geographic Pole (true north).

Figure 1-33. The earth has more than one North Pole. Which North Pole does a compass needle point toward?
A compass needle points toward the North Magnetic Pole.

The magnetic declination of a place changes over time. For this reason, constant revision of magnetic declinations is needed in mapping.

if you had a compass and followed the direction the needle pointed, you would not be going exactly true north. To go true north, you would need to take into account the difference between true north and magnetic north.

The difference between true north and magnetic north is called the **magnetic declination,** or magnetic variation. As shown in Figure 1-33, magnetic declination varies from one

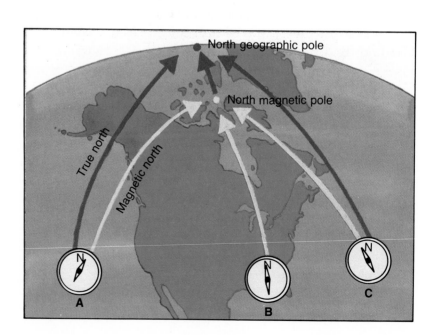

location to another. In Figure 1-33, Location A has a declination of about 20° east. To make the N on your compass point true north at Location A, you would first line up the N with the north-seeking end of the compass needle. You would then need to turn the compass about 20° to the left. Location B has no declination at all. Location C has a declination of about 20° west.

To find true north from a compass direction, you need to know the magnetic declination for your location. Some maps provide the magnetic declination for the area that is mapped out. To show magnetic declination on a map, a symbol like the one in Figure 1-34 is placed somewhere along the bottom of the map.

The earth's magnetic poles can be considered like the north and south poles of a bar magnet, with the earth itself as a giant electromagnet. The earth's magnetism may be caused by the earth's rotation acting on a liquid outer core of iron and nickel around a solid inner core of iron and nickel. The magnetic poles differ from the geographic poles for several reasons. For one, the earth's magnetic poles are continuously wandering over the polar regions. According to data from the Department of Energy Mines and Resources in Ottawa, the North Pole has journeyed northwest 800 km since 1904. Geophysicists attribute this migration to motion of the earth's fluid outer core.

Another cause of difference between the geographic poles and the magnetic poles has to do with large-scale movements of the earth's lithospheric plates. This movement will be discussed in Chapter 10, The Restless Crust.

For the benefit of navigators, it is necessary to locate the magnetic poles from time to time. In May, 1984, the average position of the North Pole was 77° north and 102.3° west. In 1973, the Pole was at 76° north and 100.6° west.

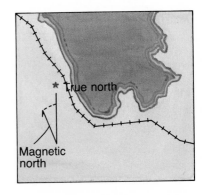

Figure 1-34. Some maps provide the magnetic declination for the area covered on the map. Is the magnetic declination shown here east or west of true north?
In answer to the caption question, the magnetic declination shown is west of true north.

Check yourself   Check yourself answers appear on the facing page.

1. If the hour hand on your watch is pointed toward the sun and it is noon, where is north?

2. To find true north from a compass direction, why is it necessary to know the magnetic declination at your location?

Science Processes: Observing; Formulating models
See also Activity Record Sheet 1-3B (Lab Manual page 10)

2½ hours   Demonstration or large group

Activity 1-3B Using a Shadow Stick to Find a North-South Line

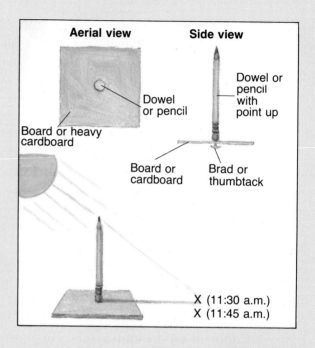

Aerial view — Dowel or pencil; Board or heavy cardboard

Side view — Dowel or pencil with point up; Dowel or pencil; Board or cardboard; Brad or thumbtack

X (11:30 a.m.)
X (11:45 a.m.)

Materials

piece of flat board or heavy cardboard

chalk

pointed stick (dowel) or sharpened pencil

nail or thumbtack

pencil for marking

protractor

Purpose

To find the geographic north-south line using shadows cast by the sun.

Procedure

1. Find a flat surface that is paved and in direct sunlight between 11 a.m. and 1 p.m. (or between 12 and 2 p.m., if you are on daylight-saving time).
2. On the pavement, mark off an outline of your board with a piece of chalk.
3. Make a dot on the pavement along one of the chalk lines. Make a corresponding dot on the board. (If the board gets moved, the dots will help you to return it to its exact position.)
4. Make a black x in the center of the board where you will put the dowel or pencil. Using the nail or tack, attach the dowel or pencil to the board as shown. You can use a protractor to make sure the dowel or pencil is straight up and down.
5. Place the board in direct sunlight about one hour before noon. Put a small x at the top of the shadow of the stick or pencil. Write the time above the x.
6. Repeat the procedure every fifteen minutes until one hour after noon.

7. After placing all the x's on the board, connect them with a smooth line. This line must be drawn carefully.
8. Mark the point on the curved line where the shadow is the shortest—that is, where the point at the end of the shadow is closest to the stick. Draw a line from this point to the stick. This is your north-south line.
9. You might want to repeat this activity later in the year.

Questions

1. At what time was the shadow the shortest? Was it exactly at noon?
2. The sun appears to move from east to west. In what direction did your shadow move?
3. Where is the sun when the shadow is the shortest?

Conclusion

A shadow stick can provide much information about the sun and the earth. Explain.

Section 3 Review   Chapter 1

Use **Reading Checksheet 1-3** TRB page 63
Skillsheet 1-3 TRB page 105
Section Reviewsheet 1-3 TRB pages 147–148
Section Testsheet 1-3 TRB page 277

Check Your Vocabulary

2	compass	15	map
14	contour interval	21	map projection
5	contour line	2	map relief
7	elevation	19	meridian
17	equator	13	North Geographic Pole
20	globe	11	North Magnetic Pole
3	hachures	4	parallel
10	latitude	23	prime meridian
9	legend	6	scale of distance
22	longitude	12	topographic map
16	magnetic declination	8	topography
18	magnetic north	1	true north

Match each term above with the numbered phrase that best describes it.

1. Toward the North Geographic Pole
2. An instrument for locating magnetic north
3. Short lines that indicate direction of slope
4. East-west line parallel to the equator
5. Line indicating the same elevation
6. Ratio of map distances and actual distances
7. Height above sea level
8. Elevations and shapes of land features
9. Key on a map that tells the scale and describes the symbols
10. Distance north or south of the equator
11. The North Pole indicated by a compass
12. A map that shows land features
13. Point where all meridians meet
14. Difference between contour lines
15. A flat representation of the earth's surface
16. Distance from true to magnetic north
17. Line that circles the earth at 0° latitude
18. Direction toward the North Magnetic Pole
19. A north-south line that crosses the equator
20. A physical model of the earth
21. An attempt to represent the earth's curved surface on a flat surface
22. Distance east or west of the prime meridian
23. The imaginary north-south line that passes through Greenwich, England
24. Difference in elevation between the highest and lowest points on a map

Check Your Knowledge

Multiple Choice: Choose the answer that best completes each of the following sentences.

1. _?_ are a simple way to indicate on a map various features on the earth's surface.
   a) Colors and symbols
   b) Arrows
   c) Parallel lines
   d) Compass directions

2. If you are at 0° latitude, you are at _?_.
   a) the equator
   b) the South Pole
   c) the North Magnetic Pole
   d) the North Geographic Pole

3. On a compass, _?_ is between northwest and southwest
   a) south   c) east
   b) north   d) west

Check Your Understanding

1. Why is it that one degree of latitude is not equal to one degree of longitude after leaving the equator?
2. Why do closely spaced contour lines indicate a steep slope?
3. Explain the difference between true north and magnetic north.

Chapter 1 Review

See also **Chapter Testsheets 1A and 1B** TRB

Concept Summary

Learning involves gathering data through observation, processing and classifying data, and forming inferences on the basis of relationships drawn from the data.

☐ Instruments enable us to learn data not available through direct observation.

☐ Classifying is a way of learning that shows relationships among observations.

☐ Learning often involves "educated guesses."

☐ Science includes all the different ways of learning.

The earth is the sum total of all earth materials and all earth processes.

☐ All three forms of matter—solid, liquid, and gas—are found on the earth.

☐ The earth can be considered in terms of different divisions or spheres.

☐ Between the different spheres, there is a constant exchange of energy and materials.

Earth science involves all the different sciences that study particular earth materials and processes.

☐ Earth science also includes astronomy, which studies the stars and planets.

☐ Within the earth sciences, there are increasingly specialized areas of scientific investigation.

The metric system is an accurate international system of measuring that is based on multiples of ten.

☐ Under the name of the International System of Units (SI), the metric system can be revised as needed.

☐ The SI units used in the metric system are based on unchanging standards of measure.

Maps are graphic representations of all or part of the earth's surface.

☐ Maps can indicate location, direction, distances, relative sizes, and various topographic features.

Putting It All Together

1. Describe how the following apply to scientific investigation: observation, instruments, evidence, classifying, inference, hypothesis, theory.

2. Name and describe four major divisions or layers of the earth.

3. Name five "earth sciences" and relate them to the major divisions, or layers, of the earth.

4. Give three requirements of a good measuring system.

5. On a separate piece of paper, copy and complete each of the following equations:
   a. $742 \text{ cm} = \underline{?} \text{ m}$
   b. $1055 \text{ mm} = \underline{?} \text{ m}$
   c. $0.85 \text{ m} = \underline{?} \text{ cm}$
   d. $6.82 \text{ m} = \underline{?} \text{ cm}$
   e. $0.43 \text{ m} = \underline{?} \text{ mm}$
   f. $128 \text{ cm} = \underline{?} \text{ mm}$

6. Explain how weight and mass are different.

7. Describe how to find the volume of an irregularly shaped object.

8. A substance has a volume of 16 cm^3 and a density of 2 g/cm^3. What is its mass in grams?

9. List three ways that meridians differ from parallels.

10. a. List two ways in which a map differs from a globe.

    b. Explain how a topographic map differs from other kinds of maps.

Apply Your Knowledge

1. Explain why making inferences is a key process of science.

2. Given: A block of aluminum has a mass of 54 g and a volume of 20 cm^3. Its density is 2.7 g/cm^3. Show that the density does not change if the block of aluminum is cut in half and you use only one half.

3. If the earth's circumference is 40 000 km, show that 1° of latitude equals about 111 km.

4. Using the sample map, answer these questions:

   a. What is the contour interval used on the map?

   b. Which is higher in elevation, location C or location D? How do you know?

   c. To reach location D, which route would you follow if you wanted the steepest climb? Which route would you pick if you wanted the gentlest climb? How do you know?

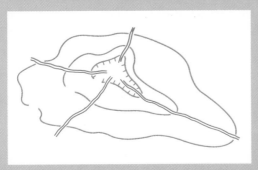

5. Draw a topographic map of the sea coast area shown at the beginning of Chapter 5, Section 3, on page 35. Assume that the highest part of the cliff is 20 m above sea level, and the highest point on the road is 54 m. Estimate the approximate levels of contour lines you could use. What altitude would the contour line be at the edge of the sea?

Find Out on Your Own

1. Make a list of direct and indirect observations for some object in the room. See if others can identify the object from your observations.

2. Observe any instrument you want. Discover as much as you can about this instrument. Report to the class about this instrument. Tell what the instrument is used for and teach others how to use it.

3. Invent your own system of measurement. Measure some common objects with your units of measure. Explain your system to the class. Describe some of the problems in making your system of measurements.

4. Eratosthenes lived over 2000 years ago. He found the circumference of the earth. Use his method and make your own measurements to determine the size of the earth.

5. Using a rubber ball, devise a system to locate positions and places.

Reading Further

Gardner, Robert. *Ideas for Science Projects.* New York: Franklin Watts, 1986.

This book proposes interesting science questions that students can try to answer on their own.

Jerrard, H. G., and D. B. McNeill. *A Dictionary of Scientific Units.* 5th ed. New York: Chapman & Hall, 1986.

This is a handy reference that gives the meaning and history of units that are used in science and technology.

Knowlton, Jack. *Maps and Globes.* New York: Crowell, 1985.

This easy-to-read guide explains how to interpret maps and globes.

Rossbacher, Lisa A. *Career Opportunities in Geology and the Earth Sciences.* New York: Arco Publishing, 1983.

Careers in all subjects of geology are clearly described in this enjoyable, informative book.

Weiner, Jonathan. *Planet Earth.* New York: Bantam Books, 1986.

This book presents current facts about the earth, showing how interesting earth science can be.

2

Student Resources		Meeting Individual Needs	
Student Text	**Laboratory Activities**		
Section 1 The Nature of Matter 58–79 Matter 59–62	Activity 2-1A Solids, Liquids, and Gases 61 Activity Record Sheet 2-1A LM 15 Investigation 2-1 Properties of Gases LM 19–20	CORE Enrichment	
Elements and Atoms 62–66 Our Science Heritage: How Did We Learn to Use Metals? 65 The Periodic Table 66–71 Isotopes 72 Compounds and Molecules 73–75 Compounds Made of Ions 75–77 Mixtures 77–78 Section 1 Review 79	Activity 2-1B Using the Periodic Table 70 Activity Record Sheet 2-1B LM 17	Reinforcement	
Section 2 Minerals 80–94 What Are Minerals? 81–84 Silicate Minerals 84–86 Nonsilicate Minerals 86–87 What to Look for in a Mineral 87–93	Investigation 2-2 Forming Crystals LM 23–24 Research Lab 2 Growing Crystals LM 29–30	Enrichment Enrichment	
	Activity 2-2A Grouping Minerals by Hardness 90 Activity Record Sheet 2-2A LM 21 Activity 2-2B Using Physical Properties to Identify Minerals 92 Activity Record Sheet 2-2B LM 22	CORE Enrichment	
Section 2 Review 94			
Section 3 Rocks 95–109 Where Does Rock Come From? 96–101 Igneous Rock 96–97 Sedimentary Rock 99–100	Activity 2-3A Forming Layers 98 Activity Record Sheet 2-3A LM 25 Investigation 2-3 Distinguishing Between Types of Sedimentary Rocks LM 27–28	Reinforcement Enrichment	
Metamorphic Rock 100–101 The Rock Cycle 101–103 What to Look for in a Rock 103–107	Activity 2-3B Determining the Class of a Rock 104 Activity Record Sheet 2-3B LM 26	CORE	
Careers: Geophysicist/Technical Secretary Section 3 Review 109			
Chapter 2 Review 110–111 Science Issues of Today: The Search for Mineral Resources 112			

Teacher Resources		Meeting Individual Needs
Teacher's Edition	**Teacher's Resource Book**	
	Essential Ideas 2-1 EI 9–10	Reinforcement
Activity Notes 56C–56D		
Demonstration 56D		
Discussion Idea 56E	Overhead Transparency S3	Enrichment
Activity Notes 56E–56F	Overhead Transparency S4	Enrichment
	Skillsheet 2-1 TRB 106	Reinforcement
Section 1 Review Answers 56F	Reading Checksheet 2-1 TRB 64	Reinforcement
	Section Reviewsheet 2-1 TRB 149–150	CORE
	Section Testsheet 2-1 TRB 278	CORE
	Essential Ideas 2-2 EI 11–13	Reinforcement
Discussion Idea 56G		
Creative Writing Idea 56G	Skillsheet 2-2 TRB 107	Reinforcement
Demonstration 56H		
Activity Notes 56J		
Activity Notes 56K		
Section 2 Review Answers 56K	Reading Checksheet 2-2 TRB 65	Reinforcement
	Section Reviewsheet 2-2 TRB 151–152	CORE
	Section Testsheet 2-2 TRB 279	CORE
Discussion Idea 56L	Essential Ideas 2-3 EI 13–14	Reinforcement
	Overhead Transparency B3	CORE
Environmental Topic 56L		
Activity Notes 56M		
	Overhead Transparency B4	CORE
	Teaching Diagram 2-3A TRB 17	CORE
Activity Notes 56N	Teaching Diagram 2-3B TRB 18	CORE
Demonstration 56P	Skillsheet 2-3 TRB 108	Reinforcement
Section 3 Review Answers 56P	Reading Checksheet 2-3 TRB 66	Reinforcement
	Section Reviewsheet 2-3 TRB 153–154	CORE
	Section Testsheet 2-3 TRB 280	CORE
Chapter 2 Review Answers 56Q–56R	Chapter 2 Testsheet TRB 319–320	CORE

2

The Nature of Matter

Learner Objectives

2-1

1. To identify the three phases of matter by their characteristics.
2. To recognize the structure and three particle types of atoms.
3. To demonstrate that the periodic table organizes elements by atomic number and hence by property.
4. To distinguish between compounds and molecules.

Concept Summary

Matter is anything that occupies space and has mass.

Activity Notes

Activity 2-1A

Solids, Liquids, and Gases   page **61**

Purpose   To show how the input of heat energy changes water from a solid to a liquid to a gas.

- **CORE** 30 minutes Groups of 4
- **Activity Record Sheet 2-1A** (Lab Manual page 15) can also be used to record this activity.
- Science Processes: Measuring; Interpreting Data.

Advance Preparation

Examine the beakers for cracks and the hot plates for frayed wires and proper functioning. Be sure there are no breaks in the thermometers.

Remind students how to read thermometers. A white card of paper behind the thermometer often improves the visibility of the indicator.

Procedure Notes

Use just enough ice to fill the beaker, otherwise when the water boils the level will be too high. Alert the students to be careful not to break the beaker when stirring the ice-water mix. The temperature variations in the beaker will make it more vulnerable. The hot plate should be set at a medium to high temperature. Thermometers should be kept in the middle of the ice water mix for consistency and accurate readings.

Safety Information

Use a stirring rod to mix the beaker's contents, not the thermometer. The latter is not designed for mixing and will crack. Once the water is warming, it's best to handle the beaker with gloves and avoid contact with the heating element, despite its degree of redness.

Disposal

In case of broken glass, use a wisk broom to collect the fragments, and discard the pieces in a suitable garbage receptacle.

If a mercury thermometer breaks, use an eyedropper and dispose of the liquid in a jar specifically labelled for this purpose. DO NOT use your hand to round up the beads of mercury and NEVER flush mercury down the sink.

Activity Notes (continued)

Answers to Questions

1. The ice melts. With increasing heat, the mixture contains increasing amounts of water in liquid phases.
2. The temperature increases with heat input, when only one phase is present. When two phases are present, an increase in heat does not result in an increase in temperature.
3. There are periods when an increase in heat causes no temperature change and periods when there is a definite increase in temperature.
4. Answers will vary.

Conclusion

At the boiling point and the melting point, an increase in heat does not change the temperature of the mixture. The temperature remains at 100°C and 0°C, respectively, until the phase change is complete, at which time an increase in heat causes an increase in temperature.

Demonstration

The Emptiness of the Atom

After the students are familiar with the basic structure of an atom, ask them to compare the nucleus and the atom in size. They will probably respond that the nucleus is nearly as large as the atom because it contains most of the atomic particles.

Take the students to the auditorium. Place a penny on the stage, informing them that this coin represents the nucleus. Ask a student to position himself/herself where the electron cloud would be. Once several students have attempted to do this, tell them that the furthest point in the auditorium from the stage would represent the electron cloud.

Penny

Provide them with an analogy. If an atom were the size of a football stadium, then its nucleus would be the size of a tennis ball (the nucleus is roughly 1/10 000 the diameter of the atom). Hence, despite the apparent solidity of the matter it forms, the atom is overwhelmingly empty space.

Science Background

The electron cloud model is based on mathematics and the way waves interact. This branch of physics is called quantum mechanics. In an atom, electrons are arranged in concentric layers known as shells or energy levels. The energy state of an electron determines which energy level it normally occupies. However, by gaining or losing a specific amount of energy an electron can move to a higher or lower energy level.

Electrons that occupy the outermost energy level of an atom are called valence electrons. The number of valence electrons in its atoms is chiefly responsible for the physical and chemical properties of an element. Most metals have one or two valence electrons. They bond by losing electrons and form positive ions. Nonmetals usually have six or seven valence electrons. They bond by gaining or sharing electrons and form negative ions.

The placement of elements in the periodic table is related to their electron structure. For example, elements in a vertical column, or family, have the same number of valence electrons. This explains why elements in a family have similar physical and chemical properties and form compounds with similar formulas.

2-1

The Nature of Matter

Student Misconception

To understand earth chemistry and the basis for physical and chemical changes of earth materials, students must have an understanding of the nature of matter. Yet, many students have difficulty with these concepts because of the abstract nature of many terms that describe matter. Making terms more concrete through visual imaging will help students overcome this barrier.

The structural relationships of atoms, elements, molecules and compounds can be visually represented to the students by using a variety of different colored shapes. For example, use a red square (■) to represent the atom hydrogen. Many red squares (■■■■) would represent the element hydrogen. Use a blue triangle (▲) to represent oxygen. Many blue triangles (▲▲▲▲) would represent the element oxygen. Combining two red squares and one blue triangle (■■▲) would represent the molecule H_2O. Several H_2O molecules grouped together (■■▲,■■▲) would represent the compound water. It is fun to assign familiar compounds to students and have them represent these to the class in this symbolic way. Class members can try to guess the mystery compound. The student who is conducting the exercise can include clues as to the physical and chemical properties of the particular substance to aid in the identification process.

Discussion Idea

Can We Change One Element into Another?

Ask the students whether we can change one element into another, such as lead into gold (transmutation). They will probably answer, "No, that only happens in science fiction."

The ancient alchemists thought transmutation was possible. In fact, Sir Isaac Newton died from mercuric fumes generated during transmutation experiments. As the science of chemistry evolved, however, this notion was increasingly seen as naive. Scientists observed that physical and chemical procedures were incapable of changing one element to another. They discovered that an element's identity was a consequence of the number of protons in its nucleus.

But it is this very fact that makes the possibility of transmutation anything but naive in today's world. Tell the students that we are now able to probe the atom's nucleus, thereby interacting with the very nature of what makes an element unique and making transmutation possible.

Ask the students what consequences such a process would have. How would our lives be changed?

Activity Notes

Activity 2-1B

Using the Periodic Table   page **70**

Purpose   To use the periodic table to identify 10 mystery elements.

- 20 minutes Individuals
- Activity Record Sheet 2-1B (Lab Manual page 17) can also be used to record this activity.
- Science Processes: Inferring; Classifying

Advance Preparation

Students may not be oriented on the Periodic Table; consequently, their search for the mystery elements may be accomplished in a highly random manner. Mentioning once again how the table is arranged, by increasing atomic number (atomic weight also increases but the increase is not uniform), might help considerably. Reacquaint the students with the location of atomic number and atomic mass within the individual element boxes of the Periodic Table.

2-1

Activity Notes (continued)

Procedure Notes

Point out that the qualification of "room temperature" refers to classifying elements according to their natural state. For example, bromine in its natural state is gaseous. In other words, at 25°C and at sea level, bromine is a gas.

Indicate that "3 less" or "2 more," in regard to atomic number, relate to lateral movement on the Periodic Table.

Answers to the Mystery Minerals

A	mercury	F	oxygen
B	iron	G	potassium
C	calcium	H	magnesium
D	silicon	I	carbon
E	aluminum	J	uranium

Answers to Questions

1. Answers should include 1) elemental state (solid, liquid, or gas), 2) Greek name, 3) atomic number, and 4) average atomic mass.
2. They can be distinguished by their physical and chemical properties. For example, sodium (Na) reacts chemically with water and aluminum (A1) does not.

Conclusion

The Periodic Table enables one to find elements that behave similarly. For example, nitrogen and oxygen differ by 1 atomic number, and yet both are highly reactive gases.

Section 1 Review Answers

Check Your Understanding
page 79

1. An element is a pure substance with unique chemical properties and is composed of a single type of atom. An atom is the smallest part of an element that still retains the characteristics of that element, but may combine with atoms of different elements to form compounds.
2. The number of neutrons equals the difference between the number of neutrons and protons, and the atomic number. Therefore, there are eight neutrons in oxygen-16.
3. The number of electrons in a neutral atom is equal to the number of protons. Hence, there are 92 electrons in the uranium atom.
4. By forming chemical bonds, atoms can lower their energy level, and become more stable.

2-1

Learner Objectives

1. To discriminate between minerals and nonminerals.
2. To describe the attributes of a mineral.
3. To understand that the physical properties of a mineral are affected primarily by the mineral's composition and structure.
4. To understand that impurities may also affect some of the physical properties of a mineral.
5. To use specific properties to identify mineral specimens.

2-2

Concept Summary

Minerals are naturally occurring, inorganic crystalline solids.

Discussion Idea

How Prevalent Are Minerals?

Ask students to name as many kinds of minerals as they can. Write the names on the board. Across from the name of each mineral, write its use or uses.

At first, students are likely to think of names of familiar rocks, individual elements, or they may think of particular gemstones. Tell them that rocks are actually combinations of minerals, and that they will learn more about rocks in Section 2. Tell them that most minerals—but not all—are made up of more than one element. Let them know that they are probably more familiar with minerals than they realize, and remind them that minerals are even important components of our diets.

Among other possibilities, your list may include iron (used for frying pans, magnets, and as an essential part of our diets); quartz (the gems amethyst and citrine, and in both sand and glass); salt; magnesium (used in traces by our bodies and an essential part of chlorophyll, needed for photosynthesis); gold; silver; diamond; corundum (ruby and sapphire); and calcium (needed by humans for strong teeth and bones).

Creative Writing Idea

The following writing exercise may help students visualize the relationship of atoms to crystal structure and develop their ability to describe three-dimensional objects.

Imagine that you are very tiny, small enough to orbit a tiny spacecraft around the nucleus of an atom. Use your spaceship to cruise along the silica tetrahedron in Figure 2-23 on page 85. Describe the pattern you travel in the same way you would describe moving through a maze. (For example, you might start with: I flew 10 minutes in a straight line heading west and then angled upward in a southeast direction and flew for 10 more minutes.) Next, choose your favorite silicate mineral and look up its crystal shape. How would the silica tetrahedrons fit together to form that shape? Describe your path as you travel outside the tetrahedrons. Sketching the way the tetrahedrons fit together may help you visualize the structure more easily.

Demonstration

Making Rock-Salt Crystals

Tell the students that minerals comprise more than gemstones or building materials; our bodies need small amounts of minerals, as well. One such mineral is sodium chloride, or salt. Tell students that this familiar crystalline compound known as table salt is made up of two elements: sodium and chlorine.

Students may be surprised to learn that the salt on our tables is mined, just like gold and silver, coal and lead. Underground salt deposits may be hundreds of feet deep. To mine the salt, sometimes it is dissolved in hot water and pumped to the surface, where it dries and forms crystals.

Show the students how to make rock-salt crystals. First, fill a large metal jar cover half full of garden soil. To 250 mL of hot tap water, add 6 to 9 teaspoons of table salt and stir thoroughly; some salt should remain at the bottom when you stop stirring.

Pour some of the clear salt water on the soil, and place the lid in a sunny location to dry. (The amount of water used will depend upon the size of your jar lid.) Next, place a 25-mm loop of copper wire on top of the mud.

After the mud has dried, you will see rock-salt crystals along the copper loop. Have students examine these crystals and note their shapes. You and your students may wish to experiment with several sizes of jar lids and varying amounts of salt.

Science Background

A property of minerals that is of scientific interest is the crystalline form. The form, or shape, is related to the way in which the atoms are packed, as shown in Figure 2-15, page 76.

Six major systems are shown in Figure 2-21. However, because of the way they are formed, not all crystals have such perfect shapes. They can be formed in two ways: 1) when molten substances cool and harden, the crystals form, and 2) they form from dissolved minerals in water when the water evaporates. In nature many crystals are pushed together, making flaws in their shapes. But in the laboratory, under controlled conditions, it is possible to make nearly perfect crystals.

The size of the crystal depends on the time it takes to form. Small crystals in lava rocks probably cooled quickly. Larger crystals resulted from a much slower cooling process. The same is true of water-formed crystals such as halite. Larger crystals will result from the slower evaporation of water.

2-2

Student Misconception

A student's first exposure to minerals generally comes from pictures and museum exhibits. These visual displays are designed to show the characteristic physical properties of minerals and often include superior photos or views of large, notable samples. While this is valuable in helping the student recognize specific properties such as crystal shape, cleavage, and fracture, it often creates a misleading impression of normally available samples.

As a result, students may have unrealistic expectations of what might be found in a typical field search.

It is unlikely that large or spectacular mineral samples can be found along the roadway or in the field. Most mineral deposits are buried by soil or may only be accessible through mining. Weathering and erosion also act to alter the size and appearance of mineral samples. Emphasize that samples depicted in a book or on display in an exhibit were probably obtained in unique geographic locations or through a mining operation. After explaining that many of these samples are specially prepared for display, students will be less likely to have mistaken impressions concerning classroom material sets and field-quality mineral samples.

2-2

Activity Notes

Activity 2-2A

Grouping Minerals by Hardness   page **90**

Purpose   To learn a way of classifying minerals by their physical properties.

- **CORE** 15 minutes Individuals or small groups
- **Activity Record Sheet 2-2A** (Lab Manual page 21) can be used to record this activity.
- Science Processes: Observing; Classifying; Comparing.

Safety Information

To avoid accidental injury while using the iron nail, the mineral sample should be placed on a desk or table, not held in the hand.

Procedure Notes

The edge of the object used for scratching should be rubbed over a small portion of the sample on the table. The scratch should then be wiped with a soft cloth and examined with a hand lens, if available. A real scratch on the surface of a mineral cannot be rubbed off with the cloth.

The students' grouping will probably conform to those that appear in Table 2-3. Using the same three informal standards, students can group additional mineral samples such as aluminum (2–2.9), agate (6–7), graphite (1–2), limestone marble (3–4), and pumice (6)—according to hardness.

Answers to Questions

1–2. Answers will vary according to the minerals studied. Check Table 2-3 for your particular minerals.

Conclusion

Minerals can be grouped, or classified, according to their physical properties, such as hardness. By consulting a table of hardness values, we can determine which group each mineral belongs to.

Going Further

You might wish to take students on a field trip to a site where they can test minerals for hardness using one of their fingernails, a copper penny, and an iron nail.

Activity Notes

Activity 2-2B

Using Physical Properties to Identify Minerals   page **92**

Purpose   To test unidentified mineral specimens for physical properties.

- 30 to 40 minutes Groups of 4–6
- **Activity Record Sheet 2-2B** (Lab Manual page 22) can be used to record this activity.
- Science Processes: Observing; Classifying; Recording data; Analyzing data; Distinguishing; Identifying.

Procedure Notes

In testing for streak, have students place the streak plate on a flat surface. Then have students hold the plate steady with one hand while rubbing the specimen across the plate.

If you have specimens of halite or galena that you are willing to break, you might let students test for cleavage by wrapping a small sample in a cloth and hitting it gently with a hammer. Students should wear safety goggles for this procedure. If a sample of mica is available, students can use a straight pin to pick it apart and study how mica cleaves.

Answers to Questions

1. Gypsum can be scratched by a fingernail.
2. Biotite mica and pyrite have a streak that is a different color from the color of the specimen. Any of the following could also have a different color streak if the sample color is not white: calcite, fluorite, gypsum, and orthoclase feldspar.
3. Clear calcite and clear gypsum can be distinguished by hardness. Gypsum can be scratched by a fingernail, and calcite cannot.
4. Galena has cubic cleavage; magnetite has no cleavage. Magnetite attracts a magnet; galena does not. Galena has a bright metallic luster; magnetite is submetallic to almost dull.
5. Answers will depend upon the specimens used, but quartz commonly has crystal faces. If fluorite has crystal faces, they are the sides of a cube and usually not very shiny.

Conclusion

A small amount of a mineral is often enough to identify it. Even in small quantities, each mineral has a combination of physical properties that forms a unique mineral.

Section 2 Review Answers

Check Your Understanding
page **94**

1. Not all minerals have the freedom and space to form crystals.
2. The sets of internal axes vary according to basic crystal types.
3. Silicate minerals, carbonate minerals, and sulfide minerals have different key elements.
4. Minerals can be identified by examining their physical properties, such as hardness, luster, cleavage.
5. The Mohs scale specifies ten minerals to use as standards for hardnesses from 1 to 10. If a mineral specimen is not scratched by quartz, you know (according to the Mohs scale) that the mineral specimen has a hardness greater than 7. You can then try topaz to see if the specimen has a hardness greater than 8, and so on.

2-2

Learner Objectives

1. To understand the major classes of rock form.
2. To understand how the earth's rocks can change from one class to another.
3. To recognize different rock textures.
4. To determine some of the more common mineral compositions of rocks.
5. To use texture and mineral composition to discriminate among igneous, sedimentary, and metamorphic rocks.

2-3

Concept Summary

Most **rocks** are combinations of two or more minerals.

Discussion Idea

The Cohesiveness of Rocks

Tell students that in this section they will learn that rocks are made from combinations of minerals. Ask: What is it that holds the rocks themselves together?

Point out to the students that they already know that some rocks seem to be held together much more tightly than others. For example, obsidian is held very tightly together, whereas you can often brush bits of sandstone off with your hand or a tool. Why?

Some kinds of rock (metamorphic and igneous) are connected by very tiny, interlocking mineral crystals. As these crystals grow and become increasingly crowded together, they fill the many tiny spaces between them like a three-dimensional puzzle. Two examples of rocks held together in this manner are marble and granite.

Rocks such as sandstone and limestone (sedimentary rocks) are connected by compaction and cementation. Under pressure, individual grains are compacted until they fuse together. When water containing minerals flows through the grains, the minerals precipitate between the grains, cementing them together. Rocks formed by compaction and cementation are less tightly held together than igneous and metamorphic rocks.

Environmental Topic

Not too many years ago, our country faced the major task of cleaning the Statue of Liberty. For over 100 years, the statue had experienced wind, rain, soot, and smog—the atmosphere of a great metropolitan area. The golden-brown copper exterior had turned green. Its smooth surface had become pitted severely.

The effects of the environment, even in less urban areas, can also be severe. Many cemeteries are dotted with gravestones whose inscriptions have long since been erased by wind and rain. Yet, nearby are other gravestones, seemingly untouched by the environment. The explanation depends on the fact that some rocks are more susceptible to weathering and erosion than others. In some climates, slate or granite gravestones may last for centuries, whereas sandstone markers may last a relatively short period of time.

Discuss with the class how such differences among rocks may affect the durability of the many "Wonders of the World," such as the Sphinx, the Parthenon, and Cleopatra's Needle. Have students determine what can be done to preserve these monuments.

Activity Notes

Activity 2-3A

Forming Layers   page **98**

Purpose   To learn how layers of sediment form and how these layers can change.

- 20 minutes Groups of 4 or teacher demonstration
- **Activity Record Sheet 2-3A** (Lab Manual page 25) can be used to record this activity.
- Science Processes: Formulating models: Observing: Comparing and contrasting; Describing; Demonstrating; Inferring.

Procedure Notes

To make a model of river sediment, mix sand, fine clay, gravel, garden soil, and water in a jar and allow it to settle into layers. Students can then compare this model to the model of mineral layers.

Answers to Questions

1. Color and, possibly, size and shape
2. Layers disappeared as materials became intermingled.
3. Materials will settle in order of density. The most dense, the iron fillings, will settle most rapidly.
4. The salt dissolved into the water.
5. Water soaked through each layer without otherwise changing the layers.
6. The iron is oxidized (rusted), and the salt layer may have partially dissolved. After evaporation, the salt should be a solid layer, rather than loose grains. Some salt may also be found throughout the sand.

Conclusion

Layers of sediment may be formed from minerals that have mixed with or dissolved in water. Denser materials may settle out from less dense materials; water may evaporate, leaving a layer of minerals behind.

Science Background

2-3

Rock or minerals that result primarily from the evaporation of water containing dissolved solids are known as evaporites. As the water becomes saturated, the ions come out of solution to form a crystalline residue.

Halite, or common table salt (sodium chloride, $NaCl$), is the most familiar evaporite mineral. Commonly, it is formed when evaporation in a bay fed by the sea occurs faster than the inflow of water. Judging from the great thickness of the renowned salt deposits of the world, the process of influx of water and evaporation must have been repeated many times over. As the Great Salt Lake deposits reveal, evaporation of an inland water body can also produce very flat rock layers.

Gypsum ($CaSO_4 \cdot 2H_2O$) is closely related to halite in origin, for it, too, is a product of the evaporation of sea water. Along with it is found an anhydrous (water-lacking) calcium sulfate ($CaSO_4$) called anhydrite.

As a body of water evaporates, the minerals precipitate out in a specific order determined by the solubility of the minerals in water—the least soluble first, the most soluble last.

Gypsum is less soluble than halite and thus precipitates first when sea water is evaporated. Both gypsum and anhydrite come out of solution after about 80 percent of the sea water has evaporated, and halite appears after 90 percent has evaporated.

Student Misconception

The identification of rock and mineral samples based on physical properties is frustrating to the beginning student. Lack of experience in recognizing specific features combined with the inability to distinguish between minerals and rocks can be frustrating. Students may misapply mineral identification tests to rock material.

Rock is a mixture of minerals. As mineral material is weathered or altered through other geophysical processes, it becomes available for incorporation into rock material. Once this occurs, specific tests used to identify minerals no longer have much meaning. Although students can use the characteristics of basic minerals in determining the composition of rocks, and in identifying rock samples, the focus of analysis must be on the texture and composition of the rock material.

Granite is particularly useful for illustrating the differences between rocks and minerals. Have students examine samples of the individual minerals that make up granite (quartz, feldspar, hornblende, and mica) and compare them with a sample of granite. Students should be able to see how distinct minerals combine to form rock material.

Activity Notes

Activity 2-3B

Determining the Class of a Rock   page **104**

Purpose   To use a key to determine the class of a rock.

- **CORE** 40 minutes Pairs of students or small groups
- **Activity Record Sheet 2-3B** (Lab Manual page 26) can be used to record this activity.
- Science Processes: Observing; Classifying; Interpreting data; Distinguishing; Reasoning.

Advance Preparation

For 10 percent hydrochloric acid, add 10 mL concentrated hydrochloric acid to 90 mL distilled water. Other amounts of acid and water can also be used as long as they are in the same proportion: one part acid to nine parts distilled water. SAFETY NOTE: *When diluting an acid,* ALWAYS *add the acid to the water. Add very slowly, stirring constantly with a glass rod.*

Safety Information

Students should wear safety goggles when using hydrochloric acid. They should carefully avoid getting any acid on their hands. If they do come in contact with the acid, they should wash their hands immediately. As a precaution, students should routinely wash their hands after using hydrochloric acid.

Procedure Notes

Once they know which sample is which, students will probably to be able to distinguish the rocks on the basis of immediately evident physical properties. For distinguishing specimens by chemical properties, however, this activity is a good exercise.

Some answers will undoubtedly be wrong, but students will learn to make valuable discriminations in the process of going through the steps.

In Step 12, cemented particles tend to "rest" on one another, whereas particles in an igneous rock fit together like an angular jigsaw puzzle. Also, cemented particles usually show signs of weathering. They are frequently bound by a cement that has some yellow, red, or brown color (caused by rust).

Conclusion

By answering a series of questons about a rock, making one decision at a time, students should see that a key makes the identification process easier.

Demonstration

A Test for Calcium Carbonate

Limestone provides a good example for showing a variety of physical properties common to rocks. Limestone comprises the floors and walls of many of our buildings, and yet it is composed of the skeletons of tiny ocean animals.

Tell students that limestone, frequently colored gray or white, is made mainly of calcium carbonate and has a hardness of between 3 and 4 on the Mohs's scale. Pure limestone is made of just one mineral: calcite.

Scrape some limestone to form a powder. Use an eyedropper to place two drops of vinegar onto the powder. (The linestone will bubble.) Ask students if they know why. (The acid making up the vinegar combines with the limestone to release carbon dioxide in the rock.)

Next, fill one beaker with cold distilled water. Fill another with cold, unflavored soda water. Stir the water until all bubbles disappear.

Place a piece of limestone in each beaker, and wait 10 minutes. Ask the students what they think will happen.

After 10 minutes, check the beakers. No change should be observable in the beaker with distilled water. However, in the beaker containing soda water you should see bubbles just above and on the limestone. This is because acids and gases in the soda water combine with the limestone to produce carbon-dioxide bubbles.

Section 3 Review Answers

Check Your Understanding
page **109**

1. Both are melted rock. Magma is found below the surface; lava is found only on the surface.
2. Igneous: Melting and cooling; Metamorphic: Mineral changes caused by intense heat and pressure; Sedimentary: Deposition, compaction, and cementation
3. Any kind of rock can form from any kind of rock, as shown in Figure 2-25. Sedimentary rock can form from any type of rock by means of weathering, erosion, deposition, compaction, and cementation of particles. Metamorphic rock can form from any type of rock that is subjected to great heat and pressure. Igneous rock can form from any rock that is melted and then cools.
4. 1) Coarse-grained: Mineral grains or crystals large enough to be seen; 2) Fine-grained: Mineral grains or crystals too small to be seen without a microscope; 3) Mixed grain: Grains or crystals of at least two different sizes; 4) Glassy: No mineral crystals, and looks like glass; 5) Layered: Crystals and grains in parallel layers throughout the rock; 6) Banded: Different minerals concentrated in different bands.
5. Hardness may be used to distinguish feldspar from quartz. The hardness of feldspar is 6, that of quartz is 7. Feldspar often can be recognized by the shine of crystal faces or cleavage planes, and quartz by the duller shine of its surfaces.

2-3

Chapter Vocabulary

Section 1

matter
energy
solid
liquid
gas
element
atom
proton
neutron
nucleus
electron
periodic table
atomic number
chemical symbol
isotope
atomic mass
compound
chemical formula
chemical bond
molecule
ion

Section 2

mineral
inorganic
crystalline solid
crystal
silicate minerals
impurities
nonsilicate minerals
cleavage
streak
luster
heft

2-3

Chapter 2 Review Answers

Putting It All Together   page 110

1. A change in temperature causes the particles that make up a substance to move faster or slower. When this increased or decreased motion causes the particles to change their relationship to each other, a change in phase occurs.

2. The silicon atom should show 14 electrons surrounding a nucleus composed of 14 protons and 14 neutrons.

3. Fluorite is composed of calcium and fluorine, with one atom of calcium for every two of fluorine.

4. To distinguish a mineral from a nonmineral, a person would need to know if the specimen is a natural, inorganic crystalline solid.

5. Cleavage and fracture relate to the basic crystalline structure. So, too, does the shape of a mineral crystal and the presence or likelihood of crystal faces.

6. Steps will vary. Here are likely choices. Look for distinguishing visible features of the specimen. Run a rough test for hardness. Look through a handbook for a likely identification, considering where the mineral was found, etc. Run other tests, as described in the handbook. Check with a rock shop or with rock collectors to see if they can tell you what the mineral is (and how they know).

7. *Igneous*—granite: quartz, feldspar, mica
Sedimentary—sandstone: quartz; shale: clay, quartz, mica
Metamorphic—granite gneiss: quartz, feldspar, mica; quartzite: quartz; schist: clay, quartz, mica

8. Limestone, dolomite, and marble are formed from nonsilicate minerals. Students may list others, depending on the specimens used in this section.

9. A rock is identified by the minerals found in the rock and by the texture of the rock. Minerals are identified on the basis of distinguishing physical properties.

10. Due to heat and pressure the crystalline structure of minerals in the rock can be altered. When that happens, a different rock results. Schists and gneisses are examples of metamorphic rocks that can form from other metamorphic rocks.

Chapter 2 Review Answers (continued)

Apply Your Knowledge   page 110

1. Among the properties that would make a mineral valuable as a gemstone are color, hardness, luster, crystal faces, size, shape, and rarity.
2. Banded, layered textures indicate metamorphic rock. A glassy texture indicates an igneous rock. A grainy texture of particles cemented together indicates sedimentary rock. Unbanded and unlayered grains that are fused together indicate igneous rock.
3. The faster the cooling, the smaller the particles.
4. Through weathering, the quartz in granite can become sand which can become sandstone. Through deep burial and heat, sandstone can be metamorphosed into gneiss. Heat in the earth's volcanic activity can melt gneiss and turn it into granite.

Chapter Vocabulary

Section 3

rock
igneous rock
sedimentary rock
metamorphic rock
magma
batholith
lava
pyroclastic deposits
porphyritic rock
laccolith
clastic rock
organic rock
chemically formed rock
metamorphosis
rock cycle
texture
mineral composition

2-3

Chapter 2

Earth Materials

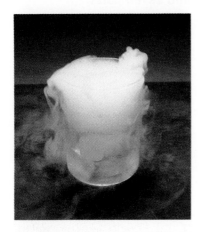

Section 1
The Nature of Matter

Matter is anything that occupies space and has mass. All matter is made of atoms, which are too small to be seen. Atoms, in turn, are made of yet smaller particles that give different types of atoms unique properties. These properties can cause certain atoms to bond with each other to form molecules. Molecules may then bond together to form compounds.

Section 2
Minerals

There are 92 elements that occur naturally on earth. These 92 elements are usually found in combinations (or compounds) called minerals. All minerals are inorganic crystalline solids. There are about 2000 different minerals in the earth's crust.

Section 3
Rocks

The earth's crust is made of rock. Under all land areas and all ocean basins is rock.

The earth's rocks are made of different combinations of the earth's minerals. Because of ongoing earth processes, the earth's rocks are being continually recycled. Some are broken down and later cemented together. Some are melted and then cooled. Some are subjected to such heat and pressure that the minerals in them are changed.

Everything on the earth is made of matter. Matter can exist as a solid, liquid, or gas. In the photo at the left, the mountains and ice are solid matter. The melting ice forms liquid matter. The air is made of gaseous matter.

The Nature of Matter   Section 1

Learner Objectives:
1. To identify the three phases of matter by their characteristics.
2. To recognize the structure and three particle types of atoms.
3. To demonstrate that the periodic table organizes elements by atomic number and by properties.
4. To distinguish between compounds and molecules, and mixtures.

Section 1 of Chapter 2 is divided into seven parts:

Matter

Elements and atoms

The periodic table

Isotopes

Compounds and molecules

Compounds made of ions

Mixtures

Figure 2-1. Matter can exist as a solid, a liquid, or a gas. The breaker contains frozen carbón dioxide (a solid, as is the beaker), water (a liquid), and carbon dioxide (a gas).

Figure 2-2. Which items above are solids? liquids? gases?
Solid: rock, beaker, aluminum foil, outside of balloon
Liquid: blue substance in beaker
Gas: substance inside balloon

There are many kinds of substances, or materials, in the world around you. As you learned in Chapter 1, each substance has its own physical and chemical properties. By observing these properties, you can classify substances into different groups, such as wood and plastic. What substances make up your desk?

The earth, too, is made of many different substances. Earth scientists have classified these substances in many different ways, using many different groupings. In this section, you will learn about the most basic ways in which scientists have classified the materials that make up the earth.

By way of introduction, you might cut an object like an apple into ever-smaller pieces (to a limit)—as Carl Sagan does with apple pie in *Cosmos*. As students conside the smaller pieces, they should have in mind questions like "Is this still an apple?"

Matter
New vocabulary: matter, energy, solid, liquid, gas

All substances have one thing in common—they are examples of **matter.** Matter is anything that takes up space and has mass. Water, rocks, air, and your body are all made of matter.

What is matter?

Heat, light, and motion, however, are not matter. They are examples of **energy.** Energy is the ability to cause change in matter. Almost everything you can think of is either matter or energy.

What is energy?

Energy can change matter in different ways. One important change caused by energy is a change in the form of matter, which is called the phase or state of matter.

Most matter can exist in three different phases. A **solid** is matter such as a rock or sheet of paper that has a definite shape. A **liquid** does not have a definite shape, but takes on the shape of the container it is in. Cooking oil is a familiar liquid. Can you think of others? Both solids and liquids also have definite volumes. The amount of space they occupy does not change much.

A **gas** is matter without definite shape or volume. A gas fills whatever space is available to it.

When does matter change phase?

Matter changes phase when heat energy is added to it or taken away from it. You have probably seen water freeze into the solid called ice when its temperature drops below 0°C or ice melt back into liquid water when it warms. Raising the temperature of water to 100°C causes it to boil and turn into a gas called water vapor. Thus water can exist in all three phases—solid, liquid, and gas.

Unlike water, most substances don't change phase under normal atmospheric temperatures. It takes large amounts of added heat energy to melt iron into a liquid. Some substances remain solid under most temperatures, and others tend to remain liquids. Still others are almost always gases. All substances, however, will change phase at some temperature.

Why does heat energy cause matter to change phase? All matter is made of tiny particles so small you cannot see them. These particles are always moving at least a little. Adding heat energy to a substance causes its particles to move faster. They move more slowly when heat is taken away. When the particles forming a piece of matter begin to move faster or slower, the physical properties of the matter begin to change. If the motion of its particles changes enough, the matter can change phase.

In a solid, the particles are locked in a specific pattern, packed closely together. They can only vibrate in place. In a liquid, the particles are packed more loosely and can slide past each other. The particles move enough to allow a liquid to change shape.

Critical Thinking

Look at the room around you. What objects occur in what phases? Describe any phase changes you can recognize.

Answers will vary.

Science Processes: Measuring, Interpreting Data

See also Activity Record Sheet 2-1A(Lab Manual page 15)
CORE   30 minutes   Groups of 4

Activity 2-1A   Solids, Liquids, and Gases

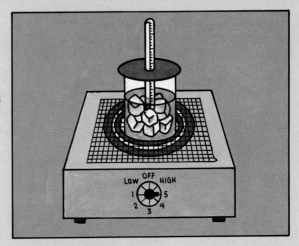

Materials

sharpened pencil	crushed ice
thermometer	glass stirring rod
clear tape	wire gauze
water	cardboard circle (9 cm in diameter)
hot plate	
250-mL beaker	watch or clock that indicates seconds

Purpose

To show how the input of heat energy changes water from a solid to a liquid to a gas.

Procedure

1. Use a sharpened pencil to poke a hole in the center of the cardboard disk. Gently ease the bulb of a thermometer through the hole. *SAFETY NOTE: Be sure the hole in the cardboard disk is large enough to allow the thermometer to be pushed through without breaking. If a thermometer is broken, avoid touching the mercury and notify your teacher.* Slide the bulb down so that when the cardboard rests on the rim of the beaker, the bulb is suspended inside the beaker. Tape the thermometer in this position and carefully put to the side. Make a table like the one shown, with spaces for 20 minutes.
2. Fill the beaker half full of water. Add enough crushed ice to fill the beaker. Do not over fill. Stir the ice and water.
3. Put the cardboard disk with the thermometer set in it over the beaker. Make sure the thermometer bulb is set in the middle of the water and ice mixture. Place the beaker on a piece of wire gauze on the cold coils of the hot plate. Set the hot plate control to medium high heat. Record the temperature of the beaker and the time.

4. Take a temperature reading every minute until the ice is melted and the water is boiling with steam evaporating. For each temperature reading, note the phase of the material—solid, liquid, or gas. If more than one phase is present at a given time, use fractions to indicate how much of each phase is present. For example, your first mixture is roughly ½ water and ½ ice.
5. Periodically remove the cardboard for a few seconds and stir the ice and water mixture.
6. Plot your data on a graph showing temperature versus time.

Questions

1. How does the solid ice respond to heat input?
2. How does the temperature change with heat input?
3. Did the temperature of your mixture change in an even way, or does your graph show bursts of temperature increase and zones of little change?
4. Cream soups undergo a phase change from solid to liquid as they are heated. What other examples of phase changes can you name?

Conclusion

What is the relationship between temperature and phase change for water?

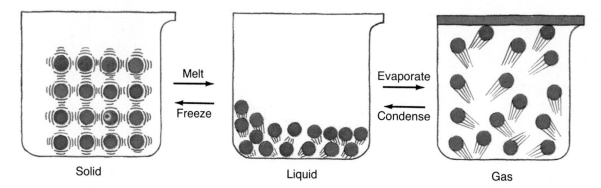

Solid   Liquid   Gas

See also Teaching Diagram 2-1A (TRB page 73).

Figure 2-3. The particles of matter are arranged differently in solid, liquid, and gas phases. How are the particles different in liquid nitrogen and nitrogen gas? In liquid nitrogen the particles are close to each other, and they lie on the bottom of their container. In nitrogen gas the particles are separated by lots of space, and they fill their container.

1. Matter is anything that takes up space and has mass.
2. The particles in a solid are locked in a specific pattern. When the solid becomes a liquid, the particles are no longer locked in a pattern and thus slide freely past each other.
3. Most gases cannot be seen because there are too few particles of the gas in a given amount of space for it to be seen.

What is matter made of?

The particles in a gas are far apart and moving very fast. If they touch, they bounce off each other. In the gas phase, there are often too few particles in a given space for us to see the matter that is there. When we can see a gas, it is often because that gas has a color. For example, chlorine gas is yellow. Most gases are colorless and cannot be seen.

Check yourself

1. What is matter?

2. How are the particles arranged in a solid? How does this arrangement change if the solid becomes a liquid?

3. Why can most gases not be seen?

Elements and atoms   New vocabulary: element, atom, proton, neutron, nucleus, electron, mass number

Grouping matter according to its phase is one way of classifying it. Each phase of a particular substance shows different physical properties. Matter can also be classified by kind. Each kind of matter has its own chemical properties.

All the matter of the universe is made up of varying amounts of different pure substances called **elements.** An element is a kind of matter with unique chemical properties. Like the primary colors blue, red, and yellow, the elements cannot be changed to simpler forms. However, just as colors can be combined to form new colors, elements can be combined to form different substances.

Some familiar substances such as aluminum and copper are made of just one element. Diamonds are made of the element carbon. Balloons that rise are filled with the element helium.

Most of the elements are *metals*. They conduct electricity well. Iron and gold are examples of metals. Metals can be drawn into wires or beaten into sheets. Some metals such as sodium and gold are soft enough to be cut with a knife.

The rest of the elements are *nonmetals*. They do not conduct electricity well. Some of the nonmetals such as chlorine and helium are gases at room temperature. Other nonmetals are brittle solids. The nonmetal silicon is the major rock-forming element.

Ninety-two different elements exist in nature. Scientists have created additional ones in the lab. Eight elements make up 98.2 percent of the earth's crust. These elements are oxygen, silicon, aluminum, iron, calcium, sodium, potassium, and magnesium. The remaining elements are relatively rare.

Elements are made of tiny particles called **atoms.** Atoms are the smallest particles of an element that have all of that element's properties. All gold atoms have the same chemical

Figure 2-4. The substances copper, sulfur, aluminum, and carbon are all elements.

Figure 2-5. Which two elements account for almost 75 percent of the elements in the earth's crust?

The elements oxygen and silicon account for almost seventy-five percent of the elements in the earth's crust.

See also Teaching Diagram 2-1B (TRB page 14).

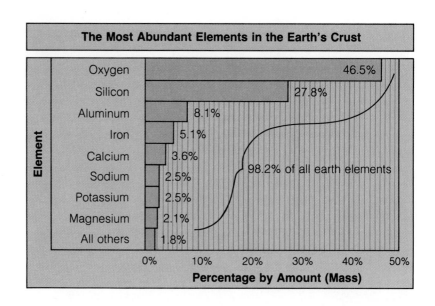

The Most Abundant Elements in the Earth's Crust

Element	Percentage by Amount (Mass)
Oxygen	46.5%
Silicon	27.8%
Aluminum	8.1%
Iron	5.1%
Calcium	3.6%
Sodium	2.5%
Potassium	2.5%
Magnesium	2.1%
All others	1.8%

98.2% of all earth elements

Library research

What elements are most abundant in the core and mantle?

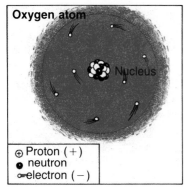

Oxygen atom

Nucleus

⊕ Proton (+)
● neutron
☌ electron (−)

Figure 2-6. Protons and neutrons are located in the nucleus of an atom. Electrons move rapidly outside of the nucleus. What charge does each particle in an atom have?
The protons have a positive charge, the electrons have a negative charge, and the neutrons have no charge.

properties, and these properties are different from those of all copper atoms. Atoms are so small it would take about a million of them lined up in a row to equal the thickness of a sheet of paper.

The structure of atoms   Atoms are not the smallest particles known. They are made up of three kinds of even smaller particles.

Protons are relatively heavy particles with a positive electrical charge (+). **Neutrons** have a mass similar to that of protons, but no electrical charge. Both particles are clustered together in the central part of an atom, forming what is called the **nucleus.** The nucleus has an overall positive charge because of the protons it contains.

Surrounding the nucleus is a cloud of rapidly moving particles called **electrons.** An electron has a much smaller mass than either of the other two particles, and it has a negative electrical charge (−). Each atom normally has as many electrons as it has protons. Thus, in a single atom, the negative charge of the electrons balances the positive charge of the protons.

The nucleus is very small compared to the atom as a whole. If the atom were as large as a football stadium, the nucleus would be the size of a pea on the 50-yd line. The rest of the atom is space that is occupied by the moving electrons.

Our Science Heritage

How Did We Learn to Use Metals?

Modern-day technology relies heavily upon the use of metals like iron, steel, copper, and aluminum. The use of metals, however, is not new. Scientists have found metal objects made by people thousands of years ago. Though no one knows for sure, the earliest use of metals probably dates back at least 8000 years.

A few metals are occasionally found alone in their natural state. Gold, silver, and copper are examples of such metals. Ancient peoples discovered that gold, copper, and silver could be shaped into a great variety of useful and beautiful objects. The oldest gold objects were made at least 5500 years ago.

Most metals are found in combination with other elements. Copper, for example, is usually found in copper ores. Iron and aluminum are found in ores, too. Ancient people probably discovered metals in ores by accident. Perhaps rocks containing copper or lead were heated in a fire.

Afterward, small amounts of copper or lead might have been found among the rocks. Iron is not easy to separate from its ore because very high heat is needed. Nevertheless, it is estimated that people have been separating iron from its ores for at least the past 4000 years.

Ancient people also discovered that metals could be combined to form new metals. These new metals, called alloys, contain very useful physical properties. Bronze, which is an alloy of copper and tin, was first discovered about 5500 years ago and played a very important part in human development.

Many of the early uses of metals were made by trial and error. As scientists learned more about the nature of matter, much more was discovered about the use of metals. As the earth's supply of certain metals is used up, scientists must look to new metals to meet the needs of the world's population.

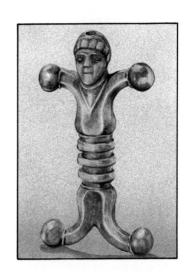

Beautiful bronze and gold work is characteristic of early Irish art. This bronze sword hilt is from the first century B.C.

Although most of an atom's volume is taken up by the electrons, the nucleus contains most of its mass. The **mass number** of an atom is the sum of the number of protons and neutrons. The mass number of carbon is 12. This is because carbon has six protons and six neutrons in its nucleus. Aluminum is a heavier atom. It has 13 protons and 14 neutrons.

Element	Symbol	The nucleus		Mass Number	Electrons	Atomic Number
		Protons	Neutrons			
Hydrogen	H	1	0	1	1	1
Helium	He	2	2	4	2	2
Carbon	C	6	6	12	6	6
Nitrogen	N	7	7	14	7	7
Oxygen	O	8	8	16	8	8
Aluminum	Al	13	14	27	13	13
Silicon	Si	14	14	28	14	14
Iron	Fe	26	30	56	26	26
Copper	Cu	29	34	63	29	29
Gold	Au	79	118	197	79	79
Uranium	U	92	146	238	92	92

Table 2-1. The composition of several important elements is shown here. For which elements is the number of electrons the same as the number of protons? All of the elements

1. An atom is the smallest particle of an element that still has that element's properties.
2. Protons, neutrons, and electrons. Protons and neutrons are found in the nucleus; electrons are found in a cloud outside the nucleus.
3. The nucleus contains most of the atom's mass.

What is the purpose of the periodic table?

Its mass number is 27. Most of the heavier elements have more neutrons than protons. Some examples are shown in Table 2-1. Notice that the number of electrons is always the same as the number of protons.

Check yourself

1. What is an atom?

2. Name the three kinds of particles in an atom. Where in the atom is each found?

3. Which part of an atom contains most of the atom's mass?

The periodic table

New vocabulary: periodic table, atomic number, chemical symbol, energy levels

Atoms of the elements have different numbers of protons, neutrons, and electrons. Atoms also have different properties. Some have a greater density than others, and some react more readily to other materials. The **periodic table** organizes the elements according to their properties. It is a handy tool for learning about the elements.

The elements are arranged in the periodic table in order of their atomic numbers. The **atomic number** of an element is the number of protons in its nucleus. Hydrogen has one proton and has an atomic number of 1. Carbon has an atomic number of 6 because it has six protons. Look at Table 2-1. The atomic numbers of the naturally occuring elements increase one by one up to the element uranium, which has 92 protons. On the periodic table (Table 2-2) the atomic number is the largest number in each box.

Each element has its own **chemical symbol**, which is a short way of writing the element's name. The large letters on the periodic table are the chemical symbols for the elements. Many of the symbols are the first letter or letters of the elements' names. For example, the symbol for hydrogen is H. The symbol for lithium is Li. Symbols that are different from the elements' names are abbreviations for Greek or Latin names. For example, the symbol for sodium is Na from the Latin word *natrium*.

The properties of an element depend on the number of electrons in the atoms and how they are arranged. The electrons are always moving rapidly. We can never tell exactly where they are or where they will be next. Electrons tend to stay in certain areas, however, and these areas are known as **energy levels**. Electrons in the energy levels close to the nucleus have less energy than electrons in energy levels farther away.

Each energy level can hold a certain number of electrons. The energy level closest to the nucleus can hold two electrons. Hydrogen (H) has one electron in this first energy level. Helium (He) has two electrons in the first energy level. Both of them are in the first row of the periodic table.

The elements in the second row of the periodic table have electrons in two energy levels. They have two electrons filling the lowest energy level. They also have one or more electrons in the second energy level. This second level can hold up to eight electrons. Elements in the third row of the periodic table fill the first two energy levels and also have electrons in the third energy level. The largest elements in the seventh row have electrons in seven energy levels.

The periodic table is an odd shape because the elements are arranged in columns as well as rows. The elements in any column of the periodic table have the same number of electrons in their outer energy level. For example, all the elements in column 1A (1) have one electron in the outer energy level. All the elements in the column 4A (14) have four electrons in their outer energy level. All the elements in column 8A (18) have a full outer evergy level. For helium (He), a full level is two electrons. For neon (Ne) and argon (Ar), a full energy level is eight electrons.

Library research

Various atomic models have been used to explain the behavior of atoms. How were the earlier models different from the current one?

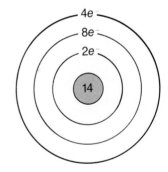

Figure 2-7. This energy level diagram represents a silicon (Si) atom. The symbol for an electron is e⁻. The energy levels are shown as circles around the nucleus. The lowest energy level can hold two electrons, and the second one can hold eight. How many electrons are in the third energy level of silicon?

Four

Table 2-2 Periodic Table of the Elements

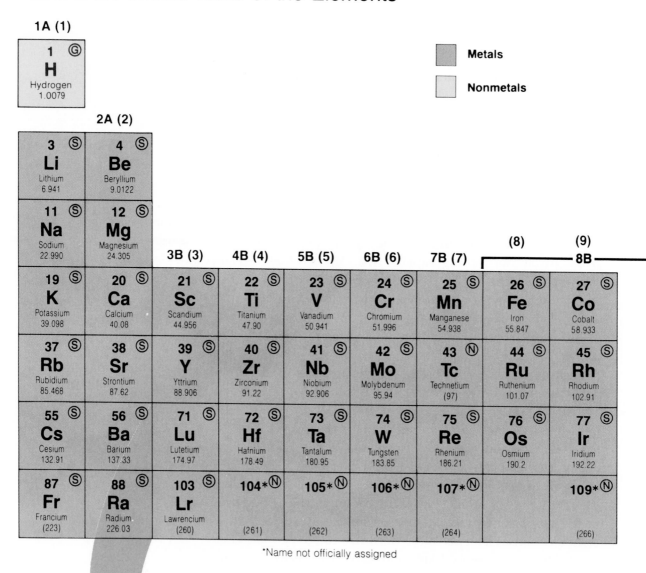

*Name not officially assigned

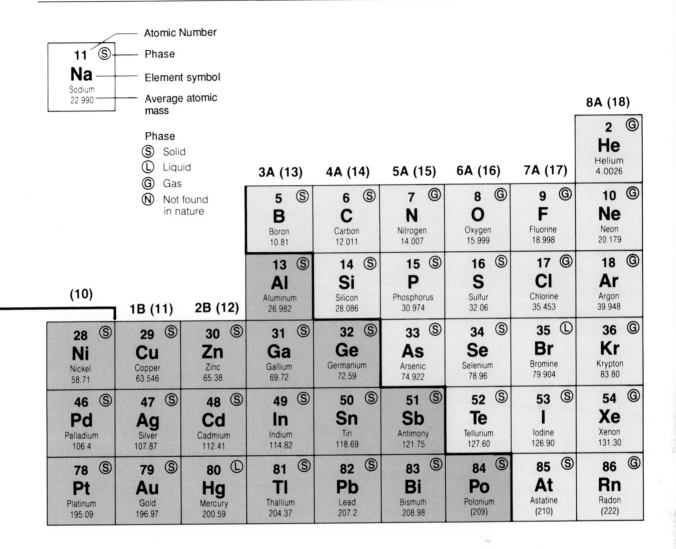

Science Processes: Observing, Classifying Data
See also Activity Record Sheet 2-1B (Lab Manual
page 17)

CORE   20 minutes   Individual

Activity 2-1B   Using the Periodic Table

Materials

periodic table
pencil
paper

Purpose

To use the periodic table to identify 10 mystery
elements.

Procedure

Make a table like the one shown. Use the periodic table and the clues given to identify each
mystery element. Write the name and the symbol of each mystery element and the clue that
helped you identify that element.

- Element A is a liquid metal at room
temperature.
- Element B has the symbol Fe taken from its
Latin name *ferrum*.
- Element C is a metal that has four energy lev-
els and two electrons in its outer energy level.
- Element D is a nonmetal with an atomic num-
ber of three less than that of chlorine.

- Element E is a solid metal with 13 protons in
the nucleus.
- Element F is a nonmetallic gas at room temperature with a single proton in the nuclei of
its atoms.
- Element G is a solid metal at room temperature represented by the symbol K.
- Element H has 12 protons and is a solid metal
at room temperature.
- Element I is a nonmetallic solid at room temperature, and has atoms with a total of 12
electons in three energy levels.
- Element J is the largest of the naturally occurring elements.

Questions

1. What types of clues were most useful in helping you identify the mystery elements?
2. Many elements are solid metals at room temperature. How can you distinguish them from
each other?

Conclusion

How does the periodic table help you understand more about a given element and how all
elements are related to each other?

Letter representing mystery element	Element identified from periodic table	Most important clue
A		
B		
C		

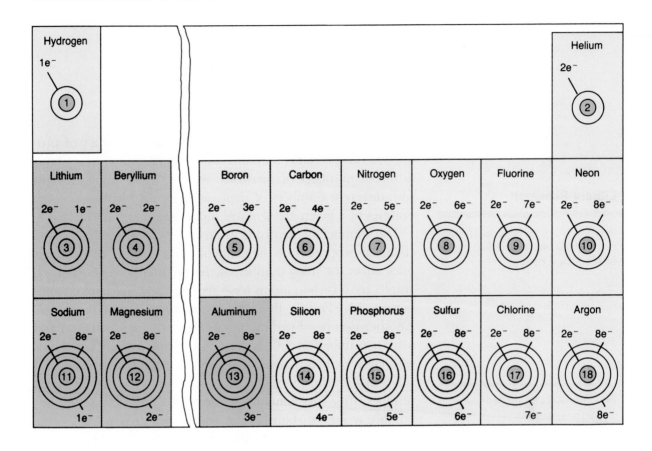

The number of electrons in the outer energy level determines the chemical properties of the element. Thus, the elements in a column have similar properties. For example, the elements in column 1A, except for hydrogen, are all soft metals. They are called the *alkali metals*. They are never found as pure metals in nature because they react violently with water. The one electron in their outer energy level tends to react with other atoms. In contrast, the elements in column 8A (18) are all gases. They are called the *noble gases* and are found in the atmosphere. They seldom react with other elements at all. This is because their outer energy level is full of electrons.

Check yourself

1. In what order are the elements arranged on the periodic table?

2. How is the atomic number related to the number of protons, neutrons, and electrons in an atom?

3. How are the elements in a column of the period table similar?

Figure 2-8. The energy level diagrams for the first 18 elements are shown here in the arrangement of the periodic table. How are the elements in any row alike? How are the elements in any column alike? The elements in any row have electrons in the same number of energy levels. The elements in any column have the same number of electrons in the outer energy level.

1. The elements are arranged in order of their atomic numbers.

2. The atomic number is the same as the number of protons and the same as the number of electrons in an atom. The atomic number is not related to the number of neutrons.

3. The elements in a column have the same number of electrons in their outer energy level, and they have similar chemical properties.

Library Research

Why are isotopes important? Find out how the isotopes of two of the elements are used.

How are isotopes named?

1. Isotopes of the same element have different numbers of neutrons. The have the same numbers of protons and electrons.
2. Most elements have two or more isotopes of different masses which are averaged.

Isotopes

New vocabulary: isotope, atomic mass

All atoms of any one element have the same number of protons. However, different atoms of the same element may have different numbers of neutrons. Atoms of the same element with different numbers of neutrons are called **isotopes**. Some isotopes of a given element are more common than others.

The number of neutrons in an isotope does not affect the chemical properties of the element. The number of neutrons does affect the mass number of the isotope, however. For example, most carbon atoms have six neutrons and a mass number of 12. This is the most common isotope of carbon. Another isotope of carbon has atoms with seven neutrons and a mass number of 13. A third isotope of carbon has atoms with eight neutrons and a mass number of 14.

Scientists write the name of an isotope by placing the mass number after the element's name. Thus, the isotopes of carbon are written carbon-12, carbon-13, and carbon-14.

The mass number only approximates the mass of an atom. A more accurate measure of an atom's mass is its **atomic mass.** The atomic mass is measured in atomic mass units, or amu. One amu is roughly equal to the mass of one proton or one neutron. The atomic mass of an element is different for each of its isotopes. The atomic mass for the element is given as an average of the masses of its isotopes. This average atomic mass is shown on the periodic table under the name of each element.

Check yourself

1. How are the atoms of two isotopes of the same element different?

2. Why is the atomic mass of most elements an average?

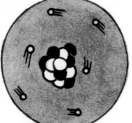
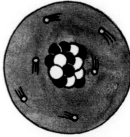

Carbon-12
6 protons
6 neutrons
6 electrons

Carbon-14
6 protons
8 neutrons
6 electrons

Figure 2-9. Carbon-12 and carbon-14 are two isotopes of carbon. How are they different? Carbon-14 has two more neutrons than carbon 12.

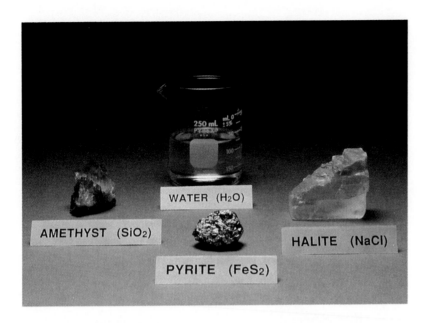

Figure 2-10. Chemical formulas show the kinds of atoms that make up a compound and the proportions of those atoms. What are the chemical formulas for water, amethyst, pyrite, and halite?
The chemical formulas are as follows:
water H_2O
amethyst SiO_2
pyrite FeS_2
halite $NaCl$

Compounds and molecules

New vocabulary: compound, chemical formula, chemical bond, molecule

Many substances, such as gold and copper, are made of pure elements. However, most earth materials are made of more than one element. Most elements tend to combine with other elements to form **compounds.** A compound is a substance made of two or more elements joined together chemically. Compounds usually have properties that are very different from those of the elements that form them.

The numbers of atoms of each element in a particular compound form a fixed ratio. For example, water is a compound formed from the elements hydrogen (H) and oxygen (O). Water is always made up of exactly twice as many hydrogen atoms as oxygen atoms. The ratio of H to O is two to one.

Scientists have special names for compounds called **chemical formulas.** A chemical formula shows both the kinds of atoms that make up a compound and their ratio. The formula for water, for example, is written H_2O. It shows that two hydrogen atoms occur for each oxygen atom.

The force that holds two atoms together in a compound is called a **chemical bond.** Chemical bonds hold together the atoms of all the substances we can see and touch.

Name the elements and the ratio of those elements that form the compound water.

Water
molecule
H_2O

Carbon dioxide   Oxygen
molecule   molecule
CO_2 O^2

Figure 2-11. All molecules are formed by the sharing of electrons.

Critical Thinking

Why is there no compound with the formula H_3O?

In H_3O, three hydrogens would each share one electron with an oxygen atom. Then the oxygen atom would have nine electrons in its outer energy level. This would be too many if one electron moved to the third energy level the atom would be unstable.

Figure 2-12. A molecule of water is formed when two hydrogen atoms share electrons with one oxygen atom. The atoms are held together by the sharing of electrons.

In one type of chemical bond, two atoms share their electrons. Atoms joined with shared electrons form **molecules** (MOL'-uh-kewlz). The atoms of a molecule stay together.

Carbon dioxide is an example of a substance that occurs as a molecule. Carbon dioxide is the gas that makes carbonated beverages bubbly. A single bubble contains many molecules of carbon dioxide. Each molecule is made up of two oxygen atoms and one carbon atom, all sharing their electrons.

Compounds form from atoms because of the actions of electrons. An atom is stable when it has an outer energy level that is full of electrons. For example, the first energy level of an atom is full with only two electrons. The element helium has two electrons in this first energy level. Helium is very stable and does not combine with other elements. By contrast, hydrogen has only one electron in this energy level. It is a very reactive element. Hydrogen forms compounds with many other elements because it is not stable alone.

Atoms tend to form compounds when they have extra electrons or not quite enough electrons for a full outer energy level. For example, oxygen has six electrons in its second energy level. It needs two more electrons to have a full outer energy level. In a water molecule two hydrogen atoms share electrons with an oxygen atom. Each hydrogen atom gets two electrons some of the time. This fills the outer energy level for each hydrogen. The two hydrogen atoms each share one electron with the oxygen. This makes a full eight electrons in its outer energy level.

By sharing electons each atom in a molecule gets a full outer energy level. The atoms stay close together because the electrons are shared. This is one type of chemical bond.

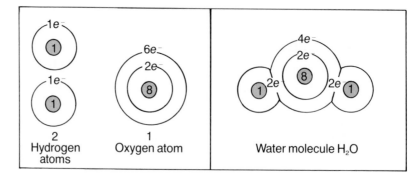

Check yourself

1. What is a compound?

2. What does a chemical formula show?

Compounds made of ions

New vocabulary: ion

In another type of bond, atoms gain or lose electrons. Then they become ions. An **ion** is an atom with a positive or negative electrical charge. An ion has more or fewer than the normal number of electrons for an atom of that element.

When an atom gains an electron it becomes a negative ion. It then has more electrons (with negative charges) than protons (with positive charges). For example, when a chlorine atom (Cl) gains an electron it becomes a chloride ion (Cl^-). These are negative ions.

Ions usually form so that the outer energy level of the ion will be full of electrons. This is a stable arrangement. For example, the chlorine atom needs to gain only one electron to form an ion. It already has seven electrons in its outer energy level. By gaining one more electron the chlorine atom (Cl) becomes a chloride ion (Cl^-). In contrast, an oxygen atom (O) has only six electrons in its outer energy level. It must gain two electrons to have a full outer energy level.

Other atoms lose electrons to become ions. For example, an aluminum atom has three electrons in its outer energy level. When it becomes an ion (Al^{3+}), it loses these three electrons. Only the inner energy levels remain. These energy levels are full. When an ion has more protons than electrons it is a positive ion.

Ions are very different from the atoms that form them. This is because of the difference in their arrangements of electrons. Figure 2-14 shows that ions can be different sizes than their atoms. They also have different chemical properties. For example, sodium *ions* are sea water. By contrast, sodium *atoms* react explosively with water.

Some compounds are made of ions. When these compounds form, electrons are transferred from one atom to another. This transfer creates the ions. The ions are held

1. A compound is a substance made of two or more different elements joined together chemically.
2. A molecule is a compound if it contains more than one element. Molecules that have two or more atoms of only a single element are not compounds.

How are the electrons usually arranged in an ion?

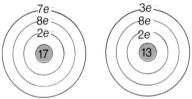

Chlorine atom, Cl   Aluminum atom, Al

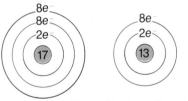

Chloride ion, Cl^- Aluminum ion, Al^{3+}

Figure 2-13. A chloride ion has one more electron than a chlorine atom. An aluminum ion has three fewer electrons than an aluminum atom.

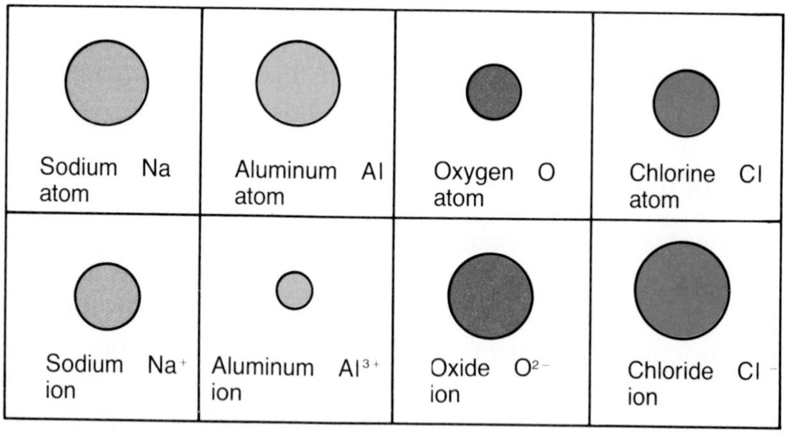

Figure 2-14. Atoms and their ions are different sizes. They also have different chemical properties.

Sodium Na atom	Aluminum Al atom	Oxygen O atom	Chlorine Cl atom
Sodium Na⁺ ion	Aluminum Al³⁺ ion	Oxide O²⁻ ion	Chloride Cl⁻ ion

together by the attraction of opposite charges. This is the second kind of chemical bond.

Halite, or rock salt, is a compound made of ions. Halite contains an equal number of sodium ions (Na^+) and chloride ions (Cl^-). They are stacked in an alternating pattern. Each positive sodium ion (Na^+) is surrounded by negative chloride ions (Cl^-). Each negative chloride ion (Cl^-) is surrounded by positive sodium ions (Na^+). They are present in equal numbers, but no two ions belong to each other.

All compounds made of ions have an orderly arrangement of the ions. They differ in the number of each type of ion. Some may have three ions of one element and two of another. Others may have four ions of one element for every two ions of another.

How are the ions arranged in rock salt?

Figure 2-15. Sodium chloride (table salt) does not contain molecules. Instead, the sodium and chloride ions are grouped in a repeating pattern. Which ion has a positive charge? Which ion has a negative charge?

The sodium ion (Na^+) has a positive charge. The chloride ion (Cl^-) has a negative charge.

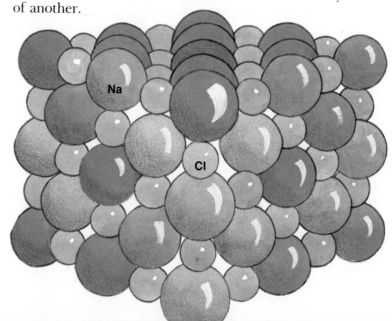

Check yourself

1. State three ways in which an ion is different from the atom it is related to.

2. Suppose an atom has two electrons in its lowest energy level and one electron in its second energy level. How many electrons will it lose to form an ion?

Mixtures
New vocabulary: mixtures

You probably can think of some substances that are neither elements nor compounds. Soil, for example, is made of clay and sand mixed with decaying plant and animal matter. Each of these parts of the soil is made of compounds. These compounds are mixed together only physically. Substances that are mixed physically, but are not joined to each other by chemical bonds, are called **mixtures.** Mixtures can contain elements, compounds, or both.

The properties of mixtures are very different from the properties of compounds. First, unlike compounds, mixtures have no fixed ratio or chemical formula. You can add or take sand away from a soil, and it remains soil.

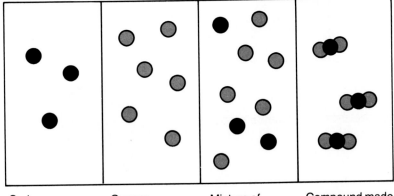

Carbon atoms | Oxygen atoms | Mixture of carbon and oxygen atoms | Compound made of carbon atoms and oxygen atoms

Figure 2-16. The atoms of two elements can form a mixture or a compound. In a mixture the atoms are physically mixed, but they still have the properties of the individual elements. In a compound the atoms are chemically bonded. A compound has different properties than its elements.

A second important difference between mixtures and compounds is that the parts of a mixture keep their physical properties. In the mixture known as chicken soup, the chicken remains recognizable by its color, texture, and taste.

Third, a mixture can be separated physically into its original parts. You can separate a mixture of sand, pebbles, and iron filings easily. No chemical bonds are broken.

Figure 2-17 shows how the mixture of salt and water can be broken down into compounds. Water is a compound made of molecules. Salt or sodium chloride is a compound made of ions. Each compound, in turn, can be broken down into its elements of hydrogen and oxygen (water) and sodium and chlorine (salt).

Check yourself

1. How are compounds and mixtures similar?
2. Name three of the differences between compounds and mixtures.

1. Mixtures and compounds are both made of more than one element.
2. Compounds have fixed proportions; mixtures do not. The elements in a compound lose their properties when the new substance is formed; components of a mixture keep their properties. Compounds must be separated chemically; mixtures can be separated physically.

Figure 2-17. The mixture saltwater is made of compounds with different types of chemical bonds. Which compound is made of ions? What is the other compound made of?
Salt is a compound made of ions. Water is made of molecules.

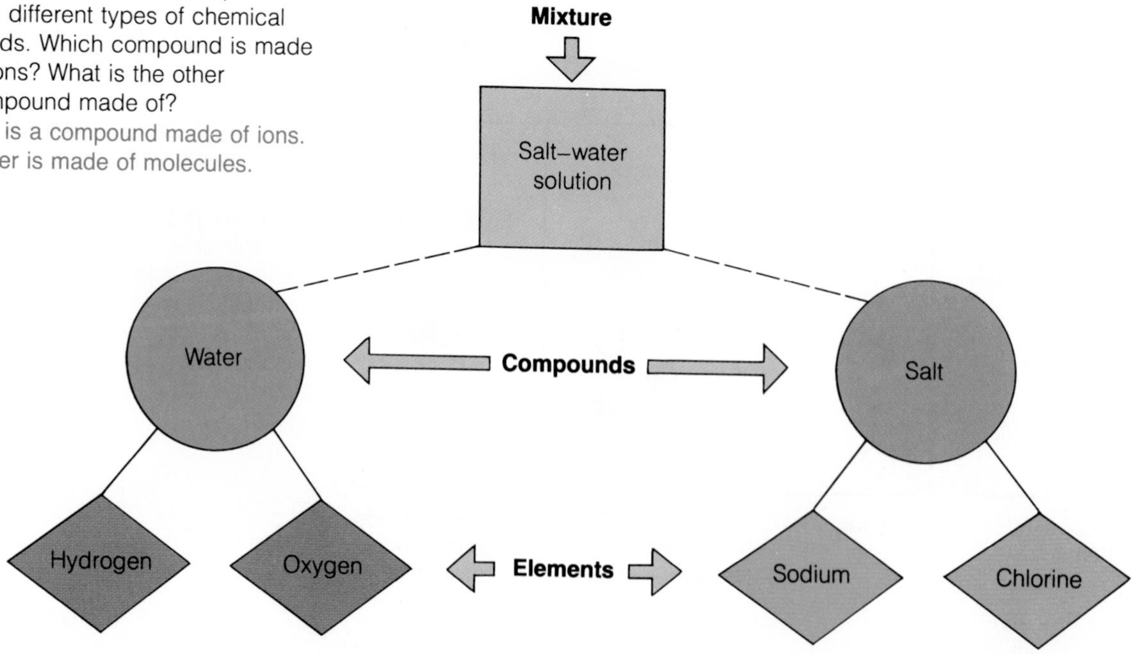

Section 1 Review Chapter 2

Use **Reading Checksheet 2-1** TRB page 64
Skillsheet 2-1 TRB page 106
Section Reviewsheet 2-1 TRB pages 149–150
Section Testsheet 2-1 TRB page 278

Check Your Vocabulary

11 atom	17 ion
15 atomic mass	6 isotope
4 atomic number	21 liquid
5 chemical bond	22 mass number
19 chemical formula	14 matter
	23 mixture
9 chemical symbol	18 molecule
1 compound	7 neutron
3 electron	20 nucleus
16 element	8 periodic table
10 energy	13 proton
24 energy level	2 solid
12 gas	

Match each term above with the numbered phrase that best describes it.

1. Substance made of chemically joined elements
2. Phase of matter with a definite shape
3. A negatively charged particle in an atom
4. Number of protons in atoms of an element
5. Force holding two atoms or ions together
6. One of at least two forms of the same element
7. Uncharged particle in an atom
8. Chart containing an arrangement of the elements
9. Short way of writing an element's name
10. Ability to cause change in matter
11. Smallest particle of an element with that element's properites
12. Phase of matter without definite volume
13. Positively charged particle in an atom
14. Anything that has mass and takes up space
15. Mass of one atom of an element
16. A pure substance with unique chemical properties
17. An atom that has lost or gained electrons
18. A group of atoms that share electrons
19. Abbreviation for the name of a compound
20. Protons and neutrons in the center of an atom
21. Phase of matter with definite volume but no definite shape
22. The sum of an atom's protons and neutrons
23. Two or more substances that can be separated by physical means
24. Areas where electrons tend to stay in an atom

Check Your Knowledge

Multiple Choice: Choose the answer that best completes each of the following sentences.

1. Matter can change phase when ⎯?⎯ is added or taken away.
   a) water b) gas c) heat energy

2. ⎯?⎯ are examples of elements.
   a) Water and air   b) Gold and copper
   c) Diamonds and balloons

3. Carbon-14 is a name for ⎯?⎯.
   a) an isotope of carbon   b) an element
   c) a chemical bond

Check Your Understanding

1. Explain the difference between an atom and an element.
2. The atomic number of oxygen is 8. Its most common isotope is oxygen-16. How many neutrons does this isotope contain?

Minerals   Section 2

Section 2 of Chapter 2 is divided into four parts:

What are minerals?

Silicate minerals

Nonsilicate minerals

What to look for in a mineral

Figure 2-18. People distinguish one mineral from another on the basis of physical properties. What physical properties do you think a person might use to describe the specimen of the mineral fluorite shown in the photograph?
Answers will vary. The visible properties most evident in the photograph involve color(s), shape, and the directions and angles of the breaks on the surface of the mineral specimen. Students might also comment on the glassy appearance of the mineral, which allows light to pass through it.

Learner Objectives
1. To discriminate between minerals and nonminerals.
2. To describe the attributes of a mineral.
3. To understand that the physical properties of a mineral are affected primarily by the mineral's composition and structure.
4. To understand that impurities may also affect some of the physical properties of a mineral.
5. To use specific properties to identify mineral specimens.

Figure 2-19. Most minerals are a mixture or combination of certain key elements. This specimen of crystalline sulfur, however, contains only the element sulfur.

What are minerals?

New vocabulary: mineral, inorganic, crystalline solid, crystal

Minerals are made of compounds that occur as natural solids in the earth's crust. There are about 2000 different known minerals on earth. As you can see from the pictures of the minerals on page 00, minerals differ from each other. They come in different sizes, shapes, and colors. Minerals differ in other ways, too. Some are harder than others. Some are heavier, or denser, than others. Some have shinier surfaces than others.

Despite the great number of minerals and despite the many differences among minerals, all minerals have four things in common. 1) All minerals are made up of key elements. 2) All minerals are natural. 3) All minerals are inorganic. 4) All minerals are crystalline solids.

What four things do all minerals have in common?

Key elements   Each mineral is a mixture or a combination of certain key elements. The mineral quartz, for example, is made up of the elements silicon and oxygen. There are a few minerals that are made up of only one element. Diamond, crystalline gold, and crystalline sulfur are single-element minerals. But single-element minerals are not very common.

Natural   Minerals are natural. They are found in nature, not made by people. People have learned how to join together the elements found in some minerals and make what is called a synthetic mineral. The word *synthetic* means that its elements were joined together in some way other than by nature. Synthetic quartz, rubies, and diamonds are made this way for use

A   Quartz

B   Feldspar

C   Mica

D   Calcite

E   Fluorite

F   Gypsum

G   Galena

H   Magnetite

Figure 2-20. Different specimens of the same mineral can differ in color. How does the color of the fluorite specimen in this figure compare with the color of the fluorite specimen in Figure 2-18 on page 80?

The colors of the two specimens are different.

System Name	Crystal Shape	Axes	Example Mineral Crystals
Isometric or cubic system Example: Pyrite	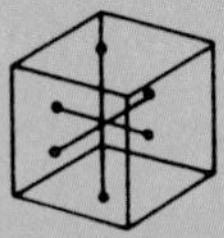	3 axes All of equal length All at right angles	
Tetragonal system Example: Vesuvitanite	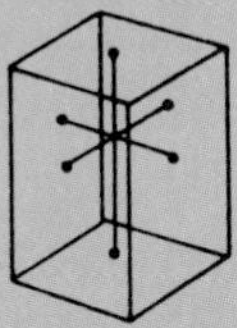	3 axes 2 of equal length All at right angles	
Hexagonal system Example: Corundum	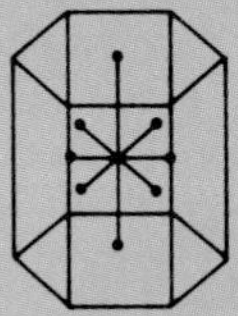	4 axes 3 of equal length The fourth one at right angles to the other three	
Orthorhombic system Example: Topaz	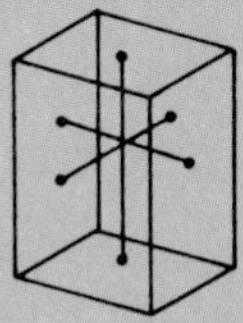	3 axes All different lengths All at right angles	
Monoclinic system Example: Orthoclase	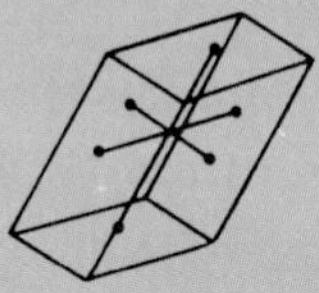	3 axes Lengths variable 2 at right angles	
Triclinic system Example: Amazonite	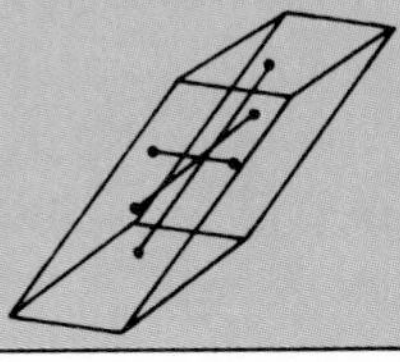	3 axes All different lengths None at right angles	

in industry. But because synthetic minerals are made by people and do not occur naturally, they are not real minerals.

Inorganic   All minerals are **inorganic,** which means they are not organic. Most compounds made by living things are organic and are not minerals. Coal is not a mineral because it is made from organic plant remains. Bones, teeth, and shells are the only common parts of living things that are made of minerals. Most minerals form from a combination of atoms without the help of plants and animals.

Crystalline solid   All minerals are **crystalline solids.** A crystalline solid is a solid substance whose atoms are locked into

Figure 2-21. Mineral crystals can be considered according to one of six general systems. To which system do topaz crystals belong? Topaz crystals belong to the orthorhombic system.

What are the only common parts of living things that are made of minerals?

See also Teaching Diagram 2-2A (TRB page 15).

It is important that students realize that not all minerals are found in crystal form. The crystal shapes in Figure 2-21 are idealized shapes. Mineral crystals from a rock shop will allow students to distinguish among minerals, even though the crystal shapes will most likely be less than perfect. The most beautiful crystal forms (as photographed in art-type books) are rare, valuable, and part of a public or private collection.

Figure 2-22. The atoms of a cube-shaped crystal line themselves up along three imaginary lines called axes. In this drawing, the three red lines represent the axes. How do the lengths of the three axes compare?

The axes of a cube-shaped crystal are all the same length.

1. Because coal is organic (formed from the remains of once-living organisms)
2. To form crystals, minerals must have the space to grow. This is not always the case. All minerals are crystalline solids, however, because they are solids whose atoms are locked into fixed patterns.

fixed patterns that repeat in three dimensions—height, width, and depth or thickness. Mineral grains form by atoms attaching themselves in a three-dimensional pattern. The three-dimensional pattern is related to one of the six systems shown in Figure 2-21. Each system is distinguished by a set of imaginary internal lines called axes. When the mineral grains have complete freedom to form in any direction, the atoms of the mineral produce a certain shape by lining up along these axes. These solid shapes are **crystals.**

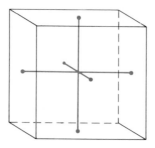

In many mineral samples that you will look at, you will see no crystals at all. Rarely are minerals found as separate crystals large enough to be seen without special equipment. Some minerals occur as masses of crystals so small that they can be seen only with a microscope. Minerals that do not have complete freedom to grow may not form crystals at all. The mineral grains, however, are still crystalline solids and can be studied with a microscope or X-rays.

Check yourself

1. Why is coal not a mineral?

2. All minerals are crystalline solids, but not all minerals are in the form of crystals. Explain.

Silicate minerals

New vocabulary: silicate minerals, impurities

Minerals can be arranged into classes according to the key elements that are found in each member of a class. The **silicate minerals** (SIL′-uh-kayt′ MIN′-er-ulz) form the most common class of minerals. All silicate minerals contain the elements silicon and oxygen.

The basic building block of all silicate minerals is a grouping made up of one silicon atom and four oxygen atoms. This grouping of atoms, shown in Figure 2-23, is known as a silica tetrahedron. The word *tetrahedron,* whose plural form is *tetrahedra,* comes from two Greek words that mean four *(tetra)* sides.

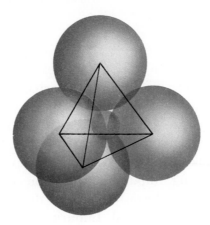

The quartz, feldspar, and mica pictured on page 82 (specimens A, B, and C) are common silicate minerals. From just those three examples, you can see that silicate minerals can look very different from each other.

Silicate minerals can look different from each other because they contain different key elements. Quartz, for example, contains oxygen and silicon. Feldspar contains oxygen, silicon, aluminum, and sodium, potassium, or calcium. Biotite mica contains oxygen, silicon, aluminum, iron, potassium, and magnesium.

Silicate minerals can also look different from each other because of the way their silica tetrahedra are arranged. In some kinds of silicate minerals, the tetrahedra occur as separate units. In other kinds of silicate minerals, the tetrahedra join together into pairs, rings, chains, sheets, or even complete box-shaped networks. Garnet and quartz, shown in Figure 2-24, are both silicate minerals. They look different, however, and are different minerals because of different chemical composition and because their atoms have joined together in different

What two elements do all silicate minerals contain?

Students can use plastic foam balls and toothpicks to construct models of the silica tetrahedron.

Figure 2-23. The basic building block of all silicate minerals is the silica tetrahedron, which is made up of four oxygen atoms and one silicon atom.

Figure 2-24. Garnet and quartz are different kinds of silicate minerals. Why are they different minerals?
Quartz and garnet are different minerals because their atoms have joined together in different ways and because their chemical composition is slightly different.

Library research

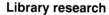

Make a list of all the different varieties of the mineral quartz and some of the ways quartz is used.

1. Composition: One silicon atom and four oxygen atoms; Arrangement: A tetrahedron, with the oxygen atom in the middle
2. 1) The way the tetrahedra are arranged; 2) Impurities
3. Impurities can cause different colors.

How have nonsilicate minerals been arranged into classes?

ways. Garnet forms according to the isometric system, and the tetrahedra are separate units. Quartz belongs to the hexagonal system, and the tetrahedra form a box-shaped network.

Silicate minerals, and all other minerals as well, can also look different from each other because of impurities. **Impurities** are atoms of elements other than the key elements of a mineral. You might think of these impurities as sneaking in while the crystals are forming. Impurities, which you can expect to find in any mineral, cause the different colors that are found among samples of the same mineral. Impurities in the mineral diamond can cause it to be pale yellow, blue, red, or even black. Regardless of color, all are the same mineral—diamond.

Check yourself

1. What is the composition and arrangement of atoms in the basic building block of silicate minerals?

2. What causes silicate minerals to be different from each other? List two causes.

3. How can impurities affect the appearance of a mineral?

Nonsilicate minerals

New vocabulary: nonsilicate minerals

Nonsilicate minerals, as their name states, are all the minerals that are not silicates. Five nonsilicate minerals (calcite, galena, magnetite, fluorite, and gypsum) are pictured in Figure 2-20 on page 82. Nonsilicate minerals have been arranged into classes according to key elements within each class. Each of the five pictured minerals is an example of a different class of nonsilicate minerals.

The carbonate minerals make up one class of nonsilicate minerals. All carbonate minerals contain the key elements carbon and oxygen. Calcite, which is calcium carbonate, is a carbonate mineral.

The sulfide minerals make up another class of nonsilicate minerals. A key element of all sulfides is sulfur. Galena, which is lead sulfide, is a sulfide mineral.

The oxide minerals are also a class of nonsilicate minerals. A key element of all oxides is oxygen. Magnetite, which is iron oxide, is an oxide mineral.

The halide minerals, which are also a class of nonsilicate minerals, can contain any one of several key elements. Fluorine, chlorine, bromine, and iodine are the most common key elements of halide minerals. The mineral fluorite, which is calcium fluoride, is a halide mineral that contains fluorine as a key element.

The sulfate minerals are a class of nonsilicate minerals, too. All sulfates contain sulfur and oxygen as their key elements. Gypsum, which is calcium sulfate and water, is an example of a sulfate mineral.

Check yourself

1. How do the nonsilicate minerals differ from the silicate minerals?

2. How (on what basis) are the nonsilicate minerals grouped into classes?

3. Sort the following minerals into two groups—silicate minerals and nonsilicate minerals: calcite, feldspar, fluorite, galena, gypsum, magnetite, mica, quartz.

What to look for in a mineral

New vocabulary: cleavage, streak, luster, heft

For an exact study of minerals, a laboratory and special equipment like microscopes and X-ray machines are used. In many cases, however, geologists can see enough with no more than a magnifying glass to identify a hand-size mineral sample. Some

Library research

Many minerals are used as precious and semiprecious gemstones. Make a list of gemstones and the minerals they come from. Also include where in the world different gem-quality minerals are found.

1. Nonsilicate minerals do not have silica tetrahedra as their basic building block.
2. On the basis of key elements

3. Silicates: feldspar, mica, quartz; nonsilicates: calcite, fluorite, galena, gypsum, magnetite

How useful is a magnifying glass to a geologist?

Figure 2-25. Mica breaks easily in one direction. What is that direction called?
The cleavage direction

physical properties to look for in a mineral sample are its cleavage, fracture, hardness, color, streak, and luster.

Cleavage   The ability of a mineral to break into smooth, parallel surfaces is called **cleavage** (KLEE′-vij). A mineral may have none, one, two, or more sets of flat breaks, each set in a different direction. Each of these sets of flat breaks represents a direction of weakness in the way the atoms of the mineral are held or joined together. Each set of flat breaks is called a cleavage direction. Mica, as shown in Figure 2-25, has one cleavage direction. Calcite, on the other hand, has three different cleavage directions.

Fracture   Different minerals break in different ways. Fracture is the manner in which minerals break that don't have cleavage. Certain minerals can be distinguished by their type of fracture. Quartz, for example, breaks along smoothly curving surfaces. This kind of fracture is glassy and conchoidal (kong-KOY′-dul). Figure 2-26 shows the conchoidal fracture of quartz.

Hardness   Certain minerals are harder than other minerals and will therefore scratch them. Hardness is the ability of a mineral to scratch another mineral. Because fluorite will scratch calcite, we know that fluorite is harder than calcite. In 1822, a German mineralogist named Friedrich Mohs chose a series of very soft to very hard minerals as a scale for hardness.

Who chose the series of ten minerals that are used as standards for testing hardness?

Figure 2-26. When quartz breaks, it breaks along smoothly curving surfaces. What kind of fracture is this called? Conchoidal fracture

Mohs' scale, which is shown in Table 2-3, is still used today to test the hardness of a mineral.

Not everyone has the ten test minerals on the Mohs' scale. Nor is such an exact measure always needed. Here are several other standards that can also be used to test for hardness: a person's fingernail = about 2½; a copper penny = about 3 to 3½; an iron nail = about 5 to 5½.

Color Color is likely to be the first physical property you notice about a mineral sample. But color may not help that much to identify a mineral. This is because many minerals can be the same color. Not only that, but because of trace elements, different samples of the same mineral often have different colors.

Streak Some minerals leave a colored powder when scratched. **Streak** is the color of the powder of a mineral against a white background. This is tested by rubbing the mineral sample on a piece of unglazed porcelain and noting the color of the powder left on the porcelain. As shown in Figure 2-27, pyrite leaves a black streak on the porcelain.

The streak test works only on minerals that are softer than porcelain. Porcelain has a hardness of nearly 7. If the mineral sample is harder than the porcelain, then the powder will be not from the mineral but from the porcelain.

Luster Different minerals reflect the light differently. The way that a mineral reflects the light is called **luster.** If the mineral reflects light like shiny metal, its luster is called metallic. Other lusters are nonmetallic and include glassy (looks like broken glass), pearly or silky (reflects light like a pearl or a piece of silk cloth), and dull (has no shine at all). Quartz, calcite, and

Science Processes: Observing; Classifying
See also Activity Record Sheet 2-2A (Lab Manual
page 21)

CORE   15 minutes   Individuals or small groups

Activity 2-2A   Grouping Minerals by Hardness

Materials

copper penny

iron nail

sample of all or some of
the following minerals:
mica, calcite, fluorite,
galena, gypsum,
magnetite, orthoclase
feldspar, quartz

Purpose

To learn a way of classifying minerals by their
physical properties.

Procedure

1. Try scratching each of the mineral samples
   with your fingernail. Remove all that your fingernail will scratch and sort into group A
   (softer than 2½).
2. After removing any samples that your fingernail will scratch, try scratching the remainder
   of the mineral samples with a copper penny.

Remove all that a copper penny will scratch
and sort into group B (harder than 2½ but
softer than 3½).
3. After removing any samples that a copper
   penny will scratch, try scratching the remaining mineral samples with an iron nail. Remove all that an iron nail will scratch and sort
   into group C (harder than 3½ but softer than
   5½).
4. After removing the mineral samples that can
   be scratched by an iron nail, label the remainder group D (harder than 5½).
5. When you have finished, check your findings
   against the hardnesses listed in Table 2-3.
   Save your findings. You will be able to use
   them in the activity on page 92.

Questions

1. Which minerals were in group A? group B?
2. Which minerals were in group C? group D?

Conclusion

How can studying the hardness of different substances help you identify them?

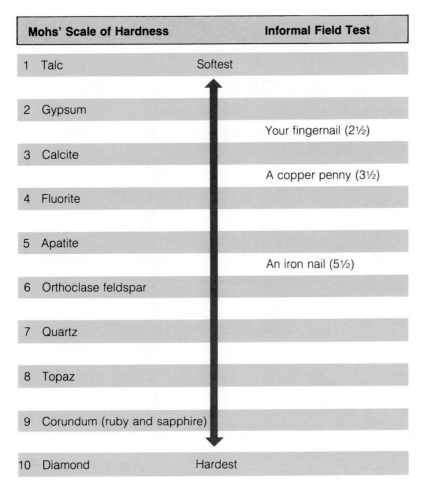

Mohs' Scale of Hardness	Informal Field Test
1 Talc Softest	
2 Gypsum	
	Your fingernail (2½)
3 Calcite	
	A copper penny (3½)
4 Fluorite	
5 Apatite	
	An iron nail (5½)
6 Orthoclase feldspar	
7 Quartz	
8 Topaz	
9 Corundum (ruby and sapphire)	
10 Diamond Hardest	

Table 2-3. The ten minerals on Mohs' scale are used as standards of hardness. Which two minerals on Mohs' scale can you scratch with your fingernail? Talc and gypsum

Figure 2-27. When rubbed against porcelain, pyrite leaves a black powder on the porcelain. What is this test called? The streak test

fluorite are likely to have a glassy luster. Gypsum is likely to look silky or pearly. Galena has a metallic luster.

Crystal faces   Crystals have smooth flat surfaces called crystal faces. Smooth crystal faces can be mistaken for cleavage surfaces. They differ because crystal faces are only on the surface of the crystal. Cleavage goes all the way through the crystal. This difference can be seen along broken edges of the mineral.

Sometimes the crystal faces and cleavages in a mineral are in the same direction. Common salt is an example of this kind of mineral.

Heft   The word *heft* means weight. **Heft** is a weight test. When you pick a mineral sample up in your hand, how heavy is it compared to an equal size piece of quartz? (Or, how does its density compare to that of quartz?) If the weight of the sample is about the same as quartz, the heft is average. Using the

Students very often confuse fluorite with quartz. Hardness sorts them. So does cleavage. Fluorite crystals can grow in shapes similar to quartz; they are not always cubes. Also, fluorite can be an octahedron, which still has cubic system symmetry.

Heft is a very rough estimate. For more precise analysis, specific gravity is used. Students might find out what specific gravity is and how it is used as a standard. They might also find out the specific gravity of various materials, including the minerals in Table 2-3.

Science Processes: Observing; Classifying
See also Activity Record Sheet 2-2B (Lab Manual page 22)

30-40 minutes   Groups of 4-6

Activity 2-2B   Using Physical Properties to Identify Minerals

Materials

magnifying glass

magnet

Mohs' Hardness Scale

numbered, unidentified
  samples of some or all
  of these minerals:
  calcite, fluorite, galena,
  gypsum, magnetite,
  mica, orthoclase
  feldspar, pyrite, quartz

streak plate

eyedropper

vinegar

Purpose

To test unidentified mineral specimens for physical properties.

Procedure

1. Set up a chart like the one at the bottom of this page. Record the number of each specimen and examine it for the physical properties listed across the top of the chart.
2. Record your findings in the appropriate column
3. Turn a mineral sample in the light so that you can see a bright reflection. This direction of flat surfaces across a break is a cleavage direction.
4. Next, turn the mineral sample in the light to see if there are other cleavage directions. If you find another, try to visualize whether it is at a 90° angle to the previous cleavage direction.

5. On your chart, record both the number of different cleavage directions and the approximate angle between each two different directions.
6. To check hardness, use the three general standards used in the activity on page 90.
7. Use the "Other" column on your chart for any unusual property that you notice, such as attraction by a magnet, crystal faces, or bubbling in vinegar.
8. For each specimen, read across the list of physical properties. Then find the mineral in Table 2-4, page 93, that has a similar series of physical properties. Write the correct mineral names in the last column of your chart.

Questions

1. Which mineral(s) can you scratch with your fingernail?
2. Which samples have a streak that is a different color from the color of the sample?
3. How can you tell the difference between clear calcite and clear gypsum?
4. In your samples of galena and magnetite, what physical properties make it easiest for you to tell which is which?
5. On which of your samples were you able to see crystal faces?

Conclusion

Do you need a large amount or a small amount of a mineral in order to identify it? Explain.

Number of Specimen	Cleavage/Fracture	Hardness	Color	Streak	Luster	Heft	Other	Mineral Name

Physical Properties of Nine Minerals							
Mineral Name	Cleavage/Fracture	Hardness	Color	Streak	Luster	Heft	Other
biotite mica	cleavage, 1 direction	2½ to 3	dark brown to black	light tan	glassy	average	forms flakes and sheets
calcite	cleavage, 3 directions, not at 90° to each other	3	white, clear, pink, blue, yellow	white	glassy	average	bubbles in dilute hydrochloric acid
fluorite	cleavage, 4 directions, not at 90°	4	colorless, purple, blue, green, yellow, brown	white	glassy	average	
galena	cleavage, 3 directions, at 90°, often bent	2½	silver or lead-gray	gray to black	metallic	heavy	cleavage surfaces often bent
gypsum	perfect in 1 direction, poor in 2; not at 90°	2	clear to white	white	pearly, silky, or dull	light to average	cleavage may not be seen
magnetite	irregular fracture	6	black	gray to black	metallic to dull	heavy	attracted by a magnet
orthoclase feldspar	cleavage, 2 directions, at 90°	6	white, red, pink	white	pearly	average	may appear to have a third cleavage direction
pyrite	irregular fracture	6 to 6½	silver-gold	black	metallic	heavy	
quartz	glassy, conchoidal fracture	7	white, clear, gray, pink	white	glassy	average	crystal faces common

heft test, gypsum will appear light to average, orthoclase average, and galena heavy.

Physical properties of quartz, orthoclase feldspar, pyrite, biotite mica, calcite, fluorite, gypsum, galena, and magnetite are listed in Table 2-4. Note how inconclusive color is as a distinguishing physical property of many minerals.

Table 2-4. Which of the nine minerals in the table above bubbles in dilute hydrochloric acid?
Calcite

Check yourself

1. How are minerals identified?

2. The streak test works only on minerals that are softer than porcelain. Explain.

1. By such physical properties as cleavage, fracture, hardness, streak, luster, presence of crystal faces, heft, and, to a limited degree, color
2. If the mineral is harder than porcelain, then the powdered streak will be from the porcelain and not from the mineral.

Section 2 Review   Chapter 2

Use **Reading Checksheet 2-2** TRB page 65
Skillsheet 2-2 TRB page 107
Section Reviewsheet 2-2 TRB pages 151–152
Section Testsheet 2-2 TRB page 279

Check Your Vocabulary

1 cleavage   11 inorganic

4 crystal   3 luster

10 crystalline solid 8 mineral

9 heft   2 nonsilicate minerals

5 impurities   7 silicate minerals

                      6 streak

Match each term above with the numbered phrase that best describes it.

1. The ability of a mineral to break into smooth, parallel surfaces

2. All minerals that are not silicates

3. The way that a mineral reflects the light

4. The shape produced when mineral grains have freedom to form in any direction

5. Atoms of elements other than the key elements of a mineral

6. The color of the powder of a mineral against a white background

7. Minerals containing silicon and oxygen

8. A compound that is natural, inorganic, a crystalline solid, and made up of key elements

9. A rough-estimate weight test for minerals

10. A solid substance whose atoms are locked together into fixed patterns; true of all minerals

11. Not organic; formed, for the most part, without the help of plants and animals

Check Your Knowledge

Multiple Choice: Choose the answer that best completes each of the following sentences.

1. All minerals are ? .
   a) organic   c) crystalline solids
   b) crystals   d) synthetic

2. The basic building block of all silicate minerals is ? .
   a) the silica tetrahedron
   b) crystalline sulfur
   c) the element fluorine
   d) the cleavage direction

3. When mineral grains have complete freedom to form in any direction, the atoms of the mineral produce a certain shape by lining up along a set of imaginary lines called ? .
   a) tetrahedra   c) carbonates
   b) fractures   d) axes

4. The ability of a mineral to break into smooth, parallel surfaces is called ? .
   a) hardness   c) cleavage
   b) fracture   d) streak

Check Your Understanding

1. Explain why not all minerals are found in crystal form.

2. Explain why the crystal forms of different minerals have different shapes.

3. Explain how silicate minerals, carbonate minerals, and sulfide minerals differ from each other.

4. Explain how minerals can be identified without using microscopes or X-ray machines.

5. Explain how Mohs' scale is used.

Rocks   Section 3

Section 3 of Chapter 2 is divided into six parts:

Where does rock come from?

Igneous rock

Sedimentary rock

Metamorphic rock

The rock cycle

What to look for in a rock

Figure 2-28. The crystal-lined structure shown is called a geode. It is a hollow rock made of silica that is filled with crystals of quartz or calcite.

Learner Objectives
1. To understand how the major classes of rock form.
2. To understand how the earth's rocks can change from one class to another.
3. To recognize different rock textures.
4. To determine some of the more common mineral compositions of rocks.
5. To use texture and mineral composition to discriminate among igneous, sedimentary, and metamorphic rocks.

How are minerals and rock related?

Critical Thinking

How are rocks grouped?

Rocks are grouped on the basis of how they were formed into three classes: igneous—from hot, molten material; sedimentary—from sediment; metamorphic—from existing rock changed by heat and pressure.

Beneath you right now, as you read the words on this page, there is a mixture of minerals called **rock.** If you happen to be sitting on a mountaintop, you might be right on solid rock. If you are in a building with soil around and under it, beneath all soil there is a layer of solid rock. If you happen to be in a boat, there is rock beneath all rivers, lakes, and oceans on the earth.

The rocks of the earth come in many different sizes and shapes and colors. But no matter what color or size or shape, each rock has a story to tell—a story about how that rock was formed. In this section, you will learn some of that story.

Where does rock come from?
New vocabulary: igneous rock, sedimentary rock, metamorphic rock

The outer layer of the earth is constantly changing. The rocky faces of mountains and cliffs are being slowly broken down into smaller particles. These increasingly smaller particles are being carried away by moving water or by wind or even by glaciers. But at the same time that parts of the earth are wearing down, other parts are building up. New rock is being formed that replaces the old. New rock is being formed from the old.

Any rock that you find on earth can be grouped into one of three classes, depending on how the rock was formed. One class of rock, called **igneous rock,** is formed from hot melted materials. A second class of rock, **sedimentary rock,** is formed from sediment, which is most often small particles of rock, such as sand and gravel. **Metamorphic rock,** a third class of rock, is formed when minerals and rocks are changed by very great heat and pressure that changes the crystal structure.

Any one of these three classes of rock can change into any other class of rock. This is because the rocky face of the earth is constantly changing. Rocks and minerals are part of a never-ending recycling process.

Check yourself

1. In what two ways is the outer layer of the earth constantly changing?

2. How is "new" rock formed?

Igneous rock

Rock that forms from **magma,** which is molten rock beneath the earth's surface, is called igneous rock. Some types of igneous rock, such as *granite,* are made of large crystals. These rock types form when the magma cools slowly beneath the surface of the earth. A large area of this type of igneous rock is called a **batholith.**

Other types of igneous rock, such as *basalt,* are made of small crystals. These rock types form on the earth's surface from **lava** that cools quickly. Lava is magma that reaches the earth's surface while it is still molten. If lava cools extremely rapidly, the atoms may not have time to form even the tiniest crystals. This results in the creation of natural glass rocks such as *obsidian.* During violent volcanic eruptions, blobs of molten lava are often ejected with great force into the air. These volcanic igneous rocks are known as **pyroclastic deposits.**

Some types of igneous rocks form at shallow depths in the earth's crust. They may cool at alternately slow and fast rates, a process that produces both large and small crystals. The resulting rocks are known as **porphyritic rock.** A large igneous formation made of this rock type is called a **laccolith.**

Check yourself

1. How does the cooling rate of an igneous rock affect the size of the crystals in the rock?

2. What is the relationship between magma and lava?

Figure 2-29. Some of the earth's rocks are formed from lava that cools on the earth's surface. What class do such rocks belong to?
Such rocks are igneous.

How are pyroclastic deposits formed?

1. The slower the cooling rate, the larger the crystals.
2. Lava is magma that has reached the earth's surface while still molten.

Science Processes: Formulating models; Inferring
See also Activity Record Sheet 2-3A (Lab Manual
page 25)

20 minutes   Groups of 4

Activity 2-3A   Forming Layers

Materials

2 test tubes, numbered
  1 and 2
test-tube rack
sand
table salt
iron filings
water

Purpose

To learn how layers of sediment form and how
these layers can change.

Procedure

1. Put the test tubes in the test-tube rack. Start
   by forming the same three layers in each test
   tube. Pour iron filings into each test tube until
   you have a layer about 1 cm thick. On top of
   the iron filings pour a 1-cm layer of table salt
   and a 1-cm layer of sand.
2. Remove Test Tube 1 from the rack. Put your
   thumb over the mouth of the test tube and
   shake the test tube hard for approximately
   10 seconds.

3. Tap the side of the Test Tube 1 near the bottom gently for several minutes.
4. Add enough water to Test Tube 1 to cover
   the sediment with 1 cm of water. Shake the
   tube gently for about 15 seconds.
5. Gently add water to Test Tube 2, but do not
   shake it. Set the test-tube rack and test
   tubes with sediments in a warm, dry, safe
   place.

Questions

1. What properties make it easy to see layers?
2. What happened to the layers when you
   shook Test Tube 1?
3. When you tapped Test Tube 1, which material settled most rapidly? Why?
4. When you covered Test Tube 1 with water
   and shook the test tube, what happened to
   the salt?
5. When water was added to Test Tube 2, what
   happened?
6. After the water has evaporated in both tubes,
   describe the layers. Where is the salt?

Conclusion

How might minerals form layers of sediments?

Step 2

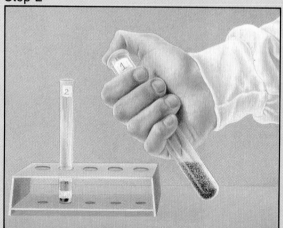

Step 5

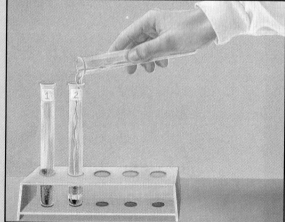

Sedimentary rock
New vocabulary: elastic rock, organic rock, chemically formed rock

The words *sediment* and *sedimentary* come from the Latin word *sedere*, which means "to sit or settle." Sedimentary rock is made from particles that have settled out of water or air. The sediments in most sedimentary rock have formed under water and later hardened into rock.

There are three ways that sedimentary rock can form. One way is from particles of minerals and rock. These particles are known as clastics, and the sedimentary rock they form is called **clastic rock.** Sandstones, shales, and conglomerates are examples of clastic rock. The particles in sandstone and conglomerate rocks are big enough to be seen, while the particles in shale are too small to see. Clastic rock forms when clastic sediments get buried deeper and deeper under newer sediments. As they are buried, they get pressed tightly together. Any dissolved elements surrounding them may act as cement

Figure 2-30. This landform, known as a butte, is made of sandstone. What class of rock does sandstone belong to?
Sandstone is a sedimentary rock.

What are the processes by which loose clastic sediments become hard rock?

1. Clastic rock—forms by compaction and cementation of loose clastic sediments; Organic rock—forms from once-living material; Chemically formed rock— formed from crystals that grow from dissolved minerals
2. Clastic: sandstone, shale, conglomerate
Organic: limestone
Chemical: halite, gypsum

Library research

Find the basic differences between contact metamorphism and regional metamorphism.

to bind the particles together. Therefore, *compaction and cementation* are the processes that change loose clastic sediments into hard rock.

Sedimentary rock also forms from the remains of plants and animals. Such rocks are known as **organic rock.** Limestone is an example of organic rock. In some limestones, skeletal remains are easily seen, while in others, the remains are unidentifiable.

The third way sedimentary rock forms is when minerals dissolved in water form interlocking crystals, which often happens as the water evaporates. This type of sedimentary rock is called **chemically formed rock.** Halite (rock salt) and gypsum are examples of chemically formed sedimentary rock.

Check yourself

1. Name the three types of sedimentary rock and the way they form.

2. Name an example of each type of sedimentary rock.

Metamorphic rock

New vocabulary: metamorphosis

Rock that has been changed from one kind of rock to another is called **metamorphic rock.** In the insect world, a butterfly completely changes its form as it goes from a caterpillar to a cocoon to an adult butterfly. This change in form is called **metamorphosis.**

Underneath the earth's surface, heat and pressure can change the minerals in a rock. Sometimes the atoms of minerals change position. Sometimes minerals lose or gain atoms. In either case, the resulting rock is a metamorphic rock.

When the atoms of a mineral change position, certain mineral grains will sometimes grow larger. Many metamorphic rocks contain very large crystals. Also, in response to pressure, the minerals in most metamorphic rocks tend to form layers. In rocks that have been under great pressure, these layers may be noticeably bent or folded.

Schist and gneiss are two examples of metamorphic rock that have undergone changes due to heat and pressure. These rocks may have originally been shale (sedimentary) or

Figure 2-31. These layers of schist were photographed at Kings Canyon National Park. What could have caused the bending and folding of the rock layers?

Great heat and pressure deep within the earth could have caused the bending and folding. (The rock could then have been uplifted to the earth's surface through a faulting process. Erosion could also have played a part in exposing the rock as it is today.)

granite (igneous) before metamorphism. Metamorphic rock itself can be further changed by more heat or pressure to form new types of metamorphic rock. Every metamorphic rock was originally some other type of rock. The original rock that metamorphosed is called the *parent rock*. Limestone, for example, is the parent rock of marble. Shale is the parent rock of slate.

Check yourself

1. What two processes can change a sedimentary rock into a metamorphic rock?

2. What is the parent rock of marble? of slate?

3. Distinguish between igneous, sedimentary, and metamorphic rock on the basis of how each forms.

1. Heat and pressure
2. Parent rock of marble is limestone; parent rock of slate is shale
3. Igneous: forms from molten magma or lava; Sedimentary: forms from particles that settled out of water or air and hardened; Metamorphic: forms beneath the earth's surface, changing existing rock with heat and pressure

The rock cycle
New vocabulary: rock cycle

Any rock you find can be grouped into one of three classes. It is either igneous, sedimentary, or metamorphic. But that rock did not always belong to the same class. The rocky face of the earth is constantly changing. Rocks and minerals are part of a huge recycling process.

Any class of rock can be changed into any other class of rock. An igneous rock, for example, can be dissolved and broken apart by weathering processes at the earth's surface. The products of weathering are either particles of rock or dissolved salts.

Library research

Expand your knowledge of rock classes to include the following: extrusive and intrusive igneous rock, clastic and nonclastic sedimentary rock, foliated and nonfoliated metamorphic rock.

See also Teaching Diagram 2-3A (TRB page 17).

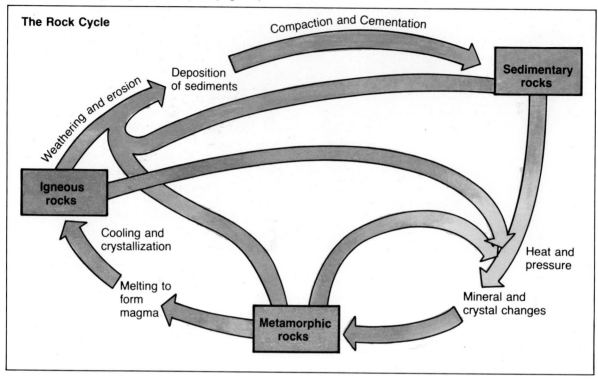

The Rock Cycle

Figure 2-32. According to this diagram of the rock cycle, how many classes of rocks can be changed into sediments by weathering and erosion?
All three classes of rocks can be weathered into sediments.

Additional Activity
Distribute a small chunk of paraffin to each student at the beginning of class. Do not explain why you have given them the paraffin. Begin to discuss the rock cycle. As the class progresses, students will write on the desk with the paraffin, make it into a ball, scratch it, bend and knead it, and find other creative methods of transforming the paraffin. Near the end of class, point out that they have applied pressure, heat, and friction to transform the paraffin, much as the earth does to rock materials.

The particles of rock and the dissolved salts are deposited and built up as layers of sediments that harden to become a sedimentary rock. The sedimentary rock can become deeply buried in the earth and changed into a metamorphic rock. The metamorphic rock can then be melted by heat within the earth and be changed into magma, which later cools and hardens into an igneous rock. This process of change from one class of rock to another is called the **rock cycle.**

In the example you just read, the igneous rock at the beginning of the cycle would probably not be the same as the igneous rock at the end. The rock cycle is a cycling in the sense of a recycling. It is a redistribution of elements and minerals from one rock type to another. The rock cycle is not the kind of cycle that returns to the same point or condition after a period of time. Nor does the rock cycle always follow the same series of changes. Figure 2-32 shows the possible changes in the rock cycle and the processes needed to bring about those changes.

Two other processes not shown in Figure 2-32 are often very important parts of the rock cycle. Rocks buried deep in the earth must be raised to the surface and exposed before they can be broken down or dissolved by the weather. And rocks near the surface must be buried to great depths in order to be exposed to the pressure and heat needed to undergo metamorphism or melting.

Check yourself

1. What are the processes that turn a sedimentary rock into an igneous rock?

2. What are the processes that turn a sedimentary rock into a metamorphic rock?

3. What are the processes that can turn a sedimentary rock into a different sedimentary rock?

The following answers are diagramed in Figure 2-32.
1. Melting (caused by heat and pressure) to form magma; cooling and crystallizing of magma
2. Subjecting to great heat and pressure that causes changes in original minerals and crystals
3. Weathering, erosion, deposition, compaction, cementation

What to look for in a rock

New vocabulary: texture, mineral composition

The first step in identifying a rock is to determine whether the rock is igneous, sedimentary, or metamorphic. This first step is very important, but it is not always easy because some very different rocks may look like each other. You therefore have to examine a rock for certain physical properties. In particular, you need to consider both a rock's texture and its mineral composition.

The **texture** of a rock is the pattern made by the size, shape, and arrangement of the particles that are in the rock. Table 2-5 defines six common rock textures. Though sometimes called by different names, those six textures will help you describe most any rock you find.

The **mineral composition** of a rock is, as its name states, a list of the minerals that make up the rock. For a start, there are a few basic minerals to look for. Recognizing those minerals will help you to make an approximate identification, which is sometimes all that a person can make without special equipment.

How can a person learn to make approximate identifications of rocks?

Most common rocks contain silicate minerals. Silicate minerals can sometimes be recognized merely by their color. Pink or red crystals are a potassium feldspar like orthoclase. Glassy, gray to purple-gray grains are quartz. Green colors are usually amphibole, pyroxene, or olivine. The micas are little flakes.

Science Processes: Observing; Classifying
See also Activity Record Sheet 2-3B (Lab Manual
page 26)

CORE   40 minutes   Pairs of students,
                                  or small groups

Activity 2-3B   Determining the Class of a Rock

Materials

numbered samples of
  unidentified rocks
iron nail
magnifying glass

metal or hard plastic rod
eyedropper
10% dilute hydrochloric
  acid

Purpose

To use a key to determine the class of a rock.

Procedure

1. Start the key at Number 1. Follow the instructions after you answer each question.
2. Record your answer (igneous, sedimentary, or metamorphic) for each sample.
3. Do not be discouraged if some of your answers are wrong. It takes practice before a person can easily answer some of these questions. Also, some rocks are so hard to identify that even experts have trouble.

Key for Determining the Class of a Rock

1. Are any of the grains or crystals large enough to see without a microscope? *If yes, go to Number 2. If no, go to Number 15.*
2. Are the grains masses of crystals that are all grown together? *If yes, go to Number 3. If no, go to Number 11.*
3. Is the overall texture banded? *If yes, go to Number 4. If no, go to Number 5.*
4. Do the bands consist of silicate minerals like quartz, feldspar, and mica? (You can use visual tests and hardness.) *If yes, the rock is metamorphic; if no, sedimentary.*
5. Are the mineral grains silicate minerals? (You can use visual tests and hardness.) *If*

yes, go to Number 6; if no, to Number 9.
6. Are there two or more abundant silicate minerals? (Consider color and hardness.) *If yes, it is igneous. If no, go to Number 7.*
7. Does the sample contain no crystal faces and consist only of quartz? (Quartz, which has a hardness of 7, will scratch glass or steel.) *If yes, the rock is metamorphic. If no, go to Number 8.*
8. Is the sample a natural glass? (Remember that glass contains no crystals.) *If yes, the rock is igneous. If no, go to Number 9.*
9. Does the sample consist entirely of calcite? (Calcite has a hardness of only 3 and will bubble in dilute hydrochloric acid.) *If yes, go to Number 10. If no, go to Number 14.*
    SAFETY NOTE: *Make sure the acid you work with is 10 percent dilute, which your teacher will provide.*
10. Is the sample white or clear? *If yes, the rock is metamorphic; if no, sedimentary.*
11. Are some of the mineral grains or crystals large enough to see? *If yes, go to Number 12. If no, go to Number 14.*
12. Are any mineral grains particles that have been cemented together? *If yes, the rock is sedimentary. If no, go to Number 13.*
13. Are the grains or crystals arranged in fine layers or bands? *If yes, the rock is metamorphic. If no, the rock is igneous.*
14. Can fine-grained parts of the rock be scratched with a nail? (Look carefully. If the nail "writes" on a very hard rock, the mark could look like a scratch.) *If yes, go to Number 10. If no, the rock is igneous.*
15. Does the rock break into thin layers when you tap it with another rock or with some other hard object? *If yes, go to Number 16. If no, go to Number 7.*
16. Does the rock have a hard, sharp, or ringing sound when you tap it with a hard rod? *If yes, the rock is metamorphic. If no, the rock is sedimentary.*

Six Common Rock Textures		
Type of Texture	Description of That Texture	Example Rocks of That Texture
coarse-grained texture	made up of mineral grains or crystals that are large enough to be seen without using a microscope	granite marble sandstone
fine-grained texture	made up of mineral grains or crystals too small to be seen without a microscope	limestone basalt
mixed-grain texture	made up of at least two very different-size grains	conglomerate
glassy texture	containing no mineral crystals at all; a natural glass	obsidian
layered texture	made up of mineral crystals all lined up in the same direction; parallel grains distributed more or less evenly within the rock	slate schist sandstone
banded texture	made up of different minerals that are concentrated in different bands rather than distributed evenly throughout the rock	gneiss

Table 2-5. How does the texture of granite differ from the texture of limestone? Granite is coarse-grained. The minerals in limestone, however, are too small to be seen without a microscope.

See also Teaching Diagram 2-3B (TRB page 18).

Library research

Find out the type of rock that each of the following is made of: Mt. Aconcagua, Mt. Everest, Pikes Peak, the Great Pyramid, Stonehenge, the Parthenon.

Biotite mica is black. Muscovite mica is clear to tan. White crystals may be any of the feldspars. If a feldspar has equal amounts of sodium and calcium, it is usually gray.

Silicate minerals can also be identified by other physical properties. To distinguish quartz from a feldspar, for instance, hardness can be used. Quartz has a hardness of 7, and feldspar has a hardness of 6. Also, feldspar crystals often have flat cleavage surfaces or crystal faces, whereas quartz usually looks like clear or gray glass filling in between other mineral grains.

Figure 2-33. Obsidian is an example of a rock with a glassy texture. How would you describe the texture of conglomerate? A conglomerate rock contains grains of very different sizes.

Answers will vary. Students should look at the size of the grains and the arrangement of the grains (scattered, in layers, or in bands), as mentioned in Table 2-3 on page 85. Many factors can cause differences in appearance: 1) different crystal or grain sizes; 2) impurities in or on the minerals; 3) the presence or absence of non-key minerals; 4) weathering of the minerals; 5) differences in lighting; 6) differences in grain orientation. The importance of these questions is to get students to see the similarities by disregarding non-essential differences.

Calcite is also a key mineral for you to be able to recognize in a rock. Limestone and marble, for instance, are made up almost totally of calcite. Calcite is easily distinguished from quartz and feldspar because calcite has a hardness of only 3. Another easy test for calcite is one drop of dilute hydrochloric acid. Calcite will bubble readily in dilute hydrochloric acid. Calcite will also bubble in white vinegar, but it may take as long as fifteen minutes for the bubbles to form in vinegar. In dilute hydrochloric acid, the bubbles form immediately.

Pictured in Figure 2-34 are pairs of common earth rocks. In each pair, the rock on the right is the metamorphic form of the rock on the left. Which textures do you think show most clearly? Looking at each pair of pictures, how would you compare the rock on the left with its metamorphic form on the right? How are they alike? How are they different? How would you describe any patterns in the arrangement of the crystals?

If you have samples of any of the rocks that are pictured in Figure 2-34, how do your samples compare with the pictures of the same kind of rock? What do you think causes differences in appearance among samples of the same kind of rock?

Check yourself answers:
1. Texture and mineral composition
2. 1) Hardness—calcite is 3, quartz is 7; 2) Acid—calcite will bubble readily in dilute hydrochloric acid.

Check yourself

1. What are the two most important physical properties to look at when identifying a rock?

2. How can you distinguish calcite from quartz in rocks?

Figure 2-34. Considered as four pairs, each rock on the right is a metamorphic form of the rock on its left.

A Granite

B Gneiss

C Sandstone

D Quartzite

E Limestone

F Marble

G Shale

H Schist

Careers   Geophysicist / Technical Secretary

For further information about a career as a geophysicist contact.

American Geophysical Union
2000 Florida Avenue NW
Washington, DC 20009

Geophysicist

These scientists use the principles of mathematics and physics to study the composition and origin of the earth. They also study the earth's forces, such as its magnetic, electrical, and gravitational fields.

The work of geophysicists may involve both field and laboratory work. In the field, they may collect information about the earth's internal structure by a technique called *seismic prospecting*. This involves using instruments that bounce sound waves off deeply buried rock layers. In the laboratory, they may use instruments such as the gravimeter and magnetometer to measure the earth's gravitational and magnetic fields.

Geophysicists often specialize in different areas. Some investigate the origins and activities of volcanoes and earthquakes. Others compile and organize data to prepare navigational charts and maps or predict atmospheric conditions. Still other geophysicists establish water supply and flood control programs and prepare environmental impact reports.

Geophysicists need to be capable of working as part of a team. They should be curious and able to communicate well. In addition to a strong background in mathematics, physics, and computer science, geophysicists need at least a bachelor's degree in geology or geophysics. Further specialized graduate degrees are often needed to obtain research positions at universities, in government agencies, or in private industries such as petroleum companies.

A technical secretary provides invaluable assistance to engineers and scientists.

Technical Secretary If working in an office appeals to you, you might like to become a secretary. Secretaries are responsible for the smooth running of an office. They answer phones, type letters and reports, keep accurate files, and make needed arrangements.

If science appeals to you, you might like to become a technical secretary. Technical secretaries work for and assist engineers and scientists. In addition to the smooth running of the office, a technical secretary may be responsible for writing routine correspondence, gathering and editing materials for scientific papers, or maintaining a technical library.

To become a technical secretary, you should learn office skills such as typing and word processing. You should also study English and science.

For further information about a career as a technical secretary, contact:

Professional Secretaries International
2440 Pershing Road, Suite G10
Kansas City, Missouri 64108

Section 3 Review   Chapter 2

Use **Reading Checksheet 2-3** TRB page 66
Skillsheet 2-3 TRB page 108
Section Reviewsheet 2-3 TRB pages 153–154
Section Testsheet 2-3 TRB page 280

Check Your Vocabulary

12 batholith
16 chemically formed rock
15 clastic rock
2 igneous rock
14 laccolith
9 lava
6 magma
4 metamorphic rock

8 mineral composition
11 organic rock
10 porphyritic rock
13 pyroclastic deposits
1 rock
5 rock cycle
3 sedimentary rock
7 texture

Match each term above with the numbered phrase that best describes it.

1. A mixture of minerals that is beneath all soil and water on the earth's surface
2. Rock that is formed from hot melted materials beneath the earth's surface
3. Rock that is formed from sediments
4. Rock that is formed deep within the earth's crust when minerals and rocks are changed by very great heat and pressure which changes the crystal structure
5. The process by which rock is changed from one class to another
6. Liquid rock melt that is found in some places beneath the earth's surface
7. The pattern made by the size, shape, and arrangement of the particles that are in a rock
8. A list of the minerals that make up a rock
9. What magma is called after it reaches the surface of the earth
10. Rock that consists of both large and small crystals
11. Rock formed from the remains of plants and animals
12. Large area of exposed rock formed of large crystals
13. Rock formed during a violent volcanic eruption
14. Formation made of porphyritic rock
15. Rock formed from particles of minerals and preexisting rocks
16. Rock formed from minerals dissolved in water

Check Your Knowledge

Multiple Choice: Choose the answer that best completes each of the following sentences.

1. Some _?_ rock is formed from minerals that were once dissolved in water.
   a) igneous
   b) sedimentary
   c) metamorphic
   d) igneous and metamorphic
2. Rocks are grouped into one of three classes, depending on how the rock was _?_.
   a) shaped   c) colored
   b) formed   d) located
3. A sedimentary rock can turn into an igneous rock by _?_.
   a) melting and then cooling
   b) weathering and deposition
   c) compaction
   d) compaction and cementation

Check Your Understanding

1. Compare lava and magma. How are they similar? How are they different?
2. Explain how the three classes of rock are formed.
3. Explain in detail the rock cycle.
4. Name and describe six common rock textures.
5. In a sample of granite, how can quartz be distinguished from feldspar?

Chapter 2 Review

See also **Chapter Testsheets 2A and 2B**

Concept Summary

Matter is anything that occupies space and has mass.

☐ Most matter can occur in three different phases—solid, liquid, and gas.

☐ Matter is considered to be made up of atoms (the smallest complete part of an element).

☐ An element is a substance that contains only one kind of atom.

☐ Atoms are made of three types of even smaller particles—neutrons, protons, and electrons.

☐ A compound is a substance that is made up of two or more elements.

☐ A chemical bond is the force that holds atoms together in a compound.

Minerals are naturally occurring, inorganic crystalline solids.

☐ Minerals are grouped into large classes on the basis of their key elements.

☐ Minerals are identified on the basis of their physical properties.

☐ Although all minerals are crystalline solids, not all minerals have the freedom to grow into visible crystals.

Most **rocks** are combinations of two or more minerals.

☐ Rocks are classified into general types by the way in which they form. These include igneous, sedimentary, and metamorphic rocks.

☐ Igneous rocks are formed from hot, melted earth material.

☐ Sedimentary rocks are formed from sediments or particles of earth material.

☐ Metamorphic rocks are formed when very great heat and pressure produces new minerals and textures in older rocks.

☐ Rocks are identified by their texture and mineral composition.

☐ Earth processes are continually changing rocks from one type to another.

Putting It All Together

1. Explain why a change in temperature can change the phase of a substance.

2. Draw a picture of a silica atom, with the correct number and placement of protons, neutrons, and electrons.

3. The chemical formula of the mineral fluorite is CaF_2. Of what elements is it composed, and in what proportion?

4. What information would a person need to distinguish a mineral from a nonmineral?

5. Explain how differences in the physical properties of minerals are related to differences in the basic blocks of the minerals.

6. Imagine that you find a mineral sample but are not sure which mineral it is. Describe what you would do to determine the mineral in your sample.

7. Make three lists of rocks, one for each general class of rocks you have studied, that contain silicate minerals. Label each list: Igneous (or Sedimentary or Metamorphic) rocks that contain silicate minerals. After naming the rocks, list the silicate minerals found in each rock.

8. What are some of the different types of rocks that nonsilicate minerals form?

9. What are the basic differences between identifying minerals and identifying rocks?

10. Describe how a metamorphic rock can be changed into a different metamorphic rock. Give an example.

Apply Your Knowledge

1. What properties of a mineral would tend to make it valuable as a gemstone?

2. Describe how texture can be a clue to the history of a rock's formation.

3. In an igneous rock, what is the relationship between crystal size and rate of cooling of the molten material?

4. Describe the processes and environments that could result in the following changes of rock types: granite → sandstone → gneiss → granite.

Find Out on Your Own

1. Scientists have discovered that neutrons and protons consist of even smaller particles known as quarks. Quarks exist in six "flavors"—up and down, truth and beauty, and strange and charm. Find out how these particles were discovered and how they are being studied.
2. Visit the nearest locality or localities where minerals can be collected. Collect several specimens. For each specimen, 1) identify the mineral, 2) specify where it was found, 3) name the person who found the specimen, and 4) list the date on which the specimen was found.
3. Using the techniques and properties you have learned, make a detailed list of each of the minerals in your collection.
4. Determine the different types of rocks that are used locally in public buildings and cemeteries.

Reading Further

Bramwell, Martyn. *Understanding and Collecting Rocks and Fossils*. Tulsa, OK: Educational Development Corp., 1983.
An easy-to-use guide to finding and identifying the most common rocks, minerals, and fossils. Also contains interesting experiments and a fine description of how rocks are formed.

Berger, Melvin. *Atoms, Molecules and Quarks,* New York: Putnam, 1986.
This is an excellent introduction to atoms, molecules, elements, and compounds.

Chesterman, Charles W. *The Audobon Society Field Guide to North American Rocks and Minerals*. New York: Alfred A. Knopf, 1978.
This field guide will interest both the beginner and the experienced rock hound.

Cvancara, Alan M. *A Field Manual for the Amateur Geologist: Tools and Activities for Exploring Our Planet*. Englewood Cliffs, NJ: Prentice-Hall, 1985.
This book is filled with useful information about how to study rocks and minerals. Included is a description of gold prospecting.

Deudney, Daniel, and Christopher Flavin. *Renewable Energy: The Power to Choose*. A Worldwatch Institute Book. New York: Norton, 1983.
Short and very readable, this book surveys renewable energy technology.

Pough, Frederick H. *A Field Guide to Rocks and Minerals*. Boston: Houghton Mifflin, 1976.
Part of the popular Peterson Field Guide Series, this handy reference book will answer almost any question about a rock or mineral.

Robbins, Manuel. *The Collector's Book of Fluorescent Minerals*. New York: Van Nostrand Reinhold, 1983.
This excellent book describes all aspects of collecting beautiful fluorescent minerals.

Science Issues of Today   The Search for Mineral Resources

Chemical analysis by Atomic Absorption Spectrophotometry involves converting the sample to an atomic vapor by using a flame or acetylene torch.

Today the most advanced equipment can measure trace amounts as small as one-billionth of a gram.

Copper, iron, zinc, tin, lead, aluminum, silver, gold, molybdenum, platinum, uranium, vanadium, titanium, and mercury are only a few of the elements obtained from rocks and minerals that are extremely important in maintaining an industrialized society. All of these elements are being mined in different parts of the world. Mining is a process that takes from nature faster than nature can replenish the earth. The more people mine these elements, the less that remains for future use.

In the early history of mining, the search for minerals was limited to looking at surface deposits that were easily seen. The deposits that were mined contained minerals extremely rich in the desired elements; these minerals had a composition that made extraction of the elements relatively simple. These easily found surface deposits have essentially been mined out so that it has become harder to find minable minerals.

The modern geologist uses many tools in searching for mineral deposits. Some of the simplest tools include topographic and geologic maps. Surface shapes and distribution of rocks are sometimes clues to what might be found beneath the earth's surface. But they are only clues, and to verify the subsurface deposits the geologist has a multitude of investigative techniques using modern technology.

Seismic exploration uses the returning echos from artificial shock waves to determine the shapes of rock masses and layers beneath the surface.

Magnetic surveys measure variations in magnetic intensity and may help to locate specific rock types or iron ore deposits.

Gravity surveys allow geologists to map very slight variations in the pull of gravity. These

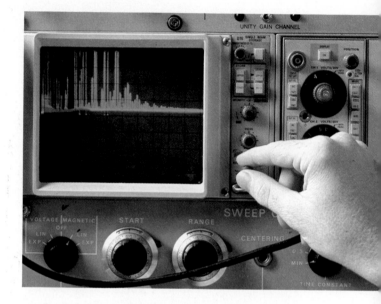

Peaks in a spectograph display help researchers identify the different elements in a prepared sample. Different elements will form peaks at different places across the screen.

variations can be caused by differences in the density or specific gravity of different rock types.

Aerial photographs and satellite imagery show large scale structural features that may be undetectable by a mapping team on the ground.

Analysis of solutions obtained from sediments and plants with an Atomic Absorption Spectrophotometer will often show very tiny amounts of elements that may indicate a nearby source for those elements.

Most successful exploration programs use several or all of the above techniques. As technology changes, so does our ability to discover new, economically valuable mineral resources.

The Earth in Space

Unit 2

On July 20, 1969, firsthand exploration of the moon began with the landing of America's *Apollo II* mission. Since then, astronauts have sampled and studied the moon's surface to learn about its early history.

The physical earth can be considered as an object in itself. The matter that makes up the earth can be considered in isolation. But certain earth processes and certain observable changes can be explained most easily when the earth is considered as a planet in motion around the sun.

Think of all the objects that appear to move across the sky. The sun and moon appear to rise and set. Winds blow. Rain and snow fall from the sky. Seasons change. Night falls. Climates vary from one place to another. Something is in motion—either the earth, or the objects other than the earth, or maybe even everything is in motion. Scientific advancement throughout recent history has enabled us to formulate a clearer description of the earth as a planet in a solar system in space.

Chapter 3
Earth Motions

Chapter 4
Beyond the Earth

Chapter 3 The System of the Earth and the Moon

3

Student Resources		Meeting Individual Needs
Student Text	**Laboratory Activities**	
Section 1 Observing the Night Sky 116–128		
Models of the Night Sky 117–118		
Locating Some Constellations 118–121		
Our Science Heritage: How Are Astronomy and Astrology Related?		
Azimuth and Altitude 121–127	Activity 3-1A Using an Astrolabe 122	CORE
	Activity Record Sheet 3-1A LM 31	
	Activity 3-1B Finding the Altitude of Polaris 124	Enrichment
	Activity Record Sheet 3-1B LM 32	
	Investigation 3-1 Mapping the Night Sky in Your Area LM 35–36	Enrichment
A Celestial Latitude and Longitude 127	Activity 3-1C Plotting the Paths of Four Stars 126	Enrichment
	Activity Record Sheet 3-1C LM 33	
Section 1 Review 128		
Section 2 Earth Motions 129–153		
The Earth Rotates 130–132		
Evidence of the Earth's Rotation 132–137	Activity 3-2A Simulating the Coriolis Effect 134	CORE
	Activity Record Sheet 3-2A LM 37	
The Time of Day 137–142	Activity 3-2B Simulating the Seasons on Earth 147	Enrichment
The Earth Revolves 142–143	Activity Record Sheet 3-2B LM 39	
Evidence of the Earth's Revolution 144–145	Investigation 3-2 Plotting the Path of the Sun Across the Sky LM 41–42	Enrichment
The Seasons 146–151		Reinforcement
Natural Timekeepers 152		
Section 2 Review 153		
Section 3 The Moon 154–165		
Characteristics of the Moon 155–157	Activity 3-3 A Way to Calculate the Diameter of the Moon 158	CORE
	Activity Record Sheet 3-3 LM 43	
Phases and Eclipses of the Moon 159–162	Investigation 3-3 Making a Moon Chart LM 45–46	Enrichment
	Research Lab 3 A Model of the Tides LM 47–48	Enrichment
Information from the *Apollo* Program 162–163		
Careers: Astronomer/Instrumentation Technician 164		
Section 3 Review 165		
Chapter 3 Review 166–167		

Chapter Planning Guide

Teacher Resources		Meeting Individual Needs
Teacher's Edition		
	Letter to Parents EI 15; Essential Ideas 3-1 EI 17–18	Enrich/Reinf
Discussion Idea 114C		
	Teaching Diagram 3-1 TRB 19	CORE
Demonstration 114C Activity Notes 114D Activity Notes 114E		
Activity Notes 114F	Skillsheet 3-1 TRB 109	Reinforcement
Section 1 Review Answers 114F	Reading Checksheet 3-1 TRB 67 Section Reviewsheet 3-1 TRB 155–156 Section Testsheet 3-1 TRB 281	Reinforcement CORE CORE
	Essential Ideas 3-2 EI 19–20 Teaching Diagram 3-2A TRB 20	Reinforcement CORE
Demonstration 114G Environmental Topic 114G Activity Notes 114H Discussion Idea 114J	Teaching Diagram 3-2B TRB 21	Reinforcement
Activity Notes 114K	Overhead Transparency B5 Skillsheet 3-2 TRB 110	CORE Reinforcement
Discussion Idea 114K	Overhead Transparency B6 Field Study 3-2 TRB 232 Overhead Transparency S5	CORE Enrichment Enrichment
Section 2 Review Answers 114K	Reading Checksheet 3-2 TRB 68 Section Reviewsheet 3-2 TRB 157–158 Section Testsheet 3-2 TRB 282	Reinforcement CORE CORE
	Essential Ideas 3-3 EI 21–22	Reinforcement
Discussion Idea 114L Activity Notes 114M Demonstration 114N	Teaching Diagram 3-3A TRB 22 Teaching Diagram 3-3B TRB 23 Projectsheet 3-3 TRB 233	CORE Enrichment Enrichment
Creative Writing Idea 114P	Skillsheet 3-3 TRB 111	Reinforcement
Section 3 Review Answers 114P	Reading Checksheet 3-3 TRB 69 Section Reviewsheet 3-3 TRB 159–160 Section Testsheet 3-3 TRB 283	Reinforcement CORE CORE
Chapter 3 Review Answers 114Q–114R	Chapter 3 Testsheet TRB 321–322	CORE

3

Observing the Night Sky

Learner Objectives

1. To use models of the night sky.
2. To use Orion to locate other constellations in the night sky.
3. To use azimuth and altitude to describe the location of a star.
4. To plot the paths of four stars at hourly intervals.
5. To recognize hourly changes in the positions of stars as evidence of motion.

Concept Summary

The **celestial sphere** is a useful model of the night sky.

Discussion Idea

How to Describe the Position of a Star

Ask students if they remember the discussion in Chapter 1 of how difficult it is to locate a place on the earth without using a system of coordinates. Ask if they can imagine how much more difficult it would be to locate a star without some kind of system, since the stars appear to move across the sky.

If possible, find pictures of celestial globe models from earlier times (such as 16th- and 18th-century versions). Have students compare these with the picture on page 117. (Student responses to the comparison will vary.)

Tell students that when stars were used for navigation, "maps" or catalogs of the stars were important. Tell them that the Greenwich observatory in England was established by King Charles II in 1675, and its first Royal Astronomer was assigned the task of compiling a catalog of the stars that would help sailors navigate. Tell students that some Polynesian societies still teach navigation by the stars to young canoeists.

Tell students that in Section 1, they will learn how to use a system of coordinates to describe the position of a star.

Demonstration

An Ancient Device to Determine Altitude

If you can find pictures of astrolabes or other astronomical instruments from earlier centuries (in encyclopedias or books about astronomy), show them to students. Explain that they will construct an astrolabe for the activity on page 122.

No classroom demonstration can replace a field trip to a planetarium or observatory. If possible, schedule one around this time.

If such a trip is impossible, ask any students who have visited a planetarium or observatory to describe their visits.

Activity Notes

Activity 3-1A

Using an Astrolabe   page **122**

Purpose   To construct an astrolabe and use it to measure the altitude of objects.

- **CORE** 30 minutes Pairs of students
- **Activity Record Sheet 3-1A** (Lab Manual page 31) can be used to record this activity.
- Science Processes: Constructing a model; Recognizing and using spatial relationships; Measuring; Calculating; Interpreting data; Inferring.

Procedure Notes

Have students read the angle between the line of sight and the string. The reading obtained is the angle in relation to the vertical. To obtain the angle of elevation (the altitude in relation to the horizontal), subtract the reading from 90°.

An alternate astrolabe can be made using a cardboard circle, a small nail, a ruler, and a long, flat stick. Have students use a protractor to make degree markings from 0° to 180° along the edge of the circle. Next, have students nail the ruler to the center of the circle, and nail the circle and ruler to a long, flat stick (such as a meter stick). The circle can be held in place on the stick with a piece of tape. The end of the meter stick should be placed in the ground in a vertical position. Students sight along the edge of the ruler, turning the ruler until it lines up with a specific object. The angle obtained with this astrolabe is the actual angle of elevation.

Answers to Questions

1. The horizon, when visible, is 0° with respect to the observer and is the starting point in measuring altitude. In the room, any object sighted in a 0° reading can be considered on the horizon.
2. The angle directly overhead is 90° and is called the zenith.
3. Readings will vary. Partners probably have different readings because they stood in different places.
4. The angle increases as the observer approaches the point where the ceiling and the wall meet.

Conclusion

Altitude is given with respect to the observer and can vary greatly depending on the location of the observer. Latitude-longitude coordinates do not vary with respect to the observer.

Science Background

Observation of objects in space began early in history. Stonehenge, in England, was evidently a carefully planned observatory that enabled ancient peoples to predict solstices and lunar eclipses. Sky observations were also used in navigation and for telling time.

The first calendars were based on phases of the moon. With the development of agriculture came the need to forecast seasons, which are more closely related to the movements of the sun and stars. As early as 2800 B.C., the Egyptians had devised a calendar with a 365-day year.

By observing and naming constellations, the ancient star-watchers also mapped the night sky. They were unaware, however, that not all stars in a constellation are near each other. Today, astronomers know that stars that appear close together are merely in the same line of vision. They are often vastly different distances apart.

3-1

3-1

Student Misconception

When asked to describe the location of an object, students frequently make reference to landmarks. While landmarks may be useful, students may fail to consider the transient nature of these reference points, as well as the subjective nature of their own position. As a result, the student may perceive he or she is giving a precise description of position, when the description is less than precise. Latitude, longitude, altitude, and azimuth are standard reference points, common to all observers, from which position can be determined.

To illustrate the need for standard frames of reference, try this exercise with your students. Divide the class into two groups. Ask the students in each group to write descriptions of the locations of several objects in the room. (Do not allow students to describe the actual objects.) Choose objects that are fixed or stationary, but whose reference points can be changed easily; for example, a particular book on a shelf, a desk, a light fixture, or an object suspended from the ceiling. (Prior to this exercise you might want to suspend a few paper stars from the ceiling.) During a time when students are not in the room, alter the reference points that surround the fixed objects. Then have the students read their descriptions to the rest of the class. From the descriptions only, is the class able to locate the objects? Discuss why or why not.

Activity Notes

Activity 3-1B

Finding the Altitude of Polaris   page **124**

Purpose   To find your latitude by measuring the altitude of Polaris.

- 20 minutes Pairs of students or small groups
- **Activity Record Sheet 3-1B** (Lab Manual page 32) can be used to record this activity.
- Science Processes: Measuring; Recognizing and using spatial relationships: Collecting data; Comparing; Inferring.

Advance Preparation

This activity uses the astrolabe constructed in Activity 3-1A on page 122.

Safety Information

You might want to suggest that students do this activity under adult supervision, especially if they are making observations in an area far from their homes.

Procedure Notes

Observations will be easier to complete in areas away from the light of big cities and large communities. Depending on location, observers may still have difficulty finding Polaris because Polaris is not very bright. Using the pointer stars in the Big Dipper, however, should help students find Polaris. Remind students to subtract their readings from 90° to obtain the angle of elevation of Polaris, and thus their latitude.

Answers to Questions

The reading for the altitude of Polaris should be the same as the latitude of your community.

Conclusion

In the Northern Hemisphere, the altitude of Polaris is always the same as the latitude of the place where an observer stands.

Activity Notes

Activity 3-1C

Plotting the Paths of Four Stars   page **126**

Purpose   To follow the paths of four stars across the sky during one evening.

- 2 to 3 hours
  20- to 30-minute followup Pairs of students or small groups
- **Activity Record Sheet 3-1C** (Lab Manual page 33) can be used to record this activity.
- Science Processes: Measuring; Collecting and analyzing data; Communicating through a chart; Recognizing and using spatial relationships; Constructing a model.

Advance Preparation

This activity calls for the astrolabe constructed in Activity 3-1A on page 122.

Safety Information

You might want to suggest that students do this activity under adult supervision.

Procedure Notes

This activity is best done when the moon is in the new phase so that its brightness does not obscure many stars.

Tell students that they might choose a planet as one of their objects. When they plot the course of their stars in class, see if they can detect which stars, if any, were planets. If you wish, use an astronomical calendar to inform students which planets are visible and their approximate times and locations.

At 30-minute intervals, it is less likely that students will have to deal with changes in sky conditions (clouds). If students use a shorter time interval, they must adjust their measurement to how far the star would appear to move in an hour. (The 5° of movement over 20 minutes will equal 15° over an hour.) Remind students to subtract their readings from 90°.

Answers to Questions

The stars move 15° in one hour and 30° in two hours. Because of possible errors, student measurements may not agree.

Conclusion

In 24 hours the stars will appear to move 360°. In 24 hours either the earth rotates once on its axis, or the stars move once around the earth.

Section 1 Review Answers

Check Your Understanding
page **128**

1. It is an imaginary sphere that surrounds the earth. To an observer, who can see no more than half the celestial sphere at any one time, it appears like the inside of a dome. The center of the celestial sphere would be at the center of the earth.
2. No, the horizon varies according to the location (latitude, longitude, elevation, etc.) of the observer.
3. Yes, the zenith is always directly over the observer's head, regardless of the observer's location.
4. North: 0° or 360°; East: 90°; South: 180°; West: 270°
5. Two indications of motion are star trails recorded on a time exposure and seasonal changes of constellations visible in the night sky.

3-1

3-2

Learner Objectives

1. To identify evidence of the earth's rotation and its revolution.
2. To explain the Coriolis effect.
3. To understand how the time of day is calculated.
4. To describe the Doppler effect.
5. To cite evidence that the earth's axis is tilted 23.5° off the vertical.
6. To relate the earth's seasons to the inclination of its axis.
7. To relate a calendar to the earth's revolution.

Concept Summary

The earth's rotation is the turning of the earth on its axis once a day.
The earth's axis is the imaginary line around which the earth spins.
The earth's revolution is the orbiting of the earth around the sun once a year.
The earth's inclination is the tilting of the earth's axis 23.5° off the vertical.

Demonstration

Implications of the Earth's Rotation

In a darkened room, shine a flashlight on a globe (or a large ball with an X marked on it). Focus the light on a particular country. Now rotate the globe in a counterclockwise direction so that your country moves from daylight to night.

Next, hold the globe or ball still and move your flashlight around it in a clockwise direction. The effect will be the same.

Explain to students why early observers could not really tell that the earth rotated on its axis. Not knowing how far away the sun was, they could not know the impossibility of its revolving around the earth every 24 hours.

Repeat the rotation of the ball, with the light shining on it (you might want to use a stationary lamp for this part). Show the students how only one half of the model earth is lighted at any one time, causing night and day; how the earth rotates from west to east in a counterclockwise direction, causing different locations to be in daytime or night, depending on their rotational position; how the sun appears to rise in the east and set in the west, although it is the earth that is actually moving.

Environmental Topic

The significance of the earth's inclination of 23.5° can be explored by having students speculate about how life as we know it would differ were the earth tilted at 45°, 70°, or even 0°.

Together with the earth's revolution around the sun, the tilt of the earth's axis is largely responsible for the seasons. Based on these seasons we plant our crops and feed our societies. What impact would an alteration in the earth's inclination have on the seasons and the production of food?

Discuss how a change in the earth's tilt might impact energy resources. Solar energy might become more economically feasible were the tilt such that a greater proportion of the earth's surface received vertical solar radiation. What effect might this change in tilt have on other energy sources?

Activity Notes

Activity 3-2A

Simulating the Coriolis Effect   page **134**

Purpose   To simulate the Coriolis effect.

- **CORE** 40 minutes Teacher demonstration or large groups
- **Activity Record Sheet 3-2A** (Lab Manual page 37) can be used to record this activity.
- Science Processes: Formulating models; Observing; Predicting; Defining operationally; Diagramming.

Procedure Notes

For the rotating platform, students can use a plastic decorating wheel (available from an art supply house), a cake plate that rotates, an old record player set at 33 rpm, or a swivel seat.

The results can be sped up by using warm water in the pie pan. Also, the smaller the holes in the cup, the more dynamic the results.

Food color will stain hands, but is not harmful and will wash off after two or three washings.

The deflection will be to the right no matter where the cup is placed. Students can observe this by using a second cup with only one hole near the base. Have students place the cup in the pie pan near the outer edge and repeat the activity.

Answers to Questions

1. No, the food coloring does not move in a straight line.
2. The food coloring moves to the right (opposite the direction of rotation) and away from the center of the rotating pie pan.
3. The apparent deflection occurs because the edge of the pie pan moves to the left faster than the center, or any other point inside the pan, does.

Conclusion

If the platform were rotated in a clockwise direction, the food coloring would deflect to the left. (This corresponds to the Coriolis effect in the Southern Hemisphere.)

Going Further

Students (in the Northern Hemisphere) may have noticed that water going down a drain spins in a clockwise direction. Have students explain how the Coriolis effect accounts for this apparent motion.

Science Background

Satellite motion is the result of two forces simultaneously acting on an orbiting object. As long as these forces are balanced, the orbit remains fixed. To get into earth orbit, for example, an artificial satellite must leave the earth's surface at a speed of 29 000 km/h (8 km/s). This speed is just great enough to balance the pull of gravity. The satellite goes around the earth as if it were on a leash. Because of its inertia (the tendency of a moving object to travel in a straight line), the satellite keeps trying to fly off into space. (Think of what happens when the string on a revolving ball breaks.) The earth's gravity acts as the leash, the inward pull that keeps the satellite in orbit.

Over millions of years, the earth's speed of rotation has been decreasing. Evidence indicates that 400 million years ago, a day on Earth was less than 20 hours long. The change is very slow. Calculations show the day is increasing by about one second every 50 000 years. Scientists believe tidal friction is responsible for this change. At the same time, the moon is slowly moving away from the earth at the rate of about 2.5 cm per year. (This is because some of the earth's angular momentum is being transferred to the moon.)

3-2

Student Misconception

Many students perceive the night sky as fixed and unchanging. Most of them inaccurately assume that the constellations have fixed positions with respect to an observer, despite the fact that the observer's position changes with the motion of the earth around the sun (revolution). Few students will have kept a yearly log of observable constellations, and thus will have no firsthand experience with the apparent migration of constellations across the night sky.

For practical and observational purposes, distant stars are considered fixed or stationary. The stars and constellations appear to move relative to the position of the observer. In reality, it is the position of the observer that changes significantly (with the revolution of the earth), not the position of the stars.

You can demonstrate this phenomenon by having students follow an elliptical path around a building that is large enough to obscure their views. The building represents the sun. As the students walk (revolve) around the building, have them sketch the landmarks (constellations) that are in their view. Remind students that the building (sun) totally obstructs their view of anything behind it. As students revolve around the sun/ building and develop their constellation/landmark maps, they will also develop a concrete understanding of how and why the constellations change on a seasonal basis.

Discussion Idea

Time Depends on Where You Are

Ask students to look at the time zone illustration on page 139. Tell them that every day at every point on the earth, there is a moment when the sun crosses the meridian (the north-south line that passes through any point on earth).

Ask students to think about what we do with the time systems we have devised. In the United States, for our convenience, every April we start calling the point when the sun crosses the meridian 1:00 p.m., so that we can have more daylight in the evening hours. The sun's time has not changed; human time has changed from noon to 1:00 p.m.

Point out that there are 24 time zones on the earth. There are 24 hours in each day. As the earth rotates through 1/24 of its cycle, each time zone goes through one hour of its time.

Discussion Idea (alternate)

The "Opposite" Seasons of the Hemispheres

Ask if any student in the class has ever lived in or visited the Southern Hemisphere. Have the student(s) describe the "opposite" seasons—Halloween in the spring, snow in July, etc. Ask the class what they know about seasons and climates in the Southern Hemisphere, the equator, the polar regions.

Ask students if they know what causes the difference between hemispheres. Tell them causes are the inclination of the earth's axis and the fact that the earth revolves around the sun. They will learn more about these causes in Section 3.

Activity Notes

Activity 3-2B

Simulating the Seasons on Earth   page **147**

Purpose   To show how the revolution of the earth and the inclination of the earth's axis cause the seasons.

- 20 minutes Groups of 4 or teacher demonstration
- **Activity Record Sheet 3-2B** (Lab Manual page 39) can be used to record this activity.
- Science Processes: Formulating models; Recognizing and using spatial relationships; Comparing and contrasting; Identifying; Demonstrating; Inferring.

Answers to Questions

1. At the autumnal equinox position, one half of the model is daylight. The earth is lighted from Pole to Pole.
2. Every place on earth gets the same amount of sunlight in one rotation at the autumnal equinox.
3. As the model is moved from the September to the December position, the hours of daylight in the Southern Hemisphere increase while those in the Northern Hemisphere decrease.
4. In the winter solstice position, the South Pole receives light all the time.
5. In the vernal equinox position, the light-dark pattern is similar to that of the autumnal equinox in September.
6. In the summer solstice position, the North Pole is lighted for one complete rotation, whereas in the winter solstice position it receives no light at all.

Conclusion

This illustrates that the sun's rays strike in different places and these places receive various amounts of sunlight.

Discussion Idea (alternate)

The "Opposite" Seasons of the Hemispheres

Ask the class what they know about seasons and climates in the Southern Hemisphere, the equator, the polar regions. Ask students if they know what causes the difference between hemispheres. Tell them causes are the inclination of the earth's axis and the fact that the earth revolves around the sun. They will learn more about these causes in Section 3.

Section 2 Review Answers

Check Your Understanding
page **153**

1. Once set in motion, a free-swinging pendulum continues to swing in the same direction. The apparent directional changes indicated by a Foucault pendulum must be caused by the motion of the earth under the pendulum.
2. This deflection is caused by differences in rotational speeds of various locations on the earth's surface below the freely moving object.
3. As the source of energy waves get closer to an observer, the frequency of the waves increases. As the source gets farther away, the frequency decreases.

3-2

The Moon

Learner Objectives

1. To compare conditions on the moon and on the earth.
2. To explain the phases of the moon.
3. To distinguish a solar eclipse and a lunar eclipse.
4. To calculate the diameter of the moon.

Concept Summary

The moon, which is the earth's only natural satellite, is like the earth in some ways and unlike the earth in other ways.

Discussion Idea

Lunar Optical Illusions

Ask students to think about properties the moon seems to have and those that it does not have. (The moon seems to give off light, but actually the light comes from the sun; the moon seems to be as big as the sun, but actually is smaller and closer to us; the moon seems to change its shape, but in fact its orbit around the earth causes us to see different parts of the lighted moon.)

Ask students if they know why the moon looks so large sometimes and so small at other times during the same night. Tell them that this apparent change in size is both an optical illusion and a psychological illusion. Optically, the moon appears larger when viewed close to the horizon, through the denseness of the earth's atmosphere. Also, the moon seems largest when it is closest to human-scale objects (trees, buildings). As it moves higher in the sky, we see the moon against the vastness of space, and it seems much smaller.

Activity Notes

Activity 3-3

A Way to Calculate the Diameter of the Moon   page **158**

Purpose   To use indirect measurement to calculate the diameters of a classroom clock and the moon.

- **CORE** Two 15-minute sessions Pairs of students
- **Activity Record Sheet 3-3** (Lab Manual page 43) can be used to record this activity.
- Science Processes: Measuring; Applying formulas; Calculating; Formulating models.

Advance Preparation

You might wish to premeasure objects to be used.

Procedure Notes

Inform students that the corresponding angles of similar triangles are equal; the proportional sides are opposite the equal angles.

Students may recall from mathematics that in a proportion the product of the means is equal to the product of the extremes (this formula is shown in the activity). It is this principle that is used to solve the equation for the unknown length.

In order to calculate the diameter of the moon, students will need to wait for the next full moon to occur. At that time, they should place two strips of masking tape at eye level on a window that has a view of the moon. Have students place the strips exactly 2 cm apart. Students should move back, away from the window, until the moon "fits" exactly between the two strips of tape. Then students should measure the distance from the window to their eyes. This measurement can then be used (in the lower formula in the box of the student page) to calculate the moon's diameter.

Answers to Questions

1. Answers will vary. If you have premeasured the clock, you will be able to inform students of the accuracy of their answers to this question.
2. Students should discuss the possibilities of mismeasuring the diameters of the coins, arithmetic mistakes, etc.

Conclusion

Modern technology provides accurate methods of measurement, such as bouncing radar beams off the moon's surface that ancient astronomers lacked.

Science Background

The earth's moon is unusual because of its size. Although four other moons in the solar system are larger, they revolve around giant planets: Jupiter, Saturn, and Neptune. The earth's diameter, however, is only four times greater than that of its moon. For this reason, and because the moon also has other characteristics of a planet, scientists now think of the earth and moon as a double planetary system.

Scientists have proposed a number of theories to explain the origin of the moon. Two of these have now been largely discredited. The fission theory pictured the moon as a chunk of matter that broke away from the earth. In the capture theory, the moon formed elsewhere in the solar system, and was later pulled into orbit by earth's gravity as it passed nearby. Still under consideration are the binary theory and the impact hypothesis. According to the binary theory, the moon and earth formed near each other at the same time. The most recent proposal, sometimes called the Big Whack, suggests that a giant planetesimal collided with the earth, melting the outer layers of both bodies and sending a huge amount of vaporized rock into orbit around the earth. As the gaseous ring cooled, its particles gradually condensed into the moon.

3-3

Student Misconception

Understanding the relationships between the movements of the earth, sun, and moon does not come easily for most students. One common misconception is that the far side and dark side of the moon are the same.

As the moon revolves around the earth it completes one full rotation. As a result, the same side of the moon always faces the earth, accounting for the near and far sides of the moon.

However, the moon's position relative to the sun is not fixed. Sunlight strikes the near and far sides of the moon as it moves around the earth. At the new moon, the near side is dark and the far side is lighted because the moon is between the earth and the sun, preventing the sun's rays from striking the near side. The opposite is true at full moon.

The concept of near side/far side can be demonstrated. Allow a desk to represent the earth. Instruct students to walk around the desk, always keeping their front toward the desk. As students complete one revolution, they will also complete one full rotation of their body, imitating the near side/far side position of the moon. By shining a light on the students as they complete the revolution, students can observe the light side/dark side effect. At new moon, the light will strike the student's back, while at full moon the light will strike the student's front.

Demonstration

In and Out of the Earth's Shadow

This demonstration will show how solar and lunar eclipses occur. Obtain a flashlight (at least 16 cm in diameter), a softball, and a golf ball, which will represent the sun, earth, and moon, respectively. (If the flashlight beam is diffuse, construct a hood from a thin piece of cardboard and attach it to the flashlight.) Trace a circle of 2-m radius on the floor, and divide the circle into 12 equal-sized arcs, each representing the spatial distance covered by the earth in a month's time.

Have a student stand in the center of the circle to direct the light. Standing on the traced circle, hold the golf ball (the "moon") in one hand and the softball (the "earth") in the other hand, 3 to 4 cm away from the golf ball. Direct the light so that the softball is in the center of the beam. Position the golf ball, either partially or totally, within the shade of the softball.

Instruct the student to keep the flashlight focused on the softball as you walk the distance of each monthly arc around the circle. As you are walking, move the moon in a circle around the earth at a 5° angle off the earth's orbital plane. When you reach the end of the arc, the moon's spatial location relative to the earth should be 30° to 40° ahead of its original position. Point out this fact to the class, as well as the fact that the moon is no longer within the earth's shadow.

Repeat the entire process, until the moon has been partially or totally enveloped in the earth's shadow several times. Explain that this event—a lunar eclipse—actually happens two to five times a year. Explain that the 5° inclination of the moon's orbit is responsible for the frequency of these eclipses.

Perform the demonstration again with the moon circling the earth at a 0° inclination. Show that under these circumstances, the moon is within the earth's shadow once a month.

Perform the demonstration once more, reversing the position of the earth and the moon. This will demonstrate a solar eclipse, during which the occluded body (the sun) is only partially shaded. Position the moon at various distances from the earth and indicate how the size of the moon's umbra is dependent upon its distance from earth. Discuss with the students the differences between a solar and a lunar eclipse.

Creative Writing Idea

The following writing assignment may help students recognize the complexity and effort involved in designing a visit to the moon.

NASA is offering grants to send individuals to the moon for a one-week visit. To qualify as a contestant, you must describe in writing how you would spend the week. Include information on what types of food you would eat and how you could prepare them in an environment with less gravity than we have on earth. Describe the types of research activities you would conduct and the equipment you would need, including types of problems you might encounter given that most of our equipment is designed for the earth. For example, would you be able to use a compass for a mapping project? NASA will be more impressed if you chose specific projects—one or two—and explain those in detail.

Section 3 Review Answers

Check Your Understanding
page **165**

1. Student diagrams should show the moon in various positions in its orbit around the earth. Diagrams should also 1) show the sun, 2) show how the half of the earth that faces the sun is lighted, and 3) show how the half of the moon that faces the sun (in each of its positions) is lighted.

2. A sidereal month is $27\frac{1}{3}$ days, the time it takes for the moon to revolve around the earth. A synodic month is $29\frac{1}{2}$ days, the time it takes for the moon to go from one new-moon phase to the next. (The additional $2\frac{1}{6}$ days between the sidereal month and the synodic month is caused by the earth's revolution around the sun, causing the moon to travel farther before it comes again to the new moon position with respect to an observer on the earth.)

3. The moon's orbit around the earth is tilted about 5° from the earth's orbit around the sun. This 5° inclination keeps the moon out of the earth's shadow as the moon revolves around the earth.

4. In a lunar eclipse, the moon becomes obscured (to an observer on the earth) by the earth's shadow as the earth passes between the sun and the moon. In a solar eclipse, the sun becomes obscured (to an observer on the earth) by the moon's shadow as the moon passes between the earth and the sun.

5. Scientists believe that the moon's interior is much like that of the earth's and that the moon and the earth are about the same age.

3-3

Chapter Vocabulary

Section 1

horizon
celestial sphere
constellation
altitude
zenith
nadir
Polaris
azimuth
right ascension
declination

Section 2

rotation
axis
time exposure
star trail
deflect
Coriolis effect
apparent solar time
mean solar time
time zone
Greenwich mean time
daylight-saving time
International Date Line
revolution
orbit
Doppler effect
inclination
Tropic of Capricorn
Tropic of Cancer
solstice
equinox
leap year

3-3

Chapter 3 Review Answers

Putting It All Together   page 166

1. Helpful models of the night sky include the interior of a planetarium theater, a star globe, star maps, and star charts.

2.

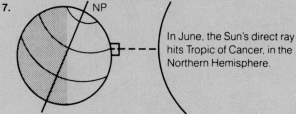

3. The earth rotates 360° in 1 day, 15° in 1 hour, and 45° in 3 hours.

4. The position of the constellation has changed with respect to the zenith and the horizon. Orion, for example, changes as follows: March—halfway between the zenith and western horizon; April—near the western horizon; May—below the western horizon (and therefore not visible in the night sky).

5. 90° on Mar 21 at the equator. 90° on June 21 at the Tropic of Cancer. 90° on Sept 21 at the equator. 90° on Dec 21 at the Tropic of Capricorn. 0° on Mar 21 at either Pole. No sun visible on Dec 21 inside the Arctic Circle. 66.5° on Sept 23 at either of the tropics.

6. If the earth's axis were upright, there would be no seasons because the altitude of the sun would remain the same all year, and therefore the strength of the sun's rays would remain the same throughout the year at any location on the earth.

7.

In June, the Sun's direct ray hits Tropic of Cancer, in the Northern Hemisphere.

8. The person will arrive in San Francisco 4:00 p.m. Eastern Time. The time in San Francisco will be 1:00 p.m. Pacific Time.

Chapter 3 Review Answers (continued)

Putting It All Together

9. The earth has an atmosphere. Therefore it has moisture and gases that support life and modify temperatures. The moon has no atmosphere, and temperature extremes are much more severe than on the earth.

10. Student diagrams should reflect the distinction between partial and total lunar eclipses shown in Figure 3-30 on page 161. In a total lunar eclipse, all of the moon is in the umbra (the darker part of the earth's shadow). In a partial lunar eclipse, part of the moon is in the penumbra.

Apply Your Knowledge   page **166**

1. You must toss the paper before you come even with the porch because the newspaper is also affected by the forward motion at which you are traveling on the bike. The porch is stationary. If you throw the newspaper when you are even with your "target," it will not hit on the target but will rather overshoot the target.

2. The sun rises directly east only on the vernal equinox (Mar 20/21) and the autumnal equinox (Sept 22/23). From the autumnal to the vernal equinox, the sun will rise south of east. From the vernal to the autumnal equinox, the sun will rise north of east.

3. You would have to reset your clock or watch 24 times, once for each of the 24 times zones around the earth. Each time you passed into a different time zone, you would have to set your clock ahead if you were traveling from west to east. You would have to set it back if you were traveling east to west.

Chapter Vocabulary

Section 3

lunar
satellite
ellipse
perigee
apogee
maria
crater
rille
phases of the moon
waxing
waning
sidereal month
synodic month
lunar eclipse
umbra
penumbra
solar eclipse
meteoroid

3-3

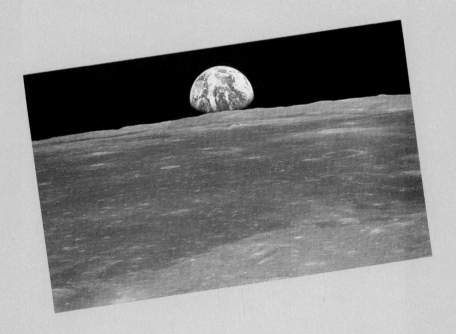

Chapter 3

The System of the Earth and the Moon

Section 1
Observing the Night Sky

Motion is detected by a change in the relative positions of two or more objects. By observing objects that are at some distance from the earth, it is evident that the relative position of the earth changes with respect to these objects. The stars and planets of the night sky have long been admired for their beauty. They do not, however, always appear to be in the same place in the night sky. Something, therefore, is moving—either the objects in the night sky or the earth, or maybe even both.

Section 2
Earth Motions

Changes in the sun's position relative to the earth seem to depend on the time of day. What is moving? the sun? the earth? both? Actually, changes in the relative positions of the earth and the objects in the sky can be explained by not one but two earth motions. One motion—the earth rotating on its axis—explains daily changes, such as morning and night. Another—the earth revolving about the sun—explains yearly changes, such as the seasons.

Through discussion, have students consider how they might use the stone structure at

Section 3
The Moon

The earth's only natural satellite, the moon, has always fascinated people. In 1969, space technology made possible one of the most exciting events of recent times. On July 20 of that year, humans actually walked on the surface of the moon itself. Through the development of scientific instruments, we now know more than ever about our nearest neighbor in space—and, in turn, about our own planet.

Stonehenge to observe changes in the positions of objects in the daytime sky and in the night sky. During the day, for example, how can shadows be used to observe motion? During the night, how can lining up the stars against the silhouettes of certain columns be used to observe motion?

Stonehenge, pictured on the facing page, is an ancient monument in England. It is believed to be a form of calendar that was based on regular changes in the sky. In this chapter, you will see how certain changes in the sky can be explained by means of earth motions.

Observing the Night Sky   Section 1

Learner Objectives
1. To use models of the night sky.
2. To use Orion to locate other constellations in the night sky.
3. To use azimuth and altitude to describe the location of a star.
4. To plot the paths of four stars at hourly intervals.
5. To recognize hourly changes in the positions of stars as evidence of motion.

Section 1 of Chapter 3 is divided into four parts:

Models of the night sky

Locating some constellations

Azimuth and altitude

A celestial latitude and longitude

Figure 3-1. Within an observatory is a telescope that is used to observe stars and planets. The roof of the observatory is dome-shaped and revolves so that, when a portion of the roof is opened, the telescope within the observatory can be pointed toward any star in the sky. When you look at the sky, what shape does it appear to have?
The sky appears to be dome-shaped, with the earth beneath the dome.

Imagine that you are at a planetarium, looking at the dome-shaped ceiling. In the center of the room is the planetarium projector, used to project the images of stars and planets onto the planetarium ceiling. As the presentation begins, the light in the room dims, and the planetarium's sun sets in a beautiful display of clouds in the west. As darkness descends, stars, planets, and the moon appear on the ceiling above you. By means of a special flashlightlike pointer, the planetarium lecturer locates many of the seasonal objects that are visible in the night sky where you live.

That same night, you look out your window at the real night sky. How do they compare—the planetarium sky and the night sky? How can you locate objects in the night sky? How can you describe their locations to someone else? In this section of Chapter 3, you will learn the answers to these and other questions about the night sky.

Models of the night sky
New vocabulary: horizon, celestial sphere

The first thing you notice when you compare the planetarium sky and the night sky is that the ceiling of the planetarium is shaped like a dome. To us, the night sky looks like a huge dome or hemisphere. And the night sky comes all the way down to the **horizon** (huh-RĪ'-zun), where the earth's surface and sky appear to meet.

The real sky looks like a dome, but it is not. When you look up into the sky, you are really looking out into endless space. The nighttime stars are really located at many distances from Earth. The idea of the sky being a dome is a convenient way to study the objects it contains. If you placed a second dome underneath the earth so that the openings of the two domes came together, you would produce a sphere. This imaginary sphere, on which all objects in the sky would appear, is called the **celestial sphere** (suh-LES'-chul SFIR).

Because the night sky appears to be dome-shaped, a star globe is the best model of the celestial sphere. A star globe has a small globe of the earth at its center. When using one, you have to imagine that you are standing on the earth globe looking at the celestial objects printed on the inside of the star globe.

In a planetarium, it is possible to represent the night sky as it will appear over your home tonight or as it appeared to the ancient Egyptians thousands of years ago. How do the objects of the sky get onto the ceiling of the theater?

Students who have visited a planetarium might discuss what it was like. A volunteer can look through an encyclopedia for pictures of a planetarium projector and theater to share with the class.

Figure 3-2. A celestial globe is the best model of the night sky. To read a celestial globe, where must observers imagine themselves to be?
Observers must imagine themselves to be inside the star globe at its center.

1. Because the night sky appears to be dome-shaped
2. An imaginary sphere of sky that surrounds the entire earth and on which all objects in the sky appear

Library research

Prepare a report on five constellations. Find out how they got their names. Then write a short history of the individual or animal that each represents.

Figure 3-3. One representation of the constellation Orion the Hunter shows a hunter carrying a shield. What is a constellation?

Check yourself

1. Why is a star globe the best model of the night sky?
2. What is the celestial sphere?

Locating some constellations
New vocabulary: constellation

In ancient times, people all over the world looked at the night sky and imagined that groups of stars formed pictures of people, animals, and things. These groups of stars are called **constellations** (kon′-stuh-LAY′-shunz). Most of the names we know the constellations by today come from the ancient Greek and Roman cultures. Many other cultures, such as the ancient Egyptians and Native American tribes, also had names for their own constellations. Today, there are 88 officially recognized constellations. A planetarium is a good place to learn about some of the better known ones.

If you were to look for different constellations, you might have a difficult time trying to find some of the pictures they are supposed to represent. But some constellations are easy to find in the night sky. One such constellation is Orion (oh-RĪ′-un) the Hunter, shown in Figure 3-3.

A constellation is a group of stars imagined to form the outline of a person or animal.

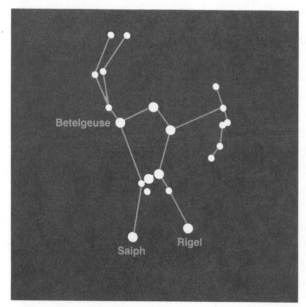

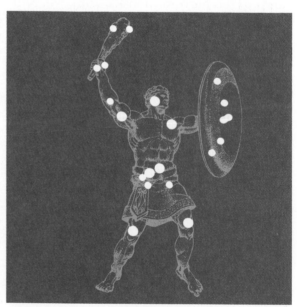

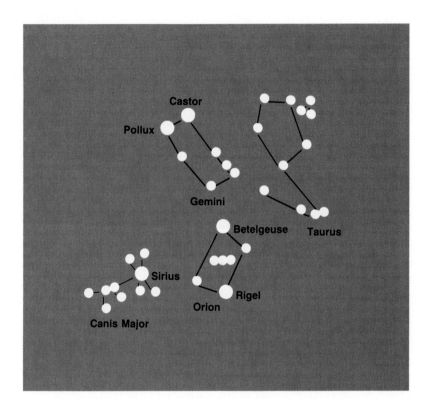

Figure 3-4. How can stars in Orion be used to locate other stars and constellations?
The last paragraph on this page and the first paragraph on the next page describe ways of using Orion to locate other constellations.

See also Teaching Diagram 3-1 (TRB page 19).

Orion is one of the most spectacular constellations because it contains many bright stars. The first thing to notice about Orion is his belt, which is made up of three bright stars that are close together in an almost straight line. Once you learn to recognize these three stars, you should have no trouble finding Orion. The best time to find Orion is about seven or eight o'clock in the evening during the winter months.

Also located in the constellation Orion are two very bright stars named Rigel (RĪ'-jul) and Betelgeuse (BET'-ul-jooz'). Reddish Betelgeuse marks Orion's right shoulder. Blue-white Rigel can be thought of as marking Orion's left foot or knee. Find Rigel and Betelgeuse on the star map in Figure 3-4.

Rigel, Betelgeuse, and the stars in Orion's belt can be used to find other stars and constellations. Using the star map in Figure 3-4, follow a straight line from Rigel through Betelgeuse. This line will lead to the constellation Gemini the Twins. The two bright stars named Castor and Pollux mark the heads of the two brothers.

Critical Thinking

Study the star charts in the Appendix on pages 622–623. Organize the stars and constellations into three groups.

Answers will vary. One possibility: stars that appear only in the April sky, stars that appear only in the August sky, and stars that appear in both April and August skys

Library research

Find out how ancient astronomers knew that there was a difference between stars and planets.

Now use the stars of Orion's belt to find two more constellations. A straight line joining these stars and extending to the left (past Orion's right foot) will point to a very bright star called Sirius (SEER'-ee-us). This star is part of the constellation Canis Major (KAY'-niss MAY'-jur), which is Latin for "big dog." Sirius, the brightest star in the night sky, is also known as the Dog Star. A line passing through Orion's belt to the right past his left shoulder leads to the constellation Taurus (TOR'-us) the Bull.

Figure 3-7 on page 131 shows a group of stars that is easy to recognize. They form the Big Dipper. The Big Dipper is

---

Our Science Heritage

How Are Astronomy and Astrology Related?

Modern astronomy is the scientific study of objects in space. But it has its roots in something that many people think is not scientific—the field of astrology. Many of the early discoveries in astronomy were made by astrologers. Ancient astrologers studied the positions of the various planets, thinking that the positions of these objects in space had an influence on people and events. Astrologers believe, for example, that an analysis of the position of the planets when a person is born will indicate the person's potential talents and personality traits.

The astrology we know today originated in Babylonia around 1000 B.C. It was very popular in ancient Greece. It was also popular in Europe throughout the Middle Ages. Astrology was so popular that many ancient astronomers became astrologers in order to support themselves. One of these ancient astronomer/astrologers was Ptolemy, who described the apparent motions of the planets. Others included Tycho Brahe and Johannes Kepler. You can, if you like, read about their accomplishments in any encyclopedia.

Modern astronomy has broken away from astrology. Most astronomers feel that there is very little evidence to support the claims of astrologers. Yet, astrology is still a popular pastime. Some people take it very seriously, while others look to it for amusement.

part of the constellation Ursa Major, the Big Bear. Ursa Major and its more familiar Big Dipper can be seen on any clear night from the United States.

Check yourself

1. Draw a simple diagram of the constellation Orion. Show how Rigel and Betelgeuse can be used to find the location of the constellation Gemini.

2. Draw a diagram of Orion. Show how the stars in the belt can be used to locate Sirius, part of the constellation Canis Major. Show how those same stars can also be used to locate Taurus the Bull.

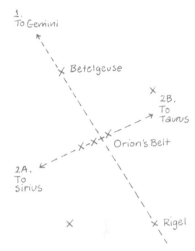

Azimuth and altitude
New vocabulary: altitude, zenith, nadir, Polaris, azimuth

Imagine that you are standing outside at night with a friend. How would you explain to your friend how to find a particular star or planet that you can see? One way would be to point and hope that he or she will find the same object you have in mind. Another way would be to use a landmark on the horizon. For example, you might say, "Follow the chimney of that house straight up until you see four stars that make a square." Your friend may or may not find the stars that you mean. Can you think of a more accurate way to locate an object in the sky?

Any location on the earth's surface can be found in terms of its latitude and longitude. If its latitude is 39° N, you know that it is located somewhere along an imaginary east-west line that circles the earth 39° north of the equator. If its longitude is 77° W, you know that it is located somewhere along an imaginary north-south line that is 77° west of the prime meridian. An object at latitude 39° N and longitude 77° W would be located where the two imaginary lines cross, which happens to be the location of Washington, D.C.

A similar method can be used to locate an object on the celestial sphere. To do this, two measurements are needed. One measurement gives the **altitude** (AL′-tuh-tood′), or height, of the object above the horizon. A star sighted on the

Students can practice trying to describe the location of one object of a set—for example, a certain desk in a roomful of desks, a certain floor tile, a certain book in a book case. Colors, etc. cannot be used as clues—only terms that describe location.

Library research

Prepare a report on a scientist who made a contribution to astronomy. Names to consider: Tycho Brache, Nicholas Copernicus, Johannes Kepler, Galileo Galilei.

Science Processes: Recognizing and using spatial relationships; Inferring
See also Activity Record Sheet 3-1A (Lab Manual page 31)

CORE   30 minutes   Pairs of students

Activity 3-1A   Using an Astrolabe

Materials

weight
rule or wood slat
string
3 thumbtacks
protractor
paper and pencil or pen

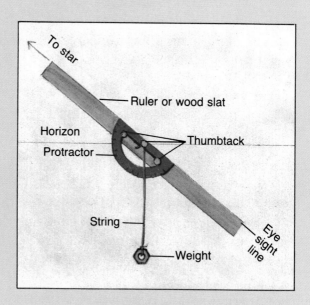

Purpose

To construct an astrolabe and use it to measure the altitude of objects.

Procedure

1. Examine the diagram on this page and construct your own astrolabe. (Attach the weight, on a string, and the protractor to the rule with a thumbtack.)
2. With a partner, measure the altitude of some objects in the room. Point the sighting edge of the stick directly at the horizon. Let your partner read the angle where the string cuts across the protractor. Subtract your reading from 90° and record it.
3. Point the sighting edge to a point directly above you. Record the angle.
4. Standing in the same place, measure the altitude of two or three other objects in the room—perhaps a light on the ceiling or a wall clock. Record your readings.
5. Standing in the same spot you've been measuring from, measure the altitude of the point where the ceiling and wall meet. Record your reading. Take four steps closer to the wall and sight again. Record this reading.

6. Let your partner repeat what you have just done, and you read the angles.

Questions

1. What angle do you get for the horizon sighting?
2. What angle do you get when you point directly above you? What is this point called?
3. What readings did you and your partner get for the classroom objects? Did the readings agree? Why or why not?
4. When you moved closer to the wall, what happened to the altitude of the point where ceiling and wall meet? Did the angle increase or decrease?

Conclusion

What can you say about the relationship between altitude and the observer? What about latitude-longitude and the observer?

horizon has an altitude of 0°, while a star sighted directly over-head has an altitude of 90°. Both of these altitude measure-ments are made with respect to the observer. This point on the celestial sphere, which is directly over the head of the ob-server, is called the **zenith** (ZEE′-nith). The point on the ce-lestial sphere directly below the observer's feet is called the **nadir** (NAY′-dur).

Where on the celestial sphere is the zenith?

Notice that the altitude of a star is given with respect to the observer. The altitude of a star can vary greatly, depending on the location of the observer. Take, for instance, the alti-tude of **Polaris** (pō-LAIR′-is), which is also called the North Star. At the earth's North Pole, Polaris is directly over the head of the observer and therefore has an altitude of 90°. At the equator, however, the altitude of Polaris is 0°. An observer standing at the equator can therefore expect Polaris to appear on the horizon.

If you recall what the latitude is at the equator and at the North Pole, you may have noticed the relationship between the altitude of Polaris and the latitude of the observer. At the equator, which is 0° latitude, the altitude of Polaris is 0°. At the North Pole, which is at 90° N latitude, the altitude of Po-laris is 90°. If you lived at 39° N latitude, you could expect to find Polaris at an altitude of 39°. Latitude in the Northern Hemisphere can be determined by measuring the altitude of Polaris above the horizon.

In the activity on page 124, students will find the altitude of Polaris and compare it with the latitude of their community.

To find all other stars on the celestial sphere from a partic-ular location on Earth, only knowing the altitude is not enough. You also need a second measurement, just as you do to locate a place on the earth's surface. A star with an altitude of 45° could be anywhere on an imaginary circle 45° above the horizon. You need to know where it is located on that imaginary circle. This second measurement used to locate a star is called the star's azimuth.

The **azimuth** (AZ′-uh-muth) of a star is its distance in de-grees around the horizon measured from true north. Azi-muth begins at true north and runs completely around the horizon, 360° in a clockwise direction, until it reaches true north again. This makes the azimuth of a star like Polaris, which is true north, either 0° or 360°.

Science Processes: Recognizing and using spatial relationships; Inferring
See also Activity Record Sheet 3-1B (Lab Manual page 32)

20 minutes

Pairs of observers

Activity 3-1B   Finding the Altitude of Polaris

Materials

astrolabe constructed for the
 Activity on page 122

Purpose

To find your latitude by measuring
the altitude of Polaris.

Procedure

1. On the next clear night, locate the Big Dipper and then find Polaris. The illustration on
   this page shows how the "pointer stars" can
   help you find Polaris.
2. Use your astrolabe to measure the altitude of
   Polaris. It would be helpful if you had someone with you to read the angle on your astrolabe. Subtract your reading from 90°.
3. Record the altitude you measure for Polaris.
4. Check with your teacher or a map of your
   area and find the actual latitude of your community.

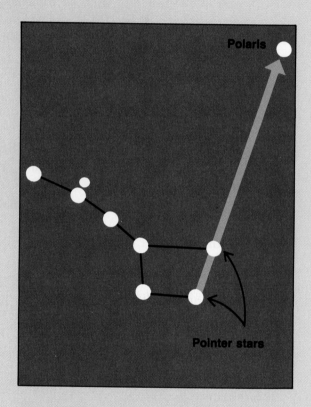

Question

How does the altitude you found for Polaris
compare with the latitude of your community?

Conclusion

Explain the relationship between the altitude of
Polaris and the latitude of a place where an observer stands.

Answers to Questions
1. The reading for the altitude of Polaris should be
   the same as the latitude of your community.
Conclusion
In the Northern Hemisphere, the altitude of Polaris is
always the same as the latitude of the place where
an observer stands.

Teaching Suggestion
Depending on location, observers may have difficulty
locating Polaris. Polaris is not that bright, even in an
area far from city lights. But using the pointer stars in
the Big Dipper should help. And the search itself will
be useful because of other inevitable conclusions.

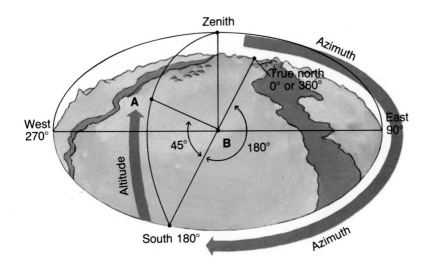

Figure 3-5. The star at Point A is located at an azimuth of 180° and an altitude of 45°. Where is the observer standing?
The observer is standing in the center, directly under the zenith.

Using altitude and azimuth to find objects on the celestial sphere has one problem. If the stars remained fixed in the same position at all times, they would be easy to find. But stars change their positions relative to the horizon throughout the night. For example, at 8:00 p.m. a star may have an altitude of 0° and an azimuth of 90°. By 2:00 a.m. it will have moved across the sky to a different altitude of about 50° and an azimuth of 180°. This movement would make it very hard for you to describe the star's location to a friend. You would have to pick a particular time of the night—and a particular date—as part of your description.

It would be even harder for you to tell a friend where to look if you and your friend lived in different parts of the country. For example, if you lived at a latitude of 43° N, Polaris has an altitude of 43°. Its azimuth is 0°. What happens if you write your friend a letter saying to look for Polaris at an altitude of 43° N and an azimuth of 0°? If your friend lives at 22° N latitude, he or she will not find Polaris at the location you described. For your friend, Polaris is only 22° above the horizon, not 43°. (Polaris has the same azimuth of 0° for all observers in the Northern Hemisphere.) Your friend would need additional information in order to locate the star that you have chosen.

By rotating a star map (see Appendix), students can get an idea of how constellations in the Northern Hemisphere move with respect to Polaris. Interested students could choose a constellation and make drawings that show how that constellation moves during a 12-hour period.

Science Processes: Communicating through a chart; Recognizing and using spatial relationships; Predicting

See also Activity Record Sheet 3-1C (Lab Manual page 33)

Activity 3-1C   Plotting the Paths of Four Stars

Materials

astrolabe constructed for use in the Activity on page 122

flashlight

Purpose

To follow the paths of four stars across the sky during one evening.

Procedure

1. Construct a table similar to the one that begins on this page.
2. On a clear night, find a place in which you can observe stars. Try to find a place with little or no outside light. Determine the location of north, south, east, and west by first finding Polaris, or the North Star.
3. Use the pointer stars in the Big Dipper to find Polaris. As you can see from Activity 3-1B, Polaris is located on a straight line with the outer two stars of the bowl of the dipper. Going in a straight line from those two stars, the first star that you come to will be Polaris. Do not be disappointed when you find Polaris. It is not very big or bright. It is just an ordinary-looking star.
4. Once you find Polaris, you know the direction of true north. Identify this direction with some type of marker (a tree, pole, etc.).
5. Choose markers that identify east, south, and west. By turning your astrolabe on its side, you can use it to locate these other directions. East is 90° to the right of north. South is directly opposite north, etc.
6. You should also mark the location on which you are standing. All your observations must be made from the same spot. (Use chalk if you are standing on a hard surface, or perhaps a rock for a grass surface.)

2-3 hours   Pairs of observers

Data Table			
Star	Location at ____ (time)	Location at ____ (1 hour later)	Location at ____ (2 hours later)
North Star (Polaris)	Azimuth: ____° Altitude: ____°	Azimuth: ____° Altitude: ____°	Azimuth: ____° Altitude: ____°

7. Select four stars that can easily be found again. One should be Polaris. The others should be very nearly east, south, and west.
8. On your chart, record the azimuth of each star. You can find the azimuth by using north as 0°, or the starting point. The azimuth of Polaris, therefore, is 0°. A star that is due east has an azimuth of 90°. The azimuth of a star due south is 180°, and the azimuth of a star due west is 270°.
9. You can find the azimuth of other positions by turning your astrolabe on its side. Use the string to measure the number of degrees the star is away from any one of the markers for north, east, south, or west.
10. Find the angle of elevation that each star is above your eye level. Sight the star with your astrolabe. Have a friend, using a flashlight, notice where the string passes the curved edge of the protractor. Always use the reading that is less than 90°. Subtract your reading from 90°. On your chart, record the altitude for each of the four stars.
11. Repeat these readings two more times, at exactly one-hour intervals. Use the same stars each time. Record all data.

Question

How many degrees of azimuth and altitude did the stars move in one hour? in two hours?

Conclusion

Can you predict how many degrees the stars will appear to move in 24 hours? What does this motion tell you?

   Locating other stars in the celestial sphere can become even more complicated. But there is a better way to find objects in the night sky—a way that uses measurements that do not change with time or your location on Earth.

Check yourself

1. In terms of describing a star's location, how do altitude and azimuth differ?

2. How can an observer in the Northern Hemisphere use the night sky to find his or her latitude?

1. Altitude: The height of the star above the horizon; Azimuth: The distance of the star in a clockwise direction along the horizon from the true north line.
2. The altitude of Polaris indicates the latitude of an observer in the Northern Hemisphere.

A celestial latitude and longitude

New vocabulary: right ascension, declination

Astronomers have borrowed the idea of using latitude and longitude to locate objects on the celestial sphere. These two new concepts are called right ascension (a-SENN′-shun) and declination (DEK′-luh-NAY′-shun). **Right ascension** is the celestial "longitude" astronomers use to find objects in the night sky. It is measured eastwards around the celestial equator from the prime meridian in units of hours, minutes, and seconds. **Declination** is the position of objects north or south of the celestial equator. It is the celestial equivalent of latitude. Declination is measured in degrees, minutes, and seconds. The celestial coordinates of Polaris would be written as right ascension 2 hours, 12 minutes, declination +89 degrees 11 minutes. The celestial coordinates of Betelgeuse are right ascension 5 hours 54 minutes, declination +7 degrees 24 minutes. Like latitude and longitude on Earth, right ascension and declination of an object in space is always the same. They make it easy for you to tell a friend how to find an object in the night sky.

What is the celestial "latitude" called?

Check yourself

1. In terms of the units in which they are measured, how do right ascension and declination differ?

2. How are right ascension and declination similar to latitude and longitude?

1. Right ascension is measured in hours, minutes, and seconds. Declination is measured in degrees, minutes, and seconds.
2. Right ascension, the celestial "longitude," is measured eastwards around the equator. Declination, the celestial "latitude," is the position of objects north or south of the equator.

Section 1 Review   Chapter 3

Use **Reading Checksheet 3-1** TRB page 67
Skillsheet 3-1 TRB page 109
Section Reviewsheet 3-1 TRB pages 155–156
Section Testsheet 3-1 TRB page 281

Check Your Vocabulary

4 altitude	1 horizon
7 azimuth	8 nadir
2 celestial sphere	6 Polaris
3 constellation	9 right ascension
10 declination	5 zenith

Match each term above with the numbered phrase that best describes it.

1. The point where, to an observer, the earth and sky appear to meet

2. The imaginary sphere on which all objects in the sky seem to be located

3. A group of stars in which some people have imagined the outline of a person or animal

4. The distance in degrees of a star above the horizon

5. The point on the celestial sphere that is directly above the head of an observer

6. The north star

7. The distance of a star in degrees on the horizon as measured from true north

8. The point on the celestial sphere directly below the observer's feet

9. Celestial "longitude," measured eastwards around the celestial eqautor

10. The position of objects north or south of the celestial equator

Check Your Knowledge

Multiple Choice: Choose the answer that best completes each of the following sentences.

1. The pointer stars in the bowl of the Big Dipper point toward __?__ .
   - a) Sirius
   - b) Polaris
   - c) Orion's belt
   - d) Canis Major

2. Rigel and Betelgeuse are __?__ .
   - a) stars
   - b) star groups
   - c) constellations
   - d) imaginary

3. Azimuth and altitude are used to describe the __?__ of a star.
   - a) brightness
   - b) latitude
   - c) color
   - d) location

4. The stars are really located __?__ .
   - a) on a huge dome
   - b) on the horizon
   - c) at many different distances from the earth
   - d) directly above an observer's head

5. At the __?__ , the altitude of Polaris is 0°.
   - a) North Pole
   - b) South Pole
   - c) equator
   - d) North or South Pole

Check Your Understanding

1. Describe the celestial sphere. Include an explanation of where the center of the celestial sphere is located.

2. Is the horizon the same for all observers? Explain.

3. Does the zenith change as the observer changes position on the earth? Explain.

4. List the azimuth of north, east, south, and west.

5. Describe two evidences of motion that are provided by the night sky.

Earth Motions   Section 2

Section 2 of Chapter 3 is divided into seven parts:

The earth rotates

Evidence of the earth's rotation

The time of day

The earth revolves

Evidence of the earth's revolution

The seasons

Natural timekeepers

Learner Objectives
1. To identify evidence of the earth's rotation and its revolution.
2. To explain the Coriolis effect.
3. To understand how the time of day is calculated.
4. To describe the Doppler effect.
5. To cite evidence that the earth's axis is tilted 23.5° off the vertical.
6. To relate the earth's seasons to the inclination of its axis.
7. To relate a calendar to the earth's revolution.

Figure 3-6. This space satellite travels in an orbit around the earth. How is the earth similar to a space satellite?
The earth is a satellite, too, traveling in orbit around the sun.

Ask students to list changes that take place in the sky once each day. Some examples: sunrise, noon, twilight, evening/night; also, movement of the moon across the sky, if it is at a phase that is visible during the day. In all instances, what appears to be moving—the earth or some object at a distance from the earth?

You have seen the sun and stars both rise and set in positions relative to the horizon during the cycle of day and night. What is moving—the earth or the sun?

Today we know that the daily rising and setting of the sun is caused by an earth motion. The earth is actually turning, or spinning around like a giant top. Once every 24 hours, the earth turns completely around on its axis.

As the seasons change, we also see apparent movement of the constellations in the night sky. But we know now that this apparent motion is actually caused by yet another movement of the earth.

The earth rotates   New vocabulary: rotation, axis, time exposure, star trail

Is the earth's axis a real line or an imaginary line?

The daily turning of the earth is called **rotation.** The earth is said to rotate on its axis. The **axis** is an imaginary line around which the earth appears to be turning. You can observe an axis by spinning a ball and looking down on the ball as it is spinning. The part of the ball that appears to have the rest of the ball spinning around it is its axis.

The question of whether or not the earth has motion has been argued for 2000 years. The followers of Pythagoras (puh-THAG′-er-is), a Greek philosopher and mathematician who lived in the sixth century B.C., believed that the earth rotates on an axis. But they could offer no proof for their belief. There are several simple ways that you can actually see the results of the earth's spinning.

One of the simplest ways we observe the earth's rotation is by experiencing night and day. Because of the solid nature of the earth's lithosphere, the sun's rays cannot pass through the earth. Therefore, only one side of the earth at any given time is in sunlight. The other side is in darkness. The "sun" side of the earth is the "day" side and the "dark" side of the earth is the "night" side. At any one instant, exactly half the earth is the night side, while the other half is the day side.

We can also infer the earth's rotation by the apparent rising and setting of the sun, moon, stars, and planets in the sky. You can see how much the earth moves by watching the stars in the night sky. For instance, if you were to stand on the equator and observe a star's location above the eastern horizon twice, once at exactly 7:00 pm and once again at 8:00 pm, you would find that the star had "risen" 15°. Likewise, at 9:00 pm it would have risen another 15°. Why is this so? This is because in the course of one day (24 hours), the earth makes one complete rotation (360°), or 15° an hour..

If you have ever looked at a star at different times on the same night, you have seen that the star changes its position in the sky. But the motion is too slow for you to watch directly. In fact, you would have to watch the position of a star relative to the horizon for about 15 minutes before you noticed that it had moved. Figure 3-7 shows how the position of the Big Dipper changes over a period of six hours. At 7:00 p.m., the handle of the Big Dipper pointed up and toward the observer's left. At 1:00 a.m., the handle of the Big Dipper pointed down toward the horizon. In another six hours, at 7:00 a.m., the Big Dipper would have completed another quarter turn. Its handle would be curving off to the observer's right.

One way to show this motion is to take a time exposure with a camera. In a **time exposure,** the shutter of the camera is kept open so that the movement of the objects is indicated by a blur on the developed film. Imagine that you took a time exposure of some stars in the sky. What would you find on the film after the shutter had been open for several hours? You would see a blurry line, or **star trail,** that is a record of the star as the earth's spinning moved it across the sky.

Figure 3-7 also shows the relationship between the Big Dipper and Polaris. You can see that the two stars that form the outside edge of the Big Dipper's bowl point to Polaris. Even as the Big Dipper changes position, those two pointer stars will still lead your eye to Polaris.

Figure 3-8 on page 132 shows a time exposure of the northern night sky. While this time exposure was being made, the camera was being pointed toward Polaris, which is located very close to the center of the star trails. Why do all the other stars who left trails on the camera's film appear to be circling Polaris? Because Polaris is located very close to the point located directly over the earth's axis.

We have made some simple observations of the earth's rotation. What is some of the proof that our planet rotates?

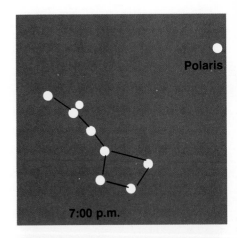

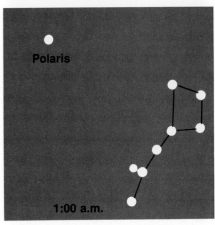

Figure 3-7. In six hours, the Big Dipper changed from the position on the top to the position on the botton. How would the Big Dipper appear in another six hours?

To see how the Big Dipper in Figure 3-6 would appear in another six hours, students can watch what happens to the 1:00 a.m. position when they rotate the book 90° in a counterclockwise direction.

Figure 3-8. The photograph is a time exposure of the night sky. What are the curved lines? The curved lines are a record of the motion of the stars during the time that the shutter of the camera was held open.

1. One half; one half
2. Star trails are curved lines made on film during a time exposure. The curved lines indicate the movement of stars over the period of time the film was exposed.

Check yourself

1. At any one moment, exactly how much of the earth is in darkness? How much is in daylight?

2. Describe how star trails are evidence of motion.

Evidence of the earth's rotation
New vocabulary: deflect, Coriolis effect

In 1851 Jean Foucault (ZHON′ foo-KO′), a French physicist, developed a device that demonstrated the earth's rotation to many people. Foucault set a pendulum swinging in a north-south line. Once a pendulum is set in motion, it will tend to continue swinging in the same direction. Foucault noticed, however, that the pendulum appeared to shift away from the north-south line in a clockwise direction. Foucault realized that it was not the pendulum that was changing direction.

seem to be deflected, or turned aside, toward their right. In the Southern Hemisphere, objects are deflected toward their left. This so-called deflection of freely moving objects was first explained in 1835 by Gaspard de Coriolis, a French mathematician. As a result, this phenomena is known as the **Coriolis effect** (kor′-ee-O′-lis uh-FEKT′).

Suppose you live in Houston, Texas, which is located at 30° north latitude. You have a friend who lives in Minneapolis, Minnesota, which is at 45° north latitude. Because you are in Houston, you are traveling at 1446 kilometers per hour (km/h) toward the east. Your friend in Minneapolis is traveling at only 1183 km/h.

Imagine that you decide to fire a rocket with a message in it due north to your friend in Minneapolis. Since you have a rotational speed of 1446 km/h, the rocket also has this sideways speed at the time it is fired. As the rocket heads north, it seems to be deflected to the east and comes down in Milwaukee, Wisconsin. Arrow B in Figure 3-10 shows this deflection, which is caused by the difference in the rotational speed of the earth at different latitudes. Minneapolis was not rotating as rapidly toward the east as Houston, where you launched the rocket.

What if your friend in Minneapolis fires a message rocket due south to you in Houston? It would seem to be deflected to the west, coming down in San Antonio, Texas. Arrow C in Figure 3-10 indicates the path of the rocket when it is fired from a slower moving location on the earth toward a faster moving location.

The Coriolis effect also causes the earth's wind patterns and ocean currents to be deflected. Both the air near the earth's surface and the oceans' currents would flow mostly north and south in straight lines. But because of the Coriolis effect, these north-south patterns seem to move in a curved path. This deflection greatly affects the weather patterns and climates of the earth.

You can see the Coriolis effect by placing a dot in the center of a piece of paper. Place your pencil on the dot and try to draw a straight line to the edge as you turn the paper quickly counterclockwise with your other hand. Any line you draw

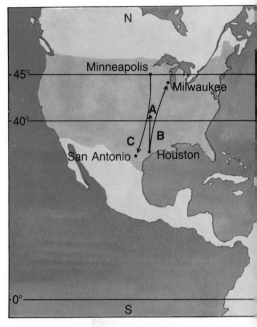

Figure 3-10. Arrow A would be the path of a rocket on a non-rotating earth. Arrow B would be the path above the rotating earth and illustrates the Coriolis effect.

As will be pointed out elsewhere in this text, the Coriolis effect also causes deflection in the earth's wind patterns and ocean currents, both of which affect climates around the earth.

How does the Coriolis effect influence wind and ocean currents?

The Coriolis effect can be demonstrated by spinning a globe or ball and tracing, with a pencil, a line in a northerly direction.

Figure 3-11. What would happen if this child let go while the merry-go-round was spinning fast? The child would go flying off onto the ground.

will curve to its right as it moves from the center of an object rotating in a counterclockwise direction.

Another effect of the earth's rotation has to do with the shape of the earth. As mentioned in Chapter 1, the earth is not a perfect sphere. Rather, there is a slight flattening at the Poles and a slight bulge at the equator. (The earth's circumference at the equator is 40 076 km. If measured around the Poles, the circumference is 40 008 km.) The bulge at the equator is very slight, as is the flattening at the earth's poles. Both the bulge and the flattening, however, are caused by the rotation of the earth.

If you have ever been on a small merry-go-round at a playground, you know what happens on a spinning object. As the merry-go-round is pushed faster, it is harder to hold on. If you let go, you would fly right off onto the ground. This same effect causes the earth to bulge slightly at the equator. This may seem hard to believe because we think of our world as a solid ball. But solids will bend if there is a great enough force applied to them over long periods of time. Also, there is evidence that the center of the earth is not solid, and that the "solid" crust we live on was at one time a liquid when the earth was young. There is also evidence that the crust we now live on is made up of huge floating plates.

The plate tectonic theory is presented in Chapter 10.

Satellites in polar orbit around the earth offer further evidence that the earth is rotating. A satellite in polar orbit crosses from one pole to the other. Each time that such a satellite recrosses a latitude between the poles, it passes farther

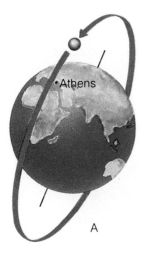

A   B   C

to the west. This indicates that our world is rotating from west to east. If you lived on a space platform, you could observe the landmasses and the oceans appear and disappear as the earth rotated on its axis below you.

Figure 3-12. A satellite in polar orbit keeps passing over the North Pole and the South Pole. In locations away from the Poles, a satellite moves to the west with each return trip.

Check yourself

1. How does the Foucault pendulum demonstrate that the earth is moving?

2. As a freely moving object travels above the earth's surface, the earth's surface is also traveling. How does the earth's motion cause an apparent deflection in the path of the freely moving object above the earth's surface?

3. Is the earth a perfect sphere? Explain.

1. A freely swinging pendulum set in motion continues to swing in the same direction. Any apparent change in direction must be caused by the motion of something other than the pendulum.
2. It causes the path of a freely moving object to appear to be curved—toward the moving object's right in the Northern Hemisphere, toward its left in the Southern Hemisphere.
3. No. The circumference around the equator is slightly more (relatively speaking) than the circumference through the poles.

The time of day New vocabulary: apparent solar time, mean solar time, time zone, Greenwich mean time, daylight-saving time, International Date Line

What time of day is it? Actually, it is possible to choose any one of several kinds of time for any place on Earth. One kind of time is measured from 12:00 noon. As shown in Figure 3-13, the noon position is when the sun crosses the north-south line for an observer. While the earth rotates from west to east, it brings more westerly cities into the noon position. Cities to the east of the noon position begin to see the sun

Figure 3-13. At any moment, a small portion of the earth is in the noon position. When is it noon for an observer in any location of the earth's surface?

It is noon for an observer when the sun crosses the north-south line for that observer (the observer's meridian).

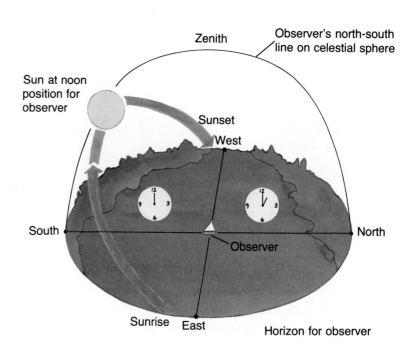

Library research

The difference between mean solar time and apparent solar time is called the equation of time. It varies 16 minutes during the year. Find out the four times each year when the correction is zero. Find out where the corrections for each day can be found.

It is important that students realize that mean solar time (the basis for the time shown on a watch or clock) is merely an average day length.

Time zone lines are bent for convenience. In many cases, towns and cities would be split into two time zones. Also, the lines generally follow state boundaries.

begin to set. Determining time by using the sun is called **apparent solar time.** *Solar* is from the Latin word for the sun.

A second method of determining time is called **mean solar time.** This is the time kept by the clocks we see all around us every day. Mean solar time is based on the average length of a day, from 12:00 noon to 12:00 noon. The average length of a day, based upon one complete rotation under the sun, is 24 hours. It is necessary to use a mean, or average, time because the earth has little variations in its rotation and other motions. These variations cause the length of a day to vary slightly. It would be annoying if we had to keep adjusting our watches every day to take these variations into account. An average day-length of 24 hours is more practical.

It is possible to tell what time it is at any place on earth because of time zones. A **time zone** is a north-south section of the earth in which all the clocks show the same time. When it is noon in Toronto, Canada, it is also noon in Havana, Cuba. As shown in Figure 3-14, Toronto and Havana are in the same time zone. But when it is noon in Toronto, it is only

Time zone lines are bent for convenience. In many cases, towns and cities would be split into two time zones. Also, the lines generally follow state boundaries.

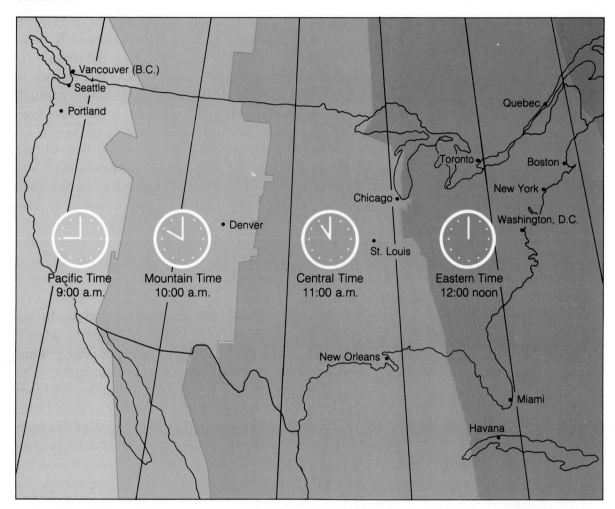

9:00 a.m. in Vancouver, Canada. That is because Vancouver is west of Toronto and is in a different time zone even though it is part of the same country.

Recall that the earth rotates 360° in 24 hours, or 15° per hour. As a result, a place with a longitude 15° west of you will have a time one hour earlier than your time. A place 15° east of you will have a time one hour later than your time. Each meridian of longitude that is a whole multiple of 15° is at the center of a time zone. Meridians 7½° east and west of the central meridian are the boundaries of the time zone. New York City is east of the 75° meridian. All points between 7½° east and 7½° west of the 75° meridian observe the same time.

Figure 3-14. Toronto and Havana are in the same time zone. What is a time zone?

A time zone is a north-south section of the earth in which all clocks indicate the same time.

Eastern time zone: Boston, Miami, New York, Philadelphia, Quebec
Central time zone: Chicago, New Orleans, St. Louis
Mountain time zone: Denver
Pacific time zone: San Francisco, Seattle, Vancouver

Library research

Find out why daylight-saving time was used during World War II. Why is it used today? Can daylight-saving time be used to save energy?

The blue line between 135° and 165° is bent so that all of the Hawaiian Islands are in the same time zone. The International Date Line is bent to allow other islands and countries to be in a single date zone.

Why is the International Date Line not a straight north-south line along the 180th meridian?

Some other times you have probably heard of are Greenwich mean time and daylight-saving time. **Greenwich mean time,** now called universal coordinated time, is the mean solar time on the prime meridian (0° longitude). As you learned in Chapter 1, the prime meridian runs north-south through Greenwich, England. Greenwich mean time is used as a standard for determining time throughout most of the world.

You can use local time and Greenwich mean time to find longitude. Suppose it is 3:00 p.m. at Greenwich and 10:00 a.m. where you live. You are five hours earlier than Greenwich mean time, so you are five time zones away. Five time zones times 15° is 75° away from Greenwich. Since your time is earlier than that of Greenwich, you are west of the prime meridian. You must be somewhere around 75° west longitude. If your time were later than that of Greenwich, you would be east of the prime meridian.

Mean solar time is a standard time that is based on the position of the sun. Standard time can be replaced by what is called daylight-saving time. During **daylight-saving time,** clocks are moved ahead one hour from standard time. This changing of the clocks does not affect the number of hours of daylight in a day. It merely shifts the whole time frame ahead one hour, causing sunrise and sunset to occur one hour later. This is done to provide one more hour of daylight *at the end* of a working day. A sunset at 5:30 p.m. standard time will occur at 6:30 p.m. daylight-saving time. In the spring, the clocks are set ahead one hour. In the fall, we move the clocks back one hour to standard time. This saying is an easy way to remember how to set your clocks: Spring forward, fall back.

Look at the times of the various meridians in Figure 3-15. You can see that it is Friday to the east of the 180° meridian, while to the west of the 180° meridian it is Saturday. From one side of this imaginary line to the other, there is a difference of 24 hours—one whole day. Since a day must begin somewhere on the earth, the nations of the world have agreed that it begins at the 180° meridian. This meridian has a special name, the **International Date Line.**

The International Date Line mostly follows the 180° meridian, which is on the opposite side of the earth from the prime meridian. In some places, however, the date line has been

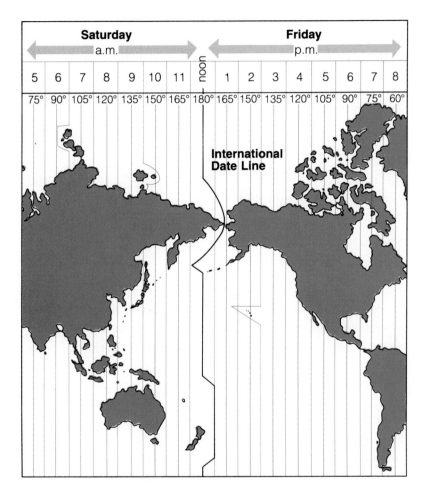

Figure 3-15. When it is Friday to the east of the International Date Line, it is Saturday to the west of the International Date Line. How does this affect the calendar of a ship sailing east across the date line?

When a ship sails east across the date line, the ship's calendar will repeat one full day.

See also Teaching Diagram 3-2A (TRB page 20).

bent to avoid problems or confusion. The Soviet Union, for instance, wanted all of Asia to be on the same side of the International Date Line. And certain islands did not want to be split by the line, so they selected to be either to the east or to the west of the date line.

When a ship sails east across the date line, the ship sails into yesterday and its calendar will repeat one full day. When a ship sails west across the date line, the ship sails into tomorrow, and its calendar moves ahead one full day. When you cross the date line, only the date—and not the time of day—changes. If you were traveling west across the date line at 2:05 p.m. on a Sunday, you would immediately find yourself at 2:05 p.m. on Monday, the day after. If you were traveling east, you would have gone from 2:05 p.m. on a Monday to 2:05 p.m. on Sunday, the day before. When thinking of the International Date Line, this saying may help: East into yesterday, west into tomorrow.

Check yourself

1. What is the difference between apparent solar time and mean solar time?

2. Explain the significance of the saying, "East into yesterday, west into tomorrow."

1. Mean solar time uses an average day-length of 24 hours. The actual day-length, based on apparent solar time, has variations that would require constant adjustment of clocks.

2. If you travel east across the International Date Line, you repeat a whole day, going back to the same time yesterday. If you travel west across the Date Line, you lose a day, jumping ahead to the same time tomorrow.

The earth revolves
New vocabulary: revolution, orbit

You saw earlier that star trails made during a time exposure photograph give evidence of a kind of earth motion that can be observed over a period of minutes and hours. A second kind of motion can be observed only over a period of weeks and months. During this time, there is a change in the stars that appear in the night sky. Some stars and their constellations can be seen only at certain times of the year. Orion, for example, will not appear on a summer night in the Northern Hemisphere. Orion will not be visible in the northern night sky until well into the fall. On pages 622–623 in the Appendix, you can see how a northern night sky in August differs from a northern night sky in April. Why do we see this kind of apparent motion in the night sky? This second apparent motion that the sun and stars exhibit cannot be explained by the earth's rotation. They can, however, be explained if the earth is revolving around the sun.

When we say that the earth rotates, we mean that it spins on an imaginary axis. The diagram on the left in Figure 3-16 shows the earth's rotation. The diagram on the right shows the earth revolving around the sun. **Revolution** is the motion of one body around another. The path that the earth follows as it travels around the sun is called the earth's **orbit.** You have seen pictures of space satellites that are orbiting the earth. At the same time that a satellite orbits the earth, the earth itself is in orbit around the sun.

What is the path called that the Earth follows around the sun?

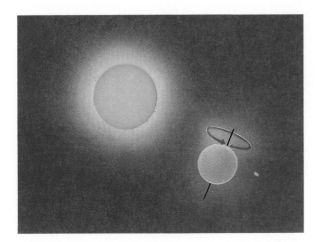 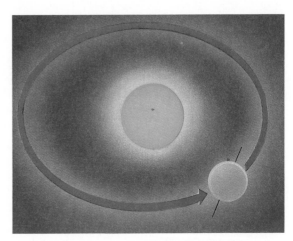

If the earth is considered to be revolving around the sun, then certain changes, like the yearly changes that take place in the night sky, are much easier to explain. Certain stars can be seen in the night sky on any clear night of the year. But many constellations can be seen only at certain times of the year. In the winter night sky, you can see such constellations as Orion, Gemini, and Canis Major. In the summer, you can see such constellations as Scorpius and Cygnus.

The earth is traveling in its orbit about 1° per day. This change in position is so small that you would not even notice it after several days had passed. After several weeks, however, the change in position is noticeable. As the earth continues its journey around the sun, new stars and constellations come into view and other constellations go out of view.

When the summer constellations appear, where are the winter contellations? They become part of the daytime sky. They cannot be seen during the day because the bright light from the sun makes it impossible.

The earth is so large that people do not have any sensation of it either rotating or revolving. Is there any evidence of the earth's revolution?

Check yourself

1. What is the difference between rotation and revolution?

2. Why are we unable to see the winter constellations on summer nights?

Figure 3-16. The diagram on the left shows the earth's rotation. What does the diagram on the right show?

The diagram on the right shows the earth's revolution around the sun.

See also Teaching Diagram 3-2B (TRB page 21).

1. Rotation is the motion of a body spinning on its axis. Revolution is the motion of one body around another.

2. During the summer, the winter constellations are still present. But they are now in the daytime sky, rather than the night sky. The sun's light prevents us from seeing them during the day.

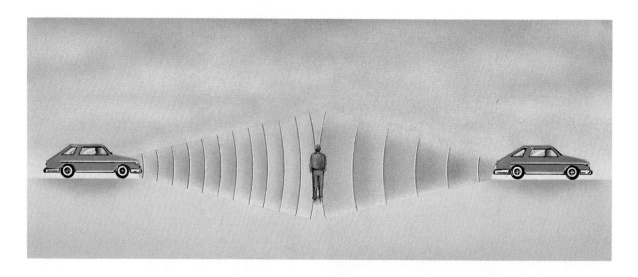

Figure 3-17. How can you tell from the sound of a car horn whether the car is moving toward you or away from you?
If the sound is rising in pitch, the car is approaching. After the car passes, the pitch will get lower.

If possible, put off any discussion about waves and wavelengths at this time. Wave motion will be discussed later in this book.

Students may have heard of the Doppler effect but never really paid attention to it. You can take a tape recorder to the street and actually tape the sound of a car horn as it approaches and then passes and travels away from you. When you play the recording in class, students will be able to visualize exactly when the car horn was even with the recorder and when it was traveling away.

You can also securely tie a tuning fork to a piece of strong cord. Strike the tuning fork, and whirl it above your head. Students will be able to hear a change in pitch as the tuning fork advances and recedes above your head.

Evidence of the earth's revolution
New vocabulary: Doppler effect

One piece of evidence known to astronomers is the **Doppler effect** on starlight. If you have ever listened to the horn of a speeding car, then you have heard the Doppler effect on sound waves. Think about that sound for a moment. How can you tell whether the car is coming toward you or traveling away from you? One clue is loudness. But the other clue is the Doppler effect. As the car speeds toward you, the sound of the horn appears to have a higher pitch, or frequency, than when it speeds away from you. After the car passes you, the pitch of the horn suddenly seems to get lower.

The Doppler effect is named after Christian Doppler, an Austrian physicist who first described it in 1842. The sound waves from a source racing toward you are crowded together, which causes them to have a higher pitch. When the source races away from you, the sound waves spread out more, causing a lower pitch. Sound waves that are closer together have a higher frequency and therefore a higher pitch than waves that are farther apart.

Light, like sound, also travels in waves. Light waves are also affected by motion. With a car, locomotive, jet airplane, or other moving source of noise, the Doppler effect causes a change in the frequency of the sound waves. With starlight, the Doppler effect causes a change in the frequency of the light waves traveling from the star.

Figure 3-18 shows how an observer on the earth can use the Doppler effect to demonstrate that the earth is revolving around the sun. The earth at Position A is traveling toward

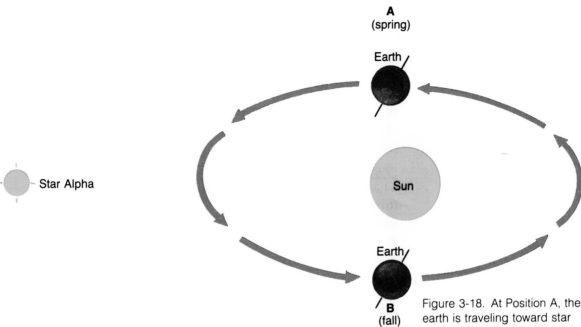

Figure 3-18. At Position A, the earth is traveling toward star Alpha. At Position B, the earth is traveling away from star Alpha. How are astronomers able to know that this is happening? As mentioned in the text, the frequency of light waves that reach the earth from star Alpha is higher at Position A than at Position B. This can be explained by the Doppler effect and by the earth at Position A traveling toward the star and at Position B traveling away from the star.

star Alpha. Six months later, the earth is on the opposite side of its orbit—at Position B—traveling away from star Alpha. The light waves from star Alpha that reach the earth at Position A are not exactly the same as the light waves that reach the earth six months later at Position B. The light waves that reach the earth at Position A have a higher frequency than the light waves that reach the earth at Position B. This change in frequency is caused by the revolution of the earth about the sun.

Astronomers can use this change in the frequency of light waves to measure the velocity of the earth in relation to a star. In Figure 3-18, star Alpha was used as an example. To chart the course and velocity of the orbiting earth, readings from many other stars are also needed.

Check yourself

1. How can you use the Doppler effect to tell whether the horn of a car is approaching you or moving away from you? Why does this happen?

2. How can the Doppler effect demonstrate that the earth is moving?

1. The sound of the horn of a car speeding toward you has a higher pitch because the sound waves are more crowded together and therefore have a higher frequency and pitch. Just the opposite happens to the sound of the horn of a car speeding away from you. The sound of the horn drops in pitch.

2. The Doppler effect also influences the frequency of light waves. Differences in frequencies of starlight are evidence of an earth motion toward and away from the star. The motion that explains this difference in frequencies of starlight and also the six-month "turning points" between toward and away from is revolution.

The seasons   New vocabulary: inclination, Tropic of Capricorn, Tropic of Cancer, solstice, equinox

If you were asked to compare the seasons, you would probably mention that in summer it is warmer than it is in winter. You might also mention that in summer there are many more hours of daylight (not counting daylight-saving time). Changes in temperature and in the length of daylight are features that are associated with the seasons. Everyone is familiar with fall, winter, spring, and summer, but few people understand what causes them.

One of the causes is the **inclination,** or tilt, of Earth's axis. Perhaps you have already noticed something about the earth's axis in the illustrations in this section of Chapter 3. It has not been pictured as straight up and down, but tilted. Look at Figure 3-19. The line from A to B represents the level, or plane, of the earth's orbit as it travels around the sun. As the earth travels in orbit around the sun, its axis is tilted 23.5° off the vertical to the plane of its orbit. It is important to remember that the direction and the amount of the tilt remain the same, regardless of the earth's position along its orbit.

Line AB in Figure 3-19 represents the plane of the earth's orbit as it travels around the sun.

Figure 3-19. The earth's axis is tilted off the vertical to the imaginary line from A to B. What does the line AB represent?

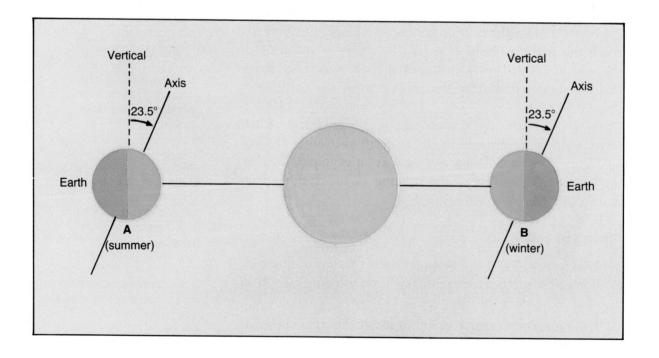

Science Processes: Formulating models; Recognizing and using spatial relationships; Inferring See also Activity Record Sheet 3-2B (Lab Manual page 39)

20 minutes   Groups of 4

Activity 3-2B Simulating the Seasons on Earth

Materials

crayon   plastic-foam ball, 5-7 cm in
light source   diameter
                    knitting needle

Purpose

To show how the revolution of the earth and the inclination of the earth's axis cause the seasons.

Procedure

1. Draw a circle around the middle of the plastic-foam ball. This represents the equator.
2. Place a knitting needle through the center of the ball at a 90° angle to the equator. The knitting needle represents the earth's axis.
3. Tilt the knitting needle to an angle of about 23.5° to represent the inclination of the earth's axis. (Upright is 90°; halfway between the horizontal and upright is 45°; move halfway again toward the upright and you are close to 23.5°.)
4. Examine Figure 3-21 on page 149, and read the text on page 150 that describes equinoxes. Place your model earth in the position of the autumnal equinox in relation to your light source, which represents the sun. Make sure that the axis of your model is pointing in the right direction. Note how much of your model earth is in daylight.
5. Slowly turn the needle so that the model earth makes one complete rotation. Compare the daylight with the darkness.
6. Move the model earth to the next position, the winter solstice. Remember not to change the direction of the earth's axis. The north end of the axis should always point in the same direction, as in Figure 3-21.
7. As you move your model slowly from the September position to the December position, observe what happens to the daylight and the darkness.

8. Turn the earth one full turn in the winter solstice position. Look for a place that receives sunlight all the time. Look for a place that receives no sunlight.
9. Move your model to the position of the vernal equinox. Compare the light-dark pattern to that of the other positions you've tried.
10. Move your model to the position of the summer solstice. Compare the North Pole at the summer solstice with the North Pole at the winter solstice. Move your model back to the position of the winter solstice, if you need to, for this comparison. Be sure the axis of your model is pointing in the right direction.

Questions

1. At the autumnal equinox position, how much of your model earth is in daylight? Is the earth lighted from Pole to Pole?
2. At the autumnal equinox, is every place on earth getting an equal amount of sunlight after one turn?
3. What happens to the daylight and the darkness as you move your model from the September to the December position?
4. At the winter solstice position, is there any place that receives sunlight all the time? Where is it?
5. At the vernal equinox position, is the pattern of light-dark similar to the pattern in any other position? Which one?
6. What is the difference between the North Pole at the winter solstice and the North Pole at the summer solstice?

Conclusion

How does this activity show that the seasons are caused by the revolution of the earth around the sun, by the inclination of the earth's axis, and by the fact that the earth's axis always points in the same direction?

Table 3-2. At what two times of the year is the sun directly overhead at the equator?
The sun is directly overhead at the equator at noon on March 20 or 21 and at noon on September 22 or 23.

	Altitude Readings of the Sun at the Equator			
Time	Date	Place	Altitude of Sun	Deviation from Vertical (See also Fig. 3-26.)
noon	March 20 or 21	equator	90°	0°
noon	June 21 or 22	equator	66.5°	23.5°
noon	Sept. 22 or 23	equator	90°	0°
noon	Dec. 21 or 22	equator	66.5°	23.5°

What evidence do we have that the earth's axis always points in the same direction?

Figure 3-20. The altitude of the sun at the equator deviates from the vertical. If the earth's axis were not tilted, the altitude of the sun at the equator would be 90° every day of the year.

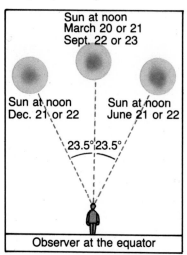

Sun at noon
March 20 or 21
Sept. 22 or 23

Sun at noon
Dec. 21 or 22

Sun at noon
June 21 or 22

23.5° 23.5°

Observer at the equator

The position of Polaris is evidence that the earth's axis points in the same direction all year long. On any night of the year, Polaris can be found on an imaginary line that extends from the end of the earth's northern axis of rotation.

For evidence that the earth is tilted on its axis, consider Table 3-2 and Figure 3-20. They show how the altitude of the sun varies through the year. At the equator, the altitude of the sun shifts from the vertical to a maximum difference of 23.5° twice a year. After each maximum change, the sun's altitude returns to the vertical.

How does this indicate that the earth's axis is tilted? Return to Figure 3-19 for a minute. Imagine what would happen if the earth's axis were shifted to the vertical. The sun would be directly over the equator on every day of the year. There would be no change from the vertical at the equator. That is why a change from the vertical at the equator is evidence that the earth's axis is not vertical to the plane of its orbit.

Two other reasons for the cycle of the seasons are the revolution of the earth around the sun and the unchanging direction of the earth's axis.

Look carefully at the earth in the December 22 or 23 position in Figure 3-21. Note that in December the North Pole is tilted away from the sun. This causes the strongest rays from the sun, or those rays that are most direct (vertical) to strike the earth south of the equator. On December 22–23, the vertical rays from the sun strike an imaginary circle called the **Tropic of Capricorn,** which is at 23.5° south latitude. At this time, the Southern Hemisphere begins its first day of summer and the Northern Hemisphere begins its first day of winter.

Consider the sun's rays in December. The most energy from the sun is reaching the earth in direct vertical rays at the Tropic of Capricorn. The altitude of the sun at the Tropic of

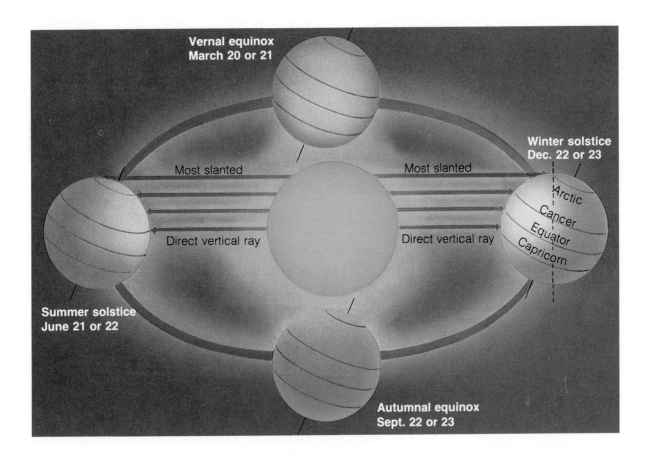

Capricorn at noon on December 22 or 23 is 90°. But in the Northern Hemisphere, the earth is receiving much more slanted—and therefore weaker—rays from the sun.

What about the length of day in December? Look for the **Tropic of Cancer,** which is at 23.5° north latitude. Then imagine where the vertical dark line crosses the earth in December. (Compare Figure 3-19 with Figure 3-21). South of the Tropic of Cancer, days are longer than nights. But north of the Tropic of Cancer, nights are longer than days. In fact, you can see that there is no sunlight at all inside the Arctic Circle on December 22 or 23. At that time, the sun never rises inside the Arctic Circle. The people who live there experience a night that is 24 hours long.

Meanwhile, at the South Pole the opposite is happening. Inside the Antarctic Circle on December 22 or 23, the sun never sets. At that time, the day is 24 hours long at any point between 66.5° and 90° south latitude.

Now look at the earth in its June 21 or 22 position. In the Southern Hemisphere it is winter, while in the Northern Hemisphere, it is summer. Direct vertical rays from the sun

Figure 3-21. This diagram illustrates three causes of seasons on the earth: 1) the earth's inclination, 2) the earth's revolution, and 3) the unchanging direction of the earth's axis.

Students should be aware that inside the Arctic Circle, it doesn't become total darkness in one day, nor is it like turning off the lights. The process is a gradual one, like the gradual dimming of lights at a planetarium.

The days of the solstices and equinoxes vary because the earth's motions are not even.

are striking the Tropic of Cancer, which is at 23.5° north latitude. North of the Tropic of Cancer, days are longer than nights. And inside the Arctic Circle there are 24 hours of daylight. South of the Tropic of Cancer, nights are longer than days. Above the Antarctic Circle, there are 24-hour nights.

June 21 or 22 and December 22 or 23 mark the periods when the sun's direct vertical rays reach their farthest points north or south of the equator. These two times of the year are known as **solstices,** from the Latin words for "the sun stands still". In the Northern Hemisphere, the solstice in June marks the beginning of summer. The winter solstice starts in December in the Northern Hemisphere.

On March 20 or 21 and on September 22 or 23, the sun's direct vertical rays strike the equator. These two times of the year, when the sun crosses the equator on its way to either the Tropic of Cancer or the Tropic of Capricorn, are known as **equinoxes.** The vernal equinox marks the start of spring, while the autumnal equinox indicates the beginning of fall. They are called equinoxes, from the Latin words for "equal night," because at these two times of the year night and day are of equal length everywhere on earth.

Near the equator, there is little change in temperature. Places near the equator receive the sun's rays more directly the year around. Daylight and darkness are almost equal all year. Temperatures near the equator remain hot throughout the year.

At higher latitudes on either side of the equator, however, seasonal changes are much greater. In summer, when the sun's rays are more nearly overhead and days are longer, average temperatures are higher than in the winter. In winter, however, the sun's rays are more slanted and the hours of sunlight are fewer. This results in much lower average temperatures for locations in the Northern Hemisphere.

1. The deviations from the vertical of the altitude of the sun at the equator. If the axis were not tilted, the noon position of the sun at the equator would never deviate from the vertical.
2. When it is winter in the Northern Hemisphere, the sun is more directly overhead in the Southern Hemisphere. Days are longer in the Southern Hemisphere then, and average temperatures are higher.
3. During the vernal and autumnal equinoxes, night and day are of equal length everywhere on Earth.

Check yourself

1. What evidence indicates that the earth's axis is tilted?

2. Why is it summer in the Southern Hemisphere when it is winter in the Northern Hemisphere?

3. What happens during the equinoxes?

Natural timekeepers

New vocabulary: leap year

The rotation and revolution of the earth, along with changing shapes of the moon, are natural timekeepers that are as old as the earth itself. Our ancestors used the changing shape of the moon to keep track of time. The time from one full moon to the next was called a month, a word derived from the word *moon*. This period of time from full moon to full moon is 29½ days. But 12 months only totals 354 days, which does not agree with the length of the year based on the sun's changing position in the sky.

Figure 3-22. Clocks, watches, and other kinds of mechanical timekeepers have been in existence for only a relatively short period of time. What are some natural timekeepers that are as old as the earth itself? The earth's rotation and revolution and the changing shapes of the moon are natural timekeepers that are as old as the earth.

Library research

Find out about other calendars in the world, such as the Chinese calendar or the Hebrew calendar. Are there any other new calendar proposals?

Critical Thinking

Classify the following terms into two groups. What is the major characteristic of each group? Axis, Coriolis effect, day, equinox, International Date Line, orbit, season, solstice, time zone, year.

The earth's rotation: axis, Coriolis effect, day, International Date Line, time zone
The earth's revolution: equinox, orbit, season, solstice, year

1. The earth's rotation (a day); 2) The earth's revolution (a year); 3) The changing shapes of the moon (a month)
2. By 1582, the vernal equinox of the Julian calendar was off by ten days from the actual equinox. This led to a date adjustment in October of 1582 and to the institution of the Gregorian calendar, which is widely used throughout the world today.

In 46 B.C., the Roman emperor Julius Caesar devised a system that was not based on the moon. Caesar determined that the length of the year was 365¼ days long. To account for the incomplete quarter day, it was decided to add an extra day to the month of February every fourth year. The year in which an extra day is added to February is known as a **leap year.** A leap year occurs in years evenly divisible by 4.

The year as measured out into the familiar weeks and month by Julius Caesar is known as the Julian calendar. But even with a year of 365¼ days, the Julian calendar is not entirely accurate. In fact, it is off by 11 minutes and 14 seconds each year. This may not seem like very much, but by the year 1582 the vernal equinox had advanced from March 21 to March 11. That year, Pope Gregory ordered the calendar to be corrected before the seasons and the calendar got even more separated. Ten days were dropped from October of 1582 so that the vernal equinox would once again occur around March 21, beginning in 1583. To accomplish this, October 5, 1582, became October 15, 1582.

Pope Gregory's calendar is known as the Gregorian calendar. To account for the extra 11 minutes and 14 seconds per year, it was decided that century years like 1800 and 1900 would be leap years only if they could be divided evenly by 400. The year 2000, then, will be a leap year, but the year 2100 will not. This eliminates three leap years every 400 years and is enough to keep the Gregorian calendar in agreement with the equinoxes and the seasons. The Gregorian calendar is used widely throughout the world.

Check yourself

1. List three natural timekeepers. What period of time does each indicate?

2. What effect did the vernal equinox have on the calendar as we know it today?

Section 2 Review   Chapter 3

Use **Reading Checksheet 3-2** TRB page 68
Skillsheet 3-2 TRB page 110
Section Reviewsheet 3-2 TRB pages 157–158
Section Testsheet 3-2 TRB page 282

Check Your Vocabulary

7	apparent solar time	20	leap year
2	axis	8	mean solar time
4	Coriolis effect	12	orbit
5	daylight-saving time	11	revolution
3	deflect	1	rotation
14	Doppler effect	18	solstice
19	equinox	21	star trail
10	Greenwich mean time	13	time exposure
15	inclination	9	time zone
6	International Date Line	17	Tropic of Cancer
		16	Tropic of Capricorn

Match each term above with the numbered phrase that best describes it.

1. The daily turning of the earth on its axis

2. An imaginary line around which the earth appears to be turning

3. Forced from a straight line of travel

4. The apparent deflection of freely moving objects above the earth's surface caused by rotational speed differences

5. An adjusted time during which clocks are one hour ahead of standard time to provide an hour more of daylight at the end of a working day

6. A day on earth starts on this imaginary line; the 180th meridian

7. Time based on the sun's actual position

8. Time that is based on the average length of a day, from noon to noon

9. A north-south section of the earth in which all clocks indicate the same time

10. The mean solar time on the prime meridian, passes through Greenwich, England

11. The motion of the earth as it travels around the sun

12. The path that an object follows as it travels around another object

13. A photographic record of an object's motion made while the camera lens was open

14. Changes sound waves as the wave source moves toward an observer

15. The tilt of the earth's axis

16. An imaginary line that circles the earth at 23.5° south latitude

17. An imaginary line that circles the earth at 23.5° north latitude

18. The time of the year when the sun's vertical rays reach farthest north or south

19. The time of the year when the sun crosses the equator on its way to the Tropic of Cancer or the Tropic of Capricorn

20. The year in every four years in which an extra day is added to February

21. Curved line on a photograph representing the apparent motion of a star over time

Check Your Knowledge

Multiple Choice: Choose the answer that best completes each of the following sentences.

1. At any one instant, _?_ of the earth has daylight.
   a) one half   c) one quarter
   b) one third   d) more than half

2. The _?_ is tilted 23.5° off the vertical.
   a) equator   c) earth's orbit
   b) earth's axis   d) star Alpha

Check Your Understanding

1. Describe how the Foucault pendulum demonstrates that the earth is moving.

2. What is the cause of the Doppler effect?

The Moon   Section 3

Learner Objectives
1. To compare conditions on the moon and on the earth.
2. To explain the phases of the moon.
3. To distinguish a solar eclipse and a lunar eclipse.
4. To calculate the diameter of the moon.

Section 3 of Chapter 3 is divided into three parts:

Characteristics of the moon

Phases and eclipses of the moon

Information from the *Apollo* program

Figure 3-23. This closeup view of an astronaut's footprint in the lunar soil was taken on July 20, 1969. From the photograph, what can you tell about the moon's surface?

The soil in the region photographed is dry and powdery. It seems to have the consistency of talcum powder.

On July 20, 1969, millions of people around the world witnessed what was originally thought to be "impossible." Two astronauts, Neil Armstrong and Edwin "Buzz" Aldrin, walked on the surface of the moon. From 1969 to 1972, television screens around the world showed the greatest exploration of human history as six *Apollo* spacecraft and their two-man crews landed on the moon.

Characteristics of the moon

New vocabulary: lunar, satellite, ellipse, perigee, apogee, maria, crater, rille

The moon has been an object of fascination in our skies since ancient times. Long before astronauts landed on its surface, information had been obtained about the moon without even leaving the earth. Although most of this information remained unchanged after the **lunar** (moon) landings of the *Apollo* spacecraft, vast amounts of new information were returned to Earth about the nature and evolution of the moon. (The word *lunar* comes from *luna,* the Latin word for the moon.)

The moon is the earth's only natural **satellite.** A satellite is an object that revolves around another body. A satellite is smaller. Many artificial satellites now travel around our world. The first of these, *Sputnik I,* was launched in 1957.

Figure 3-24. The landing module *Intrepid,* part of the *Apollo 12* expedition, begins its descent to the lunar surface. What does the word *lunar* mean?
The word *lunar* means "of the moon." The lunar surface is, therefore, the surface of the moon.

Library research

Weightlessness is an important consideration in space travel. Find out how the conditions of weightlessness are simulated on the earth.

How does the moon's gravity affect the earth's oceans?

Our moon is one of the largest natural satellites in the solar system. It has a diameter of 3476 km, about the same distance as from New York City to Denver. The moon is about one fourth the diameter of the earth. Once the diameter of the moon is known, its volume can be calculated.

The gravitational pull of the moon is one-sixth that of the earth. If you weighed 120 pounds (about 54 kg) on Earth, you would weigh 20 pounds (about 9 kg) on the moon. By knowing the gravitational pull of the moon, astronomers are able to calculate the mass of the moon. Much of this information comes from measuring the force that the moon exerts on the earth's oceans. This gravitational pull from our satellite produces tides. Since the mass and the volume of the moon are known, the density of the moon can also be calculated.

The moon is a silent, lifeless world. On Earth, the sounds we hear are transmitted through the atmosphere. The moon has no atmosphere, so there is no sound there. Without an atmosphere, there can be no life. The moon also has no water. The force of gravity on the moon is too weak to hold water molecules or an atmosphere.

Temperatures on the moon are extreme. During daylight on the moon (about 14¾ full days on the Earth), temperatures soar to +132°C, while the equally long lunar nightimes plunge to −120°C. Without an atmosphere to hold the heat, it is quickly radiated back into space from the moon's surface.

The moon travels around the earth in a path or orbit that is shaped like an ellipse. An **ellipse** is a smooth, closed curve. It is not a perfect circle. It is shaped like a slender football. If the moon traveled around the earth in a perfect circle, it would always be at the same distance from us. In an elliptical orbit, there is a point where the moon comes closest to the earth. This is called **perigee** (PEAR′-uh-jee′). When the moon reaches perigee, it is about 360 000 km from the earth. When the moon reaches its farthest point from the earth, **apogee** (AP′-uh-jee′), it is 405 000 km from Earth. The average distance between the earth and the moon is 385 000 km.

The moon's surface is very complex. Galileo Galilei, in his lunar observations over 300 years ago, was responsible for naming many of the larger features on the moon. Galileo

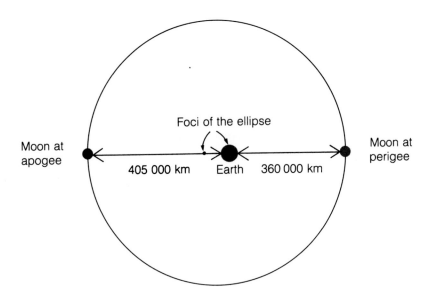

Moon at apogee

405 000 km   Earth   360 000 km

Foci of the ellipse

Moon at perigee

thought at first that the large, dark areas you can see with the naked eye to be oceans, so he named them **maria** (MAR'-ee-uh). (*Maria* is the Latin word for seas or oceans.) Today these dark, relatively level areas are still called maria even though we now know that they contain no water. They are, in fact, ancient lava flows that spread across the lunar surface and solidified.

The moon has very rugged mountains, many of which are as tall as the highest mountains on Earth. Galileo also noticed that there were craters on the lunar surface. **Craters** are holes in the moon's surface caused by chunks of material from space hitting the moon. Some of these craters have long, light-colored streaks radiating from them. Galileo called such streaks rays. Today we know that this is material flung out of the crater from the force of the impact. Galileo also noted cracks in the moon's surface. These cracks are named **rilles.**

What caused the moon's craters?

Check yourself

1. Why is the moon called a satellite?

2. How much closer to the earth is the moon at perigee than at apogee?

1. Because the moon revolves around the earth, which is larger than the moon
2. 45 000 km

Science Processes: Measuring; Using numbers;
Formulating models
See also Activity Record Sheet 3-3 (Lab Manual
page 43)

CORE   Two 15-minute sessions   Pairs of students

Activity 3-3   A Way to Calculate the Diameter of the Moon

Plan Ahead
It is recommended that you pre-measure all the
classroom objects to be used before the students do
the activity.

Procedure

dime, penny, nickel

masking tape

meter stick or metric
  tape measure

Purpose

To use indirect measurement to calculate the diameters of a classroom clock and the moon.

What to Do

1. Assume that you must calculate the diameter
   of the classroom clock but cannot measure
   it directly with the meter stick.
2. A helpful method of direct measurement
   uses similar triangles, which are triangles
   having sides in proportion. Look at the diagram of two triangles.

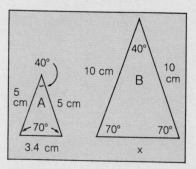

What is the length of x in triangle B? It is
found by setting up a proportion for the similar triangles, as follows:

$$\frac{5}{10} = \frac{3.4}{x}$$
$$5x = 10 \times 3.4$$
$$5x = 34$$
$$x = 6.8 \text{ cm}$$

3. You are now ready to calculate the diameter
   of the clock on the wall. Measure the distance from the wall to the point where you

are standing. It is good to be across the
room and directly opposite the clock.

4. Measure the diameter of your coin. Close
   one eye. Hold the coin at arm's length between your open eye and the clock. Move
   the coin toward your eye until it exactly covers the clock. Have a partner take the meter
   stick and measure the distance from your
   eye to the coin.
5. You now have three measurements and can
   calculate the diameter of the clock without
   actually measuring it. Calculate the diameter,
   using the upper formula in the box.
6. In a similar way, calculate the diameter of the
   moon. The average distance from the earth
   to the moon is 385 000 km. Use the lower
   formula in the box. Place two strips on the
   window as a distance comparison.

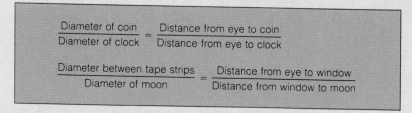

Questions

1. What diameter did you get for the clock?
2. How can you account for variations among
   different measurements of the clock?

Conclusion

Ancient astronomers knew a mathematical formula necessary for calculating the distance to
the moon and so were able to estimate the
moon's diameter. Why can we get a more accurate measurement now?

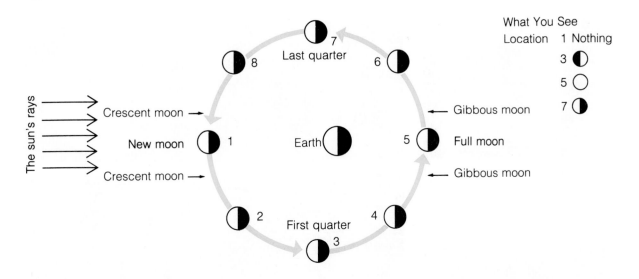

What You See
Location   1 Nothing

The sun's rays

Crescent moon →

New moon

Crescent moon →

7 Last quarter
8
6
Earth
Gibbous moon
5 Full moon
Gibbous moon
2 First quarter
3
4

3 ◐
5 ○
7 ◑

New vocabulary: phases of the moon, waxing, waneing, sideral month, synodic month, lunar eclipse, umbra, penumbra, solar eclipse

Phases and eclipses of the moon

The moon does not give off light of its own. How is it that we can see the moon? The moon, like the planets and other satellites of the solar system, reflects sunlight. Ever since ancient times, people have observed the moon's appearance change from a thin crescent shape to a full moon and back to a crescent. These changes in the amount of the moon illuminated are called **phases of the moon.**

As more and more of the moon appears to be lighted, we say that it is **waxing.** After reaching full moon, the lighted part begins to get smaller. This is called **waning.**

The reason we cannot always see a fully lighted moon has to do with its location in its orbit relative to the sun and the earth. Look at Figure 3-26. In Position 1, you will note that you cannot see any moon because the lighted side is facing away from the earth. From Earth, the moon shows no reflected sunlight, so we cannot see it. In Position 3, the right half of the moon appears lighted.

Notice that the moon is always lighted by the sun no matter where it is in its orbit. Differing amounts of the moon are seen from Earth because of changes in the location of the moon in its orbit relative to the earth. You can also see that an observer on Earth can never see the entire surface of the moon because one of its sides is always facing away from the earth.

The moon takes 27⅓ days to make one revolution around the earth. This time period is called a **sidereal month** (sy-DEER'-ee-ul). It is based upon the moon making one com-

Figure 3-26. When the moon is in Location 1, an observer on the earth cannot see any part of the moon. Why does this happen? Because the lighted half of the moon is facing away from the earth.

See also Teaching Diagram 3-3A (TRB page 22).

Figure 3-27. As described in both your text and in Figure 3-26, the moon changes phase throughout the synodic month. In order, these photographs show the moon on the following days of a synodic month: 3, 5; 8; 11; 14; 20; 23, 26

How long is a lunar day?

Figure 3-28. How often does a lunar eclipse occur each year? Two to five times

plete revolution. The moon also takes 27⅓ days to make one complete rotation. Since the rotation and revolution rates are the same, we always see the same side of the moon facing us in the night sky.

A **synodic month** (si-NOD′-ik) is based on the phases of the moon. It is the time it takes the moon to go from one new moon to the next. This takes 29½ earth days. A lunar day and night are each about 14¾ earth days in length.

The difference between the sidereal and synodic months is caused by the revolution of the earth around the sun. During the first 27⅓ days that the moon is going through its phases, the earth has been steadily moving to a new position in its orbit. The moon needs the additional time of about 2⅙ days to come back to the new moon position for observers on the earth.

The moon's orbit around the earth is tilted about 5° from the plane of the earth's orbit around the sun. As the moon revolves around the earth, this 5° inclination keeps the moon out of the earth's shadow. If it were not for this tilt, the earth's shadow would cover the moon once each month.

When the earth's shadow does happen to fall on all or part of the moon's surface, it is called a **lunar eclipse.** A lunar eclipse can take place two to five times a year. When all of the moon is in the **umbra,** the darkest part of the earth's shadow, a total lunar eclipse occurs. If part of the moon goes into the umbra and part into the lighter part of the earth's shadow,

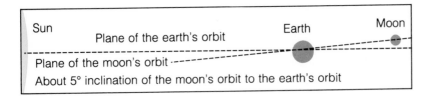

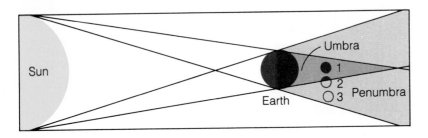

Figure 3-29. The moon's orbit around the earth is tilted about 5° from the earth's orbit around the sun.

See also Teaching Diagram 3-3B (TRB page 23).

Figure 3-30. There are three types of lunar eclipses. What happens during a lunar eclipse? During a lunar eclipse, the earth's shadow falls on the moon.

the **penumbra,** a partial lunar eclipse occurs. When all of the moon is in the penumbra, a penumbral eclipse occurs.

Each month, the moon passes between the sun and the earth. During this new moon phase (Position 1 in Figure 3-26), the moon's shadow sometimes falls on the earth, causing a **solar eclipse.** Usually the moon's shadow misses and passes either above or below the earth. When the moon's umbra falls on the earth, the sun cannot be seen from the part of the earth directly below the shadow, and a total solar eclipse occurs at that location. In order for a total solar eclipse to take place, three conditions must be met at the same time.

1) The moon must be in the new moon phase.

2) The moon must be at or near perigee so that the shadow will reach the earth.

3) The sun, moon, and earth must be exactly lined up.

Solar eclipses are not rare events, but it is much less likely for a person to observe a total solar eclipse than a total lunar eclipse. This is because the moon's umbra on the earth is never more than 260 km (162 mi) wide, and an observer must be within the narrow path of that shadow to witness a total solar eclipse.

To witness a partial solar eclipse, the observer need only be located within the penumbra of the moon's shadow. Since the penumbra covers a much larger area of the earth than the umbra, it is far more common to witness a partial eclipse of the sun that it is to witness a total solar eclipse.

Figure 3-31. In order for a total solar eclipse to occur, in what phase must the moon be? The moon must be in the newmoon phase.

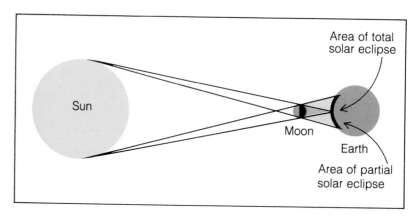

See also Teaching Diagram 3-3B
(TRB page 23).
Figure 3-32. A total solar eclipse
is caused by the moon's umbra
on the earth. What is the moon's
umbra?
The moon's umbra is the darker
shadow cast by the moon.

Check yourself

1. How does a partial lunar eclipse differ from a total lunar eclipse?

2. How does a solar eclipse differ from a lunar eclipse?

1. In a total lunar eclipse, all of the moon is in the earth's darker shadow (umbra). In a partial lunar eclipse, part of the moon is in the earth's umbra and part is in the earth's penumbra (lighter shadow).
2. In a lunar eclipse, the earth casts a shadow on the moon. In a solar eclipse, the moon casts a shadow on the earth.

Information from the *Apollo* program

New vocabulary: meteoroid

The astronauts that landed on the moon during the *Apollo* space flights set up scientific instruments, conducted investigations, and probed the interior of the moon. They mapped the surface and collected samples of rock and soil.

In Chapter 9, earth soils are described as a product of weathering. Lunar soil, however, is thought to be meteoric dust that rained down on the moon.

Evidence brought back by the *Apollo* missions indicates that the moon is covered by a layer of lunar soil that varies from 1 to 20 m in depth. Lunar soil is different from earth soils in that it did not result from the weathering and erosion of rock. Lunar soil originated from the moon's surface being broken up by impacts from objects from space.

Craters on the moon were once a center of controversy. Some astronomers thought the craters were volcanic in origin. Others believed them to be from meteoroids striking the moon. **Meteoroids** are small particles of stone or iron that drift through space. We now know that these pieces of solar system debris are responsible for most of the moon's craters. When these meteoroids strike the moon, they blast out large quantities of lunar soil.

Critical Thinking

Group the phases of the moon at least two different ways. Here's one way: In which phases is the moon waxing? In which is it waning?

Waxing phases: waxing crescent, first quarter, waxing gibbous up to full moon
Waning phases: waning gibbous, last (third) quarter, waning crescent up to new moon
Other answers will vary.

The *Apollo* missions told us much about the different kinds of moon rocks. Since the moon lacks an atmosphere and water, moon rocks are better preserved than earth rocks. Moon rocks are like the igneous rocks found on Earth. Moon rocks contain the same elements and minerals found in most earth rocks.

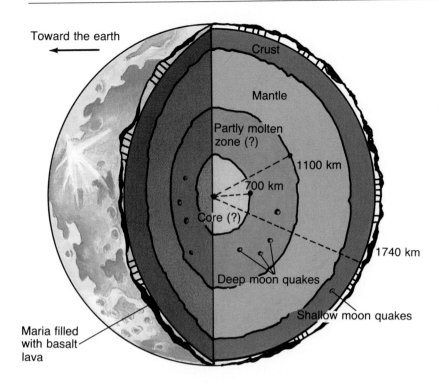

Toward the earth

Crust

Mantle

Partly molten zone (?)

1100 km

700 km

Core (?)

1740 km

Deep moon quakes

Shallow moon quakes

Maria filled with basalt lava

Figure 3-33. On the moon, the basins (maria) filled in with molten rock that rose to the moon's furface. On the earth, what are the basins filled with? Oceans/water

Carbon and water are necessary for life. The *Apollo* astronauts found only tiny amounts of carbon and carbon compounds, but no water. Therefore, astronomers have ruled out the possibility of life on the moon. Instruments were placed on the moon to find out about the moon's interior. These instruments have indicated that there are very weak "moonquakes" deep within the interior.

Astronomers believe that the moon and the earth are about the same age. The moon's surface was molten and cooled slowly, creating the lunar rocks. During this cooling period, the moon was bombarded by huge meteors that created the giant basins. The meteor bombardment subsided, leaving the features of the moon as we now know it.

Heat produced by radioactive material caused molten rock under the moon's surface. This molten rock rose and poured out onto the surface, filling in basins (maria) just as water fills our ocean basins.

Why have astronomers ruled out the possibility of life on the moon?

Check yourself

1. What is responsible for most of the craters on the moon?

2. Why are moon rocks better preserved than earth rocks?

1. The impact of many meteoroids on the moon's surface

2. They are better preserved because the moon lacks water and an atmosphere.

Careers Astronomer / Instrumentation Technician

For further information about a career as an instrumentation technician, contact:

The American Society of Mechanical Engineers
345 E. 47th Street
New York, New York 10017

By means of the computer, this astronomer is able to study data received through the observatory's powerful telescope.
For further information about a career as an astronomer, send 25 cents to
Dr. Harry Shipman
Education Officer
American Astronomical Society
University of Delaware
Newark, Delaware 19711

Astronomer Through the ages, astronomers have been responsible for new, exciting, and at times startling theories. The geologist, the meteorologist, and the oceanographer can tell us much about the earth we live on. But it is the astronomer who helps us to see the earth in relation to the countless objects that surround us in space.

Because astronomers study the sun, stars, planets, and outer space, their area of investigation is much more open to theory and to the need for very powerful and reliable instruments. The information that astronomers learn about the various stars, planets, galaxies, and nebulae is obtained by analyzing light

waves and radio waves that are being emitted from objects in space.

Regardless of the career you finally choose, you can always pursue an interest in astronomy and learn more about quasars and pulsars and black holes. But astronomy as a career is a very limited area. There are not many job openings for astronomers.

Most astronomers teach in colleges and universities or work for the aerospace industry. To prepare for a career in astronomy, or even to be able to appreciate the latest findings of astronomers, take as many courses in mathematics and the physical sciences as you can.

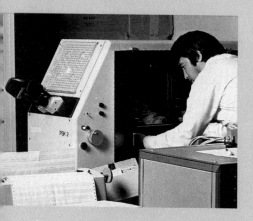

An instrumentation technician is responsible for seeing that needed equipment is kept in good repair.

Instrumentation Technician
Technicians are persons who perform many tasks that help the specialist. Scientists, astronomers, and navigators are desperately in need of instrumentation technicians, who assist specialists in using instruments for data gathering, data analysis, and record keeping. Instrumentation technicians also see to it that the various instruments, machines, and other needed equipment are kept in good running order.

To get a job as a technician, it would be necessary to have a high school education with some basic courses in science, mathematics, and English. It would also be helpful if you had good manual dexterity, some mechanical aptitude, and the ability to organize data. Technicians frequently get on-the-job training or attend technical schools or programs.

Section 3 Review   Chapter 3

Use **Reading Checksheet 3-3** TRB page 69
Skillsheet 3-3 TRB page 111
Section Reviewsheet 3-3 TRB pages 159–160
Section Testsheet 3-3 TRB page 283

Check Your Vocabulary

4 apogee	7 phases of the moon
16 crater	18 rille
2 ellipse	1 satellite
5 lunar	8 sidereal month
10 lunar eclipse	13 solar eclipse
6 maria	9 synodic month
14 meteoroids	11 umbra
12 penumbra	15 wane
3 perigee	16 wax

Match each term above with the numbered phrase that best describes it.

1. An object that revolves around a body larger than itself

2. A smooth, closed curve; not a perfect circle

3. The point in the moon's elliptical orbit when the moon is closest to the earth

4. The point in the moon's elliptical orbit when the moon is farthest from the earth

5. Having to do with the moon

6. The large, dark, relatively level areas on the moon's surface

7. Changes in the moon's appearance

8. A month based upon the moon making one complete revolution; 27⅓ earth days

9. A month based on the time between one new moon and the next; 29½ earth days

10. When the earth's shadow falls on the moon's surface

11. The dark central part of a shadow

12. The lighter part of a shadow

13. When the moon's shadow falls on the earth's surface

14. Various sized particles of stone and/or iron that travel through space

15. What the moon does as the lighted part becomes smaller and smaller

16. Holes in the moon's surface caused by the impact of material from space

17. What the moon does as the lighted part becomes larger and larger

18. Long cracks in the moon's surface caused by the impact of material from space

Check Your Knowledge

Multiple Choice: Choose the answer that best completes each of the following sentences.

1. The point where the moon is closest to earth is called ＿?＿.
   a) perigee   c) an ellipse
   b) apogee   d) a satellite

2. Maria are the dark areas on the moon. Galileo first thought these dark areas were ＿?＿.
   a) mountains   c) oceans
   b) volcanoes   d) plains

3. The dark part of the earth's shadow during a lunar eclipse is known as ＿?＿.
   a) penumbra   c) earthshine
   b) moonshine   d) umbra

4. A lunar day is ＿?＿.
   a) 14¾ earth days
   b) 27⅓ earth days
   c) 1 earth day
   d) 29½ earth days

Check Your Understanding

1. How much of the moon is lighted at any particular time? Draw a diagram that shows this.

2. Explain the difference between the sidereal month and the synodic month.

3. Why doesn't the earth's shadow cover the moon once every month?

4. Explain the difference between a solar eclipse and a lunar eclipse.

5. What do scientists believe about the moon's age and interior?

Chapter 3 Review

See also **Chapter Testsheets 3A and 3B**

Concept Summary

Earth motions, which can refer to any movements of the earth, include specifically the earth's rotation on its axis and the earth's revolution around the sun.
☐ The motions of the sun, moon, and stars across the sky are evidence that either they or the earth is moving.
☐ The sum total of movements across the sky is most easily explained if the earth is considered to be moving.

The earth's rotation is the turning of the earth on its axis once a day.
☐ The Foucault pendulum demonstrates that the earth is in motion.
☐ The earth's rotation explains day and night, hourly changes in the night sky, and the deflection of objects traveling above the earth's surface.

The earth's axis is the imaginary line around which the earth spins.
☐ The North and South Poles are sometimes considered as the points where the earth's axis passes through the earth's surface.
☐ If continued out beyond the North Pole, the earth's axis extends toward Polaris, the North Star.

The earth's revolution is the orbiting of the earth around the sun once a year.
☐ Seasonal changes are most easily explained by the earth's revolving around the sun.
☐ The Doppler effect on starlight is offered as evidence that the earth orbits the sun.

The earth's inclination is the tilting of the earth's axis 23.5° off the vertical.
☐ The earth's axis always points in the same direction, toward Polaris (or away from Polaris, if considered in reverse).
☐ The fact that the sun's direct rays do not strike the earth's surface at the equator year round is evidence that the earth's axis is tilted.

The moon, which is the earth's only natural satellite, is like the earth in some ways and unlike the earth in other ways.
☐ Both revolve in slightly elliptical orbits around larger objects.
☐ Both are thought to have similar interiors and to be about the same age.
☐ Unlike conditions on the earth's surface, conditions on the moon's surface (which include extremes of temperature and no atmosphere) do not promote life.

Putting It All Together

1. What are some models that can be used to help observe the night sky?
2. Make a diagram that shows that the azimuth of southwest is 225°.
3. How many degrees does the earth rotate in 24 hours? in 1 hour? in 3 hours?
4. A constellation is observed at the same time and from the same location each night for a month. After one month, what appears to have happened? Why?
5. From the information given, identify the latitude of an observer in each situation.

Date	Sun's Altitude	Date	Sun's Altitude
Mar 21	90°	Mar 21	0°
June 21	90°	Dec 21	no sun visible
Sept 21	90°	Sept 23	66.5°
Dec 21	90°		

6. What would happen if the earth's axis was upright rather than inclined?
7. Draw a diagram that shows how the earth's position on June 21 causes warm weather in the Northern Hemisphere.
8. If a person starts out in New York City at noon and travels west at the rate of 15° per hour, what time will it be when the person arrives in San Francisco four hours later?

9. Compare the earth and the moon as environments for life. Describe specific conditions that affect anything on the surface of either the earth or the moon.

10. Draw a diagram that shows the difference between a total lunar eclipse and a partial lunar eclipse.

11. Compare the observations of the moon made by Galileo and by the *Apollo* spacecraft. What kinds of data were gathered by each source? How was the data obtained by each source? How did the data gathered during the *Apollo* mission relate to the findings of Galileo?

Apply Your Knowledge

1. Make believe you deliver newspapers. You toss them onto doorsteps as you ride along on your bicycle. In order for a newspaper to land on a doorstep from your bicycle, when should you toss it? Why?

2. Does the sun always rise directly in the east? Explain your answer.

3. If you were travelling around the world, how many times would you have to reset your clock or watch? Why? Under what circumstance would you set the clock ahead each time? Under what circumstance would you set the clock back each time?

Find Out on Your Own

1. You can make your own planetarium with a lamp and a tin can. Many science books with projects tell how. You can actually project constellations. You can also make a slide projector with a shoe box.

2. Keep track of sunrise and sunset for 2–3 weeks. This can be obtained from a newspaper or almanac. Are the lengths of daylight getting longer or shorter? Is the amount of time from sunrise to sunrise always the same? Account for this observation.

3. Sundials were used by ancient Egyptians to indicate the time of day. Build a sundial and demonstrate how it works.

Reading Further

Adler, Irving. *The Stars: Decoding Their Messages.* New York: Crowell, 1980.
   A fine explanation of how astronomers get their information about stars, galaxies, and space.

Berger, Melvin. *Star Gazing, Comet Tracking and Sky Mapping.* New York: Putnam's, 1985.
   Featuring star charts for each month, this book explains how to enjoy looking at the night sky with the naked eye. Included are directions for making an astrolabe.

Dunlop, Storm. *Astronomy: A Step-by-Step Guide to the Night Sky.* New York: Collier, 1985.
   This is a very good reference book on star gazing. It includes tables of planet positions and eclipses that are valid through the year 2000. It also discusses astronomic photography.

Ridpath, Ian, and Wil Tirion. *Universe Guide to Stars and Planets.* New York: Universe, 1985.
   Clear text and exceptional figures of the constellations make this a valuable aid for viewing the stars.

Roth, Charles E. *The Sky Observer's Guidebook.* New York: Phalarope, 1986.
   This book suggests fun outdoor activities to help understand astronomy and meteorology.

Snowden, Sheila. *The Young Astronomer.* Tulsa, OK: Educational Development Corp., 1983.
   This excellent first reference book has outstanding illustrations.

Chapter 4 Beyond the Earth

	Student Resources		Meeting Individual Needs	
Student Text	**Laboratory Activities**			
Section 1 The Solar System 170–192 The Birth of the Solar System 171–172 A Sun-centered System 172–177	Investigation 4-1 Simulating a Planet in Orbit LM 51–52		Enrichment	
Our Science Heritage: A Model of the Solar System 176 The Inner Planets 177–182 Asteroids and Meteroids 182–183 The Outer Planets 185–190 Comets 190–191 Section 1 Review 192	Research Lab 4 Impact Crators LM 63 Activity 4-1 Constructing Scale Models of the Solar System 184 Activity Record Sheet 4-1 LM 49		Enrichment CORE	
Section 2 The Stars 193–211 Characteristics of the Sun 194–196 Characteristics of Other Stars 196–201 Different Kinds of Stars 202–204 The Hertzsprung-Russell Diagram 205–207 Clusters of Stars 207 How Far Away Are the Stars? 209–210 Section 2 Review 211	Activity 4-2A Calculating the Distance to the Sun 198 Activity Record Sheet 4-2A LM 53 Activity 4-2B Observing Magnitudes of Light Bulbs 206 Activity Record Sheet 4-2B LM 54 Activity 4-2C Observing Parallax Displacement 208 Activity Record Sheet 4-2C LM 55 Investigation 4-2 Rotation and Neutron Enrichment Stars LM 57–58		CORE Reinforcement Enrichment	
Section 3 The Galaxies and Beyond 212–225 The Milky Way Galaxy 213–214 Other Galaxies and Superclusters 214–217 Careers: Geoscience Librarian/Solar Energy Firm Owner 216 Beyond the Galaxies 217–222 Thinking Skill: Observing 218 Looking at the Universe 222–224 Section 3 Review 225	Activity 4-3 Simulating an Expanding Universe 220 Activity Record Sheet 4-3 LM 59 Investigation 4-3 Taking a Star Count LM 61–62		CORE Enrichment	
Chapter 4 Review 226–227 Science Issues of Today: Improvements in Astronomic Observations 228				

4

Teacher Resources		Meeting Individual Needs
Teacher's Edition	**Teacher's Resource Book**	
Demonstration 168C Discussion Idea 168C Teaching Thinking Skills 168E–168F Activity Notes 168D Creative Writing Idea 168F Section 1 Review Answers 168F	Essential Ideas 4-1 EI 23–24	Reinforcement
	Teaching Diagram 4-1 TRB 24	Enrichment
	Overhead Transparency S6	Enrichment
	Skillsheet 4-1 TRB 112	Enrichment
	Reading Checksheet 4-1 TRB 70	Reinforcement
	Section Reviewsheet 4-1 TRB 163–164	CORE
	Section Testsheet 4-1 TRB 284	CORE
Activity Notes 168G Discussion Idea 168H Discussion Idea 168H Demonstration 168H Activity Notes 168J Activity Notes 168K Section 2 Review Answers 168K	Essential Ideas 4-2 EI 25–26	Reinforcement
	Overhead Transparency S7	Enrichment
	Teaching Diagram 4-2 TRB 25	CORE
	Skillsheet 4-2 TRB 113	Reinforcement
	Reading Checksheet 4-2 TRB 71	Reinforcement
	Section Reviewsheet 4-2 TRB 165–166	CORE
	Section Testsheet 4-2 TRB 285	CORE
Discussion Idea 168L Activity Notes 168M Environmental Topic 168N Demonstration 168P Section 3 Review Answers 168P	Essential Ideas 4-3 EI 27–28	Reinforcement
	Overhead Transparency B9	CORE
	Skillsheet 4-3 TRB 114	Reinforcement
	Reading Checksheet 4-3 TRB 72	Reinforcement
	Section Reviewsheet 4-3 TRB 167–168	CORE
	Section Testsheet 4-3 TRB 286	CORE
Chapter 4 Review Answers 168Q–168R	Chapter 4 Testsheet TRB 323–324	CORE

4

Learner Objectives

1. To identify the role of the sun in the solar system.
2. To identify factors leading to the acceptance of a sun-centered solar system.
3. To distinguish among the planets on the basis of data gathered from space probes.
4. To construct a model of the solar system.

4-1

Concept Summary

The solar system is the sun and all the objects that revolve around the sun.

Demonstration

Illustrating the Sun's Gravitational Force

Take the class outdoors or ask them all to stand at the back of the room. Attach a plastic-foam ball to the end of a piece of string. Tell the students that you are representing the sun, and the ball represents a planet. Swing the ball around in a circle in front of you. After a few rotations, let go of the string. The ball should fly off in a straight line.

Explain to students that the gravity of the sun keeps the planets in orbit. If the sun were to lose its gravity, the planets would all escape their orbit and fly off into space.

Ask: How do rockets escape the earth's gravity? (They must reach a velocity that allows them to escape the force of the earth's gravity.) Explain that if a planet could speed up enough to overcome the force of the sun's gravity, it too could escape its orbit.

Discussion Idea

Curious Features of the Solar System

Ask students what interesting facts they know about other planets. Answers will vary. You might add information such as Venus' day (243 earth days); Venus' rotation is retrograde or backwards; and the sun rises in the west and sets in the east.

Tell students that the differences between the planets are many, and yet scientists believe they all formed at the same time, along with the sun. Explain that scientists are continually revising their theories about the solar system as spacecraft such as *Voyager 1* and *2* send back more information.

Ask students if any of them were able to view Halley's comet during its 1986 appearances. Discuss the appearance of the comet; use any news clippings or magazine articles you are able to find. Ask students if anyone knows about any new information learned from the comet's most recent appearance.

Activity Notes

Activity 4-1

Constructing Scale Models of the Solar System   page **184**

Purpose   To draw a model of the solar system.

- **CORE** 20 minutes Groups of 4
- **Activity Record Sheet 4-1** (Lab Manual page 49) can be used to record this activity.
- Science Processes: Formulating models; Converting units of measurement; Calculating; Inferring.

Advance Preparation

You will need a roll of adding machine tape for each group of students.

Procedure Notes

Instead of using astronomical units, students may mark off on the tape the distances from the sun to each planet in millions of kilometers (km). Have students use the figures in Table 4-1, page 181, letting 1 mm = 1 million km. If students let 1 cm = 1 million km, the tape roll may not be long enough to reach Pluto.

Students might draw the planets to scale (Step 4) at the scale distances determined in Step 3.

Students might also construct scale models of the planets using clay, and place their models in position along the adding machine tape.

Answers to Questions

1. Another planet might be placed between Mars and Jupiter.
2. The first four (nearest the sun) could be considered minor and the next four major, with Pluto considered as a separate object.

Conclusion

Scientists believe that a planet either exploded or never quite formed in the region between Mars and Jupiter. The asteroids provide some evidence for this.

Going Further

A class field trip to a nearby planetarium where students view solar system displays would be a valuable experience. Have students determine the scale used in the planetarium's model of the solar system and compare it with the scale they used in class.

Science Background

All the essential materials of life on the earth (such as oxygen, water, and nitrogen) are in limited supply except for one—energy. The sun sends out enormous amounts of energy. More of this energy is absorbed by the earth every day than we could possibly use.

It is important that students realize that not all sources of energy are in dwindling supply. While we have "used up" much of the earth's stores of petroleum, solar energy is a vast, largely untapped energy resource.

There are many paths by which energy reaches us, but all of these paths begin with the sun. Here is an example:

The sun emits light. → Sunlight enables plants to grow. → Cattle eat plants. → Beef comes from cattle. (The energy we get from eating beef really came from the sun.)

Energy from fossil fuels also comes from the sun:

The sun emits light. → Sunlight enables ancient sea organisms to live. → Bodies of dead sea organisms fall to the bottom of the sea as sediment. → The sediment is compressed over millions of years. → Fossil fuels form.

4-1

Student Misconception

Often students of earth-space science have little perspective on the space race between the United States and the Soviet Union that prompted the human landings on the moon. Well before their time, the *Apollo* missions and the Soviet missions seem like ancient history. Many students misperceive that explorations of planets and satellites other than the moon have involved human landings. Exploration of other planets and satellites has been restricted to satellite explorations that collect indirect data. A comprehensive listing of the various missions can be obtained from NASA.

Creating an illustrated international time line will help your students gain a perspective for the many space exploration missions. Teams of students can be assigned to research and represent a particular mission on the time line, emphasizing the purpose of the mission and any information obtained by those efforts.

Compiling this collection of mission descriptions will enable students to see the particular planets that have been explored and the nature of those missions. It should also highlight the fact that the vast majority of our information about the other eight planets has been collected by cameras, telescopes, and even less direct methods.

4-1

Teaching Thinking Skills

Observing   page 182

We usually notice only a fraction of the sights, sounds, and smells that our senses actually detect around us. Learning the skill of observation means training the mind and the senses to work together so that we are consciously aware of a greater number of things in the world.

The skill of observing can be developed in two ways. First, students can learn to more equally use all of their senses, rather than relying mostly on sight. Second, they can learn to increase the sensitivity of each sense.

When teaching the skill of observing, it is important to make a clear distinction between observing and inferring. Students often make inferences when they observe, confusing these interpretations with the "facts" of the observation.

Advance Preparation

Have ready five different kinds of powdered substances for *Learning the Skill.* The substances should be a variety of colors, and one or two should have a distinct smell. All must be safe to taste. Good choices are salt, sugar, cinnamon, cloves, powdered pudding mix, flour, gelatin powder, and cornmeal. Each will need a set of the five powders arranged in small piles on a plate or paper towel.

Applying the Skill relies on a teacher demonstration. You need 2 Bunsen burners or hot plates, 2 beakers half full of water, ice cubes or a piece of ice, and 1 or more quartz crystals.

Procedure Note

Learning the Skill should be done in groups. Provide each group with its own set of five powders. Once students have recorded their observations, use the questions on the skill page for discussion.

Perform the demonstration as follows: Place the ice in one beaker and the crystal in the other. Heat both gently (with the same flame height or heat setting) until the ice melts. It may be useful to stir the contents to make the ice and crystals easier to see. For more dramatic results, you may want to continue heating the water until it evaporates.

Possible Student Responses

Student observations of the demonstration will vary. They should state something similar to the following: "Two clear crystals were placed in beakers containing clear liquids. The beakers were heated, and one of the crystals was transformed slowly into a liquid." Any mention of ice, water, or quartz should be identified as an inference.

Teaching Thinking Skills (continued)

Discussion

Begin a discussion of the skill of observation with the following questions:

1. What sense is most used by people for observing? Why is this so? How can other senses be used more frequently than they actually are?
2. What problems might occur if scientists did not separate their inferences from their observations?

Going Further

1. Highlight the skill of observing on a field trip. Field trips present an excellent opportunity to show students how development of their observation skills can expand their world.
2. Nearly every activity in this book uses observation. Make a point of noting this explicitly for each activity, and review the steps of observing each time any kind of observation is called for.

Creative Writing Idea

The following writing assignment may be used to help students recognize that scientific theories are changed and even discarded when simpler explanations are formed, and to help students recognize that we do live in a sun-centered system.

For many hundreds of years, humans believed that the earth is the center of the universe and that the planets, sun, and other stars move around the earth. Complex systems were designed to explain how the motions of the celestial bodies accomplish this task. In the sixteenth century, an astronomer named Copernicus observed that the motions of the celestial bodies were more simply explained by having the planets orbit the sun. Many people were shocked by this concept, considering it a violation against commonly held beliefs. Pretend that you are Copernicus, and write a persuasive article to convince other people of your opinion.

Section 1 Review Answers

Check Your Understanding
page 192

1. The solar system probably began with a large cloud of dust and gas that collapsed inward, and began to flatten out. The massive, hot, innermost part became a star—our sun. Still later, pieces of rock and metal clumped together to form the inner planets. Further out, the outer planets formed from gases. Pluto's origin is not yet known.
2. 1) The orbit of each planet is elliptical, with the sun as one of the foci of the orbit. 2) As each planet, gets nearer the sun, it speeds up. 3) There is a definite proportion between the distance a planet is from the sun and the time it takes for the planet to revolve around the sun.
3. According to the law of inertia, a body in motion will remain in motion with a constant speed and in a straight line unless acted upon by an outside force. The person standing on the moving bus is moving in the same direction and with the same speed as the bus. When the bus stops, the standing person has the same forward motion as before the bus stopped and will therefore continue to move forward when the bus stops.
4. The inner planets—Mercury, Venus, Earth, and Mars—are solid bodies of rock and metal. The outer planets—Jupiter, Saturn, Uranus, Neptune—are gaseous, nonsolid objects. The outermost planet, Pluto, is believed to be a nongaseous solid body.
5. The earth is the only planet known to have an oxygen atmosphere and bodies of water.

4-1

Learner Objectives

1. To describe methods of measuring stellar distances.
2. To identify ways of describing a star's brightness.
3. To identify two kinds of motion of a star.
4. To distinguish among different kinds of stars.

4-2

Concept Summary

The sun is the star that provides the earth's energy and is the star around which all the planets revolve.

A **star** is a light- and heat-producing celestial object produced from a cloud of dust and gas.

Activity Notes

Activity 4-2A

Calculating the Distance to the Sun   page **198**

Purpose   To calculate the distance between the earth and the sun.

- 15 minutes Small groups
- **Activity Record Sheet 4-2A** (Lab Manual page 53) can be used to record this activity.
- Science Processes: Measuring; Applying formulas; Calculating.

Safety Information

Caution students never to look directly at the sun, as eye damage can result. Indirect observation, such as watching shadows, should always be used when making observations of the sun.

Advance Preparation

If students have not done the activity on page 000, have them read the part that explains how a pair of similar triangles can be used to obtain an unknown distance (length).

Procedure Notes

The lens must be facing the sun. The students can then observe the sun's image by keeping their backs to the sun and facing the screen. Either the lens or the screen may be moved to focus the image as described in Step 3.

Answers to Questions

1. The distance to the sun is 150 000 000 km.
2. Students' answers may vary because of inexactness in measuring, errors in arithmetic, etc.

Conclusion

Nuclear fusion produces so much energy on the sun that the resulting heat and light can travel great distances, reaching the earth as well as other planets.

Discussion Idea

Telescopes Expand our View of the Cosmos

Ask students to guess how many stars they can see with the naked eye on a clear night. (There seem to be innumberable stars, but actually only about 1500 are visible at a given time.) Explain that binoculars allow you to see several thousand stars; with a small telescope, you can see approximately one-half million. With larger and more complicated telescopes, scientists have gained direct evidence of over 100 billion stars.

Ask students what questions about the universe they would like scientists to be able to answer. Tell them that in Section 3 they will learn about galaxies and recently discovered kinds of stars.

Demonstration

Comparing Solar and Stellar Distances

Hold a basketball up in front of the class and tell them that it represents the sun. Explain that if the ball is the sun, then the solar system has a diameter of about 3 km. The nearest star would be represented by a basketball 8000 km away. (Ask students to find on a globe or world map a place 8000 km away from where you are.)

Ask students if they remember reading about the constellation Orion in Chapter 3. Explain to them that the nearest star to Earth in Orion is closer to the earth than it is to the farthest star in Orion.

Tell students that in Section 3 they will learn about the size of the universe, the distances to stars, and the ways we try to measure brightness from such distances.

Science Background

The sun is a medium-sized, yellow-white star. Like all stars, it was "born" in a nebula. Nebulae are dense clouds of gas and dust that float in the space between existing stars. As a protostar gains mass, gravitation packs matter ever more densely into its core. This contraction heats the core. When the core temperature and pressure are great enough, nuclear fusion reactions begin to convert hydrogen into helium and the star enters its "main sequence." During this period of its life cycle, the star's nuclear furnace burns steadily for a long time. Astronomers estimate the sun is about 5 billion years old.

A star begins to die when its hydrogen fuel is used up. This changes its internal balance. What happens then depends on the star's mass. Smaller stars become white dwarfs; massive stars explode as supernovas.

In about 5 billion years, the sun's core will begin to contract while radiation swells its outer layers. It will become a red giant. In time, the outer layers will blow off in an expanding cloud of gas called a planetary nebula, leaving a collapsed core the size of earth. Then a white dwarf, the sun will cool until it is completely dark.

4-2

Student Misconception

A *light-year* is the distance light travels in a year. It is generally expressed in miles or kilometers. The term light-year is deceiving to many students because they associate the unit "year" with the measurement of time. Many students have the misconception that a light-year is an expression of time, rather than an expression of distance.

Knowing the speed at which light travels (300 000 km/s, 186 000 mi/s) makes it possible to calculate the distance light travels in a given period of time. Have students calculate the distance light travels in one minute, one hour, one day, and one year. At each step in the calculations, emphasize that the value being calculated is a distance. Be certain to have students express the unit of measure (km, mi, etc.) along with the numerical value. This practice will facilitate the students' ability to associate the term *light-year* with the concept of distance.

The demonstration in Section 4-3 helps students see how the concept of light-year allows astronomers to understand past events in the cosmos.

4-2

Activity Notes

Activity 4-2B

Observing Magnitudes of Light Bulbs page **206**

Purpose To illustrate apparent brightness and magnitude, using light bulbs.

- **CORE** 20 minutes Teacher demonstration or large groups
- **Activity Record Sheet 4-2B** (Lab Manual page 54) can be used to record this activity.
- Science Processes: Observing; Classifying; Interpreting data; Reasoning.

Safety Information

Light bulbs, even at low wattages, heat up rather quickly. Caution students to keep their hands away from the bulbs.

Procedure Notes

You will need to darken the room for this activity. Despite differences in students' observations, they should conclude that brightness decreases with distance.

You might have students use only the lowest watt bulb and the highest watt bulb to illustrate the effect of distance on brightness. Starting with the bulbs together, students can move either bulb until they appear to be the same brightness.

Answers to Questions

1. Students may find that bulbs of the same wattage have been placed at different distances from the observer; this discrepancy illustrates the difficulty in comparing brightnesses with the human eye.
2. Students should find that the bulbs with higher wattage have been placed father from the observer than the bulbs of lower wattage.
3. Answers will vary.
4. Closing one eye makes it even more difficult to judge.

Conclusion

It cannot be very accurate when done by the human eye. We need to use instruments to get additional information.

Going Further

When students have completed the activity, you might use a photographer's light meter to take a reading near one of the bulbs. Move the light meter farther from the bulb and take another reading. Explain to the students that you have shown, with an instrument that brightness diminishes with distance.

Activity Notes

Activity 4-2C

Observing Parallax Displacement page **208**

Purpose   To see how parallax displacement works.

- 5 minutes Individuals or pairs of students
- **Activity Record Sheet 4-2C** (Lab Manual page 55) can be used to record this activity.
- Science Processes: Observing; Defining operationally; Demonstrating; Inferring.

Answers to Questions

1. The toothpick at the far end of the tabletop appears to move when you focus on the near toothpick.
2. The toothpick at the near end of the tabletop appears to move when you focus on the far toothpick.

Conclusion

In this activity, students use one eye at a time to observe parallax displacement from two different points an inch or two apart. When measuring the distance to a star, scientists stay at the same spot on earth, but the spot moves thousands of miles as the earth revolves around the sun. Thus scientists observe parallax displacement from two different points thousands of miles apart.

Going Further

Students might investigate the effect of distance on parallax displacement. Using a longer tabletop made by putting several tables together, students can place the toothpicks farther and farther apart, comparing how far the toothpicks appear to move each time.

Section 2 Review Answers

Check Your Understanding
page **211**

1. For stars that are more than 65 light-years from the earth, the parallax angle becomes increasingly more difficult to detect.
2. The magnitude of a star is based on its brightness as observed from the earth. The absolute magnitude of a star is a calculation of what the star's brightness would be if the star were 32.6 light-years from the earth.

4-2

Learner Objectives

1. To distinguish among three types of galaxies.
2. To describe the leading theory of the origin of the universe.
3. To describe a variety of ways of gaining information about the universe.

4-3

Concept Summary

A **galaxy** is a large system of stars that is held together by gravitational attraction.

The universe probably came into being through an explosion called the **Big Bang.**

Discussion Idea

Is There a Limit to the Universe?

What is beyond the furthest object in the cosmos? Are there other objects at even greater distance?

Tell the students that scientists have come to accept the notion that the universe was created in a massive explosion, or "Big Bang," some 13 billion years ago. And since that event, all the component parts from that explosion have sped away from one another at close to the speed of light. Regardless of how long this has progressed, common sense tells us that there must be a point, just beyond the furthest object, at which there is "nothing."

Ask what is means by "nothing." If nothing is the absence of "something," it cannot *be* anywhere. Point out to the students that the initial problem has become one of language, or semantics.

Activity Notes

Activity 4-3

Simulating an Expanding Universe page **220**

Purpose   To imitate the action of an expanding universe.

- **CORE** 5 minutes Pairs of students
- **Activity Record Sheet 4-3** (Lab Manual page 59) can be used to record this activity.
- Science Processes: Formulating models; Analyzing data; Defining operationally; Inferring.

Procedure Notes

Some of the evidence for an expanding universe is based on observations of the Doppler effect (pages 000 and 000), showing that the stars and galaxies are moving away from the earth. Explain that scientists believe that although the universe is expanding, the galaxies are not changing in size.

Answers to Questions

1. The farther two galaxies are from one another, the faster they move apart.
2. The labels do not change size.

Conclusion

Perhaps the universe will continue to expand forever, and galaxies will continue to move apart. Perhaps the expansion will slow down, stop, and be follwed by contraction of the universe—and its destruction. One theory holds that as the universe expands, new galaxies form.

Science Background

Using a simple telescope, Galileo observed in 1610 that the Milky Way is made up of stars. It was not until around 1930, however, that the concept of the Milky Way as a galaxy began to take shape.

The universe is a giant time machine. Because it takes time for electromagnetic waves such as light to travel from their source to the earth, we see objects in space as they appeared in the past. The sun always looks as it did eight minutes ago, for example. Because light from quasars has been traveling for billions of years, observing a quasar is looking far back into time.

Since their discovery, black holes have been the best explanation for the intense radiation given off by quasars and "active" galaxies. Recently, however, astronomers have found evidence of black holes in two "quiet" galaxies, the Andromeda galaxy and M32. They believe the Milky Way and other quiet galaxies may also have black holes at their centers. This could explain differences between galaxies: active galaxies have larger black holes that are still sucking in gas, while quiet galaxies have run out of material on which the black hole can feed.

Black holes may also hold the key to the fate of the universe. If enough of these super-dense objects exist, the mass of the universe will be great enough that its gravity will someday halt and reverse its expansion.

4-3

Student Misconception

4-3

The very nature of science is rooted in the ability to make observations. As our awareness of the universe has expanded, our need to extend our senses through the development of instruments for observation and measurement has also increased. Students may not have a clear recognition of the significance of the role technology plays in the advancement of scientific knowledge.

Many scientific theories have been advanced or rejected after receiving support or dispute from information gained by technological advances. Consider the development of the telescope, which confirmed through direct observation the presence and motion of celestial bodies. Exploring galaxies and beyond requires sophisticated technology. Cameras; laser technology; methods involving the use of radio, ultraviolet, infrared, and X-ray waves; and technology as yet undiscovered will enable us to advance or reevaluate current theories involving the universe.

Construct a bulletin board or other visual display reflecting the unaided ranges of man's senses. Add to this the ranges of observations now afforded scientists through various instruments and technologies. The display will assist students in understanding the significance of observation in the development of scientific theory and enhance their awareness of current technology.

Environmental Topic

Humans have always sought knowledge regarding what lies beyond the solar system. Until recently, travel to other worlds has been restricted to the mind. Inducement for such adventure has been the question of whether life in space exists and if this life consists of civilizations more advanced than ours. In fact, the central focus of the early 1950s film *Forbidden Planet* was the acquisition of knowledge from such a civilization, the Krell.

Today's sophisticated photographic techniques have revealed the possibilities of other solar systems. Could these solar systems be inhabited? If so, are the inhabitants intelligent and willing to share their knowledge with us? Explore with the students the feasibility of searching for life elsewhere in the universe. Discuss the technology necessary for such a mission, and acquaint students with the problems involved in developing this technology (such as traveling at near light speeds). Also point out that any information obtained would only be available to future generations because of the time involved in the technological development required and the time required to travel far beyond the solar system.

Demonstration

Looking into the Cosmic Past

This demonstration builds on the concept that light years measure distance, explored in the Student Misconception for Section 4-2, and helps students see how the measurement allows scientists to view past events in the cosmos.

Select three students. One will represent an observer on earth looking at a star ten light years away (the distance light travels in ten years). The other two students will represent the star and its light. Position the latter two students, side by side, 3 m from the "earth." For demonstration purposes, let five seconds represent a year and 1 m represent a light year. Draw a circle with a 1-m radius around the observer on earth. When the starlight is on or within this circle, the observer will see the starlight within the next second.

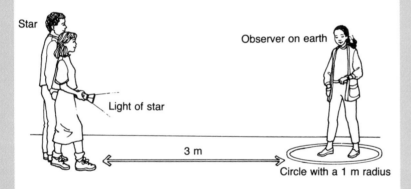

Have the student representing the starlight walk toward the earth observer, at a rate of 1 m per five seconds. Using a stopwatch with a second hand, record the number of seconds that pass before the student representing starlight reaches the circle around the earth. Point out to the students that the earth observer will have aged nine years in this amount of time. Hence, the observer will see starlight that was emitted nine years before. In effect, we can see into the past. Indicate that all this is contingent on a finite light speed, enabling time to pass while light is traveling from one point to another.

Section 3 Review Answers

Check Your Understanding
page **225**

1. The earth is a member of the solar system, which is a part of the Milky Way galaxy. It is located in one of the Milky Way's spiral arms, about 30 000 light-years from its center.

2. *Spiral galaxies* include the Milky Way, our own galaxy. They are giant pinwheels of stars and contain many nebulae. *Elliptical galaxies* range from nearly spherical to very elliptical. They seem to be older than the other types of galaxies. *Irregular galaxies* have no specific shape.

3. The Milky Way, the Andromeda galaxy, the Magellanic Clouds, and NGC 205 are all galaxies in the Local Group.

4. It indicates that quasars may be at the center of very young galaxies seen forming early in the history of the universe.

5. Because quasars formed early in the history of the universe, they are moving as fast as the material in the universe was moving when they first formed. Since quasars have the fastest speed of any object in the universe, they are farther from the center of the universe than other objects.

6. Some galaxies seem positioned as though on the outside of giant soap bubbles, with each bubble touching the one next to it. The centers of these "bubbles" of galaxies appear to be hollow.

4-3

Chapter 4   Beyond the Earth

Chapter Vocabulary

Section 1

solar system
protoplanet
retrograde motions
law of gravitation
law of inertia
greenhouse effect
asteroids
meteor
meteorite
ringlet
comet
coma
Oort cloud

4-3

Section 2

nuclear fusion
photosphere
sunspot
solar flare
aurora
solar wind
chromosphere
corona
nebulae
apparent magnitude
magnitude
true brightness
absolute magnitude
spectroscope
radial velocity
proper motion
Cepheid variable
supernova
neutron star
pulsar
black hole
Hertzsprung-Russell diagram
globular cluster
parallax
parallax angle
light-year

Chapter 4 Review Answers

Putting It All Together   page 227

1. The solar system is made up of the sun, the planets, and the satellites that revolve around the planets. Minor planets called asteroids are found in a region between the orbits of Mars and Jupiter. The solar system also includes many comets and meteoroids.

2. Newton's law of gravitation explains the force of attraction between the different objects in space. Newton's law of inertia explains how the objects in the solar system can remain in their orbits as they revolve around the sun.

3. The largest planet is Jupiter (88.7 thousand miles diameter). The smallest planet is Pluto (1.5 thousand miles diameter). Mercury is nearest to the sun (36 million miles distant). Pluto is farthest from the sun (3675 million miles distant). Venus (7.7 thousand miles diameter) is nearest in size to the earth (7.927 thousand miles diameter).

4. Mercury has an iron core that makes its surface gravity higher than that of the moon. The greater gravity means that when meteoroids collide with Mercury, the resultant debris cannot travel far from Mercury's surface. Thus Mercury has fewer and smaller craters than the moon.

5. Venus has an extremely dense carbon dioxide atmosphere, which produces the greenhouse effect. Radiation from the sun becomes trapped and cannot escape, resulting in high surface temperatures.

6. Stars are hot and glowing because of their production of thermonuclear energy through nuclear fusion.

7. By means of a telescope, scientists are able to make more detailed observations of stars from the earth. A telescope is able to make the star appear closer. By means of spacecraft, scientists are able to observe planets and satellites from space. By means of instruments on the spacecraft, close-up photographs can be transmitted back to earth. Radio telescopes are able to receive radio waves transmitted from objects in space that could not be detected by other means.

8. Stars have a proper motion, which is the change of the apparent location of a star. A star's proper motion is detected only by photographing a star against its background of stars, photographing the star again after several years, and comparing the position of the star to the stars in the background. Stars also have a radial velocity, which is the motion of the star toward or away from the earth. This motion is detected by analyzing its spectrum. A shift toward the blue or violet end of the spectrum indicates that the star is approaching the earth. A shift toward the red end indicates the star is traveling away from the earth.

Chapter 4 Review Answers (continued)

9. Scientists believe that stars begin when clouds of gases and dust begin to contract because of gravitation. As they contract, pressure and temperature increase to the point where a thermonuclear reaction occurs. Some stars end in an explosion (called a nova or supernova). Some stars become white dwarfs, expanding gradually and then collapsing inward.

10. The distance of stars within 65 light-years can be calculated by measuring the parallax angle of the star (the angle to the star from the earth at two different locations in its orbit). For stars farther than 65 light-years from the earth, their distance is determined by comparing a star's absolute magnitude (the brightness of a star if it were 32.6 light-years from the earth) with its apparent magnitude (the magnitude of the star based on how bright it appears from the earth).

Apply Your Knowledge   page 228

1. Answers will vary, depending on student interests. Provision must be made for oxygen, water, warmth, food, and light.
2. Student time lines can include 1) the observations of ancient civilizations like the Greeks, Egyptians, Persians, and Chinese; 2) the periods of Galileo, Newton, Brahe, etc.; 3) the improvements on the telescope; 4) the spacecraft/space probes that began with *Pioneer 1* (Oct 11, 1958); and 5) development and refinement of the radio telescope.
3. Bulletin board displays will vary.
4. A debate will provide a good impetus for students to decide on a problem, find out how much is currently known about aspects of the problem, and then draw inferences based on the data learned.
5. Space exploration, discoveries, and theories are occurring all the time. By means of newspapers, magazines, and TV programs, students can keep up with current space events and can devise a means (bulletin board or otherwise) for sharing this information with others in the class.

Chapter Vocabulary

Section 3

Milky Way galaxy
galaxy
Local Group
supercluster
quasar
Big Bang
Big Crunch

4-3

Chapter 4

Beyond the Earth

Section 1
The Solar System

The earth can be considered as an object in itself, with its own processes and cycles. But such a consideration would be incomplete. The earth is merely one of very many objects in space. Our understanding of the earth in relation to these other objects, and particularly in relation to the sun, will necessarily affect the way in which we consider individual aspects of the earth.

Section 2
The Stars

How far is far? Think of the things that used to be far away. At one time, the other side of a river or lake or forest was far away. As means of transportation developed, faraway places like the other side of a continent or the other side of an ocean or the other side of even the earth itself ceased to be distant.

Modern technology continues to expand our knowledge and our understanding of what is beyond us, beyond the earth, and even beyond the solar system of which we are a part.

Section 3
The Galaxies and Beyond

The Milky Way galaxy was once thought to be all that existed in the universe. Now we know that our own Milky Way is but one galaxy among many thousands. And each galaxy has billions of stars. In many of these galaxies, new stars are still being formed. Our universe did not always exist. Scientists are finding new evidence to support theories of the universe's beginning and probable end. Modern technology is an important part of our efforts to understand even space and time.

Students might mention various systems they have considered in the world of matter. Students might also mention systems they are familiar with from their knowledge of living organisms and biology.

A system is a grouping or arrangement of parts that are interrelated in some way. Systems like the galaxy (NGC 598 in Triangulum) on the facing page are very large. When you consider the earth and its processes, what other kinds of systems can you think of?

The Solar System   Section 1

Learner Objectives

1. To identify the role of the sun in the solar system.
2. To identify factors leading to the acceptance of a sun-centered solar system.
3. To distinguish among planets on the basis of data gathered from space probes.
4. To construct a model of the solar sytem.

Section 1 of Chapter 4 is divided into six parts:

The birth of the solar system

A sun-centered system

The inner planets

Asteroids and meteoroids

The outer planets

Comets

Figure 4-1. These photographs of the earth and Jupiter show their relative sizes. You can also see Jupiter's Great Red Spot, an enormous storm system.

The **solar system** is the sun and all the objects that revolve around it. You have already learned much about two of these objects, the earth and its moon. In Section 1 of Chapter 4 you will learn about the sun as a star and the planets that revolve around the sun. You also will learn about asteroids, comets, meteors, and the natural satellites of other planets within the solar system.

What is the solar system?

The birth of the solar system

New vocabulary: solar system, protoplanet

Our sun and its family of nine known planets did not exist five billion years ago. In its place was a large, cold, dark cloud of dust and gas. This cloud was one of thousands in the Milky Way galaxy. Gradually this cloud collapsed inward. As it collapsed, it began to flatten out like a giant pancake. The innermost part of the "pancake" became very massive and hot, forming our sun. Farther out from the center, pieces of rock and metal clumped together into larger and larger balls. These young worlds, or **protoplanets,** are now Mercury, Venus, Earth, and Mars. The central part of the pancake was very dense. Its outer regions were composed of gases. The protoplanets that formed there are now the giant balls of gas known as Jupiter, Saturn, Uranus, and Neptune. Pluto, as you shall see later, may have had a different origin.

As a cloud of dust and gas collapsed inward, its center (the sun) became very massive and hot. Pieces of rock clumped together to form the inner planets. Giant balls of gases made up most of the outer planets.

Figure 4-2. How might the solar system have come into being?

Dust and gas collapsing inward   Sun forming   Planets forming

Astronomers have estimated that this creation scene took place about 4.6 billion years ago. How do we know, when no one was around to see it happen? Some meteorites have been dated at 4.6 billion years. The earth's oldest rocks are dated at 3.8 billion years.

It is important to remember that no one theory for the origin of the solar system is accepted. Most astronomers agree, however, that the sun and its family of planets, satellites, comets, asteroids, and meteoroids were formed at the same time. Recent evidence has shown that some other stars are surrounded by what may be planetary systems in formation. Further observations of these stars may help us understand our own distant past.

Check yourself

1. Mercury, Venus, Earth, and Mars
2. Gases

1. Which planets are called the "inner" planets?

2. As the solar system was forming, what were the outer protoplanets composed of?

See also Teaching Diagram 4-1 (TRB page 24).

Figure 4-3. Was Ptolemy's system of planetary motions sun-centered or earth-centered? Earth-centered

A sun-centered system

New vocabulary: retrograde motions, law of gravitation, law of inertia

The sun provides us with the light and heat necessary for life. The "day star" is also what holds our solar system together. From about 500 B.C. to the second century A.D., Greek, Roman, and Egyptian philosophers such as Pythagoras, Plato,

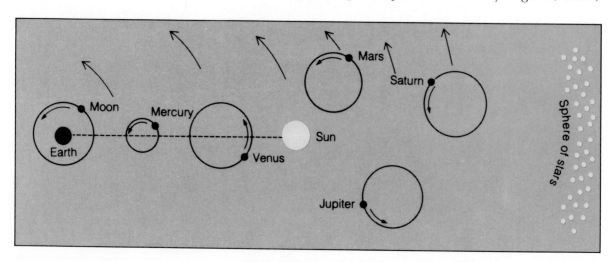

Aristotle, and Ptolemy developed a model that tried to explain the rising and setting of the sun. They tried to understand the motions of the moon, planets, and stars. Ptolemy (TOL′-uh-mee) explained these motions by saying that the earth was at or near the center of the solar system. He said that the earth did not move. All the other objects seen in the heavens moved around the earth.

We can still imagine why these people thought the earth did not move. Since one could not see or feel the earth moving, it was easy to believe that it was the other objects that were moving.

About 1300 years later, a Polish astronomer named Copernicus (ko′-PER′-ni-kis) changed the ideas of the "earth-centered" solar system to one that was "sun-centered." Copernicus studied the motions of the planets. Certain planets (Mars, Jupiter, and Saturn) seemed to reverse themselves at various times. These apparent reversals, or **retrograde motions,** could be much more easily explained if one assumed that the earth and all the other planets were revolving around the sun.

Tycho Brahe (TEA′-ko BRA′-hey), a Danish astronomer, tried to disprove the Copernican system. Brahe made many accurate measurements of the planets. He kept very detailed

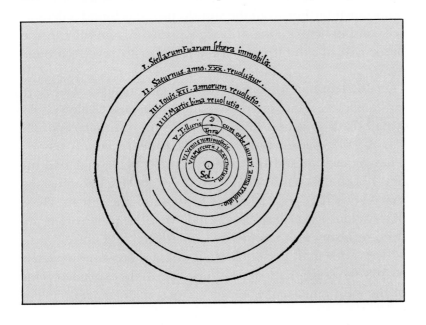

Figure 4-4. Copernicus found it easier to explain the motions of objects in the sky by assuming that the sun (*Sol*) rather than the earth (*Terra*) is at the center of the system.

Figure 4-4 is a reproduction of the diagram that appeared in Copernicus's book *De Revolutionibus Orbium Coelestium* (On the Revolutions of Heavenly Bodies), which was published in 1543. Even though Copernicus was Polish, the book was published in Latin, the language used at the time for legal and scientific works published by European scholars.

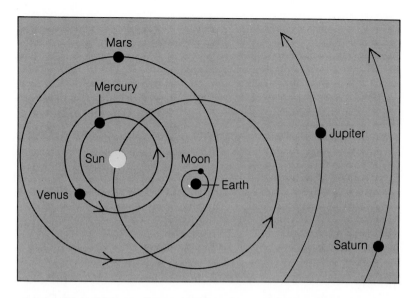

Figure 4-5. According to Brahe's system shown in this diagram, the sun revolved around the earth and all the other planets revolved around the sun.

Figure 4-6. With his telescope, Galileo observed that Venus had phases similar to those of the moon, but with apparent size changes.

1910 Sept 27

1910 June 10

1927 Oct 24

1919 Sept 25

notes of his observations. Brahe developed a theory that the sun revolved around the earth, and the other planets revolved around the sun.

Johannes Kepler (yo-HAHN'-is KEP'-ler), Brahe's assistant, inherited all of Brahe's notes when he died. After much study, Kepler found he was unable to accept Brahe's theory. In 1609 Kepler developed two important theories of his own. Kepler stated that each of the planets moved about the sun in an orbit that was slightly elliptical. He said that the sun was one of two points, or foci, that they went around.

Kepler concluded that each of the planets revolves in such a way that as it comes closer to the sun it speeds up. A planet slows down farther from the sun. Kepler also found a definite relationship between the distance a planet is from the sun and the length of time it takes for the planet to revolve around the sun.

In 1610 an important piece of evidence in support of Kepler's model was uncovered. The Italian scientist Galileo Galilei (gal-uh-LAY'-o gal-uh-LAY'-ee) made his own telescope. He was the first person to see some of Jupiter's largest moons. They moved around the planet in orbits very similar to the orbits of the planets as described by Kepler. He also observed that Venus had phases similar to those of the moon. These observations led Galileo to conclude that the planets were indeed revolving around the sun as predicted by Kepler.

It was not until the publication of Isaac Newton's *Principia* in 1687 that Kepler's conclusions were fully explained. One of the most important books in science, the *Principia* contains

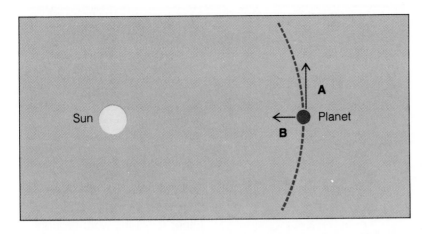

Figure 4-7. If it were not for the gravitational interaction (B) of a planet and the sun, the planet would continue in the straight line shown by A in the diagram. Because of the interaction between sun and planet, the planet remains in orbit.

Newton's famous **law of gravitation.** This law states that there is a force of attraction between every object in the universe. This force is in proportion to the product of their masses and inversely proportional to the square of the distance between two objects.

In words, this sounds complicated. The following example should help you better understand Newton's law of gravitation. Put a textbook on a table. Now place another object, such as a pencil, 1 m away. What Newton said means that there is a measurable force between the book and the pencil. The amount of this force can be found by multiplying the mass of the book times the mass of the pencil, and then dividing by the square of the distance between the two.

Why don't the book and pencil come together? The gravitational force between the table and the objects is greater than the force of attraction between the book and the pencil. The force of friction also helps to keep the book and the pencil from coming together.

Newton also discovered other important laws about the world around us. The **law of inertia** (in-ER′-shuh) is one. This law states that a body in motion will remain in motion with a constant speed in a straight line unless acted upon by another force. A body at rest will remain at rest unless acted upon by an outside force that will set it in motion. In the example mentioned above, the book and pencil are at rest on the table.

What does Newton's law of inertia state about a body in motion?

Copernicus', Kepler's, and Newton's conclusions are important in helping us understand how the solar system behaves. Surrounding the sun are nine planets and their satellites. It is their motion around the sun and their gravitational interaction with it that keeps these objects in orbit. If the pull

Perhaps a student in your class could use a rocket to illustrate the laws of gravitation and inertia.

Our Science Heritage

A Model of the Solar System

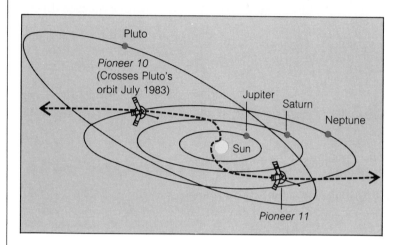

In their attempt to understand complicated processes, scientists create models which incorporate all existing data and theories as to how that data might be explained. The models can also be changed to incorporate new data and new theories.

The present model of the solar system includes nine planets that orbit the sun. In addition, satellite moons orbit the planets. When seen in motion, a working model of the solar system may seem very logical and easy to accept as a fact. But the present model represents centuries of disputes, investigations, theories, and revisions of the working model.

There is much information available about the revisions of the solar system model that have occurred over the years. One major revision had to do with placing the sun rather than the earth at the center of the system. Other revisions were brought about by the discovery of Uranus (1781), Neptune (1846), and Pluto (1930).

The existence of Neptune was predicted because of variations in the orbit of Uranus. It was felt that such variations could best be explained by the gravitational pull of another planet farther away from the sun than Uranus. A telescope directed to the location discovered the planet Neptune, just as predicted.

In 1978, the discovery of a moon circling Pluto enabled scientists to measure that planet's mass, which appears to be far less than expected and not enough to explain the orbital variations of Neptune and Uranus. Until some other massive source of gravity is found, our model of the solar system cannot be considered. Perhaps data provided from the outward-traveling spacecraft *Pioneer 10* and *11* will lead to a more complete model.

of the sun's gravity on them were to suddenly stop, the planets would go flying through space in a straight line away from it. If the sun's gravity were to increase, the planets would need to speed up in order to keep from being pulled into the sun.

Check yourself

1. How does Newton's law of gravitation explain why planets stay in their orbit?

2. What would happen to the earth if the sun suddenly had no gravity?

1. Newton's law of gravitation says that the force of attraction between the sun and planets is strong enough to hold the planets in their orbits.
2. If the sun suddenly had no gravity, the planets would fly through space in a straight line away from the sun.

The inner planets
New vocabulary: greenhouse effect

Our solar system can be divided into the first four planets, sometimes called the "inner" planets or terrestrial (earthlike) planets, the "outer" planets, and Pluto. The inner planets—Mercury, Venus, Earth, and Mars—are those closest to the sun. They are also called the "rocky" planets, because they have solid surfaces.

Beyond the asteroid belt are the outer planets: Jupiter, Saturn, Uranus, and Neptune. They are giant balls of gases, with no solid surface. Pluto is very different from those planets. Observations suggest that it is a solid body.

Mercury, Venus, Mars, Jupiter, and Saturn were all known to ancient peoples. These planets could be seen without a telescope. The planets moved across the sky from west to east against the background stars. Ancient peoples thought the planets were special stars. The word *planet* is from a Greek word that means "wanderer." Table 4-1 on page 181 gives data for all of the planets.

To supplement the data given, interested students could—for each of the planets—gather whatever additional data is available and present their findings to the class.

Mercury   Mercury is the nearest planet to the sun. Too small and close to our star to observe any details from Earth, the first close-up photographs of this planet were made by the *Mariner 10* spacecraft in 1974. Like our moon, Mercury is very stark and gray. It is covered with thousands of impact craters. However, unlike Mercury, the craters of the moon often are surrounded by many small craters, or have bright, linelike rays coming from them. The main difference is that

Figure 4-8 (*on the right*). The planet Mercury is the closest planet to the sun.

Figure 4-9 (*on the left*). Venus, the second planet from the sun, is surrounded by pale yellow clouds.

Mercury has a large iron core at its center, just like Earth. The moon does not. This iron core makes the surface gravity on Mercury higher. When a crater is created on a planet or a satellite, the force of the impact is so great that debris from the surface of the body is blown out of the hole just created. Since the surface gravity of the moon is lower, this material travels away from the new crater. Mercury's higher surface gravity does not allow this material to go very far, so we see fewer craters or rays.

How do astronomers know that Mercury has such a large iron core at its center? Confirming evidence came from *Mariner 10,* which detected magnetic fields on Mercury. Without an iron core, Mercury would not have had a magnetic field around it.

Mariner 10 also found that Mercury has a very thin atmosphere. It is so thin that even someone standing on the planet's surface would need special instruments to detect it. Like the moon, Mercury rotates very slowly. The side facing the sun is very hot and can reach temperatures of 427°C. Mercury may have pools of molten metal. There is also evidence of lava flows. Temperatures on the dark side of the planet drop to −173°C.

Venus   Venus is the second planet from the sun. It is the third brightest object in the sky, after the sun and the moon. Venus is sometimes known as Earth's twin because it has similar mass, size, and density. If we were to stand on the surface of Venus, we would quickly see that this is where the similarities end. Venus has a dense atmosphere of carbon dioxide. Its surface temperature is very high, owing to the **greenhouse effect.** This is the same phenomena that heats up your car

Library research

If you were to observe Venus at various times of the year, you would discover that it varies in brightness. Find out why.

Why is the surface temperature on Venus so high?

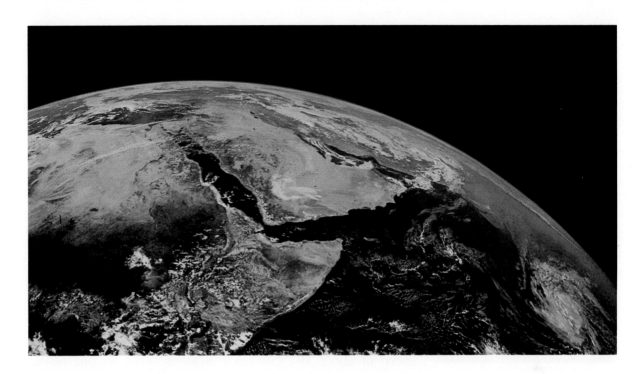

when you leave the windows rolled up on a sunny day. On Venus, radiation from the sun becomes trapped by the atmosphere and cannot escape. Temperatures soar to about 480°C. With such a dense atmosphere, the surface presure on Venus are about 90 times higher than what we are used to on Earth. It would be equal to having two diesel locomotives balanced on your head! The high clouds on Venus contain droplets of sulfuric acid. So, if you were able to step out of a spacecraft onto the surface of Venus, you would be baked by the heat, squashed flat by the atmosphere, and perhaps even burned by the acid—all at once!

Venus is surrounded by pale yellow clouds that prevent us from observing its terrain from Earth, or even from robot probes. The *Pioneer Venus* spacecraft used radar to map the planet in 1978. It found deep canyons and what appear to be volcanoes. Rocks found by unmanned probes on Venus are similar to the basalt found on Earth and the moon.

Earth   Our world is the third planet from the sun and the fifth largest in size. About four fifths of the surface of the earth is covered by water. The remaining fifth is made up of land areas of varied composition and topography. Earth is surrounded by an atmosphere of gases that process energy from the sun.

Figure 4-10. How do water and the atmosphere affect the environment on the planet Earth? Both are needed for life of the earth.

Critical Thinking

Study Figure 4-10. What are you able to observe in this satellite view of the earth that you would not be able to observe from the surface?

Answers will vary.

Because of students' experiences, it is expected that students will be able to provide much more information about the planet Earth.

Figure 4-11. In this illustration, the sun has already set on Mars. The colored rings and the white spot show where the sun has set. They were produced in the computer processing of the camera's pictures. A human eye would have seen a black night grading uniformly to a reddish glow where the sun had set.

Library research

Find out what methods have been used to change the direction of a space capsule while in flight. How are yaw, pitch, and roll accomplished? Draw diagrams.

Earth travels around the sun once every 365.25 days at a speed of about 107 826 km/h. Seasons occur on our planet because the earth is tilted on its axis, which causes different amounts of the sun's energy to reach its surface.

Earth's atmosphere and bodies of liquid water provide an environment capable of supporting life. Earth is the only planet in the solar system on which life is known to exist.

Mars   The surface of Mars is divided into three distinct sections. The Southern Hemisphere has many craters. A second region consists of a volcanic plateau 4 to 10 km in height, extending over about 4000 km. The third section is a low-level plains region found mainly in the Northern Hemisphere. The plains section is composed of a mixture of volcanic debris and windblown sediments. Mars has a thick crust, probably owing to its small size and to rapid cooling.

Besides many craters on its surface, Mars also has a giant canyon, *Valles Marineris,* that stretches along the planet's equator. If placed on the United States, *Valles Marineris* would stretch from New York to Los Angeles. By comparison, Earth's own Grand Canyon in Arizona is equal in size to only one of the small canyons seen feeding into *Valles Marineris.* Orbiting robot probes that mapped the planet also found dozens of volcanoes. Many of them are larger than any known on Earth. The largest, *Olympus Mons,* has a base wider than the state of Missouri. Three times taller than Mount Everest in the Himalayas, the vent at the top could hold the state of Rhode Island.

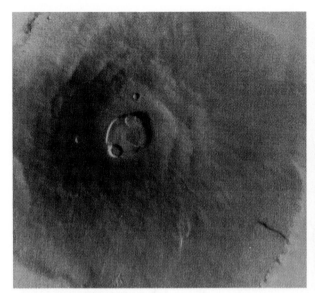

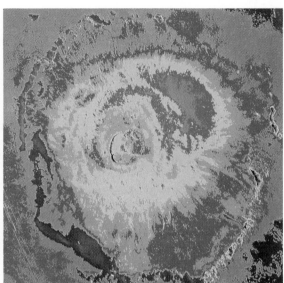

It was once popular to believe that if life were to be found on another planet, it would be found on Mars. One of the reasons for the belief is that Mars has polar ice caps similar to those on Earth. These ice caps appear to grow and shrink, indicating that Mars, like our world, has seasons. The changing seasons on Mars can be explained by the 25° inclination of its axis (tipped only 1.5° more than the earth) and its very elliptical orbit. At its closest point. Mars is 332 million km from the sun. At its farthest point from the sun, Mars is 401 million km away.

Figure 4-12. These two photographs of Mars show Olympus Mons, the largest volcano in the solar system. It is no longer active.

Table 4-1. Which planet takes more than 248 years to revolve around the sun?   Pluto

Planet	Mean Distance from the Sun		Diameter		Period of One Revolution Around the Sun (in earth days and years)	Period of One Rotation on Its Axis (days = earth days)	Number of Satellites
	in millions of km	in millions of miles	in km	in miles			
Mercury	57.94	36	4988.97	3100	87.97 days	58.66 days	0
Venus	108.26	67.27	12 391.95	7700	224.7 days	243.2 days	0
Earth	149.67	93	12 757.27	7927	365.256 days	23.93 hours	1
Mars	228.06	141.71	6759.25	4200	1.881 years	24.62 hours	2
Jupiter	778.73	483.88	142 748.81	88 700	11.862 years	9.83 hours	16
Saturn	1427.71	887.14	120 861.73	75 100	29.458 years	16.65 hours	21-23
Uranus	2871.04	1783.98	51 499.01	32 000	84.013 years	12.8 hours	15
Neptune	4498.86	2795.46	44 578.83	27 700	164.794 years	15.8 hours	2
Pluto	5914.77	3675.27	2414.02	1500	248.430 years	6.33 days	1

Figure 4-13. On February 17, 1977, *Viking 1* digs a trench up to 30 cm deep on the surface of Mars to obtain samples of Martian soil.

Figure 4-13 clearly shows the reddish dust of the Martian surface. Because of the digging, the amount of reddish dust increases greatly in the atmosphere and around the lander.

1. Both have many craters and no atmosphere.
2. Both experience the greenhouse effect: solar radiation becomes trapped, leaving no way for heat to escape.
3. Mars has polar icecaps that get larger and smaller.

The observation of what appear to be dried riverbeds on the Martian surface has suggested that once there may have been enough liquid water to support life. We know that Earth has undergone an Ice Age. Perhaps Mars is experiencing a similar change in climate. The two *Viking* spacecraft which landed on Mars in 1976 searched for signs of life, but with inconclusive results. Further exploration will be needed to prove if life was ever on Mars.

Mars has two tiny satellites, Phobos and Deimos, that revolve very close to the planet.

Check yourself

1. Name two ways in which Mercury is like Earth's moon.

2. What does Venus have in common with a closed-up car on a hot day?

3. What evidence is there that Mars has seasons?

Asteroids and meteoroids

New vocabulary: asteroid, meteor, meteorite

Between the orbits of Mars and Jupiter lies the realm of thousands of small objects orbiting the sun. These rocky and metallic objects are **asteroids.** These bodies, too small to be planets, are also known as *planetoids,* or *minor planets.* The first of these miniature worlds, Ceres, was discovered in 1801 by Giuseppe Piazzi. Ceres is the largest of the asteroids. Its diameter is estimated to be about 1000 km.

Since 1801 thousands of asteroids have been discovered. Astronomers have only calculated the orbits for 3000 of them. There may be as many as 100 000 asteroids that are bright enough to be photographed from Earth.

Where did they all come from? It has been theorized that the asteroids are the fragments of a planet that exploded or was never completely formed. They are in their present orbits because that is where the planet would have been. Some asteroids stray from the others. One possible explanation for Mars' tiny moons, Phobos and Deimos, is that they are asteroids captured by the planet's gravity.

The solar system includes many asteroids—perhaps hundreds of thousands. There are probably hundreds of times as many meteoroids as there are asteroids. As explained in Chapter 3, meteoroids are pieces of metal or rock, measuring up to a few hundred meters across. They drift through space. Like asteroids and comets, they are left over from the solar system's formation.

On a clear night you can see a few meteors streak across the sky each hour. Many people mistakenly refer to them as "shooting stars." **Meteors** are not stars, however, but meteoroids that have collided with Earth's atmosphere, burning up because of friction. The fainter ones you see are only about the size of a grain of sand. Brighter ones are about the size of a garden pea. Sometimes a meteor is large enough that it does not burn up. When it reaches the surface of the earth, it is called a **meteorite.** Some meteorites are large enough to form craters on the earth's surface. Figure 4-14 shows one of the largest meteor craters in the world. The lines along the outside of the crater are roads.

Check yourself

1. What are two theories that explain the presence of the asteroid belt?

2. Why do relatively few meteors reach the earth's surface?

Figure 4-14. This meteor crater in Arizona is among the largest in the world.

How do meteors differ from meteoroids?

1. Scientists believe that the asteroids may be fragments of a planet that exploded or never completely formed.
2. They burn up in the earth's atmosphere because of friction.

Science Processes: Formulating models; Inferring
See also Activity Record Sheet 4-1 (Lab Manual
page 49)

CORE   20 minutes   Groups of 4

Activity 4-1 Constructing Scale Models of the Solar System

Materials

adding-machine tape, 1 m long
meter stick
pencil
data from Table 4-1 on page 181
drawing compass

Purpose

To draw a model of the solar system.

Procedure

1. The distance from the earth to the sun (93 million miles or 149.67 million kilometers) is often used as a standard of comparison for measuring distances within the solar system. This distance is often referred to as one astronomical unit (1 A.U.).
2. Rounding off the distances on Table 4-1 to the nearest million kilometers, convert the distance from the sun to each planet to an astronomical unit. (Since, for example, the distance from the earth to the sun is 1 A.U., then the distance from Venus to the sun is 67 ÷ 93 or 0.7 A.U.)
3. On the adding-machine tape, plot the relative distances of the planets from the sun.

On one end of the tape, make a dot and label it as the sun. Using 1-cm distance for each astronomical unit, place each planet at the appropriate scale distance from the sun. (Earth will be 1 cm from the sun.) Label each planet.

4. Using a compass, a ruler, and the data on Table 4-1, construct scale drawings that show the relative sizes of the planets. (Let the diameter of Pluto be a 1-mm dot and stand for 1 unit of measure.) Begin your drawings at the 50-cm mark on the adding machine tape.

Questions

1. In your scale model of solar system distances, was there a place between any two planets where you feel another planet could be placed? If so, where?
2. In your scale model of solar system sizes, how could you divide the planets into two groups according to size?

Conclusion

Why is there such a big space between Mars and Jupiter? Review page 183 to see what scientists believe.

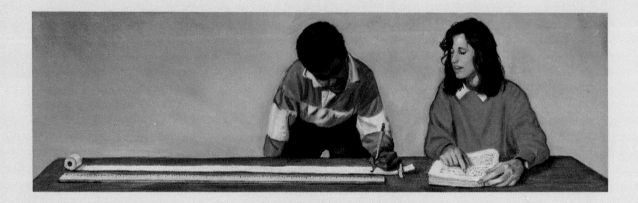

Figure 4-15. In early March, 1979, Jupiter (with the colored bands) and its four planet-size moons were photographed and assembled into this composite picture. The planet and its satellites are not to scale, but they are in their relative positions.

The outer planets
New vocabulary: ringlet

Jupiter, Saturn, Uranus, and Neptune are known as the "outer" planets. They are also called the "gas giants" because of their huge size and nonsolid bodies. Pluto is also one of the sun's outer planets, but it is different from the gas giants.

Jupiter In 1979 *Voyagers 1* and *2* sent back to the earth extensive photographs of Jupiter and its moons. Jupiter is the largest of the nine known planets. It is about 11 times larger than the earth. While it takes our world about 24 hours to make one rotation, this giant of the solar system does it in less than ten hours. Jupiter is a giant ball of hydrogen and helium gases surrounding a small, rocky core. Its rapid spinning makes it bulge noticeably at the equator. *Voyager 1* discovered a thin, flat ring of fine particles that surrounds Jupiter.

Observed for over 300 years, the Great Red Spot on Jupiter had been a mystery. Measurements by the *Voyager* spacecraft have revealed that it is actually a gigantic, spinning atmospheric storm. It turns counterclockwise once every six days. The Great Red Spot is so large that it would take about two to three earths side by side to cover it up.

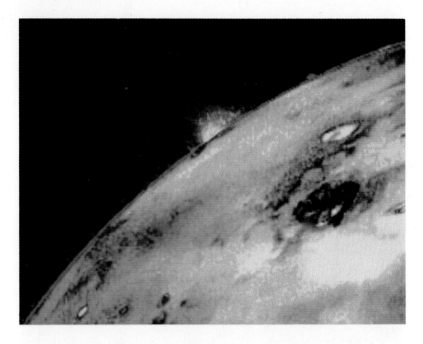

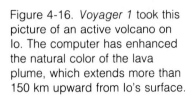

Figure 4-16. *Voyager 1* took this picture of an active volcano on Io. The computer has enhanced the natural color of the lava plume, which extends more than 150 km upward from Io's surface.

Jupiter's four largest moons are named Io, Europa, Ganymede, and Callisto. They were discovered in 1610 by Galileo, using a simple telescope he had made himself. Thanks to larger telescopes and robot spacecraft such as the *Voyager's*, we now know that Jupiter has at least 16 satellites.

One of the biggest surprises of the *Voyager* missions was the discovery of several active volcanoes on the surface of Io. Compared to the other planets and moons, Io is the most volcanically active world in the solar system.

Europa is an icy world that has been compared to a cue ball on a billiard table because it is so smooth. Observations from Earth show that the surface is covered with frozen water.

Ganymede, the largest satellite in the sun's family, is so large that it would be a planet if it were in orbit about the sun rather than around Jupiter. Ganymede is about 400 km larger than Mercury.

Callisto has many craters. It also has the largest impact feature yet discovered. Named the *Valhalla Basin,* it is a set of concentric rings 3000 km in diameter. Astronomers think it was formed about four billion years ago when an asteroid-sized body collided with Callisto. As the satellite's icy crust melted, the waves created in the newly thawed surface froze, forming the giant, bull's-eyelike pattern. The noontime temperature on Callisto is −118°C, while at night it plummets to −193°C. *Voyager 1* also discovered a thin, flat ring of fine particles that surrounds Jupiter.

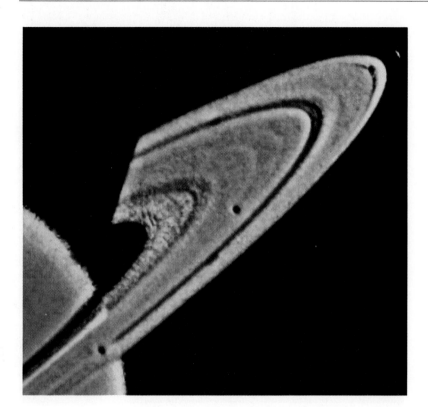

Figure 4-17. What do scientists think make up Saturn's rings and ringlets?
They appear to be made up mostly of ice.

Saturn   Everyone would probably agree that Saturn is the most beautiful planet in the solar system. As *Voyager 1* got close to Saturn, it became obvious that the atmosphere of Saturn is not as spectacular as that of Jupiter. The chemical reactions in Jupiter's atmosphere that make it so colorful are less likely to take place at Saturn's distance from the sun. It is much colder there. *Voyager 2* sent back photographs showing colored bands that represent storm systems. Most of Saturn's atmosphere is composed of hydrogen and helium. Wind velocities were found to be as high as 400 to 500 meters per second (m/s). Saturn also has a large oval spot similar to Jupiter's Great Red Spot, although it is smaller.

Voyagers 1 and *2* revealed that Saturn's five major rings are actually made up of thousands of small rings, or **ringlets.** In some photographs of the rings, the ringlets are so numerous that it looks as if one is looking at the grooves of a phonograph record. The rings are probably composed of pieces of ice. The rings are extremely thin for their width. If Saturn's rings were as wide as a football field, they would only be as thick as a page in this book!

Figure 4-18. This composite picture, a montage, combines photographs taken by *Voyagers 1* and *2* of Saturn and its major satellites.

New information on Uranus: *Voyager II* passed Uranus on January 25, 1986, and sent back information indicating that the planet has at least 10 rings and a total of 15 satellites, some of which show evidence of plate tectonic activity. *Voyager II* also furthered scientific knowledge about Uranus' "tilt" by discovering that the planet's magnetic field is at a 55° angle from its axis of rotation.

The *Voyager* spacecraft discovered many new satellites. Most are small and irregular in shape. They are composed of ice and rock. Titan, one of the nearly two dozen satellites that orbits Saturn, is so large that it has its own atmosphere.

Uranus In January 1986 *Voyager 2* reached Uranus (YOOR′-uh-nus), providing us with our first close-up look at one of the outer gas giants. Uranus was discovered by William Herschel with a homemade telescope in 1781. This discovery doubled the known size of the solar system overnight. Uranus lies twice as far from the sun as Saturn.

On a clear night, Uranus can be seen with a pair of binoculars. The atmosphere of Uranus is similar to that of Saturn and Jupiter. It is composed of hydrogen and helium, with small amounts of methane and other gases. Methane is what gives Uranus its characteristic aquamarine color.

The tilt of Uranus' axis is very different from that of any other planet. It is tipped downward at an angle of 98°, so far that Uranus seems to roll around the sun on its side. This tilt may be the result of a collision between Uranus and another body the size of the earth billions of years ago.

Prior to *Voyager 2*'s arrival in 1986, five moons had been photographed by telescopes on Earth. The robot spacecraft added ten more.

In 1977 astronomers using a telescope on board a jet aircraft observatory discovered that Uranus had a system of nine dark rings.

What surprising discovery was made about Uranus in 1977?

Neptune   Neptune was discovered in 1846. It was predicted mathematically by an Englishman named Adams and a Frenchman named Leverrier before being observed telescopically by Galle, a German. It lies beyond Uranus and has two known satellites. One of its moons, Triton, may turn out to be larger than Ganymede. Further study may reveal that Neptune has a ring system surrounding the planet.

Pluto   When Pluto was first discovered photographically by American Clyde Tombaugh in 1930, it was thought to be about the same size as Mars. Since then scientists have learned that it is actually less than 3000 km in diameter. In 1978 astronomer James Christy discovered that Pluto had a satellite that was about half the size of the planet. This moon has been named Charon.

Its small size and icy (rather than gaseous) nature suggest that Pluto may be an escaped moon of Neptune. Computer simulations have shown that the same earth-sized body that passed through the outer solar system billions of years ago may have also swept by Neptune, upsetting its system of moons. This could have sent one of Neptune's satellites out of orbit and into one of its own farther away from the sun. Pluto's orbit is very elliptical, which is what astronomers would expect to see if this theory were true. Pluto passes between the sun and Neptune for about 20 years out of its 248-year period. In fact, Pluto is currently in this part of its orbit now, making it the eighth planet from the sun and Neptune the ninth. It will cross back over Neptune's orbit in 1999.

Some astronomers have suggested that Pluto should no longer be counted as a planet because of its small size. Others have speculated that it may be a comet, an asteroid, or even a new type of solar system object. Unfortunately, we will not get a close-up look at Pluto for a long time.

1. Several active volcanoes
2. Pieces of ice
3. Pluto

Check yourself

1. What exciting discovery did the *Voyager* spacecraft find on the surface of Jupiter's moon Io?

2. Of what are Saturn's rings probably composed?

3. Which planet is eighth from the sun right now? Why?

Comets

New vocabulary: comet, coma, Oort Cloud

A **comet** is a mass of frozen gases mixed with dust and small pieces of rocky material. A good model of a comet's solid body, or nucleus, would be a dirty snowball a few kilometers in diameter. As a comet approaches the sun, its outer surface begins to vaporize, surrounding the nucleus with a cocoon of gases called a **coma.** When the comet gets close enough to the sun, the solar wind pushes these gases away from the nucleus, forming its beautiful tail. These tails can stretch for hundreds of thousands of kilometers. A comet's tail always points away from the sun because of the solar wind pushing on it.

As a comet makes each passage around the sun, it loses some of its frozen material by evaporation. Their orbits are strewn with little pieces of rock and dust that they have left behind. If the earth encounters a comet's orbit, we may see a *meteor shower* as these little pieces of comet debris burn up in our atmosphere. The best meteor shower of the year, the Perseids, occurs in mid-August. If it is a clear night and the moon is not visible, you may be able to see as many as 50 meteors each hour from this one shower.

Comets have very long and narrow ellipses for orbits. The shortest known period for a comet, that of Comet Encke, is a little over three years. Comet Kohoutek, which was visible in the mid-1970s, has a period of over 75 000 years. Comet Halley, the most famous of these solar system nomads, returns once every 74 to 76 years.

Comet Halley made its most recent flyby of the sun in 1986. Amateur and professional astronomers all over the world made thousands of observations as it slowly made its way

Figure 4-19. A comet is thought to be a mass of frozen gases mixed with rocky material. What causes the tail of a comet to glow?
The tail of a comet glows because of sunlight reflected off particles in the tail.

against the background stars. Since this was Halley's first return after the invention of spacecraft, a small fleet of five robot probes were sent to study it. While Japan's *Sakigake* and *Suisei* spacecraft observed from a distance, the Soviet Union's two *VeGa* and the European Space Agency's *Giotto* plunged into Halley's coma. They were able to send back our first photographs of a comet's nucleus. Much to everyone's surprise, it was very dark and shaped like a potato or peanut about 16 by 7.5 by 8 km in size. The dirty snowball model of a comet's nucleus fit perfectly. Observations of Halley from the spacecraft and Earth were able to tell us more about comets in a year than had been learned since the first recorded observations of these objects by the ancient Chinese. If you did not see Comet Halley this time around, you may get another chance. It will return to our skies again in the year 2061.

Why study these evaporating snowballs of frozen gas and dust? Like meteoroids and asteroids, comets are believed to be left over from the origin of the solar system. When we study these objects, we are looking at material that has been unchanged since the solar system was born. They provide important clues about our distant past. After the sun became a star, the solar wind blew most of the debris left from its birth beyond the orbits of the newly formed planets. Astronomers have suggested that a huge cloud of millions of comet nuclei surrounds the solar system some 50 000 times the earth-sun distance. Known as the **Oort cloud,** each comet begins its sunward journey here. Disturbed by the gravity of a passing star, a nucleus begins its slow plunge toward the sun. On its way in, it may get tugged on by Jupiter, causing it to go into orbit around the sun. Observations have been made from both Earth and space showing that some other stars appear to be surrounded by a cloud of material that may be made up of comets.

Check yourself

1. What are the Perseids?

2. Where is a comet's tail in relation to the sun?

Library research

Find out more about what scientists learned from the various missions to Halley's Comet.

What do comets have in common with meteoroids and asteroids?

1. A meteor shower of comet debris
2. The tail always points away from the sun.

Section 1 Review   Chapter 4

Use **Reading Checksheet 4-1** TRB page 70
Skillsheet 4-1 TRB page 112
Section Reviewsheet 4-1 TRB page 161–162
Section Testsheet 4-1 TRB page 284

Check Your Vocabulary

12	asteroids	8	meteorite
5	coma	7	Oort cloud
13	comet	10	protoplanet
6	greenhouse effect	2	retrograde motions
3	law of gravitation	11	ringlet
4	law of inertia	1	solar system
9	meteor		

Match each term above with the numbered phrase that best describes it.

1. The sun and all the objects that revolve around the sun

2. Apparent reversals in the motions of certain planets

3. A scientific law, that states that there is a force of attraction between every object in the universe

4. A scientific law that states that a body at rest will remain at rest and a body in motion will keep moving in the same direction unless acted upon by some outside force

5. A cocoon of gases surrounding the center of a comet

6. The process by which heat energy becomes trapped by a planet's atmosphere

7. A huge cloud of material in which all of the solar system's comets may begin

8. Metal or rock from space that has reached the earth's surface

9. Pieces of metal or rock that have collided with the atmosphere, burning up through friction

10. Clumps of rock and metal in the early stages of forming a planet

11. One of many bands of fine ice particles surrounding Saturn

12. Fragments of rocky objects that revolve around the sun and that are smaller than planets

13. An object with an oblong orbit that forms a long glowing tail as it approaches the sun

Check Your Knowledge

Multiple Choice: Choose the answer that best completes each of the following sentences.

1. _?_ is the scientist who changed the idea of the "earth-centered" solar system to a "sun-centered" solar system.
   a) Plato   c) Aristotle
   b) Ptolemy   d) Copernicus

2. The scientist who discovered the laws of gravitation and inertia was _?_.
   a) Kepler   c) Ptolemy
   b) Newton   d) Copernicus

3. Two planets with polar icecaps are Earth and _?_.
   a) Venus   c) Mars
   b) Mercury   d) Jupiter

Check Your Understanding

1. Describe one theory of the formation of the solar system.

2. Describe three important conclusions that Kepler formed with regard to the movement of the planets.

3. Using Newton's law of inertia, explain why a person standing on a bus falls forward when the bus stops.

4. How do the "inner" planets differ from the "outer" planets? In what important way is Pluto more like the inner planets than like the outer ones?

5. Why is Earth probably the only planet in the solar system on which life exists?

The Stars   Section 2

Learner Objectives

1. To describe methods of measuring stellar distances.
2. To identify ways of describing a star's brightness.
3. To identify two kinds of motion of a star.
4. To distinguish among different kinds of stars.

Section 2 of Chapter 4 is divided into six parts:

Characteristics of the sun

Characteristics of other stars

Different kinds of stars

The Hertzsprung-Russell diagram

Clusters of stars

How far away are the stars?

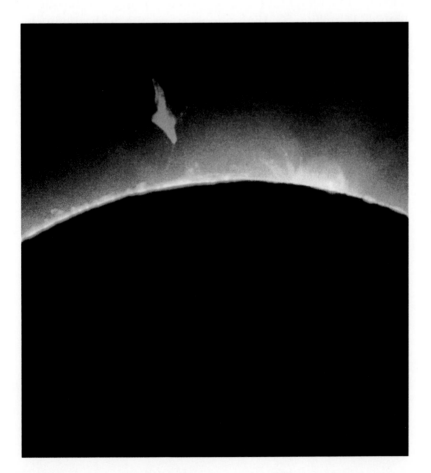

Figure 4-20. A solar prominence, which can extend hundreds of thousands of kilometers from the sun's surface, can be seen clearly in this photograph of a solar eclipse.

Characteristics of the sun
New vocabulary: nuclear fusion, photosphere, sunspot, solar flare, aurora, solar wind, chromosphere, corona

Most of us have seen pictures of the sun. We have observed it rise in the morning and set in the evening. We have also been warned never to look at the sun directly when it is shining brightly. To look at the sun when it is so bright is extremely dangerous. It can cause permanent damage to your eyes! This also applies to using binoculars and telescopes.

Where does the sun get its supply of energy to keep it shining so brightly? Is there an unlimited amount of oil or coal on the sun that provides its fuel?

Scientists are now quite sure that it is thermonuclear energy that keeps the sun hot and glowing. The sun is composed mostly of the elements hydrogen and helium. The temperature of the sun's surface has been estimated to be about 5500°C. The temperatures at the center of the sun may be as high as 15 million °C. With temperatures this high, the nuclei of the hydrogen atoms have enough energy to cause them to join, or fuse, with other hydrogen nuclei. This process is called **nuclear fusion.**

When this reaction takes place, four hydrogen nuclei are fused together to make one helium nucleus. A small amount of matter seems to disappear as part of the fusion process. However, this "missing" matter is not really lost. It has been turned into an equal amount of energy. A small amount of matter can produce a lot of energy. It is this thermonuclear process that has kept the sun shining for at least 4.5 billion years. And the sun will continue to shine for another 4.5 billion years.

To get an idea of how much energy is produced on the sun, you can think of it this way. As 0.01 g of hydrogen is converted into helium and energy, enough energy is produced from the "missing" matter to provide your home with electricity for 2000 years!

The "surface" of the sun is called the **photosphere** (FOT'-uh-sfir). It is not really a surface, but rather the highest layer of visible gases. On the photosphere are dark splotches called **sunspots.** Sunspots were first observed by Galileo in the seventeenth century. They appear dark because they are many degrees cooler than the rest of the photosphere. Sunspots can

---

Matter cannot be lost. It can, however, be changed into other matter and/or energy.

When nuclear fusion occurs, what happens to the "missing" matter?

Library research

Sunspots occur in cycles. How do sunspots affect the earth?

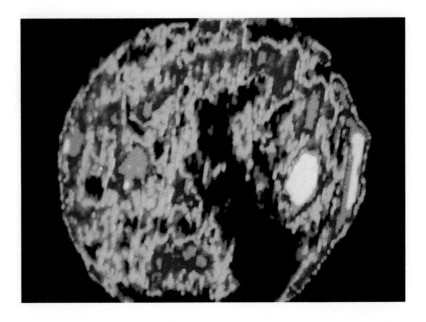

Figure 4-21. This false-color photographic representation of the sun's surface was processed from an August 20, 1973, television transmission of *Apollo* Telescope Mount from *Skylab* 3. Astronauts on board the space station could, by using monitors, control the telescope and follow changes on the sun's surface.

be observed to drift across the sun's surface as our star rotates on its axis. The sun rotates faster at its equator than it does at its Poles. As a result, sunspots move faster at its equator than at the Poles. For many years, a record has been kept of the number of sunspots seen on the sun. The number of sunspots increases for a period of 5.5 to 6 years, reaches a maximum, and then decreases for 5.5 to 6 years, on the average.

Solar flares are sudden bursts of energy given off by sunspots. They give off electrically charged particles that can interfere with radio communications on the earth. They can also cause unusually bright displays of **auroras.** The **solar wind,** mentioned in Section 1, is another kind of stream of electrically charged particles. These particles are constantly given off by the sun. The solar wind pushes comet tails in the direction opposite the sun. When electrons and protons from solar flares or wind interact with the earth's upper atmosphere, spectacular bands and streamers of colored light appear in the night sky. Sometimes referred to as the northern lights, the "aurora borealis" appears in the Northern Hemisphere. In the Southern Hemisphere, the "aurora australis" occurs.

The **chromosphere** (KRO'-muh-sfir') is a thin, colored layer that marks the change between the sun's photosphere and its corona. The **corona** (kuh-ROH'-nuh) is the outermost layer of the sun's atmosphere. Seen as a pearly sheet of light surrounding the sun's disk during a total eclipse, the corona consists of electrically charged gases with temperatures of 2 million °C.

Figure 4-22. This photograph, obtained during the 1973 *Skylab* 3 mission, reveals for the first time that helium erupting from the sun can stay together to altitudes of up to 500 000 miles (over 800 000 km).

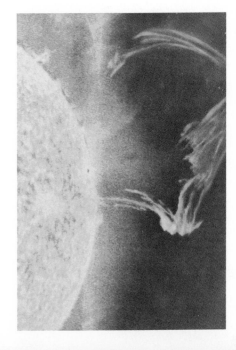

Figure 4-23. What occurrence on the sun causes spectacular light shows like this aurora borealis (northern lights) to appear in the earth's atmoshpere? The electrically charged particles that leave the sun's surface as solar wind are responsible for occurrences such as an aurora borealis, which takes place when part of the earth's atmosphere becomes electrically charged.

1. By means of nuclear fusion, a small amount of matter is changed into energy.
2. Electrons and protons from solar flares or from solar wind interact with the earth's upper atmosphere.

New vocabulary: nebula, apparent magnitude, magnitude, true brightness, absolute magnitude, spectroscope, radial velocity, proper motion

Streaming from the sun's surface are cooler eruptions of gases called *solar prominences*. These prominences appear to leap out of the sun to heights of 800 000 km. They sometimes make an arc and return to the sun's surface in another place.

Check yourself

1. How can the sun continue to give off so much energy without "burning up"?
2. What causes an aurora?

Characteristics of other stars

You learned earlier that the sun and planets were formed from a large cloud of dust and gas some 4.6 billion years ago. Such clouds are called **nebulae,** after an ancient Greek word for "cloud." Any star you see in the sky or in a photograph was formed in such a nebula at some time in the past. Since there are still thousands of these clouds floating around in the spiral arms of the Milky Way, stars are still forming today.

One such example of these special places of star birth that you can see with the naked eye can be found in the winter sky. Just below the belt of Orion hangs his sword. The center "star" is a fuzzy patch of light that is actually the Orion nebula. Astronomers have found stars within this nebula that are only a few million years old. This may seem very old to us when compared to a human lifetime. But to a star, it is still very young. While the Orion nebula looks like a small, fuzzy patch of light to the naked eye, it is actually very big. If you could make stars just like the sun from this one cloud of dust and gas, you would end up with about 10 000 stars.

When a nebula is turning into stars, planets may form. We have no proof that planets are circling other stars. But it would also be wrong to assume that we are the only planets that have ever formed in our galaxy. Several stars have been shown to have what appear to be disks or halos of material around them. These may be planets forming around a young star. One such star is Beta Pictoris (BAY′-tuh PICK′-tor-uss). Beta Pictoris has been called the best evidence for planets forming around a star other than the sun.

After all of the gas in a nebula has been turned into stars, you end up with a group of stars that gradually drift apart over tens of millions of years. An example of a nebula turned into stars is the Pleiades (PLEE′-uh-dees) star cluster in Taurus the Bull. Astronomers have estimated that these stars are about 50 million years old.

When you go outside on a clear night, it does not take long to notice that the stars overhead all seem to have different brightnesses. Some are very bright, while others are barely visible. In the second century B.C., Hipparchus (hi-PAR′-kuss) devised a way of grouping stars into classes according to their **apparent magnitude,** or how bright the stars look from the earth without using a telescope. Each of these brightness classifications is known as a **magnitude** (MAG′-nuh-tood′). Hipparchus classified the brightest stars as first-magnitude stars and those just visible as sixth-magnitude stars. Each of the other visible stars were grouped into one of the in-between magnitudes. Even though it is thousands of years later, Hipparchus' magnitude classes are still in use.

Classifying stars by apparent brightness is based on how bright the star appears to be to an observer on Earth. But this does not represent a star's **true brightness** (its luminosity), which is the amount of light it is giving off. Stars are located at different distances from the earth. You know that a light appears to get dimmer the farther you get from it. The same is true for stars. Astronomers have devised a scale that tells how bright stars really are as if they were all compared from the same distance, 32.6 light-years, from the earth. This

Point out that as the number of the magnitude decreases, the brightness increases. A star of the second magnitude, for example, is brighter than a star of the fifth magnitude. To make sure students understand how this numbering system works, ask them which is brighter, a star of the tenth magnitude or the fourth magnitude, a star of the seventh magnitude or the eighth magnitude, etc.

What is classifying stars by their apparent brightness based on?

Science Processes: Measuring; Using numbers   CORE   15 minutes   Small groups
See also Activity Record Sheet 4-2B (Lab Manual
page 54)

Activity 4-2A   Calculating the Distance to the Sun

Materials

convex lens

15-cm X 15-cm white tagboard

meter stick

lens holder

paper holder

meter stick support

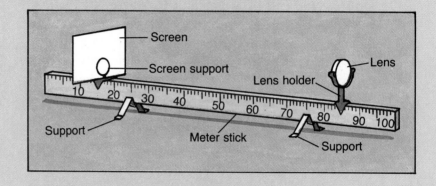

Purpose

To calculate the distance
between the earth and
the sun.

Procedure

1. In Chapter 3, you used similar triangles to calculate the diameter of the moon. In this activity, you will use similar triangles to calculate the distance from the earth to the sun.
2. Set up the apparatus as shown in the diagram above.
3. Move the lens until you get a clear, sharply defined image of the sun on your screen. *SAFETY NOTE: Never look at the sun directly. Use only shadows or some other forms of indirect observation.*
4. Measure the distance between the lens and screen. Record the information, to the nearest centimeter.
5. Measure the diameter of the sun's image on the screen. Record this information.
6. Using the diameter of the sun (which is 1 400 000 km), calculate the distance from the earth to the sun.

Questions

1. What did you calculate the sun's distance to be?
2. Did everyone get the same answer? If not, why not?

Conclusion

How can something so far away provide the heat and light that the sun does for the earth? To find out, look back at page 194.

brightness is called a star's **absolute magnitude.** To see how this works, imagine you have two glowing light bulbs. One is a 100-watt light bulb and the other a 40-watt light bulb. If you placed the 100-watt bulb 50 m away and the 40-watt bulb only 5 m away, you would say that the 40-watt bulb appears to be brighter. But, if you place them both 5 m away, you can tell that the 100-watt bulb is the brighter of the two. This is the same as comparing two stars in the sky as seen from the earth (apparent magnitude) and placing them side by side at the same distance from you (absolute magnitude).

By comparing a star's absolute magnitude to its apparent magnitude, its distance may be determined. Another factor that enters into this method of distance determination is the reddening of a star's light that is caused by dust that is found throughout the galaxy. This dust affects the color of a star observed from the earth by making it redder. As a result, the apparent light of a star can be redder than the actual light given off by that star. The farther the star is from the earth, the redder the dust will make it appear. The star's light has to travel through more dust to get to us.

In calculating a star's actual brightness, astronomers discovered relationships among the colors, sizes, and temperatures of stars. 1) A star's color is the result of its temperature. Red stars are cooler than yellow stars (our sun is a yellow-white star), which are cooler than blue-white stars, which are the hottest of all. (See Table 4-2.) If you heated a metal bar in a

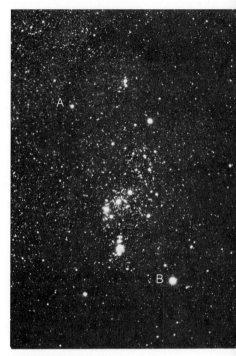

Figure 4-24. Careful observation reveals that Betelgeuse (A) is a red star and Rigel (B) is a blue-white star. In what constellation are these stars located?
Orion

Star Colors and Temperatures		
Color	Class	Temperature
Blue-white	O	50 000°C
Blue	B	20 000°C
White	A	10 000°C
White	F	7000°C
Yellow	G	6000°C
Orange	K	5000°C
Red	M	3500°C

Table 4-2. Which are hotter, red stars or blue stars?
Blue stars

fire, it would first glow red. As you continued to heat it, it would turn yellow and eventually become "white hot," indicating that it has a higher temperature. 2) In addition, the temperature determines the amount of light that an object gives off. The red hot bar would give off less light than the white hot bar. And the same bar at room temperature would give off no visible light at all. 3) Finally, a larger object gives off more light than a smaller one heated to the same temperature. So, a metal bar 4 cm across would give off more light than a metal bar 1 cm across even if they were both heated to 500°C.

Betelgeuse, which is in Orion's right shoulder, is a very large star. It is called a supergiant because of its enormous size. If you were to look carefully at it, you would see that it is orange-red in color. A star of orange-red color is very hot, and so you would think it would not give off very much light. But, being so large, Betelgeuse gives off vast quantities of its orange-red light. This is why it appears so bright to us, even though it is not a very hot star and is far away.

Rigel, in Orion's left ankle, appears just about as bright to us as does Betelgeuse. But Rigel appears to be blue-white in color. This means that Rigel is much hotter than Betelgeuse. Astronomers have determined that blue-white stars like Rigel are considerably smaller than the red supergiants like Betelgeuse. Although they appear to be about just as bright, Rigel is nearly twice as far from us as is Betelgeuse.

What are stars made of? To find out, an instrument called a **spectroscope** (SPEK′-truh-skōp′) is used. (See Figure 4-25).

Figure 4-25. What can scientists learn about a star by using a spectroscope?
A spectroscope indicated which elements make up the star.

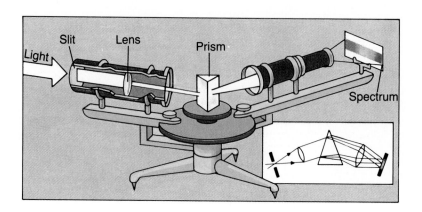

By allowing the light from a star to pass through a spectroscope's prism, the light is separated into the different colors of the spectrum. Lines in this chemical fingerprint of the star reveal the elements found in the star. Every star is about 90 percent hydrogen and 10 percent helium, with very small amounts of all the other elements.

The spectrum of a star also reveals something about its motion. All stars have two motions. One motion is called **radial velocity.** In this first motion, the star is moving in a line toward or away from the earth. The radial velocity can be determined by examining the spectrum of a star. Astronomers have observed that the lines in the spectrum of some stars shift toward the red end of the spectrum, while other stars have a spectral shift toward the blue end of the spectrum.

The cause of such a shift was first discovered with sound waves through the Doppler effect, discussed in Chapter 3. Wavelengths from an object become longer if the object is moving away from us and shorter if it is moving toward us.

Red light has the longest wavelength of the visible colors. Violet, at the other end of the visible spectrum, has the shortest. Therefore a shift toward the red end indicates that the star is moving away from the earth. A shift toward the blue end indicates that the star is approaching the earth.

The **proper motion** of a star is the change in the apparent location of the star over time. Stars are in constant motion through the galaxy. Because of the enormous distances between the earth and the stars, this change in position cannot be detected immediately. Astronomers must take a picture of a star and its location relative to the stars around it. Several months or years later, they again photograph the same star and measure its position. By comparing the position of the star in the first photograph with its position in the second, it is simple to calculate how far the star moves per year when compared to the other stars in the photograph.

Check yourself

1. How does apparent magnitude differ from absolute magnitude?

2. How can a spectroscope be used to determine a star's radial velocity?

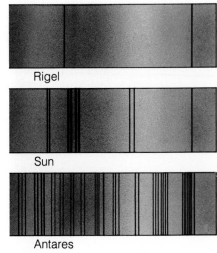

Rigel

Sun

Antares

Figure 4-26. The lines in the spectrum of a star's light reveal information about the star's motion and about elements found in the star.
Rigel (RĪ'-jil) is a bluish-white star. The sun is a yellowish star. Antares (an-TER'-eez) is a reddish star.

1. Apparent magnitude is how bright a star looks from Earth, whereas absolute magnitude indicates how bright a star would be if all stars were compared from the same distance, 32.6 light-years from the earth.

2. A star's radial velocity can be determined by examining the spectrum of the star with a spectroscope. A blue shift indicates that the star is moving away from the earth. A red shift indicates that it is moving closer.

Different kinds of stars
New vocabulary: Cepheid variable, supernova, neutron star, black hole

There are many special kinds of stars in the sky. While our star is single, there are stars that may have one or more stellar companions. Such *binary* (double) and *multiple star systems* are actually more common in the Milky Way than single stars. The stars in such systems revolve around each other. The time it takes them to orbit around one another enables astronomers to calculate their size, mass, and density. Polaris, which you learned about earlier, is an example of a famous star that also happens to be a double star. A small telescope will reveal Polaris' companion star, which orbits Polaris in many thousands of years at a distance of about 2000 times the distance between the sun and the earth.

Another special kind of star is called a **Cepheid variable** (SEF′-ee-id or SEE′-fee-id). These stars get brighter and dimmer at regular intervals of time as the star expands and then contracts. A young American astronomer named Henrietta Leavitt catalogued these special stars. She found that longer periods between when a Cepheid was brightest and dimmest indicated brighter stars. Cepheids with shorter periods were dimmer stars. This relationship is important because astronomers can use this to find the distance of other galaxies outside of the Milky Way. By noting how long it takes a Cepheid to brighten and fade in another galaxy, an astronomer can calculate how far away the object is.

Astronomers believe that stars are formed when gravitation causes clouds of dust and gas to begin to contract. This results in an increase in pressure and temperature at the center of the forming star. Eventually the temperature becomes hot enough that a thermonuclear reaction takes place. A new star forms. At this point the star begins to give off energy.

Changes occur as stars approach old age. In about 4.5 billion years, our sun will expand into a *red giant*, gobbling up Mercury and probably Venus in the process. It will then begin to shrink until it becomes a *white dwarf*. Such a star is about the size of the earth—but much hotter than the sun. White dwarfs gradually cool until they give off no more heat. They become dark, burned out cinders.

What does an astronomer learn by noting how long it takes a Cepheid to brighten and fade?

Figure 4-27. The Crab Nebula is the remains of a supernova that was first seen in the year 1054.

Stars much bigger and more massive than the sun undergo a violent death. After all of their fuel is used up, they collapse like a punctured balloon. Then a tremendous explosion called a **supernova** occurs. The star is torn apart. The explosion is so strong that it ejects most of the star's material into space. It is also so strong that it makes elements such as gold and uranium, which do not form elsewhere. If you have a gold ring or chain, you have something that was formed long ago in just such an explosion! The most famous supernova, the Crab nebula, is located in the constellation of Taurus the Bull. Chinese and Native American astronomers observed its explosion on July 4, 1054. It was so bright that it could be seen in

Interested students could find out more about why stars explode, why stars die, and how a nebula is formed. They could then present their findings to the class.

Figure 4-28. Supernova SN 1987A (in the Large Magellanic Cloud) was seen in 1987 by astonomers in the Southern Hemishpere. It was the first supernova visible to the naked eye to appear in nearly four centuries.

the daytime sky. You can still see the star's material with a telescope as it expands away from where the star once was.

Astronomers received a special surprise during the winter of 1987 when a star in the Large Magellanic Cloud, a satellite galaxy of the Milky Way, exploded. This was the first time that they had a chance to study a nearby supernova in over 300 years. The supernova was about 170 000 light-years away. Known as SN 1987A, it was an astronomer's dream come true. Telescopes all over the Southern Hemisphere studied it until it faded from view.

After a supernova explodes, the thermonuclear power plant at the center of the star shrinks. It collapses inward with such high pressures and temperatures that electrons and protons are fused together. This incredibly dense mass of neutrons is called a **neutron star.** Neutron stars may be as small as a few kilometers across. But their mass can equal or exceed the sun's. A cubic centimeter of material scooped up from such an object would weigh several billion tons. Neutron stars spin very rapidly. As they spin, we can observe a flash of light for each turn the neutron star makes. We can also hear a click of radio energy for each rotation. Neutron stars are also called **pulsars.** As the neutron star spins, it gives off a pulse. Old pulsars spin very slowly, while young ones spin very rapidly. Some spin so rapidly that they sound like a drummer in a marching band playing a roll on a snare drum. Scientists can hear this sound with a radio telescope.

If the star that became a supernova was very massive, the thermonuclear power plant at its center shrank to a size even smaller than a neutron star. Such tiny, massive objects are called **black holes.** A black hole's gravity is so strong that it pulls back in any light that is trying to leave its surface. Since we cannot see any light it is giving off, we see nothing but a "black hole" in space. A black hole can pull in the light of anything that falls directly within its gravitational field.

Check yourself

1. What is unusual about Cepheid variables?

2. Where are gold atoms formed?

3. What is a black hole?

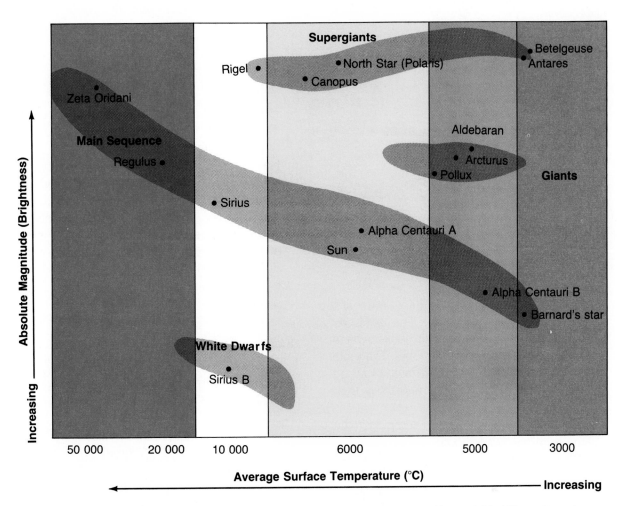

The Hertzsprung-Russell diagram
New vocabulary: Hertzsprung-Russell diagram

By the beginning of the twentieth century, astronomers had made a number of discoveries about the colors and absolute magnitudes of stars. About 1905, Danish astronomer Ejnar Hertzsprung plotted these two features on a graph. He found that they formed a regular pattern. About ten years later, American astronomer Henry Norris Russell did the same thing with similar results. Today this graph of star colors versus absolute magnitude is known as the **Hertzsprung-Russell diagram,** or simply, "H-R diagram."

Look at Figure 4-29, which is an H-R diagram showing color and absolute magnitude for a number of stars. The first thing that you notice about the H-R diagram is the band of stars that stretches from the top left to the lower right. This is called the main sequence. About 90 percent of the stars end

Figure 4-29. What can we learn about the sun in this Hertzsprung-Russell diagram? It is yellow, in the main sequence, and moderately bright, compared with other stars.

Science Processes: Observing; Classifying
See also Activity Record Sheet 4-2A (Lab Manual
page 53)

20 minutes   Demonstration, or large groups

Activity 4-2B   Observing Magnitudes of Light Bulbs

Materials

several light bulbs of different wattages (for
  example, 10 watts, 40 watts, 200 watts)

2 light bulbs of the same wattage

light sockets with long cords (Table lamps without
  shades and with extension cords will do nicely.)

Purpose

To illustrate apparent brightness and magnitude, using light bulbs.

Procedure

1. Place the light bulbs in their sockets on a
   long table at one end of the room. The table
   should be placed so that the lamps can be
   slid along the table, toward and away from
   the observer.
2. Turn off the lights in the room and plug in the
   lamps on the table. Stand across the room'
   from the table and have another student
   slide the lamps toward and away from you
   until all of them appear to be the same
   brightness.
3. Turn the room lights back on and observe
   the way the bulbs are lined up on the table.
4. Try the same activity again, keeping one eye
   closed. (Closing one eye prevents your mind
   from using parallax displacement as a way
   of determining distance.)

5. Mark the positions of the bulbs on the table.
   Then have a partner try the activity while you
   adjust the lamps.
6. Have someone else observe the light bulbs
   after you have set them up in the manner described in Step 2. But have that person close
   one eye. (As mentioned in Step 4, closing
   one eye prevents the mind from using parallax displacement as a way of determining
   distance.) With one eye closed, how do the
   bulbs compare in terms of brightness and
   distance from the observer?

Questions

1. After your partner has arranged lamps the
   way you indicate, are bulbs of the same wattage next to each other?
2. Are the bulbs that have the higher wattages
   (and so give off more light) at the far end of
   the table? Are the low-wattage bulbs at the
   near end?
3. Does your partner's arrangement agree with
   yours?
4. How does closing one eye affect the conclusions of the third observer?

Conclusion

How accurate do you think classification by
magnitude is?

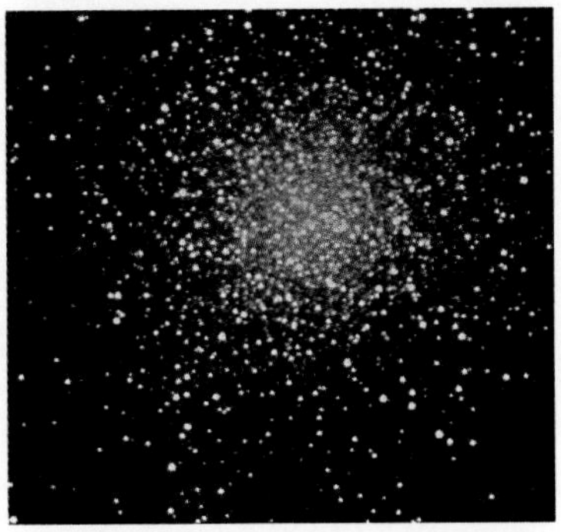

up in the main sequence when they are plotted on an H-R diagram. These stars are very stable. They use their nuclear fuel at a steady rate over billions of years. Notice the position of the sun in the main sequence. Its position on the H-R diagram tells us that it is yellow in color and moderately bright when compared to other stars.

Stars are bright at the top of the H-R diagram, and dim toward the bottom. Stars to the left side of the H-R diagram are blue-white, while those at the right side are red.

Figure 4-30. This photograph shows globular cluster M13 in the constellation Hercules.

Check yourself

1. What two star characteristics are plotted on a Hertsprung-Russell diagram?

2. The sun is in which part of the H-R diagram?

1. Color and absolute magnitude are plotted on an H-R diagram.
2. The main sequence.

Clusters of stars

You learned earlier that many stars form at one time out of a nebula of dust and gas. There are two different kinds of groups that these stars become a part of after they form. *Open,* or *galactic, clusters* are groups of up to several hundred stars that are found in the spiral arms of the Milky Way. Since there are many nebulae in a galaxy's spiral arms, we will also find many open clusters there as well. Two of the most famous open clusters are the Hyades and the Pleiades star clusters.

While such open clusters do not seem to have any shape, *globular clusters* are organized into balls of 10 000 to 100 000 or more stars. Globular clusters are found surrounding the center of the Milky Way. They formed early in the history of our galaxy and have changed very little. The oldest known globular clusters are over ten billion years old. The most famous one is M13 in the constellation of Hercules the Hero.

How old are the oldest globular clusters?

Check yourself

When and where were globular clusters in the Milky Way formed?

Globular clusters were formed early in the history of the galaxy and are in its center.

Science Processes: Observing; Inferring; Defining operationally
See also Activity Record Sheet 4-2C (Lab Manual page 55)

5 minutes   Individuals or pairs of students

Activity 4-2C   Observing Parallax Displacement

Materials

clay
tabletop or board 120 cm long
2 toothpicks

Purpose

To see how parallax displacement works.

Procedure

1. Place each toothpick upright in a lump of clay. Put one toothpick at the far end of the table. Put the other toothpick about 30 cm from the near end.
2. Standing at the near end (the end without the toothpick), crouch down until you are eye-level with the tabletop and the toothpicks. Line the two toothpicks up so that they appear even with your nose.
3. With both eyes open, focus on the near toothpick (the one 30 cm from the near end). Close first one eye and then the other.

4. Focus on the far toothpick and follow the same procedure.

Questions

1. What happens to the far toothpick when you focus on the near one?
2. What happens when you focus on the far one?

Conclusion

Compare your observation of parallax displacement in this activity with the use of parallax displacement to measure the distance to stars.

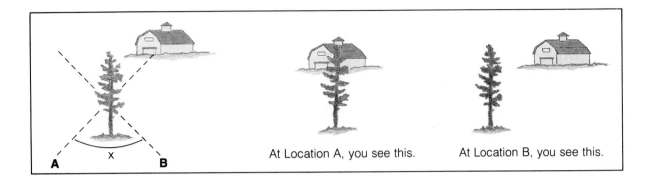

At Location A, you see this.   At Location B, you see this.

How far away are the stars?

New vocabulary: parallax, parallax angle, light-year

How far away is a star? There are two basic methods that are used to measure stellar distances. (*Stella* is the Latin word for star.) One method, discussed earlier, is based on comparing a star's apparent and absolute magnitudes of brightness. For relatively close stars, a second method is based on angles.

Angle X in Figure 4-31 shows the kind of angle that is used in measuring distances to nearby stars. It is the same way that a surveyor measures distances. Imagine yourself in the diagram. When you look at the tree from Location A, the tree and the building are lined up. When you move to Location B, the tree appears to the left of the building. The shift in the relative positions of the tree and the building is caused by the difference in the direction from which you are viewing the tree. The difference in the direction of the line of sight to an object from two different places is called **parallax** (PAIR′-uh-laks′). The resulting angle (angle X in the diagram) is called the **parallax angle.**

You can use the parallax angle and the distance between Locations A and B to calculate the distance between the observer and the tree. You can also use the parallax angle and the distance between two observation points along the earth's orbit to calculate the distance to a star.

To determine the distance of nearby stars, astronomers observe a star's position two times, six months apart. Six months after the first observation, when the earth has traveled to a point just opposite where the first observation was made, a second observation is made. A comparison is made between the star's position against the background stars for both observations. The distance that the star has moved compared to the background stars is the parallax angle. Since the distance

Figure 4-31. As you move from Location A to Location B, what will happen to the relative positions of the tree and the building?
The tree and the building appear to be farther apart.

Library research

Distances between stars are frequently expressed in parsecs. What is a parsec?

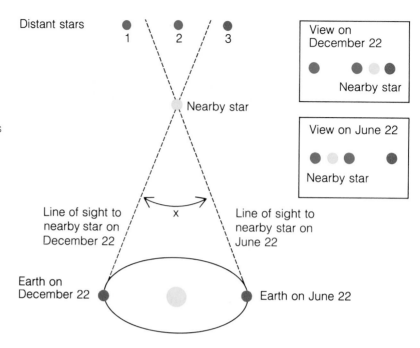

See also Teaching Diagram 4-2 (TRB page 25).

Figure 4-32. When obtaining the parallax of a "nearby" star, why are the astronomer's observations made six months apart? Observations are six months apart because after six months the earth has traveled halfway around its orbit, to a point exactly opposite its original position. The distance between the two points on the orbit is then used, along with the parallax angle, to calculate the distance to the star.

You might have students work out some comparisons, to get a better idea of distances expressed in light years. They could, for example, convert 680 light years to kilometers or to miles.

How can you use your thumb to observe parallax displacement?

The parallax method works only for relatively nearby stars because as distance increases, their parallax becomes too small to measure.

from one side of the earth's orbit to the other is known, an astronomer can calculate the distance to the star. Because stars are so far away, their distances are measured in light-years. A **light-year** is the distance light travels in one year, at the speed of 300 000 km (186 000 mi) per second. Since there are 31 557 600 seconds in a year, this means that a light-year is about 9.5 trillion km.

The parallax method of measuring stellar distances is useful only for the thousand or so stars that are within 65 light-years of the earth. As stars become more distant, other indirect methods must be used. To see how parallax is affected by distance, hold up your thumb about a foot in front of you.

By winking, look at your thumb through only your left eye and then through only your right eye. Parallax will cause the position of your thumb to change against the background of your classroom. Now have a friend across the room hold up his or her thumb. When you wink and sight your friend's thumb through one eye and then through the other, you probably will not notice any change in position. The parallax will be too small.

Check yourself

Why is the parallax method for measuring distance only useful for the thousand stars nearest the earth?

Section 2 Review Chapter 4

Check Your Vocabulary

16 absolute magnitude

15 apparent magnitude

10 aurora

21 black hole

8 Cepheid variable

6 chromosphere

7 corona

24 Hertzsprung-Russell diagram

12 light-year

13 magnitude

25 nebula

22 neutron star

2 nuclear fusion

p 1 parallax

11 parallax angle

3 photosphere

18 proper motion

20 pulsar

19 radial velocity

5 solar flare

9 solar wind

17 spectroscope

4 sunspot

23 supernova

14 true brightness

Match each term above with the numbered phrase that best describes it.

1. The difference in the line of sight to an object from two different places

2. The joining together of lightweight nuclei into a nucleus with greater mass

3. The surface of the sun

4. Dark spot on the photosphere

5. Sudden burst of energy from a sunspot

6. A thin layer that marks the change between the photosphere and the corona

7. The outermost part of the sun's atmosphere

8. A star that gets brighter and dimmer

9. Streams of electrically charged particles constantly given off from the sun

10. A natural light show caused by the effects of solar wind in the earth's atmosphere

11. The angle that results when an object is viewed from two different locations

12. The distance that light travels in one year

13. A classification of a star according to its apparent brightness

14. The amount of light a star is giving off

15. How bright a star appears from the earth

16. Brightness of a star if 32.6 light-years away

17. An instrument that analyzes light

18. Change of a star's apparent location

19. The motion of a star in a line toward or away from the earth

20. A rotating neutron star that gives off pulses

21. Not even light can escape from it

22. An extremely dense mass of neutrons

23. An explosion that occurs after a star has used up its fuel

24. A graph of star colors and absolute magnitudes

25. A large cloud of dust and gas in which stars form

Check Your Knowledge

Multiple Choice: Choose the answer that best completes each of the following sentences.

1. The brightness of a star as seen from the earth depends upon __?__.
   a) temperature, size, distance from earth
   b) temperature and color
   c) color and distance
   d) temperature only

2. Stars that get brighter and dimmer at regular intervals are called __?__.
   a) supergiants
   b) Cepheid variables
   c) white dwarfs
   d) binary stars

Check Your Understanding

1. Why is the parallax method useful for measuring the distance of only "nearby" stars?

2. How does absolute magnitude differ from magnitude?

Use **Reading Checksheet 4-2** TBR page 71
Skillsheet 4-2 TRB page 113

Section Reviewsheet 4-2 TRB pages 163–164
Section Testsheet 4-2 TRB page 285

The Galaxies and Beyond   Section 3

Learner Objectives
1. To distinguish among three types of galaxies.
2. To describe the leading theory of the origin of the universe.
3. To describe a variety of ways of gaining information about the universe.

Section 3 of Chapter 4 is divided into four parts:

The Milky Way galaxy

Other galaxies and superclusters

Beyond the galaxies

Looking at the universe

Figure 4-33. The Horsehead Nebula in Orion is among the most spectacular sights in the universe.

If you looked up at the sky on a clear night, how many stars do you think you would be able to see? On any given night you should be able to see only about 2000 stars with the un-aided eye. But with a telescope, millions of stars would be vis-ible. They are all part of the gigantic system of stars we live in known as the Milky Way.

The Milky Way galaxy New vocabulary: Milky Way
galaxy, galaxy

Our sun is but one star out of about 100 billion stars that make up the **Milky Way galaxy.** A **galaxy** is an enormous group of stars, all of which are kept grouped together by gravity. Besides the stars we can see in the sky with our eyes and with telescopes, we can also see a faint band of light that stretches across the sky. A faint band of light, the Milky Way, has been observed for thousands of years. It is best seen in summer from a dark location. Measured from edge to edge, it has a diameter of about 100 000 light-years. The sun is not located in the center of the Milky Way, but in one of its spiral

Figure 4-34. Where in the Milky Way is our solar system located? The solar system is located in one of the Milky Way's spiral arms, about 30 000 light-years from its center.

arms, about 30 000 light-years from the center. Our star revolves around the center of the galaxy, just like all the other stars in it. It takes about 250 million years for the sun, with the solar system, to make the trip once.

Check yourself

How long does it take the solar system to complete one orbit around the center of the Milky Way galaxy?

Other galaxies and superclusters
New vocabulary: Local Group, supercluster

The Milky Way galaxy was once thought to be all there was to the universe. As larger and larger telescopes were built in recent centuries, astronomers began to study objects far fainter than what their eyes alone could see. Some of these new objects were fuzzy patches of light that looked like spirals. At that time, astronomers did not have a way to measure their distances, so these puzzling objects remained a mystery. Early in this century, astronomers had found several ways to measure the distances of these spiral objects. Careful measurements showed that they were gigantic collections of stars similar to—and outside of—our own Milky Way.

Galaxies are divided into three general classes. *Spiral galaxies* are gigantic pinwheels of stars like the Milky Way. Their spiral arms contain many nebulae, so they are still making stars today over 10 to 15 billion years after their formation. The most famous spiral galaxy—after the Milky Way—is the Andromeda galaxy. At a distance of 2.3 million light-years, it is the closest large galaxy to us. The Andromeda galaxy can be seen with the naked eye in the fall. Even though it appears faint to your eye, it contains about 400 billion stars.

The second general class of galaxies are called *elliptical galaxies*. Their shapes range from nearly spherical to very elliptical. There does not appear to be any dust and gas in this kind of galaxy. No more star formation is taking place. Stars found in ellipticals are older than those observed in other types. One of the closest ellipticals to the Milky Way, called NGC 205, is also a satellite of the Andromeda galaxy. While

It takes about 250 million years for the solar system to orbit the Milky Way.

What does the absence of dust and gas in an elliptical galaxy tell scientists?

Figure 4-35. The Andromeda galaxy, 2 000 000 light-years away from our sun, is orbited by two companion galaxies that you can see in the photograph as bright spots near Andromeda.

it is small, other ellipticals are some of the largest galaxies known in the universe.

Irregular galaxies look like collections of stars without any real shape. Some star formation must still be taking place in them because they still contain some nebulae. Observers in the Southern Hemisphere can easily see the two most well known examples of this type of galaxy without even using a telescope. The Large and Small Magellanic (ma′-jel-AN′-ik) Clouds orbit the Milky Way galaxy like NGC 205 orbits the Andromeda galaxy. When first seen, you might mistake them for two small cumulus clouds in the earth's atmosphere.

You learned earlier that stars can form groups called clusters. It is also possible for galaxies to be joined together by gravity into such groups. The Milky Way and the Andromeda galaxies, the Magellanic Clouds, and NGC 205 are members of such a cluster named the **Local Group.** About 30 galaxies are a part of the Local Group. They are held together by gravity as they travel through the universe.

Some clusters of galaxies can also be part of **superclusters**.

Critical Thinking

Name and distinguish among the three major types of galaxies.

The three types are spiral, elliptical, and irregular. Our galaxy, the Milky Way, is a spiral galaxy. Stars are still being formed in both spiral and irregular galaxies. Elliptical galaxies have no dust and gases, and so stars are no longer being formed in them.

Careers Geoscience Librarian / Solar Energy Firm Owner

Geoscience librarians help scientists locate the information they need.

For further information about a career as a geoscience librarian, contact:

Special Libraries Association
235 Park Avenue South
New York, New York 10003

Geoscience Librarian Many geoscience librarians work for geological surveys and other government agencies. Others are employed by universities, petroleum and mining companies, and large public libraries.

Geoscience librarians review, purchase, and maintain collections of technical materials. These collections include information stored in computers as well as photographs, maps, books, and other printed materials.

The primary responsibility of geoscience librarians is to make the information in their collections easily available to scientists or other patrons.

They help people use the library and they do some research for them.

Geoscience librarians need a background in earth science, and they must communicate information effectively. In addition, they must use various systems of storing and retrieving information, and they must do accurate and detailed work.

To train for this career, take a college preparatory course that includes a foreign language. In college, you might major in geology or a related science. Then plan to study for a year after college to earn a master's degree in library science.

The owners of solar energy firms are involved in all aspects of running a business.

For further information about a career as a solar energy firm owner, contact:

Solar Energy Firm Owner

If you think you would enjoy being involved in all aspects of running a business, perhaps your goal is to start a company of your own. An interest in science and technology might lead you to consider establishing a business within the field of solar energy.

Solar energy is a small field today, but it is likely to grow rapidly in the next decade. Solar energy products that are currently available include various kinds of domestic heating systems. As we attempt to rely less on fossil

American Solar Energy
Association

fuels for our heating needs, the demand for these products should increase. Future technological developments should result in new solar energy applications as well.

There are no specific academic requirements for a business owner, but courses in business management would be helpful. Engineering, architecture, and science courses also would benefit a person who wants to design and manufacture solar energy products.

395 Concord Avenue
Belmont, Massachusetts 02178

Superclusters are clusters of clusters of galaxies. Such huge collections of galaxies, like clusters of galaxies, are held together by gravity. They do not mix together, but remain distinct and separate. The Local Group lies on the outskirts of one such group known as the Virgo supercluster.

Check yourself

What holds superclusters of galaxies together? Gravity

Beyond the galaxies

New vocabulary: Big Bang, Big Crunch

Galaxies extend out into the universe as far as our telescopes can see. Some photographs of the most distant galaxies look no different than photographs of a sky full of stars. They are so far away that they appear to be dim points of light. In the 1960s, astronomers found the most distant objects known, the quasars.

Quasars (KWAY′-sarz) look like stars, but they are very different. Quasars have been found to be racing away from the Milky Way at speeds higher than any other objects in the universe. A quasar is only about ten times the diameter of the earth's orbit. But it gives off as much energy as trillions of suns! What could possibly be supplying the fuel to power such objects? Some scientists once thought that quasars might get their energy from a gigantic cluster of stars at its center. Even that does not supply enough energy for what is observed. The only other object that could supply such energy might be a gigantic black hole at the center of each quasar. In fact, such a black hole would have to have a mass about a billion times that of the sun. One of the most exciting discoveries about quasars is that they are often surrounded by what astronomers call "fuzz." This fuzz looks just like the stars found in galaxies. Astronomers now think that quasars may be the centers of very young galaxies seen forming early in the history of the universe. One important question we need to yet answer about quasars is why they are racing away from us.

In the 1920s, American astronomer Edwin Hubble began to study the radial velocities of galaxies. To his surprise, he found that the farther he looked, the faster the galaxies were

Figure 4-36. The three main types of galaxies are shown, classified by shape. *Upper:* An elliptical galaxy—NGC 205 Nebula in Andromeda; *Middle:* A spiral galaxy—the Whirlpool galaxy in Canes Venatici; *Lower:* An irregular galaxy

Thinking Skill   Observing

When you see your best friend, when you hear the telephone ring, or when you feel the softness of a kitten's fur, you are gathering information with your senses. In other words, you are observing.

Scientists use observation also. But they must make observations more carefully and accurately than you do in your daily life. Scientists practice many years to learn how to observe skillfully as they collect and record data. For example, only by careful observation of the moon, stars, and sun can scientists determine the position and movement of the earth.

It is important to remember that accurate scientific observations do not include inferences. Scientists may make inferences to try to explain their observations, but only after the observations are made.

Using the following steps may help you to develop you skill of observation:
1. Examine the entire item or situation.
2. Look carefully for details using only your sense of sight.
3. Write down all of the specific details found using your sense of sight.
4. Look for details using another one of your senses, and write down the specific details you found.
5. Continue this process with all your remaining senses, if possible.
6. Write down all your observations.

Learning the Skill
Use the steps of the skill of observation to observe the five substances provided by your teacher. Record your results and be prepared to dicuss the following questions:
1. What did you observe about each substance with the sense of sight?
2. What did you observe about each substance with the sense of touch? Smell? Hearing? Taste? (SAFETY NOTE: Never taste materials unless directed to do so by your teacher.)
3. Which senses give you the most information about the substances?

Applying the Skill
Your teacher will do a demonstration. Carefully observe the beakers and their contents. Write down your observations and be prepared to discuss them with the class. Did you write down only what you actually observed?

moving away from the Milky Way. (The same thing would also be true if we were in another galaxy looking at the Milky Way. It too would appear to be rushing away.) Before the universe had always been assumed not to be moving. It now looked as though everything were rushing away from some kind of explosion.

About 15 to 20 billion years ago there was no universe as we know it today. All that is believed to have existed at this time was a very dense concentration of material. Suddenly, this material exploded in an event now called the **Big Bang,** and the universe was created. As the material expanded, it cooled. Galaxies formed, with their billions of stars. As you might have already guessed, the quasars are farthest from the Milky Way because they were created early in the universe. They travel at their high speed because that is how fast the material in the universe was moving when they were formed. Since they have the fastest speed, quasars have gone the farthest of any objects we have observed.

Other important evidence that the Big Bang actually took place is an amazing discovery made in the mid-1960s. Two American astronomers, Arno Penzias and Robert Wilson, were using a very sensitive telescope that detected radio waves when they discovered the remains of the heat left over from the Big Bang explosion. Every direction they turned their telescope, they found a signal equal to about 3 Kelvins (near $-276°C$, or absolute zero, a temperature so cold that all the

Suggest that interested students find out more about the Big Bang theory. In particular, what do scientists mean when they say that space as well as matter can be compressed?

Figure 4-37. If the universe does not contain enough mass for gravity to hold it together, what will eventually happen to it? The universe will expand forever. When all of the stars have used all of thier fuel, it will become dark and cold.

Science Processes: Formulating models; Inferring
See also Activity Record Sheet 4-3 (Lab Manual
page 59)

CORE   5 minutes   Pairs of students

Activity 4-3   Simulating an Expanding Universe

Materials
balloons
8-10 circular gummed
  labels

Purpose
To imitate the action of an expanding universe.

Procedure
1. Slightly inflate a balloon until it has a round shape. Squeeze the end together to keep the air in the balloon.
2. Have another student paste the small gummed labels at different locations on the slightly inflated balloon. The gummed labels represent different galaxies.

3. Now continue to inflate the balloon, and observe what happens to the distance between the galaxies.

Questions
1. Compare the way galaxies move apart. How do two galaxies close to each other move in comparison with two that are far apart?
2. Do the gummed labels change size?

Conclusion
Think about what a continually expanding universe might mean. Scientists aren't sure. What do you think might happen?

Step 2

Step 3

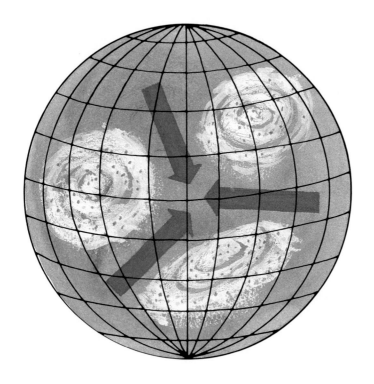

Figure 4-38. If the universe does not contain enough mass for gravity to hold together, what will eventually happen to it?
The universe will expand to the point that gravity stops the expansion. Then it may contract until it finally comes together in the Big Crunch.

motion in atoms stops). On first thought, this might not make sense; one would expect the heat from the Big Bang to be very hot. But after 15 to 20 billion years, it could easily have cooled to this very low temperature. Even though 3 Kelvins is indeed extremely cold, it is still warmer than scientists would expect the universe to be if the Big Bang explosion had never occurred. Penzias and Wilson's evidence strongly suggests that the Big Bang did occur and thus began the creation of our universe.

One of the biggest questions that astronomers are trying to answer is whether or not the universe will continue to expand forever. The answer depends on how much mass there is in the universe. This is not easy to determine because we can only see objects that give off light. There may be more dark material with mass in the universe. If there is not enough mass, gravity will not be able to hold the universe together. It will expand forever. Eventually, all of the stars in the galaxies will have used up their fuel, and the universe will become dark and cold.

Library research

What is the Very Large Array near Socorro, New Mexico? What have scientists been able to learn about radio waves from outer space?

If the universe has enough mass, it will continue to fly apart only until it reaches a point where its gravity will stop the expansion. The universe will then begin to contract until it all comes together with a crash. Some astronomers refer to this event as the **Big Crunch.** Following the Big Crunch, another Big Bang may take place, creating a whole new universe. Although it can't be proved, this cycle of Big Bang, Big Crunch, Big Bang, Big Crunch may have happened many times. The universe we see all around us today may not have been the only universe to have ever existed. It may not be the last.

The more astronomers look at the universe, the more questions seem to be raised. Are galaxies distributed evenly, or are they more clumped together in some parts than others? This question of the universe being either "smooth" or "lumpy" is an important one because it will tell us more about conditions at the time of the Big Bang. One of the most fascinating new discoveries is what is known as the "soap bubble model" of galaxy distribution. Measurements of the radial velocities of some galaxies have shown that they are positioned as if they are on the surfaces of what have been compared to giant soap bubbles. Each bubble touches the one next to it like a kitchen sink full of soap suds. The centers of the bubbles seem to be hollow, with no galaxies.

1. Quasars probably were created early in the universe's history. Their speed may represent how fast the matter in the universe was moving when they were created.
2. The Big Bang

Check yourself

1. Why do astronomers think quasars travel at such high speeds?
2. If the Big Crunch occurs billions of years from now, what event might follow it?

Looking at the universe

Astronomy has come a long way since our ancestors first looked skyward and wondered about what they saw. We can now study the universe in parts of the spectrum that we cannot even see with our eyes.

The field of radio astronomy was born in the 1930s when it was discovered that the Milky Way gave off radio waves.

Figure 4-39. This large saucerlike dish is a radio telescope. How have radio telescopes enabled scientists to expand their exploration of the universe?
A radio telescope is able to pick up radio waves from objects that were not detected by any other means.

Today some of the most detailed observations are made with radio telescopes. Since radio waves pass easily through our atmosphere both day and night, astronomers can observe objects with radio telescopes around the clock.

If an earthbound telescope can be put on a high mountaintop where there is little water in the atmosphere, it can be used to study the heat being given off by astronomical objects. Observing this infrared energy can tell us about how stars form in nebulae. In fact, very young stars have been observed in the Orion nebula that can't be seen with optical telescopes.

As bigger and better rockets were built as part of the space program, satellite observatories became possible. Satellites are above the moisture, turbulence, and molecules in the earth's atmosphere. Once in space, you can observe any part of the spectrum you want. Observation is not limited by what the earth's atmosphere will permit. In addition to infrared and visible light, satellite observatories can also be built to study objects giving off ultraviolet, X-ray, and gamma-ray portions of the spectrum. Some of the most unusual and interesting objects in the universe—black holes, supernovae, and exploding galaxies—can be studied in this way.

Figure 4-40. The IRAS infrared satellite collects information about the universe from far above the earth's atmosphere.

Figure 4-41. The *Skylab 1* space station carried humans, who performed scienfitic experiments over a two-year period.

Figure 4-42. The Hubble Space Telescope will take pictures of many celestial objects. Solar arrays, looking here like giant wings, will provide power. The information the telescope collects will be sent first to Goddard Space Flight Center and then to the Space Telescope Science Institute.

With the new knowledge that astronomers obtain from new telescopes on the earth and new satellites in space, the next few decades may lead to a better understanding of the universe.

Check yourself

Satellite observatories are above the earth's atmosphere.

What advantages do satellite observatories have over observatories on the surface of the earth?

Section 3 Review   Chapter 4

Check Your Vocabulary

4   Big Bang

7   Big Crunch

1   galaxy

5   Milky Way galaxy

3   Local Group

6   quasar

2   supercluster

Match each term above with the numbered term that best describes it.

1. An enormous group of stars held together by gravity

2. Clusters of clusters of galaxies

3. The cluster of galaxies to which the Milky Way belongs

4. The explosion of material that created the universe

5. The galaxy of which the solar system is a part

6. An object that looks like a star but produces as much energy as trillions of stars

7. The possible final contracting of the universe by gravity

Check Your Knowledge

Multiple Choice: Choose the answer that best completes each of the following sentences.

1. Astronomers think that star formation is no longer taking place in ? .
   a) the Milky Way
   b) elliptical galaxies
   c) spiral galaxies
   d) irregular galaxies

2. One important piece of evidence for the Big Bang theory was Penzias and Wilson's discovery of ? left over from the explosion.
   a) X-rays
   b) ultraviolet light
   c) heat energy
   d) water vapor

3. If the Big Bang is eventually followed by the Big Crunch, the Big Crunch will be followed by ? .
   a) another Big Bang
   b) a black hole
   c) another Big Crunch
   d) pulsar formation

4. Satellite observatories are especially useful because they ? .
   a) study radio waves
   b) are not limited by the earth's atmosphere
   c) use X-rays
   d) can see black holes

Check Your Understanding

1. If you visited another planet in another galaxy, how would you describe Earth's location to an inhabitant of that planet?

2. Describe the three general classes of galaxies. To which class does the Milky Way belong?

3. Name four members of the Local Group.

4. Why is the discovery of the "fuzz" around a quasar exciting to astronomers?

5. Why are quasars farther from the Milky Way than other celestial objects are?

6. Describe the "soap bubble" model of galaxy distribution.

Use **Reading Checksheet 4-3** TRB page 72
   Skillsheet 4-3 TRB page 114
   Section Reviewsheet 4-3 TRB pages 165–166
   Section Testsheet 4-3 TRB page 186

Chapter 4 Review

Concept Summary

The **solar system** is the sun and all the objects that revolve around the sun.
☐ Various models of a solar system have been suggested throughout history.
☐ Much evidence exists in favor of the present sun-centered model.
☐ The earth is the only planet known to support life.
☐ Information about the planets other than Earth has been obtained through the use of telescopes, spacecraft, and other instruments.
☐ Comets, asteroids, and meteoroids may be debris left over from the formation of the solar system.

The **sun** is the star that provides the earth's energy and is the star around which all the planets revolve.
☐ The sun's energy is provided by nuclear fusion.
☐ Without the sun, there could be no life on the earth.
☐ Without the gravitational force of the sun, the planets would fly off into space.

A **star** is a light- and heat-producing celestial object that has evolved from a cloud of dust and gas.
☐ Stars vary greatly in size, age, and distance from the earth.
☐ Although some stars are going out of existence, new stars are still being formed.

A **galaxy** is an enormous group of stars that is held together by gravitational attraction.
☐ Our solar system is part of the Milky Way galaxy.
☐ New stars are still being formed in two of the three main types of galaxies.

The universe probably came into being through an explosion called the **Big Bang.**
☐ The behavior of quasars is one kind of evidence supporting the Big Bang theory.

☐ If enough mass exists in the universe, gravity may one day cause it to contract, causing the Big Crunch. The Big Bang may then occur once more.

Putting It All Together

1. What objects belong to the solar system?
2. Why are Newton's laws important to a scientific understanding of the motions of the different objects within the solar system?
3. Identify each of these planets: the largest; the smallest; the nearest to the sun; the farthest from the sun; the planet nearest to the earth in size.
4. Why do we see fewer impact craters on Mercury than on the moon?
5. Explain why the surface temperature of Venus is higher than that of the earth.
6. Why is the sun—or any star—very hot and glowing?
7. Name at least three instruments used to study the stars. Tell why each is important to astronomers.
8. Describe two kinds of motion that stars have. How is each kind of motion detected?
9. How is a star created? How do stars come to an end?
10. Describe two methods that scientists use to determine stellar distances.

Apply Your Knowledge

1. Prepare a list of items you would take with you if you were going to Mars by yourself.
2. Make a time line to show the progress of the conquest of space.
3. Construct a bulletin board display to show the hazards of space travel.

4. Organize a debate that centers on a space-oriented question. Some examples: Is there life in outer space? Are there flying saucers in space?
5. Make an area on the bulletin board for space and astronomy current events. Put up interesting clippings, news headlines, and articles. Obtain an astronomical sky map and report to the class the various events that can be seen each night.

Find Out on Your Own

1. Observe a meteor shower. Prepare a report of when meteor showers occur. Make a count of how many you observed. If possible, take a time-lapse photograph.
2. Choose one planet that is visible and make an observation of that planet each day at the same time. Keep a record of its position against the star background. Explain the motion you observe.
3. Using a cardboard mailing tube or the cardboard tube from a roll of paper towels, look through the tube at the Big Dipper. Count the number of stars. Then point the tube at a section of the Milky Way and make a star count. Report your findings to the class.

Reading Further

Branley, Franklin M. *Mysteries of the Universe.* New York: Dutton, 1984.
   This short, readable book presents facts and speculations about the universe.

Couper, Heather, and Nigel Henbest. *The Sun.* New York: Franklin Watts, 1986.
   Accurate, up-to-date information about the sun is presented with good illustrations. Included are projects such as making a sundial and observing an eclipse.

Moore, Patrick. *The New Atlas of the Universe.* New York: Crown, 1985.
   The author takes us on a fascinating tour of the universe with the help of maps and photographs of the stars.

Nicks, Oran W. *Far Travelers: The Exploring Machines.* Washington, DC: NASA, 1985.
   The story of NASA's unmanned space probes is told by the director of the program.

Reeves, Hubert. *Atoms of Silence: An Exploration of Cosmic Evolution,* trans. Ruth A. Lewis and John S. Lewis. Cambridge: MIT Press, 1984.
   This book discusses the Big Bang theory and how it relates to biological evolution.

White, Jack R. *Satellites of Today and Tomorrow.* New York: Dodd, Mead & Co., 1985.
   This interesting book discusses the history of space activities, describes the many current uses of satellites, and speculates about satellites of the future.

Science Issues of Today   Improvements in Astronomic Observations

The multiple-mirror telescope is well suited to examining quasars, light-emitting bodies on the visual outer fringes of space.

In 1609, Galileo was the first person to use the newly invented telescope to make astronomical observations. His improved versions of the telescope allowed him and other naturalists to make the basic discoveries that led to the modern science of astronomy.

Always wanting to reach out further, astronomers have designed larger and more powerful telescopes. Telescopes use sophisticated lenses and mirrors that have to be precisely ground and polished to provide distortion-free images. Light-gathering ability and magnification increase with larger-diameter mirrors. The larger-diameter mirrors have traditionally been very thick and heavy because a large mirror that is too thin will eventually bend, deform, and lose its usefulness.

Even though some astronomers have sensing devices that measure types of radiation such as radio waves and X-rays, the need to reach out further for optical images still continues. For many years the 200-inch diameter mirror at Mount Palomar Observatory in California was considered the largest possible size for a telescope; the mirror alone weighed over 14 tons, and the entire instrument about 500 tons.

However, with the advent of space age materials and new designs, even more powerful telescopes are now being built. One method of making larger mirrors that are strong and much lighter in weight is to make the back surface like a honeycomb. Another technique is to use multiple mirrors which are aimed and synchronized by using computer control. One telescope of this type is currently in operation in Arizona. It uses four 295-inch mirrors and has the equivalent total light-gathering capacity of a 590-inch mirror. Two other powerful telescopes with completion dates of 1989 and 1996 are under con-

The six 72-inch mirrors of this telescope view the sky from Mount Hopkins, near Tucson, Arizona. The images of the joint Smithsonian-University of Arizona telescope are coordinated by a sophisticated video system.

struction; one is in west Texas and the other is in Hawaii. These telescopes will have the capabilities of 300-inch and 400-inch mirrors. A 300-inch mirror has over twice the light-gathering capacity of a 200-inch mirror!

The atmosphere is another limiting factor for telescopes because light forming the images is often distorted as it travels to the earth's surface. The best optical observatory should be located above the earth's atmosphere, perhaps even on the moon. With the increasing effective size and decreasing weight of mirrors, a moon-based observatory may become a reality in the twenty-first century.

All the improvements in astronomic observations provide an increased understanding of our universe and how it formed. This is one of the most exciting frontiers of modern science.

Air in Motion

Unit 3

Above the "solid" earth are two kinds of fluids. One fluid, water, fills the lakes, rivers, and oceans. The other fluid is the one that all of us live under—the gases that make up the atmosphere.

Without the earth's atmosphere, there could be no life on the earth. The earth's atmosphere filters out certain rays from the sun which are harmful. The earth's atmosphere contains the gases needed by living organisms. Much of the recycling and redistribution of the earth's water takes place in the earth's atmosphere.

Chapter 5
The Atmosphere

Chapter 6
Weather and Climate

5

Student Resources		Meeting Individual Needs	
Student Text	**Laboratory Activities**		
Section 1 Heat and the Atmosphere 232–248			
Energy from the Sun 233–235	Investigation 5-1 Analyzing Sunlight LM 67–68	Enrichment	
Energy Moves by Conduction 235–237			
Our Science Heritage: How Does the Sun Produce Energy? 236			
Energy Moves by Convection 238–239			
Energy Moves by Radiation 239–242			
Temperatures Around the Earth 242–247	Activity 5-1A Changing the Angle of Incoming Energy 244	Reinforcement	
	Activity Record Sheet 5-1A LM 65		
	Activity 5-1B Measuring the Effect of the Angle of Incoming Energy 246; Activity Record Sheet 5-1B LM 66	CORE	
Section 1 Review 248			
Section 2 Winds and the Atmosphere 249–262			
Convection Currents and Wind Belts 250–253	Activity 5-2A Forming Convection Currents 252	CORE	
	Activity Record Sheet 5-2A LM 69		
Specific Heat and Convection Currents 254–255			
Atmospheric Pressure and Winds 255–257	Investigation 5-2 Determining Wind Direction and Speed LM 71–72	Enrichment	
The Density of the Atmosphere 257–258			
Reading an Atmospheric Pressure Map 259–261	Activity 5-2B Comparing Differences in Specific Heat 260	Enrichment	
	Activity Record Sheet 5-2B LM 70		
Section 2 Review 262			
Section 3 Moisture and the Atmosphere 263–281			
Energy and the States of Water 264–265	Research Lab 5 Factors Affect Evaporating Rates LM 77	Enrichment	
Water Vapor in the Atmosphere 266–269	Activity 5-3A Finding the Relative Humidity 268	CORE	
	Activity Record Sheet 5-3A LM 73		
When Does Condensation Occur? 269–274	Activity 5-3B Finding the Dew-Point Temperature 272	Enrichment	
	Activity Record Sheet 5-3B LM 74		
Careers: Weather Forecaster/Weather Technician 270			
Condensation Near the Earth's Surface 274–275			
Condensation in the Atmosphere 276–278	Investigation 5-3 Keeping a Cloud Watch LM 75–76	Enrichment	
Precipitation 279–280			
Section 3 Review 281			
Chapter 5 Review 282–283			

Chapter Planning Guide

Teacher Resources		Meeting Individual Needs
Teacher's Edition	**Teacher's Resource Book**	
	Letter to Parents EI 29	Enrichment
	Essential Ideas 5-1 EI 31–32	Reinforcement
	Skillsheet 5-1 TRB 115	Reinforcement
	Teaching Diagram 5-1 TRB 27	CORE
	Overhead Transparency B10	CORE
Demonstration 230C; Discussion Idea 230D	Overhead Transparency B11	CORE
Activity Notes 230E		
Activity Notes 230F		
Section 1 Review Answers 230F		
	Reading Checksheet 5-1 TRB 73	Reinforcement
	Section Reviewsheet 5-1 TRB 167–168	CORE
	Section Testsheet 5-1 TRB 287	CORE
Environmental Topic 230G	Essential Ideas 5-2 EI 33–34	Reinforcement
Activity Notes 230G–230H	Teaching Diagram 5-2 TRB 28	Reinforcement
	Overhead Transparency S8	Enrichment
	Skillsheet 5-2 TRB 116	Enrichment
Demonstration 230H	Overhead Transparency S9	Enrichment
Discussion Idea; Creative Writing Idea 230J		
Activity Notes 230K	Overhead Transparency B12	CORE
Section 2 Review Answers 230K	Reading Checksheet 5-2 TRB 74	Reinforcement
	Section Reviewsheet 5-2 TRB 169–170	CORE
	Section Testsheet 5-2 TRB 288	CORE
	Essential Ideas 5-3 EI 35–36	Reinforcement
Activity Notes 230L–230M	Teaching Diagram 5-3A TRB 29	Enrichment
Demonstration 230M		
Activity Notes 230N		
Environmental Topic 230P		
	Teaching Diagram 5-3B TRB 30	CORE
	Overhead Transparency B13	CORE
Discussion Idea 230P	Skillsheet 5-3 TRB 117	Reinforcement
Section 3 Review Answers 230P	Reading Checksheet 5-3 TRB 75	Reinforcement
	Section Reviewsheet 5-3 TRB 171–172	CORE
	Section Testsheet 5-3 TRB 289	CORE
Chapter 5 Review Answers 230Q–230R	Chapter 5 Testsheet TRB 325–326	CORE

5

Heat and the Atmosphere

Learner Objectives

1. To identify effects of the earth's atmosphere on incoming radiation from the sun.
2. To discriminate among three ways in which energy moves.
3. To identify causes for temperature differences around the earth.
4. To demonstrate how the angle of incoming radiation affects the amount of energy received.
5. To recognize that sunlight (energy from the sun) is made up of a spectrum of energy waves of different wavelengths.

5-1

Concept Summary

The atmosphere is a layer of gases that surrounds the earth and that affects energy levels on the earth's surface.

The sun's energy is the energy that is radiated out into space from the sun and that powers the winds and the weather changes that occur within the earth's atmosphere.

Demonstration

The Dynamics of a Convection Current

Put the mouth of a round balloon over the top of a small soda pop bottle. The balloon will be limp. Then place the bottle in a bowl or saucepan of very hot tap water. The balloon will "stand up" as if someone were trying to blow it up.

Explain that heating causes the molecules of air to spread out. When the air in the bottle is heated it must be spread out into the balloon.

If time allows, put the bottle (with balloon still attached) in a cool place for 10 minutes (a refrigerator would be ideal). After it has cooled down, show the class that the balloon has collapsed or—if the bottle has cooled enough—been pulled into the bottle. Explain that as air cools, the molecules pull back together. If you've cooled the bottle to less than the temperature it was when you started, the volume of the air is less than it was originally.

Explain to the students that heating and cooling the bottle shows how energy moves by convection. In Section 1 they will learn about three ways energy moves and how this movement affects the atmosphere and the climate.

You can leave the bottle with balloon attached on a table for several days. Students can see how the balloon is affected by changes in room temperature. (This is most effective if the classroom temperature changes significantly during the day.)

Discussion Idea

Temperature Inversions

Collect newspaper and magazine clippings about air pollution, smog alerts, temperature inversions, etc. Put them on a bulletin board and allow students time to read them.

Explain what happens in a temperature inversion. Usually warm air near the earth rises, while cooler air drops and then is warmed and rises. There is a constant cycling of air. Occasionally the pattern changes and a warm air mass traps the cooler air, which then cannot rise. Because air masses don't rise, pollutants are not carried away. People can become very ill; those with respiratory problems are especially threatened. Plants are harmed. All activities that add pollutants to the air must be strictly curtailed until the weather changes and allows air to rise again.

Ask students if they have had any experience of pollution emergencies. Have them explain what they and their families did, or would do, in such a situation (reduce driving, use car pools and public transportation, stop using wood stoves and fireplaces, etc.). Ask what society as a whole can do (develop alternative fuels, improve public transportation systems, educate people about pollution, etc.).

Tell students that in Section 1 they will learn how our use of fuels might have a long-term effect on climate.

You might also discuss "natural" causes of air pollution, such as volcanic eruptions, dust storms, etc.

Discussion Idea (alternate)

The Threat of the Greenhouse Effect

Collect newspaper and magazine clippings that describe studies of the greenhouse effect and perhaps also some that describe theories of nuclear winter. Put them up on a bulletin board and allow students several days to examine them.

Ask students what can be done to reduce the increasing amounts of carbon dioxide in the air. (The newspaper clippings might give them some ideas; they will probably comment on the need to reduce the burning of fuels, to conserve and increase green-plant growth etc.)

This concept is further developed in The Environmental Topic for Section 6-3.

Science Background

According to the kinetic theory of matter, particles of matter are in constant motion. Moving particles have kinetic energy. As a substance gains heat energy, its particles move faster and have more kinetic energy. When a substance cools, its particles move slower and have less kinetic energy. A substance can gain or lose heat, but it does not contain heat. The total amount of energy a substance possesses is called its internal energy. Temperature is simply a measure of the average kinetic energy of the particles of a substance. It does not indicate the total amount of internal energy the substance contains.

It is important for students to understand that the term cold refers to the absence of heat, just as dark refers to the absence of light. A cold object has less internal energy than one that is warmer. Hot and cold are also relative terms. An ice cube at 0°C is relatively hot compared to liquid nitrogen at −196°C. Heat always flows from a warmer region to a cooler one. An object becomes colder because heat flows out of it. For example, houses are insulated to prevent heat from leaving or entering—not to keep "cold" in or out.

5-1

Student Misconception

5-1

Many students are not aware of the factors that affect incoming solar radiation, and they may have the misconception that all incoming radiation reaches the earth's surface.

Of all incoming solar radiation, approximately 34 percent is scattered or reflected by clouds, dust, and the earth's surface. Another 19 percent is absorbed by the atmosphere, leaving 47 percent that is actually absorbed by the earth's surface. (Even more amazing is that less than 1 percent of this solar radiation supports photosynthesis—the basis for all food on our planet.)

Make these figures real to your students through the manipulation of representative objects. Try this activity *prior to* presenting the facts. Ask students to bring in 100 small objects, such as washers, or marbles. Have students allocate washers to represent in percentages the division of incoming solar radiation (100 washers equals 100 percent). They should divide it according to the amounts of reflected radiation, atmosphere-absorbed radiation, and radiation that strikes the earth's surface.

Ask students to explain their reasoning. They may draw on their knowledge of the percentage of radiant energy reflected back by a surface, the greenhouse effect, and photosynthesis. Conclude by asking students to consider how human activities might alter the amount of solar radiation that reaches the earth's surface.

Activity Notes

Activity 5-1A

Changing the Angle of Incoming Energy   page **244**

Purpose   To see how the angle of incoming light affects energy received.

- 10 minutes Large groups or teacher demonstration
- **Activity Record Sheet 5-1A** (Lab Manual page 65) can be used to record this activity.
- Science Processes: Formulating models; Observing; Comparing and contrasting; Describing; Inferring.

Procedure Notes

This activity works best in a darkened room.

You might have students count the number of squares on the graph paper that are illuminated at each angle. This will illustrate how the same amount of energy can be spread out over a larger area.

Answers to Questions

1. A bright round circle is produced when the light strikes the paper at a 90° angle.
2. The light spreads out and is not as bright.

Conclusion

Yes. The same amount of light has been spread out over a larger area. Any point within the area that is lit by the flashlight receives more energy when the angle is 90° than it does when the angle is smaller than 90°.

Going Further

Have students predict what effect the angle of incoming energy may have on temperature. Then have students do Activity 5-1B on page 246 to test their predictions.

Activity Notes

Activity 5-1B

Measuring the Effect of the Angle of Incoming Energy   page **246**

Purpose   To see how the angle of light coming from the sun affects hearing at the earth's surface.

- **CORE** 20 minutes Large groups or teacher demonstration
- **Activity Record Sheet 5-1B** (Lab Manual page 66) can be used to record this activity.
- Science Processes: Formulating models; Measuring; Demonstrating; Comparing; Interpreting data; Inferring.

Advance Preparation

To save time, students might set up the apparatus earlier in the day.

Safety Information

Caution students not to handle the bulb while it is hot.

Procedure Notes

Both thermometers should be at the same starting temperature. The black paper should cover only the bulb of the thermometers.

You might have students set up a third thermometer at an even smaller angle. Then students can compare the three readings.

Answers to Questions

1. The vertical thermometer should show the greater change in temperature.
2. More heat is received when the angle of incoming energy is closest to 90°.

Conclusion

The equator receives the sun's rays year-round at a nearly vertical angle; it is hot at the equator year-round. The Poles receive the sun's rays at a small angle year-round, and so the Poles are always cold.

Section 1 Review Answers

Check Your Understanding
page **248**

1. 1) Some are reflected back. 2) Some are scattered throughout the atmosphere. 3) Some are filtered out. 4) Some reach the earth's surface and are absorbed. 5) Some are radiated back from the earth's surface. 6) Some reflected energy is absorbed by carbon dioxide in the atmosphere.

2. Convection: winds and ocean currents; conduction: warming the earth materials below the surface. Radiation: energy received from the sun during daylight hours and radiated from the earth at night.

3. Temperatures would rise because carbon dioxide absorbs energy radiated by the earth.

4. The hottest temperatures occur around 2:00 p.m. rather than noon (when the sun's rays are most direct) because before noon a surplus of energy has been stored in the earth's surface. Temperatures do not start to drop until after this surplus has been depleted (about two hours after solar noon). The coolest temperatures occur at night after the earth's surface has lost much of the heat it absorbed during the day.

5. Highest annual temperatures occur about six weeks after the beginning of summer. The lowest temperatures occur about six weeks after the beginning of winter.

5-1

Winds and the Atmosphere

Learner Objectives

1. To relate winds to convection currents caused by unequal heating of the earth's surface.
2. To recognize the Coriolis effect on winds in the earth's atmosphere.
3. To relate differences in the specific heat of different common earth materials to temperature changes.
4. To relate atmospheric pressure to density.
5. To interpret symbols for atmospheric pressure on a map.

Concept Summary

The atmosphere is a layer of gases that surrounds the earth and that affects energy levels on the earth's surface.

Environmental Topic

Thousands of lakes and forests in Canada, the United States, and Europe are dying. Lakes that were once healthy are now acidified, with many former lake inhabitants destroyed by the acidity. The culprit, acid rain, is largely a product of burning quantities of fossil fuels. Through a series of chemical reactions, industrial exhaust gases combine with water in the atmosphere to produce acid rain. Acid rain also damages soil and corrodes metals and carbonate building materials.

Have students investigate possible solutions to the acid rain problem, such as the reduction of fossil fuel combustion and the placement of chemical filters (scrubbers) on industrial smokestacks. Discussion questions may include: Who will pay for these preventive measures—the companies producing the exhaust gases? The consumers? What difficulties might arise when environmental problems cross national borders?

Activity Notes

Activity 5-2A

Forming Convection Currents   page **252**

Purpose   To trace the movement of a convection current in a fluid.

- **CORE** 20 minutes Groups of 4 or teacher demonstration
- **Activity Record Sheet 5-2A** (Lab Manual page 69) can be used to record this activity.
- Science Processes: Formulating models; Inferring; Communicating through a drawing; Observing; Applying concepts.

Advance Preparation

Students can set up the apparatus and fill beakers and other containers with water earlier in the day to reduce waiting time in Steps 2 and 5. The potassium permanganate crystals should be kept in their closed container until needed.

Safety Information

Be sure students wear their safety goggles for this activity.

Potassium permanganate is a strong oxidizing agent. Caution students not to let the potassium permanganate crystals come in contact with their skin or clothes. You may wish to have students wear rubber gloves.

Caution students not to dismantle the apparatus until the water in the beaker has cooled or to use beaker tongs and heat-resistant mitts.

Activity Notes (continued)

Procedure Notes

In Step 7, students should add the ice as gently as possible.

Answers to Questions

1. Drawings will vary, but it is expected that they will show the water moving upward above the source of heat.
2. Drawings will vary; movement in the water will be downward, toward the ice.
3. The dye travels in convection currents.
4. The dye shows how the water is affected by temperature changes and forms currents.

Conclusion

The model represents warm air rising above a warm surface and sinking above a cool surface.

Disposal

Potassium permanganate should not come in contact with sulfuric acid, glycerine, ethylene, or glycol. Pour the potassium permanganate down the drain and flush it with water.

Going Further

Bring a "lava lamp" to class. Ask students how it works. (The lamp contains an oily substance and water. A light bulb in the bottom warms the oil, which expands and becomes lighter than the water.)

Demonstration

An Experience with Atmospheric Pressure

Fill a glass to the brim with water and cover it with cardboard. Holding the cardboard, turn the glass to one side over a sink. Let go of the cardboard. Ask why the cardboard stays in place. (The sideways pressure of the air holds it there.)

Holding the cardboard, turn the glass upside down. Let go of the cardboard. Again, ask the class to explain why the water doesn't push the cardboard away. (The upward pressure of air is greater than the pressure exerted by the water.)

Science Background

Even though the Coriolis effect can explain why the winds blow, by no means does it tell the whole story. Equally important is the fact that various areas on the earth's surface differ widely in temperature. A blacktop parking lot will absorb much heat on a sunny day. This heat is later radiated to the air above the parking lot. The warmer air above the parking lot rises. Air from above nearby grassy areas moves in and takes the place of the warmer air. Air currents across huge areas of the earth act in much the same way, causing regional winds to build up.

The amount of heat gained or lost by a substance depends on three factors: 1) the kind of substance, 2) the amount of the substance, and 3) the temperature change that takes place. Different kinds of material require different amounts of heat to make the same temperature change. The amount of heat required to make one gram of matter increase 1°C is called the specific heat of the substance.

5-2

Winds and the Atmosphere

Student Misconception

Students are probably aware that air pressure is lower at high altitudes. Many students may not realize, however, that pressure changes with altitude at all levels, not only at high altitudes. In addition, students may fail to recognize that everyday events reflect changes in air pressure and density.

Pressure is a function of density (mass per unit volume). As the density of air increases, pressure increases. The pull of gravity on the atmosphere is greatest closest to the earth. As a result, the density of the air, and therefore its pressure, are also greatest there. As altitude increases, the effect of gravity decreases, thus density and pressure decrease with altitude. The expression "thin air" stems from this reality.

Students can be assisted in understanding the effect of pressure through a discussion of normal life experiences. For example, many students can recall experiences of "ear-popping." Explain that the eardrum is a flexible membrane that adjusts to changes in air pressure. Typical experiences of ear-popping occur in elevators, airplanes, and when climbing or riding up mountains—all places where the air pressure can change. Students should be better able to associate a change in elevation with a corresponding change in pressure as a result of this discussion.

5-2

Discussion Idea

Winds Can Bring Relief or Destruction

Ask students to look out the window and describe the breeze (or lack of it) outside. Ask what the breezes or winds usually bring to your area—cool weather, rain, warm weather, etc.

If you have a wind vane or anemometer, the class can go outdoors and determine wind direction and speed. You can then check your results with the weather bureau reports. (You may be able to get one immediately on a radio with a weather band.)

Ask what benefits the wind brings (relief from heat, needed rain, clearing of smog, etc.). Ask what problems the wind can bring (dust storms, damage to high-rise buildings and bridges, etc.).

Ask if any students have ever been in a hurricane or seen the effects of a tornado.

Tell students that in Section 2 they will learn about how winds move on earth and how atmospheric pressure affects wind.

Creative Writing Idea

The following writing assignment may help students become more aware of differences in the layers of the atmosphere and the significance of those layers to our survival.

You have a magnificently designed air vehicle that will allow you to travel through the layers of the atmosphere slowly enough to experience and observe the air at each level. The vehicle is only large enough for you, however, and the newspapers and television stations are waiting anxiously for your report on the different layers of the earth's atmosphere. Write a report describing the layers. Include information about temperature, moisture, wind, how easily you can breathe, and the types of animals and inorganic material you see.

Activity Notes

Activity 5-2B

Comparing Differences in Specific Heat   page **260**

Purpose   To compare the specific heats of water and sand or soil.

- 30 minutes Groups of 4
- **Activity Record Sheet 5-2B** (Lab Manual page 70) can be used to record this activity.
- Science Processes: Formulating models; Observing; Collecting and analyzing data; Communicating through a chart; Comparing and contrasting; Inferring.

Advance Preparation

You might wish to set out the sand (or soil) and water earlier in the day so that they are at room temperature when the activity begins.

Procedure Notes

The thermometers should be at the same starting temperature. They should not touch the sides of the containers.

Answers to Questions

1. The temperature rose more in the sand.
2. The temperature dropped more in the sand.
3. The water has the higher specific heat because it required more energy to warm it.

Conclusion

Although the sand (or soil) and water received the same amount of energy, the water maintained its temperature more steadily than the sand did. Water has a higher specific heat than sand, and water reflects radiation better than sand does. Sand absorbs and radiates radiant energy better than water does, so sand heats up and cools down faster than water. Therefore, the sand and water do not have the same amount of heat transferred in and out.

Going Further

You might want students to consider whether the kind of sand, soil, or water would make a difference in the results of the activity. Students might compare white sand and brown sand; clay soil and garden soil; fresh water and salt water. Some of these factors are considered in Activity 8-3B on page 416.

Section 2 Review Answers

Check Your Understanding
page **262**

1. Fluids can change shape and bend and spread out without breaking. Also, winds are convection currents, which occur only in fluids.
2. Prevailing westerlies are the result of deflection caused by the Coriolis effect. As shown in Figure 5-17 on page 253, the air in the diverging zone at 30° north latitude that heads back toward the North Pole is deflected toward its right. This belt of air is known as the prevailing westerlies and the deflection is caused by the Coriolis effect.
3. Objects with high specific heat absorb more heat before air temperatures are affected. That is why temperature changes over land areas are more sudden than over water. Land has a low specific heat, and warms and cools faster than water.
4. Wind is the movement of air from an area of higher pressure to an area of lower pressure.
5. You can expect a drop in temperature and less dense air and feel cooler. You will get winded more easily because there is less oxygen in the same unit volume of air.

5-2

Learner Objectives

1. To distinguish the energy content of water from one physical state to another.
2. To describe the energy transfer as water changes from one state to another.
3. To find the relative humidity of air.
4. To relate dew-point temperature to condensation in the atmosphere.
5. To explain the various forms in which precipitation occurs.

5-3

Concept Summary

The sun's energy is the energy that is radiated out into space from the sun and that powers the winds and the weather changes that take place within the earth's atmosphere.

Water is a compound made up of hydrogen and oxygen, and it can be found on the earth in any of the three physical states of matter.

Activity Notes

Activity 5-3A

Finding the Relative Humidity   page **268**

Purpose   To use a sling psychrometer to find the relative humidity of the air.

- **CORE** 20 minutes Pairs of students or groups of 4
- **Activity Record Sheet 5-3A** (Lab Manual page 73) can be used to record this activity.
- Science Processes: Measuring; Calculating; Reading a table; Collecting and interpreting data; Reasoning.

Advance Preparation

You will need to obtain from a supply house a sling psychrometer for each pair or group of students. Or students may make their own by using fine wire to securely mount two identical liquid thermometers onto a narrow board (about 2" wide). The bulb of one thermometer should extend past the edge of the board. This bulb should be covered with cotton gauze held in place with a rubber band. A loop of rope or strong cord can be attached as a handle, or the apparatus can be left stationary and air can be fanned over it.

The psychrometer will be used for the activity on page 272.

Safety Information

Caution students to stand clear of the psychrometer as it is twirled and to be careful to avoid hitting any objects in the room.

Procedure Notes

Instead of swinging the psychrometer, the same effect can be achieved by fanning air past the bulbs.

After each group has calculated the relative humidity, their findings can be compared and noticeable differences discussed. Students might compare their readings with a local weather report, and discuss reasons for any differences noted.

Answers to Questions

Answers will depend on the relative humidity at the time the activity is done.

Activity Notes (continued)

Conclusion

When less humidity is in the air, more water can evaporate from the wet bulb. The greater the difference between dry-bulb and wet-bulb readings, the lower the level of relative humidity. The lesser the difference in the readings, the higher the level of relative humidity.

Going Further

You might have students repeat this activity on a rainy day or on a particularly dry day (depending on where you live). You might also have students repeat this activity at the same time every day for a week to see how the relative humidity changes.

Demonstration

Cooling Air by Evaporation

Show the students a thermometer that records room temperature, and read them the current temperature. Put some alcohol in the palm of your hand and lay the thermometer in it, making sure that the bulb is in the alcohol. Blow on the alcohol to speed its evaporation. The temperature recorded on the thermometer should drop several degrees.

Explain to students that evaporation of a liquid removes heat from the air, thus causing a drop in temperature. Tell them that in dry regions, houses are "air-conditioned" without the need of a compression unit by using the process of evaporation. Air is blown over water that is exposed to the sun; the air cooled by the evaporation is then blown throughout the house. This method is much less expensive than refrigerated air conditioning but requires a dry climate.

Science Background

Water is the only common substance that occurs in three physical phases in the natural environment. The kinetic theory of matter explains the differences among solids, liquids, and gases.

Motion within solids is limited to the vibration of particles around a fixed point. The closely packed particles are held together by strong attractive forces. Solids have a definite shape and volume. Because the spaces between particles are small, solids have high densities and cannot readily be compressed.

Liquid particles have more kinetic energy than those of solids, and the bonds between them are weaker. As a result, the particles are farther apart and have more freedom of movement. Liquids have a definite volume, but they take the shape of their container.

The particles of a gas are much farther apart than those of a liquid or solid, and move more rapidly. There are no fixed bonds between particles. Consequently, a gas has no definite shape or volume. This also explains why gases have low densities, diffuse rapidly, and are easily compressed.

5-3

Student Misconception

Evaporation is a chilling process that involves the absorption of heat energy. Sound confusing? Any phase change involves the transfer of heat—energy is either absorbed or released. When a solid changes to a liquid, and then to a gas (evaporation), the energy for these processes comes from the environment and is stored (absorbed) in the motion of molecules. Despite the fact that evaporation produces a cooling effect, molecules are actually gaining energy. As a gas changes to a liquid (condensation), and then to a solid, the stored energy is released. During condensation, heat energy is released back into the environment.

You can relate these concepts to your students through real-life examples such as the following. When someone has a fever, a doctor may recommend sponging the body with water, which allows the water to evaporate from the skin and reduces the body temperature. The cooling effect is produced because heat from the body is absorbed by the thin layer of water on the person's skin, causing the water to change from a liquid to a gas. As a result, body temperature decreases, and the person feels cooler.

The energy that was absorbed during evaporation remains trapped in the molecules of water vapor until condensation begins. At that point, heat will be released into the environment, thus explaining the slight rise in temperature that usually accompanies rain or snow.

5-3

Activity Notes

Activity 5-3B

Finding the Dew-Point Temperature   page **272**

Purpose   To find the dew-point temperature of the air you are breathing.

- 20 minutes Pairs of students or groups of 3 or 4
- **Activity Record Sheet 5-3B** (Lab Manual page 74) can be used to record this activity.
- Science Processes: Controlling variables; Observing; Defining operationally; Calculating; Collecting and interpreting data; Reasoning.

Advance Preparation

Use the psychrometer from the activity on page 268.

Since some of the water must be at room temperature, you may wish to have it ready ahead of time.

You might wish to try this activity before the students do, as different conditions may require different procedures as described below.

Procedure Notes

If the atmosphere is very humid, very little ice (perhaps one cube) will be needed to reach the dew-point temperature.

Under dry conditions, the dew point will be very low, and you might want to save time by starting with cool water. You may need to add salt to the water to lower the temperature enough to reach the dew point.

Be sure students do not breathe on the can or jar during the activity. You may wish to discuss with them how breathing on the can could affect the results. (Their breath may be warmer and more humid than the air they are testing; the condensation they see may be from the water vapor in their breath.)

Answers to Questions

Answers to each question will vary. If students are careful in their timing and add the ice in only small amounts, their calculations will approach the actual dew-point temperature. Timing, however, is critical. It is recommended that students compare their findings and discuss any discrepancies.

Conclusion

The higher the relative humidity, the higher the dew point temperature will be.

Environmental Topic

Farmers have long been concerned about frost. Frost can devastate entire crops, resulting in multi-million-dollar losses. Until recently, the techniques of spraying crops with warm moist air, wrapping individual plants, and even blanketing whole fields have met with limited success.

In early 1987, the first field test of a genetically engineered "frost-free" bacteria was conducted on the West Coast. The test was greeted with much anxiety. Many people were concerned that a genetically-engineered organism would pose a threat outside of the laboratory. For some, the test symbolized the beginning of a new age, as people wondered what "monsters" might arise from the manipulation of genetic material.

Allow the class to explore the many pros and cons of genetic engineering. The class might consider whether the taking of such a risk is justified by a valuable end product—the protection of crops from frost damage.

Discussion Idea

The Impact of Precipitation

A day or two ahead of time, ask students to find out the average annual precipitation for their community and for any other places where they have lived.

Ask students to describe the kind of precipitation that falls in their area—snow, rain, hail, sleet, etc. Ask whether it falls fairly evenly around the year or whether there is a "wet season."

Ask how the precipitation affects the community—what benefits it brings, what hardships, etc. (Answers will vary; they might include good growing conditions, the need for flood control, the need for water conservation, the expense of snow removal, the loss of school days and working days, etc.)

Ask students who have lived in different parts of the country to describe the amount of precipitation in those places and the climatic conditions that resulted.

Section 3 Review Answers

Check Your Understanding
page 281

1. 1) Liquid (water); 2) Solid (ice); 3) Gas (water vapor)
2. Water vapor contains the most because it had to absorb its heat of vaporization. Ice contains the least because it has neither its heat of vaporization (water vapor) nor its heat of fusion (liquid water).
3. The rate of evaporation decreases with increasing humidity. This is because less humid air is farther from its saturation point and can absorb more moisture than air that is closer to its saturation point.
4. Warmer air can hold more water vapor than cooler air.
5. Similar: Both involve water that is in its liquid or solid form. Different: 1) Condensation involves a change of state/form from a gas to a liquid or a solid, but precipitation involves a change in size from smaller to larger particles; 2) Condensation does not involve the particles falling to the earth, but precipitation does.

5-3

Chapter Vocabulary

Section 1

atmosphere
electromagnetic waves
wavelength
electromagnetic spectrum
conduction
convection
radiation
fluid
convection current
oxygen-carbon dioxide cycle

Section 2

local winds
prevailing winds
wind belts
prevailing westerlies
specific heat
onshore breeze
offshore breeze
atmospheric pressure
barometer
standard atmospheric pressure
millibar
troposphere
pressure map
isobar
low-pressure center
high-pressure center

5-3

Chapter 5 Review Answers

Putting It All Together   page 282

1.

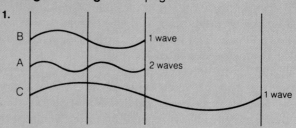

2. When a fluid is heated, its volume increases. Its mass remains the same. Its density (mass ÷ volume) decreases when only the volume increases.

3. When uneven heating takes place in a fluid, the warmer portion (which is less dense) is forced upward by the denser, cooler portion of the fluid.

4. Carbon dioxide is able to trap heat energy reradiated from the earth. If the amount of carbon dioxide in the atmosphere increases, this could increase air temperatures around the earth.

5. Because of an increase in the hours of daylight and an increase in sun's altitude, the Northern Hemisphere receives an ever-increasing amount of energy between January and June. Because of this increase in energy, the earth receives more than it radiates back into the atmosphere. This excess energy is stored in the earth as a surplus.

6. Because water has the highest specific heat of any common natural substance, water must receive a greater amount of energy before its temperature will increase 1°C. In terms of the earth's climates, the high specific heat of water means that land areas near water have less sudden changes in temperature.

7. Convection—hot air rising above a heat source like a candle, stove, or furnace. Conduction—the inside of a frying pan gets hot, but the heat source is on the outside of the pan. Radiation—light from a light bulb.

8. A dry-bulb thermometer measures air temperature. A sling psychrometer measures relative humidity. A barometer measures atmospheric pressure. An anemometer indicates wind speed. A wind vane indicates wind direction.

Chapter 5 Review Answers (continued)

Putting It All Together

9. (In the Northern Hemisphere, winds blow toward a low-pressure center in a counterclockwise direction.)

10. Clouds are condensation that occurs when air is cooled to its dew-point. Clouds often occur in a warm air mass near a boundary with a cold air mass. Clouds are evidence of a lowering temperature. They indicate that a portion of an air mass has been cooled.

Apply Your Knowledge   page **282**

1. It gets very hot inside the car. Because of the greenhouse effect, energy from the sun passes through the glass of the windows and into the car. But the energy that is re-radiated by the seats, etc. inside the car has longer wavelengths, cannot pass back through the glass, and is trapped inside the car.

2. Answers will vary.

3. Answers will vary.

4. Other things being equal, Freezer A (the freezer chest with the lift-top door) will be more efficient. The cold air inside a freezer is denser than the warm air outside the freezer. When the door of Freezer B is swung open, the cold air will pour out of the freezer (just as cold water will pour out of a container opened from the side rather than from the top).

5. The portion nearest the floor will have the least smoke because smoke rises in warm air (which is less dense than cooler air that has not been near the fire). By crawling along the floor, you can therefore lessen the danger of breathing smoke into your lungs.

Chapter Vocabulary

Section 3

water vapor
evaporation
heat of vaporization
condensation
heat of fusion
saturated air
humidity
relative humidity
sling psychrometer
saturation temperature
dew-point temperature
dew
frost
fog
clouds
stratus clouds
cumulus clouds
cirrus clouds
precipitation
rain
snow
sleet
hail
rain gauge

5-3

Chapter 5

The Atmosphere

Section 1
Heat and the Atmosphere

Without heat, temperatures on the earth would be far too cold to provide an environment for life.

The earth receives most of its heat from the sun. Even though the earth receives only a small portion of the total energy given off by the sun, the energy received is enough to power a life-supporting system.

The earth does more than just receive solar energy. It must also process that energy. This important function is performed by the earth's atmosphere.

Section 2
Winds and the Atmosphere

The atmosphere not only processes incoming energy. It also acts as a circulating system.

The air in the atmosphere is a fluid which can move from one place to another. These movements of air, which are caused by unequal heating of the earth's surface, are called winds. Winds affect temperatures around the earth.

Section 3
Moisture and the Atmosphere

Heat causes warmth. Heat also causes motion in the atmosphere.

Motion in the atmosphere can bring a warm breeze during cold weather or a cooling breeze during a hot spell. It can also bring the moisture needed to support life.

Heat powers the winds. It also powers the water cycle, causing water to enter the atmosphere in the form of invisible water vapor which later condenses and forms the raindrops and snowflakes that replenish the earth's supply of fresh water.

Sample answers to the caption question: smell—natural smells (like salty air) vs. smells from industry and machines (like automobile exhaust); touch—the warmth or dampness of a breeze; hearing—the sound of the wind blowing over the earth's surface.

The clouds in the picture on the facing page are made up of water droplets that condensed because of a change in air temperature above the earth's surface. But most of the atmosphere is invisible. What can you learn about the invisible atmosphere through your senses of smell, touch, and hearing?

Heat and the Atmosphere   Section 1

Learner Objectives

1. To identify effects of the earth's atmosphere on incoming radiation from the sun.
2. To discriminate among three ways in which energy moves.
3. To identify causes for temperature differences around the earth.
4. To demonstrate how the angle of incoming radiation affects the amount of energy received.

Section 1 of Chapter 5 is divided into five parts:

Energy from the sun

Energy moves by conduction

Energy moves by convection

Energy moves by radiation

Temperatures around the earth

Figure 5-1. The image in the photo behind the gazelle is a mirage. Mirages are visual illusions caused when light rays pass through air of different temperatures.

New vocabulary: atmosphere

Almost all the earth's energy comes from the sun. Without the sun, the earth would be a frozen wasteland. Surface temperatures would be hundreds of degrees below zero. Without the sun, there could be no life on earth.

Without the atmosphere, there could be no life on earth either. The atmosphere is the blanket of air that surrounds the earth. Air is a mixture of several different gases. On dry days, the air in the atmosphere is about ⅘ nitrogen and ⅕ oxygen. The air also contains tiny amounts of carbon dioxide, hydrogen, argon, and other gases. Another important gas found in the air is water vapor. The amount of water vapor in the atmosphere varies, depending on weather conditions.

The atmosphere is important because it filters out harmful parts of the incoming energy from the sun. The atmosphere is important because it absorbs and stores up useful energy that would otherwise be lost. The atmosphere is also important because it provides a means by which energy can be recycled and circulated around the earth.

Energy from the sun   New vocabulary: electromagnetic wave, wavelength, electromagnetic spectrum

The sun's energy that reaches the earth's atmosphere is only a small part of the energy that leaves the sun. The sun sends out energy in all directions. Yet this energy is so strong that the earth, which is about 150 million kilometers from the sun, receives enough energy to support life.

The sun's energy is carried through space by waves. These waves are similar to the waves that are produced when an electric current moves back and forth through the coil of an electromagnet. Therefore they are called **electromagnetic waves.**

As shown in Figure 5-2, waves can be of different sizes. It may help you to understand this better if you think in terms of water waves. Imagine water waves on a lake or ocean. Sometimes the waves are large and sometimes they are small. The distance between waves also differs from time to time. The distance between waves, which is measured from the top of one wave to the top of the next wave, is called a **wavelength.** In Figure 5-2, the wavelength of Wave A is twice as long as the wavelength of Wave B.

Using pictures from old magazines, students could prepare collage-type presentations that contrast the earth's surface with the surface of the moon or any of the other planets. Some pictures may show areas of the earth's surface that resemble conditions on the moon or another planet. Those pictures will be useful in discussing climate in Chapter 6. Students can pinpoint the pictured locations on a globe and consider the various factors that might cause such conditions.

How does the atmosphere affect the energy the earth receives from the sun?

In answer to the caption question, the wavelength of Wave A is twice as long as the wavelength of Wave B. Considered the other way, the wavelength of Wave B is one half as long as the wavelength of Wave A.
Figure 5-2. Waves can be of different sizes. How do the lengths of Waves A and B compare?

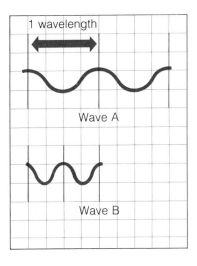

See also Teaching Diagram 5-1 (TRB page 27).

Figure 5-3. The electromagnetic spectrum contains energy waves of many different wavelengths. What kind of electromagnetic waves carry the greatest amount of energy in sunlight? The electromagnetic waves of visible light carry the greatest amount of energy.

You can demonstrate the effect of particles on light by shining a beam of bright light through water to which a drop or two of milk has been added. The milk will add particles of matter to the water. The particles will cause the light passing through to have a bluish appearance. (The same effect can be achieved by shining a beam of light through chalk dust tapped from an eraser into a flask.)

Library research

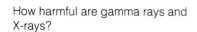

Prepare a report on the different zones within the earth's atmosphere. What are the various zones? How does each zone differ from the others? How has the data on each zone been obtained?

How harmful are gamma rays and X-rays?

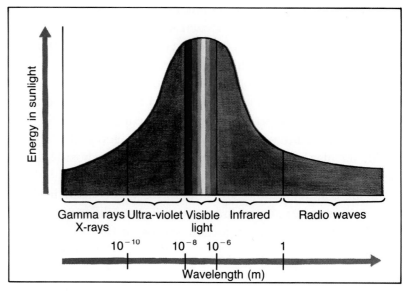

Energy from the sun comes in waves of many different wavelengths. The energy waves of all the different wavelengths together make up what is called the **electromagnetic spectrum.** Figure 5-3 shows the different energy waves in the electromagnetic spectrum. It also shows that the electromagnetic waves of visible light (the thin band in the middle of the diagram) carry the greatest amount of energy in sunlight.

Figure 5-4 shows what happens to the sun's energy that reaches the earth's atmosphere. Part of the sun's energy is reflected back into space. This is caused when incoming energy strikes dust particles or water droplets that are present in the atmosphere. (It is these dust particles that cause light to be scattered, thus giving the sky its blue appearance.) The amount of incoming energy that is reflected back into space in this way is very small.

Part of the sun's energy is scattered throughout the atmosphere. This scattering is caused by dust particles, by water droplets, and by molecules present in the atmosphere.

Part of the sun's energy is filtered out by the atmosphere. Gamma rays and X-ray waves, which would kill people, are filtered out before they reach the earth's surface. Ultraviolet waves, which produce suntans and sunburns, are also partially filtered out. Otherwise, human life would be shortened, particularly for people whose skin is sensitive to sunburn.

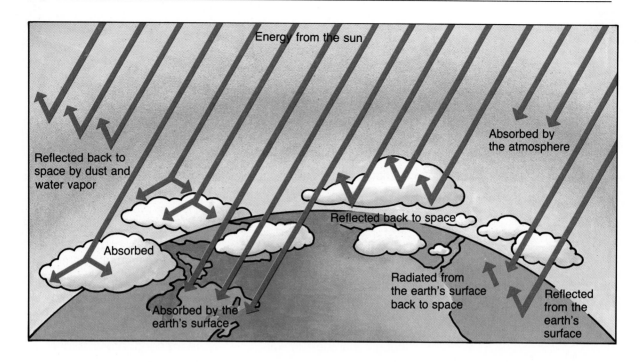

Part of the sun's energy reaches the earth's surface and is absorbed. If you have ever touched a metal surface that is in direct sunlight you have experienced an example of a solid material that has absorbed energy from the sun.

Check yourself

1. What effect does the earth's atmosphere have on incoming energy waves from the sun?

2. How necessary is the atmosphere for life on the earth? Give examples.

Energy moves by conduction

New vocabulary: conduction, convection, radiation

Energy moves in one of three ways. 1) Energy can move through a material, usually a solid object, without the material itself moving. This type of movement is called **conduction.** 2) Energy can move through a material such as a liquid or a gas because of some movement within the material. This way of moving is called **convection.** 3) Energy can move through empty space, or through a material such as air, water, or glass without the aid of the material. This way is called **radiation.**

Figure 5-4. What would happen if energy waves like gamma rays and X-rays were not filtered out by the atmosphere?
If harmful rays from the sun were not filtered out by the atmosphere, human life would be shortened. Other forms of life would no doubt also be affected.

1. It controls the amount and types of radiation that reach the earth's surface from the sun. Some rays are reflected, some filtered out, and some pass through to reach the earth's surface.
2. If the atmosphere did not filter out gamma rays and X-rays, the lives of people sensitive to sunlight would be shortened.

Our Science Heritage

How Does the Sun Produce Energy?

From earliest times, people have realized the importance of the sun. Without the light and heat from the sun, there could be no life on earth. Because the sun is so necessary, some people have considered the sun to be a god.

How does the sun produce energy? Various explanations have been suggested.

At one time, it was thought that the sun was a mass of burning material, sending out heat and light as if from a huge bonfire. But this explanation cannot be true. If the sun's energy were produced by burning, the sun would burn itself out in about two years.

Other theories were also suggested. Some people thought that the release of energy was caused by meteors crashing into the sun. In the 1800s, a theory was developed that the sun's energy was produced by a gradual shrinking of the sun.

It was not until the 1900s that scientists developed a theory of how the sun, which is thought to be over four and a half billion years old, could continue to produce such huge amounts of energy over so long a period of time.

Scientists now believe that the sun produces energy by a process of nuclear fusion. Much of the sun is made up of hydrogen gas. The heat and the force of gravity at the center of the sun are so great that particles within atoms of matter are rearranged. Atoms of one element are changed into atoms of another element which has less mass. In the process, some matter is changed into energy.

The discovery that matter can change into energy is one of the key scientific discoveries of the twentieth century. The work of many twentieth-century scientists has been concerned with the atomic structure of matter and with the relationship between matter and energy.

As for how the sun produces energy, you might want to find out more about Hans Bethe, a scientist who won the Nobel prize in 1967 for his work on energy production of stars.

When energy moves by conduction, it moves through a material without the material itself moving. If a metal bar is heated at one end, the other end will soon become hot. Heat, which is

Figure 5-5. Heat energy can move through solid material by means of conduction. Eventually, heat from the flame will warm the metal pipe, then the end of the metal tongs near the pipe, and then the handles of the tongs.

a form of energy, has been transferred from one end of the bar to the other by means of conduction. Conduction can also take place when two different things touch each other, such as a finger touching an ice cube.

Energy is transferred by conduction when fast-moving atoms or molecules of a material strike other nearby atoms and molecules. That is why energy is transferred by conduction best through a solid material. In a solid material, the atoms and molecules are closer together than they are in a liquid material or in a gas.

Heat is a form of energy. When something is heated, it is taking in energy. When you heat the end of a metal bar, heating causes the atoms in the heated end of the metal bar to speed up. These atoms strike other atoms nearby, causing them to speed up. This process continues all along the bar. In a short time, the atoms all the way along the bar are moving faster, too. The entire bar has become hot. Energy, in the form of heat, has been transferred from one end of the metal bar to the other end by means of conduction.

Check yourself

1. Why is energy by conduction best transferred through a solid material?

2. Describe an example of energy transfer by conduction.

1. Because conduction involves molecules striking each other and molecules in a solid are closer together than they are in a liquid or a gas

2. Answers may vary, but must involve heat transfer through a solid material. Some examples: Heat transfer in a bar when only one end is heated; a pan on a stove, where the whole pan gets hot even though only the bottom is heated; the floor of a ground-floor room built on a cement slab gets cold in winter because of cold temperature beneath the floor.

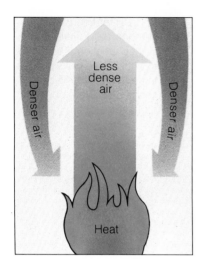

Figure 5-6. Warm air rises because it is forced upward by cooler air, which has greater density.

Energy moves by convection

New vocabulary: fluid, convection current

When energy moves by convection, it moves through a material because of some movement within the material. Convection occurs in fluids. A **fluid** is any material that can move and change shape without separating. Gases and liquids are fluids.

Convection occurs when a fluid is heated. Heating causes the atoms and molecules of a fluid to spread out. When this happens, the fluid increases in volume. But its mass remains the same, since no new matter is added. You may recall the formula

$$\text{density} = \frac{\text{mass}}{\text{volume}}$$

When a fluid increases in volume but not in mass, the fluid becomes less dense.

When a fluid is heated in one area, the portion of the fluid that is nearest the source of heat becomes less dense. (See Figure 5-6.) Gravity exerts more force on the rest of the fluid, which has greater density. The denser portion of the fluid is pulled down in under the less dense portion of the fluid, forcing the less dense portion to rise. A fluid with a low density can float on a more dense fluid.

Figure 5-7. A hot-air balloon rises because the hot air in the balloon is less dense than the cooler air outside the balloon.

The unequal densities caused by the unequal heating of a fluid cause what is called a **convection current.** Convection currents occur in oceans and lakes. Convection currents also occur in the atmosphere, where they cause winds. A hawk or condor can soar and glide great distances, carried along on convection currents of air.

Check yourself

1. Compare convection and conduction. How are they similar? How are they different?

2. Describe the causes of a convection current.

Energy moves by radiation

New vocabulary: oxygen-carbon dioxide cycle

When energy moves by radiation, it moves without the aid of any material it is passing through. Light and heat are both forms of energy. Light and heat from the sun are examples of energy that moves by radiation. Light from a light bulb is also an example of energy that moves by radiation.

Inside a light bulb is a very fine wire called a filament, which is surrounded by an empty space or a vacuum. When the light bulb is turned on, electricity causes the filament to heat up to a very high temperature. Because the filament has become warmer than its surroundings, it emits—or sends out—energy by means of radiation. The heated filament emits energy in all directions—through the empty space and through the atmosphere outside the bulb. In other words, it radiates energy. Most of the energy from a light bulb is in the form of visible light. But some energy is also emitted in the form of invisible light.

If any object that is warmer than its surroundings will emit radiation, does that mean that the earth emits radiation? Absolutely. The surface of the earth, which is warmed by energy from the sun, emits radiation back into the atmosphere (shown in Figure 5-4). The reason you cannot see this radiation is because the earth's surface is not hot enough to emit energy in wavelengths that are visible.

What causes the convection currents that occur in fluids like the atmosphere and bodies of water?

1. Similar: Both involve heat transfer and the use of a material; Different: Convection occurs because of movement of a fluid, whereas conduction occurs in a solid but not because of any movement of the solid material itself.

2. Heating one part of a fluid causes that part of the fluid to become less dense. The denser parts of the fluid are more affected by the force of gravity and are pulled down under the less dense part, causing it to rise and setting up a convection current.

In answer to the caption question, the sun and a light bulb are alike in that both give off energy by radiation.

Figure 5-8. How is a light bulb like the sun?

Figure 5-9. Our hands can detect the heat energy of a burner on a low heat setting, but our eyes cannot. Radiant energy is visible at high heat settings. Be careful not to touch burners set at a low temperature.

Have students find out about LANDSAT and infrared or infrared scopes.

What would happen if the earth radiated energy in the same wavelengths as the energy it received?

Not all wavelengths of energy can be seen. Most are too long or too short to be visible to the human eye. Figure 5-9 shows that the energy waves emitted from a burner at a low temperature setting cannot be seen while some of the energy waves emitted from a burner at a higher temperature setting can be seen. The wavelengths of energy emitted as heat are too long to be visible. The wavelengths of energy emitted as light are shorter and can be seen. At a higher temperature setting, more energy is released in the form of heat, and some is released as light. The wavelengths of energy waves radiated from the earth, like the wavelengths of heat, are too long to be visible to the human eye.

The longer wavelengths of energy emitted from the earth play an important part in maintaining comfortable temperatures on earth. The shorter wavelengths emitted from the sun pass through the earth's atmosphere and reach the earth's surface. If the earth radiated back the energy in the same wavelengths, most of the energy would pass back out into space. The longer wavelengths of energy radiated by the earth are absorbed by gases like carbon dioxide and remain in the atmosphere. This is called the greenhouse effect because a greenhouse traps heat in a similar way.

In a greenhouse, the short wavelengths of energy from the sun pass through the glass and into the greenhouse. Some of this energy is absorbed by the plants, the soil, and other objects in the greenhouse and then radiated back into the air. The energy radiated from the objects in the greenhouse has longer wavelengths than sunlight because the objects have a much lower temperature than the sun. These longer wavelengths cannot pass through the glass. The energy in these longer wavelengths is trapped inside the greenhouse where it heats the air. That is why the temperature inside a greenhouse is usually warmer than the temperature of the air on the outside.

In the atmosphere, the greenhouse effect occurs all over the earth. Because of the greenhouse effect, the earth remains a comfortable place to live. Without the greenhouse effect, the average temperature at the earth's surface would be much colder.

Some scientists are concerned that the greenhouse effect may increase to a dangerous degree in the future. The amount of carbon dioxide in the atmosphere is slowly increasing. The increase in carbon dioxide causes an increase in the greenhouse effect. Carbon dioxide is released by the respiration of

In answer to the caption question, the glass of a greenhouse permits solar energy to enter the greenhouse but traps longer-wavelength energy radiated from objects in the greenhouse. Figure 5-10. Why is the temperature inside a greenhouse usually warmer than the temperature of the air on the outside?

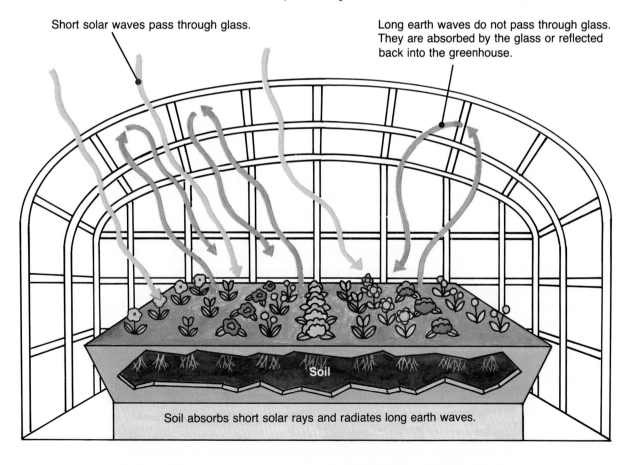

Short solar waves pass through glass.

Long earth waves do not pass through glass. They are absorbed by the glass or reflected back into the greenhouse.

Soil

Soil absorbs short solar rays and radiates long earth waves.

How do plants, as they make food for themselves, affect the amounts of carbon dioxide and oxygen in the atmosphere?

The early earth's atmosphere may not have had any free oxygen.

1. Similar: All involve the transfer of energy; Different: Radiation does not involve any material it may happen to be passing through.
2. The greenhouse effect occurs because a material (like glass in a greenhouse or gas in the atmosphere) permits shorter wavelengths of energy from the sun to pass through but traps longer wavelengths of energy reradiated by materials on the earth's surface, preventing the energy from passing back out into space.

Library research

What methods of heating buildings are used around the world? (Look for some unusual ones, too.) How do the different methods compare from one area to another? Why is one method more likely than another in a particular area? How do the different methods compare in terms of energy efficiency?

animals and by the burning of fuels. Carbon dioxide is removed from the atmosphere by plants during the food-making process. The plants give off oxygen, which is taken in by animals. These two processes together are known as the **oxygen-carbon dioxide cycle.** For hundreds of millions of years, the amounts of both these gases have remained about the same, until recently. Now, however, people are burning many more fuels than they used to—in automobiles, in factories, and in homes. More carbon dioxide is being put into the air than ever before. As we reduce the number of trees and plants and make more concrete roads and shopping malls, there are less plants to remove carbon dioxide from the atmosphere.

Check yourself

1. How is radiation similar to conduction and convection? How does it differ from conduction and convection?

2. Describe the greenhouse effect.

Temperatures around the earth

The temperature of the air at the earth's surface depends very much on energy from the sun. Energy from the sun warms the earth's surface. In turn, energy from the earth's surface warms the atmosphere.

Air temperatures vary greatly from one place to another on the earth. The air temperature at the equator is much hotter than it is at the North or South Pole. And air temperatures at the same place change from hour to hour and from season to season. Among the causes for differences in air temperature are 1) the angle at which the waves of energy from the sun strike the earth and 2) the number of hours of daylight.

The angle at which the sun's energy strikes the earth's surface affects the amount of energy, and therefore heat, that is received. Near the equator, the sun is more nearly overhead. The angle at which the sun's energy hits locations near the equator is closer to 90°. (See Figure 5-12). Thus

locations near the equator receive much energy and have high temperatures.

Near the North and South Poles, the sun's energy strikes the earth's surface at a small angle (and sometimes not at all). The same amount of energy is spread over a much larger area. This results in less heat and therefore lower temperatures. As the angle of the sun's rays of energy decreases from 90°, the amount of energy received at any location also decreases.

At any location, the angle of the sun's rays of energy changes during the day. In the morning, the angle is small. The angle increases until about noon. Then the angle begins to decrease again. This results in temperature changes throughout the day.

Air temperature is also affected by the number of hours of sunlight. In summer, there are more hours of sunlight per day. As the number of hours of sunlight increases, the amount of energy received from the sun also increases.

Figure 5-11. The angle at which the sun's energy strikes the earth's surface affects the amount of energy, and therefore heat, that is received. During Southern California's summer (left), it receives more direct energy than Antarctica (right).

As indicated in Figure 3-21, the sun does not shine within the Arctic Circle on the winter solstice (December 22 or 23) or within the Antarctic Circle on the summer solstice (June 21 or 22). At those times, the polar regions are in total darkness.

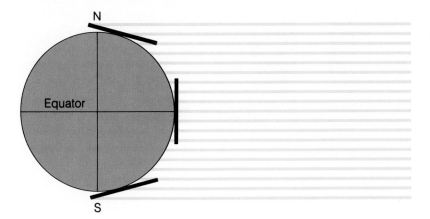

Figure 5-12. Rays of energy from the sun strike the earth's surface at different angles, depending on location and time of year. How does the angle near the equator compare with the angle near the North or South Pole?
At the equator, the sun's rays are striking the earth at a 90° angle. At the North and South Pole, the angle is much less than 90°.

Science Processes: Formulating models: Inferring
See also Activity Record Sheet 5-1A (Lab Manual
page 65)

10 minutes   Large group or demonstration

Note: This activity works best in a darkened room.

Activity 5-1A   Changing the Angle of Incoming Energy

Materials
flashlight
piece of graph paper

Purpose
To see how the angle of incoming light affects
energy received.

Procedure
1. Place the paper on a table or other flat surface. Make sure that the shades or blinds
   are drawn and lights are dimmed or turned
   off.
2. Shine the flashlight directly at a surface so
   that the light strikes the surface at a 90° angle.
3. Move the flashlight so that the light strikes
   the surface at a smaller angle.

Questions
1. What does the light look like when it strikes
   the paper at a 90° angle?
2. How does change in angle affect the size of
   the lighted area? the brightness of the
   lighted area?

Conclusion
Is the total energy striking the paper the same
both at 90° and at a smaller angle? Does the
amount of energy striking the paper at any particular point change when the angle changes?

Step 2

Step 3

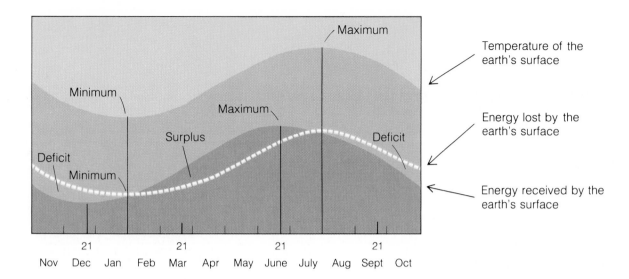

Figure 5-13. Why is there a time lag between maximum energy received and maximum temperature?

Figure 3-20 on page 148 shows the angle of the sun's rays at specific times during the year at the equator. As the sun's path increases in height, the angle of the sun's rays of energy gets closer at 90°. As the sun's path gets longer, the hours of sunlight increase. In December at the mid-latitudes, the sun appears to travel on a path that is short and low in the sky. By March, the path is higher and longer. This means that the same area is now receiving energy that is stronger since the angle has increased. The area is also receiving energy for a longer period of time each day since the hours of sunlight are increasing. For both of these reasons, temperatures in the same Northern Hemisphere location are warmer in March than they were in December.

North of the equator, the sun's path is longest and highest on June 21-22. The heating effects of the sun should therefore be greatest at that time. But, as Figure 5-13 shows, the highest temperatures do not occur until around the beginning of August. This is because the earth's temperature also depends on a third factor, the rate at which the earth's surface loses energy by radiating it back into the atmosphere.

As shown in Figure 5-13, between January and June in the Northern Hemisphere, the earth's surface receives more energy than it loses. There is a surplus of energy, which becomes stored in the earth's surface. After June 21, this stored energy keeps building up for about six weeks. Even though the days are getting shorter during this period, they are still longer than the nights. The angle of the sun's rays is still very high. During this period, therefore, average temperatures continue to rise

As explained in the text, the earth's surface in the Northern Hemisphere continues to have a surplus of energy until about six weeks after summer has begun. So long as there is a surplus of energy in the earth's surface, temperatures continue to rise.

Why, in the Northern Hemisphere, are temperatures warmer in March than in December?

Science Processes: Formulating models; Measuring; Inferring
See also Activity Record Sheet 5-1B (Lab Manual page 66)

CORE   20 minutes   Demonstration or large groups

Activity 5-1B   Measuring the Effect of the Angle of Incoming Energy

Materials

2 thermometers

3-cm-wide strip of black
  construction paper

clock or watch

modeling clay

light source with
  100-watt bulb

wooden block

cellophane tape

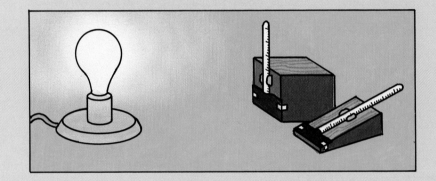

Purpose

To see how the angle of light coming from the sun affects heating at the earth's surface.

Procedure

1. Cut 2 pieces, each about 6 cm long, from the strip of black construction paper.
2. Fold the pieces in half and tape them over the bulbs of the thermometers. As shown in the illustration, the paper should cover each bulb. The paper provides a larger surface for absorbing energy.
3. Set up the equipment as shown in the illustration. Use the clay to hold the thermometers against the wooden block. One thermometer should stand vertically. The other should be at a smaller angle. The light source should be placed about 30 cm from the thermometers.
4. Set up a chart to record the temperature of each thermometer at one-minute intervals.

5. On the chart, record the starting temperature of each thermometer.
6. Turn on the light source. At the end of one minute, read and record the temperatures again. Do not turn the light off.
7. Continue taking readings every minute for ten minutes.

Questions

1. Which thermometer indicated the greater change?
2. What appears to be the relationship between heating and the angle of incoming energy?

Conclusion

Look at Figure 5-12. On the earth, the angle of the sun's rays becomes smaller as we move from the equator to the poles. How does this relate to what you observed with the two thermometers?

until a balance is reached between energy received and energy lost by the earth's surface, usually early in August. Temperatures begin to drop only after this balance has been reached.

From September to December, the earth begins to lose this stored energy. Beginning on December 21-22, energy from the sun begins to increase again. But because of the deficit between energy lost and energy received, the earth's surface continues to cool for another six weeks. It takes six weeks of increased energy (from December 21 to the end of January) before a balance of energy is reached and the earth's surface starts to warm up again.

This same kind of time lag occurs on a daily basis. <u>Though the angle of the sun is greatest in the noon position, maximum temperatures do not occur until early afternoon.</u> During the morning, the earth's surface receives more energy than it loses through radiation. This causes a heat surplus that is stored in the earth's surface until incoming energy and outgoing energy reach a balance and the earth's surface begins to cool.

Temperatures at the earth's surface, therefore, depend on three factors: 1) the angle of the energy waves coming from the sun, 2) the number of hours of sunlight, and 3) the balance between energy received by and lost by the earth's surface.

Check yourself

1. How do day length and the angle of the sun's rays affect air temperatures on the earth?

2. Why is there about a six-week time lag between the first day of summer and the highest average temperatures? between the first day of winter and the lowest average temperatures?

Figure 5-14. Because of a deficit between energy lost and energy received, the earth's surface continues to cool even after energy from the sun begins to increase.

Do highest daily temperatures occur at noon, when the sun's rays are the strongest?

1. As day length and/or the angle of the sun's rays increase, more energy is received. Air temperatures will therefore be warmer.
2. Summer: Because of a surplus of energy stored in the earth's surface, the earth's surface does not begin to cool for about six weeks. During this time, temperatures continue to rise. Winter: Because of a deficit of energy in the earth's surface, the earth's surface continues to absorb energy without warming the surrounding air until the deficit is canceled out.

Section 1 Review   Chapter 5

Use **Reading Checksheet 5-1** TRB page 73
  Skillsheet 5-1 TRB page 115
  Section Reviewsheet 5-1 TRB pages 167–168
  Section Testsheet 5-1 TRB page 287

Check Your Vocabulary

1 atmosphere

5 conduction

6 convection

9 convection current

4 electromagnetic
  spectrum

2 electromagnetic
  waves

8 fluid

10 oxygen-carbon dioxide
  cycle

7 radiation

3 wavelength

Match each term above with the numbered phrase that best describes it.

1. The blanket of air that surrounds the earth; mainly nitrogen (⅘) and oxygen (⅕)

2. Energy waves similar to the waves produced by an electromagnet; how the sun's energy travels

3. The distance between waves, which is measured from the top of one wave to the top of the next wave

4. The energy waves of all the different wavelengths of energy from the sun

5. The movement of energy through a material without the material itself moving

6. The movement of energy through a material because of some movement within the material

7. The movement of energy through a material without any aid from the material

8. Any material that can move and change shape without separating

9. The movement of a fluid caused by unequal densities of portions of the fluid that have been heated unequally

10. The cycling of oxygen and carbon dioxide that takes place in the atmosphere

Check Your Knowledge

Multiple Choice: Choose the answer that best completes each of the following sentences.

1. Almost all the earth's energy comes from __?__.
   a) water   c) the earth's interior
   b) the sun   d) carbon dioxide

2. Metal heats up after being left in the sun because it takes in or __?__ energy from the sun.
   a) reflects   c) emits
   b) radiates   d) absorbs

3. __?__ are fluids.
   a) Only gases   c) Solids and liquids
   b) Only liquids   d) Liquids and gases

4. Any object that is warmer than its surroundings will __?__.
   a) absorb heat   c) emit radiation
   b) reflect heat   d) become denser

Check Your Understanding

1. List six things that happen to the sun's energy waves that enter the earth's atmosphere.

2. Give examples of energy transfer by convection, by conduction, and by radiation that occur naturally among earth materials.

3. How would an increase in carbon dioxide in the atmosphere affect air temperatures?

4. The earth's surface radiates heat back into space. Because of this, the highest and lowest daily temperatures do not occur when a person might expect them to. Explain.

5. What effect does the earth's radiating heat back into space have on the average highest and lowest yearly temperatures?

Winds and the Atmosphere   Section 2

Section 2 of Chapter 5 is divided into five parts:

Convection currents and wind belts

Specific heat and convection currents

Atmospheric pressure and winds

The density of the atmosphere

Reading an atmospheric pressure map

Figure 5-15. The wind cannot be seen, but its presence is revealed by the smallest blade of grass. How is the wind's presence revealed in this picture?
The full sails and the waves are evidence of a wind. Students might describe how this scene would be different if there were no wind.

Learner Objectives
1. To relate winds to convection currents caused by unequal heating of the earth's surface.
2. To recognize the Coriolis effect on winds in the earth's atmosphere.
3. To relate differences in the specific heat of different common earth materials to temperature changes.
4. To relate atmospheric pressure to density.
5. To interpret symbols for atmospheric pressure on a map.

How thick is the atmosphere, the outermost layer of the earth?

Critical Thinking

Look out the window of your schoolroom. What evidence do you see to indicate there is wind?

Answers will vary.

Library research

Find out how the earth's wind belts affected navigation in the days of sailing vessels. Which areas of the ocean were particularly troublesome to navigators? for what reason(s)?

The earth, you may recall, is made up of several layers. The outermost layer is made up of invisible gases and is over 100 km thick. This layer of gases, which is called the atmosphere, is very fluid. Within the atmosphere, masses of air change shape and flow from one place to another.

Has the atmosphere ever flowed over you? Certainly. Every time you feel the wind blowing, it is really a mass of fluid air that is flowing past you as it spreads out along the surface of the earth.

In this section, you will learn the answers to various questions about the wind. What, for example, causes the winds to blow? What can a person tell about the wind by reading a weather map? And how are winds named? Does a westerly wind blow *from* the west or *toward* the west?

Convection currents and wind belts   New vocabulary: local winds, prevailing winds, wind belts, prevailing westerlies

There are two general types of winds, local winds and prevailing winds. The winds that you are most familiar with are local winds. **Local winds** may blow from any direction. **Prevailing winds,** on the other hand, almost always travel longer distances and blow from the same direction. Prevailing winds are part of much larger patterns of air circulation. These general patterns of air circulation are called **wind belts.** Wind belts circle the earth and play a very important role in determining climate and weather. (Figure 5-17 on page 253 shows the earth's wind belts, which are caused by the earth's rotation.)

Watch a television weather forecast for several days in a row. Each day, you will note that weather conditions change. Temperatures rise and fall. Rain comes, skies become cloudy, or the sky clears. But if you live in the continental United States, one thing does not change. The weather conditions that the weather forecaster describes come to your area from the west. They may come from the southwest, from due west, or from the northwest. But almost always, weather conditions over the continental United States come from some westerly direction. They generally move across the continent from the west to the east. This happens because, for the most part, the continental United States lies in the wind belt of **prevailing westerlies.**

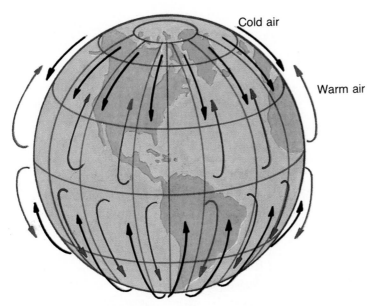

Cold air

Warm air

Figure 5-16. If the earth did not rotate, the earth's air would circulate in a generally north-south direction. What causes air to sink near the Poles? What causes air to be forced upward near the equator?
Air sinks near the poles because of cooler temperatures. Air is forced upward near the equator because warm temperatures make the air less dense, and less dense air is forced upward by cooler denser air.

(Note that westerly winds blow from the west. Winds are named for the direction from which they blow.)

Two factors affect the direction of the prevailing winds in wind belts: 1) unequal heating of the earth's surface, and 2) the earth's rotation. Figure 5-16 shows what the pattern of air circulation on the earth would be if the earth did not rotate on its axis and if all the surface was made of the same substance (water, or rock or soil, etc.). In the Northern Hemisphere, cooled air near the North Pole would sink and flow south along the surface toward the equator. Heated air near the equator, where energy from the sun is strongest, would be forced upward by the cooler, denser air moving in underneath. This warmer, less dense air would then flow north toward the North Pole, above the cooler air that is moving south. A convection current would form from this moving air. And the flow would be in a north-south direction.

In the Southern Hemisphere, the general direction would still be north-south. But the directions between the South Pole and the equator would be reversed. Air cooled near the South Pole would move north to the equator. Air warmed near the equator would move south to the South Pole.

But as you may recall from Chapter 3, the earth's rotation causes what is known as the Coriolis effect. Because of the Coriolis effect, air-borne objects in the Northern Hemisphere seem to be deflected toward their right. And air-borne objects in the Southern Hemisphere seem to be deflected toward their left. To illustrate this, you might think of a rocket fired from the North Pole. If the rocket were aimed at New York when it was

Do westerly winds blow from the west or toward the west?

On a non-rotating earth, in what direction would cool air flow?

Science Processes: Formulating models; Inferring; Communicating through a drawing
See also Activity Record Sheet 5-2A (Lab Manual page 69)

CORE   20 minutes   Groups of 4

Activity 5-2A   Forming Convection Currents

Materials

1000-mL heatproof beaker

water

wire gauze

tripod stand

Bunsen burner

spoon, tweezers, or tongue depressor

potassium permanganate

clear plastic or glass container, shoebox size (aquarium or refrigerator container will be fine)

ice cubes

Purpose

To trace the movement of a convection current in a fluid.

Procedure

1. Fill the heatproof beaker about 3/4 full of water.
2. Place the beaker on the wire gauze on the stand. Let the water sit about ten minutes. Any moving currents that resulted from pouring it will stop.
3. Place the burner near one side of the beaker. Using tweezers, spoon, or tongue depressor, drop a few crystals of the potassium permanganate into the water. Drop them at the side near the burner.
   SAFETY NOTE: *Do not touch the crystals of potassium permanganate with your bare skin. Wear safety goggles.*
4. Turn on the burner and observe what happens. Then turn off the burner.
5. Next, fill the clear container 3/4 full of water. Allow it to sit for ten minutes for the water to settle.
6. Using the tweezers, spoon, or tongue depressor, drop a few crystals of potassium

permanganate into the water near one end of the container.

7. Carefully add a few ice cubes to the water at the end away from the crystals. Try not to stir up the water. Observe what happens.

Questions

1. Make a simple drawing of the path that the dye follows in the heated water.
2. Sketch the path the dye follows in the water once the ice cubes are added.
3. How did the potassium permanganate dye travel in the water?
4. What does the path of the dye through the water show?

Conclusion

How does this model relate to the circulation of air in the atmosphere?

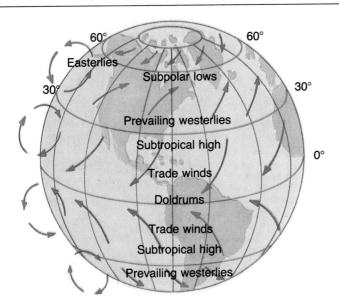

See also Teaching Diagram 5-2
(TRB page 28).

Figure 5-17. Because of the
earth's rotation, the earth's air
currents are deflected from a
generally north-south direction.
Several belts of prevailing winds
are formed. What happens to the
air at 30° north latitude?
At 30° north latitude, there is a
diverging zone where air sinks to
the surface and spreads out.
Some sinking air heads back
toward the North Pole. Some
heads toward the equator.

fired, it would land somewhere around Chicago. Figure 5-17
shows what happens to the earth's air circulation because of the
Coriolis effect. Instead of a large north-south convection current forming, several smaller currents are formed.

In Figure 5-17, you will notice that there are several zones
where air is sinking or where air is being forced upward. The
places where air is sinking and spreading out are called diverging zones. The places where air is coming together and is being
pushed upward are called converging zones. In the Northern
Hemisphere, there are diverging zones of air near the North
Pole and near 30° north latitude. Converging zones are found
near the equator and near 60° north latitude.

In Figure 5-17, you will also notice that some of the diverging air at 30° north latitude heads back toward the North Pole
and some heads toward the equator, Above 30° north latitude,
the prevailing winds are from the west to the east after the
apparent deflection caused by the Coriolis effect. As mentioned earlier, these prevailing winds are called westerlies because they come from a westerly direction. Between 30°
north latitude and the equator, the prevailing winds flow
from the northeast to the southwest. Because they flow from
the northeast, they are called the northeast trade winds.

Check yourself answers:
1. Prevailing winds are part of
much larger wind patterns that
circle the earth. Local winds
are caused by variations in
local atmospheric conditions.
2. Unequal heating of fluid
causes convection currents,
which would flow north-south if
it weren't for the earth's
rotation. But the Coriolis effect
of the earth's rotation causes
the convection currents to be
deflected in various ways,
setting up general patterns
around the earth.

What are the prevailing winds
between 30° north latitude and
the equator?

Check yourself

1. How do prevailing winds differ from local winds?

2. Explain how unequal heating and the earth's rotation affect
   the direction of prevailing winds in wind belts.

Specific heat and convection currents

New vocabulary: specific heat, onshore breeze, offshore breeze

Convection currents can form because different parts of the earth receive unequal amounts of the sun's energy. Convection currents can also form because different materials on the earth's surface absorb heat differently. At the beach on a hot summer day, you often feel a cool breeze blowing in, or flowing in, from over the water. Also, if you were in a boat out in the water, the air would be cooler than it is on the beach. These things happen because land temperatures change faster than water temperatures.

At the beach, the same amount of sunlight is shining on both the sand and the water. The surface sand becomes so hot that it burns your feet. The surface water remains cool. This indicates that it takes more energy to warm the water than it does to warm the sand. Water has what is called a higher specific heat than sand has. **Specific heat** is the amount of energy needed to raise 1 g of a substance 1°C. Water, in fact, has the highest specific heat of any common natural substance. That means that water needs to absorb a greater amount of energy before its temperature will rise.

As shown in Figure 5-18, the difference in specific heat between land materials and water causes convection currents to form along coastal areas. During the day, the surface of the water is cooler than the surface of the land. The air over the water cools, sinks, and flows toward the land. The air over the land is hotter and less dense than the cooler air pushing in from the sea. The warm air over the land is forced upward by the cooler, denser air. A sea breeze forms, flowing from the sea to the land. This breeze is called an **onshore breeze** because it blows onto the shore from out over the sea. Onshore breezes can blow inland for many kilometers.

At night, just the opposite happens. Because the land materials contain less heat than water does when both materials are at the same temperature, land materials cool off faster than water. Also, temperature differences between land materials and water are affected because the different surfaces reflect, absorb, and radiate energy in differing amounts.

At night, therefore, land temperatures become cooler than the temperature of the surface of the water. A convection cur-

---

Are sand and water warmed equally by the same amount of energy?

Interested students could prepare a chart comparing the specific heats of various materials. Such a chart could be used for various discussion purposes. For example, what is the relationship between specific heat and the use of a material for heating or insulating purposes? Which materials would make good building materials in a hot (or cold) climate? Why? What materials are cooking utensils made out of? Why?

Why do land materials cool off faster than water?

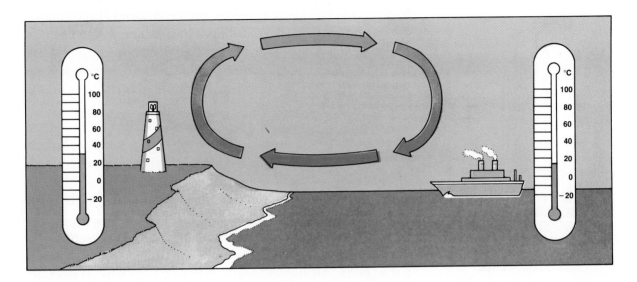

rent forms, but it flows in the opposite direction at night. Air is now cooled over the land. This cooler, denser air sinks and spreads out over the water. This time a land breeze forms, flowing from the land to the sea. This breeze is called an **offshore breeze** because it blows off or away from the shore.

Check yourself

1. How does difference in specific heat cause convection currents in coastal areas?

2. How does the direction of breezes in coastal areas change from day to night? Why does this happen?

Atmospheric pressure and winds   New vocabulary: atmospheric pressure, barometer, standard atmospheric pressure, millibar

The gases and other materials in the atmosphere have mass. Drawn to the earth's surface by the force of gravity, the atmosphere exerts pressure against the surface of the earth. This pressure, which is called **atmospheric pressure,** varies according to the density of the air. Denser air, which has a greater mass per unit volume, exerts greater pressure against the earth's surface than does less dense air.

Dense air, which exerts greater atmospheric pressure, moves in underneath less dense air. In other words, air moves from

Figure 5-18. On a summer day, the sand gets hotter than the water. How can this cause a cooling sea breeze to blow in off the water?

The air over the sand becomes warmer and less dense than the air over the water. The cooler, denser air from over the water forces its way in under the warmer, less dense air. Have students draw a diagram that shows Figure 5-18 at night. What happens to the temperatures? What happens to the wind direction?

1. Land materials warm up faster than water because they have a lower specific heat. During the day, therefore, the air over land areas is warmer than air over the water. At night, land materials cool faster. The air over the land is cooler, and the breeze reverses.

2. During the day, breezes blow onshore because air over the land is warmer and less dense. During the night, breezes blow offshore, because air over the water is warmer and less dense than air over the land.

areas of greater atmospheric pressure to areas of lower atmospheric pressure. Winds, therefore, blow from high-pressure areas to low-pressure areas. And if the difference in pressure between the two areas increases, the wind speed also increases.

Because winds blow according to differences in atmospheric pressure, it is important to be able to measure atmospheric pressure. The basic instrument for measuring atmospheric pressure is called a **barometer.** Atmospheric pressure is also called barometric pressure.

Some barometers use a liquid. As shown in Figure 5-19, a mercury barometer uses a column of mercury to measure atmospheric pressure. **Standard atmospheric pressure** is capable of balancing a column of mercury that is 760 mm high. As atmospheric pressure decreases, it cannot balance as much matter and the column of mercury falls. As atmospheric pressure increases, the column of mercury is forced upward.

In addition to mercury barometers, there are also aneroid barometers. An aneroid barometer (see Figure 5-21) does not use a liquid. Instead, it uses a sealed metal container from which nearly all the air has been removed. Changes in atmospheric pressure cause the sides of the container to move in or out. As the sides move, a pointer also moves, indicating the changes in atmospheric pressure.

An aneroid barometer can be hooked up to a revolving drum with paper on it. The pointer would be equipped with a pen point. The drum keeps a continuous record of all changes in atmospheric pressure registered by the barometer. This instrument, which is shown in Figure 5-22, is called a barograph.

"Standard atmospheric pressure," or barometric pressure, can be expressed in a variety of values. It can, for example, be expressed as "one atmosphere." In terms of a column of mercury, one atmosphere equals 760 mm (or 29.92 in.) of mercury.

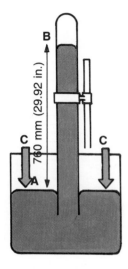

Figure 5-19. The height of the mercury column (from A to B) is determined by the atmospheric pressure (C) on the mercury.

Figure 5-20. a mercury barometer

Figure 5-21. an aneroid barometer

Figure 5-22. a barograph

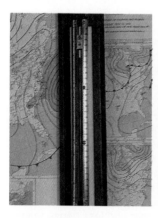

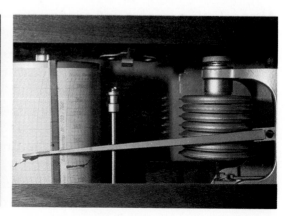

Standard atmospheric pressure can also be expressed in terms of a column of water, which is much less dense than mercury. In terms of a column of water, one atmosphere equals 1033.3 cm (or 33.9 feet) of water. Standard atmospheric pressure can also be expressed as 1013.25 millibars. **Millibars** are the unit of pressure measurement most commonly found on weather maps.

Check yourself

1. How does atmospheric pressure affect wind?

2. Explain how a mercury barometer works.

The density of the atmosphere

New vocabulary: troposphere

Standard atmospheric pressure is measured at sea level and at 0°C. That is because the density of the earth's atmosphere is affected by three factors: by moisture (water vapor), by height above sea level (elevation), and, as you have already seen, by temperature.

The amount of moisture in the air affects the density of the atmosphere. As the amount of moisture in the air increases, the air becomes less dense because molecules of water have less mass than molecules of other gases in the air. Figure 5-23 shows different layers of the earth's atmosphere. Just about all the moisture in the atmosphere is found within the **troposphere,** which extends to about 16 km above sea level. (The troposphere is also the level of the atmosphere in which all of the earth's weather is found.)

Above the troposphere is the *stratosphere,* up to 50 km above sea level. The stratosphere contains the *ozone layer,* with ozone O_3 molecules. These filter dangerous rays from the sun. Above this is the *mesosphere* up to 80 km and the *thermosphere,* an even thinner layer in the atmosphere which goes beyond 100 km above sea level. Air is extremely thin in these upper layers. However, most speeding *meteors* burn up when they enter the atmosphere here. The friction of the speeding rock against the thin air molecules produces tremendous heat.

Height above sea level affects the density of the atmosphere. Starting from the earth's surface, the atmosphere becomes less and less dense as distance above the earth's surface increases. If you were to climb a mountain a few kilometers high, you

Library research

Prepare a report that describes the development of a scientific instrument connected with energy and the atmosphere. It can be an instrument used in the past or in the present. Include dates and the names of the inventors and developers.

1. Winds are caused by differences in atmospheric pressure. Winds blow from high-pressure to low-pressure areas. As the difference in pressure increases, wind speed also increases.
2. Atmospheric pressure is capable of balancing a column of mercury. The height of the column balanced depends on the atmospheric pressure. Changes in the height of the column indicate changes in atmospheric pressure.

Why is standard atmospheric pressure measured at sea level and at 0°C?

The height of the troposphere varies with latitude and season— from about 17 km year-round at the equator to about 9 km at a pole at its coldest season or about 10 km at a pole at its warmest season.

Figure 5-23. All the earth's weather and almost all of the moisture in the atmosphere are found in the same layer. What is the name of that layer?

The earth's weather, and almost all the moisture in the atmosphere, are found in the troposphere, the layer of the earth's atmosphere closest to the earth's surface.

The troposphere is the layer of the atmosphere in which temperatures drop as altitude above sea level increases. The stratosphere is the layer in which the temperature is nearly constant. Interested students can do a vertical temperature profile for the layers of the earth's atmosphere.

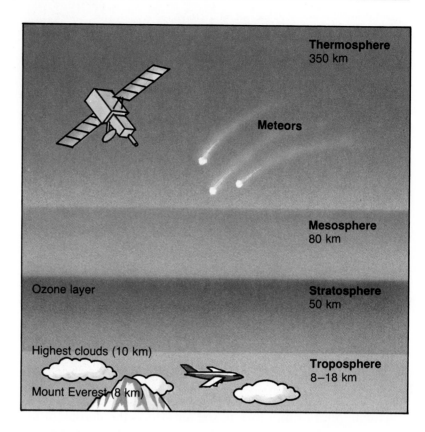

In high-flying airplanes, why must machines supply air for people to breathe?

1. Moisture decreases density because water vapor molecules have less mass than molecules of other gases in the air.
2. Air gets less dense as you go higher above sea level.

would find that you get winded more easily. The air at that altitude is thinner. With each breath, you draw in less oxygen than you do when you breathe at sea level.

About 90% of all the gas in the atmosphere is found within a few kilometers of the earth's surface. In high-flying airplanes, machines must supply air for people to breathe. The air outside the plane is too thin to support life. And beyond 100 km, very little atmosphere remains. People traveling in space must bring their own air supply with them.

Variations in the density of the atmosphere cause variations in atmospheric pressure. Variations in atmospheric pressure play a major role in determining wind speed and direction. And wind speed and direction play a major role in determining local weather patterns on earth.

Check yourself

1. How does amount of moisture affect the density of the atmosphere? Why?

2. How does height above sea level affect the density of the atmosphere?

Reading an atmospheric pressure map   New vocabulary:
pressure map, isobar, low-pressure center, high-pressure center

As mentioned earlier, variations in elevation of features on the earth's surface can be shown on a topographic map. Variations in atmospheric pressure from one location to another can be shown on a pressure map. Atmospheric pressure measurements are made at different locations. These readings are sent to central recording stations. At the stations, the readings are plotted on a map. This map, which can be called a **pressure map,** provides a picture of the pressure pattern in a state or country.

To make it easier to see the pressure pattern, locations that have the same atmospheric pressure are connected by means of a line called an **isobar.** A topographic map uses contour lines to connect points that have the same elevation. A pressure map uses isobars to connect points that have the same atmospheric pressure.

Figure 5-24 shows a pressure map with isobars. On this map, the lines form a circular pattern. The pressure decreases toward the center of the pattern. This pattern is called a low-pressure area. The letter L or the word Low is used to label a **low-pressure center,** which is the center of a low-pressure area. Since atmospheric pressure is lowest at the center of a low-pressure area, winds will tend to blow in toward and slightly to either the right or left of a low-pressure center.

If students have performed the activity on convection currents (page 252), have them relate their observations to the markings on an atmospheric pressure map. Air pressure is a difficult concept for some students to grasp. Perhaps you can think up other examples of convection currents to help students visualize movement in a fluid.

How are contour lines and isobars similar?

Due to the Coriolis effect, winds in the Northern Hemisphere tend to blow slightly to the right of a low-pressure center. In the Southern Hemisphere, winds tend to blow slightly to the left.

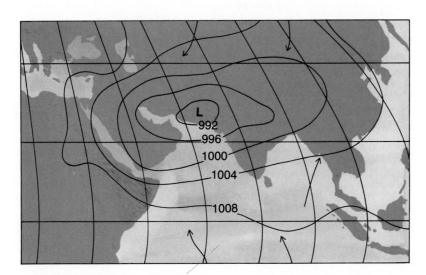

Figure 5–24. Isobars connect locations that have the same atmospheric pressure. Does the atmospheric pressure increase or decrease toward the center of a low-pressure area (indicated on a map by the letter L or the word Low)?
Atmospheric pressure decreases toward the center of a low-pressure area.

Science Processes: Formulating models;
Measuring; Communicating through a chart; Inferring
See also Activity Record Sheet 5-2B (Lab Manual
page 70)

30 minutes

Groups of 4

Activity 5-2B Comparing Differences in Specific Heat

Materials

sand or soil, at room temperature
water, at room temperature
2 plastic containers
light source
stand for light source

Purpose

To compare the specific heats of water and
sand or soil.

Procedure

1. Pour a measured amount of sand into one
   container. Pour an equal amount of water
   into the other container.
2. Insert one thermometer into the sand so that
   the bulb is just below the surface. Suspend
   the other thermometer on a string so that its
   bulb is just below the surface of the water.
3. The sand and the water should be about the
   same temperature. If they are not, wait for a
   while until they are.
4. Prepare a chart that begins like the one
   shown. Note that some of the readings are
   with the light source on and others with the
   light source off.
5. Attach the light souce to the stand and position the stand so that the light shines

equally on both containers. Do not turn the
light source on yet.

6. Take your first temperature reading for the
   sand and water. Record these temperatures
   as reading number 1 on your chart. Then
   turn the light source on.
7. Take temperature readings of the materials
   each minute until you reach reading number
   10. Record each reading on your chart.
8. After reading number 10, turn off the light
   source. Continue to take temperature readings with the light source off every minute
   until you reach reading number 20.

Questions

1. In which material did the temperature rise
   more when the light source was on?
2. In which material did the temperature drop
   more when the light source was off?
3. From the data on your chart, which material
   has the higher specific heat? Explain.

Conclusion

Which material holds a more steady temperature? Do the materials receive the same amount
of energy? What reasons can you give for your
answer? Review page 254.

Temperature with Light Source On		
Reading	Sand	Water
1		
2		
3		
4		

Temperature with Light Source Off		
Reading	Sand	Water
11		
12		
13		
14		

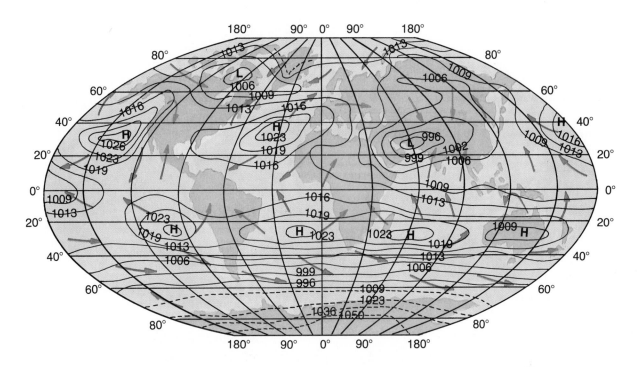

For a **high-pressure center,** which is the center of a high-pressure area, the pattern is reversed. The pressure increases toward the center. Winds will therefore tend to blow out from a high-pressure center. The letter H or the word High is used to indicate a high-pressure center.

Figure 5-25 shows a typical pressure map for July. On the map, you will notice several high-pressure and low-pressure centers. Arrows indicate the pattern of wind movement. Notice that the winds do not blow straight into a low-pressure area or straight out of a high-pressure area. The winds are deflected by the Coriolis effect that is caused by the earth's rotation.

From the map in Figure 5-25, you can draw several conclusions about winds. 1) Winds blow from regions of high pressure to regions of low pressure. 2) In the Northern Hemisphere, winds blow away from high-pressure centers in a clockwise direction. 3) In the Northern Hemisphere, winds blow toward a low-pressure center in a counterclockwise direction.

Check yourself

1. Describe a pressure map.

2. How do high-pressure areas, low-pressure areas, and the Coriolis effect influence the direction of winds that are found in the Northern Hemisphere?

Figure 5-25. In the Northern Hemisphere, in what direction do winds blow away from a high-pressure center?
In the Northern Hemisphere, winds blow away from a high-pressure center in a clockwise direction.

For display and discussion in class, have a few student volunteers find local maps that show winds and pressure centers.

1. A pressure map indicates, by means of isobars, all locations that have the same atmospheric pressure. It will also indicate centers of high and low pressure.
2. Winds blow from high-pressure areas to low-pressure areas. Because of the Coriolis effect, winds in the Northern Hemisphere blow away from a high-pressure area in a clockwise direction and toward a low-pressure area in a counterclockwise direction.

Section 2 Review   Chapter 5

Use **Reading Checksheet 5-2** TRB page 74
   Skillsheet 5-2 TRB page 116
   Section Reviewsheet 5-2 TRB pages 169–170
   Section Testsheet 5-2 TRB page 288

Check Your Vocabulary

9 atmospheric pressure	16 onshore breeze
10 barometer	4 pressure map
7 high-pressure center	14 prevailing westerlies
5 isobar	12 prevailing winds
1 local winds	15 specific heat
6 low-pressure center	11 standard atmospheric pressure
2 millibar	3 troposphere
8 offshore breeze	13 wind belts

Match each term above with the numbered phrase that best describes it.

1. Winds specific to a local area

2. The unit of atmospheric pressure measurement commonly found on weather maps

3. The layer of the earth's atmosphere closest to the earth's surface

4. A map that indicates atmospheric pressure patterns for an area of the earth's surface

5. A line that connects locations having the same atmospheric pressure

6. The center of an area of low atmospheric pressure

7. The center of an area of high atmospheric pressure

8. A breeze that blows away from the shore and out over the sea

9. The pressure the atmosphere exerts against the surface of the earth

10. The basic instrument for measuring atmospheric pressure

11. Atmospheric pressure at sea level and 0°C

12. Winds that are part of much larger patterns of air circulation than local winds

13. General patterns of air circulation that circle the earth; includes prevailing winds

14. Winds that blow from a westerly direction

15. The amount of energy needed to raise 1 g of a substance 1°C

16. A breeze that blows onto the shore

Check Your Knowledge

Multiple Choice: Choose the answer that best completes each of the following sentences.

1. Places around the earth where cool air sinks and spreads out along the earth's surface are called __?__.
   a) prevailing westerlies
   b) converging zones
   c) local winds
   d) diverging zones

2. __?__ has the highest specific heat of any common natural substance.
   a) Rock   c) Water
   b) Sand   d) Air

3. Molecules of water have __?__ mass than molecules of other gases in the air.
   a) less   c) the same
   b) slightly more   d) much more

Check Your Understanding

1. There would be no wind if the atmosphere were not fluid. Explain.

2. Explain the relationship between prevailing westerlies and the Coriolis effect.

3. How does specific heat affect air temperatures?

4. Explain the relationship between wind and atmospheric pressure.

5. As you climb a mountain, what two atmospheric changes can you expect? How will you notice these changes?

Moisture and the Atmosphere   Section 3

Section 3 of Chapter 5 is divided into six parts:

Energy and the states of water

Water vapor in the atmosphere

When does condensation occur?

Condensation near the earth's surface

Condensation in the atmosphere

Precipitation

Learner Objectives

1. To distinguish the energy content of water from one physical state to another.
2. To describe the energy transfer as water changes from one state to another.
3. To find the relative humidity of air.
4. To relate dew-point temperature to condensation in the atmosphere.
5. To explain the various forms in which precipitation occurs.

Figure 5-26. In this picture, you see the sun shining on snow in the French Alps. You know that the sun can melt snow. In this section, you will learn how the sun causes snow.

Energy from the sun provides light and warmth on the earth. Energy from the sun causes the winds that blow across the face of the earth. Energy from the sun also causes the rain that falls upon the dry land. How can the sun be the cause of both sunshine and rain? How can the sun be the cause of even the snowstorms and hailstorms that occur on the earth?

The questions will be answered in the pages that follow in this section.

Energy and the states of water  New vocabulary: water vapor, evaporation, heat of vaporization, condensation, heat of fusion

Water is a compound that is made up of the elements hydrogen and oxygen. Its chemical formula, H_2O, indicates that each molecule of water is made up of one atom of oxygen and two atoms of hydrogen.

On the earth, water can be found in any of the three physical states of matter. That means that water can be found as a liquid, as a solid, and as a gas. **Water vapor** is the name commonly used for water as a gas. Whether water is found as a liquid, solid, or vapor at a particular location depends largely on heat energy.

You are familiar with the physical properties of water as a liquid and water as a solid (ice). But what is water vapor like? Water vapor cannot be seen or tasted or smelled or felt. Water vapor is an invisible gas. Some water vapor is present in all the air that is closest to the earth's surface.

Not only does water exist as a liquid or a solid or a vapor, but water can also be easily changed from one state to another. Once again, it depends on heat energy.

The changing of a substance from a liquid into a vapor or gas is called **evaporation.** When water changes from a liquid to a vapor, it must take in energy. The amount of heat needed for 1 g of a substance to become a vapor is called its **heat of vaporization.** When liquid water is able to take in its heat of vaporization from its surroundings, the liquid water changes to water vapor. Because of the needed heat of vaporization, water vapor contains much more energy than liquid water.

The changing of a vapor into a liquid is called **condensation.** The word *condensation* comes from Latin words that mean "to make very dense." Liquid water is about one thousand times denser than water vapor.

Figure 5-27. Here are two pictures of the same puddle. The puddle at the bottom shows how evaporation caused the puddle to become smaller.

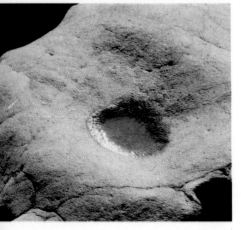

When water changes from a vapor to a liquid, it gives off energy to its surroundings. It loses the same amount of heat that it gained through its heat of vaporization.

What do you suppose happens when ice, which is water in its solid state, melts? Do you think it takes in energy or gives off energy? When ice melts, water changes from a solid to a liquid. For this to happen, solid water must take in energy. The amount of heat needed for 1 g of a solid substance to melt and become a liquid is called its **heat of fusion.** When ice is able to take in its heat of fusion from its surroundings, the solid water changes to a liquid.

When liquid water freezes, just the opposite happens. Freezing water gives off energy to its surroundings. When liquid water freezes, it loses the same amount of heat that it gained through its heat of fusion.

Check yourself

1. Water vapor contains much more energy than liquid water. Explain.

2. In terms of energy transfer, what happens when ice melts?

Figure 5-28. When liquid water freezes, does it give off energy or does it gain energy?
When liquid water freezes, it gives off energy to its surroundings. (It gives off the same amount of heat it gained through its heat of fusion.)

Library research

Find out how much of the earth's water supply is in the form of ice. Where is this ice located? Why is ice found in those regions?

1. Water vapor had to absorb heat energy (its heat of vaporization) in order to evaporate. As vapor, it contains that energy.
2. When ice melts, it must absorb heat energy from its surroundings. The amount is called its heat of fusion.

Water vapor in the atmosphere
New vocabulary: saturated air, humidity, relative humidity, sling psychrometer

Water vapor makes up a very small but very important part of the earth's atmosphere. In very moist air, only 3% of the total volume of air is water vapor. In drier air, the amount of water vapor present is less. But even in very dry areas, there is always some moisture left in the atmosphere.

Where does this moisture come from? And how does it get into the atmosphere? The water in the atmosphere evaporated from liquid water on the earth's surface. Heat energy from the sun provided the needed heat of vaporization so that liquid water could change into vapor.

Water is always evaporating from the surface of lakes, rivers, and oceans. Water evaporates from puddles. Water evaporates from the moisture in the ground. Water even evaporates from the surface of a person's skin. From the smallest puddles and drops of perspiration to the largest oceans, water is evaporating into the atmosphere day after day. Plants also release water vapor into the atmosphere. The water vapor is released through tiny openings on the undersides of the plants' leaves. This process, called transpiration, is described on page 347.

There is a limit to the amount of moisture that air can hold. When the air is holding all the moisture it can, we say that the air is saturated. **Saturated air** is air that can hold no more moisture. Once the air becomes saturated, it must return any extra moisture to the earth's atmosphere by condensation.

The amount of water vapor the air can hold depends upon the air temperature. At higher temperatures, the same volume of air can hold more water vapor. As shown in Figure 5-29, a cubic meter of air at 10°C can hold 10 g of water vapor. At 40°C, the same volume of air can hold about 50 g of water vapor.

Perhaps you have heard of the terms *humidity* and *relative humidity*. These terms have to do with the amount of moisture in the air. **Humidity** is the amount of moisture that is in the air. **Relative humidity** is a comparison between the amount of moisture in the air and the amount that the air can hold. Relative humidity is expressed as a percentage. A relative humidity of 50% means that the air contains half of the total amount of

Figure 5-29. The maximum amount of water vapor that air can hold depends on the temperature of the air. At 40°C, how many grams of water vapor can a cubic meter of air hold?

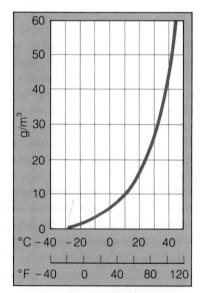

In answer to the caption question, a cubic meter of air at 40°C can hold about 50 g of water vapor.

See also Teaching Diagram 5-3A (TRB page 29).

moisture that it can hold at that temperature. When the air is saturated, its relative humidity is 100%.

One instrument that is often used to measure the amount of moisture in the air is the **sling psychrometer.** It consists of two thermometers fastened to a base. A wet cotton wick is attached to one of the thermometers. The psychrometer is swung in a circular motion. The thermometer without the wick measures the dry bulb temperature, which is the temperature of the air. Twirling the psychrometer does not affect the dry bulb reading. If the air temperature is 30°C, then the dry-bulb reading remains at 30°C when the psychrometer is twirled.

What is a sling psychrometer used for?

Figure 5-30. A sling psychrometer uses two thermometers to measure the relative humidity of the air.

The temperature of the other thermometer, the wet-bulb thermometer, drops when the psychrometer is twirled. As water evaporates from the wick, the temperature of the wet-bulb

Science Processes: Measuring; Using numbers; Interpreting data
See also Activity Record Sheet 5-3A (Lab Manual page 73)

CORE   20 minutes   Pairs of students

Activity 5-3A   Finding the Relative Humidity

Materials

sling psychrometer

water at about room temperature

clock or watch that indicates seconds

relative humidity table on page 624 of the Appendix

Purpose

To use a sling psychrometer to find the relative humidity of the air.

Procedure

1. Wet the wick of the wet-bulb thermometer of your sling psychrometer. Use water that is at or near air temperature. Record the temperatures of both the wet-bulb and dry-bulb thermometers.
2. Before twirling the psychrometer, make sure no person or object is near enough to get hit by the moving psychrometer. Then twirl the psychrometer for about 15 seconds. Record the temperature of both thermometers.
3. Twirl the psychrometer for another 15 seconds. Again record the temperatures.
4. Repeat this process until the wet-bulb temperature stops dropping. (The dry-bulb temperature should remain the same.)
5. Subtract the final wet-bulb temperature from the dry-bulb temperature to calculate the wet-bulb depression.
6. Use the relative humidity table on page 624 of the Appendix to find the relative humidity. Locate your calculated wet-bulb depression along the top of the relative humidity table. Then locate your closest dry-bulb temperature down the left side of the table. Reading across from the dry-bulb temperature and down from the wet-bulb temperature, find where the two lines intersect. You will then

Step 2

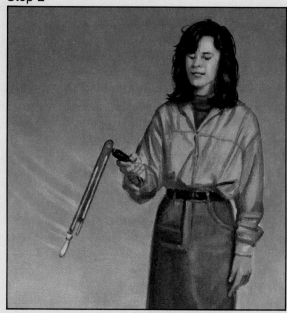

see the relative humidity for your temperature readings. For example, if your wet-bulb depression is 5°C and your dry-bulb temperature is about 20°C, then the relative humidity is about 59%.

Question

What relative humidity did you find from your measurements and calculations?

Conclusion

Look again at the relative humidity table in the Appendix. At 20°C and a 5°C wet-bulb depression, the relative humidity is 59%. At 20°C dry-bulb temperature and 1° wet-bulb depression, the relative humidity is 91%. At 20°C dry-bulb temperature and 10° wet-bulb depression, the relative humidity is 24%. The lower the wet-bulb depression is at any given temperature, the higher the relative humidity is. Can you explain this pattern? Review the discussion of evaporation on page 264.

thermometer drops because water that evaporates is taking heat energy from its surroundings. Also, the amount of moisture in the air affects the rate of evaporation. When there is less moisture in the air, more water evaporates from the wick. This causes a greater drop in the wet-bulb temperature.

The difference between the dry-bulb temperature and the wet-bulb temperature is a relative measure of the amount of moisture in the air. On a very humid day, the wet-bulb temperature may drop only one or two degrees. If, however, the air is dry, the wet-bulb temperature may drop ten degrees or more.

Check yourself

1. If the relative humidity is 50%, what does that say about the moisture content of the air?

2. Explain how a sling psychrometer indicates relative humidity.

Check yourself answers:
1. It contains half the total moisture it can hold at that temperature.
2. One thermometer of a sling psychrometer has a wet wick around its bulb. Water from the wet wick will evaporate faster when the relative humidity is low. The rate of evaporation from the wet wick is registered by the temperature drop on the wet-bulb thermometer.

When does condensation occur?
New vocabulary: saturation temperature, dew-point temperature

As mentioned already, warmer air can hold more water vapor than cooler air. Suppose the air temperature were 30°C and the air were saturated. What do you think would happen when the temperature of that saturated air starts to drop?

First, we must consider what we mean when we say that the air is saturated. We mean that the air contains all the water vapor it can hold at that temperature. Its relative humidity is 100%. When air is at its **saturation temperature,** or dew-point temperature, there is a balance between the number of molecules of water vapor entering and leaving the air. For every molecule of water vapor that enters saturated air through evaporation, one must leave. There is just no more room for extra molecules of water vapor in that mass of air as long as it stays at the same temperature.

What happens when air cools below its saturation temperature? As air cools, it can hold less and less water vapor. As the temperature of the air drops below its saturation temperature, more and more water vapor must leave the air. How does this

What is the relative humidity of saturated air?

As ocean spray enters the atmosphere, the water is evaporated, leaving behind a small particle of salt. Such particles remain suspended in the air and become condensation nuclei. (The teacher note for Figure 1-1, page 4, relates to sense observations at the seashore.)

Careers   Weather Forecaster / Weather Technician

In order to predict the weather in advance, a weather forecaster analyzes data from a variety of sources.

For information about jobs with the National Weather Service, contact:

National Weather Service
Personnel Section
Gramax Building
8060 13th Street
Silver Springs, Maryland 20910

For further information about a career as a weather forecaster, contact:

Weather Forecaster

Weather forecasters predict future weather. They work for television and radio stations, airlines, utility companies, the armed forces, and government agencies.

In order to predict the weather for more than a few hours ahead, forecasters must have weather data for a wide area. They get this information from National Weather Service maps, which indicate such data as wind speed, temperature, and humidity for locations all over the world. Forecasters are also able to use pictures of weather systems obtained from weather satellites in orbit around the earth.

American Meteorological Society
45 Beacon Street
Boston, Massachusetts 02108

Forecasters compare past and current maps to find out how weather systems are moving. They use their map analysis plus their knowledge of local weather conditions and patterns to prepare forecasts for their area.

If you are interested in becoming a weather forecaster, take math and science courses in high school. Since weather forecasters are meteorologists, you will study meteorology in college.

If you are one for immediate action, you can start with today's weather maps and conditions. Keep records. Look for patterns. Then try your hand at some short-range forecasting!

Weather technicians operate and maintain electronic equipment used for gathering weather data.

For information about a career as a weather technician, contact:

American Meteorological Society
45 Beacon Street
Boston, Massachusetts 02108

Weather Technician

Weather technicians operate and maintain weather instruments such as anemometers, barometers, and psychrometers. They also operate and maintain electronic equipment such as weather data processors.

Weather technicians measure weather conditions, plot weather data on charts and diagrams, and maintain weather data files. Some weather technicians prepare forecasts.

As a weather technician, you will be able to assist a

meteorologist in a variety of ways. You might be a weather observer, a weather chart preparer, or a weather clerk.

Training for a weather technician is available at vocational and technical schools and through specialized training courses offered to members of the armed forces. In high school, plan to take math and science courses. And all the while, of course, keep an eye on the weather!

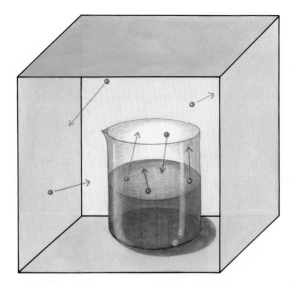
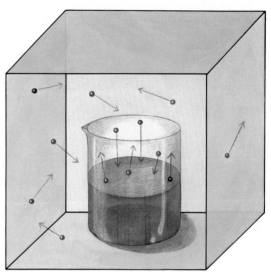

happen? Water vapor leaves the air by changing into droplets of water that form around tiny particles of matter in the atmosphere. These microscopic particles are called condensation nuclei. Salt provides many of these particles to the atmosphere.

For this changing of water vapor into liquid water, which is called condensation, three conditions are necessary. 1) The air must be cooled to its saturation temperature. 2) There must be moisture available in the form of invisible water vapor. 3) There must be a surface on which water vapor can condense. Since tiny particles or dust and other solid matter are present throughout the atmosphere, condensation readily occurs whenever air reaches its saturation temperature.

You have probably seen condensation occur on the outside of a can, glass, or pitcher containing an ice-cold liquid. Drops of moisture form on the outside of the container. The cold surface of the container cools the air near the surface of the container. The air near the surface of the container is cooled to its saturation temperature. The extra water vapor condenses on the surface of the container. If you wipe the moisture away, more will form. As long as the air near the container is being

Figure 5-31. When the air is at its saturation temperature, an equal number of molecules are escaping from and returning to the surface of the water. Which picture represents air at its saturation temperature? The picture on the right represents air at its saturation point.

Why do drops of moisture form on the outside of a container of cold liquid?

272

Science Processes: Separating and controlling variables; Measuring; Interpreting data
See also Activity Record Sheet 5-3B (Lab Manual page 74)

20 minutes   Pairs of students, or groups of 3–4

Activity 5-3B   Finding the Dew-Point Temperature

Materials

drinking glass or shiny can

water at room temperature

warm water

thermometer

ice chips or cube

sling psychrometer

Purpose

To find the dew-point temperature of the air you are breathing.

Procedure

1. Put some water in a can or glass. (The water should be at about room temperature.)
2. Slowly add ice chips to the water. Stir the water with a thermometer until drops of moisture first begin to form below the waterline on the outside of the container.
3. Record the water temperature as soon as you notice the slightest film of moisture begin to form on the outside of the container.
4. Remove the ice. Trace your finger across the outside of the container to make a clear path through the beads of moisture.
5. Slowly raise the temperature of the water inside the container to the point where no film forms in the freshly cleared area on the surface. Raise the temperature by slowly adding warm water to the water in the container, constantly stirring with the thermometer.
6. Record the temperature of the water when no drops of moisture form in a cleared area.
7. Calculate the temperature that is halfway between the two temperatures you recorded. It should be near the dew-point temperature of the air.
8. Repeat the cooling and warming several times, if time allows.

Step 5

9. Using a sling psychrometer and the dew-point temperature table on page 625 of the Appendix, find the actual dew-point temperature.

Questions

1. What dew-point temperature did you get using the cold-water/warm-water method?
2. If you repeated the activity several times, were your results nearly the same each time? Compare your results with those of others in the class.
3. How did the dew-point temperature you obtained from the table compare with your calculation?

Conclusion

Look at the dew-point temperature table. Read across from a dry-bulb temperature reading of 20°C. Recall from the activity on page 268 that the higher the wet-bulb depression, the lower the relative humidity. What relationship can you see between relative humidity and dew-point temperature if the dry-bulb temperature stays the same?

Figure 5-32. The outside of the pitcher on the right is covered with water droplets. Where did the moisture in the water droplets come from? The moisture in the water droplets came from the condensation of water vapor in the air surrounding the container.

cooled enough, then water vapor from the saturated air will condense on the surface of the container.

The temperature to which air must be cooled to reach its saturation point is called its **dew-point temperature,** or saturation temperature. The dew-point temperature is the temperature at which the air contains all the water vapor it can hold. Suppose the temperature of ice water in a pitcher is 5°C and that the air temperature around the pitcher is 30°C. Suppose also that the dew-point temperature, or saturation temperature, of the air surrounding the pitcher is 20°C. This means that when the air near the surface of the pitcher is cooled to 20°C, condensation will begin. As soon as the air in contact with the outside of the pitcher reaches 20°C, water droplets will begin to form on the surface of the pitcher.

The dew-point temperature varies with the amount of water vapor present in the air. Air containing less water vapor must be cooled to a lower temperature before it becomes saturated. As the amount of water vapor in the air decreases, the dew-point temperature drops. For this reason, the dew-point temperature also indicates something about the amount of water vapor in the air. Air with a dew-point temperature of 20°C contains more water vapor than air with a dew-point temperature of 10°C. In Figure 5-32, the surface temperature of the

Have students consider the use of a defroster when the windows of a car fog up on the inside. What does the defroster do to prevent the fogging up? (It raises the temperature of the glass so that the glass no longer causes the water vapor inside the car to condense on the windows.) Some students may also observe that the excess water vapor in the car is caused by people in the car. The air they breathe out has been warmed and can therefore hold more water vapor than the cooler air at air temperature.

Students can use the two photographs to discuss what they do not indicate. They do not indicate relative amounts of moisture in the air because, among other things, 1) they do not indicate if they are both in the same air mass, 2) they do not indicate the surrounding air temperature (the temperature on the left could be close to freezing), 3) they do not indicate the temperature of the liquid in each container.

1. The surface of the ice-water container cools the surrounding air to its dew-point temperature. Water vapor in the air then condenses on the cool surface of the container.
2. The dew-point temperature is the temperature at which moisture in the air reaches the saturation point and the air can hold no more moisture.

pitcher on the right has cooled the surrounding air below its dew-point temperature. The condensation on the outside of the container is evidence that this has occurred.

Check yourself

1. Explain why droplets of water form on the outside of a container of ice water.

2. What is the relationship between the dew-point temperature and the saturation point of air?

Condensation near the earth's surface

New vocabulary: dew, frost, fog

The part of the earth that is in night receives no energy from the sun. That part of the earth cools down. If night air near the earth's surface cools down below its saturation point, condensation will occur. Dew, frost, and fog are caused by condensation that occurs near the earth's surface.

Dew is the droplets of water that can be found on the surfaces of leaves and grass early in the morning. Dew forms because during the night the air near the earth's surface is cooled below its dew-point temperature. This happens because the earth's surface cools to a temperature below the dew-point temperature of the air. Both conditions needed for condensation are present. 1) The night or early-morning air has cooled to its saturation temperature. 2) Objects like grass and leaves provide surfaces on which the extra water vapor can condense.

Frost forms in the same way as dew. But in order for frost to form, the dew-point temperature of the air must be below 0°C, the temperature at which water freezes. When such air is cooled below its dew-point temperature, ice crystals form instead of water droplets. This produces frost rather than dew. The process of water vapor changing from a gas to a solid is called sublimation.

Dew and frost occur when water vapor condenses on objects on the earth's surface. The excess water vapor from the cooling of saturated air can also condense on tiny particles of dust and other solid matter near the earth's surface. Millions of tiny water droplets form, producing a thick fog.

Figure 5-33. What is the difference between frost and dew?

Frost is made of ice crystals that form on a solid surface. Dew is made of liquid water that condenses on a solid surface.

Fog is really just a cloud that has formed on the earth's surface.

Most fogs form at night when the earth's surface cools and heat flows from the air to the land. Also, fogs often occur near bodies of water. As you may recall, air temperatures at night are warmer over bodies of water than over the land. That is because the land, which has a lower specific heat, cools off faster. The warm air over the water can hold more moisture than the cooler air over the land. When warm, moist air moves in over the cooler land surfaces, fog often occurs.

Figure 5-34. Fog is actually a cloud near the surface of the earth. Fog can form over land or water when the air is cooled below its dew-point temperature.

1. 1) The dew-point temperature of the air must be below 0°C. 2) There must be surfaces on which frost can form.
2. Frost is ice crystals that form on a solid surface; dew is liquid water that has condensed on a solid surface; fog is water droplets that have condensed on particles in the atmosphere close to the earth's surface.

Check yourself

1. What conditions are necessary for frost to form?

2. How does fog differ from dew and frost?

Condensation in the atmosphere

New vocabulary: clouds, stratus clouds, cumulus clouds, cirrus clouds

Air may be cooled below its dew-point temperature by coming into contact with a cool surface. This is what happens when moisture forms on a pitcher of ice water. This is also what happens when dew, frost, and fog form during the night and early morning.

Air is also cooled when it is lifted above the earth in convection currents. Most of the water vapor in the atmosphere is found in the troposphere, which is the zone of the atmosphere nearest the earth's surface. In the troposphere, it normally gets colder as altitude above sea level increases.

What do you think happens when warm, moist air is forced up in a convection current? Try to imagine that body of air becoming increasingly cooler as it rises above the earth's surface. At some point, that mass of air will cool below its dew point. Condensation will occur on the tiny particles of solid matter that are present in the atmosphere. If you look at the sky right now, chances are you can see some examples of this

What happens to the temperature of air as it rises above the earth in a convection current?

The temperature of the warm air will begin to drop as the air rises. This is because the air molecules will spread out and cause the air to cool. In some cases, the warm air does not cool and remains over the cooler air. This results in a temperature inversion. (See Figure 6-5, page 293.)

Figure 5-35. Stratus clouds are horizontal layered clouds. What causes stratus clouds to form in layers?

Stratus clouds often form at the horizontal boundary between a layer of warm air that is passing over a layer of cooler air. (The clouds form in the warm air mass, after the air temperature has been cooled to or below its dew-point temperature by the cooler air mass over which it is passing.)

Figure 5-36. Cumulus clouds, which usually form from upward-moving air, can be very large. What two factors determine the size of a cumulus cloud? The size of a cumulus cloud is determined by 1) the force of the upward movement of air and 2) the amount of moisture in the air.

kind of condensation. They are called **clouds.**

Almost all clouds fall into one of two general types—stratus clouds or cumulus clouds. The word *stratus* comes from the Latin word that means "to spread out." **Stratus clouds** are horizontal, layered clouds that stretch out across the sky like a blanket. Sometimes a layer of warm, moist air passes over a layer of cool air. Stratus clouds often form at the boundary where these layers meet. Where two such layers of air meet, the warm air is cooled. If the warm air is cooled below its dew point, the excess water vapor condenses to form a blanket-like layer of stratus clouds. If the layers of air are very large, the stratus clouds may extend for many kilometers across the sky.

The word *cumulus* comes from the Latin word for a heap or a pile. **Cumulus clouds** are puffy in appearance. They look like large cotton balls. Cumulus clouds usually form when warm, moist air is forced upward. As this air rises, it is cooled. If it is cooled below its dew-point temperature, condensation will occur. The size of a cumulus cloud depends on the force of the upward movement of air and the amount of moisture in the

What are the names of two general cloud types?

Figure 5-37. Cirrus clouds are so thin that sunlight can shine through them. What are cirrus clouds made of?
Cirrus clouds are made of ice crystals.

If students were to look into the sky this very minute, they well might see a cloud that doesn't look like a stratus, cumulus, or cirrus cloud as described on these pages. Stratus, cumulus, and cirrus are three general cloud types that are useful to consider for their main features. However, as indicated in the investigation for this section (Lab Manual pages 73–74), there are combinations and variations of the three general types. Some variations (for example, altocumulus and altostratus) have to do with altitude above sea level.

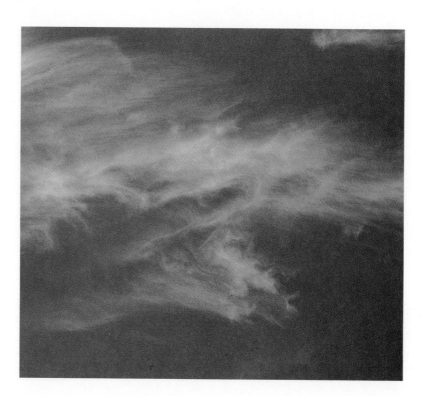

1. 1) Convection currents occur in the atmosphere. 2) As air rises in convection currents, it is cooled because temperatures drop as you go up in the troposphere.
2. Cumulus clouds are puffy because they are formed by vertical movements of air. Stratus clouds are blanket-like because they are formed by horizontal air movements.

air. The largest cumulus clouds are caused by very strong upward movements of warm, moist air. The clouds that produce heavy thunderstorms in summer are a form of cumulus clouds called cumulonimbus. Cumulonimbus clouds may extend upward for hundreds of meters.

Cirrus clouds are a third general type of cloud. The word *cirrus* comes from the Latin word for a tuft or curl of hair. **Cirrus clouds** are very wispy and feathery looking. They form only at high altitudes, about 7 km above the earth's surface. Cirrus clouds are composed of ice crystals and are so thin that sunlight can pass right through them.

Check yourself

1. What two conditions in the troposphere affect the formation of clouds?

2. How do cumulus clouds and stratus clouds differ in appearance? What causes this difference?

Precipitation

New vocabulary: precipitation, rain, snow, sleet, hail, rain gauge

Clouds form as a mass of air is cooled below its dew-point temperature. Clouds are formed of tiny water droplets that are small enough to stay suspended in the air. But as the cooling continues, more and more water vapor condenses. The size of the cloud increases. The size of the water droplets also increases as they hit against one another and become joined together. Sometimes the drops of water become too big to remain suspended in the air. When this happens, the water falls to the earth's surface.

Any form of water that falls to the earth from the atmosphere is called **precipitation.** The word *precipitation* comes from a Latin word that means "to throw down headfirst." Precipitation of water from the atmosphere can occur in several forms, depending on air temperature.

The most common forms of precipitation are rain and snow. **Rain** is merely drops of water that have become too large to remain in the air. A single raindrop is about one million times larger than a cloud particle. Flakes of **snow** form when the

What happens as an air mass containing a cloud continues to cool?

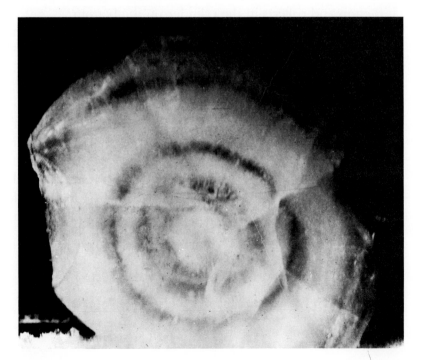

Figure 5-38. This photograph shows a cross section of the layers of ice inside a hailstone. Because of strong upward currents inside a tall cloud, hailstones can become larger than golf balls before they finally fall to the earth's surface.

Check yourself answers for page 280:
1. When air is cooled below its dew-point temperature and there are particles present for water vapor to condense on
2. Sleet forms when raindrops freeze as they fall through a layer of cold air. Snow forms not from a liquid but from water vapor, when the dew-point temperature is at or below freezing.

In answer to the caption question, a rain gauge is used to measure the amount of precipitation that falls at a particular location.

Figure 5-39. Rainwater enters this rain gauge through the opening at the top. What is a rain gauge used for?

Library research

Prepare a report or display on the crystal forms of snowflakes. Consider both the variety and the points of similarity among crystal forms.

dew-point temperature and the air temperature are at or below freezing.

Two other forms of precipitation you may have heard of are sleet and hail. **Sleet** is formed when raindrops fall from warmer air that is over very cold air and freeze into small pellets of ice. Hailstones form only in tall clouds. **Hail** starts off as tiny crystals of ice. But as the bits of ice pass through the different layers of air inside the cloud they pick up more layers of ice or water. There are strong upward currents of air inside the cloud that toss the hailstones back higher into the cumulus cloud. Each time this happens, more layers of ice are added. Eventually the hailstones can get as many layers as an onion. When they get too heavy to be held up, they fall to the earth's surface. When there are very strong upward currents of air in the cloud, the hailstones can become larger than golf balls.

How can a person tell how much precipitation falls at a certain place? The most common way is to measure the precipitation with a **rain gauge.** Rain gauges can be made of steel or plastic and come in many different sizes and shapes. In the rain gauge shown in Figure 5-39, the rain falls into an opening at the top and collects in the cylinder on the bottom.

To measure the amount of a snowfall, several methods can be used. If the snow is about the same depth all over, the simplest way is to insert a ruler into the snow and record the depth. The depth of the snow must then be changed into whatever its value would be in liquid water. Though the water content of a snowfall varies, ten units of snow commonly equals one unit of water. In such a case, 10 cm of snow would contain as much water as 1 cm of rain. The water content of a snowfall can be measured by using a rain gauge. The amount of snow that fell into the gauge is measured and then melted. The amount of water from the melted snow is then compared with the amount of snow from which it came.

Check yourself   Check yourself answers appear on page 279.

1. What causes water to fall from the sky as precipitation?

2. How does sleet form? How does this differ from the way snow forms?

Section 3 Review   Chapter 5

Use **Reading Checksheet 5-3** TRB page 75
Skillsheet 5-3 TRB page 117
Section Reviewsheet 5-3 TRB pages 171–172
Section Testsheet 5-3 TRB page 289

Check Your Vocabulary

13 cirrus clouds

21 clouds

4 condensation

12 cumulus clouds

18 dew

11 dew-point tempera-
ture

2 evaporation

20 fog

19 frost

23 hail

5 heat of fusion

3 heat of vaporization

7 humidity

14 precipitation

15 rain

24 rain gauge

8 relative humidity

6 saturated air

10 saturation temperature

17 sleet

9 sling psychrometer

16 snow

22 stratus clouds

1 water vapor

Match each term above with the numbered phrase that best describes it.

1. The name commonly used for water as gas

2. The changing from a liquid into a vapor

3. The amount of heat needed for 1 g of a substance to become a vapor

4. The changing of a vapor into a liquid

5. The amount of heat needed for 1 g of a solid substance to melt and become a liquid

6. Air that contains all the moisture it can hold

7. The amount of moisture that is in the air

8. A comparison of the amount of moisture in the air to the amount it can hold

9. An instrument that measures humidity

10. The temperature at which air is saturated

11. Same as saturation temperature

12. Puffy clouds that look like large cotton balls

13. Wispy, feathery-looking clouds

14. Any form of water that falls to the earth

15. Drops of liquid water that fall to the earth

16. Precipitation in the form of flakes

17. Small pellets of ice that form when raindrops fall through cold air and freeze

18. Droplets of water that condense on objects on the earth's surface

19. Ice crystals that form on objects on the earth's surface

20. A cloud that formed on the earth's surface

21. Droplets of water that condense on tiny particles up in the sky

22. Horizontal, layered clouds

23. Layered, round formations of ice

24. An instrument used to measure the amount of precipitation

Check Your Knowledge

Multiple Choice: Choose the answer that best completes each of the following sentences.

1. When water changes from a liquid to a vapor, it must _?_ energy.
   a) lose
   b) take in
   c) give off
   d) radiate

2. In very moist air, _?_ of the total volume is water vapor.
   a) 100%
   b) 50%
   c) 10%
   d) 3%

Check Your Understanding

1. What are the three physical states of water?

2. Which physical state of water contains the most energy? the least? Explain.

3. How does relative humidity affect the rate of evaporation? Why does this happen?

4. How does air temperature affect the amount of water vapor in the air?

5. Compare condensation and precipitation. How are they similar? different?

Chapter 5 Review

See also **Chapter Testsheets 5A and 5B**
TRB pages 325–326.

Concept Summary

The atmosphere is a layer of gases that surrounds the earth and that affects energy levels on the earth's surface.

☐ The atmosphere is made up of about ⅘ nitrogen and ⅕ oxygen.

☐ The air also contains tiny amounts of carbon dioxide, hydrogen, argon, and other gases.

☐ Gases and particles of solids in the atmosphere affect the kinds of energy waves from the sun that reach the earth's surface and that remain trapped in the atmosphere.

☐ Because the atmosphere is a fluid, it can transfer energy from one place to another by means of convection.

The sun's energy is the energy that is radiated out into space from the sun and that powers the winds and the weather changes that take place within the earth's atmosphere.

☐ Almost all the earth's energy comes from the sun.

☐ Only a tiny portion of the sun's energy reaches the earth.

☐ The sun's energy travels by means of electromagnetic waves.

☐ Heat and light are forms of energy.

☐ Energy travels by conduction, by convection, and by radiation.

☐ Energy is transferred when water changes from one physical state to another.

Water is a compound made up of hydrogen and oxygen, and it can be found on the earth in any of the three physical states of matter.

☐ Water changes from one physical state to another.

☐ As water changes from one state to another, there is a transfer of energy; energy is either taken in or given off.

☐ Most of the water in the atmosphere is found in the troposphere, the zone of the atmosphere that is closest to the earth's surface.

Putting It All Together

1. Draw diagrams that show the wavelengths of three waves (Wave A, Wave B, and Wave C). Wave A has a wavelength one half as long as Wave B. Wave C has a wavelength twice as long as Wave B.

2. When a fluid is heated, what happens to its volume? to its mass? to its density?

3. When uneven heating takes place in a fluid, what causes the warmer portion to rise?

4. More carbon dioxide is being put into the air than ever before. How can this affect conditions on the earth's surface?

5. Between January and June in the Northern Hemisphere, there is a surplus of energy that is stored in the earth's surface. Explain.

6. Water has the highest specific heat of any common natural substance. What does this mean?

7. Name the three kinds of energy transfer and give an example of each.

8. Tell what each of the following instruments measures: dry-bulb thermometer, sling psychrometer, barometer, anemometer, wind vane.

9. By means of the letter L and directional arrows, show how winds in the Northern Hemisphere move in relation to a low-pressure center.

10. How are clouds evidence of temperature differences in the atmosphere?

Apply Your Knowledge

1. A car is left in the sun. All the windows of the car are shut. What happens to the temperature inside the car? Why?

2. Study a room that you are familiar with. How does it receive heat? light? How does it lose heat? How might the room be made more energy efficient?

3. Draw a simple diagram of a solar heating unit for a house. Show how your unit involves energy transfer by radiation, conduction, and convection.
4. Freezer A is a freezer chest. The door of Freezer A is on top and lifts up. The door of Freezer B is in the front of the freezer and swings open like the door of a refrigerator. How does Freezer A compare with Freezer B in terms of energy efficiency? Explain your answer.
5. There is a fire in the building and you have to travel down a portion of a smoke-filled corridor. Which portion of the corridor will have the least amount of smoke? How can you use this knowledge to lessen the danger of breathing smoke into your lungs?

Find Out on Your Own

1. Mark the end of a shadow made out of doors by a stick or pole. Make a second mark that shows where you think the end of the shadow will be in one hour. After an hour, check to see where the end of the shadow is. How close was your prediction?
2. Place several thermometers in the sun. Place a different filter or screen in front of each thermometer. (One thermometer should be in full sun and one should be totally blocked from the sun.) How do the filters affect temperature readings on the thermometers?
3. Place thermometers in various locations in a room—near the ceiling, near the floor, near a window or door, and so forth. Predict which locations will record the highest temperature and which will record the lowest. Then measure the temperatures.
4. Measure the surface temperatures of different objects outdoors on a sunny day. Some objects should be made of different materials. Some objects should be made of the same material but be different colors. Are the temperature readings what you expected? What might explain any differences?
5. Make a wet-bulb thermometer. Experiment with different kinds of cloth, different amounts of moisture, different atmospheric conditions (in sunlight, in front of a fan, and so forth). Do any changes in condition affect the maximum temperature drop?

Reading Further

Adler, David. *World of Weather*. Mahwah, NJ: Troll Associates, 1984.
This is a comprehensive book of basic information on weather. Topics include tornadoes, hurricanes, evaporation, condensation, rain, snow, hail, and weather forecasting.

Asimov, Isaac. *How Did We Find Out About the Atmosphere?* New York: Walker, 1985.
This book takes us on an interesting tour of the history of ideas that led to our current understanding of the atmosphere.

Cosgrove, Margaret. *It's Snowing.* New York: Dodd, Mead & Co., 1980.
With wonderful illustrations, this book explains how snow is made and how crystals grow. It also describes avalanches.

Jeffries, Lawrence. *Air, Air, Air*. Mahwah, NJ: Troll Associates, 1984.
This simple text clearly explains many air phenomena. These include air composition and atmospheric pressure. In addition, it describes several investigations that can be done at home.

McFall, Christie. *Wonders of Dust*. New York: Dodd, Mead & Co., 1980.
This interesting book describes the sources of dust from within the earth to outer space. It presents problems we have with dust storms, pollution, weather phenomena—and dust as a possible cause of hailstorms.

Chapter 6 Weather and Climate

Student Resources		Meeting Individual Needs
Student Text	**Laboratory Activities**	
Section 1 Air Masses and Weather Fronts 286–297		
Air Moves in Masses 287–289	Investigation 6-1 Collecting Weather Data LM 80–81	Enrichment
Variations Within an Air Mass 289–290		
Conditions Along a Cold Front 290–291		
Conditions Along A Warm Front 291–293		
Thinking Skill: Inferring 292		
A Front on Top of a Front 293–295	Activity 6-1 Comparing Air Masses Across a Weather Front 294; Activity Record Sheet 6-1 LM 78	CORE
Stationary and Moving Fronts 295–296		
Section 1 Review 297		
Section 2 Predicting the Weather 298–314		
Recording the Local Weather Conditions 299–301		
Weather Fronts on a Map 301–303	Activity 6-2A Plotting Changes on a Weather Map 304 Activity Record Sheet 6-2A LM 82	CORE
Predicting Changes in the Weather 305		
Difficulties with Predicting the Weather 306–308	Investigation 6-2 Analyzing Weather Data LM 85–86	Enrichment
Extreme Weather Conditions 308–313	Activity 6-2B Tracking Severe Weather Conditions 309 Activity Record Sheet 6-2B LM 83	Enrichment
	Research Lab 6 Studying the Occurrence of Hurricanes LM 91–92	Enrichment
Section 2 Review 314		
Section 3 Climate 315–329		
General Types of Climates 316–318		
Factors That Affect Temperature 318–321		
Factors That Affect Moisture 321–324	Investigation 6-3 Making a Wind Rose for Your Location LM 89–90	Enrichment
Careers: Climatologist/Air-Conditioning Mechanic 323		
Our Science Heritage: Did Glaciers Really Cross the Sahara? 325		
Climate Graphs 325–327	Activity 6-3A Plotting a Climate Graph 326 Activity Record Sheet 6-3A LM 87	CORE
	Activity 6-3B Observing Effects of Climate Changes 328 Activity Record Sheet 6-3B LM 88	Reinforcement
Section 3 Review 329		
Chapter 6 Review 330–331		
Science Issues of Today: Preventing Disasters from Sudden Weather Changes 332		

6

Teacher Resources		Meeting Individual Needs
Teacher's Edition	**Teacher's Resource Book**	
Discussion Idea 284C	Essential Ideas 6-1 EI 37–38	Reinforcement
Creative Writing Idea 284C	Teaching Diagram 6-1 TRB 31	CORE
Demonstration 284D	Overhead Transparency S10	Enrichment
Teaching Thinking Skills 284E Activity Notes 284F	Overhead Transparency S11	Enrichment
	Skillsheet 6-1 TRB 118	Reinforcement
	Overhead Transparency S12	Enrichment
Section 1 Review Answers 284F	Reading Checksheet 6-1 TRB 76	Reinforcement
	Section Reviewsheet 6-1 TRB 173–174	CORE
	Section Testsheet 6-1 TRB 290	CORE
	Essential Ideas 6-2 EI 39–40	Reinforcement
Discussion Idea 284G Creative Writing Idea 284G Activity Notes 284G–284H	Teaching Diagram 6-2 TRB 32	CORE
	Skillsheet 6-2 TRB 119	Reinforcement
Demonstration 284J	Projectsheet 6-2 TRB 241	Enrichment
Activity Notes 284K		
Section 2 Review Answers 284K	Reading Checksheet 6-2 TRB 77	Reinforcement
	Section Reviewsheet 6-2 TRB 175–176	CORE
	Section Testsheet 6-2 TRB 291	CORE
	Essential Ideas 6-3 EI 41–42	Reinforcement
Demonstration; Discussion Idea 284L Environmental Topic 284M	Overhead Transparency B14	CORE
Activity Notes 284N		
Activity Notes 284P		
Section 3 Review Answers 284P	Reading Checksheet 6-3 TRB 78	Reinforcement
	Section Reviewsheet 6-3 TRB 177–178	CORE
	Section Testsheet 6-3 TRB 292	CORE
Chapter 6 Review Answers 284Q–284R	Chapter 6 Testsheet TRB 327–328	CORE

6

Learner Objectives

1. To distinguish air masses by general properties.
2. To relate air masses to the types of regions in which they form.
3. To distinguish among the different kinds of weather fronts.
4. To infer conditions from a weather map.

Concept Summary

6-1

An **air mass** is a large body of air that moves as a unit and that has more or less uniform characteristics throughout.
A **weather front** is the boundary between two air masses and often produces a change in the weather.

Discussion Idea

What Makes the Weather Change?

Ask students to describe the most recent weather change in your community. Have them describe temperature changes, clouds, winds, etc. Ask them to describe a sudden or severe change in weather that they remember.

Explain to students that weather changes occur as fronts move through an area. Tell them they will learn about weather fronts in Section 1 of Chapter 6.

Creative Writing Idea

The following writing assignment may help students develop an understanding of the relationship of fronts to local weather conditions.

You are a new radio announcer whose first assignment is to explain the variable weather conditions your community has been experiencing in terms of fronts. A moving cold front has just chased away a stationary warm front. For your listeners, describe the weather your community has experienced, and explain why the weather patterns have occurred the way they have.

Demonstration

The Difference in Density Between Warm and Cold Air

Get two identical jars—pint-size at least. Have one in the refrigerator or freezer cooling for several minutes and run hot water on the outside of the other to heat it. Have ready a thin card larger than the mouth of the jars. Also have on hand touch paper, a paper product that smokes without flame, or rolled-up pages of newspaper you can light to create smoke. You'll need one student to help you.

Light the touch paper (blow the flame out if newspaper is used). Take the cold jar out of the refrigerator and insert the smoking end of the touch paper into the jar for a few seconds. Remove the touch paper and immediately have the student put fresh paper over the mouth of the cold jar.

Leaving the paper in place, place the mouth of the hot jar down on the paper, exactly covering the mouth of the cold jar. Hold the two jars steady while the student pulls the paper out.

The smoke will stay where it is. Cold air, when underneath warm air, stays where it is.

Holding the jars together, turn them upside down and put the smoky, cold air on top. The smoke and cold air will quickly drop into the lower air. The warm air, hit by the cold air, is forced upward.

Tell students that the demonstration shows how cold air and warm air act when they meet each other. In Section 1 of Chapter 6, they will learn how large masses of cold and warm air act when they meet.

Science Background

In each hemisphere, a sharp boundary between warm tropical air and cold polar air, called a polar front, encircles the globe. The fronts usually lie within the temperature zones and account for the frequent and extreme weather changes that occur there. The position of the wavy front changes with the seasons and may even vary from day to day. High-altitude winds known as jet streams flow directly above a polar front.

A jet stream is a twisting band of strong winds found at the top of the troposphere. The air currents, about 100 km wide and 3 km high, may reach speeds of 400 km/h. They flow eastward in great loops, constantly shifting speed, direction, and position. Jet streams are normally lower, faster, and closer to the equator in winter than they are in summer. Because they control the movement of pressure systems in the lower atmosphere, jet streams are important in weather forecasting. A shift in the position of a jet stream can cause abnormal weather patterns that last for weeks.

Natural processes and human activities alter weather patterns. Volcanic eruptions, for example, form huge dust clouds that may circle the earth in the stratosphere for a year or more. These clouds reflect incoming sunlight back into space, causing cooler surface temperatures.

6-1

Student Misconception

Many students perceive changes in weather and cloud formation as random and unpredictable. Yet pressure, temperature, cloud formation, and precipitation are major indicators of frontal movement. While measurable qualities such as pressure and temperature are helpful in predicting weather patterns, observable changes are of great significance to the average person. Cloud patterns are especially useful in this respect.

Clouds signal frontal movement; for example, the appearance of cumulus and cumulonimbus clouds usually accompany the passing of a cold front. The thickening of cirrus and stratus clouds usually announces that a warm front is approaching.

Students can apply this information once they are able to recognize major cloud types.

You can introduce the three basic cloud types by associating them with the altitudes at which they form: cirrus clouds are high altitude clouds; cumulus are mid-altitude clouds; and stratus are low-altitude clouds. Have students keep a daily log describing the type of clouds present and the corresponding weather. If this procedure is carried out over a period of about a month, students should begin to see a relationship between the type of cloud and the resultant weather.

6-1

Teaching Thinking Skills

Inferring   page 292

Inferring is a more subjective skill than either observing or classifying. Inferences can be proven right or wrong, but the process of making an inference involves intuition as well as logical thought. Stress the point that inferences should be based on observed data, not on wild guesses. Make sure that students use the logical processes in Step 5 to check the intuitive processes in Step 3.

Advance Preparation

Photocopy one of the maps on pages 604 to 607 in the Appendix. Make one copy for each student.

Procedure Note

Both *Learning the Skill* and *Applying the Skill* are best done individually and followed by class discussion. Provide each student with a photocopied map for *Applying the Skill*.

Possible Student Responses

Possible inferences for the observations in *Learning the Skill:*
(1) The new mineral probably contains elements similar to that of galena. (2) Orion is not visible because it is summer (in the Northern Hemisphere). (3) The date is June 21 or 22, or December 21 or 22.

The sketches drawn for *Applying the Skill* will vary, but should demonstrate an attempt to show the relative elevation, shape, and distance from the viewer of each significant mountain or landform.

Discussion

Discuss why and how each inference was made. Encourage students to share the thought processes they used while they made their inferences. It may also be useful to compare different sketches and to discuss the differences in the kinds of inferences made in each one.

Going Further

As a classroom activity, have students work together to draw on the board a sketch of a particular view inferred from the map. Begin with an X and an arrow that everyone agrees with. Then have volunteers come to the board and each draw a part of the sketch as they see it. The point of this activity is to see what it takes for different people to agree on inferences. It will also force outspoken students to argue for their particular inferences, thus exposing their thought processes.

Activity Notes

Activity 6-1

Comparing Air Masses Across a Weather Front   page **294**

Purpose   To read a weather map and compare conditions on both sides of a weather front.

- **CORE**   20 minutes Individuals or pairs of students
- **Activity Record Sheet 6-1** (Lab Manual page 79) can be used to record this activity.
- Science Processes: Interpreting weather maps; Analyzing data; Communicating through a diagram; Communicating through a data table; Comparing and contrasting; Reasoning.

Advance Preparation

This activity calls for weather maps from recent newspapers. While students can bring in their own, you might want to have several extra on hand.

Procedure Notes

Some of the most easily recognized changes across a front include differences in temperature, wind direction, humidity (dew-point temperatures), and precipitation. There may or may not be differences in barometric (atmospheric) pressure.

Answers to Questions

1. Answers will vary. Students may find weather conditions that they did not expect to find (for example, precipitation somewhere other than along the boundary of a weather front).
2. Answers will vary. Study and discussion of various weather maps will increase student awareness of the many variables that influence weather conditions at a particular location.

Conclusion

Weather conditions on opposite sides of a front are usually very different. Noticeable changes in weather often take place as a front moves through an area.

Section 1 Review Answers

Check Your Understanding
page **297**

1. An air mass is a large body of air that is carried by prevailing winds and that, throughout its mass, contains about the same amount of moisture and is about the same temperature.
2. The same prevailing wind can bring different weather conditions on different days because 1) there can be variations within the air mass that is moving over an area, and 2) the same prevailing wind can bring different air masses to an area.
3. Because they formed in different areas (where it was warm or cold, moist or dry)
4. Incoming air masses cause weather changes because they bring the temperature changes, moisture, etc. associated with weather.
5. A cold front is the boundary where an advancing mass of cold air is pushing warm air ahead of it. The boundary along a cold front is steeper than along a warm front. Cumulus clouds form along a cold front and precipitation is likely to be heavy. Along a more gently sloping warm front, stratus clouds form and precipitation is less intense and more spread out.

Predicting the Weather

Learner Objectives

1. To interpret the information given in a station model.
2. To interpret symbols on a weather map.
3. To plot changes on a weather map.
4. To identify variables that affect weather predictions.
5. To identify causes of certain extreme weather conditions.

Concept Summary

6-2

A **station model** is a clear and simple way of recording weather conditions at a particular weather station.
A **weather map** is a representation of weather conditions over an area of the earth's surface.

Discussion Idea

How Local Features Affect Weather Conditions

Ask if students know about any features of their area that affect the weather. (Students living near the Great Lakes or Great Salt Lake may be familiar with "lake-effect snow." Students who live on one side or the other of a mountain range are probably familiar with heavy precipitation or high winds.)

Ask students which severe weather conditions might affect their area (thunderstorms, blizzards, hurricanes, tornadoes). How does their locale influence the type of weather experienced? (For instance, in a hurricane, inland areas would be affected by heavy rains, winds, and possible tornadoes rather than by high waves.)

Inform the students that the features unique to an area are among the factors that make weather prediction difficult. They will learn more about them in Section 2 of Chapter 6.

Creative Writing Idea

The following writing assignment may help students become aware of what information and equipment are necessary for making accurate weather predictions.

You have received a promotion at the radio station you work for, and you are now a meteorologist, responsible for predicting the weather for your community. The station will purchase equipment to help you predict correctly. You must write a report detailing the types of information you will need to make accurate predictions, and the equipment and materials you will use. Be complete about what you need—they may not offer you a second chance on ordering equipment!

Activity Notes

Activity 6-2A

Plotting Changes on a Weather Map   page **304**

Purpose To predict weather patterns based on weather maps.

- **CORE** 30 minutes Individuals or small groups
- **Activity Record Sheet 6-2A** (Lab Manual page 83) can be used to record this activity.
- Science Processes: Interpreting weather maps; Analyzing data; Identifying; Predicting; Using diagrams for comparison; Inferring.

Activity Notes (continued)

Advance Preparation

At least three days before doing this activity, have students start saving weather maps from a daily newspaper.

You will need blank maps for each student or group of students, and you might want to have extra weather maps on hand in case students forget to bring them. You can obtain Daily Weather Maps from the U.S. Government Printing Office, Washington D.C. 20402. For a reasonable annual subscription rate, these maps are mailed weekly and contain charts for the preceding weeks.

Procedure Notes

You may wish to discuss with students the different types of symbols used on a weather map and their meanings.

Students can write to a local chapter of the National Oceanic and Atmospheric Administration (NOAA) for copies of satellite photographs used in forecasting weather. They may compare the photos with the daily weather maps.

Answers to Questions

1. Answers will vary, but, in general, temperatures will be higher on one side of a front than on the other.
2. Winds usually blow out from a high-pressure center and in toward a low-pressure center. But there may be exceptions; any general expectations are subject to variation. Students should not be surprised by conditions that do not seem to agree with what they expected.
3. Cloudy areas are usually associated with warm air masses. They occur ahead of a cold front and behind a warm front.
4. Answers will vary. Students may be able to draw inferences about where severe storms occur, etc.
5. Answers will vary.

Conclusion

Reading weather maps makes it possible to predict such things as general movement of a front and changes in temperature. But weather maps do not show all the variables affecting the weather. More detailed, accurate predictions require information gathered by satellite and by radar.

Going Further

Students can collect weather reports and maps from the daily newspaper over a period of two weeks to see if they can detect a trend of movement of weather across the United States.

Also, students can compare daily weather predictions with the actual weather that occurs over a month. They can determine what percentage of times the predictions were correct.

Science Background

Weather satellites and computers have revolutionized weather forecasting. Since 1960, weather satellites have provided important data on large-scale weather systems. Cloud-cover photographs help meteorologists discover weather patterns and follow weather fronts. Weather satellites also carry instruments that measure atmospheric temperature and moisture at different altitudes. In addition, the satellites collect local weather information from hundreds of data-collecting platforms on land, sea, and in the air. They relay the information to ground receiving stations.

Currently, the United States has four weather satellites. Two Tiros-N satellites travel in polar orbits at an altitude of 870 km. Each scans the entire surface of the earth once every 24 hours. Two GOES satellites orbit above the equator at an altitude of 35 800 km. This geostationary orbit keeps them at fixed positions over the earth. Television weather maps come from the East Coast GOES.

Meteorologists began using computers in the early 1950s. Today, a Cyber 205 supercomputer at the National Meteorological Center in Maryland analyzes thousands of separate measurements relayed from weather satellites, helium balloons, and ground stations. Based on the computer's calculations, the center issues forecasts twice a day for the next 12, 24, 36, 48, and 72 hours. It also issues severe storm warnings.

6-2

Predicting the Weather

Student Misconception

Students often confuse hurricanes with tornadoes. Both are intense storms characterized by low pressure centers that occur when contrasting temperature and pressure gradients create strong convection currents in the atmosphere. Tornadoes form only over land, and hurricanes form only over water. Water vapor provides the "fuel" for a hurricane. Without it, the hurricane dies.

When water vapor condenses, heat is released into the environment, furthering convection. The warm, moist air rises, cools, and condenses, releasing heat and leading to further convection. As a hurricane moves inland, its fuel supply is reduced, and the storm decreases in intensity. To give your students a better understanding of hurricanes, review the following sequence of events:

1. Convection currents in the atmosphere set up a low-pressure center accompanied by the formation of cumulonimbus clouds.

2. As warm air rises, it cools, and condenses.

3. Condensation involves the release of heat, furthering the upward movement of air.

Ask students, "What will act to limit or break this cycle?" It should become obvious that the energy released during condensation fuels the storm. As a hurricane moves from over water to over land, its source of fuel is eliminated, and the storm dies.

Demonstration

How Accurate Are Weather Forecasts?

Collect weather maps and forecasts from the newspaper for several days in a row. Choose those that predict the weather for several days so that today's weather was predicted two, three, and four days ago.

Read the forecasts to the class and ask how accurate the forecast for today was. Did it change from day to day?

(If you have the use of a videotape recorder and player, then tape the television weather forecasts for several days and show them to the class).

If the forecast was accurate, ask the students to point out those factors upon which the predictions were based. If the forecast changed, ask them if they know what factors caused the meteorologists to change their forecast.

Tell students that they will learn more about weather maps and weather forecasts in Section 2 of Chapter 6. They will be able to make their own predictions.

Activity Notes

Activity 6-2B

Tracking Severe Weather Conditions   page **309**

Purpose   To understand how severe weather conditions occur and how they affect people.

- 20 minutes Small groups
- **Activity Record Sheet 6-2B** (Lab Manual page 84) can be used to record this activity.
- Science Processes: Collecting and interpreting data; Researching; Communicating through a map; Describing; Generalizing.

Advance Preparation

You might want to advise students several weeks in advance of this activity so that they can look for the information they need. Sources might include weather programs on TV, nationally distributed newspapers such as the *New York Times* and *USA TODAY*, and newsmagazines. You will need blank maps for each group of students.

Procedure Notes

If you live in an area of the country where severe weather conditions such as tornados or hurricanes occur, you might review with the class some of the safety precautions to follow under those conditions. It might also be a good time to discuss safety precautions to take during a thunderstorm accompanied by lightning. Such information can be obtained from an encyclopedia, the National Weather Service, or from a local chapter of the Red Cross.

Answers to Questions

Answers to each question will vary. This activity provides an important extension—from a consideration of local and national conditions to a consideration of atmospheric conditions at other locations on the earth.

Conclusion

Answers will vary. Students will see why understanding and predicting weather trends are so important; severe weather conditions can have devastating effects on the environment and on people.

Section 2 Review Answers

Check Your Understanding
page **314**

1. Large-scale weather maps make use of data from ground stations throughout a large area and incorporate measurements from the station models provided by those ground stations.
2. Triangles indicate a cold front. They also indicate, by the side of the line they are on, the direction in which the front is moving.
3. Student drawings should indicate that the fronts are 1) similar in that they contain symbols for both warm and cold fronts (semicircles and triangles), and 2) different in that the symbols are on the same side of the line for an occluded front, but on opposite sides of the line for a stationary front.
4. If two variables are inversely related, an increase in one causes a decrease in the other.
5. Probabilities are useful in predicting the weather because no weather prediction is 100 percent certain. Too many variables affect the total weather picture. Therefore, meteorologists weigh the possibilities and if, for example, rain is more likely than no rain at all, they may indicate how likely by saying that there is a 60 percent or 70 percent chance of rain.

6-2

Learner Objectives

1. To distinguish between weather and climate.
2. To relate general types of climate to latitude.
3. To identify factors other than latitude that affect temperature.
4. To identify factors that affect moisture.
5. To interpret a climate graph.

Concept Summary

Climate is the average weather conditions, primarily moisture and air temperature, that occur in one place over a year or longer.

6-3

Demonstration

Finding Out Where the Deserts Are

Obtain a world map with clearly defined latitude and longitude markings. Place two strips of ticker tape in an east-west direction, one at 30° N and one at 30° S. Ask students what geographical features can be found along these lines of latitude. (All the world's major deserts are found there.)

Tell the students that 30° N and 30° S are zones of diverging air. This descending air is warming up and therefore will produce very little precipitation.

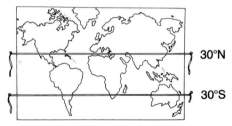

Point out that the polar regions are also deserts. Students will probably disagree because of the presence of snow and ice. Inform them that at the polar regions there is very little precipitation. What precipitation occurs remains on the surface because of the cold temperatures.

Discussion Idea

Terrestial Climate and Human Adaptation

Ask students if there are any terrestrial climates in which humans cannot live. (People have set up research settlements in Antarctica and lived there year-round; people live at the equator.) Explain that humans are usually able to adapt to climatic changes. Ask if any students have ever flown to a high-altitude area and then tried vigorous exercise (such as skiing or jogging.) Ask if they have ever found themselves underdressed in unexpected cold or overdressed in unexpected heat. Tell them that people can usually adjust to such unforseen changes in temperature but that occasionally they can be life-threatening when they are greatly beyond the range expected in a certain climate. In India people have died because of a cold spell of 15°C (59°F)—because their clothing and housing were inadequate for what we in any part of the United States would not consider a life-threatening temperature.

Tell students that in Section 3 of Chapter 6 they will learn about climate and the factors that determine it.

Environmental Topic

The scorching temperatures on Venus are caused largely by a runaway "greenhouse effect." Like the glass in a greenhouse, the dense carbon dioxide atmosphere of Venus lets solar radiation pass through to its surface but does not let the resultant heat escape from the surface and re-enter space. Thus heat remains trapped near the surface, creating temperatures of close to 480°C (800°F). It is so hot on Venus that the most recent Russian probes, *Venera 13* and *14*, melted within an hour of contact with the planet's surface. Some climatologists are concerned about a repetition of the greenhouse effect occurring on earth.

With the continued rise in fuel consumption, increasingly larger amounts of carbon dioxide are being released into our atmosphere. Predictably, there has been a significant global warming over the years. Some scientists fear that an increase in atmospheric temperature could trigger the melting of glaciers, producing a rise in sea level, and resulting in the flooding of coastal areas.

Have the class explore the effects of an increase in atmospheric temperature on climate (change in precipitation patterns, warmer oceans, etc.). Discuss what can be done now to prevent this from happening. You might also have the class consider whether there are any possible beneficial effects of global warming.

Science Background

Climate and topography determine which plants and animals live in a region. Ecologists divide the earth into large areas called biomes. The major biomes include Arctic and alpine tundras, grasslands, desert, and several kinds of forests. Each biome has a unique set of climatic conditions.

Climate also influences soil formation and how a landscape takes shape. Soil develops more rapidly in a moist region than in a dryer one. Moreover, where life is abundant, the soil usually contains more humus. Landforms in regions of moderate to heavy rainfall are shaped largely by the action of running water. In dry areas, wind plays a greater role in erosion.

Evidence indicates the earth has experienced three major ice ages during the last 600 million years. The most recent period of glaciation began about a million years ago. During this time, polar ice sheets advanced and retreated at least four times; valley glaciers also grew and shrank. When the last advance reached its peak around 20 000 years ago, glaciers covered 30 percent of the earth's land surface. The ice retreated again 10 000 years ago, as temperatures warmed. Some climatologists believe the present warm temperatures are merely another interglacial period. There are many theories about what causes ice ages, but the reasons remain unknown.

6-3

Climate

Student Misconception

As you move from a discussion of weather to an analysis of climate, it is important to recognize that students often have difficulty distinguishing between the daily weather events and averages of the numerical values of those events.

In discussing weather, emphasis is placed on the readings of temperature, precipitation, pressure, and wind. These values are viewed as distinct events. Rarely is a daily reading placed in the immediate context of seasonal averages. Climate is a study of weather patterns that occur in one place over an extended period of time. In discussing climate, emphasis is placed on the *averages* of temperature, precipitation, pressure, and winds.

You can highlight the differences between weather and climate for your students. Compile a list of the temperature ranges, extremes, and averages for your area. Based on this information, have students guess the location of the place you are describing. For example, you might say, "People living in this geographic region are likely to experience temperature ranging from _____ to _____." Students may be surprised by the variance between extremes and averages. You might extend this activity into a class research project by assigning each student a particular area that he or she must identify the characteristic weather and climate data.

6-3

Activity Notes

Activity 6-3A

Plotting a Climate Graph   page **326**

Purpose   To compare climates at three different locations.
- **CORE** 30 minutes Individuals or small groups
- **Activity Record Sheet 6-3A** (Lab Manual page 87) can be used to record this activity.
- Science Processes: Interpreting data; Communicating through a graph; Classifying; Identifying; Describing; Inferring.

Procedure Notes

Students can find the annual temperature range for each of the three locations by subtracting the lowest temperature reading from the highest.

You might have students calculate the average monthly precipitation for each location by dividing the total precipitation (given in the data table) by 12. Students can then compare these averages.

Answers to Questions

1. Student descriptions will vary. In general, Location B (Jacobabad, Pakistan), with the least precipitation and the highest temperatures, has a desert climate. Temperatures at Location A (Buenos Aires, Argentina) are not so varied as those at Location C (Memphis, Tennessee). Locations A and C receive more precipitation than Location B. The most precipitation occurs in the warmer months at Location A and in the colder months at Location C.
2. You can tell that a place like Location A (Buenos Aires) is in the Southern Hemisphere by noting that the temperatures are highest in December, January, and February.

Conclusion

From a climate graph, you can infer in which hemisphere an unnamed place is located, and the climate to which it belongs. You can perhaps tell whether its prevailing winds are maritime or continental. Students may provide other answers.

Going Further

If possible, obtain climatic data for your area from a climate map, climate atlas, or your local weather office. Have students plot a climate graph using the data. Students can then compare this graph with the graphs made in class.

Activity Notes

Activity 6-3B

Observing Effects of Climate Changes page **328**

Purpose To see how plants of the same kind are affected by different climates.

- 30 minutes plus 3 brief weekly observations Groups of 4
- **Activity Record Sheet 6-3B** (Lab Manual page 88) can be used to record this activity.
- Science Processes: Separating and controlling variables; Simulating conditions; Experimenting; Observing; Measuring; Collecting and analyzing data; Inferring.

Advance Preparation

This activity calls for transplanted/potted plants in a stabilized condition. Transplanting should be done about a week before beginning the activity in order to give the plants a chance to stabilize. (If the plants are not stabilized, students will not be able to tell whether certain changes in the plants are the result of climate changes or transplant shock.) If you are growing the plants from seeds, you might need to allow 2–3 weeks before beginning the activity.

Procedure Notes

Students might simulate a cold climate by keeping plants on ice. If a cooler or refrigerator with a glass or plexiglass door is available (to let light through), students might refrigerate some of their plants.

Answers to Questions

1. Answers will vary.
2. Answers will vary.
3. Answers will vary. It is expected that each plant will respond best to the climate conditions ideal for that type of plant. This could be a good way for students to become aware of how various kinds of plants require different amounts of moisture, sunlight, and warmth.
4. Accuracy improves with increased data. Averaging provides greater precision and overcomes differences due to irregular growth by a particular plant.
5. Answers will vary.

Conclusion

Answers will vary. Students will probably expect different plants of the same type to react similarly to climate changes. Different plant types might or might not be affected similarly.

Section 3 Review Answers

Check Your Understanding
page **329**

1. Weather and climate are similar in that both are influenced by temperature and amount of moisture. They are different insofar as weather is concerned with present conditions and climate is concerned with average weather conditions that can be expected in a particular location throughout a 12-month period.
2. Latitude affects climate because warmest air temperatures are caused by most direct (vertical) rays of the sun's energy which, in general, strike the earth at the lower latitudes (between 22.5° N and 22.5° S latitudes).
3. At the same latitude, air is warmest at sea level. In general, as you go higher above sea level, the air becomes cooler.
4. Descending air warms rapidly, causing it to lose moisture through evaporation.
5. On the east coast, ocean currents are traveling away from the equator. They therefore contain warm water that warms the air in areas near these currents. On the west coast, the ocean currents are traveling toward the equator. They contain cool water that cools the air in areas near the ocean.

6-3

Weather and Climate

Chapter Vocabulary

Section 1

prevailing winds
air mass
continental air mass
maritime air mass
polar air mass
tropical air mass
front
cold front
warm front
occluded front
stationary front

Section 2

station model
cumulonimbus cloud
thunderstorm
lightning
thunder
blizzard
tornado
hurricane

Chapter 6 Review Answers

Putting It All Together   page 330

1. C = continental, an air mass of dry air that forms over land areas. M = maritime, an air mass of moist air that forms over water. P = polar, an air mass of cold air that forms near the poles. T = tropical, an air mass of warm air that forms in the tropics (between the Tropics of Capricorn and Cancer and near the equator).

2. A. cold front

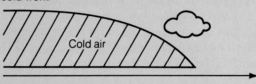

Cold air

B. warm front

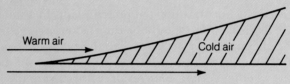

Warm air   Cold air

C. occluded front

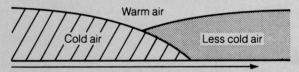

Warm air
Cold air   Less cold air

3. You would expect heavier precipitation along a cold front. Because the slope of the boundary is steeper, the warm air is pushed up more quickly. Cooling will therefore be more rapid, and result in heavier condensation and precipitation than if the cooling process were more gradual.

4. A station model is a graphic device for presenting weather measurements for a certain area. By means of numerals in certain positions, it indicates atmospheric pressure, air temperature, and dew-point temperature. By means of a circle and shading, it indicates cloud cover. By means of a staff and flags, it indicates wind direction and speed.

5. Because weather is caused by the interaction of several variables, predicting the weather can never be 100 percent accurate. Percentages offer a realistic way to indicate what the weather will probably be like and how likely it is that the prediction will occur.

6. Similar: Both involve high-speed winds traveling in a circular direction toward a low-pressure center. Different: Hurricanes affect a much wider area than tornadoes (300 km vs 100 m). Wind speeds in a tornado are considerably greater than in a hurricane (800 km/h vs 150 km/h).

Chapter 6 Review Answers (continued)

Putting It All Together   page **330 continued**

7. Because of advance warning, people can prepare for extreme weather conditions. They can reduce damage by securing property as much as they can. They can leave an area that is likely to be hit by floods or a snowslide.

8. In general, tropical climates are found near/between the tropics and are characterized by tropical air masses, which contain warm air. Polar climates are found near the poles and are characterized by polar air masses, which contain cold air. Temperate climates are found in the mid-latitudes (between the tropics and the Poles) and are affected by both polar and tropical air masses, causing more moderate temperatures than are associated with polar and tropical climates.

9. Prevailing winds are responsible for climate insofar as prevailing winds bring weather to particular locations. Climate is expressed by average monthly air temperatures and amounts of precipitation for a period of twelve months. Prevailing winds have a direct effect on air temperatures and amounts of moisture.

10. Deserts are found in areas of descending air. As air descends, it warms. As air warms, it loses moisture through evaporation. Deserts are characterized by dry air (less than 10 in./254 mm of precipitation per year).

Apply Your Knowledge   page **330**

1. Cold air masses can be expected to move in the general direction of the equator, where the cold air is able to displace warmer, less dense tropical air. Other factors (such as Coriolis effect, the location of high-pressure centers and low-pressure centers, and geographical features) also affect the direction of movement of air masses.

2. What is the barometric pressure where you live? If it is lower than the pressure where it is raining, or if it is between the area of rain and a low-pressure area, winds will blow toward that low-pressure area and can be expected to bring the rainy conditions along with them.

3. Student diagrams can indicate varying amounts of cloud cover, depending on how cloudy they want the sky to be. This sample shows 50 percent cloud cover.

4. As with any symbol or standard device, information can be given in a way that can be read and interpreted at a glance. Symbols, standard positions, and other devices make it unnecessary to surround the data with explanatory text.

5. Because of prevailing conditions, ice-covered polar regions can be characterized by very dry air masses and therefore very little precipitation.

Chapter Vocabulary

Section 3

weather
climate
tropical climate
polar climate
temperate climate
marine climate
continental climate
adiabatic change
desert
rain-shadow desert
climate graph

6-3

Chapter 6

Weather and Climate

Section 1
Air Masses and Weather Fronts

The earth's atmosphere is like an ocean of gases that surrounds the earth's surface.

The earth's atmosphere is made up of large masses of air that are characterized by similar temperatures or moisture content.

When you feel a sudden change in air temperature, or when you see a line of clouds or a thunder-and-lightning storm advancing across the sky, you know by direct observation that an air mass is on the move.

Section 2
Predicting the Weather

Anyone who is planning to do something outdoors must consider what the weather might be like. Will it be sunny or will it be raining? Will it be warm or will it be cold?

A weather report will tell you what kind of weather is likely to occur. It can also tell you how likely it is to occur. But, as with any other prediction, the outcome may not be what was expected.

Section 3
Climate

The climate of an area is determined by the amount of moisture that location receives in an average year and by the average temperatures that can be expected from month to month throughout the year.

Weather data, collected over the years, enables scientists to describe the world's climates. In some instances, the world's climate zones are related, in predictable ways, to geographical location and features. In other instances, surprising variations in climate occur at particular locations. In answer to the questions in the caption on the left, our ability to observe weather from above is due to the development of at least three general kinds of instruments: instruments that can observe the weather from above, instruments that can record, and instruments that can transmit the data to a receiving station.

Until recently, people who studied the weather had to observe it from below. The picture on the facing page shows what a hurricane looks like when seen from above. What kinds of instruments make it possible to observe weather from above. How does this kind of observation affect the ability of scientists to predict tomorrow's weather?

Air Masses and Weather Fronts   Section 1

Learner Objectives
1. To distinguish air masses by general properties.
2. To relate air masses to the types of regions in which they form.
3. To distinguish among the different kinds of weather fronts.
4. To infer conditions from a weather map.

Section 1 of Chapter 6 is divided into six parts:

Air moves in masses

Variations within an air mass

Conditions along a cold front

Conditions along a warm front

A front on top of a front

Stationary and moving fronts

Figure 6-1. A lightning storm is moving across this portion of the earth's surface. What brings local weather to an area?
Local weather is brought to an area by prevailing winds, which usually come from the same direction.

As mentioned on page 250, two types of winds circulate the atmosphere above your town or city—local winds and prevailing winds. **Prevailing winds,** which are part of much larger patterns of circulation, almost always come from the same direction. In the continental United States, the prevailing winds are westerly. They move from the west to the east across the country.

Local weather is brought to an area by the prevailing winds. Since the prevailing winds generally come from the same direction, what causes changes in the weather? How, for example, is it possible for the same prevailing wind to bring warm air and clear skies one day and cooler air and precipitation on another day?

Air moves in masses New vocabulary: air mass, continental air mass, maritime air mass, polar air mass, tropical air mass

Local weather conditions are brought in by prevailing winds. But weather conditions depend upon characteristics of the air itself. The air that is carried by prevailing winds moves as a unit. It is really a body of air that is moving. This body of air that is carried by the prevailing winds is called an **air mass.**

An air mass is large. It may extend for hundreds of kilometers. Also, the air mass is nearly uniform throughout. This means that all the air has about the same amount of moisture. It also means that all the air is at nearly the same temperature.

The characteristics of a particular air mass depend upon where the air mass forms. In general, air masses form either over land or over water and near a polar region or near the tropics. Four terms used to describe such air masses are *continental, maritime, polar,* and *tropical.* A **continental air mass** is one that forms over dry land (the continent). A **maritime air mass** is one that forms over an ocean. (*Mare* is the Latin word for sea or ocean.) A **polar air mass** is one that forms near the North or South Pole. A **tropical air mass** is one that forms near the Tropic of Cancer or the Tropic of Capricorn.

Each different air mass has its own general characteristics. A continental air mass will contain dry air whereas a maritime air mass will contain moist air, picking up moisture when it forms over an ocean. A polar air mass will contain cold air. A tropical

See also Teaching Diagram 6-1
(TRB page 31).

Table 6-1. The characteristics of
an air mass depend on where the
air mass formed. If an air mass
formed over water, would it
contain moist air or dry air?
An air mass that formed over
water would contain moist air.

Using TV weather forecasts or
newspaper weather maps,
students can track specific types
of air masses as they move
across the country. A moisture-
laden maritime tropical air mass,
for example, may continue to
produce precipitation.

There are some seasonal
patterns associated with certain
types of air masses. Interested
students should be encouraged to
research and report on this to the
class.

Type of Air Mass	Where Formed	Characteristic of Air Mass
continental (c)	over land	dry
maritime (m)	over water	moist
polar (P)	near a polar region	cold
tropical (T)	near the tropics	hot

air mass will contain warm air. A continental polar air mass will
be dry and cold. A maritime tropical air mass will contain both
characteristics also (moist and warm).

Figure 6-2 shows the common air masses that affect weather
conditions across the continental United States. Note how the
letters c (for continental), m (for maritime), P (for polar), and
T (for tropical) are used to label the different air masses. An
air mass labeled cP is a continental polar air mass. Note also
that the arrows show the general direction in which air masses
move across the continental United States. This follows the
general direction of movement of the prevailing westerlies.

The characteristics of air masses can be related to observed
weather conditions. Suppose in your area a cool dry day was
followed by a warm humid day. You might infer that a continental polar (cP) air mass was over your area on the first day.
Then a maritime tropical (mT) air mass moved in and replaced

Figure 6-2. Maritime polar air
masses, which contain cool moist
air, form over the northern Pacific
and Atlantic Oceans.

Source region

mP   Maritime polar
       (Pacific) air masses

cA   Arctic air masses

cP   Continental polar
       air masses

mP   Maritime polar
       (Atlantic) air masses

mT   Maritime tropical
       (Pacific) air masses

cT   Tropical continental
       air masses

mT   Maritime tropical
       (Gulf) air masses

mT   Maritime tropical
       (Atlantic) air masses

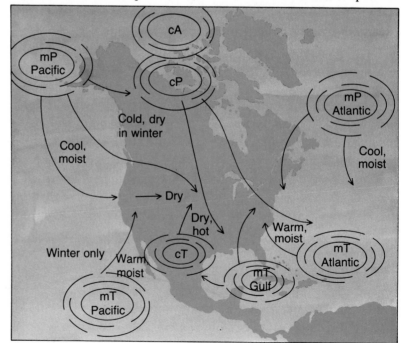

the cP air mass. Since air masses can extend for hundreds of kilometers, the same air mass may be over a particular area for several days. Several consecutive days of similar weather would be evidence of this.

As air masses slow down, they may change their characteristics. An example would be a cP air mass originating in Canada. The air would be dry and cold. As it moves south, it would warm up. If it passed over the Great Lakes, it would pick up moisture. (Note that all air masses generally follow the prevailing wind belt. For the continental United States, therefore, air masses tend to move from west to east across the land.)

Check yourself

1. How do air masses affect the weather of an area?
2. How does where an air mass forms affect the characteristics of an air mass?

Variations within an air mass

Air masses generally show up as high-pressure areas. But, as shown in Figure 6-3, there may be differences in atmospheric pressure within the same air mass. Low-pressure areas may also be found at the boundaries of an air mass.

Another characteristic of air masses is that, in general, all the air in a particular air mass has the same temperature and the same amount of moisture. Some variations, however, do exist. In Figure 6-3, note that the high-pressure area of the air mass is centered over the Hudson Bay region of Canada. That portion of the air mass would have picked up more moisture than the portion of the air mass that formed over land.

Temperatures within the same air mass can also vary. On a certain summer day, Sault Ste. Marie, Buffalo, and Detroit were located under the same air mass. Their temperatures were as follows: Sault Ste. Marie—23°C; Buffalo—27°C; Detroit—29°C.

Though temperatures and moisture content are not uniform

You might point out something about the use of the terms hot and cold in relation to air masses. When two air masses are compared—one with a temperature of 90°F and one with a temperature of 80°F—the air mass with the temperature of 80°F is, by comparison, considered cold.

1. Weather is caused by the type of air mass present in an area. An air mass can contain warm, cold, dry, or moist air— depending on the type of air mass.
2. Warm air masses form near the equator, cold ones near the poles, dry ones over land, moist ones over water.

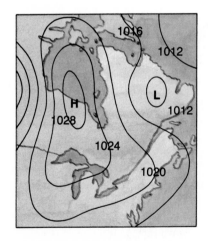

Figure 6-3. The high-pressure area of this air mass is centered over the Hudson Bay region of Canada.

Point out to students that the differences are relative. Temperatures within a tropical air mass during winter can be colder than temperatures in a polar air mass in summer.

	Air Mass	Temperature	Relative Humidity
summer	cT	27°C	52%
summer	mT	27°C	93%
winter	cP	−30°C	negligible
winter	mP	10°C	66%

Table 6-2. In general, which contain higher relative humidities—continental air masses or maritime air masses? Maritime air masses generally contain higher relative humidities than continental air masses.

throughout an air mass, a continental polar air mass is colder and contains less moisture than a maritime tropical air mass. The data in Table 6-2 provides a means of comparing variations among different types of air masses. (Note that the altitude of a city may also affect the temperature and humidity of an air mass over that location.)

Check yourself

1. What are three variations that can occur within an air mass?

2. What can explain differences in amounts of moisture within the same air mass?

1. Variations in atmospheric pressure, temperature, and amount of moisture
2. Part of the air mass may have formed over water.

Conditions along a cold front
New vocabulary: front, cold front

When listening to a weather report, you may have heard the terms *warm front* or *cold front*. A **front** is the boundary between a mass of warmer air and a mass of colder air. Whether the front is a warm front or a cold front depends on which air mass is pushing the other air mass ahead of it.

A **cold front** forms when a cold air mass pushes a warm air mass ahead of it. Cold air is denser than warm air. The warm air is therefore forced upward.

Figure 6-4 illustrates a cold front. Notice the steep slope along the boundary. The warm air is pushed up rapidly. Moisture in the warm air mass condenses to form clouds.

The clouds most commonly found along a cold front are vertical cumulus clouds. The more moisture present in the warm air mass, the larger are the cumulus clouds that form. If enough moisture is present, precipitation will occur.

Precipitation along a cold front tends to be heavy. How long the precipitation will last in an area depends upon how fast the

Library research

What kinds of weather fronts move in over the area where you live? From what direction does each usually come? How can you recognize the approach of each kind of front?

Heavy precipitation tends to occur along a cold front because the air is rising more rapidly. As it does, the moisture condenses more rapidly and produces heavier precipitation.

Figure 6-4. A cold front forms when a cold air mass pushes a warm air mass ahead of it. What characteristic of the cold air forces the warm air upward? Cold air is denser than warm air and therefore forces the warm air upward.

front is moving. A heavy thunderstorm may last only a few minutes, or it may continue for a few hours.

Check yourself

1. Describe a cold front in terms of air masses.

2. Why do clouds form along a cold front?

Conditions along a warm front
New vocabulary: warm front

A **warm front** forms when a warm air mass pushes a cold air mass ahead of it. When this happens, the warm air moves up and over the cold air mass. At the same time, the cold air mass is pushed back.

As shown in Figure 6-5, the boundary line along a warm front slopes more gently than the boundary line along a cold front. Along a warm front, the warm air does not rise as rapidly. The clouds that form along a warm front are usually stratus clouds. These clouds are thinner than cumulus clouds and usually spread over a much larger area.

Precipitation can also occur along a warm front. The precipitation is usually spread over a much larger area than the precipitation along a cold front. Also, a cold front tends to produce thunderstorms of short duration. A warm front produces a steady drizzle that may last for several hours or even longer.

Check yourself answers:
1. A cold front forms when a cold air mass pushes a warm air mass ahead of it.
2. Air in the warm air mass is cooled, causing water vapor in the warm air mass to condense and form clouds.

Critical Thinking

If you saw a warm front indicated on a weather map, what type of clouds would you expect to find along the front?

Thinking Skill Inferring

Have you ever approached one of your friends from behind, tapped him or her on the shoulder, and discovered your "friend" was a perfect stranger? If so, you have experienced making an incorrect inference.

Inferences are interpretations of observations. They may or may not be correct. In the example above, your observation of the stranger's characteristics led you to infer the stranger was your friend.

When you use the skill of inferring, you think about your observations and try to explain them. You may also try to determine the causes of what you observed, or you may make predictions based upon your observations.

When weather forecasters predict the weather, they are making inferences based upon their observations of temperature, wind direction, air pressure, and humidity. Their skills of inferring have been developed through years of training and experience dealing with the weather.

The following steps will help you make better inferences:

1. Make careful and accurate observations.
2. Determine the type of inference to be made: to *explain an observation,* to *determine the cause of an observation,* or to *make a prediction* based on an observation.
3. Based on your knowledge and experience, relate the data of the observation to an inference.
4. Test the inference, if possible.
5. Ask yourself if the inference makes sense. Is there a link between the observation and the inference? Does the inference go beyond the data you collected from observing?

Learning the Skill

Use the steps of the skill of inferring to make inferences about the following observations:

1. A new mineral has characteristics similar to those of galena. What can you infer about the elements it is made of?
2. You step out of the house to look for Orion in the night sky, but cannot see it. What can you infer about the season?
3. You are at the equator and observe the sun at an altitude of 66.5°. What can you infer about the date?

Applying the Skill

When you look at a map to get information, you make inferences about the actual topography and features based upon your observations of the map symbols.

Study the map given to you by your teacher. Use the skill of inferring to form a picture of the topography represented by this map. In pencil, place an X on one of the edges of the map. Then draw an arrow pointing toward the center of the map. Sketch the view you would see if you were standing at location X and facing the direction of the arrow.

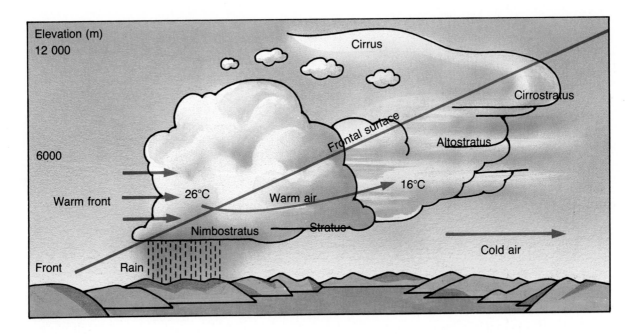

Figure 6-5. A warm front forms when a warm air mass pushes a cold air mass ahead of it. How does the slope of the boundary along a warm front compare to that along a cold front? The slope is more gentle along a warm front.

Check yourself

1. Describe a warm front in terms of air masses.

2. Why are clouds that form along a warm front thinner and more spread out than clouds that form along a cold front?

3. How does precipitation along a warm front compare with that along a cold front?

1. A warm front forms when a warm air mass pushes a cold air mass ahead of it.

2. Clouds along a warm front are thinner because the boundary slopes more gently and the warm air does not rise as rapidly as it does along a cold front.

3. Along a warm front, precipitation tends to be more spread out, less intense, and of longer duration.

A front on top of a front
New vocabulary: occluded front

There is an unusual type of front that sometimes occurs. It forms when a cold front comes up behind and overtakes a warm front. The cold air mass, which is then pushing a mass of less cold air ahead of it, is able to lift the warm air mass completely off the ground. An **occluded front** has formed because the warm front has been cut off or blocked from touching the ground. (The word *occluded* means closed off or shut in.)

Figure 6-6 shows an occluded front. An occluded front may be thought of as a warm front on top of a cold front. The warm front is located above the earth's surface.

Some of the most violent thunderstorms occur along occluded fronts because of the highly unstable air movement.

294

Science Processes: Interpreting data;
Communicating through a diagram; Communicating
through a data table
See also Activity Record Sheet 6-1 (Lab Manual
page 79)

CORE   20 minutes   Individuals, or pairs of students

Activity 6-1   Comparing Air Masses Across a Weather Front

Materials

weather map from a newspaper

Purpose

To read a weather map and compare conditions on both sides of a weather front.

Procedure

1. Find and study a weather map printed in a newspaper.
2. Choose four or six cities, half on one side of a weather front and half on the other. Look for cities with noticeable weather changes from one side of the front to the other.
3. Draw a diagram that shows the cities and the front.
4. Make a data table that gives available information for each city (for example, temperature, atmospheric pressure, cloud cover, precipitation).
5. When you have finished, cover the names of the cities on your data table. Show someone else your diagram and data table and see if she or he can match the cities with the data in the data table.

Questions

1. Does your weather map show any areas of precipitation? How are these related to weather fronts pictured on the map?
2. Are the conditions across the weather front similar to what you expected? If not, what could be the reason for any unexpected findings?

Conclusion

What does your weather map tell you about weather conditions on opposite sides of a front?

Step 1

Step 4

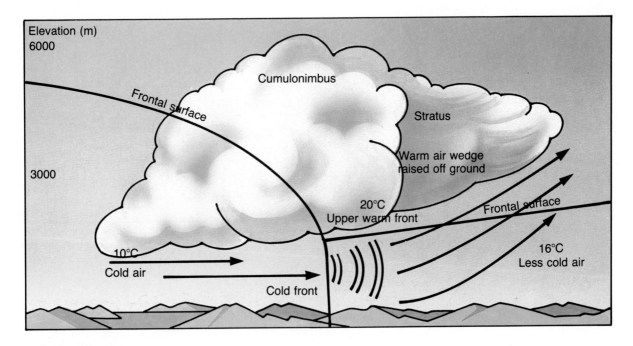

Check yourself

1. Describe an occluded front in terms of air masses.

2. If you were located directly under an occluded front, would the warmest air temperatures occur where you are on the earth's surface or would they occur at some distance above your head? Explain your answer.

Stationary and moving fronts

New vocabulary: stationary front

Sometimes the boundary between a cold air mass and a warm air mass is not moving. Such a front is called a **stationary front.** Either a warm front or a cold front can become a stationary front. This condition may last for only a few hours, or it may last for more than a day.

Often, however, a front moves. It is not difficult to tell when a front is moving through an area. All you have to do is learn to recognize the evidence. The most obvious evidence will be any noticeable changes in the weather.

Figure 6-7 shows how weather conditions change as a cold front moves across an area. At 9:00 a.m., the cold front is approaching City B. Heavy precipitation is occurring at that city. At City A, in the cP air mass, the sky is clear. At City C and City D, within the mT air mass, the sky is partly cloudy. Since City A is located in the cold air mass, temperatures at that city are lower than at City C and City D. (Weather reports for your area

Figure 6-6. Sometimes a cold air mass is able to lift a warm air mass completely off the ground. When this happens, an occluded front forms.

1. An occluded front forms when a warm air mass is lifted completely off the ground by cold air masses.
2. The warmest temperatures would be at some distance above you because that is where the warm air mass is; on the surface, you are in the cold air mass that has lifted the warm air off the surface.

What is the most obvious evidence that a front is moving through an area?

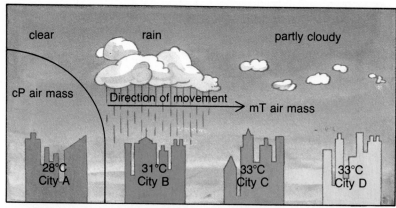

Figure 6-7. By 4:00 p.m., the rain has moved from City B to City C. What time would you expect the rain to reach City D?
The rain can be expected to reach City D between 10:00 p.m. and midnight.

9:00 a.m.

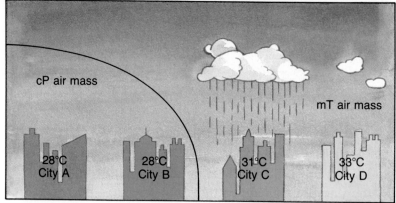

4:00 p.m.

most likely give temperatures in °F, degrees Fahrenheit, rather than in °C, degrees Celsius. In this chapter, therefore, temperatures will appear in both °C and °F.)

By 4:00 p.m., the cold front has moved and is bringing rain to City C. The skies over City B have cleared. Notice how the temperatures at City B and City C have dropped since 9:00 a.m. City A, within the cP air mass at both times, shows no change in weather conditions. But City B and City C do show changes. By 4:00 p.m., weather conditions at City C have changed to those that were at City B at 9:00 a.m. Conditions at City B have changed to those that were at City A at 9:00 a.m. Based on the pattern of changes, it is likely that the rain will reach City D between 10:00 p.m. and midnight.

1. Noticeable changes in the weather are the most obvious evidence that a weather front is moving through an area.
2. Cooler temperatures and rain often occur as a cold front passes over an area.

Check yourself

1. What is the most obvious evidence that a weather front is moving through an area?

2. Describe two changes that might occur as a cold front passes over an area.

Section 1 Review   Chapter 6

Use **Reading Checksheet 6-1** TRB page 76
   Skillsheet 6-1 TRB page 118
   Section Reviewsheet 6-1 TRB pages 173–174
   Section Testsheet 6-1 TRB page 290

Check Your Vocabulary

2 air mass	5 polar air mass
8 cold front	1 prevailing winds
3 continental air mass	11 stationary front
7 front	6 tropical air mass
4 maritime air mass	9 warm front
10 occluded front	

Match each term above with the numbered phrase that best describes it.

1. Winds that are part of large patterns of circulation and come from the same direction

2. A large body of air with about the same temperature and amount of moisture throughout

3. An air mass that forms over dry land

4. An air mass that forms over an ocean

5. An air mass that forms near the Poles

6. An air mass that forms near the Tropic of Cancer or the Tropic of Capricorn

7. The boundary between two air masses

8. A weather front that forms when a cold air mass pushes a warm air mass ahead of it

9. A weather front that forms when a warm air mass pushes a cold air mass ahead of it

10. A weather front that forms when a cold front advances on and lifts a warm front completely off the ground

11. A weather front that is not moving

Check Your Knowledge

Multiple Choice: Choose the answer that best completes each of the following sentences.

1. Warm humid air is characteristic of a(n) __?__ air mass.
   a) mP   c) cP
   b) mT   d) cT

2. Local weather conditions are brought in by __?__.
   a) prevailing winds
   b) local winds
   c) stationary fronts
   d) sea breezes

3. On a weather map, air masses generally show up as __?__.
   a) stationary fronts
   b) occluded fronts
   c) high-pressure areas
   d) low-pressure areas

4. The boundary of a(n) __?__ has a steep slope.
   a) warm front and cold front
   b) warm front
   c) occluded front
   d) cold front

5. __?__ clouds are characteristic of a warm front.
   a) Stratus   c) Cumulus
   b) Cirrus   d) Cumulonimbus

Check Your Understanding

1. What is an air mass?

2. Why can the same prevailing wind bring different weather conditions on different days?

3. Why do different air masses have different characteristics?

4. What is the relationship between air masses and weather changes?

5. How does a cold front differ from a warm front?

Predicting the Weather   Section 2

Learner Objectives

1. To interpret the information given in a station model.
2. To interpret symbols on a weather map.
3. To plot changes on a weather map.
4. To identify variables that affect weather predictions.
5. To identify causes of certain extreme weather conditions.

Section 2 of Chapter 6 is divided into five parts:

Recording the local weather conditions

Weather fronts on a map

Predicting changes in the weather

Difficulties with predicting the weather

Extreme weather conditions

Figure 6-8. Clear skies and plenty of sunshine were predicted, but an unexpected rainstorm has caused an interruption in this game. Why might the weather report have been wrong?

As will be pointed out in this section, many variables influence the movement (speed and direction) of air masses that bring changes in the weather. That is why weather predictions are often expressed as probabilities (70% chance of rain, etc.).

Figure 6-9. Weather stations continuously record atmospheric conditions at a particular location. Data from many such weather stations is transmitted to a weather center where it is processed and used to construct a picture of large-scale weather conditions.

Predicting the weather is an important task. It can help people plan their outside activities. It can also help people prepare for extreme weather conditions that can be dangerous and that can cause great damage.

You can certainly remember instances in which a weather forecast was completely wrong. What happened? Did the forecaster make a mistake? Or did something else probably happen? Why is it so difficult to predict the weather, even with the most advanced equipment? And how much confidence can a person have in any particular weather prediction?

Students might cite examples from their own experience when their plans, based on weather reports, were spoiled by an unexpected change in the weather. The questions asked in this paragraph are meant merely to get students thinking about possible answers. The questions will be answered as students progress through this section of Chapter 6.

Recording the local weather conditions
New vocabulary: station model

Weather can be defined as the condition of the atmosphere at a given place and at a specific time. What is the weather like where you are right now? You might answer with merely a general reaction like "It's great" or "Terrible" or "Raining as usual."

For a more scientific description of the weather, however, you will need to gather and record certain data. Is the sky, for example, clear or cloudy? What is the air temperature? What is the atmospheric pressure? What is the dew-point temperature? Has there been any precipitation? If so, how much? And what about the wind? What direction is it blowing from? And what is its speed?

If you were to gather the data needed to answer just these questions, you would be performing the job of an observer at

Interested students can find the locations of two or three weather stations nearest to where you live. What kinds of data are gathered at those places? (A visit to such a weather station would enable students to learn through direct observation.)

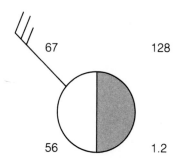

Figure 6-10. This is an example of a station model. What does the stick part of the flag indicate? As mentioned in Number 6 on the right, the position of the stick part of the flag indicates the direction from which the wind is blowing. In this case, the wind is blowing from the northwest. (You might have someone show, on the board, the conventional positions of N, E, S, and W, remembering that North is generally toward the top. The intermediate positions NE, SE, SW, and NW can then be indicated, too.)

There are other weather variables for which data is gathered (such as visibility, cloud height, etc.). These may be more important in some locations than in others.

1. A station model can indicate degrees of cloudiness, air temperature, dew-point temperature, atmospheric pressure, amount of precipitation, wind speed, and wind direction.
2. The position of the stick shows the direction from which the wind is blowing. The cross marks indicate wind speed. (Long mark = 8-10 knots; short = 3-7 knots.)

a weather station. There are many thousands of weather stations all around the world. Each of these stations continuously measures and records atmospheric conditions at that particular location. Conditions at each weather station are recorded simply and clearly by means of a set of symbols that make up a **station model.**

Figure 6-10 shows a sample station model.

1. The circle in the middle is half darkened. This means that half the sky is covered with clouds.

2. The number at the upper left is the air temperature. In this case, the air temperature is 67°F.

3. Below the air temperature is the dew-point temperature, which is 56°F.

4. At the upper right is the atmospheric pressure. It has been abbreviated. The value 128 has been shortened from 1012.8 millibars. To get the true atmospheric pressure of pressures of 1000 mb or higher from a station model, you must move the decimal point one digit to the left (changing the number from 128 to 12.8, for example) and then add 1000.

5. The number beneath the atmospheric pressure is the amount of precipitation, which is commonly measured in inches. In this case, the station model indicates that there has been 1.20 inches of precipitation.

6. The position of the stick part of the flag indicates the wind direction. In this case, the wind is blowing from the northwest.

7. The wind speed, commonly given in knots (nautical miles per hour), is indicated by the number of cross marks on the flag. Each long mark represents 8-10 knots. Each short mark represents 3-7 knots.

The symbol in Figure 6-10 indicates a wind speed of about 25 knots per hour. (1 nautical mile = 1 minute of arc of a great circle of the earth or 1852 meters or 6076.1 feet or 1.15 miles.)

Check yourself

1. What kinds of information are indicated on a station model?

2. How can you determine wind direction and speed from a station model?

Weather fronts on a map

In the United States, information from each different weather station is transmitted to central data banks. There the data is compiled and analyzed with the help of computers. In addition to ground recording stations, other sources of information are used. Radar and satellites photograph and track large-scale air movements. Weather balloons measure weather conditions higher in the atmosphere. All this information is transferred to weather maps. By means of certain symbols, a single weather map can indicate atmospheric conditions above a large portion of the earth's surface.

Figure 6-11. Satellites are able to photograph and track large-scale air movements.

Figure 6-12 shows a newspaper forecast of atmospheric conditions over part of the continental United States on Saturday, July 10. Listed below the map are meanings for the various symbols used on weather forecast maps.

Find the weather front that stretches from near San Antonio up toward Minneapolis-St. Paul. As explained below the map, the triangles indicate that this is a cold front. And the fact that the triangles are to the south of the front indicates that the cold front is moving southward. Cold air north of the front is pushing warm air south of the front.

See also Teaching Diagram 6-2 (TRB page 32).

Figure 6-12. What kind of weather front stretches from near San Antonio up toward Minneapolis-St. Paul?
A cold front (indicated by the triangles)

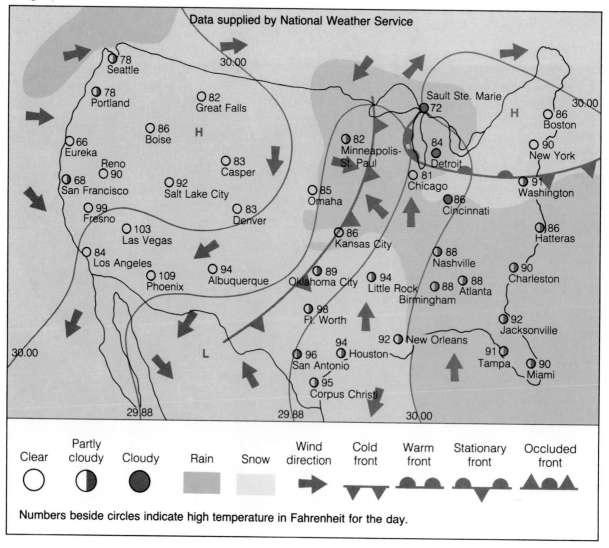

Notice how air temperatures compare across the cold front. For Little Rock, 94°F is predicted, which is ahead of the cold front. For Kansas City, at the boundary of the cold front, an 86°F temperature is predicted. And for Omaha, behind the cold front, 85°F is predicted.

Figure 6-12 also shows another type of weather front, stretching from Sault Ste. Marie south and east toward Washington, D.C. As explained below the map, the semicircles indicate that this weather front is a warm front. And the position of the semicircles along the north side of the front indicates that the warm front is moving northward. Warm air from the south is pushing cold air from the north.

Predicted air temperatures for Cincinnati, Detroit, and Sault Ste. Marie indicate lower temperatures for cities in the cold air mass that is ahead of the warm front.

Notice what happens to the weather front as it continues to the east of Washington, D.C. It changes from a warm front to a cold front. The triangles indicate that the front that extends from Washington, D.C. to the right-hand edge of the map is a cold front and that it is pushing southward.

Look at the other symbols below the map. Notice the symbols that would be used if a stationary front or an occluded front were predicted. For a stationary front, symbols for a warm front and a cold front are combined and are shown as pushing against each other. A stationary front, therefore, does not move in either direction.

The symbol for an occluded front also combines the symbols for a cold front and a warm front. But in an occluded front, the symbol shows that both the cold front and the warm front are moving in the same direction. (In an occluded front, as mentioned earlier, the warm front is located above a cold front.)

Check yourself

1. What are four sources that provide data for central weather data banks?

2. Looking at a weather front on a weather map, how can you tell on which sides of the front the warm and cold air masses are located? Mention two ways.

Data on weather maps can be used to illustrate that conditions within an air mass are not identical. There can be small variations from place to place. The temperature may be a few degrees cooler. The pressure may be several millibars greater.

What kind of weather front is indicated by semicircles?

If students become confused between symbols for a cold front (triangles) and a warm front (semicircles), they can look on the weather map to see whether the front is moving from the north or from the south. In the Northern Hemisphere, cold fronts come from the north and warm fronts come from the south.

Reading a weather map, like reading any other kind of map, becomes much easier and more meaningful once the meanings of the conventional symbols have been learned. On the chalkboard, students can practice using the symbols that indicate the different kinds of fronts.

1. Ground recording stations, radar, satellites, and weather balloons
2. Air temperatures and type of weather front (A warm air mass is located ahead of a cold front and behind a warm front.)

Science Processes: Interpreting data; Predicting
See also Activity Record Sheet 6-2A (Lab Manual
page 83)

CORE   30 minutes   Individuals, or small groups

Activity 6-2A Plotting Changes on a Weather Map

Materials

weather maps from old
  newspapers, for any
  three consecutive days

blank map of same area
  as shown on the
  weather map

3 colored pencils
  (different colors)

Purpose

To predict weather patterns based on weather maps.

Procedure

1. Look at the weather map for the first of the three days.
2. Find the high-pressure and low-pressure centers. Look at the isobars around these centers. Note how the atmospheric pressure changes as you move away from each of these centers. Draw the centers and isobars on your blank map with a colored pencil.
3. Locate and identify the weather fronts on the first map. Draw and label these fronts on your map, using the same pencil you used in step 2. Mark the colder and warmer air masses on opposite sides of each front.

4. In another color, draw the pressure centers and weather fronts for the second day. Compare the way that the pressure centers and weather fronts moved from one day to the next.
5. From what you have drawn on your map, predict where those pressure centers and weather fronts will be on the third day. Draw these predicted locations in a third color.

Questions

1. Using your first day's map, look at temperatures on opposite sides of the fronts. Do the differences in temperatures match your labeling of the air masses?
2. Which way do winds usually blow near high-pressure and low-pressure centers? Check the first day's map to see if this pattern is true in this case. Is it?
3. Where on the map do you find cities with cloudy skies? with clear skies? Is this what you would expect?
4. What other inferences can you draw about weather conditions from the first day's map?
5. How does the map you drew compare with the newspaper's weather map for the third day? Were your predictions accurate?

Conclusion

How well can you predict the weather by reading weather maps?

Step 1

Step 2

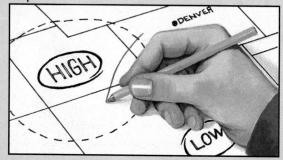

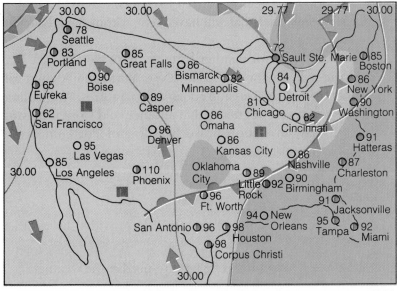

(Map symbols are explained in Figure 6-12, page 302.)

Figure 6-13. What kind of
weather front extends from near
San Antonio to near Oklahoma
City?

A stationary front (indicated by
symbols on both sides of the line)

Predicting changes in the weather

A weather map can be used to interpret current weather conditions. It can also be used to predict how the weather will
change in the next few days, especially when used along with
weather maps for the preceding day (or days) and along with
information gathered by satellites and by radar.

What are two uses for a weather
map?

As an example, let us compare weather conditions forecast-
ed for July 10 (Figure 6-12) and July 12 (Figure 6-13). Compare the position of the weather fronts on the two maps. By
July 12, you will note, the major weather front has pushed
down in a southeastward direction. From near San Antonio
to near Little Rock, the front has become stationary. From
Nashville, a cold front curves northward into Canada.

Notice also what has happened to the rainy areas. For July
12, most of the rain was once again predicted to fall ahead of
the cold front. But the advancing cold front has pushed the
area of rainfall eastward. And the high-pressure center that
was near Salt Lake City has moved eastward to Kansas City,
bringing clear skies to the cities behind the cold front.

The map in Figure 6-13 also shows how the advancing cold
.front is expected to affect air temperatures. For July 12, cooler

It may be helpful for students to
"track," on a blank map, the
changes from Figure 6-12 to
Figure 6-13 and the predictions in
the paragraph just before the
Check yourself questions on the
next page. On their maps,
students might label current
conditions and future predictions
and then use arrows to connect
the two.

Figure 6-14. As the air spreads out from heating, there are fewer molecules per unit volume to exert pressure.

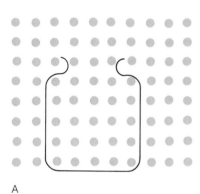

A

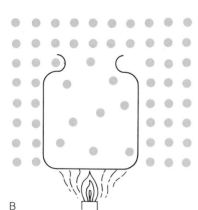

B

temperatures have been predicted for Cincinnati, Chicago, Detroit, and other cities that will have come within the advancing mass of cold air.

Based on these two weather forecast maps, you can see that within the next day or so, Boston, New York, and Atlanta will probably have clear skies and cooler temperatures. At the same time, however, you will notice that another cold front is moving in an easterly direction toward Seattle and Portland in the Pacific Northwest.

Check yourself

1. What are some types of information provided by weather maps?

2. How can weather maps be used to predict the weather?

Difficulties with predicting the weather

Predicting weather conditions is a very complex task. Many factors affect the weather. At some time, you may have observed the following occurrence. You listen to a weather forecast. It predicts rain for the following day. When the day comes, the skies are cloudy, but no rain falls. To understand what might have caused the incorrect weather prediction that you heard, it is necessary to understand something about the relationships among weather variables.

Let us begin by considering the relationship between two simple weather variables, temperature and pressure. When the air temperature becomes warmer, the air expands. When air expands, it spreads out, exerting less atmospheric pressure on the earth's surface. We may conclude that as air gets warmer, the air pressure (atmospheric pressure) drops. We may also conclude that as the air temperature drops, the air pressure increases.

We say that temperature and pressure in the atmosphere are inversely related. The word *inversely* means "in ways that are directly opposite." As one goes up, the other goes down. And as one goes down, the other goes up.

But this relationship between temperature and pressure in the atmosphere does not always happen. Let's say that you take temperature readings on Monday and Tuesday morning. Tuesday's reading shows an increase in temperature. But your measurements of atmospheric pressure taken at the same time show that the pressure has not decreased. It may have remained the same. It may even have gone up. In either case, this is not what you expect.

The explanation for this can be related to changes among other weather variables. Atmospheric pressure, for instance, is also affected by the amount of moisture in the air. If the air becomes drier, the atmospheric pressure will rise. Suppose this is what happened between your Monday and your Tuesday readings. The temperature rise caused the atmospheric pressure to drop. But the loss of moisture in the air caused the atmospheric pressure to rise. These two changes were offsetting each other. If the greater change was a loss of moisture, the overall change would be a small increase in pressure.

Relationships among air temperature, atmospheric pressure, and moisture content affect the weather. Add to this other factors such as wind direction and you can begin to see why predicting, or forecasting, the weather is not an easy task.

Given the many difficulties connected with predicting the weather, how can weather forecasts be made? They are made on the basis of probabilities. You may have heard a weather report indicate a 70% chance, or a 70% probability, of rain for the following day. At another time, the prediction may have been for a 50% chance of rain. In both cases, rain is possible. In the first case (the 70% chance of rain), the forecaster, after analyzing all the weather data, decided that it was more likely that it would rain than that it wouldn't rain.

We can never be absolutely certain about any weather prediction. Variations are always possible. It is, of course, the big variations that are most noticeable. There may, for example, have been a time when the local forecast called for clear skies with only a slight chance of rain for the next day. But then, during the night, the wind direction changed. The next day, there was a heavy thunderstorm.

Computers have allowed scientists to greatly improve the accuracy of weather forecasts. Information can be processed and

The true relationships among weather variables are far more complex than is being presented here, and, in many cases, they are still not well understood. The intent of this section is to provide students with a "feel" for this complexity so that they can appreciate why forecasting is not 100% accurate. At the same time, however, students should come to recognize that weather forecasting is much better than simple guesswork.

What factors make it difficult to predict the weather?

Figure 6-15. Computers allow scientists to process and analyze large amounts of data very quickly.

Check yourself answers:
1. Temperature, atmospheric pressure, moisture, wind direction
2. When air gets warmer, atmospheric pressure decreases.
3. When the moisture content of air increases, the atmospheric pressure decreases.
4. Over the long run, we can expect accurate forecasts to outnumber wrong ones.

All severe weather conditions, thunderstorms, tornadoes, etc. are extensions of common weather conditions. The difference between a heavy rain and a thunderstorm, for example, is the extent and speed of the upward air movement.

analyzed much more quickly. But even with future advances, we will probably never be able to forecast the weather with 100% accuracy. There are just too many small variations possible. Over the long run, however, accurate weather forecasts from professional sources will outnumber the cases in which they were wrong.

Check yourself

1. Name four variables that make predicting the weather a very complex task.
2. What happens to the atmospheric pressure when air gets warmer?
3. What happens to the atmospheric pressure when the moisture content of the air increases?
4. Over the long run, how accurate can we expect weather forecasts from reliable sources to be?

Extreme weather conditions   New vocabulary: cumulonimbus clouds, thunderstorms, lightning, thunder, blizzard, tornado, hurricane

From time to time, unusual combinations of atmospheric conditions produce extreme and dangerous weather conditions. Thunderstorms and blizzards are produced by unusual atmospheric conditions. Tornadoes and hurricanes are also produced by unusual atmospheric conditions. In all such cases, advance warning by weather forecasters can save lives and property that would otherwise be lost.

Thunderstorms   Thunderstorms are produced by large rising columns of warm moist air. You may recall that cumulus clouds are produced by condensation from warm moist rising air. Sometimes these updrafts are so strong that the cloud may extend 300 m or more. These massive clouds are called **cumulonimbus clouds.** (When *nimbus* is part of the name of a cloud, the cloud is a rain cloud.)

Cumulonimbus clouds contain huge amounts of moisture. They can produce a torrential downpour. The larger the cloud

Science Processes: Interpreting data;
Communicating through a map
See also Activity Record Sheet 6-2B (Lab Manual
page 84)

Enrichment   20 minutes   Small groups

Activity 6-2B   Tracking Severe Weather Conditions

Materials

newspapers
radio
television
blank maps

Purpose

To understand how severe weather conditions
occur and how they affect people.

Procedure

1. Severe weather conditions occur throughout
   the world. Look for reports of a severe
   weather condition somewhere on the earth.
2. Using newspaper, television, and radio reports, track the movement of the severe condition. Plot its path on a blank map.
3. Note any other accompanying weather conditions. Also note the weather in the affected
   areas both before and after the severe conditions. Record these conditions on your
   map, too.

Questions

1. How were people affected by the severe
   weather conditions? Was there any property
   damage? If so, what kind of damage? What
   was the estimated cost of the damage?
2. If some areas were affected more than others by the severe weather, was any explanation offered? If so, what?
3. What kinds of precautions were taken in the
   affected areas? Were they helpful?
4. What else might have been done to reduce
   losses?

Conclusion

What have you learned about severe weather
conditions? What do they do to the environment? to people?

Step 1

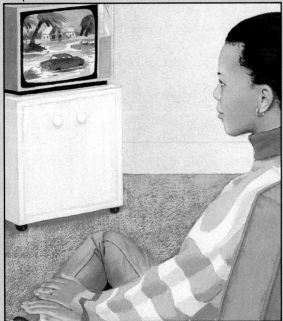

Step 2

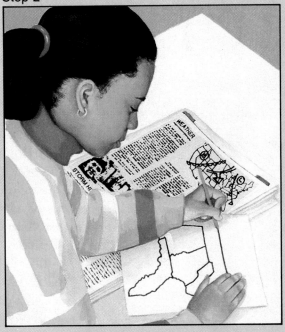

Figure 6-16. What causes lightning in a cumulonimbus cloud?
Lightning is caused by static electrical charges that build up in different parts of a cloud and then jump from one part of the cloud to another or from the cloud to the surface of the earth.

Students can learn to estimate how far away thunder is occurring. The lightning they "see" is traveling at the speed of light, which means they see it within a fraction of a second after it occurs. The thunder they "hear" is traveling at the much slower speed of sound. By counting the seconds between the time they see the lightning and hear the

and the more moisture present, the heavier will be the precipitation. When accompanied by thunder and lightning, the resulting storm is called a **thunderstorm.**

Lightning and thunder are found in a cumulonimbus cloud. **Lightning** is a flash of light produced because static electrical charges build up in different parts of a cloud. When these charges jump from one part of the cloud to another part of the cloud or to the ground, lightning results. At the same time, the lightning causes a rapid expansion of the air it passes through. This rapid expansion of air produces a loud rumbling noise called **thunder.**

Thunderstorms usually occur in the warmer summer months. The heating of the air near the ground adds to the rapid upward movement of air. The most severe thunderstorms usually occur near a cold front. Air is pushed up more rapidly along a cold front.

thunder, students can estimate how far away the storm is,

allowing one mile for each second elapsed.

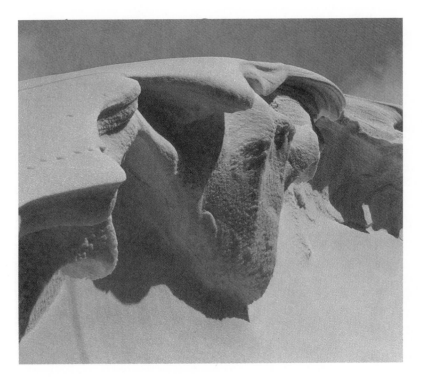

Figure 6-17. Air temperature is usually the best indicator as to whether precipitation will be in the form of rain or snow. The rapid upward air movement that produces a blizzard also is experienced near the surface. This accounts for the strong winds that people notice. The large snow drifts produced by strong winds can create more of a problem than the amount of snowfall.

Blizzards   If the air temperature is below freezing, conditions similar to thunderstorm conditions can produce a **blizzard.** During a blizzard, much snow may fall in a few hours. At the same time, strong winds can blow the snow into very deep drifts.

Tornadoes   A **tornado** is a funnel of air that extends down from a cumulonimbus cloud. The winds in a tornado travel in a circular direction at speeds of up to 800 km per hour. When a tornado touches the ground, it can cause extensive damage. The wind speeds are so great at times that cars may be lifted off the ground and the roofs of houses may be blown off. The air pressure inside the tornado is very low.

The funnel cloud of a tornado is usually only 100 m or less in diameter. Points along the direct path of the tornado may be completely leveled. At the same time, points 1 km away may be relatively untouched.

In the United States, tornadoes occur most frequently in the Midwest. More than one thousand tornadoes a year occur in

Library research

Research other extreme weather conditions such as typhoons or waterspouts. Are the extreme conditions you chose limited to certain areas of the world? to certain times of the year?

Figure 6-18. Tornadoes are funnels of air extending down from cumulonimbus clouds. How fast could the winds in this tornado be going?
The winds in this and other tornadoes could be traveling at speeds up to 800 km per hour.

What are hurricanes?

The destructive power of a tornado is usually much greater than for a hurricane because the wind speeds are usually much greater. The reason hurricanes usually cause more total damage is because they extend over a much larger area.

that area. Most of them are small or occur in relatively isolated areas. If, however, a powerful tornado hits a large city, great damage may result.

Cities and towns in the "tornado belt" usually have advance warning systems to warn the people if a tornado is approaching. This permits enough time for people to find shelter in basements or other safe underground locations.

Hurricanes **Hurricanes** are very large circular storms with wind speeds of at least 64 knots (118 km/h) and extremely low pressure at the center. Wind speeds may reach 150 km per hour or even greater. A hurricane is accompanied by dense clouds and heavy rain. The diameter of a hurricane is much larger than that of a tornado. The high winds of a hurricane may affect an area as wide as 300 km.

Being a low-pressure center, hurricane winds travel in toward the center of the hurricane. At the center, which may be several kilometers across, the air is traveling upward. As a result, weather conditions in the center, or "eye," of the hurricane may be relatively calm.

Figure 6-19. Hurricanes and typhoons can cause ships to run aground and can cause great damage along seacoasts.

Hurricanes that reach the United States form over the Caribbean Sea or over the Gulf of Mexico. They travel westward or northwestward at a rate of 10-20 km per hour. Hurricanes can cause great damage along the coasts. The strong winds produce huge ocean waves that pound the coast and flood low-lying areas. Hurricanes also cause great damage when they pass inland and travel across the land.

Some hurricanes are weak and do not last long. Such hurricanes obviously do less damage than strong hurricanes. Some hurricanes remain out over the ocean and do not approach land as they travel northward from their place of origin. These hurricanes are a much greater danger to ships on the sea than they are to people and property on the land. In any case, modern tracking methods keep a careful watch on a hurricane's position and on any changes in its force and in the course along which it is moving.

Check yourself

1. Why do thunderstorms often occur during summer months?

2. How do tornadoes and hurricanes compare in terms of wind speed, size of area affected, and air pressure at the center?

Interested students can prepare a map that shows the paths of recent hurricanes that traveled, for example, up the Atlantic coast from the Caribbean or the Gulf of Mexico.

1. Upward movement of air is increased because of warm surface temperatures.
2. 1) Wind speed: tornadoes—up to 800 km/hr; hurricanes—64 to 150 km/hr. 2) Size of area affected: tornado—path 100 m wide; hurricane—path up to 300 km wide. 3) Air pressure at center: the pressure is extremely low at the center of both a tornado and a hurricane.

Section 2 Review   Chapter 6

Use **Reading Checksheet 6-2** TRB page 77
Skillsheet 6-2 TRB page 119
Section Reviewsheet 6-2 TRB pages 175–176
Section Testsheet 6-2 TRB page 291

Check Your Vocabulary

6 blizzard	1 station model
3 cumulonimbus cloud	5 thunder
	2 thunderstorm
8 hurricane	7 tornado
4 lightning	

Match each term above with the numbered phrase that best describes it.

1. A set of symbols used to record conditions at a weather station simply and clearly

2. A storm produced by large rising columns of warm moist air and characterized by thunder, lightning, and heavy precipitation

3. A massive vertical cloud containing much moisture; associated with thunderstorms

4. A flash of light produced when static electrical charges jump from one part of a cloud to another or from a cloud to the ground

5. A noise caused by the rapid expansion of air as lightning passes through it

6. A storm produced when thunderstorm conditions occur at below freezing temperatures; characterized by heavy snow and strong winds

7. A narrow funnel of air extending down from a cumulonimbus cloud

8. A very large circular storm with wind speeds of at least 64 knots

Check Your Knowledge

Multiple Choice: Choose the answer that best completes each of the following sentences.

1. Each long mark on a station model wind speed indicator represents ?.
   a) 3-7 knots
   b) 8-10 knots
   c) 8-10 miles per hour
   d) 8-10 km per hour

2. Millibars (mb) are used to measure ?.
   a) air temperature
   b) wind speed
   c) air pressure
   d) relative humidity

3. Lower temperatures can be expected ?.
   a) behind a stationary warm front
   b) behind an advancing warm front
   c) ahead of an advancing cold front
   d) behind an advancing cold front

4. Extreme ? at the center of a tornado may cause a building to explode.
   a) amounts of snow
   b) amounts of rain
   c) high pressure
   d) low pressure

5. Weather conditions in the center a ? may be relatively calm.
   a) thunderstorm
   b) tornado
   c) hurricane
   d) blizzard

Check Your Understanding

1. How do station models affect large-scale weather maps?

2. Are triangles used to indicate a warm front or a cold front? What else do the triangles on a weather front indicate? How do they do this?

3. Draw the symbols for an occluded front and a stationary front. How are they similar? How are they different?

4. What does it mean when two variables are inversely related?

5. How are probabilities useful in making weather predictions?

Climate Section 3

Section 3 of Chapter 6 is divided into four parts:

General types of climates

Factors that affect temperature

Factors that affect moisture

Climate graphs

Figure 6-20. A crack crosses the frozen surface of McMurdo Sound, Antarctica. In Antarctica, snow and ice cover the earth's surface every day of the year, year in and year out. How does the climate of Antarctica differ from the climate where you live? Answers will vary, depending on where students live. Also, in discussing their climate, students will need to consider what it's like all year long—in winter, summer, spring, and fall.

Learner Objectives
1. To distinguish between weather and climate.
2. To relate general types of climate to latitude.
3. To identify factors other than latitude that affect temperature.
4. To identify factors that affect moisture.
5. To interpret a climate graph.

How are weather patterns related to climate?

It is important for students to grasp the concept that climate represents long-term averages. They may have observed or heard people talk about a particularly cold winter or a particularly hot summer, but even these variations are not as great as the usual day-to-day changes in weather.

Library research

Pick a region on the climate map (Figure 6-21). Research the various climate factors for that region and explain how they combine to produce the climate for that region.

As mentioned in earlier chapters, temperatures around the world are affected by the angle of incoming rays of energy from the sun. The most energy is received where the sun's rays are at or near 90°. During the year, the sun's vertical rays move between the tropics, causing highest temperatures in that region. The smallest angles of the sun's rays occur at the poles, causing low temperatures in those areas.

New vocabulary: climate

How do weather and climate differ? **Weather** is the atmospheric conditions at a particular location at a particular moment in time. Weather conditions relate to the here and now. And weather conditions are subject to sudden and very noticeable changes.

Climate, on the other hand, is not concerned with immediate weather conditions. Climate is concerned with long-term patterns. **Climate** is concerned with weather patterns that occur in one place over a period of a year or longer.

What kind of climate do you live in? What factors determine the climate where you live? And what effect does the climate have on life in your area?

General types of climates   New vocabulary: tropical climate, polar climate, temperate climate, marine climate, continental climate

Any climate of the world can be classified according to two basic factors. One basic factor of climate is temperature. Over the long run, are air temperatures at a certain location hot or cold? The other basic factor of climate is the amount of moisture or precipitation. Over the long run, is the weather wet or dry? Different combinations of hot or cold and dry or wet provide a simple way of considering the earth's major climates.

In general, temperatures are directly related to latitude. As the latitude decreases, average temperatures increase. Highest average temperatures can, in general, be expected to occur at locations near the equator (0° latitude). Lowest average temperatures can be expected to occur near the North Pole (90° N latitude) and the South Pole (90° S latitude).

Figure 6-21 shows three major climate zones, based largely on average temperatures. Temperatures in these three zones are the result of the kind of air mass commonly found there. Tropical air masses are found in a **tropical climate.** A tropical climate, therefore, has the warmest temperatures. In a tropical climate, the average temperature during the coldest month does not drop below 18°C (67°F).

Polar air masses are found in a **polar climate.** Therefore, as you would expect, a polar climate has the coldest average temperatures. In a polar climate, the average temperature during the warmest month does not rise above 10°C (50°F).

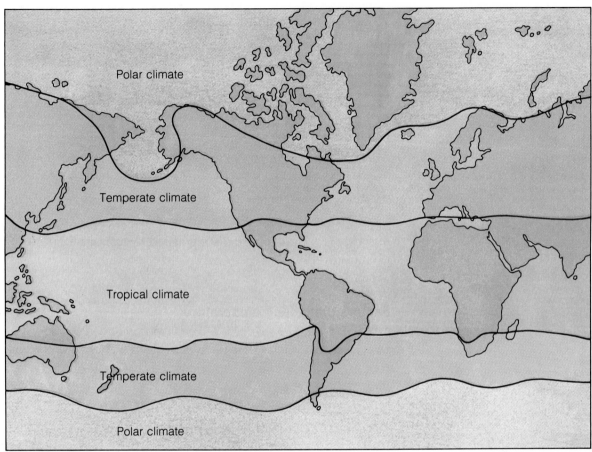

Polar climate

Temperate climate

Tropical climate

Temperate climate

Polar climate

In between these two extremes of climate, in the middle latitudes, is a **temperate climate.** Temperatures in this climate are affected by both tropical and polar air masses. Average temperatures in a temperate zone are moderate, in between the average temperatures of the polar and tropical zones.

The other basic factor that affects climate is the average amount of precipitation that falls in a certain area over a period of time. Two kinds of air masses affect the amount of precipitation an area receives: maritime air masses and continental air masses.

In general, areas that lie near large bodies of water will receive more precipitation than other areas. Maritime air masses are commonly found near large bodies of water. The climate in such areas is called a **marine climate** or oceanic climate.

The three divisions are based on average temperatures.
Figure 6-21. Here is one way of dividing the earth's climates into general zones. Are these three divisions based on average temperatures or on average amounts of moisture?

The divisions and boundaries between climate zones are somewhat arbitrary. In common usage, the zones illustrated are further subdivided. They have been simplified here to enable students to grasp the basic concepts involved. Interested and capable students may wish to pursue more advanced work on climate classification.

Students may notice that climate regions do not follow simple geographic patterns. This is caused by the influence of altitude, ocean currents, and other factors discussed in the material that follows in this section of Chapter 6.

How does a continental climate differ from a marine climate?

1. Temperature and amount of moisture or precipitation
2. Tropical, polar, and temperate
3. Marine and continental

There are also areas of land that do not receive moisture that evaporated from a large body of water. Continental air masses are commonly found in such areas. These areas experience a **continental climate,** which is a drier climate than a marine climate. The amount of moisture is the distinguishing factor between a marine climate and a continental climate.

Check yourself

1. What are the two basic factors that determine climate?

2. What three climates are distinguished by average temperatures?

3. What two climates are distinguished by average amounts of moisture?

Factors that affect temperature
New vocabulary: adiabatic change

In general, average temperatures decrease as latitude increases. There are, however, other natural factors that affect temperatures at a particular location. Two such factors are altitude and nearness to ocean currents.

Altitude   The lower layers of the atmosphere are heated by radiation from the earth's surface. Particles in the atmosphere trap this heat from the earth and exercise a kind of greenhouse effect on the layers of air closest to the earth's surface. The greenhouse effect is most noticeable at elevations close to sea level. As you go higher above sea level, the air gets colder.

The average temperatures at cities at high elevations are a few degrees cooler than they would be at sea level. Temperatures at the top of a mountain are many degrees colder than the temperatures at the base of the mountain. Because of this you can find a snow-covered mountaintop very close to the equator. It is a matter of altitude.

Students may at first be inclined to expect higher temperatures at higher elevations due to being closer to the sun. Distances in elevation on the earth are insignificant when considered in terms of the distance between the earth and the sun.

Temperatures on a mountaintop may also be affected by the fact that the land area on a mountaintop is so small in comparison to the air that surrounds it. Since the air is heated by heat from the land, less heat will be radiated back into the atmosphere from a mountaintop than from a larger surface of land.

As pointed out in the text, low elevation is only one of the factors that is responsible for Death Valley's high temperatures. Its southern location and the adiabatic heating of air descending into the valley also affect temperatures at that location.

The place with the hottest average temperatures in the United States is Death Valley, located in California. Death Valley also has the lowest elevation of any place in the United States. At its deepest, Death Valley is about 90 m below sea level.

In addition to its low elevation, Death Valley's southern location and its location in a valley surrounded by mountains also affect its temperature. Because of its southern location, all exposed land surfaces (including the surrounding mountainsides) receive more direct rays from the sun than locations farther to the north. And because Death Valley is located in a valley, the air that descends into the valley warms up as it loses altitude.

Descending air warms up because air pressure at lower altitudes is greater than at higher altitudes. As the air pressure becomes greater, the molecules of air become more closely packed together. They therefore collide into each other more

In answer to the caption question, temperatures become increasingly lower as elevation above sea level increases. In the case of the snow on Mount Rainier, one of two reasons could be involved. Either temperatures at the top are still near freezing, or else the snowpack from the winter was so heavy that even though temperatures at the top warm up in spring and summer, they never become warm enough to melt the entire snowpack.

Figure 6-22. Snow covers the top of Mount Rainier in Mount Rainier National Park, Washington. How can there be snow at the top of the mountain and blooming flowers at lower elevations?

frequently and cause the air to become warmer. If you have ever used a bicycle pump to pump up a tire and noticed the bicycle pump becoming warmer as you used it to pump up the tire, you have experienced this warming of air as pressure increases. This type of warming is called an **adiabatic change** (ad'-ee-uh-BAT'-ik) because the temperature change of the air was caused solely by a compression of the material and not by any heat exchange with other material in its surroundings.

As air rises, just the opposite happens. The atmospheric pressure decreases. The air expands. The air molecules become more spread out and collide less frequently. The air becomes cooler without any heat exchange with surrounding material. This type of cooling, which was caused solely by the expansion of the material, is also called an adiabatic change.

Ocean currents   Another factor that influences temperatures is nearness to ocean currents. The surface temperature of water affects the temperature of the air above. Cool water will cool the air. Warm water will warm the air.

Figure 6-23 shows the ocean currents of the world. Ocean currents traveling away from the equator contain warm water. Ocean currents traveling toward the equator contain cool water.

Notice the direction of the current off the southeastern coast of the United States. Off the coast of Florida and the southern states, the current is traveling away from the equator. The current is warm. Because of this current, the climate of Bermuda (an island about 930 km east-southeast of North Carolina) is warmer than locations at the same latitude on the mainland. And at Palm Beach (Florida), the closest point on the mainland to this warm current, the lowest average temperature for the coldest month is 19°C (66°F). But at Miami, which is about 105 km south of Palm Beach, the lowest average temperature for the coldest month is 15.5°C (60°F).

Now look at the ocean current off the west coast of the United States. Off the west coast, the current is traveling toward the equator. This current contains cool water. That is why a city along the southeastern coast of North America can be expected to have warmer temperatures than a city at the same latitude on the west coast.

How does warming by means of conduction, which involves a heat exchange, compare with adiabatic warming?

What causes Bermuda to have a warmer climate than locations at the same latitude on the mainland of the United States?

Students might look up the average temperatures for cities along the eastern and western coasts of the United States and compare them.

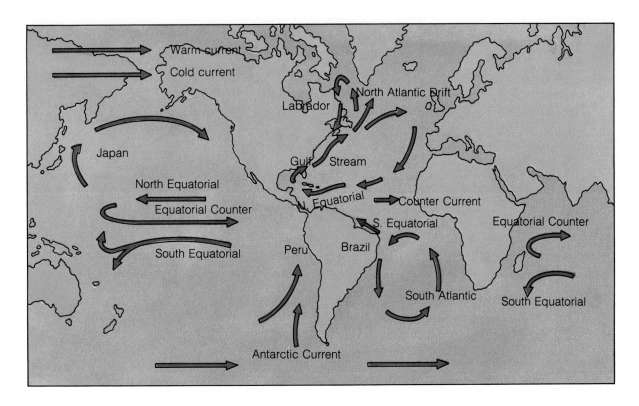

Check yourself

1. How does altitude affect climate?

2. How do ocean currents traveling northward from the equator affect temperatures along the coast?

Factors that affect moisture
New vocabulary: desert, rain-shadow desert

In general, average amounts of precipitation are affected by nearness to a large body of water. But there are natural factors that affect average amounts of precipitation at a particular location, just as there are natural factors that affect temperature. Two natural factors that affect average amounts of precipitation are prevailing winds and mountain ranges.

Prevailing winds   The Sahara Desert is one of the driest places on the earth. Yet it extends to the Atlantic Ocean. How can an area that borders the ocean be a desert? Look at the belts of prevailing winds shown in Figure 5-17 on page 253. Notice that in some locations the prevailing winds carry air from over water to land. In other cases, the prevailing winds carry air from the land to water.

Figure 6-23. Ocean currents flowing away from the equator contain warm water.

1. In general, higher elevations have lower air temperatures than other, lower locations at the same latitude.
2. Ocean currents traveling from the equator cause warmer temperatures along the coast.

You might want to review with students the effect of the earth's rotation on wind patterns (discussed on pages 251 and 253 of Chapter 5). Also, the Sahara Desert is located in a zone of diverging air. As mentioned in the third paragraph on the next page, this descending air is warming up and therefore will produce very little precipitatiion. Almost all of the earth's major deserts are located within zones of diverging air.

Figure 6-24. Near Infni, Morocco, the Sahara meets the Atlantic Ocean. Why doesn't the part of the Sahara Desert that borders the Atlantic have a moist marine climate?

The prevailing wind where the Sahara meets the Atlantic has come across the Sahara and lost most of its moisture. For a marine climate, the prevailing wind would be blowing off the water, not off the continent/land.

Air blowing from over the water to the land will have a high moisture content. Air blowing from the land to water will have a much lower moisture content. The air moving across the Sahara Desert has come across the continent. As it moved across the continent, it lost what little moisture it had. The prevailing wind direction is more important in determining whether a climate is humid or dry than its closeness to the ocean.

When you picture a desert, your first thought is probably endless expanses of sand. Actually a **desert** is defined as an area where the total annual amount of precipitation is less than 254 mm (10 in.). Some deserts extend out over oceans! There is plenty of water present, but there is hardly any precipitation.

It is not a coincidence that most of the earth's deserts lie along the Tropic of Cancer or the Tropic of Capricorn. These two areas, at 23½° N and S latitude, are regions of descending air. This air heats up as it sinks. Warming air produces very little precipitation. Even if the air is descending over the ocean, there will be very little precipitation.

Mountain ranges   Mountain ranges also affect the amount of precipitation that falls at a particular location. The mountain ranges along the west coast of the United States, for example, act as a barrier to moisture that is carried by the prevailing

Careers   Climatologist / Air-conditioning Mechanic

For further information about a career as an air-conditioning mechanic, contact:

Air-Conditioning and Refrigeration Institute
1815 N. Fort Myer Drive
Arlington, Virginia 22209

Air Conditioning Contractors of America
1228 17th Street NW
Washington, DC 20036

Maps and graphs are useful to climatologists, who study long-term weather conditions.

Climatologist Climatologists (klī′-muh-TOL′-uh-jists) are meteorologists, but they do not predict tomorrow's weather. They work with yearly and seasonal patterns of temperature, rainfall, and other weather conditions. They describe the climate of an area and identify the causes of its typical weather.

Climatologists also study changes in weather patterns, and they try to find out why these changes occur. Events on earth, such as volcanic eruptions, and events in space, such as storms on the sun, affect our weather.

Climatologists investigate all these things.

Climatologists use the information from their research to predict future weather patterns. This information helps people plan food production, design buildings, and develop heating and cooling systems.

Most climatologists have a graduate degree in meteorology. The federal government is the main employer of climatologists.

For further information about a career as a climatologist, contact:
American Meteorological Society
45 Beacon Street
Boston, Massachusetts 02108

Air-conditioning mechanics are responsible for the installation and maintenance of air-conditioning equipment.

Air-conditioning Mechanic
A central air-conditioning system has several different components. One machine cleans the air. Other machines control temperature and humidity. Ducts, or pipes, circulate the air.

These systems are installed and serviced by skilled air-conditioning mechanics. To install a system, the mechanics first read blueprints and instructions. Then they use a variety of tools to assemble the components. If a system breaks down, the mechanics find the problem and make the necessary repairs. They also work on heating and

refrigeration equipment.

Many air-conditioning mechanics learn their skills through on-the-job training. They are hired as helpers or apprentices and trained for about four years. Others study air-conditioning and refrigeration in high schools, vocational schools, or junior colleges.

If you enjoy figuring out how machines work, and if you are interested in working with heavy equipment, you might want to consider this career. Your high school preparation should include courses in physics, math, and mechanical drawing.

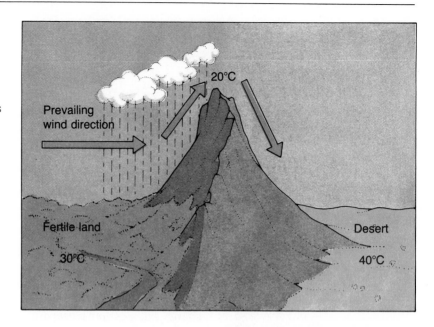

Figure 6-25. How can mountains cause deserts?
The air loses its moisture as it rises over the mountains.

Why does precipitation occur as air rises?

Interested students might compare the climates of cities on opposite sides of mountain ranges. The effect is more striking along the western coast of the United States because the prevailing winds are bringing in moisture from the ocean.

1. A desert is any place (land or water) that, on the average, receives less than 10 in. (254 mm) precipitation per year.
2. On the side of the mountains away from the prevailing winds, because the air loses most of its moisture as it ascends the windward side of the mountains.

westerly winds that carry moisture from out over the Pacific Ocean. As shown in Figure 6-25, mountains cause air to rise. As air rises, it cools and most of its moisture condenses, falling to the surface of the earth as precipitation. Cities and towns on the windward side of the mountains, between the Pacific Ocean and the coastal ranges of mountains, receive high annual amounts of precipitation.

On the side of the mountains that is sheltered from the wind, called the leeward side, conditions are very different. By the time the westerly winds reach the top of the mountains on the windward side, they have lost most of their moisture in the form of precipitation. Then, as this air descends on the leeward side, it warms up rapidly (1°C for every 100 m of elevation it loses). This temperature change is an adiabatic change, caused solely by the expansion or compression of a material.

The air that descends on the leeward side of the mountains quickly loses through evaporation whatever moisture it contained. The mountains have, in effect, produced a rain shadow, blocking rain from reaching the area on the leeward side of the mountains. If these prevailing winds continue throughout the year, a **rain-shadow desert** is produced.

Check yourself

1. How is it possible to have a desert over the ocean?

2. On which side of a mountain range would you expect to find the drier climate? Why?

Our Science Heritage

If asked to compare the climates of the Sahara Desert and Antarctica, you'd probably have little difficulty. The climate of the Sahara is hot and arid. Antarctica has a polar climate and is characterized by below-freezing temperatures and a permanent cover of ice and snow.

Descriptions of present-day climates are based on direct and indirect observations. Weather data for an area is gathered over a period of time. The data is studied. Patterns are inferred.

It is also possible to infer what climates were like long before people left written records of weather data. The earth's rocks date back billions of years and contain evidence of what the earth's climates were like in the past. Distinctive grooves in rock surfaces in the Sahara, for example, indicate that glaciers once traveled across that area. And coal deposits and fossil palm leaves in Antarctica indicate that that land surface once experienced a warm and humid climate.

What are some of the evidences? Coral and carbonate rocks like limestone and dolomite indicate that the area was probably once covered by tropical seas (warmer than 18°C and 25 m to 60 m in depth). Widespread salt deposits are evidence of a former climate that was arid and relatively warm. Coal deposits indicate former low-lying swamps of luxuriant vegetation and a warm, moist climate. Fossil forms of land and sea organisms also tell much about former conditions at a particular location.

Additional evidence of climate changes is obtained from fossils in sea cores (100 million years), the oxygen content of ice in ice cores (120 thousand years), and the rings of a bristle-cone pine (4 thousand years).

Did Glaciers Really Cross the Sahara?

Climate graphs

New vocabulary: climate graph

A **climate graph** provides a picture of the climate conditions at a particular location during the year. It depicts the average monthly temperature and precipitation conditions. Climate graphs are helpful for comparing the climates of different cities. From climate graphs, you can tell at a glance which cities have hot summers or cold winters. You can also tell which cities have dry or humid climates.

Omaha, Nebraska, and Paris, France, the two cities compared on page 327, were selected despite latitude differences because of the similarity in their average climate conditions. Another approach would be to select two cities at the same latitude and to explain reasons for differences in their climates.

Science Processes: Interpreting data;
Communicating through a graph; Inferring
See also Activity Record Sheet 6-3A (Lab Manual
page 87)

CORE   30 minutes   Individuals, or small groups

Activity 6-3A   Plotting a Climate Graph

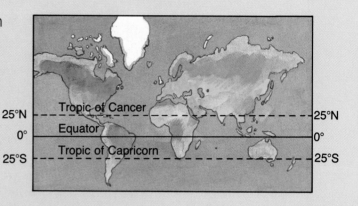

Materials

data table on this page
graph paper
world map

Purpose

To compare climates at three different locations.

Procedure

1. The data table on this page contains information about the climates of three different locations. Using the same format as the climate graphs on the facing page, plot the monthly temperatures and amounts of precipitation for each location.
2. The three locations represented are Memphis, Tennessee; Jacobabad, Pakistan; and Buenos Aires, Argentina. Match each to its respective climate graph. Find each location on a world map.

Questions

1. From your climate graphs, how would you describe the climate of each location? How would you compare them?
2. How can you tell quickly from a climate graph if a location is in the Southern Hemisphere?

Conclusion

What can you tell about an unnamed location from a climate graph?

Data Table													
	Jan	Feb	Mar	Apr	May	Jun	Jul	Aug	Sep	Oct	Nov	Dec	Year
LOCATION A													
Average Temp. (°C)	24	23	21	17	14	11	10	12	14	16	20	22	17 average
Total Precip. (mm)	104	82	122	90	79	68	61	68	80	100	90	83	1027 total
LOCATION B													
Average Temp. (°C)	15	18	24	30	35	37	35	34	32	28	22	17	27 average
Total Precip. (mm)	8	8	7	2	4	6	37	22	1	0	1	3	99 total
LOCATION C													
Average Temp. (°C)	6	7	11	17	22	26	28	27	24	18	11	7	17 average
Total Precip. (mm)	148	116	124	117	102	92	87	67	71	73	106	119	1223 total

Look at the climate graph for Omaha, Nebraska, in Figure 6-26. The solid line connects the average monthly temperatures. In April, for example, the average temperature in Omaha is about 10°C. In September, the average temperature is about 18°C.

The solid bars show the average total amount of precipitation for each month of the year. On the average, about 70 mm of precipitation falls in Omaha during the month of April. In November, the average is about 30 mm. These figures are only averages. One year, the amount of precipitation may be more. The next year, it could be less.

Now look at the climate graph for Paris, France. There the average temperatures for April and September are about 10°C and 16°C. The fall and spring temperatures are almost the same as for Omaha. But the summer and winter temperatures are very different. Average winter temperatures are colder in Omaha. In January, the average temperature is about 3°C in Paris, but it is −4°C in Omaha. Average summer temperatures are hotter in Omaha. In July, the average temperature in Paris is about 18°C. In Omaha, it is about 24°C. Though the average temperature for the year is the same for both cities (11°C), the temperature range is much greater for Omaha.

What do the climate graphs tell you about average amounts of precipitation in Omaha and Paris? Over a whole year, the total amount is fairly similar for both cities. Paris receives an average of 585 mm of precipitation, and Omaha receives an average of 700 mm. But there is a major difference in the patterns of precipitation between the two cities. In Paris, the amount of precipitation is almost the same from month to month throughout the year. But in Omaha, the amount of precipitation is high during the summer but low during the winter.

Check yourself

1. What do climate graphs show?

2. How are average monthly temperatures indicated on a climate graph? How are amounts of precipitation indicated?

3. Why is it important to consider the monthly patterns on a climate graph rather than just the totals?

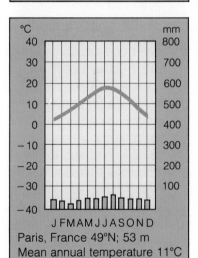

Omaha, Nebraska 41°N; 304 m
Mean annual temperature 11°C
Annual temperature range 31°C
Mean annual precip. 700 mm

Paris, France 49°N; 53 m
Mean annual temperature 11°C
Annual temperature range 16°C
Mean annual precip. 585 mm

Figure 6-26. On these climate graphs, the line toward the top plots average monthly temperatures. The bars at the bottom indicate average monthly amounts of precipitation.
On a percentage basis, the differences in the total precipitation for Omaha and Paris are not as great as the numbers may seem to indicate.

Science Processes: Separating and controlling variables; Inferring
See also Activity Record Sheet 6-3B (Lab Manual page 88)

30-minute setup plus 3 brief weekly observations
Groups of 4

Activity 6-3B Observing Effects of Climate Changes

Materials

2 or 3 large flowerpots, or other containers suitable for growing plants
6 or more small plants of one kind of local vegetation
ruler

Purpose

To see how plants of the same kind are affected by different climates

Procedure

1. Prepare the flowerpots with the plants in them. All plants should be of the same kind (for example, all the same variety of common weed or whatever other kind of local vegetation you choose). Also, each pot should contain the same number of plants.
2. If you are transplanting your plants from the ground outside, you will need to give the plants about a week to get over the shock of transplanting and to adjust to their new surroundings. Remove any that fail to adjust.
3. If you cannot obtain living plants from outside, you can obtain plants from seeds. Choose the seeds of plants that are normally found in your area. Also choose seeds that will produce seedlings easy to recognize.
4. When your plants are ready for the activity, measure and record the heights of the plants in each pot. Label one flowerpot Climate 1. Label the other flowerpot Climate 2.
5. Climate 1 will be the existing local climate. Climate 2 (and Climate 3, if you wish) will be the artificial climate conditions you create.
6. Decide how you are going to make Climate 2 different from Climate 1. Any change in temperature conditions, moisture conditions, or both can be used. If the temperature is much hotter or colder outdoors, the Climate 2 plants can be left indoors on a windowsill where they will receive sunlight. The Climate 1 plants can be left outdoors. Another possibility would be to give the Climate 2 plants a certain amount of water twice a week. A third set of plants, Climate 3 plants, might be given the same amount of water but only once a week or once every two weeks.
7. Whatever differing climate conditions you choose, they should represent different climates. Before you begin the activity, write a brief description of what the temperature and moisture conditions will be for each climate and how you plan to see that those conditions are maintained.
8. Place each set of plants in its respective climate. Once a week, for at least three weeks, measure and record the heights of the plants in each flowerpot. For each week's readings, also calculate the average height of the plants in each pot.
9. You may wish to investigate the effect of climate changes on more than one type of plant. If the flowerpots are large enough, you could grow samples of both plant types in the same pot. Otherwise, you could use more than one pot for each climate. In either case, take separate average heights for each plant type.

Questions

1. What plant type(s) did you use?
2. What type of climate did each set of plants grow under?
3. How did the growth of the plants compare?
4. Why use more than one plant in each pot? Why compare the average heights rather than the heights of individual plants?
5. In which climate did your plants grow better?

Conclusion

What do you think would have happened if you had used different plants of the same type? if you had used different plant types?

Section 3 Review Chapter 6

Use **Reading Checksheet 6-3** TRB page 78
   Skillsheet 6-3 TRB page 120
   Section Reviewsheet 6-3 TRB pages 177–178
   Section Testsheet 6-3 TRB page 292

Check Your Vocabulary

7 adiabatic change   3 polar climate
1 climate   9 rain-shadow desert
10 climate graph   5 temperate climate
6 continental climate 2 tropical climate
8 desert   11 weather
4 marine climate

Match each term above with the numbered phrase that best describes it.

1. The weather patterns that occur in one place over a period of a year or longer.

2. A climate influenced mainly by tropical air masses; characterized by the warmest temperatures

3. A climate influenced mainly by polar air masses; characterized by cold temperatures

4. A climate influenced mainly by maritime air masses; characterized by abundant precipitation; also called an oceanic climate

5. A climate influenced by both polar and tropical air masses; characterized by moderate temperatures

6. A climate influenced mainly by continental air masses; characterized by dry air

7. A temperature change that occurs because of a material's expansion or compression

8. Any area where the total amount of precipitation is less than 10 in (254 mm) per year

9. A desert caused by a mountain range that prevents prevailing winds from bringing moisture to an area

10. A graph that indicates average monthly temperature and precipitation conditions for twelve months at a particular location

11. The atmospheric conditions at a particular location at a particular moment

Check Your Knowledge

Multiple Choice: Choose the answer that best completes each of the following sentences.

1. _?_ is the atmospheric conditions at a particular location at a particular moment in time.
   a) Weather
   b) Climate
   c) The average temperature
   d) Average rainfall

2. Any climate of the world can be classified according to _?_.
   a) wet and dry
   b) hot and cold
   c) temperature and moisture
   d) polar and tropical

3. As air rises, it _?_.
   a) compresses and warms
   b) compresses and cools
   c) expands and warms
   d) expands and cools

4. Most of the earth's deserts are located _?_.
   a) along the Tropics of Cancer and Capricorn
   b) along the windward side of mountains
   c) near warm ocean currents
   d) at the same latitude as Death Valley

Check Your Understanding

1. Compare weather and climate. How are they similar? How do they differ?

2. Explain how and why latitude affects climate.

3. Explain how and why altitude affects climate.

4. Explain what happens to the moisture content of descending air. What causes this to happen?

5. How do ocean currents affect the climates of cities on the east and west coasts of the United States? Why does this happen?

Chapter 6 Review

See also **Chapter Testsheets 6A and 6B**
TRB pages 327–328.

Concept Summary

An **air mass** is a large body of air that moves as a unit and that has more or less uniform characteristics throughout.
☐ Air masses are named by the kinds of locations over which they form.
☐ Though generally uniform throughout, some variation in temperature, atmospheric pressure, and moisture content occurs within an air mass because of differences among local conditions.
☐ Air masses are responsible for the weather conditions at a particular location.

A **weather front** is the boundary between two air masses and often produces a change in the weather.
☐ Differing cloud types and precipitation patterns are associated with cold fronts and warm fronts.

A **station model** is a clear and simple way of recording weather conditions at a particular weather station.
☐ Information from station models for different locations is fed into computerized data banks and is used to obtain larger weather patterns.

A **weather map** is a representation of weather conditions over an area of the earth's surface.
☐ A weather map incorporates information from radar, satellites, and weather balloons.
☐ Patterns observed on weather maps for successive days are useful in predicting the weather.

Climate is the average weather conditions, primarily moisture and air temperature, that occur in one place over a year or longer.
☐ Climates are distinguished on the basis of average moisture and average temperatures.
☐ Average temperatures are affected by latitude, altitude, and ocean currents.
☐ Average moisture is affected by prevailing winds and nearness to large bodies of water.

Putting It All Together

1. Describe the following air masses: c, m, P, T. For each, give the name, tell where it forms, and give a general characteristic.
2. Draw a diagram of a cold front, a warm front, and an occluded front. Indicate the direction of movement of each front.
3. Would you expect heavier precipitation along a cold front or warm front? Why?
4. What is a station model? What kinds of information are given on a station model? In what form is the information expressed?
5. Explain why weather predictions are often expressed as probabilities.
6. Describe some of the similarities and differences between hurricanes and tornadoes.
7. Describe effects of advance warning in weather forecasting.
8. Relate the major climates to location and to air masses.
9. How do prevailing winds affect climate?
10. Explain the relationship between deserts and descending air.

Apply Your Knowledge

1. In what general direction would you expect a cold air mass to move? Why?
2. It is raining in a nearby city. How would you tell whether it might rain where you live?
3. Construct a station model that indicates that the sky is cloudy, the air temperature is 80°F the dew-point temperature is 48°F, the atmospheric pressure is 1015.9 mb, there is no precipitation, and the wind is blowing from the southeast at 15 knots per hour.
4. Why is it helpful for station models to use the same symbols and to indicate the same kinds of information in the same positions?
5. Explain how ice-covered polar regions can have very dry climates.

Find Out on Your Own

1. List factors that influence the climate in your area. How does each affect the climate?
2. How does the climate of your area affect the following: what is worn; what is grown; the type of construction used in buildings; energy consumption?
3. What cities or towns in other parts of the world have climates similar to yours? How do those cities or towns compare with yours in what is worn, what is grown, the type of construction used in buildings, and in energy consumption? What might explain any differences?
4. How does the climate of your area affect the type and amount of industry found in your area? What aspects of your climate might attract industrial growth? What aspects might act as a deterrent? Explain.

Reading Further

Gribbin, John. *Weather Force: Climate and Its Impact on Our World*. New York: G. P. Putnam's Sons, 1979.

Detailed data on many aspects of weather, storms, and climates. Exciting photographs. A book to browse through rather than read from cover to cover. A handy source for much out-of-the-ordinary reference-type information.

Hays, Dr. James D. *Our Changing Climate*. New York: Atheneum, 1977.

A clear and mature presentation of the earth's climates. Smooth-flowing text that interweaves data, theory, the past, present, and future.

Lambert, David. *Weather*. New York: Watts, 1983.

A well-written, informative account of most weather phenomena. Good index and illustrations.

Ross, Frank, Jr. *Storms and Man*. New York: Lothrop, Lee & Shepard Co., 1970.

A clear, informative, chapter-by-chapter presentation of different kinds of storms. Scientific information is combined with photographs and historical accounts of destructive storms of the past. Many black and white photographs.

Rubin, Louis D., with Hiram J. Herbert. *Forecasting the Weather*. New York: Franklin Watts, Inc., 1970.

Clear identification and presentation of the different elements that influence the weather. Includes photographs of various cloud sequences with explanatory text that tells what kind of weather each sequence signals.

Witty, Margot and Ken. *A Day in the Life of a Meteorologist*. Mahwah, NJ: Troll, 1981.

Presents a typical day in the life of a weather forecaster. Explains how weather information is gathered from satellite pictures, weather maps, and related equipment.

Science Issues of Today Preventing Disasters from Sudden Weather Changes

Meteorologists are able to predict and track certain types of storms by using data from remote sensing devices from satellites, from land stations, and from ocean buoys. Hurricanes can be tracked and coastal residents are often given enough warning so that they can take steps to protect themselves.

However, certain types of weather conditions are difficult, if not impossible, to accurately predict. In midsummer, 1976, twelve inches of rain fell in five hours in north central Colorado. The Big Thompson River increased its flow drastically, and the ensuing erosion and flooding killed nearly 140 people and destroyed about 250 structures.

In June, 1982, a sudden storm developed winds over 70 knots, capsized two sailboats, and destroyed a large fishing ship and its entire crew. In this case, the atmospheric pressure dropped rapidly over a short period of time. This type of pressure drop is not usually predictable with current sensing devices and computer analysis.

In May, 1985, tornadoes ripped through parts of eastern Ohio and western Pennsylvania. People were killed and many houses and businesses were destroyed.

Airplanes have experienced sudden sideways or downward bursts of wind that are very dangerous, especially during landing or takeoff. In August, 1985, at a Texas airport, a large airliner crashed while landing because of this type of wind shear.

What can be done to predict sudden shifts in wind and weather? Each of the wind or storm conditions mentioned above is thought to be caused by different conditions. Each presents its own difficulties in prediction and monitoring. These storms arise so rapidly that long-term prediction is impossible.

Detecting unusual weather conditions that may affect flying is an important concern for meteorologists.

However, short-term prediction and warning may be possible. Often, the judgment of experienced meteorologists has been all that prevented even greater disaster from rapid weather changes. One of the technologic tools that a meteorologist can use is called Doppler radar (see pages 151 and 153 for a discussion of the Doppler effect). This radar device can accurately measure changes in wind that could forewarn of certain problems like wind shear and tornadoes; but the warning time is still very short, and it would require an almost impossibly large deployment of radar units to cover all airfields and tornado-prone areas.

Scientists are studying these weather phenomena and the environmental conditions that precede them. They may find that, even with improved prediction techniques, the warning time before a disastrous wind or storm may still be very small. We may then find that the best defense is to understand the intensity of sudden bad weather, and build our houses, buildings, and roads accordingly.

Water in Motion

Unit 4

Near Bermuda, a diver releases colorful dye into the water to study the flow of the current.

Water distinguishes the earth from other planets in the solar system. Water provides the moisture needed by the cells of living organisms. Water provides an environment in which many of the earth's organisms live. Water—moving water and the alternate freezing and thawing of water—is responsible for many of the beautiful formations of the earth's landscapes.

Modern technology has enabled scientists to extend their observations to objects never seen before—the tiniest particles of matter; objects on the surface of the moon, Mars, and other planets; organisms deep below the surface of the ocean, where life occurs in total darkness. Like outer space and inner space, the earth's oceans offer exciting frontiers for scientific exploration, investigation, discovery, and progress.

Chapter 7
The Earth's Fresh Water

Chapter 8
The Ocean

Chapter 7 The Earth's Fresh Water

Student Resources		Meeting Individual Needs	
Student Text	**Laboratory Activities**		
Section 1 Water on the Ground 336–349			
Water Recycles 337–338	Investigation 7-1 Simulating the Water Cycle LM 95–96	Enrichment	
Our Science Heritage: Water and Ancient Civilizations 339			
Water Collects On the Ground 340–342			
Water Runs Off the Ground 342–345	Activity 7-1A Comparing Rainfall and Stream Discharge 344	CORE	
	Activity Record Sheet 7-1A LM 93		
Water Leaves the Earth's Surface 346–347	Activity 7-1B Observing Transpiration from a Plant 348	Enrichment	
	Activity Record Sheet 7-1B LM 94		
	Research Lab 7 Determining an Area's Water Budget LM 101–102	Enrichment	
Section 1 Review 349			
Section 2 Water in the Ground 350–363			
Pore Spaces in Rock and Soil 351–352	Investigation 7-2 Determining Permeability LM 99–100	Enrichment	
Water Soaks into the Ground 352–353			
Zones of Water in the Ground 354–357	Activity 7-2A Observing the Cohesion of Water Molecules 356	Reinforcement	
	Activity Record Sheet 7-2A LM 97		
Water Comes Out of the Ground 357–361	Activity 7-2B Simulating the Water Table 358	CORE	
	Activity Record Sheet 7-2B LM 98		
Careers: Hydrologist/Heavy-Equipment Operator 362			
Section 2 Review 363			
Chapter 7 Review 364–365			

Teacher Resources		Meeting Individual Needs
Teacher's Edition	**Teacher's Resource Book**	
	Letter to Parents EI 43	Enrichment
	Essential Ideas 7-1 EI 45–46	Reinforcement
	Overhead Transparency B15	CORE
	Teaching Diagram 7-1 TRB 34	CORE
Demonstration 334C		
Discussion Idea 334C		
Activity Notes 334D		
Activity Notes 334E	Skillsheet 7-1 TRB 121	Reinforcement
Environmental Topic 334F		
Creative Writing Idea 334F		
Section 1 Review Answers 334F	Reading Checksheet 7-1 TRB 79	Reinforcement
	Section Reviewsheet 7-1 TRB 179–180	CORE
	Section Testsheet 7-1 TRB 293	CORE
	Essential Ideas 7-2 EI 47–48	Reinforcement
Demonstration 334G	Overhead Transparency S14	Enrichment
	Projectsheet 7-2 TRB 244	Enrichment
Environmental Topic 334H		
Discussion Idea 334H	Overhead Transparency S15	Enrichment
Activity Notes 334J		
Activity Notes 334K	Skillsheet 7-2 TRB 122	Reinforcement
	Teaching Diagram 7-2 TRB 35	Enrichment
	Overhead Transparency S16	Enrichment
Section 2 Review Answers 334K	Reading Checksheet 7-2 TRB 80	Reinforcement
	Section Reviewsheet 7-2 TRB 181–182	CORE
	Section Testsheet 7-2 TRB 294	CORE
Chapter 7 Review Answers 334L–334M	Chapter 7 Testsheet TRB 329–330	CORE

7

Water on the Ground

Learner Objectives

1. To describe the water cycle.
2. To describe what happens to water that falls to the earth's surface.
3. To describe how water runs off the earth's surface.
4. To relate the time of heaviest rainfall and the time of greatest stream discharge.
5. To describe how water leaves the earth's surface.

Concept Summary

7-1

In the **water cycle,** water is continually recycled between the earth's surface and the atmosphere, changing form (through evaporation, condensation, and freezing) because of the different atmospheric conditions.

Demonstration

All Water Samples Are Not Alike

Collect samples of water from as many different sources as you can. Sources can include the school's water system, a different community's water system, rain, a lake or pond, the ocean (if possible), a well, a spring, etc.

Label each sample and ask the students to comment on the way the water looks—whether it is clear or muddy, whether it has any sediments, etc.

Ask one student to taste all those samples that you know are safe to drink. Have the student describe the taste of the samples. Ask students what they know about the source of drinking water and what treatment it undergoes.

Allow small amounts of the water samples to evaporate until dry. Discuss the results.

Discussion Idea

The Effect of Water on the Ground

Ask students if they know what watershed they live in. Where does the water flow to? Where does it start? Where is the nearest divide?

Ask students to describe the ways communities divert sheet runoff—and to explain the consequences of the diversion. (Communities often build storm sewers or other drainage systems to prevent flooding of streets, basements, etc., and to divert water to areas where it won't cause a problem.) You might want to discuss what effect such diversion has on the landscape and ecology of a region.

If you live in an area once covered by glaciers, ask students to discuss the landforms that result from the glacial advances and retreats.

Activity Notes

Activity 7-1A

Comparing Rainfall and Stream Discharge   page **344**

Purpose   To graph an amount of rainfall and the resulting amount of stream discharge.

- **CORE** 20 minutes Individuals or small groups
- **Activity Record Sheet 7-1A** (Lab Manual page 93) can be used to record this activity.
- Science Processes: Interpreting data; Communicating through a graph; Comparing and contrasting; Reasoning.

Procedure Notes

This activity may be done in class or at home. It demonstrates the role of graphing in analyzing data.

These graphs are similar to the climate graphs on pages 326 and 327, where temperature and precipitation were plotted against time of year. In this case, the amount of rainfall and the volume of stream discharge are plotted against time of day.

For comparison purposes, the vertical scale for amount of rainfall should range from 0 to 5 cm/h, at intervals of 1 cm/h. The vertical scale for stream discharge should range from 0 to 3000 m^3/sec, at intervals of 500 m^3/sec.

Answers to Questions

1. The greatest discharge occurred two hours after the heaviest rainfall. Apparently it took two hours for the precipitation to run off the ground, to be channeled into streams, and to reach the point where the stream discharge was being measured.
2. The stream discharge graph is lower. Not all the water that fell as rain reached the point in the stream where the discharge was measured. Some water passed down into the soil. Some evaporated into the air. Some could have run off without passing the stream discharge measuring point.
3. The stream discharge graph has a more gradual curve. This pattern indicates that as water runs off the earth's surface, its flow is affected by the surface. Surface features such as plants, tree trunks, rocks, slope, shape of stream channel, etc. slow down the runoff, causing the curves on the discharge graph to be more gently sloped.

Conclusion

Stream discharge increases as rainfall does, but the increase is delayed. Furthermore, not all the rainfall is channeled into the stream where it can be measured as runoff.

Science Background

Water is vital to life on earth. Although the total amount of fresh water on earth is still enough to take care of the needs of the world's population, local water shortages occur because water is not distributed evenly and because many water sources have become polluted.

Sources of water pollution can be divided into two groups, point sources and nonpoint sources. Point sources come from factories, sewage treatment plants, and other specific locations. Nonpoint source pollution has no single identifiable source. It includes agricultural runoff with its load of fertilizers, pesticides, and animal wastes, and materials washed from city streets such as motor oil.

Fertilizer that makes its way into lakes and ponds causes a process known as eutrophication. Nitrates and phosphates in the nutrient-rich water trigger an excessive growth of algae, called algal bloom. When the algae die and decay, the process uses much of the dissolved oxygen in the water. This reduces the amount of oxygen available to animal life.

Eutrophication speeds up a natural sequence of events known as succession. In ecological succession, a pond or lake gradually fills with sediments and decomposing organic materials. In time, it becomes a marsh. If left alone, the marsh will become a meadow, which may eventually develop into a climax forest.

7-1

Student Misconception

Swamps, bogs, and marshes are often viewed as wasted land, areas that should be drained to be made useful. Yet these wetlands are not only valuable because of their recreational and aesthetic dividends, but because of their necessity for wildlife and watershed management.

Students may not be aware of the distribution of wetlands across the nation or even in their own neighborhood. Soil surveys are available through your county extension agent and are very useful in identifying these important areas. Have students construct a local map showing the distribution of wetlands. Another approach is to have students develop a map of the United States or the world showing the major areas of wetlands.

7-1

Activity Notes

Activity 7-1B

Observing Transpiration from a Plant   page **348**

Purpose   To see evidence of the part transpiration plays in the water cycle.

- Two 5-minute sessions Groups of 4
- **Activity Record Sheet 7-1B** (Lab Manual page 94) can be used to record this activity.
- Science Processes: Investigating; Observing; Communicating through a data table; Interpreting data; Inferring.

Advance Preparation

For each group of students, you will need a potted plant, such as geranium or coleus, in stabilized condition. You might also have some students use other plants, such as cacti or ferns.

You may wish to have some students determine the mass of their plants and bags before and after to see whether the mass changes. If so, you will need to have a balance on hand for student use. (Some water loss may result from evaporation from the soil. Covering the soil with aluminum foil can help prevent this loss.)

Procedure Notes

Transpiration is a continuous process—it does not take place only at night. To illustrate this, you might have students fold a square of blue cobalt chloride paper so that it is in contact with both the upper and lower surfaces of a leaf; then cover the cobalt chloride paper with a piece of clear plastic to protect the paper from the moisture in the air, and fasten with a paper clip. Cobalt chloride paper is blue when dry, but turns pink when moist. Have students observe the paper every 5 minutes and record their observations.

Answers to Questions

1. Moisture collected on the inside of the bag. This is caused by transpiration.
2. When the activity is repeated, moisture will again collect on the inside of the bag. Over several days, less moisture will collect, and the plant may begin to wilt, depending on the amount of water in the soil before starting.

Conclusion

In the process of transpiration, water vapor passes out of the leaves of a plant (and condenses on the inside of the bag).

Environmental Topic

Most of northern Brazil serves as a watershed for the Amazon River. Heavy rains and hot, humid conditions have resulted in the development of extremely heavy growth called rainforest throughout much of this region. The rainforest with its vast quantity of vegetation is important in the replenishing of oxygen to the atmosphere. An extremely rich variety of life is sheltered within its thick growth.

The government of Brazil is clearing the rainforest for pasture land, industrial development, and dam construction. The latter is being designed to tap into the vast hydroelectric potential of the Amazon River. It has been estimated that by the year 2030, the rainforest will exist no more if the rate of clearing is not reduced.

Discuss with the class the serious consequences of the destruction of the rainforest environment. Include a discussion of how the loss of oxygen in the atmosphere will impact the global environment and how the extinction of even one species affects us all. You might remind students of recent efforts to preserve this complex ecosystem, such as the fast food chain Burger King deciding in 1987 to suspend funds for clearing rainforest land for cattle grazing.

Creative Writing Idea

The following writing assignment may help students think about the processes of evaporation and transpiration, and the sources of moisture in the air.

You and a friend have been hiking beside a large stream through a meadow when you come to the glacier that feeds the stream. The day is very hot so you decide to picnic on the glacier. You feel lazy after lunch and curl up to take a nap. When you awaken, you notice large clouds above your head. Your friend is surprised that clouds could show up on such a beautiful day. Assuming the clouds were not brought in by a front, explain how there could be enough moisture entering the air from the glacier and surrounding area to produce clouds.

Section 1 Review Answers

Check Your Understanding
page 349

1. Liquid—oceans, lakes, ponds, brooks, pore spaces in rock and soil, and water droplets in clouds; Solid—icebergs in oceans, glaciers and icecaps on land, ice on frozen bodies of water, and ice crystals in clouds; Gas—water vapor in the atmosphere

2. Water evaporates from the land, condenses in the atmosphere, and returns to earth as precipitation.

3. Water that falls to the earth's surface can evaporate, can collect in a body of water, can run off the surface, and can soak into the ground.

4. Transpiration can be expected to be greater over a forest, because the soil in a forest is generally moister than in a desert. Through their roots, forest trees draw moisture from the ground. This moisture is expelled by the trees through openings in the underside of their leaves. In a desert, where rain is scarce, plants conserve whatever moisture they can; loss of water through transpiration is therefore much less than in a moister area.

5. A river collects and channels water from a very large area (its watershed). The runoff from the watershed area flows toward the sea. Water from tributaries may therefore cause flooding when more water is channeled into the river than its banks can contain.

7-1

Learner Objectives

1. To distinguish between porosity and permeability.
2. To identify zones of water in the ground.
3. To distinguish among the ways in which water comes out of the ground.

Concept Summary

Infiltration is the process by which water sinks into the ground.
Porosity is the total volume of the pore spaces in a material.
Permeability is the ease with which water flows through a material.

7-2

Demonstration

How Particle Size Affects Capillary Action

Take a glass tube filled with coarse sand and stand it in a pan of water. (A capillary tube, such as those used in chemistry classes, would work well.)

Ask students if they can explain why the water rises (capillary action). In Section 1 of Chapter 7 they will learn what properties of water cause capillary action.

Take a similar tube filled with fine sand and place it in the water. Ask students if they can explain why the water does not rise as far or as fast.

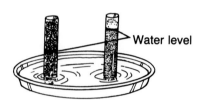

Water level

Tell students that in Section 1 of Chapter 7 they will learn that porosity and permeability of materials affect the movement of water through them. They will also learn how porosity and permeability affect ground water and the water table.

Environmental Topic

To replenish our groundwater supply, we need considerable amounts of water to soak into the ground. This is accomplished by maintaining large stretches of permeable land, such as open fields. In large cities, however, the tendency is to build on all available land. Open land becomes covered with buildings and pavements, thereby preventing rainwater from penetrating the surface and infiltrating the ground. Consequently, rainwater becomes runoff that often finds its way into the sewage system, reducing our usable water supply and increasing the frequency of floods.

Discuss the need for careful study of the terrain to plan land use that will prevent flooding and the loss of available groundwater for drinking and other uses.

Discussion Idea

The Importance of Maintaining the Water Table

Ask students if they have experienced an extended drought in their community or somewhere else. What happened to the water table? Could they see the water level drop in ponds or lakes? Did they see any differences in streams or river beds?

Ask about wells—has anyone in the class ever had a home water well go dry?

Ask what students themselves do to conserve water. What do their families do? What does the community do?

Explain that the level of the water table is usually of the utmost importance to a community; even if water comes not from wells but from reservoirs, the capacity of the reservoirs is tied to the water table. Students will learn more about ground water and the water table in Section 2 of Chapter 7.

Science Background

More than half of all Americans depend on ground water for drinking water. Two problems threaten this important source of fresh water.

In many places, ground water is being used up faster than it can be replaced by precipitation. In the western United States, for example, enormous quantities of ground water are pumped out for irrigation. The natural refilling of an aquifer, called recharging, is a slow process because ground water moves very slowly. Excessive pumping can also cause land subsidence (the formation of sinkholes).

Recently, scientists and health officials have become concerned about the quality of ground water. Water in aquifers located below septic tanks, improperly constructed landfills and industrial waste sites, and leaking underground storage tanks (such as those used in gasoline stations) have become contaminated with hazardous substances. In agricultural regions, recharge water often carries a heavy load of pesticides and fertilizers. Water purification occurs slowly in aquifers, if at all, and the contaminated water may travel far from the source of its pollution.

7-2

Water in the Ground

Student Misconception

Cohesion and adhesion are important concepts for students to comprehend if they are to understand the movement of water through soil. Many students believe that the movement of water through soil takes place only in the downward direction due to the force of gravity.

Adhesion is the attraction of molecules of different substances to each other. Cohesion is the attraction of molecules of the same substance to each other. Both forces act to move water upward through soil. Water clings, or adheres, to soil particles, drawing water up from the zone of saturation into the zone of aeration. A light film of water on soil particles attracts more water. This is due to cohesion.

A few simple demonstrations will facilitate your students' understanding of these principles. Place a few drops of water about 5 cm apart on a piece of waxed paper. Slowly edge the drops together. As the drops get very close they will merge to form one large drop. In this case, the cohesion between water molecules is greater than the adhesion between water and waxed paper. For a second demonstration, place some water in a narrow cylinder or test tube. Ask students to observe how the water clings to the side of the glass container, forming a meniscus. The adhesion force between water and glass is stronger that the cohesive force between water molecules.

Activity Notes

Activity 7-2A

Observing the Cohesion of Water Molecules   page **356**

Purpose   To see if you can make a needle stay on the surface of water.

- 20 minutes Groups of 4 or teacher demonstration
- **Activity Record Sheet 7-2A** (Lab Manual page 97) can be used to record this activity.
- Science Processes: Investigating; Observing; Defining operationally; Comparing; Reasoning.

Procedure Notes

If the needle is made slightly oily by rubbing it between the fingers, it will not get wet.

Once the needle is "floating" on the water, have students examine the surface with a hand lens. Students will see that actually the needle is sitting in a depression on the surface of the water. The weight of the needle is counterbalanced by the upward force exerted by the cohesion of the water molecules. This property of liquids is known as surface tension.

Detergents (soap powders) lower the surface tension of water, thus making it possible for water and detergent to penetrate between fibers and dirt particles.

Answers to Questions

1. Cohesion, the attraction of one molecule to other molecules of the same kind, enables the water level to go above the top of the beaker without spilling over.
2. The attraction of water molecules to each other is strong enough to support a horizontal needle placed so gently on the surface of the water that the cohesion is not disturbed.
3. The needle sinks.

Conclusion

When soap powder is added to the water, the cohesion of the water is weakened and the needle can no longer be supported on the surface.

Activity Notes

Activity 7-2B

Simulating the Water Table   page **358**

Purpose   To build a model of a water table.

- **CORE** 20 minutes Teacher demonstration or large groups
- **Activity Record Sheet 7-2B** (Lab Manual page 98) can be used to record this activity.
- Science Processes: Formulating models; Observing; Demonstrating; Diagramming; Comparing.

Procedure Notes

Layers of soil, sand, and gravel can also be used.

Answers to Questions

1. *Infiltration* is the name of the process by which water sinks down into soil. Answers will vary, depending on what materials are put in the jar.
2. The boundary line separating the saturated soil from the rest of the soil is called the water table.
3. The water level should be lower the next day because of evaporation of water from the soil. The lowering of the water table can be prevented by covering the surface of the soil, by covering the jar, or adding more water to the soil.

Conclusion

The water table in the earth rises and falls with rainfall and evaporation. The community might depend on the water table for various water uses.

Going Further

Students can observe variations in the water table by making a similar model in a baking pan. Have students dig a small hole in the "soil" until the "water table" is reached. Then students can observe what happens to the water in the hole when more water is added near the edge of the pan. (The water level rises.)

Section 2 Review Answers

Check Your Understanding
page 363

1. The permeability of a material is affected by 1) the number of pore spaces, 2) the size of pore spaces, and 3) how well the pore spaces are interconnected.
2. The porosity of a material is affected by 1) the shape of the grains of the material, 2) how packed together or loose the grains are, and 3) whether the pore spaces between the grains are empty.
3. The level of the water table can rise as more water infiltrates the ground. The level of the water table can drop as water evaporates from the soil, as water flows downward toward the level of the sea, and as ground water is removed by people and by the roots of growing plants.
4. An artesian spring is fed by water from an aquifer. Water in an aquifer is not affected by local infiltration because an aquifer is separated from local ground water by a layer of impermeable rock.
5. Water would rise higher through capillary action in earth material that is made up of small particles. The pore spaces between small particles are smaller. Attraction of water molecules to the soil particles above, through adhesion, and consequent attraction of other water molecules through cohesion, is greater where the materials are closer together.

7-2

Chapter Vocabulary

Section 1

freeze
condense
evaporate
water cycle
glacier
lake
pond
swamp
runoff
sheet runoff
stream
divide
tributaries
watershed
transpiration

7-3

Chapter 7 Review Answers

Putting It All Together   page 364

1. Liquid water is a fluid that is wet, that freezes at 0°C, that boils at 100°C, and that evaporates between 0°C and 100°C. Solid water, ice, is liquid water that has frozen into crystals. Water vapor is an invisible gas that is found in the atmosphere. Water changes from one state to another because of changes in amount of energy. When water changes from a solid to a liquid or from a liquid to a gas, it absorbs energy. When water changes from a gas to a liquid or from a liquid to a solid, it loses energy to its surroundings.

2. Student diagrams should include water evaporating from the earth's surface (liquid to vapor), water condensing and forming clouds in the atmosphere (gas to liquid), and water falling to the earth as precipitation.

3. Student diagrams should include a divide, sheet runoff to stream runoff, stream runoff through a tributary into the river, and then downstream past other tributaries and an even larger river until it enters the sea.

4. Liquid water is found in pore spaces in rock and soil, in bodies of water on the earth's surface, and in clouds in the earth's atmosphere. Solid water is found in ice on the earth's surface and ice crystals in clouds. Water vapor is found in the atmosphere.

5. Tributaries are streams that channel water into a river.

6. Student diagrams should include the main features shown in Figure 7-14 on page 354.

7. Water molecules are attracted to other kinds of molecules through a process called adhesion. As a result, water molecules are drawn up from the surface of the water table and cling to soil particles. These water molecules, in turn, attract other molecules through a process called cohesion.

8. Student diagrams should include the main features shown in Figure 7-15 on page 359.

9. Many rocks contain pore spaces and are therefore porous. Water can enter these pore spaces. If these pore spaces are interconnected or if the rock has cracks in it, water can travel through the rock, which is said to be permeable. If water cannot travel through the rock, the rock is impermeable.

10. Geysers are caused by superheated water and steam. The water and steam obtains its heat from volcanic activity in the earth's crust.

Chapter 7 Review Answers (continued)

Apply Your Knowledge   page **364**

1. All organisms need water for life. When water evaporates from the earth's surface, it is purified. Through precipitation, water falls on even the highest elevations on the earth's surface. Through infiltration, water enters the soil and can then be drawn, through a plant's root system, up into the plant.

2. Climate is determined by average monthly temperatures and amounts of precipitation. In general, in a tropical climate, much evaporation and precipitation can be expected because warm temperatures increase the rate of evaporation. Also in tropical climates the sun's rays are strongest. Much transpiration from growing plants (as in tropical rain forests) occurs in the tropics. In polar climates, cold temperatures would reduce evaporation, and therefore the condensation and precipitation that would follow. And in temperate climates, an in-between/moderate amount of evaporation and precipitation can be expected. Such expectations, however, are general and based solely on average temperatures at different latitudes. Geographic features and prevailing winds cause variations at particular locations.

3. Freezing temperatures can prevent water from infiltrating the ground. If the precipitation occurs as snow or ice, it cannot infiltrate unless/until it melts. If water in the ground is frozen, it cannot move and the soil/rock becomes impermeable to further infiltration.

4. Floods can be prevented by controlling the rate of runoff and by increasing the size of a river channel (either in width or depth) to handle the runoff. Runoff can be reduced/controlled by means of dams and by means of ground cover to reduce the velocity of sheet runoff and to promote infiltration of the soil.

5. Infiltration will be less where the surface is less permeable and where the surface slopes. Infiltration is greater in permeable material that is nearly level so that the water does not run off the surface. (Trees, terracing, etc. are used to reduce runoff/erosion and to increase infiltration on slopes.)

Chapter Vocabulary

Section 2

infiltration
pore spaces
porosity
permeability
ground water
zone of aeration
adhesion
impermeable
zone of saturation
water table
capillary action
cohesion
capillary fringe
spring
artesian system
aquifer
artesian spring
geyser

7-3

Chapter 7

The Earth's Fresh Water

Section 1
Water on the Ground

Rain may be inconvenient. It may, for instance, spoil a picnic or force the cancellation of a game. But rain is a basic earth process and part of the earth's water cycle.

The earth's fresh water cycles between the earth's surface and the earth's atmosphere. Water leaves the earth's surface through evaporation and returns through precipitation.

On the earth's surface, some of the water flows in streams and rivers. Some collects in lakes and ponds. Some collects in glaciers and icebergs.

Section 2
Water in the Ground

Part of the water that returns to the earth as precipitation flows across the earth's surface, but part of it soaks down into the earth's surface and becomes part of the earth's underground water supply.

Water comes out of the ground, sometimes in startling ways or in unexpected places. And stored deep beneath the earth's surface, meltwater from Ice Age glaciers remains cool and clear and pure.

Some students may know the sources and destinations of streams in your area. Some may even have followed a brook to visible springs that are its source. In general, streams start where water comes out of the ground or where ice or snow melts and runs off the surface. And all streams flow downhill toward the sea (or at least toward the lowest level they can).

In discussion, students can list places in your area where water is found naturally in one of its three forms. For bodies of water, bodies of salt water should be distinguished from bodies of fresh water. Where known, students should identify where the water comes from (the source of a stream or river, for example).

The earth's brooks and streams carry fresh water downhill toward the sea. Brooks and streams can be pleasant-sounding and provide a habitat for many plants and animals. If there is a stream near your home, where does the water in the stream come from, and into what larger body of water does the stream flow?

Water on the Ground   Section 1

Section 1 of Chapter 7 is divided into four parts:

Water recycles

Water collects on the ground

Water runs off the ground

Water leaves the earth's surface

Figure 7-1. In the picture, you can see liquid water (the ocean and the clouds). You can see solid water (the iceberg). But you cannot see the water in its third form, water vapor in the atmosphere, because water vapor is an invisible gas.

Learner Objectives
1. To describe the water cycle.
2. To describe what happens to water that falls to the earth's surface.
3. To describe how water runs off the earth's surface.
4. To relate the time of heaviest rainfall and the time of greatest stream discharge.
5. To describe how water leaves the earth's surface.

Only 3% of all the earth's water is fresh water. The other 97% is stored in the earth's oceans as salt water. Where does the earth's fresh water come from? And where does it go?

Water recycles
New vocabulary: freeze, condense, evaporate, water cycle

Water is a very unusual earth material because it is found in all three forms of matter. Water is found as a liquid in the oceans, in other bodies of water, in porous rocks and soil, and in the atmosphere (water droplets in clouds). Water is found as a solid in the oceans (icebergs), on the land (glaciers and icecaps), on frozen bodies of water (ice), and in the atmosphere (ice crystals in clouds). And water is found as a gas in the atmosphere. Table 6-1 shows the distribution (in volume) of water on the earth.

Distribution of Water on the Earth			
Location	Form	Volume	Percent of Total Volume
oceans	liquid	1 322 000 000 km³	97.2%
icecaps and glaciers	solid	29 200 000 km³	2.15%
on or under land	liquid	8 637 000 km³	0.635%
atmosphere	solid, liquid, gas	13 000 km³	0.001%

Not only is water found in all three forms of matter. It also changes back and forth from one form to another. At 0°C, water **freezes,** changing from a liquid to a solid. At 100°C, water boils. When air is cooled to a low enough temperature, the water vapor in the air **condenses,** changing from a gas to a liquid or even to a solid. Between 0°C and 100°C, water **evaporates,** changing from a liquid to a gas.

According to present scientific estimates, the earth formed as a planet about 4.6 billion years ago. During all the years between then and now, water has been moving continuously into and out of the atmosphere. Water vapor enters the atmo-

The earth's fresh water comes from the water cycle, which processes water into fresh water. The water may be used, or it may flow downhill toward the sea. In any case, it can be expected to find its way back into the water cycle. (As mentioned earlier, questions like these in the section openers are meant to spark initial thought and discussion about matters that will be treated in that particular section of the text.)

Table 7-1. How much of the earth's water is found in the oceans?
The oceans contain 97.2% of the total volume of the earth's water supply.

Interested students could find out the mass percentages of the water in each location. Because of differences in densities, the 0.001% (volume) in the atmosphere would be even smaller as a mass percentage.

At what temperature does water freeze?

Water can boil at less than 100°C if air pressure is reduced. If air pressure is increased, water can boil at a temperature higher than 100°C. (That is why superheated water occurs in geysers, as will be mentioned at the end of the next section of this chapter.)

See also Teaching Diagram 7-1 (TRB page 34).

The process of transpiration, in which water vapor enters the atmosphere from the leaves of living plants, is treated more fully at the end of this section of Chapter 7.

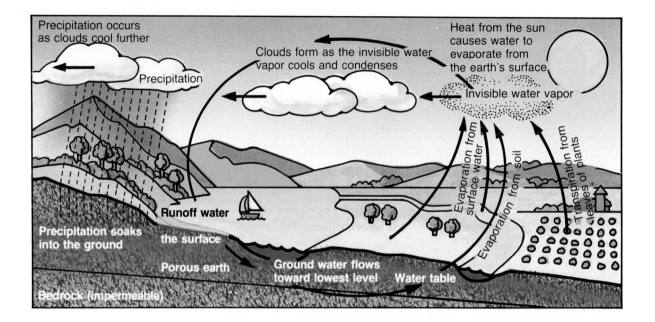

Figure 7-2. The earth's water is recycled in a combination of processes that make up the water cycle.

For a more detailed picture of the water table, see Figure 7-14 on page 354.

Library research

Edmund Halley is responsible for advancing our understanding of the water cycle. Find out more about Edmund Halley.

1. Liquid—in bodies of water, in pore spaces in rocks and soil, and in clouds; Solid—icebergs in the ocean, glaciers and icecaps on land, and ice crystals in clouds; Gas—water vapor in the atmosphere
2. Water leaves the earth's surface by evaporation and transpiration and returns by condensation and precipitation.

sphere from the oceans. Each year about 80 000 cubic miles of water evaporate from the surface of the oceans. Water vapor also enters the atmosphere from the leaves of living plants. Water returns from the atmosphere as a liquid or solid, condensing and falling back to earth. This recycling process whereby water enters the atmosphere by evaporation and transpiration, then condenses, and then returns to the earth's surface as precipitation is called the **water cycle** or the hydrologic cycle.

Much of the precipitation that returns to earth falls back into the oceans. But what happens to the water that falls on the land areas of the earth? Where does that water go? Some of it evaporates back into the atmosphere. Some of it soaks into the ground and becomes part of the underground water supply. Part of it stays on the surface of the earth, and part of it runs off.

Check yourself

1. Where on the earth is water found in each of the three states of matter?

2. Explain the changes that take place in the water cycle.

Our Science Heritage

Water and Ancient Civilizations

People cannot live without fresh water. Their body cells and body processes depend on a continual supply of fresh water. Also, the food that people eat requires water to grow.

Civilizations could not develop without the invention of farming. With farming, people could stay in one place and raise their own food rather than relocate depending on the availability of natural foods.

Evidence indicates that people in the Middle East began raising grain, goats, and sheep about 11 000 years ago. Crops were raised and animals domesticated about 9500 years ago in Southeast Asia and about 8500 years ago in what is now Mexico.

About 5000 years ago, four major civilizations arose. Each of those civilizations developed in a river valley that contained fertile soil for farming and fresh water for irrigation and for use by people. The four river valleys are the Nile (in present-day Egypt), the Tigris and the Euphrates (in present-day Iraq), the Indus (in present-day Pakistan), and the Hwang Ho, or Yellow River (located in present-day China).

Scientists who study the past feel that there is a connection between the rise and fall of civilizations and the way they used their land and other natural resources. In the case of the Sumerians, who lived in the valley between the Tigris and the Euphrates Rivers, there is evidence that they destroyed their farmlands by poor irrigation practices.

They increased the salt content of the soil to a point where crops could no longer be raised (a problem that still occurs in areas that water their crops by irrigation).

Figure 7-3. Margerie Glacier flows downhill until it meets the sea at Glacier Bay, Alaska.

Where is most of the earth's fresh water supply stored?

Water collects on the ground

New vocabulary: glacier, lake, pond, swamp

Water can return to the earth as rain, a liquid, or as snow, a solid. When the water returns in the form of snow, the snow may collect and pile up to great depths. Increasing pressure on the bottom layers of snow causes that snow to change to ice. Most of the earth's fresh water supply is stored in glaciers and other forms of ice.

A **glacier** is a moving mass of ice and snow. Glaciers flow downhill and out from their center. Glaciers usually move very slowly, gouging and reshaping the land as they go.

In order for glaciers to exist, more snow must fall than melts each year. Most of the glaciers and ice sheets are located near the North Pole and the South Pole where the energy from the sun, even in summer, is not strong enough to melt all the ice and snow.

Water collects in lakes, ponds, and swamps. A **lake** forms when water collects in a hole or depression in the earth's surface. The Great Lakes, pictured in Figure 7-4, are the largest body of fresh water on earth. They are thought to

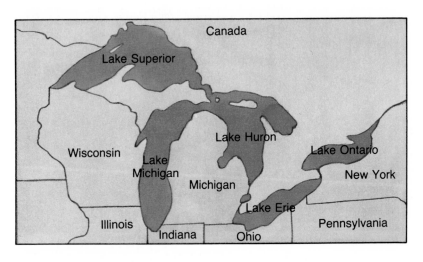

Figure 7-4. The Great Lakes form the largest body of fresh water on the earth. It is estimated that together the Great Lakes contain 22 800 cubic kilometers of fresh water, which is almost twice as much as all the water contained in the earth's atmosphere.

have been formed about 250 000 years ago, when a glacier dug the lake beds out of the rock surface. The rock and soil that were scooped out of the hollow formed natural dams. Somewhere between 11 000 and 15 000 years ago, the southern part of the glacier melted. Water from the melting glacier filled the huge hollows and formed the Great Lakes.

Many lakes of the world were formed by glaciers. Some lakes form when water fills the craters of inactive volcanoes. Crater

Figure 7-5. Volcanic lakes can be very deep. Crater Lake, which is formed in the crater of an inactive volcano in southwestern Oregon, is about 610 meters deep.
The formation of Crater Lake, which followed the violent eruption of Mount Mazama about 6600 years ago, is described in Section 1 (Volcanoes) of Chapter 10. A topographic map of Crater Lake (to be used in conjunction with the activity on page 482 of Section 1 of Chapter 10) appears in the Appendix.

Figure 7-6. Bald cypress trees grow in this water-filled swamp near Wilmington, North Carolina.

It is important for students to understand that lakes are temporary features. They may become dry or a swamp. They may fill in at one end. (Interested students could research a lake of their choice—for example, the formation of the Bonneville salt flats and the Great Salt Lake.)

Other types of lakes formed by glaciers include finger lakes, cirque lakes, tarns, chain lakes, and kettle hole lakes.

What are swamps?

1) Glaciers—moving masses of ice; 2) Lakes—bodies of fresh water in depressions in a land area; 3) Pond—body of water like a lake, but smaller and shallower; 4) Swamp—a water-soaked area, often marshy and filled with vegetation and spongy soil

Lake, pictured in Figure 7-5, is an example of a lake that formed within the collapsed crater of an inactive volcano. *Reservoirs* are lakes made by people. They are usually formed by damming a river. F. D. Roosevelt Lake is the reservoir behind the Grand Coulee Dam (Figure 12-10).

Some surface water collects in ponds as well as lakes. A **pond** is a body of water that is smaller and shallower than a lake. Ponds and lakes that are filled with water and vegetation are called **swamps**. The English word *swamp* comes from a Greek word that means sponge. If you have ever seen a swamp, you know from direct observation how well the name *swamp* fits these low-lying water-soaked marshes and bogs. Swamps provide a home for many varieties of plants and animals.

Check yourself

Name four places where fresh water collects on the earth. Give a brief description of each.

Water runs off the ground
New vocabulary: runoff, sheet runoff, stream, divide, tributary, watershed

A large amount of liquid water that falls to the earth has no place to collect. Much of this water flows directly off the surface and is known as **runoff**.

Runoff occurs in one of two ways: sheet runoff and streams. **Sheet runoff** has no channels to direct its flow. It runs off the surface as broad flat sheets of water. **Streams** are runoff that flows in channels between banks of soil, rock, or other material. The banks of the stream contain the flowing water and give it direction.

When water falls onto a mountain ridge, for example, or when snow melts on the ridge, some water will run off on one side of the ridge and some water will run off on the other. The highest land that separates the direction in which water will run off is called a **divide.** (See Figure 7-7.) A divide causes the water to run off in one direction or the other, depending on which side of the divide the water falls on.

The mightiest river systems in the world begin as small flows of water that feed into little stream channels. These little stream channels flow into larger stream channels until they eventually form a river. Streams and small rivers that empty into one large river system are called **tributaries.** Eventually the large main river empties into the sea.

A river will need a much wider channel than a stream to carry all the water that is emptying into it from its tributaries. The distance between the banks of the Mississippi River, for example, varies from 0.3 m near its beginning to over 1500 m near its end.

All the area of land that drains into a river, along with its

What are two ways in which runoff occurs?

Sheet runoff (also called sheet wash) occurs under the following conditions: 1) The ground is hard (sun-baked or frozen); 2) Excessive rain falls in a short period of time; 3) There is a steep slope.

What are the streams that empty into a large river system called?

Figure 7-7. What is a divide? A divide is the highest land that separates the direction in which water runs off the surface of the earth.

Science Processes: Interpreting data;
Communicating through a graph
See also Activity Record Sheet 7-1A (Lab Manual
page 93)

CORE   20 minutes
Individual students, or small groups

Activity 7-1A   Comparing Rainfall and Stream Discharge

Materials

data table

graph paper

black pencil

colored pencil

Purpose

To graph an amount of rainfall and the resulting amount of stream discharge.

Procedure

1. On a graph, plot the data from the data table. The vertical axis on the left side will show the amount of rainfall in cm/hour. The vertical axis on the right side will show the volume of discharge in m^3/second. Discharge is the amount of stream water that flows past a stream gauging station each second. The horizontal axis will show the time (from 12 noon to 9:00 p.m.). You will actually be plotting two graphs—one for rainfall and one for stream discharge.
2. Using a black pencil, plot the amount of rainfall recorded for each of the times indicated on the horizontal axis. Connect the plots with a line in black pencil.
3. Using a colored pencil and the vertical axis on the right side, plot the stream discharge for each of the times indicated. Connect the plots with a line in the same color.

Questions

1. About how many hours after the heaviest rainfall was the stream discharge the greatest? What might explain the time difference?
2. How do the two graphs compare in height? Which is lower? What might explain this difference?
3. How do the two graphs compare in shape? Which has more gradual curves? What does this indicate? What might explain this difference?

Conclusion

How does the amount of rainfall affect the amount of stream discharge?

Data Table					
Time	Amount of Rainfall in cm/hour	Stream Discharge in m^3/second	Time	Amount of Rainfall in cm/hour	Stream Discharge in m^3/second
12 noon	0	100	5:00 p.m.	0.2	3000
1:00 p.m.	2.6	200	6:00 p.m.	0	2000
2:00 p.m.	4.7	500	7:00 p.m.	0	1000
3:00 p.m.	4.8	1100	8:00 p.m.	0	500
4:00 p.m.	2.0	2000	9:00 p.m.	0	500
Total				14.3 cm	10 900 m^3

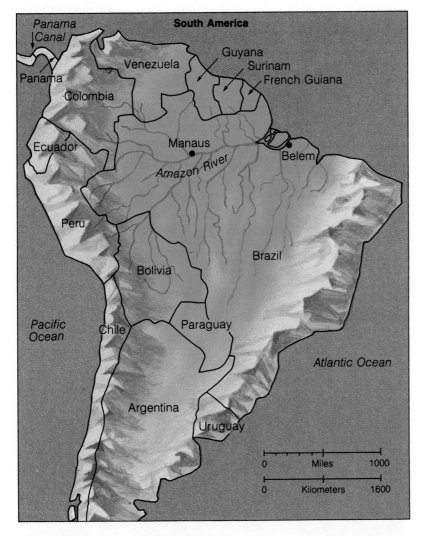

Figure 7-8. Most of Brazil serves as a source of runoff for the Amazon River. What is the name of the entire area that serves as a source of runoff for a river system?
The area that serves as a source of runoff for a river system is called a watershed.

If possible, have students trace the rivers and streams of the Amazon's watershed (or any other large watershed) on a relief map.

Critical Thinking

Predict what would happen to the Amazon River watershed if the tropical rainforests were cut down.

Answers will vary but should relate to increased runoff and less water being absorbed.

system of streams and other tributaries, is called a **watershed.** Figure 7-8 shows the watershed for the Amazon River, which is over 6000 km long. As you can see from the map, most of Brazil serves as a watershed for the Amazon.

Check yourself

1. Compare streams and sheet runoff. How are they similar? How are they different?
2. Describe a watershed in terms of boundaries and function.

1. Streams and sheet runoff are similar in that both are examples of water running off the surface. They are different because in a stream the runoff flows in channels.
2. A watershed is an entire area from which runoff collects and flows, eventually, to the sea.

Perspiration is also a temperature-regulating device. As water evaporates on the surface of the skin, it absorbs heat from the body's surface. (As mentioned in Chapter 5, water takes in from its surroundings its heat of vaporization in order to change from a liquid to a gas [that is, to evaporate].)

Figure 7-9. Through a certain process, an acre of growing corn can cause 1.8 million liters of water to enter the atmosphere as water vapor in a single growing season. What is this process called?
This process is called transpiration.

Water leaves the earth's surface
New vocabulary: transpiration

Water rises from the earth as a gas, or vapor. As you read these words, water is evaporating from many of the surfaces around you—and on you!

Water evaporates from the surface of your skin. The human body is constantly getting rid of moisture through small openings, called pores, in the skin. But this moisture, which is called perspiration, is noticeable only when it builds up on the skin.

Through transpiration, an enormous amount of water vapor is released into the atmosphere over forests, jungles, and fields of growing farm crops.

Most of the time, this moisture is removed from the skin by evaporation.

As green plants make food, they give off water vapor to the atmosphere through small openings in their leaves. This process in plants is called **transpiration** (tran′-spuh-RAY′-shun). It is estimated that a typical acre of growing corn can, through transpiration, cause 1.8 million liters of water to enter the atmosphere as water vapor in a single growing season. (For some trees, you can double the amount given for the growing corn.) Since growing trees and plants use sunlight to make food and since sunlight is strongest in the summertime, the amount of water that enters the atmosphere through transpiration is greatest in the summer.

Water evaporates from the surface of the earth, sometimes before you even realize it's there. You've probably seen it rain and right after the rain stops the streets and sidewalks are dry. This usually happens when the streets are very hot and the air has a low humidity. A strong wind will also speed the evaporation of water from the surface of the earth back into the atmosphere.

Sometimes the water falling from a cloud evaporates before it reaches the earth. It is not uncommon to see rain falling from a cloud but never reaching the surface of the earth. This can be seen frequently in dry regions such as the southwestern United States.

Water also evaporates from the area just below the surface of soil. After a rain, the soil is moist. But if soil goes for a long time without water, it dries out. Any particles of liquid water in the spaces among the grains of soil evaporate. They change to water vapor and enter the atmosphere. The surface soil is then left without moisture and must wait for the next rainstorm. In a desert area, evaporation from the soil occurs soon after the storm passes. In other areas, evaporation is not so rapid.

Check yourself

1. Describe two ways in which water leaves the surface of the earth.

2. How do heat, low relative humidity, and wind affect the rate at which water evaporates?

Critical Thinking

Where would air be more humid, over a cornfield or over a paved parking lot?

Air over a cornfield would be more humid due to transpiration.

Library research

See if you can find out how water was formed on the earth. Also, do other planets have water? If so, which ones. What is the evidence for such conclusions?

Interested students can find out more about transpiration and how evaporation is also involved in the process of transpiration.

1. Water evaporates from surfaces on the earth. Water vapor is given off by plants through the process of transpiration.
2. Heat, low relative humidity, and wind all increase the rate of evaporation.

Two 5-minute sessions

Groups of 4

Activity 7-1B Observing Transpiration from a Plant

Materials

potted plant (coleus or
  geranium works best)
large plastic bag with tie

Purpose

To see evidence of the part transpiration plays in the water cycle.

Procedure

1. Take the plastic bag and place it over the plant. Using the tie, seal the bag tightly around the stem of the plant so that no air gets in. Leave the bag over the plant overnight.
2. The next day, observe the bag around your plant. Describe what you see on a data chart like the one on this page.
3. Remove the plastic bag, put a new bag around the plant, and repeat the experiment.
4. Repeat over several more days if you wish.

Questions

1. What change happened after the plant's first night in the bag? What do you think caused the change?
2. What change(s) happened after the plant's second night in the bag? How does what you observe compare with the results after the first night? Also describe any changes in the plant.

Conclusion

Explain what you observed.

Data Chart							
Observation Number	Date	Time	Temperature in °C	Location of Plant	Description of Condensation on Inside of Bag	Changes, if any, in Plant(s)	Mass of Bag and Its Contents
1							
2							
3							
4							
5							

Conclusion
In the process of transpiration, water vapor passes out of the leaves of a plant through tiny openings.

Section 1 Review Chapter 7

Use **Reading Checksheet 7-1** TRB page 79
Skillsheet 7-1 TRB page 121
Section Reviewsheet 7-1 TRB pages 179–180
Section Testsheet 7-1 TRB page 293

Check Your Vocabulary

2 condense	11 sheet runoff
12 divide	9 stream
3 evaporate	7 swamp
1 freeze	15 transpiration
5 glacier	13 tributaries
6 lake	4 water cycle
10 pond	14 watershed
8 runoff	

Match each term above with the numbered phrase that best describes it.

1. To change from a liquid to a solid

2. To change from a gas to a liquid

3. To change from a liquid to a gas

4. The process by which water is continually recycling between the earth's surface and the atmosphere; also called the hydrologic cycle

5. A moving mass of ice and snow

6. A body of water that collects in a hole or depression in the earth's surface; larger and deeper than a pond

7. A low-lying water-soaked marsh or bog that forms when a lake or pond fills with sediment and vegetation

8. Water that flows off the earth's surface

9. Runoff that flows in a channel between banks of soil, rock, or other material

10. A body of water that is smaller and shallower than a lake

11. Water that has no channels to direct its flow as it runs off the earth's surface

12. The highest land that separates the direction in which water will run off the earth's surface

13. Streams and small rivers that empty into one large river system

14. All the land that drains into a river, with its system of streams and other tributaries

15. The process by which green plants, as they make food, give off water vapor through small openings in their leaves

Check Your Knowledge

Multiple Choice: Choose the answer that best completes each of the following sentences.

1. Water vapor is a ? .
   a) solid   c) crystal
   b) liquid   d) gas

2. Water freezes at ? .
   a) 100°C   c) 20°C
   b) 50°C   d) 0°C

3. Most of the earth's fresh water supply is found in the form of ? .
   a) vapor   c) ice
   b) liquid   d) lakes

4. Water returns to the earth's surface through the process of ? .
   a) transpiration   c) boiling
   b) evaporation   d) precipitation

Check Your Understanding

1. Describe different places where fresh water is found. For each, tell in what state of matter the water occurs.

2. Trace the steps that occur in the water cycle.

3. Describe four things that can happen to water that falls to the earth's surface.

4. Where would water vapor from transpiration be greater—over a desert or over a forest? Explain.

5. Spring rains and melting snow and ice cause the flooding of a river hundreds of kilometers downstream. Explain why this happens.

Water in the Ground   Section 2

Learner Objectives
1. To distinguish between porosity and permeability.
2. To identify zones of water in the ground.
3. To distinguish among the ways in which water comes out of the ground.

Section 2 of Chapter 7 is divided into four parts:

Pore spaces in rock and soil

Water soaks into the ground

Zones of water in the ground

Water comes out of the ground

Figure 7-10. Most of the earth's liquid fresh water is found in the ground. Springs like the one shown in the picture are fed from this underground water supply. What evidence can students offer of water in the ground near the place where they live? Is there a place where water passes down into the ground? Is there a place where it is obvious that the ground is water soaked (for example, a swamp)? Is there a place where water comes out of the ground in the form of a spring?

What indirect evidence can students offer for water in the ground (for example, plants that need water)? How do differing types of vegetation indicate amount of water (for example, cottonwoods or willows growing only along a stream/stream bed)?

Students can observe various kinds of sand under a magnifying glass. Grains of construction sand, for example, will probably not be so rounded or so even in size. Differences are caused by weathering processes (Chapter 9).

Think of all the freshwater lakes in the world. All together they certainly contain a huge amount of water. Or think of all the fresh water that is contained in the rivers of the world, including the Mississippi and the Nile and the Amazon. Once again, you are thinking of a very large amount of water.

Would you say that most of the earth's liquid fresh water is found in its lakes or in its rivers? Or would you say that most of the earth's liquid fresh water is found neither in lakes nor in rivers, but in a third place? If you chose a third place, you would be correct. Most of the earth's liquid fresh water is found in the ground. In fact, there is fifty times more liquid fresh water below ground than there is in all the lakes, rivers, and streams on the earth's surface.

How does all this water get into the ground? Does it stay in one place once it gets under the ground? Does it ever come back out of the ground? If so, what makes it do this?

Pore spaces in rock and soil
New vocabulary: infiltration, pore spaces, porosity

Water can soak into or flow into a material only when there are openings or spaces in the material and when the spaces are not already filled with water. The earth's land surface is made up of different materials. In some places, it is covered with soil. In other places, it is covered with sand or gravel or rock.

Suppose you took a graduated cylinder and filled it with sand up to the 50-mL mark. What would happen if you then poured water into the same cylinder? Could you add water without going above the 50-mL mark? If you said yes, you are correct. The water that you add will sink into the sand. This process, in which water sinks down into the ground, is called **infiltration.**

If you've ever seen sand, you know that it is made up of individual grains. If you look at grains of sand under a magnifying glass (see Figure 7-11), you will notice that the grains are rounded. You will also notice that the grains are more or less the same size. If you fill a container with round-shaped particles, there will be spaces between the particles, as shown in Figure 7-12. You can see this very easily by looking at a glass full of marbles.

Point out to students that they are now considering only liquid fresh water (the third location, "on or under land" and 0.635% by volume, as indicated in Table 7-1 on page 337). A consideration of only liquid fresh water eliminates both ocean water (97.2% by volume) and solid water in icecaps and glaciers (2.15% by volume).

The questions in the last paragraph of this introduction will be answered in this section of Chapter 7. They appear here mainly to get students thinking about these matters and to discuss what they think the answers are.

Figure 7-11. Spaces enable water to pass through sand.

Figure 7-12. Pore spaces among round-shaped particles of loose materials can account for about one third of the total volume.

To illustrate porosity, fill a beaker or graduate with marbles to the 100-mL mark. Then see how much water can be added without going over the 100-mL mark.

Library research

Some people claim they can find underground water with a stick. This is called water witching or dowsing. Prepare a report on this technique of finding water. Do you think it is scientific? Support your reasoning.

To show that sandstone is porous, mass a piece of dry sandstone. Then let it soak overnight, or several days, in water. Pat it dry and measure its mass again. Any added mass is due to water that infiltrated the rock.

Porosity is only one of the factors that affect infiltration. Infiltration is also affected by 1) slope of the land, 2) whether pore spaces are already filled with water, and 3) whether the ground is loose or hard-packed.

1. 1) There must be pore spaces in the material, and 2) the pore spaces must not already be filled with water.
2. Water will infiltrate sandstone more because sandstone most likely contains pore spaces, whereas granite consists of interlocking crystals.

What does it mean to say that sand has a high permeability?

The open spaces between particles of sand or soil are called **pore spaces.** The total volume of the pore spaces in a certain volume of material is called its **porosity.** The porosity of sand is about 35%. That means that in 50 mL of sand, there is about 17.5 mL of open pore spaces.

It is easy to recognize that loose soil, sand, and gravel have pore spaces and are therefore porous. But what about rock? Can rock also be porous? The answer is yes, but the degree of porosity varies with the kind of rock. Sandstone, for example, is quite porous. It is made of particles of sand that are cemented together by some mineral. Frequently there are pore spaces between the sand grains and the cementing material. Other kinds of rock, such as granite, which may consist of interlocking crystals or tightly pressed layers, will have a very low porosity or no porosity at all.

Check yourself

1. What two conditions are needed in order for water to be able to infiltrate a material?

2. Into which rock will more water infiltrate, sandstone or granite? Explain your answer.

Water soaks into the ground
New vocabulary: permeability

Water does not infiltrate into all materials at the same rate. Water will infiltrate into a dry sandy soil almost immediately. But water may form a puddle on top of a clay soil, infiltrating into that kind of soil very slowly. Because water can flow quickly down through sand, we say that sand has a high **permeability.** Permeability is the ease with which water flows through a material. The higher the permeability, the faster a liquid can pass through the material.

Porosity and permeability are closely related, but they are different. A rock with a high porosity does not necessarily have a high permeability. Some sediments, such as clay, can have a high porosity and a low permeability. This is because permeability depends on the number and size of the pore spaces and whether these pore spaces are interconnected.

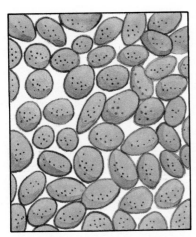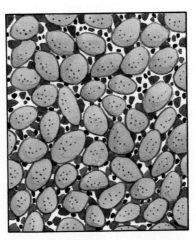

Figure 7-13. Particles of silt and clay may be many times smaller than sand particles. When they fill the pore spaces among sand particles (as shown in the picture on the right), they greatly reduce the permeability of the material.

In nature, soil can contain some round-shaped materials. It also probably contains irregularly shaped materials like clay, which is made up of flat, irregular particles that may be many times smaller than sand particles. Because of the varying amounts of materials of different sizes and shapes in soils, the number and size of pore spaces will vary.

Another factor that affects the size of pore spaces and permeability is packing. Water will pass much more quickly through loosely packed soil than it will through soil that is tightly packed. When soil is tightly packed, the flat particles of clay can fit together almost like a jigsaw puzzle. Water passes through such material very slowly, if at all. The soil becomes more tightly packed as the distance below the surface increases. It becomes more tightly packed at greater depths because the weight of the overlying materials pressing down on it is greater.

Pore spaces are not always needed for high permeability. A rock such as basalt or granite is not very porous. But if it has cracks in it, and the cracks are interconnected, water can pass through very rapidly. Basalt, granite, and other such kinds of rock would have a low porosity but a high permeability.

Check yourself

1. Describe a situation in which a material has a high porosity but a low permeability.

2. Describe a situation in which a material has a low porosity but a high permeability.

This is also true in regions where blasting has taken place, such as along highways.

1. A material can have a high porosity because it contains many pore spaces, but it may have a low permeability because the pore spaces are very small or because the pore spaces are not interconnected.

2. A material can have a low porosity because it contains few pore spaces, but it can be very permeable because of interconnected cracks that run through the material.

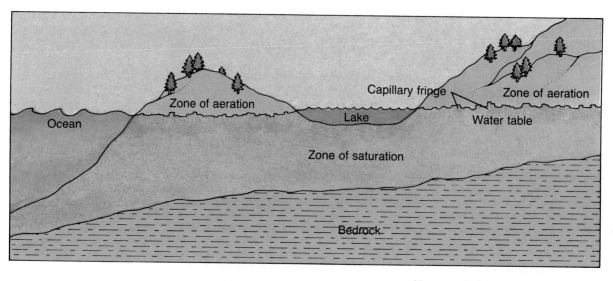

Figure 7-14. In the zone of saturation, the pore spaces are filled with water. What do the pore spaces in the zone of aeration contain?
Pore spaces in the zone of aeration contain both air and water.

To demonstrate water in the soil, you might mass a quantity of damp soil. Then heat the soil in a pie tin over a hot plate, find the mass of the soil again, and determine the amount that was water. Try again right after a rainfall and after a long period of no rain.

New vocabulary: ground water, zone of aeration, adhesion, impermeable, zone of saturation, water table, capillary action, cohesion, capillary fringe

Zones of water in the ground

The water that infiltrates the earth's surface becomes part of the huge supply of water stored in the ground. It is called **ground water.** Gravity acts on ground water, pulling it downward through the pore spaces, cracks, and other openings in the ground.

The amount of water in soil often varies, depending on the depth of the soil below the surface. After a rain has soaked into the ground, the layer of soil near the surface is usually moist, but not soaking wet. Most of the rainwater has passed down through the pore spaces of this layer and is in a lower layer of soil. But some water does remain behind, clinging to the soil particles at or near the surface. This layer of the soil is known as the **zone of aeration** (see Figure 7-14) because the pore spaces in this layer contain air as well as water.

Water clings to soil particles in the zone of aeration because water molecules are attracted to many other kinds of molecules. This attraction of water molecules to other kinds of molecules is called **adhesion.** It is this process of adhesion that keeps the soil in the zone of aeration damp long after it rains.

As long as the ground is permeable, gravity will pull ground water deeper into the earth. But at some point the ground water reaches a layer of soil or rock that is **impermeable,** or not *(im-)* permeable. It allows no water to pass through. This is known as the impermeable layer.

Once the descending ground water hits an impermeable layer (the bedrock in Figure 7-14), it begins to collect there. Ground water will fill up the pore spaces above the impermeable layer. As the pore spaces fill with water, the soil or permeable rock becomes saturated. This saturated layer of soil or permeable rock is known as the **zone of saturation.**

If you pour 10 mL of water into a cylinder containing 50 mL of sand, some of the water will gradually sink to the bottom of the cylinder, which is impermeable. Some of the water will adhere to the sand, making it damp. The descending water will then form a zone of saturation. After all water has descended to the zone of saturation, there will be a boundary where the water-filled zone of saturation meets the layer of particles above it. This boundary, which is the top of the zone of saturation, is called the **water table.**

Some water in the soil moves upward, against the downward pull of gravity. This upward movement of water in soil is called **capillary action.** You have probably seen examples of capillary action, but never realized what it was. Have you ever seen water soaked up by a sponge, a paper towel, or a blotter? If you have, then you have observed capillary action. You can observe capillary action at home by taking a small amount of water, placing the end of a paper towel in the water, and watching what happens.

Capillary action is caused by both cohesion and adhesion. **Cohesion** is the attraction of one molecule to another molecule of the same kind. Adhesion, as already mentioned, is the attraction of one molecule to a molecule of a different kind. By the process of adhesion, water molecules at the top of the water table are attracted to molecules of the soil particles above. Then, when water molecules have attached themselves to molecules of soil particles, they attract other water molecules to themselves by the process of cohesion.

In soil, these forces of adhesion and cohesion lift a little water upward from the zone of saturation to the **capillary fringe,** an area which is just above the water table. (See Figure 7-14).

The damp soil in the zone of aeration receives its moisture

Due to particle size, shape, and packing, the amount of water that can be added may vary.

Library research

Scientists have calculated how much water empties into the sea from the major rivers of the world. See if you can find this information. Make a list of these rivers and their discharge.

What causes capillary action?

To demonstrate capillary action, you could put a cut flower or a stalk of celery in water containing food coloring. The colored water will be drawn up into the flower or the celery stalk.

356

Science Processes: Defining operationally; Experimenting
See also Activity Record Sheet 7-2A (Lab Manual page 97)

20 minutes   Groups of 4, or demonstration

Activity 7-2A   Observing the Cohesion of Water Molecules

Materials

pie tin
fork
several needles
soap or detergent (granular)
beaker
water
eyedropper

Purpose

To see if you can make a needle stay on the surface of water.

Procedure

1. Put a beaker in the middle of a pie tin. Fill the beaker with water. When the water is just about even with the top of the beaker, stop.
2. Using the eyedropper, add more water to the beaker. Continue until the water is above the top of the beaker.
3. Place the needle on the fork and hold the fork so that the needle is horizontal. Try to make the needle "float" on the water by gently lowering the fork and needle to the surface of the water.
4. It is important to lay the needle on the water as gently and evenly as possible. Also, it may be necessary to make several attempts before you get a needle to stay on the surface of the water.

5. Once you get a needle to stay on the surface, begin adding a few grains of soap powder.

Questions

1. What might explain why you can add water above the edge of the beaker? Review page 355.
2. What keeps the needle from sinking to the bottom?
3. What happens to the needle when you add soap powder?

Conclusion

What did the soap powder do to the cohesion of the water molecules?

Answers to Questions
1. Cohesion, the attraction of one molecule to other molecules of the same kind, enables the water level to go above the top of the beaker without spilling over.
2. The attraction of water molecules to each other is also strong enough to support a horizontal needle placed so gently on the surface of the water that

the cohesion is not disturbed.
3. The needle sinks.
Conclusion
When soap powder is added to the water, the cohesion of the water molecules is weakened and the needle can no longer be supported on the surface.

from water that infiltrates down from the surface. The soil particles in the capillary fringe get their moisture from the zone of saturation by capillary action. If the pore spaces in the capillary fringe are small, the water will rise higher than if the pore spaces are large. The height of the capillary fringe ranges from about 2.5 cm or less in sands and gravels to as much as 60 cm or more in silty soils.

Check yourself

1. What is found in the pore spaces in the zone of aeration? in the capillary fringe? in the zone of saturation?

2. Describe what happens as a result of adhesion and cohesion in the capillary fringe.

1. In the zone of aeration, air and water; in the capillary fringe, water and air; in the zone of saturation, water (except for bubbles of trapped air)

2. Because of adhesion, water molecules on the surface of the water table are attracted to molecules of the soil particles above. By cohesion, the water molecules that have attached themselves to soil particles attract other water molecules.

Water comes out of the ground

New vocabulary; spring, artesian system, aquifer, artesian spring, geyser

In general, the water table is more or less parallel to the earth's surface. But if, as shown in Figure 7-14, the ground slopes or the impermeable layer slopes, then gravity will cause ground water to move toward the lowest level. This movement of ground water usually is very slow because of the small size of the underground pore spaces and interconnections through which it must pass.

Springs   If the water table intersects the earth's surface on a slope, the water will flow onto the surface of the land. The place where ground water flows out of the ground is called a **spring.** Sometimes the water from springs collects in hollows or basins to form marshes, ponds, and lakes. If the springs are located in the hollow, then the place where the springs come out of the ground is under the water. Many ponds and lakes are fed by underwater springs.

A spring can also feed water into a stream. This happens when the spring is not located in a hollow or basin. Then the water runs downhill off the surface, finding or creating a channel over a period of time.

What is a spring?

Science Processes: Formulating models
See also Activity Record Sheet 7-2B (Lab Manual page 98)

CORE   20 minutes   Demonstration or large groups

Activity 7-2B   Simulating the Water Table

Materials

jar
sand
gravel
water
grease pencil or
    masking tape

Purpose

To build a model of a water table.

Procedure

1. Fill the jar with a mixture of sand and gravel, using any proportions of sand and gravel that you choose. Or you may use all sand or all gravel.
2. Slowly pour water onto the mixture (soil) in the jar. Wait a few minutes. While waiting, observe what happens to the water you just poured onto the soil.
3. Add more water until a section of the soil near the bottom of the jar is saturated.
4. Wait until all the water has had a chance to sink in. With a grease pencil or strip of tape, mark the jar at the place that separates the saturated soil from the rest of the soil.
5. On a piece of paper, make a diagram of the jar. Label each of the following: impermeable layer, zone of saturation, water table. Also show where you think the capillary fringe and zone of aeration are.
6. Put your jar away and observe it in a day. Check to see if the water table is at the marker.

Questions

1. What do you call the process by which the water sinks down into the soil? How long did it take?
2. What do you call the boundary line between the saturated soil and the rest of the soil?
3. Is the water table at the marker on the second day? What do you think caused the change? How can you prevent the lowering of the water table in the jar?

Conclusion

Does the water table in the earth act like that in your jar? Does the level of the water table affect the community?

Step 1

Step 2

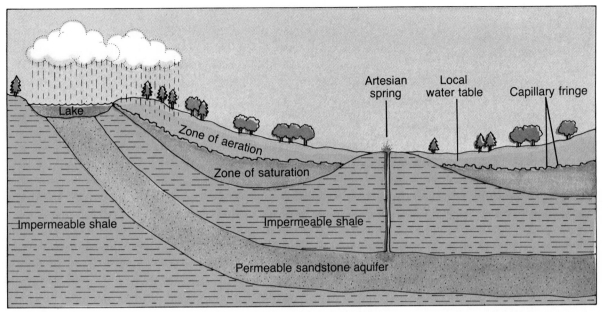

Lake

Zone of aeration

Zone of saturation

Impermeable shale

Impermeable shale

Permeable sandstone aquifer

Artesian spring

Local water table

Capillary fringe

See also Teaching Diagram 7-2 (TRB page 35)

Artesian systems   There is a type of spring that is not fed by water from the local water table. In the states of Kansas, Nebraska, Texas, North Dakota, and South Dakota, there is very little annual rain and snow to supply underground water. Yet this Great Plains region has a good water supply. Where does the water come from?

Beneath this Great Plains region and extending westward to the Rocky Mountains there is a special arrangement of underground rock layers. It is made up of three layers of rock. A middle layer of permeable rock passes between two layers of impermeable rock. This combination of rock layers is called an **artesian system.** A simple artesian system is shown in Figure 7-15. In an artesian system, the middle layer of rock is permeable. Because water passes through this layer, it is called an **aquifer.** The word *aquifer* comes from two Latin words that mean "to carry water." Aquifers are often layers of sandstone or gravel.

Water traveling through an aquifer travels through very small pore spaces in rock. Travel is therefore slow. Depending on the length of the aquifer, it may take hundreds and even thousands of years for water to travel the full length of the aquifer.

Figure 7-15. Why is the middle layer of rock in an artesian system called an aquifer?

Because it is the middle layer that carries the water, and, as mentioned in the text, an aquifer gets its name from two Latin words that mean "to carry water."

As mentioned in the next paragraph, the water comes from the Rocky Mountains.

Library research

Prepare a report on artesian wells and/or the mining of water from deep in the earth. In what areas of the world is water stored deep in aquifers? (Some water dates back to the Ice Ages.) What is the danger of entering such aquifers in search of water?

The downward flow of water in an aquifer is affected by gravity, as water seeks the lowest level. It is also affected by hydrostatic pressure caused by the weight of overlying water.

Artesian water is usually very pure. The aquifer serves as a filter and the impermeable layer(s) above the aquifer prevents polluted ground water from entering the aquifer. Artesian water is also usually cool, since it is from melted snow and ice and has been deep underground where temperatures are not affected by the sun's rays.

If people know where artesian systems are located, they will often sink wells to draw the water to the surface. As they have found out in Long Island, New York, however, this is a dangerous process, because once the impermeable layer(s) above the aquifer is penetrated, polluted water from above can then enter the aquifer and pollute the water in the aquifer from that point on.

What is an artesian spring?

Students can use a dictionary to find the origin of the word *geyser*.

The top and bottom layers of an artesian system are impermeable. These two layers of impermeable rock, between which the aquifer passes, prevent water from leaving the aquifer once the water enters it. Shale, a rock formed from particles of clay and silt, is practically impermeable. Shale is commonly found in artesian sytems.

The collecting area of an artesian system can be very far away. In the case of the sandstone aquifer (known as the Dakota sandstone) that brings water to the Great Plains, the collecting area is in the Rocky Mountains. Much of the water that enters the aquifer in the Rocky Mountains is from the snow that melts in the springtime. The water is very cool and pure.

Artesian springs   The water that enters the aquifer in the Rocky Mountains is at much higher levels than the Great Plains. The water flows downward through the aquifer because of the force of gravity. This downward flow and the weight of the water force the water in the aquifer to the surface wherever there is a crack or break in the layer of impermeable rock above the aquifer. The flow of water from an aquifer is called an **artesian spring.** Due to pressure in the aquifer, water from an artesian spring sometimes gushes up above the surface like a fountain.

Geysers   Sometimes water erupts from the earth in a spectacular way. In areas of volcanic activity, ground water may sink to great depths through very deep cracks. Here it is heated by hot magma or by hot igneous rocks. Because the pressure is much greater at these depths, the boiling point of water is raised well above 100°C. Suddenly, the superheated water changes to steam that forces the water resting on it out through openings in the rock above. Such an eruption is called a **geyser.**

Geysers can be found in New Zealand, Iceland, and Yellowstone National Park in Wyoming. One of the best known geysers is Old Faithful in Yellowstone National Park, which sends about 40 kL of water as high as 45 m into the air with each eruption. Old Faithful got its name because the time of each eruption used to be fairly predictable, erupting about once

Figure 7-16. A geyser is a spring of hot water and steam that gushes out of the ground. Where does the water in a geyser obtain its heat?
From hot magma and hot igneous rocks deep within the earth's crust

Library research

Find out how the flow of streams is measured. Explain these techniques to the class. How is the speed and volume measured? Why would a scientist want to know this information?

Geysers are self-destructive. The hot water dissolves minerals in the surrounding rock layers, causing the formation to collapse.

1. The place where the water enters the aquifer is at a higher elevation than the place where the spring is located. (Students' diagrams should show this.)
2. Similar: Both are means by which water comes out of the ground. Different: In an artesian spring, water is forced upward because of the water level in the aquifer; in a geyser, water is forced up by steam caused by heat within the earth's crust.

every 65 minutes. Most geysers, however, are very irregular in the time of their eruptions.

Check yourself

1. What causes an artesian spring to gush up out of the ground? Draw a diagram that shows this.

2. Compare an artesian spring and a geyser. How are they similar? How are they different?

Careers   Hydrologist / Heavy-Equipment Operator

For further information about a career as a heavy-equipment operator, contact:

Associated Builders and Contractors
729 15th Street NW
Washington, DC 20005

International Union of Operating Engineers
1125 17th Street NW
Washington, DC 20036

Hydrologists use instruments to measure the flow of water in streams and rivers.

For further information about a career as a hydrologist, contact:
  American Geological Institute
  5202 Leesburg Pike
  Falls Church, Virginia 22041

Hydrologist Hydrologists are scientists that map and measure water flow to and from bodies of water such as rivers and lakes. With increases in the use of water by industry and by an expanding population, many companies will be adding water experts to their staffs to advise on water problems such as how to obtain clean water, how to recycle water, and how to handle liquid wastes.

Hydrologists study the occurrence and movement of water on and below the surface of the earth. They work on problems of how to control it and develop it for use by people and industry. For example, some hydrologists work on projects such as water resources, irrigation, flood control, and soil erosion.

Students desiring to enter this career should be in good physical health and enjoy working out of doors. Biological, earth, and physical sciences should be taken in high school. Several higher level mathematics courses are also required.

The minimum requirement for entering this field is a Bachelor of Arts or Bachelor of Science degree in one of the physical or geological sciences. Graduate degrees are required for those wishing to advance in the field or for positions in research, teaching, or administration.

Heavy-equipment operators use backhoes to dig trenches for underground water pipes.

Heavy-Equipment Operator (Water Department) When a home or business needs new or additional water service, or when a pipe between a water main and a building must be repaired, the water department of the city or town does the work.

A water department crew usually consists of a supervisor, two laborers, two plumbers, and a heavy-equipment operator (HEO). HEOs primarily operate backhoes and truck cranes. A backhoe is used to dig trenches and a crane is used to put pipes into place.

HEOs must be skilled, well-coordinated, and alert. One way in which you might learn the skills of an HEO is through a union apprenticeship program in the construction industry. To be eligible for a water department HEO position, you must pass a civil service exam. You should check with your city or town, or with your state civil service office, for information about the exam.

Section 2 Review   Chapter 7

Use **Reading Checksheet 7-2** TRB page 80
Skillsheet 7-2 TRB page 122
Section Reviewsheet 7-2 TRB pages 181–182
Section Testsheet 7-2 TRB page 294

Check Your Vocabulary

7 adhesion	8 impermeable
16 aquifer	1 infiltration
17 artesian spring	4 permeability
15 artesian system	2 pore spaces
11 capillary action	3 porosity
13 capillary fringe	14 spring
12 cohesion	10 water table
18 geyser	6 zone of aeration
5 ground water	9 zone of saturation

Match each term above with the numbered phrase that best describes it.

1. The process by which water sinks into the ground

2. Spaces between particles of sand or soil

3. The total volume of the pore spaces in a certain volume of material

4. How easily water flows through a material

5. Water that has infiltrated the earth

6. The layer of soil between the water table and the earth's surface

7. The attraction of water molecules to other kinds of molecules

8. Allowing no water to pass through

9. The layer of soil below the water table

10. The boundary between the zone of aeration and the zone of saturation

11. The upward movement of water in soil due to adhesion and cohesion

12. The attraction of one molecule to another molecule of the same kind

13. An area just above the water table that receives its moisture by capillary action

14. The place where ground water flows out of the ground because the water table has intersected the earth's surface

15. A combination of rock layers in which water passes downward through an aquifer

16. A layer of permeable rock through which water travels

17. A natural flow of water from an artesian system

18. The eruption from the ground of water and steam that has been heated by hot magma or rocks in the earth's crust

Check Your Knowledge

Multiple Choice: Choose the answer that best completes each of the following sentences.

1. Because of _?_, ground water flows toward the lowest level.
   a) gravity   c) capillary action
   b) impermeability   d) shale and clay

2. An aquifer is often a layer of _?_.
   a) shale   c) clay
   b) sandstone   d) bedrock

3. Water travels through an aquifer _?_.
   a) quickly   c) very slowly
   b) fairly quickly   d) as steam

Check Your Understanding

1. What three factors affect permeability?

2. What three factors affect porosity?

3. Why is the water table not permanent in its location?

4. Explain why heavy rains have no effect on an artesian spring.

5. In which earth material would water rise higher by capillary action—particles of small size or of large size? Explain your answer.

Chapter 7 Review

See also **Chapter Testsheets 7A and 7B**
TRB pages 329–330.

Concept Summary

In the **water cycle,** water is continually recycled between the earth's surface and the atmosphere, changing form (through evaporation, condensation, and freezing) because of different atmospheric conditions.
☐ Water on the earth is found in all three states of matter.
☐ When water evaporates, it changes from a liquid to a gas (also called vapor).
☐ When water condenses, it changes from a gas to a liquid or solid.
☐ When water freezes, it changes from a liquid to a solid.
☐ On a worldwide basis, the water cycle is a balanced system in which just as much water leaves the earth's surface as returns to it.

Infiltration is the process by which water sinks into the ground.
☐ The rate at which water can infiltrate a material depends upon its porosity and permeability.

Porosity is the total volume of the pore spaces in a material.
☐ The porosity of a material is affected by the shape of the particles, the size of the particles, and how tightly the particles are packed together.
☐ Even rock can be porous, but the degree of porosity of a rock varies with the kind of rock. (Sandstone, for example, is quite porous.)

Permeability is the ease with which water flows through a material.
☐ The permeability of a material is affected by the number of pore spaces, the size of the pore spaces, and whether the pore spaces are interconnected.
☐ An aquifer is a layer of permeable rock (often sandstone) between layers of impermeable rock.
☐ The flow of water through an aquifer, even though quite permeable, can be very slow.

Putting It All Together

1. Describe each of the different states of water. Explain what causes water to change from one state to another.
2. Draw a diagram that shows what happens in the water cycle, using labels as needed.
3. Draw a diagram that traces water from precipitation out of a cloud to water in a river entering the ocean. Label the main parts of a river runoff system.
4. Where on the earth is water, in each of its physical states, found?
5. What are tributaries? How do they function in a watershed system?
6. Draw a diagram that shows the different zones of water in the ground.
7. Describe the capillary action that occurs in soil beneath the earth's surface.
8. Draw a diagram of an artesian system. Include an artesian spring.
9. Explain how water can travel through a rock. In your explanation, include the terms *porous, permeable,* and *impermeable.*
10. How and why are geysers related to volcanic activity?

Apply Your Knowledge

1. How is the water cycle important to the earth as an environment for life?
2. How are the water cycle and climate related? Describe variations that you would expect within the water cycle from one climate zone to another.
3. How can freezing temperatures affect the rate at which water infiltrates the ground?
4. In what ways can floods be prevented?
5. Explain how the nature of the earth's surface determines the amount of precipitation that will infiltrate the ground and become ground water.

Find Out on Your Own

1. What major river do you live closest to? Make a list of all the rivers and large streams that are its tributaries. Make a map of the watershed for your river, showing the river, its tributaries, and any divides.
2. Using earth materials such as sand, clay, and gravel, construct a working model of an artesian system and an artesian well. Explain the parts and their functions to the class.
3. Measure the flow of a stream. You can find the velocity of a stream by floating a cork a known distance and timing it. Try this during wet and dry periods. Report your findings to the class.
4. Visit a nearby lake or pond. Find out how it was formed. Is there any evidence that the lake was higher or lower than it was when you observed it? Is the lake filling in with sediments and plants? Where does the lake get its water? Prepare a report that answers such questions.

Reading Further

Arnov, Boris. *Water: Experiments to Understand It.* New York: William Morrow, 1980.
Thirteen experiments with exceptional drawings demonstrate the properties of water.

Bauer, Ernst. *Wonders of the Earth.* New York: Franklin Watts, 1978.
This book describes many water features, including geysers, waterfalls, and caves. It has excellent illustrations and maps.

Bramwell, Martyn. *Glaciers and Ice Caps.* New York: Franklin Watts, 1986.
Filled with excellent illustrations, this book presents a vast amount of information about glaciers and ice caps.

Dickinson, Jane. *Wonders of Water.* Mahwah, NJ: Troll, 1984.
This book discusses the water cycle and uses of water in a way that is very easy to understand.

Emil, Jane. *All About Rivers.* Mahwah, NJ: Troll Associates, 1984.
With colorful diagrams, this book discusses many aspects of the geology of rivers. These include how and where a river begins, erosion, drainage basins, deltas, the Continental Divide, and flooding.

Leopold, Luna, and Kenneth Davis. *Water.* The Life Science Library. New York: Time Incorporated, 1977.
This book describes the nature of water, what it does, and how it is used by people.

Radlauer, Ruth, and Lisa Sue Gitkin. *The Power of Ice.* Chicago: Childrens Press, 1985.
This is an enjoyable book written by a teenager who spent her summers doing research in Alaska. Its discussion of glaciers and continental ice sheets is enhanced by excellent photographs.

Reisner, Marc. *Cadillac Desert: The American West and Its Disappearing Water.* New York: Viking Penguin, 1986.
This book describes the fast-disappearing Ogalala aquifer in the American West. It discusses past and future solutions to the problems of water control.

Chapter 8 The Ocean

Student Resources		Meeting Individual Needs
Student Text	**Laboratory Activities**	
Section 1 The Bottom of the Ocean 368–384		
The Major Oceans 369–370		
Marginal Seas 370–372		
Sounding the Ocean Bottom 372–373	Investigation 8-1 Making Profiles of the Ocean Bottom LM 105	Enrichment
The Topography of the Ocean Bottom 374–381	Activity 8-1A Comparing the Density and Elevation of Floating Objects 378; Activity Record Sheet 8-1A LM 103	CORE
Our Science Heritage: The *Nautilus* and the *Challenger* 375		
Resources of the Ocean Bottom 381–383	Activity 8-1B Taking and Using Soundings 382 Activity Record Sheet 8-1B LM 104	Reinforcement
Section 1 Review 384		
Section 2 Properties of Ocean Water 385–399		
Salinity 386–389	Activity 8-2 Evaporating Salt Water 388 Activity Record Sheet 8-2 LM 107	CORE
Temperature and Density 389–391	Investigation 8-2 Comparing Salinities, Temperatures, and Densities of Water Samples LM 109	Enrichment
Sea Ice 391–394		
Thinking Skill: Analyzing 392		
Water Pressure 394–395		
Water Absorbs Light 395–397		
Resources of Ocean Water 398		
Section 2 Review 399		
Section 3 The Circulation of Ocean Water 400–417		
Directions of Motion in a Wave 401–403	Activity 8-3A Simulating Wave Motion 402 Activity Record Sheet 8-3A LM 111	CORE
The Beginning, Middle, and End of a Wave 404–406		
Careers: Marine Geologist/Computer Operator 405		
Effects of Wave Action 407–408	Investigation 8-3 Wave Action/Sand Movement LM 113–114	Enrichment
Tides 409–411		
Surface Ocean Currents 411–414		
Deep Ocean Circulation 414–415	Activity 8-3B Simulating the Effects of Heat Absorption on the Earth's Surface 416; Activity Record Sheet 8-3B LM 112	Enrichment
	Research Lab 8 Studying Models of Density Currents LM 115–116	Enrichment
Section 3 Review 417		
Chapter 8 Review 418–419		
Science Issues of Today: Aquaculture 420		

8

Teacher Resources		Meeting Individual Needs
Teacher's Edition	**Teacher's Resource Book**	
	Essential Ideas 8-1 EI 49–50	Reinforcement
	Teaching Diagram 8-1A TRB 36	CORE
	Teaching Diagram 8-1B TRB 37	CORE
Demonstration 366C	Overhead Transparency S17	Enrichment
Activity Notes 366D	Overhead Transparency B16	CORE
	Overhead Transparency S18	Enrichment
	Skillsheet 8-1 TRB 123	Enrichment
Activity Notes 366E		
Discussion Idea, Environmental Topic 366F		
Section 1 Review Answers 366F	Reading Checksheet 8-1 TRB 81	Reinforcement
	Section Reviewsheet 8-1 TRB 183–184	CORE
	Section Testsheet 8-1 TRB 295	CORE
Demonstration 366G	Essential Ideas 8-2 EI 51–52	Reinforcement
Activity Notes 366G–366H		
Creative Writing Idea 366H	Teaching Diagram 8-2 TRB 38	CORE
	Overhead Transparency S19	Enrichment
Teaching Thinking Skills 366J		
Discussion Idea; Environmental Topic 366K	Skillsheet 8-2 TRB 124	Reinforcement
Section 2 Review 366K	Reading Checksheet 8-2 TRB 82	Reinforcement
	Section Reviewsheet 8-2 TRB 185–186	CORE
	Section Testsheet 8-2 TRB 296	CORE
	Essential Ideas 8-3 EI 53–54	Reinforcement
Demonstration 366L		
Activity Notes 366M	Teaching Diagram 8-3 TRB 39	CORE
	Projectsheet 8-3 TRB 247	Enrichment
	Overhead Transparency S20	Enrichment
Discussion Idea 366N		
	Skillsheet 8-3 TRB 125	Enrichment
Activity Notes 366N–366P		
Environmental Topic 366P		
Section 3 Review Answers 366P	Reading Checksheet 8-3 TRB 83	Reinforcement
	Section Reviewsheet 8-3 TRB 187–188	CORE
	Section Testsheet 8-3 TRB 297	CORE
Chapter 8 Review Answers 366Q–366R	Chapter 8 Testsheet TRB 331–332	CORE

8

Learner Objectives

1. To distinguish oceans from marginal seas.
2. To describe features that cause marginal seas.
3. To describe main features of the ocean bottom.
4. To relate volcanic activity to features of the ocean bottom.
5. To identify resources of the ocean bottom.

Concept Summary

Oceans and seas cover nearly 71 percent of the earth's surface.
The ocean bottom has a varied topography.

Demonstration

Turbidity Currents Influence Ocean-Bottom Topography

Obtain a clear glass or plastic trough-shaped container or aquarium. Half-fill the container with salt water (35 g sodium chloride per 1 L water) and tilt the container at a 10° to 15° angle. Mix one-half part sand and one-half part sediment (soil will do). Quickly pour the sand-sediment mixture into the salt water at the upper end of the container.

Observe the turbidity current (the murky water disturbance) carrying the mixture down the container. Notice the churning affect of the current, a powerful source of ocean bottom erosion. Point out that as a consequence of this erosion phenomena, deep canyons exist under water, rivaling those on land. Finally, observe the ultimate transport of the mixture to the container's lower end, analogous to the transport of sediment to the abyssal plain.

8-1

Activity Notes

Activity 8-1A

Comparing the Density and Elevation of Floating Objects
page **378**

Purpose   To calculate the density of two different materials and then compare their elevations above water as they float.

- CORE 20 minutes Groups of 4 or teacher demonstration
- **Activity Record Sheet 8-1A** (Lab Manual page 103) can be used to record this activity.
- Science Processes: Measuring; Calculating; Observing; Collecting and analyzing data; Comparing; Inferring.

Procedure Notes

To prevent spillage from overflow, do not fill the tub or container more than halfway with water.

You might have students push each of the floating blocks under the water and note what happens to the water level. Also have them note what happens when the block is released. (When the block is pushed under the water, more water is displaced, and the water level rises. When the block is released, the water level drops.)

Answers to Questions

1. The hardwood block has the greater density.
2. The hardwood block should float lower in the water.

Conclusion

The block of wood that floats lower in the water has greater density.

Going Further

Students might repeat this activity using different concentrations of salt water. (In general, the same objects will float higher in salt water than in fresh water. The greater the concentration of salt, the higher the objects will float.)

Science Background

During the International Geophysical Year 1957–1958, ships from various countries took echo soundings of the ocean's bottoms, discovering canyons, plains, and mountain ridges. These features extend throughout the middle of the oceans.

A remarkable feature of the mid-ocean ridges is the communities found around hydrothermal vents. Scientists first discovered these in 1977 while exploring the Galapagos spreading center in the research diving submersible, Alvin. Since that time, similar colonies have been located elsewhere on the East Pacific Rise along the mid-Atlantic Ridge.

The vents themselves are chimneylike structures called "black smokers." Hot water containing minerals dissolved from the magma below pours out through these vents. When the solution mixes with the cold ocean water, fine particles of iron, copper, and zinc sulfides precipitate (forming the "smoke") and settle out. Like terrestrial hot springs, the vents are surrounded by mineral deposits.

The vent communities make up the only ecosystem known on earth that does not depend on photosynthesis. The food chain is based on bacteria that synthesize food from hydrogen sulfide and carbon dioxide. Some of the animals found there include giant tube worms, "dandelions" (a fluffy yellow jellyfish), and "spaghetti" worms that drape themselves over rocks.

8-1

Student Misconception

It is difficult for students to develop an understanding of the magnitude of sea floor features, such as seamounts and trenches, when many have yet to conceptualize the magnitude of corresponding land features. Seamounts are cone-shaped peaks of volcanic oceans that reach up from the ocean floor. They are, simply said, underwater mountains. Trenches are narrow and steep troughs that border the margins of continents or lines of volcanic islands. These sea floor features are similar to mountains and canyons on land, although the size of these features vary greatly.

Have students investigate the size of various land and sea floor features by building scale models out of clay or papier-mâché (information about the dimensions of earth features can be found in an atlas). Students might then compare these to structures such as houses and skyscrapers to make the scale more relevant.

8-1

Activity Notes

Activity 8-1B

Taking and Using Soundings   page **382**

Purpose   To take soundings of an underwater surface and to use the results to reconstruct its topographic features.

- 30 minutes Groups of 4
- **Activity Record Sheet 8-1B** (Lab Manual page 104) can be used to record this activity.
- Science Processes: Measuring; Recording and analyzing data; Identifying; Recognizing and using spatial relationships; Communicating through a map; Predicting.

Advance Preparation

Prepare mystery underwater surfaces for groups of students to use for their soundings. Do this by placing one or more irregularly shaped submersible objects on the bottom of a square or rectangular waterproof container. You might, for example, use a jar full of water and an upside-down strainer or bowl. Another object that proves a challenge is the kind of dish used for squeezing oranges. Then pour a solution of milk and water into the container until the container is nearly filled with the opaque solution. Use enough milk to make the water so opaque that the objects on the bottom cannot be seen.

Procedure Notes

You might have students compare the method used in this activity with methods used before the development of echo soundings. Discuss the disadvantages of this method in deep ocean waters. (String may not be long enough to reach bottom; dropping string or line and hauling it up could be time consuming, etc.)

Answers to Questions

1. Answers will vary.
2. Answers will vary.

Conclusion

The shape can be determined more precisely by increasing the number of soundings.

Going Further

Obtain data from an oceanography book, encyclopedia, or oceanographic institute that students can use to plot a depth profile of part of the ocean floor. Have students see what features described in the text can be seen from the profile.

Discussion Idea

The Exclusive Economic Zone

In 1983, President Reagan proclaimed that the ocean area extending from a line 3 miles off the coast of the U.S. and its territories out to 200 nautical miles was the Exclusive Economic Zone (EEZ) of this nation. This action gave our nation control over those 3.9 billion acres, an area about twice the total onshore area of the U.S. and its territories, and the impetus to conduct more extensive research of the ocean floor.

The economic significance of the EEZ can be seen in many locations. Off the southern coast of California, ocean basins are formed by tension along the San Andreas fault zone. These basins, some over 20 000 m deep, provide traps for sediment eroded from surrounding ridges. Many such traps are known to have oil reservoirs.

In the valleys of the Gorda and Juan de Fuca rift zones off the coasts of Oregon and Washington, faults provide conduits by which molten rock can rise and reach the sea floor. Cold sea water circulates downward into the hot crust, reacting with the hot rock and leaching from it such elements as manganese, zinc, silver, and cadmium. This now warm, mineral-rich water rises to the sea floor and shoots upward in a plume. This underwater "geyser" is known as a smoker. The minerals precipitate on the walls of the fault conduit and around the vent. Exceedingly high concentrations of economically valuable minerals can be found there.

Environmental Topic

Discuss with the class the effect on the ocean environment of using the ocean as a major food source. For example, Georges Bank, the body of water above the eastern continental shelf of the United States, has long been a vital fishing area. Over the past 5 to 10 years, the number of fish taken from the Georges Bank has declined. This once fertile region now suffers from overfishing. What can be done to prevent such upsets of the ocean ecosystem? Where else can we turn to feed the world's people? Have the class investigate hydroponics, hybrid crops, and fish farming (aquaculture) as sources of food.

Section 1 Review Answers

Check Your Understanding
page **384**

1. Ocean basins are formed mainly of basalt, which has a greater density than the granite and granite gneiss that form the continents.

2. A ping is sent from a ship toward the bottom of the sea. The ping hits the bottom and is reflected back toward the ship. On board the ship, a machine can determine, from the time it took the ping to return to the ship, the total distance the ping traveled. From that total, the distance to the bottom (half the total distance) can be determined.

3. The mid-ocean ridge is a very long, very high, very wide chain of mountains (the biggest on the earth) that extends along the bottom of the major ocean basins. Down the middle of this chain of mountains is a rift valley, where much volcanic activity occurs.

4. The earth is sometimes called the water planet because most of its surface (about 72 percent) is covered by water.

5. Trenches are bordered by volcanic activity (evidenced either by present volcanism or by past eruptions that caused island arcs).

8-1

Properties of Ocean Water

Learner Objectives

1. To explain salinity as a property of water.
2. To describe how salinity and temperature affect density.
3. To explain the conditions necessary for ice to form on the ocean.
4. To describe the photic, disphotic, and aphotic zones of the ocean.
5. To identify resources of ocean water.

Concept Summary

Physical properties of ocean water affect the ocean environment in many ways.

8-2

Demonstration

Characterizing Ocean Water

This first demonstration will show that pressure increases with water depth. Have on hand a piece of rubber tube about a meter long and a centimeter in diameter. Fill with water a bucket or sink that is at least 50 cm deep. Put one end of the hose just under the surface of the water and ask a student to blow bubbles through the tube. The student should find that he or she can do so with little difficulty. Then lower the tube into 50 cm of water and have the student try to blow bubbles. It should be much more difficult.

Explain that the student had to blow harder to overcome the water pressure at the bottom of the bucket. In deeper water, the pressure is greater.

To help students see the impact salinity has on density place an egg in a clear glass of tap water. It will sink to the bottom of the glass.

Pour two or more tablespoons of table salt into the water. As the salt dissolves, the egg will begin to rise.

Explain to students that the salt water of the ocean has some properties different from those of fresh water. They will learn about some of these properties in Chapter 8.

Activity Notes

Activity 8-2

Evaporating Salt Water   page **388**

Purpose   To see what happens when salt water evaporates.

- **CORE** 10 minutes plus brief followup Teacher demonstration or small groups
- **Activity Record Sheet 8-2** (Lab Manual page 107) can be used to record this activity.
- Science Processes: Investigating; Measuring; Observing; Interpreting data; Comparing; Inferring.

Activity Notes (continued)

Advance Preparation

A lightweight container, such as a clean plastic milk or bleach container with the top cut off, will be needed for each group of students. You may wish students to bring these in from home.

Answers to Questions

1. The mass of the container will be greater at the second measurement.
2. The salt from the filter was left in the container after the water evaporated.
3. The salinity at the outset was 35 parts per thousand (which is the average salinity of ocean water).
4. The rate of evaporation could have been speeded up by 1) using heat, 2) increasing the surface area of the solution, and 3) using a smaller sample (e.g., 100 mL of water and 3.5 g of salt and then multiplying the results by 10; this would, however, multiply any experimental error by a factor of 10).

Conclusion

Evaporation can be one cause of an increase in the average salinity of the ocean.

Going Further

You might discuss with students how salt obtained by evaporation can be considered a resource of the ocean. Students might also want to consider how fresh (drinking) water can be obtained from the ocean. Some students might wish to do research about desalination techniques, and report to the class when discussing ocean resources, page 398.

Creative Writing Idea

The following writing assignment may help students recognize the relationship of density and buoyancy.

While visiting in Italy near the Mediterranean Sea, you build a small boat. Describe your boat, including where the water level on the outside of your boat is in the Mediterranean. You decide to take your boat to the Red Sea and the Black Sea. Describe where the water level on your boat is in each of the seas, and explain why it is different in each of them.

Science Background

Although its total salinity varies from place to place, the chemical composition of ocean water is nearly constant. At least 72 chemical elements have been identified in sea water. All but half a dozen of these, however, are present in very small amounts.

Sources of these substances include dissolved chemicals eroded from the earth's crust, solids and gases from volcanic eruptions, and suspended sediments that wash into the water. The U.S. Geological Survey estimates the world's rivers carry 4 billion tons of dissolved salts into the ocean annually. Because the average salinity of the ocean appears to remain constant, a similar amount must be removed from the sea water each year. Most of this is probably deposited as layers of sediment on the ocean floor.

Sea life also plays a role in the mineral balance of salt water. Oysters extract calcium salts from the water to build their shells. Coral reefs are the calcium carbonate skeletons of coral animals built up in layers over millions of years. Diatoms remove silica to construct their "glass" houses. Certain seaweeds concentrate iodine from sea water in their tissues.

8-2

Student Misconception

To many people the oceans represent a vast and unlimited supply of food and raw materials that can be used to support an increasing world population. This is a serious misconception.

The world's oceans are vast, covering nearly three quarters of the earth's surface, but these waters cannot be viewed as an unlimited source of resources. Most of the ocean's resources are renewable, which means that these resources can be replaced through natural cycles. The process is a long-term one, however, sometimes taking thousands of millions of years. In addition, most of the ocean's resources lie within a narrow band along the continental margins. As a result, these resources are susceptible to exploitation or destruction by virtue of their proximity to human activities.

Have students develop a list of ocean resources. The list should include plants, fishes, mammals, fossil fuels, mineral deposits, and dissolved substances. You might also have students locate on a map where these resources are found.

Discuss how human activity affects these resources (overfishing, pollution, etc.). Students can also investigate the time it takes for these resources to renew themselves. Students should leave the discussion with the perception that ocean resources are not limitless and, in fact, will be depleted if we do not regulate their use.

8-2

Teaching Thinking Skills

Analyzing   page 392

Because analysis can be used in different ways, students may have difficulty with the first step of analyzing—determining the purpose of the analysis. If the purpose is clearly determined, the analysis will be more effective.

Advance Preparation

Secure a variety of retractable ball point pens.

Procedure Note

Both *Learning the Skill* and *Applying the Skill* are best done individually. Students should respond to the questions in each activity with written answers. Class discussion may follow.

Possible Student Responses

Typical parts of a retractable ball point pen include the following: ball point, ink cartridge, ink, spring, push button, pocket clip, outer barrel. Not every pen has the same parts. Only a ball point, ink, and ink cartridge are necessary for a pen to write. The lists of relationships between the parts will vary. Possible relationships include the following: ink cartridge holds the ink, ball point spreads the ink on the paper; push button works with spring to retract or expose the point.

The parts of the graph include the following: title, *x* axis, *y* axis, names of axes, measurement units for temperature, measurement units for month, plotted points, and the line connecting the points. (1) The surface temperature in April was 14°C. (2) There was a steady increase in surface temperature between February and August. (3) The maximum surface temperature was 28°C. (4) The temperature rises rapidly during the spring months, more slowly in the summer, and drops in the fall. The temperature is near 0°C in the winter.

Discussion

Discussion should focus on the relationships discovered in the graph. Ask students what the graph shows, and how the parts work together to show it. Point out that the plotted line is both a part of the graph and an exact description of the relationship between surface temperature and time of year. Ask students if the plotted line would make any sense without the rest of the graph's parts.

Going Further

Analyze the weather map on page 302. Ask students how the parts of the map work together, and what the map shows.

Discussion Idea

Ocean Water Supplies More Than Fish

Ask students what items in the classroom or in their homes might have originated in the oceans. (Answers will vary.)

Tell students that, in addition to oil and gas used in vehicles, homes, asnd schools, other petro-chemical products, such as plastic items, may have had their source in the ocean.

Diatomaceous earth, from diatoms—a form of algal plankton—is used in insulating materials, filtration systems, polishes, cosmetics, and even in toothpaste. Hard-shelled plankton are the original source for materials that are used in building and to produce chalk.

Seaweed is sometimes an ingredient in cosmetics, candy bars, soups, and salad dressings. Students may think of other products (sponges, food from fish).

Considering these resources, ask students to comment on pollution of the oceans.

Environmental Topic

The photic zone, extending from the ocean's surface to a depth of 200 m, supports the growth of marine life dependent on the sun's energy. Thriving here are the marine algae (phytoplankton) that form the base of the ocean food chain. All other marine organisms feed on these algae directly or indirectly.

Consequently, threats to the welfare of this region, such as oil spills, are quite serious. Oil pollution resulting from leaks, accidents, or intentional discharge not only kills sea birds and marine life, but also may cover the surface of the ocean, making it impenetrable to light. Thus the marine algae, dependent on solar radiation for photosynthesis, are threatened, which jeopardizes the complex food web of the ocean.

Discuss with the class the danger and long-range effects of placing the lowest level of the food chain at risk. What can be done to minimize pollution of the ocean by oil and toxic chemical wastes?

Section 2 Review Answers

Check Your Understanding
page **399**

1. An ocean is a saline solution because ocean water contains a mixture of salts that are dissolved in the water, thereby making ocean water a solution of dissolved salts.
2. 1) When temperatures are below freezing, ice forms readily on ponds, which contain fresh water and which are usually shallow. 2) Ice forms less readily on a deep lake (presumably a freshwater lake) than on a pond because water is denser at about 4°C than at 0°C. This causes vertical mixing, so that the whole body of water, and not just the surface water, must be cooled. 3) In a river, the motion of the water deters ice formation. 4) In the ocean, salinity and depth prevent sea ice except in certain portions of the ocean.
3. Surface waters are warmed by energy from the sun. And along the rift valley of the mid-ocean ridge system, active volcanism heats ocean water by means of heat from deep within the earth.
4. Most life is found in the photic zone, the zone closest to the surface. Enough light is received in this zone to support photosynthesis. As depth increases and light diminishes, lack of light limits the life forms that can live in that environment.
5. As depth below the surface increases, so does the pressure the water exerts on the bodies of organisms. This increase in water pressure forms barriers below which certain organisms cannot live because the pressure would be too great.

8-2

Learner Objectives

1. To identify the directions of motion in a wave.
2. To identify the parts of a wave.
3. To describe causes of unusually high waves.
4. To describe tides.
5. To describe ocean currents.
6. To describe deep water circulation.

Concept Summary

Ocean water movements affect the ocean environment, the coastline, and the climate.

8-3

Demonstration

Observing Particle Motion in a Wave

If at all possible, take students to see a ripple tank. A ripple tank may be available in the laboratory of a nearby high school or college physics department. Museums of natural history or of science and industry may also have ripple tanks.

If you are able to locate a ripple tank or substitute an aquarium, let students take turns creating waves with the tank. Then place a cork on the water's surface.

Ask students what they think will happen to the cork as a wave rolls forward. Usually, the first answer will be that the cork will move forward, too, but actually it will not. This provides a good opportunity for students to realize that the wave is not pushing the water forward; rather, the wave is going *through* the water.

If students are still doubtful about whether the water is actually moving forward with each wave, point out that even when the tide is going *out*, the waves are still coming *in!*

Tell students that they will learn much more about waves and ocean tides in Section 3 of Chapter 8.

Activity Notes

Activity 8-3A

Simulating Wave Motion   page **402**

Purpose   To use a rope to imitate the motion of a wave.

- **CORE** 20 minutes Groups of 2 or 3
- **Activity Record Sheet 8-3A** (Lab Manual page 111) can be used to record this activity.
- Science Processes: Formulating models; Defining operationally; Communicating through a diagram; Communicating through graphs; Reasoning.

Procedure Notes

This activity works well in conjunction with the ripple tank or aquarium demonstration on page 366L. The demonstration allows students to observe that although the wave moves forward, the water itself does not.

Answers to Questions

1. The speed of the wave is in direct proportion to the speed of the side-to-side motion of the hand.
2. To make higher waves, you would need to increase the distance of the side-to-side motion of the hand that is creating the wave motion.
3. The ball moves up and down. The waves move along the rope, toward the secured end and away from the source of motion.
4. The size of the ball's movement is equal to the wave height.

Conclusion

The vertical axis would be labeled "ball movement up and down" and the horizontal axis would be labeled "wave height along rope." The plots would be at (1,1); (2,2); (3,3) etc.

Science Background

Waves transmit energy from one place to another. Because many forms of wave motion (sound waves, for example) are invisible, water waves provide a convenient model. Wind is the main source of energy for ocean waves, but earthquakes, undersea landslides, and the movement of ships also create waves.

Remind students that the particles of the medium through which a wave passes (in this case, the water) do not move along with the wave front. As a wave goes by, the water molecules move up and down as well as back and forth, creating a circular pattern called orbital motion. Although this pattern varies with the kind of wave, the principle is the same: the particles of the medium never move far from their home positions.

Tides that are higher than usual, called spring tides, occur during the full moon and new moon. At these times, the sun, moon, and earth are in line; and the sun's gravitational pull combines with that of the moon. When the moon is in its first and third quarters, the sun and moon form a right angle with the earth and pull against each other. This causes weaker tides known as neap tides.

8-3

8-3

Student Misconception

The moon is largely responsible for the occurrence of tides. Few students are aware, however, that the sun's position with respect to the earth and the moon also affects tidal motions. Despite a 150 000 000 km separation between the earth and the sun, the gravitational attraction between these two masses is significant. (It is this attraction that maintains the earth in orbit around the sun.)

During full moon and new moon, the sun, earth, and moon are positioned in a straight line. At these times, the gravitational pulls of the sun and moon are combined, producing the highest high tides (spring tides). At first quarter and third quarter, the moon and sun are at right angles to each other, weakening each other's gravitational pull. This is when the lowest low tides (neaptides) occur. Simple diagrams may help your students put these forces into perspective. Instruct students to diagram the positions of the earth, sun, and moon at new moon, first quarter, full moon, and third quarter. Figure 8-30 on page 409 may help them get started. Explain that tidal forces are strongest when the sun and moon exert a combined pull on the earth. Have students identify the diagram(s) that represent this alignment. Also ask students to identify the diagram(s) that place the sun and moon at right angles. Discuss how this position acts to reduce the effect of either force.

Discussion Idea

Are Tides Important?

If the earth had no moon—and not all planets do have moons!—how might tides be different? In fact, would there be any tides at all? And, if there were no tides, would we even have life on the earth? Remember, many biologists believe that life first began in the sea. Tell students that some kinds of organisms (great white sharks, giant kelp, anemones, barnacles, etc.) seem unable to survive without the motion of the tides; moving water is apparently essential for them to obtain the oxygen or nutrients they need for life.

Activity Notes

Activity 8-3B

Simulating Effects of Heat Absorption on the Earth's Surface page **416**

Purpose   To compare the absorption of heat by different materials.

- 30 minutes Large groups or teacher demonstration
- **Activity Record Sheet 8-3B** (Lab Manual page 112) can be used to record this activity.
- Science Processes: Experimenting; Measuring; Comparing and contrasting; Communicating with data tables; Inferring.

Safety Information

State the following cautions:

1. Make sure your hands are dry before turning the lamp on.
2. Do not touch the lamp while it is on, as heat lamps get much hotter than regular incandescent light bulbs.
3. Turn the lamp off whenever it is not being used.
4. Exercise extreme caution when using the lamp (or any electrical appliance) near water. Neither the lamp nor its cord should come in contact with water at any time.

Procedure Notes

If enough lamps, timers, and thermometers are available, you might have each group of students use a different material.

A geometric progression of time (2, 4, 8 minutes) was chosen so that the measurements would show more of a difference. In the case of the water, this progression could be critical for success, depending on the precision of the thermometer.

Activity Notes (continued)

Answers to Questions

1. Water absorbs the most energy with the least change in temperature.
2. The dark-colored sand absorbs heat faster.
3. The temperature will be warmer closer to the surface except in the case of the stirred water, where the temperature should be nearly equal throughout.

Conclusion

The temperature is more even in the liquid that is being stirred. In still water, the water closer to the heat source will float on the surface, as it heats first. It is less dense than the cold water below it. By constantly moving the water, you imitate the currents that allow cold water to rise and mix with warmer water near the surface.

Going Further

Immediately after the lamp is turned off, students can measure the temperature of the air 2 cm above the surface of each material. They should then take measurements every 30 seconds for 3 to 5 minutes. Ask: What causes differences in air temperature? (The different heating and cooling rates of the land and the water affect the air temperature above the surface.)

Environmental Topic

An environmentally sensitive ocean region lies off the northwest coast of South America. Here, the Coriolis force deflects the warm surface water away from the coast. This warm water is replaced by cooler water that upwells from below the surface. This cold, oxygen-rich water contains great concentrations of dissolved nutrients that provide an ideal feeding ground for algae, fish, fowl, and—ultimately—humans.

There is a strong possibility that large petroleum deposits are situated beneath the ocean floor in this region. Such an oil discovery would bring in substantial revenue. At this time, attempts to find oil in these waters have been blocked by ecologists and others who are aware of the area's environmental value; nevertheless, the financial impetus to prospect for oil is strong.

Have students consider the ecological and economical importance to our society of ocean regions where upwelling occurs. Students might discuss the pros and cons of exploring these regions for oil and other resources.

Section 3 Review Answers

Check Your Understanding
page **417**

1. The orbital motion of the wave changes from circular to elliptical. The wavelength shortens and the wave height increases until the wave collapses because it can no longer hold its shape.
2. The length remains the same but the height is equal to the sum of the height of the two original crests.
3. Waves move along the coast in an irregular, zigzag-type movement, causing sand to be moved along the coastline.
4. 1) The speed of the moon in its orbit, which affects the high-tide bulges caused by the moon; 2) The shape of the ocean bottom, which can affect the high-tide bulges; 3) The shape of the shoreline, particularly in bays and estuaries; 4) Twice a month, at full moon and new moon, the relative positions of the sun, earth, and moon cause unusually high tides; 5) Local storms also affect tides in coastal areas.
5. In the Northern Hemisphere, currents in a major gyre circulate in a clockwise direction; in the Southern Hemisphere, currents in a major gyre move in a counterclockwise direction.

8-3

The Ocean

Chapter Vocabulary

Section 1

ocean
marginal sea
island arc
echo sounding
ocean basin
continental margin
abyssal plain
trench
Ring of Fire
mid-ocean ridge
rift valley

Section 2

salinity
water mass
freezing point
sea ice
pack ice
icebergs
water pressure
photic zone
disphotic zone
aphotic zone

8-3

Section 3

crest
trough
wave height
wavelength
wave base
swell
surf zone
rogue wave
tsunami
high tide
low tide
gyre
upwelling

Chapter 8 Review Answers

Putting It All Together   page 418

1. At 3000 m depth, the ocean environment has the following characteristics: temperature—1° to 2°C; salinity—34.5 to 34.9 parts per thousand; water pressure—300 bars; light—total darkness except for light from bioluminescence or volcanic eruptions; life—some life based on a food chain beginning with sulfur-eating bacteria.

2. The large surface currents are generally circular and circulate cold water from the polar regions and warm water from the tropics. Deep ocean currents involve a sinking of oxygen-rich water and then an upwelling of nutrient-rich water.

3. The salinity of ocean water is affected by evaporation, rain, river inflow, and vertical mixing. Hot springs near mid-ocean ridges can contain very high concentrations of salts.

4. Increases in salinity and temperature do not affect water density in the same way. An increase in salinity causes the water to become more dense. But an increase in temperature causes the water to become less dense.

5. Water pressure increases one bar for every 10 m of depth. To breathe underwater, people must have a special apparatus. And divers can only go so deep without being crushed. That is why deep-sea exploration can occur only within a submersible strong enough to withstand the great pressure of the water at those depths.

6. The continental margin includes the continental shelf, the continental slope, and the continental rise. The continental shelf is the gently sloping area nearest the land. The continental slope is the steeper part of the continental margin as it slopes down toward the deep sea floor. The continental rise is a gently sloping area at the base of the continental slope. Deep erosional valleys and canyons are found in the continental margin. Seamounts are volcanic cones that rise more than 1000 m from the ocean floor. Guyots are undersea volcanic cones less than 1000 m high. Abyssal plains are large level areas of the deep sea floor that are covered by layers of sediments from the land. Trenches are very deep areas that are sites of active volcanism and earthquakes. The mid-ocean ridge is a high, rugged mountain range that extends along the basins of the major oceans.

7. Waves and tides continually change a shoreline because of weathering, erosion, and deposition. High tides bring waves farther up onto the land where wave action can attack cliffs and other landforms and structures along the coast. Waves and tides also change beaches by depositing sand or by eroding sand, sometimes on a seasonal basis. Also, ocean currents cause waves to advance along a shore, carrying the sand along with them.

8. In the Arctic Ocean, the middle and lower layers have a high salinity that forms a barrier to the vertical mixing of surface waters. Surface water can therefore reach the freezing point before sinking all the way to the bottom.

Chapter 8 Review Answers (continued)

Putting It All Together

9. A tsunami is a group of waves that have very long wavelengths and very low wave heights. As these waves (which may be traveling at 600 km/h) approach the shore, their height can increase to 50 m, causing great damage along coastlines. The waves of a tsunami, which are caused by an underwater earthquake, are most frequently found in the Pacific Ocean, because of the earthquakes associated with that area.

10. Marginal seas can form in a rift between continents that are moving apart or moving toward each other. Marginal seas can also be formed by island arcs.

Apply Your Knowledge   page 418

1. Use and development of certain ocean resources have been hindered because they are not economically feasible or because they present dangers to the environment. Offshore drilling for oil and natural gas is promoted because of the value and need for fossil fuels, but obtaining oil in such a way has resulted in pollution of some portions of the ocean. As for minerals and heavy metals on the ocean bottom, no way has yet been found to make it sufficiently profitable to obtain certain minerals in this way because they are easier to obtain by mining the land. As for elements dissolved in ocean water or minerals found near the mid-ocean ridge system, ways must still be found for analyzing water for valuable minerals/elements and for removing the valuable elements once they have been detected.

2. A submarine traveling beneath the wave base (which is one-half the wavelength) will feel no motion from the waves on the surface.

3. The topography of the ocean bottom is a factor in deep ocean circulation because ocean basins are shallower near the continents and deeper farther out. Cold water travels along coastlines from polar regions toward the equator. Some of this cold water sinks into the deeper parts of the ocean basin and causes an east-west flow across the bottom of the deep sea floor. When this east-west flow of water reaches a continental rise on the opposite side of the ocean, the rising slope directs this flow of water upward toward the surface.

4. The velocity of a ship is affected by the velocity of the water in which it is moving. A ship traveling against a current will have to use more energy to maintain the same speed, because the ship's propellers must overcome the opposing force of the current. If sea captains can follow the water circulation patterns of the North American Gyre, they will make better time and use less energy than if they had to oppose the force of the circulating water.

5. Oceans cover about 71 percent of the earth's surface. Therefore, about 71 percent of the meteorites that strike the earth's surface can be expected to end up on the ocean bottom.

8-3

Chapter 8

The Ocean

Section 1
The Bottom of the Ocean

From the photo above, little is evident about the earth's ocean bottoms except that some colorful forms of life live and build homes on them.

Until recently, the topography of the ocean bottoms was a mystery. We now know that the earth's highest mountains and deepest canyons lie beneath the ocean. We also know that volcanic processes beneath the oceans are responsible for the shape, and the position, of the land areas.

Section 2
Properties of Ocean Water

A large portion of the earth's surface is covered by water. Many of the organisms that live on the earth are marine organisms. They live in the sea.

The ocean environment varies with location. Surface temperatures are warmer than temperatures deep below the surface. Also, as depth increases, great pressure and continual darkness limit the kinds of organisms found in those regions.

Section 3
The Circulation of Ocean Water

The water in the earth's oceans is constantly moving. On the surface, motion occurs in the form of waves. Waves, which are generally caused by storms at sea, move away from the storm center in all directions and often end up by breaking against a rocky shore or sandy beach.

Larger kinds of water movements also occur in the oceans. Huge circulation patterns, similar to the wind belts in the atmosphere, take place in the earth's oceans.

As a wave approaches the beach, the water becomes shallower. As will be explained in Section 3 of this chapter, as the water becomes more shallow, the wave cannot retain the orbital motion it had at sea. It therefore grows in height until it can no longer hold its shape. It then crashes onto the beach as a forward-breaking mass of water.

If you've ever stood on the shore and looked out over the water, you've probably noticed that waves increase in height as they approach the beach. The wave pictured on the facing page is breaking in an area near the beach known as the surf zone. What do you think causes waves to break against the shore?

The Bottom of the Ocean   Section 1

Learner Objectives
1. To distinguish oceans from marginal seas.
2. To describe features that cause marginal seas.
3. To describe main features of the ocean bottom.
4. To relate volcanic activity to features of the ocean bottom.
5. To identify resources of the ocean bottom.

Section 1 of Chapter 8 is divided into five parts:

The major oceans

Marginal seas

Sounding the ocean bottom

The topography of the ocean bottom

Resources of the ocean bottom

Figure 8-1. The topography of the ocean bottom is as varied as the topography of the land. This coral cave is located beneath the surface of the Red Sea.

Through discussion, elicit from students their ideas about what the ocean bottom is like. Also elicit sources for the students' ideas and impressions.

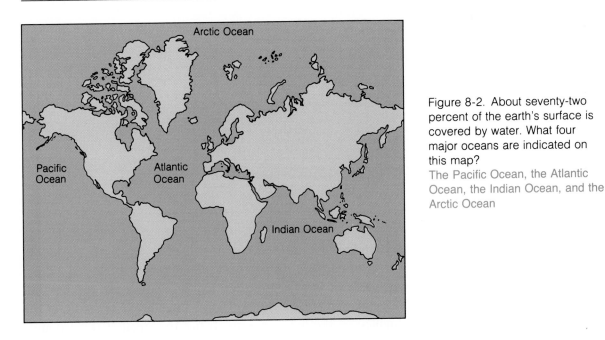

Figure 8-2. About seventy-two percent of the earth's surface is covered by water. What four major oceans are indicated on this map?
The Pacific Ocean, the Atlantic Ocean, the Indian Ocean, and the Arctic Ocean

Oceans are huge basins of rock that are filled with salt water. Why are ocean basins deeper than the land areas that are known as continents? Is the bottom of the ocean flat or does it have a varied topography just as the surface of the land does? And how have people been able to reconstruct what the deep parts of the ocean basins look like?

What are oceans?

The questions in this introductory paragraph are meant to stimulate student thought and discussion. The questions will be answered as students progress through this section of Chapter 8.

The major oceans
New vocabulary: ocean

If you look up the word **ocean** in your dictionary, you will find that the word has more than one meaning. One meaning refers to the entire body of salt water that covers much of the earth's surface. Another meaning refers to the major geographical divisions of this huge body of salt water. Each of these major geographical divisions is also called an ocean. In this earth science book, the word *ocean* is used in both senses.

As shown in Figure 8-2, much of the earth's surface is covered with water. The relationship between land surface and water surface is about 28% land and 72% water. Of the total earth's surface, nearly 71% is covered by salt water. Thus, most of the earth's surface is covered by oceans and seas, and the earth has been called by many people the water planet.

Because so much of the earth's surface is covered by salt water, the major oceans and most seas are connected. The earth's major oceans are the Pacific Ocean, the Atlantic Ocean, the

Ask students if they can think of another reason why the earth is called the water planet. As pointed out in Chapter 7, the earth's water cycle and the earth's fresh water are needed by organisms that live on the land. Without water, there could be no life on the earth. And, as mentioned in Chapter 4, there is no evidence of water on any of the other planets in the solar system. Nor is there water on the moon.

The Earth's Major Oceans				
Ocean	Surface Area	Average Depth	Volume	Percentage of the Earth's Total Surface Area (514 million km²)
Pacific	181.3 million km²	3940 m	714.4 million km³	35.3%
Atlantic	94.3 million km²	3575 m	337.2 million km³	18.3%
Indian	74.1 million km²	3840 m	284.6 million km³	14.4%
Arctic	12.3 million km²	1117 m	13.7 million km³	2.4%

Table 8-1. Which has the greater average depth—the Atlantic Ocean or the Indian Ocean? The Indian Ocean

Library research

Examine maps in various books. Which maps indicate an Antarctic Ocean?

1. 72% water and 28% land (2½ times more water area than land area)
2. Pacific, Atlantic, Indian, Arctic
3. Pacific, Indian, Atlantic, Arctic

Have students check the dictionary definition of *margin* (a border or an edge). Point out to students the relationship between *margin* and *marginal*. Marginal seas are located along the margins (that is, the borders or edges) of the earth's major oceans.

Indian Ocean, and the Arctic Ocean. As shown in Table 8-1, the Pacific Ocean is the largest major ocean. It has the largest surface area, the greatest average depth, and the greatest volume of water. The Arctic Ocean, on the other hand, is the smallest of the major oceans. It has the smallest surface area, the least average depth, and the least volume of water.

If you look at Figure 8-2, you will notice that Antarctica is surrounded by the southern parts of the Pacific Ocean, Atlantic Ocean, and Indian Ocean. The mass of water that surrounds Antarctica is sometimes referred to as the Antarctic Ocean.

The total surface area of the earth's four major oceans is 362 million square kilometers. The total surface area of all the earth's land masses (including glaciers, lakes, and rivers) is 152 million square kilometers.

Check yourself

1. What is the ratio of water to land on the earth's surface?

2. List the major oceans in order of size, from the largest to the smallest.

3. List the major oceans in order of depth, from the deepest to the shallowest.

Marginal seas

New vocabulary: marginal sea, island arc

The margins of the major oceans frequently have smaller seas. **Marginal seas** formed in one of three different ways.

Some marginal seas formed when continents came together. It may seem hard to believe that land masses as huge as continents actually move. But there is evidence that during different eras of geologic history the earth's land masses were positioned

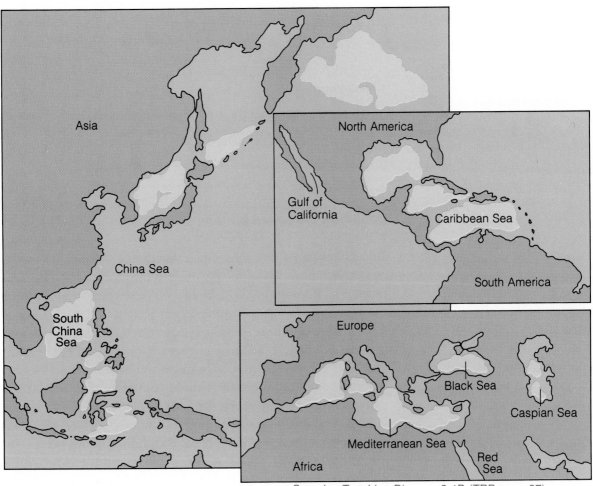

See also Teaching Diagram 8-1B (TRB page 37).

differently on the earth's surface. The Mediterranean Sea, which is between the continents of Africa and Europe, is thought to have formed when the two continents enclosed it. The Black Sea, located between Europe and Asia, is another example of a marginal sea that may have formed as the result of continents coming together.

Some marginal seas are separated from the major oceans by chains of islands. The South China Sea is separated from the Pacific Ocean by other seas, and they are all separated by series of island chains. Because the island chains are usually curved, they are called **island arcs.** The Caribbean Sea is another example of a marginal sea formed by an island arc.

Some marginal seas are thought to have formed as the result of a structural break in a land mass. The Red Sea and the Gulf of California are examples. In the case of the Red Sea, the continental crust was not only split, but it separated. Ocean crustal rocks have been found in the area of separation.

In Chapter 10, the islands forming island arcs are related to volcanic activity, seismic activity, and crustal plates.

Figure 8-3. Marginal seas formed in one of three different ways. How did the Red Sea form? The Red Sea formed when continental crust split and then pulled apart. (The shaded areas indicate the South China basin, Japan basin, Okhotsk basin, Aleutian basin, Gulf of Mexico, Yucatan basin, Venezuelan basin, Balearic basin, East Mediterranean basin, and basins in the Black Sea and Caspian Sea.)

Library research

Examine maps in various books and find the names of some island groups that separate the China Sea from the Pacific Ocean.

1. A smaller ocean somewhere along the boundary of a major ocean
2. 1) When continents came together; 2) when island arcs formed in a major ocean; 3) when a structural break occurred in a land mass
3. 1) The Mediterranean and the Black Sea formed when continents came together. 2) The China Sea and the Caribbean Sea were formed by island arcs. 3) The Red Sea and the Gulf of California were formed by structural breaks in a land mass.

Check yourself

1. What is a marginal sea?

2. Describe the three different ways marginal seas form.

3. List two examples for each type of marginal sea.

Sounding the ocean bottom
New vocabulary: echo sounding

In 1492, when Columbus sailed across the Atlantic Ocean, a common notion was that the ocean bottom was flat and featureless. The only method known to determine the depth of the ocean water was to lower a heavy weight tied to the end of a rope into the water until it hit bottom. Then the length of line was measured. Sailors were usually interested in the position of the ocean bottom only if the water became so shallow that their ship might hit the bottom. Consequently they did not carry enough rope to reach the deep ocean bottom.

Four hundred years after Columbus, people were still using the same method for measuring the depth of the ocean. By that time, however, wire had been substituted for rope, and a power-driven winch was used to lower and raise the weight on the end of the wire. Many scientists continued to believe that the ocean bottom was mostly flat. They based their belief on the fact that the bottoms of reservoirs usually become flat because of the sediment that settles out of the water.

Figure 8-4. How can sound waves be used to measure the depth of the ocean?
The depth of the ocean can be measured by means of echo sounding, described on the facing page.

In 1925, a more modern method of measuring the depth of the ocean was first used in a detailed survey of the ocean bottom. This method, which uses sound, is called echo sounding. In **echo sounding,** a sharp noise called a ping travels from the ship to the ocean bottom and bounces back from the bottom as an echo. The length of time it takes the ping to make the trip down and back is measured. By knowing how fast sound travels in water, the distance from the ship to the bottom can be calculated.

In echo sounding, a precision depth recorder makes a continuous record of ping echoes on a moving strip of paper. The pings are sent out continuously as the ship moves, and the paper record is a scale representation of the ocean bottom. An example is shown in Figure 8-5. Thousands of these types of records have shown that the ocean bottom has an even more varied topography than does the land.

Figure 8-5. Continuous records of ping echoes recorded on moving strips of paper provide profiles of the topography of the ocean bottom.

Check yourself

1. How was the depth of the ocean bottom measured before the twentieth century?

2. What type of information is produced by the precision depth recorder?

3. What did people learn about the ocean bottom from data provided by the precision depth recorder?

1. By lowering a weighted line or cable from the surface
2. A scale representation of the ocean bottom (Firmness/looseness of sediment on the bottom can also be detected.)
3. That the ocean bottom has an even more varied topography than does the land

The topography of the ocean bottom

New vocabulary: ocean basin, continental margin, abyssal plain, trench, Ring of Fire, mid-ocean ridge, rift valley

Ocean basins are quite different from the landmasses that make the continents. The most obvious difference is depth. Ocean basins are at a much lower level than the land. They sit at a lower level in the earth because they are formed mainly of ocean basin rocks, which are more dense than continental rocks. Ocean basin rocks are mostly basalt, whereas continental rocks are mostly granite and granite gneiss.

The depth of ocean basins can vary greatly from one location to another. But there are several general characteristics that will help you to get a clearer picture of the topography of the ocean bottom. Figure 8-6 shows several general regions of the ocean bottom. It also shows features that characterize each region. These regions and features are associated with certain earth processes.

Near the continents is an area that is known as the continental margin. Most sediment eroded from the land is deposited in this part of the ocean. The continental margin generally consists of a continental shelf, a continental slope, and a continental rise. Submarine valleys and canyons are erosional features of this region of the ocean bottom.

Farther from shore, and at a greater depth, is the deep sea floor. This area is affected by the earth processes of sedimen-

---

Is there much variation in the depth of ocean basins?

In answer to the caption question, the water is much deeper above an abyssal plain than it is above a continental shelf.

Figure 8-6. Is the water deeper above a continental shelf or above an abyssal plain?

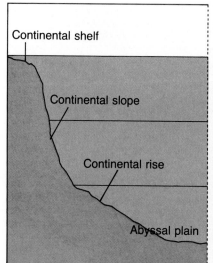
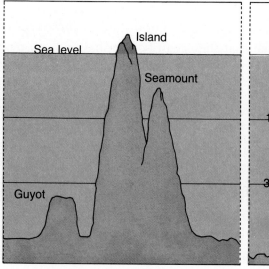
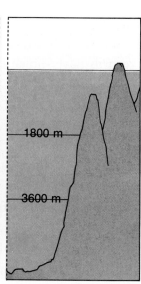

tation and volcanism. Seamounts, guyots (gee-ŌZ′), abyssal plains, trenches, and mid-ocean ridges are features that make up the deep sea floor.

In what part of an ocean basin is the mid-ocean ridge located?

Our Science Heritage

Before the twentieth century, with its invention of airplanes and its space age technology, people crossed the ocean only by ship. Some of the voyages down through history have become famous. Among those that come to mind are the voyages of Christopher Columbus, Ferdinand Magellan, James Cook (known as Captain Cook), and Charles Darwin. You can certainly think of other famous voyagers.

Some totally fictional voyages have also become quite famous. Thanks to the genius of its author, Jules Verne, many people are very familiar with the detailed account of the *Nautilus* in *Twenty Thousand Leagues Under the Sea,* published in 1870. But how many have ever heard of the *Challenger* expedition (1872–1876)?

From the resources of his remarkably creative (and in some ways prophetic) imagination, Jules Verne was able to describe an undersea world that had never been visited and a submarine that had never existed. In the world of science, however, it took considerably more time to develop a picture of the world under the sea.

In the world of science, the voyage of the *Challenger* in the 1870s represents the first organized expedition whose purpose was to gather data about the earth's ocean basins and their contents.

The *Challenger* was a surface vessel, far less exciting than the *Nautilus*. And the *Challenger* had to gather all its data by means of simple instruments like jars and nets that were lowered on wires from the surface. But after three and a half years at three hundred and fifty observation stations throughout the earth's oceans, enough data had been collected to fill fifty volumes. And the science of oceanography had been born.

The *Nautilus* and the *Challenger*

The *Challenger* collected enough data on the earth's oceans to form the basis of a new area of study in earth science.

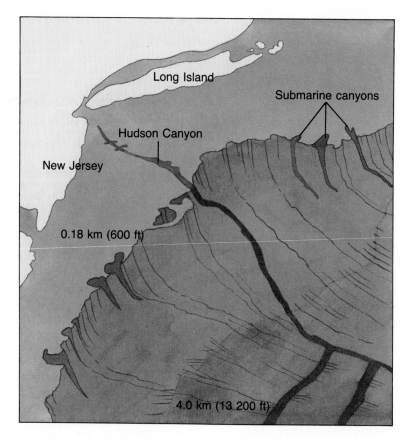

Figure 8-7. How might an underwater canyon have been formed?
An underwater canyon can be formed where a river enters the ocean. Sediment carried down the river can, by means of abrasion, wear away part of the continental margin in the same way that sandpaper can wear away the surface of a piece of wood.

How does the continental slope differ from the continental rise?

Features of continental margins   A continental margin is a region that separates a continent from the deep sea floor. The continental margin is not as deep as the abyssal plain because the continental margin is made up of continental crustal materials, rocks, and/or sediments.

Continental margins consist of several parts. The part nearest the land has, on the average, a very gentle slope and is called the continental shelf. At a depth of about 200 m, the steepness increases. This steeper part is called the continental slope. At the base of the continental slope is another, much gentler slope that leads down to the abyssal plain. This gently sloping area is known as the continental rise.

Erosional valleys and canyons cut across the continental margins. Some of these canyons are deeper and wider than the Grand Canyon in Arizona. These valleys and canyons were probably formed by rapidly flowing turbidity currents. *Turbidity currents* are rapidly flowing mixtures of sediment and water. (Flowing particles of sand and other sediments can change a rock surface in the same way that sandpaper can wear away a wood surface.) The canyons and valleys might also have been formed by glaciers during the last Ice Age.

Features of the deep sea floor   Continental margins, which border the continents, are formed of continental crustal rock, sediment, and other materials. Beyond the continental margins, the deeper parts of the ocean basins are formed of ocean crustal rock. All ocean crustal rocks are volcanic, formed by underwater eruptions of dark-colored basaltic flows.

Volcanic action at the ocean bottom causes changes in the crustal features. Among the tallest objects that rise from the deep sea floor are underwater mountains called seamounts. Seamounts are volcanic cones that grow upward from the ocean bottom, layer by layer. Seamounts usually rise more than 1000 m above the ocean floor.

Seamounts sometimes reach the ocean surface and form islands. Virtually all islands in the ocean were formed by volcanic activity. Igneous activity also takes place in the ocean crust beneath these volcanic features. This igneous activity causes additional bulges in the ocean crust.

Library research

Find out more about guyots. What is the origin of their name?

Volcanic activity is the subject of Section 1 of Chapter 10.

Figure 8-8. Tahiti is an island in the South Pacific. How were virtually all islands in the ocean formed?
As a result of volcanic activity

Science Processes: Measuring; Inferring
See also Activity Record Sheet 8-1A (Lab Manual
page 103)

CORE   20 minutes   Groups of 4, or demonstration

Activity 8-1A Comparing the Density and Elevation of Floating Objects

Materials

1 block of balsa wood
and 1 block of a
hardwood, each of the
same thickness

balance

clear jar or 500-mL
beaker

graduated cylinder

water

tub or other container
large enough to float
the blocks of wood
fork

Purpose

To calculate the density of two different materials and then compare their elevations above water as they float.

Procedure

1. Using the balance, determine and record the mass of the two blocks of wood.
2. If the blocks have a rectangular shape, measure their length, width, and height. Calculate their volume by multiplying length times width times height.
3. If the blocks have an irregular shape, calculate their volume by using the water displacement method described in Chapter 1 on page 29.
4. Calculate the density of each block by dividing its mass by its volume.
5. Pour water into the tub and float the two blocks of wood side by side in the water. Measure and record the difference in elevation of the tops of the blocks above the level of the water.

Questions

1. Which of the two wood blocks has the greater density?
2. Which block floated lower in the water?

Conclusion

What can you say about the relationship between the elevations and densities of the two blocks?

Step 1

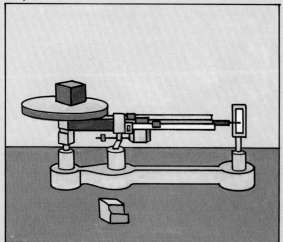

Step 3

Because of wave action or ocean crustal movement, volcanic islands can disappear beneath the surface of the sea. Volcanic islands are attacked by wave action. If the volcanoes have become extinct, then wave action is often able to erode the tops of the seamounts down to sea level. Sometimes the ocean crust beneath extinct volcanoes sinks, lowering the eroded seamounts well below the ocean's surface, forming flat-topped underwater mountains called guyots (gee-OZ′). Guyots, which are found in deeper parts of the ocean basins, can rise to nearly 1000 m above the ocean floor.

Other than erosion, a flat top can form by the growth of a coral reef as the island slowly sinks.

Sporadic flowing mixtures of water and sediments called *turbidity currents* spill off the continental margins into the deep ocean. Turbidity currents can cover abyssal hills near continental margins with hundreds of layers of sediment. These sediments can extend for hundreds of kilometers across the ocean bottom, leaving large flat areas called **abyssal plains.** Most abyssal plains make up the deeper parts of the major ocean basins at about 5 km depth. These abyssal plains are examples of the flat surface area that many scientists once thought covered the entire ocean bottom.

Library research

What unusual kinds of organisms are found in the enriched waters around active volcanic rift valleys?

A very small percent of the ocean basin has long deep **trenches** that extend from the deep ocean basin downward to about 11.5 km. Trenches are usually bordered by enough volcanic activity to create island arcs. In the case of the Peru-Chile Trench, the volcanic activity near the trench forms part of the Andes Mountains. The region of volcanic activity that surrounds the basin of the Pacific Ocean is called the **Ring of Fire** and is generally associated with deep sea trenches. (Trenches and island arcs indicate areas of collision between separate oceanic crustal plates.)

The interrelationships among the Ring of Fire, volcanic activity, trenches, island arcs, and crustal plates are discussed in Chapter 10.

The mid-ocean ridges   The rest of the ocean basin is made up of the world's biggest and longest mountain system, the **mid-ocean ridges.** The mid-ocean ridge system is about 65 000 km long. In the Atlantic Ocean, the mid-ocean ridge occupies the central third of the entire basin from the Arctic Ocean to about the latitude of the southern tip of South America. Iceland is a part of the mid-ocean ridge that became an island though volcanic growth.

As shown in Figure 8-9, the mid-ocean ridge passes between Africa and Antarctica and into the Indian Ocean, where it

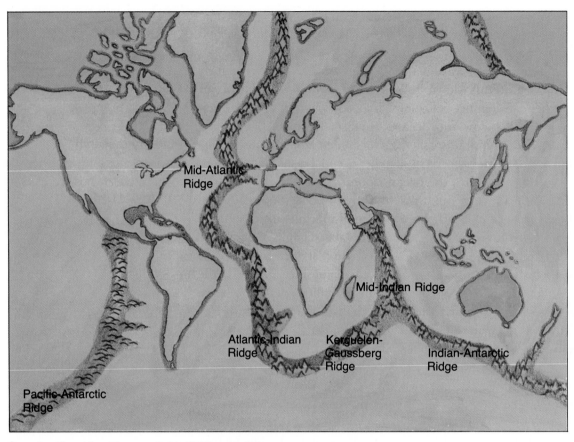

Mid-Atlantic
Ridge

Mid-Indian Ridge

Atlantic-Indian
Ridge

Kerguelen-
Gaussberg
Ridge

Indian-Antarctic
Ridge

Pacific-Antarctic
Ridge

See also Teaching Diagram 8-1A (TRB page 36).

Figure 8-9 Why, in the Pacific
Ocean, is the mid-ocean ridge
called a rise rather than a ridge?
Because in the Pacific Ocean the
mid-ocean ridge is less rugged

If possible, have students look at
a relief map/globe that shows the
topography of the ocean bottoms
in three dimensions.

splits. One branch heads north and forms the Red Sea between
Africa and Saudi Arabia. The other branch extends generally
southeast and east between Australia and Antarctica and then
across the southern portion of the Pacific Ocean.

In the Pacific Ocean, the mid-ocean ridge is less rugged. As
a result, it is called a rise. The rise continues under the southeastern part of the Pacific Ocean toward Central America. The
rise then branches. Part of it disappears near Panama. The
other part disappears near Baja California.

The mid-ocean ridge system is offset by hundreds of breaks
in the earth's crust. These breaks are fracture zones that can
extend for hundreds of kilometers. The ridge part of the system is extremely rugged. It has a fairly deep central **rift valley**
with high peaks near the rift valley, which is a site of active
volcanism. Much heat from the volcanic action in this rift valley

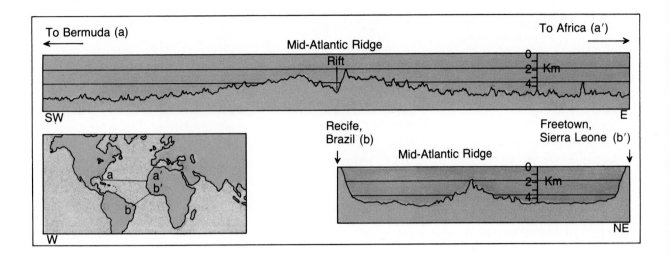

Figure 8-10. These two views show an east-west profile and a northeast-southwest profile of the Mid-Atlantic Ridge system. In which part of the mid-ocean ridge system does volcanic activity take place?
In the deep rift valley which extends down the center of the ridge system

is absorbed by ocean water. In addition, new ocean-floor crust forms at the mid-ocean ridges during volcanism.

Check yourself

1. List the ocean bottom features associated with continental margins.

2. List the ocean bottom features associated with the deep basins.

3. What type of geologic activities affect the permanence of ocean islands?

Resources of the ocean bottom

The ocean bottom contains many resources and is used in different ways.

☐ Natural gas and crude oil form and accumulate in the sediments of the continental margins.

☐ Gold, diamonds, titanium ores, and other heavy substances are often deposited on continental margins.

☐ Sand and gravel deposits in the nearshore environment are used for construction materials.

Interested students could do comparisons of the Mid-Atlantic Ridge system and the Rocky Mountain system or any other mountain system they might choose (or even something like the Grand Canyon). Profiles could be prepared from data and the findings displayed in class.

1. Continental shelf, continental slope, continental rise, erosional valleys and canyons
2. Seamounts, guyots, abyssal plains, deep sea trenches
3. Volcanic activity within the seamount and within the crustal rock on the ocean bottom (Wave action also affects the permanence of islands in the ocean.)

Science Processes: Measuring; Recognizing and using spatial relationships; Communicating through a map

See also Activity Record Sheet 8-1B (Lab Manual page 104)

30 minutes   Groups of 4

Activity 8-1B   Taking and Using Soundings

Materials

specially prepared tub
 of opaque solution

string

small metal weight that
 does not contain lead

rule

several paper towels or
 napkins

paper

pencil

	A	B	C	D	E
1					
2					
3					
4					
5					

Purpose

To take soundings of an underwater surface you cannot see and to use the results to reconstruct topographic features of the underwater surface.

Procedure

1. Obtain the specially prepared tub of opaque solution. You should not be able to see the underwater surface of the container.
2. Imagine a grid system over the tub, similar to the one shown on this page. On a blank sheet of paper, make lines that correspond to your grid system. Label all of the spaces in one direction with numbers. Label all of the spaces in the other direction with letters.
3. Tie the weight onto one end of the string.
4. Take a sounding for the area of the tub that is represented by space 1A on your grid. Lower the weighted end of the string into the tub at the proper location. Lower the string until the weight just touches the bottom at that location. The string must be kept tight and straight if you are to get an accurate reading.
5. Raise the weighted string and measure the length of string that got wet. This represents the depth of the solution at that location.

Record the depth in the appropriate space on your grid.
6. Wipe the string with a paper towel and take another sounding. Take a total of 16 to 20 soundings. In the appropriate space on your grid, record the depth of each sounding.

Questions

1. On the basis of the data in your grid, what is the shape of the bottom of the container? Draw a map of it, showing the high points and the low points.
2. Pour the liquid from your container into another container. How does your answer to Question 1 compare with the actual shape of the bottom of the container?

Conclusion

Using the same method with the string and weight, how could you determine the shape more precisely?

□ Manganese nodules are found in abundance in many places on the deep ocean floor. They contain copper, cobalt, zinc, and other metals that are valuable.

Why are manganese nodules valuable?

□ Many valuable minerals form around the hot springs associated with the central valleys of the mid-ocean ridge system.

□ The shellfish industry is a resource of the continental shelves.

□ Beaches are commonly used for recreational purposes.

□ The deep ocean floor has been used as a place to dump canisters of waste chemicals. Nerve gas and nuclear wastes are two examples.

Check yourself

1. What types of resources are found in and on the continental margins?

2. What types of resources are associated with the deep ocean floor?

1. Natural gas, crude oil, gold, diamonds, titanium ores, sand and gravel, shellfish
2. Valuable metals/minerals found in manganese nodules or around hot springs associated with the mid-ocean ridge system

Figure 8-11. Oil rigs are used to obtain oil and natural gas from beneath the sea. Where do natural gas and crude oil form and accumulate offshore?
In the sediments of the continental margins

Section 1 Review   Chapter 8

Use **Reading Checksheet 8-1** TRB page 81
　　Skillsheet 8-1 TRB page 123
　　Section Reviewsheet 8-1 TRB pages 183–184
　　Section Testsheet 8-1 TRB page 295

Check Your Vocabulary

7 abyssal plain	1 ocean
5 continental margin	6 ocean basin
4 echo sounding	11 rift valley
3 island arc	9 Ring of Fire
2 marginal sea	8 trench
10 mid-ocean ridge	

Match each term above with the numbered phrase that best describes it.

1. The entire body of salt water that covers much of the earth's surface; also, any of its major geographical divisions

2. A smaller body of salt water found along the margin of a major ocean

3. A chain of islands, usually curved, that separates a marginal sea from a major ocean

4. A method of using noise (pings) to measure the depth of the ocean

5. The region of the ocean bottom near the land areas; contains most of the sediment eroded from the land; separates a continent from the deep sea floor

6. The low-lying earth formation that contains the ocean's water; consists mainly of dense basaltic crustal rock

7. Large flat area of the deep sea floor; formed by sediment flows that spill off the continental margins

8. A long narrow depression of the deep sea floor; generally has steep sides; usually bordered by areas of volcanic activity

9. The region of volcanic activity that surrounds the basin of the Pacific Ocean

10. A system of rugged mountains that extends down the middle of the ocean basins

11. Deep valley in the center of the mid-ocean ridge; a site of active volcanism

Check Your Knowledge

Multiple Choice: Choose the answer that best completes each of the following sentences.

1. _?_ are a feature found on the continental margins.
   a) Guyots
   b) Seamounts
   c) Submarine canyons
   d) Trenches

2. An abyssal plain forms from _?_.
   a) sediments being deposited
   b) lava flows from underwater volcanoes
   c) erosion of the mid-ocean ridge
   d) erosion of guyots

3. The ocean with the least amount of water is the _?_.
   a) Arctic Ocean
   b) Atlantic Ocean
   c) Indian Ocean
   d) Pacific Ocean

4. The _?_ is an example of a marginal sea that formed because of an island arc.
   a) Black Sea
   b) Gulf of California
   c) Mediterranean Sea
   d) Caribbean Sea

5. A resource associated with the deep ocean floor is _?_.
   a) manganese nodules
   b) diamonds
   c) shellfish industry
   d) sand and gravel

Check Your Understanding

1. What causes ocean basins to be at a different level than the continents?

2. Describe the technique of echo sounding.

3. Describe the mid-ocean ridge system.

4. What is the reason the earth is sometimes called the water planet?

5. What is the relationship between trenches and volcanic activity?

Properties of Ocean Water   Section 2

Section 2 of Chapter 8 is divided into six parts:

Salinity

Temperature and density

Sea ice

Water pressure

Water absorbs light

Resources of ocean water

Learner Objectives
1. To explain salinity as a property of water.
2. To describe how salinity and temperature affect density.
3. To explain the conditions necessary for ice to form on the ocean.
4. To describe the photic, disphotic, and aphotic zones of the ocean.
5. To identify resources of ocean water.

Figure 8-12. Physical properties like salinity, temperature, and density affect the ocean as an environment for plants and animals. What is another word for *salinity*?
As mentioned on the following page, *saltiness* and *salinity* have the same meaning.

In Section 1 of this chapter, you considered dimensions and features of the ocean bottom. In this section, you will consider some properties of the ocean's water. You will also consider how those properties affect the ocean as an environment for plants and animals.

Salinity

New vocabulary: salinity

One characteristic that is common to all ocean water is saltiness. All ocean water is salty. But some samples of ocean water are saltier than other samples. Sometimes the difference is so great that you can taste the difference. Sometimes, however, the difference is not that great. For scientific purposes, there is a precise way to determine the saltiness, or salinity, of water.

The words *saline* (which means salty) and *salinity* (which means saltiness or degree of saltiness) are from the Latin word *sal,* which means salt. When speaking scientifically of the salinity of ocean water, the word *salinity* has a more precise meaning. **Salinity** is a measure of the amount of total dissolved materials in water. The salinity of ocean water is defined as grams of dissolved materials per kilogram of ocean water.

What do we know about the materials that are dissolved in ocean water? As shown in Table 8-2, six elements account for over 99% of the dissolved materials in water. Two of those

Table 8-2. What two elements make up over eighty-five percent of the dissolved materials in ocean water?

Sodium (30.6%) and chlorine (55%)

Have students, in discussion, 1) mention characteristics of the ocean as an environment, 2) compare those characteristics with the characteristics of a freshwater lake, and 3) give examples of plants and animals that live in each environment.

Elements in Dissolved Materials in Ocean Water		
Element	Form Found in Water	Percentage of Dissolved Materials
chlorine	chloride ion	55.0%
sodium	sodium ion	30.6%
sulfur	sulfate ion	7.7%
magnesium	magnesium ion	3.7%
calcium	calcium ion	1.2%
potassium	potassium ion	1.1%
Total		99.3%

seven elements, chlorine and sodium, which make up common table salt (sodium chloride), are by far the most abundant.

Average ocean water has a salinity of 35 parts per thousand, which means that it has 35 grams of dissolved materials per kilogram of water. Certain environmental changes, however, can affect the salinity of ocean water.

In the upper parts of the major oceans (less than 1 km below the surface), evaporation, rain, river inflow, and vertical mixing cause significant variations. Similar environmental changes also affect the salinity of marginal seas.

The Mediterranean Sea has few large rivers entering it. The Mediterranean Sea also has excessive evaporation, little rainfall, and limited connection to the Atlantic Ocean. Most of the Mediterranean, therefore, has a greater than average salinity of 36 to 39 parts per thousand.

The salinity of the Black Sea, on the other hand, is far less than average. The Black Sea has three major rivers flowing into it. The Black Sea has less evaporation than the Mediterranean and it has only a narrow, shallow connection with the Mediterranean. As a result, the surface salinity of the Black Sea is only 16 parts per thousand.

Library research

Find out what an ion is and why that would be the form of an element found in solution.

Critical Thinking

How do evaporation, rainfall, and river inflow affect ocean salinity?

In general, evaporation increases salinity, while rainfall and river inflow decrease salinity.

Figure 8-13. The Greek island of Naxos is located in the Aegean Sea, an arm of the Mediterranean Sea. How does the salinity of the Mediterranean Sea compare with the salinity of other bodies of salt water?
Most of the Mediterranean has a greater than average salinity (38 to 39 parts per thousand).

Science Processes: Experimenting; Measuring; Inferring
See also Activity Record Sheet 8-2 (Lab Manual page 107)

CORE   10 minutes, plus brief follow-up
Demonstration or small groups

Activity 8-2 Evaporating Salt Water

Materials

jar with about 1 L of tap water

salt

balance and standard masses

large, lightweight container (a clean plastic milk or bleach container with the top cut off will be fine)

filter paper and funnel

Purpose

To see what will happen when salt water evaporates.

Procedure

1. Put the filter paper in the funnel. Using the balance, measure 35 g of salt. Put the salt inside the filter.
2. Put the empty container on the balance. Using standard masses, find and record the mass of the empty container.
3. Add a 1-kg standard mass to the pan with the other masses.

4. Holding the filter cone with the salt in it above the empty container, pour tap water through the filter and into the container until the container and the masses balance.
5. Put the uncovered container in a place where the water can remain for a week or more until it evaporates.
6. After all the water has evaporated, put the container on the balance and find its mass.

Questions

1. How does the mass of the container after the water has evaporated compare with the mass of the container when you first measured it?
2. How do you explain the difference in mass?
3. Salinity (in parts per thousand) equals grams of salt per kilogram of solution. What was the salinity of your solution when it first began to evaporate? How does that salinity compare with the average salinity of ocean water?
4. How could this activity have been speeded up?

Conclusion

How does evaporation affect ocean salinity?

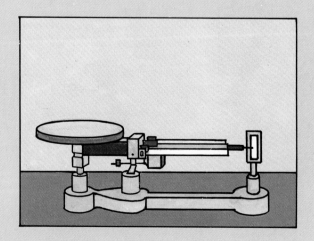

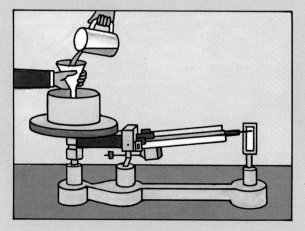

The salinity of the major oceans below 1 km depth is nearly constant at 34.5 to 34.9 parts per thousand. Along the center of the mid-ocean ridges, however, are isolated areas with hot springs called hydrothermal vents. Dissolved elements from these vents account for nearly half of all dissolved elements in ocean water. When deep-water circulation is restricted, hot water from the hydrothermal vents can form brine pools with salinities as high as 257 parts per thousand.

Check yourself

1. How is the salinity of ocean water determined?
2. What types of environmental changes can affect salinity?
3. What six elements make up over 99% of the salinity of ocean water?

What is the salinity of the major oceans below 1 km depth?

1. By measuring the grams of dissolved materials per kilogram of ocean water
2. 1) In the upper parts of the major oceans: evaporation, rain, river inflow, vertical mixing; 2) In the deep ocean: hot springs, brine pools formed by the restriction of deep water circulation
3. Chlorine, sodium, sulfur, magnesium, calcium, and potassium

Temperature and density

New vocabulary: water masses

Along with salinity, temperature is one of the most frequently measured properties of ocean water. The surface of the open ocean ranges from very cold in the polar regions to room temperature in tropical areas. This difference in temperature is caused by the variation in solar radiation at different latitudes. As shown in Figure 8-14, at the higher latitudes the sun's rays strike the earth's surface at a smaller (more oblique) angle than they do near the equator. As the angle of incoming radiation decreases, a given amount of solar radiation is spread over larger areas of the earth's surface. As a result, the amount of

Library research

What is a thermocline? Where is it located?

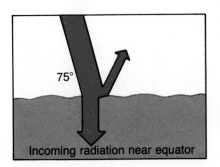

75°

Incoming radiation near equator

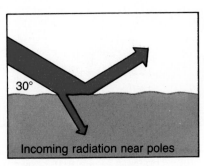

30°

Incoming radiation near poles

Figure 8-14. How does the angle of incoming solar radiation affect surface temperatures of ocean water?
At higher angles, more energy is received and surface temperatures of the water are warmer.

radiation that penetrates the same area of ocean water also decreases.

Depth also affects the temperature of ocean water. Figure 8-15 shows the distribution of water temperature with depth from north to south through the Pacific Ocean. You will note that the most rapid temperature changes take place within one kilometer of the surface in the equatorial and temperate regions. Also note that deep ocean water is about the same temperature as the surface water nearer the poles.

Another important property of ocean water is density. As mentioned in Chapter 1, certain materials are more "dense" than others. A certain volume of iron, for example, weighs more than the same volume of wood because the iron has a greater mass and is therefore more dense. Oil "floats" on water because oil is less dense than water.

The density of ocean water depends on the temperature and the salinity of the water. Figure 8-16 shows that as salinity increases, density increases. The density of river water will therefore be less than the density of ocean water since river water is generally understood to be fresh water and therefore contains less dissolved materials than ocean water.

Figure 8-16 also shows that the temperature and density of water decreases. As the water temperature rises, for instance, the water becomes less dense. Warmer surface water near the equator is therefore less dense than cooler surface water near the North Pole and South Pole.

How does deep ocean water at the equator compare in temperature with surface water near the poles?

For a discussion of density in a fluid and how it causes convection currents, refer students to page 238.

Near the surface between the Tropics of Cancer and Capricorn
Figure 8-15. Where do the most rapid temperature changes in ocean water take place?
See also Teaching Diagram 8-2 (TRB page 38).

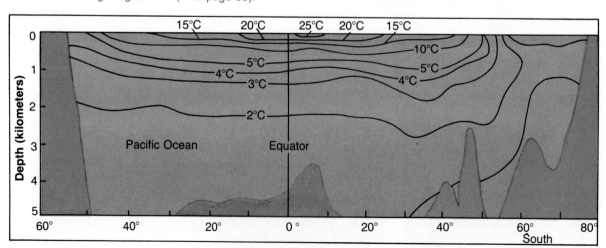

The profile in Figure 8-15 shows how the temperature of water in the Pacific Ocean varies with depth and with latitude.

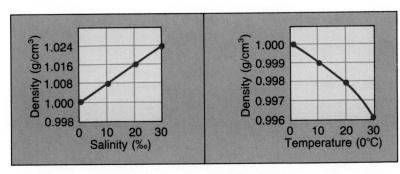

Figure 8-16. As the salinity of ocean water increases, the density also increases. What happens to the density as the temperature increases?
As the temperature increases, the water becomes less dense.

Ocean water moves in large volumes. These large volumes of water are called **water masses.** By determining temperature, salinity, and density, scientists are able to identify large water masses and to trace their movement from place to place.

Check yourself

1. What geographic variables affect the temperature of ocean water?

2. How does temperature affect water density?

3. How does salinity affect water density?

1. Latitude and depth
2. As water temperature rises, water becomes less dense.
3. As salinity increases, water becomes more dense.

Sea ice

One of the consequences of the temperature, salinity, and density relationship in ocean water is the lack of sea ice in most of the world's oceans. Salinity affects the **freezing point** of water. Pure water freezes at 0°C. Salt water freezes at a lower temperature. The saltier the water is, the colder it must be before it freezes. Water with a salinity of 35 parts per thousand freezes at −1.9°C.

Cooling of ocean water occurs at the surface because of cold winter winds. The spray from winter waves can coat the decks and rails of a ship with ice. And yet, even as ships get coated with ice, the surface of the ocean has no ice. That is because of the relationship between temperature and density. As the surface water gets colder, it becomes denser than the water beneath it. The denser surface water sinks and is replaced by less

How does the depth of the ocean affect the formation of ice on its surface?

Thinking Skill Analyzing

Often when we want to find out how something works we take it apart. A mechanic, for example, learns about a particular kind of engine by actually disassembling it. We can also use our minds to take apart information or ideas. This is what scientists do when they study the spectrum of a star's light to determine the elements found in the star. Both kinds of taking apart are examples of analysis.

Scientists usually analyze things in three separate steps. The first step involves breaking down the object or event into its parts. In the second step, the scientist determines the relationships among the parts. In the third step, the scientist determines how all the parts fit together and work as a whole.

Complete analysis may require additional data not available at the time. For example, information and moon rocks brought back by the *Apollo* astronauts helped scientists analyze the moon's composition, but much more information is needed before a complete analysis is possible.

The following steps may help you use the skill of analyzing:

1. Ask yourself, "What is the purpose of this analysis? What do I want to find out?"
2. Observe the entire object or event to be analyzed.
3. Search the object or event piece by piece to identify the parts. Make a list of the parts.
4. Study the parts to detect relationships that relate to your purpose. Write down these relationships.
5. Determine how the parts work together as a whole.
6. Write a short statement about how the whole object or event is organized.

Learning the Skill

You probably have a ball point pen with you. If you do not, borrow one for this exercise.

Use the steps of analyzing to determine how the parts of your pen work together to enable you to write with it. List all the parts and then list all the relationships between them.

1. Are there any parts not needed for actual writing?
2. Would every ball point pen have exactly the same parts?
3. What parts are needed in every ball point pen for it to be used for writing?

Applying the Skill

Scientists often analyze graphs, maps, and tables to get detailed information. Use the steps of the skill of analyzing to analyze the graph below.

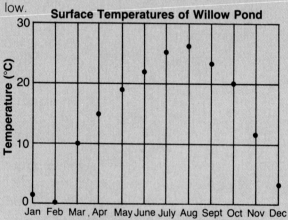

Surface Temperatures of Willow Pond

Identify the parts of the graph. Then answer the questions below to help you detect the relationships shown in the graph.

1. What was the surface temperature of the pond in April?
2. During what time period was there a steady increase in the surface temperature?
3. What was the maximum surface temperature of the pond?
4. How would you describe the relationship between time of year and surface temperature?

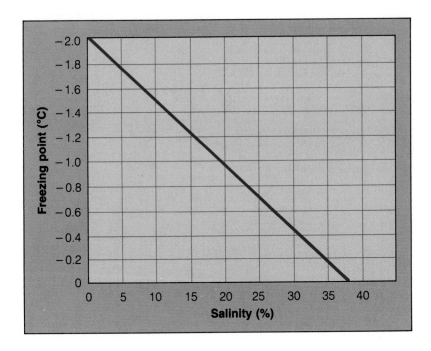

Figure 8-17. This graph shows what happens to the freezing point of water as salinity increases.

dense water, which is not as cold as the water it replaced. As this constant exchange of water continues, the cold water sinking below the surface extends deeper and deeper. This sinking water can be stopped only by the ocean bottom or by a denser water mass.

In the Arctic Ocean, the middle and lower levels have a high-salinity water mass that forms a barrier to the downward mixing of the cold surface waters. The surface water does, therefore, become cold enough to freeze and form **sea ice.** Because of the extreme cold and because of the length of the cold season in the Arctic, the sea ice eventually forms very thick masses called **pack ice.** (See Figure 8-18 on the next page.) Pack ice is ice that has been broken, pushed upward, and refrozen into jagged, irregular ridges known as pressure ridges.

The open Atlantic, Pacific, and Indian Oceans are too deep for sea ice to form. The water never gets cold enough from top to bottom to freeze. However, sea ice might form around the margins of these oceans where the bottom is shallow and where horizontal mixing is restricted. Sea ice might also form in bays and estuaries that have a salinity of less than 24.7 parts per thousand.

Bodies of water with a salinity of less than 24.7 parts per thousand form ice fairly easily during the winter months because such water does not become continuously more dense as it is cooled. The water will reach a maximum density at some

Library research

How does the salt content of sea ice compare with the salt content of the ocean water from which it formed?

Figure 8-18. Pack ice has irregular, jagged ridges. Pack ice is a common sight on Baffin Bay, an arm of the North Atlantic between Greenland and Canada.

Why does water with a salinity of less than 24.7 parts per thousand freeze more readily than saltier water?

temperature above the freezing point. Then, as the water gets colder, it becomes less dense and floats on the surface. This top layer of water gets colder and colder until it freezes. This is the same way that freshwater ponds and lakes freeze.

When you think of ice on the ocean, you might also think of icebergs. **Icebergs,** however, are not sea ice. They are not frozen ocean water. Icebergs are masses of ice that broke off freshwater glaciers that form on the land.

Check yourself

1. Where in the world's oceans does sea ice form?
2. How do icebergs differ from sea ice?
3. How cold must average ocean water be in order to start freezing?

1. 1) In the Arctic Ocean, where the middle and lower levels have a high-salinity water mass that forms a barrier to vertical mixing; 2) around the margins of the oceans (especially in bays and estuaries that have a salinity of less than 24.7 parts per thousand)
2. Icebergs are from ice that froze on land; sea ice is from frozen sea water.
3. −1.9°C

Water pressure

New vocabulary: water pressure

Another physical property of ocean water is **water pressure.** Let's say you are at sea level and standing at the edge of a swimming pool. The atmospheric pressure against your body at sea level, which can be expressed in terms of bars as well as in inches of water or millimeters of mercury, is about one bar. If you dive into the pool and swim to the bottom, you feel an increase in pressure on your body. As you go deeper below the surface, the water pressure becomes greater. Due to the mass of overlying water, the water pressure increases by one bar for every ten meters depth of water.

Some organisms cannot tolerate large changes in water pressure. For these organisms, water pressure forms barriers which limit vertical movement. The organisms simply cannot live beyond a certain depth because the pressure would be too great for them.

People are also limited by water pressure. Perhaps you have seen a swimmer breathing through a snorkel tube. A snorkel tube permits a swimmer to breathe surface air while swimming facedown on the surface of the water. But all snorkel tubes are very short. It would be impossible for a swimmer one meter below the surface to breathe surface air through a tube because the water pressure would crush the body beyond the ability of the muscles to inflate the lungs.

Divers using air tanks can swim to much greater depths than a snorkler because a regulator delivers the air to the lungs at the same pressure as the water pressure around the diver. This balances the pressure both inside and outside the body, letting the diver's muscles properly inflate the lungs. This same principle of balancing the pressure applies to a person using a diving suit attached to a pressure pump on the surface.

Figure 8-19. This swimmer is breathing through a snorkel tube. Why is the tube so short? Because at a greater depth, the water pressure would be so great that the diver could not expand the lungs to draw in air

Check yourself

1. What is the rate of pressure change with ocean depth?

2. What is the approximate atmospheric pressure (in bars) at sea level?

3. How are divers with air tanks able to breathe at depths of twenty meters?

1. The water pressure increases one bar for every ten meters depth of water.
2. One bar
3. A regulator delivers air to the lungs at the same pressure as the water pressure around the diver.

Water absorbs light
New vocabulary: photic zone, disphotic zone, aphotic zone

Sunlight that enters the ocean is a mixture of all the rainbow colors. But pictures taken underwater frequently look blue. Water absorbs light. The blue color is due to the fact that water absorbs the red, orange, yellow, green, and violet colors of the rainbow spectrum more rapidly than it absorbs blue.

Because water absorbs light, light cannot travel very far through water. In fact, light disappears rather quickly with increasing depth of water. The ocean environment can be divided into three zones, depending on the amount of light that has penetrated to that zone.

The uppermost zone of the open ocean is the zone of most light. This zone extends to a depth of 200 m and is called the **photic zone** (FŌT'-ik ZŌN). (*Photic* is from the Greek word *phōs*, which means a light.) In the upper 150 m of this photic zone, the light is strong enough to support the growth of algae, which are one-celled plants and a basic food source for many animals.

Water between 200 m and 1000 m in depth is quite dark. In this zone, the light is not strong enough to allow algae to con-

Figure 8-20. As depth below the surface increases, divers must use artificial light to observe the surroundings.

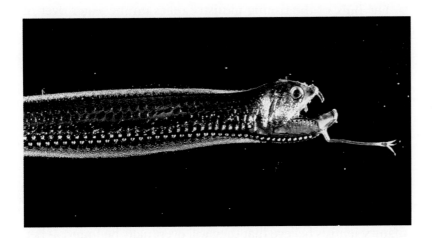

Figure 8-21. The angler fish uses bioluminescence to attract other fish. Why is bioluminescence effective below the photic zone of the ocean? Because below the photic zone there is little or no light from any other source

tinue to live. Only a very tiny, almost immeasurable amount of light in the blue color range extends into this zone, which is called the **disphotic zone** (DIS′-FŌT′-ik ZŌN). (*Disphotic* is from the Greek words for half light or reduced light.) Some of the organisms living in the disphotic zone have extremely sensitive eyes. The brightest lights in this zone are produced by animals through a biochemical process called bioluminescence. (Fireflies also produce light by the process of bioluminescence.)

The bulk of the ocean's water lies below the disphotic zone. Except for bioluminescence and underwater lava eruptions, this part of the ocean is in total darkness. Not even the smallest amount of surface light reaches into this zone, which is called the **aphotic zone** (A′-FŌT′-ik ZŌN). (*Aphotic* is from the Greek words for no light.)

Because of the light distribution in the ocean, most organisms are concentrated in the photic zone, where algae live. In the aphotic zone, however, there are some predators and scavengers and "pockets" of life based on a food chain beginning with sulfur-eating bacteria (no photosynthesis involved).

Library research

Prepare a report on planktonic, nektonic, and benthonic sea life forms.

Check yourself

1. What color of light is absorbed least rapidly in water?

2. What are the three major depth zones in the ocean, based on light penetration?

3. What are the natural sources of light in the deep ocean?

1. Blue is absorbed least rapidly.
2. 1) Photic zone—surface to 200 m; 2) Disphotic zone— 200 m to 1000 m; 3) Aphotic zone—below 1000 m
3. Bioluminescence and underwater lava eruptions

Resources of ocean water

Ocean water resources are quite important to people.

□ The bulk of the fishing industry relies on the water over or near the continental margins. Fish are concentrated in these areas because of the greater abundance of smaller organisms and nutrients in the water. Fish are used for food, oils, fertilizer, and livestock feed.

□ Ocean water is 96.5% water. Desalination plants can remove the 3.5% dissolved materials and produce fresh water from ocean water. In some coastal areas, desalination is more economical than other sources of fresh water.

Is desalination an economical way to obtain fresh water?

□ Scientists have been able to find many elements dissolved in ocean water. Although not all elements have yet been detected, many scientists believe that they will eventually be found as better analytical tests are developed. At present, only sodium chloride (table salt), magnesium, and bromine are commonly derived from dissolved elements in ocean water.

□ Differences in water temperature between the surface and the depths can be used to generate electricity. OTEC (Ocean Thermal Energy Conversion) has been tried near Hawaii and offers great promise for the future.

□ Many industries use ocean water as a coolant for their machinery and equipment. The water is circulated through heat exchangers where excess, unwanted heat is absorbed.

□ For recreational purposes, the ocean's waters offer sports fishing, swimming, diving, boating, and water skiing.

□ The ocean provides a habitat for maintaining a great number of different types of life forms. This is ecologically important in order to maintain the quality of life in general and to provide a resource base for future needs. *Pollution* has been responsible for destroying life in the ocean. Offshore oil wells have caused much pollution and destruction of life. Chemical fertilizers are washed down rivers into the ocean. Chemical wastes from factories as well as human sewage have ended up in the ocean.

1. 1) Fish; 2) Fresh water through desalination; 3) Products from dissolved elements; 4) Generation of electricity; 5) Coolant for industrial machinery; 6) Recreation; 7) Habitat for marine life

2. Sodium chloride, magnesium, bromine

Check yourself

1. List the seven major resources of ocean water.

2. What substances are presently derived from the dissolved elements in ocean water?

Section 2 Review   Chapter 8

Use **Reading Checksheet 8-2** TRB page 82
Skillsheet 8-2 TRB page 124
Section Reviewsheet 8-2 TRB pages 185–186
Section Testsheet 8-2 TRB page 296

Check Your Vocabulary

10 aphotic zone	8 photic zone
9 disphotic zone	1 salinity
3 freezing point	4 sea ice
6 icebergs	2 water mass
5 pack ice	7 water pressure

Match each term above with the numbered phrase that best describes it.

1. Saltiness; a measure of the amount of total dissolved materials in water; grams of dissolved materials per kilogram of water

2. A large volume of water characterized by a similar temperature, salinity, and density throughout its mass

3. The temperature at which a liquid freezes

4. Frozen ocean water

5. Sea ice that has been broken and then refrozen into jagged pressure ridges

6. Floating masses of ice that broke off freshwater glaciers

7. The force that a mass of overlying water exerts upon a submerged surface

8. The uppermost zone of the open ocean and the zone of most light

9. A zone of reduced light in the ocean; between 200 m and 1000 m deep

10. The part of the ocean that is in total darkness

Check Your Knowledge

Multiple Choice: Choose the answer that best completes each of the following sentences.

1. The average salinity of ocean water is _?_ parts per thousand.
   - a) 16
   - b) 30.6
   - c) 35
   - d) 38 to 39

2. _?_ are the two most abundant elements that make up the salinity of sea water.
   - a) Sodium and potassium
   - b) Chlorine and sulfur
   - c) Calcium and sulfur
   - d) Chlorine and sodium

3. _?_ is the depth zone in the ocean that contains the greatest number of organisms.
   - a) Below the photic
   - b) Aphotic
   - c) Photic
   - d) Disphotic

4. The temperature of the ocean below 1 km depth is _?_.
   - a) greater than 20 degrees C
   - b) 15 to 20 degrees C
   - c) 5 to 10 degrees C
   - d) less than 5 degrees C

5. The pressure at 100 meters depth in the ocean is _?_ bars.
   - a) 101
   - b) 100
   - c) 11
   - d) 10

Check Your Understanding

1. Ocean water is a saline solution. Explain.

2. What factors affect the formation of ice on these bodies of water—a pond, a deep lake, a river, an ocean?

3. What are two causes for increases in the temperature of ocean water? Where does each kind of heating occur?

4. How is life in the ocean affected by light?

5. How does water pressure affect life in the ocean?

The Circulation of Ocean Water   Section 3

Learner Objectives

1. To identify the directions of motion in a wave.
2. To identify the parts of a wave.
3. To describe causes of unusually high waves.
4. To describe tides.
5. To describe ocean currents.
6. To describe deep water circulation.

Section 3 of Chapter 8 is divided into six parts:

Directions of motion in a wave

The beginning, middle, and end of a wave

Effects of wave action

Tides

Surface ocean currents

Deep ocean circulation

Figure 8-22. It is afternoon as these waves approach San Francisco's Ocean Beach. What evidence suggests these waves are approaching a beach? The formation of these waves suggests that they are getting ready to break in the surf zone along a beach. As will be mentioned in this section, this occurs because the shallowness of the water prevents the wave from maintaining the shape it had at sea, which is normally a gently-curving wave that is part of a rhythmic pattern of waves called swell.

The ocean's water is like a restless person, shifting from place to place and always on the move. Some of the ocean's water moves in and out of the ocean through evaporation and precipitation. But most of the ocean's water simply moves around within the ocean environment.

Waves, tides, and currents are three major ways in which ocean water moves. The ways in which ocean water moves, the forces that cause these movements, and the effects of ocean water movements are of particular interest.

Directions of motion in a wave

New vocabulary: crest, trough, wave height, wavelength, wave base

If you have ever tried floating among waves, you are familiar with at least two directions of motion that are caused by waves. One direction of motion is up and down. As waves pass under you, they cause you to bob up and down.

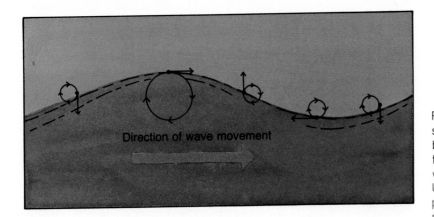

Direction of wave movement

Figure 8-23. The small arrows show directions of motion caused by wave movement. What are four directions of motion along a wave?
Up, down, forward, and back, producing an overall orbital motion

Another direction of wave motion is forward and backward. If you are floating offshore, waves will generally push you in all four directions. The combination of up, down, forward, and backward movements results in an overall circular motion. You can see in Figure 8-23 that the water in a wave does not stream forward with the wave but moves in a circular motion as the wave passes by.

Near the shore, forward wave motion dominates floating objects, causing driftwood and other debris to wash up onto the shore.

What causes driftwood to wash up onto the shore?

Science Processes: Defining operationally;
Communicating through a diagram
See also Activity Record Sheet 8-3A (Lab Manual
page 109)

CORE   20 minutes   Groups of 2 or 3 students

Activity 8-3A   Simulating Wave Motion

Materials

6.5-m length of small-
  diameter rope

chalk

meter stick

graph paper

colored pencils

plastic foam ball, 2-3 cm
  diameter, with hole
  large enough for rope
  to pass through

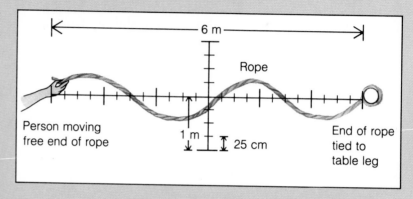

Purpose

To use a rope to imitate the motion of a wave.

Procedure

1. Working in a group of two or three students, attach one end of the rope to the leg of a chair or table. Pull the rope out straight.
2. On the floor, draw a simple grid similar to the one shown in the diagram. Use chalk and a meter stick, with the outstretched rope as a guide.
3. On a piece of graph paper, make a grid that represents the one on the floor.
4. One student should wiggle the free end of the rope from side to side to make waves.
5. The other students in each group should observe and estimate the direction, the height, and the length of the waves. During these measurements, the student making the waves should maintain a constant amount of motion in the rope.
6. On the graph paper, plot a wave that represents (in height and length) the wave you observed. With an arrow, indicate the direction of motion.
7. Now vary the speed of the waves. The student moving the rope should move the free end either faster or slower but should keep

his or her hand moving the same distance from side to side.

8. Once a different speed has been established, another set of measurements should be estimated and recorded. Plot one of these waves on the graph, using a different color line for this wave.
9. Now fasten the plastic foam ball to the center of the rope. First, tie a simple knot about halfway down the rope. Then thread the free end of the rope through the hole in the ball and move the ball along the rope to the knot. Tie a second knot on the other side of the ball to hold the ball in place.
10. Wiggle the end of the rope to set up a wave motion.

Questions

1. What is the relationship between the speed of the wave and the speed of the side-to-side motion of the hand?
2. What would need to be done to make higher waves?
3. How does the ball's motion differ from the wave's motion?
4. How does the size of the ball's movement compare with the wave height?

Conclusion

How might the answer to these last two questions be plotted on a graph? Try it.

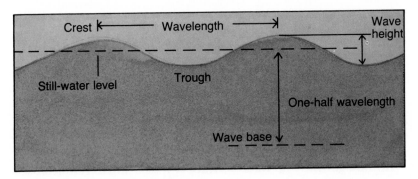

See also Teaching Diagram 8-3 (TRB page 39).

Figure 8-24. What is the relationship between wave base and wavelength?
Wave base is located at a depth of one half a wavelength below the mid-height of a wave.

Look for a minute at Figure 8-24 and familiarize yourself with the names of various parts of a wave. The **crest** of a wave is its highest point. The **trough** is the lowest point between two wave crests. **Wave height** is the vertical distance between a wave's highest and lowest points. **Wavelength** is the horizontal distance from a point on one wave to the corresponding point on the next wave. And **wave base** can, as a general rule, be located at a depth of one half a wavelength below the mid-height of the wave.

As shown in Figure 8-23, the orbit at the surface is circular and has a diameter that is equal to the wave height. As depth below the surface increases, the diameter of the orbit becomes increasingly smaller until, at a depth called the wave base, the size of the orbit is only one twenty-third of the diameter at the

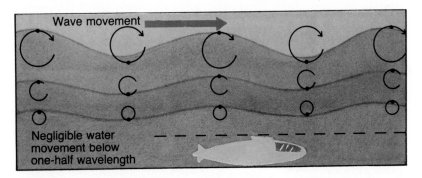

Figure 8-25. How deep must a submarine be in order to escape the orbital motion of surface waves?
Below wave base

See also Teaching Diagram 8-3 (TRB page 39).

surface. At wave base, the orbital motion of a wave nearly disappears. A submarine located below wave base will not be affected by the orbital motion of water due to surface waves.

1. Wave parts in student drawings should be similar to those in Figure 8-24 on page 403.
2. In student drawings, arrows for direction of movement should be similar to those in Figure 8-23 on page 401.

Check yourself

1. Draw and label a profile view of a wave.

2. Using arrows, show the direction(s) of movement of the water in the wave you drew.

The beginning, middle, and end of a wave

New vocabulary: swell, surf zone

Many ocean waves begin in a state of total confusion. They form in a storm area and are caused by the winds associated with the storm. The water surface under a storm center at sea has a very irregular pattern of waves. Waves of many different heights and lengths are formed by the winds within the storm center. Some of the waves exceed a height-to-length ratio of 1 to 7 and collapse. Other waves interact with each other to make the surface of the ocean even more confused. Because of irregular wave sizes and patterns and because waves are breaking and interacting on the surface of the ocean, ships have a very difficult time during a storm at sea.

Waves transmit energy. The energy transmitted across the surface of a stormy area at sea is very irregular because the energy in a wave is related to its height. To be specific, wave energy is directly proportional to the square of the wave height. A wave two meters high has four times as much energy as a wave one meter high. A wave six meters high has thirty-six times as much energy as a wave one meter high. In other words, it takes about thirty-six times as much wind energy to form a six-meter wave as to form a one-meter wave.

Why do ships have a difficult time during a storm at sea?

Figure 8-26. A storm causes hazardous conditions for this fishing boat off the coast of Scotland.

Careers   Marine Geologist / Computer Operator

For further information about a career as a computer operator, contact firms that use computers (such as banks, manufacturing and insurance firms, colleges and universities, and data processing service organizations). The local office of the state employment services is another source of information about employment and training opportunities.

Marine Geologist Marine geology is the study of the rocks and land under the ocean. It is a branch of oceanography, which also includes the study of biological, physical, and chemical aspects of the ocean.

Some marine geologists do research that is designed to increase our basic knowledge about underwater land. Some seek information about fossil fuels. Others work to find underwater mineral deposits.

Some oceanographic work is done in offices and laboratories, but much experimentation and data-gathering are done at sea. Some marine scientists use scuba gear and other underwater equipment in their work.

Approximately half of all oceanographers in the United States and Canada are employed by universities. Many others work for government agencies.

It takes many years of study to become an oceanographer. If you want to specialize in marine geology, a college degree in geology and graduate courses/study in oceanography probably would provide the best training. You will be likely to spend some of your time aboard a research ship while you are a graduate student.

Marine geologists can tell much from sediments scooped up from under the sea.
For further information about a career as a marine geologist, contact:
  American Geological Institute
  5202 Leesburg Pike
  Falls Church, Virginia 22041

Computer Operator Computer operators (or console operators) follow written instructions to set up and run jobs on large computers.

The operator loads the program, or instructions to the computer, and the data to be processed. The program and data, which are called input, may be on punch cards or magnetic tapes or disks.

The operator then monitors the computer while it is running. If the computer stops in the middle of a program, or if an error light goes on, the operator tries to identify and solve the problem. It is important for operators to be able to solve problems because many operators work at night when other employees are not available to help them.

If you enjoy following step-by-step procedures, making decisions, and working independently, you might like to be a computer operator. There are a variety of ways to prepare for this career. Some high schools offer courses in computer operating. High school graduates can learn needed skills at two-year colleges, computer schools, and in the armed forces.

This computer operator operates a group of computers that control a circular accelerator at the Berkeley Radiation Laboratory.

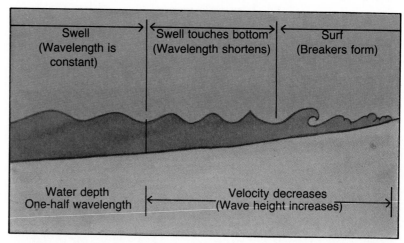

Figure 8-27. What happens to a wave as it nears the shore? As swell touches bottom, wavelength shortens and wave height increases until the wave can no longer maintain its shape.

The middle stage of a wave is much more regular than its beginning. As waves move away from a storm center, they separate according to wavelength. This happens because waves with long wavelengths travel faster than waves with short wavelengths. Eventually a regular rhythmic pattern of waves develops. This regular pattern of waves of similar wavelength is called **swell.**

Ocean swell can cover hundreds of kilometers of open ocean, with the waves all moving forward without breaking or collapsing. The orbital motion within the waves of ocean swell is circular. The energy in ocean swell is transmitted across the ocean with very little loss.

Most waves eventually end up on a beach. As ocean swell nears the shore, the water becomes shallower. Where the ocean bottom is above wave base, the orbital motion of the water in waves changes from circular to elliptical. As the water continues to become shallower, the elliptical orbit becomes flatter. At the same time, the wavelength shortens and the wave height increases until the wave can no longer maintain its shape. At this point the wave collapses, either as a foaming mass of water or as a forward-breaking mass of water. The area near the ocean's margins where breaking waves occur is called the **surf zone**.

Library research

Where in the world do the best waves for surfing occur? Why do these waves occur in those locations? What features cause surfers to desire these waves?

Check yourself

1. Confusion; regular rhythmic swell; collapse

2. Waves separate according to wavelength.

3. Winds in a storm center

1. List the three stages a wave can go through.

2. What aspect of wave motion is responsible for the development of swell?

3. What force in nature creates most ocean waves?

Effects of wave action

New vocabulary: rogue wave, tsunami

On the open sea, storms can create huge breaking waves and irregular wave patterns that are dangerous to ships and to other surface objects such as offshore oil-drilling rigs. In addition to the powerful waves of stormy seas, huge waves can form as the result of wave interference. Wave shapes are additive. When the swell from different storm centers passes through the same water and the crests and troughs coincide, a single crest forms that is equal in height to the sum of the two original crests.

When two or more high waves of about the same wavelength have their crests coincide, the resultant wave, which is called a **rogue wave**, is usually big enough to cause problems for ships. Rogue waves can form and disappear very quickly. The southeastern coast of Africa is known for fairly frequent rogue waves. Many ships have been lost or damaged because of these waves which develop heights up to twenty meters.

Along the margins of the oceans, waves can directly attack the land. The constant pounding of waves can, over long periods of time, reduce boulders and rocky cliffs to particles of gravel and sand. Waves not only directly attack the shore, but they create a movement of loose particles and water in the surf and on the beach. As shown in Figure 8-28, waves approach the shore diagonally, which causes a zigzag motion of water along the shore. The result of this zigzag motion is the movement of sand along a coastline. The sand may be moved hundreds of kilometers. If the supply of sand from rivers and eroding sea cliffs were to stop, then most of the sand beaches would eventually disappear.

Along the Pacific coast of North America, the beaches would all disappear fairly quickly if the sand supply ended. This coastline has a narrow continental shelf. In a few places, submarine canyons cut across the shelf and come fairly close to the shore. The sand that is moving along the shore slips down into these submarine canyons and drains onto the ocean bottom.

Perhaps the most rapid damage to a shoreline is caused by a huge wave called a **tsunami** (tsoo-NAH′-mee). A tsunami is actually a group of waves with fourteen or more crests and is caused by an underwater earthquake somewhere along the

Can waves combine to form larger waves?

In answer to the caption question, the angle of the waves (forming what is called a longshore current) causes sand to move along the coast.

Figure 8-28. The zigzag motion of water along the shore that causes sand to move along the coastline can be seen in this picture of Brazil's coastline.

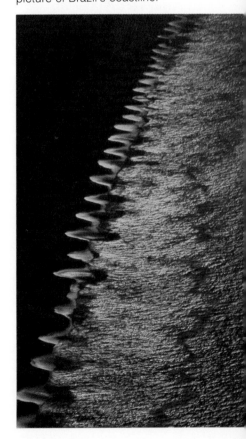

Figure 8-29. This destruction at Seward, Alaska, was caused by a group of huge waves called a tsunami. What causes a tsunami? A tsunami, popularly but inaccurately called a tidal wave, is caused by an underwater earthquake or volcano.

ocean bottom. At sea, the waves of a tsunami may have a height of only 2 m and a wavelength of up to 160 km. Because of their wavelength, it can take up to 15 minutes for successive wave crests to pass a given point on the surface of the ocean even though they may be traveling more than 600 km per hour. And because of their height-to-length ratio, these waves are scarcely noticeable out at sea.

But as the waves of a tsunami approach the shore and the water becomes shallower, they can build to a height of 50 m. A moving wall of water this high can toss railroad locomotives around like toys. Buildings can be smashed. Trees can be snapped like toothpicks. Whole villages and cities can be wiped out by a tsunami. Tsunami are most common around the margins of the Pacific Ocean because of the large number of earthquakes that are associated with that area.

Check yourself

1. 18 meters
2. Along a shoreline
3. When two or more high waves of about the same wavelength have their crests coincide

1. If a ship traveling in a nine-meter swell were hit by a rogue wave, how high might the wave be?

2. Where are tsunami destructive?

3. What causes rogue waves?

Tides

New vocabulary: high tide, low tide

If you've ever built a sand castle on an ocean beach, you've probably noticed that over a period of time the waterline moves either toward the castle or away from the castle. This happens because the level of the sea at a particular location rises and falls during the course of a day.

About once every twelve hours, the waterline reaches what can be called the high water mark. When the waterline reaches this level, the ocean at that location is said to be at **high tide**.

After the waterline reaches the high water mark, the waterline then moves back down toward the open sea until it reaches a low water mark. When the waterline reaches its lowest point, the level of the sea in that area is at **low tide**.

High tide is the result of huge bulges in the level of the ocean. The bulges are caused mainly by the relative positions of the sun, moon, and earth. Figure 8-30 shows the bulges in sea level in relation to these positions.

You will notice that there are actually two bulges. The one nearest the moon is caused by the force of gravity from the moon attracting objects on the earth's surface. The moon pulls on all parts of the earth. But the pull is strongest at the points closest to the moon. The earth's solid surface is not greatly affected by the moon's gravitational pull. But the water on the earth's surface is noticeably affected because water is fluid and can change its shape. The bulge directly opposite the moon, on the other side of the earth, is caused by the rotation of the earth and moon through space.

The fact that sea level at any location goes from high tide to low tide and back again is due to the earth rotating on its axis. The solid earth is actually rotating under the bulges of water.

Tides affect the kinds of plants and animals that can live along the margins of the oceans. Tides can cause alternate wetting and drying of land areas. Rising and falling tides create tidal currents in coastline environments. Incoming tidal currents can bring salt water into an area that has fresher water at low tide. Incoming and outgoing tidal currents also affect the temperature of an environment.

Tides also affect people who live, work, or travel near the water's edge. Tidal changes affect the depth and the water

The gravitational pull of the moon causes a bulge on the part of the ocean nearest the moon. The impact is greater during a new moon when the sun and moon combine gravitational forces.

Figure 8-30. How does the moon affect the level of the ocean's surface on the earth? When does it have a stronger impact?

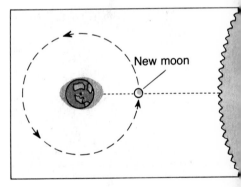

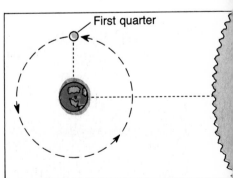

Figure 8-31. Parrsboro, Nova Scotia, is located on the Bay of Fundy, where tidal differences are extraordinary.

Library research

What conditions make cliff-diving at Acapulco such a thrilling sight to see? Why is the timing of the divers so very important?

Students can investigate effects of tides. 1) If possible, students observe and measure tidal differences at a body of water near where they live. 2) Students find out about places around the world that have unusual tides and how these tides affect life in those areas.

speed and direction in harbors and along coastlines. For that reason, ships frequently schedule their arrivals and departures to coincide with a certain tidal condition. Other nearshore and offshore activities, such as fishing and recreation, are also affected by tides.

Several factors affect the timing and the height or strength of tides.

1. Tides do not occur on a 12-hour schedule because the moon orbits the earth at a speed that is slightly faster than the earth's rotation. It therefore takes about 12 hours and 25 minutes for two successive high tides to pass the same location.

2. The shape of the ocean basins affects the timing of the tide. In some places (for example, parts of the Gulf of Mexico), the bulge opposite the moon is not developed. In that case, the cycle from high water to high water takes 24 hours and 50 minutes.

3. The shape of a shoreline affects the strength of the tide. The tides are usually weaker at the mouth (the wide end) of a V-shaped bay than at the head (the narrow end of the bay).

4. The sun's gravitational force also affects the tides. Twice a month, during full moon and new moon, stronger tides with higher and lower water can occur because of the relative positions of the sun, moon, and earth with respect to each other.

5. Local storms may also affect the timing and the strength of the tides along a coastal area.

With the exception of the effects of storms, the times at which high and low tides will occur at a given location can be predicted accurately if the history and characteristics of that location are known. Because of the number of variables, predictions are most easily made by using computers.

Check yourself

1. What is the tide?
2. How much time does it take to go from high tide to high tide?
3. How can the tides affect people's activities?
4. What types of information are needed in order to make tidal predictions?

Surface ocean currents

New vocabulary: gyre

Ocean water circulates from place to place at rates much slower than the movement of waves or tides. Oceanic circulation, although slow, moves unbelievably large quantities of water. The Antarctic Current, for example, moves about 190 times more water than all the freshwater rivers and streams on the earth.

The circulation of surface ocean water is caused primarily by the interaction of four phenomena: the wind, the Coriolis effect, the pull of gravity, and the position of the continents. Figure 8-32 shows the major patterns of water circulation on the ocean's surface.

Both wind and water tend to move in a constant direction. The earth beneath them, however, rotates. Therefore, the path of objects moving across the earth's surface appears to change. The rotation of the earth causes both atmospheric winds and ocean currents to turn to the right of their paths of motion in the Northern Hemisphere and to the left of their paths of motion in the Southern Hemisphere. This deflection of objects moving across the earth's surface is known, as you may recall, as the Coriolis effect.

Why are computers useful in making tidal predictions?

1. The rise and fall of the level of the sea because of ocean bulges which are caused by the moon's gravitation and affected by the earth's rotation
2. Normally, 12 hours and 25 minutes (Due to other factors, however, the period between high tides can be longer.)
3. Tides can affect 1) the arrival and departure of ships; 2) fishing; 3) clamming—which is done at low tide; 4) recreation —swimming, diving, boating, water-skiing, and other water sports.
4. 1) The history of tides in an area; 2) The characteristics of the basin—shape, depth, location, etc.; 3) Any unusual weather conditions, such as a storm

---

How much water moves in the Antarctic Current?

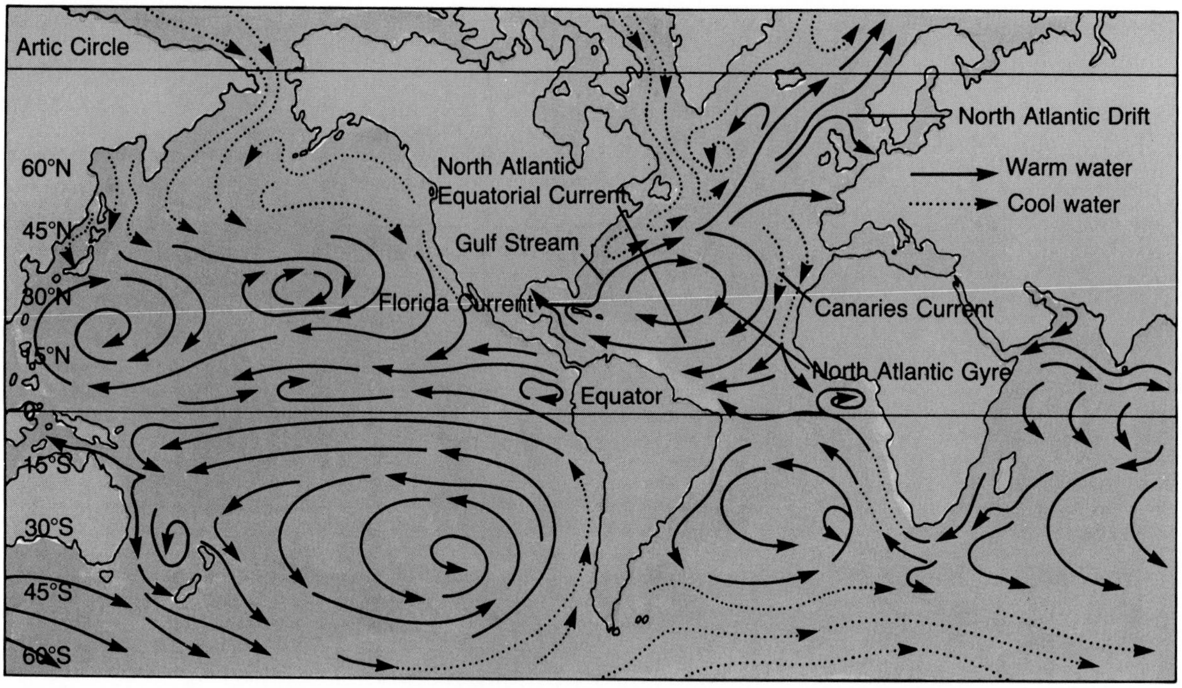

Figure 8-32. This map shows the oceans' major circulation patterns

Consider for a moment the currents in the Pacific or Atlantic Ocean. Prevailing winds cause east-west movements of water that are forced to flow north-south at the margins of the ocean basins. Several major rotating systems of currents are formed in this way. Each of these closed systems of rotating currents is called a **gyre** (JĪR), from the Greek work *guros,* which means a ring or a circle. As an example, look at the North Atlantic Gyre located to the east of Florida on the map above.

The Coriolis effect causes clockwise gyres in the oceans of the Northern Hemisphere and counterclockwise gyres in the oceans of the Southern Hemisphere. (See Figure 8-32.) Between gyres, part of the water on the western edge of the oceans returns across the oceans as an equatorial countercurrent. When this water reaches the eastern side of the ocean basin, it moves north and south and is fed back into the low latitude parts of the gyres.

Each of the gyres is made up of several ocean currents. As shown in Figure 8-32, the North Atlantic gyre contains the Florida Current, Gulf Stream, North Atlantic Drift, Canaries Current, and North Atlantic Equatorial Current.

Currents within a gyre can be recognized by their physical properties. The Florida Current, for example, is a narrow, well-defined, fairly strong current in which warm waters are moving north into cooler water. The Gulf Stream carries warm water northeast from the Florida Current into the North Atlantic, where the current starts to fan out.

As the water moves across the ocean in the North Atlantic Drift, it is constantly being cooled. It is also becoming a wider, slower current. By the time the water reaches the eastern side of the ocean basin, it has spread out and slowed down so much that the Canaries Current has no well-defined margins.

Surface ocean currents affect the climate of coastal areas. In general, ocean currents flowing from the equator contain warm water. The warm water warms the air which in turn increases air temperatures along the coast. Ocean currents flowing toward the equator generally carry cool water, which has a cooling effect on air temperatures.

Ocean currents affect climate in another way as well, because as ocean currents affect air temperature, they also affect the moisture content of the air. Warm air that blows from the ocean over the land brings not only warmer temperatures but also moisture.

How does water change as it moves in the North Atlantic Drift?

Figure 8-33. The climate of Little Sound, Bermuda, is affected by an ocean current flowing from the equator. What effect do such currents generally have on air temperatures?
Currents flowing from the equator contain warm water, which warms the air near the current.

Students can find pictures that show effects of ocean currents on coastal climates.
From details in each picture, what can other students infer about climate, geographic location, and type of ocean current for that area?

Check yourself answers:
1. 1) The wind; 2) the Coriolis effect; 3) the pull of gravity; 4) the position of the continents
2. 1) The Florida Current is a narrow, fairly strong current of warm water that moves north off the East Coast of the United States. 2) The Gulf Stream carries warm water from the Florida Current. 3) The North Atlantic Drift is a wider, slower current in which the water is cooled as it moves across the North Atlantic. 4) The Canaries Current, on the eastern side of the Atlantic basin, is slow-moving, spread out, and has no clearly defined margins. 5) The North Atlantic Equatorial Current is where water from the Canaries Current is warmed before it re-enters the gyre in the Florida Current.
3. Ocean currents flowing from the equator cause moisture and warmer temperatures in coastal areas. Those flowing toward the equator cause cool temperatures.

As an example, minor shifts in the position of the Gulf Stream that persist over several months can be correlated with either severe winters or mild winters in Europe, depending on the direction of the shift. In North America, weather patterns are likewise affected by the position of the Japanese Current in the North Pacific Ocean.

Check yourself

1. What are the four factors that cause the surface circulation in the ocean?

2. Describe the currents in the major North Atlantic gyre.

3. What effects do the gyre systems have on temperature and climate?

Deep ocean circulation
New vocabulary: upwelling

Deep ocean water also circulates in definite patterns. Most of this circulation is caused by colder polar water sinking. This sinking water contains dissolved oxygen, which is extremely important to the animals living in the deep ocean.

After sinking, the cold oxygen-rich waters travel toward the equator. The earth's rotation causes the water to follow the western edges of the ocean basins. The water eventually moves eastward across the ocean basins. It will return to the surface only near continental margins where prevailing winds push less dense surface waters away from the shoreline. Where this type of wind-caused water movement takes place over long distances of shoreline, the deeper water must rise to fill in behind the outgoing surface waters. This process by which deep, cold water comes to the surface is called **upwelling.**

In areas of upwelling, nutrients from the deep ocean are brought to the surface. As excrement and dead organisms settle from the surface to the bottom of the ocean, bacteria convert the organic matter back into a dissolved form. The dissolved matter includes the nutrients phosphorus and nitrogen. These nutrients become concentrated in deep ocean water. In

Figure 8-34. Why are some of the world's major fisheries located in areas of upwelling?
In answer to the caption question, upwelling brings many nutrients up from the deep sea floor. These nutrients support much life near the ocean surface.

1. The sinking of colder polar water, which is denser than equatorial water
2. Sinking cold water contains needed dissolved oxygen. Water rising from the deep ocean through upwelling contains phosphorus and nitrogen.
3. Cold water sinks near the poles and travels toward the equator. The earth's rotation causes water traveling toward the equator to approach and follow continental shorelines. This water then moves across the ocean bottom to the opposite side of the ocean basin, where it rises to the surface along the continental margins.

areas of upwelling, these nutrients are brought to the surface where plants and animals can use them. That is why some of the world's major fisheries are located in areas of upwelling.

Check yourself

1. What causes circulation in the deeper ocean waters?
2. Describe the transfer of dissolved nutrients both to and from the deep ocean basins.
3. Describe the circulation pattern of the deep ocean waters.

Science Processes: Experimenting; Measuring; Communicating through data tables; Inferring
See also Activity Record Sheet 8-3B (Lab Manual page 112)

30 minutes
Large groups, or demonstration

Activity 8-3B   Simulating the Effects of Heat Absorption on the Earth's Surface

Materials
timer (or clock or watch that indicates seconds)
thermometer (quick-response type preferred)
heat lamp
dishpan or similar container
light-colored sand
dark-colored sand
water
long-handled wooden or plastic spoon for stirring

Purpose
To compare the absorption of heat by different materials.

Procedure
1. Make four data tables that begin like the one shown (for light-colored sand, dark-colored sand, still water, and moving water). Extend each to include three depths: 1 cm, 3 cm, and 5 cm below the surface.
2. Pour light-colored sand into the container to a depth of at least 6 cm.
3. Place the heat lamp so that the heat source is about 20 cm above the surface of the light-colored sand. Measure the distance between the light and the sand's surface. (Maintain this distance for each material.)
4. Before turning on the lamp, take temperature readings of the sand at depths of 1 cm, 3 cm, and 5 cm. Record these readings in the appropriate spaces on your data table for light-colored sand.
5. Turn on the heat lamp. SAFETY NOTE: *Have dry hands when you turn on the lamp. Do not touch the heat source once the lamp is on. Turn off the lamp whenever it is not needed.*
6. At the end of 2, 4, and 8 minutes of heating, take the necessary temperature readings. Record them on your data table.
7. With the heat lamp off, empty the light-colored sand from the container, replace it with dark-colored sand, and repeat the experiment.
8. Repeat the experiment, this time for still water. SAFETY NOTE: *When using an electrical appliance near water, care must be taken to keep water from touching the appliance or its cord. Also, the person turning the appliance on and off must have dry hands.* Measure and record the temperatures.
9. For the moving-water experiment, refill the container with fresh water before taking the first temperature reading. Then, using the spoon, create a water circulation by continually stirring the water or by making waves on the surface. Continue this motion until the table has been completed.

Questions
1. Which material can absorb the most energy with the least change in temperature?
2. How does the color of a substance affect the absorption of heat?
3. How does depth affect temperature?

Conclusion
How does motion in the water affect the distribution of heat? Why?

Data Table for Light-colored Sand				
Depth of Temperature Reading	Temperature Before Lamp Is Turned On	Temperature With Lamp On for 2 Minutes	Temperature With Lamp On for 4 Minutes	Temperature With Lamp On for 8 Minutes

Section 3 Review   Chapter 8

Use **Reading Checksheet 8-3** TRB page 83
   Skillsheet 8-3 TRB page 125
   Section Reviewsheet 8-3 TRB pages 187–188
   Section Testsheet 8-3 TRB page 297

Check Your Vocabulary

1 crest	2 trough
12 gyre	9 tsunami
10 high tide	13 upwelling
11 low tide	5 wave base
8 rogue wave	3 wave height
7 surf zone	4 wavelength
6 swell	

Match each term above with the numbered phrase that best describes it.

1. The highest point of a wave

2. The lowest point between two wave crests

3. The vertical distance between a wave's highest and lowest points

4. The horizontal distance from a point on one wave to the corresponding point on the next wave

5. The point below the surface of water at which the orbital motion of a wave nearly disappears (1/2 a wavelength below the mid-height of the wave)

6. A rhythmic pattern of waves

7. The area where breaking waves occur

8. A very high wave that forms on the open ocean when high waves of about the same wavelength have their crests coincide

9. A huge wave caused by an underwater earthquake somewhere along the ocean bottom; barely noticeable out at sea

10. When the waterline of a body of water reaches its highest point

11. When the waterline of a body of water reaches its lowest point

12. A closed system of rotating ocean currents

13. A process by which deep, cold, nutrient-rich water is brought to the surface and replaces lighter surface water

Check Your Knowledge

Multiple Choice: Choose the answer that best completes each of the following sentences.

1. The orbital motion of a wave is greatest (largest diameter) __?__.
   a) at wave base
   b) about ½ the depth of wave base
   c) below the trough but above wave base
   d) at the surface

2. The energy in a wave is proportional to __?__.
   a) wave height squared
   b) wave length squared
   c) wave speed squared
   d) wave length

3. Tsunami are caused by __?__.
   a) wind
   b) coinciding crests of two or more different waves of about the same wavelength
   c) underwater earthquakes
   d) density differences in the water

4. The tide is caused by __?__.
   a) wind
   b) the moon's gravitational pull
   c) the rotation of the earth
   d) the moon's gravitational pull and the earth's rotation

Check Your Understanding

1. What happens to the movement of water in a wave in the surf zone?

2. How does the height-to-length ratio of waves change when they merge to form a rogue wave?

3. How is sand moved along a coastline?

4. Describe the factors that affect the timing and height (strength) of tides.

5. How do the major gyres of rotating ocean surface currents differ in the Northern and Southern Hemispheres?

Chapter 8 Review

See also **Chapter Testsheets 8A and 8B**
TRB pages 331–332.

Concept Summary

Oceans and seas cover nearly 71% of the earth's surface.
☐ The oceans are the Pacific, Atlantic, Indian, and Arctic.
☐ Marginal seas form in three different ways.
☐ The depth of the oceans is measured by echo sounding.

The **ocean bottom** has a varied topography.
☐ Continental margins connect the continents with the deep ocean basin.
☐ The mid-ocean ridge is a continuous feature that girdles the entire surface of the earth.
☐ The varied topography is formed from volcanic activity, erosion, and deposition of sediments. Ocean bottom resources are extremely varied and of great value.

Physical properties of ocean water affect the ocean environment.
☐ The salinity of sea water varies from place to place in the oceans, but the average is 35 parts per thousand.
☐ Surface temperatures are highly variable, but vary only slightly (from 5°C to less than −1°C) below 1 km depth.
☐ Density in ocean water varies as temperature and salinity change.
☐ Water pressure increases 1 bar every 10 meters depth.
☐ The ocean depths can be divided into three zones (photic, disphotic, and aphotic) on the basis of available light.

Ocean water movements affect the ocean environment, the coastline, and the climate.
☐ Water motion in most waves (which are created mainly by storms and other winds) is circular rather than forward.
☐ The rhythmic rise and fall of tides is created by the gravitational pull of the moon and the rotation of the earth.
☐ Ocean surface currents form large circular motions called gyres.

☐ Deep water circulation is caused by the sinking of cold water near the poles.
☐ Upwelling returns deep, cold, nutrient-rich water to the ocean's surface.

Putting It All Together

1. Describe the ocean environment at 3000 m depth. Include all physical and chemical features.
2. How do deep ocean currents differ from surface currents?
3. What causes changes (increases and decreases) in the ocean's salinity?
4. Do increases in salinity and temperature affect water density in the same way? Explain your answer.
5. How does water pressure affect people's activities in the ocean?
6. Describe the topographic features in the ocean.
7. Describe the effects of waves and tides on a shoreline.
8. Explain why sea ice is able to form in the Arctic Ocean.
9. Describe the formation and movement of a tsunami. Include places where one is most likely to occur.
10. How are marginal seas related to structural features of the ocean bottom?

Apply Your Knowledge

1. What types of ocean resources seem to be at cross purposes in terms of their use or development?
2. Explain how a vessel could travel across the ocean and not feel the orbital motion of the waves.
3. How might the topography of the ocean basins affect deep ocean circulation?

4. How could a captain wisely use surface current information while engaging in commercial shipping between Europe and North America?
5. What percentage of meteorites striking the earth's surface would probably end up on the ocean bottom? Explain your answer.

Find Out on Your Own

1. Using reference books, find out how OTEC works, and make a labelled diagram of an OTEC system.
2. Where in the world are the major areas of upwelling and what percentages of the world's fish catch is taken from these waters?
3. Describe the major surface gyres in all the oceans. How do the currents in these gyres compare and contrast? What types of patterns are present?
4. Make a detailed list of all the products made from menhaden (Atlantic herring).
5. What are some of the hazards for divers using air tanks?
6. What are the bends? What causes them? What can be done for a victim of the bends?
7. Find out specifics about a recent deep-sea expedition and report your findings to the class. Some possibilities: the Mariana Trench, the underwater canyon in Monterey Bay (California), the Red Sea, the Mid-Atlantic rift zone, the search for the *Titanic* or some other sunken vessel.

Reading Further

Cook, Jan Leslie. *The Mysterious Undersea World.* Washington, D.C.: National Geographic Society, 1980.
This book contains beautiful photography and descriptive text of the undersea world.

Elting, Mary. *Mysterious Seas.* New York: Grosset and Dunlap, 1983.
This is an interesting, informative book about little-known facts of life in the oceans. The section on unsolved mysteries connected with the undersea world is especially appealing. Fine illustrations, glossary, index, and pronunciation guide all aid in learning more about the ocean.

Gilbreath, Alice. *River in the Ocean: The Story of the Gulf Stream.* Minneapolis: Dillon, 1986.
This enjoyable book discusses many aspects of the Gulf Stream. It describes how the current is formed and how it influences the climate of surrounding land.

Heezen, Bruce C., and Charles D. Hollister. *The Face of the Deep.* New York: Oxford University Press, 1971.
This illustrated natural history of the deep-sea floor is a wonderful book to browse through. It contains hundreds of close-up photographs of tracks, traces, and organisms of the abyss.

Hargreaves, Pat, ed. *The Arctic.* Morristown, NJ: Silver Burdett, 1981.
Each chapter of this book describes one aspect of the ocean: waves, tides, winds, currents, continental drift. The book also describes the interaction of humans with the ocean.

Lambert, David, and Anita McConnell. *Seas and Oceans.* New York: Facts on File, 1985.
This fascinating book surveys several aspects of oceanography—physical features, islands and shorelines, life in the ocean, and human interactions. Excellent photographs accompany the text.

Science Issues of Today   Aquaculture to Help Meet the World's Hunger

The origins of aquaculture are not new; oysters have been farmed for more than 2000 years. Today, aquacultural bounty, like the trout being netted below, account for 6% of the annual fish catch.

Fish and shellfish, both marine and freshwater, have been a staple food in many parts of the world since before written history. The fishing industry is losing the ability to keep pace with an increasing demand for more food from an ever-growing world population.

The numbers of fish and shellfish and their distribution are key factors in determining whether or not commercial fishing will be successful. Basically, the population size of organisms is ever changing in response to natural gains and losses. Reproduction and growth rates are balanced by death and predation rates. Also, long-term changes in nature influence cyclic changes in population sizes. Once an organism becomes targeted as a commercially valuable species, fishing will also tend to reduce the population size. Overfishing can further reduce the numbers until the fish virtually disappear. Fish and shellfish are only abundant in areas of high productivity where nutrients, such as nitrogen and phosphorus, are also abundant. In the presence of sunlight, algae use these nutrients to grow; and the algae are the oceanic plants that other organisms eat. These types of abundant nutrients and algal growth are limited to two areas: shallow waters over the continental shelves, and upwelling areas where nutrient-rich waters from the depths of the ocean return to the surface.

Continental shelves and upwelling areas are being worked with new and more efficient fishing and fish-processing techniques every year, resulting in quicker and larger catches. Thus, the diminishing size of fish populations will very soon become a limiting factor.

One way modern science is trying to provide a consistent harvest from the ocean without harmfully decreasing the numbers of organisms

is through aquaculture. Aquaculture is to the water realm what agriculture is to the land. Shellfish can be successfully started and concentrated in very favorable marine environments, where they are tended and harvested. Several different types of fish can be penned, fed, and protected from predators in large underwater enclosures. As long as the enclosures permit free circulation of water, then the highly concentrated number of fish will be free of disease, and their body wastes will be harmlessly recycled. These same concepts can be applied to freshwater fish like trout and catfish.

Research in the areas of marine and freshwater aquaculture has to include biologic, physical, and chemical aspects of the growth environment. Some fruitful research in these areas has been done, but much more will be needed if we are to provide a continuous, ecologically sound supply of fish and shellfish to satisfy a world's hunger.

Landscapes

Unit 5

Scientists monitor temperatures of the earth near active volcanoes carefully, looking for signs that may indicate that an eruption is about to occur.

Motion and change are apparent in the earth's atmosphere. Motion and change are apparent in the earth's position relative to the sun, moon, and stars. Motion and change are apparent in the earth's oceans, rivers, streams, and lakes. Not so apparent is the fact that the earth's land masses are also subject to motion and change.

Sometimes, motion and change in the earth's crust are sudden and violent. Earthquakes and volcanoes are examples of such changes. Other times, the changes are taking place over much longer periods of time and are caused by weathering, erosion, and deposition of earth materials.

Any landscape you look at is the result of earth processes acting on earth materials. That landscape will continue to change throughout the earth's future. Such changes are part of the beauty and dynamics of earth science and the ever-changing earth.

Chapter 9
The Earth's Changing Surface

Chapter 10
The Restless Crust

Chapter 9 The Earth's Changing Surface

Student Resources		Meeting Individual Needs	
Student Text	**Laboratory Activities**		
Section 1 Weathering 424–436			
Physical Weathering 425–426	Investigation 9-1 Physical Weathering and Erosion by Running Water LM 119–120	Enrichment	
Chemical Weathering 426–428			
Mixed Weathering 428–429			
Rates of Weathering 429–431	Activity 9-1A Comparing Rates of Chemical Weathering 432	Reinforcement	
	Activity Record Sheet 9-1A LM 117		
From Rock to Soil 431–434	Activity 9-1B Comparing Samples in a Soil Profile 434	CORE	
	Activity Record Sheet 9-1B LM 118		
Careers: Geographer/Civil Engineering Technician 435			
Section 1 Review 436			
Section 2 Erosion 437–452			
Erosion by Running Water 438–441			
Our Science Heritage: Travel and World Geography 440			
The Formation of a River Valley 441–443			
Erosion by Glaciers 443–445	Investigation 9-2 Fluidity of Ice LM 123–124	Enrichment	
Erosion by More than One Agent 445–447			
Controlling Erosion 447–451	Activity 9-2 Changing the Rate of Erosion 450	CORE	
	Activity Record Sheet 9-2 LM 121		
Thinking Skill: Comparing 448			
Section 2 Review 452	Research Lab 9 Identifying Features of Alpine Glaciation LM131	Enrichment	
Section 3 Deposition 453–465			
Deposition by Running Water 454–457	Activity 9-3A Analyzing a Core Sample 456	Enrichment	
	Activity Record Sheet 9-3A LM 125		
	Investigation 9-3 Comparing Settling Rates LM 129	Enrichment	
Stream Erosion and Deposition 457–459	Activity 9-3B Stream Erosion and Deposition Patterns 458	CORE	
	Activity Record Sheet 9-3B LM 126		
Deposition by Wind 459–461			
Deposition by Glaciers 461–464	Activity 9-3C Comparing Core Samples 462	Enrichment	
	Activity Record Sheet 9-3C LM 127		
Section 3 Review 465			
Chapter 9 Review 466–467			

9

Teacher Resources		Meeting Individual Needs
Teacher's Edition	**Teacher's Resource Book**	
Discussion Idea 422C	Letter to Parents EI 55 Essential Ideas 9-1 EI 57–58 Overhead Transparency B17	Enrichment Reinforcement CORE
Demonstration 422D Creative Writing Idea 422D		
Activity Notes 422E		
Activity Notes 422F	Teaching Diagram 9-1 TRB 40 Skillsheet 9-1 TRB 126	CORE Reinforcement
Section 1 Review Answers 422F	Reading Checksheet 9-1 TRB 84 Section Reviewsheet 9-1 TRB 189–190 Section Testsheet 9-1 TRB 298	Reinforcement CORE CORE
	Essential Ideas 9-2 EI 59–60	Reinforcement
Demonstration 422G		
	Teaching Diagram 9-2 TRB 41	CORE
	Skillsheet 9-2 TRB 127	Reinforcement
Discussion Idea 422G Activity Notes 422H Environmental Topic 422J Teaching Thinking Skills 422J–422K Section 2 Review Answers 422K	Reading Checksheet 9-2 TRB 85 Section Reviewsheet 9-2 TRB 191–192 Section Testsheet 9-2 TRB 299	Reinforcement CORE CORE
	Essential Ideas 9-3 EI 61–62 Teaching Diagram 9-3A TRB 42	Reinforcement CORE
Activity Notes 422L		
Activity Notes 422M	Teaching Diagram 9-3B TRB 43	CORE
Demonstration 422N Discussion Idea 422N Activity Notes 422P Section 3 Review Answers 422P	Overhead Transparency S22 Skillsheet 9-3 TRB 128 Projectsheet 9-3 TRB 250 Reading Checksheet 9-3 TRB 86 Section Reviewsheet 9-3 TRB 193–194 Section Testsheet 9-3 TRB 300	Enrichment Reinforcement Enrichment Reinforcement CORE CORE
Chapter 9 Review Answers 422Q–422R	Chapter 9 Testsheet TRB 333–334	CORE

9

Weathering

Learner Objectives

1. To distinguish between physical and chemical weathering.
2. To identify factors that affect rates of weathering.
3. To distinguish layers in a soil profile.
4. To relate soil formation to physical and chemical weathering.

Concept Summary

Weathering is the breaking down and wearing away of earth materials.

Physical weathering occurs when earth materials are reduced in size.

Chemical weathering occurs when new substances are formed from earth materials.

Discussion Idea

Everyday Signs of Weathering

Tell students that they probably already know more about weathering of rock than they realize. For example, find out if students have ever visited a very old cemetery with stone grave markers. Ask: Were some of the headstones hard to read? If so, why? (The names and dates may have been worn away.)

Which headstones do students believe were harder to read—the youngest or the oldest? (the oldest) How did the students infer that the hard-to-read headstones were the oldest? (Of all the stones, they were the most worn away.)

Explain that they are probably right; in most cases, the most worn-away stones are indeed the oldest stones. However, it also depends upon the material of which the headstone was made. For example, marble wears away much more slowly than does sandstone or limestone.

Explain that the process of rock becoming worn away is the process of weathering. Virtually nothing on earth is immune from weathering—not headstones, roads, buildings, river beds, or even the mountains themselves.

Tell students that they will find out much more about the earth's weathering in Section 1 of Chapter 9.

9-1

Demonstration

Evidence of Chemical Weathering

Obtain and show slides of Carlsbad Caverns, New Mexico; Mammoth Cave, Kentucky; or Lehman Cave, Nevada. (Slides can be obtained commercially through chambers of commerce or through past visitors to the caves.) These famous caves provide excellent examples of chemical weathering.

Explain that such caves began long ago when the water table was much higher than it is now. In fact, each cave began under water, with highly mineralized water slowly circulating throughout the present cave area. The minerals in the water chemically dissolved portions of what is now the cave.

In time, the water table became lower. Then the relentless dripping of running water, containing dissolved carbon dioxide, dissolved more and more of the limestone that made up the cave. This in turn began the formation of the beautiful stalactites and stalagmites in the cave.

Ask students if they have ever visited a cave and, if so, where. Have them describe their experiences.

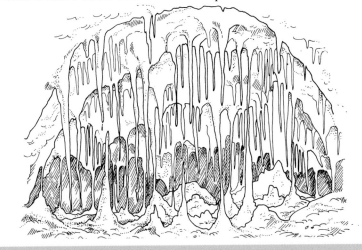

Creative Writing Idea

The following writing assignment may help students grasp the chemical weathering process of carbonization.

You are exploring caves in New Mexico, much like the one shown in Figure 9-4 on page 427, with your eight-year-old cousin. Your cousin is delighted with how beautiful the cave is and wants to make one when you go home. Explain to your cousin how the cave was formed and why it would be difficult to create one in your backyard. Describe a simple experiment to show your cousin how the process of carbonization works.

Science Background

Rocks and minerals break down at the earth's surface through a complex combination of both physical and chemical weathering. Most weathering is actually a result of this combination, rather than caused by a single process. As physical weathering (also called mechanical weathering) breaks rocks and minerals into smaller and smaller pieces, more surface area becomes available for a variety of chemical changes to occur.

The most significant type of physical weathering is caused by the 9 percent expansion that occurs when water freezes.

Oxidation is the most rapid type of chemical weathering. Typically, in a given soil profile the oxidized zone may be the most extensive one.

Chemical weathering is also important in the creation of the zone of leaching, intermediate in a soil profile. In this zone, water filtering down through the topsoil has chemically removed much of the carbonate mineralization

Minerals originally formed at the highest temperatures are the most rapidly affected by chemical weathering. For example, olivine is readily affected by chemical weathering, whereas quartz is very resistant.

9-1

Student Misconception

The concept of a changing earth is difficult for most students to grasp. Many view the earth's surface as a rather permanent entity because day-to-day weathering is slow and subtle. Signs of physical and chemical weathering are all around us; we simply fail to notice.

Create a "Weathering Alert" station in your room by having students monitor particular areas or physical features of the room over a period of several months for all subtle and obvious evidence of physical or chemical weathering. Include features that will be relatively unaffected by humans (e.g., a terrarium) and others that will be obviously affected by human behavior (e.g., a bookcase) to open discussion about human impact of weathering and erosion processes. Another useful object to observe would be a thin pane of glass placed on a high shelf with several centimeters extending past the edge. The glass will begin to "flow" downward after a few months.

Reports can take the form of news releases, written as if the event had great significance. This emphasis on the everyday physical and chemical weathering of the students' immediate environment will help to create an awareness and appreciation for the changing nature of the earth's surface.

9-1

Activity Notes

Activity 9-1A

Comparing Rates of Chemical Weathering page **432**

Purpose To compare weathering rates in different rocks.
- **CORE** 10 minutes Demonstration or groups of 4
- **Activity Record Sheet 9-1A** (Lab Manual page 117) can be used to record this activity.
- Science Processes: Experimenting; Inferring.

Safety

Know in advance where the sink or eyewash station is located. If acid does get in your eye, wash your eye out immediately. Have everyone wear goggles if they are available. If acid gets on hands or clothes, wash them immediately with water.

Advance Preparation

For 10 percent hydrochloric acid, add 10 mL concentrated hydrochloric acid to 90 mL water. SAFETY NOTE: *When diluting an acid, ALWAYS add the acid to the water. Add very slowly, stirring constantly with a glass rod.*

Procedure Notes

Reaquaint the students with reading the meniscus, and review the proper technique for using the balance. Draw attention to the use of sample fragments for this activity. Have students swirl the beakers containing the samples as often as possible to promote the reaction.

Disposal

The diluted acid (10% hydrochloric acid) is disposed of down the drain. Make sure all glassware in contact with the diluted acid is washed thoroughly.

Answers to Questions

1. The samples of carbonate rock will weather more.
2. An increase in the rate of weathering from one day to the next can be caused by a chemical breakdown of resistant materials on the surface of the sample. A decrease in the rate of weathering would indicate a chemical reaction on the surface that prevents further weathering.

Conclusion

The rate of chemical weathering is affected by the size of the fragment and by the amount of its exposed surface area. Shaking the mixture will increase weathering due to abrasion.

Activity Notes

Activity 9-1B

Comparing Samples in a Soil Profile   page **434**

Purpose To look at relationships between soils and rocks.

- 20 minutes Groups of 4
- **Activity Record Sheet 9-1B** (Lab Manual page 118) can be used to record this activity.
- Science Processes: Observing; Classifying.

Advance Preparation

Choose several road or stream cuts where the vertical sequence of rock, rocky soil, subsoil, and topsoil are visible. From each site, collect a rock sample and 2 or 3 soil samples. Label the samples according to site and level.

Alternatively, soil formation kits are available from scientific supply houses.

Procedure Notes

For Step 2, tell the students to separate the materials by any variable(s) they choose. After they have completed one set of samples, poll the students to see what variables they used and how the size of the piles changed along the vertical sequence.

Point out the dark humus in the topsoil and the characteristics of rich, valuable soil. Ask students the source of humus.

Answers to Questions

1. Answers will vary.
2. Answers will vary.

Conclusion

Answers will vary. Some soils will seem closely related to the rocks from the same road cut (for example, sand and sandstone may be present). But other rocks and soils will appear to have different origins. Layers should be obvious in most cases.

Going Further

Given the soil profile and the conditions under which it was generated, allow the students to speculate on how the soil might differ if one of several critical factors altered: temperature, moisture, topography, or soil organisms.

Section 1 Review Answers

Check Your Understanding
page **436**

1. Running water carries particles along with it. As the particles in the stream strike other particles they become smaller (physical weathering through abrasion). Water affects chemical weathering because it can dissolve substances in rock (as in the formation of limestone) and because, in some cases, it reacts with substances to form new substances in the rock (as in the formation of iron oxide from iron in a rock).

2. Because water can combine with carbon dioxide in the air, forming a weak carbonic acid that is able to dissolve limestone

3. A granite statue, because granite is an igneous rock that is not permeated by water (a weathering agent) as easily as a sedimentary rock like sandstone

4. A stone statue would undergo less chemical weathering in a dry climate. Some physical weathering, however, occurs in desert climates because of abrasion by sand particles carried by the wind.

5. The size of the particles becomes smaller due to weathering. The number of layers increases because of changes in particle size and also because of the accumulation of organic material such as humus.

9-1

Learner Objectives

1. To identify features of erosion by running water.
2. To describe the formation of a river valley.
3. To identify features of erosion by glaciers.
4. To infer type of erosion from physical characteristics of particles.
5. To consider ways of controlling erosion.

Concept Summary

Erosion involves the transport of weathered earth materials from one place to another.

9-2

Demonstration

The Impact of Erosion Caused by Running Water

Show a variety of pictures or slides of the Grand Canyon. No more spectacular example of erosion can be found on our planet! Ask students who have visited the canyon to describe their experiences.

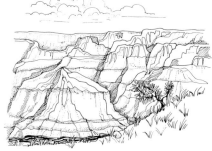

As you show the slides or pictures, tell students that the Grand Canyon is a mile deep and 8 to 12 miles wide. It is a relatively young feature of the earth's landscape, although the river that flows through it—the Colorado—is an old river. Explain that movement of the earth's crust caused changes in the landscape, resulting in formation of the Grand Canyon by the already long-present river.

Tell students that Mars also has its own "grand canyon"—but one that is 4 miles deep! Scientists question if its presence means that water once flowed on Mars.

Discussion Idea

How Erosion Can Be Curtailed

Point out to students that although erosion has been responsible for features of great beauty (such as the Grand Canyon), it has also caused great problems.

Ask students what sorts of problems they think could be caused by erosion. (Answers will vary: possible answers are crop failures, loss of homes, and loss of life as a result of floods; loss of property and lives as a consequence of landslides and avalanches, etc.)

Ask: What methods can be used to prevent problems caused by erosion? (Answers will vary; possible suggestions are damming of flood-prone rivers; improved drainage techniques to minimize flood damage; swimming lessons for residents of areas likely to flood; making certain that homes are not built on ground susceptible to landslide damage; etc.)

Activity Notes

Activity 9-2

Changing the Rate of Erosion   page **450**

Purpose   To study factors that affect rate of soil erosion.

- **CORE** 30 minutes Demonstration or large group
- **Activity Record Sheet 9-2** (Lab Manual page 121) can be used to record this activity.
- Science Processes: Formulating models.

Advance Preparation

Be sure the holes in the plastic are effectively covered with fresh tape.

Reaquaint students with the protractor so that they will be able to make quantitative angle adjustments.

Procedure Notes

You might want to have the two holes on opposite sides of the plastic container to have more control of the water flow.

Answers to Questions

1. The rate of erosion increased as the slope increased because the water is moving faster.
2. The rate of erosion increased as the volume of water increased because greater volume can exert more force on particles in the stream.

Conclusion

Increasing stream slope and increasing stream volume are two factors that can change the rate of erosion. Other factors that influence erosion rate include the nature of the material being eroded (sandstone will erode more rapidly than marble) and the size of rocks and rock fragments.

Going Further

If time allows, students could fill the container to the top and unplug both holes. How does this affect the erosion rate? Students could also design and carry out an activity to discover what effect particle size has on the rate of erosion.

Allow students to time the complete transport of sand into the bucket under a variety of conditions such as different water levels, amounts of sand, etc.

Evaluate the impact of a crinkled bedrock (using aluminum foil) on sand erosion.

Science Background

The term erosion is often used to mean both the wearing away (weathering) of a material and the removal of the weathered particles. In this text, a distinction is made between weathering and erosion, and the term erosion refers only to the transport or carrying away of weathered particles of rock.

Soil erosion is a serious environmental problem. In 1982, the U.S. Department of Agriculture estimated that the nation's farms lose about 3 billion tons of soil annually. This is more than twice the amount of soil formed each year. Loss of topsoil reduces soil fertility and crop yields. Most soil erosion is the result of poor farming and lumbering practices and overgrazing.

Terracing, contour plowing, strip cropping, cover crops, and conservation tillage are farming methods that protect topsoil. Farmers are also encouraged to remove hilly land that erodes easily from cultivation and to plant permanent vegetation such as shrubs and small trees. Planting rows of trees that serve as windbreaks reduces wind erosion.

Soil conservation has other benefits. It increases the amount of precipitation absorbed by a watershed and decreases the amount of sediment carried into lakes and rivers. By reducing runoff, soil conservation helps control flooding. Planting trees and shrubs on land unsuitable for cultivation provides habitat for wildlife.

9-2

Student Misconception

Students often do not realize that soil is a valuable natural resource. Controlling erosion is a significant aspect in maintaining soil. To understand the significance and nature of erosion control measures, students need a basic understanding of soil types and of the physical and chemical properties of each soil group.

Many human activities contribute to soil erosion. Soil surveys, which are reference manuals developed for every county, contain information on the capabilities of each soil type along with aerial maps and photographs keyed to the various soil types.

Using the soil survey for their county, students can identify the soil type of their home or school area. They can research the limitations and capabilities of that specific soil type and understand the presence or absence of particular structural features or uses of the soil. An excellent project is to assign students a particular tract of land and have them report on the soil conditions in that area and make recommendations as to the development of the area based on those properties. Soil surveys are available through most county extension agents.

9-2

Environmental Topic

The deserts of the western United States are a unique and fragile part of the country's landscape. Desert plants, animals, and soils are easily damaged and are slow to recover. Because of the desert's beauty and mineral resources, many people want to use desert lands for recreation and mining. But these activities are often harmful to the desert.

Environmental groups have strongly urged the mining industry to look elsewhere for mineral resources. Many people are also trying to restrict the use of off-road vehicles such as campers, motorcycles, and dune buggies on desert lands. The struggle over how to use desert lands pits two groups who feel strongly about their views against each other.

Discuss the conflict between allowing public and commercial access to desert lands and protecting its wildlife and landscape. Ask: How might this conflict be resolved?

Teaching Thinking Skills

Comparing   page 448

Comparing two or more things is related to classifying them—in both cases you find similarities. Comparing, however, requires an equal focus on finding differences. Students may sometimes have difficulty discovering similarities among seemingly different things, or discovering differences among apparently similar things. The teacher should make sure the students are using both parts of this important skill.

Reporting the findings of a comparison is often not as straightforward as it may seem at first. The best way to report the findings of a comparison depends on what is compared. In some cases, a table will do. When the similarities and differences are more complex, writing a paragraph is the best way to carry out Step 5.

Advance Preparation

For *Learning the Skill,* have ready examples of several different kinds of paper, such as construction paper, 25 percent cotton typing paper, onionskin paper, glossy photographic or printing paper, paper towels, and so on. The paper can be cut into small pieces to provide each student or group with a sample of each kind of paper.

For *Applying the Skill,* have ready samples of biotite mica, calcite, and fluorite (other minerals may be substituted if necessary). Each student or group will need a set of the three minerals.

Teaching Thinking Skills (continued)

Procedure Note

Learning the Skill should be done individually or in groups. Ask students to make a table to report their findings. Students should list the general features they identify on the left-hand side of the table and how each feature specifically applies to each type of paper on the right hand side. For example, for the feature "thickness," construction paper is "thick" and onionskin is "thin."

Applying the Skill can also be done individually or in groups. The challenge in this activity is to use the table of physical properties to write a clear paragraph comparing these minerals.

Possible Student Responses

Possible features of paper include thickness, color, smoothness of surface, strength, ease of tearing, absorption, fiber content, erasability, and so on. How the different papers are compared according to these features will vary.

Paragraphs comparing the minerals will vary. They should not simply describe each mineral's characteristics, but compare them. Statements such as "Calcite and fluorite are similar in color, streak, and luster, but differ in hardness and cleavage" indicate understanding of the skill of comparing.

Discussion

In a class discussion, have students compare the two comparisons they did for this skill. What is similar and different about reporting results in a table and in a paragraph? What problems occur with tables but not with paragraphs?

Going Further

Have students write a paragraph based on the table they made in *Learning the Skill*. You may also want to extend the comparison of minerals in *Applying the Skill* to include two or more additional minerals.

Section 2 Review Answers

Check Your Understanding
page **452**

1. Wind, running water, ice, and gravity
2. Gravity is the cause of all erosion. Gravity causes the winds to blow, running water and glaciers to move downhill, and particles of a solid to fall downhill (as in a landslide or rockslide).
3. As steepness increases, water speed increases and therefore more erosion takes place.
4. Particles carried in suspension are chemically separate from the water and can be filtered out or will settle out when the water slows down enough. Particles in solution are dissolved in the water and will not settle out. They can be removed only through evaporation or a chemical process of some kind.
5. In a glacier, both ice and gravity are involved. And at the foot of a glacier, meltwater causes erosion by running water. In a stream, both water and gravity are involved. In a sandstorm, there could be no wind without gravity. In a landslide, rockslide, avalanche, or snowslide, water or snow often triggers the motion that gravity causes to continue. In addition, landscapes (such as a desert scene) show evidence of erosion by wind and water.

9-2

Section 3 Deposition

Learner Objectives

1. To identify features of deposits left by running water.
2. To relate particle size and stream velocity to sorting.
3. To distinguish core samples of deposits left by running water and by glacial action.
4. To observe patterns of erosion and deposition in a river.
5. To identify landscape features caused by glacial action.

Concept Summary

Deposition occurs when particles of earth materials are deposited by an agent of erosion.

Activity Notes

Activity 9-3A

Analyzing a Core Sample   page **456**

Purpose   To examine a geologic core sample.

- 10 minutes Groups of 4
- **Activity Record Sheet 9-3A** (Lab Manual page 125) can be used to record this activity.
- Science Processes: Observing; Inferring

Procedure Notes

Tell students that examination of core samples is frequently used in the petroleum industry to learn the most likely places where oil reserves may be found. Core samples are useful for other mineral industries as well.

Point out any repetition in sequence revealed in the core sample. Ask students what such repetition might indicate. Alert the students' attention to the shape of the particles within each layer for clues about the depositional process involved.

Answers to Questions

1. The oldest deposits pictured are at the bottom right because deposits build on top of one another.
2. The three major colors of particles shown are black, white, and brown.
3. Yes, there are size differences related to the color differences. The brown sand has the largest particles, the white sand has the second largest, and the black sand has the smallest particles.
4. The fine-grained black particles were probably deposited in the silt area of Figure 9-18, the white in the sand area close to the silt, and the brown in the sand near the pebbles. The significant factor in the environments is the velocity of the water as the particles are deposited.

Conclusion

Examining a core sample can quickly provide information about a very long period of time in the earth's history. Many years of deposition can be viewed at once in a way that is not possible from only looking at the earth's surface.

Going Further

You might familiarize the students with the process of acquiring a core sample in the field. Present the students with core samples and encourage them to explain the samples.

Activity Notes

Activity 9-3B

Stream Erosion and Depositional Patterns   page **458**

Purpose   To learn where erosion and deposition patterns occur in a stream.

- **CORE** 30 minutes Demonstration or large groups
- **Activity Record Sheet 9-3B** (Lab Manual page 126) can be used to record this activity.
- Science Processes: Separating and controlling variables; Formulating models.

Advance Preparation

In selecting sand for this activity, construction sand works well because it is medium grained. Particle size affects the amount of time necessary for meanders to form. It may take 20 minutes to an hour (or even longer) with coarse sand. Soil meanders can form within a few minutes, but soil is messy to use.

Procedures Notes

Be sure to distribute the sand evenly over the pan surface.

To aid in the formation of meanders, the tubing can be angled so that it does not aim directly down the slope. Keep water velocity slow for the formation of meanders.

Answers to Questions

1. The stream begins to erode, and meanders begin to form.
2. Erosion takes place on the outside of meanders because the speed of the water is faster there.
3. Particles are deposited on the inside of meanders because the speed of the water is slower there.
4. The smallest particles; they are picked up first and carried farthest.
5. As water volume and speed increase from the second siphon, the rate of erosion also increases. (If the increase is too great, however, meanders may be destroyed.)

Conclusion

At the bends in meanders, the change of water speed provides conditions favorable for erosion (where the water is faster) or for deposition (where the water is slower).

Going Further

In repeating the exercise, find the critical siphon angle or slope that inhibits meander formation.

Science Background

Dry areas such as deserts contain much material that has been deposited by winds. Deserts often contain a wide variety of materials and particle sizes because they are a mixture of soils from many places, depending on the direction of the wind.

Soils deposited by the wind are known as loess soils (LES or LŌ'-is) and are often quite rich for growing crops because of their varied composition. Often they contain lava particles from volcanic eruptions. Particles from eruptions of Mount St. Helens probably can be found in most soils throughout North America today.

The segregation of many vital minerals results from sedimentary processes. The sedimentary deposits form when metal particles or gemstones are weathered from rock at higher elevation and carried downstream. Because they are heavy, these particles are among the first to settle out when the water speed decreases (where the stream gradient is reduced). The discovery of a sedimentary deposit of heavy ore, or placer deposit, is often the first clue to valuable minerals upstream. Prospectors found the Kimberly diamond mines in South Africa by exploring the area upstream from a placer deposit. Large amounts of native gold have been recovered from placer deposits in California.

9-3

Deposition

Student Misconception

A common misconception is that resources are distributed throughout the earth's crust in a rather random nature. While this may be true for some substances, the distribution of many of the earth's resources is tied to geophysical and geochemical processes that act to concentrate particular substances in given areas. For example, one of the most important sources of sulfide ore concentrations is found near the base of "layered intrusives," which form as minerals crystallize from a magma melt and settle to the floor of a magma chamber in distinct layers. One large body of this type, found at Sudbury, Ontario, contains great quantities of layered nickel, copper, and iron sulfide near its base.

Have the students examine Figure 12-5, a resource map showing the location of major deposits. Relate each deposit to a geophysical and/or geochemical process. Some resources that are related directly to these processes include coal, oil, natural gas, salt, ores, and manganese nodules.

Demonstration

The Impact of Wind Deposition on the Landscape

Bring in pictures or slides of sand dunes and other evidence of wind deposition. (If you live near a desert or beach area, a brief field trip would be even better.) In addition to photos of such places as White Sands, New Mexico, and the Sahara Desert, try to include photos of the "Great Dust Bowl" of the 1930s and of ash from the 1980 eruption of Mount St. Helens.

Explain to students that each of the above has had a profound effect on the environment of deposition. For example, the dust storms across the Great Plains of the United States in the years between 1933 and 1937 ruined millions of acres of farmland. Ironically, these storms were a combination of erosion and deposition resulting from several near-rainless years and overfarming.

The ash resulting from the eruption of Mount St. Helens in May 1980 fell on hundreds of square miles of Washington and Oregon. In fact, volcanic eruptions can force enough windblown particles into the air to be noticed globally.

Tell students that wind-blown sand is a major factor in the creation of a desert landscape. Unlike the deposits of running water, however, the particles deposited by wind have a very limited size range. Ask the students why this is so. (Because wind—unlike water—cannot carry large particles.)

Discussion Idea

Glaciers Are Agents of Erosion and Deposition

Point out that erosion and deposition work together to change the landscape. A good example is a glacier, which deposits materials as it abrades the surface that it crosses.

Ask students if they have ever seen a glacier. (Glacial ice can be seen in Alaska, Canada, north-central United States, the Alps, and the Andes.) If so, did it seem different from other snow and ice? Ask if the students saw rocks, rock fragments, and boulders deposited by the glacier.

Rocks and boulders can be carried by a glacier for hundreds of kilometers. When the glacier retreats, the boulders are deposited, often on bedrocks of a very different nature. Geologists refer to such deposits as *erratics*.

Activity Notes

Activity 9-3C

Comparing Core Samples   page **462**

Purpose   To infer geologic history by comparing two model core samples.

- 10 minutes Groups of 4
- **Activity Record Sheet 9-3C** (Lab Manual page 127) can be used to record this activity.
- Science Processes: Observing: Inferring.

Procedure Notes

Reacquaint the students with how core samples are taken in the field.

Alert the students to the differences in particle shape (angular versus rounded) that characterize a particular sample.

Answers to Questions

1. In sample A, particles are sorted by size and are more rounded than those in sample B. In sample B, particles are unsorted and many are angular.
2. Sample B was most likely formed by glaciers; if running water has formed this sample, layers would most likely have been distinct, and a higher number of particles would have become rounded.
3. Sample A was most likely formed by running water; layers of water-deposited particles are very evident.

Conclusion

Analysis of an area's rock and soil deposits can often help to determine which agent or agents (glaciers, volcanoes, running water, etc.) of erosion and deposition were once active in a particular area.

Section 3 Review Answers

Check Your Understanding
page **465**

1. The largest and densest particles settle out first. The smallest particles settle out last, farthest from the place where a river meets the sea. This happens because the size of the particles a stream can carry depends on the volume and speed of the water. As the water slows down, those requiring the greatest force from the stream (the largest/densest) will settle out first.
2. The bank on the outside of a meander is steep. Erosion takes place here because the water speeds up on the outside of a curve. On the inside of a meander, the bank slopes more gently because the water moves more slowly here, causing deposition to occur in this part of the river.
3. The wind removes sand from the windward side of the dune and carries it over the crest of the dune where it is deposited on the slope of the slip face.
4. Glacial deposits are easy to identify because the fragments vary greatly in size and because some fragments can be as large as boulders.
5. Sorting of glacial deposits can take place only on the outwash plain because sorting can be caused by erosion of particles carried by running water but not by erosion of particles carried by solid ice.

9-3

The Earth's Changing Surface

Chapter Vocabulary

Section 1

weathering
physical weathering
chemical weathering
bedrock
topsoil
humus
leaching
subsoil

Section 2

erosion
stream load
flood plain
levee
meanders
base level
oxbow lake
valley glacier
continental glacier
erratics
abrasion

9-3

Section 3

deposition
sorting
transported soils
residual soils
slip face
moraine
end moraine
terminal moraine
glacial lobe
outwash plain
till
stratified drift
drumlin
kettle lake

Chapter 9 Review Answers

Putting It All Together   page 466

1. Sandstone is a sedimentary rock formed from grains of sand that have been compacted and cemented together. Through chemical weathering, water is able to break down the cement that holds the particles together. Physical weathering of sandstone also takes place through abrasion, as particles of sand and/or rock pass along the surface of the cliff. In either case, gravity causes the weathered particles to fall to the base of the cliff.

2. A fully developed soil profile contains four layers. The lowest layer is the original bedrock. Above the bedrock is a layer of large fragments that have, through weathering, become separated from the bedrock. As weathering of the particles continues, a layer of smaller particles is formed at the top of the developing profile. And finally, in a fully developed profile, organic matter called humus is added to the smallest particles (which are on top) to form a layer of topsoil. Beneath the topsoil layer is a layer of subsoil. Minerals removed through leaching from the topsoil layer accumulate in the subsoil layer.

3. Answers will vary. Physical weathering will occur wherever abrasion or expansion and contraction take place. Chemical weathering will occur in the presence of water or other moisture. Discoloration is often a sign of chemical weathering.

4. Before the erosional process, weathering is primarily chemical and involves the formation of fragments and particles from larger pieces of solid material. During the erosional process, physical weathering through abrasion takes place. If liquid water is involved in the erosional process, chemical weathering will also further break down the particles and fragments.

5. On a desert, erosion can be either by wind (a sandstorm) or running water (runoff after a rainstorm).

6. A flood plain and a delta are similar insofar as both are formed by the deposition of particles from running water. They differ in that a flood plain is formed in level areas along the course of a river when a river overflows its banks and then recedes after the flood stage passes. A delta forms at the end of a river where particles that have been carried down the river are continually being deposited as the velocity of the river slows when it enters a body of water like a large lake or ocean.

7. The size of particles that can be carried along by running water depends on the velocity and volume of the stream. Layers of different size particles indicate changes in the stream's volume or velocity. No such sorting takes place in deposition by wind (where particles are all small) or by glaciers (where particles are totally unsorted and vary greatly in size).

8. Student diagrams should include the main features of Figure 9-20 on page 457. The riverbank curves more steeply along the outside because water moves faster along the outside of the curve and causes erosion to take place there. Deposition takes place along the inside of the curve, where the water moves more slowly. That is why the bank is much less steep along the inside of a meander.

Chapter 9 Review Answers (continued)

Putting It All Together

9. Student diagrams should contain the main features indicated in Figure 9-22 on page 460.

10. Student diagrams should contain the main features shown in Figure 9-24 on page 463.

Apply Your Knowledge   page 466

1. In a forest, you would expect the soil to be deeper because there is more liquid water and therefore more weathering. You would also expect the soil in a forest to be richer in humus, because leaves, pine needles, etc. from the trees of the forest fall to the ground, decompose, and become part of the topsoil layer. Near the North Pole where tundra conditions predominate, there is little vegetation and little liquid water. Soils are poor, dry, and not deep.

2. Continued watering leaches nutrients from the soil in a flowerpot. To prevent or offset this occurrence, plant food can be mixed with the water that is used to water the plant. Also, care must be taken to give only as much water as is needed to moisten the soil. (Some students may mention watering the plant from below, so that the water is drawn up into the soil. In such cases, the water not absorbed within a certain time must be discarded. A plant that sits in water constantly can drown because the soil becomes totally saturated with water and there is no room for air in the soil.)

3. When a sandstone cliff weathers, minerals that hold particles together are dissolved by water through a process of chemical weathering. The dissolved minerals are then washed away with the water and are deposited in the soil or wherever evaporation takes place. Particles that are not dissolved outright become dislodged, fall with the sand particles, and may dissolve at a later time. If the particles are not soluble, they will remain as particles along with the sand particles.

4. Scientists can infer the number of periods of deposition in a river delta by analyzing a core sample. Each period of deposition will be indicated by a sequence of layers of sorted particles that indicate changes in the volume and velocity of the stream flow.

5. Scientists can infer that glaciers once passed over an area because glacial erosion is different from erosion by running water. Scientists can also infer how far glaciers advanced by the presence of moraines and outwash plains.

9-3

Chapter 9

The Earth's Changing Surface

Section 1
Weathering

The earth's face is constantly changing. The part of the earth's surface that is water moves in a variety of ways. Water on the land flows downhill toward the sea. Water in lakes and oceans moves in waves and currents.

The part of the earth's surface that is covered with vegetation grows and dies and decomposes.

The part of the earth's surface that is rock is constantly being broken down into smaller pieces and into different combinations of elements.

Section 2
Erosion

Gravity causes wind, water, and glaciers to move constantly over the surface of the earth, carrying along with them any particles they are able to.

Glaciers carry particles that vary greatly in size. The size of the particles that water can carry depends on the speed and volume of the water. Wind carries only small particles.

Section 3
Deposition

As part of the earth's surface is being broken down, other parts of it are being built up. The particles of the earth's surface that are broken down and carried away become deposited somewhere else. There they can build up to very thick layers and become cemented into rock.

The wearing down and building up of earth surfaces are part of the balance in which earth materials are recycled. The materials may change form and location and composition. But the elements remain the same.

As will be discussed in this chapter, deposition caused the layers of sand which formed the sandstone. Weathering and erosion—most likely by running water, which is not visible in the photograph—caused the canyon to form down through the rock surface.

Various landforms cover the earth's surface. In some of them, the effects of earth processes are more evident than in others. What earth process(es) do you think might have shaped the walls of Jada Canyon, Arizona, pictured on the facing page?

Weathering   Section 1

Learner Objectives
1. To distinguish between physical and chemical weathering.
2. To identify factors that affect rates of weathering.
3. To distinguish layers in a soil profile.
4. To relate soil formation to physical and chemical weathering.

Section 1 of Chapter 9 is divided into five parts:

Physical weathering

Chemical weathering

Mixed weathering

Rates of weathering

From rock to soil

Figure 9-1. When people want a structure to last, they build it out of rock. But not even rock lasts forever.

Ask students to tell what they know of the pyramids and other ancient stone structures. For example, how old are they? What condition is their exterior in? What is causing any deterioration of the exterior?

Then have students relate this kind of deterioration to the earth's rock surfaces. Do mountains, for example, deteriorate? What factors affect the rate of deterioration? What happens to the parts of mountains that are worn away?

Answers to questions like these will be answered in the chapter. At this time, the main purpose of the questions is to get students thinking, in general, about the earth processes of weathering, erosion, and deposition.

Students can give other examples of expansion and contraction, like 1) the clearance in a roadbed at either end of a bridge, 2) the curling of a hot cookie sheet one end of which has been put under cold running water, etc.

If you leave a bicycle out in the rain, parts of it will probably rust. If you want a wooden building to last long, you keep a coat of paint on it to protect it from the sun and the weather. Roadways crack, split, and wash away. Bridges rust and corrode. Stone buildings, monuments, and statues are worn away. Nothing on the earth's surface escapes the effects of the atmosphere, not even the highest and hardest mountains.

Physical weathering
New vocabulary: weathering, physical weathering

The weather in the earth's atmosphere acts upon the surface of the earth, causing even the hardest of rocks to change. By means of water, wind, and chemicals, the atmosphere attacks the land and breaks down its rock surface. This breaking down and wearing away of the earth's rocks by the earth's atmosphere is called **weathering.**

One kind of weathering changes only the size of the rock. Large rock masses are broken down into smaller pieces of the same rock material. An example would be pieces of granite at the foot of a granite cliff. This type of weathering is called **physical weathering.** The size of the rock is changed, but the kind of rock is not changed.

What causes physical weathering on the surface of rocks? One cause has to do with changes in temperature. The high temperatures of summer cause the rock material to expand, or get larger. In winter, the low temperatures cause the rock material to contract, or get smaller. Over the years, this expanding and contracting weakens the rock material, causing it to crack and to break off. Because rock is a poor conductor of heat, this expanding and contracting occur mostly on the surface of the rock. It is the surface rock material, therefore, that is most affected by temperature changes.

Another cause is known as *frost wedging,* or *hydrofracturing.* Water in tiny cracks in rocks freezes from the outside surface toward the inside. Due to this kind of freezing, the pressure from the ice and trapped water increases as the water continues to freeze deeper into the rock. This pressure can, by means of countless tiny fractures, actually split the rock.

Are even the highest and hardest mountains changed by the earth's atmosphere?

Other examples can be given in which objects must be shielded from the weather by paint or some other protective coating. What, for example, happens to metal (bridges, ships, appliances) or wood (fences, docks and piers) that is left unprotected?

Figure 9-2. Fragments of granite at the base of a granite formation are an example of what type of weathering?
Fragments of granite below a granite formation are an example of physical weathering, in which only the size of a material is changed.

In any given seasonal change, several cycles of freezing and thawing occur. The repetition, almost on a daily basis, greatly enhances the breaking apart of rock.

How can even animal burrows promote physical weathering?

1. Temperature changes cause rock to expand and contract. This weakens rock and causes it to crack and break into smaller pieces.
2. The roots of plants that grow in cracks in rock push against the sides of the cracks as the plant grows. This can weaken the rock and cause pieces to break off.

In answer to the caption question, rusting is an example of chemical weathering, because there is a change in substance (from iron to iron oxide)

Figure 9-3. Is rusting an example of physical weathering or chemical weathering?

The roots of shrubs and trees also cause physical weathering. Some plants can grow in between the cracks in rocks. As the plant roots grow, they push against the sides of the cracks in the rock surface. The surface of the rock weakens and pieces of rock finally break off. As more and more rock pieces break off, the crack becomes larger. This allows even more room for water to collect or roots to grow. Animal burrows also promote physical weathering by removing some of the underlying support of rocks.

Temperature changes and the roots of shrubs and trees can break down a large rock mass into a pile of smaller pieces of the same rock material. The many small pieces are the results of physical weathering.

Check yourself

1. How can temperature changes cause physical weathering?

2. How can the roots of plants cause physical weathering?

Chemical weathering
New vocabulary: chemical weathering

Physical weathering changes only the size of the rock material. But there is a kind of weathering that changes the material itself. You have most likely seen patches of rust on a steel wool pad, cast-iron frying pan, bicycle, or other object that contains iron. The rusting of iron is actually a form of weathering. In this kind of weathering, a change takes place in the material itself. It is no longer the same material that it was before the weathering took place.

When rust forms, iron combines with oxygen from the air to form iron oxide, a new substance with different properties than either iron or oxygen. Iron, for example, is attracted by a magnet, but the iron oxide in rust is not. This kind of weathering, in which a different substance is formed, is called **chemical weathering.**

Sometimes you can observe orange discoloration in a rock. The rock may have become brittle. Pieces can easily be chipped off. The orange color is probably a sign of iron oxide in the rock. The original rock contained iron or minerals with iron.

A form of chemical weathering known as oxidation has changed the iron to iron oxide.

Sometimes when the outer layer is chipped away, the inner rock appears to be a different color. The outer rock layer has undergone chemical weathering, but the inner layer has not. Different minerals have been formed in the outer layer.

There is some evidence that the freezing of water in rocks creates ideal conditions for chemical weathering. As water freezes, it expands 9%. The resulting pressure can force films of water into micropores and crevasses within the crystal structure of the rock. There the water can weaken the rock chemically.

A form of chemical weathering known as carbonization causes caves to form in rock material. Carbon dioxide from the air dissolves in water to form carbonic acid. This weak acid reacts slowly with some minerals found in rocks. One rock that is affected is limestone. Huge limestone caves can be formed over long periods of time by running water that contains dissolved carbon dioxide. The water flows through underground cracks in the limestone. The carbonic acid continues to dissolve more and more of the limestone along the surface of the cracks until a cave is formed. As years pass, the cave becomes larger and may be many meters high and many kilometers long.

Library research

Prepare a report on sink holes such as those that have occurred in the state of Florida. What causes them? Can anything be done to reduce the amount of damage that is caused by them?

Figure 9-4 shows a portion of Dolls Theatre, Carlsbad Caverns National Park, New Mexico. As mentioned in the text, carbonic acid forms in nature when carbon dioxide from the air dissolves in water.

Figure 9-4. Limestone caves form when carbonic acid dissolves the limestone. How does carbonic acid form in nature?

If a small amount of an acid is dropped onto a piece of limestone, gas bubbles can be observed on the limestone surface. A chemical reaction is occurring. The rock releases carbon dioxide gas as the acid reacts with the limestone or calcium carbonate mineral in the limestone rock. Can you imagine what would happen if you continued to add acid to the limestone? In a limestone cave, the chemical reaction is much slower, but it has been going on for thousands of years.

Check yourself

1. How does chemical weathering differ from physical weathering?

2. Explain the formation of limestone caves as an example of chemical weathering.

Mixed weathering

In nature, it is hard to separate chemical from physical weathering. Both often occur at the same time.

The longer that weathering takes place, the smaller the rock pieces become. Physical weathering continues when pieces of rock fall onto other pieces of rock and smash them into smaller bits. It continues as the pieces of rock get smaller when rubbed against each other, as during a landslide or while being carried along by a stream.

Chemical weathering often takes place at the same time as physical weathering. Freezing water forces films of water into very tiny pores in rock where the water reacts chemically with the rock. Running water or weak acid dissolves some of the minerals in rock fragments that are being physically weathered. The roots of growing plants, in addition to exerting pressure against rock, also have a chemical effect on the rock. As pieces of rock become smaller, more and more of the rock material itself is also being changed.

Have you ever wondered where the sand at a natural beach comes from? In most cases, the sand comes from the weathering of nearby rock layers. The sand at most beaches is made of small grains of the mineral quartz. Because of its hardness,

quartz resists weathering more than any other common mineral. Quartz remains when weathering removes less resistant minerals that were present in the rock. If you examine the rock layers near such a beach very carefully with a magnifying glass, you can observe the grains of quartz.

Check yourself   Check yourself answers appear in the margin below.

1. What is the relationship between chemical weathering and physical weathering?

2. What mineral is beach sand often composed of? Why does this occur?

Rates of weathering

In arid and semiarid climates, limestone is very resistant to weathering and forms mountains. In humid climates, limestone usually forms valleys.

Not all weathering of rock takes place at the same rate. The speed at which a rock weathers depends on several things: 1) the type and hardness of the minerals in the rock, 2) the type of rock, 3) the climate, 4) the topography, and 5) the exposure of the rock.

Figure 9-5. Where in this picture can quartz probably be found? As mentioned in the student text, quartz is commonly found in beach sand and in nearby rock layers from which the sand may have weathered. (Along some beaches, however, the water brings the sand from elsewhere by moving it along the coast. This process is described on page 407 of Chapter 8, where effects of wave action of ocean waves are discussed.)

Check yourself answers:
1. Both often occur together. As particles become smaller through physical weathering, it is easier for chemical weathering to occur because more surface areas are exposed.
2. Quartz, because it is more resistant to weathering than most other minerals, which are removed in the weathering process

If physical weathering predominates, sandstone will weather faster than granite. If chemical weathering predominates, granite can—depending on the solubility of the cement in the sandstone—weather faster than the sandstone.

Figure 9-6. In the past one hundred years, the obelisk called Cleopatra's Needle has weathered more than it did in the previous three thousand years.

How do substances found in the air in New York City affect the rate of chemical weathering?

What kinds of rock in your area are used for building stone? What kinds of rock are used for carved statues? Why are these kinds of rock used? How does weathering vary among the different kinds of rocks used?

The minerals in a rock affect the rate at which the rock weathers. Rocks made up of minerals that dissolve easily in water weather faster than rocks made of water-resistant minerals. Rocks made up of minerals that react with acids and with substances dissolved in water also weather faster. Limestone, as you have seen, is one example of a rock that weathers quickly when acid is present.

Of the three types of rock, sedimentary rock generally weathers faster than igneous or metamorphic rock. Most sedimentary rocks form from grains that have been cemented together. Sedimentary rock is therefore more porous than igneous or metamorphic rock. Water can permeate the rock more easily. Often the cement is a mineral that water can easily dissolve. That is why sandstone, for example, tends to weather faster than granite.

The climate of an area also affects the rate of weathering. The more precipitation in an area, the faster is the rate of weathering. Rocks weather fastest in a humid climate with a wide range in annual temperatures. In the United States, for example, rocks weather faster along the East Coast than they do in the dry Southwest.

Around 1500 B.C., the people of ancient Egypt built tall stone monuments called obelisks. Even though 20 m or greater in height, each obelisk was carved from a single piece of rock (usually red granite from a quarry at Aswan). The builders also carved writings on the sides of these granite obelisks.

A little over a hundred years ago, in 1880, one of these obelisks came to New York City as a gift to the American people. Before coming to New York, this obelisk (now called Cleopatra's Needle) had been exposed to the climate of Egypt for over 3000 years. Even so, the writing on its sides had weathered very little. But in the hundred years or so in New York City, the writing has been almost completely weathered away.

One key to explaining what happened to the writing on the sides of Cleopatra's Needle lies in the difference in climate between the two locations. Egypt is warm or hot all year long, and very dry. New York City has cold winters and hot summers and much more precipitation than Egypt. Another key has to do with substances found in the air in New York City which increase the rate at which chemical weathering occurs.

Check yourself

1. Why does sedimentary rock weather faster than igneous or metamorphic rock?

2. How can climate affect physical weathering? How can it affect chemical weathering?

From rock to soil   New vocabulary: bedrock, topsoil, humus, leaching, subsoil

Physical and chemical weathering are important in the formation of soil, the loose material on the surface of the earth that supports plant life. Profiles 1, 2, 3, and 4 in Figure 9-7 show how soil forms when rock is weathered.

Profile 1 shows the solid layer of rock from which soil will form. This layer of rock, which is under every soil, is called **bedrock.** In Profile 1, very little weathering has taken place.

Profile 2 shows the first stages of soil formation. Weathering has caused large fragments of rock to break off from the solid rock. Water can easily penetrate to the bedrock, which is now below the surface.

In Profile 3, zones of different particle sizes have formed. The particles near the surface are the smallest because they have weathered the longest. The particles near the bedrock are larger because weathering has begun there more recently.

Profile 4 shows a fully developed soil profile. Nearest the surface is a layer of **topsoil.** This layer contains **humus,** which is a dark brown or black substance that is formed when dead plants and animals decay. Humus is very rich in materials which plants need for growth. Because of humus, plants grow readily in topsoil.

Humus is an organic material. All organic materials contain the element carbon, an element found in all living things. Humus contains carbon because humus is formed from the remains of plants and animals that were once alive.

Chemical weathering of soil changes its mineral content. Water filtering down through the topsoil removes some of the minerals. This process is called **leaching.** In the zone of leaching (the topsoil layer), only the minerals that are most resistant to weathering remain unchanged.

1. Sedimentary rock, which is usually made up of grains that are cemented together, is more porous than metamorphic and igneous rock and therefore tends to weather faster.

2. Climate can affect physical weathering because extremes of temperature can increase the expansion and contraction of rock, which weakens it. Climate can also increase the rate of chemical weathering when there is more precipitation.

Library research

Present-day conditions are speeding up the weathering of ancient and priceless stone statues and buildings in Greece and Italy. Find out what is being done to preserve these statues and buildings from weathering.

Science Processes: Experimenting; Inferring
See also Activity Record Sheet 9-1A (Lab Manual
page 117)

10-minute setup plus 5 follow-up observations
Demonstration or groups of 4

Activity 9-1A   Comparing Rates of Chemical Weathering

Materials

chips of carbonate rock fragments (marble, limestone, dolomite), sandstone, granite, and any other rock you'd like to try

250-mL beakers or jars (1 for each sample)

laboratory balance

10% dilute hydrochloric acid   wire screen

graduated cylinder   water

Purpose

To compare weathering rates in different rocks.

Procedure

1. Pour enough fragments of each sample into a beaker to fill it ¼ full.
2. Rinse the fragments in each beaker with water to remove any loose, tiny grains. Turn on the faucet and let water run slowly into the beaker. When full, place the wire screen on top of the beaker to prevent any fragments from falling out when you pour off the water. Repeat several times for each sample.
3. Next, use the balance to find the combined mass of the beaker and rock fragments for each sample. Record the data on a table like the one shown.
4. Using a graduated cylinder, measure out 100 mL of dilute hydrochloric acid and pour it over the rock fragments in the first beaker. Add an equal amount to each of the other beakers, too. Put the beakers aside until the next day.

   SAFETY NOTE: *Do not handle concentrated hydrochloric acid. Make sure the acid you work with is 10 percent dilute, which your teacher will provide. Do not get any of this dilute acid on your body. If you do, wash with plenty of clear water.*
5. On the second day, pour off the acid from each beaker, using the wire screen to keep the fragments from falling out. Pour the acid down the drain.
6. Rinse and drain the fragments in each beaker several times with fresh water from the faucet, as you did the previous day.
7. Carefully measure and record the combined mass of each beaker and fragments.
8. As before, add 100 mL of dilute acid to each sample and set aside until the next day. Then follow Steps 4–7.
9. At the end of the activity, rinse all fragments thoroughly to remove any dilute acid.

Questions

1. Which rock sample weathered more? How does your data explain your answer?
2. What change, if any, was there in the amount of weathering from one day to the next? What might explain this?

Conclusion

In addition to rock type, what else might influence the rate of chemical weathering?

Rock Sample	Combined Mass Day 1	Combined Mass Day 2	Combined Mass Day 3	Combined Mass Day 4	Combined Mass Day 5
A					
B					
C					
D					

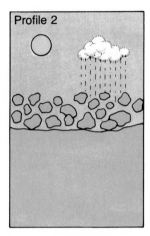
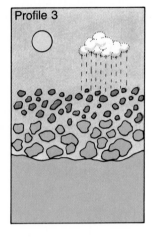

⬛ Topsoil (zone of leaching)	Zone of partially decomposed bedrock
Subsoil (zone of accumulation)	Unweathered bedrock
Partially weathered rock	

Figure 9-7. What is the name of the layer of rock that is under every soil and that appears in all four of these profiles?
(Unweathered) bedrock
See also Teaching Diagram 9-1 (TRB page 40).

As shown in Profile 4, a layer of **subsoil** is found under the topsoil in a fully developed profile. Clay and other substances that have filtered down from the zone of leaching accumulate in this layer of the soil. The soil in this zone of accumulation contains few of the elements needed by plants for growth. If the topsoil is removed from an area and the subsoil is exposed, plants will not grow readily in the exposed subsoil.

Because climate affects the rate of weathering, it also affects the formation of soil profiles. In areas where the climate is humid and there is much precipitation, a soil profile several meters thick can develop in a period of a few thousand years. In desert regions, however, where there is very little water, weathering takes place much more slowly. Soil found in a desert is usually sandy and the particles are much larger than the tiny soil particles of a fully developed soil profile.

Does climate affect the formation of soil profiles?

1. The particles on top are smallest because they have weathered the longest.
2. Humid climates promote the formation of thick, fully developed soil profiles in a few thousand years. In dry climates, weathering is much slower. As a result, soil particles are larger and profiles are less fully developed.

Check yourself

1. In a soil profile, where are the smallest particles found? Why?

2. How does climate affect the formation of soils?

Science Processes: Observing; Classifying
See also Activity Record Sheet 9-1B (Lab Manual page 118)

CORE   20 minutes   Groups of 4

Activity 9-1B   Comparing Samples in a Soil Profile

Materials

2 or 3 soil samples from
  different levels of a
  road cut
rock sample from lowest
  part of road cut
several sheets of blank
  white paper
toothpick (or teasing
  needle)
magnifying glass

Purpose

To look at relationships between soils and rocks.

Procedure

1. Pour a small quantity of soil from the sample from the highest level of the road cut onto a piece of paper.

2. Using the teasing needle and a magnifying glass, separate the sample into piles of similar materials.

3. Do the same for each of the other soil samples.

Questions

1. When examining the first sample, how did you decide which fragments were the same material? (Size, color, shape, and so forth?)

2. How do the different piles of materials compare—from the level nearest the surface to the deepest level?

Conclusion

How does the soil compare with the rock? Would you say that the soil formed from the rock or from other sources? Explain.

Careers   Geographer / Civil Engineering Technician

Geographer Geography has often been described as the beginning of the sciences. The word *geography* means "earth description." Many years ago, students studied geography. Now it is called earth science.

A geographer conducts research on the nature and use of the many areas of the earth, as well as on the distribution of people and resources. There are many special areas in which a geographer may work. Some of these are soils, climates, mineral resources, water resources, and their relation to people.

If you were to enter this field, it would be necessary to complete college. You should have a well-rounded background in the sciences but not necessarily a great deal of science.

You could expect to find job vacancies in colleges and universities. The federal government employs geographers in intelligence agencies. Local and state governments, market research firms, and travel groups also employ geographers.

For further information about a career as a geographer, contact:

A geographer's tasks may require working out-of-doors, in offices, or in laboratories. Travel is frequently necessary.
Association of American Geographers
1710 16th Street NW
Washington, DC 20009

Civil Engineering Technician
Engineers and engineering technicians use scientific and mathematical discoveries to solve practical problems in many different areas of modern life. Civil engineering is the branch that deals with the design and construction of highways, bridges, water supply systems, and similar structures.

Functions that may be performed by civil engineering technicians include the preparation of cost estimates, materials specifications, and construction schedules. They may also assist with surveying, drafting, and designing.

If you enjoy technical work, a career in civil engineering may interest you. To prepare, take science and math courses in high school. Then you might attend a technical institute, community college, or vocational school. Some engineering technicians have learned their skills through on-the-job training, but, in general, those with some education after high school have greater job opportunities.

Civil engineers and technicians are employed primarily by government agencies and by the construction industry.
For further information about a career as a civil engineering technician, contact:

The plan and profile this civil engineering technician is preparing will be used to improve drainage and reduce erosion.

American Society of Civil Engineers
345 E. 47th Street
New York, New York 10017

Section 1 Review   Chapter 9

Use **Reading Checksheet 9-1** TRB page 84
Skillsheet 9-1 TRB page 126
Section Reviewsheet 9-1 TRB pages 189–190
Section Testsheet 9-1 TRB page 298

Check Your Vocabulary

4 bedrock   8 subsoil

3 chemical weathering   5 topsoil

6 humus   1 weathering

7 leaching

2 physical weathering

Match each term above with the numbered phrase that best describes it.

1. The breaking down and wearing away of the earth's rocks by the earth's atmosphere

2. A kind of weathering in which a material is changed only in size, becoming smaller as a result of the weathering action

3. A kind of weathering in which different substances are formed

4. A layer of solid rock that is under every soil

5. The layer of soil that contains humus; found in a fully developed soil profile

6. An organic substance rich in materials that plants need for growth

7. The removal of minerals in the topsoil layer by water that is filtering down through the soil

8. The layer of soil that is found under the topsoil of a fully developed soil profile; contains few elements needed by plants for growth

Check Your Knowledge

Multiple Choice: Choose the answer that best completes each of the following sentences.

1. Expansion and contraction are caused by __?__.
   a) rusting
   b) chemical weathering
   c) changes in temperature
   d) rain

2. Oxidation and carbonization are examples of __?__.
   a) physical weathering
   b) leaching
   c) chemical weathering
   d) subsoils

3. As water __?__, it expands.
   a) condenses   c) falls
   b) freezes   d) infiltrates

4. In the formation of limestone caves, __?__ and carbon dioxide in the air combine to form weak carbonic acid.
   a) red granite
   b) calcium carbonate
   c) clay
   d) water

5. Because of its __?__, quartz resists weathering more than any other common mineral.
   a) permeability   c) porosity
   b) hardness   d) cement

Check Your Understanding

1. How does water affect physical weathering? How does it affect chemical weathering?

2. Why do caves generally form in areas where there is limestone?

3. Which will retain fine details longer—a sandstone statue or a granite statue? Why?

4. In which type of climate would a stone statue probably undergo the least weathering? Why?

5. As time passes, what happens to the size of the particles in a soil profile? What happens to the layers (number and size) in a soil profile? Why?

Erosion   Section 2

Section 2 of Chapter 9 is divided into five parts:

Erosion by running water

The formation of a river valley

Erosion by glaciers

Erosion by more than one agent

Controlling erosion

Learner Objectives
1. To identify features of erosion by running water.
2. To describe the formation of a river valley.
3. To identify features of erosion by glaciers.
4. To infer type of erosion from physical characteristics of particles.
5. To consider ways of controlling erosion.

Figure 9-8. Rocks that fall into a stream can be changed by the running water. How can they be changed in terms of their size, shape, composition, and location?
Size—they become smaller; shape—they become rounded; composition—soluble minerals in the rock are dissolved by the water; location—over time and as they become smaller, the rocks are moved farther and farther from the bedrock that is their source.

New vocabulary: erosion

Rock fragments are found at the base of a rock cliff. A closer look reveals that the fragments are composed of the same minerals as the rock cliff. Chemical and physical weathering have caused the fragments to break off the cliff. When you look at the cliff, you may notice that more of the cliff has been weathered away than can be explained by the fragments at its base.

What happened to the other rock fragments? They were most likely carried away by a natural agent such as running water. If there is a stream in the area, you will probably find rock fragments in the stream bed that contain the same minerals as the rock cliff.

The transporting of the products of weathering is called **erosion** (i-RŌ′-zhin). Four common agents of erosion are running water, glaciers, gravity, and wind.

Erosion by running water
New vocabulary: stream load

In almost all areas, running water is the dominant agent of erosion. When it rains, loose material is picked up and carried along by the rainwater running off the surface. (Even the splash of raindrops can loosen surface material.) As the runoff enters streams, it carries some of the loose weathered material along with it as mud, silt, sand, and pebbles. How far that material is carried depends on both the size of the particles of material and the force of the moving water.

You may have seen rocks or pebbles at the bottom of a stream. Chances are that they were carried to the stream by runoff water or that they fell into the stream because of gravity. The rocks and pebbles probably entered the stream closer to the stream's source and are being slowly carried downstream by the water. Furthermore, rocks with rounder edges have probably been carried farther by the stream.

The rocks and pebbles may not appear to be moving. But little by little, because of gravity and the force of the running water, the fragments and particles move downstream. Large fragments of rock may move only very short distances. Smaller fragments, like pebbles and gravel, travel much greater distances. Very small particles keep moving until the stream or river empties into a lake, reservoir, or sea.

Suggest that students observe a stream bed for particle sizes and distribution. Students might even bring sample stones and other size particles back to class for examination. How do the students' findings compare with what they expected to find?

Figure 9-9. The mud in this river is being carried in suspension. What will happen to the particles of mud when they reach a part of the river where there is little or no water movement?
The particles will settle to the bottom.

All the material transported by a river or stream is called the **stream load.** The smallest particles, which are too small to be seen with the naked eye, are being carried in solution. That is, they are dissolved in the water. In most rivers and streams, the water looks clear. Suppose you collected a sample of clear water and let the water evaporate. You would probably notice some very fine material that remained on the sides and bottom of the container. This material, which had been dissolved in the water, was being carried unseen in solution.

Other small particles are carried in suspension. That is, they are suspended in the water by the movement of the water. When they reach a point where the water stops moving, they settle to the bottom. Muddy water contains small particles of clay that have been stirred by the moving water and are suspended in the water. Suppose you collected a jar of this water and left it to stand. Soon, the water would start to clear as particles in suspension settled to the bottom of the container.

The process of weathering continues while erosion is taking place. The particles carried by a stream strike each other and strike particles on the stream bed. The farther downstream they are carried, the smaller, rounder, and smoother they become. Through physical weathering, large fragments eventually break into bits small enough to be carried along in suspen-

How much of the material transported by a stream makes up the stream load?

Review with students the difference between particles in solution and particles in suspension. Particles in solution (for example, salt in salt water) have been dissolved, have become part of the solution, and will pass through a filter. Particles in suspension (mud in muddy water, for example) are still separate from the liquid and can be filtered out. They are merely being carried along by the water.

Students should be aware that, as particles are being eroded, the weathering process is also continuing to act on these particles.

How do particles of rock change as they are carried farther downstream?

Our Science Heritage

Travel and World Geography

Two thousand years ago, the Greek geographer Strabo observed and described the countries around the Mediterranean Sea.

Today, if people want to know what it's like in China, they can start to find out at their nearest library. There they will find many resources, including atlases, descriptive nonfiction works, and the various kinds of publications for which organizations like Time-Life, Incorporated, and the National Geographic Society are famous.

Such was not always the case. The total picture of the earth, which we can now take for granted, is the result of centuries of travels, explorations, observations, and the keeping of accurate records and journals.

The ancient Greeks were the first people to want to know why different peoples lived differently. And they kept records of what they observed. Strabo, a Greek geographer and historian who lived from 63 B.C. to 24 A.D., traveled throughout the lands surrounding the Mediterranean Sea. His 17-volume geography describes all parts of the world known to the ancient Greeks and is still available and recognized as the best source of geographical information on the Mediterranean countries as they were 2000 years ago.

As you become more familiar with world geography and world history, you will come to appreciate the part various travelers, writers, naturalists, and geographers have played in extending our knowledge of the world out to its present boundaries.

---

sion. Through chemical weathering, some of the minerals in the fragments dissolve and are carried along in solution.

The amount of material carried by a stream (that is, the stream load) depends on the speed of the water and the volume of the water in the stream. A fast-moving stream can carry larger particles than a slower-moving stream. The amount of material transported also depends on the amount of water that is moving along. A slow-moving, large river can carry far more material than a fast-moving mountain stream.

Check yourself

1. How do particles in solution differ from particles that are in suspension?

2. What two factors affect stream load?

The formation of a river valley

New vocabulary: flood plain, levee, meanders, base level, oxbow lake

Almost everywhere on the earth you can find landscapes carved by running water. One of the most common examples is a river valley that is formed between two mountains. The three states shown in Figure 9-10 are typical of what happens.

At Stage 1, a fast-moving stream or river tumbles down the steep slopes between the sharp peaks of the two mountains. It begins to carve a valley between the peaks. Rainwater flows down the mountainsides, carrying small particles weathered from the rocky mountainsides. Eroded pieces, fragments, and particles of rock from the mountain peaks become the stream load and are transported down the slopes by water.

As time passes, the valley becomes wider and wider. Running water continually removes material from the sides of the mountains. The mountain peaks become lower and rounder because of the weathering and eroding action of the water. As the river erodes the mountain, it cuts its channel to a lower elevation. More streams form, capturing and draining water from a larger area into the river valley.

During Stage 2, the steepness of the river channel decreases, and the river valley becomes wider as the river curves and flood plains start to develop. A **flood plain** is a fairly flat area next to a river and nearly at river level. A flood plain is created by sideways erosion on the outside and deposition on the inside of a river's curve.

Even though the river is getting wider, it cannot contain the increased flow volumes that occur after heavy precipitation and runoff. At such times, the river overflows its banks and leaves deposits of sediments. The coarser sediments fall out of the flood waters as they first move out of the riverbed and over the bank. These deposits form a natural **levee** (LEV′-ee) on both sides of the river.

Library research

Find out the importance of the investigations of Nicolas Desmarest regarding the formation of river valleys.

What is a flood plain?

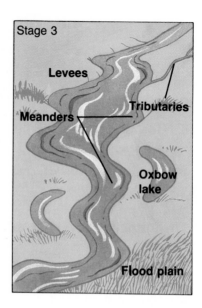

Figure 9-10. At which of the
three stages in the formation of a
river valley is the water moving
the slowest?
In answer to the caption question,
the water is moving the slowest at
Stage 3, which is why a flood
plain can develop at this stage.

See also Teaching Diagram 9-2
(TRB page 41).

Regarding the formation of oxbow
lakes: the reason meanders are
cut off—whether it happens
through normal erosion or during
a flood—is because the cut-off
shortens the length of the
channel, effectively increasing the
gradient (rate of descent) of the
river.

Can the climate of an area affect
the type of river valley that forms?

As the steepness of the river channel decreases, the river's course forms bends called **meanders** (mee-AN'-derz). Although the river is still eroding downward, the sideways erosion is increasing. The surrounding slopes are becoming less steep and the valley is being widened. River water velocity in non-desert climates stays the same or slightly decreases from Stage 1 to Stage 3. The energy in the moving water from Stages 1 to 2 to 3 is gradually shifted from downward erosion to sideways erosion. Every river has a limit to its downward erosion. This limit is the level of a lake or ocean that the river empties into, and it is called **base level.**

By Stage 3, the valley has become very wide and approaches base level. The river has such large meanders that they sometimes intersect each other, and the river flow then bypasses the cut-off meander. Sediment slowly fills in both ends of the cut-off meander, forming what is known as an **oxbow lake.** The wide, Stage 3 flood plain makes excellent farmland because the deposits from floods continually add nutrients to the soil.

The climate of an area can affect the type of river valley that forms. As examples, consider the Susquehanna Valley and the Grand Canyon. Both landscape systems have been forming for millions of years. Both have been produced by running water. But both are very different in appearance.

The Susquehanna Valley is located in an area with a high annual rate of precipitation. It has a very wide flood plain. The

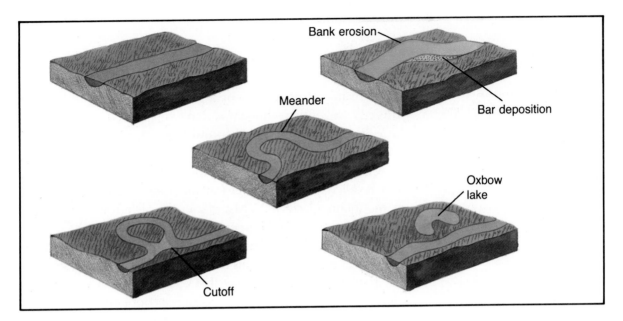

mountains that form this valley have gently sloping sides. Precipitation can increase rates of erosion and weathering, which cause a valley to widen. Humid climates with high annual amounts of precipitation often produce wide river valleys with gently sloping mountainsides.

The Grand Canyon, on the other hand, is narrow with steep walls. Its flood plain is very small. The Grand Canyon is located in a very arid climate, where there is little rainfall. Arid climates produce deep and narrow river valleys with steep canyon walls.

Figure 9-11. A portion of a meandering river can become separated from the river by sediment. What is the resulting blocked-off body of water called? The resulting blocked-off body of water is called an oxbow lake.

Check yourself

1. How does the steepness of the riverbed and the speed of the water change from Stage 1 to Stage 2 to Stage 3 in the formation of a river valley?

2. Why wouldn't a flood plain develop at Stage 1?

1. From Stage 1 to Stage 2 to Stage 3, both steepness of the riverbed and the speed of the water decrease.
2. Because the riverbed is too steep and the water is moving too fast

Erosion by glaciers

New vocabulary: valley glacier, continental glacier, erratic

The influence of glaciers, which are moving masses of ice, is confined to the cold regions where they are found. In these regions, snow does not completely melt in summer and thus builds up from season to season. In time, the mass of the snow on the top changes the snow on the bottom to ice. Under great pressure from its own weight, the ice begins to flow. A glacier has formed.

Library research

Find out more about John Wesley Powell and his contributions to our knowledge of the geology and landscape features of the American Southwest.

How much does a glacier move in a day?

The rate of movement of a glacier is too slow to be seen directly. Scientists, however, have measured the rates of movement of glaciers and found them to move a few centimeters or more each day.

A glacier may flow down a mountainside. This kind of glacier is called a **valley glacier** (or sometimes an alpine glacier or a mountain glacier). Valley glaciers, which follow old river channels, flow down between walls of rock.

A glacier may flow outward from its thick center over wide regions of a landscape. This kind of glacier is called a **continental glacier** and is an ice sheet that covers much of a continent. The ice sheet that covers Antarctica is a continental glacier.

Thousands of years ago, huge ice sheets covered the northern part of North America. As these glaciers moved down from the north, they carried with them loose material frozen in the ice. When the ice melted, the loose material was left behind. In some cases, the material included boulders 1 m or more in diameter. (These large water-worn and ice-borne boulders are known as **erratics** (i-RAT'-iks).

How can scientists infer that a boulder was carried by a glacier? The scientists can study the boulder to see what kind of rock it is and what minerals it contains. They can then look for layers of rock that match that of the boulder. In many cases, the matching rock layers are many kilometers away. The scientists then study the slope between the boulder and the matching rock layers to see if a gravity-caused rockslide could explain the movement of the boulder. If gravity is unlikely, then glaciers are the only other agent of erosion capable of moving a boulder such a great distance.

Figure 9-12. In a Stage 1 stream (on the left), the valley bottom is completely filled with flowing water. A flood plain and oxbow lake (on the right) are characteristic of Stage 2 to Stage 3 development of a river valley.

Figure 9-13. Some glaciers flow down a mountainside. How does the shape of this glacier-carved valley compare with the valleys shown in Figure 9-12?
The glacier-carved valley is smoother on the sides, and its cross-sectional shape is U-shaped rather than V-shaped (as in Figure 9-12, left).

The erosion produced by a glacier is different from the erosion produced by running water. Running water can carry only small particles. Glaciers can carry particles of all sizes—from tiny grains to large boulders. Also, in the case of a valley glacier, the glacier extends up the sides of the valley and erodes the valley walls at the same time it is eroding the base, changing a V-shaped valley to a U-shaped valley. A river of running water, on the other hand, flows along the floor of the valley.

Check yourself

1. How does a valley glacier differ from a continental glacier?

2. How does a valley formed by a river differ from a valley shaped by a glacier?

1. A valley glacier flows in a channel (an old riverbed), whereas a continental glacier flows outward from its center in any direction possible.
2. Rivers form V-shaped valleys. Glaciers form U-shaped valleys.

Erosion by more than one agent
New vocabulary: abrasion

Often a landscape has been shaped by more than one agent of erosion. The landscape in a desert area, for example, is often the work of both running water and the wind. The sand dunes in a desert show the effect of the wind as an agent of erosion. During a windstorm, particles of sand may be carried many meters from their original location. But one period of rainfall

What two agents of erosion commonly shape a desert landscape?

Figure 9-14. Both wind and running water have eroded this landscape. What effect does the agent of erosion have on the size of the particles that are eroded? As particles are eroded, they also become smaller through the process of abrasion.

in a desert can produce more erosion than several months of wind action. (Also keep in mind that physical weathering and erosion occur together. As particles are eroded, they also become smaller by the physical weathering process of **abrasion** (uh-BRAY'-zhin), in which particles rub and scrape and hit against each other.

Evidence of erosion may suggest which agents were active. It may not be possible, however, to determine which of the agents had the greater effect. In a landslide, it may appear that gravity is the only agent. But the landslide could have been started by rainwater running off the mountainside. In that case, both running water and gravity were the agents of erosion.

Where glaciers are active, the erosional system usually involves both glacial action and running water. The glacier carries the material down the side of the mountain. At the base of the glacier, running water from the melting ice carries some of the material farther along.

Gravity as an agent of erosion is most evident in landslides, rockslides, or snowslides. In a rockslide, weathering weakens the rock surface along a cliff. Fragments of rock break off. Gravity causes the fragments to fall to the base of the cliff.

Gravity is also the underlying force behind all erosion. It is gravity that causes water to run downhill. It is gravity that causes glaciers to flow. And it is gravity that produces winds by pulling heavy colder air down beneath lighter warmer air.

Check yourself

1. Using glaciers as an example, show how an erosional system usually involves more than one agent of erosion.

2. How is gravity also involved in erosion caused by running water, by glaciers, and by wind?

Controlling erosion

The activities of people can have a marked effect on the erosion of weathered material from the earth's surface. For example, the trees, shrubs, and grasses of undeveloped areas prevent soil erosion. When the land is stripped of this natural vegetation, there is nothing to prevent wind and water from eroding valuable topsoil.

The roots of natural vegetation hold the soil in place. The stems of grasses and other plants act to slow down the flow of runoff. The leaves break the force of falling raindrops. Slower runoff can mean that more water soaks into the ground. And less runoff means less erosion.

Farmers play an important role in maintaining the soil. The best farming methods are those that help to preserve topsoil. If farmers decide not to plant crops on a field, they will let wild vegetation grow. Lumber companies also play an important role when they replant forest areas after cutting down trees for lumber. In replanting, people act to preserve valuable soil and watersheds.

People also affect erosion when they build dams in rivers. Dams, which provide sources for inexpensive electrical power,

Library research

Prepare a report on erosion by wind. Using examples, show how it affects the landscape. What, if anything, can be done to prevent it?

Check yourself answers:
1. Erosion by a glacier involves the glacial action (abrasion/transport) of the moving glacier and running water at the base of the glacier.
2. Gravity causes glaciers and water to move downhill. It also causes denser, cooler air to move in under warmer, less dense air, thus producing winds.

Critical Thinking

Classify the following terms as components of water, glacial, wind, or gravity erosion: ice, stream load, dust, rockslide, flood plain, sand dunes, landslide, erratics.

Water: stream load, flood plain
Glacial: ice, erratics
Wind: dust, sand dunes
Gravity: rockslide, landslide

How does replanting affect valuable soil and watersheds?

Thinking Skill Comparing

When you compare different objects or events, you are finding similarities and differences. The skill of comparing helps you to focus and organize your observations. Once you have compared a group of objects or events, you will know more about each item in the group.

For example, you might compare two clouds. You observe that they are similar because they are both rain clouds. But they are different because one is tall and puffy and the other is spread out like a blanket. Your comparison of the clouds helps you classify them—the first is a cumulus cloud and the second is a stratus cloud.

Both similarities and differences must be considered when comparing. The following steps may help you improve your skill of comparing:

1. Examine all the objects or events to be compared.
2. Carefully observe the characteristics of each object or event.
3. Identify each characteristic as a similarity or a difference among the objects or events.
4. Write down the similarities, and then write down the differences.
5. Report your findings.

Learning the Skill

Use the steps of the skill of comparing to compare the different kinds of paper provided by your teacher. Besides thickness and color, how many kinds of features, or characteristics, does paper have? Can you think of titles that describe these features clearly?

Applying the Skill

Compare the following minerals: biotite mica, calcite, and fluorite. You may use the table on page 93.

To report your findings, write a paragraph describing the similarities and differences among these minerals. Begin with characteristics they all share and end with those unique to each mineral.

biotite mica

calcite

fluorite

create lakes where rivers once flowed. The flow of water in the river below a dam can be controlled. Seasonal flooding can be prevented by dams that trap and store much of the sudden increases in water coming from the watershed areas.

There are many places in the world where canals have been dug to provide artificial waterways and irrigation channels. Diverting the water in a river reduces the amount of water flowing in the river. This in turn reduces the amount of erosion that occurs farther down the river.

The erosion that takes place along coastlines is much harder for people to control. Over a long period of time, ocean waves erode the coastline. People who have built homes near the coast try to prevent this from happening. In most cases, such attempts have not been successful. Houses built back from the coast have actually fallen into the sea because of erosion by ocean waves.

Library research

Do a report on the channelization of a river (for example, the Missouri River) to control flooding and to stabilize its banks.

Figure 9-15. How does natural vegetation help to prevent erosion?
The roots of plants hold soil in place. The stems act to slow down the flow of runoff. The leaves absorb some of the force of the falling raindrops so that they have less impact on the soil.

Science Processes: Formulating models
See also Activity Record Sheet 9-2 (Lab Manual
page 121)

CORE   30 minutes   Demonstration or large groups

Activity 9-2   Changing the Rate of Erosion

Materials

plastic or metal trough

large plastic container
  with two holes, one
  above the other, near
  the bottom

bucket

measuring cup or
  beaker

fine sand

water

marking pencil

protractor

books or blocks or wood
  to use as props

1 sheet of plastic

masking tape

Purpose

To study factors that affect rate of soil erosion.

Procedure

1. Using the books, the sheet of plastic, and the trough, set up the trough as shown in the picture. The plastic should cover the books so that they won't get wet. Start with a slope of 10° on the trough.
2. With the marking pencil, mark the side of the measuring cup about 2/3 of the distance from the bottom.
3. Fill the cup to the mark with sand, and empty this sand into a pile about midway down the trough.
4. With the marking pencil, mark the large plastic container about 2/3 of the way from the bottom.
5. Put masking tape over each hole near the bottom of the container. Make sure both holes are completely and tightly covered.
6. Fill the container to the 2/3 mark with water.
7. Put the bucket at the bottom of the trough. Position it so that it will catch any water and sand that comes down the trough.
8. The student who is holding the container should remove the bottom strip of tape and let the water run down the trough. (One or two trial runs may be necessary.)

9. When all of the water has left the container, note how much (if any) of the sand is left in the trough. Record the results.
10. Increase the stream slope 5° or 10°. Repeat the procedure and record your results.
11. With the marking pencil, make a second mark on the container half way between the top mark and the bottom of the container.
12. After making sure that both holes are securely covered with tape, fill the container to the lower mark.
13. Using the smaller slope, repeat the procedure with water flowing through only the bottom hole of the container.
14. Now use a single strip of tape to cover both holes. Fill the container to the lower mark. Remove the tape so both holes are open.

Questions

1. What happened to the rate at which the sand was eroded when the stream slope was increased? Explain.
2. What happened to the rate at which the sand was eroded when the stream volume was increased? Explain.

Conclusion

What factors have you studied that can change the rate of soil erosion? What other factors might change the rate of erosion?

Figure 9-16 How can a shopping mall affect the runoff pattern of an area?
A shopping mall creates an impermeable surface which prevents water from soaking into the ground. This water then runs across the roofs and parking lots, increasing the amount of runoff in that area.

Wherever people are, the landscape changes. To make roadways, hills are leveled and stripped of vegetation. Mountains are tunneled through. Swamps are filled. Wide paths are cleared through forests. To make room for homes and shopping centers, schools and factories, huge tracts of land are cleared.

Think of how a shopping mall can change the runoff pattern of an area. The impermeable surface of the rooftops and paved parking lots permits no rainfall to soak into the ground. All of this water can collect on the surface as runoff and be channeled into a potentially erosive stream. The large areas of impermeable surface can act as funnels, causing a rapid build-up of water and increasing the likelihood of a flash flood.

Urban development greatly affects the landscape. It also affects how the agents of erosion will change that landscape in the future. Urban developers must therefore effectively plan for the discharge of water from paved and developed areas.

How can large areas of impermeable surface increase the likelihood of a flash flood?

1. Erosion can be prevented by replanting areas stripped of vegetation and by reducing or controlling the flow of water in a stream (as through channels, canals, and dams).
2. Erosion can become more likely if soil is stripped of its ground cover and if soil is covered by an impermeable substance, both of which increase the amount of runoff.

Check yourself

1. What are two ways in which people can help prevent erosion?

2. What are two ways in which people can increase the likelihood of erosion?

Section 2 Review   Chapter 9

Use **Reading Checksheet 9-2** TRB page 85
Skillsheet 9-2 TRB page 127
Section Reviewsheet 9-2 TRB pages 191–192
Section Testsheet 9-2 TRB page 299

Check Your Vocabulary

10 abrasion	6 levee
11 base level	4 meanders
8 continental glacier	5 oxbow lake
1 erosion	2 stream load
9 erratics	7 valley glacier
3 flood plain	

Match each term above with the numbered phrase that best describes it.

1. The transporting of the products of weathering
2. All the material transported by a stream
3. The level area between the banks of a river and the foot of the mountains
4. Curves and bends in a stream or river
5. A lake that forms when sediment fills in both ends of a cut-off meander
6. A natural embankment formed on both sides of a river
7. A glacier that flows down a mountainside
8. An ice sheet that flows outward from its center over wide regions of a landscape
9. Larger water-worn boulders that have been deposited by a glacier
10. The physical weathering process in which particles hit against each other
11. The level of a lake or ocean that a river empties into

Check Your Knowledge

Multiple Choice: Choose the answer that best completes each of the following sentences.

1. In almost all areas, _?_ is the dominant agent of erosion.
   a) glaciers
   b) wind
   c) running water
   d) gravity

2. Through _?_, some of the minerals in rock fragments dissolve in the water and are carried along in solution.
   a) abrasion
   b) chemical weathering
   c) evaporation
   d) physical weathering

3. As the steepness of a river decreases, the speed of the water _?_.
   a) decreases
   b) increases slightly
   c) remains the same
   d) increases greatly

4. The soil in a flood plain is _?_.
   a) full of erratics
   b) rich in nutrients
   c) not fertile
   d) impermeable

5. _?_ can carry particles of all sizes.
   a) Wind
   b) Running water
   c) Glaciers
   d) Runoff

Check Your Understanding

1. What are four common agents of erosion?
2. What effect does gravity have on erosion?
3. What effect does the steepness of a riverbed have on erosion?
4. How do particles that are carried in suspension differ from particles that are carried in solution?
5. Using examples, explain how in most erosional systems there are two or more agents active.

Deposition   Section 3

Section 3 of Chapter 9 is divided into four parts:

Deposition by running water

Stream erosion and deposition

Deposition by wind

Deposition by glaciers

Figure 9-17. This photograph of Mendenhall Glacier (near Juneau, Alaska) shows ground deposits left fifty years ago by the receding valley glacier. What size particles would you expect to find in the deposit left by a receding glacier?
Receding glaciers leave deposits with a wide mixture of particle sizes—ranging from clay-size particles to large boulders. Streams and rivers formed from the melting glacier leave deposits of small particles, well sorted by size.

Learner Objectives
1. To identify features of deposits left by running water.
2. To relate particle size and stream velocity to sorting.
3. To distinguish core samples of deposits left by running water and by glacial action.
4. To observe patterns of erosion and deposition in a river.
5. To identify landscape features caused by glacial action.

New vocabulary: deposition

Suppose you find a deposit of earth materials many meters thick. The bottom layers contain a wide range of particle sizes. The particles are angular and of different shapes. The upper layers contain particles that are the same size and that are rounded, with smooth surfaces. This evidence provides clues to what happened in that area.

The deposits left by each agent of erosion differ greatly. In the example just mentioned, the evidence indicates both glacial deposits (the lower layers) and deposits eroded by running water (the upper layers). As you might have inferred, **deposition** means the process whereby particles and fragments of earth materials are deposited or laid down by an agent of erosion.

Deposition by running water

New vocabulary: sorting, transported soils, residual soils

Deposits formed from running water contain layers of different particle sizes. Also, the particles deposited from running water are rounded rather than angular. As the particles are carried along by the water, they become round and smooth from striking each other.

Rivers and streams carry particles of weathered earth materials like soil and rock downstream. The size of the particles a stream can carry depends on the volume and speed of the water. When a river reaches the sea, the water slows down. As the flow of the water slows down, the particles begin to settle to the bottom. In a process called **sorting,** the largest and densest

---

What kinds of evidence in a deposit of earth materials provide clues to the agents of erosion that were active in that area?

Through discussion, explore ideas about the effects of erosion and deposition in your area. What forms/agents of erosion are active in your area? What landforms in your area might be the result of materials brought there by some agent of erosion? (Soil and the formation of flood plains were discussed earlier in this chapter. Other landforms will be discussed in this section of Chapter 9.)

In answer to the caption question, the smallest particles are carried the farthest distance by moving water.

Figure 9-18. This diagram shows a profile of the deposits of material near the mouth of the stream. Why are the smaller particles found further into the ocean?

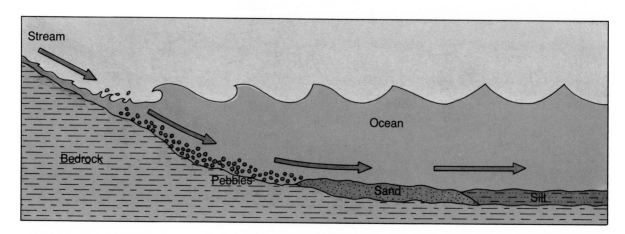

Figure 9-19. The rich farmland in this valley is made up of transported soils. What natural agent of erosion transports soils from one place to another? Running water transports soils from one place to another. (Wind can remove exposed soil, but such particles are widely dispersed by the wind, rather than deposited in a thick layer.)

particles settle out first. As the flow becomes slower and slower, increasingly smaller particles settle out until all material has been deposited except the material in solution.

As deposits build up near the mouth of a river, the slope of the riverbed decreases. This further slows down the speed of the water. Smaller and smaller particles settle out in layers as the speed of the flow decreases. That is why a cross section of the deposits near the mouth of a river will show the largest particles near the bottom of the deposit. The particles become smaller and smaller toward the top of the deposit.

Along the coasts of continents, layers of deposits build up wherever rivers flow into the sea. Deposits from large rivers can cover many square kilometers and can be hundreds and even thousands of meters thick.

As a river enters the sea, the particles carried by the river are deposited in the shape of a fan. Because of its shape, a deposit near the mouth of a river is called a delta (from Δ, which is the capital form of *delta*, the third letter of the Greek alphabet).

Delta regions contain rich soils that have formed from materials deposited from the water. Soils formed from eroded materials are called **transported soils.** (Other soils, which remain near the bedrock from which they have weathered, are called **residual soils.**)

Transported soils have often determined the location of human civilizations. Farming has always been important because it provides the food needed for life. Due to heavy precipitation in the fall or spring, the volume of some rivers increases

Library research

The ancient Egyptians relied on the Nile to flood each year to provide fertile land for farming. Prepare a report on the good and bad effects of rivers flooding.

Science Processes: Observing; Inferring
See also Activity Record Sheet 9-3A (Lab Manual page 125)

10 minutes   Groups of 4

Activity 9-3A   Analyzing a Core Sample

Materials

the model core sample
 shown on this page

Purpose

To examine a geologic core sample.

Procedure

1. One way that earth scientists learn what materials have been deposited in a certain location is to drill a hole into the earth and pull out the material. This material is called a core sample. Examine closely the core sample shown on this page.
2. Each layer represents a different period of deposition. Note the different types of materials and the order in which they are deposited in the sample.

Questions

1. If the rocks in top left corner were closest to the surface of the earth, where are the oldest rocks in this core sample?
2. What are the three major colors of particles shown here?
3. Are there size differences related to the color differences? Why might the layers show different particle sizes? (Hint: How might the size of the particle be related to water speed?)
4. What types of environment would these rocks be deposited in? Figure 9-18 may help you decide.
5. The mixture of black and white particles at the left was caused by animals burrowing in the mud. What types of animals might live in the environments in which these rocks were deposited?

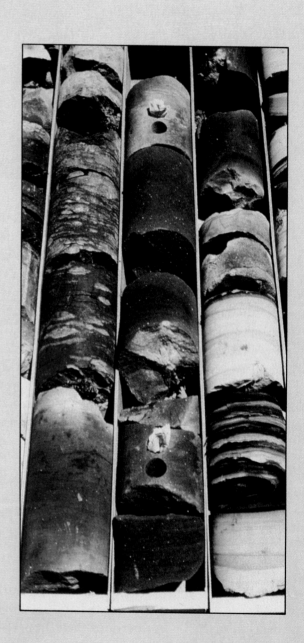

Conclusion

How can looking at a core sample help you learn the geologic history of an area?

greatly. These rivers overflow their banks at least once a year. Figure 9-19 shows a valley where this happens. The soil in such a valley is very rich from material deposited by the overflowing river. Some of the earliest civilizations developed in such regions because the soil was good for farming.

Check yourself

1. As a river begins to slow down, which particles settle first?

2. How do transported soils differ from residual soils?

1. The largest and densest particles settle out first.
2. Transported soils result from deposition of materials carried by an agent of erosion. Residual soils form at the site of the weathering and are not brought from someplace else.

Stream erosion and deposition

In some places in a stream or river, it is possible to observe evidence that erosion and deposition are both taking place at the same time. One such place is at a curve, or meander, in a river or stream, as shown in the top view in Figure 9-20.

When the water in a river reaches a meander, the speed of the water changes. Along the outside of the meander, the speed of the water increases. The increase in speed causes erosion. That is why the riverbank along the outside of the meander (labeled A in the diagram) is steeper than the riverbank along the inside. Along the outside of the meander, it is possible to observe material being eroded away from the riverbank.

The speed of the water is greater along the outside of a meander, causing erosion to occur in that area. Along the inside of a meander, the water slows down, causing particles to settle out of the water.

Figure 9-20. Erosion is the dominant process on the outside of a meander. Deposition is the dominant process on the inside. What causes erosion and deposition to occur?

See also Teaching Diagram 9-3B (TRB page 43).

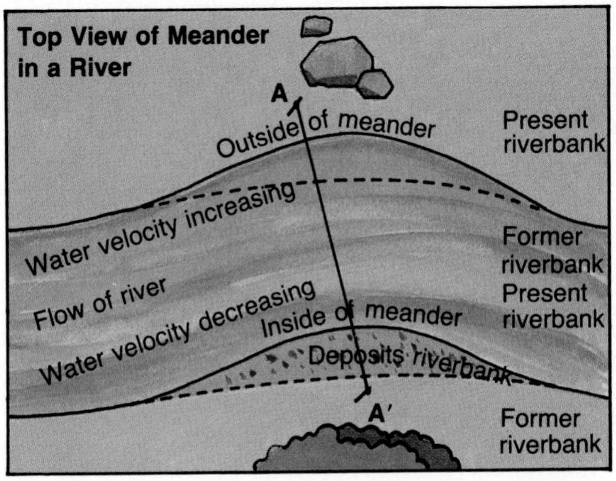

Top View of Meander in a River

A
Outside of meander
Present riverbank
Water velocity increasing
Flow of river
Former riverbank
Present riverbank
Water velocity decreasing
Inside of meander
Deposits riverbank
A′
Former riverbank

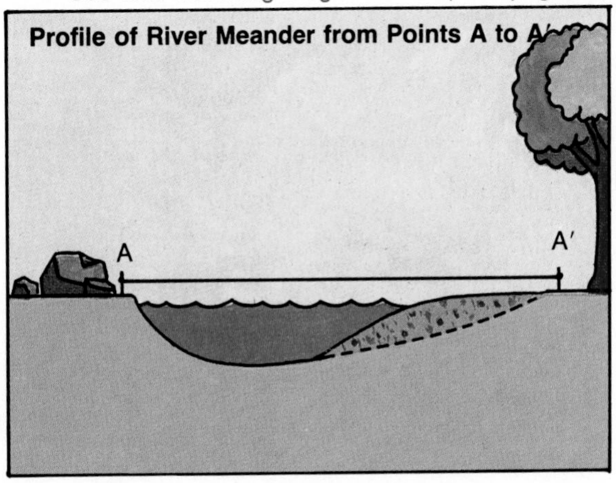

Profile of River Meander from Points A to A′

A   A′

Science Processes: Separating and controlling variables; Formulating models
See also Activity Record Sheet 9-3B (Lab Manual page 126)

CORE   30 minutes   Demonstration or large groups

Activity 9-3B   Stream Erosion and Deposition Patterns

Materials

stream table, or large pan with a hole at one end

2 plastic buckets

rubber or plastic tubing

ordinary sand like that used in construction (soil works well but is messy)

books or blocks of wood to use as props

a few pebbles

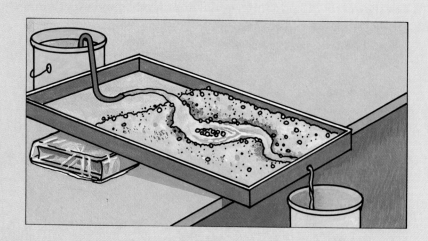

Purpose

To learn where erosion and deposition patterns occur in a stream

Procedure

1. Spread a layer of sand or soil across the stream table as shown in the picture. Include a few pebbles. They will add interesting effects to the stream erosion.
2. Place the stream table on a very small slope. (A steep slope will inhibit the formation of meanders.)
3. Fill the bucket at least half full of water. (You can add more water later if necessary.)
4. Using the rubber or plastic tubing as a siphon, allow the water to run over the sand or soil, forming a model stream. Note the results.
5. After examining the effects of your stream,

add a second siphon to the system and note the results.

Questions

1. What happens to the path of the stream as the water first flows from the original siphon?
2. As the water continues to flow, at what point(s) along the stream are particles being eroded? Why?
3. Where are particles being deposited? Why?
4. What size particles are eroded first? Why?
5. What effect does adding the second siphon have on erosion and deposition in the stream?

Conclusion

In general, where do erosion and deposition patterns occur in a stream? (Hint: See Figure 9-20 on the preceding page.)

Along the inside of the meander of a river or stream, the water slows down. This decrease in speed causes material to be deposited along the inside of the meander. That is why the riverbank along the inside of the meander slopes more gently than the steeper bank on the outside of the meander.

Check yourself

1. At a meander, where does the most erosion take place? Why?

2. How can both erosion and deposition take place at the same meander?

Deposition by wind
New vocabulary: slip face

Winds can carry only very small particles. Therefore, deposits formed by winds contain particles that are all small and all about the same size. Also, the surfaces of particles carried by wind become scratched from striking each other.

On a worldwide basis, the effects of wind erosion and deposition are more limited than those of running water and glaciers. In a desert, however, it is often possible to see the distinctive effect of wind on the shaping of the landscape. The most

Check yourself answers:
1. Most erosion takes place on the outside of the curve because the speed of the water increases along the outside curve.
2. Erosion takes place on the outside of the curve. Deposition occurs on the inside of the curve where the water slows down, causing particles to be deposited.

With the exception of areas that have sand dunes, desert features are usually shaped and modified by moving water during brief periods of rainfall, which may occur a few times a year or maybe only once every several years.

Figure 9-21. Sand dunes like this one at White Sands National Monument, New Mexico, are a wind-formed feature of a desert landscape.

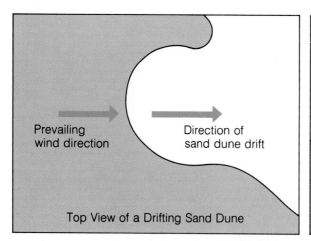

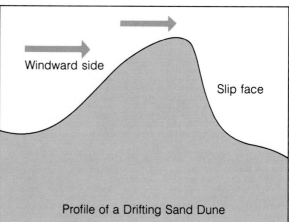

Figure 9-22. The steeper side of a sand dune, the side away from the wind, is called the slip face.

The rock layers are formed from buried sand dunes whose particles have become cemented together.

Figure 9-23. Why aren't the rock layers in this sandstone formation horizontal?

distinctive wind-formed feature of a desert landscape is the sand dune. As shown in Figure 9-21, the sand dune is commonly a crescent-shaped mound of sand.

Figure 9-22 illustrates how a sand dune drifts. Wind carries the sand up and over the gentle slope of the windward side of the sand dune. The sand is then deposited along the steeper slope of the **slip face,** which is the side away from the wind. This erosion and deposition causes the sand dune to "move" in the direction that the wind is blowing. This is what is meant when people refer to drifting sand dunes in a desert.

Figure 9-23 is a close-up photograph of rock layers in Utah's Zion National Park. These rock layers are really buried sand

dunes whose grains have been cemented into rock. If you look closely you can see the slanted sides of what formerly were sand dunes. The rock layers are hundreds of meters thick. Just imagine how long it must have taken for all of those sand dunes to build one on top of another.

Check yourself

1. What are three characteristics of particles deposited by the wind?

2. A sand dune involves both erosion and deposition. Explain.

1. All particles tend to be small, to be about the same size, and to have scratched surfaces.
2. Wind erodes sand from the windward side of the dune and deposits it on the other side of the dune (the slip face).

Deposition by glaciers

New vocabulary: moraine, end moraine, terminal moraine, glacial lobe, outwash plain, till, stratified drift, drumlin, kettle lake

Glacial deposits are easy to identify. They may contain a wide range of particle sizes—from tiny grains to large boulders. When a glacier moves, it picks up and carries particles of all sizes. This mixture is deposited when the glacier melts. Because the particles are carried frozen in the ice, they do not become rounded and sorted like particles carried by running water.

The deposits of material made by advancing or retreating glaciers along their margins (or edges) are called **moraines.** The deposit formed at the foot or end of the glacier is called an **end moraine.** If that point is the farthest south that the glacier advanced, this end moraine is called a **terminal moraine.** At some locations in the United States, there are terminal moraine deposits with a thickness of 30 m or more.

Sometimes a **glacial lobe** will form along the side of a continental glacier. This lobe of ice, which sticks out like a tongue from the main ice mass, may be more than 30 km wide.

The melting ice at the foot of the glacier forms rivers and streams that carry with them the smaller particles. Most of this material is deposited and sorted within a few kilometers of the foot of the glacier, as the speed of the running water decreases. This area of deposition is called an **outwash plain.**

Figure 9-24 shows the outwash plain at the foot of a glacier. Most of the earth material, including all the large particles, is

What size particles do glacial deposits contain?

This discussion of glaciation refers solely to continental glaciers, which were prevalent in the northern parts of the Eastern and Central United States during the last ice ages.

Library research

Find out about a present-day glacier. How does the data you discover relate to the ideas about prehistoric glacial deposition presented in this section?

What is an outwash plain?

Science Processes: Observing; Inferring
See also Activity Record Sheet 9-3C (Lab Manual page 127)

10 minutes   Groups of 4

Activity 9-3C   Comparing Core Samples

Materials

the model core samples
 shown on this page

Purpose

To infer geologic history by comparing two model core samples.

Procedure

1. The two model core samples on this page (labeled A and B) represent samples taken from two different locations. At one location the major agent that shaped the landscape was glaciers. At the other, the major agent was running water. You are to figure out which core sample shows the work of which agent.

2. Examine the material in each sample. Record all observations that you think might help.

Questions

1. How do the particles in each sample compare in arrangement, size, and sorting?
2. Which sample came from a landscape formed by glaciers? Explain your reasoning.
3. Which sample came from a landscape formed by running water? Explain your reasoning.

Conclusion

One of the first steps to take in interpreting the history of a landscape is to analyze any deposits that are present. Why is this so important?

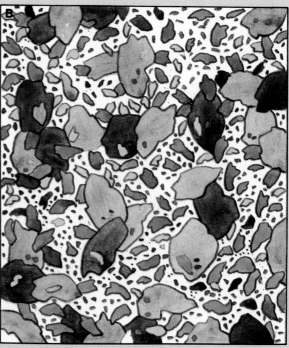

deposited at the foot of the glacier. The smaller particles are carried away from the foot of the glacier and deposited on the outwash plain, which has a gentle slope.

The material in a glacial moraine is called **till.** Till can easily be distinguished from river deposits because it contains such a wide variety of unsorted and unrounded particles that range in size anywhere from boulders to tiny fragments.

The material that is carried away from the glacial moraine by meltwater and deposited in the outwash plain is called **stratified drift.** Stratified drift is similar to river deposits in that the particles are well sorted. As the meltwater slows down, the largest particles settle out first. Farther out on the outwash plain, particles are deposited in increasingly smaller size.

In what order are particles deposited on an outwash plain?

Continental glaciers produce many interesting and unique landscape features. Figure 9-25 shows a series of **drumlins,** which are smoothly rounded hills of glacial till. From the air, drumlins are more or less teardrop-shaped. The narrow end of the "teardrop" points in the direction in which the glacier was moving. (The word *drumlin* comes from the Irish word *druim,* which means "a narrow ridge.")

Figure 9-24. How do the particles deposited at the foot of a glacier differ from those deposited on the outwash plain?

How drumlins formed is something of a mystery. One theory suggests that drumlins solidified from a fluid mass of rock, soil, ice, and water that flows along with and under an advancing glacier. Increases in pressure, caused perhaps by rocks or other obstructions on the earth's surface, "squeeze" the water

See also Teaching Diagram 9-3A (TRB page 42).

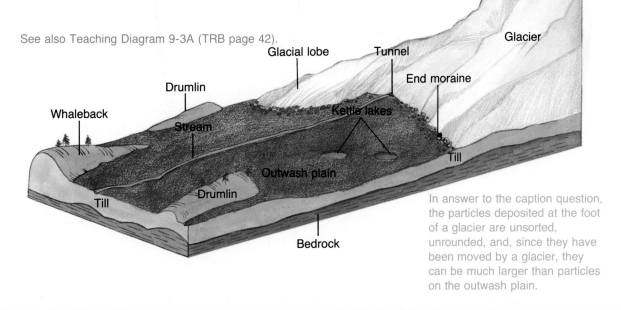

In answer to the caption question, the particles deposited at the foot of a glacier are unsorted, unrounded, and, since they have been moved by a glacier, they can be much larger than particles on the outwash plain.

Figure 9-25. The small, deep pool of water in this picture is a kettle lake. How do kettle lakes form?

Kettle lakes form when large blocks of ice break off from a glacier, become buried under overlying deposits, and melt.

1. River deposits are sorted by the speed of the running water, with larger particles settling out first and the smallest particles settling out last.
2. Similar: Both moraine and stratified drift result from glaciers. Different: Moraine is unsorted. Stratified drift is sorted because it is deposited out of meltwater flowing from the edge of a glacier.

out of the fluid mass and cause it to solidify. The abrasive action caused by the glacier's continued movement over this solid mass would tend to explain why the surface of this kind of glacial deposit is so well rounded.

Sometimes large blocks of ice break off from a glacier and become buried under large masses of overlying deposits. When the ice melts, a large cavity in the deposit is left behind. The cavity, which fills with water from the melting ice, forms a **kettle lake.** Kettle lakes are usually round and very deep.

Check yourself

1. River deposits are said to be well sorted. How are they sorted? What causes the sorting?

2. Compare a moraine with stratified drift. How are they similar? How are they different?

Section 3 Review   Chapter 9

Use **Reading Checksheet 9-3** TRB page 86
Skillsheet 9-3 TRB page 128
Section Reviewsheet 9-3 TRB pages 193–194
Section Testsheet 9-3 TRB page 300

Check Your Vocabulary

1 deposition	8 residual soils
12 drumlin	3 slip face
5 end moraine	2 sorting
7 glacial lobe	11 stratified drift
13 kettle lake	6 terminal moraine
4 moraine	10 till
9 outwash plain	14 transported soils

Match each term above with the numbered phrase that best describes it.

1. The process whereby particles and fragments are deposited by an agent of erosion

2. The process by which fragments of earth materials are deposited from running water in order of size

3. The side of a dune away from the wind

4. The deposit of material made along its margins by an advancing or retreating glacier

5. A deposit formed at the foot of a glacier

6. The deposit that marks the farthest advance of a glacier

7. A tongue-like mass of ice that sticks out from the main mass of a glacier

8. Soils that remain near the bedrock from which they have weathered

9. A gently sloping area of deposition at the foot of a glacier

10. The material in a glacial moraine

11. Sorted particles that have settled out of meltwater on an outwash plain

12. A teardrop-shaped hill of glacial till

13. A lake that formed when a large block of buried glacial ice melted

14. Soils formed from eroded materials

Check Your Knowledge

Multiple Choice: Choose the answer that best completes each of the following sentences.

1. Deposits formed from _?_ contain layers of different particle sizes.
   a) continental glaciers
   b) valley glaciers
   c) landslides
   d) running water

2. Sorting takes place in moving water because of differing _?_ of the water.
   a) temperatures
   b) volume and speed
   c) solutions
   d) lobes

3. Along the outside of a meander, the speed of the water _?_.
   a) decreases a little
   b) increases
   c) decreases noticeably
   d) does not change

4. Particles deposited by wind are _?_.
   a) large
   b) unsorted
   c) all about the same size
   d) unscratched

Check Your Understanding

1. How are particles carried along by a river deposited where a river enters the sea? Why does this happen?

2. How do the river banks on either side of a meander compare? How can this difference be explained?

3. How can a sand dune drift?

4. Why are glacial deposits easy to identify?

5. Why could the sorting of glacial deposits take place only on the outwash plain?

Chapter 9 Review

See also **Chapter Testsheets 9A and 9B**
TRB pages 333–334.

Concept Summary

Weathering is the breaking down and wearing away of earth materials.
☐ Weathering can change the size of a material, the substance of a material, or both.
☐ Soils are formed from the weathering of rock.

Physical weathering occurs when earth materials are reduced in size.
☐ Physical weathering is caused by temperature changes and the abrasion that occurs when rock fragments strike each other.

Chemical weathering occurs when new substances are formed from earth materials.
☐ Chemical weathering often takes place at the same time as physical weathering.

Erosion involves the transport of weathered earth materials from one place to another.
☐ Four common agents of erosion are running water, wind, glaciers, and gravity.
☐ Particles carried by erosion vary greatly in size—from substances dissolved in water to large boulders.
☐ Running water is the dominant agent of erosion.
☐ Most erosion involves more than one agent.
☐ In addition to being an agent of erosion, gravity is also the underlying force behind all other forms of erosion.

Deposition occurs when particles of earth materials are deposited by an agent of erosion.
☐ Sorting of particles by size indicates deposition from running water.
☐ Unsorted particles that vary greatly in size indicate a glacial deposit.

Putting It All Together

1. Explain the formation of beach sand from a sandstone cliff. Include physical and chemical weathering in your explanation.

2. Explain the formation of a fully developed soil profile.
3. Give examples of physical and chemical weathering that occur where you live.
4. What is the relationship between weathering and erosion before the erosional process and during the erosional process?
5. What erosional processes take place on a desert? What agents of erosion are involved?
6. Compare a flood plain and a delta. How are they similar? How are they different?
7. Explain why sorting indicates deposition by running water.
8. Draw a diagram that shows what happens along the inside and outside curves of a meander. Why does this happen?
9. Draw a profile of a drifting sand dune, distinguishing between the windward side and the slip face.
10. Draw a diagram that shows the relative positions of end moraine, stratified drift, and drumlins. Then, with a colored pencil, show where the glacier would have been before it melted.

Apply Your Knowledge

1. How would the kind of soil that forms near the North Pole compare with the kind of soil that forms in a forest?
2. Describe what happens to the soil in a flowerpot after continued watering. What can be done so that plant growth is not affected?
3. When a sandstone cliff weathers, what happens to the minerals that held the particles of sand together?
4. How can scientists infer that there have been many different periods of deposition in a river delta?
5. What can scientists infer about ice sheets once covering areas of North America?

Find Out on Your Own

1. Find three different kinds of soils that formed naturally near where you live. How do the soils differ from each other? What might explain the differences?
2. Find examples of erosion that are taking place near where you live. When does the erosion occur? What if anything is being done to prevent the erosion?
3. Find examples of deposition that are taking place near where you live. What is causing the deposition? How long can the deposits be expected to remain? What will probably happen to the deposits?
4. What about the geology of the area where you live? What landscape formations are the result of erosion? What formations are the result of deposition?
5. What if anything is being done that affects erosion and deposition where you live? Why is this being done?

Reading Further

Bates, D.E.B., and J.F. Kirkaldy. *Field Geology in Color*. New York: Arco Publishing, 1977.
This is an excellent field guide to geologic formations. Color photographs of field occurrences vary from close-ups of mud cracks to distance shots of large formations. It's a handy reference book to have on a field trip.

Chronic, Halka. *Pages of Stone*. Seattle: The Mountaineers, 1984.
This is a book to take along when visiting our national parks and monuments. It contains geological descriptions and attractive photographs of 16 locations.

Doolittle, Jerome, and the Editors of Time-Life Books. *Canyons and Mesas*. The Time-Life American Wilderness Series. New York: Time Incorporated, 1974.
This is a guided tour of an area whose land formations speak for themselves. It includes descriptions of the earth processes that shaped the unforgettable sights of this vast wilderness.

Jones, Philip. *The Forces of Nature*. Chicago: Childrens Press, 1982.
This interesting account of the formation of the earth also describes changes of weather: clouds, rain, wind, snow, ice, thunder, and lightning. It includes beautiful photography of ice crystals.

Marcus, Elizabeth. *All About Mountains and Volcanoes*. Mahwah, NJ: Troll Associates, 1984.
This easy-to-read book explains how mountains are formed and how they affect weather. A section on erosion is included. The diagrams are excellent.

Chapter 10 The Restless Crust

Student Resources		Meeting Individual Needs
Student Text	**Laboratory Activities**	
Section 1 Volcanoes 470–483 The Power of a Major Volcanic Eruption 471–475 Why Some Eruptions Are So Violent 475–477 Volcanic Landforms 477–479 Where Volcanoes Occur 480–481 Section 1 Review 483	 Activity 10-1A Inferring Lava Viscosity 478 Activity Record Sheet 10-1A LM 133 Activity 10-1B Reconstructing the Topography of a Volcanic Cone 482; Activity Record Sheet 10-1B LM 134 Investigation 10-1 Observing Lava Rocks LM 135–136	 Enrichment CORE Enrichment
Section 2 Stress, Structure, and Earthquakes 484–500 Rocks Under Stress 485–489 Movement Along a Fault 489–494 What Is an Earthquake? 494–496 Earthquake Damage 497–499 Section 2 Review 500	 Activity 10-2A Simulating Anticlines and Synclines 488 Activity Record Sheet 10-2A LM 137 Activity 10-2B Making a Fault Model 490 Activity Record Sheet 10-2B LM 138 Activity 10-2C Simulating Faults 492 Activity Record Sheet 10-2C LM 139 Investigation 10-2 Determining the Epicenter and Time of an Earthquake LM 141–142 Research Lab 10 Constructing a Seismograph and Measuring P- and S-waves LM 147	 Reinforcement CORE Enrichment Enrichment Enrichment
Section 3 Plate Tectonics 501–517 The Interior of the Earth 502–504 The Theory of Continental Drift 504–508 Our Science Heritage: From Hypothesis to Theory 506 The Theory of Plate Tectonics 508–511 Pangaea 511–516 Careers: Seismologist/Construction Inspector 515 Section 3 Review 517	Investigation 10-3 Simulating the Earth's Magnetism LM 145–146 Activity 10-3A Reconstructing Pagaea 514 Activity Record Sheet 10-3A LM 143 Activity 10-3B Simulating Sea-Floor Spreading 516 Activity Record Sheet 10-3B LM 144	Enrichment Reinforcement CORE
Chapter 10 Review 518–519 Science Issues of Today: Predicting Earthquakes 520		

10

Chapter Planning Guide

Teacher Resources		Meeting Individual Needs
Teacher's Edition	**Teacher's Resource Book**	
Discussion Idea 468C	Essential Ideas 10-1 EI 63–64 Overhead Transparency S24	Reinforcement Enrichment
Demonstration 468D		
Activity Notes 468E	Overhead Transparency B18 Skillsheet 10-1 TRB 129	CORE Reinforcement
Activity Notes 468F	Teaching Diagram 10-1 TRB 44 Overhead Transparency S25	CORE Reinforcement
Section 1 Review Answers 468F	Reading Checksheet 10-1 TRB 87 Section Reviewsheet 10-1 TRB 195–196 Section Testsheet 10-1 TRB 301	Reinforcement CORE CORE
	Essential Ideas 10-2 EI 65–66	Reinforcement
Activity Notes 468G	Teaching Diagram 10-2A TRB 45; Skillsheet 10-2 TRB 130 Overhead Transparency S26	Reinforcement Enrichment
Activity Notes 468H	Teaching Diagrams 10-2B, 10-2C TRB 46, 47 Overhead Transparency S27	CORE Enrichment
Activity Notes 468J		
	Overhead Transparency S28 Overhead Transparency S29	Enrichment Enrichment
Demonstration 468J Discussion Idea; Environmental Topic 468K Section 2 Review Answers 468K	Reading Checksheet 10-2 TRB 88 Section Reviewsheet 10-2 TRB 197–198 Section Testsheet 10-2 TRB 302	Reinforcement CORE CORE
	Essential Ideas 10-3 EI 67–68 Teaching Diagram 10-3A TRB 48 Overhead Transparency S30	Reinforcement CORE Enrichment
Demonstration 468L	Overhead Transparencies S31, S32, S33 Teaching Diagram 10-3B TRB 49 Skillsheet 10-3 TRB 131 Projectsheet 10-3 TRB 253 Overhead Transparency S34	Enrichment CORE Reinforcement Enrichment Enrichment
Discussion Idea 468L		
Activity Notes 468M		
Activity Notes 468N–468P Creative Writing Idea 463P Section 3 Review Answers 468P	Reading Checksheet 10-3 TRB 89 Section Reviewsheet 10-3 TRB 199–200 Section Testsheet 10-3 TRB 303	Reinforcement CORE CORE
Chapter 10 Review Answers 468Q–468R	Chapter 10 Testsheet TRB 335–336	CORE

10

Section 1   Volcanoes

Learner Objectives

1. To define what is meant by volcanic activity.
2. To identify factors that affect the violence of a volcanic eruption.
3. To identify three basic types of volcanic mountains.
4. To relate volcanic activity to certain areas of the world.
5. To draw inferences from specimens of volcanic rock.

Concept Summary

Volcanic activity occurs when lava, gas, or solid fragments come out of a vent in the earth's crust.

Discussion Idea

Volcanic Activity Can Be Beneficial

Tell students that many things in life can appear at first glance to be all harmful or all beneficial. For instance, volcanoes may be extremely destructive, but they may also bring benefits to those who live near. The country of Iceland is a land of contrasts—not only does it have glaciers, but it has a chain of volcanoes. (In fact, some of Iceland's glaciers are capping volcanoes!) The people of Iceland have learned to benefit from their volcanoes in many ways.

Ask the students if they can think of how Iceland might benefit from its volcanoes.

In Iceland, the major benefit of volcanic activity is a great deal of geothermal energy that can be harnessed for the country's use. This energy is used to obtain hot water, for heating and electricity, and even for use in Iceland's important fish-packing industry.

Geothermal wells in Iceland provide heating for three-fourths of its population. Parts of Iceland have had geothermal plants since 1928. It hasn't been easy; some of the wells have proven too hot for use and have had corrosive chemicals in the water. And Iceland has experienced severe damage from volcanic eruptions from time to time. But with research and hard work, Iceland's inhabitants have learned to turn the mighty force of volcanoes to good use.

Ask: If the residents of Iceland could get rid of the volcanoes, do you think they would? Why or why not?

In Section 1 of Chapter 10, students will find out about volcanoes and volcanic landforms.

10-1

Demonstration

The Difference Between Magma- and Lava-Formed Rocks

Bring in specimens of granite, rhyolite, basalt, and andesite volcanic rocks. (Science supply houses, rockhound shops, or the geology department of any university can supply these easily, if they are not already in your teaching collection.) Pass the samples and a magnifying glass around the classroom.

Tell the students that each of the rocks being passed around is a type of igneous rock. Tell them that rhyolite, basalt, and andesite were formed from lava. Ask: What is lava? (molten rock when it is on the surface on the earth)

Remind them that the granite, however, formed from magma. Ask: What is magma? (molten rock when it is *below* the surface of the earth)

Explain to the students that the lava-formed rocks—the rhyolite, basalt, and andesite—are called *igneous-volcanic*. Magma-formed rocks—in this case, the granite—are called *igneous-plutonic*. (A *pluton* is any body of igneous rock formed by cooling of magma below the earth's surface.) Plutonic rock cools more slowly than volcanic rock, and thus crystals in plutonic rock can grow to visible size.

Students may be able to see small crystals of such minerals as feldspar, quartz, and biotite in the granite.

Tell students they will learn much more about volcanic rocks in Section 1 of Chapter 10.

Science Background

Volcanic eruptions are perhaps the most dramatic events in the earth's history. While most are caused by the pressure of molten material under the earth's crust, they can be triggered by water seeping down. In 1915, Mount Lassen erupted as a result of this phenomenon. The water became trapped over the magma chamber beneath the mountain. Steam pressure built up until it finally broke through, forming an open crater on top of the mountain.

Most volcanoes erupt skyward. The recent eruption of Mount St. Helens was a rare lateral eruption. Pressure from magma rising inside the mountain pushed out a bulge on its north side. The eruption began when a 5.1 magnitude earthquake shook the volcano so violently the bulge crumbled and slid away. The sudden release of pressure caused superheated water inside the volcano to flash into steam. Because much of the mountain's north side was gone, the blast was directed laterally.

The initial explosion and ensuing avalanches of hot rock, called pyroclastic flows, destroyed all life on the north side of the mountain. Elsewhere, most of the damage resulted from torrential mudflows that began when heat from the blast melted snow and ice on the upper slopes. In places as far away as Yakima, Washington, the fallout of ash from the eruption was a foot thick.

10-1

468D

Volcanoes

Student Misconception

It is difficult for students to accept the fact that rock can melt, changing from a solid to a liquid. Temperatures of hundreds to more than a thousand degrees Celsius exist within the earth's mantle and, when combined with great pressure, create conditions that can melt rock. You can remind students that lava is liquid rock that hardens into a solid when it cools.

Few students understand that melting and freezing points vary with the substance being considered, and thus they mistakenly associate the melting and freezing points of water with the behavior of other materials. To illustrate the wide range of temperatures involved, you might have students look up the melting and freezing points of various substances in a chemistry book.

You can also demonstrate the melting points of other materials in the classroom, such as congealed soup or gelatin.

10-1

Activity Notes

Activity 10-1A

Inferring Lava Viscosity   page **478**

Purpose   To infer lava viscosity from volcanic materials.
- 10 minutes Small groups
- **Activity Record Sheet 10-1A** (Lab Manual page 133) can be used to record this activity.
- Science Processes: Observing; Inferring.

Advance Preparation

Basalt samples should be available through geological supply stores. Obtain a set of at least three different samples.

Procedure Notes

Encourage the use of a magnifying glass to discern minute details of the rock samples.

Answers to Questions

1. The nonvesicular basalt indicates a less viscous lava.
2. The vesicular basalt probably had a higher silica content and so was more viscous.

Conclusion

By looking at basalt, you can tell whether the lava was relatively free-flowing. If so, it is likely to be a low silica lava, which has a smoother texture. If not, it is probably a lava, which has a high silica porous texture.

Going Further

Highly viscous lavas often trap gas bubbles. These lavas have lower densities than lavas with less viscosity. For example, pumice is light enough to float; it is full of holes from gases once trapped in the rock.

Have students determine the densities of the rocks. Remind students that density $= \dfrac{\text{mass}}{\text{volume}}$. Measure the amount of water displaced in a beaker to find the volume. Weigh the rocks to determine mass.

Activity Notes

Activity 10-1B

Reconstructing the Topography of a Volcanic Cone   page **482**

Purpose To learn to translate a topographic map of a volcanic cone into a profile view.

- **CORE** 30 minutes Individuals or small groups
- **Activity Record Sheet 10-1B** (Lab Manual page 134) can be used to record this activity.
- Science Processes: Interpreting data; Inferring.

Advance Preparation

Remind students that topographic maps represent vertical features of the landscape by contour lines and that we often need to translate a topographic map into a profile map.

Procedure Notes

It is vitally important to line up the folded edge of the graph paper with the contour map. The use of tape would keep the edge in place. Encourage the students to record the elevation at each point to reduce errors. Connect the points. The more contour lines used, the smoother the line will be.

Answers to Questions

1. It is expected that profiles that run in the same direction will be similar.
2. To make the profile more closely represent the cone, the number of readings per profile can be increased. The number of profiles can also be increased to get a better idea of what the mountain's profile looks like when calculated for another direction.

Conclusion

It is expected that the outline will show Orr Mountain to be a cinder cone, which is relatively small and has steep slopes.

Going Further

Take the newly constructed profile map and regenerate a topographic map of Orr Mountain.

Take profiles for another direction placing the folded edge at the desired location on the topographic map.

Using the other topographic maps in the Appendix, reconstruct the profiles of Odell Butte and Crater Lake. For Crater Lake, extend outward about 2½ miles from the rim and include Wizard Island in the profile.

Section 1 Review Answers

Check Your Understanding
page **483**

1. 1) Extruded material (ash, heated mud, lava, searingly hot gases) can destory all life that it touches. 2) Structures and even whole towns have been covered by extruded material. 3) Dust clouds from major eruptions can reduce the amount of the sun's energy that reaches the earth's surface. 4) An explosive eruption changes the shape of the earth's surface, destroying even the tops of mountains along with anything else present on that surface when the eruption occurs.

2. 1) A shield cone is formed from lava flow and has gently sloping sides. 2) A cinder cone is formed from cinder and ash, has steep sides, and is relatively low (usually less than 450 m). 3) A composite cone is formed from gently sloping lava flows near the base with a greater percentage of steeper ash and cinder formation toward the top, is characterized by a beautifully symmetrical shape, and can reach 4 km in height.

3. Plateau basalts form thick, horizontal layers of basaltic lava that flow from fissures in the ground.

4. The chemical composition of the magma—especially the amounts of silica and water—controls how violent or calm a volcanic eruption is.

5. Volcanic activities are most commonly found 1) along the Ring of Fire that circles the Pacific Ocean and 2) along the mid-ocean ridge that extends along the basins of the major oceans.

10-1

Stress, Structure, and Earthquake

Learner Objectives

1. To describe how rocks are changed by stress within the earth's crust.
2. To relate synclines, anticlines, domes, and basins to stresses within the earth's crust.
3. To distinguish among different types of faults.
4. To use arrival times of S-waves and P-waves to determine the epicenter and time of occurrence of an earthquake.
5. To compare the Richter scale and the Mercalli scale.
6. To make models of faults.

Concept Summary

Folded structures are caused by shape changes in rocks.
Faults are breaks in the earth's crust along which the rocks have moved.
Earthquakes are caused by movement along a fault or by volcanic activity.

10-2

Activity Notes

Activity 10-2A

Simulating Anticlines and Synclines   page **488**

Purpose   To study the relationship between synclines and anticlines.

- 5 minutes Pairs of Students
- **Activity Record Sheet 10-2A** (Lab Manual page 137) can be used to record this activity.
- Science Processes: Formulating models.

Advance Preparation

When doing this activity, have students refer to Figure 10-13 (page 487) to note how rock layers are affected by the compressional stress of syncline and anticline formation.

Procedure Notes

Point out to students that synclines and anticlines are very often created in tandom.

It would be advantageous for the students to fold the paper several times and create more than one syncline and anticline.

Answers to Questions

1. The tops of the folds represent anticlines.
2. The bottoms of the folds represent synclines.

Conclusion

Both anticlines and synclines can occur together, in alternating sequence, as a result of compressional stress.

Going Further

Have students make a three-layer clay model of a rock sequence, using a different color of clay for each layer. Compress the model to produce synclines and anticlines. Discuss how the clay folds and fractures. Explain that rocks compress and expand in a similar manner.

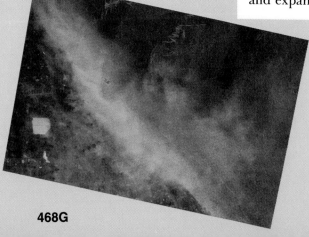

Activity Notes

Activity 10-2B

Making a Fault Model   page **490**

Purpose   To make a model of a geologic fault.

- **CORE** 15 minutes Small groups or demonstration
- **Activity Record Sheet 10-2B** (Lab Manual page 138) can be used to record this acitivity.
- Science Processes: Formulating models; Measuring: Communicating.

Advance Preparation

Have rulers available, so that students can measure the length and width of the fault model.

Procedure Notes

Knead clay to remove the air bubbles that might disturb the fault surface.

Hold blocks tightly and cut clay in one stroke. The fault angle is to be approximately 45°. Show the students how to approximate this.

Safety

Hands should be on the blocks and not the wire when making the cut. As you unwind, hold on to both the wire and the block of wood.

Answers to Questions

1. The three types of stress that might affect the fault are compressional stress, tensional stress, or shear stress.

2.

Footwall

Hanging wall

Conclusion

Normal faulting would lengthen the earth's crust. Reverse faulting would shorten it.

Going Further

Contrast the fault model created at a fault angle of 10° with that at 45°.

Science Background

On pages 508–511 of this chapter, the theory of plate tectonics is described. According to that theory, the earth's surface is divided into a series of large platelike sections. These plates are gradually moving in relation to each other. The boundaries of the plates are huge cracks in the earth's surface called faults.

The North American Continental Plate and the Pacific Plate come together on the West Coast of North America. The San Andreas fault in California makes part of this boundary. Movements along this fault caused the San Francisco earthquake of 1906. But since that earthquake, there has not been much movement along the San Andreas fault. Pressures have been building up. This has made geologists believe that sooner or later there will be another great earthquake in California.

Within the past 20 years, scientists have learned much about the occurrences of earthquakes, but they still cannot predict them exactly. The information they are now collecting will probably lead to a successful way of predicting earthquakes in the future.

10-2

Student Misconception

As students attempt to visualize the geophysical process of folding, they are likely to perceive that folding results in obvious and corresponding surface features; anticlines form hills and synclines form valleys. Students may fail to consider the effects of erosion and deposition on the folded rock material. Over time, the surface expressions of anticlines and synclines may be eroded away entirely.

Have students construct clay models of layers of sedimentary rock. Instruct students to apply compressional stress to the models so that they fold, forming anticlines and synclines. Then have students alter the models to show the effects of erosion and deposition. As the models are altered, students will be able to see that anticlines and synclines exist beneath the earth's surface, as well as at the surface (as hills and valleys).

10-2

Activity Notes

Activity 10-2C

Simulating Faults   page **492**

Purpose   To simulate a variety of geologic faults.

- 15 minutes Small groups or demonstration
- **Activity Record Sheet 10-2C** (Lab Manual page 139) can be used to record this activity.
- Science Processes: Measuring; Inferring; Defining operationally.

Procedure Notes

Provide the students with rulers to measure the width and length of the fault models made in Activity 10-2B. Students need to be careful when measuring the length and width of the model, since the differences might be small.

Answers to Questions

1. The canal is broken vertically when the part of the canal on the hanging wall drops. A normal fault has been simulated.
2. The canal is broken vertically when the part of the canal on the footwall drops. A reverse fault has been simulated.
3. The canal is at the same height but is no longer continuous. It has been broken into two segments by the horizontal movement. A transform fault has been simulated.
4. Transverse faulting offsets the canal sideways.

Conclusion

A normal fault is caused by tensional stress. A reverse fault is caused by compressional stress.

Demonstration

The Severity of Earthquake Damage

Bring in photos of the results of major earthquakes, such as the September 1985 disaster in Mexico City and the 1906 San Francisco earthquake.

Ask students if they remember hearing about the Mexico City earthquake on the radio or on television.

Tell them that the earthquake, which registered 7.8 on the Richter scale, was one of the most severe earthquakes of our time. It caused millions of dollars in damage and enormous loss of life. It raised portions of California almost one inch and caused a tidal wave that reached Hawaii.

Discussion Idea

How to Prepare for an Earthquake

Ask students if they have ever felt an earthquake. Have them describe their experiences to their classmates: How long did it last? What did it feel like? Was anyone hurt? Did any property damage occur?

Almost everyone either lives in a place likely to have an earthquake or knows someone who does. Discuss safety measures that governments, architects, builders, and individuals should take. (Have flexible buildings with low centers of gravity, easy-access fire escapes, safety glass in windows and glass doors, well-posted building exits, no interior furnishings such as unstable bookcases that could readily topple over onto people, etc.)

If you live in an area in which an earthquake is possible (or perhaps probable), discuss specific safety precautions to take both at school and at home. Make a list on the chalkboard. (Keep jugs of sterile water at home; keep a supply of canned food; make sure fires are never left unattended; turn off all electrical lights and appliances when not in use; keep essential papers in a single fireproof box; know where all exits are at home, at school, and in the workplace.)

Environmental Topic

Earthquake damage is real and frightening. The prediction of earthquakes is a sophisticated science that is still not far advanced. Even if earthquakes could be predicted accurately, the problems associated with large-scale evacuation of an area must be considered.

An alternative to prediction and evacuation is the actual control of earthquakes. Any technique to avert an earthquake must somehow relieve the tension along a fracture zone.

Allow the class to explore the possibilities for controlling and/or lessening the impact of earthquakes. These possibilities include the injection of fluid to ease slippage and the deliberate triggering of many small earthquakes to relieve stress.

Section 2 Review Answers

Check Your Understanding
page **500**

1. The location of an earthquake can be determined by comparing the arrival times of the earthquake's shock waves at three or more different seismograph stations. A seismographic record also shows the amount of energy released at the time of the movement in the earth.

2. Fractures often develop along the top of an anticline or bottom of a syncline. These fracture zones are more subject to weathering and erosion.

3.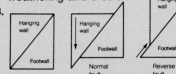

4. Compressional stress causes the folding of the earth's surface into synclines and anticlines and the upward movement of the hanging wall in a reverse fault. Tensional stress causes the downward movement of the hanging wall in a normal fault. Shear stress causes the horizontal movement that occurs along a transform fault.

5. Mountain valleys can be formed by the erosion of anticlines, leaving the synclines as ridges. Upward-arching domes can be formed by upward-pushing pressures associated with igneous activity. Downward-arching basins are caused by sinkage of a portion of the earth's crust. Mountains and plateaus can be caused by fault movement.

10-2

Learner Objectives

1. To identify the layers of the earth, based on the strength and rigidity of the rocks.
2. To relate Alfred Wegener to the theory of continental drift.
3. To describe the theory of plate tectonics.
4. To relate Pangaea to the theory of plate tectonics.
5. To relate magnetic reversals to sea floor spreading.

Concept Summary

The interior of the earth is made of layers of different densities and rigidity.
The theory of continental drift states that the continents have moved around the surface of the earth over the top of the oceanic crust.
The sea floor spreading theory states that ocean basins spread apart as the ocean crust grows at the mid-ocean ridges.
The plate tectonic theory states that the earth's lithosphere is constantly forming and being destroyed, and that the continents are slowly carried around on top of the lithosphere.

10-3

Demonstration

Our Changing View of the Earth's Surface

Show the students a modern globe and, if possible, a globe that is printed with ancient maps. From the library, also bring in photographs of maps made many centuries ago. Help them to compare and contrast the appearance of the various maps.

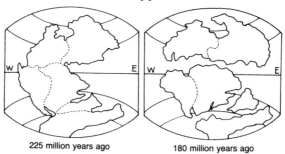

225 million years ago   180 million years ago

Tell students that, over the years, we have had to revise our ideas of the formation and the shape of the earth many times. Each time, people were resistant to the new ideas.

Ask: What ideas about the earth can you think of that we no longer believe to be true? (The earth is flat; dragons await unwary travelers at the edge of the earth; etc.)

Tell students that in Section 3 of Chapter 10 they will learn about the *theory of plate tectonics,* scientific theory that has been doubted by scientists in our own time. As is true with any new idea, the concept of plate tectonics required time for acceptance.

Discussion Idea

The Impact of a New Pangaea

Tell students that in Section 3 of Chapter 10 they will learn about the earth's former "supercontinent," called Pangaea, believed by many geologists to have been in existence more than 200 million years ago. Pangaea included younger versions of all of the continents on the earth today.

Some geologists believe that the earth is once again forming a new supercontinent, although it would take millions of years for this gradual change to occur.

Ask: If a new supercontinent were to form and if humans were still on the earth, how might things be different from the way they are today? (Depending upon where the continent formed, climate could change radically; political boundaries would have to be renegotiated; no oceans would separate the continents; etc.)

Activity Notes

Activity 10-3A

Reconstructing Pangaea   page **514**

Purpose   To study the relationships between the present continents and Pangaea.

- 20 minutes Individuals or small groups
- **Activity Record Sheet 10-3A** (Lab Manual page 143) can be used to record this activity.
- **Science Processes:** Observing; Classifying; Using space/time relations; Inferring.

Advance Preparation

Make sure the map the students use is very clear, because some detail will be lost in tracing. Make sure that the scissors are not dull.

Procedure Notes

The students need to tape down the tracing paper before they begin.

Remind the students to remove all post-Paleozoic features, to ensure a good fit. Care must be taken when cutting out the continents.

Answers to Questions

Answers will vary; students should note similarities and differences as they compare their maps.

Conclusions

Answers will vary; students should observe that by actually moving maps of the modern continents to approximations of their original locations, they can gain additional perspective on the movement of crustal plates.

Going Further

Ask: What accounts for the rotation of landmasses, relative to the center from which they originally separated?

Science Background

Tectonic processes include spreading, subduction, collision, faulting, and accretion. All of these played a part in the geologic history of western North America.

About 200 million years ago, the North American plate separated from the African plate and the Atlantic Ocean was born. As the North American plate drifted slowly westward, it overran a series of Pacific Ocean plates. Magma from the subducting oceanic crust fed volcanoes that built up the Columbia Plateau and the Cascade Range.

During the past 90 million years, the continent has drifted slowly over the volcanically active area known as the Yellowstone hot spot. Geologists know this because lavas grow younger from the eastern border of Oregon to Yellowstone Park. Idaho potatoes grow in the fertile soil of the Snake River plains, once a giant lava field.

As the North American plate overrode the Pacific seafloor, pieces of land, called terranes, adhered to the western coast. This process, known as accretion, added substantial amounts of land to the continent. The pieces included sea mounts, island arcs, micro-continents, submerged plateaus, and sediments from the continent shelf.

The collision of the Pacific Ocean plate and North American plates also raised the Rocky Mountains 65 to 45 million years ago.

10-3

Student Misconception

In their normal course of study, students have been taught to identify the major landmasses and oceans on the earth. Through this process, students begin to view these as distinctly separate features, rather than as different portions of the lithosphere, the rigid portion of the earth's surface that consists of the crust and upper mantle. As a result, students often have the misconception that plate boundaries match the outlines of continents and that oceans divide and separate the continents.

A simple demonstration can eliminate this misconception. On a hard-boiled egg, draw or paint the earth's major landmasses and oceans. Explain that the shell of the egg represents the lithosphere. Gently crack the shell of the egg. Ask students to describe the fracture pattern. Do the individual pieces reflect the divisions between continents and oceans? Students should be able to see that the earth's lithosphere contains the features of the earth—continents and oceans.

10-3

Activity Notes

Activity 10-3B

Simulating Sea-Floor Spreading   page **516**

Purpose   To simulate sea-floor spreading.
- **CORE** 30 minutes Groups of 4 or demonstration
- **Activity Record Sheet 10-3B** (Lab Manual page 144) can be used to record this activity.
- Science Processes: Formulating models; Inferring.

Advance Preparation

You may wish to obtain scapels for cutting in this exercise to prevent accidents with razor blades.

Setup: The central slot represents the center position of the mid-ocean ridge, where new ocean crust is formed.

Step 5: Labeling the paper with N's or R's creates a record which simulates the direction of magnetism the rocks would pick up as the lavas at the center of the mid-ocean ridge cool into basalt.

Step 6: The total width of the exposed portions of paper on both sides of the central ridge area represents the width of the ocean basin.

Step 7: The sheet of waxed paper that is just long enough to stretch across both of the labeled sheets of paper (the width of the ocean basin of Step 6) represents the sediments and the remains of animals and algae that sink to the bottom of the ocean and accumulate.

Step 8: Cutting the waxed paper completely in half represents the fracturing of the crust along the midocean ridge that allows lava to rise up and form new crust.

Step 9: Exposing 3 or 4 cm of unmarked paper on each side of the slot represents the growth of the plates by spreading and extrusion of lava at the position of the central valley of the mid-ocean ridge.

Procedure Notes

Safety Note: To prevent blades from slipping, provide students with a hard surface on which to cut. Remind them to cut in a direction away from and never toward their bodies, or parts of their bodies.

If razor blades are used, have a disposal jar available. It is very important that the students carefully cut the wax paper in half and pull equally on both ends of the typing paper. Point out the symmetry across the cardboard slot.

Activity Notes (continued)

Answers to Questions

1. Patterns of reversal on one side of the rift are a mirror image of the patterns on the other.
2. The layer of waxed paper in direct contact with the marked paper and farthest from the rift represents the oldest sediment.
3. The age of the waxed paper in direct contact with the marked paper increases as it gets farther from the rift. This indicates that the newest ocean crust is near the rift, that the oceanic crust is moving apart, and that some accommodation must be made for the oldest layers. Either they are subducting or uplifting, or else they are moving along with the continental crust.

Conclusion

Cutting the waxed paper in half represents crustal fracturing along the mid-ocean ridge. This fracturing allows lava to rise up from below and thus form new crust.

Creative Writing Idea

The following writing assignment may help students recognize that plate tectonics is an ongoing, changeable process, rather than a static, completed occurrence.

Imagine that the directions of crustal plate movement were reversed (that is, the subduction zones became areas of sea floor spreading and mid-oceanic ridges became subduction zones). Describe the major changes that would take place in landforms associated with plate boundaries. Be specific, using Figure 10-33 to help you locate current plate boundaries.

Section 3 Review Answers

Check Your Understanding
page 517

1. According to the theory of continental drift, the continents are drifting over the top of oceanic crust.
2. According to the sea floor spreading theory, huge sections of the sea floor are being pushed or pulled in opposite directions, creating a rift that becomes filled with molten material that rises from the earth's interior and cools into igneous rock.
3. According to the plate tectonic theory, the earth's surface is made up of seven major plates and several smaller plates. These lithospheric plates are rigid and slow-moving. At the boundaries of these plates, one of several things occurs. 1) Plates that are being pulled apart (as along the mid-ocean ridge) grow larger because of molten material that rises in the rift zone and cools into igneous rock. 2) Where plates collide, plate edges can be uplifted to form mountains. 3) Where plates collide, plate edges can be forced downward into the asthenosphere, creating deep trenches on the surface of the lithosphere. 4) Plates can also move most past each other with a horizontal shearing motion.
4. "Impossible" theories can stimulate thought and lead to debate, additional data gathering, and new syntheses/theories that offer more satisfactory explanations.
5. Scientists have discovered a low-velocity zone in the earth's upper mantle by studying the arrival times of P-waves and S-waves from an earthquake.

10-3

The Restless Crust

Chapter Vocabulary

Section 1

caldera
lateral eruption
volcanic activity
vent
magma
lava
volcano
fumarole
viscosity
shield cone
cinder cone
composite cone
fissure
plateau basalts
island arc

Section 2

plastic deformation
folded rock
syncline
anticline
fracture
compressional stress
tensional stress
shear stress
fault
hanging wall
footwall
normal fault
reverse fault
thrust fault
transform fault
earthquake
focus
P-wave
S-wave
seismograph
epicenter
seismologist
Richter scale
Mercalli scale

10-3

Chapter 10 Review Answers

Putting It All Together   page 518

1. The Ring of Fire is found along the edges of plate boundaries.
2. 1) The focuses of earthquakes follow a definite pattern along a subducting plate. Shallow focus earthquakes occur near deep sea trenches. As distance from the trench increases, the focus of the earthquake becomes deeper, which indicates that the subducting plate is being forced deeper and deeper into the earth. 2) The location of earthquakes around the world also relates to the plate tectonic theory insofar as earthquakes occur along the boundaries of plates. The occurrence of these earthquakes is most easily explained by the grinding motion of these huge plates as they move past each other.
3. Compressional stess occurs where plates collide head-on. One of two results is possible—uplifting to form mountains (e.g., the Himalayas) or the subduction of one plate under another, as is happening along the west coast of South America.
4. Folded mountains are caused by compressional stress which occurs when two lithospheric plates collide head-on.
5. The theory of continental drift and the plate tectonic theory might involve low-probability aspects. For example, no known forces can explain how land masses as huge as continents could be moving. Another example of overcoming an improbability is the interrelationship between the sea floor spreading theory and the studies of the earth's magnetism and the evidence of magnetic reversals throughout the earth's history.
6. As shown in Figure 10-35, 180 million years ago, an east-west break separated Pangaea into Laurasia and Gondwanaland. Then, 60 million years ago, North America moved away from Europe, and South America moved away from Africa.
7. Lava flows occurred in the eastern United States during the Triassic Period (about 230 million years ago). Lava flows are associated with plate boundaries.
8. Movement along the San Andreas fault causes earthquakes that affect the San Francisco and Los Angeles areas.
9. Along the mid-ocean ridge system, faulting and volcanism are near the surface. A trench area indicates a place where a plate is subducting. Along the subducting plate, shallow focus earthquakes occur nearest the trench. As distance from the trench increases, the subducting plate is deeper below the earth's surface and the focus will be deeper.
10. Student diagrams should contain the main features shown in Figures 10-31, 10-32, and 10-34 (pages 508, 509, and 511, respectively).

Chapter Planning Guide

Chapter 10 Review Answers (continued)

Apply Your Knowledge   page 519

1. Earthquakes are dangerous insofar as they cause structures to fall. Such hazards can be reduced by careful choice of construction sites and by the choice of construction methods and building materials.
2. Mountains can be formed by faulting and uplifting of lithospheric plates. They can also be formed by volcanic activity.
3. The mid-ocean ridge system consists of high mountains formed by volcanic activity. The deeper ocean basins are plates of dense basaltic crust that are moving away from the rift zones of the mid-ocean ridges. The depth of the ocean basins is caused by the density of the crustal rock and by the weight of overlying layers of sediment. The depth of the trenches is caused because of the subduction of one plate under another.
4. Along the San Andreas fault, the whole western part of the state is moving northward with respect to the eastern part of the state. This motion is a grinding motion of two plates sliding past each other and not the kind of motion that would cause a part of the state to fall into the ocean. It might be possible that some day Los Angeles would be much closer to San Francisco but that would take millions of years.

Chapter Vocabulary

Section 3

low-velocity zone
discontinuity
oceanic crust
continental crust
rigidity
lithosphere
asthenosphere
mesosphere
theory of continental drift
plate tectonic theory
rift zone
sea floor spreading
subduction

Chapter 10

The Restless Crust

 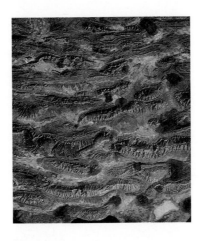 

Section 1
Volcanoes

To an observer viewing some of the earth's landforms, the earth's crust may appear to be solid and stable. But deep below the surface, there is pressure that is great enough to bend rock and heat that is great enough to melt rock.

Sometimes this underground activity merely changes the earth's crustal rocks. At other times, however, this below-the-surface activity breaks through to the earth's surface and is then known as volcanic activity, which can vary greatly in form and intensity.

Section 2
Stress, Structure, and Earthquakes

Rocks in the earth's crust will melt when subjected to great heat. Rocks in the earth's crust will also fold and bend, break and slide because of pressures that build up within the earth's crust.

Sometimes the pressure is released through many small earthquakes. At other times, however, pressure in the earth's crust continues to build, and the pressure can be released only through a major earthquake.

Section 3
Plate Tectonics

Earthquakes and volcanoes are very powerful, and they can cause great damage. Scientists, therefore, are looking for ways to predict when a major eruption or earthquake might occur.

Earthquakes and volcanoes are much more likely to occur in certain parts of the world than in others. The Pacific Ocean, for example, is circled by areas of volcanism and faulting. Beneath the Atlantic Ocean there is another area of active volcanoes.

In discussion, students can explore any ideas they have about how mountains form. As will be pointed out in this chapter, some mountains are formed by volcanic activity. Others are formed by uplifting.

The mountains pictured on the facing page are part of the Himalayan range that rises between India and China. The Himalayas are the highest landforms on the earth. What do you think might be causes for the earth's mountain ranges, which are among its most beautiful and spectacular landforms?

Volcanoes   Section 1

Section 1 of Chapter 10 is divided into four parts:

The power of a major volcanic eruption

Why some eruptions are so violent

Volcanic landforms

Where volcanoes occur

Figure 10-1. This volcano is located on Heimaey Island, Iceland. What two causes of volcanic activity exist within the earth's crust?
As mentioned on the facing page, volcanic activity is caused by tremendous heat and pressure that exist within the earth's crust.

Learner Objectives
1. To define what is meant by volcanic activity.
2. To identify factors that affect the violence of a volcanic eruption.
3. To identify three basic types of volcanic mountains.
4. To relate volcanic activity to certain areas of the world.
5. To draw inferences from specimens of volcanic rock.

Of all the earth processes, volcanic activity is certainly among the most powerful. By means of volcanic activity, people are able to witness the active transfer of earth materials and the active re-formation of the earth's surface. By means of volcanic activity, people are able to get some idea of the tremendous heat and pressure that exist within the earth's crust, where the heat is great enough to melt rock and the pressure is great enough to blow the top off a mountain.

As will be developed in this section of Chapter 10, volcanic activity involves a transfer of earth materials. The materials include fluids (lava), solids (rock fragments, cinder, ash), and gases.

The power of a major volcanic eruption

New vocabulary: caldera, lateral eruption

History contains accounts of over five hundred major volcanic eruptions and thousands of minor eruptions. Some have been described in great detail. Some have been photographed. Some have happened so recently that the details can be obtained directly from eyewitnesses.

The eruptions of Mount Mazama, Mount Vesuvius, Krakatau, Mount Pelée, Mount Lassen, Parícutin, and Mount St. Helens provide examples of the power of a major volcanic eruption. In addition, you can use your library as a resource for other accounts of volcanic eruptions.

Mount Mazama   The Cascade Mountains of the northwestern United States have been the site of much volcanic activity. Of all the volcanoes in the Cascade Range (which extends from northern California to Canada), the one that may have had the largest eruption was probably Mount Mazama (muh-ZAH′-muh) in southern Oregon.

Prior to its eruption about 6600 years ago, Mount Mazama had a height of over 1800 m. During that eruption, 49 cubic km of mostly ash and pumice were blown into the air and extruded (forced or pushed) out and down the sides, spreading over 896 000 square km. Beneath the mountain, the magma chamber that had been emptying during the eruption became even larger as the remaining magma drained back into the depths of the earth. The mountaintop collapsed into the empty magma chamber, leaving a large circular depression 916 m in diameter.

Through eruption and collapse, Mount Mazama lost 70 cubic km of its top. The remaining rim now rises only 450 m

Figure 10-2. In some eruptions, the mountaintop collapses into the empty portions of the magma chamber beneath the mountain, forming a caldera.

Figure 10-3. Crater Lake is located in a caldera that formed after a violent eruption of Mount Mazama. How long ago did that eruption occur?
The eruption of Mount Mazama took place about 6600 years ago.

What is the hole in a collapsed crater called?

A translation of Pliny's account can be obtained from a library.

Krakatau is also commonly referred to as Krakatoa (krah'-kuh-TŌ'-uh). Sometimes it is called Rakata (the local Malay name).

Students can locate these volcanoes on a map or globe. Some have been indicated on the map in Figure 10-8 on page 480.

above the surrounding countryside. This type of a collapsed volcanic crater is called a **caldera** (kal-DIR'-uh). Three small volcanic cones were later formed in the floor of the collapsed crater. Water has since accumulated to a depth of about 610 m inside the caldera. The area is known today as Crater Lake National Park.

Mount Vesuvius　　A seventeen-year-old young man by the name of Pliny (PLIN'-ee) has provided us with an eyewitness account of the eruption of Mount Vesuvius (vuh-SOO'-vee-is) on August 24, A.D. 79. The eruption of Mount Vesuvius took place across the bay from present-day Naples. In that A.D. 79 eruption, three towns were buried under more than 18 m of heated mud and ash. About ten percent of the population of the three towns was killed during the eruption.

Krakatau　　In 1883, a volcanic mountain erupted on Krakatau (krah'-kah-TOW'), a small island between Java and Sumatra in present-day Indonesia. The noise from the eruption was heard as far away as Australia. The force of the eruption blew off much of the mountain and created a large caldera (a example of what probably happened to Mount Mazama 5600 years earlier). The eruption also produced a huge dust cloud that circled the earth at altitudes of over twenty-seven kilometers. For three years following the eruption, the volcanic dust cloud caused the solar radiation level in Europe to be ten percent below average. The dust cloud also provided years of spectacular sunsets all over the earth.

Mount Pelée   In 1902, on the island of Martinique in the West Indies, Mount Pelée (puh-LAY′) erupted. The eruption did not come out of the top of the volcanic mountain because the top was plugged with volcanic rock from a previous eruption. Instead, the eruption broke through a weakened side of the volcano. Hot ash, cinders, gas, and rock rubble roared down the slope toward the seaport of St. Pierre at a speed of nearly 90 km per hour. Mount Pelée's eruption killed 28 000 people. Only two people survived. One of the two survivors was a prisoner in a dungeon, and the other was in his basement at the time of the eruption.

Library research

Find and compare eyewitness accounts of several major volcanic eruptions. Which account do you find the most interesting? Why?

Figure 10-4. When Mount Pelée (the mountain in the background) erupted on May 8, 1902, 28 000 people were living in the seaport of St. Pierre (Martinique, West Indies). How many people survived?
Only two people survived.

What is a lateral eruption?

Mount Lassen   In 1914, another period of volcanic activity took place in the Cascade Mountains. A **lateral eruption** (an eruption from the side of the mountain) took place on Mount Lassen, located in northern California.

Mount Lassen's eruptive period lasted from 1914 to 1921. An ash cloud rose over 9000 m. Several centimeters of volcanic ash accumulated on the streets of Reno, Nevada, 216 km away. The lateral eruption extended for several kilometers away from the mountain and involved lava that spilled down the sides of the mountain, melted snow, and created floods filled with large volcanic boulders.

Parícutin   In February, 1943, a volcano named Parícutin (pah-REE'-koo-ten') began as a small opening in a farmer's field in Mexico. At first, Parícutin was a curiosity that drew visitors and attracted scientific interest. As the volcanic material grew into a mountain, however, the farmer had to abandon the farm. In time, people in nearby towns had to leave their homes because the entire area became filled with ashes and lava. Parícutin was no longer a curiosity. It had destroyed two towns and the surrounding countryside. In one town, only the top of a church steeple showed above the thick lava deposits.

How destructive was the eruption of Parícutin?

Mount St. Helens   In May, 1980, an eruption of Mount St. Helens in the state of Washington set off huge ash falls, mudslides, and floods. More than six people were killed, and property damage was set at $2.7 billion.

In one large explosion, the upper 400 m (about 4 cubic km) of Mount St. Helens blew away. Much of the explosion propelled broken rock, ash, and mud laterally down the side of the mountain, scorching and smothering the land and every living thing in its path. The debris filled in valleys and created dams. As a result, the level of Spirit Lake near the base of Mount St. Helens is about 115 m higher than it was before the eruption.

The blast from the eruption stripped trees of limbs and laid the trees over onto the ground. From high in the air, the ground appeared covered with matchsticks. But these matchsticks represented nearly 590 square km of formerly thickly forested land.

Mount St. Helens has had a long history of activity. Four hundred years ago, volcanic activity reshaped the cone into one

A photograph of the Mount St. Helens eruption appears in Figure 1-5 on page 13.

of the most symmetrically shaped cones in the world. Between 1831 and 1957, the mountain was again active with minor eruptions. However, even though the volcano had been intermittently active, the 1980 eruption was unexpectedly violent.

An area of over 400 square km of the Mount St. Helens region has been designated a National Volcanic Monument and attracts many visitors. The bleak landscape has an eerie quality and is a reminder of the awesome power and death-dealing nature of volcanoes.

Loss of life and property is common with volcanic eruptions. But even with all the dangers, people often repopulate devastated landscapes. The slopes of Mount Vesuvius, for example, have people living there today.

Figure 10-5. Volcanic eruptions can occur very rapidly. This series of pictures shows beginning stages of eruption of Mount St. Helens on May 18, 1980. The first picture was taken at 8:27:00 am. The second picture, showing the lateral blast, was taken at 8:32:41 am. The furious surge of volcanic material shown in the third picture was taken at 8:32:51 am.

Check yourself

1. How do volcanic eruptions in inhabited areas affect people?

2. How far into the atmosphere can volcanic eruptions reach? Give an example.

3. List and describe three examples of major volcanic eruptions.

1. Volcanic eruptions in inhabited areas destroy property and can kill people.
2. 27 km, as evidenced by the dust cloud that circled the earth following the 1883 eruption of Krakatau.
3. Answers will depend on which three eruptions students choose and which details they include for each eruption.

Why some eruptions are so violent   New vocabulary: volcanic activity, vent, magma, lava, volcano, fumarole, viscosity

Volcanic activity includes all earth processes in which molten rock, gases, or fragments of solid material come out of a **vent,**

Probably the students have a clear notion of the distinction between lava and magma. In Investigation 10-1 (Lab Manual pages 135–136), igneous rock that forms from lava is termed igneous volcanic. Igneous rock that forms from magma deep within the earth is termed igneous Plutonic. (*Plutonic* comes from *Pluto*, the name of the god who, according to Greek and Roman mythology, was the god of the underworld.)

What are four sources of heat within the earth?

Library research

Find out more about the causes and effects of the earth's interior heat.

Students should be aware of the relationship between viscosity and the consistency of a fluid. The more viscous a fluid is, the thicker it is and the slower it flows. Through discussion, have students offer sequences of fluids that progress from least viscous to most viscous—for example, water to syrup to catsup to mustard, etc.

which is an opening in the earth's crust. (As you may recall, molten rock below the surface of the earth is called magma; molten rock on the surface of the earth is called lava. Sometimes the lava or fragments spread out almost flat. Sometimes the volcanic material from the vent builds up to form a mountain. Either the vent or the mountain is known as a **volcano.**

Volcanic material is hot. Gases and lava may reach 1200°C. The source of heat within the earth can be from several different earth processes. One source would be heat left over from when the earth was first formed. A second source of heat would be from the friction of rocks bending or sliding past other rocks deep within the earth. A third source is radioactive elements found within the earth that undergo spontaneous change and release heat. Other sources such as chemical reactions associated with the forming and re-forming of different minerals may contribute minor amounts of heat.

One of the concerns of people has been the violent nature of volcanoes. The Valley of 10,000 Smokes in Alaska was at one time a volcanic mountain, Mount Katmai (KAT′-mī). In 1912, Mount Katmai exploded, leaving a huge valley with thousands of fumaroles. A **fumarole** (FYOO′-muh-rōl′) is a volcanic vent or opening out of which gases and smoke come.

What causes some eruptions like Mount Katmai and Mount St. Helens, to be violent and others, like those of Hawaii or Iceland, to be relatively quiet? To a large degree the chemical composition of the magma—especially the amounts of silica and water—controls how violent or calm an eruption will be.

The amount of silica in a magma controls its viscosity. **Viscosity** (vis-KOS′-uh-tee) is a measure of how easily a liquid flows. A magma containing more than about 60 percent silica is viscous and flows slowly. This is because the silica bonds together to form chains of molecules. These chains slow down the magma's movement.

The presence of water in a viscous magma can lead to a violent eruption. In a magma of low viscosity, water can escape, allowing for a calm eruption. In a magma of high silica content, the silica chains hold the water under pressure. As the water becomes superheated, it boils and breaks through those bonds. The result is often an explosive eruption.

Figure 10-6. These erosion patterns were photographed in the Valley of the 10,000 Smokes, Alaska. How and when was this valley formed? The Valley of the 10,000 Smokes was formed by the explosion of Mount Katmai in 1912.

Check yourself

1. What earth processes are considered volcanic activities?
2. List the three major sources of heat that contribute to the heat in the earth.
3. How hot are volcanic gases and molten rock?

1. Any activity in which molten rock, gases, or fragments of solid material come out of an opening in the earth's crust
2. 1) Left over from when the earth was formed; 2) Friction caused by moving rock; 3) Radioactive decay
3. Can reach 1200°C

Volcanic landforms   New vocabulary: shield cone, cinder cone, composite cone, fissure, plateau basalts

Volcanic eruptions can develop into three different types of volcanic mountains, depending on the nature of the volcanic material. The three types of volcanic mountains are shield cones, cinder cones, and composite cones.

A **shield cone** is a volcanic mountain that is built almost entirely of lava flow. The slopes of a shield cone volcano are very gentle and rounded like a warrior's shield. (The slopes of such a volcano have an average angle of 2°.) The islands of Iceland and the Hawaiian Islands are examples of shield cones. The island of Hawaii is a shield cone volcano that rises from the ocean floor. That volcano is more than 10 km high from its base on the ocean bottom to its highest point above the sea.

A **cinder cone** is a volcanic mountain that is built entirely of volcanic cinders and ashes. Cinder cones are small (usually less than 450 m high) and have steep sides. The slopes of such a volcano have an average angle between 30° and 40°. Examples of cinder cones are the volcanic cones of Parícutin in Mexico, Cerro Negro in Nicaragua, and Wizard Island in Crater Lake, Oregon.

The different types of volcanic cones are related to viscosity. The steepest cone is formed from cinder and ash, which is not a fluid and therefore doesn't flow. The most gently sloping cones are shield cones, formed of lava flows. (Lava is a fluid whose viscosity varies with temperature. The activity on the following page explores the relationship between temperature and the viscosity of lava.)

If possible, show students a shield or a facsimile of a shield. Have students imagine the gently sloping sides when the shield is laid flat on the ground. (A convex lens could also be used for comparison of slope.)

Science Processes: Observing; Inferring
See also Activity Record Sheet 10-1A (Lab Manual page 133)

10 minutes   Small groups

Activity 10-1A   Inferring Lava Viscosity

Materials

specimens of basalt
  from two different kinds
  of lava flows:
  vesicular basalt
  nonvesicular basalt

Purpose

To infer lava viscosity from volcanic materials.

Procedure

1. Examine your lava specimens. They are made of basalt, one of the most widespread of volcanic igneous rocks. Basalt rock occurs as massive lava flows, which can accumulate to the astounding size of large landforms known as plateau basalts, or basalt floods.
2. Note the texture of your specimens. Are they smooth or porous? The small holes are known as *vesicles,* and the sample with vesicles is known as a vesicular basalt. Vesicles form as water and other gases escape from hot lava. What does that tell you about the chemical contents of the two magmas?

Questions

1. Which kind of basalt lava indicates a less viscous (that is more freely flowing) lava?
2. Which kind of basalt lava probably had a higher silica content and was more viscous (less free flowing)?

Conclusion

What does looking at basalt tell you about the viscosity of the lava from which it was made?

A

B

C

A **composite cone** is built of alternate layers of lava flows and volcanic cinders and ashes. Composite cones are volcanic mountains with beautifully symmetrical shapes. Mount Fuji in Japan and Mount Shasta in California are two examples of composite cone volcanoes. Mount St. Helens, a composite cone, had a more symmetrical shape before its last eruption.

Composite cone volcanoes can reach 4 km in height. The gentle slopes near the base of a composite cone are generally lava flows. These lower slopes have an average angle of 5°. The steeper parts of a composite cone contain larger percentages of cinders and ash. The upper slopes have an average angle of 30°.

Some volcanic activity does not produce a cone. Sometimes the lava flows from a **fissure** (FISH′-er), which is a long crack in the ground. Thick buildups of horizontal layers of basalt may form as a result of lava flows from fissures in the ground. These types of thick deposits on the continents are called **plateau basalts.** Much of eastern Washington and Oregon and parts of Idaho are covered by plateau basalts. In India, the Deccan plateau basalts cover more than 500 000 square kilometers. In South America, the Parana plateau basalts of Brazil and Paraguay cover more than 750 000 square kilometers.

Check yourself

1. List examples of three types of volcanic mountains.

2. What are the relative sizes of the three types of volcanic mountains?

3. How do plateau basalts form?

4. List three examples of areas of plateau basalts, and indicate their size.

Figure 10-7. (A) Mauna Kea, Hawaii, shield cone. (B) Cinder cone in a volcanic field near Sonora, Mexico. (C) Mount Fuji, Japan, composite cone.

Interested students could prepare reports on striking erosional landforms that are remnants of volcanic activity. Some sample locations: Shiprock, New Mexico; Devil's Tower, Wyoming; the Palisades along the Hudson River.

What are plateau basalts?

1. 1) Shield cone: Hawaiian Islands, Iceland; 2) Cinder cone: Parícutin, Cerro Negro, Wizard Island; 3) Composite cone: Mount Fuji, Mount Shasta, Mount St. Helens before its last eruption

2. 1) Shield cone—more than 10 km high; 2) Composite cone—up to 4 km high; 3) Cinder cone—usually less than 450 m high

3. From lava flows from fissures, which are long cracks in the ground

4. 1) Much of eastern Washington and Oregon, and parts of Idaho; 2) The Deccan plateau basalts in India—more than 500 000 km²; 3) The Parana plateau basalts of Brazil and Paraguay—more than 750 000 km²

Where volcanoes occur   New vocabulary: Ring of Fire, island arc, mid-ocean ridge

Volcanic activity is more likely to occur in certain regions of the earth than in others. Two regions of volcanic activity are the Ring of Fire and the mid-ocean ridge.

The Ring of Fire   Many active and inactive volcanoes are located around the rim of the Pacific Ocean. This entire group of volcanoes makes up what is called the **Ring of Fire.** A glance at Figure 10-8 will show you why this group of volcanoes is called a ring.

The Ring of Fire includes the volcanic mountains near the edges of North America, Central America, and South America. It also includes the volcanic islands that are found in the North and West Pacific. These volcanic islands form curve-shaped groups called **island arcs.** The Mariana Islands and Japan in the West Pacific and the Aleutian Islands in the North Pacific are examples of island arcs. The Aleutians curve south and west from Alaska and form the southern boundary of the Bering Sea.

There is a relationship between the volcanoes of the Ring of Fire and trenches in the Pacific Ocean. Along the bottom of the ocean, volcanoes that are part of the Ring of Fire are

The Ring of Fire is also mentioned in Chapter 8 (page 379) in conjunction with features of the ocean bottom.

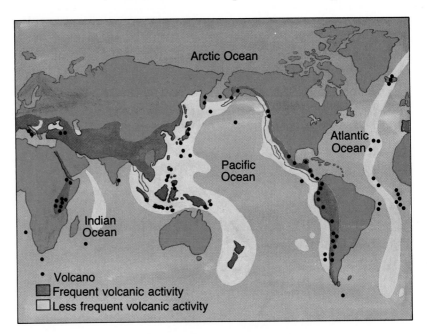

Figure 10-8. Many volcanoes are located around the edge of the Pacific Ocean and form what is called the Ring of Fire. Where are many volcanoes of the Atlantic Ocean?
Along the mid-ocean ridge

See also Teaching Diagram 10-1 (TRB page 44).

found near trenches. The volcanoes of the Aleutian Islands, for example, are along the Aleutian Trench, which is 3700 km long and 7.7 km deep. On the continent of South America, the volcanoes of the Andes Mountains are parallel to the Peru-Chile Trench. In Central America, the volcanoes are near the Middle America Trench.

The mid-ocean ridge   Much volcanic activity takes place along the mid-ocean ridge. The **mid-ocean ridge** is a system of tall, rugged, submerged mountains that form the single most dominant feature of the ocean bottoms. As shown in Figure 8-9 (page 380), the mid-ocean ridge extends down the center of the Atlantic Ocean, around the tip of Africa, and into the Indian Ocean. In the Indian Ocean, the mid-ocean ridge splits into a Y shape. One part of the Y extends northward toward the Gulf of Aden where it splits into a Red Sea branch and an African rift system branch. The other part extends southeastward—passing south of Australia, across the southern Pacific Ocean, and up toward Central America. Active volcanoes are found along many parts of this mid-ocean ridge system. Although most of the volcanic activity along the ridge is below the ocean's surface, some volcanic mountains form islands like Iceland and the Azores in the Atlantic Ocean.

Check yourself

1. Describe the Ring of Fire.

2. Describe the volcanic nature of the mid-ocean ridge.

3. What do the Japanese Islands and the Aleutian Islands have in common?

Figure 10-9. Surtsey, off the southern coast of Iceland, is located along the mid-ocean ridge, a site of much volcanic activity.

Critical Thinking

What are the similarities and differences between the Ring of Fire and the mid-ocean ridge?

They are similar in that they are both volcanic mountain ranges. They differ in location.

1. The Ring of Fire includes the volcanic mountains near the edges of the Americas; it also includes volcanic islands like the Aleutians, Japan, and the Marianas.
2. Active volcanoes continually erupt along many parts of the ridge system. Most eruptions take place below the ocean surface. Some parts of the ridge system (for example, Iceland and the Azores) are above sea level.
3. Both are island arcs that formed from volcanic eruptions.

Science Processes: Interpreting data; Inferring
See also Activity Record Sheet 10-1B (Lab Manual
page 134)

CORE   30 minutes   Individuals or small groups

Activity 10-1B Reconstructing the Topography of a Volcanic Cone

Materials

the three topographic
 maps reproduced in
 the Appendix

graph paper

pencil

Purpose

To learn to translate a topographic map of a volcanic cone into a profile view.

Procedure

1. Fold the graph paper along one of the lines. Place the folded edge of the paper across the topographic representation of Orr Mountain. The folded edge should be down, running east to west, and passing through the Lookout on the mountaintop. The southern half of the mountain should be visible.
2. Reading across the folded edge, determine the lowest elevation that the folded edge passes through at the bottom of the mountain. (The lowest elevation can be on either side of the mountain. Also, because the base lines are irregular, you can use the lowest numbered contour line as your starting point.)
3. Record the lowest elevation in the margin of your paper. Also record the highest elevation (the mountaintop) that the folded edge passes through.
4. In ascending order, number horizontal lines to match the numbered intervals used on the map (200 feet). Number the line on the folded edge with the lowest numbered elevation. Number a line above the folded edge to match the next elevation, in ascending order (4600, 4800, etc.) until you reach 6000 (the next interval above the peak).

5. Along the folded edge, make a check mark at each location where the folded edge crosses a numbered, darker contour line. Next to the check mark, record the elevation.
6. Directly above each check mark, draw a dot on the line with the same elevation. Connect the dots with a smooth curve.

Questions

1. How does the profile you drew compare with those drawn by others in the class? Are they all more or less similar in outline?
2. How could you make your profile more closely represent the cone of the topographic map?

Conclusion

From the shape of your outline, would you say that Orr Mountain is a shield cone, a cinder cone, or a composite cone?

Section 1 Review   Chapter 10

Use **Reading Checksheet 10-1** TRB page 87
Skillsheet 10-1 TRB page 129
Section Reviewsheet 10-1 TRB pages 195–196
Section Testsheet 10-1 TRB page 301

Check Your Vocabulary

1 caldera	8 magma
11 cinder cone	14 plateau basalts
12 composite cone	10 shield cone
13 fissure	4 vent
6 fumarole	7 viscosity
15 island arc	3 volcanic activity
2 lateral eruption	5 volcano
9 lava	

Match each term above with the numbered phrase that best describes it.

1. A large circular depression that forms when a volcanic mountaintop collapses into the magma chamber beneath the mountain
2. An eruption from the side of a volcano
3. Any earth process by which molten rock, gases, or fragments of solid material come out of an opening (called a vent) in the earth's crust
4. An opening in the earth's crust from which volcanic materials pass to the earth's surface
5. A vent or mountain from which volcanic materials pass to the earth's surface
6. A volcanic vent or opening that gases and smoke come out of
7. A measure of how easily a liquid flows
8. Molten rock below the surface of the earth
9. Molten rock on the surface of the earth
10. A volcanic mountain with gently sloping sides; built almost entirely of lava flow
11. A small volcanic mountain with steep sides
12. A mountain built of alternate layers of lava flows and volcanic cinders and ashes
13. A long crack from which lava flows
14. Thick buildups of horizontal layers of basalt on continents that form as a result of lava flows from fissures
15. A curve-shaped group of volcanic islands

Check Your Knowledge

Multiple Choice: Choose the answer that best completes each of the following sentences.

1. _?_ is not a source of heat for volcanic activities.
   a) Internal friction in the earth
   b) Radioactive decay in rocks and minerals
   c) Underground burning of coal
   d) Leftover heat from the earth's formation
2. A magma and lava with high water content will contribute to _?_.
   a) the building of a larger volcanic mountain
   b) an increase in explosive activity
   c) a less viscous lava
   d) a compositional change in the crustal rock that forms

Check Your Understanding

1. Explain how different volcanic activities can be destructive.
2. Describe the differences among each of the three types of volcanic mountains.
3. How do plateau basalts form?
4. Describe the three factors that determine the violence of a volcanic eruption.
5. Where are volcanic activities most commonly found on the earth's surface?

Stress, Structure, and Earthquakes   Section 2

Section 2 of Chapter 10 is divided into four parts:

Rocks under stress

Movement along a fault

What is an earthquake?

Earthquake damage

Figure 10-10. This area of the Zagros Mountains, Iran, shows evidence of folding, erosion, and lava flow. What causes folded mountains to form?
As mentioned on the facing page, stresses within the earth's crust can cause rocks to change in volume and shape. The stresses that cause bends and folds occur deep within the earth. As will be pointed out later in this section, stresses nearer the surface cause breaks in rocks.

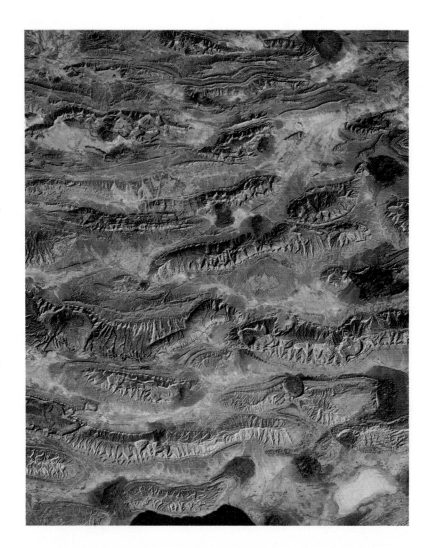

Learner Objectives
1. To describe how rocks are changed by stress within the earth's crust.
2. To relate synclines, anticlines, domes, and basins to stresses within the earth's crust.
3. To distinguish among different types of faults.
4. To use the arrival times of S-waves and P-waves to determine the epicenter and time of occurrence of an earthquake.
5. To compare the Richter scale and the Mercalli scale.
6. To make models of faults.

The rocks that make up the earth's crust are under great pressure or stress. Sometimes, this stress causes observable movement. Volcanic activity, for example, is caused by tremendous pressure and heat within the earth's crust. Earthquakes, where sections of the earth's crust can be felt or seen to move, are caused by the release of stress within the earth's crust.

Sometimes, however, stress and movement within the earth's crust can only be inferred. By studying certain changes in the earth's crust, it is possible to infer the causes of those changes.

Rocks under stress   New vocabulary: plastic deformation, folded rock, syncline, anticline, fracture, compressional stress

When you apply pressure to a piece of wood, one of several things will happen. 1) If the piece of wood is thick and strong, there will probably be no noticeable change in the wood. 2) If the piece of wood is thin like a ruler and the pressure is not too great, the piece of wood will bend. 3) If you keep putting more pressure on the ruler, the piece of wood will bend only so far, and then it will break.

Rocks, too, respond to stress and pressure in a number of ways. Rocks buried deep in the earth's crust experience strong confining pressure and heat. Forces within the earth cause stresses to build up in the rocks. As the stresses get stronger, the rock will change. Rock can change in volume, in shape, or in both volume and shape. Figure 10-11 shows simple changes in volume and shape.

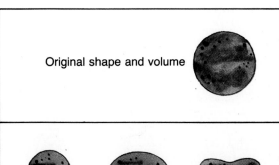

Original shape and volume

Change in volume

Changes in shape and volume

Library research

Find photographs of landforms that are clear examples of folded rock structures.

The volume of a rock can be changed by the elimination of pore spaces when the mineral grains in the rock are forced closer together. Under extreme pressure and heat, atoms in the minerals will rearrange themselves into new and denser minerals. This is the kind of change that takes place when metamorphic rock is formed.

The shape of a rock can be changed when stresses are put on rocks under high confining pressures. When this happens, many of the rocks will bend, flow, and deform like modeling clay. Geologists call this type of change in rocks **plastic deformation.**

Rocks that have been bent by high confining pressure are called **folded rocks.** The two most common types of folds in rocks are synclines (SIN'-klīnz) and anticlines (AN'-ti-klīnz). Figure 10-12 shows a block diagram of rock layers that have been folded into a syncline and an anticline. A **syncline** is a downward-arching fold in rocks. An **anticline** is an upward-arching fold in rocks.

The layers of an anticline slope downward and away from the highest point of the fold in the same way that the sides of a sloped roof slant away from the ridge that runs along the top of the roof. The layers of a syncline, on the other hand, slope downward and inward towards the lowest point of the fold.

Synclines and anticlines extend lengthwise and vary in size. In width, a syncline or anticline can be anywhere from microscopic to several kilometers. In length, synclines and anticlines can extend for many kilometers. In fact, great mountain systems like the Alps in Europe and the Appalachians in North America contain synclines and anticlines.

Figure 10-12. Which is an upward-arching fold in rocks —a syncline or an anticline? An upward-arching fold is an anticline.

See also Teaching Diagram 10-2A (TRB page 45).

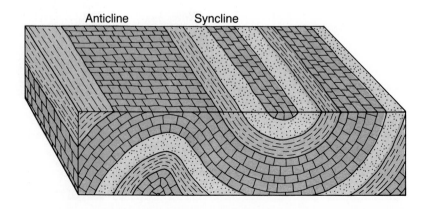

Anticline   Syncline

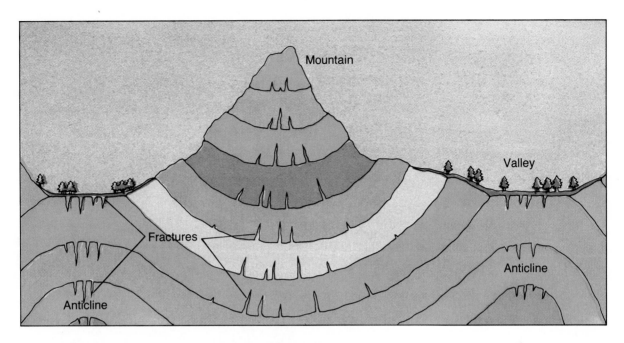

As rocks are folded into synclines and anticlines, the rocks may develop cracks called **fractures** (FRAK′-cherz). These fractures frequently occur where the bending is the strongest— along the bottom of a syncline or the top of an anticline. These fracture zones are zones of weakness that may experience rapid weathering and erosion. Commonly, valleys develop along the tops of eroded anticlines. This is evidenced by the pattern of streams which is controlled by the underlying structure.

Figure 10-13 shows the relationship among synclines, anticlines, mountains, and valleys. As shown in the diagram, fractures along the tops of anticlines can lead to the erosion of a valley. And the erosion of the tops of anticlines on both sides of a syncline can leave the syncline elevated as a long mountain ridge.

Different kinds of stress exist within the earth's crust. Taking the ruler as an example, one kind of stress is applied when you push in on the two ends of the ruler. If the ruler is thin enough, the ruler will bend in the middle. This form of stress, in which matter is being pushed together or compressed, is called **compressional stress.** Synclines and anticlines are caused by compressional stress.

Upward and downward stresses also exist within the earth's crust. Using the ruler as an example, it is possible to apply stress to the ruler by pushing down or up on the ruler. If this kind of pressure is applied to the middle of the ruler, the ruler will bend one way or the other.

Figure 10-13. How can valleys form in anticlines?
Fractures which form in anticlines are subject to rapid weathering and erosion. In time, valleys are formed by the weathering and erosion.

See also Teaching Diagram 10-2A (TRB page 45).

In what part of an anticline do fractures occur?

488

Science Processes: Formulating models
See also Activity Record Sheet 10-2A (Lab Manual
page 137)

5 minutes   Pairs of students

Activity 10-2A   Simulating Anticlines and Synclines

Materials

sheet of paper

marker pens, 2 different
 colors

Purpose

To study the relationship between synclines and
anticlines.

Procedure

1. Working in pairs, one person cradles a sheet
   of paper between his or her hands (as
   shown in the picture) and then slowly pushes
   the hands together to create folds in the paper.
2. Using the two marker pens, the other person
   marks the tops of the folds with one color
   and bottoms of the folds with the other color.

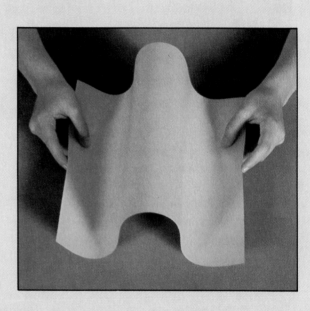

Questions

1. Which folds represent anticlines?
2. Which folds represent synclines?

Conclusion

How are anticlines and synclines related? What
type of force created the folds?

In the earth's crust, upward and downward stresses are responsible for the formation of folded structures called domes and basins. Domes and basins are circular or oblong when seen from the air. A dome is a large, up-arched structure with a diameter at the base from 8 to 160 km. In cross section, each of the individual rock layers of a dome would look like an upside-down bowl. The upward-pushing pressures that cause domes are sometimes associated with igneous activity.

A basin is just the opposite of a dome. A basin is a rock structure that is bent downward. In cross section, each of the individual rock layers of a basin would look like a bowl right side up. Basins are created by the sinking of the earth. As the earth sinks, more sediments pour into the basin and cause the rock layers of the basin to sink deeper.

Figure 10-14. A cloud of dust rose from this fault, which is part of the San Andreas fault system, during the October 2, 1987, earthquake near Los Angeles.

Library research

Find the location of the earthquake fault closest to where you live. What kind of fault is it? When was the last time that movement took place along that fault?

Check yourself

1. What types of changes in rocks can be caused by stresses in the earth's crust?

2. What is plastic deformation?

3. What are the differences among anticlines, synclines, basins, and domes?

4. How does change in volume due to pressure create metamorphic rocks?

Movement along a fault

New vocabulary: tensional stress, shear stress, fault, hanging wall, footwall, normal fault, reverse fault, thrust fault, transform fault

Rocks that fold when deep in the earth may break when put under stress nearer the surface. Breaks in rocks can be caused by compressional stress, tensional stress, or shear stress.

1. Changes in shape or volume or both

2. A change in the shape of rocks that flow like modeling clay when under great pressure

3. Anticlines and domes are up-arched structures; synclines and basins are down-arched.

4. The chemical elements are forced into patterns of closer spacing. In order to do this, the minerals break down and new minerals form, resulting in metamorphic rock.

What kinds of stresses cause breaks in rocks near the surface?

Science Processes: Formulating models;
Measuring; Communicating
See also Activity Record Sheet 10-2B (Lab Manual
page 138)

CORE   15 minutes   Small groups, or demonstration

Activity 10-2B   Making a Fault Model

Materials

modeling clay, three
different colors

pencil

thin wire, 3/4 to 1 m long

2 small pieces of wood

Purpose

To make a model of a geologic fault.

Procedure

1. To make the model, form three flat layers of modeling clay, each a different color and each about 1 cm thick. Stack the layers on top of one another.
2. Use the blocks of wood and the wire to make a cutter similar to a cheese cutter. Wrap a few turns of wire around one of the pieces of wood until it is tight and won't slip. Do the same with the other piece of wood and the other end of the wire. Leave a length of wire between the pieces of wood that is just a few centimeters longer than the width of the stacked clay layers.
3. Make a canal across the width of the top layer of clay by pressing a pencil lengthwise halfway into the top clay layer.
4. To create the fault, use the wire to cut completely through the clay layers at a 45° angle.
5. Measure and record the width and length of the block. (Note: Be sure to save your model and your measurements for use in another activity later in this section.)

Questions

1. What three kinds of stress might affect the fault model you have made?
2. Draw a cross section of your fault model and label the hanging wall and the footwall.

Step 1

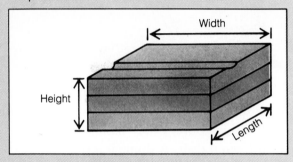

Step 2

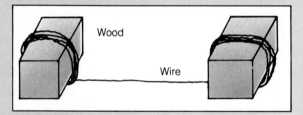

Step 3

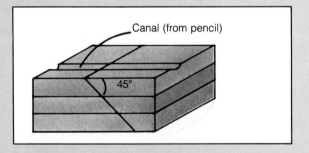

Conclusion

Now that you have made your model, which type of faulting would you predict would stretch your model? Which type would shorten it? (Hint: see page 493.)

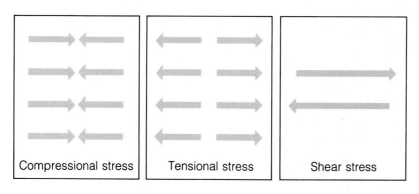

Figure 10-15. When you stretch a rubber band, are you applying compressional, tensional, or shear stress?
Tensional stress

Stretching a rubber band is an example of applying a **tensional stress.** Rubbing your hands past one another is an example of **shear stress.** Figure 10-15 shows the directions of the forces in compressional stress, tensional stress, and shear stress.

You may have heard of faults or perhaps you have heard about a particular fault, such as the San Andreas fault that passes near the city of San Francisco, California. A **fault** is a break or fracture in rocks along which the rocks move. Compressional and tensional stresses cause an up-down movement along a fault. Shear stress causes horizontal movement along a fault.

What is a fault?

Figure 10-16 shows a cross section of a fault that is not at 90° to the surface. The rock masses on either side of such a fault are known as the hanging wall and the footwall. The **hanging wall** is the mass of rock that is above the fault. The **footwall** is the mass of rock that is below the fault. (The names are from mining. Normally, miners walk on the footwall and hang their lanterns on the hanging wall.)

The motion along this fault was probably horizontal because the rocks show no vertical movement. Hanging wall/footwall terminology remains consistent whether the motion is vertical, horizontal, or a combination.

Faults are classified according to the direction in which the rocks move on either side of the fault. A **normal fault,** shown in Figure 10-17, is one in which the hanging wall has moved

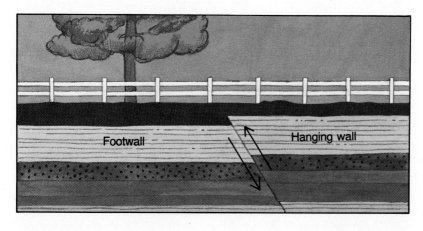

Footwall   Hanging wall

It is the hanging wall that is above the fault.
Figure 10-16. Which mass of rock is above a fault—the hanging wall or the footwall?

Science Processes: Measuring; Inferring; Defining operationally
See also Activity Record Sheet 10-2C (Lab Manual page 139)

15 minutes   Small groups, or demonstration

Activity 10-2C Simulating Faults

Materials

Fault model made in previous activity,
 "Making a Fault Model"

Purpose

To simulate a variety of geologic faults.

Procedure

1. From the hanging wall block of your fault model, remove the bottom layer of clay. Then put the hanging wall back against the footwall as shown in illustration A.
2. Measure and record the length and width of the clay model.
3. Next, replace the bottom clay layer you removed in step 1. From the footwall block, remove the bottom layer of clay. Then put the footwall back against the hanging wall as shown in illustration B.
4. Measure and record the length and width of the clay model.
5. Replace the bottom layer of clay removed in step 3.
6. Move the hanging wall block laterally by using a shear stress as shown in illustration C.
7. Measure and record the length and width of the clay model.

Questions

1. When you followed the directions in step 1, what type of fault did you simulate? Describe what happened to the canal.
2. When you followed the directions in step 3, what type of fault did you simulate? Again, describe what happened to the canal.
3. When you followed the directions in steps 5 and 6, what type of fault did you simulate? What happened to the canal?
4. Which type(s) of faulting offsets the canal sideways?

A

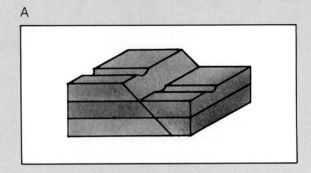

B

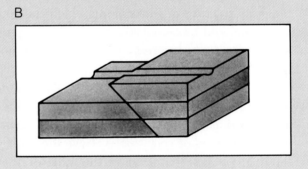

C

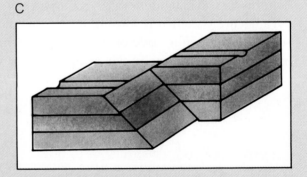

Conclusion

You have simulated several kinds of faults. Which type of stress (compressional or tensional) would create reverse faults? Which would create normal faults?

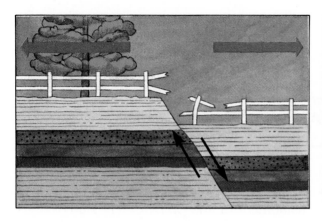 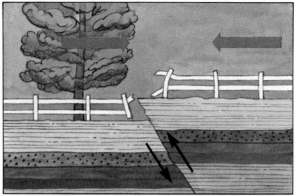

See also Teaching Diagram 10-2B (TRB page 46).

down with respect to the footwall. In a normal fault, movement along the fault is caused by tensional stress in the crust.

A **reverse fault,** shown in Figure 10-18, is one in which the hanging wall has moved up with respect to the footwall. In a reverse fault, movement along the fault is caused by compressional stress in the earth's crust.

A **thrust fault** is a special type of reverse fault. In a thrust fault, the fault surface is at a very low angle or even horizontal in some places. As with other reverse faults, movement along a thrust fault is caused by compressional stress.

A **transform fault** is a fault along which there is a horizontal movement similar to that when you rub your hands together. Movement along a transform fault is caused by shear stress. Most transform faults are found in the ocean crust. A few, however, extend onto the land and are rather significant. The San Andreas fault, which runs through the state of California, is an example. Along this fault, the whole western part of the state is moving northward with respect to the eastern part of the state. The great San Francisco earthquake of 1906 was caused by movement along this fault.

The up-down movement of rock masses along faults has

Figure 10-17 (left). A normal fault.

Figure 10-18 (right). A reverse fault.

Figure 10-19. Fault-block mountains (horsts) form when areas of crust sink between two faults. The lowered area, called a graben (GRAH'-bin), forms a valley.

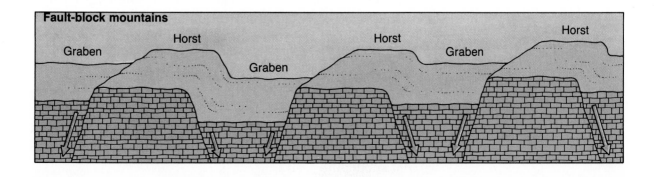

Do the Appalachian Mountains
consist of folds or faults or both?

1. Tensional, compressional, and
   shear stress
2. Relative positions of the
   hanging wall and footwall in
   the students' drawings should
   be as shown in Figure 10-16.
3. In a normal fault, the hanging
   wall moves down relative to
   the footwall. In a reverse fault,
   just the opposite movement
   occurs.
4. A transform fault caused by
   shear stress

See also Teaching Diagram 10-2C
(TRB page 47).

caused a variety of different kinds of landforms on the earth's surface. The Appalachian Mountains, for instance, consist not only of folds but also of numerous reverse faults and thrust faults. The Basin and Range Province of the western United States, with its fault-block mountains, is another example. And the large step-like plateaus of northern Arizona and southeastern Utah are still another example of a different kind of landform caused by the movement of rock masses along faults.

Check yourself

1. What kinds of stresses can create faults?

2. Draw a cross section of a fault, and label the hanging wall and the footwall.

3. How does the movement in a normal fault differ from that in a reverse fault?

4. What type of fault is the San Andreas fault?

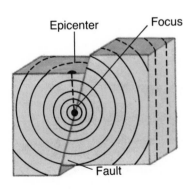

Figure 10-20. P-waves and S-waves radiate from the focus, the center of the earthquake. The focus is located within the earth. The epicenter is on the earth's surface directly above the focus.

The difference between stress and strain is very important, and the two terms should not be confused. Stress is applied force; strain is the deformation that results when force is applied.

What is an earthquake?   New vocabulary: earthquake, focus, P-wave, S-wave, seismograph, epicenter, seismologist, Richter scale

An **earthquake** is a motion, trembling, or vibration of the ground. An earthquake is caused by the release of stress that has been slowly building up in the earth's crust. An earthquake can be caused by sudden movement along a fault. An earthquake can also be caused by volcanic activity.

When an earthquake occurs, stress energy that has been building up in the earth's crust changes to wave energy. Earthquakes originate in the earth's crust or upper mantle. The point of origin of an earthquake, where stress energy changes to wave energy, is called the **focus** of the earthquake. The focus is the center of an earthquake. From this center or focus, waves spread out through the earth in all directions.

Most earthquakes occur at a shallow depth, somewhere between the earth's surface and 70 km depth. These earthquakes are said to have a shallow focus. Some earthquakes have an intermediate focus, between 70 km and 300 km depth. Only a very few earthquakes have a deep focus, between 300 km and 700 km depth.

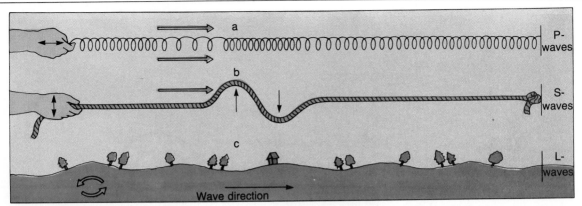

Earthquake vibrations produce two major kinds of waves, P-waves and S-waves. **P-waves** are primary waves. A primary wave is a longitudinal wave. In a longitudinal wave, the particles of material through which the wave is traveling move in the same direction that the wave is traveling. A longitudinal wave is also called a compressional wave because the wave compresses and then stretches the particles of material in the same direction that the wave is moving. (See Figure 10-21.)

S-waves, or secondary waves, are transverse waves. In a transverse wave, the particle motion is perpendicular to the direction in which the wave is moving. The motion is similar to a guitar string, which is set in motion by being plucked in a direction that is perpendicular to the string. Adjacent points in the direction of transverse or S-wave motion move sideways to one another as the wave passes. This motion is called shear, and S-waves are sometimes called shear waves.

Both S-waves and P-waves move outward from the focus. But an S-wave causes the ground to vibrate sideways or perpendicular to the direction in which the wave is traveling. A P-wave compresses and then stretches the ground in the same direction that the wave is traveling. When P-waves and S-waves reach the surface of the earth, surface waves are set in motion. One type of surface wave is an *L-wave*. L-waves cause broad up-and-down motion that may open and close cracks in the earth.

Earthquake waves are recorded on instruments called **seismographs** (SĪZ′-muh-grafs). Many seismograph stations are located around the world. Shock waves from an earthquake arrive at different stations at different times, depending on how far away the station is from the focus. By comparing the arrival times recorded by seismographs at three or more different stations, the exact position of the focus of an earthquake can be determined. The earthquake's **epicenter,** which is the point or area on the earth's surface directly above the focus, can also be determined. (See Figure 10-22.)

Figure 10-21. P-waves compress and stretch the earth in the direction of the wave movement. S-waves move material up and down like the wave on the rope. L-waves flow along the earth's surface like ripples on water.

What kind of wave motion occurs when you pluck a guitar string?

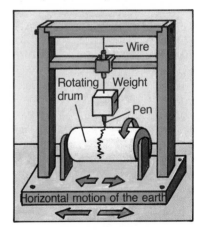

Figure 10-22. Seismographs record earthquake waves by measuring how much the rotating drum moves against the motionless pen. The pen is motionless because it is weighted and suspended by a wire. What does the seismograph measure besides the amount of energy in a wave?
A seismograph also measures the arrival time of a wave.

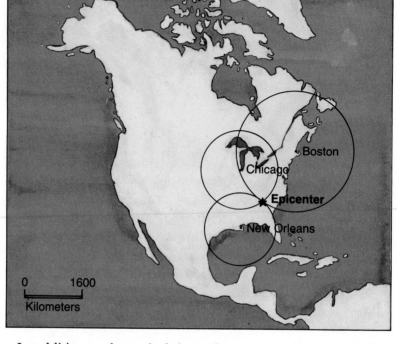

Figure 10-23. By comparing the arrival times recorded by seismographs at three or more different stations, the exact position of the focus of an earthquake can be determined. What is the relationship between the focus and the epicenter of an earthquake?

The focus is the center, or point of origin, of an earthquake. The epicenter is the point on the surface directly above the focus.

See also Teaching Diagram 10-2C (TRB page 47).

What two kinds of information are provided by a seismograph?

1. Sudden movement along a fault, or volcanic activity
2. By using a seismograph, and then expressing the intensity of the quake in terms of the Richter scale
3. P-waves and S-waves
4. 70 km to 300 km

In addition to the arrival time of a wave, a seismograph also shows the amount of energy in the wave. From this record, the amount of energy released at the time of the movement in the earth can be calculated. The units used to measure the strength of an earthquake are based on a system devised in 1935 by Charles Richter, an American **seismologist** (a scientist who studies earthquakes). This system, known as the **Richter scale,** uses a numerical scale from 1 to 10 to measure the amount of energy released at the focus. Each of the numerical steps in the Richter scale represents a ten-fold increase in the amount of energy released. For example, a reading of 3 on the Richter scale indicates the release of 10 times more energy than would be indicated by a reading of 2 on the Richter scale. And a reading of 7.5 on the Richter scale indicates the release of 1000 (10 times 10 times 10) times more energy than would be indicated by a reading of 4.5.

Check yourself

1. What natural earth processes can cause earthquakes?

2. How is the energy in an earthquake measured?

3. What are the two major kinds of waves an earthquake produces?

4. What is the depth range of intermediate focus earthquakes?

Earthquake damage

New vocabulary: Mercalli scale

Scientists estimate that the earth produces, on the average, an earthquake every 32 seconds. Many of these are so weak that they cannot even be felt. Others, however, do great damage. During some earthquakes, the movement of the earth's crust causes buildings and bridges to crack and collapse. Roadways are split. Landslides are set in motion and cliffs tumble into the sea.

The Richter scale measures the energy contained in a wave. It does not indicate the amount of damage that has been done. Another type of scale, the **Mercalli scale**, is used to show damage. Table 10-1 shows six of the twelve steps in the Mercalli scale, which was created in 1902 by Giuseppe Mercalli, an Italian seismologist. The Mercalli scale is still widely used to describe the amount of damage caused by an earthquake.

Figure 10-24. On Thursday, September 19, 1985. Mexico City was heavily damaged by an earthquake. With a force of 8.2 on the Richter Scale, the shock waves were felt as far away as Houston, Texas.

Table 10-1. At what step on the Mercalli scale do cracks form in the ground?
At step IX, cracks form in the ground.

Some Steps in the Mercalli Scale of Earthquake Damage	
Step	Extent of Earthquake Damage
I	The earthquake is felt by only a few people near the epicenter.
III	The earthquake is felt in buildings, but usually only on the upper levels.
V	Windows and fragile objects are broken.
VII	People run out of buildings, and some masonry breaks.
IX	Cracks form in the ground, and all buildings are damaged.
XII	Objects are thrown into the air, and all structures are destroyed.

Library research

Provide data for five earthquakes that occurred within the last ten years. For each, give the date, location, intensity according to the Richter scale, brief description of the earthquake damage, and the source of your information.

The amount of damage caused by an earthquake depends on several factors.

1. The amount of damage depends in part on the amount of energy in the earthquake waves.

   a. Usually the damage is greatest at the epicenter and becomes less severe as the earthquake waves get farther away from the epicenter.

   b. In areas where fault movement is fairly frequent, earthquakes are usually not strong enough to cause severe damage. But in areas where the movement along a fault is rare, stresses in the earth may build up to such a strength that, when the earth does slip, a great amount of energy is released and can cause heavy damage.

2. The amount of damage depends on the type of rock or sediment through which the earthquake waves are moving. Soft sediment will allow more damage than a solid bedrock such as granite. That is why buildings constructed on loose sediment 100 km from an epicenter may experience more damage than buildings built on granite at the site of the epicenter.

3. The amount of damage depends on the type of building materials and the type of construction used in the area that is experiencing the earthquake. (Wood frame buildings, for example, may suffer less damage than buildings made of materials that are cemented together.) In an earthquake, some flexibility within the individual structures is desirable.

In some cases, the earthquake-caused breaking of water and sewer pipes is a greater threat to a community than is the initial shock damage. During the great San Francisco earthquake in

1906, most of the damage was caused by fires that could not be put out because the water pipes had all been broken. And the health hazard due to unsafe water and disrupted sewage lines often causes greater loss of life than falling buildings.

The most deadly earthquake in history, killing 830 000 people, occurred on January 24, 1556, in Shenshi Province, China. China also experienced disastrous earthquakes on December 16, 1920, and July 28, 1976.

When and where did the most deadly earthquake in history occur?

Earthquakes are common along active fault zones. And certain types of earthquakes are associated with volcanic activity. In an area of volcanic activity, for example, many shallow-focus earthquakes immediately precede an eruption. These particular earth movements are probably caused by the movement of magma just beneath the surface of the earth. Knowing that earthquakes are associated with fault zones and with volcanic activity, engineers and scientists can predict in a general way where earthquakes are most likely to occur on a regular basis. In some cases, the amount of energy that might be released can also be predicted. With this kind of information, construction sites and building codes can be designed that will give maximum safety to people living in earthquake areas.

Some very destructive earthquakes occur in places where they are least expected. In 1811 and 1812, the interior of the United States was rocked by a series of earthquakes that were centered near New Madrid, Missouri. (These earthquakes rocked the Mississippi Valley so violently that for a short time the Mississippi River flowed north!) And in 1866 the epicenter of a severe earthquake was located near Charleston, South Carolina. For people living in areas like these, which are outside the obvious earthquake zones, it is difficult to prepare for an earthquake because several generations may pass between one earthquake and the next.

What caused the Mississippi River to flow in the opposite direction?

Check yourself

1. How is the amount of damage done by an earthquake related to the amount of energy?

2. Besides energy, what other factors affect the amount of damage done by an earthquake?

3. What is the Mercalli scale?

1. In general, the more energy, the greater the damage.
2. The type of rock or soil and the type of building construction
3. It is a scale of earthquake damage that has twelve steps.

Section 2 Review   Chapter 10

Use **Reading Checksheet 10-2** TRB page 88
Skillsheet 10-2 TRB page 130
Section Reviewsheet 10-2 TRB pages 197–198
Section Testsheet 10-2 TRB page 302

Check Your Vocabulary

10 anticline	13 plastic deformation	
7 compressional stress	24 P-wave	
	4 reverse fault	
22 earthquake	17 Richter scale	
21 epicenter	20 seismograph	
8 fault	16 seismologist	
23 focus	15 shear stress	
12 folded rock	19 S-wave	
6 footwall	9 syncline	
11 fracture	14 tensional stress	
5 hanging wall	1 thrust fault	
18 Mercalli scale	2 transform fault	
3 normal fault		

Match each term above with the numbered phrase that best describes it.

1. A special type of reverse fault
2. A fault with horizontal movement
3. A fault in which the hanging wall has moved down with respect to the footwall
4. A fault in which the hanging wall has moved up with respect to the footwall
5. The mass of rock that is above a fault
6. The mass of rock that is below a fault
7. Stress when matter is pushed together
8. A fracture along which rocks move
9. A downward-arching fold in rocks
10. An upward-arching fold in rocks
11. A crack in folded rocks
12. Rock bent by high confining pressure
13. When rocks deform like modeling clay
14. Stress when material is pulled apart
15. Stress when rocks slide past each other
16. A scientist who studies earthquakes
17. A system that measures the amount of energy released at the focus of an earthquake
18. Describes the amount of earthquake damage
19. A secondary wave
20. Measures and records earthquake waves
21. The point directly above the focus
22. A motion or trembling of the earth
23. The point of origin of an earthquake
24. A primary wave

Check Your Knowledge

Multiple Choice: Choose the answer that best completes each of the following sentences.

1. Shear stress can be represented by these arrows: __?__.
   a) $\longrightarrow \longleftarrow$ c) $\longrightarrow \longrightarrow$
   b) $\longleftarrow \longrightarrow$ d) $\longrightarrow$
                                              $\longleftarrow$

2. In terms of earthquake protection, it is best to construct a building on __?__.
   a) loose sand   c) clay
   b) granite   d) hard-packed sand

Check Your Understanding

1. How can the location and strength of an earthquake be determined?
2. How can folded rocks affect weathering and erosion?
3. Draw and label a normal fault and a reverse fault. Use arrows to show the directions of movement of the hanging wall in relation to the footwall.
4. How are tensional and compressional stresses related to faulting and folding?
5. Describe and give examples of how faults and folds are related to different landforms.

Plate Tectonics   Section 3

Section 3 of Chapter 10 is divided into four parts:

The interior of the earth

The theory of continental drift

The theory of plate tectonics

Pangaea

Figure 10-25. The Golden Gate Bridge (San Francisco, California) could never have been built if it weren't anchored into "solid earth." Just how solid is the earth? This question is meant to elicit students' ideas as they begin this section on plate tectonics. No specific answer is expected at this time. By the end of this section, students will be better able to formulate an answer to such a question as this.

Learner Objectives

1. To identify the layers of the earth, based on the strength and rigidity of the rocks.
2. To relate Alfred Wegener to the theory of continental drift.
3. To describe the theory of plate tectonics.
4. To relate Pangaea to the theory of plate tectonics.
5. To relate magnetic reversals to sea floor spreading.

What two kinds of people would especially appreciate setting foot on solid earth again?

Imagine what it must be like for an astronaut to return to the earth after walking on the moon and being in space for eight days or more. Or imagine how it would feel to reach land safely after surviving a storm at sea. How good it would feel to set foot again on solid earth!

The solid earth is a term frequently used to describe the land, especially landmasses that are as large as continents. In this section of Chapter 10, you will learn more about just how solid the earth really is. You will also learn about a theory that explains volcanic activity and earthquakes and the formation of some of the most spectacular landforms on the earth.

The interior of the earth

New vocabulary: low-velocity zone, discontinuity, oceanic crust, continental crust, rigidity, asthenosphere, mesosphere

Properties of earthquake waves have enabled scientists to learn much about the earth's interior. P-waves will travel through both solid and liquid, although P-waves slow down when they pass through a liquid. S-waves will travel through a solid but not through a liquid. And both types of waves slow down when they approach a material that has the consistency of putty.

Figure 10-26. How have scientists determined that the outer part of the earth's core behaves as a liquid? Scientists determined that the outer core behaves as a liquid because it blocks out S-waves. (S-waves travel through a solid but not through a liquid.)

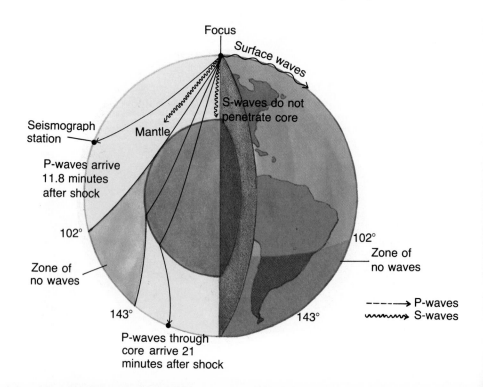

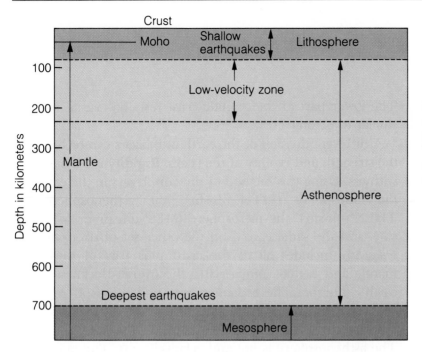

Figure 10-27. Why is the low-velocity zone called by that name?
The low-velocity zone has the ability to slow down both S-waves and P-waves.

By studying the arrival times of P-waves and S-waves, scientists have been able to determine that the earth consists of different layers. These layers are called the crust, the mantle, and the core. Scientists have also determined that the outer part of the core behaves as a liquid because it blocks out S-waves. The inner core behaves as a solid, which scientists can determine because of the change in speed by P-waves traveling through the liquid outer core and then through the inner core.

By studying earthquake waves, scientists have discovered another zone within the upper mantle. This zone has the ability to slow down both P-waves and S-waves and is called the **low-velocity zone.** The low-velocity zone is where intermediate focus earthquakes originate.

By studying the arrival times of earthquake waves, scientists have also determined that the densities of the materials in the different layers in the earth increase toward the core.

The divisions of crust, mantle, and core within the earth are based on earthquake wave velocities. Boundaries between these divisions show sharp changes in earthquake wave velocity. These boundaries between the divisions of the earth's interior are called **discontinuities.**

The earth's crust is mostly made of two different types of materials, basalt and granite. **Oceanic crust** is basaltic, denser than continental crust, and about 5 km thick. **Continental crust** is granitic and varies in thickness between 20 and 60 km.

Library research

What is the Mohorovicic discontinuity (Moho for short)? How did it get its name?

What have scientists learned about the densities of the earth's layers?

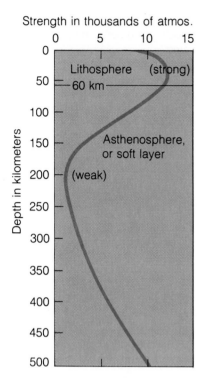

Strength in thousands of atmos.

Lithosphere (strong)

60 km

Asthenosphere, or soft layer

(weak)

Depth in kilometers

Figure 10-28. This diagram gives a rough estimate of the rigidity of rock in the earth's lithosphere and asthenosphere. In which layer is the rock most rigid?
In the lithosphere (which is most rigid about 25 km from the surface)

Check yourself answers:
1. They are discontinuities caused by changes in density.
2. Both P-waves and S-waves slow down when passing through this zone.
3. Lithosphere, asthenosphere, mesosphere, and core

How did plant and animal fossils influence the theory of drifting continents?

The lower part of the granitic crust rests on crustal material similar to oceanic crust.

A different division of the earth into layers can be based on the strength and rigidity of the rocks. **Rigidity** is a measure of stiffness. Using this method of division, layers in the earth are the lithosphere (LITH′-uh-sfir), the asthenosphere (as-THEN′-uh-sfir), the mesosphere (MES′-uh-sfir or MEZ′-uh-sfir), and the same core as in the other set of divisions. The *lithosphere* includes all of the crust plus part of the upper mantle and is thin compared to the overall thickness of the earth's interior. The **asthenosphere** and **mesosphere** correspond to the rest of the mantle below the lithosphere. The lithosphere is relatively cool and rigid. (See Figure 10-28.) The asthenosphere is hot and relatively soft. The mesophere is in between the asthenosphere and lithosphere in terms of rigidity but is very hot and under very high pressure.

Check yourself   Check yourself answers appear in the margin below.

1. What are the boundaries between the core, mantle, and crust?

2. What gives the low-velocity zone its name?

3. Name the earth's layers, as based on strength and rigidity.

The theory of continental drift
New vocabulary: theory of continental drift

In 1620, the Englishman Francis Bacon noted that the shape of the coastlines on both sides of the Atlantic Ocean was such that the continents could fit together like a jigsaw puzzle and that the continents had possibly drifted apart. During the nineteenth century, several observations seemed to support the concept that the continents had drifted apart.

1. Rocks on opposite sides of the Atlantic Ocean were of similar types, ages, and sequences of layers in those areas that would meet if the continents were pushed together.

2. Included in some of those rocks were plant and animal fossils. Their distribution pattern was most logically explained on the basis that all the continents had been together at one time.

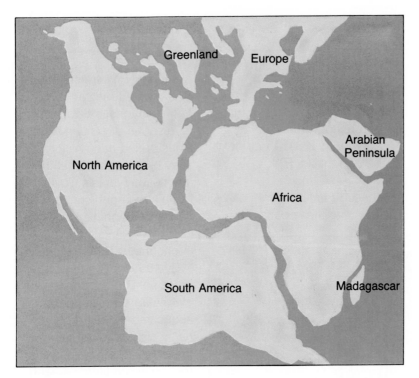

Figure 10-29. What did Francis Bacon, in the year 1620, note about the shape of the Atlantic coastlines? Francis Bacon noted that the shape of the coastlines on both sides of the Atlantic was such that the continents could fit together like a jigsaw puzzle and that the continents had possibly drifted apart.

3. Another type of evidence was that certain mountains and faults lined up if the continents were pushed together.

Any of these observations standing alone was not sufficient evidence to prove that the continents had been together at one time. In a court of law, when several pieces of circumstantial evidence all point to the same conclusion, the case becomes much stronger. Statistically, this is also true for scientific observations. The cumulative evidence for drifting continents was quite strong.

How strong was the cumulative evidence in support of drifting continents?

Many different evidences for continental drift were first brought together in 1915 in a book written by Alfred Wegener, a German geologist, meteorologist, and explorer. The title in English of Wegener's book is *The Origin of Continents and Oceans.* In that book, Wegener, who is credited with being the founder of the **theory of continental drift,** envisioned the continents drifting over the top of the oceanic crust.

Library research

Other scientists, however, considered the theory of continental drift to be impractical or even impossible. No known forces were strong enough to overcome the friction between the two crustal rock types. In 1931, an English geologist by the name of Arthur Holmes speculated that continental drift might be

Find out more about sea floor sediments. How are they important to our understanding of the plate tectonic theory?

Our Science Heritage

From Hypothesis to Theory

In the early 1960s, some puzzling variations in magnetic patterns above the ocean bottom were observed. In 1963, a pair of British scientists, F. J. Vine and D. H. Matthews, proposed the following solutions to these patterns.

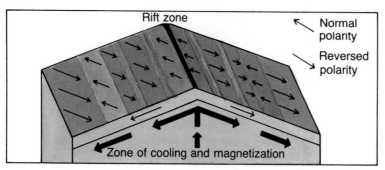

First of all, they suggested that the crustal rock under the oceans was formed from a molten basaltic material from the earth's mantle. As the molten basalt cools, it becomes permanently magnetized in the direction of the prevailing magnetic forces that are associated with the North and South Magnetic Poles.

Secondly, Vine and Matthews suggested that the earth's magnetic field reversed in direction several times during earth history. They hypothesized that the magnetic reversals would explain the north-south bands of magnetic variations observed above the floor of the northeast Pacific Ocean.

By 1966, ocean crust age dates verified the concept of magnetic reversals and suggested a pattern of reversals for the preceding three and a half million years (during which time the earth appears to have reversed polarity at least nine times).

The working hypothesis that Vine and Matthews had proposed as a way to explain certain observations led to a more detailed understanding of the ocean bottom. This in turn led to further discoveries and played an important part in the development of the plate tectonic theory.

---

caused by convection currents beneath the earth's crust and that the oceanic crust was acting like a slowly-moving conveyor belt. But because of lack of evidence, Holmes's idea did little to make the theory more acceptable to other scientists.

During the 1940s, scientists studying the ocean bottom learned many new things about the ocean crust. Then, in 1961 and 1962, Harry Hess and Robert Dietz proposed a theory of sea floor spreading similar to that of Holmes, but Hess and Dietz had more supporting evidence. In addition, Hess and

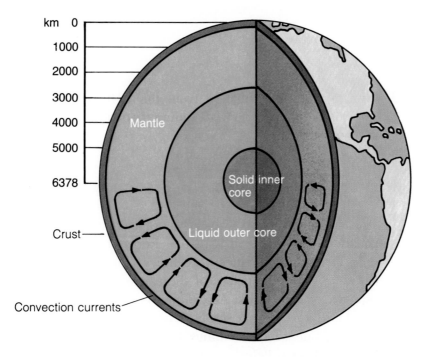

Crust—

Convection currents—

Figure 10-30. What did Arthur Holmes offer, in 1931, as a possible explanation for continental drift?
Holmes speculated that continental drift might be caused by convection currents beneath the earth's crust and that the oceanic crust was acting like a slowly-moving conveyor belt.

Dietz expanded the theory to include the destruction of ocean floor material where ocean crust meets continental crust.

How did Hess and Dietz expand Holmes's theory of sea floor spreading?

In 1965, with the addition of magnetic studies of the ocean's crust, J. Tuzo Wilson consolidated the concept of sea floor spreading and the theory of continental drift into the theory of plate tectonics. Wilson described the basic nature of plates and plate boundaries.

One of the lessons that can be learned from this sequence of events is that "impossible theories" may be very important in the development of scientific concepts. The theory of continental drift produced vigorous debate during Wegener's time. Even though other scientists clearly showed that the theory was impossible, the impossible theory stimulated thought, led to more data gathering, and continued to be a focal point of debate. And the result was well worth the effort. All this data gathering and debate finally led to a new synthesis, a synthesis considered by many scientists to be the great unifying theory of geology. This great unifying theory is known as the theory of plate tectonics.

Critical Thinking

Identify the different features of the theory of continental drift. How are these features related? Write a statement that summarizes all the relationships.

Answers will vary.

Check yourself

1. In which century was the idea of continental drift first mentioned?

2. What was Wegener's contribution to the idea of continental drift?

1. In the early seventeenth century (1620)
2. He published a book in which he brought together many evidences that supported the idea.

3. New knowledge about the ocean bottom and oceanic crust, including magnetic studies

3. What types of information from the 1940s through the 1960s led to the sea floor spreading theory and the theory of plate tectonics?

The theory of plate tectonics   New vocabulary: plate tectonic theory, rift zone, sea floor spreading, subduction

The plate tectonic theory, which was first described in 1965, is a relatively recent scientific theory. Roots of the theory extend back into the seventeenth century. The **plate tectonic theory** states that the surface of the earth consists of several lithospheric plates of rock. According to the theory, the plates are rigid and moving very slowly. Where different plates meet each other, one of three things happens. The plates grow larger, the plates collide, or the plates move past each other with a shearing motion.

How do crustal plates grow?

Plates grow by the addition of molten material along great faults. This is what happens along the mid-ocean ridge. The central part of the mid-ocean ridge, which is called a **rift zone,** is a zone of tensional stress. Huge sections of the sea floor are being pushed or pulled in opposite directions. To fill the gap in the ocean crust, molten material rises from deep in the earth and cools into igneous rock. Tensional stress eventually causes a fault to form in this new rock and the process is repeated. This faulting and movement of growing plates away from a central rift zone (plates can move up to 9 cm per year) is what is known as **sea floor spreading.**

When plates collide head-on, one of two results is possible. One possibility is that the edges of the plates, or the plate margins, can buckle up and form mountains. Another possibility is that one of the plate margins can be forced downward into the asthenosphere. This type of downward movement is called **subduction.**

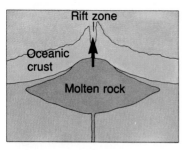

Figure 10-31. Molten rock rises in the rift zone of a mid-ocean ridge and forms new ocean crust.

Subduction of oceanic plates causes the formation of deep ocean trenches. A subducting plate is destroyed by the time it reaches the mesosphere. Rock in the subducting edge will eventually be recycled back to the surface, either through extremely slow convection motion of hot rock within the asthenosphere or by magma pushing up to form volcanoes. This magma pushing up to form volcanoes is the source of the vol-

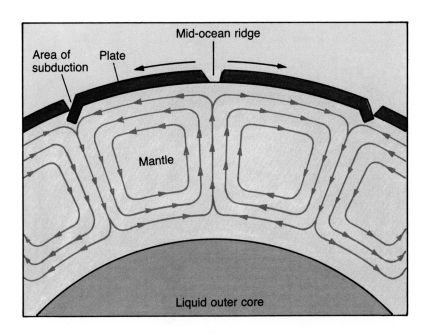

Figure 10-32. In sea-floor spreading, lithospheric plates fault, grow, and move away from a central rift zone. Eventually the plates can be forced downward into the asthenosphere. What is this type of downward movement called?
Subduction

See also Teaching Diagram 10-3A (TRB page 48).

canism along the mid-ocean ridge and near the deep sea trenches.

The rigidity of the lithospheric plates allows them to carry sediments and rock that are on top of them. Therefore, the continents are carried along as part of the moving plates. Also, because of the rigidity of the plates, great fractures are developed across the mid-ocean ridge. These fractures may extend for hundreds of kilometers across the oceanic crust. When the ridge and rift zone are offset along these fractures, a transform fault develops between the offset rift zones, and the rocks on opposite sides of the fault grind past each other as the plates move. In some places, the transform fault may be a few hundred kilometers long and form margins or boundaries between plates. The Cayman Trough in the Caribbean Sea and its extension into Central America as the Montagua fault in Guatemala is an example.

Seven major plates and several smaller plates make up the earth's surface. Figure 10-33 shows the location of the plates with their boundaries. The arrows indicate directions of movement. Plate boundaries are zones where earthquake and volcanic activity are concentrated.

Much evidence supports the plate tectonic theory. Here are some of the most recent evidences:

1. Direct observation has been made of oceanic crust being formed through volcanic activity along the central rift zone of the mid-ocean ridge.

Library research

Find a map that shows fractures in oceanic crust.

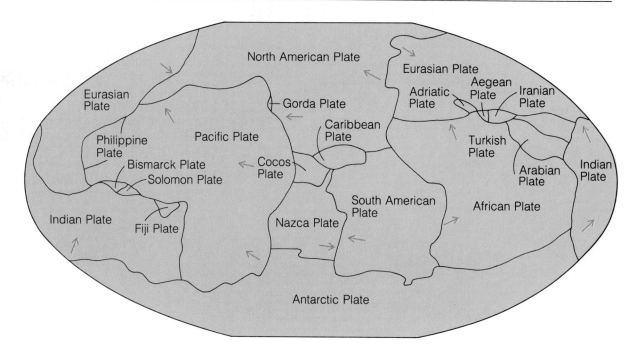

Figure 10-33. The earth's surface is made up of seven major plates and several smaller plates. What do the arrows indicate?
The arrows indicate directions of movement.

See also Teaching Diagram 10-3B (TRB page 49).

What does a shallow-focus earthquake indicate about the depth of a subducting plate?

Library research

What are magnetic field anomalies? Find a picture that shows actual anomalies over a ridge (for example, the Reykjanes ridge south of Iceland).

2. The youngest rocks in the sea floor are in the rift zone. The rocks get older with increasing distance away from the central rift zone.

3. Ocean sediments increase in thickness and age with increasing distance away from the central rift zone.

4. Studies of rock magnetism show a symmetrical pattern on both sides of the central rift zone. This pattern can best be explained by sea floor spreading.

5. The focuses of earthquakes follow a definite pattern along a subducting plate. (See Figure 10-34.) Shallow-focus earthquakes are produced nearest a deep sea trench. The shallow focus indicates an area of subducting plate that is above the low-velocity zone of the earth's upper mantle. Earthquakes of intermediate focus occur farther from the trench. This indicates that at this location the plate is deeper, in the low-velocity zone. Deep-focus earthquakes occur farthest from a trench and indicate that the subducting plate is below the low-velocity zone.

6. Detailed mapping of rock formations in western North America, from Alaska to Baja California, reveals a pattern of growth for the North American continent. Some rocks appear to have formed originally as part of a different continent. Others are from oceanic volcanic islands or large chunks of sea floor. This pattern of "foreign" rocks along the margin of a continent presumably is the result of convergence between two plates. At the juncture, low-density rock fragments will tend to

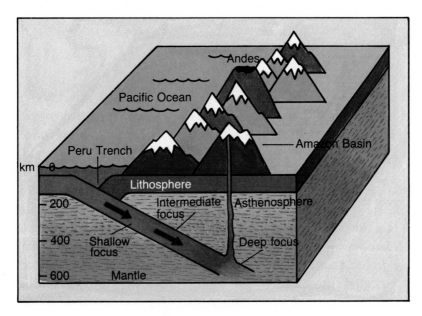

Figure 10-34. Which earthquakes occur farthest from a trench—shallow-focus or deep-focus earthquakes?
Deep-focus earthquakes.

float on denser, subducted crust. These fragments are, in effect, scraped off one plate to become mountains on the other.

The concept of sea floor spreading resolved Wegener's greatest theoretical problem—the friction of continents drifting over the ocean crust. No force was or is known which could overcome so much friction. According to the sea floor spreading concept, continents do move, but not by drifting. They are rafted along by basaltic ocean crust which continually forms at mid-ocean ridges from a molten state. Friction is significant at crustal plate boundaries only. The force that causes plate movements, however, is poorly understood but is believed to be heat-related convection movement in the asthenosphere. (See Figure 10-30 on page 507.)

According to the sea floor spreading theory, how do continents move?

Check yourself

1. What are the plates of the plate tectonic theory?
2. What are the seven major plates on the earth's surface?
3. Describe briefly the different types of plate boundaries.

Pangaea

According to the plate tectonic theory and Wegener's theory of continental drift, at the end of the Paleozoic Era, the continents came together and formed one single continent, a supercontinent called, by Wegener, Pangaea (pan-JEE'-uh). As rift valleys formed and extended across continental

1. Large sections of the earth's lithosphere, which is the crust and part of the upper mantle
2. The Pacific Plate, the North American Plate, the South American Plate, the African Plate, the Eurasian Plate, the Indian Plate, the Antarctic Plate
3. 1) Rift zones where molten material rises to fill gaps in plates moving away from each other; 2) Mountainous areas where colliding plate edges have buckled up, and deep sea trenches where one plate is forced down into the asthenosphere; 3) Places where plates move past each other with a shearing motion

Into what two land masses did Pangaea first break?

masses, the lithospheric plates started moving apart, ocean crust formed, and ocean water spread between land masses. The breakup of Pangaea followed the patterns shown in Figure 10-35.

According to the theory, Pangaea first broke into two large land masses called Laurasia and Gondwana. If you check your dictionary, you will find that the word *Laurasia* is made from parts of words that refer to North America, Europe, and Asia. Those three land masses were originally part of Laurasia. And Gondwana, according to the theory, included the present-day land masses of India, Australia, Africa, South America, and Antarctica. As shown in the diagram for 180 million years ago (Diagram B) in Figure 10-35, the equator serves as the dividing line between Laurasia and Gondwana. (Laurasia is to the north; Gondwana is, for the most part, to the south.)

Present-day landforms stretch back to the formation and breakup of Pangaea. Examples include the Appalachian Mountains, the Himalayan Mountains, and the Red Sea.

1. The Appalachian Mountains formed during the mid to late Paleozoic Era. The compressional forces responsible probably were caused when Africa and Europe converged on North America as Pangaea was forming.

2. The Himalayan Mountains were formed when India and Asia collided in the Cenozoic Era. After the breakup of Pangaea, India converged with Asia and part of India subducted under Asia. Because of the double thickness of continental crust, the Himalayas are the highest landforms on the earth.

3. The Red Sea was formed twenty million years ago when a

Table 10-2. The earth's history can be divided into different time groupings which are called eras. During which era were the Appalachian Mountains formed? How many millions of years ago might that have been?
Mid to late Paleozoic. Anywhere from 430 to 255 million years ago.

Major Divisions of Earth Time	
Era	Length of Time
Cenozoic	From 65 million years ago to the present
Mesozoic	From 255 million years ago to 65 million years ago
Paleozoic	From 600 million years ago to 255 million years ago
Precambrian	From the beginning of the earth to 600 million years ago

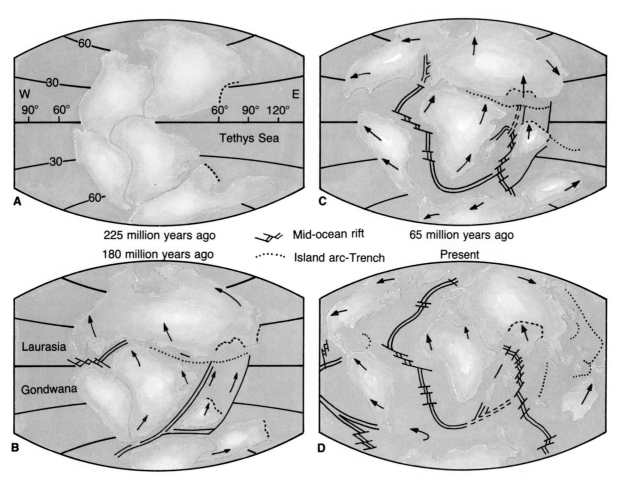

225 million years ago   ⤝⤟ Mid-ocean rift   65 million years ago

180 million years ago   ⋯⋯⋯ Island arc-Trench   Present

rift valley developed between Africa and Arabia. In the future, the Red Sea may widen into a major ocean. As it does, the rift valley of Africa, which is still above sea level, may be split enough to form a new seaway.

The collision and moving of plates has probably been taking place throughout most of earth history and will probably continue as long as there is heat and motion in the asthenosphere. While the movement continues, continents will split and collide, mountains will be uplifted, volcanoes will erupt, and earthquakes will occur. And most of this activity will be concentrated along plate boundaries.

Check yourself

1. What was Pangaea?

2. What mountain range formed as Pangaea formed?

3. What has been the history of the Red Sea, and what might it become in the future?

Figure 10-35. How did the position of India change from Pangaea to the present? India moved in a generally northeasterly direction from 60° S latitude to its present position north of the equator and part of Asia.

1. A supercontinent that formed during the late Paleozoic Era
2. The Appalachians (and others, like the Atlas Mountains in North Africa)
3. The Red Sea is young, only twenty million years old. It formed as a rift between Africa and Arabia. It may widen into a major ocean over the next several tens of millions of years.

Science Processes: Recognizing and using spatial relationships; Formulating models; Inferring
See also Activity Record Sheet 10-3A (Lab Manual page 143)

20 minutes   Individuals or small groups

Activity 10-3A   Reconstructing Pangaea

Materials

map of world today

tracing paper

scissors

glue, rubber cement, or cellophane tape

map of Pangaea (See Figure 10-35 on page 513.)

Purpose

To study the relationships between the present continents and Pangaea.

Procedure

1. Trace and label the continents as they appear today from a world map.
2. Cut out the continents at the seaward edge of the continental margins.
   a) Separate India from Asia, cutting along the Himalayan Mountains.
   b) Separate Saudi Arabia from Eurasia.
   c) Separate Greenland from North America.
3. Cut away the following post-Paleozoic features:
   a) Parts of southeast Asia, including Indonesia, Malaya and Borneo.

b) The Afar triangle (in East Africa on the Gulf of Aden at the entrance to the Red Sea).

c) The part of Central America from Guatemala to South America.

4. The "Y" between Spain and France was opened up since the Paleozoic. Reconstruct the late Paleozoic position of Spain by cutting between France and Spain and rotating Spain.

5. Reconstruct Pangaea by putting the pieces together, using a map of Pangaea as a guide. Tape or glue your pieces in place, after you are sure of the position of each piece.

Question

How does your finished reconstruction compare with those made by other students in your class?

Conclusion

How does constructing a model help to show relationships between the modern continents and Pangaea?

Step 2

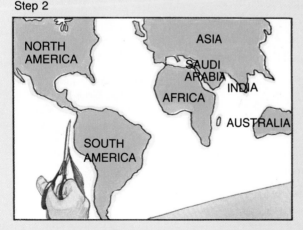

Step 5

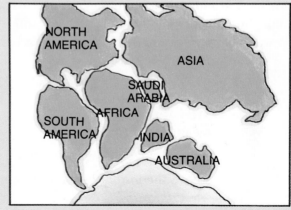

Careers Seismologist / Construction Inspector

For further information about a career as a seismologist, contact:

American Geological Institute
5202 Leesburg Pike
Falls Church, VA 22041

Seismologist Seismologists (sīz-MAHL'-uh-jists) study waves in the earth that are produced by earthquakes and other disturbances. They use instruments such as the seismograph, which magnifies movements in the earth and records the data on a graph.

Seismologists locate earth-quakes and seek methods for predicting and controlling them. They also learn about the structure of the earth, explore for oil and minerals, and provide information to the construction industry.

Many seismologists work in the field. They might set off explosions and measure waves reflected from the rocks beneath the earth's surface. Others perform their work in laboratories and offices.

Seismology is a branch of geophysics, which is the physics of the earth and its atmosphere. To become a seismologist, work toward a college degree in geology, physics, or geophysics. Your high school preparation should include math, physics, and earth science.

Seismologists can tell much from the data recorded on a seismograph.

Construction Inspector
Federal, state, and local governments employ inspectors for all types of construction. There are inspectors for electrical systems, mechanical systems (such as plumbing), public works (such as roads), and buildings.

Construction inspectors who specialize in buildings first review the plans for a building. They make sure that the plans follow building codes and zoning regulations. They indicate any special construction techniques such as would be necessary in earthquake-prone areas. They also determine whether the building might cause any harm to the environment.

Inspectors usually visit a construction site several times. If they find something wrong and it is not corrected quickly, they can issue a "stop-work" order. They write a report after each inspection.

To become a construction inspector, you should take math, drafting, and English in high school. Then you might work in the construction industry for a few years before applying to be an inspector. You will increase your opportunities if you take some college courses in engineering or architecture.

Construction inspectors visit construction sites to make sure that buildings are constructed properly.

For further information about a career as a construction inspector, contact: International Conference of Building Officials, 5360 South Workman Mill Road, Whittier, CA 90601; Building Officials and Code Administrations International, Inc., 17926 Halstead Street, Homewood, IL. 60430; Southern Building Code Congress International, Inc., 900 Montclair Road, Birmingham, AL. 35213.

Science Processes: Formulating models; Inferring
See also Activity Record Sheet 10-3B (Lab Manual page 144)

CORE   30 minutes   Group of 4, or demonstration

Activity 10-3B Simulating Sea-Floor Spreading

Materials

2 large pieces of corrugated cardboard

6 sheets of typewriter paper

single-edge razor blade or sharp knife

bar magnet

magnetic compass

colored markers or pencils, black and red

roll of waxed paper

cellophane tape

Purpose

To simulate sea-floor spreading.

Procedure

1. Set up the model as shown in the diagram. Tape 3 sheets of typewriter paper together into a sheet 28 cm wide by 65 cm long.
2. Label one edge of the cardboard north, making sure that the slot points in a north-south direction relative to your label.
3. Slide the paper sheets through the slot. Leave about 5 cm of paper showing on the surface on each side of the slot.
4. You will now perform a series of steps which you will repeat six times. First, note that the unmarked paper on each side of the slot represents ocean crust that has formed during a time when the earth's magnetic field was in a constant direction. Have a member of your team close her or his eyes, pick up the bar magnet, and place it on the paper with the length of it parallel to the slot. (The purpose is to place the magnet randomly so

that it does not have the same end always pointing in the same direction.)

5. Place the compass on top of the bar magnet and note which way the north end of the needle points. If it points toward the north on your cardboard, label the paper with black N's (for normal polarity). If the needle points toward the south, label with red R's (for reverse polarity).
6. Measure and record the total width of the exposed portions of paper on both sides of the central ridge area.
7. Tear off a sheet of waxed paper just long enough to stretch across both of your labeled sheets of paper (the width of the ocean basin of Step 6). Tape the waxed paper securely to the paper beneath it. (Each succeeding time you do this step, you will need a longer piece of waxed paper to cover any previously laid-down waxed paper as well as the area just formed.)
8. Carefully cut the waxed paper right down the middle of the slot. The waxed paper has to be cut completely in half. A team member can keep the waxed paper stretched tight while another member cuts the paper.
9. Grasp each sheet of paper and pull them apart, exposing another 3 or 4 cm of unmarked paper on each side of the slot.
10. Return to Step 4. Repeat 4-9 six times.

Questions

1. How do the patterns of magnetic reversal compare on each side of the slot?
2. Which layer of waxed paper represents the oldest sediment?
3. What happens to the age of the waxed paper that is in direct contact with the marked paper from the slot position outward?

Conclusion

Why did you need to cut the waxed paper completely in half as part of your simulation? (Hint: see page 508.)

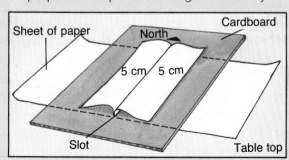

Sheet of paper   North   Cardboard
5 cm 5 cm
Slot   Table top

Section 3 Review Chapter 10

Use **Reading Checksheet 10-3** TRB page 89
Skillsheet 10-3 TRB page 131
Section Reviewsheet 10-3 TRB pages 199–200
Section Testsheet 10-3 TRB page 303

Check Your Vocabulary

9	asthenosphere	1	rift zone
8	continental crust	5	rigidity
12	discontinuity	2	sea floor spreading
13	lithosphere	3	subduction
11	low-velocity zone	6	theory of continental drift
10	mesosphere		
7	oceanic crust	4	theory of plate tectonics

Match each term above with the numbered phrase that best describes it.

1. The central part of the mid-ocean ridge where molten material rises from the earth's interior and cools into igneous rock

2. The faulting and movement of growing plates away from the central rift zone

3. The downward movement of a colliding plate margin that is being forced down toward the asthenosphere

4. A theory that views the earth's surface as composed of slowly-moving rigid plates that grow larger, collide, or move past each other with a shearing motion

5. A measure of the stiffness of a material

6. A theory that envisions the continents drifting over the top of the oceanic crust

7. Crustal rock that is basaltic, denser than granite, and about 5 km thick

8. Crustal rock that is granitic and that is between 20 and 60 km thick

9. The layer of the earth immediately below the lithosphere; includes the low-velocity zone; hot and relatively soft

10. The layer of the earth immediately below the asthenosphere; very hot and under very high pressure; moderately rigid

11. A zone in the earth's upper mantle that can slow down both P-waves and S-waves

12. A boundary between two divisions of the earth's interior; indicated by sharp changes in earthquake wave velocity

13. The earth's crust plus part of the upper mantle; relatively cool and rigid

Check Your Knowledge

Multiple Choice: Choose the answer that best completes each of the following sentences.

1. The earth layer that behaves like a liquid is the ___?___.
   a) mantle   c) inner core
   b) crust   d) outer core

2. Subduction occurs along ___?___.
   a) trenches
   b) transform faults
   c) rift zones
   d) mid-ocean ridges

3. ___?___ is credited with being the founder of the theory of continental drift?
   a) J. Tuzo Wilson
   b) Alfred Wegener
   c) Arthur Holmes
   d) Robert Dietz

Check Your Understanding

1. Describe the theory of continental drift.

2. Describe the sea floor spreading theory.

3. Describe the plate tectonic theory.

4. What is the value of "impossible" theories in science?

5. How can you tell which of the earth's layers (lithosphere, asthenosphere, mesosphere) corresponds to the low-velocity zone?

Chapter 10 Review

See also **Chapter Testsheets 10A and 10B** TRB pages 335–336.

Concept Summary

Volcanic activity occurs when lava, gas, or solid fragments come out of a vent in the earth's crust.

☐ Explosive activity is caused by viscous lavas, granitic-composition lavas, or lavas containing superheated water.

☐ Volcanic landforms include shield volcanoes, cinder cones, and composite cones.

Folded structures are caused by shape changes in rocks.

☐ Anticlines and synclines are elongate folds caused by compressional stress.

☐ Domes and basins are circular or oblong folds caused by up and down motion due to stress.

☐ Anticlines and domes are upward-arched structures, and synclines and basins are downward-arched structures.

Faults are breaks in the earth's crust along which the rocks have moved.

☐ In a normal fault, the hanging wall moves down relative to the footwall.

☐ In a reverse fault, the hanging wall moves up relative to the footwall.

☐ A thrust fault is a low angle reverse fault.

☐ Transform faults are sideways offsets in the crust associated with shear stress.

Earthquakes are caused by movement along a fault or by volcanic activity.

☐ Compressional (P-waves) and shear waves (S-waves) are two types of motion produced in an earthquake.

The **interior of the earth** is made of layers of different densities and rigidity.

☐ The layers are studied indirectly by using earthquake waves.

☐ The crust, the mantle, and the core are based on density differences.

☐ The lithosphere, the asthenosphere, the mesosphere, the outer core, and the inner core are based on differences in rigidity.

The theory of continental drift states that the continents have moved around the surface of the earth over the top of the oceanic crust.

The sea floor spreading theory states that ocean basins spread apart as the ocean crust grows at the mid-ocean ridges.

The plate tectonic theory states that the earth's lithosphere is constantly forming and being destroyed, and that the continents are slowly carried around on top of the lithosphere.

☐ The mid-ocean ridge is the site of ocean crust formation.

☐ The trenches are sites of subduction of the lithosphere.

☐ The continents were together as a single land mass called Pangaea.

Putting It All Together

1. How does the Ring of Fire relate to lithospheric plate boundaries?

2. How does earthquake activity relate to the plate tectonic theory?

3. What types of plate boundaries would most likely experience compressional stress? Give specific examples.

4. How do folded mountain belts relate to the plate tectonic theory?

5. How can events with a low probability be used to create a theory? Give an example.

6. Describe a sequence of events that probably occurred during the formation of the Atlantic Ocean basin.

7. The Palisades along the Hudson River in New Jersey, and the ridges in and around Gettysburg, Pennsylvania, are dark colored basaltic material that is upper Triassic in age. How might these rocks be related to the plate tectonic theory?

8. What causes the earthquake activity in the California areas around Los Angeles and San Francisco?

9. Earthquakes along the mid-ocean ridge are all shallow focus, whereas earthquakes near trenches are shallow, intermediate, and deep focus. What causes these differences in earthquake activity?

10. Make a cross-sectional diagram of the earth, showing lithospheric plates, low-velocity zone, and motion of the plates (use arrows). Label areas of plate growth, plate convergence, and plate destruction.

Apply Your Knowledge

1. Describe the hazards of an earthquake, and how the hazards might be avoided or made less severe.

2. What types of earth processes can create mountains?

3. What types of inner earth activities might cause variations in ocean basin depths (specifically, the mid-ocean ridge system, the deeper ocean basins, and the trenches)?

4. Some reports have indicated that California is going to split apart and fall into the ocean. Describe what will really happen to California according to the plate tectonic theory, and how long it may take at the present rates of change.

Find Out on Your Own

1. Using reference books, find out how the Hawaiian Islands relate to the plate tectonic theory.

2. Find out what types of rock structures are within a 300-km radius of your home, and relate this to the plate tectonic theory.

3. Make a list of the kinds of activities that people do that can create earthquakes. Include the magnitude of the earthquakes that can be generated by each of these activities.

Reading Further

Asimov, Isaac. *How Did We Find Out About Volcanoes?* New York: Walder, 1981.

This book explains the nature of volcanic activities, including accounts of major volcanic eruptions. The young reader is inspired by the process of discovery.

Bramwell, Martyn. *Volcanoes and Earthquakes.* New York: Franklin Watts, 1986.

This attractive, informative book provides in-depth knowledge about volcanoes and earthquakes. It contains numerous color photographs and diagrams.

Golden, Frederic. *The Trembling Earth: Probing and Predicting Quakes.* New York: Scribner's, 1983.

Earthquake lore—past, present, and future—is presented in this interesting book. It has an excellent discussion of the development of plate tectonic theory, as well as current methods of earthquake prediction.

Lauber, Patricia. *Volcano: The Eruption and Healing of Mount St. Helens.* New York: Bradbury, 1986.

Excellent illustrations and text describe the eruption of Mount St. Helens in 1980, and the return of life to this devastated mountain. The Ring of Fire is also discussed.

Lane, Frank W. *The Violent Earth.* Topsfield, MA: Salem House, 1986.

Earthquakes and volcanoes are among the violent phenomena described in this book. The author discusses the relationship between the forces of nature and the course of human history. Color photographs accompany the text.

Rydell, Wendy. *All About Islands.* Mahwah, NJ: Troll Associates, 1984.

This easy-to-read and enjoyable book about the formation of a volcanic island contains many colorful illustrations.

Science Issues of Today   Predicting Earthquakes

The first seismograph was invented in China before 132 A.D. by philosopher Chang Heng. There were eight bronze dragons spaced around the central device like points on a compass rose. The photograph below shows a cross-sectional reconstruction of the device.

A changing earth is inevitable. Slow changes are of no particular hazard to people on a day to day basis. But slow changes such as lithospheric plate movements of 4 to 10 cm per year can lead to a buildup of stress in the earth's crust. Most crustal rocks are fairly rigid, and the friction between them allows the stress to build to rather high levels. A sudden release of the stress causes crustal movements of rock along fault zones, and the resulting energy travels to and around the earth's surface in the form of shock waves. These shock waves can be highly destructive. An earthquake in Guatemala in 1976 killed over 22 000 people and injured another 70 000. Another earthquake later in the same year in China killed nearly 650 000 people!

Predicting earthquakes is important in saving people's lives and preventing injuries. One successful prediction in 1975 in a highly populated part of China resulted in little personal injury despite widespread destruction of buildings; the people were instructed to get out of the buildings and stay outdoors. The prediction and mobilization of people came only a few hours before the earthquake struck the area.

To be most useful, earthquake predictions need to accurately determine the time of the tremor and its intensity. Several phenomena seem to be helpful in making predictions, but none of them is foolproof. For each specific locality, a detailed understanding of the local and regional geology and of historical patterns of events that precede earthquakes is essential in earthquake prediction.

Water can play a role in triggering earthquakes. In 1962 and 1963, Denver, Colorado, had over 700 small to medium earthquakes. The number of tremors was unusually high for the area. The tremors started within an 8 km radius

of some wells that were being used for injecting liquid wastes into the ground. When the injection was stopped, so did the earthquakes. Resumption of injection was accompanied by a resumption of tremors. Water, evidently, can lubricate a fault zone and make it easier for the built-up stress to cause movement. Some scientists speculate that water injection in other fault zones might allow small movements of rock, thus releasing stress in small, non-destructive pulses. But scientists also fear that introducing water into a fault zone that has not moved in a long time might trigger a massive release of energy and cause much destruction.

Lithospheric plates are constantly creating stress in the earth's crust. As long as earthquakes are a threat to our safety, scientists will continue to study ways to decrease the danger.

Past, Present, and Future

Unit 6

The earth's past stretches back billions of years. Preserved in the earth's rocks are records of changes that have taken place over that enormous expanse of time. Changes in life forms, changes in the earth's crust, changes even in the relative positions of the earth's continents can be detected or inferred from a study of the earth's rocks.

The earth's present and future will also be shaped by natural earth processes. Increasingly, however, the human population is having an effect on the earth as a planet, as a source of needed materials, as an environment for life. In a sense, the present use of the earth is determining the earth of the future.

Chapter 11
The Earth's Geologic History

Chapter 12
Environmental Concerns

Chapter 11 The Earth's Geologic History

Student Resources		Meeting Individual Needs
Student Text	**Laboratory Activities**	
Section 1 Unraveling the Rock Record Uniformitarianism 525–526 Assumptions in Science 526–527 The Principle of Superposition 527–530	Activity 11-1A Verifying the Principle of Superposition 528 Activity Record Sheet 11-1A LM 149 Investigation 11-1 Predicting Settling Rates LM 151–152	Reinforcement Enrichment
The Principle of Original Horizontality 530–532 The Principle of Faunal Succession 532–535 Darwin's Theory of Evolution by Natural Selection 535–537 Interpreting Rock Formations 538–539 Section 1 Review 540	Activity 11-1B Reading a Rock Record 534 Activity Record Sheet 11-1B LM 150	CORE
Section 2 Dating the Rock Record Early Scientific Investigations 542–545 Our Science Heritage: Smith, Cuvier, and Geologic Time 544 Radiometric Dating 545–550 Thinking Skill: Evaluating 548 Careers: Petrologist/Refinery Operator 546 The Amino Acid Method 550–551 Geologic Time 552–555 Section 2 Review 557	Activity 11-2 Approximating Half-Life Decay 556 Activity Record Sheet 11-2 LM 153 Investigation 11-2 Making a Geologic Time Scale LM 155–156	CORE Enrichment
Section 3 A Parade of Life Forms The Fossil Record 559–563 Precambrian Life Forms 563–566	Activity 11-3A Making a Fossil Mold 564 Activity Record Sheet 11-3A LM 157 Investigation 11-3 Making a Biological Time Scale LM 159–160 Research Lab 11 Identifying Areas of the Country That Were Once Ancient Sea Beds LM 161–162	Reinforcement Enrichment Enrichment
Paleozoic Life Forms 566–571 Mesozoic Life Forms 571–573 Cenozoic Life Forms 574–575 Section 3 Review 577	Activity 11-3B Distinguishing Fossils and Inferring Ancient Environments 576 Activity Record Sheet 11-3B LM 158	CORE
Chapter 11 Review 578–579		

11

Teacher Resources		Meeting Individual Needs
Teacher's Edition	**Teacher's Resource Book**	
Discussion Idea 522C; Demonstration 522D Activity Notes 522E	Letter to Parents EI 69; Essential Ideas 11-1 EI 71–72	Enrich; Reinf Enrichment
	Overhead Transparency S35	Enrichment
	Overhead Transparency S36	
Activity Notes 522F		
	Teaching Diagram 11-1 TRB 50	CORE
	Overhead Transparency B19	CORE
	Overhead Transparency S37; Skillsheet 11-1 TRB 132	Enrichment
Section 1 Review Answers 522F	Reading Checksheet 11-1 TRB 90	Reinforcement
	Section Reviewsheet 11-1 TRB 201–202	CORE
	Section Testsheet 11-1 TRB 304	CORE
	Essential Ideas 11-2 EI 73–74	Reinforcement
Discussion Idea 522G Creative Writing Idea 522G		
	Teaching Diagram 11-2 TRB 51	CORE
	Skillsheet 11-2 TRB 133	Enrichment
Teaching Thinking Skills 522H		
	Teaching Diagram 11-2B TRB 52	Enrichment
	Overhead Transparency S38	Enrichment
Activity Notes 522J Demonstration 522K Section 2 Review Answers 522K	Reading Checksheet 11-2 TRB 91	Reinforcement
	Section Reviewsheet 11-2 TRB 203–204	CORE
	Section Testsheet 11-2 TRB 305	CORE
	Essential Ideas 11-3 EI 75–76	Reinforcement
Discussion Idea 522L Activity Notes 522M	Projectsheet 11-3 TRB 256	Enrichment
Demonstration; Environmental Topic 522N Activity Notes 522P	Teaching Diagram 11-3 TRB 52	Enrichment
	Skillsheet 11-3 TRB 134	Reinforcement
Section 3 Review Answers 522P	Reading Checksheet 11-3 TRB 92	Reinforcement
	Section Reviewsheet 11-3 TRB 205–206	CORE
	Section Testsheet 11-3 TRB 306	CORE
Chapter 11 Review Answers 522Q–522R	Chapter 11 Testsheet TRB 337–338	CORE

11

Unraveling the Rock Record

Learner Objectives

1. To recognize that science is based on certain assumptions.
2. To recognize the importance of the assumption of uniformitarianism in re-creating the earth's past.
3. To identify other assumptions used in determining the relative ages of materials from the earth's past.
4. To determine the relative ages of rock layers in profile.
5. To relate Darwin's theory of evolution by natural selection to the record of life forms found in the earth's rocks.

Concept Summary

An **assumption** is the taking for granted that a certain process or scientific law remains constant through time and place.
Theories are working statements that are intended to be tested, modified, added to, or replaced.
The rock record is the history of the earth as recorded in its crustal rocks.

Discussion Idea

The Risk and Necessity of Making Assumptions

Explain to students that scientists often have ideas or theories that later turn out to have been partly right and partly wrong; scientists must take risks, and even the best are not always correct in their every assumption.

Ask students to think of times when they were partly right and partly wrong about an idea. What was the occasion? What happened?

For example, late in the eighteenth century many scientists known as "Neptunists" believed that all of the earth's rocky layers had been laid down very long ago by one large sea that covered the entire earth. They thought that the water then subsided, revealing the various rock layers.

The German founder of Neptunism was a scientist named Abraham G. Werner. He also thought that volcanoes were the result of coal seams in the earth that were bursting into flame.

Werner and his colleagues were right about some of their ideas and wrong about others. For example, Abraham Werner was the scientist who established the first useful geological timetable. Also, we know now that the Neptunists were right in their belief that the earth was much older than assumed by many other scientists at that time. But all layers were not caused by a single continuous sea, and volcanoes are not the result of combustive coal seams.

Tell students they will find out more about past and present assumptions of earth scientists as they read Section 1 of Chapter 11.

Demonstration

Illustrating the Principle of Faunal Succession

Bring in a variety of plant and animal fossils for the students to examine. Try to provide examples of kinds of organisms that are now extinct (for example, trilobites) and of kinds of organisms that are still alive (clams, snails, petrified wood, etc.). Tell them that some of these organisms were on earth at a particular point in time but no longer are.

While the students examine the fossils, ask them to think of other kinds of organisms that are now extinct. (dinosaurs, saber-toothed tigers, mammoths, etc.) Ask them also to think of animals that might become extinct in our lifetime. (California condors, giant pandas, whooping cranes, etc.)

Tell students that the concept of organisms existing in a certain time sequence on earth is called the *principle of faunal succession.* They will learn much more about this principle in Section 1 of Chapter 11.

Science Background

Over the years, Darwin's theory of evolution has been modified by discoveries that indicate evolution also takes place in sudden leaps. For example, scientists now know that plants and animals produce offspring with completely new traits because of mutations, permanent changes in hereditary material. In the 1970s, two paleontologists, Stephen Jay Gould and Niles Eldredge, proposed that the greatest effects of evolution occur rapidly. According to this theory of "punctuated equilibrium," a species changes quickly when its environment changes rapidly. Sometimes the species evolves into a new species. The new species may then experience very little change during the rest of its existence. Mass extinctions may set the stage for periods of such rapid evolution.

Student Misconception

While many students enjoy interpreting the order of events in a particular rock sequence, few develop an appreciation for unconformities in the rock record through this process. Students tend to focus on those layers or events actually shown in the illustration rather than examining the sequence for gaps in the record.

An unconformity is merely a break in the rock record. It represents a period of erosion and subsequent burial. As a result, rocks above and below an unconformity will vary in age, composition, and fossil content.

The idea of an unconformity will become more obvious to your students if they are required to describe a sequence of events that result in a rock sequence, then construct a diagram of that sequence. Their description must include a period of erosion that will, in their diagram, be represented as an unconformity. By reversing the process of analysis, students will be forced to account for the unconformity or period of erosion in the actual rock sequence.

11-1

Activity Notes

Activity 11-1A

Verifying the Principle of Superposition   page **528**

Purpose   To examine the principle of superposition.

- 10 minutes Pairs of students
- **Activity Record Sheet 11-1A** (Lab Manual page 149) can be used to record this activity.
- Science Processes: Formulating models; Inferring.

Advance Preparation

Be sure to check all clocks for stopwatch action.

Procedure Notes

Point out to the students that the top-down, young-old assumption holds only under ideal conditions. An upheaval that tilts the sequence is likely to disturb the assumption. Also, the longer the period between depositions, the greater the possibility of an upheaval.

Answers to Questions

1. This very simple activity is important insofar as it provides a concrete example of layering and relative ages. As first dropped, the oldest card is on the bottom and the youngest is on the top.
2. The first list will be in the same order as the order in which the cards were first sequenced on the book. The second list will be in the opposite order.
3. When the pile is turned on edge or turned upside down, the oldest layer will no longer be on the bottom.

Conclusion

Students should realize that such upheavals are found in the earth's crust. (Chapter 10 discusses faulting, folding, and other forms of crustal movement and stress.)

Going Further

Ask: How can scientists tell whether a particular geologic profile has had an upheaval in the past? (Subsequences within the profile might be compared with similar ones found elsewhere.)

Activity Notes

Activity 11-1B

Reading a Rock Record   page **534**

Purpose To learn to examine a geologic cross-section for clues to faunal succession.

- **CORE** 20 minutes Individuals or small groups
- **Activity Record Sheet 11-1B** (Lab Manual page 150) can be used to record this activity.
- Science Processes: Interpreting data; Inferring.

Advance Preparation

Reacquaint the students with the rock types and the forces that create them.

Point out to the students that geologic cross-sections offer vital clues to faunal succession, as a consequence of the principles of superposition and original horizontality.

Procedure Notes

Alert the students the restriction of some species to one sediment layer.

Answers to Questions

1. The horizontal marks within each rock illustrate horizontal layers originally formed/deposited.
2. Animal *c* lived only in clay muds. Animal *d* lived only in sand. Animal *b* lived only in lime muds. Animal *a* lived in three different environments.
3. Animals *c* and *d* lived during time zone T0-T1. Animals *a*, *b*, *c*, and *d* lived during time zone T1-T2. Animals *b*, *c*, and *d* lived during time zone T2-T3. Animals *b*, *c*, and *d* also lived during time zone T3-T4.
4. Fossil *a* is found in only one time zone and is an index fossil.

Conclusion

The sandstone layers on the left side of the diagram are older than the layers on the right.

Going Further

How is it possible for one species to be restricted to one sediment type?

If two geologic shifts had occured to the cross-section studied in this exercise, would it still be readable?

Section 1 Review Answers

Check Your Understanding
page **540**

1. Uniformitarianism is the basic assumption held by scientists that earth processes occurring today are the same processes that have been occurring throughout the earth's history.
2. Assumptions are basic to science. Every time scientists apply a scientific principle or law to a past or future occurrence, they are making an assumption. Were it not for assumptions, science would be locked into present time and into data gained only through direct observation.
3. Scientists determine the relative ages of different rocks by using the basic assumptions of superposition, original horizontality, faunal succession, and by studying angular relationships and unconformities.
4. According to the principle of faunal succession, the different forms of animals throughout the earth's past are thought to have occurred in a definite order or sequence.
5. The scarcity of intermediate organisms in the fossil record means that Darwin's theory of evolution by natural selection cannot account for many of the changes seen in the fossil record. Therefore, other theories of evolution must be proposed and tested.

11-1

Dating the Rock Record

Learner Objectives

1. To distinguish relative age from absolute age.
2. To understand radiometric dating as a method of determining the ages of earth materials.
3. To measure the radioactivity of certain objects.
4. To compare radiometric dating to other forms of age dating.
5. To identify the eras and periods of geologic time.

Concept Summary

Absolute age determinations estimate the age of the earth in years. Such age determinations have been made in many ways.

Geologic time is a method of age determination that dates the earth's history not by years but by eras and periods of time.

11-2

Discussion Idea

An Early Estimate of the Earth's Age

Explain to students that scientists have worked for centuries to determine the age of the earth and of earth materials. From 1650 until the late 18th century, the prevailing theory was that of Anglican Archbishop James Ussher of England. By examining biblical data, Ussher determined that the earth was created at 9:00 in the morning, October 26, 4004 B.C.

Tell students that, while such a specific number sounds strange to us today, Ussher was a well-educated man who believed he had determined the most reasonable possibility. Considering the lack of available data, he had every reason to believe his estimate was a good one. In the mid-1600s scientists and scholars did not have access to the kind of geologic age-dating equipment that scientists do now, of course.

Ask: Can you guess how old the earth might be? What did you base your guess on? (Answers will vary; list on the blackboard.)

Remind students that scientists no longer believe that the earth is only 6000 years old. As students will learn in Section 3 of Chapter 11, most earth scientists believe that the earth is approximately 4.6 *billion* years old.

Creative Writing Idea

The following writing activity may help students visualize the life forms and conditions on earth in other geologic time periods.

You have been granted a round trip, one-week visit to a previous geologic time period. Choose the time period you would like to investigate and describe your experiences during that period. Include information about special equipment you might need to survive. You will not have enough room to pack all the food you will need, so describe the food that you will have to obtain and how you will obtain it.

Teaching Thinking Skills

Evaluating   page 548

Evaluating differs from other thinking skills because it involves subjective judgements. The teacher should discuss the concept of *criteria* and its subjective nature when introducing this skill to students.

Advance Preparation

None.

Procedure Note

Both *Learning the Skill* and *Applying the Skill* should be done individually and followed by group discussion. The teacher should remind students that information about the elements used for radiometric dating may be found on pages 547 and 549.

Possible Student Responses

Evaluations of the automobiles will vary. Students should be able to explain what criteria they used to make their selections.

Evaluations of the best element to use for radiometric dating will also vary. However, the elements a scientist would be most likely to choose are the following: (A) Carbon-14, (B) Uranium-238, (C) Potassium-40, and (D) Carbon-14. Students should be able to explain and justify their choices based on specific criteria.

Discussion

Ask students how evaluating is similar to and different from the other thinking skills they have learned in this text. Why may evaluating be more difficult to use than the other thinking skills?

Going Further

Have students evaluate one or more of the following:

1. The theory of plate tectonics;
2. The threat posed by acid rain;
3. The efforts being made to control destruction of the earth's ozone layer.

Before the class evaluates these issues, the teacher may want to present additional information, or have student volunteers make presentations of background material. Students can also evaluate these issues in short research projects.

Science Background

Radioactive atoms are unstable forms of ordinary atoms. They are often referred to as radioisotopes. About 70 radioisotopes occur in nature. They make up a small part of rocks, soil, air, and water.

The process by which radioisotopes break down is called radioactive decay. In this process, particles and/or energy are ejected from unstable nuclei. Three different kinds of nuclear radiation–known as alpha, beta, and gamma radiation–have been observed.

Carbon-14 was the first isotope to be used in radioactive dating. Ordinary carbon atoms have 12 particles in their nuclei, 6 protons and 6 neutrons. These stable atoms are called carbon-12. All materials that contain carbon also have some unstable carbon-14 atoms. Their nuclei are made up of 6 protons and 8 neutrons.

Carbon-14 is a valuable isotope in dating organic materials such as wood. It cannot be used to date objects older than about 70 000 years. Scientists use uranium and other radioactive elements to date inorganic materials.

11-2

Student Misconception

Many students have misconceptions regarding the difference between absolute and relative dating in the establishment of a geological time scale. Relative dating gives information about the age of an object in relation to other objects. Thus relative dating methods produce only comparisons, not actual dates.

In the establishment of a relative geological time scale, scientists compared rock layers on the basis of their fossil content. To do this, they first determined the order of deposition in one region and, on the basis of index fossils (short-lived fossils), compared this sequence with another at a different location. Through the application of the law of superposition, it was possible to determine, at least locally, which fossils were older than others. As more sequences of rocks were correlated, it became possible to establish a chronological order on the basis of the fossils in the rock.

Absolute dating, which relies on several long "half-life" radioisotopes (most commonly, uranium-235, potassium-40, and carbon-14) and the extent of their radioactive decay, establishes the age of an object in years. It has enabled scientists to refine the geological time scale, determining rates of evolution and time spans for mountain formation.

The refined geologic time scale is often referred to as the "absolute", or "radiometric" time scale to distinguish it from the relative geological time scale.

11-2

Activity Notes

Activity 11-2

Approximating Half-Life Decay   page **556**

Purpose   To simulate half-life decay of radioactive elements.

- **CORE** 30 minutes Groups of 4
- **Activity Record Sheet 11-2** (Lab Manual page 153) can be used to record this activity.
- Science Processes: Communicating; Defining operationally.

Procedure Notes

In a geometric progression, the type of change that represents half-life decay, the ratio is the same at each interval. In the case of the perfect half-life decay, the ratio of change to nonchange at each interval is 1 to 1. That means that during each interval (half-life) 50 percent of a radioactive material undergoes a change. This investigation merely approximates the type of change called half-life decay because chance affects the results and prevents the ratio from being the same at each interval.

Remind the students that the coin flip is only an approximation. If the coin is a tail, let's say, then the radioactive element has decayed into a nonradioactive form. If the coin is a head, then the radioactive element is still radioactive.

In any given number of trials, students will rarely see 50 percent heads when flipping the coins. If the students have a string of low-probability events, you may wish to repeat the activity.

Answers to Questions

1.

Half-Life number	Percentage of original material that remains unchanged
1	50%
2	25%
3	12.5%
4	6.25%
5	3.13%
6	1.56%
7	0.78%

2. Answers will vary.
3. Column D
4. Seven years

Conclusion

25 divided by 32 = 0.78%

Demonstration

Exploring Geologic Time

Show students a geologic time chart that includes drawings of the life forms that existed during different eras. Begin to familiarize students with the names of the geologic eras and periods. (Many students may be surprised to learn that humans and dinosaurs never overlapped in time.)

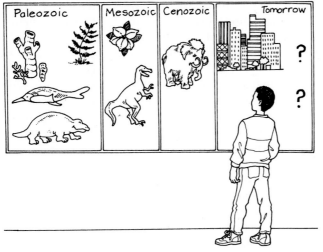

Tell students that understanding how the many organisms which have populated the earth fit into the planet's history has been a difficult job. Scientists are still working hard to learn more about geologic age dating.

As you show the chart(s), ask students if they have been to a museum of natural history and if they have seen dinosaurs and other fossils. Have them describe their experiences. (If possible, of course, visiting a natural-history museum would be an invaluable teaching for this section.)

Tell students that they will find out some of the ways in which scientists have dated rocks and fossils in Section 2 of Chapter 11.

Section 2 Review Answers

Check Your Understanding
page **557**

1. During the mid- to late-nineteenth century, several types of investigations were conducted in relation to the age of the earth. These investigations were based on 1) the amount of dissolved salt in the ocean, 2) the thickness of sediments on the earth, 3) the life spans of different types of sea animals preserved as fossils in rock layers, 4) the cooling rates of rock materials, and 5) the amount of heat flow that is coming from within the earth.

2. By the amount of radioactive decay that certain radioactive elements have undergone

3. Answers may vary, depending on how students choose to compare the lengths of time. One possibility: Let the Cenozoic Era (the past 65 million years) = X.
   Then the Mesozoic = 2.5X
       the Paleozoic = 5.8X
       the Precambrian = 61.5X

4. Igneous, metamorphic, and sedimentary rocks can be dated by radiometric techniques. Charcoal, wood, and shells can also be dated by these methods.

5. 1) Any rocks representing the first 600 000 years of earth history would have been subsequently metamorphosed or remelted, and their age date would give a younger age.
   2) Possibly some rocks older than the oldest rock now known (3.9 billion years) exist but are yet undiscovered. 3) Perhaps the earth was molten for much of that first 600 000 years, and rocks did not stay solid until the end of that time.

11-2

A Parade of Life Forms

Learner Objectives

1. To distinguish fossils and nonfossils.
2. To identify limitations of the fossil record.
3. To make a fossil mold.
4. To infer details of life forms from the fossil record.
5. To identify major changes among life forms that occurred in earth history.

Concept Summary

The fossil record is the record of former life forms as preserved in the earth's rocks.

11-3

Discussion Idea

The Causes of Major Extinctions

Tell students that scientists have long wondered at the cause of the major extinctions that have taken place on earth over hundreds of millions of years. A number of theories have been proposed, but we still do not know what happened with certainty.

For example, many theories have been put forth to explain the extinction of the dinosaurs. One current theory suggests that a collision of the earth and an asteroid caused long-term reduction of sunlight and temperature. Another theory proposes that a super nova (an exploding star) elsewhere in the galaxy may have caused great amounts of X-ray radiation to strike the earth, resulting in a severe temperature drop. A third theory states that the extinction of the dinosaurs might have been caused by reversal of the earth's magnetic poles, caused in turn by inconsistencies in the earth's spin.

In 1983, a fourth theory emerged. A careful analysis of the fossil records of marine animals over the past 250 million years led two scientists to infer that large-scale extinctions occur at regular intervals—about every 26 million years. This theory has touched off a new debate: What kind of enormous cycle could explain this pattern? One possibility is the periodic passage of a companion star of the sun, dubbed the "death star."

Ask: What kinds of events can you think of that might eventually cause extinction of various organisms living today? (Nuclear war; pesticides, which can inhibit reproductive ability through thinning of birds' eggs; overhunting, such as that which endangers whales and other species; severe reduction of habitat, such as that which threatens the California condor; major climate changes; etc.)

Activity Notes

Activity 11-3A

Making a Fossil Mold   page **564**

Purpose   To learn to distinguish between a fossil mold and a fossil cast.

- 2 30-minute sessions Small groups
- **Activity Record Sheet 11-3A** (Lab Manual page 157) can be used to record this activity.
- Science Processes: Observing; Classifying; Inferring.

Advance Preparation

This activity relates closely to the activity at the end of this section of Chapter 11 (page 576), in which students distinguish fossils from nonfossils and infer ancient environments.

Procedure Notes

Help the students to make the plaster of Paris the correct consistency. When mixed, it should resemble heavy cream.

Be sure that students use petroleum jelly to lubricate the cup, the seashell, and (when forming the cast) the mold.

Answers to Questions

The fossil cast will look more like the original seashell. The mold is a "negative" of the seashell; the recessed parts are elevated, and the raised parts are recessed.

Conclusion

A fossil mold is formed from covering an organism or part of an organism. A fossil cast forms from the inside of a mold and thus takes on the shape of the original fossil.

Science Background

Fossils are most common in layers of sedimentary material. Limestone and calcareous shale are particularly important sources of fossils. Many fossils originally formed in sediments that collected on the bottom of a river or a lake. Over time, such layers build up—each layer younger than the one beneath it.

The discovery of the rock layers that make up the Grand Canyon was probably one of the greatest revelations of geological history. The Colorado River, over several million years, carved out a canyon in layers of rocks that had taken hundreds of millions of years to develop.

These layers were found to be rich with fossil specimens; they once made up the bottom of an ancient sea. The Grand Canyon, more than any other site, provides a rich panorama of once-living history and the sequence of living organisms.

11-3

A Parade of Life Forms

Student Misconception

Students very often take the presence of oxygen in the atmosphere for granted. Few can visualize a world without oxygen. How would it appear? Curiously, this was precisely the state of affairs early in the history of our planet.

Hydrogen is the most abundant element in the cosmos, driving the sun's nuclear furnace and filling the space between the stars. This fact has led scientists to conclude that the early atmosphere was hydrogen-rich, or reducing. Theories abound as to how an oxygen-rich atmosphere came into existence.

One popular theory proposes that oxygen was produced as a byproduct of hydrogen respiration by primitive bacterial organisms (similar to the release of carbon dioxide that occurs with oxygen respiration). After millions of years, oxygen came to represent a large proportion of the atmosphere's content. By that time, according to the theory, some mutant strain(s) or organisms had become capable of breathing oxygen. Now the vast majority of organisms are oxygen consumers. This is in part due to the greater energy efficiency of oxidation over reduction, and the failure of organisms dependent on reduction to compete effectively with oxygen-breathing organisms, in the vast majority of ecological niches.

Encourage the students to explore alternative theories as to the development of our oxygen-rich atmosphere.

11-3

Demonstration

The Dinosaurs Were a Diverse Group

Bring in one or several current library books on dinosaurs. Discuss the pictures. Ask students to describe what they already know about dinosaurs. Make a list on the blackboard.

Explain to students that dinosaurs ranged in size from less than one-half meter in length to more than 30 m. Fossils of more than 300 kinds of dinosaurs have been found. Dinosaurs were on earth during the Mesozoic Era, a period of about 160 million years!

Tell students that they will find out about an entire parade of life forms that lived over hundreds of millions of years as they read Section 3 of Chapter 11.

Environmental Topic

The fossil record shows that extinction is a natural process. Of all the life forms that have ever existed, far more have died out than exist today. Scientists and environmentalists are concerned that large numbers of organisms are currently threatened with extinction because of human behavior.

Discuss why saving organisms from extinction is an important environmental concern. In prehistory, extinctions resulted from natural changes in climate. Today, however, humans seem to be causing the changes that are leading to the extinction of many plants and animals. The use of pesticides and the destruction of natural environments such as rain forests have contributed significantly to the extinction of a number of species. If humans are causing these changes, should they be responsible for saving the threatened organisms?

Activity Notes

Activity 11-3B

Distinguishing Fossils and Inferring Ancient Environments
page **576**

Purpose To distinguish different types of fossils and infer their original environments.

- **CORE** 30 minutes Groups of 4
- **Activity Record Sheet 11-3B** (Lab Manual page 158) can be used to record this activity.
- Science Processes: Observing; Classifying; Inferring.

Advance Preparation

Review with the students the different formation environments and how they dictate the type of fossil formed.

Procedure Notes

Point out the sharp differences in details between a cast and a mold. Also point out the hardness of petrified wood compared with that of carbonized wood.

Answers to Questions

1. Answers will depend on specimens observed.
2. The fossilized wood specimens probably represent material that has been replaced by some mineral. You can tell by analyzing the mineral composition of the fossil.
3. The difference between the two different kinds of fossilized wood could be caused by 1) the presence or absence of ground water and 2) the depth of burial. Petrified wood is caused by pore-filling and replacement by silica from ground water. Carbonized wood is caused by heat and pressure owing to deep burial as sediments accumulated.
4. Answers will depend on specimens observed. A cast has the shape of the original fossil. A mold is a "negative," or impression, of the original.

Conclusion

Fossils are impressions formed by minerals other than those that made up part of the original organism. Fossils, which are formed by mineral replacements, are different in appearance from recent bones, shells, etc.

Answers will vary but may include the following: Knowing that clams, many brachiopods, and crabs live in salt water, it is a reasonable inference that they were also fossilized there. Wood may be fossilized in both wet and dry environments.

Section 3 Review Answers

Check Your Understanding
page **577**

1. The fossil record is made up of the remains or traces of organisms that lived on the earth long ago. These remains or traces are preserved in rock layers. Their ages are determined by the ages of the rock layers they are found in.
2. Most of the fossils found are of organisms that 1) lived in or near water and therefore were covered by sediment, or 2) had hard, skeletons or shells.
3. 1) The appearance of organisms with hard parts marks the boundary between the Precambrian and Paleozoic Eras. 2) A major time of extinction of most land and ocean dwellers marks the boundary between the Paleozoic and Mesozoic Eras. 3) Another period of extinction marks the boundary between the Mesozoic and Cenozoic Eras.
4. Answers may vary. Highlights include the following. Precambrian—microscopic bacteria and algae. Paleozoic—organisms with hard parts; fish; first reptiles and insects; plants and swampland forest. Mesozoic—dinosaurs, flowering trees. Cenozoic—modern fish and mammals, hominids.
5. The following stages in the progression of vertebrates are mentioned in the student text. *Ordovician Period*—Some strange looking fish *Devonian Period*—Amphibians and other land dwellers that have developed skeletons

11-3

Chapter Vocabulary

Section 1

uniformitarianism
assumption
principle
principle of superposition
principle of original horizontality
principle of faunal succession
fossil
index fossil
evolve
theory
formation
unconformity
dike
sill

Section 2

absolute age
radioactivity
radioactive decay
radiometric dating
half-life
amino acids
geologic time
era

Section 3

life form
fossil record
paleontologist
sexual reproduction
living fossils
extinct

11-3

Chapter 11 Review Answers

Putting It All Together   page 578

1. Because of the principle of uniformitarianism, scientists assume that the earth processes which are occurring in the present are the same as those that have been occurring back through the ages of the earth's history. Geologists, therefore, are able to use their understanding of such present geologic processes as weathering, erosion, deposition, volcanic activity, and earthquakes when they study the earth's crust. From studying the layers, rock types, and fossils, scientists are able to reconstruct what probably led to the formations that are present in the rock record.

2. According to the law of faunal succession, the different forms of animals occurred in a definite order or sequence. The law of faunal succession, therefore, provides the structure for any theory of evolution. A theory of evolution would have to work within the framework of faunal succession and try to explain the sequence or order, taking into consideration any irregularities in that sequence.

3. Acceptance and application of Darwin's theory has been hindered by the fact that not as many in-between life forms have been found as Darwin had predicted.

4. Formations are units of rock that have certain characteristics. Formations are used to sequence events in the earth's past and to assign relative ages to those events.

5. Some unconformities represent a gap in earth history, caused by the absence of a portion of the rock record that either never existed (because of a period of no sedimentation) or that was eroded away. Other unconformities (like dikes and faults) are caused by volcanic activity or earthquakes. Unconformities indicate past processes of sedimentation, erosion, volcanism, and faulting.

6. Radiometric dating is based on relative amounts of radioactive elements and their decay elements. In order for this type of dating to be accurate, scientists assume that the specimen chosen has not been subject to addition or loss of radioactive elements anywhere back throughout the earth's history. Scientists must also assume that the rate of radioactive decay has remained the same throughout the earth's history.

7. Carbon-14 dates can be checked by using the amino acid method, based on the ratio of left-handed to right-handed molecules.

8. Answers will vary. Following are merely highlights mentioned for each period.
Precambrian (Era)—Organisms with soft bodies. Grinding glaciers at the end of the Precambrian Era.
Cambrian—Organisms with hard parts.
Ordovician—Some land pokes up above sea but landscape is barren and very few land organisms; most live in the sea.
Silurian—Armored fishes, land plants, the first fossil land animals (scorpion-like arachnids).

Chapter 11 Review Answers (continued)

Putting It All Together

Devonian—Predatory fish, swamps and forest, the first land vertebrates (amphibians) with skeletons for support, skin to keep from drying up, and ability to breathe air.

Carboniferous (Mississippian and Pennsylvanian Periods)—Swampland forest that led to abundance of winged insects, the first reptiles (which are amphibian-like).

Permian—Oceans recede; there is an abundance of land organisms and an increase in the amount of land; ends with the extinction of many organisms. Only the fish show little change.

Triassic—Cephalopods (good index fossils); the continental masses begin to separate. Small dinosaurs and rodents.

Jurassic—Gigantic dinosaurs; the first true birds, the first flowering trees; climate of whole earth is warm.

Cretaceous—Reefs form, oceans rise, land masses decrease, then land masses rise again. Reef-forming ends in another major time of extinction. Clams disappear.

Tertiary—Earth's climates become cooler; conebearing evergreens become more abundant; mammals and fish begin to look familiar. The first hominids appear.

Quaternary—Glaciers; modern human forms.

9. Precambrian Era (from the earth's beginning 4.6 billion years ago to 600 million years ago). Paleozoic Era (from Cambrian Period which began 600 million years ago through the Permian Period which ended 225 million years ago). Mesozoic Era (from the Triassic Period which began 225 million years ago through the Cretaceous Period which ended 160 million years ago). The Cenozoic Era (from the beginning of the Tertiary Period 65 million years ago to the present day).

10. Water, chemical action in moist sediment, the movement of sediment through erosion, and the weight of overlying layers of sediment all hinder the formation of fossils of soft-bodied organisms.

Apply Your Knowledge   page 579

1. Fossils are most likely to be found in sedimentary rock.
2. To obtain more reliable dates in the 70 000- to 100 000-year range, advances would have to be made in the precision and accuracy of the laboratory procedures and the instruments used.
3. Answers will vary. Consider swampy areas and areas where deposition (probably by running water, possibly by wind) are occurring.
4. Answers will vary. Consider any area where erosion is taking place, where normal deposition processes are being interrupted, where there is earthquake activity and subsequent uplifting along a fault, or where there is volcanic activity.
5. People 20 000 years from now will presumably reconstruct our present environment by searching and studying the earth's crust. Urban environments will presumably be uncovered layer by layer by archeologists much as ancient cities are being unearthed today. Natural environments will be reconstructed by means of core samples, etc. of soils and sediments in a layer dating back to that time.

11-3

Chapter 11

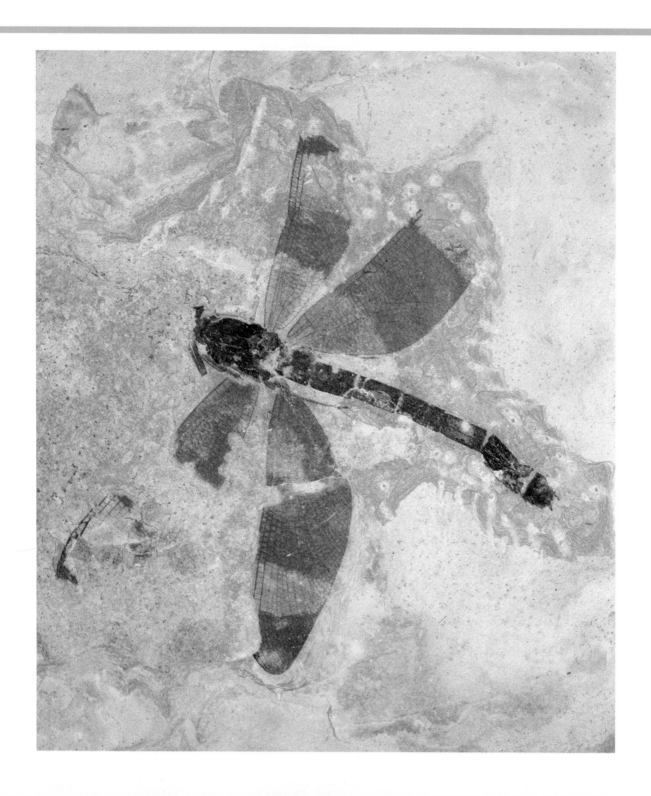

The Earth's Geologic History

Section 1
Unraveling the Rock Record

Assumptions play an important part in science. Even the most scientific of conclusions will often involve one or more assumptions.

For example, in order for scientists to interpret the rock formations in the earth's crust, scientists assume that the earth processes that occur today have been occurring throughout earth history.

In this chapter, you will become acquainted with some of the basic assumptions underlying our present understanding of earth history.

Section 2
Dating the Rock Record

Throughout human history, various estimates have been offered for the earth's age. Some estimates expressed the earth's age in thousands of years. Other estimates expressed the earth's age in millions of years. The most recent scientific methods place the earth's age at about 4.6 billion years. To try and imagine the length of time indicated by 4.6 billion years is no easy task.

Through fossils like the one pictured on the facing page, scientists can learn about life forms that lived in the earth's past. Scientists can, for example, provide an approximate age for

Section 3
A Parade of Life Forms

By means of certain assumptions, scientists have been able to reconstruct earth processes that are presumed to have been occurring throughout earth history. By means of assumptions, scientists have also been able to reconstruct a sequence of life forms that have been found on the earth at various periods of the earth's long history. Scientists have also attempted to explain changes which have occurred among life forms over long periods of time, taking into consideration processes that are being observed to take place in and among present-day life forms.

the dragonfly by determining the age of the rock it is in. And the details in the fossil enable scientists to compare this prehistoric dragonfly to present-day forms.

For our knowledge of life forms that occurred in the earth's distant past, we must examine the earth's rocks. The fossilized dragonfly pictured on the facing page was found in the Green River Formation, Garfield County, Colorado. What kinds of information can scientists learn from such a fossil?

Unraveling the Rock Record   Section 1

Section 1 of Chapter 11 is divided into seven parts:

Uniformitarianism

Assumptions in science

The principle of superposition

The principle of original horizontality

The principle of faunal succession

Darwin's theory of evolution by natural selection

Interpreting rock formations

The cave paintings of Lascaux are not prehistoric because they are a record that was made by people. Prehistory is the period that stretches back beyond any such records.

The scientific method is illustrated by the entire content of Section 1 of Chapter 11.

Figure 11-1. These animals were painted on the inside of a cave in Lascaux, France, about 17 000 years ago. They are one of the earliest records left by long-vanished people. The rock on which the paintings appear, however, traces back much farther into the earth's distant past.

Learner Objectives
1. To recognize that science is based on certain assumptions.
2. To recognize the importance of the assumption of uniformitarianism in re-creating the earth's past.
3. To identify other assumptions used in determining the relative ages of materials from the earth's past.
4. To determine the relative ages of rock layers in profile.
5. To relate Darwin's theory of evolution by natural selection to the record of life forms found in the earth's rocks.

The story of the earth's past stretches way back into prehistory—the period before the earliest drawings and writings left by long-vanished peoples. Even though there are no historical records of the earth's distant past, there are records of prehistoric events in the rocks of the earth's crust. From these geologic records, it is possible to reconstruct how the earth probably appeared in prehistoric times.

Uniformitarianism

New vocabulary: uniformitarianism

In science, certain rules or principles are followed in the study of nature. Scientists observe and record nature, gathering their data or information through direct observations. But direct observations are made only in the present. How, then, is it possible for science to say anything about the earth as it was before observations were recorded?

Scientists do more than just record observations. They also study and compare observations made by others. Sometimes patterns become evident. We may safely assume that some of these patterns have held true throughout all of earth history. For example, certain physical, chemical, and biological processes are the same today as they were during the time of scientists who lived hundreds of years ago.

In the earth sciences, it is assumed that past earth processes such as volcanism and erosion can be explained by the same chemical and physical laws used to explain earth processes in the present. In fact, many of the same earth processes directly observed today probably occurred in the past. This kind of sameness or uniformity through time of earth processes that scientists take for granted is called **uniformitarianism.**

Uniformitarianism is an assumption that scientists make. Scientists assume that the earth processes occurring today are the same as those that have always occurred. Time machines that would take us into the past or the future do not exist. The only direct evidence that scientists have of the earth's past is the pattern of the earth's rocks. Whenever a scientist can connect patterns in the rock record to an earth process—rocks in layers to repeated flooding, for example—that scientist can go beyond the present of direct observation.

What period of time does the word *prehistory* refer to?

Ask students for their ideas about records of prehistoric events in the earth's rocks. What do such records look like? How are such records formed?

As will be developed in this chapter, the reconstruction of prehistoric life forms is based on the fossil record. Fossils are commonly found in sedimentary rock. And the relative ages of rock layers, and therefore of the fossils they contain, are determined by means of certain basic scientific assumptions.

What kind of uniformity is taken for granted in the assumption of uniformitarianism?

If students take the word *uniformitarianism* slowly and a syllable at a time, they will find it less formidable. Someone might also show how the word is related to *uniform* (one form) and *uniformity* (sameness). A dictionary will show the various related forms and how each form differs from another. In most cases, it's merely the part of speech that changes (for example, adjective to noun). The basic meaning, however, carries through all forms.

The assumption that the laws of chemistry and physics are constant through time and place is one of the primary assumptions of all science. It forms the basis of the way that scientists study and explain past and present events and predict future events.

Check yourself

1. How is uniformitarianism used by scientists?

2. List the kinds of processes that uniformitarianism refers to.

3. What kinds of activities are used in a scientific investigation?

1. Uniformitarianism is used to interpret the past and to predict the future.
2. Chemical, physical, biological
3. In a scientific investigation, scientists make direct and indirect observations, record data, study and compare their observations with other people's observations, note patterns, and extrapolate to the past or future, using the assumption of uniformitarianism.

Assumptions in science
New vocabulary: assumption, principle

It may surprise you to think that scientists can accept something as far reaching as uniformitarianism. Once they do that, then a lot of other assumptions can be made. In fact, each time a process in the present is applied to the past or the future, scientists are making an **assumption.**

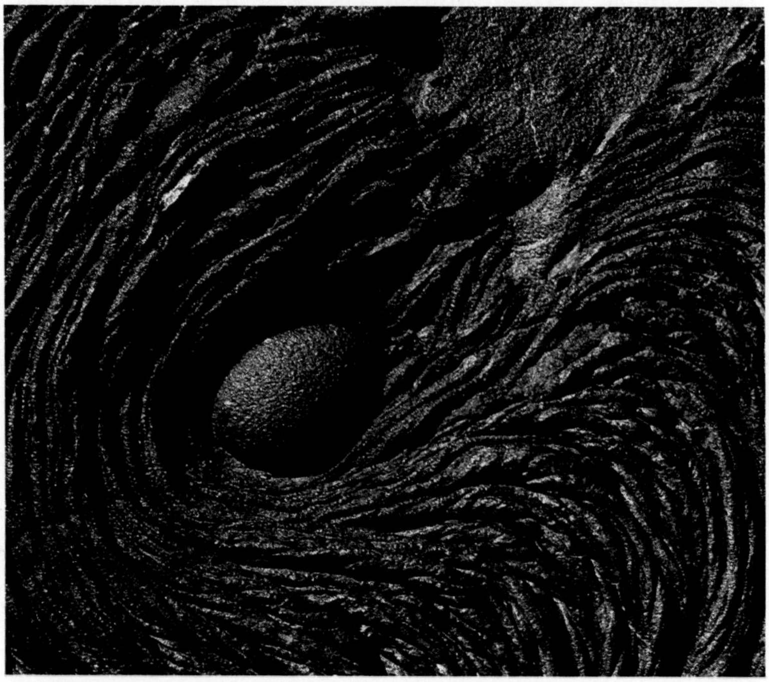

Figure 11-2. This rock formation (on James Island, Galapagos) was caused by a lava flow. Scientists assume that the volcanic activity that caused this lava flow has been occurring throughout the earth's history.

Scientists have no way to prove that an assumption like uniformitarianism is true. Does this mean that making assumptions in science is bad? Not at all, as long as everyone recognizes that they are assumptions. Whether or not a person wants to accept an assumption is a personal matter. If people could not remember the past or anticipate the future, then there would be no need for science. But people are capable of such thought processes. So, in order to understand science, it is important that people know the basic assumptions of science. Also, it is important to realize that some assumptions may need to be changed. It is always possible that more observations or further thinking will cause scientists to revise certain assumptions.

Some assumptions in science are more obvious than others. Certain assumptions have even become so well accepted that they are considered to be **principles** or laws. This is true of many assumptions that are basic to an understanding of the earth's history. Uniformitarianism is perhaps the most basic and therefore the least changeable assumption in earth science. Three other assumptions now basic to understanding the earth's long past are 1) the principle of superposition, 2) the principle of original horizontality, and 3) the principle of faunal succession. We shall examine how each of these three principles is used repeatedly to connect the patterns in the rock record to earth processes.

Check yourself

1. How do assumptions help a scientist?

2. Describe the relationship between an assumption and a principle or law.

3. What can cause a scientist to change an assumption?

The principle of superposition
New vocabulary: principle of superposition

Information about the earth's history is contained in rocks. Rock that forms the earth's crust is often formed in layers. When geologists study rock formations, they need to know the relative ages of the layers of rock. Which layer is the oldest? Which layer is the youngest?

Library research

Who were the Plutonists and the Neptunists and how do they relate to our present understanding of the earth's rocks?

It is important that students realize this relationship between science and assumptions. They should also realize that even though assumptions cannot be proven to be true, their reliability can be constantly tested, and they can be revised to incorporate new thinking and discoveries.

What is a scientific principle or law?

1. Assumptions are used by scientists to make predictions of the future and interpretations of the past. They help understand present processes, and they provide the basis for further investigation.
2. A principle or law is nothing more than an assumption that is widely accepted in the scientific community, and believed to be fact by most people.
3. Additional observations or data can cause a scientist to modify or change an assumption.

528

Science Processes: Formulating models; Inferring
See also Activity Record Sheet 11-1A (Lab Manual
page 149)

10 minutes

Pairs of students

Activity 11-1A Verifying the Principle of Superposition

Materials

4 playing cards (No two should be the same.)
textbook
clock or watch that indicates seconds

Purpose

To examine the principle of superposition.

Procedure

1. Choose which partner will be the recorder and which will drop cards onto the textbook one at a time.
2. Begin to drop the cards. Make sure that the second card is dropped on top of the first card. Each succeeding card should be on top of the previous card.
3. The recorder will record each card and the time that it landed on the book or other card, to the nearest second.
4. After all four cards have been dropped and the times recorded, list the sequence of cards on the book.

5. Now, holding the cards tightly against the book, turn the cards and the book upside down and list the sequence. (Remember, the book is now on the very top.)

Questions

1. When you first drop the cards, which card is the "oldest" card? Which card is the "youngest" card?
2. How do your two sequence lists compare in the ordering of the cards from top to bottom?
3. What would happen to the top-bottom relationship of the cards if the book and cards were tilted upright and held in a vertical position?

Conclusion

How might you relate this activity to movement in the earth's crust?

Step 2

Step 5

Card Dropped	Time of Landing
1.	
2.	
3.	
4.	

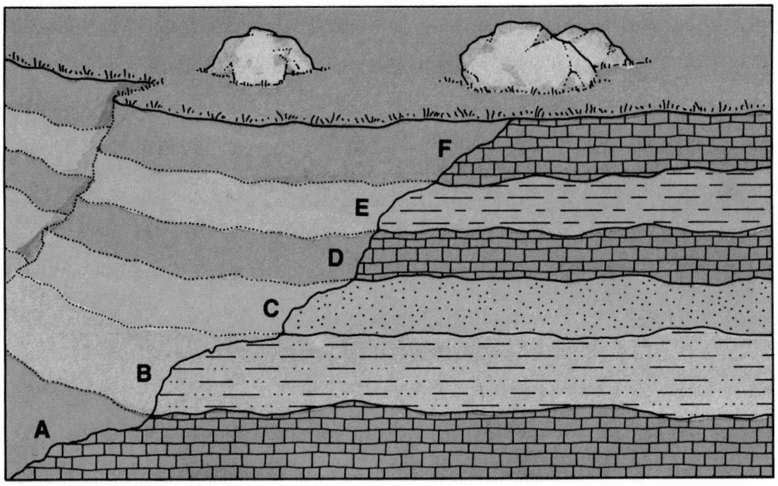

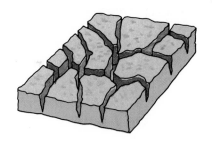

Figure 11-3. Which rock layer is the oldest—Layer A or Layer F? Layer A is the oldest rock layer.

According to the **principle of superposition,** the oldest rock in any undisturbed sequence of rocks is the rock on the bottom, if the rocks are lying in a nearly original position. According to this principle, Layer A in Figure 11-3 is the oldest layer of rock. That is to say, Layer A was the first layer to be deposited. It had to be in place before the next layer above could be deposited. Therefore, each rock layer that has rock layers above and below has younger rock above and older rock below.

In an undisturbed sequence of rock layers, which layer is the oldest?

The word *superposition* comes from two Latin words that mean to place above *(super)*. One of the basic assumptions behind the principle of superposition is that rock forms on top of previously existing rock. This is true of sedimentary rock. This is also true of lava flows, which occur on the earth's surface. But it is not true of magmas. Although related to lava, magmas can squeeze in between layers of previously formed rock and harden, forming a new layer of rock between older layers. Another exception is that the principle of superposition is not necessarily true for metamorphic rocks.

If rock layers have been upended or turned upside down by movements within the earth's crust, the principle of superposition may be difficult to apply. Scientists can check for this by carefully studying the rocks, both in the field and in the laboratory. Mud cracks and ripple marks made by waves are often preserved in the rocks. These are useful tools that help in telling tops from bottoms of rock layers. As shown in Figure 11-4, mud cracks are widest at the top, and form a V shape downward. As shown in Figure 11-5, wave-created ripple marks have sharp ridges. If buried beneath other rock layers, these ridges always point toward younger rock. When originally formed, the ridges pointed up. If you found rock

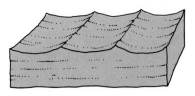

Figure 11-4. The points of V-shaped mud cracks point downward.

Figure 11-5. The points of ripple marks point upward toward younger rock.

1. The principle of superposition states that the oldest rocks are on the bottom and the youngest rocks are on the top.
2. Mud cracks form a "V," with the open end up. Wave-created ripple marks form sharp points that point upward. Both mud cracks and ripple marks can be preserved as part of sedimentary rocks.

layers in which wave ripples pointed down, you would know that those layers had somehow been turned upside down.

Check yourself

1. What basically does the principle of superposition say about the ages of rocks?
2. What features indicate if rock layers are right side up?

The principle of original horizontality

New vocabulary: principle of original horizontality

Sedimentary rocks were originally formed by sediments that were deposited, usually by wind or water. According to the **principle of original horizontality,** it is assumed that the sed-

Figure 11-6. These sand dunes are located in the Namib Desert, South West Africa. Very little of a sand dune's surface is horizontal.

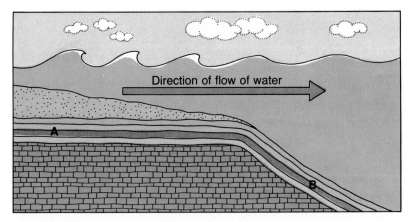

Figure 11-7. Are the layers of sediment in a delta horizontal where the river first enters a lake or ocean, or are they horizontal farther out?
The layers are horizontal where the river first enters a lake or ocean (Point A).

iments were deposited in layers that were parallel to the earth's horizon. By comparing the rock layers to the earth's horizon, you can see that the rock layers in Figure 11-3 on page 529 are horizontal.

In order for the layers to be horizontal, the rate of deposit is assumed to be the same over the extent of the rocks. It is also assumed that the surface on which each layer of sediments was deposited was horizontal to begin with. These assumptions require circumstances that were fairly common in many parts of the world during earth history. There are, however, two common exceptions: sand dunes and deltas.

In sand dunes, the layers of sediment are parallel to the top surface of the dune. The wind blows the sand up one side of the dune. The sand particles fall down the other side, which is sheltered from the wind. As shown in Figure 11-6, very little of a sand dune is in a horizontal position.

In deltas, most of the sediments are deposited where a stream or river enters a lake or ocean. There, the underwater surface of the delta is nearly horizontal. But farther out in the ocean, where less sediment is falling and the ocean bottom is dropping, the layers are angled downward. The sediment layers are formed parallel to the surface of the delta. As a result, some of the layers of deposit are horizontal, and some are not.

Where are most of the sediments in deltas deposited?

Over great distances, deposition of sediments is usually not consistent. In some cases, this is obvious because layers become thinner or thicker or have sloping surfaces. In other cases, however, the change is so minor over such great distances that it is discovered only by careful fieldwork and mapping.

1. Generally, only sedimentary rocks and some lava flows (igneous rocks) would agree with the principle of original horizontality.
2. The surface of deposition has to be horizontal, and deposition must proceed more or less evenly over that surface.

What does the word *fauna* mean?

What are fossils?

Index fossils are a very fast way for scientists to identify similar layers of rock in different parts of the earth's surface. Encourage interested students to research this further and to explain to the class how this process of age determination works.

Check yourself

1. What rock types agree with original horizontality?
2. What conditions are assumed for original horizontality?

The principle of faunal succession
New vocabulary: principle of faunal succession, fossil, index fossil

Throughout the vast stretches of the earth's past, animals of many different kinds and sizes and shapes have appeared on the earth's surface. Some forms of animals survived on the earth for a long period of time while other forms of animals survived for only a relatively short period of time. Some forms became extinct while other forms developed into animals that are still living on the earth today. According to the **principle of faunal succession,** the different forms of animals throughout the earth's past are thought to have occurred in a definite order or sequence. (The word *fauna* means "all the animals that live or lived together at a certain time or in a certain place.")

Information about faunal succession is based on the fossil record found in the earth's rocks. When animals die, their skeletal remains may become preserved in sediments that in time are turned into sedimentary rocks. An impression of the animal remains can be preserved in the rock even though the animal remains have long since disappeared. Skeletal remains or impressions of previously living life forms in rock that formed before written history are called **fossils.**

Hard parts of animals are the most common fossils. Fossils of shelled sea animals are common. Fossil jellyfish are rare. This suggests that most fossils were formed slowly. Yet there are fossils of earthworms and other soft-bodied organisms, which may have died in a place protected from decay organisms. Or sometimes, when a volcano erupts, living organisms become covered over. As the volcanic material hardens, the organism becomes a fossil in rock.

Fossils are often used to identify the relative ages of rock layers in widely separated locations around the earth. Sediments that were deposited one hundred years ago contain the remains of animals that died one hundred years ago. Sediments that were deposited five thousand years ago contain the remains of animals that died five thousand years ago, and so forth.

Certain kinds of fossils serve as index fossils or guide fossils. They provide a fast way for geologists to determine the age of rock layers relative to other rock layers. To serve as an **index fossil,** a fossil must meet two requirements. First of all, the fossil must be of a life form that appeared on the earth during only a relatively short period of time. That way, any layer of rock containing that fossil can be identified as belonging to a certain period of time in the earth's past. And secondly, an index fossil is one that must appear in rock layers in distant places around the earth. That way, relative ages of rock layers in widely separated areas can be established.

One example is a fossil trilobite (TRĪ′-lō-bīt′) that was found in a layer of shale in the Grand Canyon. The trilobite belongs to a particular variety resembling those found in rock layers in Wales that have been identified as Cambrian (a time period of the earth's past between 500 million and 600 million years ago.) The trilobite fossil in the Grand Canyon therefore serves as an index fossil that leads scientists to infer that the shale layer in the Grand Canyon is about the same age as the Cambrian rock layers in Wales.

Another useful feature of index fossils is that some of them accumulated in many different environments. These index fossils are especially valuable because they are now found in many different types of sedimentary rocks. These index fossils enable scientists to identify similarities in the age of rock layers that differ widely in other outward appearances.

In order to apply the principle of faunal succession, scientists first make the following four assumptions:

1. The general sequence of fossils in the earth's rocks will be similar everywhere.

2. Rock layers of different ages will contain different groups of fossils.

3. The principle of original horizontality is a valid assumption.

4. The principle of superposition is a valid assumption.

Using the four assumptions just listed as rules to govern their thinking, the scientists have made the following inferences:

1. Rock layers of the same type and age in different parts of the world contain similar types of fossils.

2. Rock layers that contain similar groups of fossils are about the same age.

There are problems with the principle of faunal succession and with the use of index fossils. Both are based on the assumption that all of the same type of organisms lived and died about the same time in earth history everywhere on the earth.

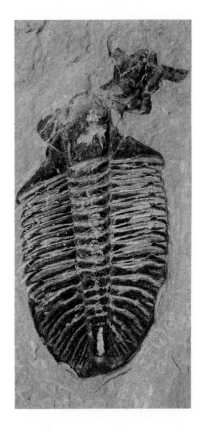

Figure 11-8. Fossil trilobites have been found in rock layers in distant places around the world.

Science Processes: Interpreting data; Inferring
See also Activity Record Sheet 11-1B (Lab Manual
page 150)

CORE   20 minutes   Individuals or small groups

Activity 11-1B Reading a Rock Record

Materials

diagram and key that accompany this activity

Purpose

To learn to examine a geologic cross-section for clues to faunal succession.

Procedure

Examine this cross-sectional view through some rocks. Notice that the boundaries between the different types of rocks (shale, sandstone, and limestone) are not parallel to the time lines T0 through T4. This is caused by a geographic shifting of the environments through time and is found often in nature.

Questions

1. What do the horizontal marks within each rock illustrate?

Key

 Shale (formed from clay muds in a bay or lagoon where the water was quiet and there was little wave action)

 Limestone (formed offshore from lime muds)

 Sandstone (formed from beach sands or shallow-water sands in an area where there was much wave action)

2. What letter represents a fossil or an animal that lived only in clay muds? Of an animal that lived only in a sandy beachlike environment? Of an animal that lived only in the lime muds? Of an animal that lived in three different environments?
3. What letter(s) represents fossils that are found during time zone T0-T1? During time zone T1-T2? During time zone T2-T3? During time zone T3-T4?
4. What letter represents a fossil that is found in only one time zone? What name is given to this type of fossil?

Conclusion

How does the age of the sandstone change from the left side of the diagram to the right side?

T0 to T4   Time lines (sequenced from oldest [T0] to newest [T4])

a   Fossil of one kind of animal

b   Fossil of a second kind of animal

c   Fossil of a third kind of animal

d   Fossil of a fourth kind of animal

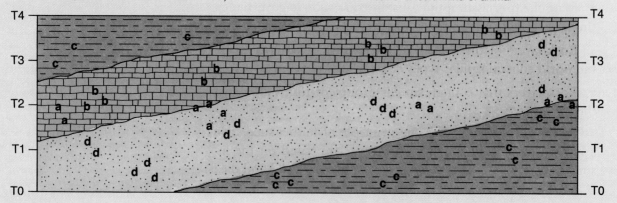

For some fossils, this assumption may not be valid over geologic periods of time. That is because organisms will migrate to new areas as environmental conditions change. Once they have migrated, their remains probably will not be accumulating in the area they left. Depending on the type of organism and the speed of the environmental change, the migration may be slow or fast. Because of these types of changes, determining whether or not a fossil is an index fossil requires careful investigation and evaluation of the rock record over a wide area.

Check yourself

1. On what four assumptions is the principle of faunal succession based?

2. What are the two basic inferences of the principle of faunal succession?

3. What is a fossil?

4. List the special properties of an index fossil.

Darwin's theory of evolution by natural selection
New vocabulary: evolve, theory

For the last two centuries, scientists have been searching and studying fossils in an attempt to unfold the story not just of the geologic earth but of the life forms on the earth. Based on a vast amount of data and research, these scientists have concluded that many species of living things have changed, or **evolved,** over time. They have also concluded that modern species of plants and animals have descended from earlier forms.

What could cause such a great change in living organisms over so many millions of years? What made it come about? Several theories have been proposed during the last two centuries. (A theory is a working statement that is intended to be tested and modified, added to, or replaced.) One of the most widely accepted up to now has been Charles Darwin's theory of evolution by natural selection as explained in his book *Origin of Species* (It is said that the entire first edition, which appeared in 1859, sold out in one day.)

Library research

What other examples of in-between life forms have been found in the rock record?

1. Four assumptions for the principle of faunal succession: 1) similar overall sequence of fossils in rocks everywhere; 2) different age rocks contain different fossil assemblages; 3) the validity of the principle of horizontality; 4) the validity of the principle of superposition

2. Two basic inferences of the principle of faunal succession: 1) similar age and types of rocks containing similar fossils world-wide; 2) similar age for rocks containing similar fossils

3. A fossil is the remains or imprint of an organism in rocks that formed before any records made by people.

4. Index fossils have 1) worldwide distribution, and 2) limited vertical distribution in rocks.

Based on fossil evidence, what have scientists concluded about life forms on the earth?

Figure 11-9. Charles Darwin published *Origin of Species* after he returned from his discovery voyage on the H.M.S. *Beagle*.

Library research

Archaeopteryx and *Dimetrodon* are capitalized and printed in italic type. What does this indicate?

Scientists have been testing Darwin's theory of evolution by searching the rock record for intermediate characteristics and forms. In addition, they have performed lab and field experiments on living organisms that have relatively short life spans and found that natural selection is very important at that level for some populations of organisms. In addition, scientists study geographically isolated groups that are related, like Darwin's original observations on finches in the Galapagos Islands.

In 1831, at the age of 22, Darwin set sail aboard the H. M. S. *Beagle* on a five-year voyage that took him from his native England to islands in the Pacific, to the coast of South America, and to Australia. During his extensive study of the plants and animals observed on his voyage on the *Beagle*, he noticed certain likenesses and differences among members of closely related species. To explain his findings, he developed a theory of evolution by natural selection. The main ideas of Darwin's theory of evolution by natural selection are as follows:

1. Individual differences are always occurring among members of the same species. For example, certain birds might have sharper beaks, better vision, or better hearing than other members of the same species.

2. Members with certain features, or traits, may be able to satisfy their needs better than others. If the individuals that have these helpful traits are more successful in producing offspring, then, in time, more and more members of the species will have these helpful traits.

3. Eventually, most members of the species in a certain area will have these helpful traits, causing a significant change in the species, or even becoming a new species.

Fairly definite evidence favoring Darwin's theory has been found among microorganisms and, to some extent, among insects. Huge populations of bacteria with different traits (usually resistance to a certain drug) develop very quickly, replacing others that do not possess the trait. Another example can be found among housefly populations that were subjected to the insecticide DDT. Those flies most resistant to the insecticide survived and passed this resistance on to their offspring. Now entire populations of flies are unaffected by DDT.

Darwin's theory of evolution by natural selection leads a person to expect that in-between life forms occurred in the development of a species. Some scientists believe *Archaeopteryx* (ar'-kee-OP'-ter-iks') to be such an in-between form. (See Figure 11-10.) *Dimetrodon* (dī-MET'-ruh-don') appears to be another example of an experimental life form. *Dimetrodon*, pictured in Figure 11-28 on page 570, was a reptile that had a temperature-regulating mechanism, although quite unlike that found in birds and mammals.

Figure 11-10. *Archaeopteryx* was an ancient organism that had feathers and limb structures like a bird. It also had a skull, teeth, and solid bones like a reptile.

Archaeopteryx may have been somewhere between a true reptile and a true bird. But not many in-between life forms of this type have been found in the fossil record. Among larger plants and animals, scientists have not found as many in-between life forms as Darwin had predicted. For that reason, scientists are proposing and testing other theories of evolution. Some scientists, for example, are exploring the possibility that great changes among most species may have taken place much faster than Darwin thought, leaving few or no intermediate forms in the fossil record.

In the future, it is likely that Darwin's theory will be only one of several theories that are necessary to explain the evolution of life forms.

Check yourself

1. What are the main ideas of Darwin's theory of evolution?

2. Describe one example that seems to support Darwin's theory of evolution.

3. How does fossil evidence influence concepts of evolution?

Check yourself answers:
1. The main ideas of Darwin's theory of evolution by natural selection: 1) Variation occurs in organisms. 2) Some variations are beneficial in the environment. 3) If the beneficial variations are passed on to offspring, then these variations may in time become a general part of the population, and the general population may be different than it was before.
2. One of the following, which are mentioned in this subsection: 1) the development of a housefly population resistant to DDT; 2) *Archaeopteryx*, thought to be an in-between life form which had some features of a bird and some of a reptile; 3) *Dimetrodon*, thought to be an in-between life form which was a reptile with a temperature-regulating device
3. Fossil evidence is the only direct evidence of what really happened in the past. Without fossil evidence, theories of evolution are little more than guesses. As new fossil evidence is found, theories will have to be modified or augmented with new theories.

Interpreting rock formations

New vocabulary: formation, unconformity, dike, sill

Within the earth's crust are many thousands of different rocks. Geologists group rocks into units called **formations.** Rocks in a particular formation share some common properties that are widespread enough to be easily recognized and mapped.

Rocks can look similar but belong to formations of different age. Geologists distinguish similar rocks by their position in a sequence of several formations.

By observing and studying the rocks and by mapping formations, geologists interpret earth history. In some places, the earth's crust has been disturbed very little over long periods of time. These areas have formations that are in their original positions. If sedimentary in origin, these areas may represent nearly continuous accumulation of sediment.

In other places, the earth's crust may have been repeatedly disturbed by vertical movement and erosion. Each time some rock is removed by erosion, a part of the earth's history is lost. A surface of erosion between rocks represents a gap in earth history and is called an **unconformity.** Figure 11-11 shows three unconformities—A, B, and C.

In a sequence of sediments, if sedimentation stopped for a period of time, even though there was no erosion, part of earth history would be missing. This type of unconformity (A and B in Figure 11-11) may not be easy to detect. This is especially true if the unconformity represents a very small time gap in the rock record.

What are two ways in which the rock record in the earth's crust can be disturbed?

Figure 11-11. An unconformity is an incomplete surface between rock layers and represents a gap in earth history. Why is Unconformity C easier to detect than either A or B?

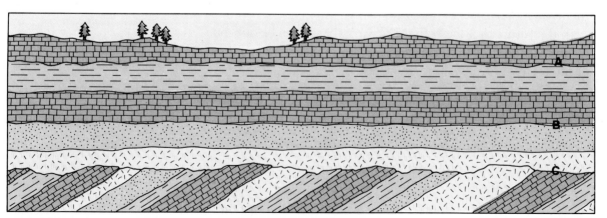

In answer to the caption question, Unconformity C is easier to detect because the layers on either side of that unconformity are at different angles to each other.

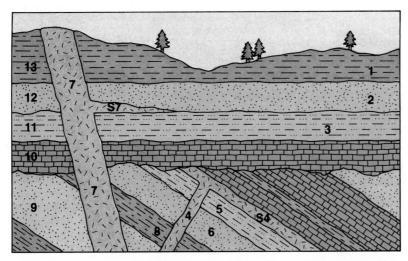

Not all unconformities are so hard to detect. Sometimes the layers above an unconformity may be at a definite angle to the layers below the unconformity (C in Figure 11-11). This angular relationship makes an unconformity easy to see.

Some other angular relationships of formations also simplify the interpretation of earth history. Whenever earth movements cause breaks that cut across crustal rocks, the crustal rocks are obviously older than the breaks. Magma sometimes forces its way along the breaks or between layers of crustal rock, forming igneous rock when it cools.

If the resulting igneous rock is at an angle to the layers of older rocks, it is called a **dike.** Layers 7 and 4 in Figure 11-12 are dikes. A dike is younger than all the rock layers, or formations, that it cuts across.

If the resulting igneous rock is parallel to and in between layers of two other rocks, it is called a **sill.** Layers S7 and S4 in Figure 11-12 are sills. A sill is younger than either of the rock layers that surround it.

By carefully mapping rock formations and by using the assumptions mentioned in this section, geologists have been able to piece together the sequence of events that led to the formation of the earth's crust as we know it today.

Check yourself

1. In Figure 11-12, which are older—dike and sill 7 and S7 or dike and sill 4 and S4?

2. List the numbered layers of rock in Figure 11-12 in increasing order of age, from the youngest (at the top of your list) to the oldest.

See also Teaching Diagram 11-1 (TRB page 50).

Figure 11-12. In this cross section of the earth's crust, the boundary below Layer 10 represents an unconformity. Layers 7 and 4 represent dikes. What do layers S7 and S4 represent? S7 and S4 represent sills.

How can igneous rock form in breaks between other crustal rocks?

1. Dike and sill 4 and S4 are older than 7 and S7.
2. The layers of rock from youngest to oldest: 7 and S7, 13, 12, 11, 10, 1, 2, 3, 5, 6, 8, 9. Layers 4 and S4 could have been formed any time after 3 and before 10.

Section 1 Review   Chapter 11

Use **Reading Checksheet 11-1** TRB page 90
Skillsheet 11-1 TRB page 132
Section Reviewsheet 11-1 TRB pages 201–202
Section Testsheet 11-1 TRB page 304

Check Your Vocabulary

2 assumption

11 dike

14 evolve

9 formation

7 fossil

8 index fossil

3 principle

6 principle of faunal
   succession

5 principle of original
   horizontality

4 principle of
   superposition

12 sill

13 theory

10 unconformity

1 uniformitarianism

Match each term above with the numbered phrase that best describes it.

1. An assumption that the earth processes occurring today have always occurred

2. The taking for granted that certain processes and scientific laws are constant through time and place; for example, the laws of chemistry

3. A widely accepted assumption that has become basic to scientific thinking; a law

4. The scientific principle that states that the oldest rock in any undisturbed sequence of rocks is the rock on the bottom

5. The scientific principle that assumes that the sediments forming sedimentary rocks were deposited in layers that were parallel to the earth's horizon

6. The scientific principle that assumes that the different forms of animals throughout the earth's past occurred in a definite order

7. The skeletal remains or impressions of previously living life forms in rock

8. A guide fossil that geologists can use to determine the relative age of rock layers

9. A unit of rocks grouped together because of common properties that are widespread enough to be easily recognized and mapped

10. A surface of erosion between rocks that represents a gap in earth history

11. A layer of igneous rock that is younger than and at an angle to the other rock layers in a formation

12. A layer of igneous rock that is younger than, parallel to, and in between two other rock layers in a formation

13. A working statement that is intended to be tested and modified, added to, or replaced

14. Undergo changes over a period of time

Check Your Knowledge

Multiple Choice: Choose the answer that best completes each of the following sentences.

1. __?__ are gaps in the rock record that represent some missing earth history.
   a) Index fossils   c) Ripple marks
   b) Assumptions   d) Unconformities

2. The principle of superposition says that __?__ rock is on top of all the other rocks.
   a) igneous   c) the oldest
   b) the youngest   d) sedimentary

3. Darwin's theory of evolution is based on the concept of __?__.
   a) very rapid changes in organisms
   b) no in-between life forms
   c) slow changes and natural selection
   d) index fossils and unconformities

Check Your Understanding

1. Describe the concept of uniformitarianism.

2. What is the role of assumptions in science?

3. How do geologists determine the relative ages of different rocks?

4. Describe the principle of faunal succession.

5. What does the scarcity of intermediate organisms in the fossil record mean in terms of evolution?

Dating the Rock Record   Section 2

Section 2 of Chapter 11 is divided into four parts:

Early scientific investigations

Radiometric dating

The amino acid method

Geologic time

Figure 11-13. Layering, weathering, and erosion are evident among the rock layers in this formation in Theodore Roosevelt National Park, North Dakota. Using the principle of original horizontality, what can you tell about the layers? According to the principle of original horizontality, 1) the oldest layer is at the bottom, 2) the newest layer is at the top, and 3) the layers were horizontal (parallel to the earth's horizon) when the original sediments were deposited. The principle of original horizontality can be used to determine the relative ages of layers in a formation.

Learner Objectives
1. To distinguish relative age from absolute age.
2. To understand radiometric dating as a method of determining the ages of earth materials.
3. To measure the radioactivity of certain objects.
4. To compare radiometric dating to other forms of age dating.
5. To identify the eras and periods of geologic time.

Through discussion, name the oldest structures (and other objects made by people) that are located in your area. How can you tell how old each is? Extend the discussion to structures in other parts of the world. How does the oldest structure anyone can think of compare to the age of the earth (4.6 billion years)?

Figure 11-14. One method of age-dating the earth was based on the amount of dissolved salt in the ocean. This method assumed that the oceans began as fresh water. Where did this method assume the salt in the present-day oceans came from?
From the weathering of rocks

Time machines exist and function only in science fiction. Time cannot be seen—either by microscope, telescope, or the unaided eye. No scientist knows a perfect method of observing or calculating the age of the earth. Nevertheless, many have tried.

Early scientific investigations
New vocabulary: absolute age

How old is the earth? How old are the earth's rocks? People have tried to answer these questions for many centuries. In earlier times, answers were often based on wild guesses and superstitions. In modern times, scientists largely base their answers on the results of scientific investigations.

The accuracy of scientific investigations has improved over time. Better scientific instruments have been developed and scientists are always learning more about natural changes that are occurring. During the mid to late nineteenth century, several types of scientific investigations were conducted. Among them, they provided a wide range of possible **absolute ages,** which are ages expressed in years, for the earth.

One early method of determining the age of the earth was based on the amount of dissolved salt in the ocean. This method assumed that the oceans were all fresh water in the beginning. It further assumed that the dissolved salt in ocean water came from the weathering of rocks. This method concluded that the age of the earth could be determined by comparing how fast salt is being added to the oceans to the total amount of salt in the oceans. Using this method, different scientists calculated ages for the earth that range from 9 million to 2.5 billion years. This method failed to take into account that ocean salt is removed by natural processes and added through volcanic eruptions.

Another method of age determination involved the thickness of sediments on the earth. Assuming that sediments had accumulated at an average rate equal to present-day rates, then the absolute age of the earth could be calculated by knowing the total thickness of sediments around the world. Using this method, different scientists of the late nineteenth century obtained ages for the earth that ranged from 3 million to 1.5 billion years. We now know that sediment deposition rates are extremely variable. Also, a great number of hard-to-detect unconformities make age estimates based on sediment thickness rather inaccurate.

Another age-dating method used the life spans of different types of sea animals that were preserved in the rocks as fossils. Using this method, one scientist estimated the age of some fossil-bearing rocks at 240 million years, and these rocks were on top of many older rocks.

The most scientifically convincing method of the time was determined by Lord Kelvin, one of the world's leading physicists. This method used the cooling rates of rock material and the measured heat flow coming from within the earth. Using this method, Lord Kelvin estimated the age of the earth to be not more than 100 million years. He felt that an age of 20 to 40 million years was probably the most reasonable estimate. He based his estimate on the assumption that all the heat from within the earth was present when the earth first formed from a molten state. He did not know that the earth has been warmed by its own radioactivity and internal friction throughout its history.

Library research

What natural processes remove salt from the ocean?

Using the thickness-of-sediment method, what ages did scientists calculate for the earth?

Ask students how they think the age of any of the earth's rocks can be determined. Then have the students, from just the headings (at the top of the student page) for the four parts of this section, tell what they think they will learn in this section. Can anyone, for example, guess what radiometric dating is, or what geologic time is? Just mulling over such questions will help clarify purposes for student reading of the section that follows.

Our Science Heritage

Smith, Cuvier, and Geologic Time

The observations of the English geologist William Smith (1769-1839) led to a breakthrough in understanding the earth's rock layers.

Classification can lead to new and better understanding of relationships among events. The systems that are used in the geologic time scale are a good example of how important classifying is to a scientist.

Geologists studying the earth's rocks had tried to come up with possible ways of sequencing the rock layers in the earth's outer crust and explaining the formation of the earth's crust. Scientists of the 1700s had tried to determine the age of a rock based on its composition. But that did not work.

An important breakthrough occurred in the 1790s when William Smith, an English surveyor who was working on the Somerset Coal Canal, happened to observe that the layers of sedimentary rocks contained characteristic types of fossils. After his work on the canal was finished, Smith continued to work as a geologic engineer throughout England. In his work, he noted that, in addition to characteristic fossils for each layer, the fossils in the layers were in order of age. He also noted that fossils in any layer did not change much from one place to another. Based on

his findings, Smith published (in 1815) the first geological map of England and Wales.

Smith's publication, based on faunal succession, represents a turning point in the knowledge and understanding of the earth's rocks. He had discovered that rock layers (strata) could be identified by the fossils they contained. This discovery made it possible for scientists to determine similar ages of rock layers in different places around the world.

Smith's system of using fossils to classify rock layers was employed and confirmed in the early 1800s by Georges Cuvier, a French expert on marine animals.

In 1912, Cuvier showed that many fossil invertebrates had no known counterparts living today. He had made an important discovery. Many once-living organisms had become extinct.

The system of classification proposed by Smith and then refined by Cuvier provided the basis on which all the rock layers of the geologic time sequence in use today were later identified and named.

In all of the early methods of age determination, scientists based their work on different assumptions. The assumptions used in the cooling-earth model were considered better than those of the other age-dating methods because they were based on physical laws that could be verified in the laboratory. However, even Lord Kelvin's basic assumption had to be put aside shortly after radioactivity was discovered in 1896 by the French physicist Henri Becquerel.

Check yourself

1. List the different scientific methods that were used for age estimates of the earth in the nineteenth century.

2. Describe the method Lord Kelvin used to estimate the earth's age.

Why were the assumptions of the cooling earth method considered better than those of other age-dating methods?

1. 1) The amount of dissolved salt in the ocean; 2) the thickness of sediments on the earth; 3) the life spans of sea animals preserved in rock as fossils; 4) measuring the earth's heat
2. Lord Kelvin used the cooling rates of rock materials and the measured heat flow coming from within the earth.

Radiometric dating   New vocabulary: radioactivity, radioactive decay. radiometric dating, half-life

Radioactivity is the ability of an element to change spontaneously into a different element by losing or gaining matter from the nucleus of an atom. The first announcement that radioactivity produced heat came from Pierre Curie and Albert Laborde in France in 1903. In Canada in that same year, Ernest Rutherford showed that the amount of heat given off is directly related to the number of atoms that are changing. Radioactivity represents a new source of heat for the earth's interior. Scientists quickly realized that the basic assumption used in the cooling earth model was not valid. They further realized that the earth might be even older than Lord Kelvin's upper limit of 100 million years.

In 1905, radioactivity was used to obtain the ages of some minerals. Some of these ages indicated an earth history many times greater than that of nearly all previous estimates. A startling revolution had begun. The age of the earth's beginning was pushed further back in time as more minerals and rocks were investigated. One of the oldest dated earth rocks comes from Greenland and has an age of 3.9 billion years!

How is radioactivity used in obtaining such ages? What are the basic assumptions behind the age-dating processes? How long is 3.9 billion years? And how old is the earth? These questions are answered in the text that immediately follows.

Careers   Petrologist / Refinery Operator

For further information about a career as a petrologist, contact:

Society of Petroleum Engineers of AIME
6200 North Central Expressway
Dallas, Texas 75206

(AIME = American Institute of Mining, Metallurgical, and Petroleum Engineers)

Petrologists can tell much about a rock just by looking at it.

Petrologist Petrologists (pi-TROL'-uh-jists) are scientists who specialize in the study of rocks. They obtain their samples from and below the surface of the earth. They have even obtained samples from the moon!

Petrologists work for colleges and universities, government agencies, oil companies, mining companies, and as private consultants.

People prepare themselves for this profession by many years of study. They usually major in geology in college and then complete further studies for advanced degrees in petrology. They also have to have a good background in mineralogy, chemistry, physics, mathematics, and statistics. Many petrologists got an early start by developing an interest in collecting rocks as a hobby.

Preparing to become a petrologist involves developing skills in science, math, reading, and good writing. The two most important attributes of any scientist apply to becoming a petrologist: 1) a person must be willing to work hard; and 2) a person should have an unending curiosity to know and understand more.

Refinery operators are in charge of processing crude oil into more usable forms.

For further information about a career as a refinery operator, contact:

Refinery Operator Refinery operators are employed by petroleum refineries. They are in charge of a processing unit, which converts crude oil (oil as it is drilled from the ground) into gasoline, heating oil, and other products. The processing, or refining, is accomplished by heating the oil and then separating it into different parts. The oil is sent through a complicated system of pipes, a furnace, a distillation (separation) tower, and other components.

Refinery operators and their helpers check on all the aspects of the processing, and they make adjustments in the rate of oil flow, temperature, and pressure. They take measurements and make adjustments by using computers and other instruments.

To become a refinery operator, you should apply for an entry-level job in a refinery after high school. From that position, you can be transferred to the operating department, where you will receive on-the-job training. Some refineries also offer classes in plant operation. You will qualify to be promoted to refinery operator when you are an experienced worker.

Society of Petroleum Engineers of AIME

6200 North Central Expressway
Dallas, Texas 75206

The changing of a radioactive element into a different element is called **radioactive decay.** Scientists assume that the rate of radioactive decay for any given element has been the same throughout all of earth history. Chemical and physical experiments on radioactive elements in laboratories have not changed the decay rates.

As radioactive elements decay, the amount of radioactive element compared to other elements decreases. Some of the other elements in the mineral come from the decay process or are related to the radioactive elements in some measurable way that allows scientists to calculate an age for the mineral. This method, which measures radioactive decay of radioactive elements, is called **radiometric dating.**

Radioactive decay is expressed in half-lives. One **half-life** is the time that it takes for one half of the radioactive material to decay. Half-lives are determined from laboratory analyses of radioactive elements. Table 11-1 lists the half-lives of five commonly used radioactive elements.

As shown in Table 11-2 on the top of page 549, the age of any object older than one hundred years can be determined. The useful range of radiometric dating varies with the different radioactive elements. The dating range is limited only by the precision and accuracy of the laboratory procedures and instruments used in the analysis.

What method of age dating measures the radioactive decay of radioactive elements?

See also Teaching Diagram 11-2 (TRB page 51).

Table 11-1. A half-life is the time it takes for one half of a radioactive material to change to its decay element through radioactive decay. What decay element forms from uranium-238? Lead-206 forms from uranium-238.

Data Table for Five Elements Commonly Used for Radiometric Dating			
Radioactive Element	Half-life	Decay Element	Material That Can Be Dated by the Radioactive Element
uranium-238	4.5 billion years	lead-206	igneous and metamorphic rocks
uranium-235	713 million years	lead-207	igneous, metamorphic, sedimentary rocks
potassium-40	1.3 billion years	argon-40	igneous, metamorphic, sedimentary rocks
rubidium-87	47 billion years	strontium-87	igneous, metamorphic, sedimentary rocks
carbon-14	5730 years	nitrogen-14	charcoal, wood, shells

Thinking Skill Evaluating

When you evaluate an item or situation, you try to determine its value, or worth. You use the skill of evaluating whenever you call something "good" or "bad."

Have you ever considered how you make such judgments? Evaluations are based upon specific criteria, or standards, against which you compare what you are evaluating.

For example, you might want to buy a new portable tape player. How will you decide which one to buy? You evaluate your possible choices based on specific criteria that are important to you. The criteria you use might include speaker size, sound quality, color, and cost. After you evaluate all the tape players you select the one that is best for you.

Scientists evaluate ideas, hypotheses, theories, and experiments. Evaluating is not always easy to do. Different criteria may be important at different times and for different people.

Evaluations are never "right" or "wrong." The following steps, however, may serve as a guide for making better evaluations:

1. Examine the items or situations to be evaluated.
2. Identify the criteria to be used in the evaluation.
3. Determine how well the items or situations match the criteria.
4. Make a judgment about the items or situations based upon how they compare with the criteria.

Learning the Skill

Which of the following motor vehicles would you buy? Use the steps of evaluating to make your selection.

Car	Color	Horsepower	Mpg	Type	Cost
A	red	350	10	sports	$20 000
B	blue	85	41	compact	$10 000
C	white	100	32	sedan	$12 000
D	silver	120	25	pickup	$18 000

What criteria were most important to you in making your selection?

Applying the Skill

A scientist collected the following samples for radiometric dating. For each sample, use the skill of evaluating to decide which radioactive element would be best for the scientist to use to date the sample.

Sample	Description
A	Seashells found in a recent rock strata
B	Igneous rocks estimated to be 4 billion years old
C	Sedimentary rock with no estimated age
D	Burned wood from a cave entrance

What criteria did you use in your selection of radioactive elements?

Dating Ranges of Five Radioactive Elements		
	Dating Range	
Radioactive Element	From	To
carbon-14	from 100 years ago	to 70 000 years ago
potassium 40	from 100 000 years ago	to the earth's beginning
uranium-238	from 10 million years ago	to the earth's beginning
uranium-235	from 10 million years ago	to the earth's beginning
rubidium-87	from 10 million years ago	to the earth's beginning

Table 11-2. Which radioactive element can be used to date materials only a few hundred years old?
Carbon-14

Most minerals contain only very small amounts of radioactive elements. And as they decay, the amount decreases. (See Figure 11-15.) If a clam shell is very old and the amount of radioactive carbon in it is so little that it can no longer be measured accurately, then the clam shell cannot be dated by the carbon-14 method. Also, the age cannot be determined if the shell is so young that the amount of decay cannot be measured.

In order to use the half-life method to obtain an accurate age for the specimen, scientists assume a closed system where there has been no addition or loss of either radioactive elements or the other elements used in the laboratory analysis. If this assumption is not true for a given sample, then the age determination would be wrong. It would be too long or too short, depending on which element was added or lost. Additions or losses can occur by weathering or by the movement of

How much radioactive material do most minerals contain?

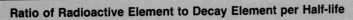
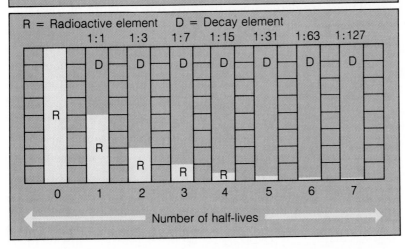

Ratio of Radioactive Element to Decay Element per Half-life

R = Radioactive element   D = Decay element

1:1   1:3   1:7   1:15   1:31   1:63   1:127

Number of half-lives

Figure 11-15. If the half-life of a radioactive element is 100 years, and the ratio of radioactive element to decay element in a mineral is 1:63, how old is the mineral? How old would a sample be if the ratio of uranium-238 to lead-206 was 1:1? (Refer to Table 11-1.)

Answer to first question: 600 years (6 half-lives); answer to second question: 4.5 billion years (1 half-life)

How do scientists minimize errors in age determination?

fluids and gases within the earth. Scientists try to minimize such errors by selecting their samples very carefully.

Different minerals are not affected equally by weathering or by ground fluids and gases. Scientists will therefore use more than one type of mineral and radioactive element in an age analysis of a rock. If all the ages from different minerals in a single rock are the same, it is likely that the assumption of a closed system is valid.

How good are radiometric dates? Half-lives have been determined and verified to be about 98% accurate, which is very good for scientific proof. Laboratory techniques in most cases are equally as good. The logic and mathematics of the techniques are accepted as correct. The dates, then, seem to be very accurate as long as the basic assumptions are valid.

Check yourself

1. 1) Consistent decay rate throughout time; 2) a closed system
2. Accuracy and precision of laboratory instruments and techniques; also, the condition of the sample (that is, does it have a reasonable chance of agreeing with the assumption of a closed system?)
3. Only by using other elements for dating the same sample
4. Only as good as the assumptions
5. Carbon-14

1. What are the basic assumptions for radiometric dating?
2. What are the limitations in obtaining radiometric dates?
3. How can the accuracy of a radiometric date be checked?
4. How good are radiometric dates?
5. Which dating method has the shortest dating range?

The amino acid method
New vocabulary: amino acid

Most ages are determined by using one or more of the radiometric age-dating methods. However, other methods for determining ages are being discovered. These newer methods may provide means of checking or verifying radiometric dates.

One of these newer methods uses certain compounds that form within living organisms. These compounds are called **amino acids.** For dating purposes, amino acids can be divided into two types of mirror-image molecules, those that are right-handed and those that are left-handed. (See Figure 11-16.) While an organism is alive, the molecules are all left-handed. After the organism dies, the left-handed molecules are unstable. They change to right-handed molecules at a rate that can vary with temperature. By determining the ratio of left-handed

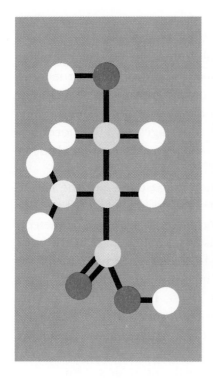

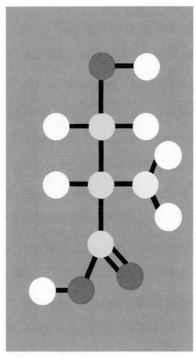

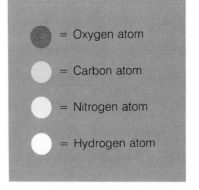

= Oxygen atom

= Carbon atom

= Nitrogen atom

= Hydrogen atom

to right-handed molecules and by correcting for temperature changes, the age can be determined. This dating method can be used on some of the same age materials as carbon-14.

The amino acid method of age dating has similarities to the radiometric method of dating and is also based on certain assumptions. Two of the assumptions for amino acid dating are 1) a constant rate of change that cannot be altered by environmental factors other than temperature and 2) a closed system.

Whenever possible, scientists try to make age determinations with different methods. Each method provides a check on the others.

Figure 11-16. These simplified drawings show, in two dimensions, differences between a left-handed molecule (on the left) and a right-handed molecule of the amino acid serine. In reality, such molecules are three-dimensional.

Check yourself

1. Describe the basic principles of amino acid dating.

2. What environmental factor must be known or estimated to use the amino acid method of dating?

3. What types of materials can be dated by using the amino acid method? 3. Materials that contain remnants of organisms that were once alive; can usually also be dated by using the carbon-14 method.

1. When an organism is alive, amino acids in that organism are all left-handed. After the organism dies, the left-handed molecules change to right-handed molecules at a rate that can vary with temperature. Amino acid dating, therefore, is based on the ratio of left-handed to right-handed molecules, with necessary corrections made for temperature changes.

2. Temperature

Geologic time

New vocabulary: geologic time, era

If the basic assumptions are valid, then the date of 3.9 billion years for the rock from Greenland would be more or less correct. But this rock from Greenland is a metamorphic rock. The age of a metamorphic rock is a measure of the age of the minerals that formed during the last stages of metamorphism. How much older was the rock before metamorphism? Indeed, how much older might the earth be?

Most scientists using radiometric age dates put the earth's beginning around 4.6 billion years ago. This age is based on the age of several meteorites and some moon soil. The meteorites probably came from the asteroid belt, a part of the solar system that is believed to have formed at the same time as the earth. As for the moon soil, environmental changes on the moon are unlike those on the earth. Because of the moon's small size, for example, it has no atmosphere to cause chemical weathering. The ages of some moon rocks and moon soil are much older than rocks and soils on the earth and may also reflect the beginning age of the earth and solar system.

How can you get some idea of an age of 3.9 billion or 4.6 billion years? Let one second represent a year. This means that each minute represents 60 years and that an hour represents 3600 years. How many seconds would it take to represent your age?

If each second represents a year, then the oldest rock would be represented by 3.9 billion seconds, which is 123.5 years. The age of the earth would be represented by 4.6 billion seconds, or nearly 146 years.

The age of the earth, or **geologic time**, can also be represented by a physical distance. Look at a ruler with millimeters indicated on it. Let one millimeter represent one year. What distance on the ruler represents your age? What distance on the ruler represents one hundred years?

Using the rate of one millimeter per year, how far do you think the 4.6 billion years of geologic time would stretch? Across an entire state? Halfway across the United States? All the way across the United States? Figure 11-17 shows you just how far 4.6 billion years would stretch, at the ratio of one millimeter per year.

What does the age of a metamorphic rock indicate?

The questions at the end of the previous paragraph are answered in the text that immediately follows.

What might be indicated by the age of moon rocks and moon soil?

Answers will vary, depending on students' ages.

Have students compare their ages (about 15 seconds) with the proportionate age of the earth (146 years).

1.5 cm (15 mm) on the ruler represents 15 years. 10 cm (100 mm) on the ruler represents 100 years.

Distance/time lengths are plotted on the map in Figure 11-17.

Interested students could convert the eras and periods of earth history into parts of a year, with the beginning of the earth on January 1, etc.

During geologic time, many physical and biological events occurred. Examples of these events are mountain building, erosion, the opening of ocean basins, and the development and extinction of many different organisms. The evidences of these events are rocks and the fossils that the rocks contain.

Figure 11-17. The geologic age of the earth can be represented by a physical distance.

Part of Journey		Distance (mm)	Distance from Boston (mm)	Geologic Era or Event (comparable)
From	**To**			
Boston, MA	Providence, RI	65 million	65 million	Cenozoic
Providence, RI	Long Island, NY	160 million	225 million	Mesozoic
Long Island, NY	Baltimore, MD	375 million	600 million	Paleozoic
Baltimore, MD	Durango, CO	2.7 billion	3.3 billion	Precambrian
Durango, CO	Lake Mead, NV/AZ	600 million	3.9 billion	(oldest rock)
Lake Mead, NV/AZ	San Francisco, CA	700 million	4.6 billion	(estimated age of earth)

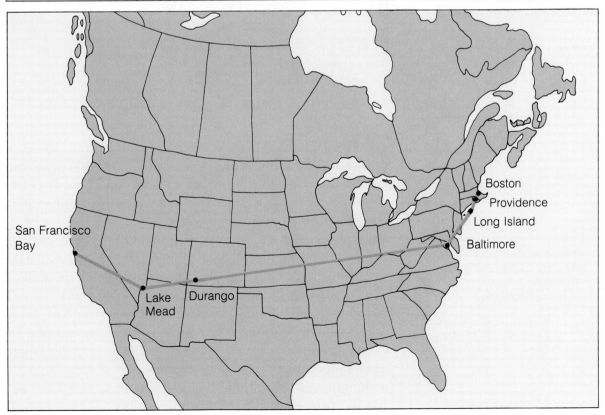

Table 11-3. The earth's history has been divided into four large units of time called eras. What kind of organisms are found in rocks from the Precambrian Era? The fossils of only soft-bodied organisms are found in Precambrian rocks.

The Eras of Geologic Time		
Age	Types of Organisms	Era
present	(most recent life forms) 'proliferation of birds and mammals	Cenozoic
65 million years ago	(middle life forms) the age of dinosaurs	Mesozoic
255 million years ago	(ancient life forms) first fish, amphibians, reptiles, and shelled ocean organisms	Paleozoic
600 million years ago	(everything before Paleozoic) soft-bodied organisms only	Precambrian
3.3 billion years ago	oldest known fossil	
4.0 billion years ago	oldest known earth rock	
4.6 billion years ago	estimated age of the earth	

On the map on the previous page, what location represents the present? What location represents the earth's beginning?

Geologic time has been divided into units of time, based on the history of life forms found as fossils in the rocks. The four large units of geologic time are called **eras.** Table 11-3 lists dates and types of organisms for each of the four eras of geologic time.

To get some idea of the relative lengths of the geologic eras, look again at the map in Figure 11-17 on page 553. Boston represents the present. From Boston to Providence (65 million mm) represents the Cenozoic Era. From Providence to Long Island (160 million mm) represents the Mesozoic Era. From Long Island to Baltimore (375 million mm) represents the Paleozoic Era. San Francisco Bay represents the earth's beginning, so it requires the entire cross-country distance of 4000 million mm (4 billion mm) from Baltimore to San Francisco Bay to represent just the Precambrian Era.

The Eras and Periods of Geologic Time			
Age	Era	Period	Duration
Present	Cenozoic	Quaternary Tertiary	65 million years
65 million years ago	Mesozoic	Cretaceous Jurassic Triassic	160 million years
225 million years ago	Paleozoic	Permian Carboniferous Pennsylvanian Mississippian Devonian Silurian Ordovician Cambrian	375 million years
600 million years ago 4.6 billion years ago (the earth's beginning)	Precambrian		4 billion years

*The terms *Mississippian* and *Pennsylvanian* are used only in North America. Combined together these periods represent the *Carboniferous Period*, which is the term used throughout the rest of the world.

Table 11-4. Much of the earth's coal was produced during the Carboniferous Period. In which era is the Carboniferous Period located?
The Paleozoic Era

Three of the four eras of geologic time are divided into smaller units of time called periods. Table 11-4 lists the eras and periods of geologic time. It also gives radiometric dates for the various units of time.

Check yourself

1. How can scientists justify the use of meteorites and moon soil to determine the age of the earth?

2. List the four eras and the kinds of animals that characterize the eras.

3. Calculate the percentage of earth time for the length of each era. (% earth time = length of each era divided by the age of the earth. Then multiply times 100.)

Check yourself answers:
1. 1) Scientists believe meteorites came from a part of the solar system that formed at the same time as the earth. 2) Moon rocks and soil, which undergo less weathering than rocks and soil on the earth, have been age-dated as older than earth rocks and may closely reflect the beginning age of the earth and the solar system (since the earth is presumably as old as the moon).
2. From the oldest to the most recent: 1) Precambrian—soft-bodied organisms; 2) Paleozoic—fish and shellfish, amphibians, reptiles; 3) Mesozoic—dinosaurs; 4) Cenozoic—birds and mammals
3. 1) Precambrian = 4000 ÷ 4600 million years × 100 = 86.96%
2) Paleozoic = 375 ÷ 4600 million years × 100 = 8.15%
3) Mesozoic = 160 ÷ 4600 million years × 100 = 3.48%
4) Cenozoic = 65 ÷ 4600 million years × 100 = 1.4%

Science Processes: Communicating; Defining operationally
See also Activity Record Sheet 11-2 (Lab Manual page 153)

CORE   30 minutes   Groups of 4

Activity 11-2   Approximating Half-Life Decay

Materials

64 equal-size coins   1 small box or plastic container, with lid

Purpose

To simulate half-life decay of radioactive elements.

Procedure

Make a data table similar to the one on this page for ten trials. Complete your data table according to the following directions:

For Columns A and B of your data table.

1. Put all the coins in the bottom of the container, date side facing up.
2. Put the lid on the container.
3. Shake the container.
4. Dump the coins onto a tabletop.
5. Separate the date-side-up coins from the opposite-side-up coins.
6. Count the number of opposite-side-up coins. Record this number in the appropriate box in Column A.
7. Remove the opposite-side-up coins from the tabletop. They will not be used again in this same series of trials.
8. Count the number of date-side-up coins that are remaining. Record this number in the appropriate box in Column B.
9. Put the date-side-up coins back into the container, date side facing up.
10. Repeat steps 2 through 9 five more times,

or until there are fewer than two date-side-up coins remaining.

For Column C of your data table.

11. Divide the number in Column A by the total number of coins used for that trial. (For the first trial, the total number used is 64. For any other trial, the total number is the number found in Column B for the preceding trial.) Then multiply the result of the division by 100 to convert it to a percentage.

For Column D of your data table.

12. Divide the number in Column B by the total number of coins used for that trial. Multiply the result by 100 to obtain a percentage.

For Column E of your data table.

13. Divide the number in Column B by 64.

Questions

1. Assuming a perfect half-life decay, what percentage of the original amount would be left after each half-life, to seven half-lives?
2. How do the percentages in Column E of your data table compare with your answer to Question 1?
3. Which column on your data table shows the percentage of date-side-up coins that remain date-side-up with each trial?
4. If the half-life of a radioactive material were one year, how many years would have passed after seven half-lives?

Conclusion

Using your answer to Question 1, how much of the original material would be left unchanged after seven half-lives?

Data Table				
	A	**B**	**C**	**D**	**E**
Trial Number	Total Opposite-side-up Coins per Trial	Total Date-side-up Coins per Trial	% of Opposite-side-up Coins per Trial	% of Date-side-up Coins per Trial	% of Original 64 Date-side-up Coins Left After Each Trial
1					

Section 2 Review   Chapter 11

Use **Reading Checksheet 11-2** TRB page 91
    Skillsheet 11-2 TRB page 133
    Section Reviewsheet 11-2 TRB pages 203–204
    Section Testsheet 11-2 TRB page 305

Check Your Vocabulary

8 absolute age   4 half-life

5 amino acids   2 radioactive decay

7 era   1 radioactivity

6 geologic time   3 radiometric dating

Match each term above with the numbered phrase that best describes it.

1. The ability of an element to change spontaneously into a different element by losing or gaining matter from the nucleus of an atom

2. The changing of a radioactive element into a different element

3. A method of age determination that measures radioactive decay of radioactive elements

4. The time it takes for one half of a radioactive material to decay

5. Compounds that form within living organisms and that can be used for age determination of certain earth materials

6. The age of the earth as revealed in its rocks; expressed in eras and periods of time rather than in years

7. One of the four large units of geologic time

8. Age expressed in years

Check Your Knowledge

Multiple Choice: Choose the answer that best completes each of the following sentences.

1. The ultimate truth of any radiometric date depends on the _?_.
   a) size of the sample
   b) type of substance that the sample is made of
   c) precision and accuracy of lab techniques and equipment
   d) validity of the basic assumptions

2. Of all the nineteenth-century estimates of the earth's age, the most acceptable one was formulated by Lord Kelvin and put an upper limit of _?_ years on the age of the earth.
   a) 9 million   c) 100 million
   b) 20 million   d) 2.5 billion

3. Lord Kelvin based his calculations of the earth's age on _?_.
   a) the cooling rate of the earth
   b) the amount of salt in the ocean
   c) radioactive measurements
   d) the thickness of sediments

4. If a radioactive element has a half-life of 1 000 000 years, and the ratio of radioactive element to decay element is 1:7, the specimen is _?_ years old.
   a) 3 000 000   c) 8 000 000
   b) 7 000 000   d) 14 000 000

5. The age of the earth is _?_ and it was determined by using _?_.
   a) 3.3 billion/fossils
   b) 4.6 billion/sediment thickness
   c) 3.9 billion/Greenland rocks
   d) 4.6 billion/meteorites

Check Your Understanding

1. How did nineteenth-century scientists determine the age of the earth?

2. How do modern scientists determine the age of the earth?

3. Compare the length of the different eras.

4. What kinds of materials can be dated by radiometric techniques?

5. Explain the absence of any earth rocks representing the first 600 000 years of earth history.

A Parade of Life Forms   Section 3

Learner Objectives

1. To distinguish fossils and nonfossils.
2. To identify limitations of the fossil record.
3. To make a fossil mold.
4. To infer details of life forms from the fossil record.
5. To identify major changes among life forms that occurred in earth history.

Section 3 of Chapter 11 is divided into five parts:

The fossil record

Precambrian life forms

Paleozoic life forms

Mesozoic life forms

Cenozoic life forms

Figure 11-18. Life forms like *Gorgosaurus* no longer live on the earth. But evidence in the fossil record shows that they are part of the earth's history. The skeleton in Figure 11-18, reconstructed of fossil bones, was photographed at the Field Museum in Chicago. A visit to a museum of natural history would add another dimension to the content of this section and would relate what students read to actual objects that have been reconstructed.

Figure 11-19. This paleontologist is cleaning sandstone away from bones of *Diplodocus* at Dinosaur National Monument, Utah. (The formation is Morrison sandstone.)

When students think of life in prehistoric times, what life forms do they visualize? In discussion, have them list plants and animals that come to mind and tell where they got their ideas from (books, magazines, TV programs, movies, museums, and so forth).

New vocabulary: life form

4.6 billion years of geologic time extends back far beyond written history. Yet it has been possible for geologists, studying the earth's rocks, to reconstruct life forms from prehistoric times. (A **life form** is the body form that characterizes a fully grown organism.) The results of the geologists' findings make up what can certainly be called a truly amazing parade.

The fossil record

New vocabulary: fossil record, paleontologist

Geologic time has been divided into eras and periods, based on the **fossil record** of life forms found in crustal rocks. Fossils can be either the remains or traces (tracks, burrows, or other evidence of behavior) of organisms that lived on the earth long ago.

The fossil record is the only direct evidence that scientists have of former life forms. Fossils represent an amazing parade of organisms through time. Inferences made from fossils and rocks lead to the reconstruction of ancient environments in which the organisms lived.

Scientists who reconstruct prehistoric life from plant and an-

How does the work of paleontologists affect the parade of organisms?

imal fossils are called **paleontologists** (pay′-lee-on-TOL′-uh-jists). Paleontologists find fossils and make inferences that make the parade of organisms more complete and easier to understand. Like all geologists, paleontologists work within the limitations of the rock record.

One specific limitation that paleontologists find in the rock record is a variable preservation of detail. X-ray photographs of a few trilobites show not only preserved soft body parts but even stomach contents of these prehistoric animals whose fossil record spans the Paleozoic Era. However, most trilobites are preserved only as hard, skeletal fragments. Fossils of *Archaeopteryx* (reconstructed in Figure 11-10 on page 537) show the feathers in great detail. And yet, only three specimens with such detail have ever been found. Some dinosaur remains have been found that include mummified skin. But reconstructing a dinosaur from fossil remains is generally difficult because the bones are usually scattered and broken.

Paleontologists make use of comparison and contrast when

Figure 11-20. How do the forms of prehistoric Irish elk on this and the facing page illustrate the work of a paleontologist? The painting is a reconstruction, based on the skeleton and other evidence and inferences. The skeleton is made of fossil bones that were found in rock, removed, and carefully put together so as to give an impression of the animal's size, etc.

they make inferences. The structure of an extinct reptile, for example, is either observed directly (in the fossil record) or it is inferred. If inferred, it is based on what is known 1) about living reptiles, 2) about better-known extinct reptiles, and 3) about other organisms living and extinct. Paleontologists use this same principle when making inferences about functions performed by different body parts or ways in which the organism adapted to changes in its environment.

Paleontologists enjoy an excellent fossil record for many types of organisms. Though the record is sparse in certain areas, in other areas it is remarkably complete. Microscopic fossils, for example, are ideal because they are abundant, widespread, and sensitive to environmental change.

The parade of organisms that paleontologists have reconstructed through changing environments and time is admittedly somewhat incomplete because most of the fossils represent sea-dwelling organisms that had hard, mineralized skeletons or shells. As for soft-bodied forms, only a few isolated

How can scientists make inferences about extinct reptiles for which there are no fossils?

Figure 11-21. The fossil bones above are being removed from an outcrop of rocks. Once removed, paleontologists are able to put bones together again, and reconstruct the skeleton of an animal such as on the facing page.

groups of fossil occurrences have been found. Certain worms may leave behind their hard teeth, but it is difficult to reconstruct the size and shape of a worm from its teeth.

Paleontologists realize that their studies also have other limitations. Among these limitations are the following:

1. Not all organisms are easily turned into fossils.

2. Of those organisms that do become fossils, they may not be where scientists can find them. Many fossils are buried far below the earth's surface.

3. Of those fossils that are found, many of the skeletons or shells have been changed by ground water, pressure, and/or heat. Sometimes the change is so great that the fossil loses its identity.

4. As a rule, the older time periods are represented by fewer available rocks because of burial or erosion. Also, older rocks have often been exposed to longer histories of changes due to ground water, pressure, and heat. Therefore, the fossil record of these older rocks is not as good as that of younger rocks.

Working carefully with and from the fossil record, paleontologists have been able to piece together an amazing parade of organisms through time. Put yourself in the reviewing stand and watch the parade go past. As you know, parades come in

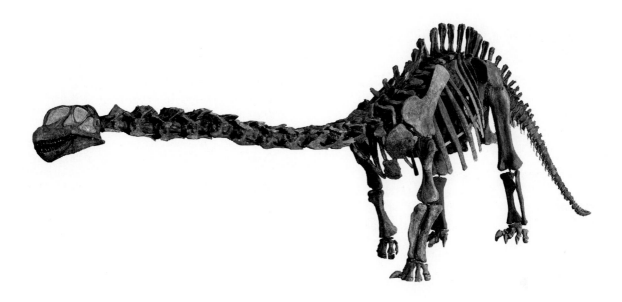

different lengths. This parade is very long. It starts 3.3 billion years ago, in the Precambrian Era.

Check yourself

1. List five limitations that affect the studies of paleontologists.
2. Describe in detail one limitation that affects a paleontologist's studies.
3. On what do paleontologists base inferences about fossils?

Precambrian life forms

New vocabulary: sexual reproduction

The organisms of 3.3 billion years ago are very tiny. Under the microscope, they look like blue-green algae and bacteria. After parading along for 200 million years, some of the blue-green algae form into large mats that grow on top of each other. This strange assortment of bacteria, algae, and algal mats continues on for another 1 billion years. (Similar mats are known to exist today in shallow tide pools in Australia.)

Noticeable changes become more evident. The algal mats are becoming more abundant. During the next 1.2 billion years, colonial bacteria, algal tubes, and cells with a nucleus join the

Library research

What is an organism? Give examples of different kinds of organisms.

1. 1) Variable preservation of detail; 2) not all organisms make good fossils; 3) many fossils may never be found; 4) many fossils have become distorted by water, heat, and pressure; 5) the fossil record of older rocks is much more sparse than for younger rocks.
2. Answers will vary, based on which of the limitations is chosen.
3. On what is known 1) about related living organisms, 2) about better-known related organisms that are extinct, 3) about other types of organisms both living and extinct.

Science Processes: Formulating models; Defining operationally
See also Activity Record Sheet 11-3A (Lab Manual page 157)

Three 10-minutes sessions   Small groups

Activity 11-3A   Making a Fossil Mold

Materials

seashells	plaster of Paris
petroleum jelly	stirring rod
graduated cylinder	food coloring
water	small plastic cup
mixing container	screwdriver

Purpose

To learn to distinguish between a fossil mold and a fossil cast.

Procedure

Part 1

1. Coat the outside of your seashell with a thin layer of petroleum jelly.
2. Pour 80 mL of water into the mixing container.
3. Pour plaster of Paris slowly into the water, mixing with the stirring rod, until it is the consistency of heavy cream. If your mixture is too thick, add water. If it is too thin, add plaster. Add enough food coloring to color the plaster.
4. Pour the plaster mixture into your plastic cup, leaving at least an inch at the top. If air bubbles are present, tap the cup to release them.

5. Press the greased outside of your seashell into the plaster. Make sure that the plaster does not flow into the shell.
6. Leave the shell in the plaster overnight.

Part 2

1. Remove the shell from the plaster. Coat the entire surface of the hardened plaster with petroleum jelly.
2. Make a second batch of plaster using the directions from Part 1. Use only 50 mL of water. Do NOT use food coloring.
3. Pour the fresh plaster onto the hardened plaster. Let set overnight.

Part 3

1. Carefully separate the two plaster blocks, using a screwdriver if necessary.

Question

Which looks more like the original seashell the fossil mold or the fossil cast? Explain.

Conclusion

What is the difference between a fossil mold and a fossil cast?

Step 5

Step 7

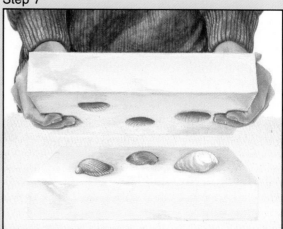

parade. This leads, during the next 200 million years, to some **sexual reproduction** in cells (that is, reproduction that involves the joining together of male and female germ cells).

Mixed into the parade at this time are fungi and threadlike blue-green algae. So far, none of the organisms in the parade has a hard skeleton or shell.

The parade has been very long. So far, 2.6 billion years have gone by, and it has been relatively quiet. Then, from southern Australia comes a wondrous group of jellyfish, corals, worms, an echinoderm (i-KĪ′-nuh-derm′), and maybe even a mollusk. All are still entirely soft-bodied. But in that 100 million year interval they are indeed a colorful addition.

Toward the end of the Precambrian Era, much of the land becomes covered with glacial ice, grinding ice and rock against rock in its downhill movement.

This brings the parade to the end of the Precambrian Era and the beginning of the Paleozoic Era.

Figure 11-22. Algal mats like these (in present-day Shark Bay, Western Australia) resemble algal mats that formed billions of years ago.

Figure 11-23. The scallop (left) and snail (right) are mollusks. The starfish (middle) is an echinoderm.

1. 3.3 billion years
2. Algae, bacteria, cells with a nucleus, fungi
3. Jellyfish, corals, worms, echinoderms, mollusks—all softbodied

Check yourself

1. How old are the very first fossil organisms?

2. List the types of organisms that are found as fossils in the first 3.8 billion years of Precambrian time. (Remember, the Precambrian is 4 billion years in duration, starting from the earth's formation 4.6 billion years ago.)

3. What types of organisms appear as fossils in the last 100 million years of Precambrian time?

Paleozoic life forms

New vocabulary: living fossil, extinct

What marks the boundary between the Precambrian Era and the Paleozoic Era is perhaps the most unique and impressive change in life forms throughout all of earth history. There, like a line of medieval knights wearing armor, are thousands of hard-shelled trilobites from all over the world. These are accompanied by a few scatterings of brachiopods (BRAYK'-ee-uh-podz'), echinoderms, sponges, and sponge-like organisms. All have hard parts.

What caused these organisms to develop hard parts? Were there some chemical changes in the oceans or in the atmosphere? Paleontologists are still pondering these questions!

Figure 11-24. The trilobites and brachiopods of the Paleozoic Era represent a unique change in the life forms that occurred down through the earth's history.

Along with all the wonder and splendor of body armor and support systems, there is a group of organisms from the middle Cambrian period of British Columbia that consists of a large variety of soft-bodied animals. These fossils are preserved as thin carbon films in rocks that were once ocean bottom sediments. Soft-bodied organisms are only rarely preserved as fossils, even though they probably have been abundant since before the beginning of the Paleozoic Era.

As the Ordovician Period of the Paleozoic Era passes by, all the animals mentioned so far are represented in the parade. Even some strange-looking fish are swimming around.

The parade so far has been a very wet parade because all the organisms live in the oceans. Areas of land poke up here and there along the parade route, but there are no plants or animals living much above the splash of the waves. The landscape is barren except for small sea-level fringes of ground-hugging algae and tiny animals, both struggling against the elements for survival. Even the air is barren, for there are no flying insects.

Silurian seas were populated with diverse armored fishes. Some were very fierce in appearance. As the parade reaches the late Silurian Period (about 425 million years ago), the first land plants, which are very small, start to appear. Scorpion-like arachnids, the first fossil land animals, are quick to follow. Trilobites are on the decline.

Library research

What is an arachnid? How does it differ from an insect?

Point out to students that the strange-looking fish of the Ordovician Period are the first vertebrates mentioned in this parade. Ask students what a vertebrate is. (It's an animal that has a backbone.)

What are conditions on the land like during the Ordovician Period?

Figure 11-25. Scorpions first appeared more than 4 million years ago. Some forms still live on the earth.

When did amphibians, the first land vertebrates, appear?

Through discussion, students can compare adaptations needed by water dwellers so that they can live in their respective environments.

Figure 11-26. Some very remarkable predatory fishes lived in the Devonian seas.

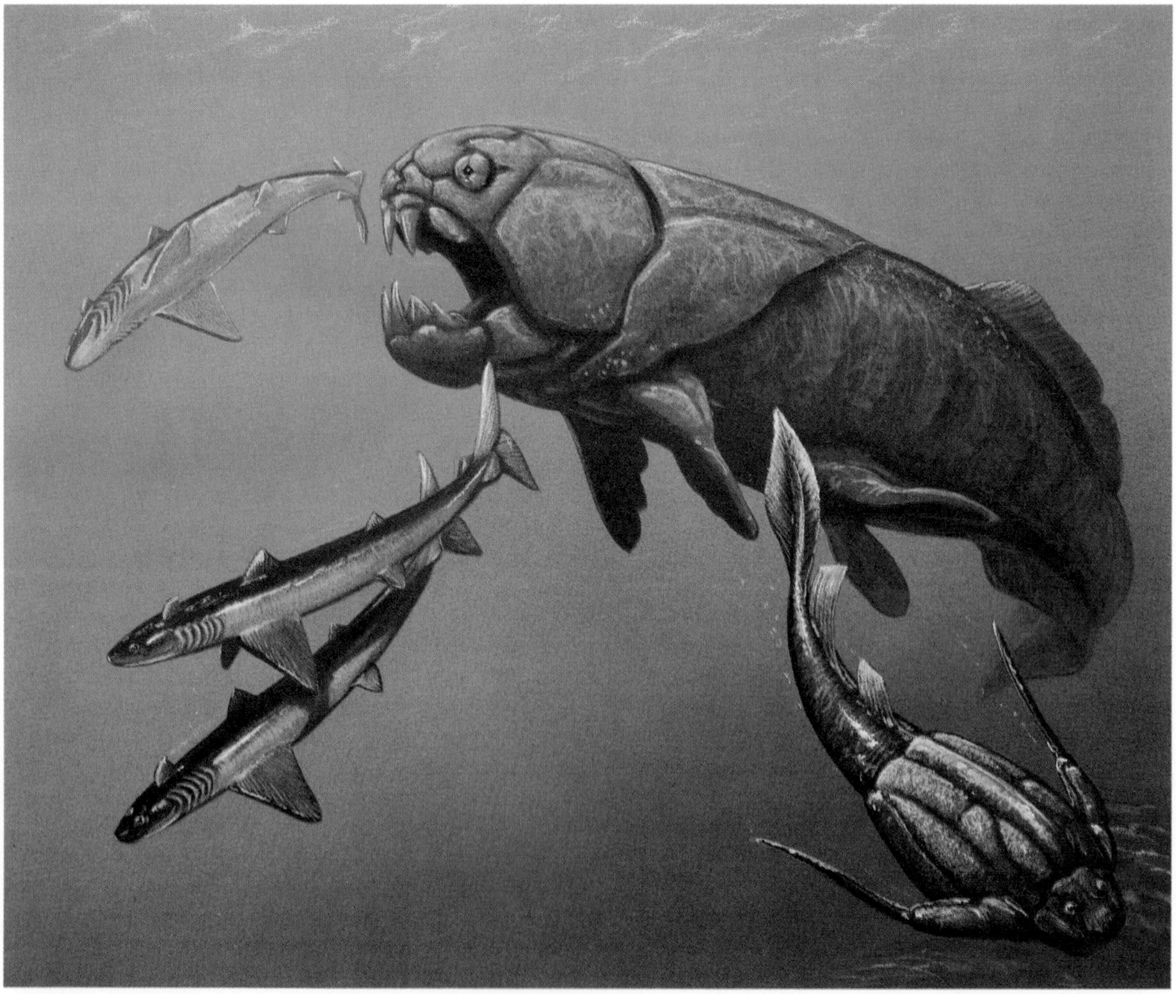

Devonian seas, like Silurian seas, contain some very remarkable predatory fishes, both sharks and bony fish. By the end of the Devonian Period, the land takes on a new appearance with swamps and forests. Also, late in the Devonian Period there is another type of movement on the land—amphibians! Land vertebrates have joined the parade.

Invasion of the land is by a select group of organisms, and it is not an easy transition. Life developed in the oceans where water keeps organisms moist and where water provides support and protection. A floater like the jellyfish cannot survive on land. Because the jellyfish cannot support itself on dry land, it cannot move, breathe, or eat. And it will finally dry up. Land

Cladoselache   *Dinicthys*

Bothriolepsis

dwellers in the Devonian Period had developed skeletons that gave support. They also developed protection from drying up and a way to use oxygen from air rather than from water.

During the Mississippian and Pennsylvanian Periods, swampland forests covered much of the land. The plants that grew in these swamps died, were buried, and changed to coal (a form of carbon) in great amounts. (Modern relatives of these swamp trees can be found as small forest and pondside forms.) Also during this time, called the Carboniferous time, dragon-flies, cockroaches, and other winged insects are abundant. It is at this time that the first reptiles, which are amphibian-like, appear in the parade.

Why is a skeleton needed by a land dweller?

The Carboniferous time includes two periods, the Mississippian and the Pennsylvanian. Suggest that students check their dictionary for the etymology of the word *carboniferous*.

Figure 11-27. By the end of the Devonian Period, swamps and forests are found on the land.

Clubmoss   Tree fern

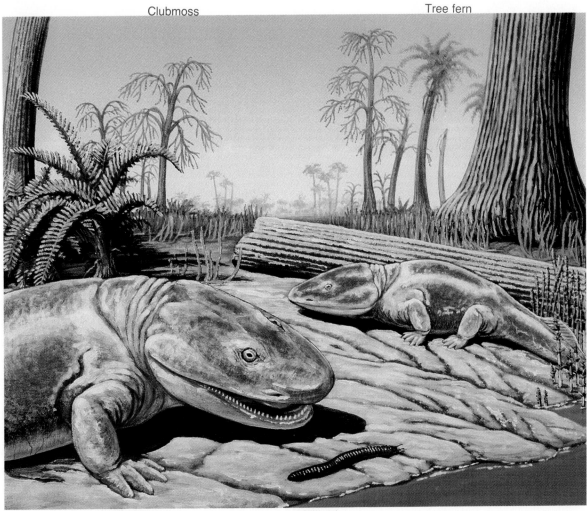

Ichthyostega   *Milliped*

Dimetrodon

Diplocaulus   *Seymouria*

Figure 11-28. By the Permian Period, many different types of animals are found on the land.

Through discussion, review what it means to become extinct. It means that a whole species of organisms disappears from the earth forever (remaining, if at all, only in the fossil record). It occurs when the last members of the species die out without leaving any descendants. There is a bumper sticker that points up the irreversible finality: Extinct Is Forever.

What is a living fossil?

The Paleozoic Era ends in the Permian Period. By this time, the land has become forested with many types of trees although none of them is a flowering tree. Land animals are abundant, with many different types of amphibians, reptiles, and insects. Some dragonflies are as big as present-day blackbirds. Some of the reptiles have features like the spiny fin on *Dimetrodon*, which aids in the control of body temperature.

The dominant sea dwellers are no longer trilobites as in the early Paleozoic Era. Seas in the late Paleozoic Era contain many fish and brachiopods.

Gradually the amount of land increases. Populations in the oceans are changing, sometimes gradually and sometimes rather abruptly. Some kinds of organisms that pass by are never seen again. They become extinct. Other organisms persist. If these persistent organisms still have living representatives today, they are referred to as **living fossils.**

Then another abrupt change occurs. Most of the land and ocean dwellers are seen for the last time. Land organisms like the lycopod trees and seed fern trees become **extinct,** which means they die out without leaving any descendants on the earth. Major groups of all animals, including trilobites and many brachiopods, become extinct. Only the fish show little change.

This major time of extinction marks the end of the Paleozoic Era and the beginning of the Mesozoic Era. It occurred at a time when the oceans had receded and much of the land was dry. Some fossil tracks have been found in Permian rocks formed from desert deposits.

During the Paleozoic Era, the continental masses of the earth's crust were assembled into one large landmass, or a supercontinent. Following the Permian Period, the continental masses began to separate. During the Mesozoic Era, we witness the continued breakup of supercontinents into the ones we know today.

Check yourself

1. What spectacular development in organisms marks the beginning of the Paleozoic Era?

2. What were the first types of land vertebrates, and when did they appear?

3. Describe the history of land plants during the Paleozoic Era.

4. What types of events end the Paleozoic Era?

Students can find out 1) what other classes of animals (in addition to cephalopods) are mollusks and 2) how each class of mollusks differs from

Mesozoic life forms
the other classes of mollusks. This type of classification research could be extended to include organisms other than mollusks.

The parade changes character in the early Mesozoic Era because of all the disappearances at the end of the Paleozoic Era. Only persistent organisms continue on. Although there are only a few different types of organisms, they are present in great numbers. Then begins a succession of many new kinds of animals, some of which come and go rapidly.

Some of the mollusks have worldwide distribution in the oceans but live only a short time before becoming extinct. It is as though they line themselves up from one side of the watery parade to the other. Each line is a new and different type, never to be seen again after passing by. These particular mollusks are a type of cephalopod (SEF'-uh-luh-pod'), distant relatives of modern squid. One day, these cephalopods will provide excellent index fossils for scientists.

What happened to the oceans at the end of the Paleozoic Era?

The breakup of the supercontinent is discussed on pages 511-512 of Chapter 10.

1. Hard parts (like the hard shells of trilobites)
2. Amphibians, late in the Devonian Period
3. Late Silurian Period—land plants appear; Mississippian and Pennsylvanian Periods—swampland forests and plants; Permian Period—many types of nonflowering trees; end of Paleozoic Era—disappearance of most land plants
4. 1) Extinction of most organisms; 2) oceans receded, leaving the land masses high and dry; 3) at the end of the Permian Period, the continental masses begin to separate.

Figure 11-29. This Boreal squid is a member of the class of animals called cephalopods.

Rhamphorhynchus *Icthyosaurus* (fish lizards) *Plesiosaurus*

Ferns *Ornitholestes* *Compsognatnus* *Camptosaurus*

Figure 11–30. Dinosaurs were the largest dwellers ever to populate the land. During what geologic period do they disappear from the land? Dinosaurs disappeared during the Cretaceous Period.

Library research

What is a vertebrate? How does it differ from an invertebrate? Give examples.

Land masses are still populated by various insects and plants. Many of them survived the changes at the end of the Paleozoic Era.

New kinds of land vertebrates keep appearing as the parade continues. Chicken-size and dog-size dinosaurs and small rodent-like mammals come along late in the Triassic Period. By the middle of the Jurassic Period, the dinosaurs become the largest dwellers ever to populate the land. Along with the land giants of the Jurassic Period are the first true birds. Except for feathers and proportionally larger brains, the first birds have teeth and are structurally similar to small dinosaurs.

Mixed in with the birds and giant dinosaurs are the first flowering trees. Because the climate of the whole earth is quite warm, the flowering trees spread far toward the North and South Poles.

Where the large plant-eating dinosaurs roam, there are moderate-sized meat-eating dinosaurs in pursuit. As the parade passes into the Cretaceous Period, the plant eaters get smaller and the meat eaters get bigger. Any mammals in this part of the parade are small and very primitive.

Brachiosaurus   *Stegosaurus*   *Allosaurus*   Conifers

Cycads   *Pterodactylus*   *Archaeopterx*

In the warmer, shallower parts of the oceans, corals and clams form reefs. The land becomes greatly flooded by the oceans, and only small land masses are seen.

Then, late in the Cretaceous Period, the land masses begin to rise again. Suddenly, the reef-forming clams disappear. The group of cephalopods that will be such good index fossils disappear. Most swimming reptiles disappear. The dinosaurs disappear. Many types of organisms also disappear, including microscopic ocean-drifting forms.

Another major time of extinction changes the character of the parade. And the Mesozoic Era ends.

Check yourself

1. What types of changes occurred in land-dwelling animals during the Mesozoic Era?

2. How did plants change during the Mesozoic Era?

3. What events in life forms occurred at the end of the Mesozoic Era?

The Cretaceous Period comes at the end of what geologic era?

1. New kinds of vertebrates appear: small-size dinosaurs and rodent-like mammals, then large dinosaurs and the first true birds, which have teeth and are structurally similar to small dinosaurs.
2. The first flowering trees appear.
3. Many types of organisms disappear, including reef-forming clams, cephalopods, swimming reptiles, dinosaurs, and microscopic ocean-drifting forms.

Cenozoic life forms

The word *cenozoic* comes from the Greek words for recent life. The Tertiary Period (from 135 million years ago to 10 million years ago) is a time of great development among mammals. By the Miocene Epoch (which began 25 million years ago), mammals began to acquire modern characteristics. Interested students could construct an illustrated chart showing the development of mammals during the Tertiary Period.

Figure 11-31. Modern human forms appeared during the Pleistocene Epoch. In what geologic period is the Pleistocene Epoch found?
The Quaternary Period

The change in life forms at the beginning of the Tertiary Period is accompanied by a change in temperature that affects the distribution of flowering trees. As the earth's climates become cooler, cone-bearing evergreens become more abundant in the colder areas.

Marine organisms increase in numbers and kind. Fish take on a modern aspect. And mammals, which have been in the parade for some time, start to become more abundant. In many cases, the mammals are also increasing in size. Progressing through the Tertiary Period, the mammals begin to look more and more familiar. By the end of the Tertiary Period, hominid (human-like) forms appear.

The Tertiary Period passes, and we now see the Quaternary Period, which is divided into two smaller divisions of time called *epochs* (Pleistocene and Recent). During the Pleistocene Epoch, glaciers covered much of the Northern Hemisphere.

The glaciers grew and melted several times, causing changes in the land environment and in sea level and water temperature. Although land dwellers were affected significantly, organisms living in the sea were relatively unaffected.

How did Pleistocene glaciers affect land dwellers and sea dwellers?

As the parade progresses through Pleistocene time, modern human forms appear. Gradually the entire parade becomes a scene that catches up to us in time. We must now leave the reviewing stand and take our place in the parade.

Check yourself

1. The Cenozoic has been called the age of mammals. What types of changes make the Cenozoic the age of mammals?

2. What parts of the environment were affected most by the Pleistocene ice age?

3. How did the earth's climate change at the very beginning of the Tertiary Period?

1. Mammals become more abundant and increase in size.
2. Organisms of the land environment of the Northern Hemisphere were most affected.
3. The earth's climates became cooler.

Science Processes: Observing; Classifying; Inferring

See also Activity Record Sheet 11-3B (Lab Manual page 158)

CORE   30 minutes   Groups of 4

Activity 11-3B Distinguishing Fossils and Inferring Ancient Environments

Materials

clam shell

fossil brachiopod

crab carapace

trilobite

wood

carbonized wood

petrified wood

casts and/or molds of fossils

Purpose

To distinguish different types of fossils and infer their original environments

Procedure

1. Divide the specimens into two sets, fossils and nonfossils.
2. Divide the fossils into sets, based on similarities and differences that you observe. Use any possible features that you can see or test (color, mineral or tissue composition, hardness, density, and so forth).
3. For each set and/or specimen, write down the differences.

Questions

1. Which of the fossil specimens might contain the original skeletal material?
2. Which of the fossil specimens probably represent material that has been replaced by some mineral? How can you tell?
3. What environmental differences could cause the differences between the two different kinds of fossilized wood?
4. Which specimens are casts? Which are molds? How can you tell the difference?

Conclusion

How did you decide which specimens were fossils and which were not? What general types of environmental differences could you infer about your fossils?

Going Further

From the types of fossils and the types of sediments or rock particles, what can you infer about the specific ancient environment in which each of your fossil specimens formed? Use the data table below for reference.

Environment	Depth of Water	Temperature of Water	Type of Sediment or Rock Particle	Type of Fossil
1. carbonate bank	shallow	warm	lime mud	algae, mollusks
2. coral reef	shallow	warm	broken skeletal fragments	corals, bryozoans, sea fans, shells
3. river delta	shallow	warm or cool	sand and silt	some mollusks or brachiopods
4. sand beach	shallow to above water	warm to cold	sand	shells and shell fragments
5. continental shelf	to 350 m deep	warm to cold	sand and silt	burrowing shells
6. deep sea basin	deep ocean	cold	silt and clay	burrowing organisms
7. volcanic area	all depths	warm to cold	volcanic rocks and fragments	usually none
8. swamp or marsh	very shallow	warm to cold	mud (sand, silt, and clay)	plants and either freshwater or saltwater animals

See also Teaching Diagram 11-3 (TRB page 52).

Section 3 Review   Chapter 11

Use **Reading Checksheet 11-3** TRB page 92
Skillsheet 11-3 TRB page 134
Section Reviewsheet 11-3 TRB pages 205–206
Section Testsheet 11-3 TRB page 306

Check Your Vocabulary

5 extinct	4 living fossils
1 fossil record	2 paleontologist
6 life form	3 sexual reproduction

Match each term above with the numbered phrase that best describes it.

1. The record of former life forms as preserved in the earth's rocks

2. A scientist who reconstructs prehistoric life from plant and animal fossils that are found in the rock record

3. Reproduction that involves the joining together of male and female germ cells

4. Fossils of organisms that have representatives still living today

5. Died out completely, without leaving any descendants on the earth

6. The body form that characterizes a fully grown organism

Check Your Knowledge

Multiple Choice: Choose the answer that best completes each of the following sentences.

1. The oldest known fossils are ___?___.
   a) trilobites and brachiopods
   b) algae and bacteria
   c) fungi and algae
   d) worms and jellyfish

2. The oldest known fossils are ___?___ years old.
   a) 4.6 billion   c) 3.3 billion
   b) 3.9 billion   d) 1.2 billion

3. The beginning of the Paleozoic is marked by ___?___.
   a) organisms with hard parts
   b) extensive glacial deposits
   c) fish and fungi
   d) a great number of desert deposits

4. The first reptiles occurred during the ___?___ Period.
   a) Ordovician
   b) Carboniferous
   c) Triassic
   d) Tertiary

5. All ___?___ became extinct at the end of the Paleozoic Era.
   a) dinosaurs   c) flowering plants
   b) fish   d) trilobites

Check Your Understanding

1. What is the nature of the fossil record?

2. Some organisms are more easily fossilized than others. What characteristics of the organisms would favor fossilization?

3. What types of events mark the boundaries between the eras? Be specific.

4. How would you characterize the life forms of each era?

5. Describe the progression of vertebrates through time, listing the periods and the types of vertebrates.

Chapter 11 Review

See also **Chapter Testsheets 11A and 11B**
TRB pages 337–338.

Concept Summary

An **assumption** is the taking for granted that a certain process or scientific law remains constant through time and place.

☐ Assumptions are necessary in science.

☐ Uniformitarianism is the basic assumption of all sciences.

☐ Scientific principles and laws are merely well accepted assumptions.

☐ The principles of original horizontality, superposition, and faunal succession are used in interpreting the rock record.

Theories are working statements intended to be tested, modified, added to, or replaced.

☐ Darwin's theory of evolution appears valid in a limited number of cases.

☐ Other theories of evolution are proving to be useful in complementing Darwin's theory.

☐ Data from nature is the raw material for testing scientific theories.

The **rock record** is the history of the earth as recorded in its crustal rocks.

Absolute age determinations estimate the age of the earth in years. Such age determinations have been made in many ways.

☐ Nineteenth-century estimates included sediment thickness, salt content of oceans, life spans of fossils, and the cooling rate of the earth.

☐ Radiometric dating assumes a constant decay rate and a closed system.

☐ Radiometric dates showed the earth to be 4.6 billion years old, much older than the nineteenth-century estimates.

Geologic time is a method of age determination that dates the earth's history not by years but by eras and periods of time.

The **fossil record** is the record of former life forms as preserved in the earth's rocks.

☐ The fossil record spans 3.3 billion years of the earth's 4.6 billion year age.

☐ The most common fossils are of those organisms that had hard parts like shells or bones.

☐ The Precambrian Era contains fossils of soft-bodied organisms only. For example, algae, bacteria, worms, and jellyfish.

☐ The Paleozoic Era starts with organisms having hard shells. For example, trilobites and brachiopods.

☐ All major groups of organisms are represented by fossils before the end of Ordovician time. (Vertebrates would be a major group, for example.)

☐ The ends of the eras are marked by major times of extinction.

☐ The Mesozoic Era was the age of the dinosaurs, the first true birds, and the first flowering tree.

☐ The Cenozoic Era is marked by the expansion of mammals and the development of modern fish.

Putting It All Together

1. How does uniformitarianism apply to geology?

2. How would the law of faunal succession help in evaluating theories of evolution?

3. What are the main scientific objections to applying Darwin's theory of evolution to all organisms?

4. How are formations of rock used in studying earth history?

5. What kinds of information about earth history can be obtained from unconformities?

6. Explain in detail the assumptions and principles of radiometric dating.

7. How can carbon-14 dates be checked?

8. List the periods of geologic time, and opposite each period indicate a new or abundant life form or major event of earth history that occurred then.

9. Add to your list of periods the names of the eras and the absolute ages of the boundaries between eras.
10. What aspects of the environment make it difficult for soft-bodied organisms to be preserved as fossils?

Apply Your Knowledge

1. What types of rocks would you most likely find fossils in?
2. What technologic or scientific changes would have to occur in order to obtain reliable radiometric dates in the 70 000 to 100 000 year range?
3. What geologic processes in your community are adding to the rock record? Be specific about locations.
4. What geologic processes in your community are contributing to a future unconformity? Be specific.
5. If all written history became destroyed and lost, how would people 20 000 years from now reconstruct the twentieth-century environment?

Find Out on Your Own

1. From a library, obtain geologic maps and descriptions of your area. Describe the geologic history of your area, including environments and unconformities.
2. Collect rocks (or use the rocks collected for Chapter 2), label them, and describe the type of ancient environment that each of them might represent.
3. Collect fossils and determine which of them are marine or non-marine. Use library sources to help you. Also, label them according to type and relative age (Cambrian, Ordovician, . . .).

Reading Further

Benton, Michael. *The Story of Life on Earth: Tracing Its Origins and Development Through Time.* New York: Warwick, 1986.

This is a very attractive, easy-to-understand book. Its topics include geologic eras, fossils, evolution, radiometric dating, and theories of dinosaur extinction. It is well organized with many color illustrations.

Colbert, Edwin H. *The Great Dinosaur Hunters and Their Discoveries,* rev. ed. New York: Dover, 1984.

This fascinating book teaches about dinosaurs by relating the stories of the people who discovered them.

Hallam, A. *Great Geological Controversies.* New York: Oxford University Press, 1983.

Major geological controversies, including uniformitarianism and the earth's age, are presented. This interesting book shows how geology has developed in the past two centuries.

Raymo, Chet. *Biography of a Planet: Geology, Astronomy, and the Evolution of Life on Earth.* Englewood Cliffs, NJ: Prentice-Hall, 1984.

Geology, astronomy, and evolution come together in this book that discusses how the earth has changed since its formation. Theories of evolution and extinction are explored.

Rydell, Wendy. *Discovering Fossils.* Mahwah, NJ: Troll Associates, 1984.

This excellent book explains what a fossil is and how old the earth is. It describes some of the great fossil discoveries, such as the woolly mammoth in Siberia. It also tells how you can hunt fossils.

Reader, John. *The Rise of Life: The First 3.5 Billion Years.* New York: Knopf, 1986.

With beautiful illustrations, this book takes us on a journey through the development of life—from chemical soup to humans.

Student Resources		Meeting Individual Needs	
Student Text	**Laboratory Activities**		
Section 1 Using Earth Materials 582–601 Using Minerals and Rocks 583–590 Using Fossil Fuels 589–592	Activity 12-1A Separating Earth Materials 587 Activity Record Sheet 12-1A LM 163	Reinforcement	
Using the Wind and the Sun 592–594 Using Water 594–597 Using Atoms 597–600 Section 1 Review 601	Research Lab 12 Alternative Energy Sources: Solar Heating LM 171–172 Activity 12-1B Simulating Ore Reserves and World Demand 600 Activity Record Sheet 12-1B LM 164 Investigation 12-1 Investigating Ore Samples LM 165–166	Enrichment CORE Enrichment	
Section 2 Preserving the Environment 602–616 Taking from the Earth 603–607 Our Science Heritage: Improving the Environment 604 Heaping Up upon the Earth 608–611 A Suitable Environment for Life 611–614 Careers: Range Manager/Petroleum Geologist 613 Section 2 Review 616	Activity 12-2A Considering the Economics of Recycling 609 Activity Record Sheet 12-2A LM 163 Investigation 12-2 Comparing the Biodegradability of Waste Materials LM 169–170 Activity 12-2B Evaluating Alternative Energy Sources on Klar 615 Activity Record Sheet 12-2B LM 168	CORE Enrichment Enrichment	
Chapter 12 Review 617–618 Science Issues of Today: Extinction Patterns and Rates 619			

12

Teacher Resources		Meeting Individual Needs
Teacher's Edition	**Teacher's Resource Book**	
Discussion Idea 581C Demonstration 581C Activity Notes 581D Activity Notes 581E	Essential Ideas 12-1 EI 75–76 Overhead Transparency S39	Reinforcement Enrichment
	Skillsheet 12-1 TRB 135 Teaching Diagram 12-1 TRB 53 Overhead Transparency B20	Enrichment CORE CORE
Environmental Topic 581F Section 1 Review Answers 581F	Reading Checksheet 12-1 TRB 93 Section Reviewsheet 12-1 TRB 207–208 Section Testsheet 12-1 TRB 307	Reinforcement CORE CORE
	Essential Ideas 12-2 EI 77–78	Reinforcement
Discussion Idea 581G	Skillsheet 12-2 TRB 136 Teaching Diagram 12-2 TRB 54	Enrichment Enrichment Enrichment
Demonstration 581G Activity Notes 581H	Overhead Transparency S40	Enrichment
Activity Notes 581J Creative Writing Idea 581K Environmental Topic 581K		
Section 2 Review Answers 581K	Reading Checksheet 12-2 TRB 94 Section Reviewsheet 12-2 TRB 209–210 Section Testsheet 12-2 TRB 308	Reinforcement CORE CORE
Chapter 12 Review Answers 581L–581M	Chapter 12 Testsheet TRB 339–340	CORE

12

Learner Objectives

1. To understand the relationships between earth materials and finished products.
2. To realize that there is a limit to the amount of earth materials.
3. To identify some of the economic limitations involved in obtaining and processing earth materials.
4. To be aware of the various factors involved in decisions regarding the use and recycling of earth materials.
5. To identify energy sources and their limitations.

Concept Summary

Earth materials consist of all the matter found on earth.

12-1

Discussion Idea

Our Dependence on Vital Earth Materials

Ask: How might our lives be different if we completely ran out of gasoline? (We might have to walk a lot! Or perhaps gasohol would run our automobiles by then; some countries are already using it almost exclusively.) Besides cars, what modes of transportation would be affected? (boats, buses, etc.)

What if we ran out of uranium? (Reactors and atomic weapons would cease to work.) What implications can students come up with for a human future without uranium?

Suppose there were no gold? (The world's money standard would have to change. Jewelry would be different. Even dental fillings would be different!)

And if there were no silicon? (There would be no sand, no glass, and none of the current generation of computers.)

Have students suggest other earth materials whose absence would powerfully affect life on earth. While most such losses are not likely, it will help students to realize the unique value of each element, mineral, or substance.

Demonstration

Constructing a "Rock"

Tell students that one of the earth materials commonly used for many purposes can be viewed as a human-made "rock." This material is concrete. Concrete is primarily made of a mixture of clay and limestone. Remind students that concrete is very strong. Ask them to think of some of its many uses.

To make a slab of this "rock" combine one part Portland cement (from the hardware store) with two parts clean sand and three parts clean pebbles. Mix the dry ingredients together very well in a shallow container. Then begin to add water a little at a time until the mixture has a pastelike consistency.

Pour your concrete into a wooden or heavy cardboard box, already located in a place where it will not be disturbed. Let the concrete harden for several days. Then remove your dry concrete from the box. Ask students what the texture is like.

Activity Notes

Activity 12-1A

Separating Earth Materials   page **587**

Purpose   To learn three ways to separate earth materials.

- 20 minutes Groups of 4
- **Activity Record Sheet 12-1A** (Lab Manual page 163) can be used to record this activity.
- Science Processes: Inferring; Classifying; Observing.

Procedure Notes

Sugar may be used instead of salt. The hot water need not be boiling water.

Answers to Questions

1. The iron filings were attracted to the magnet. Iron is magnetic.
2. The iron settled to the bottom. Iron has a greater density than sand.
3. Salt crystals were left after the water evaporated. Salt dissolves in water and sand does not.

Conclusion

Salt and sand cannot be separated with a magnet because they are not magnetic. They cannot be separated by the addition of cool water because neither settles into individual layers. Iron and sand cannot be separated by evaporation because neither will dissolve. Students will see that not all earth materials have the same physical properties.

Science Background

Since man first learned to fashion tools from stone, the technology of using earth materials has been an important part of the history of humankind. The use of metals began about 8000 years ago. Metals that occur uncombined in nature—such as copper, silver, and gold—were the first to be used. Later, methods of smelting copper and iron ores and of alloying metals such as copper and tin ushered in the Bronze and Iron Ages. Today, dozens of metals play important roles in Space Age technologies.

Other useful earth materials include nonmetals and metalloids. Sulfur, a nonmetal, collects around volcanic vents. It is recovered commercially from large underground beds along the Gulf coast. Vast quantities of sulfur are used in the manufacture of sulfuric acid, the world's leading industrial chemical. The electronics industry depends on silicon, a metalloid found in ordinary sand. It is a key ingredient in computer chips and solar cells.

Many important earth materials are chemical compounds or mixtures of compounds. Fossil fuels are mixtures of organic compounds. Because of the importance of fossil fuels as chemical feedstocks, or raw materials, for so many useful products (such as plastics), they are considered by some to be too valuable to burn as fuel.

12-1

Student Misconception

The concept of rock as a reservoir for oil and natural gas may be difficult for students to grasp. They may view rock as being hard with no openings to allow for the movements of liquids or gases. It may not be obvious to students that a solid substance can be porous.

Sedimentary rock is made of many small particles cemented together. Pores are created when individual particles touch, but because of their shape, do not fit precisely together. This can easily be demonstrated by having students apply small amounts of water (using a dropper) to various solids—some porous, some impermeable. Materials that are useful include sponge, sandstone, limestone, slate, marble, and plexiglass. This activity will allow students to see how solid, yet porous, rock can serve as a reservoir for fossil fuels.

12-1

Activity Notes

Activity 12-1B

Simulating Ore Reserves and World Demand   page **600**

Purpose   To learn about the supply of and demand for the world's metal ores.

- **CORE** 40 minutes Groups of 3
- **Activity Record Sheet 12-1B** (Lab Manual page 164) can be used to record this activity.
- Science Processes: Using models; Keeping records; Analyzing data; Researching.

Background Information

Ore reserves increase at very slow rates, measured in millions of years in most cases. Our present available reserves are the result of accumulation since the formation of the earth, 4.6 billion years ago.

Industry uses these reserves at a much faster rate than they are being replenished. From the industrial revolution up to nearly 1980, the rate of use of reserves has increased at a geometric rate; i.e., a doubling every few years.

Ore usage is tied very closely to economics. In times of worldwide recession or depression, ore usage drops. During affluent times, the usage returns to an ever-increasing rate. The overall doubling rate is not constant in terms of years, but is nonetheless predictable. The world will run out of many ores within the next century or two, unless: 1) technologies change, allowing costs of mining and processing to decrease; 2) selling prices increase; and 3) new reserves are found.

Procedure Notes

Students might plot the amounts in column C of their chart in one colored pencil and the amounts from column D in another color. At what point do the colored lines cross? How does this compare with their answer to question 3?

Answers to Questions

1. 125
2. Because the output begins to increase at a rapid rate
3. During the eighth minute

Conclusion

Student answers will vary, but each answer should include the idea that nature cannot replace natural resources at the rate we are currently consuming them. We will have to conserve what we have and learn to rely on alternatives where possible.

Environmental Topic

One of the greatest environmental problems that we face to-day is the disposal of dangerous, radioactive wastes. These wastes have been mounting up since the nuclear industry began in the late 1940s. Most such wastes are now stored underground in stainless steel tanks in nuclear power plants and munitions factories. However, this kind of storage is only satisfactory for the short term. Many of the nuclear wastes have half-lives of thousands of years and could cause serious danger to people and the environment in the future.

Scientists and politicians have difficulty agreeing on a safe method of disposing of these wastes that will keep them isolated from the rest of the environment for centuries to come. Some low-yield wastes were placed in metal containers and dumped into the ocean. Would this be a safe, long-term practice? Other proposals have included firing the waste into space toward the sun. This idea might be plausible some day, but at present it is highly dangerous. If a rocket carrying these wastes were to crash on earth, tremendous environmental pollution could result.

France has placed large amounts of wastes deep underground in a mine shaft. Scientists are concerned about this procedure because of possible future upheavals of the earth's crust occurring in this highly populated area in Europe.

Two more plans have received considerable attention in recent times. One has been to convert the wastes into a solid form—a kind of glass. This material would then be placed in a salt diapir in a geologically stable, lightly populated area. Salt diapirs can only exist in very dry places, since the flow of water through them would dissolve the salt. Some exist in the western United States that are millions of years old and are expected to remain unaffected far into the future. However, research indicates that the diapirs may not be as isolated from the water table as initially was hoped.

The second plan is to sink the wastes into a tectonic trench; that is, a fault that separates two tectonic plates. Subduction along the trench would force the wastes farther underground until they reached the earth's mantle, a plasticlike material on which the plates are floating. Here, the radioactive substances could eventually disperse among material beneath the earth's crust that is already mildly radioactive. A possible problem is that the increased radioactivity would raise the temperature along the fault, increasing volcanic and earthquake activity.

No consequence-free method of storing the materials is presently known. Have students examine the alternatives, discussing the advantages and costs of each.

Section 1 Review Answers

Check Your Understanding
page **601**

1. Metals conduct heat and electricity, and they can be shaped without breaking. In some instances, their low melting points and their luster may be important. Students may also mention other qualities—for example, that some metals have great strength.
2. Nonmetals are used as gemstones; building and ornamental stone; and in the production of such things as cement, glass, silicon chips, china and pottery, plaster and wallboard, and fertilizers.
3. Geologists look for an impermeable rock layer beneath the earth's surface that might be blocking natural gas and petroleum trapped in porous rock below it. Their explorations often lead to rocks that have formed on the ocean bottom.
4. A river is dammed, raising the level of the water behind the dam. Gravity pulls the water through the turbines of electrical generators at the base of the dam.
5. When part of the nucleus of the atom is split away, the atom is changed from one element into another and tremendous amounts of heat energy are released.

12-1

Learner Objectives

1. To describe effects of farming, mining, and lumbering on the landscape.
2. To describe ways of disposing waste materials.
3. To recognize that there are limits to the earth and to its resources.
4. To consider the economics of recycling.
5. To consider the economics of different energy sources.
6. To consider how our past use of earth materials has affected the quality of life and how our present use of earth materials affects this quality.

Concept Summary

The earth's resources are limited and must be preserved because they are necessary for all life on earth.

12-2

Discussion Idea

Conservation: How You Can Make a Difference

Ask students to keep track of electricity, water, and gas/heating oil use in their home in one day. Ask them to note if any lights were left on unnecessarily, if showers were longer than necessary, if thermostats were set too high or low, or if more automobile trips were made than were necessary.

Ask students to think about and comment on how difficult it would be to change the family's patterns so that conservation was a natural part of daily life. (Answers will vary.) Ask them to imagine how difficult it would be to get an entire community, state, or nation to change its habits.

Tell students that in Chapter 12 they will learn that the energy crisis of the early 1970s forced people to look for alternative energy sources. Conservation remains important as we develop other sources of energy.

Demonstration

Ways to Minimize Waste

Collect a day's trash from your classroom and spread it out over a large table that has been covered with plastic.

Ask the students to comment on what was "wasted." (Paper could have been used further or recycled, or glass and aluminum could have been recycled. If any food was thrown away, it might have been appropriate for a compost pile.)

Ask students to determine if any contents are not biodegradable or recyclable. How much? Ask what can be done to reduce the amount of such material used and disposed of. (Answers will vary.) Ask students if they think consumers can affect the use of packaging materials, perhaps by letter-writing campaigns or boycotts.

Ask students if they know how their community's waste is disposed of, where landfills in the community are located, and what plans the community has for disposal in the future.

Activity Notes

Activity 12-2A

Considering the Economics of Recycling   page **609**

Purpose To see if a recycling program can pay for the cost of waste disposal and provide an affordable source of raw materials.

- **CORE** 15 minutes Individuals or pairs of students
- **Activity Record Sheet 12-2A** (Lab Manual page 167) can be used to record this activity.
- Science Processes: Using numbers; Inferring.

Advance Preparation

Familiarize the students with the recycling process. Describe for them the sequence of events during the recycling of paper, for example.

Procedure Notes

Note the amount of paper recycled and how little money it brings in. Compare the data for the other recycled material with the data for paper.

Answers to Questions

1. The total income for the material recovered ($1.27 billion) cannot pay for the total cost of disposal and land for dumping sites ($7.35 billion).
2. The total disposed of in Part A is less than the total disposed of in Part B because the total in Part A includes only paper, glass, scrap iron, and aluminum. The total in Part B includes everything that is to be disposed of in addition to food scraps and all other forms of garbage.

Conclusion

Recycling means that smaller amounts of earth materials (ores, trees, etc.) are required to meet the same production needs. Recycling also means that less material is dumped into a disposal site. So, in addition to considering income versus cost, we must consider these two environmental factors when discussing the economics of a recycling program.

Going Further

Suggest ways of making products more easily compacted or recycled. (Consider going back to bottled milk.) Would tax incentives to major corporations for such changes be feasible?

Consider other ways of removing waste.

Science Background

All life depends upon the earth. In turn, the earth is changed by the life forms that inhabit it. For example, most of the oxygen in our atmosphere comes from the life processes of photosynthetic organisms. Only in recent decades have people become aware of the intricate, delicate balance that exists between the earth and its many life forms.

More than any other species, *Homo sapiens* has the ability to change the earth. Today a growing human population faces the challenge of learning to live in greater harmony with the planet's resources. Science and technology will play important roles in this struggle to preserve our environment.

The metaphor of the earth as a spaceship is helpful in understanding the need for earth's life-support system. Like a spaceship, the earth is a closed system with limited resources. And like decisions made by the inhabitants of a spaceship, what affects one, affects all. Human decisions regarding air, land, and water use can affect the rapidity with which natural changes occur. Furthermore, the effects of many of these decisions are cumulative; what we do today affects the environment of generations to come.

Decisions about resource use comprise ethical considerations, economic factors, human convenience, and politics. Students need to understand that humankind is less the *owner* of the planet than a *part* of the environment.

12-2

Student Misconception

Students tend to believe that public land can take care of itself. That may be true, but the fact remains that the land is rarely left alone for this to happen. Different groups of people would like to use the land for their own purposes. Livestock associations, miners, and lumber companies would like to exploit public lands with little restraint. Conservationists, are concerned about watershed protection, wildlife conservation, and wilderness preservation. Other groups are primarily interested in utilizing the land for recreational purposes.

About one third of the land in the United States is public land—that is, owned and managed by the federal government. The majority of this land is administered jointly by the Bureau of Land Management and the U.S. Forest Service.

Federal lands are rich in resources. For example, it is estimated that these lands hold 20 percent of the country's known oil reserves, 30 percent of the natural gas, and 40 percent of the coal. In addition, substantial amounts of uranium ore and oil shale are found on public lands. Have students cite ways in which resources have been removed without serious damage to the environment.

The Bureau of Land Management or the U.S. Forest Service may be able to provide a speaker to introduce students to the interplay of forces that must be juggled in the administration of public lands.

Activity Notes

Activity 12-2B

Evaluating Alternative Energy Sources on Klar   page **615**

Purpose   To select the best fuel for a new power plant on the imaginary planet Klar.

- 20 minutes Individuals or small groups
- **Activity Record Sheet 12-2B** (Lab Manual page 168) can be used to record this activity.
- Science Processes: Using numbers; Interpreting data.

Advance Preparation

Go over with the students the steps involved in evaluating the energy sources. Explain the pollution index.

Procedure Notes

Point out that for nuclear fuel the pollution index is low but that nuclear facilities require water to cool the reactor, thereby heating up nearby water sources.

Point out that the low cost of solar fuel and the disproportionately high plant and equipment costs.

Answers to Questions

1. For Fuel 1, annual costs are: plant, 100; special equipment, 25; pollution-control equipment, 10. For Fuel 2: plant, 100; special equipment, 25; pollution-control equipment, 20. For Fuel 3: plant, 200; special equipment, 20; pollution control equipment, 5. For Fuel 4: plant, 200; special equipment, 100; pollution-control equipment, 0.
2. Total annual costs: Fuel 1, 285; Fuel 2, 245; Fuel 3, 305; Fuel 4, 350.

Conclusion

Answers will vary. Students will probably mention the pollution-free nature of solar energy; the possible hazards of radioactive fuels; the nonrenewable nature of fossil fuels, etc. As in the activity on page 590, they may conclude that dollar cost is not the most important factor.

Going Further

Encourage the students to generate other factors to consider in evaluating potential energy sources.

12-2

Creative Writing Idea

The following writing assignment may help students recognize some of the complexity and difficulty involved in making environmentally sound choices.

You live in a community near an area that looks much like the scene in Figure 12-16. A neighboring city has leased the land to build a garbage dump such as that shown in Figure 12-21. The state government has approved the site because the present dump is filled past regulation standards for safety. Write a letter to your senator or representative indicating your opinions and feelings on the approval of the dumpsite. If you do not approve of the site location, make suggestions of how the garbage could be handled. How would your letter change if you were a city dweller whose garbage could no longer be picked up regularly because of an overfilled dump?

Environmental Topic

Energy is needed to operate many facets of our modern society. The mainstay of our energy resources, petroleum, is expected to run out in the twenty-first century. Thus, there has been an increased effort toward finding alternative sources of energy, such as geothermal and hydroelectric energy. However, both of these sources take a toll on the environment. The use of thermal energy requires the building of a facility to process the earth's heat, and therefore requires the destruction of vital land ecosystems, such as tropical rainforests. Hydroelectric power requires the flood of irreplaceable wilderness and farmland areas in the construction of dams.

Discuss with the students these and other invisible costs incurred in the pursuit of alternative energy sources.

Section 2 Review Answers

Check Your Understanding
page 616

1. Increased population puts ever greater demands on the earth and its resources. People are being forced to realize that the earth's surface and earth materials are limited, and that how they are used today affects what will be available for use in the future.
2. Modern technology has increased the number and kinds of manufactured goods that people use. An increase in manufactured goods means that more earth materials are used, a process that can reduce the quality of the earth's air and water. Increased use of manufactured goods increases the problem of disposing of these items.
3. Solid-waste disposal is becoming a greater problem for several reasons. 1) Increased population means increased consumption and an increase in material discarded. 2) Technology increases the number of items available, and modern processes often make it cheaper to replace an item rather than to repair it. 3) Increasing use is being made of materials that are not biodegradable.
4. Recycling can reduce the amount of material that is discarded as garbage and it can reduce the amount of raw materials removed from the earth to meet the needs of industrial processes.
5. By acquiring land, the government can ensure that natural earth processes can continue on that land—land which otherwise could be developed, mined, stripped of its vegetation, or put to other uses.

12-2

Environmental Concerns

Chapter Vocabulary

Section 1

ore
mine
fossil fuels
petroleum
natural gas
trap
petrochemicals
coal
solar energy
hydroelectric energy
geothermal energy
atomic energy
fission
fusion

Section 2

reforestation
recycled
incinerate
air pollution
acid rain
landfill
wetlands

Chapter 12 Review Answers

Putting It All Together   page 617

1. Diagrams will vary. Among likely metals are copper, steel, aluminum. Nonmetals include sheetrock, cement, glass, and wood.
2. Economics is the major factor determining whether a rock or mineral deposit is classified as an ore. The rock or mineral deposit must be valuable—and its value depends upon the cost of removing and refining the ore and the value of the ore in marketable form.
3. Merits: Both fission and fusion are able to generate huge amounts of energy by means of only a small amount of material. Drawbacks: Fission involves radioactivity during the reaction and radioactive waste materials afterwards. In addition, no successful way has yet been found to control the fusion process.
4. The process of planting new seedlings as trees are removed, or reforestation, preserves vital soil and guarantees a future supply of trees for the production of such necessary items as wood and paper.
5. Recycling is one way of disposing of solid waste. Current efforts have focused on recycling glass, aluminum, and newspapers, since these materials can be easily broken down and used again.

    Incinerating, or burning, solid waste is another often-used method. A considerable reduction in waste mass results from this method, since most solid waste is flammable.

    Burying solid waste in landfills is an option used by many cities. A large pit is dug and filled with garbage. Both biodegradable and some nonbiodegradable materials decompose after prolonged burial.

    Disposing of solid waste in the ocean is the remaining option used by some cities. Since the potentially hazardous consequences of this method are being recognized, disposal of waste into the ocean is currently less favored.
6. People have responded by recycling, reforesting, exploring alternative energy sources, and advocating protection of undeveloped land such as wetlands.

12-3

Chapter 12 Review Answers (continued)

Apply Your Knowledge   page 617

1. Answers will vary but should include the following: 1) Food—Is the community agriculturally self-sufficient or does it depend on other communities? 2) Water—Is water obtained from local sources such as wells, recycled within the community, or channeled in from outside sources such as reservoirs? 3) Energy—what fuels will the community rely upon? Hydroelectric, solar, gas, coal, or others? 4) Shelter—What geological resources, such as rock and wood, does the community have for construction of shelter? 5) Waste disposal—Will the community use landfills, incineration, ocean disposal, or recycling methods?

2. Answers will vary but should include the following: 1) Increased food production and/or increased dependency upon outside food sources, resulting in increased grazing and farming of surrounding land and possibly increased food transporation costs; 2) Increased amounts of water needed, possibly resulting in depletion of local and outside water sources, and exploration of alternative water sources: 3) Increased energy needs, resulting in possible depletion of the community's natural energy sources and exploration of alternative energy sources; 4) Increased construction of shelter, resulting in reduction of local geological resources such as rock and wood; and 5) Increased waste disposal, resulting in large areas of land being devoted to landfill or incineration operations, possible water and air pollution, and recycling efforts.

3. Acid rain will weather rock containing calcite (limestone, marble, etc.) faster than it will weather rock containing silicate minerals.

4. If the animals are not provided with supplemental food sources or alternative grazing lands, they may experience the following: increased competition for available food sources; increased susceptibility to diseases; migration in search of better grazing lands; and an increased death rate.

    People can alter the situation by carefully planning and controlling the use of the land for farming and raising cattle. We can also monitor our water use and recycle water.

12-3

Chapter 12

Environmental Concerns

Section 1
Using Earth Materials

We rely on the earth's resources for nearly everything we make. We use minerals and rocks for constructing buildings, transportation systems, and items of daily use, such as eating utensils.

Our energy needs are met by such earth materials as fossil fuels, radioactive minerals, and water. We also use earth materials to capture the energy of the sun and the wind.

Section 2
Preserving the Environment

The earth's rocks, minerals, and other materials have been recycling for billions of years. People's use of these materials affects this cycle. Some materials are being used faster than they can be replaced by natural earth processes.

For a time, the supply of earth materials was treated as if unlimited. Today, however, people are becoming aware of the balance between what is removed from the earth and what remains in the earth for the future.

Cities are a combination of both the natural and the manufactured. In the picture of Rio de Janeiro, Brazil, on the facing page, which objects occurred naturally? Which were made by people?

In discussing the photograph on the facing page, students should first distinguish between natural and manufactured objects. Once the natural landforms have been identified, have students discuss the earth materials involved. Then have students consider the manufactured objects and what materials might be used in each.

Using Earth Materials   Section 1

Section 1 of Chapter 12 is divided into five parts:

Learner Objectives
1. To understand the relationships between earth materials and finished products.
2. To realize that there is a limit to the amount of earth materials.

Using minerals and rocks

Using fossil fuels

Using the wind and the sun

Using water

Using atoms

Figure 12.1 This picture shows part of a Chrysler robot assembly line. Which of the objects in the picture could have been made without the use of earth materials?
None. As mentioned in the student text on the following page, every product involves the use of earth materials, either directly (made from earth materials) or indirectly (made from synthetic materials derived from earth materials). Earth materials are involved in the machinery used to make the products and in obtaining the energy needed to run the machines.

3. To identify some of the economic limitations involved in obtaining and processing earth materials.
4. To be aware of the various factors involved in decisions regarding the use and recycling of earth materials.
5. To identify energy sources and their limitations.

Think of any object around you that did not just happen naturally. That object, which was made by people, might be a roadway, a building, a chair, a magazine, or a pair of jeans. No matter which object you consider, that object could not have been made without earth materials.

Most products that we use are made from earth materials. Earth materials are also the source of the energy needed to run the machines that make products. The products themselves may be the very latest and most up to date. The machines and energy sources may also be very new. But the earth materials, on which the whole process depends, are very old. Earth materials have been recycling for millions of years.

How old are the earth materials used in making the most up-to-date product?
Students might consider products in the classroom, identifying through discussion the various earth materials involved in each product.

Using minerals and rocks

New vocabulary: ore, mine

Minerals and rocks are the source for most of the earth's metals. A few metals, such as copper and gold, can be found as pure elements in nature. But most are found as mineral compounds of either oxygen (oxide minerals) or sulfur (sulfide minerals). Metals such as chromium, tin, magnesium, aluminum, and iron come from oxide minerals. Other important metals, such as nickel, lead, zinc, and copper, come from sulfide minerals.

Metals are an important group of elements because of properties that nearly all of them possess. In general, metals melt easily. They conduct heat and electricity. They can be hammered or pressed into different shapes without breaking. And they have a certain kind of luster, or shine.

Metals are widely used today. Steel, which is made mostly from iron, has great strength. Tall buildings, long bridges, ocean liners, jet planes, and automobiles depend on steel, aluminum, and other metals for their strength. Most metals have many uses. Copper and aluminum, for example, are made into wire because they are good conductors of electricity. You can certainly think of many other products that make use of the earth's metals.

Minerals and rocks also provide a source for important nonmetals. Nonmetals, as their name indicates, are substances that are not metals. Sand, for example, is a nonmetal that is used in

Figure 12-2. In the pictures above, each metal object on the right could be a product of the ore to its left. Specimen A is an iron ore (hematite). Specimen C is an aluminum ore (bauxite). Specimen E is a copper ore (bornite).

making cement. Sand is also used in making glass and the silicon chips used in computers. Clay, another common nonmetal, is used in making china and pottery. Gypsum is used in making plaster and wallboard. Limestone is used in making cement, an important building material. And compounds of phosphorus

(phosphates) and of nitrogen (nitrates) are used in making fertilizers. Other uses of nonmetals include building stone, ornamental stone, and gemstones for jewelry.

Any mineral or rock from which a needed substance can be removed cheaply enough and easily enough is called an **ore.**

Figure 12-3. In the pictures above, each earth material on the left is used in the manufacture of the nonmetal product to its right. The earth materials are sand (A), clay (C), and limestone (E).

Figure 12-4. In this photograph, you can see that part of an open-pit phosphate mine in Florida has been restored and is being used as pasture land for animals. What factors affect the total cost of obtaining and refining ores? The factors include the cost of 1) removing the ore, 2) transporting the ore, 3) refining the ore, 4) losing the mined land for other uses, and 5) restoring the land.

Library research

Make a list of the rocks or minerals that are ores for each of the following metals: iron, aluminum, copper, lead, chrome, titanium, mercury.

Both metals and nonmetals are obtained from ores. Ores are taken from the ground by a process called mining. The place the ore comes from is called a **mine.**

There are two basically different types of mines—surface mines and underground mines. Both types of mines can be small or large. Open-pit mines are surface mines. Copper and aluminum ores are frequently mined this way. Strip mining is another type of surface mining. Large earthmoving equipment removes the surface materials to get down to the ore or fossil fuel. Coal is frequently mined this way.

A mined ore must be processed in order to obtain a useful substance. For some substances, such as gold or gravel, a simple crushing or washing is all that is needed. For other substances such as iron, copper, or aluminum, the ore must be further treated with heat, chemicals, or electricity to obtain the metal. These processing methods are referred to as refining the ore.

Not all minerals and rocks that contain a needed substance are used as sources for that substance. Much depends on cost. Sometimes it costs too much to remove the rock or mineral

Science Processes: Inferring; Classifying
See also Activity Record Sheet 12-1A (Lab Manual
page 163)

20 minutes   Groups of 4

Activity 12-1A Separating Earth Materials

Materials

sand or sandy soil	magnet
iron filings	2 jars
water (hot and cool)	2 glass pie plates
salt	plastic rod or ruler to use as stirrer

Purpose

To learn three ways to separate earth materials.

Procedure

1. In a pie plate, mix together some iron filings and some sand.
2. Drag a magnet through the mixture and note what happens.
3. In a jar, mix together more iron filings and sand and add cool water to cover the mixture to a depth of about 5 cm or more.
4. Stir the mixture rapidly and then let the sand and iron settle out.
5. In a jar, mix together some sand and some table salt. Add hot water to cover the mixture to a depth of 2-3 cm. Stir the mixture well.
6. Pour off the water into a pie pan. Let the water evaporate until the pan is completely dry.

Questions

1. When you dragged the magnet through the iron and sand mixture, what happened to the iron? What property of iron allows you to separate it from sand in this way?
2. When you added water to the iron and sand mixture, what happened to the iron? What property of iron allows you to separate it from sand in this way?
3. When you added hot water to sand and table salt, what was left in the pie pan? What property of salt enables you to separate it from sand in this way?

Conclusion

Why won't just one method work to separate these earth materials?

Step 2

Step 6

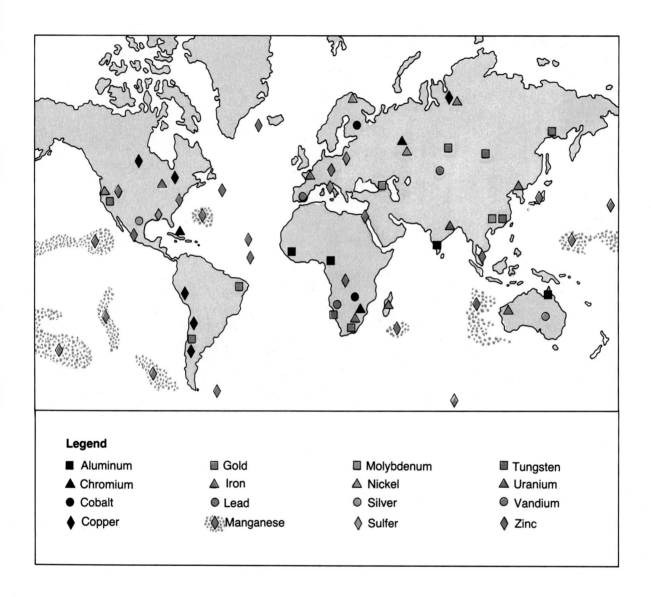

Legend

■ Aluminum	■ Gold	■ Molybdenum	■ Tungsten
▲ Chromium	▲ Iron	▲ Nickel	▲ Uranium
● Cobalt	● Lead	● Silver	● Vandium
◆ Copper	◆ Manganese	◆ Sulfer	◆ Zinc

Figure 12-5. This illustration shows the worldwide locations of major ore-producing areas.

from the earth. Sometimes it costs too much to remove the needed substance from the mineral or rock through a refining process. Sometimes it costs too much in terms of what removing the material does to the earth's surface.

The total cost of obtaining and refining ores is, therefore, influenced by several factors: 1) the cost of removing the ore from the earth, 2) the cost of transporting the ore to a refinery, 3) the cost of refining the ore, 4) the cost involved because of the loss of the mined area for other purposes, especially where open-pit mining and strip mining are involved, and 5) the cost of restoring the mined area to something more closely resembling its original condition.

Check yourself

1. List physical properties of metals that distinguish them from nonmetals.

2. Describe how useful substances are obtained from rocks and minerals. Include the terms *ore, mining,* and *refining.*

1. 1) Melt easily; 2) Conduct heat and electricity; 3) Can be shaped without breaking; 4) Metallic luster

2. Rocks that can be a profitable source of useful substances are called ore. Ore is removed from the ground by mining. Useful substances are removed from ore through a process of refining.

Using fossil fuels   New vocabulary: fossil fuel, petroleum, natural gas, trap, petrochemical, coal

Plants and animals that lived and died long ago have been a source of very important products called **fossil fuels.** Fossil fuels are fuels that are brought up out of the earth. Three fossil fuels are petroleum (oil), natural gas, and coal.

Petroleum (puh-TRŌ'-lee-um) and **natural gas** are fossil fuels that are found in rock. Petroleum, whose name comes from the Greek words for rock and oil, is a liquid. Natural gas is a gas. Both petroleum and natural gas can occupy the tiny spaces between grains of sediment. Both can also fill pores and cracks in rocks. And both are frequently found next to each other.

Water is also able to penetrate nearly all pore spaces and cracks in rocks, even to great depths below the surface. Figure 12-6 shows areas of a porous rock layer whose pore spaces are saturated with water, petroleum, and natural gas. The rock layer containing the water, petroleum, and natural gas has been bent by some movement of the earth's crust. You will note, however, that the layers of pore spaces that are filled with water or petroleum or natural gas do not bend with the rock layer. Rather, the layers of water, petroleum, and natural gas tend to seek their own levels.

In Figure 12-6, the petroleum is located above the water be-

Where do all fossil fuels come from?

See also Teaching Diagram 12-1 (TRB page 53).

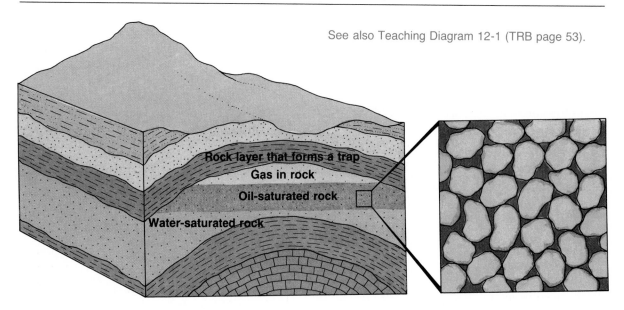

Rock layer that forms a trap
Gas in rock
Oil-saturated rock
Water-saturated rock

Figure 12-6. This cross section shows water, oil, and gas in some bent layers of solid rock. 1) How can water, oil, and natural gas be in solid rock? 2) Why don't the levels of water and oil bend with the rock layer?
1) Rock contains pore spaces, which water, oil, and gas can penetrate. 2) Water and oil are fluids that seek their own levels.

Library research

Make a list of the major petroleum producing areas in the world and the amount of known reserves. Find out what the world consumption rate of petroleum is now, and what it is expected to be in the future. Also, estimate how soon our known reserves could run out.

cause petroleum tends to float on water, even underground. And the natural gas, the least dense of the three materials, is located above the petroleum. Petroleum and natural gas move slowly up through sediments and rocks until they are blocked by a material that is too solid to let them pass through. This kind of blockage is called a **trap.** A trap is what geologists look for when they explore for petroleum and natural gas.

No one knows for sure how petroleum and natural gas formed. The most common theory is that they formed from the remains of microscopic plants and animals that lived in the earth's oceans. As the plants and animals died, their remains accumulated on the bottom of the sea. Bacteria in the water caused the plant and animal remains to decay. At the same time, the decaying material was covered with sediment that washed into the sea from the land. Over a long period of time, the sediment piled up to great depths. This caused heat and pressure on the decayed material beneath the sediment. All four factors—time, heat, pressure, and decay by bacteria—may have changed the plant and animal remains into petroleum and natural gas.

Petroleum has more uses than just about any other substance on earth. From it are made many forms of fuel and lubricating oils. From it are also made hundreds of chemical products called **petrochemicals.** Petrochemicals are used to make fertilizers, insecticides, plastics, synthetic fibers, and many other products that are in wide use throughout the world.

Coal is a solid fossil fuel that is mined both at the surface and underground. Coal is thought to have formed from layers of plant material, called peat, that became buried in a wet environment, failed to decay completely, and then changed through heat and pressure into coal.

In the formation of coal, the plant material passes through a number of stages. With each stage, the plant material increases in hardness and in heat value. Heat value is the amount of heat given off by a certain amount of fuel. As the peat becomes buried under successive layers of overlying material, heat and pressure change the peat, which is very soft, into lignite. Lignite is a soft coal that has a low heat value. Continued and increasing heat and pressure turn the lignite into a better grade of soft coal called bituminous coal. Finally, the great heat and pressure associated with deep burial produces a hard coal called anthracite coal, which has the highest heat value of the various forms of coal.

Coal has many uses. It can be processed to make artificial gas. It is burned to produce steam, which is then used to produce electrical power. It is used to make various chemical products. Also, bituminous coal is especially valuable because it can be changed into coke, a fuel used in making steel.

Check yourself

1. Describe how petroleum and natural gas become trapped beneath the earth's surface. In your description, include the terms *water, pore spaces, blockage,* and *trap.*

2. Describe how petroleum and natural gas may have formed.

3. Describe how coal is formed. In your description, include the terms *anthracite, heat value, heat,* and *pressure.*

Using the wind and the sun
New vocabulary: solar energy

The wind can be used to push a sailboat. The wind can also be used to turn the blades of a windmill. In both cases, people use the wind to do work for them.

People's use of the wind has played an important part in the development of the world as it is today. Up through the nineteenth century, sailing ships were the main means of carrying

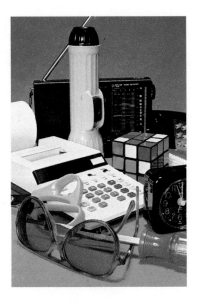

Figure 12-7. Parts of all of these products are made of plastic. How is plastic related to petroleum?
Plastics are made from petrochemicals. Petrochemicals are made from petroleum.

1. Water is found in pore spaces beneath the earth's surface. Petroleum and natural gas will rise through water-filled spaces until they meet a trap, which is a layer of rock that contains no pore spaces. This trap, which prevents the petroleum and natural gas from rising, causes a blockage.

2. Time, heat, pressure, and decay changed the remains of microscopic oceanic organisms into petroleum and natural gas.

3. Layers of plant material that failed to decay completely became buried. As sediment piled up on top, increasing heat and pressure cause the coal to increase in hardness and heat value until anthracite forms.

Figure 12-8. By means of
windmills, people can make the
wind do work for them. What
kinds of work can windmills do?
Windmills can pump water, grind
grain, and generate electricity.

products and people over the oceans. And windmills have long
been used to pump water from the ground and to grind the
grain needed for flour. At present, windmills are also being
used to generate electrical energy.

Energy from the sun, or **solar energy,** is obviously not an
earth material. But earth materials are used to capture this energy and to store it for future use.

Solar energy can be used for heat. Energy from the sun is
called radiation. Some of this radiation is called sunlight. Glass,
a product of earth materials, can be used to trap radiation.
Sunlight will pass through the glass and warm any objects that
are behind the glass. As the objects warm up, they in turn radiate heat. This heat is trapped behind the glass because it will
not pass through glass as sunlight will.

On a sunny day, a closed structure with a lot of glass will heat
up rapidly. This is the way greenhouses keep warm from sun-

Figure 12-9. These solar panels are able to capture energy from the sun. Solar energy can be used for heating purposes. It can also be used to generate electricity.

light. Some people are able to heat their houses the same way, using the sun to heat water or rocks. The heat stored in the water or rocks can later be used to heat the house when the sun is not shining.

Solar energy can also be used to generate electricity. Silicon and traces of a few other earth materials are used in making solar cells that change sunlight into electricity. Because solar cells are very expensive to make, electrical energy from solar cells costs much more to produce than electrical energy from other sources.

What do solar cells do?

Check yourself

1. How has the wind been used to do work?

2. How are earth materials used to trap energy from the sun?

1. Sailing ships and windmills
2. Water and rock absorb energy from the sun; glass, made from earth materials, traps energy from the sun.

Using water

New vocabulary: hydroelectric energy, geothermal energy

People have learned to use the earth's water as a source of energy. Two types of energy that depend on water are hydroelectric energy and geothermal energy.

Solar energy is powered by the sun. **Hydroelectric energy** is powered by both the sun and gravity. Because of the sun, water reaches even the highest locations on the earth's surface. The sun causes water on the earth's surface to evaporate, changing from a liquid to a gas called water vapor. The water vapor passes into the atmosphere. Cooler temperatures high in the atmosphere cause this water vapor to condense, changing from a gas to a liquid or even to a solid such as snow or ice. This liquid or solid water then returns to the earth's surface.

Because of gravity, the water that falls from the atmosphere flows from higher to lower levels on the earth's surface. This flowing water, which is being pulled downward by gravity, can be directed into a channel. Once channeled, the flowing water can be used to turn the blades of a turbine. A water turbine is a modern version of a water wheel. As the turbine spins, it turns a generator that makes electricity.

Figure 12-10. In Washington, the Grand Coulee Dam uses water from the Columbia River to provide hydroelectric energy.

From deep within the earth
Figure 12-11. This geothermal power station is located in Wairakei, New Zealand.

Most turbines and generators are built into dams across rivers. That way the water level will be very high behind the turbine. Also, the flow of water through the turbine will be constant all year long, even during times of little rainfall.

Hydroelectric energy is also generated by using the tides, which are the regular rise and fall of the level of the sea. A dam is built across the mouth of a bay. The rise and fall of the ocean water, powered by the moon's gravitational pull, causes a difference in water level on opposite sides of the dam. Letting the water through the dam spins the turbines.

Can the rise and fall of the tides be used to generate hydroelectric energy?

Another type of energy that uses water is geothermal energy. **Geothermal energy** is powered by heat from deep within the earth's crust. This heat is believed to come from radioactive elements in minerals and from the friction of internal movements. The outer part of the earth's core may be molten, and this heat adds to the other heat sources.

Where does the heat within the earth's crust come from?

1. The sun's energy causes water to evaporate into the atmosphere, where it condenses and falls back to the earth. Gravity pulls water on the earth's surface from higher to lower elevations. This running water can be channeled and used to turn the turbines of generators that generate electricity.

2. Geothermal energy is energy from heat within the earth. It is brought to the earth's surface by water, in the form of hot water (which can heat buildings) and steam (which can be used for heat and to turn the turbines of electrical generators).

The heat in the earth is high enough in some places to melt rock and form magma. In such places, any water will be in the form of steam, which can be brought to the earth's surface and used to turn the turbines of electrical generators.

If no water is present, two wells can be drilled down into the rock. Cold water can be forced down one well, heated by the rock, and brought back to the surface in the other well. In some places, the rocks at depth may not be hot enough to produce steam. Even so, the returning water from such wells is hot enough to heat buildings.

Check yourself

1. Describe how hydroelectric energy is produced. In your description, include the terms *sun, gravity, water, turbine,* and *generator.*

2. Describe geothermal energy, how it is obtained, and how it can be used.

Using atoms

New vocabulary: atomic energy, fission, fusion

Atomic energy is energy that is derived from the atoms of certain earth materials. Because this type of energy involves the nucleus, or central part, of the atom, it is also known as nuclear energy.

One way of getting nuclear energy is called **fission.** The word *fission* comes from a Latin word that means to split apart. In nuclear fission, part of the nucleus of an atom is split away. During this splitting of the atom, heat energy is released and the atom is changed from one element into another element. The tremendous amounts of heat released are used to heat water. The hot water is then used to turn the turbines of electrical generators.

Nuclear fission occurs when certain large, unstable atoms are made to split apart. These large, unstable atoms are said to be radioactive. Radioactive atoms are atoms that are gradually breaking down. As they do, they give off energy and tiny nuclear particles.

What are radioactive atoms?

Figure 12-12. This photograph was taken at the San Onofre nuclear-powered generating plant near San Clemente, California. What are two ways of obtaining energy from the nucleus of an atom?
Fission and fusion

Library research

Using library sources, make a list of all the different types of ways we generate electrical energy. Make a list showing the relative ranking of which methods are used most, second most, etc. Indicate the earth material that is used to produce the energy for each type of electrical power. In considering the radioactivity of earth materials, students might find the following interesting. A chunk of everyday common granite placed in a container that completely isolates the granite from its surroundings (a superinsulator) will melt from the heat of natural radioactive decay in about eleven million years. In other words, a chunk of igneous rock (particularly granite) has enough radioactive element content to melt itself if no heat escaped.

Some elements containing radioactive atoms occur naturally in the earth's crust. These produce much of the heat within the earth. One of these elements is uranium, which is found in several minerals. Uranium and plutonium, another radioactive substance, are commonly used for producing nuclear fission. Plutonium is not found in nature, but it can be produced in a laboratory from certain uranium atoms.

Another type of nuclear reaction involves **fusion.** The word *fusion* means fused together or joined together in some way. In

Does plutonium occur naturally?

Figure 12-13. Uraninite (pitchblende) and carnotite are uranium ores. How is uranium related to nuclear energy? Uranium is used in nuclear fission.

Critical Thinking

What are the two groups of nuclear reactions called? What are the most important characteristics of each?

Fission: atoms split
Fusion: atoms fuse together

What is preventing nuclear fusion from being used as a source of electrical energy?

nuclear fusion, atoms of an element are fused together to form atoms of a different element, one with greater mass. Forms of the element hydrogen are commonly used in nuclear fusion research. The fusion of atoms of hydrogen, which has the least mass of any element, requires less heat and pressure than the fusion of atoms of elements with greater mass.

Nuclear fusion generates great amounts of heat, but it occurs only under extremely high temperature and pressure. Nuclear fusion occurs naturally in the sun and the stars. The pull of gravity in the sun and the stars creates enough pressure and heat to produce a fusion reaction. The light and heat that the earth receives from the sun are the result of a nuclear fusion reaction on the sun.

As with any of the other forms of energy, there are problems connected with the use of nuclear reactions. In the case of nuclear fission, there is the problem of radioactivity, which is harmful to living things. In nuclear fission, radioactivity is involved both during the reaction and in the radioactive wastes that are produced. In the case of nuclear fusion, there is the problem of control. Scientists have not yet been able to create a controlled nuclear fusion reaction from which electrical energy can be generated. But if they do succeed, nuclear power generation should become much less of an environmental

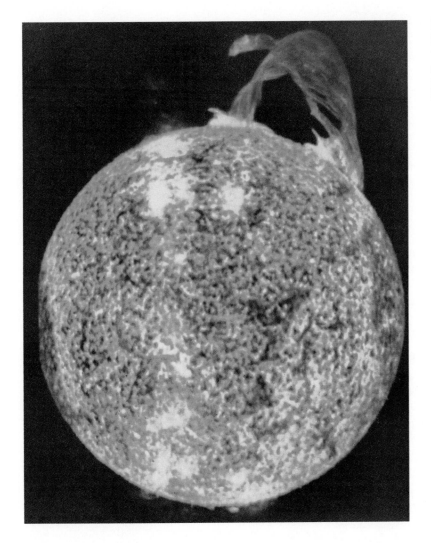

Figure 12-14. This photograph of the sun was taken December 19, 1973, by NASA's *Skylab 4*. Light and heat from the sun are produced by nuclear fusion on the sun.

hazard because fusion reactions produce very little radioactive waste material. The problem can, indeed, be compared to that of harnessing a piece of a star on earth.

Check yourself

1. Distinguish between the process of nuclear fission and the process of nuclear fusion.

2. Describe the problems connected with using nuclear fission and nuclear fusion as sources of energy.

1. Nuclear fission: An atom is split and the atom is changed from one element to another; Nuclear fusion: Atoms are fused together to form atoms of an element with greater mass

2. Nuclear fission: Radioactivity during the reaction and in the radioactive wastes; Nuclear fusion: Inability to control the reaction, which involves tremendously high temperatures and pressure

Science Processes: Formulating models; Inferring
See also Activity Record Sheet 12-1B (Lab Manual
page 164)

CORE   40 minutes   Groups of 3

Activity 12-1B Simulating Ore Reserves and World Demand

Materials

clock or watch that   152 pennies per group
indicates seconds

Purpose

To learn about the supply of and demand for the world's metal ores.

Procedure

Before you begin, read all of the following steps. Make sure you understand what you are to do.

1. Each person in a group assumes one of these roles:
   Ore Reserves   Nature   World Demand
2. Ore Reserves forms a pile of 120 pennies.
   This pile stands for the copper ore reserves that nature built up before people started to mine copper ores.
3. Nature forms a pile of 32 pennies.
   This pile contains the amount of copper that will be concentrated to form new copper ores during the game.
4. Begin the game when the indicator on your watch or clock passes the 60-second mark.
5. Fifteen seconds after the game has begun, Nature adds a penny to Ore Reserves' pile. Every 15 seconds for the rest of the game, Nature adds another penny to that pile.
   This stands for the constant rate at which copper is concentrated into new ores in the real world.

6. At the end of the first minute of the game, World Demand removes a penny from Ore Reserves' pile. At the end of each succeeding minute, World Demand doubles its demand. At the end of the second minute, it removes two pennies; at the end of the third minute, four pennies; then eight, and so forth.
   This stands for the real situation in which increasing numbers of people put ever greater demands on the earth's supply of copper.
7. Continue to play until Ore Reserves can no longer meet the demands of World Demand.
8. Note how long it took for World Demand to remove all the pennies from Ore Reserves.
9. Record what happened in a chart that begins like the one on this page. The first two minutes of play have already been recorded. Complete the chart for the entire game.

Questions

1. What is the greatest Total in Ore Reserves (column E of your chart)?
2. Why does the Total in Ore Reserves (column E) decrease rapidly after four minutes?
3. During which minute of time elapsed does the Subtotal in Ore Reserves (column C) become too small to meet the output demanded by World Demand (column D)?

Conclusion

How does supply and demand affect world requirements for metal ores?

Number of Minutes Elapsed	A Total in Ore Reserves (E) at Beginning of Each Minute	B Input from Nature (4 per minute)	C Subtotal in Ore Reserves (A + B)	D Output to World Demand	E Total in Ore Reserves at End of Each Minute
1	120	+4	124	−1	123
2	123	+4	127	−2	125

Section 1 Review   Chapter 12

Use **Reading Checksheet 12-1** TRB page 93
　　Skillsheet 12-1 TRB page 135
　　Section Reviewsheet 12-1 TRB pages 207–208
　　Section Testsheet 12-1 TRB page 307

Check Your Vocabulary

12	atomic energy	2	mine
8	coal	5	natural gas
13	fission	1	ore
3	fossil fuels	7	petrochemicals
14	fusion	4	petroleum
11	geothermal energy	9	solar energy
10	hydroelectric energy	6	trap

Match each term above with the numbered phrase that best describes it.

1. Any mineral or rock from which a needed substance can be removed cheaply enough and easily enough

2. The place that ore comes from

3. Fuels formed from the remains of plants and animals that lived and died long ago

4. A liquid fossil fuel

5. A fossil fuel that is a gas

6. A kind of blockage formed by nonporous rock that traps petroleum and natural gas

7. Chemical products made from petroleum

8. A solid fossil fuel

9. Energy from the sun

10. Electricity produced by generators powered by moving water

11. Energy powered by heat from deep within the earth's crust

12. Energy derived from the atoms of certain earth materials; also called nuclear energy

13. Atomic energy that is produced when certain large, unstable atoms are made to split apart to form atoms of a different element

14. Atomic energy that is produced when atoms of an element are fused together to form atoms of a different element

Check Your Knowledge

Multiple Choice: Choose the answer that best completes each of the following sentences.

1. Steel, copper, and aluminum are examples of _?_.
   a) phosphates
   b) nonmetals
   c) metals
   d) nitrates

2. Petroleum, natural gas, and water travel through _?_.
   a) lava
   b) porous rock
   c) nonporous rock
   d) no rock at all

3. Natural gas and _?_ are frequently found next to each other.
   a) petroleum
   b) lignite
   c) coal
   d) petrochemicals

4. _?_ can change sunlight into electricity.
   a) Greenhouses
   b) Gravity
   c) Tides
   d) Solar cells

5. The light and heat that the earth receives from the sun is the result of _?_.
   a) nuclear fusion
   b) nuclear fission
   c) geothermal energy
   d) hydroelectric energy

Check Your Understanding

1. Describe properties of metals that make them important.

2. Give five important uses of nonmetals.

3. Describe the kind of trap that geologists look for when they explore for petroleum and natural gas.

4. Describe how hydroelectric power is obtained. Include the types of construction and machines needed.

5. Describe what happens when an atom is split.

Preserving the Environment   Section 2

Section 2 of Chapter 12 is divided into three parts:

Taking from the earth

Heaping up upon the earth

A suitable environment for life

Figure 12-15. What natural processes are taking place here? Runoff occurs in the stream as part of the water cycle. Weathering and erosion are taking place as part of the rock cycle.

Students can discuss evidence of earth processes found in the Sahalie Falls scene. It should be noted that there is no evidence of human development that would interfere with natural earth processes.

Learner Objectives
1. To describe effects of farming, mining, and lumbering on the landscape.
2. To describe ways of disposing of waste materials.
3. To recognize that there are limits to the earth and to its resources.
4. To consider the economics of recycling.
5. To consider the economics of different energy sources.
6. To consider how our past use of earth materials has affected the quality of earth as an environment for life and how our present use of earth materials affects this quality.

Figure 12-16. What natural earth processes produced this farmland in Jackson, Wyoming? Farmland results from weathering, erosion, and deposition. Students might also mention the decomposition of dead grasses and other plant materials, which improves the quality of the soil and provides it with nutrients.

People are putting ever greater demands upon the earth's materials. Many resources that we take from the land are *nonrenewable resources*. Once used up these can never be replaced. Oil is a nonrenewable resource. *Renewable resources* such as wood can be replaced, but are often taken too rapidly.

Taking from the earth
New vocabulary: deforestation, reforestation

Huge areas of the earth's surface have been laid waste because of overuse or misuse. In the past, it may have been possible to move on to another location, ignoring the damage that had been done to the earth. Today, however, it is becoming increasingly clear that the earth's environment is irreplaceable.

In addition to urban development and suburban sprawl, farming and lumbering have had particularly marked effects on the environment.

Farming   The people of the world need food to live. Part of the earth's surface will, therefore, always be needed to obtain food. In their search for food, however, it is possible for people to abuse the land and render it useless.

One area of abuse has to do with the excessive removal of ground water. Great technological advances make it possible

---

Our Science Heritage

Improving the Environment

Pollution is not new. From the mummy of a woman who died in China more than 3000 years ago, scientists were able to determine that she had a lung condition known as pulmonary emphysema. In addition, her lungs contained deposits of various metallic elements, carbon, and silicon dust. Researchers believe that the carbon deposits indicate the environment was polluted from "the smoke that came with the burning of wood, animal carcasses, and other combustible material."

Pollution may not be new. That does not mean nothing can be done about it. Much, in fact, has been done. But much remains to be done.

In the area of technology, pollution-controlling devices have been invented and are being used to reduce the amount of the pollutants that are introduced into the

environment. The numbers, types, and uses of such devices change rapidly. Only a newspaper, magazine, or almanac can keep up with the latest technological advances.

The most important advances, however, might have been those that have taken place in the area of public awareness. Ten or fifteen years ago, far fewer people were even aware of the problems. Such terms as *habitat* and *food chain* were unfamiliar. And many warnings went unheeded.

The condition of the environment has now become a matter of public concern. And more and more individuals are beginning to realize that each of us shares the responsibility for maintaining the earth as a life-supporting planet.

What are two harmful effects of the heavy use of ground water?

to pump water from very deep underground. Heavy use of ground water to irrigate arid land has caused land to sink. In some areas, underlying geologic formations have been so weakened that the land has settled 10 m or more.

In addition to land sinking, excessive removal of ground water can also introduce dissolved salts from the sea. Near bodies of salt water, heavy use of ground water can cause salt water to infiltrate the underground water supply. The addition of substances to the underground water supply that make it unfit to drink is an example of *water pollution*.

Figure 12-17. The plant cover of this South African field can provide food for a limited number of grazing animals and, at the same time, continue to replenish itself.

Another area of abuse has to do with overgrazing and overproducing. In those instances, the soil can be drained of nutrients needed by plants for life. Huge areas of land can lose their vegetation and even their soil cover. Such exposed soil is likely to be lost through erosion by water or wind.

Figure 12-18. This area of Etosha National Park, South West Africa, shows the effects of overgrazing.

Are water and land resources?

A lesson to be learned is that better use must be made of land as a resource. There must be greater planning and control in the use of the land for farming and for raising cattle. Greater care must also be taken in how the water supply is used. Limits must be placed on water use, and there must be more water recycling.

We must also learn to control human population growth in many areas. Sometimes the population density becomes too great to be supported by the available resources. The water supply may be insufficient, or there may not be enough land available for farming or grazing. These factors are important

Figure 12-19. Near Olympic National Park, Washington, an area of forest has been clear cut of trees. To prevent soil erosion and to restore the forest cover, the cleared area will be replanted with seedling trees.

Figure 12-20. These rows of seedling ponderosa pines will be used to replant clear-cut forest areas. Ponderosa pines are valued for their timber.

to consider because of their impact on the environment and the health of all living things. Taking all these factors into consideration is called *land use planning.*

Lumbering   Over time, the need for wood products increased. Deforestation, or the stripping of millions of acres of forest land, led to extensive soil erosion. In the past, little effort was made to conserve this renewable resource because many felt that the supply of forest land was unlimited. Today, better practices are followed. Removing trees from forests is a much more selective process. As trees are removed, seedlings are planted. Such a program of **reforestation** (ree'-for-ist-AY'-shin) has two positive effects: 1) the soil in forest lands is preserved, and 2) a future supply of trees for wood and paper products is ensured.

Check yourself

1. Why are farming and lumbering necessary activities?

2. How have farming and lumbering affected the earth's surface? In each case, how can the effects be offset by some kind of restoration?

1. Because people need food to eat; wood for building, furniture, and paper; and minerals/rock for industry and construction

2. 1) Farming—original ground cover (forest, prairie, etc.) is removed so crops can be raised; nutrients are taken from the soil; ground water is removed from the soil; the soil is laid bare and is easily removed by wind and water; restoration would involve replacement of ground cover, nutrients, and ground water.
2) Lumbering—ground cover is removed and soil is subject to erosion; restoration would involve replacement of trees and other ground cover.

Heaping up upon the earth

New vocabulary: recycled, incinerate, air pollution, acid rain, landfill

It has often been said that we live in a "throw away society." By this it is meant that we throw things away after we've used them only once or perhaps a few times. For example, many of the beverages we drink (milk, soda, juice, etc.) come in disposable containers. Once used, these containers are thrown away. But prior to about thirty years ago, many of these same beverages were packaged in reusable glass containers that were used again and again, as deposit bottles are today.

The same is true for other items. In the past, broken radios, toasters, and other small appliances were repaired. Today, it is often cheaper to buy a new item than to pay the cost of repairing the broken one. Such practices create huge amounts of discarded materials called *solid waste,* or "garbage."

How much garbage does accumulate? Suppose for each member of your family 0.5 kg of garbage is disposed of each day. This would include food scraps, empty containers, newspapers, cartons, broken appliances, etc. Now suppose you live in a medium-size city of about 100 000 people. This means that each day 50 000 kg of garbage must be disposed of. For one year, this would amount to 18.25 million kilograms (or 18.25 thousand metric tons). Add to this all the waste disposed of by industrial and retail operations, abandoned automobiles and trucks, and the total amount can probably be doubled.

To give you an idea just how much solid waste this is, consider a compact-size automobile to weigh about one metric ton. This means that for our model city the annual solid waste disposal is equal in mass to about 18 000 compact automobiles. That is a lot of garbage!

What do we do with all that garbage? A small amount from industrial and retail operations is **recycled,** meaning broken down and reused. Some cities and towns have also established recycling programs for such materials as glass, aluminum, and old newspapers. These materials can be broken down and used again. But the process is costly.

At the present time, most solid waste is not being recycled. Most solid waste is **incinerated** (in-SIN′-uh-rayt′-id), or completely burnt up. Since much of this solid waste will burn, the total mass of solid waste is greatly reduced after incineration.

Interested students can find pictures and data about the most up-to-date incinerators and report their findings to the class.

Are reusable glass containers in use at the present time?

Library research

How many tons of paper, glass, metals, food scraps, and other waste materials were generated in the last year of the most recent estimate you can find? How does this compare with twenty years ago and with the population growth since then?

Science Processes: Using numbers; Inferring
See also Activity Record Sheet 12-2A (Lab Manual
page 167)

CORE   15 minutes   Individuals or pairs of students

Activity 12-2A   Considering the Economics of Recycling

Materials
data table on this page

Purpose
To see if a recycling program can pay for the cost of waste disposal and provide an affordable source of raw materials.

Procedure
1. Using the data in Part A of the data table, calculate on a piece of paper the amount of money received for each material and the total for all recovered materials.
2. Using the data in Part B, calculate the cost for disposal and for land. Add those two costs to determine the total cost of waste disposal.

Questions
1. Can the material recovered pay for the cost of disposal? Give evidence for your conclusion.
2. The total disposed in Part A does not equal the total disposed in Part B. What do you think accounts for the difference?

Conclusion
What other factors, if any, should be considered when discussing the economics of a recycling program?

Data are representative rather than exact.

Data Table			
A. Material Recovery Income	Material	Total Disposed (tons)	Payment Rate ($ per ton)
	paper	50 000 000	5
	glass	15 000 000	12
	scrap iron	12 000 000	20
	aluminum	1 500 000	400
B. Cost of Waste Disposal	Item	Total Disposed (tons)	Disposal Cost ($ per ton)
	disposal	150 000 000	43
	land (for dumping)	150 000 000	6

Answers to Questions
1. The total income for the material recovered ($1.27 billion) cannot pay for the total cost of disposal and land for dumping sites ($7.35 billion). (Calculations appear on page T112 in the front of this book.)
2. The total disposed of in Part A is less than the total disposed of in Part B because the total in Part A includes only paper, glass, scrap iron, and aluminum. The total in Part B includes everything that is to be disposed of and includes food scraps and all other forms of garbage.

Conclusion
Recycling means that smaller amounts of earth materials (ores, trees, etc.) are required to meet the same production needs. Recycling also means that less material is dumped into a disposal site. So, in addition to considering income versus cost, we must consider these two environmental factors when discussing the economics of a recycling program.

Figure 12-21. How much solid waste must a city of 100 000 dispose of in a year if each person disposes of 0.5 kg of garbage per day?
0.5 kg times 100 000 equals 50 000 kg per day.
50 000 kg times 365 equals 18.25 million kg per year.

Many cities and towns burn their garbage in incinerators. But this is not an ideal solution because some products add contaminants to the air when they are burned. **Air pollution** occurs when excessive amounts of contaminants are added to the air. Common contaminants include carbon monoxide, sulfur dioxide, oxides of nitrogen, and fine particles of ash. Some of these substances dissolve in water droplets in the air. They cause the water droplets to become acidic. These water droplets may then fall as **acid rain.** When acid rain falls into a freshwater lake over a long period of time, the water in the lake becomes increasingly acidic. The increasing acidity may cause fish and other organisms in the lake to die. Acid rain may also cause injury and disease to trees. In some parts of the world, large areas of forest are dying. Many scientists believe this may be due to the effects of acid rain.

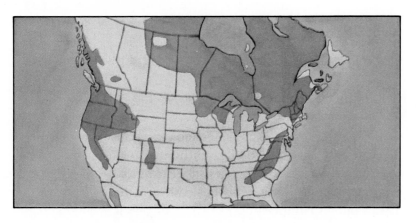

Figure 12-22. The shaded areas on this map are endangered by acid rain.

Some waste products can be buried in a **landfill,** a large pit in the ground that is filled with layer upon layer of garbage. The heat and pressure of the overlying layers cause biodegradable materials to decompose. Cans made of iron and tin also decompose through chemical processes over time.

Some materials, however, present more of a problem. Many of the cans used today are made of aluminum. Aluminum oxidizes much more slowly than iron, but eventually it too will break down. Plastic and rubber products are also a problem because they do not decompose.

In a large city, a landfill area several kilometers in diameter may be filled in less than twenty years. Eventually, the mounds of garbage become too high to permit additional dumping. New sites must be found.

Some coastal cities attempted to resolve the problem by carting the garbage out into the ocean in barges. There the garbage was dumped. Unfortunately, studies have shown that this causes more pollution than was first expected.

Great advances have been made in the incineration of solid wastes. For one, modern incinerators cause much less air pollution than their predecessors. These incinerators operate at much higher temperatures than their predecessors. At these higher temperatures any hazardous materials that were formerly released into the atmosphere are broken down.

Check yourself

1. What are three ways in which waste products and materials are disposed of?

2. Describe the different things that happen to waste materials buried in a landfill area.

Have students find out how garbage is disposed of in your area. Also, what happens to it after it has been disposed of? Does it, for example, decompose or break down further?

1. Recycling, burning in an incinerator, burying in a landfill area so that biodegradable materials will decompose
2. Materials like food scraps decompose rapidly. Some metal materials (like those made of iron and tin) readily decompose through oxidation. Other metals (like aluminum) will oxidize and decompose, but much more slowly than iron and tin. And some materials (like plastic and rubber) merely accumulate because they do not decompose.

Library research

For the most recent year you can find, how much waste material was disposed of in landfills? in incinerators? in the ocean? What kinds of materials were disposed of in each way?

Library research

Since 1900, how much open land has been converted to other uses? What are the uses? What is the outlook for the future?

A suitable environment for life

New vocabulary: wetlands

In the past 150 years, great technological advances have resulted in an array of products unthought of just a short time ago. Everywhere you look, you will see examples of those items. But every one of those items has cost something—not only in money but also in the supply of earth materials.

In recent years, it has become increasingly evident that there are limits even to the earth's resources. There is just so much to go around. And once those supplies are depleted, people will be forced to find and use something else.

The oil crisis of the early 1970s forced industrialized nations to realize how much of their economies was based on cheap and plentiful supplies of oil. For the first time, people came to recognize in a forceful way that supplies of energy are not limitless. In some places, gasoline was rationed, and people had to wait in long lines to purchase gasoline when it was available. Even after the crisis was over, the price of gasoline remained much higher than before.

A lesson had been learned. Greater efforts would have to be made to find other sources of energy. When energy was cheap, there was little incentive to develop new sources of energy. Now, however, alternate sources such as solar energy are being explored.

Because of the energy crunch, people have come to realize that other of the earth's resources are also limited. Governments can have a powerful effect by acquiring land and protecting it from development. In that way, the earth's natural processes will be allowed to continue. As an example, consider the government acquisition of wetlands.

Wetlands are coastal and freshwater swamps. They serve as breeding grounds for thousands of plant and animal species. They also help to filter pollutants from surface water. Many of these wetlands are located near heavily populated areas. In many cases, this makes the land itself very valuable.

Almost a third of the wetlands in the United States have been filled in and converted for other use. Houses, factories, airports, and parking lots have been built over land that was formerly wetlands. But now, through the efforts of local, state, and federal agencies, attempts are being made to stop this process.

Careers   Range Manager / Petroleum Geologist

For federal government careers related to range management, contact:

U.S. Department of Agriculture
Forest Service
P.O. Box 2417
Washington, DC 20013

Range Manager

Rangelands cover over 2 billion acres in North America. They have important economic uses such as ranching and mining. They also serve as recreational areas and provide a habitat for wildlife.

Range managers work to increase the productivity of the land while protecting the environment. They help ranchers increase cattle or sheep production, and they reclaim areas that have been damaged by strip-mining. Range managers spend much of their time on the range. They also do office work and frequently work with other people.

Range managers must have an understanding of biology, chemistry, physics, math, and communication skills. Knowledge of forestry, hydrology, and fish and wildlife management is desirable.

The best preparation for this career is a bachelor's degree in range management or range science. Summer jobs in range management or ranching can provide practical experience. Range managers may work for government agencies, mining companies, and large ranches.

Range managers spend much of their time on the range.

Petroleum Geologist

Petroleum geologists participate in different activities— some in the field and some in the laboratory. They explore and interpret the earth's crust in an attempt to discover more petroleum.

Some of the work involves interpretation of the earth's crystal rocks and structures. Many techniques are used— field mapping, working with photographs taken from airplanes, working with information transmitted from satellites, and using sophisticated electronics equipment to gather data in the field.

Exploratory wells are drilled in likely looking areas, and the geologist interprets the rock samples from the different depths in the wells. The samples are analyzed for their age, fossil content, rock type, and possible relationship to other rocks in the area. Much of the analysis of the fieldwork and exploratory drilling is done in laboratories with a range of equipment, from simple rock crushers to elaborate computers and electron microscopes.

Petroleum geologists usually work for oil companies. Most of the petroleum geologists have a geology degree from a college. Many also complete one or more graduate degrees.

A petroleum geologist uses a microscope in the laboratory to analyze rock samples taken in the field.

Figure 12-23. Earth processes can continue uninterrupted on wetlands like this salt marsh in northwest Florida.

People have come to appreciate the value of wetlands as a preserve for many living species and for their value in fighting water pollution. On a much larger scale, people are coming to appreciate the role that the entire earth plays in providing a suitable environment for life. The depletion and pollution of earth materials and the interruption of earth processes affect all living organisms.

1. People came to realize that the earth's natural resources are limited.
2. Government acquisition of wetlands keeps wetlands from being destroyed by development and permits natural earth processes to continue to take place in those areas.

Check yourself

1. What effect did the oil crisis of the early 1970s have on people's attitudes toward the earth's natural resources?

2. How is government acquisition of wetlands important to the environment?

Science Processes: Using numbers; Interpreting data
See also Activity Record Sheet 12-2B (Lab Manual page 168)

20 minutes   Individuals or small groups

Activity 12-2B Evaluating Alternative Energy Sources on Klar

Materials

data table on this page

Purpose

To select the best fuel for a new power plant on the imaginary planet Klar.

Procedure

1. Imagine that you are the regional utility manager on an imaginary planet called Klar. As a result of population growth, a new power plant must be built. You have four fuels to select from. They are listed on the data table.
2. On a separate piece of paper, calculate the annual costs for items A, B, and C. (For each, divide the total cost by the years of use.)
3. Also find the total annual cost (the sum of annual costs for items A through E) for each energy source.

Questions

1. For Fuel 1, what is the annual cost of items A, B, and C? For Fuel 2? Fuel 3? Fuel 4?
2. What is the total annual cost for Fuel 1? Fuel 2? Fuel 3? Fuel 4?

Conclusion

Using data and other considerations you feel important, recommend a fuel and give reasons for your choice.

Data are representative rather than exact.

Data Table for Evaluating Alternative Energy Sources			1 (a liquid that is burned)	2 (a solid that is burned)	3 (a radioactive fuel)	4 (solar energy)
A. Cost of Plant	total cost		3000	3000	4000	6000
	years of use	100	30	100	30	200	20	200	30
B. Special Equipment	total cost		500	500	400	2000
	years of use	25	20	25	20	20	20	100	20
C. Pollution-Control Equipment	total cost		100	200	50	0
	years of use	10	10	20	10	5	10	0	
D. Operating Expenses	annual cost	50	50	50	50	50	50	50	50
E. Fuel Costs	annual cost	100	100	50	50	30	30	0	0
F. Pollution Index Value			1.0	1.5	0.2	0

285   245   305   350

Section 2 Review   Chapter 12

Use **Reading Checksheet 12-2** TRB page 94
  Skillsheet 12-2 TRB page 136
  Section Reviewsheet 12-2 TRB pages 209–210
  Section Testsheet 12-2 TRB page 308

Check Your Vocabulary

4 incinerate   1 reforestation

5 landfill   2 acid rain

7 air pollution   6 wetlands

3 recycled

Match each term above with the numbered phrase that best describes it.

1. Replanting a forest with new seedlings as trees are removed

2. Precipitation that is contaminated with pollutants

3. Changed into a usable form and used again

4. To burn up completely

5. A large pit in the ground which is filled with layer upon layer of garbage

6. Coastal and freshwater swamps

7. Toxic chemicals that are in the atmosphere

Check Your Knowledge

Multiple Choice: Choose the answer that best completes each of the following sentences.

1. The earth's natural landscapes are the result of ?.
   a) farming
   b) suburban sprawl
   c) natural processes
   d) mining

2. At the present time, recycling takes care of ? of the solid waste materials.
   a) most   c) none
   b) about half   d) a small amount

3. In a landfill area, the heat and pressure of ? cause the biodegradable materials to decompose.
   a) incinerators
   b) old automobiles
   c) overlying layers of solid waste
   d) fires

4. Disposing of ? is also a problem because they do not decompose.
   a) iron and tin cans
   b) plastic and rubber products
   c) paper goods and food scraps
   d) dead plant materials

Check Your Understanding

1. How has the change in population affected our attitude toward the earth and its resources?

2. How has our present way of life increased the demands that are being placed on the earth as a source of needed materials?

3. Why is solid-waste disposal becoming an increasingly greater problem?

4. How can the recycling of waste materials affect the environment?

5. How can government acquisition and protection of land benefit the environment?

Chapter 12 Review

Concept Summary

Earth materials consist of all the matter found on earth.
- Earth materials include rocks, minerals, fossil fuels, and water.
- Nearly everything people use is made either from or by using earth materials.
- The cost of using earth materials involves more than the cost of obtaining and processing the material; it also involves restoration costs for the landscape.
- Energy can be produced from such earth materials as radioactive minerals, fossil fuels, and water.
- Solar energy and wind energy are captured by using earth materials.

The earth's landscapes are all of the physical features that can be seen on the earth's surface.
- The earth's landscapes are the results of earth processes that have been recurring for billions of years. These landscapes have been scarred by the indiscriminate removal of earth materials from the earth's surface.
- Mineral and energy shortages and population growth are forcing people to realize that the earth and its materials are limited. Care must be taken to preserve the earth as a suitable environment for life.

Putting It All Together

1. Draw a diagram of a building. Label various earth materials (metals and nonmetals) used in the building.
2. How can you recognize whether a mineral deposit is an ore?
3. What are the relative merits and drawbacks of the different types of atomic energy?
4. How does a reforestation program protect the earth?
5. Describe the ways that we have of handling solid waste.
6. In recent years, what are some of the ways people have responded to the awareness that resources are limited?

Apply Your Knowledge

1. Design a small community (10 000 people) in terms of its resources. Provide for earth resources, biological resources, and waste disposal.
2. Double the size of the community you designed in Question 1. Describe how the increased population impacts resource production and use. Be specific about the limited resources and the control of waste products.
3. Which types of building stones weather fastest from acid rain?

4. What will happen to animals that live on overgrazed land, such as that shown in Figure 12-18, without human intervention? What could people do to alter the situation?

Find Out on Your Own

1. What types of minerals and rocks are mined within a 75- to 150-km radius of your home? Determine how these materials are processed and used.

2. If an oil company were to drill a well in your community, what sequence of rocks would it find beneath the ground? Which of these rocks might be a good reservoir for oil?

3. What types of energy does your community use? Contact your local power company to find out its major sources of energy. Determine if individual homes or companies are using renewable sources such as wind, water, or energy from the sun.

4. What evidence of land use do you see within a 75 km to 150 km radius of your home? What are the major resources received from this use? What impact does the use have on the environment?

5. Research how waste products are handled in your community. Are recycling programs available? What is the approximate annual solid waste disposal for your community?

6. Acid rain is becoming a worldwide problem. Research what causes acid rain and how it impacts the environment.

Reading Further

Branley, Franklyn M. *Feast or Famine? The Energy Future.* New York: Crowell, 1980.
This book contains a wealth of information on the uses, sources, and forms of energy as well as assesses various energy options.

Cheney, Glen Alan. *Mineral Resources.* New York: Franklin Watts, 1985.
In an interesting way, the distribution, refinement, and use of specific minerals are described.

Douglas, John H., and the Editors of Crolier. *The Future World of Energy.* New York: Franklin Watts, 1984.
Excellent photographs and artwork enhance this interesting book about energy possibilities for the future.

Deudney, Daniel, and Christopher Flavin. *Renewable Energy: The Power to Choose.* A Worldwatch Institute Book. New York: Norton, 1983.
This very readable moderately short book surveys renewable energy technology. It provides up-to-date coverage of a fascinating subject without burdening the reader with nonessential detail.

Leon, George de Lucenay. *Energy Forever: Power for Today and Tomorrow.* New York: Arco Publishing, 1982.
This book defines energy and discusses the various renewable and nonrenewable sources that can provide us with the energy we need in the future.

Satchwell, John. *Energy at Work.* New York: Lothrop, Lee and Shepard, 1981.
Difficult concepts are made easy to understand in this extremely readable book on the world energy crisis. It contains suggestions for conservation and is highly recommended.

Science Issues of Today   Extinction Patterns and Rates

The humpback whale calf pictured below is hitching
a ride on its mother's back. Humpbacks and other
whales have been protected since 1986 by an
international moratorium on commercial whaling.

The Geologic Time Scale is mostly based on divisions in earth history that are characterized by different life forms. Trilobites mark the beginning of the Paleozoic Era, and become extinct near the end of that time. But throughout the Paleozoic Era many different species of trilobites developed, thrived, and then became extinct. The Mesozoic Era was the age of the dinosaurs. Many of these magnificent reptilian species developed and became extinct, with the last species surviving until the end of the Mesozoic Era.

This pattern of life forms developing, living, and becoming extinct has been repeated tens of thousands of times with different types of organisms. This pattern is a part of the natural processes of life on earth.

What causes the extinctions? No single answer can be given to this question because many natural phenomena can cause extinctions. Large meteorites striking the earth can create dust clouds that block the sun and cause major weather changes. Disease can ravage populations. Periods of excessive volcanism can cause instant kills and longer-term weather changes. Variations in continental positions on the earth's surface due to plate tectonic movements can change environments and climate patterns. Genetic changes in response to solar radiation or chemicals entering the environment from the weathering of rocks and minerals also affect organisms. Glacial epochs are accompanied by a lowering of sea level and a change in temperature. The development of a predator or competitor in the environment can rapidly destroy a species. The number of possibilities goes on and on.

Rates of extinction for different species can be determined from an examination of the rock record. The extinction rate is highly variable depending upon the type of organism involved.

A humpback cow and her calf stay close together for at least a year.

Species of reptiles, for example, might have longer life spans than species of crabs. Most organisms are unaware of extinction patterns and rates.

People, however, are in the unique position of not only knowing about other organisms, past and present, but also of being able to drastically alter the environment and extinction rates. This gives us the responsibility to learn how we are affecting the environment and its life forms. One of our single greatest challenges is to understand our environment and protect it, so that we will beautify and enhance the earth and its living creatures.

Appendix

The Night Sky in August   622

The Night Sky in April   623

Relative Humidity Table (°C)   624

Dew-Point Temperature Table (°C)   625

Topographic Map of Orr Mountain   626

Topographic Map of Odell Butte   627

Topographic Map of Crater Lake   628

Seismographic Records of a Hypothetical Earthquake   630

P-Wave Arrival Time for a Hypothetical Earthquake   631

The Night Sky in August

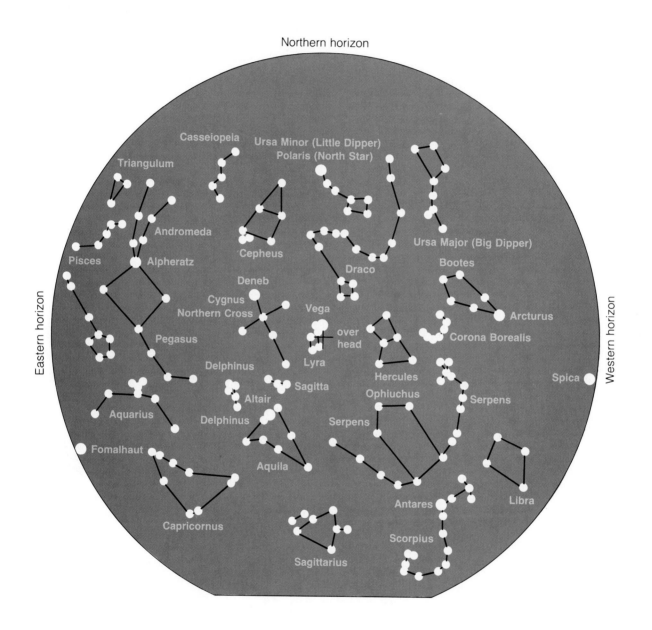

Northern horizon

Casseiopeia

Ursa Minor (Little Dipper)
Polaris (North Star)

Triangulum

Andromeda

Ursa Major (Big Dipper)

Pisces

Cepheus

Bootes

Alpheratz

Deneb

Draco

Cygnus

Vega

Arcturus

Northern Cross

over head

Corona Borealis

Pegasus

Delphinus

Lyra

Hercules

Spica

Sagitta

Ophiuchus

Serpens

Altair

Aquarius

Delphinus

Serpens

Fomalhaut

Aquila

Libra

Antares

Capricornus

Scorpius

Sagittarius

Eastern horizon

Western horizon

West is to the right of North
because when the chart is lifted
above the observer's head, the
compass points are in their
normal orientation.

The Night Sky in April

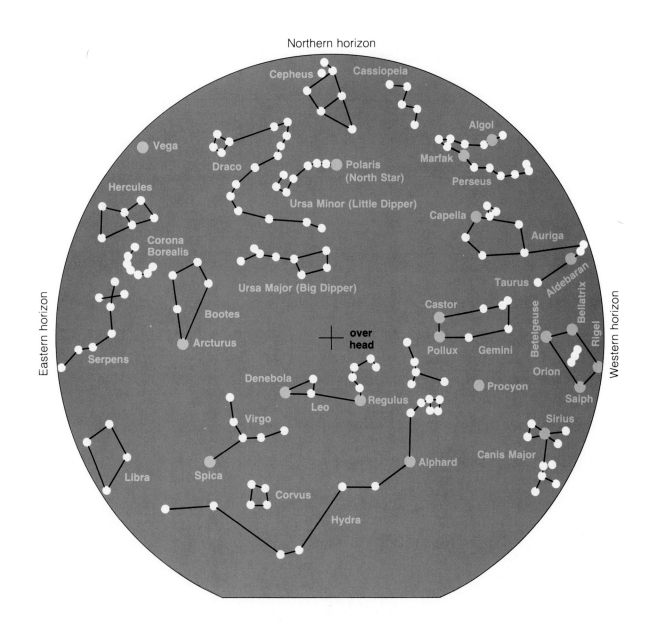

Relative Humidity Table: Celsius

Wet-Bulb Depression (°C) (Dry-bulb temperature minus wet-bulb temperature)

Dry-Bulb Temperature(°C)	1	2	3	4	5	6	7	8	9	10	11	12	13	14	15	16	17	18	19	20
−10	67	35																		
−8	71	43	15																	
−6	74	49	25																	
−4	77	55	33	12																
−2	79	60	40	22																
0	81	64	46	29	13															
2	84	68	52	37	22	7														
4	85	71	57	43	29	16														
6	86	73	60	48	35	24	11													
8	87	75	63	51	40	29	19	8												
10	88	77	66	55	44	34	24	15	6											
12	89	78	68	58	48	39	29	21	12											
14	90	79	70	60	51	42	34	26	18	10										
16	90	81	71	63	54	46	38	30	23	15	8									
18	91	82	73	65	57	49	41	34	27	20	14	7								
20	91	83	74	66	59	51	44	37	31	24	18	12	6							
22	92	83	76	68	61	54	47	40	34	28	22	17	11	6						
24	92	84	77	69	62	56	49	43	37	31	26	20	15	10	5					
26	92	85	78	71	64	58	51	46	40	34	29	24	19	14	10	5				
28	93	85	78	72	65	59	53	48	42	37	32	27	22	18	13	9	5			
30	93	86	79	73	67	61	55	50	44	39	35	30	25	21	17	13	9	5		
32	93	86	80	74	68	62	57	51	46	41	37	32	28	24	20	16	12	9	5	
34	93	87	81	75	69	63	58	53	48	43	39	35	30	26	23	19	15	12	8	5
36	94	87	81	75	70	64	59	54	50	45	41	37	33	29	25	21	18	15	11	8
38	94	88	82	76	71	66	61	56	51	47	43	39	35	31	27	24	20	17	14	11
40	94	88	82	77	72	67	62	57	53	48	44	40	36	33	29	26	23	20	16	14

Dew-Point Temperature Table: Celsius

Wet-Bulb Depression (°C) (Dry-bulb temperature minus wet-bulb temperature)

Dry-Bulb Temperature (°C)

	1	2	3	4	5	6	7	8	9	10	11	12	13	14	15	16	17	18	19	20
−10	−15	−22																		
−8	−12	−18	−30																	
−6	−9	−14	−23																	
−4	−7	−11	−17	−30																
−2	−5	−8	−13	−20																
0	−2.5	−6	−10	−15	−25															
2	−0.5	−3	−7	−11	−18	−30														
4	2	−1	−4	−7.5	−12	−17														
6	4	1.5	−1	−4	−8	−14	−22													
8	6	4	1	−1.7	−4.5	−9	−15	−20												
10	8	6	4	1	−1.5	−5	−9.5	−15	−28											
12	10	9	6	4	1	−2	−5.5	−10	−16	−30										
14	12	11	8	6	4	1	−2	−6	−10	−17.5										
16	14	12.5	10.7	8.5	6	4	1	−2	−6	−10	−18									
18	16	14.5	13	11	9	6.5	4	1	−2	−4.5	−10	−18								
20	18	16.7	15	13	10.5	9.5	7	4.5	2	−1	−5	−10	−18							
22	20	18.7	17	16	13.5	11.5	10	7.5	5	2	−1.5	−5	−10	−18						
24	22	20.7	19	17.5	16	14	12	10	8	5	2.5	−1	−5	−10	−18					
26	24	22.7	21	19.5	18	16.5	15	13	10.5	8	6	3	−1	−5	−10	−18				
28	26	24.7	23	22	20	19	17	15	13	11	9	6	3	−1	−5	−10	−18			
30	28	26.7	25	24	22	21.5	20	18	16	14	12	10	6	3	−1	−5	−10	−18		
32	30	28.7	27	26	24	23	22	20	18	17	15	13	10	6	3	−1	−5	−10	−18	
34	32	30.7	29	28	26	25	24	22	20	19	17	15	13	10	6	3	−1	−5	−10	−18
36	34	32.7	31	30	28	27	26	24	22	21	19	17	15	13	10	6	3	−1	−5	−10
38	36	34.7	33	32.5	30	29	28	26	24	23	21	19	17	15	13	10	6	3	−1	−5
40	38	36.9	35	34	32	31	30	28	26	25	23	21	19	17	15	13	10	6	3	−1

Topographic Map of Orr Mountain

(adapted from a USGS map for Bray, California)

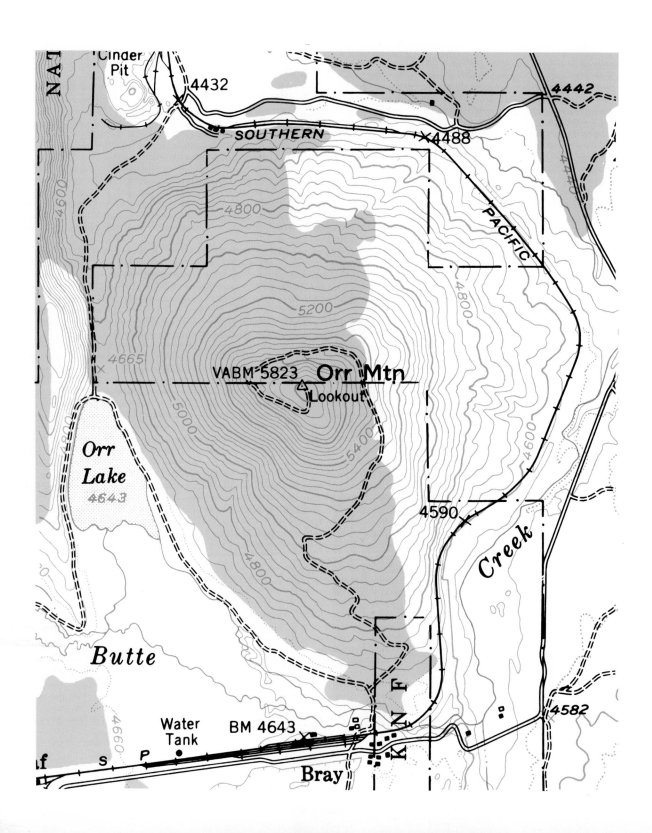

Topographic Map of Odell Butte

(adapted from USGS maps for Crescent Lake, Oregon, and Odell Butte, Oregon)

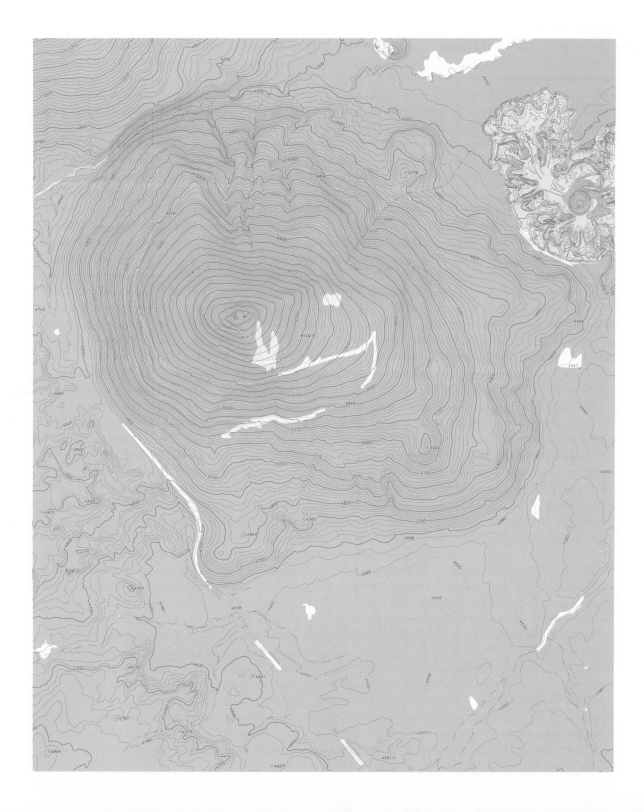

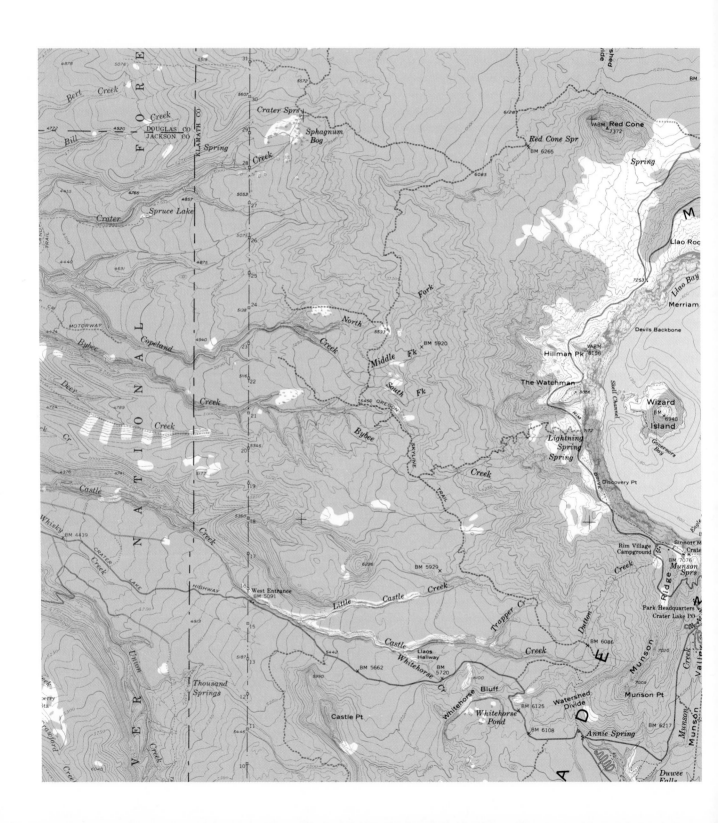

Topographic Map of Crater Lake

(adapted from a USGS map for Crater Lake National Park and Vicinity, Oregon)

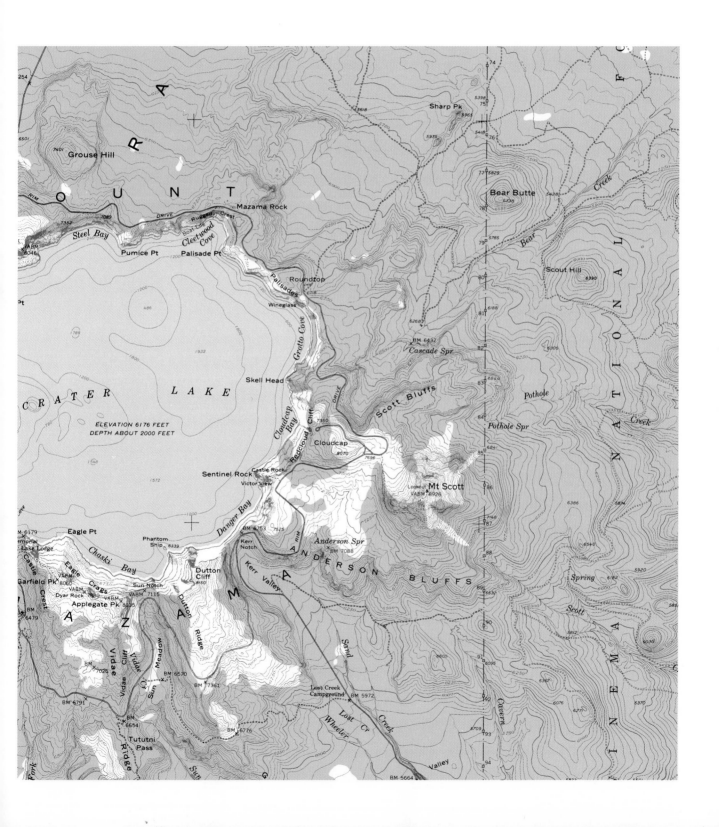

Seismographic Records of a Hypothetical Earthquake

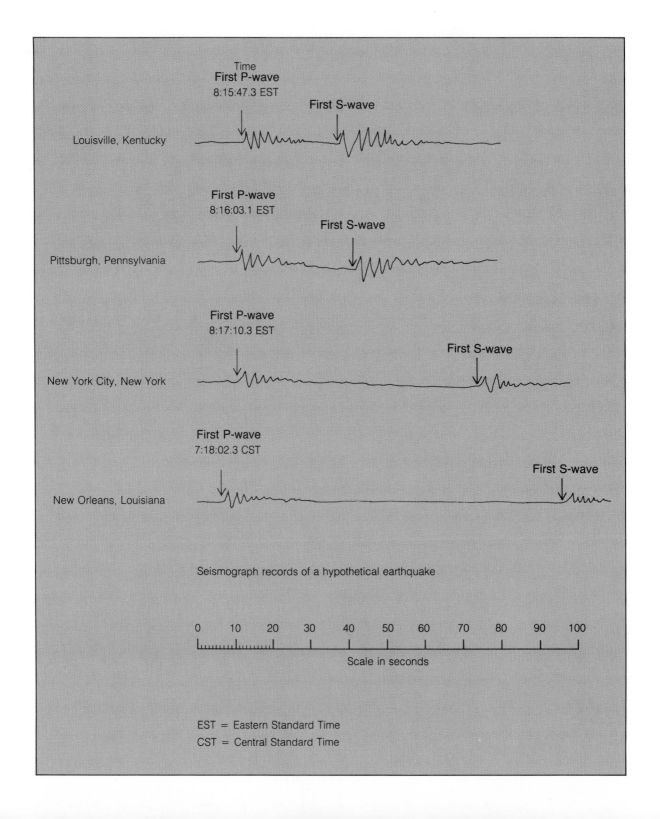

Seismograph records of a hypothetical earthquake

P-Wave Arrival Time for a Hypothetical Earthquake

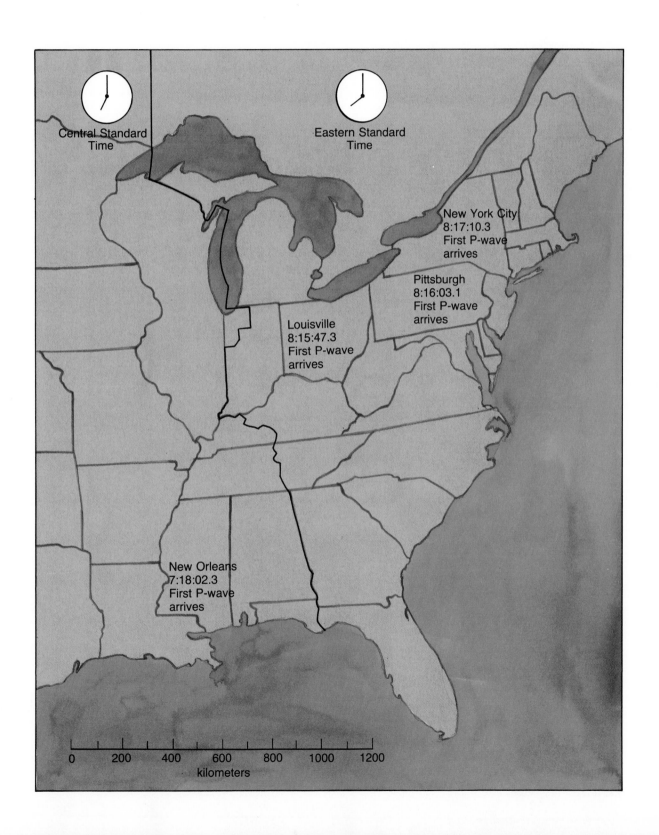

Central Standard Time

Eastern Standard Time

New York City
8:17:10.3
First P-wave
arrives

Pittsburgh
8:16:03.1
First P-wave
arrives

Louisville
8:15:47.3
First P-wave
arrives

New Orleans
7:18:02.3
First P-wave
arrives

0   200   400   600   800   1000   1200

kilometers

Glossary
Pronunciation Key

A simple, phonetic pronunciation is given for words that may be unfamiliar or hard to pronounce. (ad′-ee-uh-BAT′-ik), for example, indicates how to say the word *adiabatic*.

Capital letters followed by an accent mark indicate the syllable that receives the heaviest stress (*bat* in the word *adiabatic*). An accent mark following a lowercase syllable (the first syllable in the representation for *adiabatic*) indicates a syllable that receives a secondary stress.

Most of the time, the phonetic pronunciations can be interpreted without referring to the following key, which gives the sound of letters that are commonly used for more than one sound.

Pronunciation Key

a	c**a**t	i	h**i**m	oy	b**oy**
ah	f**a**ther	ī	k**ī**te	s	**s**o
ar	c**ar**	j	**j**am	sh	**sh**ine
ay	s**ay**	ng	si**ng**	th	**th**ick
e, eh	h**e**n	o	fr**o**g	ŦH	**th**en
ee	m**ee**t	ō	h**o**le	u, uh	s**u**n
eer	d**eer**	oo	m**oo**n	z	**z**ebra
ew	n**ew**	or	f**or**	zh	plea**s**ure
g	**g**rass	ow	n**ow**		

Glossary

abrasion (uh-BRAY'-zhin) The physical weathering process in which particles rub and scrape and hit against each other. (p. 446)

absolute age Age expressed in years. (p. 542)

absolute magnitude The apparent brightness that a star would have if it were 32.6 light years from the earth. (p. 199)

abyssal plain (uh-BIS'-ul) A large flat area of the deep sea floor, formed by sediment flows that spill off the continental margins. (p. 379)

acid rain Pollutants combined with moisture in the air, coming to earth as rainfall. (p. 610)

adhesion (ad-HEE'-zhin) The attraction of water molecules to other kinds of molecules. (p. 354)

adiabatic change (ad'-ee-uh-BAT'-ik) A change in temperature that occurs solely because of the expansion or compression of a material and not because of any heat exchange between different materials. (p. 320)

air mass A large body of air that has about the same amount of moisture and about the same temperature throughout. (p. 287)

air pollution An atmospheric condition in which toxic chemicals are in the air. Common pollutants include carbon monoxide, sulfur dioxide, oxides of nitrogen, and fine particles of ash. (p. 610)

altitude (AL'-tuh-tood') The distance in degrees of a star above the horizon. (p. 121)

amino acid (uh-MEE'-no AS'-id) A compound that forms within living organisms and that can be used for age determination of certain earth materials. (p. 550)

anticline (AN'-ti-klīn') An upward-arching fold in rocks. (p. 486)

aphotic zone (a'-FOT'-ik ZŌN) The part of the ocean that is in total darkness. (p. 397)

apogee (AP'-uh-jee') The point of the moon's elliptical orbit farthest from the earth. (p. 156)

apparent magnitude The measure of a star's brightness as it appears from the earth, as seen by the naked eye. (p. 197)

apparent solar time Time as determined by using the actual position of the sun. (p. 138)

aquifer (A'-kwuh-fer) A layer of permeable rock through which water travels. (p. 359)

artesian spring (ar-TEE'-zhin) A natural flow of water from an artesian formation. (p. 360)

artesian system (ar-TEE'-zhin) A combination of rock layers in which water passes downward through a permeable rock layer that is between two layers of impermeable rock. (p. 359)

assumption (uh-SUM'-shin) The taking for granted that certain processes and scientific laws are constant through time and place, such as the laws of chemistry and physics. (p. 526)

asteroid (AS'-ter-oid) Fragments of rocky objects that revolve around the sun and that are smaller than planets. (p. 182)

asthenosphere (as-THEN'-uh-sfir) The layer of the earth immediately below the lithosphere. The asthenosphere includes the low-velocity zone. (p. 504)

astronomical unit (as'-truh-NOM'-i-k'l) The distance between the earth and the sun (93 million mi; 149.67 million km), often used as a standard of comparison for measuring distances within the solar system. (p. 184)

astronomy (uh-STRON'-uh-mee) The science that is concerned with the size, composition, structure, and movement of all objects in space. (p. 18)

atmosphere (AT'-muh-sfir') The blanket of air and other materials that completely covers the earth's lithosphere and hydrosphere; mainly nitrogen (4/5) and oxygen (1/5). (p. 17)

atmospheric pressure (at'-mus-FER'-ik PRESH'-er) The pressure that the atmosphere, which has mass, exerts against the surface of the earth; also called barometric pressure. (p. 255)

atom (AT'-um) The smallest complete part of an element which contains all the properties of that element. (p. 63)

atomic energy (uh-TOM'-ik) Energy that is derived from the atoms of certain earth materials; also called nuclear energy. (p. 596)

atomic mass The average mass of each element. This number is given in atomic mass units, or amu. One amu is approximately equal to the mass of one proton. (p. 72)

atomic number The number of protons in one atom of a particular element. In the modern periodic table, elements are arranged in order of atomic number. (p. 66)

aurora (uh-ROR'-uh) A natural light show that is caused by the effects of solar wind in the earth's upper atmosphere. (p. 195)

axis (AK'-sis) An imaginary line around which the earth appears to be turning. (p. 130)

azimuth (AZ'-uh-muth) The distance of a star in degrees on the horizon as measured in a clockwise direction from true north. (p. 123)

barometer (buh-ROM'-uh-ter) The basic instrument for measuring atmospheric pressure. (p. 256)

base level The limit to the downward erosion of a river. It is established by the level of the body of water into which the river flows. (p. 442)

batholith (BATH'-uh-lith) A huge intrusion of igneous rock exposed at the earth's surface. (p. 97)

bedrock A layer of solid rock that is under every soil. (p. 431)

Big Bang The theory that the universe was formed from a fireball of matter which exploded. As the material expanded, it cooled. Then galaxies formed, with their billions of stars. (p. 219)

Big Crunch An event that may occur when gravity stops the expansion of the universe. The universe will then begin to contract until it all rapidly comes together. (p. 222)

biosphere (BI'-uh-sfir) The region near the earth's surface where all life is found. (p. 17)

black hole A very dense object with such strong gravitational force that not even light can escape from it. (p. 204)

blizzard A thunderstorm occurring at temperatures below freezing. Blizzards are characterized by heavy snow and strong winds. (p. 311)

caldera (kal-DIR'-uh) A large circular depression that forms when a volcanic mountaintop collapses into the magma chamber beneath the mountain. (p. 472)

capillary action (KAP'-uh-ler'-ee) The upward movement of water in soil due to adhesion and cohesion. (p. 355)

capillary fringe (KAP'-uh-ler'-ee) An area just above the water table that receives its moisture from the zone of saturation by capillary action. (p. 355)

celestial sphere (suh-LES'-chul SFIR) The imaginary sphere on which all objects in the sky appear to be located. (p. 117)

Cepheid variable (SEF'-ee-id) or (SEE'-fee-id) A star that gets brighter and dimmer at regular intervals. (p. 202)

chemical bond A force that holds two atoms together in a compound. (p. 73)

chemical formula A shorthand method used to show the kinds of atoms that make up a compound and their proportions. p. 73)

chemically formed rock A sedimentary rock formed when minerals that are dissolved in water create interlocking crystals. Chemical rock formation often occurs as the water evaporates, leaving the crystals. (p. 100)

chemical property (KEM'-uh-kul PROP'-er-tee) A feature of the way one substance reacts with another substance. The fact that silver tarnishes is a chemical property of silver. Compare physical property. (p. 9)

chemical symbol An abbreviated way of writing an element's name. For example, the chemical symbol of cobalt is Co. (p. 67)

chemical weathering (KEM'-uh-kul) A kind of weathering in which different substances are formed. (p. 426)

chromosphere (KRŌ'-muh-sfir') A thin layer that marks the change between the photosphere and the corona. (p. 195)

cinder cone A small volcanic mountain with steep sides. (p. 477)

circumference (ser-KUM'-fer-ins) The distance around a circular object. (p. 33)

cirrus cloud (SIR'-us) Wispy, feathery looking cloud that is so thin sunlight can pass through it. (p. 278)

classifying The grouping of similar events or objects, based upon observed properties or characteristics. (p. 7)

clastic rock Sedimentary rock that is formed from particles of minerals and rock. (p. 99)

cleavage (KLEE'-vij) The ability of a mineral to break into smooth, parallel surfaces. (p. 88)

climate (KLI'-mit) The weather patterns that occur in one place over a period of a year or longer. Climate is determined primarily by average amounts of precipitation and average temperatures. (p. 316)

climate graph A graph that indicates average monthly temperature and precipitation conditions for twelve months at a particular location. (p. 325)

cloud Droplets of water that condense on tiny particles of dust and other solid matter in the sky above the earth's surface when the air is cooled below its dew point. (p. 277)

coal A solid fossil fuel. (p. 590)

cohesion (ko-HEE'-zhin) The attraction of one molecule to another molecule of the same kind. (p. 355)

cold front A weather front that forms when a cold air mass pushes a warm air mass ahead of it. (p. 290)

coma The cloud of dust and gas surrounding the nucleus of a comet, formed by the outer surface of the comet vaporizing. (p. 190)

comet (KOM'-it) An object with a long elliptical orbit that forms a long glowing tail as it approaches the sun. (p. 190)

compass (KUM′-pis) An instrument with a needle that points to the North Magnetic Pole. (p. 49)

composite cone (kum-POZ′-it) A volcanic mountain built of alternate layers of lava flows and volcanic cinders and ashes. (p. 479)

compound A substance that is made up of two or more elements that are joined together in fixed proportions. (p. 60)

compressional stress A form of stress in which matter is pushed together. (p. 487)

condensation (kon-den-SAY′-shin) The changing of a vapor into a liquid. (p. 264)

condense (kun-DENS′) To change from a gas to a liquid. (p. 337)

conduction (kun-DUK′-shin) The movement of energy through a material without the material itself moving. (p. 235)

constellation (kon′-stuh-LAY′-shin) A group of stars in which some people have imagined the outline of a person or animal. (p. 118)

continental air mass An air mass that forms over dry land. (p. 287)

continental climate A climate influenced mainly by continental air masses; characterized by dry air. (p. 318)

continental crust Crustal rock that is granitic and that is between 20 and 60 km thick. (p. 503)

continental glacier An ice sheet that flows outward from its thick center over wide regions of a landscape. (p. 444)

continental margin The region of the ocean bottom near the land areas. The continental margin contains most of the sediment eroded from the land and separates a continent from the deep sea floor. (p. 374)

contour interval (KON′-toor IN′-ter-vul) The difference in elevation between any two contour lines on a topographic map. (p. 46)

contour line (KON′-toor) A line that connects places that have the same elevation, indicating at the same time the shapes of land features at various elevations. (p. 45)

convection (kun-VEK′-shin) The movement of energy through a material because of some movement within the material. (p. 235)

convection current The movement of a fluid caused by unequal densities of portions of the fluid that have been heated unequally. (p. 239)

core The innermost layers of the earth, consisting of both the outer core and the inner core. (p. 16)

Coriolis effect (kor′-ee-Ō′-lis) The apparent deflection of an object that is traveling above the earth's surface; it is caused by differences in rotational speeds on the earth's surface. (p. 135)

corona (kuh-RŌ′-nuh) The outermost part of the sun's atmosphere. (p. 195)

crater Hole in the moon's or a planet's surface caused by the impact of material from space. (p. 157).

crest The highest point of a wave. (p. 403)

crust The thin, outermost layer of the earth. (p. 16)

crystal The solid shape produced when mineral grains have complete freedom to form in any direction. (p. 84)

crystalline solid (KRIS′-tuh-lin) A solid substance whose atoms are locked together into fixed patterns that repeat in three dimensions—height, width, and depth or thickness. All minerals are crystalline solids. (p. 83)

cumulonimbus cloud (kyoom′-yuh-lo-NIM′-bus) A massive vertical cloud containing huge amounts of moisture; they are associated with thunderstorms. (p. 309)

cumulus cloud (KYOOM′-yuh-lis) Puffy cloud that looks like a large cotton ball. (p. 277)

data (DĀT′-uh) or (DAT′-uh) A collection of observations. (p. 7)

daylight-saving time An adjusted time during which clocks are one hour ahead of standard time to provide an hour more of daylight at the end of a working day. (p. 140)

declination (DEK′-luh-NAY′-shun) The position of objects north or south of the celestial equator. Declination is the celestial equivalent of latitude and is measured in degrees, minutes, and seconds. (p. 127)

deflect (di-FLEKT′) Force from a straight line of travel. (p. 133)

density The mass of 1 cm^3 of a material. (p. 31)

deposition (dep′-uh-ZISH′-un) or (dee′-puh-ZISH′-un) The process whereby particles and fragments of earth materials are deposited, or are laid down, by an agent of erosion. (p. 454)

derived unit A unit of measure that is derived from two or more base units. (p. 28)

desert Any area where the total amount of precipitation is less than 10 inches (254 mm) per year. A desert can even be an area on the surface of the ocean. (p. 322)

dew Droplets of water that condense on objects on the earth's surface when night air is cooled below its dew-point temperature. (p. 274)

dew-point temperature The temperature to which air must be cooled to reach its saturation point. Dew-point temperature is the same as saturation temperature. (p. 273)

dike A layer of igneous rock that is younger than and at an angle to the other rock layers in a formation. (p. 539)

direct observation Information that is received by means of one or more of the five senses. (p. 5)

discontinuity (dis'-kan-tuh-NOO'-uh-tee) A boundary between two divisions of the earth's interior. Discontinuity is indicated by sharp changes in earthquake wave velocity. (p. 503)

disphotic zone (dis'-FŌT'-ik ZŌN) A zone of reduced light in the ocean; between 200 m and 1000 m below the surface. (p. 397)

divide The highest land that separates the direction in which water will run off the earth's surface. (p. 343)

Doppler effect (DOP'-ler) Changes in sound waves or light waves as one object moves toward or away from another object. (p. 151)

drumlin A smoothly rounded teardrop-shaped hill of glacial till. (p. 463)

earthquake A motion, trembling, or vibration of the earth; caused by the release of stress that has been slowly building up in the earth's crust. (p. 494)

echo sounding A method of using noise (pings) to measure the depth of the ocean. (p. 373)

electromagnetic spectrum (i-lek'-tro-mag-NET'-ik SPEK'-trum) The energy waves of all the different wavelengths of energy from the sun. (p. 234)

electromagnetic wave (i-lek'-tro-mag-NET'-ik) Energy waves similar to the waves produced by an electromagnet; how the sun's energy travels. (p. 233)

electron (ih-LEK'-tron) A rapidly moving particle that surrounds the nucleus in clouds. It is smaller than both a proton and a neutron; it has a negative electrical charge. (p. 64)

element (EL'-uh-mint) A substance that contains only one kind of atom. (p. 62)

elevation (el'-uh-VAY'-shun) Height above sea level. (p. 45)

ellipse (i-LIPS') A smooth, closed curve that is not a perfect circle. (p. 156)

end moraine (muh-RAYN') A deposit formed at the foot of a glacier. (p. 461)

energy (EN'-er-jee) The ability to cause change in matter. (p. 59)

epicenter (EP'-uh-sen'-ter) The point on the earth's surface directly above the focus. (p. 495)

equator (i-KWAYT'-er) An imaginary line that circles the earth halfway between the North and South Poles, at zero degrees latitude. (p. 37)

equinox (EE'-kwuh-noks') The time of the year when the sun crosses the equator on its way to the Tropic of Cancer or the Tropic of Capricorn. (p. 151)

era (IR'-uh) or (AIR'-uh) One of the four large units of geologic time. (p. 554)

erosion (i-RŌ'-zhin) The transporting of the products of weathering. (p. 438)

erratics (i-RAT'-iks) Large water-worn boulders that have been deposited by a glacier. (p. 444)

evaporate (i-VAP'-uh-rayt') To change from a liquid to a gas. (p. 337)

evaporation (i-vap-er-AY'-shin) The changing of a substance from a liquid into a vapor. (p. 264)

evolve (i-VOLV') To undergo changes over a period of time. (p. 535)

extinct (ik-STINGKT') Died out without leaving any descendants. (p. 570)

fault A break or fracture in rocks along which the rocks move. (p. 491)

fission (FISH'-in) Atomic energy that is produced when certain large, unstable atoms are made to split apart to form atoms of a different element. (p. 596)

fissure (FISH'-er) A long crack in the ground from which lava flows. (p. 479)

flood plain The level area between the banks of a river and the foot of the mountains. (p. 441)

fluid (FLOO'-id) Any material that can move and change shape without separation. (p. 238)

focus (FŌ'-kis) The point of origin of an earthquake. (p. 494)

fog Droplets of water that condense on tiny particles of dust and other solid matter near the earth's surface when the air is cooled below its dew point. (p. 275)

folded rock Rock that has been bent by high confining pressure. (p. 486)

footwall The mass of rock that is below a fault. (p. 491)

formation A unit of rocks grouped together because

of common properties that are widespread enough to be easily recognized and mapped. (p. 538)

fossil The skeletal remains or impressions of previously living life forms in rock that formed before written history. (p. 532)

fossil fuels Fuels formed from the remains of plants and animals that died long ago; fossil fuels include oil, coal, and natural gas. (p. 589)

fossil record The record of former life forms as preserved in the earth's rocks. (p. 559)

fracture (FRAK′-cher) A crack that develops when rocks are folded. (p. 487)

freeze To change from a liquid to a solid. (p. 337)

freezing point The temperature at which a liquid freezes. (p. 391)

front The boundary between two air masses. (p. 290)

frost Ice crystals that form on objects on the earth's surface when the dew-point temperature of the air is below 0°C and the air is cooled below its dew point. (p. 274)

fumarole (FYOO′-muh-rōl′) A volcanic vent or opening that releases gases and smoke. (p. 476)

fusion (FYOO′-zhin) Atomic energy that is produced when atoms of an element are fused together to form atoms of a different element. (p. 194)

galaxy (GAL′-ik-see) A large system of stars that is held together by gravitational attraction. (p. 213)

gas Matter that has neither a definite shape nor a definite volume. (p. 60)

geologic time (jee-uh-LOJ′-ik) The age of the earth as revealed in its rocks; expressed in eras and large periods of time rather than in years. (p. 552)

geology (jee-OL′-uh-jee) The science that is concerned with the structure of the earth's lithosphere, its composition, and what causes it to change. (p. 18)

geothermal energy (jee′-o-THER′-mul) Energy powered by heat from deep within the earth's crust. (p. 595)

geyser (GĪ′-zer) The eruption from the ground of water and steam that have been heated by hot magma or hot igneous rocks in the earth's crust. (p. 360)

glacial lobe (GLAY′-shul) A tongue-like mass of ice that sticks out from the main mass of a glacier. (p. 461)

glacier (GLAY′-sher) A moving mass of ice and snow. (p. 340)

globe A ball-shaped physical model of the earth. (p. 36)

globular cluster (GLAHB′-yuh-luhr) A ball of 10 000 to 100 000 or more stars. Globular clusters are found surrounding the center of the Milky Way. (p. 207)

greenhouse effect The warming of the atmosphere that takes place because gases like carbon dioxide in the atmosphere are able to absorb energy in the wavelengths in which it is radiated from the earth. (p. 178)

Greenwich mean time (GREN′-ich) The mean solar time on the prime meridian; now called universal coordinated time. (p. 140)

ground water Water that has infiltrated the earth's surface. (p. 354)

gyre (JĪR) A closed system of rotating ocean currents. (p. 412)

hachures (huh-SHOORZ′) or (HASH′-oorz) Short lines drawn from a contour line to indicate direction of slope. (p. 46)

hail Layered formations of ice that build up as they are tossed through different layers of air within tall clouds; can become larger than golf balls before they finally fall to the earth's surface. (p. 280)

half-life The time it takes for one half of a radioactive material to decay. (p. 547)

hanging wall The mass of rock that is above a fault. (p. 491)

heat of fusion (FYOO′-zhin) The amount of heat needed for 1 g of a solid substance to melt and become a liquid. (p. 265)

heat of vaporization (vay′-per-uh-ZAY′-shin) The amount of heat needed for 1 g of a substance to become a vapor. (p. 264)

heft A rough-estimate weight test that compares the weight of a mineral sample to an equal-size sample of quartz. (p. 91)

Hertzsprung-Russell diagram A chart of the relationship between colors and absolute magnitudes of stars. (p. 205)

high-pressure center The center of an area of high atmospheric pressure; indicated by the letter H or the word High on a pressure map. (p. 261)

high tide When the waterline of a body of water reaches its highest point. (p. 409)

horizon (huh-RĪ′-zun) The point where, to an observer, the earth and sky appear to meet. (p. 117)

humidity (hyoo-MID′-uh-tee) The amount of moisture that is in the air. (p. 266)

humus (HYOO'-mis)   An organic substance rich in materials that plants need for growth. (p. 431)

hurricane (her'-uh-KAYN')   A very large circular storm with wind speeds of at least 64 knots; accompanied by dense clouds and heavy rain. (p. 312)

hydroelectric energy (hī'-dro-uh-LEK'-trik)   Electricity produced by generators powered by moving water. (p. 593)

hydrology (hī-DROL'-uh-jee)   The science that is concerned with the earth's entire hydrosphere, including the water below the earth's surface and the water in the earth's atmosphere. (p. 18)

hydrosphere (HĪ'-druh-sfir)   All the water found on the earth, including the water that is below the ground and the water that is found in the atmosphere. (p. 17)

hypothesis (hī-POTH'-uh-sis)   A possible answer to a question or a possible solution to a problem, based on observations. The plural form of hypothesis is hypotheses. (p. 11)

icebergs   Floating masses of ice that broke off freshwater glaciers. (p. 394)

igneous rock (IG'-nee-is)   Rock that is formed from hot melted materials. (p. 96)

impermeable (im-PER'-mee-uh-bul)   Allowing no water to pass through. (p. 354)

impurities (im-PYOOR'-uh-teez)   Atoms of elements other than the key elements of a mineral. (p. 86)

incinerate (in-SIN'-uh-rayt')   To burn up completely. (p. 608)

inclination (in'-kluh-NAY'-shin)   The tilt of the earth's axis. (p. 146)

index fossil   A guide fossil that geologists can use to determine the age of rock layers relative to other rock layers. (p. 533)

indirect observation   An observation that requires the use of an instrument. (p. 6)

inference (IN'-fer-ins)   An interpretation of observations. (p. 9)

infiltration (in'-fil-TRAY'-shin)   The process by which water sinks into porous earth materials like soil or porous rock. (p. 351)

inner core   The solid, innermost layer of the earth. (p. 16)

inorganic (in-or-GAN'-ik)   Not organic; formed, for the most part, without the help of plants and animals. (p. 83)

instrument   A scientific invention that extends the five senses by such means as magnifying, record-

ing, and providing standard units of measurement. (p. 6)

International Date Line   An imaginary line agreed upon as the starting point for a day on the earth; the 180th meridian. (p. 140)

ion   An electrically charged atom that has either lost or gained electrons. (p. 75)

island arc   A chain of volcanic islands, usually curved, that separates a marginal sea from a major ocean. (p. 371)

isobar (Ī'so-bar)   A line that connects points on the earth's surface having the same atmospheric pressure. (p. 259)

isotope (Ī'-suh-tōp)   Any of the atoms of the same element with different numbers of neutrons, and hence different masses. (p. 72)

kettle lake   A lake that formed when a large block of buried glacial ice melted. (p. 464)

laccolith (LAK'-uh-lith)   A large igneous formation that pushes overlying rocks into an arch. (p. 97)

lake   A body of water that collects in a hole or depression in the earth's surface; larger and deeper than a pond. (p. 340)

landfill   A large pit in the ground which is filled with layer upon layer of garbage. (p. 611)

lateral eruption (LAT'-er-ul i-RUP'-shin)   An eruption through a weakened side of a volcano. (p. 474)

latitude (LAT'-uh-tood')   The distance that any point is north or south of the equator. (p. 37)

lava (LAH'-vuh) or (LAV'-uh)   What magma is called after it reaches the surface of the earth; molten rock on the surface of the earth. (p. 97)

law of gravitation (grav'-uh-TAY'-shin)   A scientific law, introduced by Isaac Newton, that states that there is a force of attraction between every object in the universe. (p. 175)

law of inertia (in-ER'-shuh)   A scientific law, introduced by Isaac Newton, that states that a body at rest will remain at rest and a body in motion will keep moving in the same direction unless acted upon by some outside force. (p. 175)

leaching (LĒCH'-ing)   The removal of minerals in the topsoil layer by water that is filtering down through the soil. (p. 431)

leap year   The year in every four years in which an extra day is added to February. (p. 152)

legend   A key that explains what symbols on a map represent. (p. 43)

levee (LEV'-ee)   A natural embankment formed on

both sides of a river by coarser sediments that settle out of flood waters as they first move over the banks of the river. (p. 441)

life form The body form that characterizes a fully grown organism. (p. 559)

lightning A flash of light produced when static electrical charges jump from one part of a cloud to another or from a cloud to the ground. (p. 310)

light-year The distance that light travels in one year. (p. 210)

liquid Matter that has a definite volume but takes the shape of the container it is in. (p. 60)

lithosphere (LITH′-uh-sfir) The solid part of the earth that is made up of rock and soil; the earth's crust plus part of the upper mantle; relatively cool and rigid. (p. 16)

living fossil Fossil of organism that has representatives still living today. (p. 570)

Local Group A cluster that has about 30 galaxies, including the Milky Way and the Andromeda galaxy, the Magellanic Clouds, and NGC 205. (p. 215)

local winds Winds specific to a local area; may blow from any direction. (p. 250)

longitude (LON′-juh-tood′) The distance that any point is east or west of the prime meridian. (p. 37)

low-pressure center The center of an area of low atmospheric pressure; indicated by the letter *L* or the word *Low* on a pressure map. (p. 259)

low tide When the waterline of a body of water reaches its lowest point. (p. 409)

low-velocity zone A zone in the earth's upper mantle that has the ability to slow down both P-waves and S-waves. (p. 503)

lunar (LOO′-ner) Having to do with the moon. (p. 155)

lunar eclipse (LOO′-ner ee-KLIPS′) When the earth's shadow falls on the moon's surface, so that that part of the moon cannot be seen from the earth. (p. 160)

luster The way that a mineral reflects the light; can be metallic, glassy, pearly, or dull. (p. 69)

magma (MAG′-muh) Liquid rock melt that is found in some places beneath the earth's surface. (p. 476)

magnetic declination (mag-NET′-ik dek′-luh-NAY′-shun) The difference between true north and magnetic north; also called magnetic variation. (p. 50)

magnetic north The direction toward the North Magnetic Pole from any place on the earth; the di-

rection in which a compass needle points. Compare with true north. (p. 49)

magnitude (MAG′-nuh-tood′) A classification of a star according to its apparent brightness. (p. 197)

mantle A layer of earth that extends from the bottom of the crust to the earth's core. (p. 16)

map A representation, on a flat surface, of all or part of the earth's surface. (p. 39)

map projection An attempt to represent the earth's curved surface on a flat surface. (p. 39)

map relief The difference in elevation between the highest and lowest points on a map, represented by contour lines. (p. 46)

marginal sea A smaller body of salt water found along the margin of a major ocean. (p. 370)

maria (MAR′-ee-uh) The large, dark, relatively level areas on the moon's surface. (p. 157)

marine climate (muh-REEN′) A climate influenced mainly by maritime air masses, characterized by abundant precipitation; also called an oceanic climate. (p. 317)

maritime air mass (MAIR′-uh-tīm′) An air mass that forms over an ocean. (p. 287)

mass The amount of material in something. Mass is the same everywhere and does not vary with gravity. Compare with *weight.* (p. 26)

matter Anything that takes up space and has mass. (p. 59)

meander (mee-AN′-der) Curve or bend in a stream or river. (p. 442)

mean solar time Time that is based on the average length of a day, from noon to noon. (p. 138)

Mercalli scale (mer-KAL′-ee) A system of twelve steps that are used to describe the amount of damage caused by an earthquake. (p. 497)

meridian (muh-RID′-ee-in) A north-south line that extends between the North and South Poles and that crosses the equator at a right angle. (p. 37)

mesosphere (MES′-uh-sfir) or (MEZ′-uh-sfir) The layer of the earth immediately below the asthenosphere. It is very hot, under very high pressure, and moderately rigid. (p. 504)

metamorphic rock (met′-uh-MOR′-fik) Rock that is formed when minerals and rocks are changed by very great heat and pressure which changes the crystal structure. (p. 96)

metamorphosis (met′-uh-MOR′-fuh-sis) A change in an organism from one stage of development to another. (p. 100)

meteor (MEET′-ee-uhr) A meteoroid that has collided with the earth's atmosphere, burning up because of friction. (p. 183)

meteorite (MEET'-ee-uh-rīt)   Meteors that strike a planet or other object. (p. 183)

meteoroid (MEET'-ee-uh-roid)   A relatively small particle of stone and/or iron that drifts through space. When meteoroids strike the moon, they blast out craters. (p. 162)

meteorology (meet'-ee-uh-ROL'-uh-jee)   The science that is concerned with the composition and structure of the earth's atmosphere and with the many changes that are constantly taking place in the atmosphere. (p. 18)

meter   A standard unit for measuring length, based originally on dividing the distance between the North Pole and the equator into small, equal units. (p. 23)

mid-ocean ridge   A system of tall, rugged, submerged mountains that extends down the middle of the ocean basins and forms their single most dominant feature. (p. 379)

Milky Way Galaxy   The galaxy in which the earth's solar system is located, in which our sun is but one star out of about 100 billion stars. (p. 213)

millibar (MIL'-uh-bar)   The unit of atmospheric pressure measurement most commonly used on weather maps. (p. 257)

mine   The place from which metal ore is removed from the earth. (p. 586)

mineral (MIN'-er-ul)   A compound that is found as a natural solid within the earth's crust. All minerals are 1) natural, 2) inorganic, 3) crystalline solids, and 4) made up of key elements. (p. 81)

mineral composition   The minerals that make up a given rock. (p. 103)

Mohorovicic discontinuity or **Moho**   The boundary between the earth's outermost layer and the mantle. (p. 16)

molecule (MOL'-uh-kewl)   A unit of matter that is formed by atoms sharing their electrons. (p. 74)

moraine (muh-RAYN') or (maw-RAYN')   The deposit of material made along its margins by an advancing or retreating glacier. (p. 461)

nadir (NAY'-dur)   The point of the celestial sphere directly below the observer's feet. (p. 123)

natural gas   A fossil fuel that is a gas rather than a liquid or a solid. (p. 381)

nebula (NEB'-yuh-luh)   A huge cloud of dust and gases in space. (p. 196)

neutron (NOO'-tron)   A neutral particle that is one of the two kinds of particles (the other is the proton) that make up the nucleus of an atom. (p. 64)

neutron star   An incredibly dense mass of neutrons formed by the inward collapse of matter after a supernova. (p. 204)

nonsilicate minerals (non-SIL'-uh-kit)   All of the minerals that are not silicates. (p. 86)

normal fault   A fault in which the hanging wall has moved down with respect to the footwall. (p. 491)

North Geographic Pole   The point in the Northern Hemisphere where all the meridians, or lines of longitude, meet. Compare *North Magnetic Pole.* (p. 49)

North Magnetic Pole   The North Pole that a compass needle points toward. It is about 1600 km from the North Geographic Pole. (p. 49)

nuclear fusion (NOO'-klee-er FYOO'-zhin)   The joining together of lightweight nuclei into a nucleus with greater mass. (p. 194)

nucleus (NOO'-klee-us)   The central part of an atom. The nucleus has an overall positive charge because of the protons it contains. (p. 64)

occluded front (uh-KLOO'-did)   A weather front that forms when a cold front advances on and lifts a warm front completely off the ground. (p. 293)

ocean   The entire body of salt water that covers much of the earth's surface; also, any of its major geographical divisions. (p. 369)

ocean basin   The low-lying earth formation that contains the ocean's water. It consists mainly of dense basaltic crustal rock. (p. 374)

oceanic crust (o'-shee-AN'-ik)   Crustal rock that is basaltic, denser than granite, and about 5 km thick. (p. 503)

oceanography (o'-shuh-NOG'-ruh-fee)   The science that is concerned with the earth's oceans and their boundaries. (p. 18)

offshore breeze   A breeze that blows away from the shore and out over the sea. (p. 255)

onshore breeze   A breeze that blows onto the shore from out over the sea. (p. 254)

Oort cloud   A huge cloud of millions of comet nuclei that astronomers think surrounds the solar system. Each comet, it is believed, begins its sunward journey there. (p. 191)

orbit   The path that an object follows as it travels around another object. (p. 142)

ore   Any mineral or rock from which a needed substance can be removed cheaply enough and easily enough. (p. 585)

organic rock Sedimentary rock that is formed from the remains of plants and animals. (p. 100)

outer core The liquid layer of the earth surrounding the inner core. (p. 16)

outwash plain A gently sloping area of deposition at the foot of a glacier. (p. 461)

oxbow lake (OKS'-bō) A lake that forms when sediment fills in both ends of a cut-off meander. (p. 442)

oxygen-carbon dioxide cycle (OKS'-uh-jin KAR'-bin dī-OK'-sīd SĪ'-kul) The cycling of oxygen and carbon dioxide that takes place in the atmosphere owing to the food-making process of plants, which use carbon dioxide and produce oxygen; also, the respiration of animals and the burning of fuels, which use oxygen and produce carbon dioxide. (p. 242)

P-Wave A primary wave; specifically, a longitudinal earthquake wave. (p. 495)

pack ice Sea ice that has been broken and then refrozen into jagged pressure ridges. (p. 393)

paleontologist (pay'-lee-un-TOL'-uh-jist) A scientist who reconstructs prehistoric life from plant and animal fossils. (p. 560)

parallax (PAIR'-uh-laks) The difference in the direction of the line of sight to an object from two different places. (p. 209)

parallax angle The angle that results when an object is viewed from two different locations. It can be used to calculate distances to stars. (p. 209)

parallel (PAIR'-uh-lel') An east-west line or ring that circles the earth parallel to the equator. (p. 37)

penumbra (pi-NUM'-bruh) The lighter part of a shadow. (p. 161)

perigee (PER'-uh-jee') The point in the moon's elliptical orbit when the moon is closest to the earth. (p. 156)

periodic table A chart that organizes the elements according to the number of protons contained by each atom of the element. (p. 66)

permeability (per-mee-uh-BIL'-uh-tee) The ease with which water flows through a material. (p. 352)

petrochemicals (pet'-ro-KEM'-uh-kulz) Chemical products made from petroleum. (p. 590)

petroleum (puh-TRŌ'-lee-um) A liquid fossil fuel. (p. 589)

petrology (puh-TROL'-uh-jee) The part of geology that specializes in rocks. (p. 18)

phases of the moon (FAY'-ziz) Recurring changes in the moon's appearance. (p. 159)

photic zone (FŌT'-ik) The uppermost zone of the open ocean; the zone of most light. (p. 396)

photosphere (FŌT'-uh-sfir') The surface of the sun. (p. 194)

physical property (FIZ'-uh-kul PROP'-er-tee) A feature of a substance itself. Features like color and softness are physical properties. Compare *chemical property*. (p. 9)

physical weathering (FIZ'-uh-kul) A kind of weathering in which a material is changed only in size, becoming smaller as a result of the weathering action. (p. 425)

plastic deformation When rocks bend, flow, and deform like modeling clay, owing to stresses and high confining pressures in the earth. (p. 486)

plateau basalts (pla-TO' buh-SAWLTS') Thick buildups of horizontal layers of basalt on continents that form as a result of lava flows from fissures. (p. 479)

plate tectonic theory (tek-TON'-ik) A theory that views the earth's surface as composed of slow-moving rigid plates that grow larger, collide, or move past each other with a shearing motion. (p. 508)

polar air mass An air mass that forms near the North or South Pole. (p. 287)

polar climate (PŌ'-ler) A climate influenced mainly by polar air masses. It is characterized by the coldest temperatures. (p. 316)

Polaris (pō-LAIR'-is) The North Star. (p. 123)

pond A body of water that is smaller and shallower than a lake. (p. 342)

pore spaces Open spaces between particles of sand or soil. (p. 352)

porosity (por-OS'-uh-tee) The total volume of the pore spaces in a certain volume of material. (p. 352)

porphyritic rock Igneous rocks that form at shallow depths in the earth's crust. They may cool at alternately slow and fast rates, a process that produces both large and small crystals. (p. 97)

precipitation (pri-sip'-uh-TAY'-shin) Any form of water that falls to the surface of the earth from the atmosphere. (p. 279)

pressure map A map that indicates atmospheric pressure patterns for an area of the earth's surface. (p. 259)

prevailing westerlies Prevailing winds that blow from a westerly direction. They affect most of the continental United States. (p. 250)

prevailing winds Winds that are part of much larger patterns of air circulation than local winds.

They almost always blow from the same direction and travel farther than local winds. (p. 250)

prime meridian (muh-RID′-ee-in) The meridian that passes through Greenwich, England. (p. 37)

principle (PRIN′-suh-pul) An obvious assumption that has become so widely accepted that it is basic to scientific thinking; also called a law. (p. 527)

principle of faunal succession (FAW′-nul suk-SESH′-in) The scientific principle that assumes that the different forms of animals through the earth's past occurred in a definite order or sequence. (p. 532)

principle of original horizontality (uh-RIJ′-uh-nul hor′-uh-zon-TAL′-uh-tee) The scientific principle that assumes that the sediments forming sedimentary rocks were deposited in layers that were parallel to the earth's horizon. (p. 530)

principle of superposition (soo′-per-puh-ZISH′-in) The scientific principle that states that the oldest rock in any undisturbed sequence of rocks is the rock on the bottom. (p. 529)

proper motion The change of the apparent location of a star. (p. 201)

proton (PRŌ′-ton) A positively charged particle in the nucleus of an atom. (p. 64)

protoplanet The early stage of a planet, when pieces of rock and metal are clumping together to form a large ball. (p. 171)

pulsar (PUL′-sar) A rotating neutron star that gives off pulses of energy (radio waves). (p. 204)

pyroclastic deposits The blobs of molten lava that erupt from volcanoes and cool rapidly. (p. 97)

quasar (KWAY′-sar) or (KWAY′-zar) An object in space that appears to be as large as a very large star but gives off energy comparable to a thousand galaxies. (p. 217)

radial velocity (RAY′-dee-ul vuh-LOS′-uh-tee) The motion of a star in a line toward or away from the earth. (p. 201)

radiation (ray′-dee-AY′-shin) The movement of energy through a material without any aid from the material; also, the movement of energy through empty space. (p. 235)

radioactive decay The changing of a particular radioactive element into a different element. (p. 547)

radioactivity (ray′-dee-ō-ak-TIV′-uh-tee) The ability of an element to change spontaneously into a different element by losing or gaining matter from the nucleus of an atom. (p. 545)

radiometric dating (ray′-dee-ō-MET′-rik) A method of age determination that measures radioactive decay or radioactive elements. (p. 547)

rain Drops of water that fall to the earth because they have become too large to remain in the air. (p. 279)

rain gauge (GAYJ) An instrument used to measure the amount of precipitation. (p. 280)

rain-shadow desert A desert caused by a mountain range that prevents prevailing winds from bringing moisture to an area. (p. 324)

recycled (ree-SĪ′-kuld) Changed into a usable form and then used again. (p. 608)

reforestation (ree′-for-ist-AY′-shin) Replanting a forest with new seedlings as trees are removed. (p. 607)

relative humidity A comparison between the amount of moisture in the air and the amount of moisture that the air can hold. It is expressed as a percentage. (p. 266)

residual soils (ri-ZIJ′-oo-wul) Soils that remain near the bedrock from which they have weathered. (p. 455)

retrograde motions (RET′-ruh-grayd MŌ′-shinz) Apparent reversals in the motions of certain planets. (p. 173)

reverse fault A fault in which the hanging wall has moved up with respect to the footwall. (p. 493)

revolution (rev′-uh-LOO′-shin) The motion of the earth around the sun. (p. 142)

Richter scale (RIK′-ter) A system that measures, on a scale of 1 to 10, the amount of energy released at the focus of an earthquake. (p. 496)

rift valley Deep valley in the center of the mid-ocean ridge; a site of active volcanism. (p. 380)

rift zone The central part of the mid-ocean ridge where molten material rises from the earth's interior and cools into igneous rock. (p. 508)

right ascension (a-SEN′-shun) The celestial "longitude" astronomers use to find objects in the night sky. It is measured eastwards around the celestial equator in units of hours, minutes, and seconds. (p. 127)

rigidity (ri-JID′-uh-tee) A measure of the stiffness of a material. (p. 504)

rille Cracks in the moon's surface. (p. 157)

ringlet The thousands of small rings that make up Saturn's five major rings. (p. 187)

Ring of Fire The region of volcanic activity that surrounds the basin of the Pacific Ocean; same as Circum-Pacific Ring of Fire. (p. 379)

rock A mixture of minerals that is beneath all soil and water on the earth's surface. (p. 96)

rock cycle The process by which rock is changed from one class to another. (p. 102)

rogue wave (RŌG) A very high wave that forms on the open ocean when the crests of two or more high waves of about the same wavelengths coincide. (p. 407)

rotation (rō-TAY'-shin) The daily turning of the earth on its axis. (p. 130)

runoff Water that flows off the earth's surface can occur as sheet runoff, which is merely across a sloping surface, and stream runoff, which follows a channel. (p. 342)

S-wave A secondary wave; a transverse earthquake wave; sometimes called a shear wave. (p. 495)

salinity (suh-LIN'-uh-tee) Saltiness; a measure of the amount of total dissolved materials in water; grams of dissolved materials per kilogram of water. (p. 386)

satellite (SAT'-ul-īt') An object that revolves around a body larger than itself. (p. 155)

saturated air (SACH'-er-ay'-tid) Air that contains all the moisture it can hold. (p. 266)

saturation temperature (sach'-er-AY'-shin) The temperature at which the air is saturated and can hold no more moisture. (p. 269)

scale of distances A ratio that shows how a distance on a map compares to the actual distance on the earth's surface. (p. 44)

sea floor spreading The faulting and movement of growing plates away from the central rift zone. (p. 508)

sea ice Frozen ocean water. (p. 393)

sedimentary rock (sed'-uh-MEN'-ter-ee) Rock that is formed from sediments. (p. 96)

seismograph (SĪZ'-muh-graf) An instrument that measures and records earthquake waves. (p. 495)

seismologist (sīz-MOL'-uh-jist) A scientist who studies earthquakes. (p. 496)

sexual reproduction Reproduction that involves the joining together of male and female germ cells. (p. 565)

shear stress The stress caused when adjacent materials slide past one another. (p. 491)

sheet runoff Water that has no channels to direct its flow as it runs off the earth's surface. (p. 343)

shield cone A volcanic mountain with gently sloping sides; built almost entirely of lava flow. (p. 477)

SI International System of Units; a system of measuring that uses seven base units; it is based on the metric system. (p. 22)

sidereal month (sī-DIR'-ee-ul) A month that is based upon the moon making one complete revolution; 27 1/3 earth days. (p. 159)

silicate minerals (SIL'-uh-kit' MIN'-er-ulz) Minerals that contain the elements silicon and oxygen; the most common class of minerals. (p. 84)

sill A layer of igneous rock that is younger than, parallel to, and in between two other rock layers in a formation. (p. 539)

sleet Small pellets of ice that form when raindrops fall through a layer of very cold air and freeze. (p. 280)

sling psychrometer (sī-KROM'-uh-ter) An instrument that measures humidity. (p. 267)

slip face The side of a sand dune that is away from the wind. (p. 460)

snow Precipitation that occurs in the form of flakes when the dew-point temperature and the air temperature are at or below freezing. (p. 279)

solar eclipse (SŌ'-ler ee-KLIPS') When the moon's shadow falls on the earth's surface, blocking out the sun in that portion of the earth's surface. (p. 161)

solar energy (SŌ'-ler) Energy from the sun. (p. 592)

solar flares Sudden bursts of energy that are given off from sunspots. (p. 195)

solar system The sun and all the objects that revolve around the sun. (p. 171)

solar wind Streams of electrically charged particles constantly given off from the sun. (p. 195)

solid Matter that has a definite shape and volume. (p. 60)

solstice (SOL'-stis) or (SŌL'-stis) The time of the year when the sun's direct vertical rays reach their farthest point north or south of the equator. (p. 151)

sorting The process by which fragments of earth materials are deposited from running water in order of size, with the largest particles settling first. (p. 454)

specific heat The amount of energy needed to raise 1 g of a substance 1°C. (p. 254)

spectroscope (SPEK'-truh-skōp') An instrument that analyzes the light given off by stars. (p. 200)

spring The place where ground water flows out of the ground because the water table has intersected the earth's surface. (p. 357)

standard atmospheric pressure Atmospheric pressure at sea level and at °C; capable of balancing a column of mercury that is 760 mm (29.92 inches) or 1033.3 cm (33.9 feet) Of water; also expressed as 1013.25 millibars. (p. 256)

star trail Curved line caused by the apparent movement of a star while a time-exposure photograph was being taken. (p. 127)

stationary front A weather front that is not moving. (p. 295)

station model A set of symbols that are used to record conditions at a weather station simply and clearly. (p. 301)

stratified drift (STRAT′-uh-fīd) Sorted particles that have settled out of meltwater on an outwash plain. (p. 463)

stratus clouds (STRAT′-is) Horizontal, layered clouds that stretch out across the sky like a blanket. (p. 277)

streak The color of the powder of a mineral against a white background. (p. 89)

stream Runoff that flows in a channel between banks of soil, rock, or other material. (p. 343)

stream load All the material transported by a river or stream. (p. 439)

subduction (sub-DUK′-shin) The downward movement of a colliding plate margin that is being forced down toward the asthenosphere. (p. 508)

subsoil The layer of soil that is found under the topsoil of a fully developed soil profile; contains few of the elements needed by plants for growth. (p. 433)

sunspot Dark spot in the photosphere. (p. 194)

supercluster Clusters of clusters of galaxies, though they do not mix. They are held together by gravity. (p. 215)

supernova The explosion of a supergiant star. (p. 203)

surf zone The area near the ocean's margins where breaking waves occur. (p. 406)

swamp A low-lying water-soaked marsh or bog that forms when a lake or pond fills with sediment and vegetation. (p. 342)

swell A rhythmic pattern of waves of similar wavelength. (p. 406)

syncline (SIN′-klīn) A downward-arching fold in rocks. (p. 486)

synodic month (si-NOD′-ik) A month that is based on the time the moon takes to go from one new moon to the next; 29½ earth days. (p. 160)

temperate climate (TEM′-per-it) A climate influenced by both polar and tropical air masses; characterized by moderate temperatures. (p. 317)

tensional stress (TEN′-shuh-nul) The stress caused when material is pulled apart. (p. 491)

terminal moraine (TER′-muh-nul muh-RAYN′) The deposit that marks the farthest advance of a glacier. (p. 461)

texture (TEKS′-cher) The pattern made by the size, shape, and arrangement of the particles that are in a rock. (p. 103)

theory (THEE′-uh-ree) or (THEER′-ee) A way of explaining how or why something happened, on the basis of generally accepted hypotheses. A working statement that is intended to be tested and modified, added to, or replaced. (p. 14)

theory of continental drift A theory that envisions the continents drifting over the top of the oceanic crust. (p. 505)

thrust fault A special type of reverse fault in which the fault surface is at a very low angle. (p. 493)

thunder A loud rumbling noise caused by the rapid expansion of air as lightning passes through it. (p. 310)

thunderstorm A storm produced by large rising columns of warm moist air and characterized by thunder, lightning, and heavy precipitation. (p. 310)

till The material in a glacial moraine. (p. 463)

time exposure (ik-SPŌ′-zher) A photograph that records the motion of a moving object because the lens of the camera was kept open. (p. 131)

time zone A north-south section of the earth in which all clocks indicate the same time; 24 time zones circle the earth. (p. 138)

topographic map (tōp′-uh-GRAF′-ik) A map that shows the shapes and elevations of the earth's surface features. (p. 45)

topography (tuh-POG′-ruh-fee) The elevations and shapes of land features on the earth's surface. (p. 45)

topsoil The layer of soil that contains humus; found in a fully developed soil profile. (p. 431)

tornado (tor-NAY′-dō) A narrow funnel of air extending down from a cumulonimbus cloud; characterized by high winds traveling in a circular direction around an extremely low pressure center. (p. 311)

transform fault A fault along which there is horizontal movement. (p. 493)

transpiration (tran′-spuh-RAY′-shun) The process by which green plants, as they make food, give off water vapor to the atmosphere through small openings in their leaves. (p. 347)

transported soils Soils formed from eroded materials. (p. 455)

trap A kind of blockage formed by nonporous rock that traps petroleum and natural gas that would otherwise rise all the way to the earth's surface. (p. 590)

trench A long narrow depression of the deep sea floor; generally has steep sides; usually bordered by areas of volcanic activity. (p. 379)

tributaries (TRIB′-yoo-tair′-eez) Streams and small rivers that empty into one large river system. (p. 343)

tropical air mass An air mass that forms near the Tropic of Cancer or the Tropic of Capricorn. (p. 287)

tropical climate (TROP′-uh-kul) A climate influenced mainly by tropical air masses; characterized by the warmest temperatures. (p. 316)

Tropic of Cancer (KAN′-ser) An imaginary line that circles the earth at 23.5° North latitude. (p. 149)

Tropic of Capricorn (KAP′-ruh-korn) An imaginary line that circles the earth at 23.5° South latitude. (p. 148)

troposphere (TRŌP′-uh-sfir′) or (TRO′-puh-sfir′) The layer of the earth's atmosphere that extends from the earth's surface to about 16 km above sea level; the layer of the atmosphere in which all of the earth's weather is found. (p. 257)

trough (TRAWF) The lowest point between two wave crests. (p. 403)

true brightness The amount of light that a star is actually giving off; its luminosity. (p. 197)

true north The direction toward the North Geographic Pole from any place on the earth. Compare *magnetic north.* (p. 49)

tsunami (tsoo-NAH′-mee) A huge wave caused by an underwater earthquake somewhere along the ocean bottom; barely noticeable out at sea. (p. 407)

umbra (UM′-bruh) The dark, central part of a shadow. (p. 160)

unconformity (un-kun-FOR′-muh-tee) A surface of erosion between rocks that represents a gap in earth history. (p. 538)

uniformitarianism (yoo′-nuh-for′-muh-TAIR′-ee-uh-niz′-um) An assumption that the earth processes occurring today are the same as those that have always occurred. (p. 525)

upwelling A process by which deep, cold, nutrient-rich water is brought to the surface and replaces lighter surface water. (p. 414)

valley glacier A glacier that flows down a mountainside. (p. 444)

vent An opening in the earth's crust from which volcanic materials pass to the earth's surface. (p. 475)

viscosity (vis-KOS′-uh-tee) A measure of how easily a liquid flows. (p. 476)

volcanic activity Any earth process by which molten rock, gases, or fragments of solid material come out of an opening (called a vent) in the earth's crust. (p. 475)

volcano A vent or mountain from which volcanic materials pass through the earth's crust to the earth's surface. (p. 476)

volume (VOL′-yum) The amount of space that an object takes up. (p. 28)

waning When the sunlit part of the moon begins to appear smaller and smaller to observers on earth due to the moon's relative orbit to the earth. (p. 159)

warm front A weather front that forms when a warm air mass pushes a cold air mass ahead of it. (p. 291)

water cycle The process by which water is continually recycling between the earth's surface and the atmosphere; also called the hydrologic cycle. (p. 338)

water mass A large volume of water characterized by a similar temperature, salinity, and density throughout its mass. (p. 391)

water pressure The force that a mass of overlying water exerts upon a submerged surface. (p. 394)

watershed All the area of land that drains into a river, along with its system of streams and other tributaries. (p. 345)

water table The boundary between the zone of aeration and the zone of saturation. (p. 355)

water vapor (VAY′-per) The name commonly used for water as gas; cannot be seen, tasted, smelled, or felt. (p. 264)

wave base The point below the surface of water at which the orbital motion of a wave nearly disappears (1/2 a wavelength below and midheight of the wave). (p. 403)

wave height The vertical distance between a wave's highest and lowest points. (p. 403)

wavelength The horizontal distance from a point on one wave to the corresponding point on the next wave. (p. 233)

waxing When the sunlit part of the moon begins to appear larger and larger to observers on earth due to the moon's relative orbit to the earth. (p. 159)

weathering (WETH'-er-ing) The breaking down and wearing away of the earth's rocks by the earth's atmosphere; see *chemical weathering* and *physical weathering*. (p. 425)

weight The pull of gravity on an object. The weight of the same object can vary depending on gravity. Compare with *mass*. (p. 26)

wetlands Coastal and freshwater swamps. (p. 612)

wind belts General patterns of air circulation that circle the earth; includes prevailing winds. (p. 250)

zenith (ZEE'-nith) The point on the celestial sphere that is directly above the head of an observer. (p. 123)

zone of aeration (air-AY'-shin) The layer of soil between the water table and the earth's surface; its pore spaces contain both air and water. (p. 354)

zone of saturation (sach'-er-AY'-shin) The layer of soil below the water table; its pore spaces are filled with water. (p. 355)

Index

Note: **Boldface** numerals denote definitions.

Abrasion, **446**
Absolute age, **542**
Absolute magnitude, of stars, **199**
Abyssal plains, 379
Acid rain, **610**
Adhesion, **354,** 355
Adiabatic change, **320**
Air, 233
  saturated, **266**
  see also Atmosphere
Air-conditioning mechanic, 323
Air masses, **287**
  comparing, 287–290, 294
  weather fronts and, 290–296
Air pollution, **610**
Air temperatures, 242–243, 245, 247,
  303
Aleutian Trench, 481
Algal mats, 563, 565
Alkali metal, 71
Alloys, 65
Alpha, 145
Alpine glacier, 441
Altitude, **121,** 123, 125
  of Polaris, 124
  of sun, 148
  temperature and, 318–320
Aluminum, 64–65, 583, 586
Amazon River, 345
Amino acids, **550**–551
Ampere, 24
Amphibole, 103
Analyzing, 392
Aneroid barometers, 256
Antarctica, 325
Antarctic Circle, 149
Antarctic Current, 411
Antarctic Ocean, 370
Anticline, **486**–487, 488
Aphotic zone, **397**
Apogee, **156**
Apollo programs, 155, 162–163
Appalachian Mountains, 512
Apparent brightness, of stars, 197
Apparent magnitude, **197**
Apparent solar time, **138**
Aquifer, **359**–360
Archaeopteryx, 536–537, 560
Arctic Circle, 149
Arctic Ocean, 370, 379, 393
Aristotle, 12, 173
Artesian springs, **360**
Artesian system, **359**–360
Assumption, 525, **526**–527
Asteroids, **182**–183
Asthenosphere, **504**
Astrolabe, 122
Astronomic observations, improvements
  in, 228
Astronomical unit, 184
Astronomy, **18,** 120, 222–224

Atlantic Ocean, 369–370, 379, 393,
  480
Atmosphere, **17, 18, 233**
  carbon dioxide in, 241–242
  condensation in, 276–278
  density of, 255, 257–258
  greenhouse effect in, 240–241
  radiation in, 235, 239–242
  sun's energy in, 233–235
  temperatures in, 242–243, 245, 247
  water vapor in, 233, 257, 266–269,
    276–278
  wind belts in, 250–251, 253
Atmospheric pressure, **255**–257
  temperature and, 306–308
Atmospheric pressure map, **259,** 261
Atom, **63**
  mass number of, 64–65
  structure of, 64
Atomic energy, **596**–599
Atomic mass, **72**
Atomic mass unit (amu), 72
Atomic number, **66**–67
Aurora, **195**
Autumnal equinox, 150
Azimuth, **121,** 125

Bacon, Francis, 504, 505
Barograph, 256
Barometers, **256**
Barometric pressure; *see* Atmospheric
  pressure
Basalt, 97, 353, 374, 479
Base level, **442**
Basin, 489
Batholith, **97**
Beagle, 536
Beam balance, 28
Becquerel, Henri, 545
Bedrock, 354, 355, **431**
Betelgeuse, 119, 200
Bethe, Hans, 236
Big Bang, **219,** 221
Big Crunch, **222**
Big Dipper, 120–121, 131
Binary stars, 202
Bioluminescence, 397
Biosphere, **17**
Biotite mica, 85, 93, 105
Black holes, **204**
Black Sea, 371, 387
Blizzards, **311**
Brachiopods, 566, 570
Brahe, Tycho, 120, 173–174
Bronze, 65

Caesar, Julius, 152
Calcite, 82, 87–89, 106
Caldera, 471, **472**
Callisto, 186
Cambrian Period, 555, 567
Canaries Current, 412–413
Canis Major constellation, 120, 143
Capillary action, **355**

Capillary fringe, 354, **355,** 357
Carbon, 64, 66
Carbonate minerals, 87
Carbon dioxide, 74, 241–242
Carboniferous Period, 555, 569
Carbonization, 427
Careers
  air-conditioning mechanic, 323
  cartographer, 48
  civil engineering technician, 435
  climatologist, 323
  computer operator, 405
  construction inspector, 515
  earth scientist, 48
  geographer, 435
  geophysicist, 108
  geoscience librarian, 216
  heavy-equipment operator, 362
  hydrologist, 362
  marine geologist, 405
  petroleum geologist, 613
  petrologist, 546
  range manager, 613
  refinery operator, 546
  seismologist, 496, 515
  solar energy firm owner, 216
  technical secretary, 108
  weather forecaster, 270
  weather technician, 270
Cartographer, 48
Celestial sphere, **117**
Celsius, 296
Cenozoic Era, 554
Cenozoic life forms, 574–575
Centimeter, 24
Cephalopod, 571, 573
Cepheid variables, 202
Chemical bond, **73,** 74
Chemical formula, **73**
Chemically formed rock, **100**
Chemical property, **9**
Chemical symbol, **67**
Chemical weathering, **426**–428, 434,
  440
Christy, James, 189
Chromium, 583
Chromosphere, **195**
Cinder cone, **477,** 479
Circumference, **33**
Cirrus clouds, 278
Civil engineering technician, 435
Classifying, **7,** 9, 10
Clastic rock, **99**–100
Clay, 352, 584
Cleavage, **88,** 91
Cleavage direction, 88, 91
Climate, **316**
  altitude and, 318–320
  changes in, 328
  mountain ranges and, 322, 324
  ocean currents and, 320
  prevailing winds and, 321–322
  types of, 316–318
  weathering of rocks and, 430

Climate graphs, **325**–327
Climatologist, 323
Clouds, 276, **277**–278, 279, 308
Clusters, of stars, 207
Coal, 586, **590**–591
Coarse-grained texture, 105
Cohesion, **355,** 356
Cold front, **290**–291, 302–303
Color, of minerals, 89
Coma, **190**
Comet, **190**–191
Comparing, 448
Compass, **49**
Compass directions, 44, 49–51
Composite cone, **479**
Compound, **73**–74
Compressional stress, **487**
Computer operator, 405
Computers, and weather forceasting, 307, 309
Conchoidal fracture, 88, 89
Condensation, **264**
    in atmosphere, 276–278
    near earth's surface, 274–275
    occurrence of, 269, 271, 273–274
    see also Precipitation
Condense, **337**
Conduction, **235**–237
Constellations, **118**–121, 131
Construction inspector, 515
Continental air mass, **287**–288, 318
Continental climate, **318**
Continental crust, **503,** 507
Continental drift, theory of, 504, **505**–507
Continental glacier, **444,** 463
Continental margin, **374,** 376, 377
Continental rise, 374, 376
Continental shelf, 374
Continental slope, 374, 376
Contour interval, **46**–47
Contour line, **45**–47
Convection, 235, 238–239
Convection currents, **239,** 506
    atmospheric condensation and, 276
    forming of, 251–253, 254–255
    specific heat and, 254–255
    winds and, 251, 253
Coordinates, 36
Copernicus, 173
Copper, 31, 65, 583, 586
Core, **16**
Core samples
    analysis of, 456
    comparison of, 462
Coriolis, Gaspard de, 135
Coriolis effect, 134, **135**
    ocean currents and, 411–412
    simulation of, 134
    winds and, 251, 253, 261
Corona, **195**
Crater, **157**
Crater Lake, 341–342, 472, 477
Crest, **403,** 407

Cretaceous Period, 555, 572–573
Crust, **16**
Crystal faces, 91
Crystalline solids, **83**–84
Crystals, **84,** 91
Cumulonimbus clouds, 278, 308–310, 311
Cumulus clouds, **277**–278, 290
Curie, Pierre, 545
Currents, ocean, 411–415
Cuvier, Georges, 544

Dams, 447, 449, 594, 595
Darwin, Charles, 535–537
Darwin's theory of evolution by natural selection, 535–537
Data, 7
    classifying, 7, 9
    collecting of, 7
    graphing of, 8
Date Line (International), **140**–142
Dating
    amino acid method of, 550–551
    early methods of, 542–545
    radiometric, 545, **547,** 549–550
Day lengths, comparison of, 149, 151
Daylight saving time, **140**
Death Valley, 319
Declination, **127**
Deductive method, 11, 13
Deep sea floor, 374–377, 379–381
Deflected, **133,** 135
Delta, 455, 531
Density, **31**
    of atmosphere, 255, 257–258
    determination of, 31, 32
    of earth, 33
    of floating objects, 378
    of ocean water, 390–391, 393–394
Deposition, **454**
    by glaciers, 461, 463–464
    by running water, 454–455, 457
    stream erosion and, 457–459
    by wind, 459–461
Derived unit, 28
Desert, **322,** 459–460
    rain-shadow, **324**
Devonian Period, 555, 568–569
Dew, **274**
Dew-point temperature, **273**–274
    see also Saturation temperature
Diamond, 86
Dietz, Robert, 506–507
Dike, **539**
Dimetrodon, 536, 570
Dinosaur, 9, 11, 559, 560, 563, 572, 573
Diplodocus, 559
Direct observation, **5**
Discontinuities, **503**
Disphotic zone, **397**
Diverging zones, 253
Divide, **343**
Dome, 489

Doppler, Christian, 144
Doppler effect, **144**–145, 201
Doppler radar, 332
Drumlins, **463**–464
Dry-bulb temperature, 267, 269
Dry-bulb thermometer, 267

Earth, 179–180, 181
    age of; *see* Dating; Geologic time
    atmosphere of, 17, 257–258
    circumference of, 33, 136
    core of, 16
    density of, 33
    history of; *see* Rock record
    interior of, 16, 502–504
    magnetic field of, 506
    mantle of, 16
    measurement of, 33
    roundness of, 12, 33
    structure of, 15–17
    surface of; *see* Deposition; Erosion; Maps; Rocks
    temperatures around, 242–243, 245, 247
Earth materials
    atoms, 596–599
    fossil fuels, 589–591
    water, 593–596
    wind and sun, 591–593
Earthquakes, 6, 13–14, **494**–496
    damage, 497–499
    focuses of, 494, 510
    predicting, 520
    radon gas and, 13–14
    tsunami and, 407
Earth's axis, **130**
    inclination of, 147–148, 160, 161
Earth science, 18–19
Earth scientist, 48
Earth's crust, **16**
    faults in, 489–494
    makeup of, 136
    under stress, 485–489
Earth's revolution, **142**–143
    Doppler effect of, 144–145
    evidence of, 144–145
    seasons and, 146–150
Earth's rotation, **130**–131
    Coriolis effect and, 134, 135, 253
    day and night and, 130
    evidence of, 132–137
    magnetism of, 51
    time of day and, 137–142
Echinoderm, 565
Echo sounding, **373**
Eclipses, 12, 159–162
Electromagnetic spectrum, **234**
Electromagnetic waves, **233**
Electron, **64**
Element, **62**–63
Elevation, **45**–46
Ellipse, **156**
Elliptical galaxy, 214–215
Elliptical orbit, 156, 157

End moraine, **461**
Energy, **59**
  alternative sources of, 612, 615
  angle of incoming, 244, 246
  atomic, **596**–599
  geothermal, **595**–596
  hydroelectric, **593**–595
  matter and, 59–60
  in ocean waves, 404, 407
  solar, **592**–593
  states of water and, 264–265
  storing in earth's surface, 245, 247
Energy level, **67,** 71
Energy movement
  by conduction, 235–237
  by convection, 235, 238–239
  by radiation, 235, 239–242
Environment
  farming and, 603–606
  improvement of, 604
  lumbering and, 607
  resource conservation and, 612, 614
  solid waste disposal and, 608, 610–611
Epicenter, **495,** 498
Equator, **37**–39
  bulge at, 33, 136
  seasons at, 151
  sun's altitude at, 148
Equinoxes, **150**
Eras, 554–555
Eratosthenes, 12
Erosion, **438**
  control of, 447, 449–451
  deposition and, 457–459
  by glaciers, 443–445, 446
  by more than one agent, 445–447
  rate of, 450
  by running water, 438–440, 446
Erratics, **444**
Europa, 186
Evaluating, 548
Evaporate, **337**
Evaporation, **264,** 266, 346–347, 388
Evolution, Darwin's theory of, 535–537
Evolve, **535**
Extinct, **570**
Extinction, 619

Fahrenheit, 296
Faults, 489–490, **491**–494
Faunal succession, principle of, **532**–533, 535
Feldspar, 82, 85, 93, 103, 105
Fine-grained texture, 105
Fission, **596**–597
Fissure, **479**
Flash flood, 451
Floating objects, 378
Flooding, 449, 451
Flood plain, **441**
Florida Current, 412–413
Fluid, **238**
Fluorite, 80, 82, 87, 88, 91, 93
Focus, **494**

Fog, 274–**275**
Folded rocks, **486**–487
Food chain, 604
Footwall, **491**
Formations, **538**–539
Fossil fuels, **589**–591
Fossil mold, 564
Fossil record, **559**–563
Fossils, 11, **532**–533, 535, 576
  living, **570**
Foucault, Jean, 132
Foucault pendulum, 132–133
Fractures, 88, 89, **487,** 491
Freeze, 265, **337**
Freezing point, **391,** 393
Front, **290**
  see also Weather front
Frost, **274**
Fuji, Mount, 479
Fumarole, **476**
Fusion, **194, 597**–599
  heat of, **265**

Galaxies, **213**–217
Galena, 82, 87, 91, 93
Galilei, Galileo, 156, 157, 174, 186, 194
Gamma rays, 234
Ganymede, 186
Garnet, 85–86
Gas, **60,** 61, 62
Gemini constellation, 119, 143
Geographer, 435
Geography, 435, 440
Geologic eras, **554**–555
Geologic periods, 555
Geologic time, 544, **552**–555
Geologic Time Scale, 619
Geology, **18**
Geophysicist, 108
Geoscience librarian, 216
Geothermal energy, **595**–596
Geyser, **360**–361
Glacial lobe, **461**
Glacier, 325, **340**–341, 453
  deposition by, 461, 463–464
  erosion by, 443–445, 446
Globe, **36,** 40
Globular cluster, **207**
Gneiss, 100
Gondwana, 512
Graduated cylinder, 28, 29
Gram, 24, 31
Grand Canyon, 442–443, 533
Granite, 96, 101, 353, 374, 425, 430
Graphic scale of distances, **45**
Graphing, 8, 32
Gravitation, law of, **175**
Gravity
  erosion by, 446–447
  weight and, 26–27
Great Lakes, 340–341
Greenhouse effect, **178**–179, 240–241, 318
Greenwich mean time, **140**

Gregorian calendar, 152
Gregory, Pope, 153
Ground water, **354**–355, 357, 603–604
Guide fossil, 532
Gulf Stream, 412–413, 414
Guyots, 379
Gypsum, 82, 87, 100
  luster of, 91
  physical properties of, 93
  uses of, 584
Gyre, **412**–413

Habitat, 604
Hachures, **46,** 47
Hail, 279–**280**
Half life, **547,** 549–550, 556
Halide minerals, 87
Halite, 100
Halley's Comet, 190–191
Hanging wall, **491**
Hardness, of minerals, 88–89, 90, 91
Heat
  as form of energy, 236–237
  sources of, 476
  specific, **254**–255, 260
  see also Air temperatures
Heat absorption, simulating effects of, 416
Heat of fusion, **265**
Heat of vaporization, **264,** 265
Heat value, 591
Heavy-equipment operator (HEO), 362
Heft, **91,** 93
Helium, 74
Herschel, William, 188
Hertzsprung, Ejnar, 205
Hertzsprung-Russell (H-R) diagram, 205, 207
Hess, Harry, 506–507
High-pressure area, 261, 289
High-pressure center, **261**
High tide, **409**
Himalayan Mountains, 512
Hipparchus, 197
Holmes, Arthur, 505–506, 507
Horizon, **117**
Hubble, Edwin, 217
Humidity, **266**
  in air masses, 290
  measurement of, 267–269
  relative, **266**–269
  see also Precipitation
Humus, **431**
Hurricanes, **312**–313, 332
Hydroelectric energy, **593**–595
Hydrofracturing, 425
Hydrogen, 66, 74
Hydrologist, 362
Hydrology, **18**
Hydrosphere, **17,** 18
Hydrothermal vents, 389
Hypothesis, **11,** 13–14, 506

Ice, 60
Icebergs, **394**

Igneous rock, **96**
  formation of, 96–97, 377, 539
Impermeable, **354–355**
Impurities, **86**
Incinerate, **608,** 610–611
Inclination, **146**–148
Index fossil, 532–**533**, 535
Indian Ocean, 370, 393
Indirect observation, 5–**6**
Inductive method, 11, **13**
Inertia, law of, **175**
Inferences, **9**, 11
Inferring, 292
Infiltration, **351**
Inner core, **16**
Inorganic, **83**
Instruments, **6**
International Bureau of Weights and
    Measures, 26
International Date Line, **140**–142
International System of Units (SI), 22–
    24
  base units of, 23–24
  prefixes in, 24, 26
Io, 186
Ion, **75**–76
Iron, 63
  discovery of, 65
  refining of, 586
  rusting of, 426–427
  sources of, 583
Irregular galaxy, 215
Island arcs, **371, 480**
Isobar, **259**
Isotope, **72**

Japanese Current, 414
Julian calendar, 152
Jupiter, 181, 185–186
Jurassic Period, 555, 572

Kelvin, Lord, 543, 545
Kelvin, 24
Kepler, Johannes, 120, 174
Kettle lake, **464**
Kilo, 24, 26
Kilogram, 24, 26
Kilometer, 25, 26
Krakatau, 472–473

Laborde, Albert, 545
Laccolith, **97**
Lakes, **340**–341
  kettle, **464**
  oxbow, **442**
Landfills, **611**
Land use
  farming, 603–606
  lumbering, 607
  planning of, 606–607
  resource conservation and, 612, 614
  solid waste disposal, 608, 610–611
Lassen, Mount, 474
Lateral eruption, **474**

Latitude, **37**–39, 42, 121, 123, 127
Laurasia, 512
Lava, **97, 476,** 478, 526
Law of gravitation, **175**
Law of inertia, **175**
Leaching, **431**
Lead, 583
Leap year, **152**
Leavitt, Henrietta, 202
Legend, **43**
Length, measurement of, 25–26
Levee, **441**
Life forms, **559**
  Cenozoic, 574–575
  Mesozoic, 571–573
  Paleozoic, 566–571
  Precambrian, 563, 565
Light, 239, 395–397
Lightning, **310**
Light waves, 144–145, 234
Light-year, **210**
Lignite, 591
Limestone, 100, 101
  chemical weathering of, 427–428,
    430
  identification of, 106
  uses of, 584
Liquid, **60,** 61
  volume of, 28–29
Liter, 29
Lithosphere, **16**–17, 18, 504
Living fossils, **570**
Local Group, **215,** 217
Local winds, **250**
Longitude, **37**–39, 42, 127, 139
Longitudinal wave, 495
Low-pressure area, 259, 261, 289
Low-pressure center, **259,** 312
Low tide, **409**
Low-velocity zone, **503**
Lunar, **155**
  see also Moon
Lunar craters, 157
Lunar eclipse, 12, **160**–161
Luster, **89,** 91
L-waves, 495

Magma, 96–97, **476,** 529, 539
Magnesium, 583
Magnetic declination, **50**–51
Magnetic north, **49**–51
Magnetite, 82, 87, 93
Magnitude, **197**, 206
Mantle, **16**
Map projections, **39**–41
Map relief, **46**
Maps, **39**, 42
  colors and symbols on, 41, 43
  latitude and longitude on, 37–39
  north on, 43–44
  pressure, 259, 261
  scale of distances on, 44–45
  topographic, **45**–47
  weather, 301–303, 304, 305–306

Marble, 106
Marginal seas, **370**–371
Maria, **157**
Marine climate, **317**
Marine geologist, 405
Mariner 10, 177, 178
Maritime air mass, **287**–288, 317
Mars, 180–182
Mass, **26**–28, 31
Mass number, **64**–65
Matter, 59–62
Matthews, D. H., 506
Mazama, Mount, 471–472
Meanders, **442,** 457, 459, 443
Mean solar time, **138**
Measurement, 22–33
  of density, 31–32
  of earth, 33
  International System of Units, 22–24
  of length, 25–26
  of mass, 26–28
  use of base units in, 23–24
  of volume, 28–29
Mediterranean Sea, 371, 387
Mercalli, Giuseppe, 497
Mercalli scale, **497**, 498
Mercator projection, 40, 41
Mercury (planet), 177–178, 181
Mercury barometers, 256
Meridians, **37**–39, 43, 44
  date and, 140
  time zones and, 139–140
Mesosphere, 257, 258, **504**
Mesozoic Era, 554
Mesozoic life forms, 571–573
Metals, 63, 65, 583, 586
Metamorphic rock, **96**
  formation of, 100–101, 486
  principle of superposition and, 529
Metamorphosis, 100
Meteor, **183,** 257
Meteorite, **183,** 552
Meteoroid, **162**
Meteorologist; see Climatologist;
    Weather forecaster
Meteorology, **18**
  see also Weather prediction
Meteor shower, 190
Meter, **23,** 24, 26
Metric system, 22–23, 25, 26, 30
Mica, 82, 85
  cleavage direction on, 88
  color of, 103, 105
Middle America Trench, 481, 508–509
Mid-ocean ridges, **379**–381
Milky Way galaxy, 196, **213**–214
Millibars, **257**
Milliliters, 29
Millimeters, 24
Mineral composition, of rock, **103,** 105–
    106
Mineral resources, search for, 112
Minerals, **81**
  common properties of, 81–84
  identification of, 92

mining of, 586–589
nonsilicate, **86**–87
physical properties of, 87–93
radioactive dating of, 549–550
refining of, 586, 588–589
silicate, **84**–86, 103, 105
synthetic, 81, 83
uses of, 583–589
Mines, **586**–589
Minutes, 39
Mississippian Period, 555, 569
Mississippi River, 343
Mixed-grain texture, 105
Mixture, **77**–78
Moho, **16**
Mohorovicic discontinuity, **16**
Mohs, Friedrich, 88
Mohs' scale, 88–89, 91
Molecule, **74**
Mollusks, 565
Moon
  age of, 163
  characteristics of, 155–157
  diameter of, 156, 158
  eclipses of, 160–161
  phases of, 159
  surface of, 156–157, 162–163
Moonquakes, 163
Moraines, **461,** 463
Mountain glacier, 444
Mountain ranges, 322–324
Moving front, 295–296
Muscovite mica, 105

Nadir, **123**
Natural gas, **381,** 589, 590
Natural selection, Darwin's theory of,
  535–537
Nautilus, 375
Nebula, **196**–197
Neptune, 176, 181, 189
Neutron, **64**
Neutron star, **204**
Newton, Isaac, 174–175
Nickel, 583
Night sky
  altitude in, 121, 123–125
  azimuth in, 123, 125
  constellations in, 118–121
  Doppler effect and, 144–145
  models of, 117
  paths of stars in, 126
  yearly changes in, 142–143
Nitrates, 585
Noble gas, 71
Nonmetals, 583–586
Nonrenewable resources, 603
Nonsilicate minerals, **86**–87
Noon position, **137,** 138
Normal fault, **491,** 493
North
  on a map, 43–44
  ways of finding, 49–51
North Atlantic Drift, 412–413
North Atlantic Equatorial Current, 412

North Atlantic Gyre, 412
Northeast trade winds, 253
Northern hemisphere
  air temperature in, 245
  seasons in, 148–149, 151
  winds in, 251, 253
North Geograpic Pole, **49**
North Magnetic Pole, **49**
North Poles, 49
North Star; *see* Polaris
Nuclear energy, 596–599
Nuclear fission, **596**–597
Nuclear fusion, **194,** 597–599
Nucleus, **64**

Observations, 218
  assumptions and, 525, 526–527
  direct, **5**
  hypotheses and, 11, 13
  indirect, 5–**6**
  inferences and, 9, 11
Obsidian, 97, 106
Occluded front, **293,** 295, 303
Ocean basins, **374**
Ocean bottom
  resources of, 381, 383
  sounding of, 372–373, 382
  topography of, 374–377, 379–381
Ocean crustal rock, 377
Ocean currents
  deep, 414–415
  deflection of, 135
  surface, 411–414
  temperature and, 320, 321
Oceanic crust, **503,** 507
Oceanography, **18**
Oceans, **369**–370
Ocean swell, **406**
Ocean tides, 409–411
Ocean trenches, 379, 480, 508
Ocean water
  density of, 390, 393–394
  elements in 386–387
  light absorption in, 395–397
  resources of, 398
  salinity of, 386–389
  temperature of, 389–390
  water pressure of, 394–395
Ocean waves
  directions of motion in, 401–403
  effects of, 407–408
  simulation of, 402
  tides, 409–411
Offshore breeze, **255**
Olivine, 103
Onshore breeze, **254**
Oort cloud, **191**
Open-pit mines, 586, 589
Orbit
  of earth, **142**–143
  of moon, 156, 157
Ordovician Period, 555, 567
Ore, 65, **585**–589, 600

Organic rock, **100**
Original horizontality, principle of, **530**–
  531
Origin of Continents and Oceans, The,
  505
Origin of Species, 535
Orion constellation, 118–119, 142, 143,
  196
Orthoclase feldspar, 93, 103
Outer core, **16**
Outwash plain, **461**
Oxbow lakes, **442**
Oxidation, 427
Oxide minerals, 87, 583
Oxygen-carbon dioxide cycle, **242**
Ozone layer, 257

Pacific Ocean, 369–370, 379, 380, 390,
  393, 408, 480
Pack ice, **393,** 394
Paleontologists, **560**–562
Paleozoic Era, 511–512, 554
Paleozoic life forms, 566–571
Pangaea, 511–513, 514
Parallax, **209**–210
Parallax angle, **209**
Parallax displacement, 208
Parallels, **37**–39, 40, 43, 44
Parent rock, **101**
Parícutin, 474, 477
Peat, 591
Pelée, Mount, 473
Pennsylvanian Period, 555, 569
Penumbra, **161**
Penzias, Arno, 219
Perigee, **156**
Periodic table, **66**–71
Periods of geologic time, 555
Permeability, **352**–353
Permian Period, 555, 570
Peru-Chile Trench, 379, 481
Petrochemicals, **590**
Petroleum, **589**–590
Petroleum geologist, 613
Petrologist, 546
Petrology, **18**
Phases of the moon, **159**
Phosphates, 585
Photic zone, **396**
Photosphere, **194**
Physical properties, **9**
  of minerals, 87–93
Physical weathering, **425**–426, 439,
  446
Pioneer 10 and *11*, 176
Pioneer Venus, 179
Planetoids, 183
Planets
  Earth, 179–180, 181
  Jupiter, 181, 185–186
  Mars, 180–182
  Mercury, 177–178, 181
  Neptune, 176, 181, 189
  Pluto, 176, 181, 189

Saturn, 181, 187–188
Uranus, 176, 181, 188–189
Venus, 178–179, 181
Plastic deformation, **486**
Plateau basalts, **479**
Plate tectonic theory, 506, **508**–511
Plato, 172
Pleiades star cluster, 197, 207
Pleistocene Epoch, 574–575
Pliny, 472
Pluto, 176, 181, 189
Plutonium, 597
Polar air mass, **287**–288
Polar climate, **316**
Polaris, **123**, 202
  altitude of, 124
  position of, 123–125, 131, 148
Poles, flattening at, 33, 39, 136
Pollution, 604, 610
Polyconic projection, 40–41
Pond, **342**
Population growth, 606
Pore spaces, 351–**352**, 353, 486
Porosity, **352**
Porphyritic rock, **97**
Pecambrian Era, 554
Precambrain life forms, 563, 565
Precipitation, **279**–280
  mountain ranges and, 322, 324
  prevailing winds and, 321–322
  along weather fronts, 290–291
Pressure map, **259,** 261
Prevailing westerlies, **250**–251, 253
Prevailing winds, **250**–251, 253, **287,**
  321–322
Prime meridian, **37,** 38
  date and, 140–141
  time zones and, 140
Principle, **527**
Principle of faunal succession, **532**–
  533, 535
Principle of original horizontality, **530**–
  531
Principle of superposition, 527, 528,
  529–530
Proper motion, of stars, **201**
Proportional scale of distances, **44**–45
Proton, **64**
Protoplanet, **171**
Psychrometer, sling, **267**
Ptolemy, 37, 120, 173
Pulsars, **204**
P-waves, **495,** 502–503
Pyrite, 93
Pyroclastic deposits, **97**
Pyroxene, 103
Pythagoras, 130, 172

Quarternary Period, 555, 574
Quartz, 81, 82
  appearance of, 85, 105
  color of, 103
  elements in, 85
  fracture of, 88

hardness of, 105, 428–429
luster of, 89
physical properties of, 93
Quasars, **217**

Radial velocity, of stars, **201**
Radiation, **235,** 239–242, 592
Radioactive atoms, 596–599
Radioactive decay, **547**
Radioactivity, 547, 549–550, 596–599
Radio astronomy, 222–223
Radiometric dating, 545, **547,** 549–550
Radio telescope, 223
Radon gas, 13–14
Rain, **279,** 280, 309–310, 610
Rain gauge, **280**
Rain-shadow desert, **324**
Range manager, 613
Recycling, **608,** 609
Red giant, 202
Red Sea, 371
Refinery operator, 546
Refining, 546, 586, 588–589
Reforestation, **607**
Relative humidity, **266**–269
Renewable resources, 603
Reservoir, 342
Residual soils, **455**
Retrograde motions, **173**
Reverse fault, **493**
Revolution, **142**
  see also Earth's revolution
Richter, Charles, 496
Richter scale, **496,** 497
Rift valley, **380**–381
Rift zone, **508**–510
Right ascension, **127**
Rigidity, **504**
Rille, **157**
Ringlet, **187**
Ring of Fire, **379,** 480–481
Rivers, 343, 454–455, 457
River valley, 441–443
Robot, 582
Rock cycle, 101, **102**–103
Rock formations, **538**–539
Rock record
  fossil record and, 532–533, 535
  principle of faunal succession and,
    532–533, 535
  principle of original horizontality and,
    530–531
  principle of superposition and, 527–
    530
  reading of, 534
  uniformitarianism in, 525–526
  see also Dating; Life forms
Rocks, **96**
  chemically formed, **100**
  chemical weathering of, 426–428
  clastic, **99**–100
  determining class of, 104
  faults in, 489–494

formation of, 96–101
identification of, 103–107
igneous, **96**–97, 377, 539
metamorphic, **96,** 100–101, 486, 529
mineral composition of, 103, 105–106
mining of, 586
on moon, 162
ocean crustal, 377, 506
organic, 100
parent, **101**
permeability of, 352–353
physical weathering of, 425–426
pore spaces in, 351–352
porphyritic, **97**
rates of weathering of, 429–430
refining of, 586, 588–589
sedimentary, **96,** 99–100, 529, 530–
  531
soil formation and, 431, 433
under stress, 485–487, 489
texture of, 103, 105
uses of, 583–589
volcanic, 377
Rogue wave, **407**
Rotation, **130**
  see also Earth's rotation
Runoff, **342**–345
Russell, Henry Norris, 205
Rusting, 426–427
Rutherford, Ernest, 545

Sahara Desert, 321, 322, 325
St. Helens, Mount, 13, 474–475, 479
Salinity, **386**–389
San Andreas fault, 491, 493
Sand
  origin of, 428
  permeability of, 352
  uses of, 583–584
Sand dune drifts, 460
Sand dunes, 459, 460–461, 530, 531
Sandstone, 99, 352, 430
Sandstone aquifer, 360
Satellites, 136–137, **155**
Saturated air, **266**
Saturation temperature, **269,** 271–274
  see also Dew-point temperature
Saturn, 181, 187–188
Scale of distances, 44–45
Schist, 101
Science, assumptions in, 525, 526–527
Science heritage
  astronomy and astrology, 120
  climate changes on Sahara Desert,
    325
  energy production by the sun, 236
  finding shape of earth, 12
  geologic time, 544
  history of metal use, 65
  from hypothesis to theory, 506
  improving the environment, 604
  model of solar system, 176
  Nautilus and Challenger, 375

travel and world geography, 440
water and ancient civilizations, 339
Science issues
  aquaculture, 420
  earthquake prediction, 520
  extinction patterns and rates, 619
  improvements in astronomic observations, 228
  preventing weather-related disasters, 332
  search for mineral resources, 112
Scientific method, 5–14
Sea floor spreading, **508,** 509, 511, 516
Sea ice, **393**–394
Sea level, 46
Seamounts, 377, 379
Seas, marginal, **370**–371
Seasons, 146–151
Sedimentary rock, **96**
  formation of, 99–100, 530–531
  principle of superposition and, 529
  weathering of, 430
Seismographs, 6, **495**–496
Seismologist, **496,** 515
Sexual reproduction, **565**
Shadow stick, 52
Shale, 99, 101, 360
Shasta, Mount, 479
Shear stress, **491,** 493
Shear waves, 495
Sheet runoff, **343**
Shield cone, **477,** 479
SI (International System of Units), **22**–24
Sidereal month, **159**–160
Silicate minerals, **84**–86, 103, 105
Silicon, 593
Sill, **539**
Silurian Period, 555, 567
Silver, properites of, 9
Silver sulfide, 9
Sirius, 120
Skylab 1, 224
Sleet, **280**
Sling psychrometer, **267**
Slip face, **460**
Smith, William, 544
Snow, 19, **279**–280, 311
Soil profile, 432
Soils
  formation of, 431–433, 455, 457
  permeability of, 352–353
  pore spaces in, 351–352, 353
  preservation of, 447
  residual, **455**
  transported, **455**
Solar cells, 593
Solar eclipse, **161,** 162
Solar energy, 233–235, 236, **591**–593
Solar energy firm owner, 216
Solar flares, **195,** 599
Solar prominences, 196
Solar system, **171**
  asteroids, 182–183
  birth of, 171–172

comets, 190–191
"inner" planets of, 177–182
meteors, 183
models of, 176, 184
"outer" planets of, 185–189
sun, 172–177
Solar time, 138
Solar wind, **195**
Solid, **60,** 61
Solid waste disposal, 608, 610–611
Solstices, **150**
Sorting, **454**–455
Sounding, 372–373, 382
Sound waves, 144
Southern hemisphere, 148–149, 151, 251
Specific heat, **254**–255, 260
Spectroscope, **200**–201
Spiral galaxy, 214
Spring, **357,** 359–360
Spring scale, 27
Standard atmospheric pressure, **256**–257
Stars, 19
  altitude of, 121, 123–125
  azimuth of, 123, 125
  characteristics of, 196–201
  clusters of, 207
  colors of, 199–200, 205, 207
  composition of, 200–201
  constellations of, 118–121
  distance to, 209–210
  Doppler effect and, 144, 201
  earth's rotation and, 130–131, 142, 143
  kinds of, 202–204
  magnitude of, 197, 199
  paths of, 126
Star trail, **131**
Stationary front, **295,** 303
Station model, **300**
Steel, 583
Strabo, 440
Stratified drift, **463**
Stratosphere, 257, 258
Stratus clouds, 276, **277**
Streak, **89**
Streak test, 89
Stream discharge, 344
Stream erosion, 438–440, 457–459
Stream load, **439**
Streams, **343,** 454–455
Stress, 485–487, 489
Strip mines, 586, 589
Subduction, **508**
Subsoil, **433**
Sulfate minerals, 87
Sulfide minerals, 87, 583
Sulfur, 87
Summer solstice, 150
Sun
  air temperatures and, 242–243, 245, 247
  altitude of, 146, 148
  angle of, 242–247

calculating distance to, 198
as center of solar system, 172–177
characteristics of, 194–196
path of, 245
production of energy by, 194, 233–235, 236
see also Solar energy
Sunlight, 592
Sunspots, **194**–195
Supercluster, **215,** 217
Supernova, **203**–204
Superposition, principle of, 527, 528, **529**–530
Surface mines, 586
Surface waves, 495
Surf zone, **406**
Susquehanna Valley, 442–443
Swamp, **342**
S-waves, **495,** 502–503
Swell, 400, **406**
Syncline, **486**–487, 488
Synodic month, **160**
Synthetic minerals, 81, 83

Taurus constellation, 120, 197, 203
Technical secretary, 108
Telescopes, 6, 223, 228
Temperate climate, **317**
Temperature
  air, 242–243, 245, 247, 303
  in air masses, 289–290
  altitude and, 318–320
  atmospheric pressure and, 306–307
  convection currents and, 254
  dew-point, 272, **273**–274
  dry-bulb, 269
  of moon, 156
  ocean currents and, 320
  of ocean water, 389–390
  saturation, **269,** 271–274
  seasonal changes in, 148–149, 151
  of stars, 199–200
  of sun, 194
  wet-bulb, 269
Tensional stress, **491,** 508
Terminal moraine, **461**
Tertiary Period, 555, 574
Tetrahedron, 85
Texture, of rock, **103,** 105
Theory, **14,** 506, **535**
Theory of continental drift, 504, **505**–507
Theory of evolution by natural selection, 535–537
Theory of plate tectonics, 506, **508**–511
Thermometer
  dry-bulb, 267
  wet-bulb, 267, 269
Thermosphere, 257, 258
Thinking skills
  analyzing, 392
  classifying, 10
  comparing, 448

evaluating, 548
inferring, 292
observing, 218
Thrust fault, **493**
Thunder, **310**
Thunderstorms, 309–**310**
Tides, 156, 409–411
Till, **463**
Time
  of day, 137–142
  geologic, 544, **552**–555
  of year, 152–153
Time exposure, **131**
Time zone, **138**–140
Tin, 583
Tombaugh, Clyde, 189
Topographic maps, **45**–47
Topography, **45**
Topsoil, **431**
Tornado, 19, **311**–312, 332
Trade winds, 253
Transform fault, **493**, 509
Transpiration, 266, **347**, 348
Transported soils, **455**, 457
Transverse wave, 495
Trap, **590**
Trench, **379**, 480, 508
Triassic Period, 555, 572
Tributaries, **343**
Trilobite, 533, 560, 566, 567, 619
Triton, 189
Tropical air mass, **287**, 288
Tropical climate, **316**
Tropic of Cancer, **149**, 150, 322
Tropic of Capricorn, **148**–149, 322
Troposphere, **257**, 258
Trough, **403**, 407
True brightness, of stars, **197**, 199
True north, **49**–51
Tsunami, **407**–408
Turbidity currents, 376, 379
Turbine, 594–595

Ultraviolet waves, 234
Umbra, **160**–161, 162
Unconformity, **538**–539
Underground mines, 586
Uniformitarianism, **525**–526
Universe
  expansion of, 220, 221–222
  formation of, 219, 221
  simulating expansion of, 220
Upwelling, **414**–415, 420
Uranium, 66, 597
Uranus, 176, 181, 188–189
Ursa Major, 121

Valley glacier, **444**
Vaporization, heat of, **264**, 265
Vent, **475**–476
Venus, 178–179, 181
Vernal equinox, 149, 151

Vertebrates, 568
Vesuvius, Mount, 472
Viking spacecraft, 182
Vine, F. J., 506
Viscosity, **476**, 478
Volcanic activity, **475**–476, 485
Volcanic cones, 477, 479, 482
Volcanic landforms, 477, 479
Volcanic rocks, 97, 377
Volcanoes, 19, **476**
  power of, 471–475
  regions of, 480–481, 508–509
  violent nature of, 475–476
Volume, **28**–29, 31
Voyager missions, 185, 186, 187, 188,
  189

Waning moon, **159**
Warm front, **291**, **293**, 303
Waste materials, disposal of, 608, 610–
  611
Water
  ancient civilizations and, 339
  density of, 32
  deposition by, 454–455, 457
  erosion by, 438–443
  evaporation of, 346–347
  forms of, 60, 337–338
  ground, **354**–355, 357, 589–590,
    603–604
  ground infiltration by, 351–353
  runoff, 342–343, 345
  states of, 264–265
  surface, 340–342
  transpiration of, 266, 347, 348
  from underground, 357, 359–361
  use of, 593–596
  zones of, 354–355, 357
  see also Ocean water
Water cycle, 337–**338**
Water displacement method, 29
Water masses, **391**
Water molecules, 74
  adhesion of, 354, 355
  cohesion of, 355, 356
Water pollution, 604
Water pressure, **394**–395
Watershed, **345**
Water table, **355**, 357, 362
Water turbine, 594–595
Water vapor, 60, **264**
  in atmosphere, 233, 257, 266–269
  condensation of, 269, 271, 273–278
  evaporation and condensation of wa-
    ter to, 594
  see also Precipitation
Wave base, **403**
Wave height, **403**
Wavelength, **233**–234, 239–241, 403,
  406
Waves; *see* Ocean waves
Waxing moon, **159**
Weather, **316**
Weather balloons, 301

Weather conditions
  extreme, 309–313
  local, 299–300
  preventing disasters from, 332
  tracking severe, 308
  see also Climate
Weather data, collection of, 299–300
Weather forecaster, 270
Weather front, **290**
  air masses and, 294
  cold, **290**–291, 302–303
  on maps, 301–303
  moving, 295–296
  occluded, **293**, 295, 303
  stationary, **295**, 300
  warm, **291**, 293, 303
Weathering, **425**
  chemical, **426**–428, 432, 440
  mixed, 428–429
  physical, **425**–426, 439, 446
  rates of, 429–430, 434
  soil formation by, 431–433
Weather maps, 305–306
  fronts on, 301–303
  plotting changes on, 304
Weather prediction
  difficulties with, 306–307, 309
  extreme conditions, 309–313
  predicting changes, 305–306
  recording local conditions, 299–300
  weather fronts and, 301–303
Weather stations, 299–300
Weather technician, 270
Wegener, Alfred, 505, 511
Weight, **26**–27
Wet-bulb temperature, 269
Wet-bulb thermometer, 267, 269
Wetlands, **612**, 614
White dwarfs, 202
Wilson, J. Tuzo, 507
Wilson, Robert, 219
Wind, 591–592
  atmospheric pressure, and, 255–257
  convection currents and, 251, 253
  deflection of, 135
  deposition by, 459–461
  direction of, 250–251, 253, 256
  ocean currents affected by, 411–412
  in pressure centers, 259, 261
  types of, 250–251, 253
  see also Air masses
Wind belts, **250**–251, 253
Windmills, 592
Winter solstice, 148–149, 151
Word scale of distances, **44**–45

X-ray waves, 234

Year, measurement of, 151–152

Zenith, **123**
Zero elevation, 46
Zinc, 583
Zone of aeration, **354**
Zone of saturation, **355**

Acknowledgments

Illustrations

Barbara Hack Barrett: 8, 28, 33, 36, 38, 43, 44 (bottom), 45, 46 (both), 55, 64, 149, 209, 243, 492, 503

Brenda Booth: 32, 44 (top), 71, 118, 119 (left), 124, 131, 139, 141, 157, 159, 161, 162, 172, 174, 175, 176, 201, 210, 233, 240, 245, 266, 300, 302, 305, 306, 327, 351, 369, 371, 391, 402, 460, 490, 504, 510, 551, 553, 608, 609

Carl Buell: 566, 567, 568, 569, 570, 572–573

Leslie Dunlap: 317, 321, 324, 354, 374, 381, 388, 390, 406, 409, 412, 443, 454, 471, 486, 487, 493 (bottom), 529 (all), 531, 534, 538, 539, 588, 590

Valerie Felts: 67, 74 (both), 75, 76 (top), 77, 78

Aleta Jenks: 30, 52, 122, 184, 206, 220, 244, 268, 272

Christa Keiffer: 574–575

Kathie Kelleher: 47, 50 (bottom), 51, 62, 72, 76 (bottom), 83, 102, 125, 133, 134, 135, 138, 145, 146, 171, 205, 219, 221, 234, 259, 271, 288, 289, 296, 326, 341, 353, 372, 376, 380, 389, 393, 401, 403 (both), 442, 443, 462, 463, 480, 485, 491, 493 (top), 494, 496, 502, 505, 506, 611

Jim McConnell: 119 (right)

Masami Miyamoto: 16, 17, 27, 28, 31, 40, 41, 50, 61, 148, 163, 198, 200, 235, 241, 246, 251, 252, 253, 255, 256, 258, 261, 291, 293, 295, 338, 345, 348, 359, 378, 388, 450, 457, 458, 495, 507, 509, 511, 513

P&A/Barbara Massey: 70, 208, 294, 304, 309, 358, 587

P&A/Angela Parsons: 98, 240, 564

Linda Ruls: 42, 243, 375

Joel Snyder: 325, 356, 514, 516, 528

Tom Wilson: 29, 65, 137, 143, 144, 149

Art on pages 372, 409, 502 has been modified with permission from *Earth Science* by Bill W. Tillery. Copyright © 1985 D.C. Heath and Company.

Art on page 611 was adapted with permission from *Environmental Science* by Daniel D. Chiras. Copyright © 1985 Benjamin/Cummings.

Special thanks to the California Academy of Sciences for the use of the mineral specimens appearing on page 83.

Photo Acknowledgments for Interleaved Teacher's Pages

2F	Clyde Smith/Peter Arnold, Inc.
2H	Stephen Frisch*
2J	Larry Lefever/Grant Heilman Photography
2L	Breck P. Kent/Earth Scenes
2M	The Bettmann Archive
2R	Byron Crader/Tom Stack, & Associates
56C	Janice M. Sheldon*
56F	Janice M. Sheldon*
56G	Stephen Frisch*
56K	Janice M. Sheldon*
56L	Breck P. Kent/Earth Scenes
56Q	Stephen Frisch*
56R	Bruce Molnia/Terragraphics/BPS
114C	James Sugar/Black Star
114F	Stephen Frisch*
114L T	Hale Observatories
114L BL	Mount Wilson & Las Campanas Observatories, Carnegie Institution
114L BC	Hale Observatories
114L BR	Hale Observatories
114P	NASA
114R	NASA
168C	NASA
168G	© 1980 Royal Observatory, Edinburgh
168K	© 1959 California Institute of Technology
168L	NASA/Grant Heilman Photography
168N	Stephen Frisch*
168R	© California Institute of Technology
230C	Dieter Blum/Peter Arnold, Inc.
230G	Runk-Schoenberger/Grant Heilman Photography
230H	Runk-Schoenberger/Grant Heilman Photography
230K	Melinda Berge/Photographers Aspen
230L	Peter Smallman/Taurus Photos
230M	Peter Smallman/Taurus Photos
230P	Stephen Frisch*
230R	D. Wilder/Tom Stack & Associates
284C	National Oceanic & Atmospheric Administration/ Environmental Data and Information Service/ National Climatic Center
284F	Roy Johnson/Tom Stack & Associates
284G	Stephen Frisch*
284L	Kevin Schafer/Tom Stack & Associates
284M L	Bruno Barbey/Magnum Photos
284M R	Alan Pitcairn/Grant Heilman Photography
334C	Jay Spurr/Bruce Coleman Inc.
334E	W. Hodge/Peter Arnold, Inc.
334G	Bill Kleeman/Tom Stack & Associates
334M	Grant Heilman Photography
366C	Robert Fried
366F	Zig Leszczynski/Animals Animals
366G	Brian Parker/Tom Stack & Associates
366L	Bob Evans/Peter Arnold, Inc.
366R	Roger Archibald/Earth Scenes
422C	Tom Bean/Tom Stack & Associates
422G	Ed Cooper Photography
422K	L. L. T. Rhodes/Earth Scenes
422L	Grant Heilman Photography
422P	U.S. Geological Survey
422R T	Vance Henry/Taurus Photos
422R C	Caroline W. Coleman/William E. Ferguson
422R B	Stouffer Productions/Earth Scenes
468C	Regina P. Simon/Tom Stack & Associates
468E	W. Hodge/Peter Arnold, Inc.
468G	George Rose/Gamma-Liaison
468J	Stephen Frisch*
468N	Stephen Frisch*
468R L	Pedro Meyer/Black Star
468R R	Joe Brannery/Bruce Coleman, Inc.
522C L	Rene Burri/Magnum Photos
522C R	Carol Hughes/Bruce Coleman Inc.
522D	E. R. Degginger/Earth Scenes
522G	Stephen Frisch*
580C	Stephen Frisch*
580D	William Felger/Grant Heilman Photography
580G	T. W. Bennett/Taurus Photos
580K	Stephen Frisch*
580L L	Lynn M. Stone/Bruce Coleman Inc.
580R	E. Cawthra/Earth Scenes
580M L	© 1982 Thomas Ives
580M R	Jonathan Wright/Bruce Coleman Inc.

*Photographs provided expressly for the publisher.

Photographs

Unit 1

1	Stock Imagery
2	NASA
3 L	Clyde Smith/Peter Arnold, Inc.
3 C	Larry Lefever/Grant Heilman Photography
3 R	Paul Chesley/Photographers Aspen
4	Clyde Smith/Peter Arnold, Inc.
10	Courtesy of California Closet Company ®
11	David Hiser/Photographers Aspen
13	James Mason/Black Star
15	R. S. Virdee/Grant Heilman Photography
19 TL	E. R. Degginger/Earth Scenes
19 TR	Ron Church/Tom Stack & Associates
19 BL	Byron Crader/Tom Stack & Associates
19 BC	Nicholas Devore III/Photographers Aspen
19 BR	E. R. Degginger/Earth Scenes
21	Larry Lefever/Grant Heilman Photography
31	Russ Kinne/Comstock
35	Paul Chesley/Photographers Aspen
37	The Bettmann Archive
56	Jason Rubinsteen/Earth Scenes
57 R	Breck P. Kent/Earth Scenes
81	Allen B. Smith/Tom Stack & Associates
95	Breck P. Kent/Earth Scenes
97	E. Cawthra/Earth Scenes
99	Hartman, DeWitt/Comstock
101	Bruce Molnia/Terragraphics/BPS
112	Walter Bibikow/The Image Bank West

Unit 2

113	NASA/Taurus Photos
114	John Serafin/Peter Arnold, Inc.
115 L	James Sugar/Black Star
115 C	NASA
115 R	NASA
116	James Sugar/Black Star
120	Culver Pictures
129	NASA
132	David F. Malin/© 1977 Anglo-Australian Telescope Board
154	NASA
155	NASA
160 TL	Hale Observatories
160 TC	Hale Observatories
160 TR	Hale Observatories
160 CL	Mount Wilson & Las Campanas Observatories, Carnegie Institution
160 C	Hale Observatories
160 CR	Hale Observatories
160 B	J. W. Hinds/Light Images
161	National Optical Astronomy Observatories
168	© California Institute of Technology
169 L	NASA
169 C	Dennis di Cicco/Peter Arnold, Inc.
169 R	© 1980 Royal Observatory, Edinburgh
170	NASA
174	Lowell Observatory
178 L	Jet Propulsion lab
178 R	NASA
179	NASA
180	Jet Propulsion Lab
181	NASA
182	Jet Propulsion Lab
183	Breck P. Kent/Earth Scenes
185	Jet Propulsion Lab
186	NASA
187	NASA
188	Jet Propulsion Lab
190	© Hans Vehrenberg/Hansen Planetarium
193	Dennis di Cicco/Peter Arnold, Inc.

195	NASA
196	Michio Hoshino/Earth Scenes
199	Mount Wilson & Las Campanas Observatories, Carnegie Institution
203	© 1959 California Institute of Technology
204	National Optical Astronomy Observatories
207	U.S. Naval Observatory
212	© 1980 Royal Observatory, Edinburgh
213	National Optical Astronomy Observatories
215	NASA/Grant Heilman Photography
217 T	Mount Wilson & Las Campanas Observatories, Carnegie Institution
217 C	Lick Observatory Photo
217 B	Lick Observatory Photo
223 B	Greg Vaughn/Tom Stack & Associates
224 T	NASA
224 B	Space Telescope Science Institute
228	Smithsonian Astrophysical Observatory

Unit 3

229	Gene Anthony/Light Images
230	Mark Newman/Earth Scenes
231 L	Dieter Blum/Peter Arnold, Inc.
231 C	Melinda Berge/Photographers Aspen
231 R	H. Gritscher/Peter Arnold, Inc.
232	Dieter Blum/Peter Arnold, Inc.
236	The Bettmann Archive
238	Mike & Carol Werner/Comstock
243 L	D. Wilder/Tom Stack & Associates
243 R	James Brandt/Earth Scenes
247	Frank Balthis
249	Melinda Berge/Photographers Aspen
256 L	Runk-Schoenberger/Grant Heilman Photography
256 C	Runk-Schoenberger/Grant Heilman Photography
256 R	E. R. Degginger/Earth Scenes
263	H. Gritscher/Peter Arnold, Inc.
265 L	Peter Smallman/Taurus Photos
265 R	Peter Smallman/Taurus Photos
274 T	Mark S. Carlson/Tom Stack & Associates
274 B	John Shaw/Bruce Coleman Inc.
275	Richard Oglesby/CLICK Chicago
279	National Oceanic & Atmospheric Administration
284	National Oceanic & Atmospheric Administration/ Environmental Data and Information Service/ National Climatic Center
285 L	Roy Johnson/Tom Stack & Associates
285 C	Focus on Sports
285 R	Kevin Schafer/Tom Stack & Associates
286	Roy Johnson/Tom Stack & Associates
298	Focus on Sports
301	National Oceanic & Atmospheric Administration/ Environmental Data and Information Service/ National Climatic Center
310	Runk-Schoenberger/Grant Heilman Photography
311	H. Gritscher/Peter Arnold, Inc.
312	Edi Ann Otto
313	Brian Fox/Taurus Photos
315	Kevin Schafer/Tom Stack & Associates
319	Alan Pitcairn/Grant Heilman Photography
322	Bruno Barbey/Magnum Photos
332	Tom Grill/Comstock

Unit 4

333	Laurence Gould/Earth Scenes
334	Mike Ederegger/Peter Arnold, Inc.
335 L	Jay Spurr/Bruce Coleman Inc.
335 R	Grant Heilman Photography
336	Jay Spurr/Bruce Coleman Inc.

339	The Bettmann Archive
340	Grant Heilman Photography
341	Bjorn Bolstad/Peter Arnold, Inc.
342	W. Hodge/Peter Arnold, Inc.
343	Jim Pickerell/Black Star
346	R. Tompkins/Tom Stack & Associates
350	Grant Heilman Photography
361	Bill Kleeman/Tom Stack & Associates
366	Kaz Mori/Taurus Photos
367 L	Robert Fried
367 C	Zig Leszczynski/Animals Animals
367 R	Roger Archibald/Earth Scenes
368	Robert Fried
377	Nicholas Devore/Bruce Coleman Inc.
383	C. B. Jones/Taurus Photos
385	Zig Leszczynski/Animals Animals
387	Steven Monti/Bruce Coleman Inc.
394	E. R. Degginger/Earth Scenes
396 L	Brian Parker/Tom Stack & Associates
396 R	Howard Hall/Tom Stack & Associates
397	Oxford Scientific Films/Animals Animals
400	Roger Archibald/Earth Scenes
404	Jonathan Wright/Bruce Coleman Inc.
407	Nicholas Devore III/ Photographers Aspen
408	Keith Gunnar/Bruce Coleman Inc.
410	Breck P. Kent/Earth Scenes
413	Norman Tomalin/Bruce Coleman, Inc.
415	Bob Evans/Peter Arnold, Inc.
420	Mark Sherman/Bruce Coleman Inc.

Unit 5

421	Greg Davis/Black Star
422	Tom Bean/Tom Stack & Associates
423 L	Vance Henry/Taurus Photos
423 C	Ed Cooper Photography
423 R	Grant Heilman Photography
424	Vance Henry/Taurus Photos
425	Caroline W. Coleman/William E. Ferguson
426	Craig Engle/Light Images
427	Ed Cooper Photography
430	S. Craig/Bruce Coleman Inc.
437	Ed Cooper Photography
439	Animals Animals
440	The Bettmann Archive
444 L	Stephenie S. Ferguson/William E. Ferguson
444 R	Dennis Geaney/Light Images
445	Ed Cooper Photography
446	L. L. T. Rhodes/Earth Scenes
449	Clyde H. Smith/Peter Arnold, Inc.
451	Grant Heilman Photography
453	Grant Heilman Photography
455	Stouffer Productions/Earth Scenes
456	U.S. Geological Survey
459	Ed Cooper Photography
460	Brian Parker/Tom Stack & Associates
464	Dr. E. R. Degginger
468	C. B. Frith/Bruce Coleman Inc.
469 L	Vance Henry/Taurus Photos
469 C	Grant Heilman Photography
469 R	Norman Tomalin/Bruce Coleman Inc.
470	Vance Henry/Taurus Photos
472	Ed Cooper Photography
473	American Museum of Natural History
475	© 1980 Gary Rosenquist, Earth Images/Hansen Planetarium
477	Joe Brannery/Bruce Coleman Inc.
478 L	Grant Heilman Photography
479 L	Nicholas Devore/Bruce Coleman Inc.
479 C	Stewart Green/Tom Stack & Associates
479 R	W. Hodge/Peter Arnold, Inc.
481	Regina P. Simon/Tom Stack & Associates
484	Grant Heilman Photography
485	William E. Ferguson
489	George Rose/Gamma-Liaison
497	Pedro Meyer/Black Star
501	Norman Tomalin/Bruce Coleman Inc.
520	Photri, Inc.

Unit 6

521	Michael Collier/Stock, Boston
522	Charles Palek/Earth Scenes
523 L	Rene Burri/Magnum Photos
523 C	John Elk III
523 R	Courtesy, Field Museum of Natural History, Chicago. Photography by Ron Testa
524	Rene Burri/Magnum Photos
526	Gerald A. Corsi/Tom Stack & Associates
530	Carol Hughes/Bruce Coleman Inc.
533	E. R. Degginger/Earth Scenes
536	The Bettmann Archive
537	American Museum of Natural History
541	John Elk III
542	Grant Heilman/Grant Heilman Photography
544	The Bettmann Archive
558	Courtesy, Field Museum of Natural History, Chicago. Photography by Ron Testa
559	Grant Heilman Photography
560	Painting by Charles Knight, photography by Ron Testa. Courtesy, Field Museum of Natural History, Chicago
561	Courtesy, Field Museum of Natural History, Chicago. Photography by Ron Testa
562	Courtesy, Field Museum of Natural History, Chicago
563	Courtesy, Field Museum of Natural History, Chicago
565 T	William E. Ferguson
565 BL	Fred Bavendam/Peter Arnold, Inc.
565 BC	Breck P. Kent/Animals Animals
565 BR	R. Mendez/Animals Animals
571	Fred Bavendam/Peter Arnold, Inc.
580	Gary Milburn/Tom Stack & Associates
581 L	Dick Durrance II/Woodfin Camp & Associates
581 R	T. W. Bennett/Taurus Photos
582	Dick Durrance II/Woodfin Camp & Associates
586	William Felger/Grant Heilman Photography
593	Liz Jaquith/Tom Stack & Associates
594	Brian Parker/Tom Stack & Associates
595	Eric Young/Tom Stack & Associates
597	Pierre Kopp/West Light
599	NASA
602	T. W. Bennett/Taurus Photos
603	Jonathan Wright/Bruce Coleman Inc.
604	William E. Ferguson
605 T	L. L. Rue III/Animals Animals
605 B	Keith Gunnar/Bruce Coleman Inc.
606	Zig Leszczynski/Earth Scenes
607	Mary L. Baer/Tom Stack & Associates
614	Lynn M. Stone/Bruce Coleman Inc.
619	Ed Robinson/Tom Stack & Associates

The following photographs were provided expressly for Addison-Wesley:

Stephen Frisch: 6, 9, 25, 48, 57C, 80, 82, 86, 88, 89, 91, 108B, 117, 136, 151, 164, 216, 223T, 237, 239, 264, 267, 270, 276, 277, 278, 280, 299, 308, 323, 351, 362, 395, 405, 429, 435, 448, 488, 515, 546, 584, 585 TL, TR, CL, BL, and BR, 591, 592, 598, 610, 613
Wayland Lee/Addison-Wesley Staff: 482
Janice M. Sheldon: 23, 57L, 58, 59, 63, 73, 83, 90, 106, 107, 108T, 218, 273, 434, 478R, 585CR

Periodic Table of the Elements

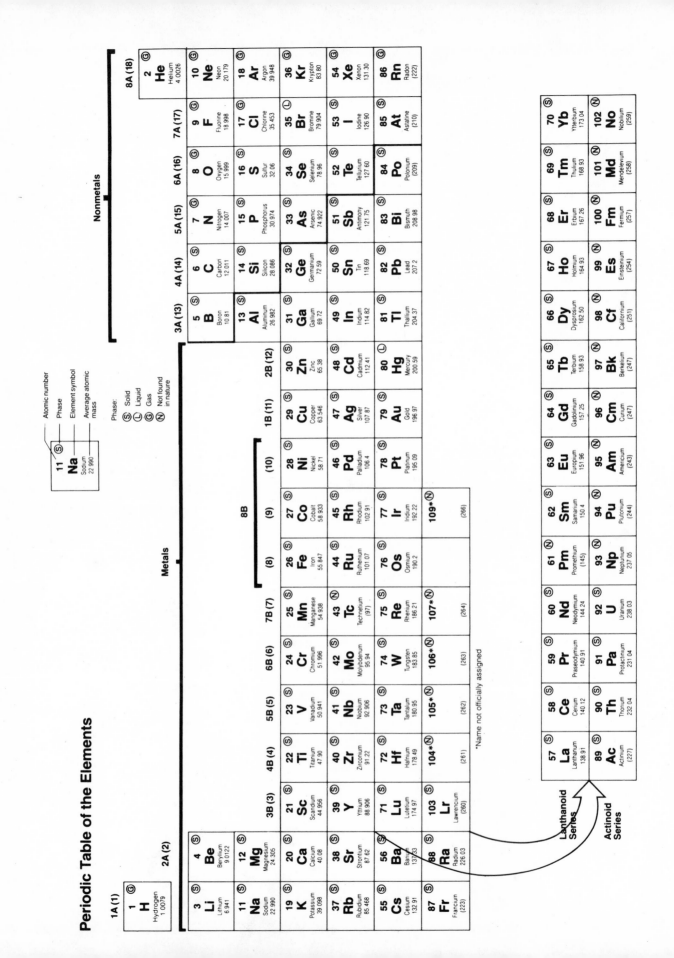